Java Programming

From the Ground Up

Ralph Bravaco
Stonehill College

Shai Simonson
Stonehill College

Boston Burr Ridge, IL Dubuque, IA New York San Francisco St. Louis
Bangkok Bogotá Caracas Kuala Lumpur Lisbon London Madrid Mexico City
Milan Montreal New Delhi Santiago Seoul Singapore Sydney Taipei Toronto

JAVA PROGRAMMING: FROM THE GROUND UP

Published by McGraw-Hill, a business unit of The McGraw-Hill Companies, Inc., 1221 Avenue of the Americas, New York, NY 10020.

This book is printed on acid-free paper.

1 2 3 4 5 6 7 8 9 0 VNH/VNH 0 9

ISBN 978–0–07–352335–4
MHID 0–07–352335–6

Global Publisher: *Raghothaman Srinivasan*
Director of Development: *Kristine Tibbetts*
Developmental Editor: *Lora Neyens*
Senior Marketing Manager: *Curt Reynolds*
Project Manager: *Melissa M. Leick*
Senior Production Supervisor: *Laura Fuller*
Senior Media Project Manager: *Tammy Juran*
Associate Design Coordinator: *Brenda A. Rolwes*
Cover Designer: *Studio Montage, St. Louis, Missouri*
(USE) Cover Image: © *Getty Images*
Lead Photo Research Coordinator: *Carrie K. Burger*
Compositor: *Macmillan Publishing Solutions*
Typeface: *10/12 Times Roman*
Printer: *R. R. Donnelley, Jefferson City, MO*

Library of Congress Cataloging-in-Publication Data

Bravaco, Ralph.
Java programming : from the ground up / Ralph Bravaco, Charles Simonson. -- 1st ed.
p. cm.
Includes index.
ISBN 978–0–07–352335–4 --- ISBN 0–07–352335–6 (hard copy : alk. paper)
1. Java (Computer program language) I. Simonson, Charles. II. Title.
QA76.73.J38B68 2010
005.13'3--dc22

2008047782

www.mhhe.com

DEDICATION

For Kathryn and Emily
—R.B.

For Andrea, Zosh, Yair, and Yona
—S.S.

CONTENTS

Chapter 20

PREFACE

Java Programming: From the Ground Up begins with the fundamentals of programming, moves through the object-oriented paradigm, and concludes with an introduction to graphics and event-driven programming. The broad coverage of topics as well as the modularity of the text makes the book suitable for both introductory and intermediate-level programming courses. The text requires no prerequisites other than an enthusiasm for problem solving and a willingness to persevere.

KEY FEATURES OF THE TEXT

The style of this text is based on the following four principles:

1. **Fundamentals first**

   Our approach is neither "objects first" nor "objects late"; it's "fundamentals first." Our method is bottom up, starting with the basic concepts common to most programming languages: variables, selection, iteration, and methods. Once students understand the basic control structures, they can use them to build classes. Programming tools such as iteration, selection, and recursion are not the exclusive property of the object-oriented paradigm. Virtually every programming language, from Ada to ZPL, provides these tools. The text discusses these common features first before using them to build classes.

   Our experience in the classroom convinces us that this bottom-up approach is pedagogically sound and the best way to teach the material. Certainly, one learns how to use the tools of carpentry before building a house. We believe that the same principle applies to building classes. You might say that we present Java from the "grounds" up.

2. **Independent presentation of fundamental programming concepts, object-oriented concepts, GUIs, and event-driven paradigms**

   The text is modular. We first tackle basic programming structures, then the fundamentals of object-oriented programming, followed by graphics, GUIs, and events. The separation of graphics from basic programming structures is especially helpful to beginners, who when presented early with programs that mix fundamentals with GUI design, events, and OOP, have difficulty separating these concepts.

   Because the text is modular, it is appropriate for a variety of courses. For example, a course that teaches Java as a second language can proceed directly to "Part 2: Principles of Object-Oriented Programming." The basics common to most programming languages (selection, iteration, recursion, methods, arrays) are covered in Part 1 and not spread throughout the text. A student familiar with another language, such as C++, can easily find the Java counterpart to any fundamental control structure.

3. **Examples, examples, and more examples**

   Examples lead to understanding. Understanding leads to abstraction. Expecting students to immediately digest an abstraction that took a professional perhaps years to distill is unrealistic. Regardless of how clever or articulate the presentation, the practical teacher quickly resorts to examples so that the student can extract the general principles in context. Our text contains dozens of examples in the form of fully implemented programs. Moreover, our experience teaching introductory courses convinces us that students rarely read examples spanning four or five pages. With that in mind, we have tried to keep our examples short, succinct, and occasionally entertaining.

4. **Independent and parallel presentation of related computer science topics**

   We present a variety of computer science topics that expand upon and enhance the study of a particular part of the Java toolbox. Optional "Bigger Picture" sections appear after the exercises of most chapters and are independent of each other. These optional segments provide an introduction to more advanced topics such as fractals, computer architecture, artificial intelligence, computer theory, bioinformatics, and trees.

PEDAGOGICAL FEATURES

Each chapter contains the following features:

1. **Objectives**—Each chapter begins with a list of concepts that the student will learn in that chapter.
2. **Just the Facts**—At the conclusion of each chapter, a summary of the fundamental ideas of the chapter can be reviewed at a glance.
3. **Bug Extermination**—At the end of each chapter is a short section on debugging with a summary of some commonly occurring bugs, and hints for how best to avoid them.
4. **Examples**—Examples permeate each chapter. Almost every numbered example is a standalone program. Many examples are dissected line by line. Each example follows the same easy-to-understand format: a problem description, a Java solution, typical output, and finally a discussion of the solution.
5. **Exercises**—Each chapter contains a variety of exercises and programming problems. The style and difficulty of the exercises and problems vary. There are:
   - crossword puzzles that test terminology,
   - short answer questions that check basic understanding,
   - debugging and tracing exercises that do not require a computer,
   - short programming problems that reinforce the concepts of the chapter, and
   - longer programming assignments that require some creativity and algorithm development.
6. **The Bigger Picture**—Following the exercises, a section entitled *The Bigger Picture* builds upon and extends the ideas covered in the chapter. Topics range from two's complement number representation, to the halting problem, to DNA sequencing. The material in *The Bigger Picture* sections is not prerequisite to any subsequent section of the text. Furthermore, one *Bigger Picture* segment does not depend upon another. Each stands entirely on its own. These sections may be included, assigned as supplemental reading, used in a closed lab setting, or skipped entirely, depending on the audience or time constraints. However, students who choose to tackle some or all of these sections will find a wealth of topics, each opening new roads of inquiry into computer science. The effort will provide students with a larger framework of ideas that extend beyond the study of programming.

THE CONTENTS

The text is divided into four parts:

1. The Fundamental Tools; 2. Principles of Object-Oriented Programming; 3. More Java Classes; and 4. Basic Graphics, GUIs, and Event-Driven Programming

Part 1: The Fundamental Tools

Part 1 consists of the standard programming constructs that exist in most programming languages: storage and control structures.

1. **Introduction to Computers and Java**
   Chapter 1 is a brief introduction to the hardware and software of a computer system. The chapter includes a discussion of programming languages, compilers, and the Java Virtual Machine.
2. **Expressions and Data Types**
   Chapter 2 begins with a few applications that display string output and moves gradually to examples that evaluate expressions. The chapter includes an introduction to the primitive data types: int, double, char, and boolean.
3. **Variables and Assignment**
   Variables are introduced in this chapter. Specifically, Chapter 3 addresses three questions:
   - How does an application obtain storage for data?
   - How does an application store data?
   - How does an application utilize stored data?

   Java's Scanner class is used for interactive input.
4. **Selection and Decision: if Statements**
   Chapter 4 covers selection via
   - the if statement,
   - the if-else statement, and
   - the switch statement.

   The chapter also includes a discussion of nested if statements.
5. **Repetition**
   Repetition is first introduced with the while statement, then the do-while statement, and finally the for loop. The chapter explains the stylistic differences among the loops and when each type of loop may be appropriate. There is a discussion of common errors that may lead to infinite loops or loops that are "off by one." The chapter includes examples of applications with nested loops.
6. **Methods**
   Methods are introduced as "black boxes" that accept input and return a value. Here, we present a number of methods from Java's Math class. The bulk of the chapter deals with "home grown" methods. Because we have not yet introduced classes and objects, all methods are static.
7. **Arrays and Lists: One Name for Many Data**
   This chapter covers arrays and array instantiation. Here, we first introduce the concept of a reference. The chapter includes an introduction to sorting and searching. After discussing two-dimensional arrays, the chapter concludes with a case study: *The Fifteen Puzzle.* The case study uses most of the concepts introduced in Part 1.
8. **Recursion**
   Recursion is the final topic of Part 1. The chapter begins with a simple example that does no more than print a message. Subsequent examples grow in complexity, leading to a discussion of tail recursion versus "classic" recursion as well as the Quicksort algorithm. A final case study, *The Design of an Anagram Generator,* ties the concepts together. The chapter emphasizes *recursive thinking.*

Part 2: Principles of Object-Oriented Programming

The heart of Part 2 is the object-oriented paradigm. With the tools of Part 1 mastered, students can concentrate on the principles of object-oriented programming. The concepts of Parts 1 and 2 are not in any way tied to building GUIs or event-driven programming. No side trips to loop-land or "by-the-ways" are necessary. Part 2 is comprised of the following chapters:

9. **Objects and Classes I: Encapsulation, Strings, and Things**
   Chapter 9 introduces encapsulation, classes, and objects. This first introduction to classes and objects is accomplished with examples of several Java classes, including:
   - Random
   - String
   - StringBuilder
   - File
   - DecimalFormat

   Here, students learn how to use text files for simple I/O.
10. **Objects and Classes II: Writing Your Own Classes**
    In Chapter 9, students learn about objects and classes by using a few prepackaged classes. In this chapter students learn how to write their own classes. The chapter discusses encapsulation and information hiding and gives meaning to a few mysterious words, such as public and static, that have been used in previous chapters. A final case study builds a simple audio player, which we dub a *myPod*.
11. **Designing with Classes and Objects**
    The sole topic of Chapter 11 is program design. This chapter consists of a single case study: an interactive poker game. We formulate a methodology for determining the appropriate classes and objects and how these objects interact. Our focus here is not the syntax, semantics, or mechanics of Java but problem solving and object-oriented design.
12. **Inheritance**
    We introduce inheritance as the second principle of object-oriented programming. Here, we contrast inheritance and composition. We also discuss the Object class and those Object methods inherited by all classes. The chapter includes a discussion of abstract classes and interfaces.
13. **Polymorphism**
    The final chapter of Part 2 is a discussion of polymorphism. If inheritance emphasizes the "sameness" of classes in a hierarchy, then polymorphism underscores the differences. The chapter discusses dynamic binding, using polymorphism with interfaces, and polymorphism as it relates to Object.

Part 3: More Java Classes

Part 3 is the most technical section of the text. Here, we examine the wrapper classes, exception classes, stream classes, and classes for random access files. We also introduce generics and several elementary data structures such as stacks, queues, and linked lists. Part 3 ends with a discussion of the Java Collections Framework.

14. **More Java Classes: Wrappers and Exceptions**
    Chapter 14 begins with a discussion of the wrapper classes. The chapter includes a discussion of auto-boxing and unboxing. The remainder of the chapter is

devoted to Java's Exception hierarchy. The chapter explains the throw-catch mechanism, the finally block, checked and unchecked exceptions, the throws clause, and how to create an Exception class.

15. **Stream I/O and Random Access Files**
    By far the most technical chapter of the text, Chapter 15 is a selective discussion of some of the Byte Stream and Character Stream classes as well as the connection between the Byte Stream hierarchy and the Character Stream hierarchy. The chapter contrasts text and binary files, gives examples of binary file I/O, and discusses object serialization. Random access files are also covered in this chapter.
16. **Data Structures and Generics**
    Chapter 16 begins with an introduction to Java's ArrayList class and generics. This leads to a discussion of several elementary data structures: stacks, queues, and linked lists. An implementation for each type of data structure is discussed.
17. **The Java Collections Framework**
    By examining the implementations of several classes in the Java Collections Framework, this chapter demonstrates how choosing the "wrong" class an lead to an inefficient application.

Part 4: Basic Graphics, GUIs, and Event-Driven Programming

Part 4 introduces graphics, graphical user interfaces, and event-driven programming.

18. **Graphics: AWT and Swing**
    Chapter 18 discusses Swing and AWT. The chapter emphasizes frame layout and discusses several layout managers. Here, we explain how to arrange graphical components within a window. We also include an introduction to the Graphics class.
19. **Event-Driven Programming**
    Event-driven programming is discussed in terms of the delegation event model. Applications that include buttons, labels, text fields, text areas, dialog boxes, checkboxes, radio buttons, mouse events, and menus fill out the rest of the chapter.
20. **A Case Study: Video Poker, Revisited**
    Chapter 20 revisits the case study of Chapter 11. Here the focus is on the design and implementation of a GUI for the text-based poker game developed in Chapter 11. The objective of this chapter is an understanding of the design principle that entails the separation of the data model from the interface, or more simply, the model from the view.

Appendix A: Java Keywords

Appendix B: The ASCII Character Set

Appendix C: Operator Precedence

Appendix D: Javadoc

This appendix describes how to use Sun's Javadoc tool to automatically generate documentation from Java source files.

Appendix E: Packages

Appendix E focuses on the use of packages to better organize large-scale applications with many classes.

TO THE INSTRUCTOR

How to Use This Book

This book is flexible and is designed to serve several audiences:

- For a college-level introduction to programming in Java, Parts 1 and 2 can be used alone or followed by Part 4 with selections from Part 3, depending on the pace and focus of the course. In a first course, we would omit the chapter on Stream classes (Chapter 15). Basic text file I/O is covered in Chapter 9.
- A course for students who already know a programming language can begin with Part 2 and refer to Part 1 as needed. This same approach could be used by an instructor who prefers "objects early."
- For high school students in an AP course, Parts 1 and 2 and selections from Part 3 cover the required Java topics. Chapter 15 can be skipped entirely.

Recursion appears as Chapter 8 at the conclusion of Part 1, prior to our introduction to object-oriented programming. We present recursion independent of object-oriented programming because recursion is a fundamental concept of program control independent of the programming paradigm. Although recursion appears at the end of Part 1, the topic can be delayed until the end of Part 2, or skipped entirely. Any example or exercise in the book that requires recursion is explicitly marked **(R)** so that an instructor can choose whether or not to assign it.

Arrays are storage structures common to most programming languages. Consequently, we have included the topic of arrays in Part 1. On the other hand, Java arrays are objects. The book is structured so that arrays (Chapter 7) can be covered at the end of Part 1, or delayed until after Chapter 9, *Objects and Classes I: Encapsulation, Strings, and Things*. Chapter 7 includes a discussion of two-dimensional arrays. These sections can be postponed without loss of continuity.

Simple data structures (stacks, queues, and linked lists) and the Java Collections Framework are covered at the end of Part 3 because the implementation of data structures is heavily dependent on the object-oriented paradigm.

Chapter Dependency Chart

The following chart gives general chapter prerequisites. The chart can be used to configure many different types of courses. Although Chapters 1 through 6 are shown as prerequisite to Chapter 9, for those instructors eager to start with objects, a course might begin with Chapters 1–3, skip to 9, and cover the material in 4–6 as needed.

Online Resources

Online resources to accompany *Java Programming* are available on the text's website at www.mhhe.com/bravaco. Some of those resources include:

- Code and data for all program examples in the text
- Lecture PowerPoint slides
- An image library of all line art in the text
- An instructor's manual containing solutions to exercises

To access these resources, contact your McGraw-Hill representative.

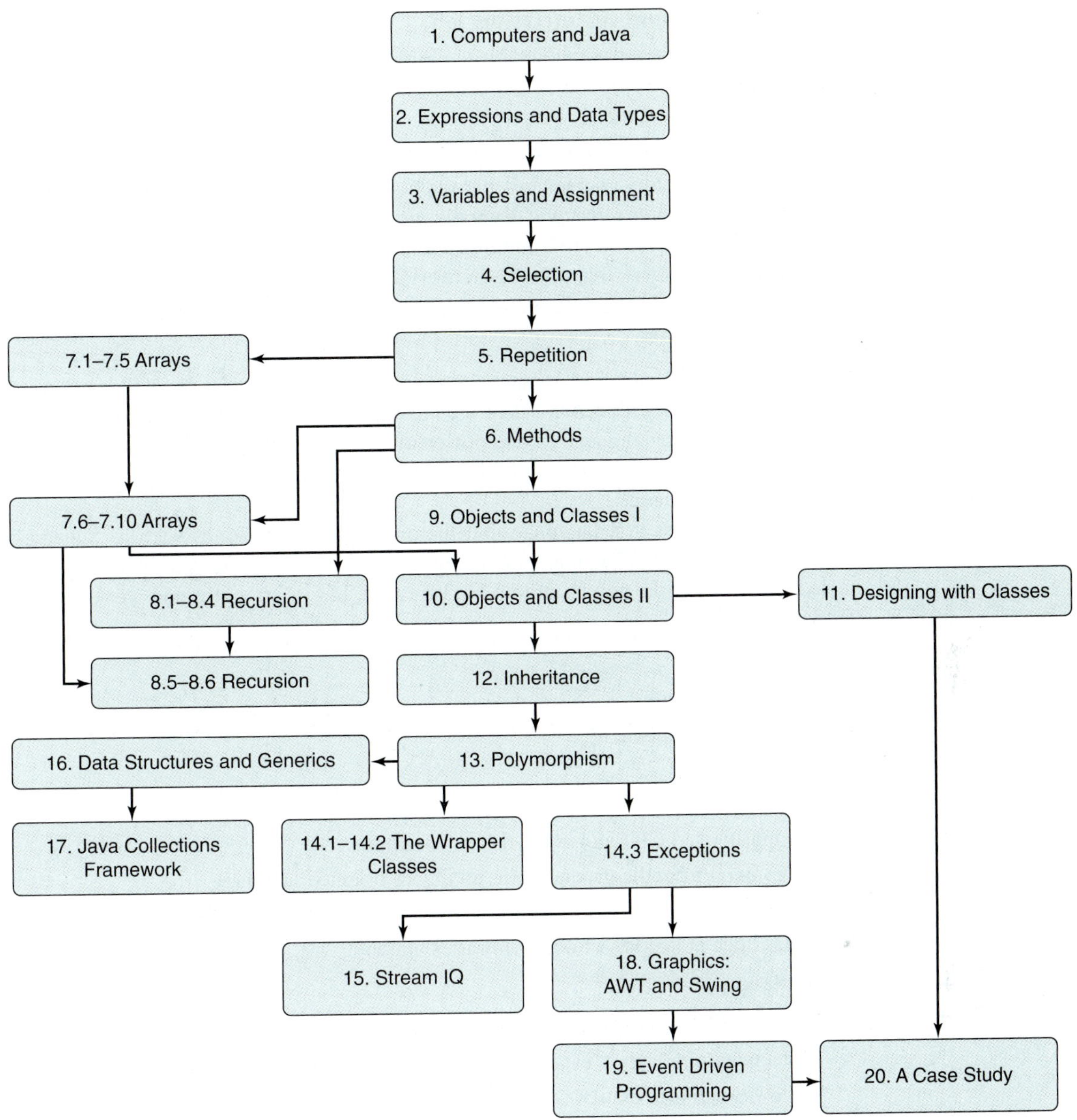

TO THE STUDENT

You are about to study Java, a popular object-oriented programming language. There are many reasons why you may be studying Java:

- **Knowledge of Java and computer programming is required in your discipline (business, information technology, science, etc.).**

  Programming is a useful tool. Even if you do not become a programmer yourself, this text will provide you with an appreciation for what a programmer does. Long after you have forgotten the details in this book, the principles that you have learned will allow you to communicate better with programmers.

- **You hope to secure an interesting job.**

  Proficiency in Java is a marketable skill. Many interactive websites are written using Java. There is much to learn and Java's learning curve is steep, but greater proficiency comes with experience.

- **You are beginning a college major in computer science.**

  Unlike introductory courses in other sciences such as chemistry and physics, a first course in computer science is generally *not* an overview of the discipline but an intense introduction to programming and the *tools* of the discipline. While there are breadth-first courses that provide an overview of computer science, these courses are rare, and most computer science programs have retained the tradition of teaching programming first.

Java may very well be the first of many programming languages that you will learn. A good first language is one with a rich set of features that enables you to learn other languages quickly. A good first language is one powerful enough to implement sophisticated algorithms without tedious effort. A good language gives you enough power to easily implement an abstract concept.

There is no best first language, but there are many good ones such as Scheme, C, C++, C#, Visual Basic, Python, and of course, Java. Each language has its fans as well as its detractors. Java, like any programming language, has its strengths and weaknesses as a first language.

Strengths:

- Internet friendly
- Platform independent
- Reliable
- Secure
- Sophisticated GUI and event-driven paradigm
- Designed from the ground up as an object-oriented language
- Widely used
- Has huge collection of object libraries allowing fast, efficient reuse of code

Weaknesses:

- Huge collection of object libraries is intimidating to beginners.
- Steep learning curve, especially for GUI and event-driven models.
- Slow execution relative to standard compiled languages.

There is no perfect choice, but Java is certainly a good one. Thousands of people consider Java their "native" programming language, and Java will not likely disappear soon from industry or the classroom. Java is an excellent first language.

The only way to become fluent in Java is to write programs. You can and should listen to lectures; you can and should read the text. And, unquestionably, you must do the exercises. With practice and perseverance, you can become a skilled and successful programmer and have a bit of fun along the way. Enjoy your journey.

Electronic Textbook Option

This text is offered through CourseSmart for both instructors and students. CourseSmart is an online resource where students can purchase the complete text online at almost half the cost of a traditional text. Purchasing the eTextbook allows students to take advantage of CourseSmart's web tools for learning, which include full text search, notes and highlighting, and email tools for sharing notes between classmates. To learn more about CourseSmart options, contact your sales representative or visit www.CourseSmart.com.

ACKNOWLEDGMENTS

Many people have contributed to the development of this book. We owe a debt of gratitude to our reviewers, who graciously gave of their time and expertise:

Suzanne Balik, North Carolina State University
Julia I. Couto, Georgia Gwinnet College
Jeanne Douglas, University of Vermont
William E. Duncan, Louisiana State University
H. E. Dunsmore, Purdue University
Joseph D. Hurley, Texas A & M University
Dennis Kellermeier, Wright State University
Lorrie Lehman, University of North Carolina, Charlotte
Kathy Liszka, University of Akron
Mark Llewellyn, University of Central Florida
Hunter Lloyd, Montana State University
Blayne E. Mayfield, Oklahoma State University
Robert J. McGlinn, Southern Illinois University, Carbondale
Rodrigo A. Obando, Columbus State University
Kevin O'Gorman, California Polytechnic Institute of Technology
Rayno D. Niemi, Rochester Institute of Technology
Juan Pavón, Facultad de Informática
Cyndi Rader, Colorado School of Mines
Michael D. Scott, University of Texas at Austin
Harish Sethu, Drexel University
Monica Sweat, Georgia Institute of Technology
Bahram Zartoshty, California State University, Northridge

We also wish to thank the members of the academic administration at Stonehill College for their encouragement and support, especially Provost and Academic Vice President Katie Conboy, Dean Karen Talentino, and Dean Joseph Favazza.

Colleagues, friends, and students who helped us along our way include Ryan Amari, Tanya Berger-Wolf, Jennifer Burge, Kathy Conroy, Robert Dugan, Matthew Fuller, Thomas Gariepy, Michael Haney, Andrew Harmon, Matthew Hinds, Antonio "Thumbs" Martinez, Nan Mulford, Elizabeth Patterson, Annemarie Ryan, Bonnie Troupe, and Thomas Wall.

Our gratitude goes to our students at Stonehill College and to the participants in our NSF Java workshops. You have contributed to this book in ways great and small.

Our editorial, production, and marketing staff helped this book take shape and we thank them all: Alan Apt, Carrie Burger, Kevin Campbell, Bonnie Coakley, Edwin Durbin, Tammy Juran, Melissa Leick, Rebecca Olson, Curt Reynolds, Brenda Rolwes, Michael Ryder, Raghu Srinivasan, and most especially Lora Kalb-Neyens, who patiently guided us throughout the creation of this book.

Lastly, we thank our families, Kathryn Kalinak and Emily Bravaco, and Andrea, Zosh, Yair, and Yona Simonson, for their love, their encouragement, and their endless patience without which this book would not have been possible.

Java Programming

From the Ground Up

PART 1

The Fundamental Tools

CHAPTER 1

An Introduction to Computers and Java

"I think there is a world market for maybe five computers."
—Thomas Watson, IBM (1943)

"Computers in the future may weigh no more than 1.5 tons."
—Popular Mechanics (1949)

"There is no reason anyone would want a computer in their home."
—Ken Olson, Digital Equipment Corp (1977)

Objectives

The objectives of Chapter 1 include an understanding of

- the basic components of a computer system: hardware and software,
- high-level languages and compilation,
- Java's place among programming languages, and
- the concept of an algorithm.

1.1 INTRODUCTION

In 1946, the *ENIAC* (Electronic Numerical Integrator and Computer), weighing 30 tons and filling a 1000-square-foot room was the world's first electronic digital computer. Today, computers far more powerful than the ENIAC weigh just a few pounds and can fit inside a briefcase with room to spare. And, contrary to the predictions of yesteryear, computers are everywhere: in homes, offices, schools, bus terminals, bookstores, and even coffee shops and cafes. Is there anyone who hasn't used a word processor, sent email, or played a computer game? And who has not "googled" for some information? Today, computer usage is as common as driving a car, reading a book, or watching television. So what exactly *is* a computer? What's going on inside the "little box" that processes data so quickly? What are "bits and bytes"? What is a computer program? This chapter addresses such questions. We begin with a general overview of a computer system: both the hardware—the physical components of a computer—as well as the software—the programs that manipulate the hardware. We conclude with a discussion of programming languages, and in particular, the programming language Java. Software development using Java is the focus of this book. And, as you will see in subsequent chapters, Java is a very powerful programming language, easy to learn, and undeniably fun.

1.2 WHAT IS A COMPUTER?

A *computer* is a machine that performs computations, logical operations, or more generally, data manipulation according to some prescribed sequence of instructions called a *computer program*. The physical components of a computer are termed *hardware* and the programs *software*.

Hardware and software work in tandem to perform tasks as varied as word processing, playing chess, finding the fastest route to your destination, or even calculating π to three hundred and seventy-eight decimal places. Together the hardware and software comprise a *computer system*.

1.3 THE HARDWARE

Although computer hardware consists of many complex parts, the major hardware components are:

- the central processing unit (CPU),
- primary or random access memory (RAM),
- secondary or long-term memory, and
- input and output devices (I/O devices).

1.3.1 The Central Processing Unit

The CPU is the heart, muscle, and brain of the machine.

The CPU does the computing, the processing, the bulk of the work.
The most important components of the CPU are

- the arithmetic and logic unit (ALU),
- the control unit (CU), and
- the clock.

The ALU performs calculations, billions per second, and the CU controls or coordinates which calculations the ALU performs. If the ALU is the heart and muscle of the computer, pumping data throughout the system and tirelessly executing calculations, then the CU is the brain that directs or orchestrates the actions of the ALU according to a prepared script, that is, according to the instructions of a program.

The CPU clock, by sending electronic pulses throughout the system, determines how frequently the computer hardware executes instructions. A system's hardware components are synchronized with the clock. Every time the clock ticks, another hardware action occurs. Of course, the clock speed depends on the amount of time required by the slowest of the CPU's actions. This is called the *critical state* of the machine. Moving the clock any faster than the time needed for the critical state would cause the next action to occur too soon, before the data from the previous action would be processed. This would make the computer unpredictable and useless.

Speeding up the critical state in the hardware allows a system to utilize a faster clock. This can be accomplished by designing smaller and more efficient circuitry. During the past thirty years, clock speeds have increased from thousands of ticks per second to billions of ticks per second.

1.3.2 Primary or Random Access Memory

How Data Is Stored

Computers store data in binary format; that is, every piece of information, including characters, numbers, and even program instructions, is stored as a sequence of 0's and 1's or, as these two binary digits are commonly called, *bits*.

For example, a lowercase 'a' is represented by `1100001` and a 'b' is encoded as `1100010`. This particular encoding is used to identify a character's *ASCII code* (American Standard Code for Information Interchange). Every character that appears on your keyboard has its own 7-bit ASCII sequence or code. However, each character is typically stored using 8 bits, a leading 0 followed by the character's 7-bit ASCII code. Thus, character 'a' is stored as **0**`1100001`.

A sequence of eight bits is called a *byte*.

A long enough sequence of bytes can be used to store text of any size.

Like character data, every decimal number also has a binary representation. The decimal numbers 0 through 15 in binary format are:

0	`0`
1	`1`
2	`10`
3	`11`
4	`100`
5	`101`
6	`110`
7	`111`
8	`1000`
9	`1001`
10	`1010`
11	`1011`
12	`1100`
13	`1101`
14	`1110`
15	`1111`

Can you determine the binary representation for 16? 17? 18?

Binary numbers are not really very different than the ordinary base-10 or decimal numbers that you use every day. As you know, a number such as 1234 can be expressed as

1 thousand +

2 hundreds +

3 tens +

4 ones

That is,

$$\begin{aligned}1234 &= 1 \times 1000 + 2 \times 100 + 3 \times 10 + 4 \times 1\\ &= 1 \times \mathbf{10^3} + 2 \times \mathbf{10^2} + 3 \times \mathbf{10^1} + 4 \times \mathbf{10^0}.\end{aligned}$$

The binary number system works similarly except that the only allowable digits are 0 and 1 (rather than 0, 1, 2, 3, 4, 5, 6, 7, 8, and 9) and the base is not 10 but 2. Thus

$$\begin{aligned} \texttt{1101}_{\text{base 2}} &= 1 \times \mathbf{2^3} + 1 \times \mathbf{2^2} + 0 \times \mathbf{2^1} + 1 \times \mathbf{2^0} \\ &= 1 \times 8 + 1 \times 4 + 0 \times 2 + 1 \times 1 \\ &= 13_{\text{base 10}} \end{aligned}$$

In other words, the binary number `1101` is equivalent to the decimal number 13. If you do the arithmetic, you'll see that `10011010010` is the binary representation of the decimal number 1234.

Long sequences of numbers are used to represent audio, video, financial transactions, and many other forms of data. With enough bits, there is no limit to the number of songs, movies, or bank account transactions you can store. Indeed, since every character is encoded with an ASCII value between 0 and 127, text can also be considered a sequence of numbers.

Where Data Is Stored

When the CPU executes a program, the program instructions, along with relevant data, are stored in *primary memory*.

> Primary memory is also known as *random access memory* (RAM) because data may be retrieved or accessed in random, rather than sequential, order.

You can conceptualize RAM as a collection of storage cells or boxes, each capable of holding just a single byte of information. A unique number, or *memory address*, identifies each such storage cell. Figure 1.1 depicts a small portion of memory with addresses 1000, 1001, 1002, 1003, etc. Of course, in practice, these addresses are expressed as binary and not decimal numbers.

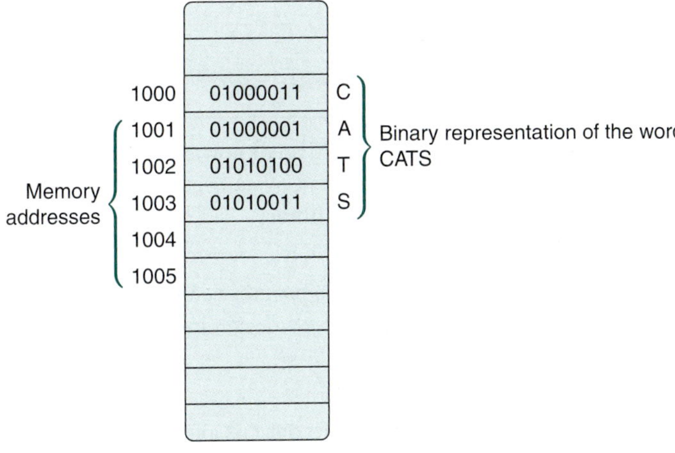

FIGURE 1.1 Primary memory

> Primary memory is *volatile*.

This means that shutting down your computer causes all data in primary memory to be erased. For example, when you work with a word processor, both the word processing program and your document are loaded into primary memory. If your computer shuts down before you have had a chance to save your work, your document may be lost forever. Long-term storage is achieved with secondary memory. When you save a document, it is saved in secondary memory.

1.3.3 Secondary Memory

Secondary memory is used for long-term or even permanent storage.

Secondary memory devices include hard disks, tapes, CDs, DVDs, and flash memory sticks. The programs that you use every day such as word processors, spreadsheets, and games are permanently stored on secondary storage devices.

Compared to RAM, secondary memory is, in general, cheaper (per bit), slower, larger, electro*mechanical* rather than electronic, and persistent: secondary memory devices do not lose their values when you turn off the computer.

Before executing a program, the CPU first copies the program instructions along with any necessary data from secondary memory to RAM. To execute the program, the instructions are fetched and executed one by one from RAM. Each instruction may be executed many thousands of times. Fetching data and instructions that are stored in electronic RAM is much faster than retrieving information from a mechanical device such as a hard disk.

1.3.4 Input/Output Devices

A computer communicates with a human user through input and output devices. Standard input devices are keyboards, mouses, joysticks, stylus pens, cameras, and microphones for audio input. Typical output devices include monitors, printers, and speakers.

1.4 THE SOFTWARE

The programs that run on a computer are collectively known as *software*. Word processors, Internet browsers, editors, database management systems, computer games, and spreadsheets are all part of your computer's software library.

When you turn on or boot your computer, a program called the *operating system* automatically runs. This special program provides an interface between you and your computer.

The operating system is the "concierge" of your computer. It manages the computer's resources and activities. If you wish to use your word processor or perhaps play solitaire, you inform the operating system, and the operating system carries out your request. If you'd like to erase or rename a file, you tell the operating system. Indeed, the operating system affects all the programs that run on a computer. Today, the most popular operating systems are Windows (various dialects), GNU-Linux, Unix variants, and MAC OS X.

You can buy many different types of software, but of course, you can create your own software, too. And doing so is precisely the topic of this book.

1.4.1 In the Beginning There Was Machine Language...

Each computer, or more specifically each CPU, executes instructions encoded in its own unique native *machine language*.

Moreover, each machine language instruction consists of a sequence of bits. For example, a hypothetical instruction for adding one number to another might have the form

```
10010010        00000001        00000001        10101101
```

Certainly, programming in machine language is both tedious and time-consuming. Machine languages tend to have instructions that operate at a level of detail too low to allow a programmer to keep perspective and maintain productivity. Furthermore, because each individual CPU understands only its own native machine language, proficiency in one machine language does not translate into proficiency in the language of another machine. Imagine trying to master a new binary-based language for each new CPU on the market!

In the early days of computers, machine language was the only option for programmers. However, in the 1960s, the first *high-level language*, FORTRAN, was invented, and no longer were programmers forced to devise programs with binary instructions. FORTRAN instructions use an English-like syntax. Today, hundreds of high-level languages are available, with dozens in mainstream use, including Fortran 2003, COBOL, Lisp, Visual BASIC, C, C++, C#, Java, Perl, Python, PHP, and Javascript.

A typical instruction coded in a high-level language, such as BASIC, might be

```
if income > 1000000 then
    print "You are rich!"
```

This is certainly more comprehensible than a sequence of bits, and easier to program.

Still, if each computer speaks but one language, its native machine language, how does a computer understand a Fortran 2003, BASIC, or C++ program? Before a program that is written in a high-level language can be executed on a particular computer, the program must be translated into the machine language of that computer.

Translation is the job of a program called a *compiler*.

You can think of the compiler as a black box that accepts a program written in a high-level language such as C++, the *source program*, and produces a translation into the *target* machine language. See Figure 1.2.

FIGURE 1.2 A compiler translates a C++ program into a machine language.

Once a compiler translates the source program into machine language, the machine's CPU can execute the resulting target program. A programmer can conveniently write just one program and translate it into several different machine languages. You need one compiler to translate your C++ program into a machine language for an Intel processor Windows machine, and another to translate it for a Mac that uses a PowerPC processor, but you write only one C++ program.

1.4.2 Then, Along Came Java

Java is a general-purpose language developed by Sun Microsystems in the early 1990s. Java was originally designed to program smart consumer electronic devices. Java's creators identified three main goals for their new language:

- Platform independence—Java programs should be capable of running on any computer.
- Security—Java programs should not be susceptible to hackers' code and dangerous viruses.
- Reliability—Java programs should not "crash."

Although Java was intended for use with consumer electronic devices, such devices did not become its destiny. Serendipitously, the Web provided Java with the perfect environment for the goals of platform independence, security, and reliability. Since its invention, Java has evolved into arguably the most important programming language for developing e-commerce and other Web-driven applications. Its application base is growing daily and includes dynamic Web-content generation with servlet technology, the building of business components with Enterprise JavaBeans, the creation of cross-platform user interfaces with Swing, and much more.

The Java Virtual Machine

In order to make Java a cross-platform programming language, Java's creative team designed an abstract computer implemented in software called the *Java Virtual Machine* (JVM). You cannot go to a store and buy a JVM computer. Instead you install software on your computer that *simulates* a JVM computer. The JVM is not a piece of hardware, but it pretends to be one. The machine language of the JVM is called *bytecode*. Java programs are first compiled into bytecode, and then executed.

Typically, the *Java interpreter*, which is part of the JVM, executes each bytecode instruction, one by one. However, to speed up execution, some versions of the JVM are equipped with a "just in time compiler" that compiles some bytecode directly to native machine code at runtime, that is, during execution. But regardless of how the JVM deals with the bytecode, the important point is that every Java program compiles into bytecode, the native language of the Java Virtual Machine. See Figure 1.3.

FIGURE 1.3 The JVM is a simulated computer that executes bytecode.

Bytecode provides an extra layer of abstraction between source code and execution. Once a Java program is translated into bytecode, the bytecode can run on any computer that has installed the JVM. A Java program needs to be compiled into bytecode just once. Proponents of Java often use the slogan "compile once, run anywhere."

The JVM allows every computer to act *as though* it were built to execute native bytecode. Therefore, once you compile a program into bytecode, it can be run on any machine with the JVM installed. The program never needs to be recompiled in order to run on a different machine. Behind the scenes, the JVM and bytecode are run in the native machine language of the target machine, but that is invisible to the programmer. Essentially, separate compilation for each machine is replaced by the flexibility of the JVM. Of course, this all works provided that the same version of the JVM is installed in each computer on which one intends to run the program.

How to Compile Java Programs

There are many different "integrated development environments" (IDEs), each complete with a slick graphical interface that facilitates the development of Java programs. Most of these IDEs provide:

- a text editor for writing programs,
- file browsing,
- a "debugger" that assists in finding program errors, and
- push-button compilation and execution.

Many of these systems such as Eclipse, JDEE, BlueJ, JGrasp, and Dr. Java are free. Because each IDE is very different, we restrict our discussion to Sun's bare bones compiler.

You do not need an IDE to write and run Java programs. If you prefer, you can write a program using *any* text editor, such as Notepad or Emacs, and compile your program with the Java Development Kit (JDK), which you can download free from Sun. Installation instructions are available on Sun's website.

The installation process places the Java compiler, javac.exe, in a newly created directory, unless you specify otherwise. In a Windows environment, the location of javac.exe is most likely

C:\Program Files\Java\jdk1.6.0_01\bin

(The version of the development kit (1.6.0_01) will probably be different, however.) If you do not know the location of the Java compiler, search for javac.exe.

Figure 1.4 shows the Windows directory C:\Program Files\Java\jdk1.6.0_01\bin, which includes the Java compiler, as well as a number of other programs that support Java.

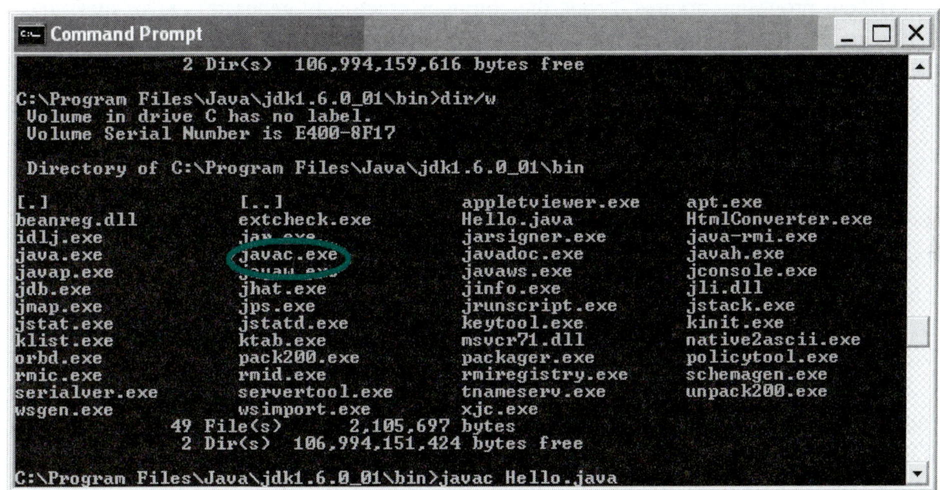

FIGURE 1.4 C:\Program Files\Java\jdk1.6.0_01\bin contains the compiler, *javac.exe.*

You can invoke the Java compiler from the command prompt with the directive

C:\Program Files\Java\jdk1.6.0_01\bin**javac**

Of course, using a fully qualified name becomes tiresome very quickly. To invoke the Java compiler from any directory with the one-word command javac, you must add the location of the Java compiler to the PATH variable of your machine. The PATH variable tells your system where to find the Java compiler. How you set the PATH variable depends on your system, and directions are readily available on the Web. If you do not set the PATH variable, you can still invoke the Java compiler with its fully qualified name. But surely, the one-word command javac is more appealing.

Once the Java Development Kit is installed, and the PATH variable set, you are ready to write and compile programs. At least in the beginning, it is a good idea to keep all of your Java programs in a folder named JavaPrograms, MyPrograms, JavaStuff, or some variation of that.

To create a program:

- Open a text editor, such as Notepad or Emacs.
- Type your program.
- Save the program in a file with a .java extension such as Hello.java or myProgram.java. (We discuss restrictions to the program name in Chapter 2.)
- Exit or minimize the text editor.

To compile the program:

- Open a command window. If you are running Windows:
  - click Start;
  - click Run;
  - in the text box that appears, type cmd;
  - click OK.
- Navigate to the directory where you have saved your program.
- Type the command

  javac *programName.java*,
  e.g., javac Hello.java or javac MyProgram.java.

If your program contains errors, the compiler graciously generates "error messages" indicating where the errors exist. In this case, you must reopen the program in the editor, fix the errors, save the program, and compile the program again. If the program has no errors, the compiler creates a *class file* using the same name as your program but with a .class extension, for example, Hello.class. This file contains the bytecode that runs on the Java Virtual Machine.

To run the program (execute the class file), type the command

java *programName*,

where *programName* is the name of your program, for example, java Hello. Notice that you do not include the .class extension. The java command executes the bytecode on the Java Virtual Machine.

A text editor along with the javac and java commands are all you need to compile and run Java programs. Nonetheless, most people rely on the convenience of an IDE. And most IDEs use Sun's compiler under the hood, so whether you click a button or type a command, you are most likely using the same compiler and building the same class file.

This book teaches you how to write and design Java programs. You are on your own to choose one of the myriad variety of systems that make compiling and debugging more convenient. Some IDEs are simple and some have a steep learning curve. There are many. The choice is yours.

1.5 PROGRAMMING AND ALGORITHMS

Mastery of a programming language such as Java is certainly a noble achievement that is part of a bigger picture that includes problem solving and the study of *algorithms*.

An *algorithm* is a finite, step-by-step procedure for accomplishing some task or solving a problem.

Algorithms are everywhere. Every time you query Google, a Web-mining algorithm runs; every time you use Mapquest for directions, a shortest-path algorithm runs; and every time you use a spell-checker, a string-searching algorithm runs. Creating correct and efficient algorithms is an art and a science, which takes both practice and creativity. Whether you need to calculate the average of five numbers, sort a list of two million names, or guide a rocket, an algorithm lurks in the background; the solution to your problem is an algorithm. The study of algorithms is a cornerstone of computer science.

A programming language is your tool, a tool that you can use to investigate and implement algorithms. With a programming language, such as Java, you can turn algorithms into programs so that a computer finds the average, sorts the list, or guides the rocket. Programs implement algorithms; programming makes algorithms come to life. As you work through the problems and exercises in this text, you will hone your problem-solving skills, design and implement your own algorithms, and, along the way, discover that programming with Java is fun.

1.6 IN CONCLUSION

In this chapter, you have seen the basic structure of a computer system: the hardware and the software. Just as the ENIAC has evolved into the powerful, easy-to-use personal computer of today, software has progressed from primitive machine language instructions to sophisticated, high-level programming languages such as Java. Hardware and software do not exist in isolation. A computer without software can do nothing. The remainder of this book deals with software development using Java. And, although we begin with the simplest of programs, by the end of the book you will be able to write applications that computer pioneers never dreamed of implementing.

Just the Facts

- A *computer* is a machine that performs computations, logical operations, and data manipulation according to some prescribed sequence of instructions called a *computer program*.
- The physical components of a computer are called *hardware*.
- The programs that run on a computer are called *software*.
- The *central processing unit* (*CPU*) is that part of the computer that performs most calculations and makes decisions.
- The *arithmetic and logic unit* (*ALU*) is the part of the CPU that performs arithmetical calculations.
- The *control unit* (*CU*) coordinates the calculations of the ALU and the movement of data between the CPU and RAM.
- The *clock* determines how frequently the computer hardware executes instructions.
- A computer stores data in *binary format*, i.e., as a sequence of 0's and 1's.
- A single 0 or 1 is called a *bit*; a sequence of eight bits is called a *byte*.

- *Primary* or *random access memory* (*RAM*) is composed of a collection of storage cells, each capable of holding one byte of information. Each cell has a unique numerical address.
- RAM is *volatile*; when the computer is turned off, all data in RAM is erased.
- Secondary memory is used for long-term or permanent storage. Retrieving data from secondary memory is slower than retrieving data from RAM.
- The *operating system* is a program that manages all the resources of a computer. All requests such as running a program, deleting a file, and printing a document are made through the operating system.
- Each CPU understands just a single language, its unique native machine language. Machine language programs are written in binary format.
- A program written in a high-level language, such as C or BASIC, cannot run on a computer until the program is translated into that computer's machine language. A program that does this translation is called a *compiler*.
- The *Java Virtual Machine* (*JVM*) is a simulated computer that is implemented in software. The machine language of the JVM is called *bytecode*. Once the Java compiler translates a program into bytecode, the bytecode can run on any computer that has installed the JVM.
- At minimum, to write, compile, and run a Java program you need a text editor, the JVM, a terminal window, and a command line. However, there are also many full-featured IDEs (integrated development environments) that facilitate the writing, compiling, execution, and debugging of Java programs.
- Downloading the newest version of JDK (Java Development Kit) from Sun is the way to get the complete functionality of the JVM. A subset of JDK called JRE (Java Runtime Environment) allows you to execute bytecode but not to compile your own programs.
- An *algorithm* is a step-by-step procedure for solving a problem. A computer program implements an algorithm so that a computer can accomplish the procedure.

EXERCISES

LEARN THE LINGO

Test your knowledge of the chapter's vocabulary by completing the following crossword puzzle.

Across

2 1111 in decimal (word)
4 101 in decimal (word)
7 Memory cells are identified by a unique ________.
9 One of the first computers
11 Invokes the Java compiler
15 Performs arithmetical calculations
16 Abstract computer implemented in software
17 Step-by-step procedure for solving a problem
20 Primary memory is electronic, secondary memory is ________.
23 Long-term memory
27 Interface between the user and the computer
29 Computer programs
30 Primary memory is ________ (two words) memory.

Down

1 RAM is ________: when the computer is turned off, all memory is erased.
3 First high-level language
5 A sophisticated system for writing and compiling programs
6 Physical components of a computer
8 The "brain" of a computer
10 Translates a program into native code
12 Output device
13 A binary digit
14 Primary memory
18 Each computer speaks a unique ________ language.
19 Computers store data in ________ format.
21 Determines how fast hardware executes instructions
22 Java programs are compiled into ________.
24 Eight bits
25 Secondary memory device
26 The Java compiler creates a file with a .________ extension.
28 Input device

SHORT EXERCISES

1. **True or False**
   If false, give an explanation.
   a. Retrieving data from RAM usually takes more time than retrieving data from a hard drive.
   b. The ALU performs arithmetical calculations.
   c. Primary memory (RAM) is addressable in units of one bit.
   d. The clock speed of a computer has nothing to do with how fast programs execute.
   e. The CU determines the next instruction that executes.
   f. An operating system is a fundamental part of the hardware of a computer.
   g. Executing the same C++ program on two machines with different CPUs requires two compilers.
   h. Bytecode is the native language of most Windows machines.
   i. Java is compiled directly to a machine's native language, and then translated line by line to bytecode.
   j. Any computer you purchase can execute Java bytecode without any special downloading of software.

2. **Binary to Decimal**
   Convert each of the following binary numbers to its decimal equivalent.
   a. `10101`
   b. `00101`
   c. `100100101`

3. **Decimal to Binary**
   Determine the binary representation of
   a. `128`
   b. `235`
   c. `66`

4. **Adding and Multiplying in Binary**
   When does 1 + 1 = 10? When you are adding binary numbers. Addition of binary numbers is much the same as with decimal numbers. For example, decimal numbers 23 and 15 in binary format are 10111 and 01111, and their sum is calculated as

```
  10111
 +01111
 ------
 100110
```

   As you see, sums are simple as long as you remember to carry a 1 whenever you add 1 + 1. Multiplication is just as simple:

```
     10111
     01111
     -----
     10111
    10111
   10111
  10111
 00000
 ---------
 101011001
```

   Find the following binary sums and products:
   a. `11111 + 00001`
   b. `101010101 + 010101011`

c. `111100011101 + 01001011111`
d. `(111) × (101)`
e. `(1010) × (0101)`
f. `(11111) × (11111)`

5. **Octal and Hexadecimal Numbers**
Octal numbers use 8 as a base and digits 0, 1, 2, 3, 4, 5, 6, and 7. Hexadecimal numbers use 16 as a base and digits 0, 1, 2, 3, 4, 5, 6, 7, 8, 9, A, B, C, D, E, and F. Conversions between binary and octal numbers can be done easily three bits at a time. Conversions between binary and hexadecimal numbers can be accomplished quickly four bits at a time. There is no need to make any interim conversions to decimal numbers. For example, 76 hexadecimal equals the binary number 0111 0110, because 7 is 0111 and 6 is 0110. There is no need to first convert 76 hexadecimal to its decimal equivalent 118 and then back to binary.

Calculate the following:

a. the decimal equivalent of the octal number `3427`
b. the octal equivalent of the binary number `100100101`
c. the hexadecimal equivalent of the binary number `00011010111101011001`
d. the binary equivalent of the hexadecimal number `A03`

6. **ASCII Encoding**
The ASCII code for uppercase 'A' is `01000001` (decimal 65); the code for 'B' is `01000010` (decimal 66); for 'C' it is `01000011` (decimal 67), etc.
Decode the following sequence of nine bytes.
`010010100100000101010110010000010100100101010011010001100101010101001110`

7. **Encoding Opcodes**
One part of a machine language instruction is the opcode (Operation Code). A typical opcode might signify the "Add" operation, another "Subtract," and another "Exit." If there are typically 120 different opcodes and each opcode is represented by a string of bits, how many bits are required to uniquely encode or represent each opcode?

8. **Java Translation**
Choose your favorite IDE, and investigate how it executes bytecode on your computer. For example, does it execute the bytecode directly, or does it translate bytecode into machine code using a JIT compiler?

9. **Compilers**
What distinguishes a high-level programming language from machine language?

10. **Assembly Language**
Assembly language is a low-level language like machine language. Do a little research and describe the format and purpose of assembly language. How does assembly language differ from machine language?

11. **Compile Once, Run Anywhere**
Does the Java slogan "compile once, run anywhere" come with any "fine print?" Explain exactly what this phrase means.

12. **Bytecode**
Programs written in a language such as C++ are compiled directly into the machine language of a particular computer. Java programs are first compiled into bytecode and then interpreted by the JVM. What are the disadvantages and advantages of using Java versus C++ with respect to compilation and execution times?

THE BIGGER PICTURE

1. MACHINE LANGUAGE AND COMPUTER ARCHITECTURE

The following equation is commonly used for expressing a computer's performance ability:

$$\frac{\text{time}}{\text{program}} = \frac{\text{time}}{\text{cycle}} \times \frac{\text{cycles}}{\text{instruction}} \times \frac{\text{instructions}}{\text{program}}$$

This equation means that the time necessary to run a program equals the time it takes for the CPU clock to tick once (time/cycle), times the number of different hardware steps required to perform an instruction (cycles/instruction), times the number of instructions in the program (instructions/program). Each of these values depends on the machine language and the computer's CPU design (or architecture).

Two major competing paradigms in CPU design are *reduced instruction set computer* (RISC) and *complex instruction set computer* (CISC)[1]. The CISC approach creates a machine language with complex instructions. For example, a single instruction might be sufficient to add the contents of two memory locations and store the result in a third. The same action in a RISC language might take four separate instructions: two to move the data from memory (RAM) to the CPU, one to add them in the ALU, and one to move the answer back to RAM. However, the single CISC instruction might take 21 clock cycles, while each of the four RISC instructions use just five clock cycles, for a total of only 20 cycles.

In general, CISC machines tend to minimize the number of instructions per program, sacrificing the number of cycles per instruction, while RISC machines do the opposite, reducing the cycles per instruction at the cost of the number of instructions per program. The clock in RISC machines tends to be faster than the clock in CISC machines because the RISC hardware is simpler.

Exercises

1. A program that compiles into 2,000,000 machine language instructions on a CISC computer requires 7,000,000 instructions on a RISC computer. The clock on the RISC computer ticks 3,000,000,000 times each second, and the clock on the CISC machine ticks 2,400,000,000 each second. The average cycles/instruction on the CISC computer is 12.5, and the average cycles/instruction on the RISC machine is 4.8. How much time does it take to run the program on each machine? Which machine runs your program faster?
2. A CPU architect is able to increase the clock speed on the RISC machine to 3,300,000,000 cycles per second, while keeping the average cycles/instruction at 4.8, but at the cost of increasing the number of instructions to 7,100,000. How much time does it take to run the program on each machine? Which machine runs your program faster?

2. ALGORITHMS

An algorithm is a step-by-step procedure for solving a problem. The following algorithm describes a procedure that converts a decimal number to a binary number. The binary number is computed from right to left. That is, the rightmost bit is written down first.

Let x be a positive decimal number.

Repeat the following steps until x has the value zero:

1. If x is even, then write down 0, otherwise write down 1.
2. Change the value of x to $x/2$, dropping the remainder, if necessary.

Let's look at this algorithm in action when $x = 17$.

$x = 17$
17 is odd, so write `1`.
Divide 17 by 2 and drop the remainder; x is now 8.
8 is even, so write `0`.
Divide 8 by 2; x is now 4.
4 is even, so write `0`.
Divide 4 by 2; x is now 2.
2 is even, so write `0`.
Divide 2 by 2; x is now 1.
1 is odd, so write 1.
Divide 1 by 2, drop the remainder; x is now 0.
Because x is 0, stop.
The final binary number is: `10001`.

Discovering and testing new algorithms is an important part of computer science, but it is a separate skill from learning how to implement an algorithm in Java. In upcoming chapters, you will learn how to turn a simple algorithm like this into a Java program. You may not have been able to discover this algorithm yourself, and even now that you have seen the algorithm, it may not be obvious why it works. Nonetheless, you can still explore some simpler algorithms such as those described in the following two exercises.

Exercises

1. Write an algorithm to convert a binary number into a decimal number.
2. The ASCII values for the digits 0–9 are 48–57, respectively. Write an algorithm that, given a positive integer x, constructs a sequence of values in the range 48–57, representing the ASCII values of the digits of x. For example, if $x = 104$, the resulting sequence is 49 48 52, since the ASCII values for 1, 0, and 4 are 49, 48, and 52, respectively.

3. STORING INTEGERS

This section describes how Java represents and stores negative numbers using bits. After reading this section, you may wonder whether any of this material is really essential to a Java programmer. A beginner can certainly get by without much behind-the-scenes knowledge, but as you gain experience as a programmer, you will find that a deeper understanding of how Java works is crucial. For example, a program that correctly encodes credit card numbers requires a thorough understanding of arithmetic overflow and number representations. This section introduces the basics.

Base 10 Numbers

In olden days everyone knows,
Folks would count on their fingers and toes.
They'd get up to twenty,
Then, twenty was plenty.
"Now, heaven knows, anything goes."

Mathematical folklore postulates that the base-10 number system which came about during the Renaissance found favor because humans possess just ten fingers for counting. Fact or fiction, we use exactly ten digits (0–9) to signify any decimal or base-10 number.

The first ten non-negative integers require just one digit: 0, 1, 2, 3, 4, 5, 6, 7, 8, or 9. Next, we add a *tens column*, put a 1 in it, and get the integer 10. You are probably so familiar with decimal numbers that you rarely notice the 10s, 100s, and 1000s columns. You know implicitly that the number 6123 consists of 6 thousands plus 1 hundred plus 2 tens plus 3 ones:

$$\begin{aligned} 6123 &= (6 \times 1000) + (1 \times 100) + (2 \times 10) + (3 \times 1) \\ &= (6 \times 10^3) + (1 \times 10^2) + (2 \times 10^1) + (3 \times 10^0) \end{aligned}$$

Unsigned Numbers

As you have read in this chapter, a computer stores integers as binary numbers. Unlike a base-10 system that requires ten symbols (0–9), a binary system needs just two: 0 and 1. In contrast to the columns of a decimal system, the column values of a binary system (right to left) have place values that are powers of 2: 1, 2, 4, 8, 16, 32, 64, 128, and so on. Thus the binary number 1111011, which is 123 in the decimal system, consists of:

1 sixty-four *plus* 1 thirty-two *plus* 1 sixteen *plus* 1 eight *plus* 0 fours *plus* 1 two *plus* 1 one.

Exercises

1. Write 37 in binary.
2. Write 137 in binary.
3. What is the value of 100110 in decimal?
4. What is the value of 100111 in decimal?
5. What happens to the value of a binary number when you append a zero to the right end?
6. What happens to the value of a binary number when you append a one to the right end?

Using a single bit you can form just two binary numbers, 0 and 1 with two bits, there are four binary numbers, 00, 01, 10, and 11, and with three bits there are eight, 000, 001, 010, 011, 100, 101, 110, and 111. With every additional column, the number of binary integers doubles. For example, the four two-bit numbers are:

```
00
01
10
11
```

To construct all three-bit binary numbers, prefix each two-bit number with a 0 and also with a 1, in effect doubling the number of possible binary numbers and giving eight bit patterns:

```
000   100
001   101
010   110
011   111
```

To construct all four-bit numbers, add 0 to the left of every three-bit number, and do likewise with 1, yielding 16 binary numbers with four bits:

```
0000   0100   1000   1100
0001   0101   1001   1101
0010   0110   1010   1110
0011   0111   1011   1111
```

These last numbers represent the positive values 0 through 15 ($2^4 - 1$). In general, n bits can store positive numbers in the range 0 through $2^n - 1$ inclusive. Such binary numbers, because they have positive values, are called *unsigned* numbers.

Exercises

7. The smallest unit of "addressable memory" in a computer is a collection of 8 bits, called a byte. How many different binary numbers are possible using 8 bits?
8. What is the largest unsigned number you can represent with 8 bits?
9. What is the range of values for a 7-bit ASCII code?
10. How many binary numbers can you create using 16 bits (two bytes)?
11. What is the largest unsigned number (in decimal) that you can make with 16 bits?
12. The largest unit of addressable memory in a computer is 32 bits (four bytes). How many binary numbers are possible using four bytes?

Negative Numbers and Two's Complement

You have probably noticed that we have not discussed negative numbers. How then are negative numbers expressed in a binary number system? Java uses a system of representation called *two's complement*. In a two's complement scheme, half the bit patterns of an integer represent positive numbers; the other half signify negative numbers. If a number begins with zero, the number is positive, and if a number starts with one, then it is negative. The leftmost bit is called the *sign bit*. For example, the byte 00010011, as you would expect, is equivalent to the decimal number 19 ($16 + 2 + 1 = 19$). The sign bit is 0, so the number is positive. However, the number 10010011, with a leading 1, is not equivalent to −19. It actually corresponds to −109. How does this work?

To simplify the discussion, we consider three-bit numbers. As you know there are 8 such binary numbers. Figure 1.5 shows both the unsigned decimal (no sign bit) value and the two's complement decimal value of each bit pattern. That is, a pattern of bits is interpreted two different ways.

Bit pattern	Decimal Value Unsigned representation No sign bit	Decimal Value Two's complement representation Left bit is sign bit
`000`	0	0
`001`	1	1
`010`	2	2
`011`	3	3
`100`	4	−4
`101`	5	−3
`110`	6	−2
`111`	7	−1

FIGURE 1.5 Three-bit number representations: unsigned and two's complement

We focus on the negative numbers. Notice that binary number `101` is both the two's complement representation of –3 and also the *unsigned* binary representation of 5. In general, the two's complement version of the 3-bit *negative* number $-x$ is the same as the unsigned binary representation of $8 - x$. So the bit pattern for −1, in the two's complement world, is the same as the unsigned bit pattern for $8 - 1 = 7$, and that's `111`; the two's complement representation for -2 is the unsigned pattern for $8 - 2 = 6$, which is `110`.

Let's generalize to bytes. A byte consists of 8 bits, and there is a total of $2^8 = 256$ different bit patterns. Therefore, byte-sized two's complement binary numbers can represent 128 non-negative numbers (0 to 127) and 128 negative numbers (-128 to -1). The negative number $-x$ has the same bit pattern as the unsigned representation of $256 - x$. Thus, a two's complement system stores -109 as `10010011` because $256 - 109 = 147$, which as an unsigned binary number is `10010011`.

We have discussed two's complement as a method for signifying negative numbers. That is so. It is also an *operation* that you can perform on a binary number. Indeed, performing two's complement on a binary number is the operation of negation.

The *two's complement* of any unsigned n-bit number x is $2^n - x$.

For example, to compute the two's complement of `011` (3 decimal): compute $8 - 3 = 5$ or `101`, which we saw is also, the two's complement representation of –3. Symmetrically, the two's complement of `101` is $8 - 5$, and that is `011`. Thus, the two's complement operation on `011` (3 decimal) gives `101` (-3) and the two's complement of `101` (-3) yields `011` (3). Computing a number's two's complement is akin to multiplication by -1, i.e., the two's complement operation is negation.

Figure 1.6 shows the results of the two's complement operation of each three-bit number.

Bit pattern	Result of the two's complement operation
000	000
001	111
010	110
011	101
100	100
101	011
110	010
111	001

FIGURE 1.6 Two's complement operation

There is a simpler method for calculating the two's complement of an n-bit number. Just toggle all the bits (change `0`'s to `1`'s and `1`'s to `0`'s) and add 1. For example,

the two's complement of `101` is `010 + 1 = 011`, and
the two's complement of `011` is `100 + 1 = 101`.

And, the two's complement of `10101010` is `01010101 + 1 = 01010111`.

You can understand this trick by once again considering the case of 3-bit numbers. First notice that toggling the bits of x is the same as subtracting x from 7 (111). For example,

```
 111            111
-101    and    -011
 010            100
```

Subtracting from 7 and then adding 1 is no different than subtracting from 8, which is what we have been doing all along in the previous examples.

Java uses two's complement representation for all integers.

Other languages such as C++ allow you to specify whether or not an integer is two's complement or unsigned. An unsigned byte value ranges from 0 through 256. The unsigned byte `10010011` is equivalent to decimal 147, but as you know, `10010011` is the two's complement representation of −109. The byte has different values depending on whether the language considers it unsigned or two's complement. There are applications such as cryptography where unsigned integers are necessary, and this lack of flexibility in Java forces some awkward code to simulate unsigned integers.

Exercises

13. Using two's complement representation, what is the decimal value of the byte `11101110`?

14. Assume that a system stores all integers as bytes using two's complement representation. What is the value of 1 + 127?

15. Using two's complement representation, what is the decimal value of the 16-bit integer `1111110111111101`?

16. Using two's complement, what range of integers can be represented with 16 bits? 32 bits? 64 bits?

17. What is the two's complement of the two's complement of x?

18. What are the decimal values of the following 32-bit, two's complement integers: `11111111111111111111111101011100` and `00000000000000000000000010001111`?

Why Two's Complement?

There are other ways to represent negative integers besides two's complement. A much simpler method uses the leftmost bit to signify the sign of the number and the remaining bits to indicate the magnitude of the number. This method is called *sign-magnitude*. For positive numbers, sign-magnitude representation is the same as two's complement, but for negative numbers it's different. For example, `10010011` = −19 in sign-magnitude and −109 in two's complement. Why choose one method over the other?

Although there are circumstances where sign-magnitude representation is preferable (multiplication circuitry), it is safe to say that the standard representation of negative integers in a computer is two's complement. And two's complement is the representation that Java uses.

There is a very important reason why Java uses two's complement representation for negative integers. A *carry-lookahead adder* is a circuit that that performs addition in a computer. Surprisingly, this same circuit does subtraction! Using two's complement representation allows the adder to do both addition and subtraction. There is no need to design a separate circuit to perform subtraction.

Addition of binary numbers is no different than addition of decimal numbers except that a carry occurs with a sum of 2 or more rather than a sum of 10 or more. Just remember `1 + 1 = 10`. For example, adding `1101 + 1101` is performed as

```
Carry →   1 1
          1101
         +1101
         11010
```

Here is how to do binary subtraction using addition. We use one byte for each number. You can verify that the binary form of 108 is `01101100` and that `00000011` signifies 3. We calculate `01101100 - 00000011`, i.e., 108 − 3.

THE BIGGER PICTURE

The calculation is simple: negate 0000001 and add. As you know, the two's complement operation is really negation. So, the two's complement of `00000011` is `11111100 + 1 = 11111101`. Thus `01101100 - 00000011` is:

```
 01101100
+11111101
101101001
```

If you ignore the leftmost bit, the remaining bits give the correct answer `01101001`, which is equivalent to 105.

Ignoring the leftmost 1 is automatic in a computer because if there is no room to store the leftmost bit, it just disappears. Similarly, to subtract `00000111 - 00000011` (7 − 3):

a. Compute the two's complement of `00000011`: `11111100 + 1 = 11111101`.
b. Add: `00000111 + 11111101 = 100000100`. (Notice that there are nine bits.)
c. Drop the leftmost bit, giving `00000100`, which is equivalent to 4.

In the following exercises, we ask you to investigate this method of subtraction.

Exercises

19. Assuming 8-bit two's complement integers, compute the binary subtraction `01100011 - 00011000` by adding the two's complement of `00011000` to `01100011`. Verify the calculation in base 10. Assuming 16-bit two's complement integers, add the two values `1001000000001011 + 0110100010010111` and write down the binary result. Verify that the result is correct by converting the values to decimal. What subtraction is being done by this "addition"?

20. The *ten's complement* of an n-bit decimal number x is defined to be $10^n - x$. For example, the ten's complement of 198 is $10^3 - 198 = 802$. A fast way to calculate the ten's complement of 198 is to subtract 198 from 999 and then add 1. Subtracting from 999 is easy because for every digit i that you subtract, each resulting digit is simply $9 - i$. Calculate the ten's complement of 1872, 192, 981652, and 19734.

21. Let's do decimal subtraction using just addition. To subtract 198 from 217, simply add the ten's complement of 198 to 217. Why does this work? Recall that the ten's complement of 198 is $1000 - 198$. Therefore, adding the ten's complement of 198 to 217 gives $1000 - 198 + 217 = 1000 + 217 - 198 = 1019$. This answer is exactly 1000 too high, so by ignoring the extra 1 in the fourth column, we get the correct answer of 19.

a. Compute $78612 - 12832$ by adding the ten's complement of 12832 to 78612.

b. Compute $8012 - 2318$ by adding the ten's complement of 2318 to 8012.

---

[1]See David A. Patterson and John L. Hennessy, *Computer Organization and Design : The Hardware/Software Interface*. Morgan Kaufmann Publisher, Third Edition, 2007.

CHAPTER 2

Expressions and Data Types

"Can you do addition?" the White Queen asked. "What's one and one and one and one and one and one and one and one and one and one?" "I don't know," said Alice. "I lost count."

—Lewis Carroll

Objectives

The objectives of Chapter 2 include an understanding of

- simple Java programs that utilize print and println,
- Java style comments,
- string literals,
- primitive data types: char, int, double, and boolean,
- numerical, relational, and boolean operators,
- operator precedence,
- expressions composed of primitive data types, and
- expressions that mix data types.

2.1 INTRODUCTION

A *computer program* or *application* is a set of instructions, written in a programming language that enables a computer to perform some specified task.

An application can play championship chess, control interplanetary probes, manage the tunes on your iPod, or navigate the Internet. This chapter does not teach you how to write a chess-playing program or even how to design a simple application that balances your checkbook. In this chapter, our goals are more modest: you will learn how to display text on your computer's screen and also how to instruct a computer to perform simple arithmetic calculations. "Everything comes gradually and at its appointed hour."—Ovid

2.2 IN THE BEGINNING . . .

We begin our discussion with the simplest of examples: an application that displays a single line of text.

EXAMPLE 2.1 **Problem Statement** Write a program that displays the line of text

Peter Piper picked apart a pithy program

Java Solution

```
1. // This application prints "Peter Piper picked apart a pithy program." on the screen
2. public class TongueTwister
3. {
4.     public static void main(String[] args)
5.     {
6.         System.out.println ("Peter Piper picked apart a pithy program.");
7.     }
8. }
```

Output

Peter Piper picked apart a pithy program.

Discussion Taking a cue from Peter, let's pick apart the program and analyze it, line by line. Line numbers are not part of a Java program and appear only for reference.

Line 1

Line 1 is a *comment*.

> Programmers use *comments* to explain or clarify the meaning of some section of a program.

This program is not complicated. Even a novice programmer would understand its purpose without the comment. With more complex and intricate programs, comments are extremely important for explaining the programmer's intentions. Since programs are continually updated or changed, well-written, succinct comments can save a programmer many hours of frustration. Comments are optional in the sense that they are not required to make the program work correctly, but stylistically, they are mandatory. Comments may be placed anywhere within a Java program. As your programs become increasingly more complex, you will see that well-placed comments can save you programming time and improve the readability and clarity of your programs.

> A *single-line comment* begins with the compound symbol // (two forward slashes) and continues until the end of the line.

The text of the comment is not executable and is ignored by the compiler. Once the compiler recognizes the beginning of a single-line comment, the compiler skips all subsequent text on that line. A comment may begin anywhere on a line. Line 1 is a single-line comment.

Java also provides *multi-line comments*. A multi-line comment begins with the compound symbol /* and ends with the compound symbol */. Between these markers you may include any text whatsoever—except another multi-line comment symbol.

The compiler ignores all text between these two symbols. Consequently, if you forget to "close" or terminate a multi-line comment, parts of your program might be ignored. Here is the program of Example 2.1 rewritten with a multi-line comment.

```
/* This application prints the sentence
"Peter Piper picked apart a pithy program."
on the screen */

public class TongueTwister
{
   public static void main (String[] args)
   {
      System.out.println ("Peter Piper picked apart a pithy program.")
   }
}
```

Line 2

Line 2 begins with two special words—public and class—that you will see over and over again. In later chapters, these words will have greater meaning for you. For the present, it is more convenient to just remember that all of your programs must begin with these two words. In fact, you might think of "public class" as synonymous with "program." This is indeed a gross simplification, and soon you will see that a program or application usually consists of many "classes," public or otherwise. For now, each of our applications consists of a single named class. The third word on line 2, TongueTwister, is the name of the class. Although the programmer chooses the class name, that name must be a *valid Java identifier*.

A *valid Java identifier* is a "word" of arbitrary length composed of letters and/or digits and/or two special characters $ (dollar sign) and _ (underscore), where the first character must be a letter.

For example, R2D2, HarryPotter, and MyProgram are valid Java identifiers. Hamlet is a valid identifier but 2BorNot2B is not.

Java is case sensitive. The name TongueTwister is considered different than tonguetwister and TONGUEtwister. Also, Java assigns special meanings to certain words and, as such, these words may not be used as Java identifiers. Such words are called *keywords* or *reserved words*. The words public and class are keywords. A list of Java keywords is shown in Figure 2.1. Finally, the words true, false, and null, although not keywords, have very specific meanings in Java and may not be chosen as identifiers.

abstract	continue	for	new	switch	assert	default	goto	package	synchronized
boolean	do	if	private	this	break	double	implements	protected	throw
byte	else	import	public	throws	case	enum	instanceof	return	transient
catch	extends	int	short	try	char	final	interface	static	void
class	finally	long	strictfp	volatile	const	float	native	super	while

FIGURE 2.1 Java keywords

By convention, a *class* name begins with an uppercase letter.

Because spaces may not be part of a name, uppercase letters are commonly used to separate "words" within a name. Some class names that follow these practices are TongueTwister, MyProgram, or TweedledumAndTweedledee. This style is called *camelCase*, because of the "bumps" in the middle of the word, suggestive of the humps on a camel.

Lines 3 and 8

The curly braces "{" and "}" on lines 3 and 8 mark the beginning and the end of the TongueTwister class that comprises our application.

A group of statements or instructions enclosed by curly braces is called *a block.*

The body or executable section of a class is contained within these matching braces. Thus, the general structure of a class is:

```
public class ProgramName
{
    // class body
    //This class body is a block

}
```

where *ProgramName* is a valid Java identifier. Again, an application usually consists of one or more classes.

Lines 4, 5, 7

The line

```
public static void main ( String[] args)
```

is certainly a mouthful of Java-speak. This line is the first line or the heading of the class's main method.

Generally speaking, a *method* is a section of a class that performs a task.

More specifically, a method consists of a *named* list of statements that a program carries out or *executes*. You might think of a statement as an instruction or a directive. A method might contain a single statement or several dozen. Although the sample program has but a single method (named main), a more complicated class usually has many methods, each with its own name. The main method, however, is special among methods.

When a Java program starts, the main method is automatically executed. That is, the statements of the main method are executed first. The main method is the starting point of every program.

Consequently, every application must have a main method. And every main method begins with the same (albeit, for now, mysterious) first line.

The curly braces of lines 5 and 7 mark the beginning and the end of the main method. The actions that the main method performs are included between these curly braces.

Thus far, a Java program has the following skeletal format:

```
public class ProgramName
{
        public static void main (String args [])
        {
              // executable statements go here
        }
}
```

Notice that we have aligned the matching braces of a block and indented statements within matched braces. This program format is a matter of style and not syntax. The application would run even if it were typed on a single line.

Another common style of program layout is

```
public class ProgramName  {
      public static void main (String[] args){
         // executable statements go here
      }
}
```

However, the programs in this text use the first style, which aligns matching pairs of curly braces.

Line 6
Line 6 is the only statement or instruction of the main method. The statement

```
System.out.println ("Peter Piper picked apart a pithy program");
```

instructs the computer to print Peter Piper picked apart a pithy program on the screen. The quoted text ("Peter Piper picked apart a pithy program") is called a *string literal* or more simply a *string*. A string literal must be contained on a single line. The quotation marks are not part of the string literal. The quotation marks indicate the beginning and the end of the string.

The statement

```
System.out.println ("Peter Piper picked apart a pithy program.");
```

instructs the computer to display the string literal on the screen. The statement also prints the *newline* character, that is, it advances the cursor to the next line. Printing the newline character ensures that the next item that is printed begins on a new line. Printing the newline character is akin to pressing the Enter key.

> The *newline* character causes the cursor to advance to the start of the next line.

The words (and periods) System.out.println will become more meaningful in subsequent chapters. But, for the present, you should accept System.out.println (or simply println) as the instruction that prints text followed by the newline character. The word println is actually the name of a method that Java provides for output. We refer to the string supplied to this println method as an *argument*. That is, "Peter Piper picked apart a pithy program." is an argument supplied to the println method. Previously, we stated that a method performs a task. Specifically, the task of the println method is to print its argument.

You will notice a semicolon at the end of the statement in line 6.

Java dictates that all statements are terminated with a semicolon. The semicolon is not optional. Forgetting semicolons is often the bane of beginning programmers.

Finally, the program *must* be saved in a file named TongueTwister.java. In general, if a class name is ClassName, you must save the class in a file called ClassName.java.

The application of Example 2.1 displays a string. At this point some questions about strings may come to mind. If quotation marks are used to indicate the beginning and the end of a string literal, can a string contain a quotation mark? How does an application print the string

"Oh, so they have Internet on computers now!" exclaimed Homer Simpson

with its two quotation marks?

The erroneous statement

```
System.out.println (" " Oh, so they have Internet on computers now! "exclaimed
Homer Simpson ");
```

does not do the job. The second quotation mark within the string falsely signals the end of the string, and results in a syntax error. The Java solution is simple. To include quotation marks within a string literal, use the *escape sequence*, \" (backslash, quote) as in the following Java statement:

```
System.out.println (" \" Oh, so they have Internet on computers now! \" exclaimed
Homer Simpson ");
```

The previous statement produces the following output:

"Oh, so they have Internet on computers now! " exclaimed Homer Simpson

The print method is a variation of println. The next example illustrates the single difference between these two methods.

EXAMPLE 2.2 **Problem Statement** Using print rather than println, write a program that displays the sentence

Peter Piper picked apart a pithy program.

Java Solution

```
// This program prints the sentence "Peter Piper picked apart a pithy program." on the screen

public class AnotherTongueTwister
{
    public static void main( String[] args)
    {
```

```
        System.out.print ("Peter Piper picked apart  ");  // print NOT println
        System.out.print ("a pithy program.");
    }
}
```

Output

Peter Piper picked apart a pithy program.

Discussion The application has two statements within the main method. Notice that these statements are of the form

System.out.**print**

rather than

System.out.print**ln**

Here, unlike the println method of Example 2.1, the statement

System.out.print ("Peter Piper picked apart ");

does *not* print the newline character following the string literal. Consequently, the program's output is

Peter Piper picked apart a pithy program.

Both string literals appear on a single line. The two strings are displayed next to each other. No newline characters are generated.

Here is one final example that uses both System.out.println and System.out.print.

EXAMPLE 2.3

Blaise Pascal (1623–1662) is often credited with the design of one of the first "computers." Pascal's computer, actually a calculating machine constructed of cogs, gears, and wheels, was capable of addition and multiplication. Subtraction and division could be accomplished only through a rather tedious and indirect method. The following program displays a little bit of that computer history. Program output is produced on four separate lines. Notice the use of both print and println.

Java Solution

```
public class ComputerHistory
{
    public static void main(String[] args)
    {
        System.out.print ("A guy named Pascal had a scheme");
        System.out.println();                    // prints the newline character
        System.out.print ("For building an adding machine");
        System.out.println();
        System.out.print ("        Too bad, his contraption");
        System.out.println();
        System.out.print ("        Could not do subtraction");
        System.out.println();
        System.out.print ("Subtraction remained just a dream ");
        System.out.println();
    }
}
```

Output

A guy named Pascal had a scheme
For building an adding machine
    Too bad, his contraption
    Could not do subtraction
Subtraction remained just a dream.

Discussion As you know, output from the statement, System.out.print("...") does *not* include a newline character. However, System.out.println() outputs the newline character and only the newline character. No string argument is supplied to println, so no string is printed.

2.3 DATA TYPES AND EXPRESSIONS

Although displaying tongue twisters and limericks might be momentarily intriguing, the fascination wears thin rather quickly. So, let's move ahead to applications that actually perform some computation. Again, we begin with a rather simple example.

EXAMPLE 2.4 The song "Seasons of Love" from the musical play *Rent* repeatedly declares that there are 525,600 minutes in a year. For most years, that's just fine, but what about leap years?

Problem Statement Write an application that calculates the number of minutes in a leap year.

Java Solution

```
1. //Calculates the number of minutes in a leap year

2. // Uses the fact that there are 525,600 minutes in a 365 day year
3. public class LeapYearMinutes
4. {
5.     public static void main(String[] args)
6.     {
7.         System.out.print( "The number of minutes in a leap year is ");
8.         System.out.println( 60 * 24 + 525600);  // 60 min/hr times 24 hr/day + 525600 min
9.     }
10. }
```

Output

The number of minutes in a leap year is 527040

Discussion Lines 7 and 8 are the only instructions or executable statements of the application. As you already know, the instruction on line 7 displays the string The number of minutes in a leap year is on the screen. Line 8 requires some explanation. Again, you see the now familiar println method. In this case, however, the argument supplied to the println method is not a string literal (look, no quotes!) but a numerical *expression:* 60 * 24 + 525600.

An *expression* is a sequence of symbols that denotes, represents, or signifies a value.

The *value* of the expression 60 * 24 + 525600 is 527040. In this case, 60 and 24 are multiplied ("*" signifies multiplication) and the product is added to 525600. The value of the computation, 527040, is supplied to the println method, and that number is displayed on the screen.

In the expression 60 * 24 + 525600, the symbols * and + are called *operators* and the numbers 60, 24, and 525600 are called *operands*. We say that the expression 60 * 24 + 525600 *evaluates to* 527040.

Example 2.4 involves the multiplication and addition of integers. Of course, Java allows computation and manipulation of other types of data such as floating-point numbers and even alphabetical characters. Each type of data is identified with a specific *data type*.

A *data type* is a set of values together with an associated collection of operators for manipulating those values.

We begin with four *primitive* data types: int, double, char, and boolean. There are others, which we discuss in subsequent chapters.

2.3.1 Type *int*

The values associated with the data type int are integers in the range −2,147,483,648 to 2,147,483,647. This range of numbers will make more sense later. And, as you will see, Java can handle even larger numbers.

The associated operators that manipulate integers are:

+	addition
−	subtraction
*	multiplication
/	division
%	modulus

The +, −, and * (times) operators function as they do in ordinary arithmetic. Thus the expression 4 + 6 evaluates to 10; 3 − 5 has the value −2; and 12 * 10 has the value 120. The / operator, however, denotes *integer* division; that is, a / b evaluates to a divided by b, discarding any remainder. Java specifies that the quotient of two integers is always an integer. Thus, 5 / 2 evaluates to 2; –23 / 6 evaluates to –3; and 4 / 43 has the value 0.

The *modulus* operator % may be new to you. The expression a % b evaluates to the *remainder* of a divided by b. The value of a % b has the same sign as a. Consequently, 5 % 2 has the value 1; −23 % 3 the value −2; and 47 % (−43) the value 4. The modulus operator is used more often than you might think. For example, we can use the modulus operator to determine whether an integer is odd or even. If x % 2 is 0 then x is even, otherwise x is odd. Also, you can use "%10" to extract the smallest digit of an integer. For example, 23657 % 10 evaluates to 7, the units digit of 23657.

The expressions a/b and a % b evaluate respectively to the quotient and *remainder* of a divided by b.

Example 2.5 illustrates both integer division and the modulus operator.

EXAMPLE 2.5 Each year, Betting Betty sets aside her spare pennies for an annual jaunt to Las Vegas. Betty bets exclusively at the quarter slot machines. This year, Betty has saved a total of 23,478 pennies.

Problem Statement Devise an application that displays the number of quarters that Betty can get from her bankroll and how many pennies remain for next year's excursion.

Java Solution

```
1. //Calculates the number of quarters and the remaining pennies obtained from 23478 pennies

2. public class BettysBundle
3. {
4.    public static void main(String[] args)
5.    {
6.       System.out.println( "In 23478 pennies there are: ");
7.       System.out.print( 23478/25);          // how many quarters?
8.       System.out.println( " quarters.");
9.       System.out.print( 23478%25);          // how many pennies remain?
10.      System.out.println( " pennies remain");
11.   }
12. }
```

Output

```
In 23478 pennies there are:
939 quarters.
3 pennies remain
```

Discussion The division on line 7 determines how many quarters are in Betty's bundle. Remember this is integer division. The remainder gives the number of pennies left over. The remainder is calculated on line 9 using the modulus operator %.

Of course, integer expressions may contain several operators. The expression 2 * 3 + 4 * 5 has three operators and a value of 26. The order in which operations are performed is the same as in ordinary arithmetic. That is, for integer expressions, operations are performed according to the *precedence* (priority) rules of Figure 2.2.

Operator			Associativity
*	/	%	Left to right
+	−		Left to right

high ↑ low

FIGURE 2.2 Operator precedence

Figure 2.2 implies that

1. *, /, and % have the highest precedence and are performed before + or −.
2. *, /, and % are equal in precedence.

3. + and − are equal in precedence but lower than *, /, and %.
4. Operations of equal precedence have left-to-right *associativity*. Thus 6 − 3 − 1 is evaluated as (6 − 3) − 1 = 3 − 1 = 2 and *not* 6 − (3 − 1) = 6 − 2 = 4. And, 8 / 3 * 4 is processed as (8 / 3) * 4 = 8, and *not* 8 / (3 * 4) = 0.

You may explicitly change the order of operations by inserting parentheses into an expression. An expression enclosed by parentheses must always be fully evaluated before it can be used in a larger expression. Thus, you might say that parentheses have the highest precedence. For example, the two multiplications of the expression 2 * 3 + 4 * 5 are performed before the addition:

```
2 * 3 + 4 * 5 =
6     + 4 * 5 =
6     + 20    =
26
```

However, the parentheses of 2 * (3 + 4) * 5 force the addition to be performed first:

```
2 * (3 + 4) * 5   =
2 * 7 * 5         =
14 * 5            =
70
```

The program in Example 2.6 uses an integer expression that is a bit more complex than those we have seen so far.

EXAMPLE 2.6

Superstitious Sam has recently suffered a streak of bad luck. In light of some recent unfortunate events and because his birthday is May 13, 1988, Sam speculates that perhaps he was born on a Friday, yes, the fearsome Friday the 13th. Certainly, that would explain Sam's unhappy circumstances.

Being mathematically savvy, Sam knows that, using a method developed by the Rev. Christian Zeller (1822–1899), he can find the day of the week for any date (month/day/year) with the following formula:

```
Day of the week =    ((day +
                          (13 * ((month + 9) % 12 + 1) − 1) / 5
                          + year % 100
                          + year % 100 / 4
                          + year / 400
                          − 2 * (year / 100) ) % 7 + 7) % 7 + 1
```

where

- Day of the week is a number between 1 and 7 representing the day of the week (Sunday = 1, Monday = 2 . . . , Saturday = 7),
- day is the day of the month (1 through 31),
- month is encoded as January = 1, February = 2 . . . December = 12, and
- year is the four-digit year in question.

Look over the formula and make sure that you understand the operations and the order of operations. It *is* rather complicated.

Problem Statement Write an application that determines whether or not Sam's birthday, May 13, 1988, occurred on a Friday.

Java Solution

```
// Displays the number of the day (1-7) on which May 13, 1988 occurred.

public class DayFinder
{
   public static void main(String[] args)
   {
      System.out.print  ("May 13, 1988 fell on day number ");
      // Uses the Zeller formula
      System.out.println(  ((13+ (13*((5+9)%12+1) -1)/5   // day = 13, month = 5
                           + 1988%100                     // year = 1988
                           + 1988%100/4
                           + 1988/400
                           - 2*(1988/100))%7 +7) %7+1 );
   }
}
```

The output confirms Sam's worst suspicions.

Output

```
May 13, 1988 fell on day number 6
```

Discussion If you look closely at the program, you might think that parentheses are unnecessary in the term 2 * (1988 / 100). That is not the case. If Java used "ordinary" (decimal) division, 2 * (1988 / 100) = 2 * 19.88 = 39.76 and (2 * 1988) / 100 = 3976 / 100 = 39.76, the parentheses would not matter. However, using integer division, 2 * (**1988 / 100**) = 2 * **19** equals 38, while (**2 * 1988**) / 100 = **3976** / 100 has the value 39. The parentheses in 2 * (1988 / 100) make a difference.

2.3.2 Type *double*

The values associated with data type double are decimal numbers in the range -1.7×10^{308} . . . 1.7×10^{308} with 14 significant digits of accuracy.

You can express a number of type double in two ways:

1. Decimal notation
2. Scientific or exponential notation

Numbers like 123.45 or .05 are numbers written in decimal notation. Scientific notation may be a little less familiar to you. The term 2.3E2 (or 2.3e2) is an example of a number expressed in scientific notation. The number 2.3E2 is numerically the same as 2.3×10^2. Thus,

$$2.3\text{E}2 = 2.3 \times 10^2 = 230.00.$$

Similarly,

$$3.2\text{E}3 = 3.2 \times 10^3 = 3200.00$$

and

$$234.567\text{E}1 = 234.567 \times 10 = 2345.67.$$

In general, a number of the form xEy (or xey), where y is an integer, means $x \times 10^y$. The number x is called the *base* and y is called the *exponent*.

As in ordinary mathematics, an exponent may be negative. Recall that $10^{-n} = 1/10^n$. Thus

$$4.63\text{E-}2 = 4.63 \times 10^{-2} = 4.63 \times 1/10^2 = 4.63 \times 1/100 = .0463$$

You may have noticed that when converting from scientific notation to decimal notation, a positive exponent, n, necessitates moving the decimal point to the right n places and a negative exponent, -n, necessitates moving the decimal n places to the left. Zeroes are added, if necessary. Thus, to convert 4.56789123E5 to decimal notation, move the decimal five places right. The equivalent number is 456789.123. Similarly, 55.2E-4 is equivalent to .00552.

The operators associated with type double are

+	addition
–	subtraction
*	multiplication
/	division

Here the division operator (/) denotes decimal or floating-point division rather than integer division; so 5.0 / 2.0 has the value 2.5 but 5 / 2 has the value 2. The % operator can also be used with numbers of type double, e.g., 5.5 % 2.5 = .5, but its use is usually restricted to integers.

EXAMPLE 2.7

Does intelligent life, capable of interplanetary communication, exist? Astronomer Frank Drake may have an answer. Drake's equation provides a method for estimating the number of intelligent civilizations capable of interplanetary communication that may exist in our galaxy. Drake's equation is usually expressed as:

$$N = R \times f_p \times n_e \times f_l \times f_i \times f_c \times L$$

where

N is the number of extraterrestrial civilizations capable of interplanetary communication,
R is the average rate of star formation in our galaxy (number per year),
f_p is the fraction of stars with planets,
n_e is the average number of planets in a solar system that can support life,
f_l is the fraction of suitable planets where any type of life develops,
f_i is the fraction of life bearing planets that have intelligent life,
f_c is the fraction of planets with intelligent life on which the interplanetary communication develops, and
L is the average lifetime (in years) of a civilization that develops technology.

Each of these values is either a rate or a fraction, so each can be represented by a number of type double. Of course, no one can determine these numbers with any certainty, and conjecture abounds.

Problem Statement Write an application that determines N given some typical default values: 20.0, .5, .5, .5, .2, .2, and 500.00 for R, f_p, n_e, f_l, f_i, f_e, and L.

Java Solution

```
1.  // An application of Drake's Equation with default values
2.  // R=20.0, f_p=.5, n_e=.5, f_l=.5, f_i=.2, f_c=.2 and L=500.00

3.  public class ET
4.  {
5.     public static void main(String[] args)
6.     {
7.        System.out.print("The number of civilizations capable of interplanetary communication is ");
8.        System.out.println( 20.0*.5*.5*.5*.2*.2* 500.00);
9.     }
10. }
```

Output

The number of civilizations capable of interplanetary communication is 50.0.

Discussion Each of the constants shown on line 8 contains a decimal point, so each is of type double. Consequently, the product is of type double.

It appears that we are not alone. ET phone home!

2.3.3 Type *char*

Computer applications do much more than numerical calculations. Programs manipulate large databases of names and addresses, manage inventory files, and facilitate word processing. Such applications must handle alphabetical or character data.

Type char is the set of all characters found on the standard keyboard (in addition to thousands of other characters that are used for displaying text in languages that do not use the English alphabet). A value of type char is enclosed in single quotes. Thus 'A' denotes a value of type char as do '%' and '$'. Note that

'5' is a value of type char,

"5" is a string literal, and

5 is an integer.

They are all different. The integer expression 1 + 5 has the value 6 but, as you will see later, the expression 1 + '5' has the value 54, and the expression 1 + "5" has the value "15".

> Computers store characters as non-negative numbers. Every character has a code number called its *ASCII value*. Even "control characters" such as the backspace and the tab have assigned codes.

So, what determines a character's internal code number? The ASCII (**A**merican **S**tandard **C**ode for **I**nformation **I**nterchange) code assigns a non-negative integer between 0 and 127 to each character found on a standard English language keyboard. For example, 'A' is assigned 65, 'B' is assigned 66, 'Z' is assigned 90, '5' is assigned 53, '6' is assigned 54, and backspace is assigned 8. Like all data, these values are stored as binary numbers, typically a leading `0` followed by a 7-bit code number between 0 and 127 inclusive. For example, 'A' is stored as `01000001`, which is the binary equivalent of 65; and the code for the backspace is `00001000`, the binary representation of 8.

> ASCII values can be stored using a single byte of memory; that is, one character requires just one byte of storage.

The ASCII character set can be found in Appendix B.

Although an ASCII value requires just one byte of storage, Java uses the *Unicode* character set and allocates two bytes of memory for each character. A one-byte scheme allows up to 255 different code numbers, of which ASCII uses half. Using two bytes expands the range significantly to 65,536 characters. Consequently, using two bytes instead of ASCII's one byte allows the Unicode character set to include not only English characters but also characters for many other languages such as Greek, Chinese, Arabic, Japanese, and Hebrew. By design, the ASCII character set is a subset of Unicode. So, for example, the character 'A' has the code value 65 in both ASCII and Unicode. The ASCII code for 'A' is stored as `01000001` (one byte), while the Unicode representation is `0000000001000001` (two bytes). Throughout this text, we will restrict our use of characters to the ASCII subset of Unicode.

In addition to standard alphanumeric characters, the value set of type char includes several special characters that are represented by an escape sequence or escape character. You have already seen the escape sequence \", which designates a double quotation mark. Other common escape sequences are:

\n	newline
\t	tab
\b	backspace
\r	carriage return
\'	single quote
\\	backslash

Like the escape sequence \", any escape character may be used within a string literal as Example 2.8 illustrates.

EXAMPLE 2.8

Returning to the history lesson of Example 2.3, we point out that Blaise Pascal's mechanical computer, dubbed the *Pascaline*, was not a colossal success. Pascal's quasi-failure is noted in the output of the following program.

Java Solution

```
public class ComputerHistoryToo
{
    public static void main(String[] args)
    {
        System.out.print ("Undaunted, Blaise built his machine\n"); // note the escape character, \n
        System.out.print ("Which came to be called \"Pascaline\"\n ");
        System.out.print ("\tBut when he unveiled it\n");
        System.out.print ("\tSome critics assailed it\n");      // \t is a tab
        System.out.print ("Reviews ranged from mean to obscene ");
    }
}
```

Output

```
Undaunted, Blaise built his machine
Which came to be called "Pascaline"
        But when he unveiled it
        Some critics assailed it
Reviews ranged from mean to obscene
```

Discussion Notice the use of print in conjunction with the newline character (\n) on lines 5 through 8. This combination is equivalent to using the single println instruction. The tab character (\t) appears twice in the program (lines 7 and 8) to effect indentation.

2.3.4 Type *boolean*

Type boolean has but two values, true and false.

The associated operators are not the standard +, −, *, and / operators but

&&, ||, and !

signifying *and, or,* and *not*, respectively.

The type name boolean honors the 19th century English mathematician George Boole, who revolutionized the study of logic by making logic more like arithmetic. He invented a method for calculating with truth values (true and false) as well as an algebra system for reasoning about such calculations. Boole's methods are used extensively today in the engineering of hardware and software systems.

Type boolean may seem somewhat peculiar at first since the values, true and false, are perhaps less familiar to you than numbers or characters. To acquire some intuition for boolean values, consider each of the following statements. Like an arithmetic expression, each statement has a value—either true or false. Read each statement and convince yourself that you understand the logic of each assigned value.

Statements 1–4 are simple assertions that we accept as either true or false:

Statement	Value
1. Snow is white.	true
2. Snow is red.	false
3. The sky is blue.	true
4. The sky is green.	false

Statements 5–14 in Figure 2.3 are compound statements with values, true or false, which can be derived from the values of statements 1–4. Read each statement and try to determine its value: true or false.

Statement	Value	Comparable *boolean* expression
5. Snow is white **and** The sky is blue	true	true && true
6. Snow is white **and** The sky is green	false	true && false
7. Snow is red **and** The sky is blue	false	false && true
8. Snow is red **and** The sky is green	false	false && false
9. Snow is white **or** The sky is blue	true	true || true
10. Snow is white **or** The sky is green	true	true || false
11. Snow is red **or** The sky is blue	true	false || true
12. Snow is red **or** The sky is green	false	false || false
13. It is **not** the case that Snow is white	false	!true
14. It is **not** the case that the sky is green	true	!false

FIGURE 2.3 *Boolean* operations

Just as an integer expression such as 2 * 4 + 3 has the value 11, the boolean expression true && true (statement 5) has the value true; the expression false || true (statement 11) has the value true; and !true (statement 13) has the value false. Figure 2.4 summarizes Java's boolean operators.

x	y	x && y (and)	x || y (or)	!x (not)
true	true	true	true	false
true	false	false	true	false
false	true	false	true	true
false	false	false	false	true

FIGURE 2.4 *Boolean* operators

Notice that the expression x && y has the value true only if *both* operands, x and y, are true. The expression x || y is false only if *both* operands are false. Among boolean operators, ! (not) has the highest precedence, followed by && and finally ||.

Example 2.9 uses electrical circuits to illustrate the type boolean.

EXAMPLE 2.9

A switching circuit through which electricity flows consists of wires and switches. Assume that electricity flows from terminal A to terminal B. When a switch, X, is open, the flow of electricity is stopped; when X is closed electrical flow is uninterrupted. See Figure 2.5.

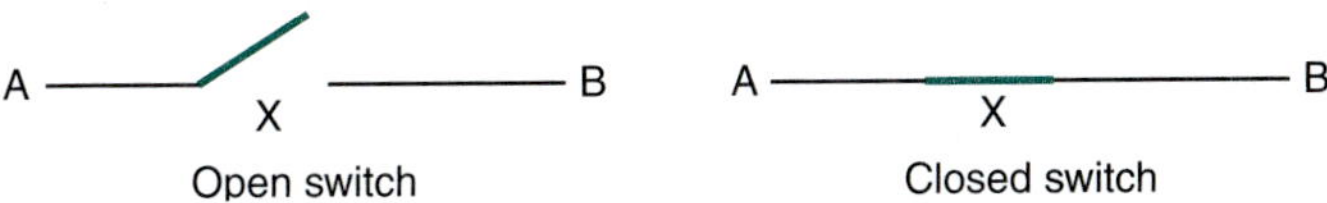

FIGURE 2.5 Electricity flows when X is closed

A light switch is a simple illustration of a switching circuit. If a light switch is turned on (closed) electricity flows to the bulb, but when the switch is off (open) the flow of current is interrupted and electricity cannot reach the bulb.

Two simple circuits are displayed in Figure 2.6.

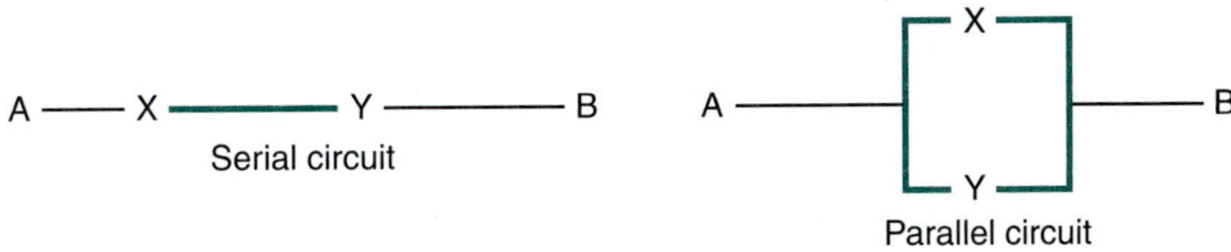

FIGURE 2.6 Two circuits

Electricity flows from A to B through the serial circuit of Figure 2.6 if and only if *both* X and Y are closed. Electricity flows from A to B through the parallel circuit if and only if *either* X or Y is closed (or both are closed).

If we assign a closed switch the value true and an open switch the value false, Figures 2.7 and 2.8 illustrate the possible scenarios for the serial and parallel circuits. A value of true in the third column (Flow) indicates that the current is uninterrupted.

X	Y	Flow = X && Y
true (closed)	true (closed)	true (flows)
true (closed)	false (open)	false (does not flow)
false (open)	true (closed)	false (does not flow)
false (open)	false (open)	false (does not flow)

FIGURE 2.7 Serial

X	Y	Flow = X || Y
true (closed)	true (closed)	true (flows)
true (closed)	false (open)	true (flows)
false (open)	true (closed)	true (flows)
false (open)	false (open)	false (does not flow)

FIGURE 2.8 Parallel

Notice that, for the serial circuit, when X && Y has the value true, electricity flows from A to B; for the parallel circuit when the expression X || Y is true, electricity flows.

Figure 2.9 shows a more complex circuit with terminal points A and B and four switches X, !X, Y, and !Y. (Note that !X is a switch that is open when X is closed and closed when X is open. !Y is similar.). The switches of Figure 2.9 can be either open or closed. A boolean expression that models this circuit is:

(X && !Y || !X && !Y || !X && Y) && (!Y || X)

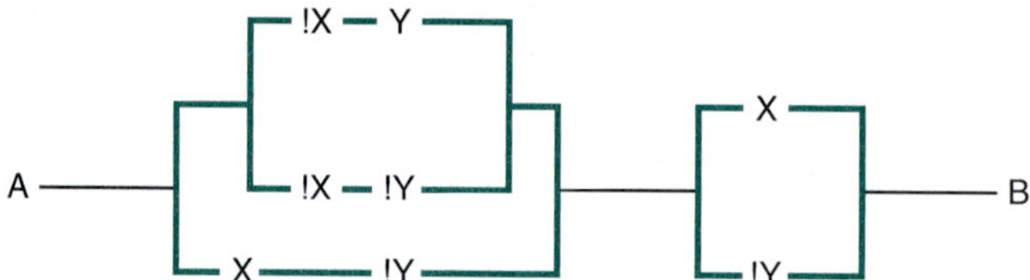

FIGURE 2.9 A more complicated circuit

Of the four possible switch configurations of the circuit:

1. X closed, Y closed (so consequently, !X open, and !Y open)
2. X closed, Y open (!X open, !Y closed)
3. X open, Y closed (!X closed, !Y open)
4. X open, Y open (!X closed, !Y closed)

two (2 and 4) let the electricity flow from A to B. The dark lines in Figure 2.10 show the flow through the circuit when X is closed and Y is open (configuration 2).

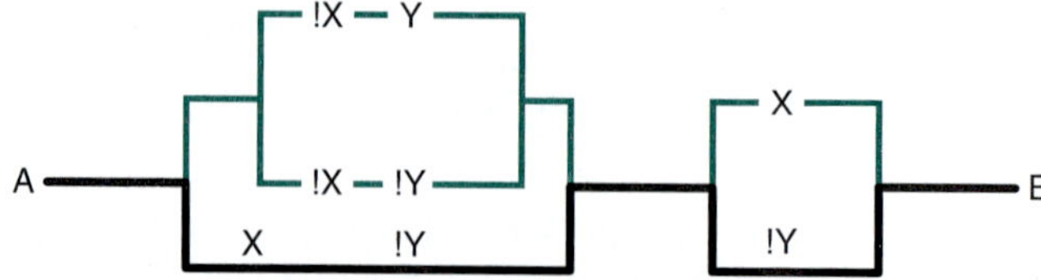

FIGURE 2.10 Flow through the circuit when X is closed and Y is open

Problem Statement Write a program that demonstrates that the electricity flows from A and B whenever

- X is closed and Y is open, that is, when X = true and Y = false, or
- X is open and Y is open, that is, when X = false and Y = false.

More simply, electricity flows from A to B whenever Y is open.

Java Solution

```
// Evaluates the four possible switch configurations:
// closed-closed, closed-open, open-closed, and open-open
// for the circuit modeled by the boolean expression
//                  (X && !Y || !X && !Y || !X && Y) && (X || !Y)
// the application displays true or false for each configuration indicating whether
// or not an electrical current can flow through the circuit

public class Circuit
{
  public static void main (String[] args)
  {
    System.out.print("If X is closed and Y is closed. Flow: ");    // X=true; Y=true
    System.out.println((true && !true ||  !true && !true || !true && true) &&(true ||!true));

    System.out.print("If X is closed and Y is open. Flow: ");    // X=true; Y=false
    System.out.println((true && !false || !true && !false || !true && false) && (true ||!false));

    System.out.print ("If X is open and Y is closed. Flow: ");    // X=false; Y=true
    System.out.println((false && !true || !false && !true || !false && true) &&(false || !true));

    System.out.print("If X is open and Y is open. Flow: ");    // X=false; Y=false
    System.out.println((false && !false ||!false&& !false || !false && false) &&(false ||!false));
  }
}
```

Output

```
If X is closed and Y is closed. Flow: false
If X is closed and Y is open. Flow: true
If X is open and Y is closed. Flow: false
If X is open and Y is open. Flow: true
```

2.3.5 Relational Operators

In addition to the operators &&, ||, and !, Java provides a set of *relational operators*, used in expressions that evaluate to true or false. Each relational operator requires two operands, which may be two integers, two decimal numbers, or two characters. The relational operators are:

<	less than
<=	less than or equal
>	greater than
>=	greater than or equal
==	equals (has the same value)
!=	not equal

Character data are compared using Unicode (ASCII) integer values. For example, because 'A' has the code value 65, and 'C' the value 67, the expression 'A' < 'C' evaluates to true since 65 < 67. The ASCII encoding purposely encodes letters so that they are ordered alphabetically. Similarly, '1' < '2' has the value true, as you would expect, because 49 < 50. You should be careful when comparing characters of different case, however. The numerical value of 'a' is 97, so the expression 'a' < 'C' (97 < 67) evaluates to false as does 'a' == 'A' since 97 does not equal 65.

The order of operations is performed according to the precedence table of Figure 2.11.

high ↑

<table>
<tr><th colspan="4">Operator</th><th>Associativity</th></tr>
<tr><td></td><td></td><td></td><td></td><td></td></tr>
<tr><td>!</td><td></td><td></td><td></td><td>Right to left</td></tr>
<tr><td>*</td><td>/</td><td>%</td><td></td><td>Left to right</td></tr>
<tr><td>+</td><td>−</td><td></td><td></td><td>Left to right</td></tr>
<tr><td><</td><td><=</td><td>></td><td>>=</td><td>Left to right</td></tr>
<tr><td>==</td><td>!=</td><td></td><td></td><td>Left to right</td></tr>
<tr><td>&&</td><td></td><td></td><td></td><td>Left to right</td></tr>
<tr><td>||</td><td></td><td></td><td></td><td>Left to right</td></tr>
</table>

low

FIGURE 2.11 Operator precedence

Figure 2.11 indicates that the ! (not) operator is right associative. This means that an expression such as !!!true is evaluated from right to left as !(!(!true)). The ! operator is called a *unary* operator because ! operates on only one value. All the other operators that we have discussed are *binary* operators because they operate on two values.

The following expressions illustrate the relational operators as well as some relational expressions.

1. 5 < 3 || 6 > 2 — false || true has the value **true**
2. 1 + 14 % 5 == 0 — **false**
3. 'A' < 'B' — **true** (code for 'A' is 65; for 'B' it is 66: 65 < 66)
4. 'Z' < 'a' — **true** (code for 'Z' is 90 and for 'a' it is 97: 90 < 97)
5. 1 + 1== 2 || 1 + 1 == 3 — true || false has the value **true**
6. 37 / 3 > .3333 — **true**
7. 2 < 3 && 4 < 5 || 7 <= 5 && 2 == 3 — true || false has the value **true**
8. 2 < 3 && (4 < 5 || 7 <= 5) && 2 == 3 — true && true && false has the value **false**
9. false == false — **true**
10. true != false — **true**

Expressions such as $2 < 3 < 4$ make no sense in Java. Java attempts to evaluate this expression as

(2 < 3) < 4
true < 4.

The expression true < 4 is invalid and generates an error. The Java equivalent of $2 < 3 < 4$ is

(2 < 3) && (3 < 4).

EXAMPLE 2.10

A leap year is any year divisible by four except those years divisible by 100 unless the year is also divisible by 400. For example, 2000 was a leap year but 1900 was not.

In researching her family tree, Jeannie Ology has discovered that her great-great-great grandmother's birth certificate records the date of birth as February **29**, 1800. Jeannie is a bit suspicious of the date. Was 1800 a leap year? Jeannie, being a skilled programmer but an error-prone mathematician, has devised a program to determine whether or not Granny's birth certificate is in error. Her program displays true or false depending upon whether or not 1800 was a leap year.

When you read the program, be certain that you understand the boolean expression on line 9 and how that expression satisfies the leap year conditions. The expression includes boolean operators as well as several relational operators. Parentheses are not necessary. Can you determine the order of the operations?

Problem Statement Write a program that determines whether or not 1800 was a leap year.

Java Solution

```
1. // A leap year is a year that is divisible by 4 but not 100 unless it is divisible by 400
2. // This program determines whether or not 1800 meets all conditions of a leap year

3. public class LeapYear
4. {
5.     public static void main(String[] args)
6.     {
7.        System.out.print("The year 1800 is a leap year? True or false: ");
8.        // (divisible by 4 and not by 100) or (divisible by 400)
9.        System.out.println( 1800%4 ==0 && 1800 %100 !=0 || 1800%400 == 0);
10.    }
11. }
```

Output

```
The year 1800 is a leap year? True or false: false
```

Discussion So, it appears that the birth certificate is in error.

There are no awards for programming with the least number of parentheses, and obscure code should never be a matter of pride. To make your code easier to read, regardless of whether it is technically required, include parentheses in your expressions. Here is a fully parenthesized version of the expression on line 9:

```
(((1800%4) ==0) && ( (1800 %100) !=0)) || ((1800%400 ) == 0 )
```

This version is preferable to the one we used on line 9.

2.3.6 Short Circuit Evaluation

Consider the following partial boolean expressions, where something and something_else have boolean values

1. (3 > 5) && (something)
2. (2 < 9) || (something_else)

Expression 1 always has the value false, regardless of the value of something. If something is true, expression 1 is false; if something is false, expression 1 is false. This is because the first operand (3 > 5) is false. No further evaluation need be performed after the first operand is evaluated since "false && something" always has the value false. The value of something is irrelevant. Expression 2 has the value true regardless of the value of something_else. If one operand has the value true, expression 2 is true.

The value of each expression can be determined without evaluating the entire expression. The term on the left is first evaluated, and evaluation stops because the value of the entire expression is determined from this term. This method of evaluation is called *short circuit evaluation*.

> Java uses *short circuit evaluation* to evaluate expressions involving the boolean operators && and ||.

This means that Java stops the evaluation of an expression once the value of the expression is determined. For example, consider the expression

1 < 2 || 2 < 3 || 3 < 4

The value of this expression is true. Notice that this value can be determined after evaluating 1 < 2. Consequently, no more of the expression need be considered.

Similarly,

(1 > 2) && (1 < 2 || 2 < 3 || 3 < 4)

has the value false because the first item (1 > 2) is false. No other evaluation within the expression is necessary. Surprisingly, (1 > 2) && (1 > 3 / 0) causes no error, despite division by zero in the second operand. Because 1 > 2 has the value false and the short circuit operator && evaluates its left operand first, the value of the expression is false regardless of the second term. The division by 0, 3 / 0, is ignored. On the other hand, the value of the boolean expression (1 < 2) && (3 < 4) cannot be determined without evaluating the entire expression.

In subsequent chapters, you will see that exploiting short circuit evaluation has its advantages.

2.3.7 Mixing Data Types in a Numerical Expression

A Java expression can be constructed from data of several different types. For example, the expression (22 + 3.0) / 4 contains both integers (int) and decimal numbers (double). Is the value of this expression 6, 6.0, or 6.25? It's 6.25. How about an expression like 'A' + 1, which mixes character data with integer data? Is the value of this expression 'B' or, since the Unicode (ASCII) value for 'A' is 65, is the value 66? Or, does the compiler consider such an expression an error?

> When evaluating a binary expression with operands of different data types, Java first *promotes* or *casts* the operand of the "smaller" data type to the data type of the other operand.

"Smaller" data type? The range of values determines the "size" of a data type. Thus char is smaller than int, which, in turn, is smaller than double.

EXAMPLE 2.11

The expression (22 + 3.0) / 4 has the value 6.25.

The expression is evaluated as follows:

(22 + 3.0) / 4	The expression consists of decimal and integer types.
(22.0 + 3.0) / 4	The integer 22 is cast to 22.0 (an int is cast to a double).
25.0 / 4	This is floating-point addition—22.0 + 3.0.
25.0 / 4.0	The integer 4 is cast to 4.0.

This is floating-point division.

The expression 'A' + 1 has the value 66.
The expression is evaluated as follows:

'A' + 1	The expression consists of character and integer data.
65 + 1	The character 'A' is cast to the integer 65—its ASCII code value.
66	This is integer addition.

The expression 'A' + 1.0 has the value 66.0.
The expression is evaluated as follows:

'A' + 1.0	The expression consists of character and a decimal data.
65 + 1.0	The integer 65 is the ASCII code for 'A', that is, 'A' is stored as 65.
65.0 + 1.0	The integer 65 is cast to 65.0.
66.0	This is floating-point addition.

The / operator, which denotes both integer and floating-point division, can often be the source of subtle bugs. For example, consider the formula that converts degrees Fahrenheit to degrees Celsius:

$$C = \frac{5}{9}(F - 32)$$

If $F = 212.0$, the mixed expression

(5 / 9) (212.0 − 32)

evaluates to 0, not 100.0.

This miscalculation is caused by the omission of a decimal point. The value of (5/9) is calculated using integer division, and consequently (5/9) evaluates to 0. The correct conversion formula should be written as

(5.0/9.0)(212.0 − 32), **(5.0/9)**(212.0 − 32), or **(5/9.0)**(212.0 − 32.)

With each expression, division is correctly performed as floating point.

Numerical operators can also be used with character operands. In this case, both operands are treated as integers.

EXAMPLE 2.12 The expression 'A' + 'Z' has the value 155 since the ASCII values for 'A' and 'Z' are 65 and 90, respectively. Similarly, 'A' − 'Z' has the value −25.

On the other hand, the expression "A" + "B" does not have the value 155. In this case, "A" and "B" are not character data but strings. The + operator may be used with strings but, as you will see in the next section, the result is not an integer.

2.3.8 The + Operator and Strings

In Example 2.12, we state that the + operator has a special meaning when used with string data:

> If both operands A and B are strings, then the expression A + B evaluates to another string, which is the *concatenation* (joining together) of A and B. If only one operand is a string, then the other operand is first cast to a string and the value of the expression is the concatenation of two strings.

Example 2.13 gives several variations on the + operator and string data.

EXAMPLE 2.13

a. Joining two strings

The expression "Bibbidi " + "Bobbidi " evaluates to a new string "Bibbidi Bobbidi ", which is formed by joining, that is, *concatenating*, "Bibbidi " and "Bobbidi ".

"Bibbidi " + "Bobbidi " + "Boo" evaluates to the string "Bibbidi Bobbidi Boo", which is formed by first joining "Bibbidi " and "Bobbidi " and then concatenating the result with "Boo". The idea is quite simple; there's no magic.

b. Joining a string and a number

The expression

2147483647 + " is not only the largest value of type int but also a prime number!"

evaluates to the string

"2147483647 is not only the largest value of type int but also a prime number!"

Here, the first operand is the integer 2147483647, which is cast to the string "2147483647" and then the two strings are concatenated.

c. Joining a string and a numerical expression

The expression "The sum of the two dice is " + (5 + 2) evaluates to the string

"The sum of the two dice is 7"

Notice that the expression in parentheses is evaluated first. Parentheses can force a change in the usual precedence because the expressions inside them must be evaluated first. However, if the parentheses are omitted, then the expression

"The sum of the two dice is "+ 5 + 2

evaluates to the string

"The sum of the two dice is 52."

Evaluation proceeds as in the following sequence. Here parentheses have been added for emphasis.

("The sum of the two dice is " + 5) + 2	
("The sum of the two dice is " + "5") + 2	The integer 5 is cast to string "5".
("The sum of the two dice is 5") + 2	"The sum of the two dice is " and "5" are joined.
("The sum of the two dice is 5") + "2"	The integer 2 is cast to "2".
"The sum of the two dice is 52"	"The sum of the two dice is 5" is concatenated with "2".

Notice that numerical addition is not performed.

In contrast, the expression

"The product of the two dice is " + 5 * 2

evaluates to the string

"The product of the two dice is 10".

The * operation is performed first since * has higher precedence than +.

Finally, the expression

"The difference of the two dice is" + 5 − 2

is ill formed and causes an error. Since + and − are of equal priority and are associated (grouped) left to right, the expression is evaluated as:

("The difference of the two dice is " + 5) − 2
("The difference of the two dice is "+ "5") − 2
"The difference of the two dice is 5"− 2

An error now occurs because the minus (−) operator cannot be applied to strings. The Java compiler detects this error.

2.4 IN THE BEGINNING . . . AGAIN

We have come full circle, and we return to the print and println methods introduced at the beginning of the chapter. You may have noticed that in previous examples we used several println methods to generate a single line of output. Typically to produce the output

```
The cost of 15 wickets is 375 dollars
```

an application might include three instructions:

```
1. System.out.print("The cost of 15 wickets is ");
2. System.out.print( 15 * 25);
3. System.out.println(" dollars");
```

Java specifies that the print and println methods accept a *single* argument of any type.

In statements 1 and 3 (above), that argument is a string literal; in statement 2 the argument is an integer (375).

Conveniently, the previous three lines of code can be condensed to a single line

```
System.out.print("The cost of 15 wickets is " + (15 * 25) + " dollars");
```

Notice that the mixed expression

"The cost of 15 wickets is " + (15 * 257) + " dollars");

evaluates to the *string:*

"The cost of 15 wickets is 375 dollars"

and it is this string that is the argument to the println method.

EXAMPLE 2.14 Test your understanding of various data types and operators and determine the value of each of the following expressions:

1. 'A' + 'B'
2. 'A' + "B"
3. "A" + "B"
4. "" + 'A' + 'B'
5. 'A' + 'B'+""
6. 3 + 4 +""
7. ""+ 3 + 4

1. Answer: 131 (int)

   The expression 'A' + 'B' is evaluated as (65 + 66).

2. Answer: AB (string)

   Since the second operand "B" is a string, 'A' is cast to the string "A". The final value is the concatenation "A" + "B" ("AB").

3. Answer: AB (string)

   "A" + "B" is the concatenation of two strings.

4. Answer: AB (string).

   The pair of double quotes positioned one after the other denotes the *empty string*, that is, the string with no characters. The evaluation is accomplished as

("" + 'A') + 'B'	
("" + **"A"**) + 'B'	'A' is cast to string "A".
"A" + 'B'	"" and "A" are concatenated to "A".
"A" + **"B"**	'B' is cast to "B".
"AB"	"A" and "B" are concatenated.

5. Answer: 131 (string)

   Here, the first + signifies addition and not string concatenation. Thus, the evaluation proceeds as

   ('A' + 'B') + ""
   (65 + 66) + ""
   131 + "" =
   "131" + ""
   "131"

6. Answer: 7 (string)
   Associativity for + is left to right, so first 3 + 4 evaluates to 7. Next, 7 + "" evaluates to the string "7".

7. Answer: 34 (string)
   The integer 3 is cast to "3" and string concatenation ("" + 3) is effected. Next, 4 is cast to "4" and "3" + "4" evaluates to "34".

EXAMPLE 2.15

The International Civil Aviation Organization has devised a formula that calculates the amount of rest (in days) needed to recover from the mental fatigue of jet lag:

1. Divide the length of the trip (in hours) by 2.
2. Subtract 4 from the number of time zones crossed.
3. Determine your departure and arrival time coefficients according to the following chart:

Local time	Departure time coefficient	Arrival time coefficient
8:00 a.m.–12:00 p.m.	0	4
12:00 p.m.–6:00 p.m.	1	2
6:00 p.m.–10:00 p.m.	3	0
10:00 p.m.–1:00 a.m.	4	1
1:00 a.m.–8:00 a.m.	5	3

   Note: if a time is "on the border" then the average of the two coefficients is used. So if a departure time is 6:00 p.m., the departure coefficient is (1 + 3) / 2 = 2.

4. Add the values in steps 1–3 and divide by 10 to get the number of days needed to recover from jet lag.

Suppose that Zip flies from New York at 4:00 p.m., arriving in Frankfurt at 5:00 a.m.
The length of the trip is 7 hours.
The number of time zones crossed is 7, so the number of time zones in excess of 4 is 3.
The departure time coefficient is 1.
The arrival time coefficient is 3.

Problem Statement Write a program that calculates the recommended number of recovery days for Zip's trip.

Java Solution Thus the number of recommended days of rest can be computed as:

(7.0 / 2 + 3 + 1 + 3) / 10

This is a mixed-type expression. The result is a value of type double.

```
//Calculates the number of days of jetlag recovery for a flight between New York and Frankfurt
//restDays= (flightLength/2 +timeZones-4 + departureCoefficient +arrivalCoefficient)/10
//where flightLength = 7, timeZones = 7, departureCoefficient = 1, arrivalCoefficient = 3

public class JetLag
{
   public static void main(String[] args)
```

```
7.   {
8.       System.out.println("Recommended rest: "+(7.0/2 + 3 + 1 + 3)/10+ "days");
9.   }
10. }
```

Output

Recommended rest: 1.05 days

Discussion Notice that all output is accomplished with one statement using the string concatenation operator. The expression on line 8 is mixed. The division 7.0 / 2 is computed using floating-point division and has the value 3.5. The subsequent sum is thus evaluated as 3.5 + 3.0 + 1.0 + 3.0 (= 10.5). Finally, the floating-point division 10.5 / 10 gives the value 1.05. Again, this final division is floating-point division because the numerator is a double.

2.5 IN CONCLUSION

This chapter presents the basics of screen output as well as a discussion of data types and expressions. Using the methods of the chapter, you can write programs that print virtually any text on the screen as well as compute all types of arithmetic and logical expressions. On the other hand, the programs of this chapter do lack a certain flexibility: all data are "hardwired" into these programs, and no program accepts input from a user. For example, the program of Example 2.10 that determines whether or not 1800 is a leap year cannot do the same for 1984 or 2968 without our rewriting and recompiling the program. In Chapter 3 you will learn how to accept data from outside an application as well as how to store that data in the computer's memory and retrieve it for later use.

Just the Facts

- Single-line comments in Java begin with // and continue to the end of the line.
- Multi-line comments in Java begin with /* and end with */.
- Comments may be placed anywhere within a program.
- For the present, applications have the following format:

```
public class ClassName
{
   public static void main(String[] args)
   {
      //Java statements go here
   }
}
```

  where *ClassName* is a valid Java identifier chosen by the programmer. The class must be saved in a file *ClassName.java*.
- A *block* is a group of statements enclosed in curly braces.
- System.out.println(...) is used to display data followed by a newline character.
- System.out.print(...) is used to display data without a newline character.

- A string literal consists of text enclosed by quotation marks. A string literal must be contained on a single line.
- If both operands A and B are strings, then the expression A + B evaluates to another string, which is the *concatenation* (joining together) of A and B. If only one operand is a string, then the other operand is first cast to a string and the value of the expression is the concatenation of two strings.
- A *data type* is a set of values together with an associated collection of operators for manipulating those values.
- Java data types include int, char, double, and boolean.
- Type int includes integer values and operators +, –, *, /, and %.
- Integer division discards the remainder.
- The modulus operator % gives the remainder of an integer division. The sign of a % b is the same as the sign of a.
- Type double includes decimal numbers and the operators +, –, *, and /. The modulus operator is available but rarely used.
- Type char includes all Unicode characters. Java stores character data using 2 bytes, that is, 16 bits.
- ASCII code numbers and Unicode values coincide. Unicode is a superset of ASCII.
- Type boolean includes just two values, true and false.
- Boolean operators are && (and), || (or), and !(not).
- The relational operators <, <=, >, >=, ==, and != return boolean values.
- The order of operations is based on operator precedence. (See the precedence chart in this chapter.) Parentheses override precedence.
- Boolean expressions are evaluated left to right until the value of the expression is determined. This is called *short circuit evaluation.*
- Data of different types can be combined in a single expression. Smaller data types are promoted to larger data types. The hierarchy of data types from smallest to largest is char, int, double.

Bug Extermination

> As soon as we started programming, we found to our surprise that it wasn't as easy to get programs right as we had thought. Debugging had to be discovered. I can remember the exact instant when I realized that a large part of my life from then on was going to be spent finding mistakes in my own programs. —**Maurice V. Wilkes, British computer scientist, 1949**

Initial versions of almost every program commonly contain errors or *bugs*. There are three categories of errors:

1. Compilation errors
2. Runtime errors
3. Logical errors

A *compilation error* occurs when a program violates one of the rules of Java, such as the omission of a semicolon, a string's quotation mark, or a closing curly brace. The compiler flags the error and tells you where the error occurs. A program must be free of such errors before it can be translated into bytecode.

As the name suggests, a *runtime error* occurs during program execution. A runtime error can occur when the program attempts some invalid operation such as division by zero. A runtime error results in program termination.

Even if the Java compiler detects no errors and a program runs to completion, a program may not do what it is supposed to do. For example, a program that converts degrees Fahrenheit to degrees Celsius using the erroneous expression

(1) **(5 / 9)**$(F - 32)$, where F represents a Fahrenheit temperature;

rather than

(2) **(5.0 / 9.0)**$(F - 32)$

may compile. However, because (5 / 9) is evaluated using integer division, the result of expression (1) is always 0. The compiler may "approve" the program but a bug obviously exists. Such a program contains a *logical error*. Uncovering logical errors can be difficult and time consuming. One primitive, yet effective, method for finding bugs is to trace the program with paper and pencil, performing each of the steps that the computer performs. Other methods include generating additional output or using a tool called the debugger.

Because our programs, thus far, are quite simple, most of the bugs that you will encounter will be syntax errors. Here are some common sources of errors:

- Using an illegal name. Remember the rules for forming a valid Java identifier.
- Omitting the parentheses with the empty println() method. Use println() not println;
- Using the wrong case. Java is case sensitive. Public and public are not interchangeable.
- Omitting a quotation mark for a string literal.
- Stretching a string literal over two lines.
- Forgetting to close a multi-line comment.
- Using a quotation mark within a string. (Use \")
- Using print when you intend to use println.
- Omitting the semicolon at the end of a statement.
- Using integer division when floating-point division is required.
- Using double quotation marks instead of single quotation marks to denote a character.
- Errors with operator precedence. When in doubt, use parentheses to ensure that the expression you type does the computation you intend it to do. Even when not in doubt, it is good style to fully parenthesize expressions.
- Using = when you mean ==. (In Chapter 3, you will see that the equals sign has its own meaning.)
- Using incompatible types with an operator. For example, the expressions (3 + true), (3 < true), and (4 && true) all result in syntax errors. To check whether 3 < 4 < 7, you must use (3 < 4) && (4 < 7). The expression 3 < 4 < 7 generates a syntax error because (3 < 4) is a boolean expression and 7 is an integer.
- Using // in the middle of an instruction, effectively hiding the remainder of the instruction from the compiler.

EXERCISES

LEARN THE LINGO

Test your knowledge of the chapter's vocabulary by completing the following crossword puzzle.

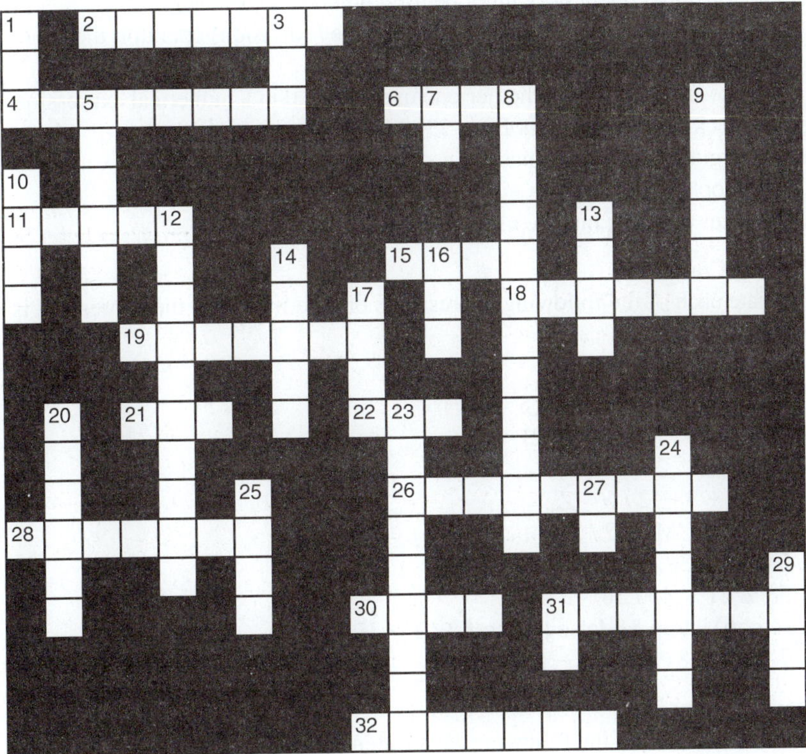

Across

2 Adds clarity to a program
4 4 in 52E4
6 Used for string concatenation
11 One-byte character code
15 Convert from one type to another
18 Java programs may consist of several _____
19 Character set with thousands of characters
21 5 * 4 / 3 (word)
22 \t
26 Statement terminator
28 ! has ____ precedence among boolean operators
30 5 * (4 / 3) (word)
31 A string literal must be contained on (two words)
32 The word public is a _____

Down

1 22 % 7 (word)
3 !
5 Built one of the first computers
7 Add to print to get a new line
8 Method of evaluating boolean expressions
9 Decimal data type
10 A program begins execution here
12 The name of a class must be a valid Java ____
13 Data type of 'X'
14 A group of statements enclosed by curly braces
16 &&
17 Associative rule for +
20 Separates System from out
23 To group operations
24 Computes the remainder
25 Symbol for multiplication
27 ||
29 6 / 10
31 Boolean operator with lowest precedence

SHORT EXERCISES

1. **True or False**
   If false, give an explanation.

   a. Integer and decimal numbers can be mixed in an expression.
   b. Integers can be added to character data.
   c. Boolean data can be cast to integer data.
   d. The relational operators cannot be used with character data.
   e. If only one decimal number is used with the / (division) operator, the result is an integer.
   f. It makes no difference whether one uses 5 or 5.0 in a numerical expression.
   g. The decimal form of 23.00E6 is 2300.00.
   h. The argument to println must be a string.
   i. Two boolean expressions may be compared using <.
   j. The plus operator may be used with two strings.

2. **Playing Compiler**
   Evaluate each of the following expressions or determine that the expression is ill formed.

   a. 3 + 4.5 * 2 + 27 / 8
   b. true || false && 3 < 4 || !(5 == 7)
   c. true || (3 < 5 && 6 >= 2)
   d. !true > 'A'
   e. 7 % 4 + 3 − 2 / 6 * 'Z'
   f. 'D' + 1 + 'M' % 2 / 3
   g. 5.0 / 3 + 3 / 3
   h. 53 % 21 < 45 / 18
   i. (4 < 6) || true && false || false && (2 > 3)
   j. 7 − (3 + 8 * 6 + 3) − (2 + 5 * 2)

3. **Playing Compiler**
   Determine which of the following Java statements/segments are incorrect. If a statement is correct, give the output. If incorrect, explain why.

```
a. System.out.print  ("May 13, 1988 fell on day number  ");
b. System.out.println( ((13 + (13 * 3 − 1) / 5
                        + 1988 % 100
                        + 1988 % 100 / 4
                        + 1988 / 400
                        − 2 * (1988 / 100)) % 7 + 7) % 7 );
c. System.out.print  ("Check out this line  ");
d. System.out.println(  "//hello there " + '9' +  7 );
e. System.out.print( 'H' + 'I' +  " is " +  1 + "more example");
f. System.out.print( 'H' + 6.5 + 'I' +  " is " +  1 + "more example");
g. System.out.print("Print both of us", "Me too");
h. System.out.print( "Reverse " + 'I' + 'T' );
i. System.out.print("No! Here is" + 1 + "more example");
j. System.out.println  ("Here is " + 10*10)) // that's 100 ;
k. System.out.println("Not x is " + true); // that's true.
l. System.out.print();
m. System.out.println;
n. System.out.print("How about this one" + '?' + 'Huh? '  );
```

4. **Playing Compiler**
Find and correct the errors in the following program:

```
public class LeapYear;
{
public static void main(String args)
{
        System.out.print("The year 2300 is a leap year? " + "True or false: ");
        // (divisible by 4 and not by 100) or (divisible by 400) //
        System.out.println( 2300 % 4 = 0 && 1800 % 100 != 0 || 1800 % 400 == 0);
}
```

5. **Parentheses and Operator Precedence**
Fully parenthesize each of the following expressions to reflect operator precedence.
   a. 2 + 3 + 4+ 5
   b. 3 * 4 + 5 / 6 − 7
   c. 2 + 3 * 4 * 5
   d. 9 % 2 / 2 * 3
   e. 7 + 6 * 4 % 2 + 3 * 5
   f. true || false || true && !true

6. **Boolean Expressions**
Compute the value of each of the following boolean expressions. Recall that Java uses short circuit evaluation. For each expression determine how much of the expression Java must evaluate to determine a value.
   a. true && false &&true || true
   b. true || true && true && false
   c. (true && false) || (true && ! false) || (false && !false)
   d. (2 < 3) || (5 > 2) && !(4 == 4) || 9 != 4
   e. 6 == 9 || 5 < 6 && 8 < 4 || 4 > 3

7. **Boolean Expressions**
Write a Java boolean expression that models each of the following circuit diagrams. See Example 2.9.

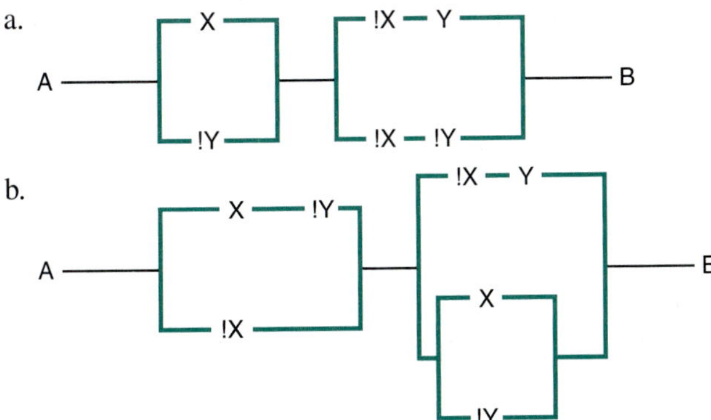

8. **Playing Compiler**
Determine which of the following expressions are valid. For each valid expression give the data type of the resulting value.
   a. 27 / 13 + 4
   b. 27 / 13 + 4.0
   c. 42.7 % 3 + 18
   d. (3 < 4) && 5 / 8

e. 23 / 5 + 23 / 5.0
f. 2.0 + 'a'
g. 2 + 'a'
h. 'a' + 'b'
i. 'a' / 'b'
j. 'a' && !'b'
k. (double)'a' / 'b'

9. **DeMorgan's Law**
DeMorgan's Laws for boolean expressions state that

```
!(a && b) is equivalent to !a || ! b, and
!(a || b) is equivalent !a && ! b
```

Use DeMorgan's Laws to simplify the following boolean expressions:

a. !(a || !b)
b. !(!a && !b)
c. !(!a || !b)
d. ! ((a &&b) || (!a && !b))

10. **What's the Output?**
Determine the output of the following program

```
public class Memory
{
  public static void main(String[] args)
  {
     System.out.print ("There once was a girl named Elaine\n");
     System.out.print ("With a microchip lodged in her brain\n");
     System.out.print ("\tHer friends were amazed\n");
     System.out.print ("\tBedazzled and dazed\n");
     System.out.print ("By the facts that Elaine could retain\n");
  }
}
```

11. **What's the Output?**
Determine the values of each of the following Java expressions:

a. 7 / 3 * 2
b. 7 / (3 * 2)
c. 7.0 / 3 * 2
d. 7 / 3 * 2.0
e. 7 / (3 * 2.0)
f. 7.0 / 3.0 * 2.0
g. (7 / 3) * 2
h. (7.0 / 3) * 2

12. **Comments**
Debugging a program can be a long and intricate process. Can you think of how you might use Java comments as an aid to debugging? What are some other ways that you might use Java comments?

PROGRAMMING EXERCISES

1. **Celsius to Fahrenheit**
The temperature F in Fahrenheit equals $(9 / 5)C + 32$ where C is the Celsius temperature. Write a program that computes and displays the temperatures in Fahrenheit for Celsius values −5, 0, 12, 68, 22.7, 100, and 6.

2. **Uptime**
The *uptime* command of the UNIX operating system displays the number of days, hours, and minutes since the operating system was last started. For example, the UNIX command *uptime* might return the string

Up 53 days 12:39

Write a program that converts the 53 days, 12 hours, and 39 seconds to the number of seconds that have elapsed since the operating system was last started.

3. **Java Competency**
The average person needs approximately four million three hundred and fifty thousand seconds of study and experience to qualify as a competent Java programmer. Write a program that calculates and prints the number of days, hours, minutes, and seconds necessary for Java competency.

4. **Logical Calculations**
Silly Sammy studies when both Serious Stuart and Studious Selma study, or when neither studies. Selma studies every day except Sunday. Stuart studies every day except Saturday. Write a program that determines, for each day of the week, whether or not Silly Sammy studies.

5. **Baseball Expenses**
A baseball game has nine innings. Freddie Fanatic likes to buy a beer before every odd-numbered inning, nachos before every even-numbered inning, and a scorecard when he first arrives for batting practice before the game begins. Beer costs $6, nachos $4, and a scorecard is $3. Write a program that prints a summary of the items that Freddie buys at the ballpark. Your program should display the name each item, the number of each item, the total cost of each item, and Freddie's total expenditures.

6. **Pictures**
Write a program that prints the triangle:

```
*
* *
* * *
* * * *
* * * * *
* * * * * *
```

7. **More Pictures**
Write a program that prints a triangle with your initials somewhere in the middle:

```
*
* *
*   *
*  S  *
*    R   *
* * * * * *
```

8. **Your Own Art**
Write a program that prints your own version of a smiley face.

9. **Your Own Header**
   Write a program that displays a box containing a line of text. Here is an example. Try to make yours look better!

```
------------------------------
*                            *
*                            *
*  Abra Varcolph and Hasim Sonsoni  *
*                            *
*                            *
------------------------------
```

10. **ASCII Name**
    Write a program that prints the letters of your name followed by the ASCII value of each letter. For example:

```
K   75
r   114
a   97
m   109
e   101
r   114
```


THE BIGGER PICTURE

1. BINARY ENCODING I—ASCII ENCODING

Decimal numbers are constructed from the digits 0, 1, 2, 3, 4, 5, 6, 7, 8, 9 but binary numbers contain only digits `0` and `1`. The digits making up a binary number are called *bits* (short for *bi*nary digi*ts*). For example, `010110` is a binary number. Although there are ten different single-digit decimal numbers (0, 1, 2, 3, 4, 5, 6, 7, 8, 9), there are just two single-bit binary numbers: `0` and `1`. Similarly, there are ninety decimal numbers with two digits (10, 11, 12 . . ., and 99) but merely four binary numbers with two bits: `00, 01, 10`, and `11`. With three bits, there are just eight different binary numbers: `000, 001, 010, 011, 100, 101, 110, and 111.`

Exercises

1. How many different binary numbers are there with 4 bits? 10 bits? n bits?
2. How many different characters are included in the ASCII coding scheme?

Although each ASCII code number uses just 7 bits, for practical reasons having to do with hardware, the number is *stored* using 8 bits (one byte) with the leftmost bit always set to `0`. For example, `01111111` and `01101010` require one byte of memory and have the leftmost bit set to `0`.

3. Many electronic devices, such as calculators and digital clocks, display no symbols other than the digits 0 through 9. With only ten possible symbols, the 7-bit ASCII code is overkill. We can use fewer than 7 bits per digit. How many bits can be used to encode a digit in a calculator or clock? Using this number of

bits per digit, how many digits can be stored in one byte? This type of encoding is called BCD, or binary coded decimal, and it is twice as compact as ASCII encoding.

4. How many different characters can be represented using the 16-bit Unicode system? Explain your answer.
5. Considering Hebrew, Arabic, Cyrillic, Greek, Sanskrit, and Kanji symbols, conjecture whether the number of Unicode values is reasonably large enough to include all the characters that humans use for written communication. Can you think of any reasons for converting to a 64-bit character code?

Like the characters 'A', 'B', 'C', and so on, the digit characters '0' through '9' also have ASCII codes. The ASCII code for zero is 48 (decimal) or `0110000` (binary). The ASCII codes for the other digits increase in order, 49 for '1', 50 for '2', and so on.

6. Determine the ASCII code for the four-digit string "1026". Use one byte for each digit.
7. Determine the binary equivalent of the decimal number 1026.
8. What are the advantages and disadvantages of storing a string of digits using ASCII rather than its binary number encoding?
9. How do you think digits in a Java program are stored? For example, are digits that are part of a class name stored in the same way as the digits that comprise an integer in an arithmetic expression? Use the following example to explain your answer.

What are the differences between the internal representations of 23748 in the following three lines of Java code?

```
public class MyClass23478
{
    System.out.println ( "In 23478 pennies there are: ");
    System.out.println( 23478 + 12);
}
```

2. BINARY ENCODING II—DECIMAL ENCODING

As you know, the digits of a decimal number *X* represent the number of ones, tens, hundreds, thousands, and so on in *X*. For example, 358 consists of 8 ones, 5 tens and 3 hundreds. Similarly, the bits of a binary number tell us the number of ones, twos, fours, eights, sixteens, and so on. For example, the binary number `1101` has 1 one, 0 twos, 1 four, and 1 eight. Furthermore, each binary number can be considered a unique decimal number and vice versa. For example, the binary number `1010001` is equivalent to the decimal number 81: $1 \times 1 + 0 \times 2 + 0 \times 4 + 0 \times 8 + 1 \times 16 + 0 \times 32 + 1 \times 64 = 81$, which incidentally is also the ASCII code for the letter 'Q'. The Unicode for the letter 'Q' is `0000000001010001`—16 bits with the leftmost 8 bits set to `0`.

Exercises

1. Give the decimal equivalents of `1011100, 1111111`, and `0000000001011100`.
2. Which characters are encoded by the ASCII and Unicode values in exercise 1?
3. Determine the 7-bit binary equivalent of 64.
4. What is the 16-bit binary equivalent of 10,000?
5. Repeat Programming Exercise 10 and include a third column with the binary equivalent of each integer in the third column. For now, you'll have to calculate

the binary numbers by hand and use the println method to display them. Typical output is:

```
R    82     1010010
a    97     1100001
l    108    1101100
p    112    1110000
h    104    1101000
```

3. BOOLEAN TYPES

Boolean values and operators have an unusual algebra that resembles the algebra of integers with || instead of +, and && instead of ×. For example, the distributive law states that if *a*, *b*, and *c* are integers, then

$$a \times (b + c) = (a \times b) + (a \times c)$$

Similarly, if a, b, and c are type boolean, then

```
a && (b || c) = (a && b) || (a && c)
```

Exercises

For each problem, if true, explain why, and if false, give a counterexample.

1. Is it true that if a, b, and c are boolean then

   a || (b && c) is equivalent to (a || b) && (a || c)?

2. Is it true that if *a*, *b*, and *c* are integers then

   $a + (b \times c)$ is equivalent to $(a + b) \times (a + c)$?

3. The *exclusive-or* (XOR) operation on two Boolean operands is defined to be true whenever *exactly* one of the two operands is true. Write a Java boolean expression that calculates the *exclusive-or* of two boolean operands x and y.

THE BIGGER PICTURE

CHAPTER 3

Variables and Assignment

"One man's constant is another man's variable"
—Alan Perlis

Objectives

The objectives of Chapter 3 include an understanding of

- the concept of a variable as a named memory location,
- variable declarations and initializations,
- assignment and Java's assignment operators: =, +=, −=, *=, /=, and %=,
- the use of a Scanner object for interactive input,
- the advantages of using final variables,
- type compatibility and casting, and
- the increment and decrement operators.

3.1 INTRODUCTION

The programs of Chapter 2 perform tasks that can just as easily be accomplished with a no-frills calculator. Indeed, most calculators provide memory and allow you to *store* and *retrieve* data. In this chapter, we explain how data can be stored by a program and later retrieved for output or further computation. Specifically, we address three questions:

1. How does a program obtain storage for data?
2. How does a program store data?
3. How does a program use stored data?

We begin with the concept of a variable.

3.2 VARIABLES

A *variable* is a named memory location capable of storing data of a specified type.

You might visualize a variable as a labeled box, container, or memory cell capable of holding a single value of a specific data type. Figure 3.1 illustrates three variables. Figure 3.1a shows a variable named quantity that holds the integer 7; Figure 3.1b shows another named cost with value 250.75, a double; and Figure 3.1c shows a variable, quality, that contains a single character, 'A'.

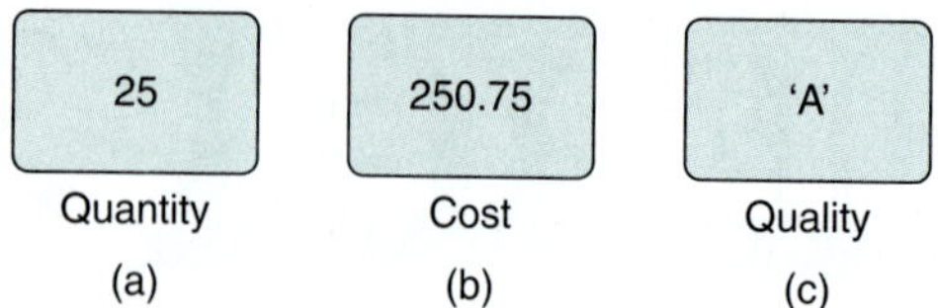

FIGURE 3.1 A visualization of three variables

You can store a value in a variable, change the contents of a variable, and also retrieve and use a stored value. The program of the following example utilizes five different variables. Read through the program and the subsequent explanation. For now, do not concern yourself with syntax or minute details. We will come back to those issues. Try to understand the role that variables play in the application.

EXAMPLE 3.1 We begin with an age-old nursery rhyme/riddle:

As I was going to St. Ives,
I met a man with seven wives,
Each wife had seven sacks,
Each sack had seven cats,
Each cat had seven kits:
Kits, cats, sacks, and wives,
How many were there going to St. Ives?

Well, technically, the answer to the question is "one." Only the narrator was going to St. Ives. The others presumably were traveling in another direction.

Problem Statement Write a program that calculates the number of people, sacks, cats, and kits that the narrator of this "polygamous poem" encountered on his/her journey.

Java Solution

```
// How many people, sacks, cats and kits were encountered on the road to St. Ives

public class StIves
{
   public static void main (String[] args)
   {
      int wives = 7;          // a variable named wives that holds the value 7
      int sacks;              // holds the number of sacks
      int cats;               // holds the number of cats
      int kits;               // number of kits
      int total;              // sum of man, wives, sacks, cats and kits

      sacks = 7*wives;                         // each wife had seven sacks
      cats  = 7*sacks;                         // each sack had seven cats
      kits  = 7*cats;                          // each cat had seven kits
      total = 1+wives+sacks+cats+kits;         // "1" counts the man

      System.out.println("Wives: "+ wives);
      System.out.println("Sacks: "+ sacks);
      System.out.println("Cats:  "+ cats);
      System.out.println("Kits:  "+ kits);
      System.out.println("Man, wives, sack, cats and kits:  "+ total);
   }
}
```

Output

Wives: 7
Sacks: 49
Cats: 343
Kits: 2401
Man, wives, sacks, cats and kits: 2801

Discussion We begin our dissection of the program at line 6.

Line 6: int wives = 7;
The statement on line 6 is a *variable declaration*. The declaration accomplishes three tasks.

1. It instructs the compiler to set aside or *allocate* enough memory to hold one integer (int).
2. It labels the allocated memory location with the name wives. The program can use the name wives to refer to this memory location.
3. It stores the number 7 in this memory location.

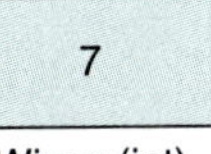

Wives (int)

FIGURE 3.2 The variable *wives*

Wives is a variable, a named memory location that can store a single number of type int. Currently, this memory cell holds the integer 7. See Figure 3.2.

In Chapter 1, you learned that every memory cell has a unique numerical address. Conveniently, a program refers to a variable by its name and not by its address. In fact, Java hides the address of a variable from the programmer. Figure 3.3 steps through the remainder of the program.

wives	sacks	cats	kits	total
7				

Lines 7–10: int sacks; int cats; int kits; int total;
Here we have four additional variable declarations. Each variable can hold one integer (int). However, in contrast to wives, no values are assigned to these variables. The variables are *uninitialized*. The uninitialized variables hold no meaningful values at this point, and we denote an uninitialized variable with an empty box.

wives	sacks	cats	kits	total
7	49			

Line 11: sacks = 7 * wives;
The value stored in the variable wives (7) is used to compute the number of sacks. The result (49) is stored in the variable sacks.

wives	sacks	cats	kits	total
7	49	343		

Line 12: cats = 7 * sacks;
The value of sacks (49) is used to compute the number of cats. This product (343) is saved in the variable cats.

wives	sacks	cats	kits	total
7	49	343	2401	

Line 13: kits = 7 * cats;
Similarly, the value 343 stored in cats is used to calculate the number of kits. The number of kits is 2401 and that is the value placed in variable kits.

wives	sacks	cats	kits	total
7	49	343	2401	2801

Line 14: total = 1 + wives + sacks+ cats + kits;
The sum of the values stored in wives, sacks, cats, and kits plus 1 (for the narrator) is computed and stored in total. Notice that it is unnecessary to re-compute the numbers of sacks, cats, and kits because these values are saved in variables.

Lines 15–19:
The numbers stored in wives, sacks, cats, kits, and total are displayed.

FIGURE 3.3 A line-by-line analysis of StIves

The simple program of Example 3.1 illustrates much of what you need to know about variables. We now fill in a few details and expand the explanation.

3.3 VARIABLE DECLARATIONS: HOW A PROGRAM OBTAINS STORAGE FOR DATA

Lines 6 through 10 of Example 3.1 illustrate an important rule.

A variable must be *declared* before it can be used.

A variable declaration specifies

- the type of data that the variable can hold, for example int or double, and
- the name of the variable.

The syntax of a variable declaration is:

Type name1, name2, name3,...;

where *Type* is a data type (int, double, char, boolean) and *nameX* is a valid Java identifier.

As the syntax indicates, several variables of the same type may be declared with a single statement. Some sample variable declarations are:

```
int cats;                              // cats can store a single integer (int)
double radius, area, circumference;    // commas separating the names are mandatory
                                       // the three variables separated by commas are
                                          all double
boolean done;                          // done can hold either true or false
```

When naming a variable, you should choose a name that is meaningful.

For example, the names used in Example 3.1 (wives, sacks, cats, kits, and total) are far more descriptive than a, b, c, d, and e or even the abbreviations w, s, c, k, and t. It is common practice to begin the name of a variable with a lowercase letter and use an upper case letter to begin any subsequent "words" of a variable name. For example, the names myVariable, numberOfPeople, and hokusPokus all follow this convention. As noted in Chapter 2, this style is called camelCase, for the uppercase "humps" in the intermediate words.

Although a variable can store an integer, a floating-point number, a character, or a boolean value, there are notable differences among the storage requirements for these different data types.

3.3.1 Integers

The declaration

```
int total;
```

instructs the compiler to allocate enough memory to store one number of type int. A value of type int requires 32 bits or four bytes of memory. With 32 bits of storage, a variable of type int can hold a value in the range −2,147,483,468 to 2,147,483,467.

In addition to type int, Java provides three other integer data types: byte, short, and long. The storage requirements and the range of values for all integer types are as follows:

byte	8 bits (1 byte)	2^7 to $2^7 - 1$ (-128 to 127)
short	16 bits (2 bytes)	2^{15} to $2^{15} - 1$ ($-32{,}768$ to 32,767)
int	32 bits (4 bytes)	2^{31} to $2^{31} - 1$ ($-2{,}147{,}483{,}468$ to 2,147,483,467)
long	64 bits (8 bytes)	2^{63} to $2^{63} - 1$ ($-922{,}337{,}203{,}685{,}475{,}808$ to 922,337,203,685,475,807)

The declaration

```
long bigNumber;
```

allocates 8 bytes of memory for bigNumber and the declaration

```
short smallNumber;
```

sets aside just two bytes for smallNumber. Only numbers between $-32{,}768$ and 32,767 inclusive can be stored in smallNumber; 1,000,000, for example, doesn't fit.

3.3.2 Floating-Point Numbers

Type double is used for decimal numbers. In addition to type double, Java provides a second, smaller type, float, that also denotes floating-point or decimal numbers. The storage requirements and the range of values for variables of these decimal types are:

float	32 bits (4 bytes)	$-3.4e^{38}$ to $3.4e^{38}$ (with 6 to 7 significant digits)
double	64 bits (8 bytes)	$-1.7e^{308}$ to $1.7e^{308}$ (with 14 to 15 significant digits)

3.3.3 Characters

Variables of type char require 16 bits or 2 bytes of memory. A character is stored as a 16-bit Unicode integer.

3.3.4 Boolean values

The boolean type has just two values: true and false. A boolean value requires just a single bit of storage.

3.4 HOW A PROGRAM STORES DATA: INITIALIZATION AND ASSIGNMENT

A variable can be given a value via an *initialization statement* or an *assignment statement*. We begin with initialization.

3.4.1 Initialization

> A variable may be declared and given an initial value with a single *initialization statement*.

The following statements declare and also initialize several different variables:

```
double pi = 3.14159;
int number = 10, sum = 0, total = 125;
boolean done = true;
char firstLetter = 'A', lastLetter = 'Z';
```

This technique of declaration together with initialization appears on line 6 of Example 3.1:

```
int wives = 7;
```

Be careful, however. The following initialization causes a syntax error:

```
short smallNumber = 100000;
```

Recall that a variable of type short can store a 16-bit number, which is a number between −32,768 and 32,767. The integer 100,000 exceeds the capacity of smallNumber.

Be cautious when using floating-point numbers. The data type of a floating-point constant is double. This means that a floating-point constant requires eight bytes, or 64 bits of storage. Consequently, the seemingly innocuous declaration

```
float decimal = 3.14;  // The data type of 3.14 is double; decimal is type float
```

generates a syntax error because the data type of 3.14 is double but the variable decimal is type float. A float variable has just four bytes and is not large enough to hold a value of type double, which demands eight bytes.

To be safe, you might declare all floating-point variables as double.

3.4.2 Assignment

Values may be stored in a previously declared variable using an *assignment statement*. An *assignment statement* has the following format:

variable = expression;

where *variable* is a declared variable and *expression* is a valid Java expression. The symbol = is the *assignment operator*.

Notice that the left-hand side of an assignment statement consists of a single variable.

Assignment is accomplished in two steps:

1. *expression* is evaluated.
2. The value of *expression* is stored in *variable*. That is, the value of *variable* is changed.

For example, consider the following declaration and assignment:

```
int sum;                      // a variable declaration: sum is type int.
sum = 1 + 2 + 3 + 4 + 5;      // assignment: sum gets the value 15.
```

First, the expression 1 + 2 + 3 + 4 + 5 is evaluated (15); then 15 is assigned to (stored in) the variable sum.

An assignment statement is also an expression.

So, like any expression, an *assignment expression* has a value. The value of the assignment expression is the value computed on the right-hand side of the = operator. For example, the assignment expression

```
number = 1 + 2 + 3 + 4 + 5;
```

not only assigns 15 to number but also evaluates to 15. Usually, the value of an assignment is discarded, but sometimes, the value can be used. For example, in the following output statement,

```
System.out.println(number = 1 + 2 + 3 + 4 + 5);
```

the value 15 is assigned to variable number and then is passed as an argument to System.out.println(...), which prints 15.

Conveniently, using the value of an assignment statement allows assignments to be chained. For example,

```
int number1, number2, number3;
number1 = number2 = number3 = 2 + 4 + 6 + 8;
```

Here, the sum on the right is evaluated first (it's 20); next, 20 is assigned to number3, then to number2, and finally to number1. As this segment illustrates, assignments are performed right to left. That is, the assignment operator (=) is right associative.

Assignments can be chained, but initializations cannot. This is because an assignment statement is also an expression but an initialization statement is not. For example, the statement

```
int x = y = z = 3;  // ERROR!
```

causes a compile time error. Correct initialization can be accomplished with

```
int z = 3, y = 3, x = 3;
```

or

```
int z = 3, y = z, x = y;  // note the left to right execution
```

The syntax of initialization can be confusing. For example, what do you think the following statement accomplishes?

```
int x, y, z = 0;
```

You might guess that all three variables x, y, and z are set to zero. In fact, the statement creates three variables: x and y are uninitialized, and only z is initialized to zero. To initialize all three variables, use the statement:

```
int x = 0,  y = 0,  z = 0;  // initialization
```

The values of x, y, and z can subsequently be changed to 3 using the chained assignment statement:

```
x = y = z = 3;  // assignment
```

3.5 HOW A PROGRAM USES STORED DATA

Once a variable has been assigned a value, you can use the variable's name in an expression, provided that the data type of the variable makes sense in the expression.

For example, consider the following code snippet:

```
int number1 = 10;
int  number2 = 20;
int sum;
sum = 5 * number1 + 2 * number2;
```

The computation on the last line uses the value 10 for number1 and 20 for number2. Consequently, sum is assigned the value 90.

However, the following group of statements is *not* acceptable:

```
boolean bool  = true;
int number = 10;
int sum;
sum = number + bool;  // ILLEGAL!
```

Here, the expression number + bool is illegal because the data type of bool is boolean, and addition involving boolean data is not a legal operation.

The value stored in a variable may be changed as Example 3.2 illustrates.

EXAMPLE 3.2

Problem Statement Write a program that exchanges the values in two variables.

Java Solution

```
1.  // switches the values stored in two variables
2.  public class Swap
3.  {
4.       public static void main (String[] args)
5.       {
6.           int a = 7;
7.           int b = 100;
8.           int temp; // uninitialized

9.           System.out.print("Before -- ");
10.          System.out.print("a: "+ a);
11.          System.out.println(", b: "+ b);

12.          temp = a;   // store the current value of a in temp
13.          a = b;      // store the value of b in a
14.          b = temp;   // store the original value of a  in b

15.          System.out.print("After -- ");
16.          System.out.print("a: "+ a);
17.          System.out.println(", b: "+ b);
18.      }
20. }
```

Output

```
Before -- a: 7, b: 100
After -- a: 100, b: 7
```

Discussion Figure 3.4 steps through the program.

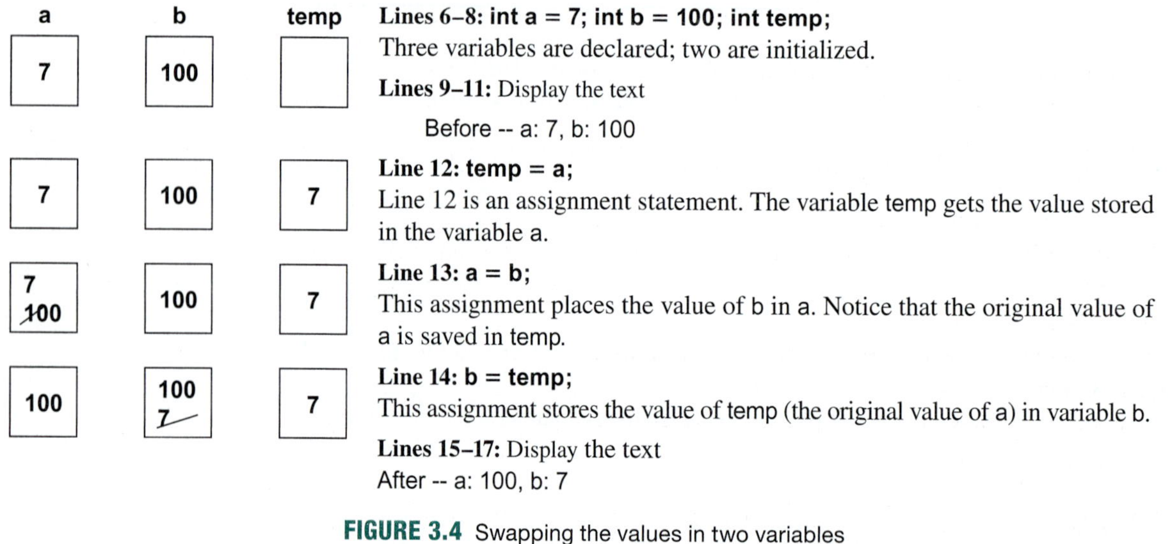

Lines 6–8: int a = 7; int b = 100; int temp;
Three variables are declared; two are initialized.

Lines 9–11: Display the text

Before -- a: 7, b: 100

Line 12: temp = a;
Line 12 is an assignment statement. The variable temp gets the value stored in the variable a.

Line 13: a = b;
This assignment places the value of b in a. Notice that the original value of a is saved in temp.

Line 14: b = temp;
This assignment stores the value of temp (the original value of a) in variable b.

Lines 15–17: Display the text
After -- a: 100, b: 7

FIGURE 3.4 Swapping the values in two variables

3.6 OBTAINING DATA FROM OUTSIDE A PROGRAM

In most cases, the data that a program uses come from outside the program, perhaps from a file or from a user who interacts with the program. The following application demonstrates one very simple mechanism available for interactive input, a Scanner object.

EXAMPLE 3.3

According to the *Farmer's Almanac*, you can estimate air temperature by counting the number of times per minute that a cricket chirps. To compute the air temperature (Celsius), divide the number of chirps/minute by 6.6 and add 4.

Problem Statement Write an application that calculates the air temperature given the number of cricket chirps per minute. A user supplies the number of chirps per minute.

Java Solution

```
1. // calculates the air temperature (Celsius) from cricket chirps/minute
2. import java.util.*;
3. public class Cricket
4. {
5.     public static void main (String[] args)
6.     {
7.         int chirps;                              // chirps per minute
8.         double temperature;                      // Celsius
9.         Scanner input = new Scanner(System.in);

10.        System.out.print("Enter the number of chirps/minute: ");
11.        chirps = input.nextInt();
12.        temperature = chirps/6.6 + 4;
13.        System.out.println("The temperature is "+temperature+"C");
14.    }
15. }
```

Output

Enter the number of chirps/minute: **99**
The temperature is 19.0C

Discussion We begin our explanation with line 7.

Line 7: int chirps;
On line 7, we declare an integer variable, chirps, that is intended to hold the number of chirps per minute.

Line 8: double temperature;
The statement on line 8 is also a variable declaration. The variable temperature holds the air temperature. Because the computation of the temperature requires division by 6.6, temperature is declared as double.

Line 9: Scanner input = new Scanner(System.in) ;
The statement on line 9 is something that you have not previously seen. The name input refers to a "Scanner object." Objects and object-oriented programming are discussed in later chapters.

For the present, we say that a Scanner object is a mechanism or "black box" used for reading data interactively from the keyboard.

This particular Scanner object has the name input. The choice of the name input is arbitrary and could just as well be any valid Java identifier such as keyboard, console, or even chirpReader. The somewhat mysterious statement on line 9 should be included in every program that uses a Scanner object for interactive input.

Line 10: System.out.print("Enter the number of chirps/minute: ");
Line 10 is an output statement that prompts the user for data. A "user friendly" program should always supply a prompt when interactive input is required. It is also a good idea to remind the user of the type of units that are expected, that is, chirps/minute rather than chirps/second.

Line 11: chirps = input.nextInt();
The statement on line 11 demonstrates the Scanner object in action. The Scanner object, input, accepts or reads one integer from the keyboard. In fact, the program pauses indefinitely until the user types an integer and presses the Enter key. Once the user supplies an integer, that number is assigned to the variable chirps. The Scanner object, input, expects an integer (input.**nextInt()**). If the user enters a decimal number or a character other than whitespace (spaces, tabs, or new lines), a runtime error terminates the execution of the program and the system issues an error message. Because the Scanner object skips leading whitespace, a user can legally enter "   77"—the spaces are ignored.

Line 12: temperature = chirps/6.6 + 4;
The value stored in chirps is used to compute the air temperature. The result of the computation is assigned to the variable temperature.

Line 13: System.out.println("The temperature is "+temperature+"C");
The program displays the value stored in temperature along with some explanatory text.

You've probably noticed that we've given no explanation of line 2 (import java.util.*). Interactive input is not simple to effect. In fact, there is an enormous amount of code lurking beneath the Scanner. This code is contained in a system *package* called java.util. A system package is a collection of code available for use in any program.

The statement import java.util.* instructs the compiler to include the java.util package in the program, and with it, the code that implements a Scanner.

This statement is necessary whenever a program uses a Scanner object for interactive input. Notice that this statement, called an *import statement*, appears outside the class declaration.

3.7 A SCANNER OBJECT FOR INTERACTIVE INPUT

Before using a Scanner object for input you must:

- Include the import statement: import java.util.*;
- Declare a Scanner object as

  Scanner *name* = new Scanner(System.in)

where *name* is a valid Java identifier such as input or keyboardReader.
Once a Scanner has been declared you can use the following methods to read data:

- *name*.nextInt()
- *name*.nextShort()

- *name*.nextLong()
- *name*.nextDouble()
- *name*.nextFloat()
- *name*.nextBoolean()

where *name* is the declared name of the Scanner.

A Scanner object cannot read data of type char.

Other Scanner methods are available, but for now, these six suffice. Like the println() method, which displays text, each of these methods accomplishes a task: each reads one value from the keyboard and supplies or *returns* that value for further computation. For example, if input is the name of a Scanner object, then the statement

```
int number = input.nextInt();
```

reads one integer from the keyboard and stores that value in the variable number.

You do not need to declare a new Scanner object for each data type.

An unlimited number of input values of different types can be read using a single Scanner object.

The program of Example 3.4 uses a Scanner object to read two double values that are supplied by a user.

EXAMPLE 3.4

Do you get more bite for your buck with a 14-inch pizza or a 10-inch pizza?

Problem Statement Write a program that calculates the price per square inch of a round pizza, given the diameter and price.

Java Solution

```
// Calculates the price/sq.in. of a round pizza using area = π r²
// Uses the diameter and the price
import java.util.*;       // to use Scanner
public class Pizza
{
   public static void main (String[] args)
   {

      Scanner input = new Scanner(System.in); //declare a Scanner
      double diameter, area, radius;
      double price;
      double pricePerSquareInch;

      System.out.print("Enter the diameter of the pizza in inches: ");
      diameter = input.nextDouble(); // use Scanner object, read a double

      radius = diameter/2.0;
      area = 3.14159*radius*radius; //area = π r²

      System.out.print("Enter the price of the pizza: ");
      price = input.nextDouble(); // use Scanner object, read a double
```

```
18.         pricePerSquareInch = price/area;
19.         System.out.println("The price per square inch of a "+ diameter
                                   + " inch pizza is $" + pricePerSquareInch);
20.     }
21. }
```

Using some real data obtained from a local pizza shop, we ran the program three times.

Output

```
Enter the diameter of the pizza in inches: 10.00
Enter the price of the pizza: 6.50
The price per square inch of a 10.0 inch pizza is $0.0827606403127079

Enter the diameter of the pizza in inches: 12.00
Enter the price of the pizza: 10.50
The price per square inch of a 12.0 inch pizza is $0.09284046188925567

Enter the diameter of the pizza in inches: 14.00
Enter the price of the pizza: 12.50
The price per square inch of a 14.0 inch pizza is $0.08120157016552973
```

Discussion Lines 3, 8, 13, and 17 contain the necessary statements for interactive input using a Scanner object. The name input (line 8) can be any valid Java identifier such as nextData or priceGrabber.

Program output shows that the 14-inch pizza is the most economical, the 10-inch pizza comes in second, and the 12-inch pizza is the most costly.

3.8 FINAL VARIABLES

The program of Example 3.4 includes the calculation

```
area = 3.14159*radius*radius.  // Line 15, Example 3.4
```

The number 3.14159 is an approximation of what is probably the world's most famous constant, π. Although most people would recognize 3.14159 as "a piece of π," a statement such as

```
area = PI*radius*radius,
```

adds greater clarity to the application.

The following revised version of Example 3.4 replaces 3.14159 with a *final* variable, PI.

> A *final* variable is a variable that is assigned a permanent value.

A final variable may be assigned a value just once in any program, and once assigned, the value cannot be altered. Its value is, well, "final." In Example 3.5, the value 3.14159 is assigned to PI as part of the declaration. It is a good practice to initialize a final variable when it is declared.

By convention, names of final variables are comprised of uppercase letters with underscores separating the "words" of a name. For example, PI, TAX_RATE, and FIDDLE_DEE_DEE adhere to this practice.

EXAMPLE 3.5

Problem Statement Write a program that performs the same task as the program of Example 3.4 using a final variable (PI) with value 3.14159.

Java Solution

```
1. import java.util.*;
2. public class MorePizza
3. {
4.    public static void main (String[] args)
5.    {
6.       Scanner input = new Scanner(System.in);   // declare a Scanner object
7.       final double PI = 3.14159;                // PI cannot be changed
8.       double diameter, area, radius;
9.       double price;
10.      double pricePerSquareInch;
11.      System.out.print("Enter the diameter of the pizza in inches: ");
12.      diameter = input.nextDouble(); //use Scanner object
13.      radius = diameter/2.0;
14.      area = PI * radius * radius;
15.      System.out.print("Enter the price of the pizza: ");
16.      price =input.nextDouble();
17.      pricePerSquareInch = price/area;
18.      System.out.println("The price per square inch of a " + diameter
                            + " inch pizza is $" + pricePerSquareInch);
19.   }
20. }
```

Discussion The variable PI is declared and initialized on line 7. Because PI is declared as final, its value cannot be changed. PI is a constant. PI is used in the computation on line 14.

A final variable is often called a *named constant* or simply a *constant*. Named constants add to the clarity of your programs. Using named constants eliminates "mystery numbers." In Example 3.5, there is no uncertainty about the number 3.14159; this decimal number represents π. Named constants also make your program easier to change. Suppose that, to increase accuracy, you decide to change the approximation of PI from five decimal places to eight. If a program uses the constant PI in several places, you can change all occurrences by altering just one line. Otherwise, you would have to search for each occurrence of 3.14159 and change each, one by one.

The use of final variables also prevents the accidental changing of a permanent value. If your code attempts to change the value of a final variable, the compiler complains.

3.9 TYPE COMPATIBILITY AND CASTING

In Chapter 2, you saw that before evaluating a binary expression with operands of different data types, Java *promotes* or *casts* the operand of the "smaller" data type to the data type of the other operand. For example, the value of the expression 2 + 3 is 5 (int) but the expression 2 + 3.0 evaluates to 5.0 (double) because the integer 2 is cast to 2.0 (double) and the subsequent addition is performed on two numbers of type double. Assignment is no different.

> The value of a smaller numerical data type may be *assigned* to a variable of a larger numerical data type.

When you assign a value of a smaller data type to a variable of a larger type, the value of the smaller type is promoted, or cast, to the larger type. The pecking order of the numeric data types from smallest to largest is:

- byte
- short
- int
- long
- float
- double

Thus, the segment

```
double decimalNumber;
decimalNumber = 100;  // a value of type int is assigned to a variable of type double
System.out.println( decimalNumber);
```

prints 100.0.

The value stored in decimalNumber is 100.0, a double, not 100. Before copying a value into decimalNumber, Java *casts* 100 (int) to 100.0 (double).

On the other hand, the following assignment is illegal:

```
int wholeNumber;
wholeNumber = 37.2;     // cannot assign 37.2 (double) to an integer variable
```

Java does *not automatically* cast 37.2 to the integer 37 because the cast results in a loss of precision. However, such an assignment can be accomplished with an *explicit* cast.

3.9.1 Explicit Casts

> If value is a number or variable of a numeric data type, then the expression
>
> (*X*)value, where *X* is a numeric data type,
>
> *explicitly* casts value to type *X*.

For example, the expression (int)3.1459.2 casts a floating-point number to an integer. The value of the expression is the integer 3. Similarly, (float)3.14159 casts 3.14159 from double to float.

The following segment demonstrates how you can use an explicit cast (line 3) to assign a value of type double to a variable of type int.

```
1. int wholeNumber;
2. double decimalNumber = 37.2;
3. wholeNumber = (int)decimalNumber;      // decimalNumber is explicitly cast to int
4. System.out.println("wholeNumber: "+ wholeNumber);
5. System.out.println("decimalNumber: "+ decimalNumber);
```

When embedded in a complete program, the output of this fragment is:

```
wholeNumber: 37
decimalNumber: 37.2
```

Before decimalNumber is assigned to wholeNumber (line 3), the value stored in decimalNumber (37.2) is explicitly cast to 37 (int), and 37 is stored in wholeNumber. The cast *truncates* 37.2, that is, the fractional part of 37.2 is removed. No rounding occurs. The cast does *not* change the value stored in decimalNumber; that value remains 37.2.

Likewise, the declaration

```
float pi = 3.14159; // cannot assign a double to a float
```

generates a syntax error because the data type of 3.14159 is double and a value of type double cannot be assigned to a variable declared as float, a smaller type. An explicit cast "down to float" allows the assignment:

```
float pi = (float)3.14159;
```

Coupled with this declaration of pi, the statement

```
float twoPi = 2.0 * pi;  // double * float results in double
```

causes an error, but

```
float twoPi = 2 * pi;    // int * float results in float
```

does not. Can you see why? In the first statement, the data type of the expression 2.0 * pi is double and a value of type double cannot be assigned to the variable twoPi, which is declared as float. In the second statement, the data type of 2 * pi is float because the data type of the product of 2 (int) and pi (float) is float, the larger type. The statement

```
float twoPi = ((float)2.0) * pi;
```

accomplishes the same result.

3.9.2 Character and Boolean Data Types

Character data may be assigned to a variable of type short, int, long, double, or float. When this is done, the ASCII (or Unicode) value is assigned to the numerical variable. Thus the code fragment

```
double  x = 'A';
System.out.print(x);
```

produces the output

```
65.0
```

because the ASCII value of 'A' (65) is cast to the double 65.0.

Of course, the segment

```
double  x = 'A';
System.out.print((char)x);
```

which casts x down from double to char, changes the output. This revised segment displays the character 'A'.

Boolean values cannot be cast to other types, nor can the values of numeric types be cast to boolean. Unlike languages such as C or C++, boolean values in Java are not considered integers.

3.9.3 Cast with Caution

An explicit cast to a smaller type can produce unexpected results. It may surprise you that the segment

```
byte x = (byte)512;        // explicit cast:  int to byte
System.out.print(x);
```

prints 0. As explained in Section 3.3.1, the integer 512 is stored as the four-byte or 32-bit binary number:

```
00000000 00000000 00000010 00000000.
```

Because a byte consists of just eight bits, the explicit cast, (byte)512, discards the three leftmost bytes of the binary representation of 512. Only the rightmost byte, `00000000`, is stored in x. Consequently, x gets the value 0.

In practice, you should avoid casts like the one described above. Such casts can lead to bugs that are often subtle and difficult to uncover.

3.10 A FEW SHORTCUTS

As you know, the assignment operator (=) does not imply mathematical equality. Although a statement such as

```
count = count + 1;
```

makes no mathematical sense, it is an acceptable Java statement. Execution of this statement involves the following two actions:

1. count+1 is evaluated, and
2. the resulting value is stored in count.

Thus, the statement count = count + 1 adds 1 to the value of count.

The statement reads "count is assigned the value count +1" rather than "count equals count +1." In Example 3.6, the variable cost is adjusted in a similar manner.

EXAMPLE 3.6 At Pepino's Pizza Parlor, pizzas are $12.00 each. Each additional topping is $1.50. Tax is 5 percent.

Problem Statement Write an application that prompts for the number of pizzas and the number of toppings. The program should calculate the price of the pizza (including sales tax) and print a receipt.

Java Solution

```
import java.util.*;
public class OrderPizza
{
  public static void main (String[] args)
  {
    Scanner input = new Scanner(System.in); // declare a Scanner object

    // some constants
    final double PRICE_OF_PIZZA = 12.00;
    final double PRICE_OF_TOPPING = 1.50;
    final double TAX_RATE = .05;

    int numPizza, numTopping;
    double cost= 0.0;
```

```
13.        // determine the number of pizza and adjust the cost
14.        System.out.print("Enter the number of pizzas: ");
15.        numPizza = input.nextInt();
16.        cost = cost + numPizza * PRICE_OF_PIZZA;

17.        // determine the number of toppings and adjust the cost
18.        System.out.print("Enter the total number of toppings: ");
19.        numTopping = input.nextInt();
20.        cost = cost + numTopping * PRICE_OF_TOPPING;

21.        // add tax
22.        cost = cost + TAX_RATE * cost;

23.        System.out.println();
24.        System.out.println("Receipt: ");
25.        System.out.println("Number of Pizzas:  " +numPizza);
26.        System.out.println("Number of Toppings: " +numTopping);
27.        System.out.println("Cost (incl tax):  " +cost);
28.    }
29. }
```

Output

```
Enter the number of pizzas: 4
Enter the total number of toppings: 6

Receipt:
Number of Pizzas:  4
Number of Toppings: 6
Cost (incl tax):  59.85
```

Discussion On line 12, cost is initialized to 0.0. Subsequently, the value of cost is adjusted three times: on lines 16, 20, and 22. The statement on line 16 adds the cost of the no-topping pizzas to cost. On line 20, the cost of the toppings is added to the current value of cost. Finally, the assignment statement on line 22 adds the tax to the value of cost.

Would the application run correctly if cost had been initialized to 0 rather than 0.0? Yes it would, because the declaration on line 12 ensures that the data type of cost is double. Consequently, 0 is automatically cast to double. What do you think would happen if cost had not been initialized at all? If you do not know, try compiling and running the program without initializing cost.

Statements such as those on lines 16, 20, and 22 occur often. As a convenience, Java provides the following shortcut assignment operators:

Operator	Shortcut	For
+=	x += 10	x = x + 10
−=	x −= 10	x = x − 10
*=	x *= 10	x = x * 10
/=	x /= 10	x = x / 10
%=	x %=10	x = x % 10

With these shortcut assignment operators, the assignment statements on lines 16, 20, and 22 of Example 3.6 can be rewritten respectively as:

```
cost += numPizza* PRICE_OF_PIZZA;
cost += numTopping* PRICE_OF_TOPPING;
cost += taxRate*cost;
```

The following example uses the += and the %= operators.

EXAMPLE 3.7 Here's a simple trick that may start you on a career as a "math-magician." Ask an unsuspecting friend to pick a number from 1 to 1000. Now, instruct your friend to divide the secret number by 7 and report the remainder. Then tell him/her to do the same with 11 and finally 13.

You can discover your friend's secret number with the following algorithm:

1. Multiply the first remainder by the magic multiplier 715.
2. Multiply the second remainder by the magic multiplier 364.
3. Multiply the third remainder by the magic multiplier 924.
4. Add the three products.
5. The secret number is the remainder when the sum is divided by 1001.

Problem Statement Write a program that allows the computer to play the role of math-magician. The program should prompt the user for the appropriate remainders and display the player's secret number.

Java Solution

```
// Determine a number from 1 to 1000 given
// the remainders when the number is divided by 7, 11, and 13
import java.util.*;
public class MagicalMath
{
    public static void main (String[] args)
    {
        Scanner input = new Scanner( System.in);

        // constants used in the calculation of the mystery number
        final int MAGIC_MULTIPLIER1 = 715;
        final int MAGIC_MULTIPLIER2 = 364;
        final int MAGIC_MULTIPLIER3 = 924;
        final int FINAL_DIVISOR = 1001;

        int mysteryNumber = 0; // eventually holds the secret number
        int remainder;

        System.out.println("Think of a number from 1 to 1000");

        System.out.print("Divide by 7 and tell me the remainder:");
        remainder =input.nextInt() ;
        mysteryNumber +=remainder * MAGIC_MULTIPLIER1;

        System.out.print("Divide by 11 and tell me the remainder:");
        remainder =input.nextInt() ;
```

```
22.     mysteryNumber += remainder* MAGIC_MULTIPLIER2;
23.     System.out.print("Divide by 13 and tell me the remainder:");
24.     remainder = input.nextInt();
25.     mysteryNumber +=remainder * MAGIC_MULTIPLIER3;

26.     mysteryNumber %= FINAL_DIVISOR; // the secret number
27.     System.out.println("You secret number is " + mysteryNumber);

28.   }
29. }
```

Output

Think of a number from 1 to 1000
Divide by 7 and tell me the remainder: **2**
Divide by 11 and tell me the remainder: **1**
Divide by 13 and tell me the remainder: **10**
You secret number is 23

Discussion Lines 19, 22, 25, and 26 are assignment statements that utilize shortcut operators. Line 19:

```
mysteryNumber +=remainder * MAGIC_MULTIPLIER1;
```

is equivalent to

```
mysteryNumber = mysteryNumber  + remainder * MAGIC_MULTIPLIER1;
```

And, line 26

```
mysteryNumber %= FINAL_DIVISOR;
```

is a compact version of

```
mysteryNumber = mysteryNumber  % FINAL_DIVISOR;
```

Figure 3.5 traces the actions of the program when the secret number is **23**.

mysteryNumber	remainder	
0		**Line 14**: Declare and initialize mysteryNumber to 0. **Line 15**: Declare remainder (uninitialized)
0	2	**Line 18**: 23 % 7 = 2, so the variable remainder gets the value 2.
1430	2	**Line 19**: The variable mysteryNumber gets the value 0 + remainder * 715 which is 1430.
1794	1	**Line 21**: remainder = 23 % 11 = 1. **Line 22**: mysteryNumber = 1430 + remainder * 364 = 1794.
11034	10	**Line 24**: remainder = 23 % 13 = 10. **Line 25**: mysteryNumber = 1794 + remainder * 924 = 11034.
23	10	**Line 26**: mysteryNumber = mysteryNumber % 1001 = 23.

FIGURE 3.5 A trace of *MagicalMath*

3.11 INCREMENT AND DECREMENT OPERATORS

In later chapters, you will see a variety of applications that systematically add 1 to the value of a variable. Typically, this can be done with a statement such as

```
number = number + 1;
```

or

```
number += 1.
```

Because this operation is so common, Java provides a special *increment operator*, ++ , which accomplishes the same effect. In fact, the ++ operator has two forms: *prefix* and *postfix*. The following statements illustrate both forms: the first statement uses the prefix form of ++ and the second statement the postfix form.

1. ++number; // **prefix** form, adds 1 to number
2. number++; // **postfix** form, adds 1 to number

Used in standalone statements such as (1) and (2), there is no apparent difference between the prefix and postfix versions of ++. Both accomplish the same task. For example, the output of the following two segments is identical.

```
int number = 5;
++number;    //prefix
System.out.println(number);
```

```
int number = 5;
number++;    //postfix
System.out.println(number);
```

In each case, number increases by 1 and the output is 6.

However, like + or *, the ++ operators can be used in a numerical expression. When used as part of an expression, the postfix and prefix versions operate differently. For example, consider the following code segments:

```
// segment 1

1. int number = 5;
2. int result;
3. result = 3 * (++number);
4. System.out.println(result);
```

```
// segment 2

1. int number = 5;
2. int result;
3. result = 3 * (number++);
4. System.out.println(result);
```

The output of segment 1 is 18 but the output of segment 2 is 15.

Segment 1 uses the prefix version of ++ (line 3) and the following actions occur in sequence:

1. The value of number increases from 5 to 6.
2. The new value of number (6) is used in the expression 3*(++number).

See Figure 3.6.

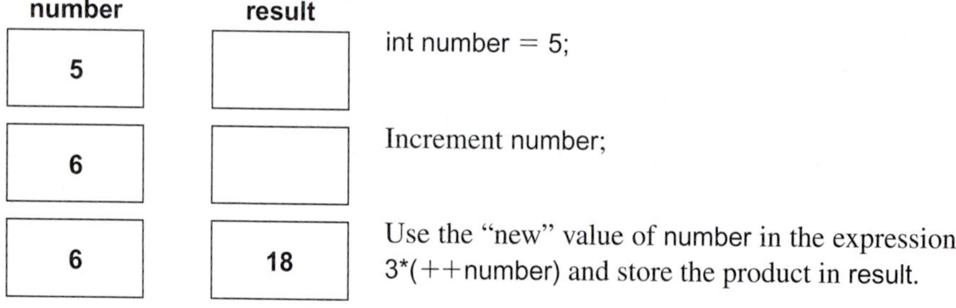
number
result
5
int number = 5;
6
Increment number;
6
18
Use the "new" value of number in the expression 3*(++number) and store the product in result.

FIGURE 3.6 Prefix operator

Segment 2 uses the postfix version of the ++operator (number++). The sequence of actions is a bit different.

1. The current value in number (5) is retrieved and stored for use in the expression.
2. The value of number increases from 5 to 6.
3. The expression is evaluated using the "old" value (5) and consequently 3 * 5 = 15 is assigned to result.

See Figure 3.7.

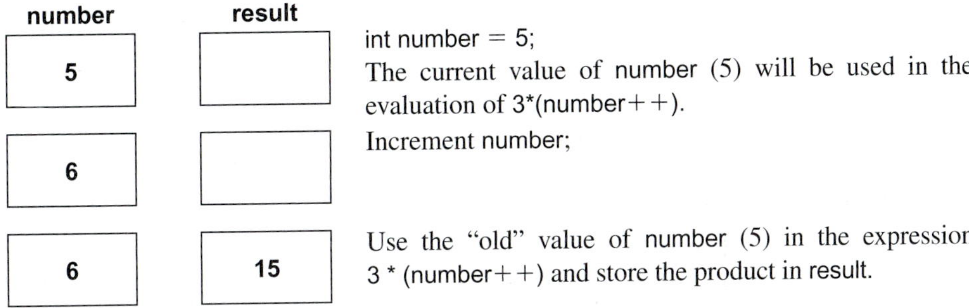
number
result
5
int number = 5;
The current value of number (5) will be used in the evaluation of 3*(number++).
Increment number;
6
6
15
Use the "old" value of number (5) in the expression 3 * (number++) and store the product in result.

FIGURE 3.7 Postfix operator

In general, when using a variable with the prefix operator in an expression:

1. The value of the variable is first increased by 1.
2. The new value is used in the expression.

Alternatively, when using a variable with the postfix operator in an expression:

1. The current value of the variable is retrieved for use in the expression.
2. The value of the variable is increased by 1.
3. The "original value" of the variable is used in the expression

In addition to the increment operator, Java provides *a decrement operator* --, which subtracts 1 from its operand. As you would expect, the decrement operator can be used as a prefix or postfix operator.

The increment and decrement operators, like the operators +=,−=,*=, /=, and %=, are shortcuts, "convenience operators," and not essential. Moreover, the increment and decrement operators are usually used in standalone statements and not within expressions. Thus, it is common to see statements such as

```
int x = 20;
...
x++;
```

However, an expression such as

```
5 + 3 * (x++)    // AVOID!
```

is obtuse and confusing, and should be avoided. This type of coding practice is begging for problems.

And now, you can probably guess how the language C++ got its name.

3.12 AN EXPANDED PRECEDENCE TABLE

We conclude the chapter with an expanded operator precedence chart that includes the assignment operators of this chapter. Notice that the increment and decrement operators have the highest priority. See Figure 3.8.

high

Operator	Associativity
! ++ --	Right to left
(*type*) [cast operator e.g. (int)]	Right to left
* / %	Left to right
+ -	Left to right
< <= > >=	Left to right
== !=	Left to right
&&	Left to right
||	Left to right
= += -= *= /= %=	Right to left

low

FIGURE 3.8 Operator precedence

3.13 STYLE

Although good programming style is partly personal preference, many practices are universally accepted. Here is a short list of stylistic conventions. As you learn more about Java and programming, this list will grow.

- Use meaningful variable names.
- If the purpose of a variable is not immediately clear, use a comment to clarify its purpose.
- Avoid trivial or gratuitous comments such as x = x + 1; // increments x.
- Avoid complex, "clever" expressions in favor of simple, straightforward ones. Shortcut operators have their place, but use them sparingly.
- Use indentation and line spacing to make your program more readable.
- Initialize variables whenever possible.
- Use explicit casts and parentheses to clarify meaning, even when not technically necessary.

3.14 IN CONCLUSION

In this chapter, you have seen a very powerful programming concept: the variable. Programs manipulate data; variables store data. The ideas and techniques of this chapter have added a new level of flexibility to your programming toolbox. Variables allow your programs to store values in the computer's memory as well as retrieve those values from memory. Moreover, variables facilitate interactive input. In Chapter 4, we show that programs can do more than evaluate expressions and manipulate variables. Programs can make decisions.

Just the Facts

- A *variable* is a named memory location capable of storing data of a specified type.
- You can store a value in a variable, change its contents, and retrieve and use the variable's stored value.
- All variables must be declared.
- A variable declaration specifies (1) the type of data that the variable can hold, and (2) the name of the variable.
- The Java syntax for a variable declaration is:

  Type name1, name2, name3, . . .;

  where *Type* is a Java data type (int, double, char, boolean) and *nameX* is a valid Java identifier.
- A variable may be declared and initialized (given an initial value) with a single statement. For example:

  int sum = 0;
- Values may be stored in a variable using an *assignment statement*.
  An *assignment statement* has the following format:

  variable = expression
- An assignment statement is also an expression and, as such, evaluates to the value calculated on the right-hand side of the = operator.
- An assignment is an expression while an initialization statement is not. Therefore, assignment statements may be chained; initialization statements may not. For example,

  x = y = z = 5;

  is legal, but

  int x = y = z = 5;

  is not.
- The assignment statement a = b; does *not* alter the value of b.
- A variable's name can be used in an expression, provided that the data type of the variable makes sense in the expression, and the variable has been assigned a value.
- A Scanner object can be used for interactive input. One Scanner object can be used for an unlimited number of input values.
- Before using a Scanner object for input, you must:

  Include the import statement: import java.util.*;

  Declare a Scanner with the statement

  Scanner *name* = new Scanner (System.in);

  where *name* is a valid Java identifier (e.g., input).
- A variable may be declared as final so that its initial value may not be changed. For example:

  final double PI = 3.14159;

  Final variables are also called *constants*. The name of a final variable is traditionally composed of uppercase letters, digits, and underscores.

- To assign a value of a larger data type to a variable of a smaller type, a cast must be used. For example

```
int x;
   double y = 3.1987;
   x = (int)y;
```

- Explicitly casting a variable does *not* change the contents of that variable. For example:

```
double y = 2.5;
int x = (int) y;
```

  gives x the value 2 but leaves y equal to 2.5.

- Java provides a number of shortcut assignment operators:

  x *op*= y; is a shortcut for x = x *op* y;
  where *op* is +, − , *, /, or %.

- The prefix increment operator ++x first adds 1 to the value of x and then returns the altered value of x.
- The postfix increment operator x++ first returns the value of x and then adds 1 to the value of x.
- In addition to the increment operator ++, Java provides prefix and postfix decrement operators (--x and x--).
- The increment and decrement operators can be applied to a variable of type byte, short, int, long, float, double, or char but not to a boolean variable.

Bug Extermination

When we use variables, some common errors that the compiler can catch are:

- Using a variable before it has been declared.
- Using illegal variable names such as: 3examples, this-is-no-better, or ba_hum_bug! Stick with the (optional) Java camelCase convention: begin every variable name with a lowercase letter and each succeeding word in a name with an uppercase letter. For example, threeExamples, thisIsBetter, and baHumBug all conform to the standard.
- Type mismatch in an assignment statement. Java will not automatically cast a larger data type to a smaller one. If x is of type short then

```
x = 5;
```

  is a type mismatch because the data type of 5 is int.

- Initialization type error:

```
double x = 9;
```

  is okay, but

```
int y = 23.9;
```

  is not. Java does not automatically cast a double to an int.

- Using a variable before it has been given a value. For example:

```
int x;
x = x + 1;      // Look! an attempt to use an uninitialized variable.
```

- Omitting parentheses around a casting operator. For example, float x = float 3.14; // Error
- Using a reserved word as a variable name. For example, int final = 6; // Error

- Chaining initializations. int x = y = 3; // Illegal
  int x = 3, y = 3; or int x = 3, y = x; // Legal
- Using +=, ++, or other such shortcuts in declaration statements.
  int x = 3, y = x; is okay, but
  int x = 3, y += x; is not.
- Failing to import a necessary Java package, e.g., import java.util.*;

Although the Java compiler can detect errors of the types just listed, the resulting error message may be misleading or cryptic. For example, the erroneous initialization

```
float x = float 3.14159
```

results in the compiler message:

```
java:38: '.class' expected
float x = float 3.14159;
```

Be aware of the common errors and pitfalls; don't rely on the compiler to do all the work for you.

Logical errors are certainly more elusive than compile time errors. A few common errors that the compiler does not detect are:

- Reversing the shortcut operator. For example: using =+ as a shortcut instead of +=. The statements

  ```
  x -= 5;
  ```

  and

  ```
  x =- 5;
  ```

  are both valid but with very different meanings.
- Misusing operator precedence. When in doubt (and sometimes even when not) use parentheses.
- Confusing prefix and postfix operators. For example,

  ```
  x = 3;
  y = x++;
  ```

  gives y the value 3, but

  ```
  x = 3;
  y = ++x;
  ```

  gives y the value 4. It is wise to avoid using ++ and -- in expressions.
- Mixing data types can cause surprising results. For most common tasks, stick with types int and double when using numerical data.
- Confusing = with ==. The former is assignment; the latter is comparison. For example, the statement

  ```
  x = true;
  ```

  assigns true to x, and as an *expression*, always has the value true; but

  ```
  x == true;
  ```

  evaluates to either true or false, depending on the value of x. Depending on its context, this error will *sometimes* be detected by the compiler, but not always.

EXERCISES

LEARN THE LINGO

Test your knowledge of the chapter's vocabulary by completing the following crossword puzzle.

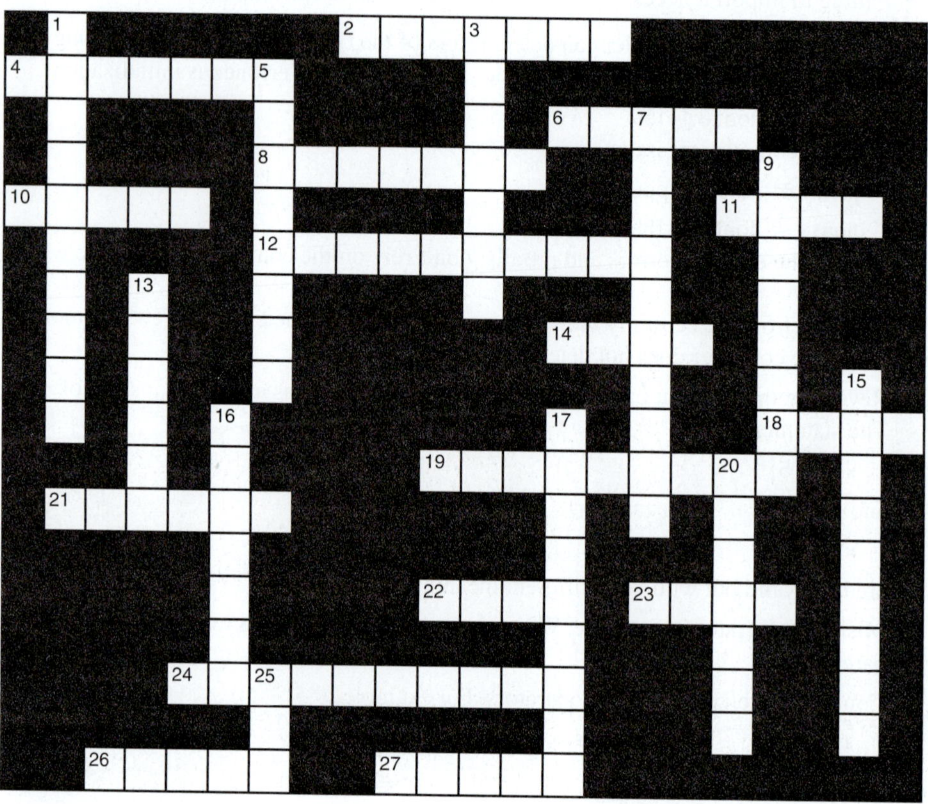

Across

2 Used for interactive input
4 A variable name cannot be a ______
6 Operator || has ___ precedence than &&
8 Named constants add to the ____ of a program
10 A variable that cannot be altered
11 A variable is accessed via its ______
12 Statement that places a value in a variable
14 Java will not automatically ____ a larger type to a smaller one
18 Largest integer type
19 Constant names should be _____
21 Like main() and println(), nextInt() is a _____
22 A variable declaration must specify the _____
23 Smallest integer type
24 Give a value in a declaration
26 Assignment is ____ associative
27 Smaller decimal type

Down

1 Choose variable names that are_______
3 Scanner method
5 Every variable must be _____
7 A Scanner object skips _______
9 Named memory location
13 To use a Scanner you must ____ java.util.*
15 ++ denotes the _____ operator
16 Type that does not allow casting
17 – – operator
20 Number of bits in a short integer
25 If x is of type byte then x + 1 is of type___

SHORT EXERCISES

1. **True or False**
   If false, give an explanation.
   a. If x has type int and y has type float, then the assignment y = x; is legal.
   b. You may declare and initialize a variable in the same statement.
   c. The statement x = 2 * y = z; generates an error.
   d. The statement x = y = 2 * z; generates an error.
   e. The statement int byte = 350; generates an error.
   f. The statement int byt = 350; generates an error.
   g. The statement byte x = 350; generates an error.
   h. Variables of type double are stored using 32 bits.
   i. The two expressions 3 * 5 / 4 and 3.0 * 5 / 4 evaluate to the same number.
   j. The two expressions 3 * 5 / 5 and 3.0 * 5 / 5 evaluate to the same number.

2. **Expressions**
   Give the value and data type of each of the following expressions or explain why the expression results in an error.

   Assume the following declarations:

```
int x = 3, w, v;
double y = 2.5;
short z = 's';
boolean m = true;
```

   a. 2 + 7 − x
   b. 2 + y − z
   c. (2 * z + x) / 100
   d. w = y * 2
   e. v = (int)5 * y
   f. 17 % (int)(10 / y) + 6.2
   g. (y == 2.5) || (m && false)
   h. (x > 2.0) && m
   i. (z < 'T') || (m == false)
   j. z *= 2 * 2

3. **Playing Compiler**
   Determine the syntax errors, if any, in each of the following statements. What error messages are issued by the Java compiler?
   a. int wives = sacks = cats = 7;
   b. int total; total += total = 7;
   c. int total = 7; total += total += 7;
   d. int wives, cats, sacks; wives = sacks = cats = 7;
   e. wives + 1 = wives;
   f. int x = 7.3;
   g. System.out.println("Wives; "+ wives);
   h. System.out.println("Sacks"; + sacks);
   i. System.out.println("Man, + wives, + sack, cats and kits: "+ total+7);
   j. System.out.println("Man, + wives, + sack, cats and kits: "+ total+ "7");

4. **What's the Output?**
   Find and correct all the syntax errors in the following program. Determine the output of the program after you fix the errors.

```
public static class Huh()
{
        public static int main(String Myname())
        {       int public = public2 = 8;
                double x = 4.7;
                public2 = (int) x++ ;
                System.out.Println("I love this stuff " + public2 + "ever");
                public =--x;
                System.out.println("I hate this stuff " + (int) x + "ever");
                System.outprintln("That is the question")
        }
```

5. **What's the Output?**
   Determine the output of the following code segments or point out the error.

   a. `int num = 5;`
      `num = num++;`
      `System.out.println(num);`
   b. `int num = 5;`
      `num = ++num;`
      `System.out.println(num);`
   c. `int num = 5;`
      `num = num++ = ++num;`
      `System.out.println(num);`
   d. `int num = 5;`
      `num /= 3;`
      `System.out.println(num);`
   e. `int num = 5;`
      `System.out.println(num += 5);`
   f. `int num = 5:`
      `System.out.println(++num + num++);`

6. **Parentheses**
   Fully parenthesize each of the following expressions so that each expression returns the specified value. Some of the expressions contain syntax errors that can be fixed with parentheses.
   Assume the following declarations:
   `int a = 1, b = 2, c = 3, d = 4;`
   `boolean x= true, y = false;`

a. ! a <= b || a != b || c == d	value: true
b. ! a <= b || a != b || c == d	value: false
c. a + b * c + d / b %3	value: 2
d. a + b * c + d / b %3	value : 3
e. a + b * c + d / b %3	value : 9
f. a + b * c + d / b %3	value: 0
g. 10 * d / c / 3 * b / 2 * a	value: 40
h. 10 * d / c / 3 * b / 2 * a	value: 4
i. 10 * d / c / 3 * b / 2 * a	value: 3
j. 10 * d / c / 3 * b / 2 * a	value: 0

7. **Playing Compiler**
   Which of the following assignments are legal?

   a. `long number = 145;`
   b. `long number = 145.0;`

c. float pi = 3.14;
d. float pi = 314e-2;
e. short number = (byte) 120;
f. short number = (byte) 150;
g. byte number = 150;
h. short number = 150;
i. char letter = 123;
j. int a; int b = a = 5;
k. int a; int b = a = 5; boolean c = a = = b;

8. **Expressions**
If variables a, b, and c are type double, are the values a * b / c and a * (b / c) always the same? If not, give an example where they are different.

9. **Expressions**
If a, b, and c are type int, are the values a * b / c and a * (b / c) the same? If not, give an example where they are different.

10. **Types and Expressions**
You may be surprised to learn that the statements x++; and x = x + 1; are not necessarily equivalent. Although the following segments appear to be performing identical tasks, segment (a) produces output and segment (b) does not compile.

(a)
```
byte x = 1;
x++;
System.out.println(x);
```

(b)
```
byte x = 1;
x = x + 1;
System.out.println(x);
```

What is the output of (a)? What is the problem with (b)? Hint: Consider data types.

11. **Types and Expressions**
Recall that a variable of type byte can store values in the range −128 to 127. The statements

```
byte x  = 127;
x++;
```

cause a "byte overflow." Some languages consider this an error, but Java computes x++; by "wrapping around" to negative numbers. For example, 127 + 1 is −128.
Determine the output of the following segment:

```
1. byte x = 127;
2. int y = x;
3. x++;
4. y++;
5. System.out.println(x);
6. System.out.println(y);
```

Does changing line 3 to x = x + 1; generate a syntax error? If not, what is the output? Does changing line 4 to y = y + 1; cause an error? If not, what is the output?

12. **Types and Expressions**
The following statement is supposed to increment the integer variable, x, but it does not work.

```
x = x++; // NOT SO CLEVER
```

If x is initialized to 5, what is the value of x after the statement executes? Explain what is going on here.

Hint: Recall that what really happens with x++; is equivalent to this:

```
w = x;                    // w is a hidden variable you never see.
x is incremented;
return w;
```

PROGRAMMING EXERCISES

1. **Powers of Two**
   Write a program that displays the first 6 powers of 2. The output should have the form:

   ```
   2^0 = 1
   2^1 = 2
   ...
   2^5 = 32
   ```

2. **Average**
   Write a program that accepts five values of type double and displays their average. Do not declare five different variables.

3. **Integer Average**
   Write a program that accepts five integers and displays their average as a double.

4. **Area**
   Write a program that prompts a user for the dimensions (double) of a room in feet (length, width, and height) and calculates the total area (walls, floor, and ceiling) of the room.

5. **Shipping Charge**
   Write a program that prompts for two double values,
   - the weight of a package in pounds, and
   - a shipping price per pound,

   and calculates the shipping charge. Your program should print dollars and cents with two decimal places such as $32.85, and not $32.8467777. (*Hint:* You can round a floating-point value x to the nearest hundredth by adding .005, multiplying by 100, casting to an integer, casting back to a double, and dividing by 100.)

6. **Extract Digits**
   Write a program that requests a 5-digit integer and displays the digits one at a time. For example, given 38145, you program should print:

   First digit: 3.
   Second digit: 8.
   Third digit: 1.
   Fourth digit: 4.
   Fifth digit: 5.

   Hint: Use the % and / operations to extract the digits.

7. **Tricky Last Digit**
   Write a program that prompts a user for an integer $n > 0$ and determines the last digit of 3^n.
   Hint: The last digit depends on the value n % 4. If $x = n$ % 4, then the last digit of 3^n is: $-2x^3 + 8x^2 - 4x + 1$. Note that this problem is simpler to do after you have read Chapter 4.

8. **Sums**
   The sum of the first $n > 0$ positive integers is $\frac{n(n+1)}{2}$. For example,

$$1 + 2 + 3 + 4 + 5 = \frac{5(6)}{2} = 15.$$

   The sum of the squares of the first $n > 0$ positive numbers is $\frac{n(n+1)(2n+1)}{6}$. For example,

$$1^2 + 2^2 + 3^2 + 4^2 + 5^2 = \frac{5(6)(11)}{6} = 55$$

   The sum of the cubes of the first $n > 0$ positive integers $\frac{[n(n+1)]^2}{4}$. For example,

$$1^3 + 2^3 + 3^3 + 4^3 + 5^3 = \frac{(5(6))^2}{4} = 225$$

   Write a program that prompts for a positive integer n and displays the three sums:

$$1 + 2 + \ldots + n,$$
$$1^2 + 2^2 + \ldots + n^2, \text{ and}$$
$$1^3 + 2^3 + \ldots + n^3,$$

9. **Baseball**
   Serious baseball fans know that the batting average is a misleading statistic. A better predictor of a player's run productivity is the OBAS: on-base average times slugging percentage. On-base average is defined to be (hits + walks + hit by pitch)/ (atBats + walks + hit by pitch + sacrifice flies). Slugging percentage is defined to be totalBases / atBats. Write a program that prompts for six integers: a player's atBats, walks, singles, doubles, triples, home runs, and calculates the player's OBAS. Note that a single is a one-base hit, a double is a two-base hit, a triple is a three-base hit, and a home run is a four-base hit. Walks do not count in totalBases. Assume that the number of hits by pitch and sacrifice flies are both zero.

10. **Larger or Smaller**
    Write a program that accepts five integers, and for each integer following the first, prints true or false depending on whether or not that integer is greater than the previous one. This program can be written more simply after reading Chapter 4.

11. **Running Sums**
    Write a program that accepts ten integers $n1, n2, \ldots, n10$ and prints a running sum—that is, your program should display ten sums: $n1$, $n1 + n2$, $n1 + n2 + n3$, and so on. For example, if the input is 3, 28, 5, 8, 9, 10, 12, 2, 1, -19 then the output is:

    Running sum:
    3
    31
    36
    44
    53
    63
    75
    77
    78
    59

12. **Investment Interest**
    Write a program that calculates and displays the amount of money that you have in the bank three, four, five, and ten years after you have invested initialMoneyInvested

at an annual rate of interestRate, where initialMoneyInvested and interestRate have type double.

Hints: If P is the initial amount invested, then after n years an investment is worth $P(1 + r)^n$, where r is the interest rate. The method Math.pow(x,n) gives the value of x^n. For example, the following statement calculates 5^3 and stores the result in variable x:

```
int x = Math.pow(5,3);
```

13. **Compound Interest**
Write a program that calculates and displays the amount of money that you have in the bank after one, three, and five years if interest is compounded monthly. Your program should prompt for two numbers (double): the initial investment and the annual interest rate.

Hints: If P is the initial amount invested, then after n years an investment is worth $P(1 + r/12)^{12n}$, where r is the interest rate and interest is compounded monthly. As in programming exercise 12, use Math.pow(x,n) to obtain the value of x^n.

14. **A Magic Trick**
Write a program that plays the following interactive "magician's" game. Your program should prompt a player for a four-digit number and permute the digits to form two numbers. For example, if a player enters 1267 then the two permutations might be 2176 and 7612. Your program should display these two numbers. Next, instruct the player to

a. calculate the positive difference between the two numbers,
b. secretly choose any digit in the difference except a zero, and
c. enter the remaining three digits in any order.

Your program will dazzle the player by supplying the secret digit.

Here is a sample run:

Enter a four-digit number: **1267**
I have scrambled your number into two numbers: 2176 and 7612.
Now subtract the smaller from the larger, and secretly pick a non-zero digit from the difference.
Enter the other three digits of the difference: **3 6 4**
The secret digit is 5!

Hint: The sum of the digits in the difference must be a multiple of 9. Use the % operator.

15. **Coconuts—A Famous Puzzle**
Here is a variant of a famous old puzzle published originally in *The Saturday Evening Post*, 1926, in a short story entitled "Coconuts," by Ben Ames Williams.

Five sailors, stranded on an island, spent their first day collecting coconuts. In the evening, they put all the coconuts into a single pile and went to sleep.

Sailor One, distrustful of his fellow sailors, woke up during the night, took one fifth of the coconuts, and went back to sleep. Then, a hungry monkey shimmied down a tree and took 1 coconut. A bit later, Sailor Two awoke and took a fifth of the remaining coconuts. Again, the monkey came down and took a coconut. Later, the third, fourth, and fifth sailors did likewise and the monkey took a coconut each time. In the morning, when the five sailors tried to divide the remaining coconuts into five equal piles, they had one coconut left, which they tossed to the ever-hungry monkey. How many coconuts were in the original pile?

There is an infinite number of solutions to this puzzle. Each solution is of the form:

number of coconuts = 12495 + 15625*a, where a = 0,1,2,3. . . .

For example, if a = 0, then the original number of coconuts is 12495 + 15625*0 = 12495; and if a = 1 the number is 12495 + 15625*1 = 28120. Your job is to write a program that accepts *a non-negative integer a,* calculates the initial number of coconuts and displays how many coconuts each man takes, as well as how many they share in the morning. Here is typical output:

Enter a non-negative integer a : **0**
The initial number of coconuts is 12495.
Man 1: 2499 coconuts; Monkey: 1 coconut.
Man 2: 1999 coconuts; Monkey: 1 coconut.
Man 3: 1599 coconuts; Monkey: 1 coconut.
Man 4: 1279 coconuts; Monkey: 1 coconut.
Man 5: 1023 coconuts; Monkey: 1 coconut.
4091 coconuts remain, each gets 818 and 1 for the monkey.

16. **A Pointy Problem**
The following problem is somewhat difficult and has even appeared as a question in programming competitions. Interestingly, it requires no more programming power than the assignment statement!

Given three non-collinear points (x_1, y_1), (x_2, y_2), and (x_3, y_3), calculate the point equidistant to all three.

Hints: Consider the triangle formed by the three given points. The point equidistant to all three points is the intersection of the perpendicular bisectors of the lines of the triangle. You may assume that all the x and y coordinates are distinct in order to avoid having to check for the special case of a vertical perpendicular bisector.

THE BIGGER PICTURE

BITWISE OPERATORS, BOOLEAN OPERATORS, AND AN INTERESTING PUZZLE

Java provides a set of operators that manipulates bits. These so-called *bitwise logical operators* are & (*and*), | (*or*), ~ (*complement* or *not*), and ^ (*exclusive-or*). If you regard the `0` bit as false, and `1` as true, then the operators &, |, and ~ operate on bits exactly as the standard logical operators &&, ||, and ! work with boolean values. For example:

a. `0 & 1` = 0 just as false && true = false;

b. `0 | 1` = 1 as false || true = true;

c. `~0` = 1 as !false = true.

In fact, you can use the bitwise operators & and | with boolean operands true and false. So for example, true & false has the value false, and true | false returns true. The only difference between the bitwise operators, & and |, and the boolean operators, && and ||, is that the boolean operators perform short circuit evaluation but the bitwise operators do not.

Also, the bitwise ~ operator cannot be applied to a boolean operand, that is, ~true or ~false generates a syntax error.

The fourth bitwise operator, ^, the *exclusive-or* operator, has no counterpart among the standard boolean operators. The exclusive-or operator returns 1 if *exactly* one operand is 1 and returns 0 otherwise:

x	*y*	*x ^ y*
1	1	0
1	0	1
0	1	1
0	0	0

Like & and |, the exclusive-or operator, ^, can be applied to boolean operands. So true ^ false returns true but true ^ true returns false. The following exercises will help you become a "bit" more familiar with the *exclusive-or* operator.

Exercises

1. Using a table like the one above, show that x ^ y is equivalent to (x || y) && !(x && y).
2. Show that x ^ y is equivalent to (x && !y) || (!x && y).
3. Write a program that verifies the identities in (1) and (2).

The program of Example 3.2 uses an additional temporary variable, temp, to exchange the values of two variables x and y:

```
temp = x;
x = y;
y = temp;
```

Indeed, this is the standard method used to swap the values in two variables. However, it is possible to exchange the values stored in two variables without an extra variable!

Exercise

4. Show that the sequence of three statements

   ```
   x = x ^ y;
   y = x ^ y;
   x = x ^ y;
   ```

   exchanges the values of the boolean variables x and y

   a. by tracing the execution of these statements by hand on all possible input, and

   b. by writing a program that executes these statements.

Because the bitwise operators applied to boolean values behave like the standard boolean operators, you will probably never need to use the operators & and | in boolean expressions. However, unlike &&, ||, and !, the bitwise operators can also be applied to integer data.

Although the expression 123 && 234 does not even compile, the expression 123 & 234 is perfectly legal. Recall from Chapter 1 that Java stores an integer as a sequence of bits. When applied to integers, &, | , ^, and ~ operate on *corresponding pairs of bits*. For example,

- 00001101 | 00010001 = 00011101
- 00001101 & 00010001 = 00000001
- 00011101 ^ 00001101 = 00010000
- ~00001101 = 11110010

THE BIGGER PICTURE

Consequently, the same three statements that exchange the values of boolean variables (see exercise 4) exchange all the bits of two integer values.

Exercises

5. Write a program to verify that the three statements

```
x = x ^ y;
y = x ^ y;
x = x ^ y;
```

exchange the values of the integer variables x and y. Note that no extra "temp" variable is required for this swap.

6. Now here is a puzzle to ponder: Using just the integer operators + and −, determine a set of three assignment statements that exchanges the values stored in two integer variables without using a third temporary variable.

Using the exclusive-or operator to exchange the values of two variables without an extra "temp" variable is a neat trick, but using a temporary variable is the more common and direct way to accomplish the task.

Are the bitwise operators useful for anything practical? Indeed they are. The power to change a single bit in an integer from 0 to 1 or vice versa, *does* come in handy. For example, a word processing program may offer you the following five independent formatting features:

a. **boldface**,
b. *italics*,
c. underlining,
d. subscripting, and
e. ~~strikethrough~~.

With a single mouse click, you can turn each of these features on or off. Of course, a word processing application must keep track of which features are on and which are off. This bookkeeping can be done quite simply by manipulating the bits of a single integer.

Use the five rightmost bits of an integer (or a single byte) to store information about which options (a through e) are turned on. For example:

00011111 indicates all five properties are turned on; the five rightmost bits are 1.

00000101 indicates that boldface (a) and underlining (c) are turned on.

00001000 indicates that subscripting is turned on; fourth bit from the right is 1.

To implement this scheme, declare five final variables:

```
final int BOLDFACE      = 1;    // 00000001 (shows just the last byte)
final int ITALICS       = 2;    // 00000010
final int UNDERLINE     = 4;    // 00000100
final int SUBSCRIPT     = 8;    // 00001000
final int STRIKETHROUGH = 16;   // 00010000
```

and another variable to hold the information about which features are on or off.

```
int format = 0;   // stored as 00000000 indicates that initially all features are off
```

You can use the exclusive-or operator to change any particular bit of the variable format from 0 to 1 or from 1 to 0. For example, to store the fact that the boldface and italics features are active, use the statements:

```
format = format ^ BOLDFACE    // 00000000 ^ 00000001 = 00000001
format = format ^ ITALICS     // 00000001 ^ 00000010 = 00000011
```

Notice that format has the value 3, which is stored as 00000011. To "turn off" the boldface option, use the exclusive-or again.

```
format = format ^ BOLDFACE    // 00000011 ^ 00000001 = 00000010
```

Exercise

7. Write a program that prompts for an integer that is stored in variable format. The program should:

a. "turn on" the **boldface**, *italics* and underlining features.

b. determine, for each feature, whether the feature is on or off and print true or false, indicating *on* or *off*. Use five println statements to do this. Each statement should print true or false for one particular bit. *Hint:* Use another bitwise operator to determine the value of a bit. This trick is called *masking*.

c. "turn off" underlining and "turn on" $_{\text{subscripting}}$, and ~~strikethrough~~.

d. print true or false, indicating the values of the underline, subscript, and strikethrough bits.

Output:

boldface: true
italics : true
underline: true
subscript: false
strikethrough : false

underline: false
subscript: true
strikethough: true

CHAPTER 4

Selection and Decision: *if* Statements

"If I had to live my life again, I'd make the same mistakes, only sooner."
—Tallulah Bankhead

"If I could drop dead right now, I'd be the happiest man alive."
—Samuel Goldwyn

Objectives

The objectives of Chapter 4 include an understanding of

- selection as a mechanism for controlling the flow of a program,
- the if statement, the if-else statement, and the switch statement,
- nested selection statements,
- the dangling else problem,
- the else-if construction, and
- the differences between the switch statement and the else-if construction.

4.1 INTRODUCTION

Is there anyone who has never used an ATM machine? Typically, a bank offers ATM customers several options: withdraw cash, make a deposit, check a balance, and so on. A customer chooses a transaction and the ATM software responds accordingly. Indeed, the ATM machine (or more precisely, the software controlling the machine) accepts the user's decision and implements it.

Similarly, a poker or blackjack program may ask a player whether she would like another card dealt. If the player responds "yes," she receives another card; otherwise she does not. Once again, the computer *selects* the next action (to deal or not to deal) based upon the player's response.

When ordering a CD from an online vendor, a buyer supplies his credit card number. If the number is valid, the vendor's software processes the order; if the entry is invalid, the program prompts the customer to re-enter the number. The program *selects* its response or subsequent action based on the validity of the credit card number that a customer submits.

In each scenario, a computer program selects the next action based upon predetermined criteria or *conditions*. In this chapter, you will learn how to add *selection* to your programs using Java's three selection (or conditional) statements:

1. the if statement,
2. the if-else statement, and
3. the switch statement.

Each option adds the capability of choice and decision-making to a program. In fact, just about every program that you write from now on will utilize at least one of these statements.

4.2 THE *if* STATEMENT

We begin with a very simple situation where selection is absolutely necessary to accomplish the required task.

EXAMPLE 4.1 When you buy an item from an online vendor, a $5.00 shipping fee is waived for purchases of $25.00 or more.

Problem Statement Write a program that calculates the final cost of an item, including sales tax and shipping, if applicable. Sales tax is 8% of the purchase price.

Java Solution A decision statement appears in bold on lines 18–22.

```
1.  // Given the price of an item, this program calculates the 8% sales tax, adds a $5.00 shipping fee
2.  // for items costing less than $25.00 and prints the total cost of the item.

3.  import java.util.*;

4.  public class BillCalculator
5.  {
6.    public static void main(String[] args)
7.    {
8.      Scanner input = new Scanner(System.in);
9.      double sale, taxes, total;

10.     final double TAX_RATE = 0.08;         // notice TAX_RATE is a constant
11.     final double SHIPPING_FEE = 5.00;  // another constant

12.     System.out.print("Enter the item price: ");
13.     sale = input.nextDouble();
14.     taxes = sale* TAX_RATE;
15.     total = sale + taxes;
16.     System.out.println("Sale: $" + sale);
17.     System.out.println("Tax:  $" + taxes);

18.     if ( sale < 25.00)
19.     {
20.       total += SHIPPING_FEE;
21.       System.out.println("Shipping is $5.00");
22.     }
23.     System.out.println("Final cost: $" + total);
24.   }
25. }
```

Running the program twice produces the following output:

Output 1

```
Enter the item price: $34.00
Tax:  $2.72
Final cost: $36.72
```

Output 2

```
Enter the item price: $16.00
Tax:  $1.28
Shipping is $5.00
Final cost: $22.28
```

Discussion The first display shows the total cost without a shipping fee. The sale is more than $25.00, so shipping is free. However, when the program runs a second time, because the sale is just $16.00, a $5.00 shipping fee is added to the order.

Most of the code in the preceding program is straightforward and requires no elaboration. The following lines, however, add a new dimension and require a bit of explanation:

```
if (sale < 25.00)
{
   total += SHIPPING_FEE;
   System.out.println("Shipping is $5.00");
}
```

These lines comprise a single if statement. Execution of this statement proceeds as follows:

1. The boolean expression sale < 25.00 is evaluated.
2. If the boolean expression is true, the two statements enclosed by the curly braces are executed.
3. If the boolean expression is false, the statements enclosed by the braces are skipped.

It's that simple. If the price of an item is $34.00 (see Output 1), then the expression sale < 25.00 is false and no shipping fee is incurred. On the other hand, if an item costs $16.00, then sale < 25.00 has the value true. Consequently, a shipping fee is added to the total and the string "Shipping is $5.00" is displayed.

The syntax for an if statement is:

```
if (boolean-expression)
{
        statement-1;
        statement-2;
        ...
        statement-n;
}
```

As Example 4.1 illustrates, *boolean-expression* is evaluated first. If the value of *boolean-expression* is true then all of the statements enclosed by the braces (*statement-1, statement-2,…,* and *statement-n*) are executed; if *boolean-expression* is false then the block of statements within the curly braces is skipped. See Figure 4.1.

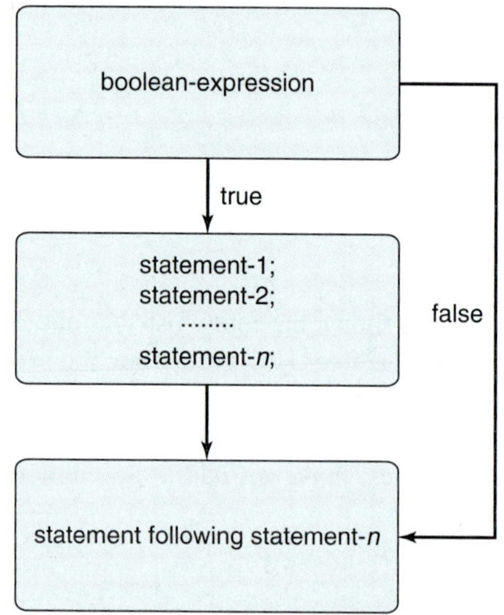

FIGURE 4.1 The *if* statement

Some terminology is in order:

- An if statement is also termed a *conditional* or *selection* statement.
- The phrase if (*boolean-expression*) is called the *if clause*.
- The boolean expression is also called a boolean *condition* (or simply a *condition*).
- The statement-list enclosed by curly braces comprises a *block* or *compound statement*.

A *block* is a group of statements enclosed by matching curly braces.

If the statement-list consists of a single statement the braces may be omitted. A single statement without the braces is not considered a block.

The following code fragment which determines the largest of three integers (a, b, and c) is an example of an if statement that does not contain curly braces.

```
int max = a;            //a is biggest so far

if (b > max)            // is b bigger than the current maximum?
      max = b;          // if so, set max to b

if (c > max)            // is c bigger than the current maximum?
      max = c;          // if so set max to c

System.out.println ("The maximum value is " +max);
```

Suppose that a, b, and c have the values 3, 5, and 4, respectively. Let's step through the fragment:

	a	b	c	max
Line 1: Variable max is set to 3. So, the "current" maximum value is 3.	3	5	4	**3**
Line 2: The boolean condition b > max is true (since 5 > 3) so the statement on line 3 executes	3	5	4	3
Line 3: Variable max is set to 5. Thus, the current maximum is 5.	3	5	4	**5**
Line 4: The boolean condition c > max is false so the statement on line 5 is skipped.	3	5	4	5
Line 6: The string "the maximum value is 5" is displayed	3	5	4	5

Alternatively, the same fragment can be written using curly braces:

```
int max = a;
if (b > max)
{
   max = b;
}
if (c > max)
{
   max = c;
}
System.out.println("The maximum value is "+max);
```

A Few Caveats

- The parentheses surrounding the boolean expression of the if clause are mandatory.
- Do not insert a semicolon after the boolean expression of the if clause.

  Your program may compile, but you will not get the results that you expect. For example, consider the following erroneous code fragment:

```
if (sale < 25.00);            // notice the misplaced semicolon
{
        total += shippingFee;
        System.out.println("Shipping is $5.00");
}
```

  The semicolon placed after the if clause is a statement terminator that signals the end of the entire if statement. The semicolon makes this particular if statement equivalent to:

```
if (sale < 25.00)
{
        // do nothing
}
```

  The two statements

```
total += SHIPPING_FEE;
System.out.println("Shipping is $5.00");
```

  are not a part of the if statement—even though they are enclosed in braces. Together they comprise a block of two statements that follows an empty if statement. Both statements *always* execute, regardless of the value of the boolean expression sale < 25.00.

- Do not neglect to use curly braces when the statement-list consists of more than one statement.

Yes, your program may compile and run, but the results may surprise you. For example, suppose that the curly braces are omitted from the if statement of Example 4.1.

```
if (sale < 25.00)
    total += SHIPPING_FEE;
    System.out.println("ShippingFee is $5.00);
```

The output produced by two typical program runs might be:

Output 1:
Enter the item price: $**34.00**
Tax: $2.72
Shipping is $5.00
Final cost: $36.72

Output 2:
Enter the item price: $**16.00**
Tax: $1.28
Shipping is $5.00
Final cost: $22.28

In both cases, the string Shipping is $5.00 appears in the output. In the first case, the message should not appear because a $34 item incurs no shipping fee. Because the curly braces are omitted, the complete if statement is really:

```
if (sale < 25.00)
   total += SHIPPING_FEE;
```

The subsequent statement:

```
System.out.println("Shipping Fee is $5.00)
```

is not part of the if statement and is *always* executed. Many consider it good practice to always include curly braces even when there is just a single statement attached to an if clause. This example shows the danger of not doing so.

4.3 THE *if-else* STATEMENT

As you have seen, an if statement allows a program to decide whether to execute or ignore a particular group of statements.

> The *if-else* statement provides an alternative: if the boolean condition is true, one group of statements executes, but if the condition evaluates to false, a different group is selected.

The following example uses an if-else statement in a program that converts U.S. dollars to euros, and euros to dollars based upon user input.

EXAMPLE 4.2

Problem Statement Assume that one euro costs $1.31. Write a program that converts dollars to euros or euros to dollars based upon user input.

Java Solution The application prompts the user for an integer: 1 or 2. If the user enters "1," a dollar amount is requested and the application displays the equivalent number of euros. If the user enters "2" or any other integer, euros are converted to dollars.

```
1.  import java.util.*;
2.  public class CurrencyConverter
3.  {
4.     public static void main (String[] args)
5.     {
6.        Scanner input = new Scanner(System.in);
7.        final double DOLLARS_PER_EURO = 1.31; // exchange rate
8.        int transactionType;
9.        double euros, dollars;

10.       System.out.print("Enter 1 to convert from dollars to euros and 2 from euros to dollars: " );
11.       transactionType = input.nextInt();

12.       if (transactionType == 1) // dollars to euros
13.       {
14.          System.out.print("Number of dollars: ");
15.          dollars = input.nextDouble();
16.          euros = dollars/DOLLARS_PER_EURO;
17.          System.out.println("Number of euros: " + euros);
18.       }
19.       else    // otherwise euros to dollars
20.       {
21.          System.out.print("Number of euros: ");
22.          euros = input.nextDouble();
23.          dollars = euros* DOLLARS_PER_EURO;
24.          System.out.println("Number of dollars: " + dollars);
25.       }
26.    }
27. }
```

Two sample executions of the program produce Output1 and Output 2.

Output 1

Enter 1 to convert from dollars to euros and 2 from euros to dollars: **1**
Number of dollars: **335.36**
Number of euros: 256.0

Output 2

Enter 1 to convert from dollars to euros and 2 from euros to dollars: **2**
Number of euros: **6908**
Number of dollars: 9049.48

Discussion Lines 12 through 25 constitute a single if-else statement. Line 12 (transactionType == 1) is a boolean condition. If this condition is true, as it is with

Output 1, then the statements on lines 14 through 17 are selected and those on line 21 through 24 are skipped. If the boolean condition is false, as it is with Output 2, then the block consisting of lines 14 through 17 is ignored and the block of statements on lines 21 through 24 executes.

The syntax of the if else statement is:

```
if (boolean-expression)
        statement-list-1
else
        statement-list-2
```

where *statement-list-1* and/or *statement-list-2* can comprise single statements or a block. If *boolean-expression* is true then *statement-list-1* is executed and *statement-list-2* is skipped; otherwise, *statement-list-1* is skipped and *statement-list-2* is executed. Every time an if-else statement is encountered, one of the two statement-lists always executes. See Figure 4.2.

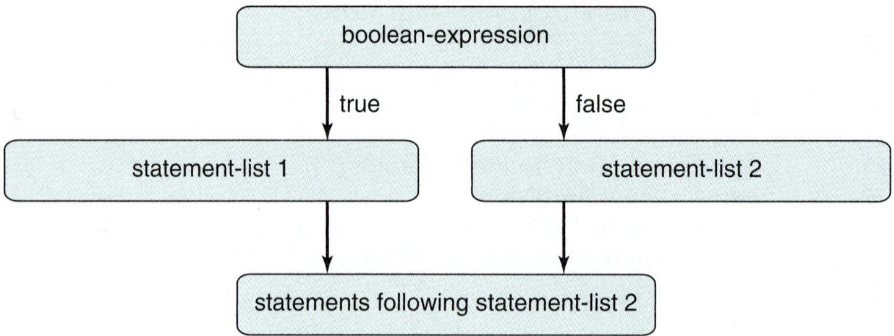

FIGURE 4.2 The *if-else* statement

4.3.1 Nested *if-else* Statements

An if-else statement can be nested inside another if-else statement, which can be nested inside another if-else statement, and so on. For example, consider the following fragment:

```
int grade = input.nextInt(); //user supplies a grade
if ( grade >= 70 )
{
   if ( grade >= 90)
      System.out.println( "High pass");
   else
      System.out.println("Pass");
}
else
      System.out.println("Fail");
```

Here, an if-else statement (lines 4–7) is nested within an if-else statement so that several paths of execution are possible, depending on the value of grade.

- If, for example, the value of grade is 65, the condition on line 2 is false and the corresponding else clause of line 10 executes. The output is "Fail." Notice that the if-else statement on lines 4–7 is skipped.
- If grade is 75, the boolean condition on line 2 is true. As a result, the if-else statement on lines 4–7 executes and the else clause on line 9 is skipped. Because *grade* is not greater than or equal to 90, the boolean condition of line 4 is false and the else clause of line 7 executes. The output is "Pass."
- If grade has the value 95, the condition of line 2 is true, so the if-else statement of lines 4–7 executes and the else clause on line 9 is skipped. This time grade is greater than or equal to 90, so the condition on line 4 is true and the println(...) statement on line 5 executes. The output is "High pass."

It is good programming practice to test every path through a nested if-else statement.

The preceding code fragment was a fairly simple example of nested if statements. Example 4.3 presents a more complex illustration with several levels of if-else nesting.

EXAMPLE 4.3

Rock-Scissors-Paper is a game played in schoolyards and even electronically in casinos. The following version pits human against computer. To play the game, enter a number: 0 (rock), 1 (scissors), or 2 (paper). The computer then randomly selects its play, also 0, 1, or 2. The game results in a win, loss, or tie based on the following rules:

- Rock breaks Scissors (Rock wins).
- Paper covers Rock (Paper wins).
- Scissors cut Paper (Scissors wins).
- If both players choose the same letter, it's a tie.

For example, if you choose Rock and the computer Paper, the computer wins because "Paper covers Rock." On the other hand, if you choose Rock and the computer Scissors, then you win because "Rock breaks Scissors."

Problem Statement Write a program that simulates a game of Rock-Scissors-Paper. Assume that input supplied by a player is correct.

Java Solution The application first prompts the player for a number, 0, 1, or 2, signifying the player's choice: Rock, Scissors, or Paper. Next, the computer chooses a random number (0, 1, or 2) representing its choice. How is that done? The rather mystifying, if not magical, expression

```
(int)(3*Math.random())
```

accomplishes the task. You will learn more about random numbers in Chapter 6.

After the player and computer make their choices, the game is scored. An algorithm for the scoring of the game is shown in Figure 4.3.

```
if the player and the computer make the same choice
    it's a tie
else
    if the player chooses rock
        if the computer chooses scissors, the player wins
        else the computer wins  // the computer chooses paper
    else  //  player chooses scissors or paper
        if the player chooses scissors
            if the computer chooses rock, the computer wins
            else the player wins // the computer chooses paper
        else  //  the player chooses paper
            if the computer chooses rock, the player wins
            else the computer wins // the computer chooses scissors
```

FIGURE 4.3 The logic for scoring Rock-Scissors-Paper

The following program implements the algorithm of Figure 4.3.

```
import java.util.*;
public class RockScissorsPaper
{
   public static void main(String[]  args)
   {
      Scanner input = new Scanner(System.in);
      final int ROCK = 0, SCISSORS = 1, PAPER = 2;     // constants representing options

      int player, computer; // human vs. computer
      System.out.print("Rock:0; Scissors:1; Paper:2 -- Choose: ");
      player = input.nextInt();
      computer = (int)(3*Math.random()) ; // a random number 0, 1, or 2
      System.out.println("The computer chooses " + computer );
      System.out.println("************************************************");

      if (player == computer)  // both choose the same value
         System.out.println("It's a tie!");
      else
         if (player == ROCK)
            if (computer == SCISSORS)
                System.out.println( "Player: rock\nComputer: scissors\nPlayer wins");
            else                        // computer chooses paper
```

```
21.                 System.out.println("Player: rock\nComputer: paper\nComputer wins.");
22.           else                          // player chooses scissors or paper
23.              if (player == SCISSORS)
24.                 if (computer == ROCK)
25.                    System.out.println("Player: scissors\nComputer: rock\nComputer wins.");
26.                 else                    // computer chooses paper
27.                    System.out.println("Player: scissors\nComputer: paper\nPlayer wins.");
28.              else                       //player chooses paper
29.                 if (computer == ROCK)
30.                    System.out.println("Player: paper\nComputer: rock\nPlayer wins.");
31.                 else                    //computer chooses scissors
32.                    System.out.println("Player: paper\nComputer: scissors\nComputer wins.");
33.    }
34. }
```

The following display gives three rounds of play:

Output 1

```
Rock:0; Scissors:1; Paper:2 -- Choose: 1
The computer chooses 2
************************************************
Player: scissors
Computer: paper
Player wins.
```

Output 2

```
Rock:0; Scissors:1; Paper:2 -- Choose: 2
The computer chooses 1
************************************************
Player: paper
Computer: scissors
Computer wins.
```

Output 3

```
Rock:0; Scissors:1; Paper:2 -- Choose: 0
The computer chooses 0
************************************************
It's a tie!
```

Discussion The application contains several if-else statements, some of which are nested inside others. The layout of the program shows how the various ifs and elses pair up. For example, the if on line 17 pairs with the else on line 22; the if on line 23 matches the else on line 28; and the if on line 29 pairs with the else on line 31. Figure 4.3 illustrates this logic.

Starting with the prompt on line 9, we trace round 1, line by line:

Line	Action
9:	Prompts player for a number.
10:	Player chooses **1,** that is, Scissors.

11: The computer randomly chooses a number, 0, 1, or 2.

12: The computer has chosen 2 (Paper).

14: The boolean condition player == computer is false, so ignore line 15 and continue with the else clause on line 17.

17: The boolean condition player == rock is false, so ignore lines 18–21 and continue at line 22.

23: The boolean condition player == scissors is true, so continue to line 24.

24: The boolean expression computer == rock is false, so continue at line 27.

27: Print

```
Player: scissors
Computer: paper
Player wins.
```

As an exercise (see Short Exercise 4), trace through the other two rounds of the game.

4.3.2 An Ambiguity—The "Dangling *else*" Problem

In the application of Examples 4.2 and 4.3, each if was matched with a corresponding else. The code segment

```
if (a > 1)
if (b > 10)
   System.out.println("D'oh!");               // says Homer Simpson
else
   System.out.println(" What's up, Doc?"); // says Bugs Bunny
```

that possibly displays either the wisdom of Homer Simpson or the curiosity of Bugs Bunny, illustrates a classic ambiguity.

If you look closely at this small fragment, you may wonder:

which if clause, (a > 1) or (b > 10), is associated with the single else clause?

Two possible interpretations of this if-else construction are reasonable (as emphasized by the braces):

Interpretation 1:

```
if (a > 1)
{
   if (b > 10)
         System.out.println( "D'oh!"); //Homer Simpson
   else
         System.out.println(" What's up, Doc?"); //Bugs Bunny
}
```

In this case, the single else clause is paired with the second if clause.

Interpretation 2:

```
if (a > 1)
{
   if (b > 10)
         System.out.println( "D'oh!");         //Homer Simpson
}
else
   System.out.println(" What's up, Doc?"); //Bugs Bunny
```

Here, the else clause belongs to the first if clause.

To emphasize the difference between the two if-else pairings, consider the following four cases:

1. a = 3; b = 20;
2. a = 3; b = 5;
3. a = 0; b = 20;
4. a = 0; b = 5;

With each of these assignments (1–4), interpretation 1 produces the following output:

1. D'oh!
2. What's up, Doc?
3. //No output is displayed
4. //No output is displayed

If we use interpretation 2, the results are different:

1. D'oh!
2. //No output is displayed
3. What's up, Doc?
4. What's up, Doc?

So, which if clause owns the else? How does Java pair an if with an else?

> An else is paired with the innermost if.

Thus, interpretation 1 is correct. Of course, you can force interpretation 2 by including the appropriate braces, but without braces the else is paired with the innermost if.

4.3.3 The *else-if* Construction

A special, perhaps simpler, case of nested if-else statements is the else-if construction, which is illustrated by Example 4.4.

EXAMPLE 4.4

Are you competitive? Are you always punctual? Do you always feel rushed? If so, psychologists might say that you have a "Type A" personality. On the other hand, are you a slow talker? Do you procrastinate? Well, then perhaps your personality is "Type B." Or maybe your personality is a combination of both types.

Problem Statement Write a program that administers a short, if unscientific, personality test, scores the test, and determines whether or not the user's personality is Type A, Type B, or somewhere in between.

Java Solution The following application prompts a user for a response to each of eight questions. Each answer is an integer in the range 1 to 5, where 1 means *never* and 5 *always*. The answers are added and, based on the final sum, a "diagnosis" is offered. Lines 33–42 illustrate the else-if construction.

```
1. import java.util.*;
2. public class PsychologyTest
3. {
4.   public static void main (String[] args)
5.   {
6.     Scanner input = new Scanner(System.in);
7.     int score = 0;

8.     //administer the test and keep track of the score
9.     System.out.println("Answer each of the following questions with a number from 1 to 5");
10.    System.out.println("such that 1 means 'NEVER' and 5 means 'ALWAYS'\n");

11.    System.out.print("1. I am competitive: ");
12.    score = score + input.nextInt();

13.    System.out.print("2. I am annoyed by people who are late for appointments: ");
14.    score = score + input.nextInt();

15.    System.out.print("3. I perform several tasks simultaneously: ");
16.    score = score + input.nextInt();

17.    System.out.print("4. I am ambitious: ");
18.    score = score + input.nextInt();

19.    System.out.print("5. I rush to get tasks completed: ");
20.    score = score + input.nextInt();

21.    System.out.print("6. I worry about the future: ");
22.    score = score + input.nextInt();

23.    System.out.print("7. I am in a race with time: ");
24.    score = score + input.nextInt();

25.    System.out.print("8. I speak very rapidly: ");
26.    score = score + input.nextInt();

27.    System.out.println();

28.    //determine the personality type based on the score:
29.    // 35-40 Type A
30.    // 21-34 Between A and B, tending towards A
31.    // 12-20 Between A and B, tending towards B
32.    // 8-11  Type B
33.    if (score >= 35)
34.      System.out.println("Score: " + score + ". Your personality is Type A");
35.    else
36.      if (score >= 21)
37.        System.out.println("Score: " + score + ". You are between A and B tending towards A");
38.    else
39.      if (score >= 12)
40.        System.out.println("Score: " + score + ". You are between A and B tending towards B");
41.      else
42.        System.out.println("Score: " + score + ". Your personality is Type B");
43.  }
44. }
```

Output

Answer each of the following questions with a number from 1 to 5
such that 1 means NEVER and 5 means ALWAYS

1. I am competitive: **3**
2. I am annoyed by people who are late for appointments: **4**
3. I perform several tasks simultaneously: **3**
4. I am ambitious: **4**
5. I rush to get tasks completed: **2**
6. I worry about the future: **2**
7. I am in a race with time: **3**
8. I speak very rapidly: **4**

Score: 25. You are between A and B tending towards A

Discussion First, look at lines 11 and 12. These lines

1. prompt the user with an assertion (line 11) and
2. add the answer to the contents of variable score (line 12).

These actions are repeated on lines 13–26, once for each "test question." You should have no difficulty understanding the statements on these lines.

Lines 33–42 contain a nested if-else construction. Figure 4.4 shows the if-else parings; each else is paired with the closest if. Let's trace through the code using various values for score: 38, 25, 15, and 10.

```
33 if (score >= 35)
34    System.out.println("Score:" + score + ". Your personality is Type A");
35 else
36    if (score >= 21)
37       System.out.println("Score:" + score + ". You are between A and B tending towards A");
38    else
39       if (score >= 12)
40          System.out.println("Score:" + score + ". You are between A and B tending towards B");
41       else
42          System.out.println("Score:" + score + ". Your personality is Type B");
```

FIGURE 4.4 Each *else* is paired with the nearest *if*.

- **38**. Since 38 > 35, the boolean expression on line 33 evaluates to true, and consequently, line 34 executes. That's it. There is no more. The remainder of the code (36–42) belongs to the else clause on line 35 and that code is skipped.
- **25**. Because score has the value 25, the condition on line 33 is false and line 34 is skipped. Next, the condition on line 36 evaluates to true. The statement on line 37 executes and the remainder of the code is ignored.

- **15**. The condition on line 33 has the value false. Next, the condition on line 36 is also false. Finally, the condition on line 39 evaluates to true and the statement on line 40 executes.
- **10**. The condition on line 33 has the value false. Next, the condition on line 36 is false. And the condition on line 39 also evaluates to false. The statement attached to the final else (line 42) executes.

Unlike the programs in Chapters 1 through 3, the execution of a program with if-else statements can follow different paths. Notice that the sample data that we chose for Example 4.4 (38, 25, 15, and 10) test every branch of the if-else statement.

It is a good practice to test your programs with data that will demonstrate the flow of the program through every possible path of execution.

You may have noticed the following features of the nested if-else statements in Example 4.4:

- The if clauses are examined sequentially, one after the next.
- The first time a boolean condition has the value true, the statement (block) attached to that if clause executes and all subsequent code of the nested if-else statement is skipped.
- If none evaluates to true, the statement attached to the final else clause executes.

To emphasize the semantics of the nested if-else statements, programmers usually format such statements as

```
if (boolean-expression1)
        statement-list-1;
else if (boolean-expression2)
        statement-list-2;
else if (boolean-expressionlist-3)
        statement-list-3;
...
else
      statement-list-n;
```

For example, lines 33–42 of Example 4.4 are more commonly (and preferably) formatted as:

```
if (score >= 35)
   System.out.println("Score: " + score + ". Your personality is Type A");
else if (score >= 21)
   System.out.println("Score: " + score + ". You are between A and B tending towards A");
else if (score >= 12)
   System.out.println("Score: " + score + ". You are between B and B tending towards B");
else
   System.out.println("Score: " + score + ". Your personality is Type B");
```

The logic of the Rock-Scissors-Paper application (Example 4.3) can also be transformed into a more lucid "else-if layout." The following fragment does just that, and it also includes an error check for invalid data. Although the fragment is longer than the code shown in Example 4.3, it is indeed more clear and complete.

```
if (player == computer)
        System.out.println("It's a tie!");
else if ( player == ROCK && computer == SCISSORS)
        System.out.println( "Player: rock; Computer: scissors; Player wins");
else if ( player == ROCK && computer == PAPER)
        System.out.println( "Player: rock; Computer: paper; Computer wins");
else if ( player == SCISSORS && computer == ROCK)
        System.out.println( "Player: scissors; Computer: rock; Computer wins");
else if ( player == SCISSORS && computer ==PAPER)
        System.out.println( "Player: scissors; Computer: paper; Player wins");
else if ( player == PAPER && computer == ROCK)
        System.out.println( "Player: paper; Computer: rock; Player wins");
else if ( player == PAPER && computer == SCISSORS)
        System.out.println( "Player: paper; Computer: scissors; Computer wins");
else
        System.out.println("Invalid choice: " + player);
```

Example 4.5 illustrates the else-if construction with an application that models a primitive ATM machine.

EXAMPLE 4.5

Problem Statement Write a program that simulates a rather simple ATM machine. The program prompts a customer for a transaction code:

- 1—withdrawal,
- 2—deposit,
- 3—check balance, or
- 4—exit.

The application subsequently carries out the customer's request. Use the else-if construction. Assume that the beginning balance is \$5423.00.

Java Solution The application implements the following algorithm:

```
prompt the user for a transaction
if the transaction is 1               // withdrawal
    prompt for an amount

    if the withdrawal amount exceeds the balance
        display a message and do not process the transaction
    else
        adjust the balance and display the new balance

else if the transaction is 2          // deposit
    Adjust the balance and display the new balance

else if  the transaction is 3         // a balance request
    display the balance

else if the transaction is 4          //exit
    display a "Thank you" message
```

```
else
   display : "invalid transaction code"
```

```
import java.util.*;
public class ATM
{
    public static void main (String[] args)
    {
        Scanner input = new Scanner(System.in);
        double deposit, withdrawal;
        double balance = 5423.00;          //initial balance
        int transaction;
        System.out.println("Welcome! Enter the number of your transaction");
        System.out.println("Withdraw cash:     1");
        System.out.println("Make a deposit:    2");
        System.out.println("Check your balance: 3");
        System.out.println("Exit:              4");
        System.out.println("--------------------");
        System.out.print("Transaction number:  ");
        transaction = input.nextInt();

        if (transaction == 1)
        {
           System.out.print("Enter amount: ");
           withdrawal = input.nextDouble();
           if ( withdrawal > balance)
              System.out.println("Invalid  withdrawal amount");
           else
           {
             balance -= withdrawal;
             System.out.println("Your  new balance is $" + balance);
           }
        }

        else if (transaction == 2)
        {
           System.out .print ("Enter amount of deposit: ");
           deposit = input.nextDouble();
           balance += deposit;
           System.out.println("Your new balance is $" + balance);
        }

        else if  (transaction == 3)
           System.out.println("Your balance is $" +  balance);

        else if (transaction == 4)
           System.out.println("Thank you.");

        else
           System.out.println("Invalid transaction");
    }
}
```

Running the program twice produces the following output:

Output 1

```
Welcome! Enter the number of your transaction
Withdraw cash:      1
Make a deposit:     2
Check your balance: 3
Exit:               4
--------------------
Transaction number: 3
Your balance is $5423.0
```

Output 2

```
Welcome! Enter the number of your transaction
Withdraw cash:      1
Make a deposit:     2
Check your balance: 3
Exit:               4
--------------------
Transaction number: 2
Enter amount of deposit: 1000.00
Your new balance is $6423.0
```

Discussion Consider Output 1. When prompted, the user enters **3** as the transaction number. Consequently,

- the boolean condition of line 18 (transaction == 1) is false and the subsequent block (lines 19–29) is skipped.
- Next, the boolean condition of line 30 is also false and lines 31–36 are skipped.
- Finally, the boolean condition of line 37 is true and the statement on line 38 executes.

At this point, because one of the boolean conditions is true, the testing proceeds no further. Testing skips from one boolean condition to the next until one condition evaluates to true. If none evaluates to true, the statement of the final else clause executes.

4.4 THE *switch* STATEMENT

Java's switch statement sometimes offers a more compact alternative to the else-if construction.

The following else-if segment displays a one-word description for each letter grade A through F.

```
if ( grade == 'A')
   System.out.println("Excellent");
else if (grade == 'B')
   System.out.println("Good");
else if (grade == 'C')
   System.out.println("Average");
```

```
else if (grade == 'D')
   System.out.println("Passing");
else
   System.out.println("Failure");
```

As you know, each boolean condition is evaluated in turn. When a condition evaluates to true, the corresponding println(...) statement executes and the else-if construction terminates.

The following switch statement accomplishes the same task.

```
switch(grade)
{
   case 'A': System.out.println("Excellent"); break;
   case 'B': System.out.println("Good"); break;
   case 'C': System.out.println("Average"); break;
   case 'D': System.out.println("Passing"); break;
   default : System.out.println(Failure");
}
```

The switch statement works as follows:

- The value of grade is compared to each "case value" ('A', 'B', 'C', and 'D') until a match is found.
- If one of the case values matches the value of grade, the corresponding println(...) statement executes and the break statement terminates the switch statement.
- If no case value matches the value of grade, then the statement of the default case executes.

The switch statement behaves in a manner similar to the else-if construction. Example 4.6 accomplishes the same task as Example 4.5 using a switch statement rather than the else-if construction.

EXAMPLE 4.6 **Problem Statement** Write a program that simulates an ATM machine. Use a switch statement rather than an else-if construction.

Java Solution

```
import java.util.*;

public class ATMMachine
{
  public static void main (String[] args)
  {
    Scanner input = new Scanner(System.in);
    double balance = 5423.00, deposit, withdrawal;
    int transaction;
    System.out.println("Welcome! Enter your the number for your transaction");
    System.out.println("Withdraw cash:      1");
    System.out.println("Make a deposit:     2");
    System.out.println("Check your balance: 3");
    System.out.println("Exit:               4");

    System.out.print("Transaction number: ");
    transaction = input.nextInt();
```

```
16.    switch (transaction)
17.    {
18.       case 1: System.out.println("Enter amount");
19.               withdrawal = input.nextDouble();
20.               if ( withdrawal > balance)
21.                     System.out.println("Invalid amount");
22.               else
23.               {
24.                  balance -= withdrawal;
25.                  System.out.println("Your new balance is $" + balance);
26.               }
27.               break;
28.       case 2: System.out .println("Enter amount of deposit: ");
29.               deposit = input.nextDouble();
30.               balance += deposit;
31.               System.out.println("Your new balance is $" + balance);
32.               break;
33.       case 3: System.out.println("Your balance is $" +  balance);
34.               break;
35.       case 4: System.out.println("Thank you.");
36.               break;
37.       default: System.out.println("Invalid transaction");
38.    }
39.  }
40. }
```

Discussion The preceding application produces output identical to the output of Example 4.5. However, this program accomplishes its task using a switch statement (lines 16–38) rather than the else-if construction.

We begin with line 16:

switch (transaction)

The variable transaction, enclosed by parentheses and following the keyword switch, is called the *switch expression*. Following line 16, and enclosed in curly braces, you will notice a number of *cases*. Each case includes a possible value for this switch expression followed by a colon. In this example, these values are 1, 2, 3, or 4. (See lines 18, 28, 33, and 35.) When the switch statement executes,

- each case value is examined in turn;
- if the value of transaction matches one of the case values, the code associated with that case is executed and the break statement terminates the switch statement;
- if the value of transaction does not match any of the case values, then the code associated with the default case (line 37) executes.

So, for example, if an ATM customer chooses transaction number 3 (line 15), then the value of transaction is 3. That's the value of the switch expression. This value 3 is compared to the case value on line 18, which is 1. There is no match. Next, the value is tested against the second case value (line 28); again no match. Finally the third case is tried. This time the value of the switch expression and the case value are both 3 and do, in fact, match. Consequently, the code associated with this case value (line 33) is executed, and the output is:

Your balance is $5423.0

No further testing is attempted. The break statement on line 34 terminates the switch statement.

Now suppose that a customer inadvertently enters 6. Again each case value is tested, but none matches 6. This time the code for the default case (line 37) executes and the output is:

```
Invalid transaction.
```

The break statement that appears after the code belonging to each case (lines 27, 32, 34, and 36) causes the program to exit ("break out of") the switch statement. To demonstrate the necessity of the break statements, suppose that the break statements had been omitted from the preceding switch statement:

```
1.  switch (transaction)
2.  {
3.      case 1:  System.out.println("Enter amount");
4.               withdrawal = input.nextDouble();
5.               if ( withdrawal > balance)
6.               System.out.println("Invalid amount");
7.               else
8.                   balance -= withdrawal;
9.                   System.out.println("Your  new balance is $" + balance);
10.              }
11.     case 2:  System.out .println("Enter amount of deposit: ");
12.              deposit = input.nextDouble();
13.              balance += deposit;
14.              System.out.println("Your new balance is $" + balance);
15.     case 3:  System.out.println("Your balance is $" +  balance);
16.     case 4:  System.out.println("Thank you.");
17.     default: System.out.println("Invalid transaction");
18. }
```

Again, assume that a customer chooses transaction 3. As before, the first two case values (lines 3 and 11) do not match, but the third case value (line 15) does match. The output may be surprising to you:

```
Your balance is $5423.0
Thank You.
Invalid transaction
```

What happened? Once case 3 is selected, the code belonging to case 3 executes, and so does all the code attached to any subsequent case (i.e., case 4 and the default case). To avoid executing this extraneous code, a break statement must be placed after the code attached to each case value. The break statements cause the switch statement to terminate. However, you will soon see situations where you might purposely omit some break statements.

In its simplest form, the syntax of the *switch* statement is:

switch (*switch-expression*)
{
    case *casevalue-1: statement;*
            statement;
            ...
            statement;
            break;

```
        case casevalue-2: statement;
                          statement;
                          ...
                          statement;
                          break;
        ...
        case casevalue-n: statement;
                          statement;
                          ...
                          statement;
                          break;

        default:          statement;
                          statement;
                          ...
                          statement;
}
```

The switch statement works as follows:

- *switch-expression* is evaluated.
- The list of case values (*casevalue-1, casevalue-2, … , casevalue-n*) is searched in order until one of the case values matches the value of *switch-expression*.
- If a match is found, the statements associated with that case execute, and the break statement causes the termination of the switch statement.
- If no match is found, the statements of the default case execute.

The default case is optional. If you omit the default case and none of the case values match *switch-expression*, then the switch statement performs no action. The break statements are also optional, as you will soon see.

A few amplifications, variations, and warnings are in order.

- The value of *switch-expression* must be an integer or character type; *switch-expression* cannot evaluate to a floating-point or boolean type.
- The case values must be constants.
- Although the switch expression of Example 4.6 is a variable, any integer or character expression is permissible, as the following segment indicates:

```
// test1, test 2, and test3 are each integers with values
// in the range 0-4.
switch ((test1 + test2 + test3)/3 )     // integer division
   {
        case 4: System.out.println("Grade: A");
                break;

        case 3: System.out.println("Grade: B");
                break;

        case 2: System.out.println("Grade: C");
                break;
```

```
        case 1: System.out.println("Grade: D");
                break;

        default: System.out.println("Grade: F);
    }
```

- The break statement can be used in other contexts, independent of the switch statement. You will see further uses of the break statement in later chapters.

There are circumstances when you might want to omit some break statements from a switch statement. One such situation arises when the same action is appropriate for several case values. For example, when playing the game craps, a player rolls two dice. If the value shown on the dice is 7 or 11, the player wins; if the value is 2, 3, or 12, the player loses. Any other value is called the player's "point" and the game is not (yet) resolved. The following code fragment uses a switch statement to display the outcome of the first toss of the dice in craps.

```
switch (diceValue)
{
        // 7 or 11 is a win
        case 7:
        case 11: System.out.println("You rolled " + value + " you win!);
                 break;

        //2, 3, or 12 is a loss
        case 2:
        case 3:
        case 12: System.out.println("You rolled "+ value + " you lose!");
                 break;

        // 4, 5, 6, 8, 9, or 10 is the "point"
        default: System.out.println("You rolled " + value + "that's your point!");
}
```

If a player tosses a 7, that is, diceValue is 7, there is a match with case 7. Since there is no break statement attached to case 7, execution continues until either a break statement is encountered or the switch statement terminates. Thus, if diceValue equals 7, the following output is displayed:

```
You rolled 7. You win!
```

This same message is also displayed if diceValue is 11. The case values 7 and 11 both require the same action. Similarly, a value of 2, 3, or 12 causes execution of the statement belonging to case 12.

An equivalent else-if construction is:

```
if (diceValue == 7 || diceValue == 11)
        System.out.println("You rolled " + value + " you win!);
else if (diceValue == 2 || diceValue == 3 || diceValue == 12)
        System.out.println("You rolled "+ value + " you lose!");
else
        System.out.println("You rolled " + value + "that's your point!");
```

One version is no better than the other; the choice is a stylistic decision. On the other hand, sometimes there is just good style and bad style. For example, although the else-if construction of Example 4.4 *can* be written as a switch statement, the else-if version is certainly preferable and less cumbersome. Compare the two:

The *else-if* Version

```
if (score >= 35)
        System.out.println("Score: " + score + ". Your personality is Type A");
else if (score >= 21)
        System.out.println("Score: " + score + ". You are between A and B tending towards A");
else if (score >= 12)
        System.out.println("Score: " + score + ". You are between A and B tending towards B");
else
        System.out.println("Score: " + score + ". Your personality is Type B");
```

The *switch* Version

```
switch (score)  // every value must be enumerated!
{
        case 40:
        case 39:
        case 38:
        case 37:
        case 36:
        case 35: System.out.println("Score: " + score + ". Your personality is Type A");
                 break;
        case 34:
        case 33:
        case 32:
        case 31:
        ......
        case 21: System.out.println("Score: " + score + ". You are between A and
                 B tending towards A"); break;

      //etc.
}
```

Although the choice between switch and else-if is often a matter of preference, convenience, or style, there are situations when the else-if construction is the only reasonable option. Example 4.7 presents such a case.

EXAMPLE 4.7

The following is a variation of the *Prisoner's Dilemma,* a famous logic puzzle. Two rather inept crooks, Bozo and Bongo, have been arrested. The district attorney presents their options:

- If one but not the other confesses, the one who confesses will go free but the other will get 10 years in prison.
- If neither confesses, then they will both get a one-year term for pretty theft.
- If both confess, they will each get a five-year term.

Each crook must separately and independently report his decision to the DA.

Problem Statement Write a program that accepts the decisions of prisoners Bozo and Bongo and reports the result.

Java Solution

```
1.  import java.util.*;
2.  public class PrisonersDilemma
3.  {
4.     public static void main (String[] args)
5.     {
6.        Scanner input = new Scanner(System.in);
7.        boolean prisoner1Confesses = true;
8.        boolean prisoner2Confesses = true;
9.        int response;

10.       // Enter data for Prisoner 1
11.       System.out.println("For each prisoner enter 1 for a confession and 0 otherwise");
12.       System.out.print("Prisoner1: ");
13.       response = input.nextInt();
14.       if (response == 0) // Prisoner 1 does not confess
15.          prisoner1Confesses = false;

16.       // Enter data for Prisoner 2
17.       System.out.print("Prisoner2: ");
18.       response = input.nextInt();
19.       if (response == 0)  // Prisoner 2 does not confess
20.          prisoner2Confesses = false;

21.       if (prisoner1Confesses && prisoner2Confesses) //both confess
22.          System.out.println("Both confessed. Each gets 5 years!");

23.       else if (prisoner1Confesses && !prisoner2Confesses) // 1 confesses; 2 does not
24.          System.out.println("Prisoner 1 goes free; Prisoner 2 gets 10 years.");

25.       else if (!prisoner1Confesses && prisoner2Confesses)  // 2 confesses; 1 does not
26.          System.out.println("Prisoner 2 goes free; Prisoner 1 gets 10 years.");

27.       else  // neither confess
28.          System.out.println("Neither confessed. Each gets one year.");

29.    }
30. }
```

Output

```
For each prisoner enter 1 for a confession and 0 otherwise
Prisoner1: 1
Prisoner2: 0
Prisoner 1 goes free; Prisoner 2 gets 10 years.
```

Discussion The else-if construction on lines 21–28 enumerates the four possibilities. Recall that the switch expression and the case values must be integer or character types. Consequently, this particular else-if construction cannot be converted *directly* to a switch statement, because the conditions that are tested are boolean expressions and not integer or character expressions. On the other hand, the else-if construction can be converted *indirectly* to a switch statement using integer case values to encode the prisoners' responses. However, you may find that the necessary encoding entails an unwieldy style.

4.5 IN CONCLUSION

Your programs are now capable of making decisions, and Java provides you with several decision-making options: the if statement, the if-else statement, and the switch statement. By nesting these selection statements, your programs can implement some rather complex logic, as you have seen in the program of Example 4.3 that plays the game Rock-Scissors-Paper. Nonetheless, that program runs just once and stops. Wouldn't it be more user friendly to ask a player whether he/she would like to play the game again, and again, and perhaps again? The Rock-Scissors-Paper program does not have that capability.

In Chapter 5, we show you how to include repetition in your programs so that your Rock-Scissors-Paper application can be continually played 10, 100, or even 1000 times.

Just The Facts

- An if statement has the following form:

```
if (boolean-expression)
{
        statement-1;
        statement-2;
        ...
        statement-n;
}
```

- The *boolean-expression* in an if statement is also called a *condition*.
- The group of statements enclosed by curly braces is called a *block*.
- If the condition of an if statement evaluates to true then the block executes; otherwise the block is skipped.
- An if-else statement has the following form:

```
if (boolean-expression)
    statement-list-1
else
    statement-list-2
```

  where *statement-list-1* and *statement-list-2* can be blocks or single statements.

- The if-else statement works like this:
  If *boolean-expression* is true then
  statement-list-1 is executed and *statement-list-2* is skipped;
  otherwise
  statement-list-1 is skipped and *statement-list-2* is executed.

Every time an if-else statement is encountered, exactly one of the two statement-lists, *statement-list-1* or *statement-list-2,* always executes.

- An else clause is paired with the innermost if.
- The else-if construction has the following form:

```
if (boolean-expression-1)
        statement-list-1;
else if (boolean-expression-2)
        statement-list-2;
else if (boolean-expression-3)
        statement-list-3;
...
else
        statement-list-n;
```

- The else-if construction works like this:

  The boolean expressions are evaluated in turn. When *boolean-expression-i* evaluates to true, the corresponding block (*statement-list-i*) executes and the if-else statement terminates. If none of the boolean expressions is true, *statement-list-n* executes. The else-if construction is a special case of a nested if statement.
- It is a good practice to test your programs with data that will demonstrate the flow of the program through every possible path of execution.
- The switch statement has the following form:

```
switch (switch-expression)
{
        case casevalue-1: statement;
                          statement;
                          ...
                          statement;
                          break;          //optional
        case casevalue-2: statement;
                          statement;
                          ...
                          statement;
                          break;          //optional
        ...
        case casevalue-n: statement;
                          statement;
                          ...
                          statement;
                          break;          //optional
        default:          statement;      //optional
                          statement;      //optional
                             ...
                          statement;      //optional
}
```

- The switch statement works like this:

  switch-expression is evaluated. The value of *switch-expression* is compared to the case values, in turn. If a match exists, the code associated with that case value executes. If no match is found, the code of the default case is selected.

- The *switch-expression* must evaluate to an integer or a character. It may not evaluate to a boolean or floating-point type.
- The break statement terminates a switch statement. Omitting a break statement causes execution of the code of subsequent cases.
- The case values in a switch statement are constants.
- The default case of a switch statement is optional. If no default case is included and the value of *switch-expression* matches none of the case values, then no action is taken.
- The break statements are optional. There are times when purposefully omitting a break statement is useful.
- An else-if construction can easily do the job of any switch statement, but not vice versa. The choice of which statement to use is a matter of both style and technique.

Bug Extermination

The Java compiler can detect many of the errors associated with if and if-else statements. For example, the omission of parentheses surrounding the boolean condition is an easy mark for the compiler. However, many common errors cannot be flagged as easily by the compiler and may produce some rather strange output.

For example, the segment

```
if (x < 5)
        System.out.println("too small");
        x++;
```

is very different from

```
if (x < 5)
{
        System.out.println("too small");
        x++
}
```

The first segment *always* increments x, while the second segment does not.

> Indentation does not take the place of braces.

A semicolon immediately following the boolean condition is another common bug that goes undetected by the compiler. The semicolon following the condition

```
(x < 5);
```

looks perfectly fine to the compiler, but it is probably not what you intend. The semicolon signals the end of the if statement. Indeed, the statement

```
if (x < 5);
```

is equivalent to

```
if (x < 5)
   { // do nothing}
```

The following list enumerates some common errors that occur when using if and if-else statements. Some of these errors are easily detected by the compiler, but many are not.

- Omitting parentheses surrounding the boolean condition of an if statement.
- Mistakenly inserting a semicolon after the if clause but before the block of an if statement.
- Neglecting to enclose a block in matching curly braces.
- Omitting the semicolon after the last line in the block. The closing brace does not terminate a statement.
- Mismatching curly braces in a deeply nested if-else statement.
- Using = instead of == in a boolean condition.
- Incorrect operator precedence in a boolean condition. Use parentheses to be sure!
- Unintentionally omitting break statements in a switch statement.
- Intentionally but incorrectly omitting break statements.
- Incorrectly closing or omitting the closing brace of a switch statement.
- Using variable expressions instead of constants for a case value in a switch statement.
- Using floating-point or boolean expressions in a switch condition.

EXERCISES

LEARN THE LINGO

Test your knowledge of the chapter's vocabulary by completing the following crossword puzzle.

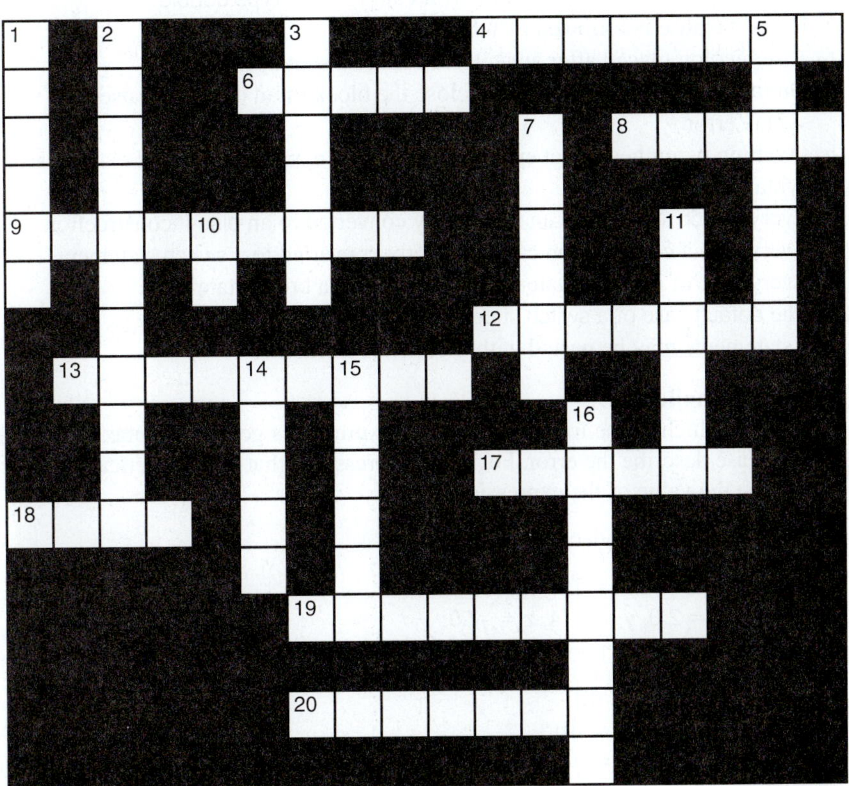

Across

4 A case value must be a ________
6 Statements in curly braces
8 Terminates the switch statement
9 The boolean expression of an if clause
12 Optional in a switch statement
13 An if statement is also called a ________ statement
17 Every switch statement includes ________
18 Keyword with switch statement
19 Do not place a ________ after the if clause
20 Data type of a condition

Down

1 Alternative to else-if construction
2 The condition of an if statement is enclosed by________
3 Nested if construction
5 An else is paired with the ________ if
7 if statements inside if statements inside if statements
10 Every else must have an ________
11 A case value cannot be a ________
14 Follows a case value
15 if statement with an alternative
16 A classic ambiguity: the ________ else

SHORT EXERCISES

1. **True or False**

   If false, give an explanation.

   a. Every if clause has a matching else clause.
   b. By default, an else clause is paired with the closest if clause.
   c. switch (x > 5) causes a syntax error.
   d. The case values of a switch statement cannot be of type double.
   e. Every if clause is followed by a block.
   f. A semicolon placed after an if clause causes a syntax error.
   g. Omitting the curly braces that enclose the block of an if clause causes a syntax error.
   h. Omitting parentheses that enclose the boolean expression of an if clause causes a syntax error.
   i. Every switch statement can be directly converted to an else-if construction.
   j. Every else-if construction can be directly converted to a switch statement.
   k. Every case of a switch statement must include a break statement.
   l. The default case of a switch statement is optional.
   m. if statements may be nested within other if statements.

2. **Playing Compiler**

   Determine which of the following boolean expressions generate syntax errors, and in each case describe the error. For those expressions that are syntactically correct, determine the value of the expression.

   Assume the following declarations:

```
int a = 2, b = 4, c = 7;
double x = 2.0, y = 3.14, z = –7.0;
boolean m = true, n = false;
```

```
a. ((a > 7) || (b < 6))
b. ((a > 7) && (b < 6))
c. ((x > 2.5) || (a == 2) && (c < 7))
d. ((x = 2.0) && (c == 7))
e. (m = (!n && (m || n)))
f. (m == ((y == y/2) && (a == b)))
g. ((m == 0) || (z == 7.0))
h. (m && n && (a == b))
i. (c == -z)
j. (m == a)
k. (( b/2 == x) && (2 * a == b))
l. ((int) (b/2) == (double) x)
m. (x + y + z + 1.86 != 0)
n. (a == x++)
o. ((int) m == 0)
p. ((x > z) || (m < n))
```

3. **What's the Output?**

   Consider the following two unformatted code segments where variables a and b have been declared as boolean:

   (i)

```
if (a)
if (b) System.out.println("Hello");
else System.out.println("Goodbye")
```

(ii)
```
if (a)
{if (b) System.out.println("Hello");}
else System.out.println("Goodbye");
```

Determine the output of each segment, (i) and (ii), assuming:

a. a = true, b = true
b. a = true, b = false
c. a = false, b = true
d. a = false, b = false

4. **Tracing**
For the program of Example 4.3, trace the execution of Output 2 and the execution of Output 3.

5. **What's the Output?**
Determine the output of the following three code segments:

(a)
```
int a = 3;
if (a++ == 3 )
        System.out.println("Three");
else
        System.out.println("Four");
```

(b)
```
int a = 3;
if (++a == 3 )
        System.out.println("Three");
else
        System.out.println("Four");
```

(c)
```
int a = 3;
a = a++;
if (a == 3 )
        System.out.println("Three");
else
        System.out.println("Four");
```

6. **What's the Output?**
Determine the output of the following poetic switch statement or point out the errors.

```
int a = 3;
switch (a)
{
   case 1: System.out.println(" Once upon a midnight dreary, while I pondered weak and weary, ");
   case 2: System.out.println(" Over many a quaint and curious volume of forgotten lore, ");
   case 3: System.out.println(" While I nodded, nearly napping, suddenly there came a tapping, ");
   case 4: System.out.println(" As of some one gently rapping, rapping at my chamber door ");
   case 5: System.out.println(" Tis some visitor, I muttered, tapping at my chamber door, ");
   default: System.out.println(" Only this, and nothing more. ");
}
```

7. **What's the Output?**
Determine the output of the following rather complicated Java fragment for each of the declarations (a) through (j).

```
if (a > b)
{
   b++;
   if (b > c)
      c++;
   if (y == x)
      y++;
    else z ++;
   if (!m)
   {
      System.out.println("You may find yourself ");
      System.out.println("Living in a shotgun shack ");
      System.out.println(a + b);
      System.out.println(y + a);
   }
   else
   {
      System.out.println("You may ask yourself ");
      System.out.println("Well - How did I get here? ");
      System.out.println(a + b);
      System.out.println(x + y);
   }
}
else
{
   a = b + c;
   if (x != 0)
      x = y + z;
   if (a != c)
      c = c - 1;
   else
      c = c + 1;
   if (c == 5)
      System.out.println("Same as it ever was " + a);
   else if (c == 6)
      System.out.println("Same as it ever was " + b);
   else if (c == 7)
      System.out.println("Same as it ever was " + c);
   else
      System.out.println("Same as it ever was " + x);
}
```

a. int a = 2, b = 4, c = 7; double x = 2.0, y = 3.14, z = −7.0; boolean m = true;
b. int a = 7, b = 1, c = 5; double x = 2.0, y = 2.0, z = 4.5; boolean m = false;
c. int a = 8, b = 2, c = 6; double x = 0.0, y = 0.0, z = 2.5; boolean m = true;
d. int a = 7, b = 3, c = 4; double x = 12.1, y = 1.2, z = 2.8; boolean m = false;
e. int a = 3, b = 9; c = 2; double x = 4.0, y = 4.0, z = 1.5; boolean m = false;
f. int a = 2, b = 7, c = 1; double x = 2.7, y = 2.7, z = 1.1; boolean m = true;

g. int a = 9, b = 9, c = 9; double x = 9.0, y = 9.0, z = 0.0; boolean m = false;
h. int a = −3, b = −3, c = 0; double x = 1.1, y = 1.2, z = 1.3; boolean m = true;
i. int a = 5, b = 2, c = 8; double x = 0.0, y = 0.0, z = −2.5; boolean m = false;
j. int a = 0, b = 1, c = 1; double x = 1.5, y = 2.5, z = 1.0; boolean m = false;

8. **Style**
Explain why, at least stylistically, you would not use a switch statement to accomplish the same task as the following else-if construction. Assume the variable grade is an integer in the range 0–100.

```
if (grade >= 90)
        System.out.println('A');
else if (grade >= 80)
        System.out.println('B');
else if (grade >=  70)
        System.out.println('C');
else if (grade >= 60)
        System.out.println('D')
else
        System.out.println('F');
```

9. **Find the Error**
What, if anything, is incorrect with the following switch statement:

```
Scanner input = new Scanner(System.in);
int number;

switch (number == input.nextInt % 2)
{
        case 0: System.out.println("Even"); break;
        default: System.out.println("Odd");
}
```

10. **Find the Error**
Is the following statement syntactically correct? If not, describe the error, otherwise give the output when answer == 'Y' and also when answer == 'N' . You may assume that answer is declared elsewhere as char.

```
if (answer == 'Y'); else System.out.println(" Hello");
```

PROGRAMMING EXERCISES

1. **Sort Three**
Write a program that accepts three integers and displays the numbers in order from lowest to highest.

2. **Taxes**
Write a program that calculates the Minnesota state income tax according to the following rules:

Income	**Tax Rate**
\$0–\$19,440	5.35%
\$19,441–\$63,860	7.05%
Over \$63,860	7.85%

All data are type double.

3. **Positive Sum**
   Write a program that prompts for five integers and calculates the sum of those that are positive.

4. **A Vending Machine**
   Write a program that simulates a vending machine. The machine holds six items numbered 1 through 6, with prices \$1.25, \$.75, \$.90, \$.75, \$1.50, and \$.75, respectively. The input to your program is an integer and a floating-point number representing an item number and a sum of money. If the money is enough to buy the item, your program should print:

   "Thank you for buying item *X*. Your change is *Y*."

   If the money inserted is insufficient, then your program should say so. The following display gives typical output:

   Enter an item number and a sum of money: **3 1.00**
   Thank you for buying item 3. Your change is \$.10

   Enter an item number and a sum of money: **6 0.25**
   Please insert another \$.50

5. **Medical Diagnosis**
   Write a program that helps people self-diagnose the symptoms of an earache according to the following self-help chart. Your program should ask questions and suggest a diagnosis based on a user's replies. Use 1 for a "yes" answer and 0 for a "no."

   Does the pain get worse when you pull at your earlobe?
   Yes: You probably have an infection of the outer ear canal.
   No: Do you have a blocked-up feeling in your ear that cannot be cleared by swallowing?
   - Yes: Did the pain begin after an airplane flight?
     - Yes: Changes in air pressure may have damaged your inner ear.
     - No: Has your hearing become worse over the past few weeks?
       - Yes: You may have wax blockage.
       - No: You may have an acute middle ear infection.
   - No: Is there a sticky yellow-green discharge?
     - Yes: You may have an infection of the outer ear canal or middle ear.
     - No: Do you have a cold?
       - Yes: Earache is a common symptom of colds.
       - No: Do you also have pain your teeth or jaw?
         - Yes: Tooth or gum trouble is sometimes felt as ear pain—contact your dentist.
         - No: Unable to suggest a diagnosis—Contact your physician.

6. **Tricky Last Digit Revisited**
   Write a program that accepts an integer $n > 0$ and determines the last digit of 3^n. *Hint:* The last digit depends on n % 4. The last digit is 3, 9, 7, or 1 depending on whether n % 4 is 1, 2, 3, or 0, respectively.

7. **Craps**
   In the casino version of the game craps, a player rolls two dice. If he bets on the "don't pass" line, he

   - loses with a 7 or 11
   - wins with 2 or 3
   - neither wins nor loses with 12 (and must begin the game again)
   - continues rolling with 4, 5, 6, 8, 9, or 10.

Write an application that generates two random integers between 1 and 6 inclusive, and determines whether or not the player wins, loses, starts over, or keeps rolling. Use an else-if construction.

Hint: To generate a random integer in the range 1–6 use the expression

```
(int)(6 * Math.random() + 1)
```

8. **Toll-Free Numbers**
As of the year 2008, a 10-digit phone number that begins with either 800, 888, 877, or 866 is toll free. Write a program that reads in a 10-digit phone number and displays a message that states whether or not the number is toll free. For example:

input: 8005651009
output: 800-565-1009 is a toll-free number.

Hint: Read the number as a 10-digit integer of type long and break the number into pieces using the operators / and %.

9. **Unusual Encoding**
Write a program that reads 10 single-digit integers and displays a string consisting of 10 characters using the coding scheme:

Digit	Corresponding Character
0	a
1	b
2	c
...	...
9	j

For example, if input consists of the 10 digits 1 8 6 1 0 3 1 8 5 5, the application responds with "bigbadbiff."

10. **Market Price**
The price of produce is marked down by 10% if you buy more than three pounds, and it is reduced by 20% if you buy over six pounds. Write a program that prompts a user for the price per pound of fruit (double) and the desired number of pounds (double). The program should print the total price for the produce rounded to the nearest penny.

11. **Grade Conversion**
A certain school assigns numerical grades ranging from 0 to 100. Write a program that queries the user for a numerical score and converts the score to a letter grade according to the following criteria:

0–59: F; 60–69: D; 70–72: C−; 73–76: C; 77–79 C+; 80–82: B−; 83–86: B; 87–89: B+; 90–92: A−; 93–96: A; 97–100: A+.

12. ***Friendly* Numbers**
A five-digit integer is said to be *friendly* if the leftmost digit is divisible by 1, the leftmost two digits are divisible by 2, the leftmost three digits are divisible by 3, the leftmost four digits are divisible by 4, and the leftmost five digits (the five-digit number itself) is divisible by 5. For example, the number 42325 is friendly because 4 is divisible by 1, 42 is divisible by 2, 423 is divisible by 3, 4232 is divisible by 4, and 42325 is divisible by 5. Write a program that prompts for a five-digit integer and determines whether or not the number is "friendly."

13. **Stock Commission**

Write a program that accepts a value (double) representing a stock sale and calculates the commission according to the following table:

Stock Sale	Commission
< $100	$20
$100–$999	$20 + 1% of price over $99
$1000–$9999	$30 + .5% of price over $999
$10000–$99999	$75 + .25% of price over $9999

14. **Bowling**

A game of tenpin bowling consists of 10 frames. In each frame you are given at most two chances to knock over all 10 pins with a bowling ball. Each frame is scored based on the number of pins that you knock over. If, in any frame, all 10 pins fall on the first roll of the ball, you've made a strike, and the score for that frame is 10 plus the number of pins that you knock over on your next two rolls. If you knock down some pins on the first roll and the remainder on the second roll, that's a spare and the score for the frame is 10 plus the number of pins that fall on the first roll of the next frame. If you don't knock over all the pins with two rolls of the ball, your score for the frame is the number of pins you did knock down. If you get a strike in the tenth frame, then you get a bonus of two extra rolls, and if you get a spare in the tenth frame, you get one extra roll.

For example, the following cumulative score assumes that your throws in one game are:

Frame	Roll1	Roll2		Score (cumulative)	
1	10		strike	20	(10 + 9 + 1)
2	9	1	spare	37	(10 + 7)
3	7	2		46	(7 + 2)
4	4	6	spare	56	(10 + 0)
5	0	10	spare	74	(10 + 8)
6	8	1		83	(8 + 1)
7	10		strike	106	(10 + 10 + 3)
8	10		strike	123	(10 + 3 + 4)
9	3	4		130	(3 + 4)
10	7	3	spare	149	(10 + 9)
Extra	9		bonus		

Write a program that accepts a sequence of integers (such as 10, 9, 1, 7, 2, 4, 6, 0, 10, 8, 1, 10, 10, 3, 4, 7, 3, 9) representing the number of pins knocked down each time a players rolls the ball, and determines the final score. Your output should be similar to the following:

Frame 1—Ball 1: **10**
Frame 2—Ball 1: **9**
Ball 2: **1**
Frame 3—Ball 1: **7**
Ball 2: **2**
Frame 4—Ball 4: **4**
Ball 2: **6**
Frame 5—Ball 1: **0**
Ball 2: **10**
Frame 6—Ball 1: **8**
Ball 2: **1**

Frame 7— Ball 1: **10**
Frame 8— Ball 1: **10**
Frame 9— Ball 1: **3**
Ball 2: **4**
Frame 10—Ball 1: **7**
Ball 2: **3**
Extra— Ball 1: **9**
Your total score is 149.

In Chapter 5, you will see that this problem has a more compact solution.

THE BIGGER PICTURE

"GO TO" STATEMENT CONSIDERED HARMFUL

In the earliest days of programming (1950s), before the advent of high-level languages, programmers wrote code exclusively in machine language. Every instruction in machine language had an associated number, and the instructions were executed in numerical order. One of the most commonly used instructions was the branch or "go to" statement. The instruction goto 100 meant that the computer, rather than continuing execution in sequential order, should instead jump to the instruction labeled 100 and continue sequentially from there. Some of the early high-level programming languages borrowed their features from machine language, and "go to" statements were prevalent in BASIC and Fortran.

In 1968, Edsger W. Dijkstra published a now famous paper "Go To Statement Considered Harmful." The article begins: "For a number of years I have been familiar with the observation that the quality of programmers is a decreasing function of the density of **go to** statements in the programs they produce."

Dijkstra went on to explain why:

"The unbridled use of the **go to** statement has an immediate consequence that it becomes terribly hard to find a meaningful set of coordinates in which to describe the process progress."

Here is a program written in an early version of BASIC. It accepts three integers, and its semantics should be self-explanatory.

```
10 print "Input 3 numbers"
20 input x
22 input y
24 input z
30 if x > y goto 60
35 if x > z goto 80
40 if y > z goto 75
50 goto 90
60 if y > z goto 90
65 if x > z goto 75
68 print x
70 goto 95
```

THE BIGGER PICTURE

```
75 print z
77 goto 95
80 print x
85 goto 95
90 print y
95 print "is the answer."
100 End
```

Exercises

1. What is this program computing?
2. Write a simple and clear version of this program in Java using nested if-else statements.
3. Describe in your own words why "go to" statements might be considered harmful.
4. What do you think the phrase "spaghetti code" means?

CHAPTER 5

Repetition

"There is repetition everywhere, and nothing is found only once in the world.
—Goethe

"I don't mind the moonlight swims, it's the loop-the-loop that hurts"
—from *Bye Bye Birdie*

Objectives

The objectives of Chapter 5 include an understanding of

- repetition and loops: the while, do-while, and for statements,
- the differences and similarities among the while, do-while, and for statements,
- the types of errors that occur with ill-formed loops: infinite loops and "off by one" errors,
- nested loops, and
- the break statement used to exit a loop.

5.1 INTRODUCTION

Computers, unlike humans, are tireless, experiencing neither boredom nor fatigue. Repeating an operation millions of times presents no problem to a computer with an internal clock that ticks billions of times every second. In this chapter, we present three Java constructions that allow repetition in programs:

1. the while statement,
2. the do-while statement, and
3. the for statement.

We begin our discussion with the while statement.

5.2 THE *while* STATEMENT

As we saw in Chapter 4, conditional statements allow programs to make choices and decisions. Yet, even with such powerful tools, we cannot write an application that calculates the sum of an arbitrary list of integers. We can write a program that adds *exactly* 5 integers and a different (albeit tedious) application that sums exactly 50 integers. But, can we write a program flexible enough to add 5 integers, 50 integers, 50,000 integers, or even 50,000,000 integers?

With a while loop, the addition of 50 numbers can be achieved as easily and compactly as the addition of 5 or 50,000 numbers. The following segment adds 50 numbers with just a few lines of code. There is nothing special about 50, and we can just as easily add 500,000 numbers.

```
1. int sum = 0;
2. int count = 0;
3. while(count < 50)
4. {
5.      sum = sum + input.nextInt();
6.      count++;
7. }
8. System.out.print("Sum is " + sum);
```

The statements on lines 3–8 execute as follows:

1. The condition on line 3 (the boolean expression, count < 50) is evaluated.
2. If the condition, count < 50, is true, continue to line 5:
   a. A number is accepted from the keyboard and added to sum (line 5).
   b. Variable count is increased by 1 (line 6).
   c. Program control returns to the "top of the loop" (line 3), and the process repeats.
3. However, if the condition on line 3 is false,
   a. The statements on lines 5 and 6 are skipped.
   b. Program control passes to line 8 and the sum is displayed.

The assignment statement

```
sum = sum + input.nextInt()   // line 5
```

executes 50 times. Repetition is second nature to a computer.

Figure 5.1 shows the logic of the loop. Example 5.1 incorporates a similar loop into a full application.

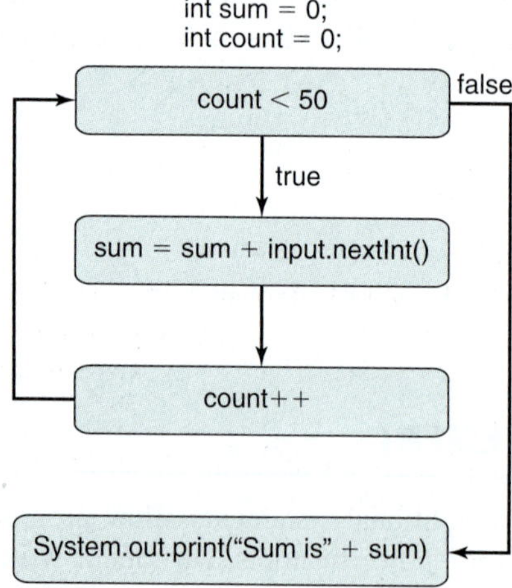

FIGURE 5.1 A loop that adds 50 integers

EXAMPLE 5.1

Problem Statement Write a program that sums a list of integers supplied by a user. The list can be of any size. The program should prompt the user for the number of data.

Java Solution The following application utilizes three variables: size, sum, and count.

- size is the number of data;
- sum holds a running sum of the numbers supplied by the user so that each time the user enters a number, that number is added to sum; and
- count keeps track of the number of data.

Variables sum and count are initialized to 0; the value of size is supplied by the user. The addition is accomplished using a while loop similar to the loop in the segment that precedes this example.

```
import java.util.*;
public class AddEmUp
{
     // adds an arbitrarily long list of integers
     // the user first supplies the size of the list
  public static void main (String[] args)
  {
     Scanner input = new Scanner(System.in);

     int sum = 0;                 // Running sum
     int count = 0;               // Keeps track of the number of integers
     int size ;                   // Size of the list

     System.out.print("How many numbers would you like to add? ");
     size = input.nextInt();
     System.out.println("Enter the " + size + " numbers");

     while (count < size)  // while the number of data is less than size repeat:
     {
       sum = sum + input.nextInt(); // read an integer, add it to sum
       count++;                     // keep track of the number of data
     }

     System.out.println("Sum: " + sum);
  }
}
```

Below, we display output generated from a list of three numbers followed by output obtained from a list of 12. Notice that the data of Output 1 are entered on separate lines, while Output 2 shows data entered on a single line terminated by pressing Enter. In each case, data values are separated by whitespace, and the specific input format is not important.

Output 1

```
How many numbers would you like to add? 3
Enter the 3 numbers
5
7
9
Sum: 21
```

Output 2

```
How many numbers would you like to add? 12
Enter the 12 numbers
23 45 65 23 43 12 87 56 34 31 84 90
Sum: 593
```

Discussion The program through line 14 is fairly simple. Lines 15 through 19 comprise a while loop. Following the keyword while and enclosed in parentheses is a boolean expression or condition (line 15), followed by a block (lines 16–19). If the condition is true, the block executes, otherwise it is skipped.

In this regard, the action of a while statement mimics the behavior of the if statement. However, in contrast to the if statement, after the block executes, program control returns to line 15. Once again, the condition is tested, and if the condition is true, the block executes again. This repetition continues until the condition, count < size, is false. With each iteration, count increases by 1, so eventually count exceeds size, the condition evaluates to false, and the repetition stops.

Figure 5.2 shows the action of the loop.

```
while (count < size)
{
   sum = sum + input.nextInt();    } Repeat these statements as long as the
   count++;                        } boolean condition(count < size)is true
}
```

FIGURE 5.2 The actions of a *while* loop

Figure 5.3 traces through the program using the data of Output 1.

The condition (count < size) may seem perplexing. Shouldn't the condition be count <= size? Well, that depends on the initial value of count. On line 10, count is initialized to 0. If, for example, size has the value 5, the loop executes exactly 5 times: when count has the values 0, 1, 2, 3, and 4. When count finally reaches 5, the loop already has performed the required 5 iterations. The loop terminates, and count retains the value 5, which is also the number of data.

On the other hand, we could initialize count to 1 rather than 0. In this case, the correct condition is, in fact, count <= 5. If size is 5, the loop executes 5 times: for values of count equal to 1, 2, 3, 4, and 5. When count reaches 6, the loop stops. Although counting from 1 seems more natural, the final value of count is 6, which is one more than the number of data.

sum	count	size	
0	0		The statements on lines 9–11 declare three variables and initialize two of them to 0.
0	0		The print statement on line 12 displays a prompt for the user. How many numbers would you like to add?
0	0	3	Line 13 is an assignment. The value 3 (entered by the user) is assigned to variable size.
0	0	3	The statement on line 14 prompts the user to enter the data: Enter the 3 numbers
5	1	3	The program reaches the while loop. The first. action of the loop is the evaluation of the expression on line 15. In this case, the expression (count < size) is true. Consequently, the block on lines 16 through 19 executes: The user enters the number 5, 5 is added to sum, (sum is 5), and count increases to 1.
12	2	3	Following line 19, control returns to line 15, i.e., the program loops back to line 15. Since the condition on line 15 (count < size) again evaluates to true, the statements of lines 16 through 19 execute again: The user enters 7, 7 is added to sum (sum is 12), and count increases to 2.
21	3	3	For a third time, control returns to line 15 and again the expression count < size is true. So one more time, the block on lines 16 through 19 executes: The user enters 9, 9 is added to sum (sum is 21), and count increases to 3.
21	3	3	Finally, control returns one last time to line 15. This time, however, because count and size are both equal to 3, the expression is false, so the block is skipped. Control passes to line 20, a println statement, which displays the value of sum: Sum: 21

FIGURE 5.3 A trace of *AddEmUp*

In the program of Example 5.1, the user supplies the number of data, which is stored in the variable size. The variable count keeps track of the number of data entered. When the condition

count < size

evaluates to false, the loop terminates.

Another mechanism used to terminate a loop is a *flag* or *sentinel*.

> A *flag* or *sentinel* is a value appended to a data collection that signals the end of the data.

A sentinel cannot be a number that is a feasible data value. For example, if all data are positive integers, you might use −1 as a flag and a list of data might have the form 234, 564, 567, 128, 123, **−1**. Example 5.2 is a revision of the previous program using a *sentinel* instead of a counter to terminate the loop.

EXAMPLE 5.2

Problem Statement Write a program that computes the sum of a list of integers that is supplied by a user. The end of data is signaled by the value -999. This value is used only as a flag and is not included in the sum.

Java Solution

```
import java.util.*;
public class AddEmUpAgain
{
    // adds an arbitrarily long list of integers
    // −999 signals the end of data
  public static void main (String[] args)
  {
    Scanner input = new Scanner(System.in);

    final int FLAG = −999;          // signals the end of data

    int sum = 0;                    // Running sum
    int number;                     // holds the next integer to be added
    System.out.println("Enter the numbers. End with " + FLAG);

    number = input.nextInt();
    while (number != FLAG)          // FLAG signals the end of data
    {
      sum += number;                // add the current integer to sum
      number = input.nextInt();     // read the next integer
    }

    System.out.println("Sum: "+ sum);
  }
}
```

Output 1

Enter the numbers. End with -999
5 6 7 −999
Sum: 18

Output 2

```
Enter the numbers. End with −999
−999
Sum: 0
```

Discussion Notice the differences between the programs of Examples 5.1 and 5.2.

- The constant FLAG (line 9) serves as a sentinel that signals the end of data. This is in contrast to the counter used in Example 5.1.
- The first datum is read *outside* the while loop (line 13). Indeed, if the statement on line 13 is omitted, the compiler generates an error message on line 14:

  variable *number* might not have been initialized.

  If the first datum happens to be FLAG, the program never enters the loop and correctly determines that the sum is 0.
- The last action of the loop is an input statement. Consequently, when the user enters –999, the sentinel value is read but not included in the sum.
- More generally, the program might prompt the user for the sentinel value rather than forcing the use of –999. This improvement is easily accomplished by replacing

  ```
  final int FLAG = −999;          // signals the end of data
  ```

  with

  ```
  System.out.println("Enter sentinel value: ");
  final int FLAG = input.nextInt();
  ```

The syntax of the while statement is:

```
while (condition)
{
   statement-1;
   statement-2;
      ...
   statement-n;
}
```

As is true with the conditional statement, the curly braces may be omitted if there is only one executable statement.

In general, the while statement executes as follows:

1. *condition,* a boolean expression, is evaluated.
2. If *condition* evaluates to true,
   a. *statement-1*, *statement-2*, . . . , *statement-n* execute.
   b. Program control returns to the top of the loop.
   c. The process repeats (go to step 1).
3. If *condition* evaluates to false,
   a. *statement-1*, *statement-2*, . . . , *statement-n* are skipped.
   b. Program control passes to the first statement after the loop.

Repetition of the block in a while loop continues until the condition evaluates to false, so you must be certain that the condition of every loop eventually evaluates to false.

Figure 5.4 shows the semantics of the while statement.

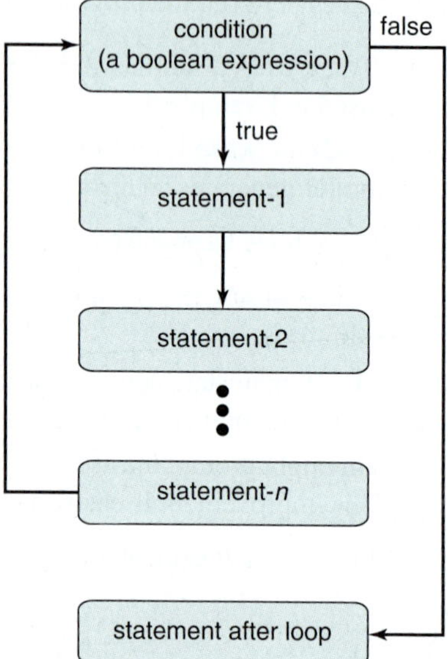

FIGURE 5.4 The semantics of the *while* statement

5.3 LOOPS: A SOURCE OF POWER, A SOURCE OF BUGS

Two common bugs that frequently find their way into programs that contain while loops are:

1. The infinite loop
2. The "off by one" error

5.3.1 The Infinite Loop

This is the song that never ends,
It just goes on and on, my friends,
Some people started singing it, not knowing what it was
And they'll continue singing it forever, just because....
(repeat)

—campfire song popularized by children's entertainer, Shari Lewis

Like the song that never ends, an infinite loop continues forever. An infinite while loop exists if the loop's terminating condition fails to evaluate to false. For example, consider again the loop in the application of Example 5.1.

```
while (count < size)
{
   sum = sum + input.nextInt();
   count++;
}
```

This loop ends when count equals size. However, if the statement count++ is inadvertently omitted, then count remains 0; count *never* equals size, and the loop never terminates. The program contains an *infinite loop*.

If you suspect that a program contains an infinite loop, for debugging purposes, include a temporary output statement that displays the contents of the variables in the loop condition.

For example, the following infinite loop includes a debugging statement that displays the value of count:

```
while (count < size)
{
    sum = sum + input.nextInt();
    System.out.println("count = "+ count); // debugging statement
}
```

When the loop executes the following output is displayed:

```
count = 0
count = 0
count = 0
count = 0
count = 0
etc.
```

From this output, you can see that the problem is a failure to increment count. Of course, once you discover the flaw, you should remove the debugging statement from your program.

At the other end of the spectrum, a loop may *never* execute. For example, consider the loop of Example 5.1, but suppose that the condition is erroneously coded as count > size rather than count < size:

```
while (count > size)
{
    number = input.nextInt();
    sum += number;
    count++;
}
```

In this case, since count is initialized to 0, and the user presumably enters a positive integer for size, then the expression count > size evaluates to false, and the statements of the loop never execute.

5.3.2 The "Off by One" Error

At some time, virtually every programmer has coded a loop that is "off by one." This error occurs if a loop executes one too many or one too few times. Example 5.3 is a classic illustration.

EXAMPLE 5.3

The following erroneous program is intended to calculate the sum of the first n positive integers: $1 + 2 + 3 + \ldots + n$. The user supplies a value for n.

```
1. import java.util.*;
2. public class AddUpToN // WITH AN ERROR!
```

```
{
    public static void main (String[] args)
    {
        Scanner input = new Scanner(System.in);

        int sum = 0;                // Cumulative sum
        int number;                 // find sum 1 + 2 + . . . + number
        int count = 1;              // counts 1 to number

        System.out.print("Enter a positive integer: ");
        number = input.nextInt();       // read the next integer
        while (count < number)          // here's the bug
        {
            sum += count;
            count++;
        }

        System.out.println("The sum of the first " + number + " positive integers is " + sum);
    }
}
```

(Erroneous) output

Enter a positive integer: **5**
The sum of the first 5 positive integers is 10

Discussion It is not too difficult to determine that the loop executes four rather than five times. The obvious error lies in the condition, which should be count <= number rather than count < number.

The next example also contains an ill-formed loop with an "off by one" error, although the exit condition is correctly formulated.

EXAMPLE 5.4 The following program is *supposed* to calculate the average of a list of numbers terminated by the sentinel value −999. *The program does not work correctly.* It mistakenly includes the sentinel as part of the data.

```
import java.util.*;
public class Average  // PRODUCES FAULTY OUTPUT!
{
    public static void main (String[] args)
    {
        Scanner input = new Scanner(System.in);
        final int FLAG = -999;
        double sum = 0;                 // running sum
        double number;                  // holds the next integer to be added
        int count = 0;                  // counts the number of data
```

```
      double average;
      System.out.println("Enter the numbers. End with " + FLAG);
      number = input.nextDouble(); // read the next number

      while (number != FLAG)
      {
         count++;
         number = input.nextDouble();      // read the next number
         sum += number;                    // add the current integer to sum
      }
      average = sum/count;
      System.out.println("Average: " + average);
   }
}
```

(Erroneous) output

```
Enter the numbers. End with −999
1
2
3
−999
Average: −331.3333333333333
```

Discussion In this case, the sentinel value (−999) is included in the sum and the first number (1) is not, that is, sum is computed with the values 2, 3, and −999.

Reversing the last two lines of the loop corrects the problem:

```
while (number != FLAG)
{
      count++;
      sum += number;
      number = input.nextDouble
}
```

Although the number of loop iterations remains the same, the sentinel −999 is no longer included in the sum. The value of sum is correctly calculated as 1 + 2 + 3 = 6.

5.4 THE *do-while* STATEMENT

Although the while loop is sufficient for any task requiring repetition, Java provides two alternative statements: the do-while loop and the for loop.

If the condition of a while loop is initially false, the body of a while loop never executes. In contrast, a do-while loop always executes the body of the loop at least once before checking the terminating condition.

A do-while loop checks the condition at the end of the loop body.

For example, the following segment, which screens for bad input, is a natural application of a do-while statement.

```
1. int x;  // must be positive
2. do
3. {
4.     System.out.println("Enter a number > 0");
5.     x = input.nextInt();
6. }while (x <= 0); // if negative, repeat
```

The loop executes as follows:

- The statement on line 4 prompts the user for a positive number.
- The statement on line 5 reads a value and assigns that value to variable x.
- The condition (x <= 0) on line 6 is evaluated. If the condition is true, the loop repeats the actions of lines 4 and 5; if the condition is false, the loop terminates.

Notice that the body of the loop (lines 4 and 5) executes once before the condition is tested. A do-while loop is guaranteed to execute at least once. This is not the case with a while loop.

Example 5.5 is yet another version of Example 5.1. This time we use a do-while loop to screen for bad input.

EXAMPLE 5.5 **Problem Statement** Write a program that calculates the sum of a list of integers that is interactively supplied by a user. The program should prompt the user for the number of data. The program should ensure that each number supplied by the user is positive.

Java Solution

```
import java.util.*;
public class DoWhileAdd
{
    public static void main (String[] args)
    {
        Scanner input = new Scanner(System.in);
        int size;                       // the number of integers to add

        do                              // repeat until size is positive
        {
            System.out.print("How many numbers would you like to add? ");
            size = input.nextInt();
        } while (size <= 0);

        System.out.println("Enter the " + size + " numbers");
        int sum = 0;                    // the running sum
        int count = 0;                  // keeps track of the number of data
        while (count < size)
        {
            sum = sum + input.nextInt();    // read the next integer, add to sum
            count++;                        // increment counter
        }
        System.out.println("Sum: "+ sum);
    }
}
```

Output

```
How many numbers would you like to add? 0
How many numbers would you like to add? −3
How many numbers would you like to add? 3
Enter the 3 numbers
5
7
9
Sum: 21
```

Discussion Lines 8 through 12 comprise a do-while loop. Notice that the condition (size <= 0) appears on line 12, at the *end* of the loop. There is no "gatekeeper" at the top of the loop. When program control reaches line 8, the block of executable statements (lines 10 and 11) executes, regardless of any condition. The condition on line 12 is evaluated *after* the block executes. If the condition (size <= 0) evaluates to true, control passes back to line 10 and the loop executes again; if the condition is false, the loop terminates.

The while loop on lines 15–19 of Example 5.1 could have been written as a do-while loop:

```
int count = 0, sum = 0;
do
{
        sum = sum + input.nextInt();
        count++;
}
while (count < size)
```

Either construction accomplishes the task.

5.4.1 Which Loop?

How does the do-while construction differ from that of the while loop?

> The while loop is *top-tested*, that is, the condition is evaluated before any of the loop statements executes. If the condition of a while loop is initially false, the loop never executes. The do-while loop, on the other hand, is *bottom-tested*, that is, the condition is tested after the first iteration of the loop. A do-while loop always executes at least once.

Let's take a second look at Example 5.2, this time using a do-while loop.

EXAMPLE 5.6

Problem Statement Rewrite Example 5.2 using a do-while loop rather than a while loop.

Java Solution

```
import java.util.*;
public class DoWhileAddEmUpAgain
{
        public static void main (String[] args)
        {
```

```
6.          Scanner input = new Scanner(System.in);
7.          final int FLAG = −999;
8.          int sum = 0; // Running sum
9.          int number;  // holds the next integer to be added
10.         System.out.println("Enter the numbers end with " + FLAG);
11.         number = input.nextInt();

12.         do
13.         {
14.             sum += number; // add the current integer to sum
15.             number = input.nextInt();
16.         } while (number != FLAG);

17.         System.out.println("Sum: " + sum);
19.     }
20. }
```

Discussion The program works correctly except when the user enters the sentinel (−999) as the first value. In that case:

- The sentinel is stored in the variable number (line 11).
- The sentinel is added to sum (line 14).
- The user is prompted for another integer (line 15).

Certainly, this is not acceptable. In contrast, if the program is written using a while loop and the initial datum is the sentinel, because the while loop is top-tested, the loop does not execute and the value of sum remains 0.

We can fix Example 5.6 without losing the do-while loop, but the change requires some inelegant code. The following version of the program correctly handles the situation that occurs when the first value entered is the sentinel.

```
1.  public class DoWhileAddEmUpAgainTwo
2.  {
3.  public static void main (String[] args)
4.  {
5.     Scanner input = new Scanner(System.in);
6.     final int FLAG = −999;
7.     int sum = 0;                        // Running sum
8.     int number;                         // holds the next integer to be added
9.     System.out.println("Enter the numbers end with " + FLAG);
10.    do
11.    {
12.        number = input.nextInt();
13.        if (number != FLAG)             // here's the fix, not too nice!
14.            sum += number;              // add the current integer to sum
15.    } while (number != FLAG);
16.    System.out.println("Sum: " + sum);
17. }
18. }
```

Notice that each number is checked to see whether or not it is the sentinel:

```
13. if (number != FLAG)
14.     sum += number;
```

This is neither particularly elegant nor efficient. Indeed, with this "fix," every value is checked against FLAG *twice*, once on line 13 and again on line 15. You can often "patch" bad code, but the result is usually not very satisfying. Although this program can be written with either loop construction, the top-tested while loop is clearly preferable to the do-while.

In general, if it the possibility exists that a loop may never execute, opt for the while loop.

The syntax of the do-while statement is:

```
do
{
        statement-1;
        statement-2;
          . . . ;
        statement-n;
} while (condition);
```

As always, *condition* is a boolean expression and, if the block consists of single executable statement, the curly braces may be omitted.

Execution of the do-while statement proceeds as follows:

1. *statement-1, statement-2, . . . , statement-n* execute.
2. *condition* is evaluated.
3. If the *condition* is true, the process repeats (go back to *statement-1*).
4. If *condition* is false, the loop terminates and program control passes to the first statement following the loop.

See Figure 5.5.

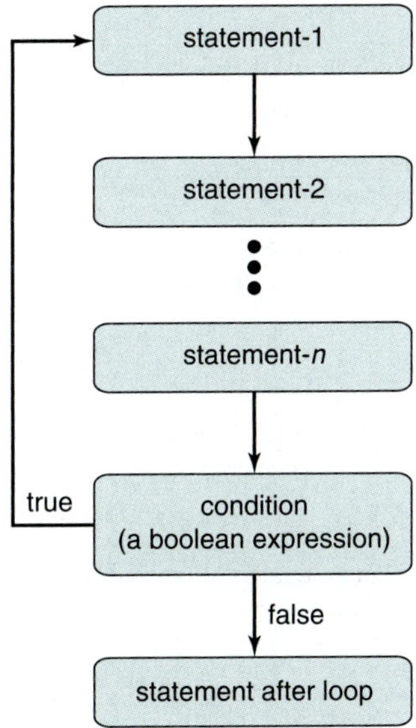

FIGURE 5.5 The semantics of the *do-while* statement

5.5 THE *for* STATEMENT

Java provides a third alternative for repetition: the for statement.

Use a for statement when you can count the number of times that a loop executes.

The following program segment uses a for loop to print the verse of a familiar, if boring, song exactly three times:

```
1.  for (int i = 1; i <= 3; i++)
2.  {
3.      System.out.println("Row, row, row your boat, gently down the stream,");
4.      System.out.println("Merrily, merrily, merrily, merrily; life is but a dream");
5.      System.out.println();
6.  }
```

The loop executes as follows:

1. The variable i is declared and initialized to 1 (int i = 1); i keeps track of the number of iterations; i counts.
2. The condition i <= 3 on line 1 is evaluated.
3. If the condition i <= 3 is true:

   Lines 3, 4, and 5 execute. // Sing along if you wish!

   The statement i++ on line 1 executes.

   Go to step 2 (check whether or not i <= 3).
4. If the condition i <= 3 is false, the loop terminates.

The variable i keeps track of the number of iterations. Before the body of the loop executes, the terminating condition (i <= 3) is checked. Once the body of the loop completes execution, the value of i is increased by 1.

Conveniently,

- the initial value of i, (i = 1),
- the loop condition, (i <= 3), and
- the update statement for i, (i++)

all appear together on line 1.

Figure 5.6 shows the program flow of this segment.

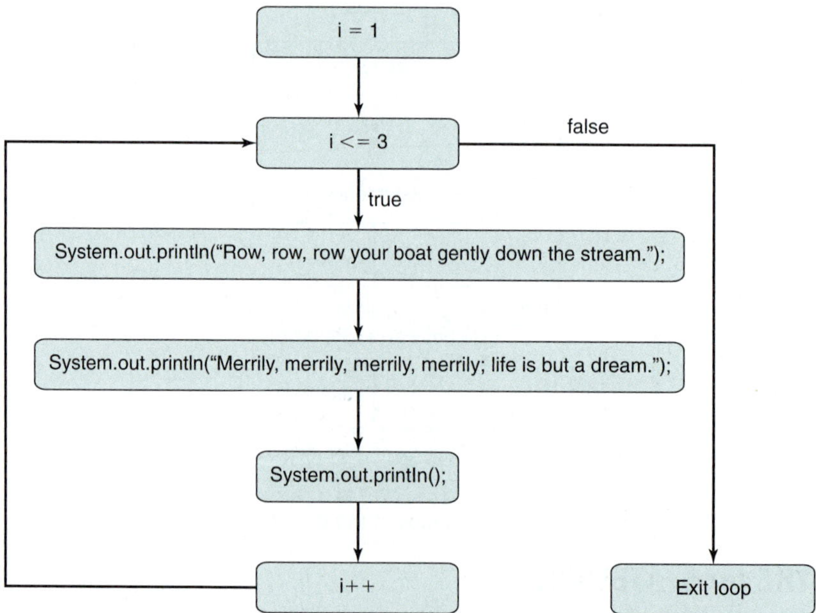

FIGURE 5.6 A *for* loop that displays the verse of a song three times

Example 5.7 rewrites the while loop of Example 5.1 as a for loop and gives a bit more detail about the inner workings of the for statement.

EXAMPLE 5.7

Problem Statement Using a for statement, write a program that sums a list of integers. The program should prompt the user for the size of the list.

Java Solution

```
1.  import java.util.*;
2.  public class ForAddEmUp
3.  {
4.     public static void main (String[] args)
5.     {
6.           Scanner input = new Scanner(System.in);

7.           int sum = 0;                  // Cumulative sum
8.           int size;                     // Number of integers to add
9.           int number;                   // holds the next integer to be added

10.          System.out.print("How many numbers would you like to add? ");
11.          size = input.nextInt();
12.          System.out.println("Enter the " + size + " numbers");

13.          for (int count = 1; count <= size; count++)     // for i = 1 to count
14.          {
15.             number = input.nextInt(); // read the next integer
16.             sum += number; // add the current integer to sum
17.          }

18.          System.out.println("Sum: " + sum);

19.    }
20. }
```

Output

```
How many numbers would you like to add? 4
Enter the 4 numbers
3
5
7
9
Sum: 24
```

Discussion The "header" of the for statement, displayed on line 13, may appear a bit daunting at first glance. Notice that the header consists of three parts:

1. the **initialization statement**, int count = 1,
2. the **loop condition** (a boolean expression), count <= size, and
3. the **update statement**, count++.

The for statement proceeds as follows:

1. The initialization statement executes.

In this case, the variable count is *both* declared and initialized to 1. The variable count is called the *control variable*. Because count is declared within the for statement, count is accessible only within the loop. Consequently, if line 18 were written as

```
System.out.println("The sum of the "+ count +" numbers is "+ sum),
```

the compiler would issue an error message to the effect that the variable count is unknown.

2. The loop condition, count <= size, is tested.
3. If the loop condition is true, then:
   a. The block (lines 14–17) executes.
   b. The update statement executes (count++, line 13).
   c. The process repeats from step 2 (Is the loop condition still true?).

   If the loop condition is false, then:
   a. The loop terminates.
   b. Program control passes to the first statement after the loop (line 18).

The for statement is a compact version of the while statement. Indeed, the for statement on lines 13 through 17 can be rewritten as:

```
int count = 1;             // the initialization statement
while (count <= size)  // loop condition
{
   number = input.nextInt();
   sum += number;
   count++;                // update statement
}
```

However, in contrast to the for statement of lines 13–17, the variable count, declared outside the while loop of the previous segment, exists after the loop terminates.

The syntax of the for statement is:

for (*initialization*; *loop condition*; update *statement(s)*)
{
  statement-1:
  statement-2;
  . . .
  statement-n:
}

As usual, the braces may be omitted if the statement block consists of a single statement.

The semantics of the for statement are:

1. The *initialization* statement executes.
2. The *loop condition* (a boolean expression) is evaluated.
3. If the *loop condition* is true, then:
   a. *statement-1, statement-2, . . . , statement-n* execute,
   b. The *update-statement(s)* executes,
   c. Go to step 2.

4. If the *loop condition* is false, then program control passes to the first statement following the block consisting of *statement-1, statement-2, . . . , statement-n.*

You should note that:

- The initialization is performed exactly once.
- The loop condition is always tested before the statement block executes.
- The update statement always executes *after* the *actions* of the statement block.
- The declared, initialized variables disappear after the for loop completes execution.

Figure 5.7 shows the semantics of a for loop.

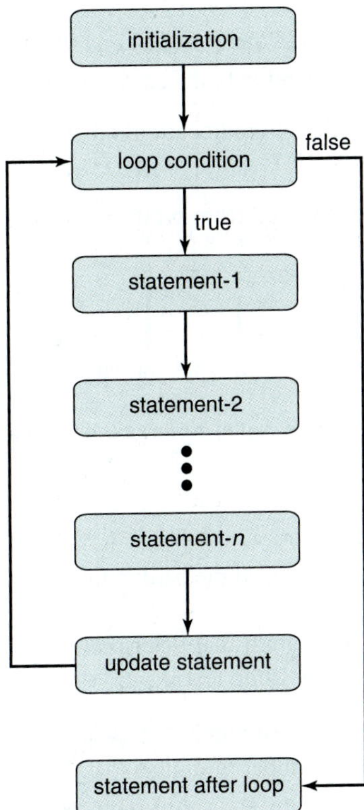

FIGURE 5.7 The semantics of the *for* statement

> Without examining the body of a for loop, you can understand its termination structure. A for loop gathers this information in one place:
>
> for (*initialization; loop condition; update statement*)
>
> The while loop and do-while loop scatter this information throughout the body of the loop.

Example 5.8 includes an application that utilizes a for statement to check the validity of a credit card number.

EXAMPLE 5.8 When you supply your credit card number to an online vendor, data input errors are checked before your credit card is validated. For example, credit cards issued by Visa all have numbers beginning with the digit 4, and those issued by American Express begin with 34 or 37.

Another method of validation is the *Luhn algorithm*. The Luhn algorithm detects some, but not all, invalid numbers. Thus, this algorithm can alert a vendor to some bad numbers but it cannot guarantee that a credit card number is valid.

The method works as follows:

1. Beginning with the second-rightmost digit and moving right to left, double every other digit. If the doubling process produces a value greater than 9, subtract 9 from that value.
2. Form a sum of all the products ("new" digits) and the unchanged digits.
3. If the sum of step 2 does not end in 0, the card is invalid.

For example, to check the validity of credit card number 5113 4765 1234 8002 proceed as follows:

1. Double alternate digits. Subtract 9 from products exceeding 9. See Figure 5.8.

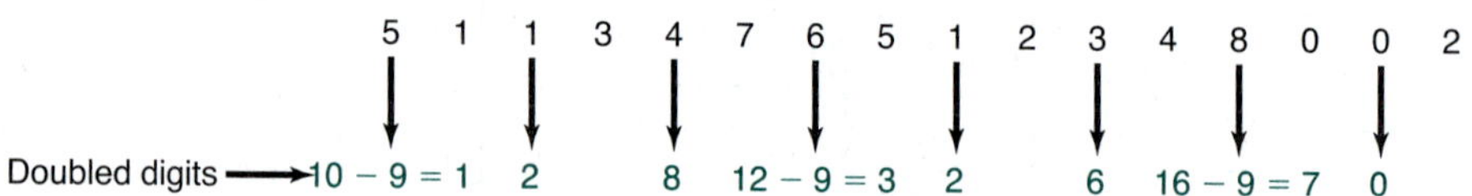

FIGURE 5.8 Double alternate digits; subtract 9 if the result is greater than 9

2. Form the sum

$$\mathbf{1} + 1 + \mathbf{2} + 3 + \mathbf{8} + 7 + \mathbf{3} + 5 + \mathbf{2} + 2 + \mathbf{6} + 4 + \mathbf{7} + 0 + \mathbf{0} + 2 = 53$$

3:. The sum 53 does not end in zero, so the card number is invalid.

Problem Statement Write a program that determines whether a credit card number with 16 (or fewer) digits passes the Luhn test.

Java Solution Since most credit card numbers consist of 16 or fewer digits, our solution assumes that the maximum number of digits is 16.

An implementation of the Luhn algorithm requires that we extract the digits of a card number, digit by digit, right to left. To extract the digits and move right to left through a number, the following solution utilizes the mod operator (%) and integer division. Using the mod operator, we can easily extract the rightmost digit from a number:

$$1234\mathbf{5} \ \% \ 10 = \mathbf{5}.$$

And, with integer division, we can remove the rightmost digit from a number to obtain a "new" number without the rightmost digit:

$$\mathbf{12345}/10 = 1234.$$

These techniques are used in the following application that implements the Luhn algorithm.

```
import java.util.*;
public class CheckCreditCard
{
  public static void main (String[] args)
```

```
5.  {
6.    Scanner input = new Scanner(System.in);
7.    final int MAX_DIGITS = 16;   // maximum number of digits for a credit card
8.    long number;                 // credit card number
9.    long sum = 0;                // the final value of sum must end in zero
10.   long digit;

11.   System.out.print("Enter Credit Card Number:" );
12.   number = input.nextLong();

13.   for (int i = 1; i <= MAX_DIGITS; i++) // for each digit, i counts digits
14.   {
15.      digit = number % 10;            // extract the rightmost digit
16.      if (i % 2 == 0)                 // double every other digit
17.      {
18.         digit = digit*2;
19.         if (digit > 9)               // subtract 9 if the product is larger than 9
20.            digit -= 9;
21.      }
22.      sum += digit;                   // add the digit to the running sum
23.      number = number/10;             // remove the rightmost digit
24.   }
25.   if (sum % 10 != 0)                 // check the rightmost digit of sum
26.      System.out.println("Invalid number");
27.   else
28.      System.out.println("Credit card number passes test");
29. }
30. }
```

Running the program twice produces the following output:

Output 1

```
Enter Credit Card Number: 5113476512348002
Invalid number
```

Output 2

```
Enter Credit Card Number: 123456789876543
Credit card number passes test
```

Discussion The program works for all numbers of 16 digits or less. The first credit card number contains 16 digits, but the second contains just 15 digits. For credit card numbers with fewer than 16 digits, after the last digit is extracted, the variable number gets the value 0, which contributes nothing to the sum.

The if statement on line 16 determines whether or not i is even, so that we "process" alternate digits. As an exercise, you might consider an alternative, perhaps simpler and more efficient, method for doing this (see Programming Exercise 1).

5.5.1 A Few More Notes on the *for* Statement

Programmers sometimes twist and contort the for statement to fit just about any situation that requires a loop. Remember, a for statement is really a compact while statement.

The following illustrations demonstrate the flexibility of the for statement. Be forewarned, however, that too much "cleverness" can sometimes be difficult to comprehend and can lead to bugs.

- Each of the three parts in the header of a for statement (initialization, loop condition, update statement) is optional. Indeed, the following for loop, equivalent to while (true), is legal, albeit infinite!

```
for ( ; ; ) // Look! No statements!
{
    System.out.println("This is the song that never ends,");
    System.out.println("It just goes on and on, my friends.");
    System.out.println("Some people started singing it, not knowing what it was");
    System.out.println("And they'll continue singing it forever, just because . . . ");
}
```

This next segment, which prints the lyrics to a familiar song, uses no explicit increment statement. The loop terminates after 100 iterations.

```
for (int i = 100; i > 0; )                          // no increment statement
{
    System.out.println(i + "bottles of beer on the wall " + i + "bottles of beer");
    System.out.println("Take one down, pass it around");
    System.out.println( --i + " bottles of beer on the wall.\n"); // i is decremented here
}
```

Notice that the last statement updates the control variable.

- More than one statement may be used in the initialization or update section of a for statement. For example, the following loop initializes and increments two variables, i and j:

```
for (int i = 1, j = 2; i < 10; i++, j += 2)
        System.out.println (i * j);
```

Multiple initializations in the header of a for statement are separated by commas. The same is true for multiple update statements.

- The update statement may be *any* executable statement. The for loop of Figure 5.9, consisting of a single line, is equivalent to the preceding loop, which prints the values 2, 8, 18, 32, 50, 72, 98, 128, and 162.

```
for (int i = 1, j = 2;  i < 10;  System.out.println (i * j), i ++, j += 2 );
```

Initialization **Update**

FIGURE 5.9 Update statements are flexible

- The control variable of a for loop is *usually* declared within the loop:

```
for (int i = 1;...;...)
```

When declared as such, the control variable is unknown outside the loop. On the other hand, the control variable *may* be declared outside the loop:

```
int i;
for (i = 1;...;...)
```

In this case, the variable i is known and is accessible after the loop terminates. Indeed, the following code does not compile:

```
for(int i = 1; i <= 100; i++)                    // i is declared within the loop
        System.out.println(i * i);
System.out.println("Final value of i is " + i);  // i is unknown here
```

This next segment, however, does compile and run:

```
int i;                                           // i is declared outside the loop
for(int i = 1; i <= 100; i++)
        System.out.println(i * i);
System.out.println("Final value of i is " + i); // i is accessible here
```

The last line of output from this segment is:

```
Final value of i is 101
```

Example 5.9 uses a for statement to calculate the *integer square root* of a non-negative whole number. The loop uses multiple initializations.

EXAMPLE 5.9

The *integer square root* of a non-negative whole number is the integer part of the "real" square root. For example, the square root of 56 is approximately 7.4833; so the integer square root of 56 is 7.

To find the integer square root of a non-negative integer *n*, add the odd positive integers, one at a time, 1 + 3 + 5 + 7 + 9 + . . . , continuing the addition as long as the next sum is less than or equal to *n*. Now, count the odd numbers used to form the sum. That's the integer square root. For example, 3 is the integer square root of 12:

```
1 + 3 + 5 = 9                        // 3 odd numbers in the sum.
```

But one more addition makes the sum too large:

```
1 + 3 + 5 + 7 = 16                   // 16 exceeds 12.
```

The integer square root of 56 is 7:

```
1 + 3 + 5 + 7 + 9 + 11 + 13 = 49     // 7 odd numbers in the sum.
```

But,

```
1 + 3 + 5 + 7 + 9 + 11 + 13 + 15 = 64  // 64 exceeds 56.
```

Problem Statement Write a program that uses a for loop to determine the integer square root of any positive whole number.

Java Solution

```
import java.util.*;
public class IntegerSquareRoot
{
    public static void main (String[] args)
    {
      Scanner input = new Scanner(System.in);
      System.out.print("Enter a non-negative integer: ");
      int num = input.nextInt();
      int count = 0;                    // counts the number of odds in the sum
```

```
10.     for (int sum = 0, odd = 1; (sum + odd) <= num; sum += odd, odd += 2)
11.             count++;

12.     System.out.println("The integer square root of " + num + " is " + count);
13. }
14. }
```

Output

Enter a non-negative integer: **150**
The integer square root of 150 is 12

Discussion

- The for statement on lines 10 and 11 perform the bulk of the work.
  - The loop initialization declares and initializes two variables. The variable sum is set to 0, and odd is assigned the first odd number 1. Notice the comma separating the initializations.
  - The loop condition checks whether the current sum plus the next odd number exceeds num. If this is not the case, then odd is added to sum in the update section of line 10, and odd is set to the next odd number.
  - Finally, the number of odds, count, is increased in the body of the loop (line 11).
- The output statement of line 12 displays the value count, which is the number of odds that comprise the sum. This value is the integer square root.

The for statement of the program is a compact version of the following while loop:

```
int count = 0;
int sum = 0;
int odd = 1;
while ((sum + odd) <= num)
{
        sum += odd;
        count++;
        odd += 2;
}
```

There is one difference between the for loop on lines 10–11 and the while loop of the previous segment. Variables sum and odd, declared in the heading of the for statement, are not accessible outside the for statement. Their counterparts, declared outside the while loop, exist after the while loop terminates.

5.6 NESTED LOOPS

It should come as no surprise that loops may be nested within loops. The snippet of code in Figure 5.10, although not very interesting, clearly illustrates the workings of nested loops.

Outer loop "i-loop"

```
for( int i = 1;  i <= 4;  i++)
{
    for(int j = 21;  j <= 23;  j++)
    {  //the inner curly braces are unnecessary
        System.out.println(i + "    " + j);
    }
    System.out.println();
}
```

Inner loop "j-loop"

FIGURE 5.10 Nested loops

Notice that the inner "j-loop" (lines 3 through 6) is nested within the outer "i-loop" (lines 1 through 8). For each value of i (1, 2, 3, and 4), the j-loop executes once. Consequently, the println statement on line 5 executes 4 × 3 = 12 times. The empty println statement (line 7) is not part of the inner loop, so this statement, which prints a blank line, executes just four times, once for each value of i. Annotated output appears in Figure 5.11.

```
        output
         1  21
i = 1 {  1  22  } j = 21, 22, 23
         1  23

         2  21
i = 2 {  2  22  } j = 21, 22, 23
         2  23

         3  21
i = 3 {  3  22  } j = 21, 22, 23
         3  23

         4  21
i = 4 {  4  22  } j = 21, 22, 23
         4  23
```

FIGURE 5.11 Tracing through a nested loop

Written as nested while loops, the code of Figure 5.10 has the following form (Figure 5.12):

```
            int i = 1;
            while (i <= 4)
            {
               int j = 21;
               while (j <= 23)
               {
Outer loop        System.out.println(i+" "+j);      Inner loop
                  j++;
               }
               System.out.println();
               i++;
            }
```

FIGURE 5.12 The code of Figure 5.10 rewritten using nested *while* loops

In Example 5.10, we use a nested for loop to calculate a series of averages.

EXAMPLE 5.10

Problem Statement Write a program that prompts an instructor for

1. the number of students in his/her class, and
2. the number of grades assigned to each student,

and determines the average grade for each student. Grades are whole numbers, but an average may be a decimal number.

Java Solution

```
1. import java.util.*;
2. public class GradeAverage
```

```
{
    public static void main(String[] args)
    {
        Scanner input = new Scanner(System.in);
        int numStudents, numGrades;
        int grade;     // an individual grade
        int sum = 0; // sum of one student's grades
        double average;
        // prompt for number of students and grades per student
        System.out.print("Number of Students: ");
        numStudents = input.nextInt();
        System.out.print("Number of Grades: ");
        numGrades = input.nextInt();
        System.out.println();

        for (int i = 1; i <= numStudents; i++) // for each student
        {
          sum = 0;
          System.out.println("Grades for student " + i);
          for (int j = 1; j <= numGrades; j++)
          {
              System.out.print("  " + j + ":");
              grade = input.nextInt();
              sum += grade;
          }
          average = (double)sum/ numGrades;   // for one student
          System.out.print("Average: " + average);
          System.out.println();
        }
    }
}
```

Outer loop (lines 17–30)

Inner loop (lines 21–26)

Output

Number of Students: **3**
Number of grades/student: **4**

Grades for student 1
  1: **90**
  2: **80**
  3: **70**
  4: **60**
Average: 75.0

Grades for student 2
  1: **75**
  2: **85**
  3: **95**
  4: **100**
Average: 88.75

Grades for student 3
  1: **88**
  2: **77**
  3: **99**
  4: **66**
Average: 82.5

Discussion Take a look at the output. There are three students and each has four grades. The outer loop (lines 17–30) executes three times, once for each student. For each iteration of the outer loop, the inner loop (lines 21–26) executes four times. The inner loop accepts the grades for each student and calculates a running sum of the student's grades. Notice that the variable sum must be set back or *reinitialized* to 0 before grades are processed for the next student. This is done in the outer loop (line 19). The average is also calculated in the outer loop (line 27) because there is just one average per student.

Example 5.11 utilizes nested while loops. The calculation in this example is similar to the previous example, except that flags are used to indicate the end of data.

EXAMPLE 5.11

Problem Statement Write a program that computes grade averages. Unlike the program of Example 5.10, the user need not supply the number of students. Moreover, the number of grades per student may vary. Use two numerical sentinels: the integer 1000 to indicate the end of all data, and the number 999 to indicate the end of a grade list for a single student. For example, data for three students might be entered as:

90 80 70 60 **999**
76 87 78 97 88 66 84 **999**
79 87 **999**
1000

Java Solution

```
import java.util.*;
public class GradeAverage1
{
   public static void main (String[] args)
   {
      Scanner input = new Scanner(System.in);
      final int END_OF_DATA = 1000;          //to indicate end of all data
      final int END_OF_GRADES = 999;         // to indicate end of a grade list
      int student = 1, numGrades = 0, grade;
      int sum = 0;

      System.out.println("\nEnter Grades for student " + student + " or 1000 to end. ");
      System.out.print("Grade list must end with 999. \n: ");
      grade = input.nextInt();

      while ( grade != END_OF_DATA) // while more data remain
      {
         while (grade != END_OF_GRADES)      // process grades for one student
         {
            sum += grade;
            numGrades++;   // each student has a different number of grades
            System.out.print(": ");
            grade = input.nextInt();
         }

         // If no grades were entered, do not divide by 0
```

```
24.          if (numGrades != 0)
25.             System.out.println("Average: " + sum/numGrades);
26.          else
27.             System.out.println("No grades entered for student " + student);
28.          student++;

29.          // reset sum and numGrades for the next student
30.          sum = 0;
31.          numGrades = 0;
32.          // get first grade for next student ( or 1000 to end the program)
33.          System.out.println("\nEnter grades for student " + student + " or 1000 to end. ");
34.          System.out.print("Grade list must end with 999.\n: ");
35.          grade = input.nextInt();
36.       }
37.    }
38. }
```

Output

```
Enter grades for student 1 or 1000 to end.
Grade list must end with 999.
: 80
: 90
: 70
: 999
Average: 80.0

Enter grades for student 2 or 1000 to end.
Grade list must end with 999.
: 75
: 85
: 95
: 65
: 100
: 999
Average: 84.0

Enter grades for student 3 or 1000 to end.
Grade list must end with 999.
: 1000
```

Discussion As in the previous example, the inner loop (lines 16 through 22) processes a grade list for each student. Because the number of grades varies for each student, a variable numGrades keeps track of the grade count. Conceivably, you could enter an empty grade list (one consisting of the sentinel 999) so that numGrades is 0, resulting in a division by 0 when computing the average. The conditional statement:

```
24. if (numGrades != 0)
25.    System.out.println("Average: " + sum/numGrades);
26. else
27. System.out.println("No grades entered for student "+ student);
```

handles this case. The following display shows output that includes one empty grade list.

Output

Enter grades for student 1 or 1000 to end.
Grade list must end with 999.
: **90**
: **84**
: **86**
: **77**
: **999**
Average: 84.25

Enter grades for student 2 or 1000 to end.
Grade list must end with 999.
: **999**
No grades entered for student 2

Enter grades for student 5 or 1000 to end.
Grade list must end with 999.
: **1000**

Finally, if a user accidentally enters 1000 before the sentinel 999, then 1000 is counted among the grades and the average is erroneous and inflated. A better action would terminate the program with an appropriate error message or ask the user to re-enter the last grade. We leave these improvements as an exercise (see Programming Exercise 13).

From the previous examples, you probably surmised that nested loops are handy for computations where each datum is associated with one or more other attributes. For example, in the application of Example 5.11, each grade is associated with a student. The outer loop counts students, and the inner loop counts grades of a particular student. The loops are related.

Example 5.12 also utilizes a nested loop construction. However, the relationship between the loops is not as intricate. The outer loop allows the user to repeat a computation and has no bearing on the inner loop. That is, the outer loop has no attribute that appears in the inner loop.

EXAMPLE 5.12

"I am thinking of a number between 1 and 100. What is it?"
"Is it 35?"
"Higher"
Is it 60?"
"Lower"
"50?"
"Lower"....
And so goes a typical guessing game.
Did you know that the number can be discovered with at most seven such questions? And, if the "secret number" is between 1 and 1,000,000, no more than 20 guesses are necessary.

Problem Statement Write a program that asks a player to discover a secret number between 1 and n, where n is any positive number that the player chooses. Each time the player guesses a number, the application responds "correct," "too high," or "too low." The program should report the number, of guesses used to unearth the secret number. Finally, the player should be given the option to play the game again.

Java Solution To begin play, the application must generate a "secret" random integer between 1 and n. In Chapter 4, you learned that

```
(int)(3 * Math.random())
```

gives a random number in the range 0 through 2, that is, 0, 1, or 2. Similarly,

```
(int)(n * Math.random())
```

generates a random integer between 0 and $n - 1$ inclusive, and

```
(int)(n * Math.random()) + 1
```

gives a random number between 1 and n, inclusive.

For example,

```
(int)(100 * Math.random()) + 1
```

evaluates to a random number between 1 and 100 and

```
(int)(1000000 * Math.random()) + 1
```

provides a number between 1 and 1000000.

The following class, which implements the guessing game, gives one more example of nested loops.

```
import java.util.*;
public class Guess
{
   public static void main(String[] args)
   {
   Scanner input = new Scanner(System.in);
   int answer;                                 // 1 for play again; 0 for quit

   do                                          // repeat the game if answer == 1
   {
     System.out.println("You will guess a secret number between 1 and n");
     System.out.print("Give me a value for n: ");
     int n = input.nextInt();                  // number is in the range 1..n
     System.out.println ("OK, I am thinking of a number between 1 and " + n);
     int number = (int)(n * Math.random()) + 1; // a random int between 1 and n
     int guess;                                // player's guess
     int numGuesses = 0;

     do // play the game
     {
       System.out.print("Your guess: ");
       guess = input.nextInt();
       numGuesses++;
       if (guess > number)
          System.out.println("Too high");
       else if (guess < number)
          System.out.println("Too low");
       else
          System.out.println("That's it!");
     } while (number != guess);
     System.out.println("Score: " + numGuesses + " guesses");

     do                                        // repeat until answer is 0 or 1
     {
       System.out.print("Play again? 1 for YES; 0 for NO: ");
       answer = input.nextInt();
       System.out.println();
     } while (answer != 0 && answer != 1);

   } while( answer == 1);
```

```
37.   System.out.println("Thanks for playing :) ");
38.  }
39. }
```

Output You will guess a secret number between 1 and n

Give me a value for n: **100**
OK, I am thinking of a number between 1 and 100
Your guess: **50**
Too high
Your guess: **25**
Too low
Your guess: **35**
Too high
Your guess: **30**
That's it!
Score: 4 guesses
Play again? 1 for YES; 0 for NO: **1**

You will guess a secret number between 1 and n
Give me a value for n: **100**
OK, I am thinking of a number between 1 and 100
Your guess: **50**
Too low
Your guess: **75**
Too low
Your guess: **87**
Too low
Your guess: **94**
Too low
Your guess: **97**
Too high
Your guess: **96**
That's it!
Score: 6 guesses
Play again? 1 for YES; 0 for NO: **0**
Thanks for playing :)

Discussion Like the program of Example 5.11, this application utilizes nested loops. The outer do-while loop (lines 8–36) gives the player the option of playing the game as many times as he/she chooses. Nested inside this do-while loop are two additional do-while loops that are not nested inside one another, that is, one follows the other sequentially.

- The loop on lines 17–28 plays the guessing game, executing its code until the player guesses the secret number.
- The do-while loop on lines 30–35 checks whether or not the player gives a valid response when asked if he/she would like to play again. No doubt, you have occasionally supplied incorrect data to a program, either producing erroneous results or crashing the program. Although this loop screens invalid numerical input, character data causes the program to crash. We are not yet at a position where we can make our programs *completely* immune to every possible input error, but with a simple loop, we can do some basic input checking.

5.7 THE *break* STATEMENT REVISITED

You have seen the break statement used within the context of the switch statement. When a break statement executes within a switch statement, the switch statement terminates and program control passes to the first statement following the switch statement. Similarly, a break statement can be used to terminate, or "break out of" a loop.

> When a *break* statement executes within a loop, the loop terminates and program control passes to the first statement following the loop.

Example 5.13 uses a break statement to terminate a while loop.

EXAMPLE 5.13 If 366 people gather in a room, the probability that two of them have the same birthday (month and day) is 1, that is, 100%. It's a certainty. (We'll pretend that there is no leap year!) Surprisingly, with a group as small as 50 people, the probability that at least two people have the same birthday is .97—close to certain! In general, the probability that at least two people in a group of *r* people share the same birthday can be computed as:

$$1 - \frac{365 \times 364 \times 363 \times \ldots \times (365 - r + 1)}{365^r}.$$

For example, the probability that, of five people, at least two have the same birthday is:

$$1 - \frac{365 \times 364 \times 363 \times 362 \times 361}{365^5} = 1 - \frac{365 \times 364 \times 363 \times 362 \times 361}{365 \times 365 \times 365 \times 365 \times 365}$$
$$= 1 - .973 = .027$$

Notice that the numerator and denominator of the fractional term each have five factors. In general for *r* people, both the numerator and denominator have *r* factors.

We now pose the following question:

> Given a probability, *p*, such as .97, how many people are necessary so that the probability that two or more of them have the same birthday is at least *p*? For example, how may people are required so that the chances are at least 50-50 ($p = .5$) that two or more people have the same birthday? Or, how many people are necessary so that there is at least a 99% chance that two or more have the same birthday? What about a 75% chance?

Problem Statement Write a program that accepts a probability *p* between 0 and 1 and determines the minimum number of people required so that the probability that two or more of them share the same birthday exceeds *p*.

Java Solution Suppose that .95 is the probability supplied interactively by the user. How many people do we need so that the probability that at least two have the same birthday exceeds .95?

The application computes the following probabilities, one by one:

- the probability that, in a room with two people, both have the same birthday;
- the probability that, in a room with three people, at least two have the same birthday;

- the probability that, in a room with four people, at least two have the same birthday;
- the probability that, in a room with five people, at least two have the same birthday;
- etc.

When the computed probability exceeds .95, it is known how many people are required and the computations stop. The following application computes these probabilities in the while loop on lines 25–34. A break statement terminates the loop.

```
1.  import java.util.*;
2.  public class Birthday
3.  {
4.     public static void main (String[] args)
5.     {
6.        Scanner input = new Scanner(System.in);
7.        int answer;                    // 1 to run the computation again
8.        int numPersons;
9.        int days;                      // counts down from 365
10.       double probability;            // 1 - probability is the probability that at least two share the same b-day
11.                                      // where probability = [365 × 364 × 363 × . . .× (365 - r + 1)]/ 365^r
12.       double inputProbability;  // input probability from the user

13.       do
14.       {
15.          do // ask user for a probability and check validity of the response
16.          {
17.             System.out.print("\nEnter a probability - at least two people share the same B-day: ");
18.             inputProbability = input.nextDouble();
19.          } while (inputProbability <= 0 || inputProbability >= 1.0); // repeat on incorrect data


20.          // Each iteration of the following loop increases the number of people by 1
21.          // and determines the probability that two share a birthday
22.          numPersons = 0;
23.          days = 366;
24.          probability = 1;
25.          while (days > 0) // days has been initialized to 366 but is decremented before its use
26.          {
27.             numPersons++;
28.             days--;
29.             probability *= days/365.0; // [365 × 364 × 363 × ... × (365 - r + 1)] / 365^r

30.             // stop when the probability that two people
31.             // share the same b-day exceeds the input probability
32.             if (1 - probability > inputProbability)
33.                break;
34.          }
35.          System.out.println(numPersons + " people are required");
36.          System.out.println("The probability that two or more have the same birthday is " + (1 - probability));
37.          System.out.print("\nRun again? 1 for yes, any other number for no: ");
38.          answer = input.nextInt();
39.       } while (answer ==1);
40.    }
41. }
```

Output

```
Enter a probability – at least two people share the same B-day: .5
23 people are required
The probability that two or more have the same birthday is 0.5072972343239857

Run again? 1 for yes, any other number for no: 1

Enter a probability – at least two people share the same B-day: .75
32 people are required
The probability that two or more have the same birthday is 0.7533475278503208

Run again? 1 for yes, any other number for no: 1

Enter a probability – at least two people share the same B-day: .95
47 people are required
The probability that two or more have the same birthday is 0.9547744028332994

Run again? 1 for yes, any other number for no: 1

Enter a probability – at least two people share the same B-day: .99
57 people are required
The probability that two or more have the same birthday is 0.9901224593411699

Run again? 1 for yes, any other number for no: 2
```

Discussion We examine the loop that does the work:

```
while (days > 0)                 // days is initialized to 366
{
      numPersons++;              // numPersons is initially 0
      days--;
      probability *= days/365.0; // [365 × 364 × 363 × ... ×(365–r+1)]/ 365^r
      if( 1 – probability > inputProbability)
            break;
}
```

Suppose that you enter a probability of .025. How many persons are necessary so that there is a 2.5% chance that at least two of them have the same birthday?

The loop operates as follows:

days	numPersons	probability	1 – probability
365	1	365/365 = 1	1 – 1 = 0
364	2	(1)(364/365) = .997	1 – .997 = .003
363	3	(.997)(363/365) = .992	1 – .992 = .008
362	4	(.992)(362/365) = .984	1 – .984 = .016
361	5	(.984)(361/365) = .973	1 – .973 = **.027**

At this point, the loop terminates (i.e., the break statement executes) because when numPersons equals five, the probability that at least two of those five people share a birthday is .027 (>.025). The control variable days never reaches 0 (the value in the test condition). After the break statement executes, program control passes to the first statement following the loop:

```
System.out.println(numPersons + " people are required");
```

5.8 IN CONCLUSION

Java provides three statements that effect repetition: the while statement, the do-while statement, and the for statement. All three statements are equally powerful, but each is best suited for specific kinds of applications. A loop that always executes at least once is usually implemented with a do-while statement, and one that may never execute with a while statement. A loop that counts iterations is usually constructed with a for statement. The choice is a matter of style, technique, and convenience.

Repetition, however, is not a convenience but a programming necessity. Repetition allows programs to perform any task multiple times. With repetition and selection, your programs can implement most any complex algorithm. No other control structures are necessary. But as your programming tasks become more complex, so do your programs. In Chapter 6, we introduce a programming mechanism that allows you to divide complicated problems into smaller, more manageable, and less complicated subtasks.

Just The Facts

- Java provides three statements that effect iteration or repetition: while, do-while, and for.
- An iterative statement includes a block of statements that repeats. These statements are enclosed in curly braces. If there is only one statement in the block, then the braces may be omitted.
- An iterative statement checks a condition before the next iteration.
- Any of the three iterative statements is powerful enough to simulate the others. Each is available for the programmer's convenience.
- An iterative statement can be nested inside the block of another iterative statement. There is no limit on the number of nesting levels.
- Nested loops are handy for computations where each datum has several attributes.
- A while statement first tests its condition and if true, then executes its block.
- A do-while statement tests its condition at the end of the block, so the corresponding block always executes at least once.
- The most important feature and advantage of a for loop is that without examining the body of the loop, we can understand its termination structure.
- A for statement is convenient when you know in advance the number of times the loop should execute.
- A for statement executes its initialization statement just once, prior to the first iteration, tests the condition at the start of each iteration, and executes its update statement at the end of each iteration.
- A for statement can count forwards or backwards, and can increment the control variable each time by an arbitrary amount.
- A for statement is extremely flexible and need not be used exclusively for "counting" loops. A for statement can use *any* condition, and *any* update statement. A for statement can declare more than one variable and can have more than one update statement.
- A break statement can be used to escape from a loop.

Bug Extermination

Every programmer has struggled with infinite loops. A simple and effective way to test the correctness of an infinite loop is to add println statements to your program. For example, a println statement that, each time through the loop, displays the values of each variable appearing in the condition might be all you need. Printing intermediate calculations can help you to see that your loop is not doing what it is supposed to do or that the termination condition will never evaluate to false. Debugging statements should be removed from a program once they are no longer needed. Also, be sure that the loop does, in fact, contain a statement that alters the variables of the termination condition.

The "off by one" error is a common bug that is simple to fix. This error usually arises from an incorrect initialization. Should the initial value be 0 or 1? This bug also rears its head when <= is used instead of <, or vice versa. Remember, the loop

```
for (int i = 1; i < n; i++)
    do something
```

executes n – 1 times, not n times. Using temporary println statements can help uncover these "off by one" bugs. Often, pencil-and-paper simulation is enough to spot the error.

Printing intermediate results can help uncover elusive bugs, but *don't print too much*. A screen full of too much data can be as bewildering as an infinite loop. First, add a few println statements and then if the results do not help, remove these println statements before adding others. Avoid screen clutter.

Following is a list of a few common bugs that occur with the use of loops. The Java compiler will catch many of these but not all.

- Placing a semicolon after the condition of a while statement:

  ```
  while (condition);
      do something;
  ```

  This results in an infinite loop. The compiler will not catch this since it is perfectly legal syntax.

- Placing a semicolon at the end of the heading of a for statement:

  ```
  for (int i = 0; i <= n; i++);
      do something;
  ```

  In this case, the "loop" consists of incrementing i until i reaches n. Then, do something executes just once. This, too, is not a syntax error.

- Building complicated conditions with several &&'s and/or ||'s. What you think evaluates to false may not.
- Using a do-while statement when there are cases for which the loop should not execute. Use a while statement instead.
- Omitting a statement in the loop body that changes the condition from true to false.
- Initializing a loop counter to 1 when it should be initialized to 0, or vice versa. This is often the cause of an "off by one" error.
- Omitting parentheses around the expression following while.
- Mistakenly using the keyword do in a while loop, such as,

  ```
  while (x < 1) do {...}
    // This generates a syntax error.
  ```

  Java provides a do-while statement and a while statement but *not* a while-do statement.

- Omitting the semicolon after the last statement in the loop block before the closing curly brace.
- Using commas instead of semicolons to separate the three sections of the for loop header.
- Using semicolons instead of commas to separate initialized variables within the first section of the for loop header.
- Missing or mismatching braces in multi-nested loops.
- Forming (incorrect) expressions by misusing operator precedence or confusing = and ==. Remember, the assignment operator = does not mean "equals."

EXERCISES

LEARN THE LINGO

Test your knowledge of the chapter's vocabulary by completing the following crossword puzzle.

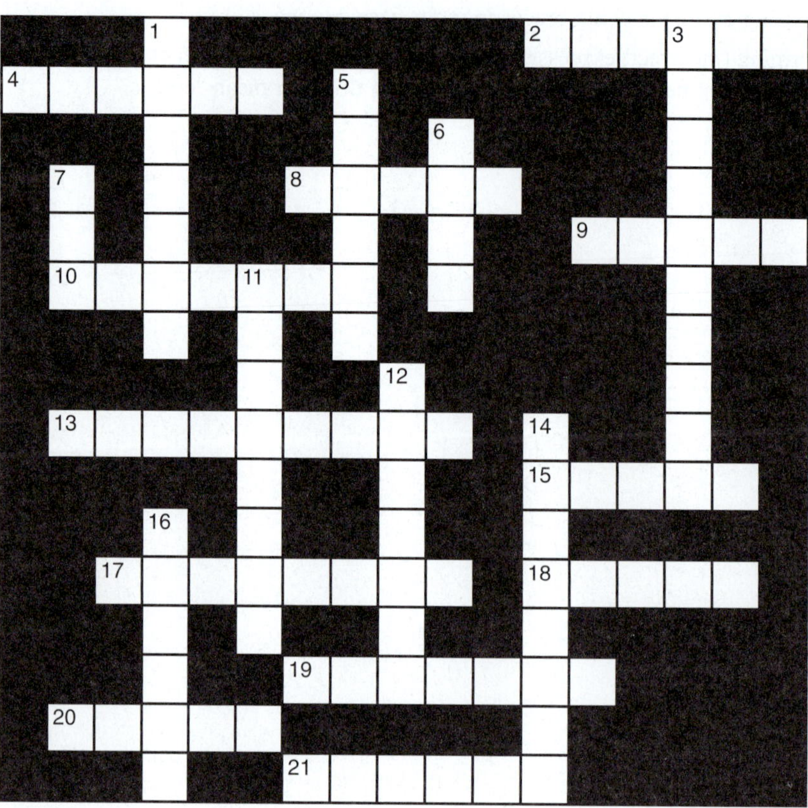

Across

2 Third part of a for statement header
4 A for loop ______ the number of iterations
8 A good way to debug a program is to include temporary ______ statements
9 Loop that may never execute
10 Loop that always executes once
13 Second part of a for loop header
15 An infinite loop can occur if the loop's terminating condition never evaluates to ________
17 Signals the end of data
18 Group of statements enclosed by braces
19 Variable in a for loop that keeps count
20 Statement that exits a loop
21 The for loop condition is tested ______ the block executes

Down

1 Variables declared in the header of a for statement are ______ beyond the loop
3 Nested loops are convenient when each datum has several ________
5 A do-while loop is often used to filter or ______ input
6 Every do-while loop must execute ________
7 You can extract the last digit of an integer with the ______ operator
11 Non-terminating loop
12 The type of the test condition
14 Common loop error (three words)
16 Loops inside loops inside loops

SHORT EXERCISES

1. **True or False**

   If false, give an explanation.

   a. To implement a loop that always repeats 100 times, it is easier to use a for statement than a while statement.
   b. Any operation that you can perform with a for statement you can also implement with a while statement.
   c. Any operation that you can perform with a while statement you can also accomplish with a for statement.
   d. A while statement always executes the loop body at least once.
   e. You cannot nest a for loop within a while loop.
   f. The data type of *condition* in while (*condition*) must be boolean.
   g. Using the number 0 as a sentinel value is one way to signal the end of a list of integers.
   h. The nesting depth of for loops is limited to at most three.
   i. The statement

   ```
   for (int i = 1; i <= 10; i++)
       {i = i − 1;}
   ```

   results in an infinite loop.
   j. The statement

   ```
   for (int i = 1; i <= 0; i++)
       {i = i − 1;}
   ```

   results in an infinite loop.

2. **Playing Compiler**

   Find the errors in the following statements. If a statement has no errors, then say so. If a statement contains errors, correct them. In each case describe the action of the loop.

   a.
   ```
   for (int i = 1; i <= 10; i++)
   {
     i = i − 1
   }
   ```
   b.
   ```
   int j = 7;
   while (j > 1)
   {
    system.out.println ("again");
    j = j % 2
   }
   ```
   c.
   ```
   int j = 1;
   while (j = 1)
   {
     System.out.print("try again");
   }
   ```
   d.
   ```
   for (int k =1, k == 20; k++) {}
   ```
   e.
   ```
   for (float h = 0.0; h < 5.0; h = h + .01)
       System.out.println(h);
   ```

f.
```
for (double h = 0.0; h < 5.0; h = h + .01)
{
  System.out.println(h);
}
```
g.
```
do
{
 int k = 3;
 System.out.print(k);
} while (k != 3);
```
h.
```
int k = 3; do
{
  System.out.print(k);
} while (k != 3);
```
i.
```
do
{
  System.out.println("This looks correct")
} while {true};
```
j.
```
while (true)
{
 int x = x + 1;
}
```
k.
```
int m = 2;
while (m > 0) do
{
  m = m -1;
};
```
l.
```
int m = 2;
while (m > 0) do
{
 m = m -1;
 System.out.println(m);
};
```
m.
```
int m = 2;
while (m > 0)
{
 m = m -1;
 System.out.println(m);
} while (false);
```
n.
```
int k;
for (k = 0; k = 1; k++)
{
  System.out.print(k = 1);
}
```
o.
```
int x = 7;
do
  (System.out.println(x); x--)
while {x < 2};
```
p.
```
for (int k = 0; k < 100; k = ++k)
  System.out.println(k)
```
q.
```
for (int k = 0; k < 100; k = ++k)
  System.out.println(k);
```

r.
```
for (int k = 0; k < 100; k = k++)
    System.out.println(k);
```
s.
```
for (int k = 0; k < 100; k = ++k)
    System.out.println(k++);
```
t.
```
for (int k = 0; k < 100; k = ++k)
    System.out.println(--k);
```

3. **What's the Output?**
Determine the output of each of the following segments.

a.
```
short x = 15000;
short y = 15000;
int z;
for (int i = 0; i < 30000; i++)
  x++;
System.out.println(x);
System.out.println(y + 30000);
z = y + 30000;
System.out.println(z);
```
b.
```
int x = 3, y = 7;
while (x < y)
{
  System.out.println(10 * x);
  for (int i = 0; i < y ; i++)
     System.out.println(10 * i);
  x *= 2;
}
```
c.
```
for ( int j = 0; j < 5; j++)
{
   for ( int k = j; k > 0 ; k--)
     System.out.println(k);
   System.out.println(j);
}
```
d.
```
boolean flag = true;
int k = 1;
int j = 1024;
while (flag)
{
      System.out.println(k);
      do
      {
            System.out.println(k);
            k = 2*k;
      } while (k < j);
      k = 1;
      j = j / 2;
      flag = (k == j);
}
```
e.
```
int m = 0, k = 0, j = 100;
while (m < j)
{
        m++;
```

```
        System.out.println(j);
        System.out.println(k);
        for (k = 0, j = 10; k != j; k++, j--)
            System.out.println(k + " and " + j);
        j++;
    }
```

4. **Variations for the header of a for loop**
   There are eight variations for the header of a for loop obtained by omitting one or more of the three parts in the header:

Initialization	Condition	Update Statement
no	no	no
no	no	yes
no	yes	no
no	yes	yes
yes	no	no
yes	no	yes
yes	yes	no
yes	yes	yes

   Under what circumstances would each case be appropriate? Give examples.

5. **Which Loop?**
   Write code segments to solve each of the following problems. Choose the loop that you feel is most natural: for, while, or do-while.
   a. On April 1, Sally Saver deposits one cent in her piggy bank. As an April Fools Day resolution, Sally decides to double the previous day's amount each day for one month. So, on April 2, Sally saves two cents; on April 3, four cents, and so on. How much will Sally have saved by April 30?
   b. On April 1, Sally Saver deposits one cent in her piggy bank. Each day she doubles the amount from the previous day. When will Sally have saved $1,000,000?

6. **Loop Rewriting**
   Rewrite the following while statements as for statements. Assume that input (a Scanner) has been previously declared.
   a.
```
int count = 0;
int sum = 0;
while ( count < 10)
{
  sum += input.nextInt();
  count = count + 1;
}
```
   b.
```
int count = 1;
while ( count <= 15)
{
  int num = 1;
  int sum = 0;
  while ( num <= 5)
  {
```

```
        sum += input.nextInt();
        num += 1;
      }
      System.out.println("Sum number " + count + " is " + sum);
      count++;
    }
```

7. **Loop Rewriting**

   Rewrite the following for statements as while statements.

   a.
   ```
   for (int i = 0, sum = 0; i < 10; i++)
      sum = sum + i * i;
   ```
   b.
   ```
   int sum;
   for (int i = 0; i < 10; i++)
   {
       sum = 0;
       for (int j = 0; j <= i; j++)
           sum = sum + j;
       System.out.println(sum);
   }
   ```
   c.
   ```
   int i, sum;
   for (i = 0, sum = 0; i < 10; sum += i++);
   System.out.println(sum);
   ```

8. **Find the Error**

   Fix all syntactical and logical errors in the following segments. Assume that input (a Scanner) has been previously declared.

   a.
   ```
   int count = 0;
   int number;
   int sum = 0;     // sum of the positive numbers among the first 15 numbers entered interactively
   while count < 15
   {
       number = input.nextInt();
       if (number > 0)
          sum = sum + number;
   }
   ```
   b.
   ```
   for (int i = 10, sum = 0; i > 5; i++)     // sum of the squares of 5 numbers entered interactively
   {
       int number = input.nextInt();
       sum = number * number;
   }
   ```
   c.
   ```
   for (int i = 1, sum = 0; i <= 10; i++)
       sum += i * i;
   System.out.println ('The sum of the first 10 squares is " + sum);
   ```
   d.
   ```
   // adds numbers entered interactively using -999 as a flag.
   while (input.nextInt() != -999)
     sum = sum + input.nextInt();
   ```

9. **Tracing**

   How many times does the third line execute in each of the following loops? Assume m, n, and product are declared as int. Your answers may be expressed in terms of m and n.

a.
```
for (int i = 1; i <= n; i++)
    for (int j = 1 ; j <= m; j++)
        product = i * j;
```
b.
```
for (int i = 1; i <= 8; i++)
    for (int j = 1 ; j <= i; j++)
        product = i * j;
```
c.
```
for (int i = 1; i <= m; i++)
    for (int j = 1 ; j <= i; j++)
        product = i * j;
```
d.
```
int max = 1;
for (int i = 1; i <= n; max *= 2, i++);
for (int i = max; i >=1; i = i / 2)
    System.out.println(i);
```

PROGRAMMING EXERCISES

1. **Credit Card Revisited**
   Rewrite Example 5.8, using a for loop index that increases the loop counter by two with each iteration, that is, use a loop such as the following

   ```
   for (int i = 1; i < MAX_DIGITS; i += 2) {...}.
   ```

   Why might this improve the performance of the program?

2. **Pictures**
   Write a program that accepts an integer *n* and prints the following right triangle with base and height *n*.

   ```
   1    X
   2    XX
   3    XXX
        ...
   n    XXX...X (n times)
   ```

3. **More Pictures**
   Write a program that accepts an integer *n* and prints the following picture of a diamond with $2n - 1$ rows.

   ```
   1              X
   2             XXX
   3            XXXXX
                 ...
   n          XXX ...   X (2n − 1 times)
                 ...
                XXXXX
                 XXX
   2n − 1         X
   ```

4. **A Bank Account Record**
   Write a program that reads a list of numbers representing deposits to and withdrawals from a savings account. Positive entries represent deposits and the negative entries withdrawals. Your program should calculate the sum of all deposits and the sum of all withdrawals. Use the sentinel zero to signal the end of the data.

5. **Prime Numbers**
   Write a program that accepts an integer *n* and displays all the prime numbers between 2 and *n*. A prime number is a positive integer divisible only by itself and 1.

6. **Coin Flipping**
   Write a program that simulates flipping a coin 100,000 times and reports the longest consecutive sequence of heads. Use (int) (Math.random() + .5) to generate a random integer, 0 for heads and 1 for tails.

7. **Greatest Common Divisor**
   The greatest common divisor of two numbers *a* and *b* is the largest number that evenly divides both *a* and *b*. For example, the greatest common divisor of 36 and 30 is 6. Write two programs to compute the greatest common divisor of two integers *a* and *b* according to the following two algorithms:

   - Brute Force: Assume that $a > b$. Start with *b* and try every integer less than or equal to *b* until you find a common divisor:

   ```
   divisor = b;
   while ( divisor does not divide both a and b)
       divisor--;
   print divisor;
   ```

   - Euclid's Algorithm: Euclid proved in 300 BCE that, if $a > b$, then the greatest common divisor of *a* and *b* equals the greatest common divisor of *b* and *a* % *b*. Hence, the greatest common divisor of 138 and 36 equals the greatest common divisor of 36 and 30 (138 % 36), which equals the greatest common divisor of 30 and 6 (36 % 30), which equals the greatest common divisor of 6 and 0 (30 % 6), which is 6.

8. **Perfect Numbers**
   A perfect number, *p*, is a positive integer that equals the sum of its divisors, excluding *p* itself. For example, 6 is a perfect number because the divisors of 6 (1, 2, and 3) sum to 6. Write a program that prints all perfect numbers less than 1000. There are not many!

9. **General Average**
   Write a program that calculates the average of *n* test scores, such that each score is an integer in the range 0 through 100. Your program should first prompt for an integer *n* and then request *n* scores. Your program should also check for invalid data. If a user enters a number outside the correct range, the program should prompt for another value. Round the average to the closest integer.

10. **Modified Average**
    Write a program that accepts a list of *n* test scores in the range 0 through 100 and finds the average of the $n - 1$ highest scores on the list—that is, the lowest score is not included in the average. For example, if the test scores are 90, 80, 70, and 60, the average is computed as $(90 + 80 + 70)/3 = 80.0$. The low score of 60 is excluded.

    Your program should first prompt for an integer *n*, and then request *n* scores. Your program should also check for invalid data. If a user enters a number outside the correct range, the program should prompt for another value.

11. **Infinite Series**
    The infinite series 1 + 1/2 + 1/3 + 1/4 + 1/5 + 1/6 … *diverges*. This means that the finite sums

$$
\begin{array}{lll}
1 + 1/2 & = 3/2 & = 1.5 \\
1 + 1/2 + 1/3 & = 11/6 & \approx 1.833 \\
1 + 1/2 + 1/3 + 1/4 & = 25/12 & \approx 2.0833 \\
1 + 1/2 + 1/3 + 1/4 + 1/5 & = 137/60 & \approx 2.2833 \\
\ldots & & \\
1 + 1/2 + 1/3 + 1/4 + 1/5 + \ldots + 1/n & &
\end{array}
$$

can be made arbitrarily large by including more and more fractions. For example, if n is large enough, the sum $1 + 1/2 + 1/3 + 1/4 + 1/5 + \ldots + 1/n$ grows greater than 100,000,000,000.

However, because a computer's accuracy with floating-point numbers is limited, very small fractions will eventually be indistinguishable from zero. Consequently, you will discover that the sum

$$1 + 1/2 + 1/3 + 1/4 + 1/5 + \ldots + 1/n$$

when calculated by a computer may not grow as large as you would expect!

Write a program that accepts an integer n and computes the sum of the series through $1/n$. Experiment with large values of n to see how large you can actually make a sum. Can you make the sum grow larger than 20? 30?

12. **Credit Cards**
The Capital One credit card limits a single charge to \$900 and the total monthly charges to \$3000. Write a program that accepts an integer n representing the number of transactions for one month, followed by the dollar/cent values of each of the n transactions (double). Your program should compute and print the minimum, maximum, and sum of all transactions for the month. If you exceed either limit (a single transaction over \$900, or total over \$3000) then the program displays the appropriate message(s).

13. **Grade Processing Revisited**
Rewrite the grade processing program of Example 5.11 using just a single loop with an embedded if statement. If the user enters 1000 before entering the sentinel for any set of grades, the program terminates and does not report the information for that last student.

14. **World Series Odds**
Once a year, the two top American baseball teams play a best-four-out-of-seven-games World Series. If the teams are evenly matched, then the probability that the series lasts for all seven games is $1/2 \times 3/4 \times 5/6 = 15/48 = 5/16$. In general, the probability that a competition of $2n + 1$ games, $n > 0$, between evenly matched teams will "go all the way" and last for all $2n + 1$ games is $1/2 \times 3/4 \times 5/6 \times 7/8 \times \ldots \times (2n - 1)/(2n)$. Write a program that accepts an integer n and calculates the probability that a competition of $2n + 1$ games will go all the way.

15. **Checkbook Balancing**
Write a program that balances a checkbook. Input to the program should be a sequence of numbers representing checks and deposits. A negative number indicates a check and a positive number a deposit. A zero signals the end of data. After each entry, "echo print" the entry, and print the current balance. Make the first entry the starting balance. For example, if the entries are 100.00, −50.00, −30.00, 200.00, 0 the output should be:

Transactions	**Current Balance**
Enter entry: **100.00**	
100.00	Starting Balance: \$100.00
Enter entry: **−50.00**	
−50.00	\$50.00
Enter entry: **−30.00**	
−30.00	\$20.00
Enter entry: **200.00**	
200.00	\$220.00
Enter entry: **0**	
0	Final Balance: \$220.00

16. **A Multiplication Table**
Write a program to generate a multiplication table such as the following "9 times table":

```
        0    1    2    3    4    5    6    7    8    9

   0    0    0    0    0    0    0    0    0    0    0
   1    0    1    2    3    4    5    6    7    8    9
   2    0    2    4    6    8   10   12   14   16   18
   ...
   9    0    9   18   27   36   45   54   63   72   81
```

17. **Craps Simulation**
To play craps, a player rolls two dice repeatedly until he wins or loses. If he makes a 7 or an 11 on the first roll, he wins immediately. An initial roll of 2, 3, or 12 results in a loss. If he tosses a 4, 5, 6, 8, 9, or 10 on his first roll, then that number becomes his "point." After a player makes a point, he continues rolling the dice and wins or loses according to the following rules: if he makes his point before rolling a seven, he wins; but if he rolls a seven first, he loses. No other values, including 2, 3, 11, or 12, affect the game's outcome once the player has established his point.

Write a program that plays craps. Your program should allow a user to play more than one game. Typical output appears below:

Enter 0 to roll the dice: **0**
You rolled a 7
You win
Play again? Enter 1 for yes: **1**

Enter 0 to roll the dice: **0**
You rolled a 4.
Your point is 4. Continue rolling.
Enter 0 to roll the dice: **0**
You rolled a 3
Enter 0 to roll the dice: **0**
You rolled a 5
Enter 0 to roll the dice: **0**
You rolled a 7
You lose
Play again? Enter 1 for yes: **0**
Bye

Hint: To roll a single die, generate a random number between 1 and 6 inclusive. You can do this with (int)(6 * Math.random()) + 1.

18. **A Digital Puzzle**
There is only one 10-digit number that contains every digit 0 through 9 exactly once and has the property that each number formed from the leftmost *j* digits is divisible by *j*. For example, the number 9876543210 is close but does not qualify. The number contains each digit once, the first digit 9 is divisible by 1, the number 98 is divisible by 2, 987 is divisible by 3, 9876 is divisible by 4, 98765 is divisible by 5, and 987654 is divisible by 6. However, the number 9876543 is *not* divisible by 7. Note that 98765432 *is* divisible by 8, 987654321 *is* divisible by 9, and 9876543210 *is* divisible by 10, so this number fails only because 9876543 is not divisible by 7.

Write a program that accepts a 10-digit integer, *n*, containing each of the digits 0 through 9, and determines how many such divisions can be performed. For example, on input 9876543210 your program should report 9 divisions (only 9876543 fails);

for 2159730648 the number of divisions is just 1; and for the number 3816547290 (and only this number) the result is 10. (*Warning*: The largest value of data type int is $2^{31} - 1 = 2{,}147{,}483{,}647$, too small for many 10-digit numbers. An integer of type long can be as large as $2^{63} - 1$.)

19. **Rectangles in a Grid**

The number of rectangles that can be formed in an n by n grid can be calculated in three equivalent ways:

1. $(1 + 2 + \ldots + n)^2$
2. $(n(n + 1)/2)^2$
3. $1^3 + 2^3 + \ldots + n^3$

For example, there are $(1 + 2)^2 = (2 \times 3)/2)^2 = (1^3 + 2^3) = 9$ rectangles of various sizes that can be formed in a 2-by-2 grid. The shaded areas of Figure 5.13 show the nine rectangles. Similarly, there are $(1 + 2 + 3)^2 = (3 \times 4)/2)^2 = 1 + 8 + 27 = 36$ rectangles of various sizes in a 3-by-3 grid.

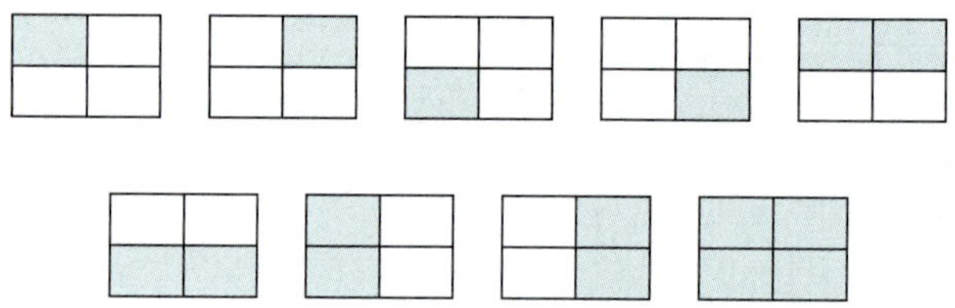

FIGURE 5.13 Nine different rectangles can be formed in a 2-by-2 grid.

Verify the identities $(1 + 2 + \ldots + n)^2 = (n(n + 1)/2)^2 = 1^3 + 2^3 + \ldots + n^3$, for $n = 1$ to 20 by writing a program to compute and display the following table.

n	$(1 + 2 + \ldots + n)^2$	$(n(n + 1)/2)^2$	$1^3 + 2^3 + \ldots + n^3$
1	1	1	1
2	9	9	9
...	...	...	...
20	44100	44100	44100

20. **Investments**

At some time, everyone eventually borrows money, perhaps for a new car, a house, or to finance a start-up business. The amount of interest that you pay over the life of a loan may surprise you. For a 30-year, $200,000 loan at 6% annual interest, the total interest is more than $230,000.

Write a program that calculates the monthly payment as well the portion of each monthly payment that is interest. The program should prompt the user for

1. the amount borrowed in dollars,
2. the annual interest rate as a percentage, and
3. the term of the loan in years.

The program should be able to run any number of times with different data.

The monthly payment is calculated with the following formula:

$$payment = \frac{(amount) \times (rate)}{1 - \left(\frac{1}{1 + rate}\right)^m}$$

where *amount* is the amount borrowed in dollars, m is the total number of *monthly* payments, and *rate* is the *monthly* interest rate. For example, if the annual interest rate is 6%, and the term of the loan is 30 years, then $m = 12 \times 30 = 360$, and $rate = .06/12 = .005$ or 0.5%.

The amount of the loan cannot exceed $1,000,000; the interest is given as a percentage between 2.0 and 15.0 inclusive, for example, 6.5 or 5.75; and the term of the loan is no more than 30 years. Your program should check input to ensure that these restrictions are met.

Your program should display the monthly payment followed by a month-by-month table showing the interest and principal paid each month. The interest paid each month equals the rate times the remaining balance of the loan. The remainder of the monthly payment goes to principal.

The loan balance begins with the amount borrowed. The remaining balance of the loan should be updated each month by subtracting the principal paid that month from the previous remaining loan balance. For convenience, round interest to the nearest dollar. This can be accomplished with

```
Math.Round(interest).
```

Finally, display the total amount of interest, rounded to the nearest dollar, paid over the life of the loan.

THE BIGGER PICTURE

1. FLOATING-POINT ARITHMETIC

The nefarious infinite loop is one of the hazards of ill-formed iterative statements. It might surprise you that careless use of floating-point numbers can be a source of infinite loops as well. Indeed, incorrect usage of floating-point numbers can result in some very subtle and unsightly bugs.

For example, on the surface, the segment

```
double x = 0.0;
while (x != 1.0)
{
    x = x + 0.1;
    System.out.println(x);
}
```

seems perfectly innocuous. Ten additions should stop the loop. Well, execute these statements and you may be surprised by the outcome. Yes, it is an infinite loop! The problem is that floating-point arithmetic is not exact.

Here's another "simple" code segment that utilizes floating-point arithmetic:

```
double x = 2.0, y = 3.14, z = −7.0;
System.out.println(z + y + x + 1.86);
```

Surprisingly, the sum z + y + x + 1.86 does not evaluate to 0.0. If you embed these statements into a program, you will see that the expression z + y + x + 1.86 evaluates to 2.220446049250313E-16, an extremely small number but certainly not the correct value of 0.0. Interestingly, the expression x + y + z + 1.86 returns 6.661338147750939E-16, a different small number but also not 0.0. Perhaps even more surprising is that the expression x + 1.86 + y + z *does* indeed evaluate to 0.0. Yes, z + y + x + 1.86, x + y + z + 1.86, and x + 1.86 + y + z all have different values! Is Java ignorant of the laws of simple arithmetic? Try a bit of experimentation with the following exercises.

Exercises

1. Write a program to test the anomalies described above.
2. Find floating-point examples of your own that exhibit a violation of the associative or commutative laws of addition.

Similar situations abound. The output from the following code segment may surprise you.

```
double number = 0.0;
for (int i = 1; i <= 10; i++)
      number += 0.1;
System.out.println(number);
```

The segment displays not 1.0 but 0.9999999999999999. Close, yes; exact, not really. The same thing happens if you add 0.01 to the variable number 100 times; the value of number still falls short of 1.0.

The explanation for these irregularities has to do with the way that Java evaluates expressions, and also how Java stores floating-point values. Java uses an encoding called the IEEE 754 standard to represent floating-point numbers in binary. Although the details of this encoding scheme are not relevant here, the consequences of using the IEEE 754 standard are:

- Floating-point arithmetic executed by a computer is not exact. You can expect accurate answers to within a very small margin of error, but you cannot always expect an exact answer.
- Floating-point arithmetic is not necessarily associative or commutative.

As a simple precaution, do not compare double (or float) values for equality. Instead, subtract one from the other and compare their difference to a small number: For example,

```
if (Math.abs(x – y) <.000001).   // Math.abs(z) computes the absolute value of z
```

is safer than

```
if (x == y)
```

where x and y are both type float or double.

Exercises

3. Alter the condition of the while statement of the first code segment of this section so that the program does not fall into an infinite loop. The program should stop when x is within 0.00001 of 1.0.
4. Consider the Birthday Paradox of Example 5.13. Recall that the formula that calculates the probability that at least two people in a group of five share the same birthday is:

$$1 - \frac{365 \times 364 \times 363 \times 362 \times 361}{365 \times 365 \times 365 \times 365 \times 365} = 1 - \frac{365}{365} \times \frac{364}{365} \times \frac{363}{365} \times \frac{362}{365} \times \frac{361}{365}$$

   The general formula for r people has r fractions instead of five. Write two programs that calculate the probability that at least two people in a group of r share the same birthday. Your program should implement the formula two ways.

THE BIGGER PICTURE

a. The first program calculates the product of r fractions, fraction by fraction, that is, (365/365) × (365/364) × (363/365) … × ((365 − r +1)/365), as is illustrated on the right side of the preceding equation, for r =5. Declare all variables, except loop counters, of type double.

b. The second program computes the numerator (365 × 364 × 363 × … × (365 − r +1)), using one loop, the denominator 365^r using a separate loop, and divides the two products at the end, as illustrated on the left side of the preceding equation. Declare all variables, except loop counters, of type double.

Run your programs for all values of r in the range 1 to 15. Print and compare the results of the two programs. Do the two methods give the same result?

Change your programs so that r ranges from 1 to 25. Did you encounter any errors with the second program? If so, what do you think caused these errors?

What do you think would happen if, in the second program, you declared the numerator and denominator to have type int and cast them to type double before performing the division?

As a final illustration of some of the pitfalls of floating-point arithmetic, we present a simple algorithm for estimating the square root of a number. To calculate the square root of 150.0 the algorithm works as follows:

- Begin with an estimate or guess for the square root of 150.0. We use 10.0, but any other number would also work.
- Divide 150.0 by 10. The quotient is 15.0, and because 10.0 × 15.0 = 150.0, the estimate 10.0 is too low and the square root of 150.0 lies between 10.0 and 15.0.
- As a second estimate of the square root of 150.0, take the average of 10.0 and 15.0. That's (10.0 +15.0)/2 = 12.5
- Divide 150.0/12.5. The quotient is 12.0, so the square root of 150 lies between 12.0 and 12.5.
- Use the average of 12.0 and 12.5 (12.25) as the next estimate.
- Divide 150 by 12.25. The quotient is approximately 12.2474489795918.
- Continue the process until two consecutive estimates are "equal," that is, the two estimates agree up to a number of decimal places—limited by the computer's accuracy.

Here is the algorithm in Java-like pseudocode for finding the square root of any positive number x:

```
oldGuess = x;
newGuess = 10.0;    // There is nothing special about 10.
                    // Any number is fine for the first guess.

while (oldGuess != newGuess)
{
    oldGuess = newGuess;
    newGuess = (oldGuess + x/oldGuess)/2.0; // calculates the average
}
```

The problem with this pseudocode is the expression (oldGuess != newGuess). The inaccuracies of floating-point arithmetic *could* bring the algorithm to a stage where the values of oldGuess and newGuess oscillate, causing this loop to run forever. Using the expression Math.abs(oldGuess – newGuess) < 0.000001 instead of oldGuess != newGuess is safer. This continues the loop until the difference between the last two guesses is small enough.

Exercises

5. Write a Java program that calculates the square root of a non-negative number. The program should prompt for the number and an initial guess. Display all intermediate estimates. Use Math.abs(oldGuess – newGuess) < 0.000001 in place of the condition oldGuess != newGuess.
6. Run the program in of Exercise 5 a few times. Examine the sequence of intermediate estimates, and describe whether or not they oscillate.
7. Replace Math.abs(oldGuess – newGuess) < 0.000001 with oldGuess != newGuess. Run your program again and try to find input that forces the program to loop forever.

Finally, be aware that floating-point arithmetic is not only a cause of infinite loops but also the root of other bugs. An if statement that compares two doubles can be just as bug-prone as a while statement.

2. LOOPS AND COMPUTABILITY

The Java compiler can scan a program and determine any number of errors: a missing semicolon, an uninitialized variable, a mismatched type, an unbalanced set of parentheses, and dozens of other syntax errors. One pesky programming error that a compiler does not flag is the infinite loop. Can a compiler determine whether or not a program will ever fall into an infinite loop? As it turns out, it is impossible to write a computer program, compiler or otherwise, that correctly determines whether other programs loop forever. This phenomenon is known as the *halting problem*, a well-known topic in theoretical computer science.

The Halting Problem: Given a program P together with some initial input, can it be determined whether P will stop or fall into an infinite loop?

In 1936, Alan Turing (1912–1954), one of the great pioneers of computer science, proved that an algorithm that determines whether or not a program halts on arbitrary input cannot exist. Turing demonstrated that the existence of a "halting program" leads to an impossible conclusion. In the following discussion, we briefly summarize Turing's argument.

We begin with the (possibly fallacious) assumption that there does, in fact, exist a program that can determine whether or not another program stops on arbitrary input. For lack of a better name, we call this program Loopy. See Figure 5.14.

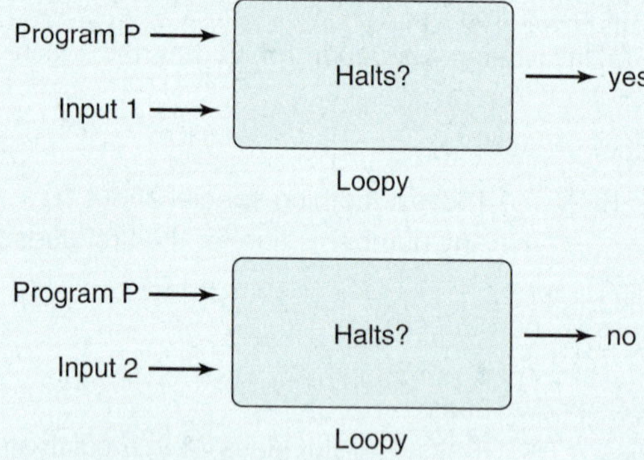

FIGURE 5.14 The Loopy program

Is there such a program as Loopy? Does Loopy exist or is Loopy just wishful thinking, the dream of some mad computer scientist? We now prove that *if* Loopy can, in fact, be written, then pigs fly, fish walk, and white rabbits carry pocket watches. That is, the existence of Loopy implies the impossible, proving there is no Loopy.

Here is the proof: Assume that Loopy does, indeed, exist—that is, there is a program that determines whether or not another program halts or continues forever. We show that this assumption leads to an absurd conclusion, the creation of an impossible program called Paradox. What is Paradox? The input to Paradox is any program P. Paradox uses Loopy to do its job. Here is how Paradox operates on program P.

a. Paradox runs Loopy using P as both input parameters, that is, Loopy will check whether or not P halts on itself.
b. If Loopy reports *no* (P does not stop with itself as input), then Paradox halts.
c. If Loopy reports *yes* (P halts on itself) then Paradox loops forever.

That is, Paradox runs according to the following algorithm:

```
if (Loopy says that P loops forever on itself)
    break;        // Paradox stops
else if (Loopy says that P stops on itself)
    while(true) ; // Paradox goes into an infinite loop
```

Figure 5.15 illustrates the operation of the program Paradox.

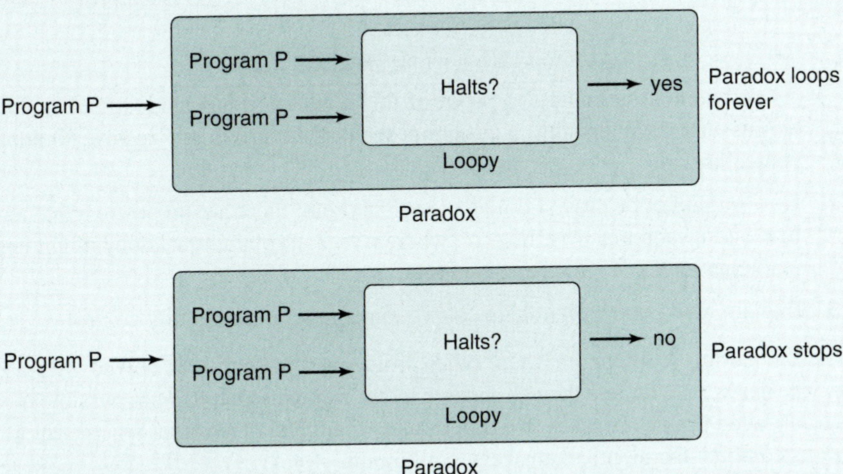

FIGURE 5.15 The Paradox program runs with program P as input

Now, what happens if the input to Paradox is Paradox itself? That is, what if P is the program Paradox? Figure 5.16 shows the two possible outcomes.

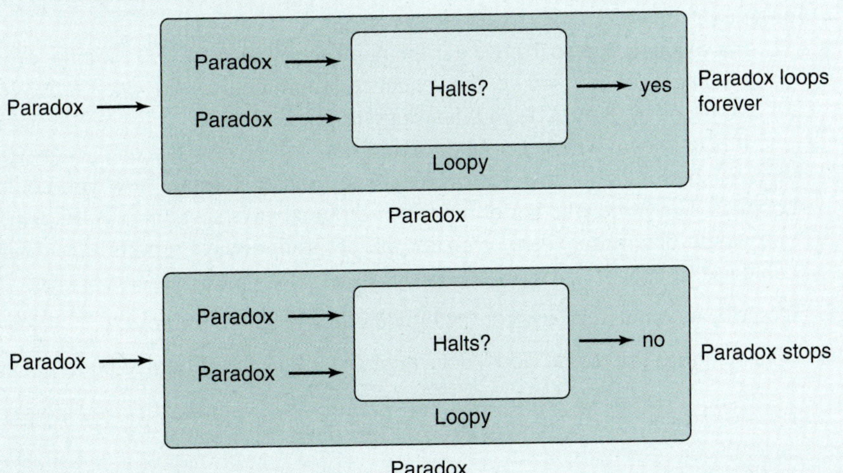

FIGURE 5.16 The Paradox program runs with itself as input

THE BIGGER PICTURE

The two possible scenarios are:

- If Loopy says that Paradox halts (on itself), then Paradox runs forever.
- If Loopy says that Paradox runs forever (on itself), then Paradox halts.

These conclusions may make sense in a world created by Lewis Carroll, Neverland, or perhaps The Twilight Zone, but in our world both possibilities are clearly impossible. Thus, we conclude that program Loopy, which is the foundation of Paradox, cannot exist.

Exercises

1. In the 18th century, Christian Goldbach (1690–1764) conjectured that every even number greater than 2 is the sum of two prime numbers. For example:

$$\begin{aligned} 4 &= 2 + 2, \\ 6 &= 3 + 3, \\ 8 &= 5 + 3, \\ 10 &= 7 + 3, \\ 12 &= 5 + 7, \\ &\dots \\ 120 &= 41 + 79, \text{ etc.} \end{aligned}$$

As simple as it is to state, a proof of this conjecture has eluded mathematicians to this day. Explain how a program such as Loopy might resolve Goldbach's conjecture.

2. How might Loopy prove Fermat's Last Theorem: there are no positive integers a, b, c, and n such that $a^n + b^n = c^n$, where $n > 2$. Explain how Loopy might help mathematicians prove other theorems.

3. Explain how Loopy might help software manufacturers' quality control.

Besides the halting problem, are there other problems that cannot be solved with a computer? The answer is yes, and they all involve loops. For example, it is not possible to write a program called Equal that takes two programs as input and determines whether or not the programs compute the identical answers to all inputs.

Exercises

4. Write a program that takes a positive integer as input and repeats the following steps in a loop until the integer becomes 1: If the integer is even, divide it by 2; and if it is odd, multiply it by 3 and add 1. If the program eventually hits 1, the program prints *success*.

For example: given 10, we get the numbers 5, 16, 8, 4, 2, 1, and the program prints *success*. With 7, we get the sequence of numbers 22, 11, 34, 17, 52, 26, 13, 40, 20, 10, 5, 16, 8, 4, 2, 1, and the program prints *success*.

It is unknown whether or not the program will always say *success* or whether there is some number that will make it run forever. Explain how you could use Loopy to determine whether or not the program always says *success*. Explain how you would determine whether or not the program always reports *success* if you could use Equal.

5. Describe a commercial use for the hypothetical program Equal.

6. (Challenging) Prove that Equal does not exist. *Hint:* Use Equal to build Loopy.

CHAPTER 6

Methods

"Though this be madness, yet there is method in 't."
—From Hamlet (II, ii, 206)

"There is more madness to my method than method to my madness."
—Salvador Dali

Objectives

The objectives of Chapter 6 include an understanding of

- the concept of a method as a "black box,"
- the methods of Java's Math class,
- how to construct methods that carry out simple tasks,
- the differences between void methods and methods that return a value,
- the scope of a name, and
- method overloading: advantages and potential pitfalls.

6.1 INTRODUCTION

Not too long ago, in the pioneer days of programming (that's circa 1966), mathematicians Corrado Bohm and Guiseppe Jacopini proved that *any* computer program can be written using just three basic structures:

1. sequence (statements in a program are executed sequentially),
2. selection (if-else statements), and
3. repetition (loops).

These three fundamental ideas are the principal concepts of Chapters 2 through 5. So, at least *theoretically*, you can put aside this text and implement any program that you dare to dream up! You have the tools.

Needless to say, complex computer programs are built with tools more sophisticated than three simple, albeit powerful, structures. Indeed, a carpenter could theoretically build a house using nothing more than nails, a saw, a hammer, and some lumber; but the task wouldn't be easy, and the finished product may be unsightly. As a carpenter needs more powerful equipment, the programmer requires tools beyond sequence, selection, and repetition. One such programming construct is the *method.*

A *method* is a named sequence of instructions that are grouped together to perform a task.

Complicated programs perform many different tasks. Methods enable the programmer to organize various tasks into neat, manageable, independent bundles of code. Every Java application that we have written contains one method; its name is main and its instructions appear between the opening and closing braces of main.

> Every Java application must have a main method, and the execution of every Java application begins with the main method.

Other methods that we have used are print(...), println(...), and Math.random().

In this chapter you will learn about a few more prepackaged methods provided by Java as well as how to construct your own methods. We begin with a "black box" view of a method.

6.2 JAVA'S PREDEFINED METHODS

Imagine a mathematical, if not magical, "black box" that works in such a way that whenever you supply a number to the box, the box gives or *returns* the positive square root of that number. See Figure 6.1a.

FIGURE 6.1a A *square root* box

Figure 6.1b illustrates a similar mechanism that accepts two numbers, perhaps the length and width of a rectangle, and returns the area of the rectangle.

FIGURE 6.1b An *area* box

Or can you fathom a gizmo that receives a character and returns the integer (ASCII) value of that character? See Figure 6.1c.

FIGURE 6.1c An *ASCII converter* box

Such a "box" is a metaphor for a *method*. A method is very much like a mathematical function—a black box that computes an output given some inputs.

> The values that you supply or *pass* to the method are called *arguments*. The value computed by the method is the *returned value*.

Later, you will see that a method may perform a task without accepting arguments or returning a value.

Java comes bundled with an extraordinary number of methods. Each of these built-in methods is comprised of Java code that performs some specific task. Fortunately, the programmer need not know *how* these Java-supplied methods work "inside the box" or "under the hood," but simply how to use them.

How do you use these methods? Where do you get them? Let's start with a simple example.

6.2.1 The Square Root Method

EXAMPLE 6.1

Imagine that you are standing on a beach gazing out at the sea. What is the distance to the horizon? How far ahead can you see? How far can you see if you are standing on a cliff above the beach?

In general, the distance to the horizon (in miles) can be estimated as follows:

- Determine the distance (in feet) from sea level to your eyes.
- Compute the square root of that distance.
- Multiply the result by 1.23.

Problem Statement Write a program that prompts a user for the distance measured from the ground to his/her eyes and calculates the distance to the horizon.

Notice that the following program must calculate a square root. This calculation is performed compliments of the method Math.sqrt(x)—a black box.

Java Solution

```
1.  import java.util.*;
2.  public class DistanceToHorizon
3.  {
4.     public static void main(String[] args)
5.     {
6.        Scanner input;
7.        double distanceToEyes;           // measured from the ground
8.        double distanceToHorizon;
9.        int answer = 1;                  // used to repeat the calculation
10.       input = new Scanner(System.in);
11.       do
12.       {
13.          System.out.print("Distance from the ground to your eyes in feet: ");
14.          distanceToEyes = input.nextDouble();
15.          distanceToHorizon = 1.23 * Math.sqrt(distanceToEyes);
16.          System.out.println("The distance to the horizon is " + distanceToHorizon + "mi.");
17.          System.out.print("Again? Enter 1 for YES; any other number to Exit: ");
18.          answer = input.nextInt();
19.       }while (answer == 1);
20.    }
21. }
```

Output

```
Distance from the ground to your eyes in feet: 16.0
The distance to the horizon is 4.92 mi.
Again? Enter 1 for YES; any other number to Exit: 1

Distance from the ground to your eyes in feet: 5.25
The distance to the horizon is 2.8182840523978414 mi
Again? Enter 1 for YES; any other number to Exit: 0
```

Discussion On line 15, the program utilizes the method

```
double Math.sqrt(double x)
```

to calculate the square root of distanceToEyes. The method Math.sqrt(...) hides the details of its implementation. *How* the square root of a number is calculated is hidden from the programmer. The method functions as a black box, and the programmer simply *uses* this method in the program.

> The *argument* passed to the method is distanceToEyes (a double), and the returned value (a double) is the square root of distanceToEyes.

For example, if distanceToEyes has the value 16.0, then Math.sqrt(distanceToEyes) returns the value 4.0 and that value is used in the expression

```
distanceToHorizon = 1.23 * Math.sqrt(distanceToEyes);
```

That's all there is to it.

The program of Example 6.1 utilizes the Math.Sqrt(...) method. To understand how a Java method works, let's take a closer look at the mechanics of this particular method.

Consider the statement

```
double root = Math.sqrt(25.0);
```

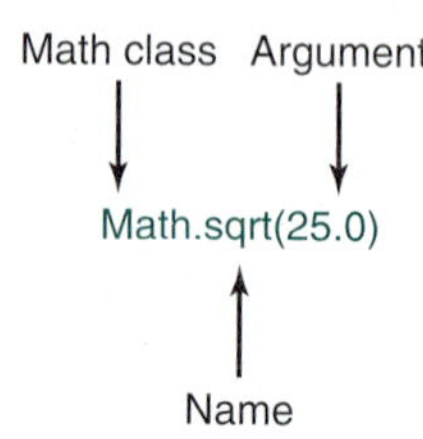

FIGURE 6.2 The *sqrt* method of the *Math* class

The effect of this statement is that variable root is assigned the value 5.0, the square root of 25.0.

This method, which calculates square root, is a member of Java's Math class. The Math class is a Java-supplied collection (or library) of methods that performs mathematical tasks or functions. Math.sqrt(...) is one of several methods in the Math class. The name of the method is sqrt, and the argument that is supplied to the method is the number 25.0. Notice the period that separates the class name Math from the method name, sqrt. See Figure 6.2.

In the statement

```
double root = Math.sqrt(25.0)
```

the Math.sqrt(...) method is *called* (or *invoked*) with the argument 25.0 and *returns* the value 5.0 (the square root of 25.0), which is subsequently assigned to the variable root. This action is similar to that of the statement:

```
double sum = 5.0 + 8.0;
```

Here, the expression 5.0 + 8.0 evaluates to (or returns) 13.0, which is assigned to sum.

The argument that is passed to a method may be a constant, an expression, or a variable. And a method call may be used within an expression. The following are valid method calls:

```
System.out.println(Math.sqrt(456));   // prints the square root of 245 ( double)

double w = Math.sqrt(input.nextInt()); // here input is a Scanner object

double x = input.nextDouble();

double y = input.nextDouble();

double z = 3.14 * Math.sqrt(x + y);   // method is used within an expression
```

A method is described by its *header,* which has the following form:

return-type **name(*parameter-list*)**

- The *return-type* specifies the data type of the value returned by the method.
- The *parameter-list* enumerates the number (implicitly) and type (explicitly) of the arguments that must be passed or given to the method.
- The names in the parameter-list are called *formal parameters,* or simply *parameters*.

For example, the header of Figure 6.3 tells us that the method named Math.sqrt accepts one argument of type double and returns a double. Parameter x is a (formal) parameter.

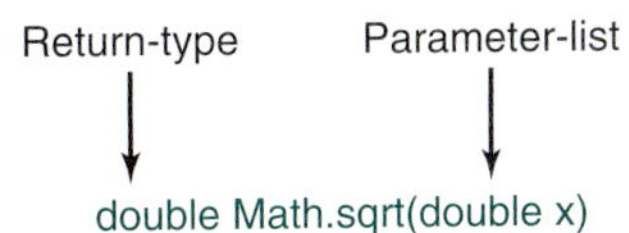

FIGURE 6.3 The header for *Math.sqrt(...)*

Although the header specifies that the argument passed to the Math.sqrt(...) be of type double, an argument of any data type may be used, provided that the argument can be automatically cast to type double. Thus, the argument of

Math.sqrt(25)

is first cast to the double 25.0. The returned value is 5.0 (not 5). The returned value is always type double regardless of the argument. To obtain an integer, you can perform an explicit cast on the method's return value:

```
(int)Math.sqrt(25);
```

Figure 6.4 lists some useful methods found in the Math class. In each case, the first two columns comprise the header for each method.

Return Type	Method	Description	Example
double	abs(double x)	absolute value	Math.abs(−3.1) returns 3.1
int	abs(int a)	absolute value	Math.abs(−25) returns 25
double	ceil(double x)	returns the smallest whole number (as a double) greater than or equal to x	Math.ceil(3.14159) returns 4.0
double	cos(double x)	cosine function, x is in radians	Math.cos(3.141592653589793) returns −1.0 ($\cos(\pi) = -1$)
double	exp(double x)	the exponential function, e^x	Math.exp(0.0) returns 1.0 ($e^0 = 1$)
double	floor(double x)	returns the largest whole number (as a double) less than or equal to x	Math.floor(3.14159) returns 3.0
double	log(double x)	natural logarithm, $ln(x)$	Math.log(1.0) returns 0.0 ($\ln(1) = 0$)
double	max(double x, double y)	returns the greater of x and y	Math.max(3.0,4.0) returns 4.0
int	max(int a, int b)	returns the greater of x and y	Math.max(3,4) returns 4 (int)
double	min(double x, double y)	returns the lesser of x and y	Math.min(3.0,4.0) returns 3.0
int	min(int a, int b)	returns the lesser of a and b	Math.min(3,4) returns 3 (int)
double	pow(double x, double y)	x^y	Math.pow(2.0,5.0) returns 32.0
double	random()	returns a random number x such that $0.0 <= x < 1$	Math.random() may return 0.2345676889 or perhaps 0.654678756
long	round(x double)	rounds to the nearest whole number (long)	Math.round(3.14) returns 3 (long) Math.round (5.67) returns 6 (long)
double	sin(double x)	sine function, x is in radians	Math.sin(3.141592653589793) returns 0.0 ($\sin(\pi) = 0$)
double	sqrt(double x)	square root	Math.sqrt(144.0) returns 12.0
double	tan(double x)	tangent function, x is in radians	Math.tan(3.141592653589793) returns 0.0 ($\tan(\pi) = 0$)

FIGURE 6.4 Methods of the *Math* class

6.2.2 A Method that Computes Powers

The next example uses the method

double Math.pow(double x, double y)

to calculate x^y.

Notice that the parameter list of the header specifies that the method requires two arguments of type double. For example, Math.pow(5.0,2.0) returns $5.0^{2.0}$, that is, 25.0. See Figure 6.5.

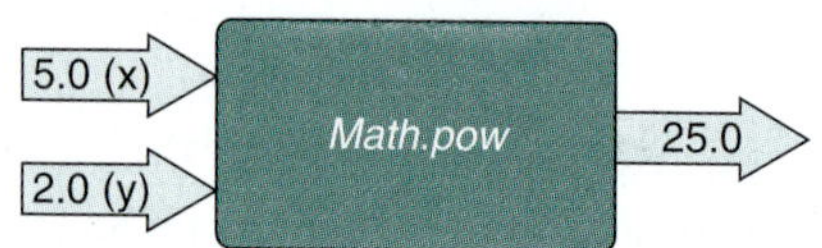

FIGURE 6.5 The power method, *Math.pow(...)*

EXAMPLE 6.2 Legend tells us that approximately 380 years ago Peter Minuit purchased the island of Manhattan for the grand sum of 60 Dutch guilders (approximately $24). If Mr. Minuit had instead deposited his $24 in the local bank at 5% interest, compounded daily, what would his money be worth today? Was his real estate investment a wise one?

To calculate the present value of Peter Minuit's original $24, we use the interest formula:

$$value = amount(1 + rate/360)^{360*years}$$

where *value* represents the present value, *amount* is the initial investment, *rate* is the yearly interest rate, and *years* is the time (in years) of the investment. Thus, for the problem at hand, *value* is calculated as

$$value = 24(1 + .05/360)^{360*380}$$

Here, we use 360 days (a 30-day month) for a "bank year," rather than 365.

Problem Statement Write a program that prompts the user for:

- the initial investment,
- the interest rate, and
- the term in years,

and calculates the present value. To perform the calculation, we use Java's "power method," Math.pow(x,y), which calculates x^y.

Java Solution

```
import java.util.*;
public class Interest
{
    public static void main(String[] args)
    {
        Scanner input;
        double value;
        double amount;
        double rate;
        double years;
        final int DAYS = 360;                  // one year
        // prompt for initial investment
        input = new Scanner(System.in);
```

```
14.     System.out.print("Initial amount: ");
15.     amount = input.nextDouble();
16.     // prompt for yearly interest rate
17.     System.out.print("Interest rate: ");
18.     rate = input.nextDouble();
19.     // prompt for number of years
20.     System.out.print("Time in years: ");
21.     years = input.nextDouble();
22.     // value = amount * (1 + rate / DAYS)^(DAYS*years) – standard interest formula
23.     value = amount * Math.pow (1 + rate / DAYS, DAYS * years); // (1 + rate / DAYS)^DAYS*years
24.     System.out.println("Present value $" + value);
25.   }
26. }
```

Output (Using the Minuit Data)

```
Initial amount: 24.00
Interest rate: .05
Time in years: 380
Present value $4.2779275332526875E9
```

Discussion The method Math.pow(...) is invoked on line 23 with two arguments, both expressions. Notice that the present value is displayed in scientific notation. In decimal notation, that's about $4,277,927,533. Considering the value of real estate in Manhattan, it appears that Peter made a very wise investment.

6.2.3 Random Numbers

The

```
double Math.random()
```

method returns a random number that is greater than or equal to 0.0 and strictly less than 1.0. Notice that Math.random() requires no parameter or argument.

For example, the first time that a program invokes Math.random(), the returned value might be 0.8787954399107227, and the next time it might be 0.31799656386438013. Each subsequent number returned by Math.random() is supposedly unpredictable. The following small program calls Math.random() ten times. There is no discernible pattern to the output . . . it's random.

```
public class TenRandomNumbers
{
   public static void main(String[] args)
   {
      for (int i = 1; i <= 10; i++)
         System.out.println(Math.random());
   }
}
```

Output

```
0.6516831128923004
0.3159760705754926
0.945877632966408
0.04538322890407964
0.8815999823052094
```

```
0.07672479266883347
0.04423548066038108
0.4441137107417066
0.15348060768674676
0.1833850393131755
```

Random numbers are indispensable for performing simulations. Such simulations are useful in all kinds of applications, including earthquake modeling, epidemic predictions, rocket testing, and games. For example, a card game that uses a deck of 52 cards might associate each card with a number from 1 to 52. Dealing a card amounts to nothing more than choosing a random number in that range. Or, a program might use a random integer, either 0 or 1, to simulate the toss of a coin: 0 for heads and 1 for tails.

Using Math.random() to Generate Integers

With a little hocus pocus we can use Math.random() in all sorts of situations. For example, to simulate the roll of a single die, a program requires a random integer between 1 and 6 inclusive. We can use Math.random() to generate integers in the range 1 through 6 by "magnifying" its 0 through 1 range.

If

```
r = Math.random();
```

then r is of type double and

$0.0 \le r < 1.0.$

Therefore,

$0.0 \le 6 * r < 6.0$ (multiplying the inequality by 6), and
$1.0 \le 6 * r + 1 < 7.0.$ (adding 1 to each value in the inequality)

Thus 6* Math.random() + 1 is a number greater than or equal to 1 but strictly less than 7.

For example, if

$$r = 0.8929343993861253, \text{ then}$$
$$6 * r = 5.3576063963167518, \text{ and}$$
$$6 * r + 1 = 6.3576063963167518.$$

To obtain an integer value, cast $6 * r + 1$ to an integer, effectively dropping the fractional part. Thus,

```
(int)(6 * Math.random() + 1)
```

returns a random integer between 1 and 6, inclusive. Similarly, (int)(52 * Math.random() +1) returns a random integer between 1 and 52, inclusive. You can use this trick to generate random integers in any range. For example, (int)(10 * Math.random() + 15) returns an integer between 15 and 24, inclusive.

Example 6.3 uses Math.random() to simulate a simple casino dice game.

EXAMPLE 6.3 Probably the simplest of all casino bets is the "over-under" bet. Two dice are rolled, and a player has the option of betting whether the sum of the spots displayed on the dice will be:

1. over 7,
2. under 7, or
3. exactly 7.

Bets (1) and (2) pay even money. So if a player bets \$1, a win pays his money back plus \$1. Bet (3) pays 4 to 1. Thus if a player bets \$2 on 7, a win pays him back his \$2 plus \$8.

Problem Statement Write a program that simulates the over-under game. If the player wins, the winning amount (not including the returned original bet) is reported, and if the player loses, a message is printed.

Java Solution

```
import java.util.*;
public class Dice
{
   public static void main(String [] args)
   {
      Scanner input;
      int bet;
      int wager;
      int die1,die2;
      int sum;
      input = new Scanner(System.in);

      // Place your bet
      System.out.print("Enter your bet\n (1) Over 7 \n (2) Under 7 \n (3) Exactly 7\n: ");
      bet = input.nextInt();
      System.out.print("Enter your wager (whole number): ");
      wager = input.nextInt();

      // Roll the dice
      die1 = (int)(6 * Math.random() + 1) ; // random integer 1..6
      die2 = (int)(6 * Math.random() + 1);
      sum = die1 + die2;
      System.out.println("The sum of the dice is " + sum);

      // Check for a win
      if ((sum > 7) && (bet == 1) || (sum < 7) && (bet == 2))
         System.out.println("You win $" + wager);
      else if ((sum == 7) && (bet == 3))
         System.out.println("You win $" + (4 * wager));
      else
         System.out.println("You lose!");
   }
}
```

Output (Two Games)

```
Enter your bet
 (1) Over 7
 (2) Under 7
 (3) Exactly 7:
2
Enter your wager (whole number): 3
The sum of the dice is 8
You lose!

Enter your bet
 (1) Over 7
 (2) Under 7
 (3) Exactly 7:
```

```
1
Enter your wager (whole number): 6
The sum of the dice is 9
You win $6
```

Discussion The expressions on lines 18 and 19 simulate the roll of a single die. As explained above, even though Math.random() returns a *floating*-point number that is greater than or equal to 0 and strictly less than 1, this Java method can be used to generate random *integers*.

6.3 WRITING YOUR OWN METHODS

Although there are thousands of methods in Java's extensive libraries, Java certainly cannot provide a method for every imaginable task. Fortunately, you can create your own methods that do whatever task you fancy—be it a method to calculate your taxes or one to determine your weight on the moon. Like Java's methods, a method that you create:

- has a name,
- may accept arguments,
- may return a value, and
- may be used as part of an expression.

The difference between a Java method and one of your own creation is that with your own method *you* must program the "black box." You are the designer, the architect and the builder. (Well, you can't expect Java to do *everything*.) In the following examples, we illustrate two types of Java methods: those that return a value and those that do not.

6.3.1 Methods that Return a Value

Many of the prepackaged methods that we have encountered perform a computation and return the result of the computation to the caller. For example, Math.sqrt(double x) returns the square root of x, and Math.random() returns a random number. The following application includes a method that returns a value but, unlike Math.sqrt(...) or Math.random(), this method is *not* part of Java's library.

EXAMPLE 6.4 Rapid Rick runs races regularly. Although Rick is determined to keep in shape, he does enjoy an occasional slice of cheesecake. If Rick knows approximately how many calories he burns while running, well, he just might treat himself to a little more dessert with a little less guilt.

The number of calories used while running depends on the runner's weight as well as the distance that he/she has run. A common rule of thumb used to estimate the number of calories burned is:

$$calories = .653 \times weight \times distance$$

where *weight* is the runner's weight in pounds and *distance* is in miles.

Problem Statement Write a program that calculates the number of calories burned as a function of weight and distance. Include a method

double caloriesBurned(double weight, double distance)

that accepts two arguments of type double and returns a value of type double. See Figure 6.6.

FIGURE 6.6 The method *double caloriesBurned(double weight, double distance)*

Java Solution

```
1. import java.util.*;
2. public class RunnersCalculator
3. {

4.   public static double caloriesBurned(double weight, double distance)
5.   {

6.   // returns the number of calories burned using the formula
7.   // calories = .653 × weight × distance
8.     double calories = .653 * weight * distance;
9.     return calories;
10.  }

11.  public static void main(String[] args)
12.  {
13.    Scanner input;
14.    double myWeight, myDistance, totalCalories;

15.    input = new Scanner(System.in);
16.    System.out.print("Enter weight in pounds: ");
17.    myWeight = input.nextDouble();
18.    System.out.print("Enter distance in miles: ");
19.    myDistance = input.nextDouble();

20.    totalCalories = caloriesBurned(myWeight, myDistance);
21.    System.out.println("Calories burned: " + totalCalories);
22.  }
23. }
```

Output

Enter weight in pounds: **165.0**
Enter distance in miles: **6.0**
Calories burned: 646.47

Discussion Like all Java applications, RunnersCalculator begins execution with main(...) (lines 11–22). The main(...) method is similar to the main(...) method of any other program that we've written. You should notice, however, that within main(...) there is a call to the method caloriesBurned(...) on line 20:

totalCalories = **caloriesBurned(myWeight, myDistance);**

A call to caloriesBurned(...) is really no different than the call to Math.sqrt(...) in Example 6.1 or the call to Math.random() in Example 6.3. The method call to calories-Burned(...) has two arguments: myWeight and myDistance; the returned value is assigned to the variable totalCalories.

The instructions of the method caloriesBurned(...) are specified on lines 8 and 9. Unlike Math.sqrt(...) or Math.random(), we can now look "inside the box," so to speak. So let's do just that.

Line 4 is the header of the method:

```
public static double caloriesBurned(double weight, double distance)
```

For now, you can ignore the keywords public and static. They are necessary and soon they will make more sense to you. The remainder of the header specifies:

- the data type of the return value: double,
- the name of the method: caloriesBurned, and
- the parameters: weight and distance.

The parameters specify the type and number of the arguments that must be passed to the method. When this method is invoked with two arguments, the value of the first argument is assigned or passed to weight and the value of the second argument is passed to parameter distance. For example, if the method call is

```
caloriesBurned(155.5, 3.5)
```

the parameter weight gets the value 155.5, and distance the value 3.5. See Figure 6.7.

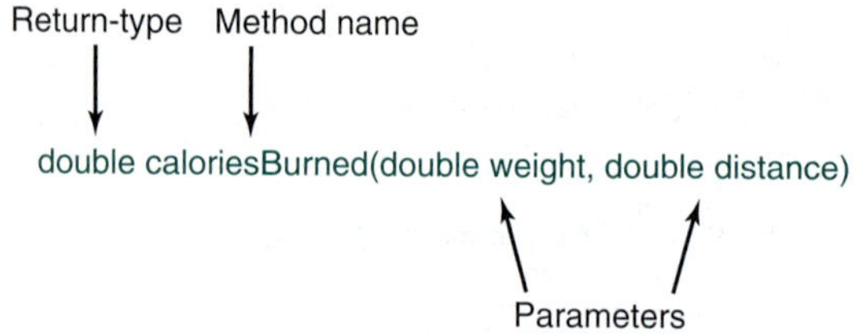

FIGURE 6.7 Parts of a method header

The block consisting of lines 5 through 10 contains the instructions of the method caloriesBurned(...).

- Line 8 is an expression that calculates the number of calories burned.
- Line 9 is a return statement. The return statement has the form:

return *expression*

> The return statement has two purposes:
> 1. It specifies the value that the method returns to the caller.
> 2. It terminates the method and returns program control to the caller.

That's all there is to it.

Figure 6.8 steps through the execution of the program. As you can see, the program executes main(...) sequentially, with a side trip to caloriesBurned(...) on line 20.

Variables	Action
myWeight: (empty), myDistance: (empty), totalCalories: (empty)	Line 14: Declare three variables, myWeight, myDistance, and totalCalories.
myWeight: 165.0, myDistance: (empty), totalCalories: (empty)	Line 17: Obtain a value for myWeight.
myWeight: 165.0, myDistance: 6.0, totalCalories: (empty)	Line 19: Obtain a value for myDistance.
myWeight: 165.0, myDistance: 6.0, totalCalories: (empty)	Line 20: Call caloriesBurned(...). Pass values of the arguments myWeight and myDistance to parameters weight and distance, respectively.

Program control passes to caloriesBurned(...).

Variables	Action
weight: 165.0, distance: 6.0	Line 4: The parameters weight and distance are initialized with the values of arguments myWeight and myDistance.
weight: 165.0, distance: 6.0, calories: 646.47	Line 8: Declare the variable calories. Calculate the number of calories burned, and initialize calories to that value.
weight: 165.0, distance: 6.0, calories: 646.47	Line 9: Return the value of calories to the caller and exit.

Program control returns to the assignment on line 20.

Variables	Action
myWeight: 165.0, myDistance: 6.0, totalCalories: 646.47	Line 20 (resumed): Assign the returned value to totalCalories.
myWeight: 165.0, myDistance: 6.0, totalCalories: 646.47	Line 21: Print the results.

FIGURE 6.8 A trace of *RunnersCalculator*

For the correct values to be passed to the appropriate parameters, the order of the arguments is crucial. When caloriesBurned(...) is invoked, the values stored in the two arguments, myWeight and myDistance, are assigned, or passed, to the parameters specified in the header of caloriesBurned(...): weight and distance, respectively. See Figure 6.9.

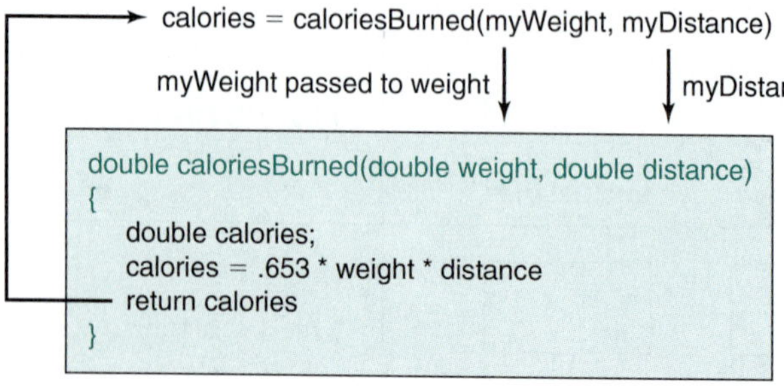

```
calories = caloriesBurned(myWeight, myDistance)

myWeight passed to weight        myDistance passed to distance

double caloriesBurned(double weight, double distance)
{
    double calories;
    calories = .653 * weight * distance
    return calories
}
```

FIGURE 6.9 Arguments are passed to parameters: *weight* gets the value of *myWeight*, and *distance* the value of *myDistance*

The values of myWeight and myDistance that are passed to caloriesBurned(...) are the values used in the expression

.635 * weight * distance

on line 8.

The arguments myWeight and myDistance supply values to the parameters weight and distance. The arguments initialize the parameters. The parameters weight and distance are considered variables of the method. Once the arguments, myWeight and myDistance, pass their values to weight and distance, the role of the arguments is complete. Variables myWeight and myDistance have no further jobs in caloriesBurned(...). Indeed, if caloriesBurned(...) were to alter weight or distance, the change would not affect myWeight or myDistance. Except for the initial copying of argument values to parameters, there is no link between the parameters and the arguments.

When the *value* of an argument is copied to a parameter, the argument is said to be *passed by value.*

6.3.2 *void* Methods

A method can perform a task without returning a value. Such a method is called a void method. You have already seen two void methods: print(...) and println(...). Each method displays text but neither returns a value.

To specify a void method, use the reserved word void in place of the return type in the method header.

For example,

void drawSquare(int size)

might be the header of a method that draws a square on the screen and does not return a value. Because a void method does not return a value, it makes no sense to incorporate a void method into an expression. The expression

5 * Math.sqrt(25)

is certainly meaningful and has the value 25.0, but

```
5 * drawSquare(25)
```

makes no sense because drawSquare(25) does not return a value.

A call to a void method is a "standalone" statement consisting of the method name along with any arguments that must be passed to the method, such as

```
System.out.println("Print me!");
```

or

```
drawSquare(10);
```

In Example 6.5, coinChanger(...) is a void method: coinChanger(...) performs a task but does not return a value.

EXAMPLE 6.5

Problem Statement Write a program that includes a void method

```
void coinChanger(int amount)
```

that accepts a single integer argument between 1 and 100 that represents an amount of money between $.01 and $1.00. The method makes change for that amount using the minimum number of coins. Coins are in denominations of half dollars, quarters, dimes, nickels, and pennies.

To ensure that the smallest number of coins is used, first compute the maximum number of half dollars, followed by the maximum number of quarters, and so on. For example, if the initial amount is 83 cents, we first calculate, in order, the number of half dollars, quarters, dimes, nickels, and pennies:

- from 83 cents: 1 half dollar, 33 cents remain;
- from 33 cents: 1 quarter, 8 cents remain;
- from 8 cents: 0 dimes, 8 cents remain;
- from 8 cents: 1 nickel, 3 cents remain;
- finally, 3 pennies remain.

These calculations are accomplished using the / (integer divide) and % (remainder) operators.

Java Solution

```
import java.util.*;
public class MoneyChanger
{

   public static void coinChanger (int amount)
   {
      // calculates the minimum number of half dollars, quarters, dimes, nickels
      // and pennies in amount

      int halfDollars, quarters, dimes, nickels, pennies;

      System.out.println();
      System.out.println(amount + " cents can be converted to:");

      halfDollars = amount / 50;       // determine number of half dollars
      amount = amount % 50;            // how much remains?
      quarters = amount / 25;          // determine number of quarters
```

```
14.         amount = amount % 25;           // how much remains?
15.         dimes = amount / 10;            // determine the number of dimes
16.         amount = amount % 10;           // how much remains?
17.         nickels = amount / 5;           // determine the number of nickels
18.         pennies = amount % 5;           // remainder is the number of pennies
19.         System.out.println("Half Dollars: " + halfDollars);
20.         System.out.println("Quarters : " + quarters);
21.         System.out.println("Dimes : " + dimes);
22.         System.out.println("Nickels : " + nickels);
23.         System.out.println("Pennies : " + pennies);
24.         return;                         // return statement is optional here
25.     }

26.     public static void main(String[] args)
27.     {
28.         Scanner input;
29.         input = new Scanner(System.in);
30.         System.out.print("Enter a value between 1 and 100: ");
31.         int money = input.nextInt();
32.         coinChanger(money);             // call to method coinChanger
33.     }
34. }
```

Output

Enter a value between 1 and 100: **83**

83 cents can be converted to:
Half Dollars: 1
Quarters : 1
Dimes : 0
Nickels : 1
Pennies : 3

Discussion The program prompts the user for an initial amount of money and invokes the method coinChanger(...) with that value as an argument. Because coinChanger(...) does not return a value, the call to coinChanger(...) is not called within an expression. The method call is the Java statement (line 32):

```
coinChanger (money);
```

The parameter amount of coinChanger(...) accepts the value of the argument money, which is supplied interactively. Next, the number of half dollars is calculated, as well as how much remains after the half dollars have been removed from amount (lines 11 and 12). Likewise, the numbers of quarters, dimes, and nickels are determined. After calculating the number of nickels, the final remainder represents the number of pennies (line 18).

Take note of the return statement on line 24. Unlike the method of Example 6.4, this return statement does not include a return value or an expression. In this situation, the return statement merely causes the method to exit; no value is returned to the calling method.

> Execution of a return statement in a void method causes the method to exit without returning a value to the caller.

Indeed, the return statement on line 24 is unnecessary. After a void method executes its last statement, the method automatically returns; no final return statement is necessary. In contrast to a method that returns a value, a void method is not required to have *any* return statements.

6.3.3 Putting It All Together

Let's take a more general look at the components of a method and fill in a few details.

> A Java method consists of a
> - *header* followed by a
> - *method block.*
>
> The *parameters* in the header specify the number and type of the *arguments* that must be *passed* to the method. When a method is invoked, the values stored in the arguments are copied to the parameters.

In Example 6.4, weight and distance are parameters, and myWeight and myDistance are arguments. In Example 6.5, the parameter is amount and the argument is money. The parameters are sometimes called *formal parameters* and the arguments *actual parameters*.

The form of the *header* is:

***modifiers return-type name*(*parameter-list*)**

where:

- *modifiers* (for now) are the keywords public and static;
- *return-type* is the data type of the value that the method returns, or void if the method does not return a value;
- *parameter-list* is a (possibly empty) list of parameters that receive values from arguments passed to the method when the method is invoked.

The *method block* is a sequence of statements enclosed by curly braces:

```
{
      statement-1;
      statement-2;
      statement-3;
         . . .
      statement-n;
}
```

For example, Figure 6.10 shows a method that calculates the volume of a box.

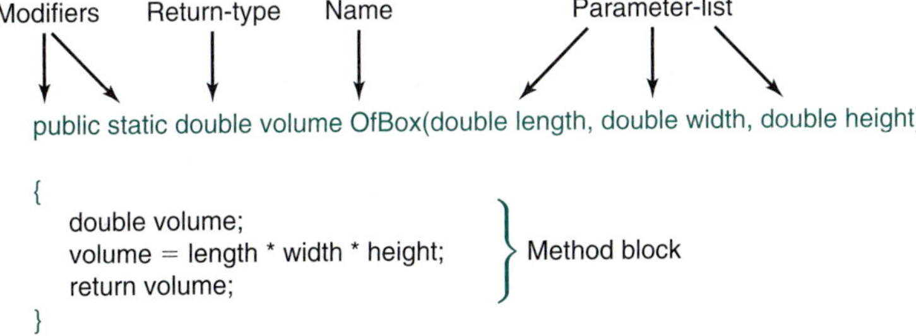
Modifiers
Return-type
Name
Parameter-list
public static double volume OfBox(double length, double width, double height)
{
double volume;
volume = length * width * height;
return volume;
}
Method block

FIGURE 6.10 A method that calculates the volume of a box

That's the big picture, but a few details are in order:

1. **Method Name.** The name of a method must be a valid Java identifier. Moreover, a method name should convey the method's purpose, function, or task. For example, the name volumeOfBox is more suitable than the name myMethod or box. Standard Java convention specifies that the name of a method begins with a lowercase letter and

starts each succeeding word in the method name with an uppercase letter. For example, the names volumeOfBox and caloriesBurned both follow this convention; the names VolumeOfBox and volumeofbox do not.

2. **Parameter-List.** A method's *parameter-list* consists of pairs of the form:

   type parameter-name

separated by commas. Figure 6.11 shows the parameter-list of the method volumeOfBox.

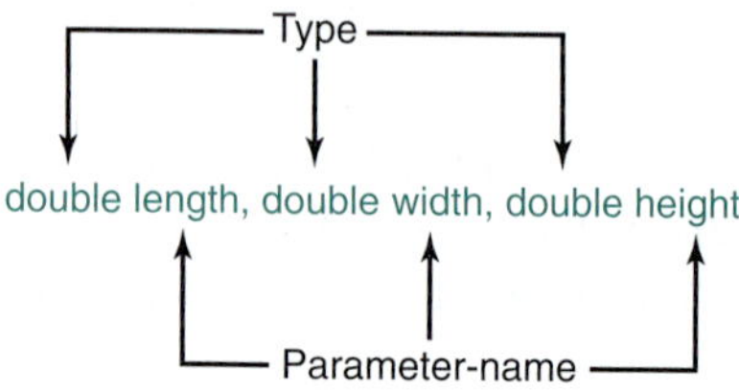

FIGURE 6.11 A parameter-list

For example:

- The parameter-list of method caloriesBurned in Example 6.4 is:

  double weight, double distance

- The method Math.random() has no parameter-list. Math.random() neither requires nor accepts any arguments. The parameter-list is empty.

3. **Argument Passing.** When calling a method, the caller passes arguments to the parameters. The calling statement must provide a type-suitable value for each parameter. If a method has five parameters, five arguments are required. Supplying more or fewer arguments than parameters is an error that the compiler can detect.

   - For example, the method

     double volumeOfBox(double length, double width, double height)

     has three parameters each of type double. The following are valid calls to volumeOfBox(...):

     ```
     volumeOfBox(2.34, 5.765, 4.678)  // three doubles are passed
     volume of box(l, w, h)           // l, w, and h are type double
     volumeOfBox(3, 4, 5)             // an integer can be expanded to a double
     volumeOfBox(3.0*l, 1.5*w, 2.7*h); // expressions are OK
     ```

     In contrast, if

     int volumeOfBox(int length, int width, int height)

     is a method with integer parameters, then the call

     volumeOfBox(3.0, 4.0, 5.0)

     is unacceptable because a value of type double cannot be automatically cast to an integer.

   - Finally, note that the invocation

     ```
     volumeOfBox(2.3, 4.5) // INVALID.
                           // Wrong number of arguments
     ```

     is illegal: only two values are passed and volumeOfBox(...) requires three.

4. **Pass by Value.** All arguments are passed "by value." This means that the arguments are evaluated and *values* of the arguments are copied to the parameters of a method. Subsequently, modifying the parameters in the method has no effect on the value of any variables passed as arguments.
5. **Method Block.** The statements of the *method block* accomplish the task of the method.
6. **The return Statement.** A method that returns a value *must* include a return statement. The form of the return statement is

   return *expression*

   If the data type of the returned value (as specified in the method header) is T, then the data type of *expression* should also be type T (or a type that is automatically cast to T). For example, the following method header specifies that the return type of method gimmeFive is double.

   double gimmeFive()

   The methods

```
double gimmeFive()        and  double gimmeFive()
{                              {
        return 5.0;                    return 5; // an integer is cast to double
}                              }
```

   both contain valid return statements. However, the following method,

```
int gimmeFive()
{
        return 5.0;   // cannot cast a double to an int
}
```

   does not have a valid return statement because the double 5.0 does not match the int return type of the method, and 5.0 is not automatically cast to an integer.

   When a method executes the return statement,

   - the method terminates,
   - program control passes back to the caller, and
   - any statements following the return statement are ignored.
7. **Local Variables.** Variables that are declared within a method are called the *local variables* of that method. Local variables exist and are known only within the method in which they are declared. When a method exits, the local variables are destroyed. Local variables do not exist beyond the life of a method call. We now look at local variables in a bit more detail.

6.3.4 Local Variables

In Example 6.4, the parameters weight and distance, as well as the variable calories that is declared on line 8, are known only within the method caloriesBurned(...), that is, between the curly braces surrounding the statements of the method. The main(...) method can neither see nor access these variables. Similarly, myWeight, myDistance, totalCalories, and even input are known only in main(...). The memory cells, myWeight, myDistance, and totalCalories of Figure 6.8, are not visible when program control passes to caloriesBurned(...).

> When a method is invoked, memory for local variables is allocated, and when a method exits, that memory is de-allocated.

Consequently, a method's local variables do not retain values from call to call. When a method exits, its local variables no longer exist.

Example 6.6 includes three methods. Each method has its own collection of local variables. Notice that the same name is used for more than one variable, yet the computer is not at all confused.

EXAMPLE 6.6

Rapid Rick of Example 6.4 runs in all weather, rain or shine, and in all seasons, hot or cold. The actual heat or cold he experiences depends on more than the outdoor temperature. The Summer Sizzle Index, *SSI*, measures what the temperature actually feels like on a hot day by taking into account the relative humidity. The Wind Chill Temperature, *WCT*, does the same for a cold day by taking wind speed into consideration. On a hot, sticky summer evening when the temperature is a not-so-balmy 80°F and the relative humidity is 77%, the *SSI* is 94.5°F. On a blustery winter day, when the temperature is a crisp 23°F and the wind speed is 20 mph, the *WCT* is 8.2°F.

The Summer Sizzle Index (*SSI*) and Wind Chill Temperature (*WCT*) are calculated as follows:

$$SSI = 1.98 * (T - (0.55 - 0.0055 * H)*(T - 58)) - 56.83$$
$$WCT = 35.74 + 0.6215 * T - 35.75 * V^{0.16} + 0.4275 * T * V^{0.16}$$

where T is the temperature (in Fahrenheit), H is the relative humidity (as a percent), and V is the wind velocity (miles per hour).

Problem Statement Write a program that, given the temperature and relative humidity, calculates both the Summer Sizzle Index or, given the temperature and wind speed, computes the Wind Chill Temperature.

Java Solution

```
import java.util.*;
public class HotAndCold
{
   public static double summerSizzleIndex(double temperature, double relativeHumidity)
   {
      // calculates and returns Summer Sizzle Index
      // temperature is in degrees Fahrenheit; relative humidity is a percent
      double SSI = 1.98 *
               (temperature – (0.55 – 0.0055 * relativeHumidity) * (temperature – 58)) – 56.83;
      return SSI;
   }

   public static double windChillTemperature(double temperature, double windSpeed)
   {
      // calculates and returns Wind Chill Temperature
      // temperature is in degrees Fahrenheit; wind speed is mph
      double windChill = 35.74 + .6215 * temperature – 35.75 *
               Math.pow(windSpeed, 0.16) + 0.4275 * temperature * Math.pow(windSpeed, 0.16);
      return windChill;
   }

   public static void main(String[] args)
   {
      Scanner input = new Scanner(System.in);
      double temperature, SSI, windChill, relativeHumidity, windSpeed;

      System.out.print("To calculate SSI enter 1; to calculate Wind Chill enter 2: ");
      int reply = input.nextInt();
```

```
24.      System.out.print("Temperature: ");
25.      temperature = input.nextDouble();
26.      if (reply == 1)
27.      {
28.        System.out.print("Relative Humidity: ");
29.        relativeHumidity = input.nextDouble();
30.        SSI = summerSizzleIndex(temperature, relativeHumidity);
31.        System.out.println("Summer Sizzle index: " + SSI);
32.      }
33.      else
34.      {
35.        System.out.print("Wind Speed: ");
36.        windSpeed = input.nextDouble();
37.        windChill = windChillTemperature(temperature, windSpeed);
38.        System.out.println("Wind chill temperature: " + windChill);
39.    }
40.  }
41. }
```

Output

To calculate SSI enter 1; to calculate Wind Chill enter 2: **1**
Temperature: **80**
Relative Humidity: **75**
Summer Sizzle index: 95.58049999999999

To calculate SSI enter 1; to calculate Wind Chill enter 2: **2**
Temperature: **25**
Wind Speed: **15**
Wind chill temperature: 12.623095109603938

Discussion The HotAndCold class has three methods, each with a number of local variables, as shown in Figure 6.12.

summerSizzleIndex	windChillTemperature	main
temperature (parameter)	temperature (parameter)	temperature (line 21)
relativeHumidity (parameter)	windSpeed (parameter)	SSI (line 21)
SSI (line 8)	windChill (line 15)	windChill (line 21)
		relativeHumidity (line 21)
		windSpeed (line 21)
		input (line 20)
		reply (line 23)

FIGURE 6.12 Local variables in three methods

Although several local variables have the same name, the variables are, in fact, distinct. For example, each method has a variable named temperature. The three temperature variables may have the same name but each has its own storage location. They are independent and distinct. Of course, too many variables with the same name can lead to confusion and bugs. In general, try to give variables unique names.

The concept of local variables is tied to the broader topic of *scope*, which we discuss in the next section.

6.3.5 Scope

The *scope* of a variable is that section of the program in which a variable can be accessed or referenced.

For example, consider the following void method that computes the sum and product of the first *n* positive integers:

```
1. void sumAndProduct(int n)
2. {
3.    int sum = 0;
4.    int product = 1;
5.    for (int i = 1; i <= n; i++)
6.    {
7.       sum += i;
8.       product *= i;
9.    }
10.      System.out.println( "Sum of the first " + n + " positive integers is " + sum);
11.      System.out.println("Product of the first " + n + " positive integers is " + product);
12. }
```

The method sumAndProduct has several local variables: n, sum, product, and i. The scope of each of these variables is as follows:

- The scope of parameter n is the entire method.
- The scope of sum begins with its declaration on line 3 and extends to the end of the method.
- Similarly, the scope of product extends from its declaration on line 4 to the method's end.
- As you already know, the variable i does not exist beyond the block of the for-loop. Thus, the scope of variable i is lines 5 through 9. Outside of the for-loop, i is inaccessible and unknown.

In general, the scope of a variable begins with its declaration and extends to the end of the *block* in which it is declared.

Recall that a block is a group of statements enclosed by curly braces { and }; so if you declare a variable in the outermost block of a method, its scope extends from the declaration to the end of the method. On the other hand, the scope of a variable declared within an inner or nested block begins at the declaration and terminates at the end of that block. In the segment

```
if (purchase > 200)
{
      double discount = .20 * purchase;
      double discountPrice = purchase – discount;
      tax = .05 * discountPrice;
      total = discountPrice + tax;
}
else
{
      tax = .05 * purchase;
      total = purchase + tax;
}
```

the scope of the variables discount and discountPrice extends from their definitions to the end of the "if block." Thus, neither variable is known within the "else block."

The scope of a variable declared in the header of a for loop is the entire for loop. In the segment

```
for (int i = 0; i <= 50; i++)
{
        // statements
}
```

The control variable i is unknown once the loop terminates.

Example 6.7 illustrates a few of these general scope rules.

EXAMPLE 6.7

Player Polly is quite a fan of the board game Monopoly. When it is Polly's turn to roll the dice, if she rolls "doubles," (i.e., both dice show the same number of spots), Polly gets another toss of the dice. However, if she unfortunately tosses doubles three times in a row, then Polly must "go to jail." Polly frequently plays Monopoly and has landed in jail more than a few times. So, Polly was wondering how likely it is that she tosses doubles three consecutive times and lands in Monopoly prison.

Problem Statement Write an application that prompts the user for an integer, numTurns representing some number of Monopoly turns. Using random numbers, the program simulates rolling the dice for that many turns. Each turn consists of one, two, or three rolls of the dice, depending on whether or not doubles appear. The program keeps track of the number of simulated turns that results in three tosses of doubles and reports the number of jail terms as well as the percentage of jail terms incurred.

Java Solution

```
import java.util.*;
public class GoDirectlyToJail
{
  public static int jailTerms(int turns)
  {
   // returns the number of turns that result in three rolls of doubles

    int threeDoubles = 0;                    // number of turns that result in three Doubles
    for (int i = 1; i <= turns; i++)         // for each turn
    {
      int numDoubles = 0;                    // counts the number of doubles on any one turn
      for (int toss = 1; toss <= 3; toss++) // up to three tosses/turn
      {
        // die1 and die2 are local to the inner block
        int die1 = (int)(6 * Math.random() + 1);
        int die2 = (int)(6 * Math.random() + 1);
        if (die1 == die2 )                   // do the dice show the same number?
          numDoubles++;
        else
          break; // not doubles, so end the turn
      }
      if (numDoubles == 3)                   // oops, go to jail
        threeDoubles++;
    }
    return threeDoubles;                     // the number turns giving three doubles
  }
```

```
26.  public static void main(String[] args)
27.  {
28.    Scanner input;
29.    input = new Scanner(System.in);
30.    int numTurns;
31.    int numJailTerms;                    // three doubles on any turn
32.    System.out.print("How many Monopoly turns would you like to simulate?");
33.    numTurns = input.nextInt();
34.    numJailTerms = jailTerms(numTurns);
35.    System.out.println("Number of times you got three doubles:" + numJailTerms);
36.    System.out.println("Percent of times you went to jail:" +
                        100 * (((double)numJailTerms/numTurns)) + "percent");
37.  }
38. }
```

Output

```
How many Monopoly turns would you like to simulate? 100000
Number of times you got three doubles: 454
Percent of times you went to jail: 0.45399999999999996 percent
```

Discussion The simulation indicates that the probability of landing in jail is less than one-half of a percent. (In fact, the actual probability is 1/216, or about 0.46296 percent).

We now look at the local variables and the scope of each. The scope of each variable declared in main(...) extends from its point of declaration to the end of the method. However, the variables of the method jailTerms(...) are a bit more interesting. Figure 6.13 lists those variables along with the scope of each.

Local Variable	Scope
turns (parameter)	the entire method jailTerms(...)
threeDoubles	the entire method jailTerms(...)
i (line 8)	the entire for loop (lines 8–23)
numDoubles (line 10)	from the declaration on line 10 to the end of the block (lines 10–23)
toss (line 11)	the entire for loop (lines 11–20)
die1 (line 14)	from the declaration on line 14 to the end of the block (lines 14–20)
die2 (line 15)	from the declaration on line 15 to the end of the block (lines 15–20)

FIGURE 6.13 Scope of variables

6.3.6 Multiple *return* Statements

A method may have more than one return statement, but only one executes before the method terminates.

The first return statement that executes terminates the method. In Example 6.8, the method isPrime(...) contains several return statements. The return statement that executes, and thereby terminates the method, depends on the input data.

EXAMPLE 6.8

A prime number p is a positive integer greater than 1 that has no positive integer divisors other than 1 and p. For example, 101 is a prime number since no positive integers other than 1 and 101 divide 101 evenly. The integers 2, 3, 5, 7, and 37 are all prime numbers. On the other hand, 100 is not a prime number because 5 is a divisor of 100. With the exception of 2, all prime numbers are odd.

Prime numbers have fascinated mathematicians for centuries. In approximately 300 BCE, Euclid proved that there is an infinite number of primes. Even today, prime numbers are the foundation of modern cryptography. Indeed, factoring large numbers into primes is a task necessary for cracking modern cryptographic codes. "New" prime numbers are discovered every year. Currently, the largest known prime number is $2^{43,112,609} - 1$, which has 12,978,189 digits. Of course, a larger prime may be unearthed tomorrow, if that hasn't happened already!

Deciding whether or not an integer with 12,978,189 digits is prime is not an easy task. That said, a rather naïve, yet intuitive, scheme for determining whether or not a positive integer, n, is prime might check all possible divisors of n that are greater than 1 and less than n. If n has no divisor, then n is prime. This simple algorithm executes quickly for small values of n, but it is hopelessly slow for large values like $2^{43,112,609} - 1$ and the large numbers used in cryptography.

Problem Statement Write a program that prompts a user for a positive integer and determines whether or not the number is prime. Include a method

```
boolean isPrime(int p)
```

that accepts an integer p as a parameter and returns true if p is prime; otherwise false. See Figure 6.14.

FIGURE 6.14 The *isPrime* (...) method

Java Solution

```
import java.util.*;
public class PrimeChecker
{
  public static boolean isPrime(int p) // returns true if p is a prime number
  {
    if (p <= 1)              // 0, 1, and all negatives are not prime
      return false;
    else if (p == 2)         // if p is 2; return true (exit) because 2 is prime
      return true;
    else if ( p % 2 == 0)    // if p is even and not 2, return false (exit);
      return false;

      // so p is odd; check for odd divisors
      // if a divisor is found, return false and exit

      for (int i = 3; i < p; i += 2) // i = 3, 5, 7, 9...
        if (p % i == 0)              // if p % i == 0 then i divides p so p is not prime
          return false;

      // if the method reaches this point, p is prime,
      return true;
  }
```

```
20.  public static void main(String[] args)
21.  {
22.     int number;
23.     Scanner input;
24.     input = new Scanner(System.in);

25.     System.out.print("What number would you like to test? ");
26.     number = input.nextInt();
27.     if (isPrime(number))
28.        System.out.println(number + " is a prime number");
29.     else
30.        System.out.println(number + " is not prime");
31.  }
32. }
```

Output

What number would you like to test? **6317**
6317 is a prime number

What number would you like to test? **7163**
7163 is not prime

Discussion The logic behind the method isPrime(...) is described in the comments on lines 6, 8, 10, 12–15, and 17.

The method isPrime(...) contains no less than five return statements. When any one return statement executes, the method exits and program control passes back to the caller. For example:

- If parameter p has the value 22, the condition on line 10 is true, and the return statement on line 11 executes, returning false and terminating the method.
- If p has the value 35, the loop of line 14 executes, and when i attains the value of 5, the return on line 16 executes, returning false (because 35 % 5 == 0, i.e., 35 is divisible by 5).
- If p is 23, then none of the conditions of the else-if statement is true nor does the condition on line 15 evaluate to true. Consequently, the return statement on line 18 returns true, that is, 23 is prime.

6.4 METHOD OVERLOADING

Java allows two or more methods of the same class to share the same name. This practice is called *method overloading*.

For example, Java's Math class has several overloaded methods, including Math.max(...), which has two forms:

1. int Math.max(int x, int y)
2. double Math.max(double x, double y)

Notice that the parameter lists of the two methods differ. The first version of Math.max(...) accepts two integer parameters and the second version accepts two double parameters.

So that the Java compiler can distinguish between methods of the same name, overloaded methods *must* differ in the types and/or number of parameters.

Because of this rule, Java (usually) has no difficulty deciding which version of a method to execute. For example, consider the four calls to Math.max(...) shown in Figure 6.15.

Method Call	Returns	Argument Types		Version
Math.max(10,5)	10	two int		1
Math.max(10.0, 5.0)	10.0	two double		2
Math.max(10.0, 5)	10.0	two double	(5 is automatically cast to 5.0)	2
Math.max(10, 5.0)	10.0	two double	(10 is automatically cast to 10.0)	2

FIGURE 6.15 Four calls to the overloaded *Math.max(...)* method

Overloading can make your programs more readable and less cluttered, but there are also hazards and pitfalls. Example 6.9 illustrates the benefits as well as some of the pitfalls of method overloading.

EXAMPLE 6.9

Problem Statement Carrie Cash shops only at stores that offer deep discounts. Write a method,

double cost(double price, double discount)

that provides Carrie with help in calculating the sale price of an item. The cost(...) method accepts two arguments: the price of an item and the discount (both double), and it returns the marked-down price. Include the method in an application called Sales.

Java Solution

```
1. public class Sales
2. {
3.   public static double cost(double price, double discount) // 0.0 < discount < 1.0
4.   {
       // returns the marked down price, i.e. price after discount
5.     return price - discount * price;            // marked down price
6.   }
7.
8.   public static void main(String[] args)
9.   {
10.    System.out.println("Cost is" + cost( 25.50, 0.10 ));
11.  }
12. }
```

Output

Cost is 22.95

Discussion The method cost(...) accepts two double parameters signifying the retail price of an item and the discount rate (a decimal number less than 1). The method returns the reduced or marked-down price. The method is simple to understand and simple to use.

Now consider another rather common scenario in which a 10% discount is passed to cost(...) not as the decimal 0.10 but as the integer 10, that is, change line 10 to:

System.out.println("Cost is " + cost(25.50, **10**)).

The program compiles, runs, and produces the following erroneous output:

Cost is −229.5

What happened? The argument 10 is automatically converted to a double 10.0 when it is passed to the (double) parameter discount. Consequently, the method calculates the marked-down price as

$$22.50 - \mathbf{10.0} * 22.50 = -229.5$$

To provide the flexibility of passing both integer and double arguments to cost(...), you can provide several versions of cost(...). The following program has four different versions of cost(...) that accommodate any combination of decimal and/or integer arguments

```
1.  public class SalesTwo
2.  {
3.    public static double cost(double price, double discount)  // version 1 – double, double
4.    {
5.      return price – discount * price;
6.    }

7.    public static double cost (int price, int discount)        // version 2 – int, int
8.    {
9.      double dollarsPrice = price / 100.0;                     // convert to dollars and cents
10.     double decimalDiscount = discount / 100.0;               // convert to decimal
11.     return dollarsPrice – dollarsPrice * decimalDiscount;
12.   }

13.   public static double cost(double price, int discount)      // version 3 – double, int
14.   {
15.     return price – price * (discount / 100.0);
16.   }

17.   public static double cost(int price, double discount)      // version 4 – int , double
18.   {
19.     return (price / 100.00) – (price / 100.0) * discount;
20.   }

21.   public static void main(String [] args)
22.   {
23.     System.out.println("Cost is " + cost(25.50, 0.10));  // double, double
24.     System.out.println("Cost is " + cost(2550, 10));     // int, int
25.     System.out.println("Cost is " + cost(25.50, 10));    // double, int
26.     System.out.println("Cost is " + cost(2550, 0.10));   // int double
27.   }
28. }
```

The program produces the following output:

```
Cost is 22.95
Cost is 22.95
Cost is 22.95
Cost is 22.95
```

The four calls to cost(...) on lines 23–26 invoke versions 1–4, respectively. Any variation of argument types is acceptable. Thus, a single method name accommodates four situations. Certainly, this is simpler and clearer than using four different method names such as cost1, cost2, cost3, and cost4.

The previous program illustrates the niceties of overloading; nonetheless, method overloading does not come free of problems. For example, the following program with just two versions of cost(...) does not compile.

```
public class SalesToo
{
  public static double cost(double price, int discount) // double and int
```

```
4.  {
5.     return price - price * (discount / 100.0);
6.  }
7.  public static double cost (int price, double discount) // int and double
8.  {
9.     return (price / 100.00) – (price / 100.0) * discount;;
10. }
11. public static void main(String[] args)
12. {
13.    System.out.println("Cost is " + cost( 25.50, 10 ));   // double, int
14.    System.out.println("Cost is " + cost(2550, 0.10));   // int, double
15.    System.out.println("Cost is " + cost( 25.50, 0.10)); // double, double
16.    System.out.println("Cost is " + cost(2550, 10));     // int, int
17. }
18. }
```

Two of the calls to cost(...) in main(...) create problems. The first two calls, on lines 13 and 14, are perfectly legal. The argument types—(double, int) and (int, double)—match the types in the parameter-lists declared on lines 3 and 7, respectively. However, the call on line 15 with two double arguments generates a compiler error. Each cost(...) method requires one integer argument. Java does not automatically cast a double to an int. The compiler generates the following message indicating that there is no version of cost(...) that satisfies the call:

cannot find symbol
symbol : method cost(double,double)

Finally, the call to cost(...) on line 16 is also problematic but for a different and more subtle reason. Because both arguments are integers, the compiler issues the following error message:

reference to cost is ambiguous, both method cost(int,double) in SalesToo and method cost(double,int) in SalesToo match cost(2550, 10))

The ambiguity occurs because Java can, in fact, choose either method. On one hand, the Java compiler *could* cast argument 2550 to 2550.0 and choose the first method (line 3). On the other hand, the second argument 10 might be cast to 10.0 to accommodate the second method (line 7). Java has a choice of two methods; each method appears suitable. Wisely, Java refuses to make an arbitrary choice and generates an error message. In general, if an ambiguous choice exists, a program does not compile.

The overloaded methods of Example 6.9 are distinguishable because the data types of their parameter lists differ. Overloaded methods can also differ in the *number* of arguments that they accept. For example, you might have two versions of a method max(...):

1. int max(int x, int y)
2. int max(int x, int y, int z)

Version 1 returns the greater of x and y, and version 2 the greatest of x, y, and z. The method call

```
max(a,b)
```

with only two arguments invokes method 1 and the call

```
max(a,b,c)
```

with three arguments, invokes method 2. The number of arguments determines the version.

Example 6.10 includes two methods, both named OnBasePercentage, that calculate the percentage of times during a season that a baseball player gets to first base. The first method accepts four integer arguments and the second method expects five.

EXAMPLE 6.10 Baseball uses many different statistics to measure the performance of a hitter. The *On Base Percentage* is the percentage of times that a batter reaches first base. Historically, two formulas have been used to calculate this statistic: one that was developed during the 1950s and a more modern version created in 1984.

The method developed in the 1950s computes the On Base Percentage as:

$$(hits + walks + hbp) /(atBat + walks + hbp)$$

The 1984 version performs the calculation:

$$(hits + walks + hbp) /(atBat + walks + hbp + \boldsymbol{sacrifices})$$

where

atBat is number of times a player gets a hit or makes an out,
hits is the number of times a player gets a hit,
walks is the number of times a player walks,
hbp is the number of times a player was hit by a pitch, and
sacrifices is the number of times a player makes a sacrifice fly.

Problem Statement Write a program with two methods, each named OnBasePercentage, that calculate this statistic. The first method uses the older formula and the second uses its more modern counterpart.

In the following program, the main(...) method of the class Baseball displays the 1920 season statistics for Babe Ruth, including both calculations of "The Babe's" On Base Percentage.

Java Solution

```
public class Baseball
{

   public static double OnBasePercentage(int atBat,int hits,int walks,int hbp)
   // old method from the 1950's
   {
     return (double)(hits + walks + hbp) / (double)(atBat + walks + hbp);
   }

   public static double OnBasePercentage(int atBat,int hits,int walks, int hbp,int sacrifices)
   // new method from 1984
   {
     return (double)(hits + walks + hbp) / (double)(atBat + walks + hbp + sacrifices);
   }

   public static void main(String [] args)
   {

          System.out.println("1920 statistics for Babe Ruth:");
          System.out.println("At bat: 458");
          System.out.println("Hits: 172");
          System.out.println("Walks: 150");
```

```
20.         System.out.println("Hit by pitch: 3");
21.         System.out.println("Sacrifice flies: 5");
22.         System.out.print("Babe's On Base Percentage (old method): ");
23.         System.out.println(OnBasePercentage(458,172,150,3)); // Babe Ruth's statistics
24.         System.out.print("Babe's On Base Percentage (new method): ");
25.         System.out.println(OnBasePercentage(458,172,150,3,5)); //Babe Ruth's statistics
26.   }
27. }
```

Output

```
1920 statistics for Babe Ruth:
At bat: 458
Hits: 172
Walks: 150
Hit by pitch: 3
Sacrifice flies: 5
Babe's On Base Percentage (old method): 0.5319148936170213
Babe's On Base Percentage (new method): 0.5275974025974026
```

Discussion The class Baseball contains two methods named OnBasePercentage, declared on lines 3 and 8. The first method requires four integer arguments and the second method five. Because the two parameter lists differ in the number of parameters, the Java compiler can easily choose a method based on the number of arguments the caller passes. The call on line 23 passes four arguments, and the call on line 25 passes five.

Examples 6.9 and 6.10 present two very simple variations of method overloading. As Example 6.9 illustrates, method overloading based on different data types can lead to problems when automatic type conversion occurs. On the other hand, overloading via a different number of parameters is much safer.

Finally, it is not legal to overload a method based on the type of the return value. The Java compiler does *not* consider

```
int      MyMethod(int x) and
double   MyMethod(int x)
```

two distinct methods. If two such declarations appear in the same class, a compilation error, complaining that MyMethod(...) is already defined, occurs.

> Attempting to overload a method based on the return type is a common error.

As in the two previous examples, overloaded methods must differ in the types and/or number of parameters. The return value is not a player.

Many of Java's library methods are overloaded. Figure 6.4 gives several examples such as:

Math.max(int a, int b) and Math.max(double a, double b)

or

Math.abs(int a) and Math.abs(double a).

Indeed, the methods appearing most often in this book, Java's print(...) and println(...) methods, are also overloaded. Each can take an argument of any data type.

6.5 IN CONCLUSION

In this chapter we describe a *method* as a black box that performs some singular task. Some methods accept arguments and some do not; some methods return a value, some do not; some methods are prepackaged with Java and others are written by the programmer. In all cases, however, methods simplify your programming tasks by separating a large problem into simpler components.

In Chapter 7, we present another programming structure, the *array*, which provides another method of program simplification, but in a very different way.

Just the Facts

- A *method* is a named sequence of instructions that are grouped together to perform a task.
- The name of a method must be a valid Java identifier. By convention, the name of a method begins with a lowercase letter and each succeeding "word" in the name begins with an uppercase letter.
- Every Java application must have a main(...) method, and every Java application begins execution with main(...).
- A Java method consists of a *header* followed by a *method block*:

```
modifiers return-type name (parameter-list) // the header
{
    // the method block
}
```

- The modifiers of a method header (for now) are the words public and static.
- A method's *parameter-list* consists of pairs of the form *type parameter* separated by commas. For example, int x, double y. Parameters are sometimes called *formal parameters*.
- The values passed to a method are called *arguments* or *actual parameters.*
- Arguments may be expressions.
- All arguments in Java are passed "by-value." This means that the values of the arguments are initially copied to the parameters of a method. Subsequently modifying the parameters in the method has no effect on the value of any variables passed as arguments.
- The method block performs the task of the method.
- The method block must include a return statement unless the method is a void method. A void method includes an implicit return, the last statement.
- When a return statement executes, the method exits and program control returns to the caller.
- The *scope* of a variable is the section of the program in which a variable can be accessed or referenced. The scope of a variable begins with its declaration and extends to the end of the block in which it is declared. For example, a variable declared in the header of a for statement is known only in the block of the for statement.
- Variables declared in the method block are the method's *local* variables and are inaccessible outside the block.

- Java allows two or more methods of the same class to share the same name. This practice is called *method overloading*. Overloaded methods must differ in the types and/or number of parameters.
- Method overloading based on different data types can lead to problems when automatic type conversion occurs. Overloading based on different numbers of parameters is safer.
- Java does not distinguish two methods based on the type of the value returned. Thus, method overloading based on the type of the return value is not allowed.

Bug Extermination

A method usually performs a single well-defined task. A method that performs several jobs is probably too complicated. Complex methods can lead to bugs that are hard to uncover. Keep things simple.

If an application includes several methods, you should implement and test them, one method at a time. When method A is working correctly, then implement and test method B. Write a method; compile it; test it. Then start the process again with the next method. Simulate data to test each method. When you are satisfied with one method then begin work on another. Bugs are easier to find when they are confined to ten lines rather than one hundred and ten.

The following list enumerates some of the more common bugs associated with methods:

- Omitting the keyword void from the header of a method that does not return a value.
- Omitting a return statement from a method that returns a value. Your method may have indeed computed the required value, but the return statement is necessary to send the value back to the caller.
- Misplacing a return statement. Once a return statement executes, the method exits. Make sure that return statements are correctly placed in a method block. If they are not, code that you intended to execute may not execute.
- Specifying your arguments incorrectly. Multiple declarations are not allowed in a parameter list:

  public void example(int a, int b, double c) is correct.
  public void example(int a, b, double c) is not.

- Overloading a method based on the return type. The return type does not distinguish one method from another. The parameter-lists of overloaded methods must differ.
- Attempting a method call with the incorrect number of arguments.
- Passing arguments of the wrong type to a method. The arguments must match the parameter-list not only in number but also in type.
- Passing arguments to a method in the wrong order. For example, when calling

  ```
  double area( double length, double width) // area of a rectangle
  ```

  the first argument of the call should signify the length of a rectangle and the second, the width. If you reverse the arguments, your program will compile and run, but your results will not necessarily be correct.
- Omitting the empty parentheses () when invoking a method with no arguments.
- Overloading a method based on data type that results in an ambiguous choice for the compiler. When, due to automatic casting, there is a choice of more than one method to match a method call, the compiler issues a syntax error. When overloading methods, be sure that no ambiguity exists about which method is appropriate.

EXERCISES

LEARN THE LINGO

Test your knowledge of the chapter's vocabulary by completing the following crossword puzzle.

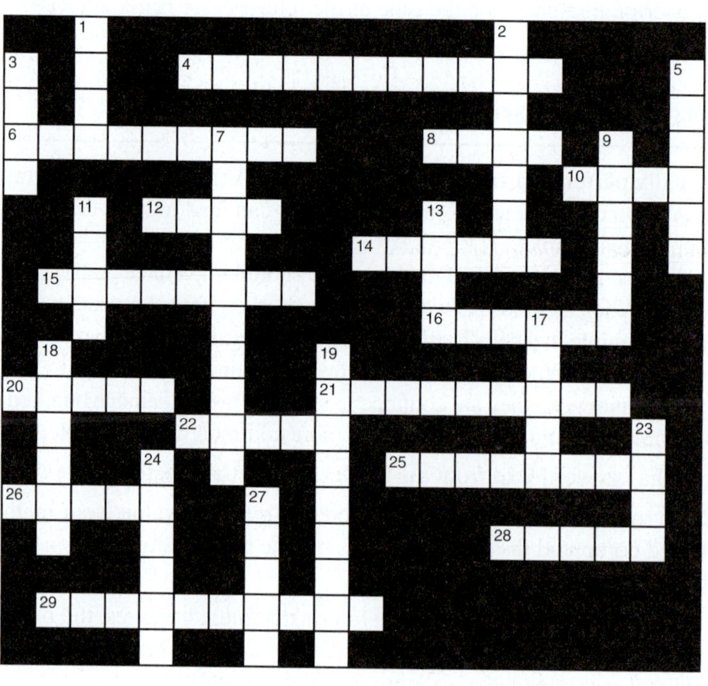

Across

4 A non-void method must specify a _____(two words)

6 The words public and static are ________

8 If the data type of the return type is T, then the type of the returned value must be T or a type that can be automatically _____ to T

10 Java library containing random()

12 Overloaded methods differ by the _____ or number of parameters

14 A method's ______ gives its name and parameter list

15 Used to pass a value to a method

16 The parameter-list specifies the type and _____ of arguments that must be given to a method

20 The _____ of a variable is the section of the program in which a variable can be accessed

21 If the choice of an overloaded method is _____ the compiler issues an error message

22 By convention, the name of a method begins with a(n) _____-case letter

25 Metaphor for a method

26 When a method is invoked, the _____ of an argument is passed to the method

28 Java-supplied void method

29 _____ methods share the same name

Down

1 Method that does not return a value

2 A variable declared in a block is unknown _____ that block

3 Local variables declared in different methods of the same application may have the same ________

5 Named set of instructions that performs a task

7 An argument may be a(n) ________

9 When a method exits, control returns to the ________

11 Java method for square root

13 Method that is always executed first

17 The statements of a method comprise the method ________

18 Another name for an argument is a(n) _____ parameter

19 Receives a value passed to a method

23 A return statement causes a method to ________

24 Not necessary in a void method

27 Variable declared in a method

SHORT EXERCISES

1. **True or False**
   If false, give an explanation.
   a. myMethod(...) may be overloaded as:
      int myMethod(int x, int y) and float myMethod(int x, double y).
   b. yourMethod(...) may be overloaded as:
      int yourMethod(int x, int y) and int yourMethod(int x, double y).
   c. hisMethod(...) may be overloaded as:
      int hisMethod(int x, int y) and float hisMethod(int x, int y).
   d. herMethod(...) may be overloaded as:
      int herMethod(int x, int y) and int herMethod(int x, int y, int z).
   e. Every Java application begins execution with main(...).
   f. main(...) can invoke at most three other methods.
   g. A method can call a method that in turn calls another method.
   h. Overloaded methods must have a different number of parameters.
   i. Overloaded methods must return the same type of data.
   j. The parameters in the header of a method are called the *actual* parameters.
   k. Arguments can be expressions or constants.
   l. The type of each parameter must match the type of its corresponding argument.
   m. The scope of a parameter in a method extends to the end of the method.
   n. The scope of a local variable extends to the end of the method in which it is defined.
   o. Every method returns a value.
   p. The name of a method cannot begin with an uppercase letter.
   q. Methods provide a programmer with a mechanism to segment a complicated application into simpler and easier-to-debug components.
   r. A method can use the same name for a local variable and a formal parameter.

2. **Playing Compiler**
   Determine the errors in each of the following segments. Fix the errors and then determine the output. Unusual formatting is not an error.
   a.
```
public class WhatTheHey
{
     public static int method1(int x,y)
    {
       return x + y;
    }

    public int method2(double x, double y)
    {
      return int(x − y);
    }

    public static void main(String[] args)
    {
      System.out.println("The output is: ", method1(method2(7.1, 6.2), method1(2, 3))
      "years of bad luck" );
    }
}
```

b.
```
public class TheBookOnLove
    {
        public static void method1()
        {
            System.out.println("I wonder who wrote the book on love");
        }
        public static void method1(int x)
        {
            for (i = 0; i < x; i++)
            System.out.println("I wonder who wrote the book on love") + i;
        }
        public static void main(String[] args)
        {
            int i; for (i = 0; i < 6; i++)
            {
                System.out.println(int i);
                method1();
                method(i);
            }
        }
    }
```

c.
```
public class ThisComputesSomeWeirdStuff
  {
    public static int method1(int a, int b)
    {
      if (a%2 == 0) return (a) else return (b)
    }
    public static int method2(int a, int b)
    {
      while (a != 1) {b++; a = a / 2;} return (b);
    }
    public static void main{String[] args}
    {
      System.out.println(method2(method1(3, 10), method1(16, 57)));
      System.out.println(method2(method1(190, 10), method1(16, 57)));
      System.out.println(method2(method2(3, 10), method1(16, 57)));
      System.out.println(method1(method2(3, 10), method2(16, 57)));
    }
  }
```

d.
```
public class ThisOneIsPrettyCool
  {
    public static int method1(int w)
    {
      int count = 0;
      while (w != 1) if (w % 2 == 0)
      {
        w = w / 2;
        count++;
      }
```

```
        else
            w = 3 * w + 1;
        return count;
    }
    public static void main(String[] args)
    {
        System.out.println(method1(10));
        System.out.println(method1(7));
    }
}
```

e.
```
public class OkIveHadEnough
{
    public static double method1(int a) { return a / 2;}
    public static double method1() {return 1.0;}
    public static int method2(double x) {return 3 * (int)x;}
    public static int method2() {return 0;}
    public static void main(String[] args)
    {
        System.out.println(method2(method1()));
        System.out.println(method1(method2()));
        for (int j = 0; j < 10; j++)
        {
            System.out.println(method2(method1(j));
            System.out.println(method1(method2(j)));
        }
    }
}
```

3. **Method Acting**

   Methods can be used to accomplish each of the following tasks. Write only the method *headers* for each example. Overload a method name, if appropriate.

   a. Calculate the largest of 2, 3, or 4 integer values.

   b. Calculate your federal income tax percentage based on the following chart:

Adjusted Gross Income Range			Percentage
\$0	–	\$7,300.00	10%
\$7,300.01	–	\$29,700.00	15%
\$29,700.01	–	\$71,950.00	25%
\$71,950.01	–	\$150,150.00	28%
\$150,150.01	–	\$326,450.00	33%
\$326,450.01	–	and up	35%

   Allow the income to be expressed in dollars and cents, or simply rounded to the nearest thousand dollars. That is, an adjusted gross income of 52,736.98 may alternatively be expressed as 53.

   c. Calculate the percentage score on an exam. You are given the number of questions on the exam, and the number that are correct.

d. Calculate your risk factor (*RF*) for auto insurance in MA, NY, and NJ. Your risk factor is either a, b, c, d, or e. In MA, *RF* depends on your age, the number of charged accidents on your record, and the number of traffic violations. In NY, *RF* depends on your age, your driving points (an integer between 6 and 35, inclusive), and the total dollars paid out to you in charged accident claims. In NJ, *RF* depends on your age, the distance from your home to the NY border (rounded to the nearest mile), the number of traffic violations on your record, and the number of people under 30 years of age in your family.

e. Decide whether or not you are eligible to become president. Eligibility is determined by your year of birth, the first letter of the country in which you were born, and the number of years that you have been a U.S. resident.

4. **Overloaded Methods**

a. Method add(...) is overloaded as follows:

```
static double add( int a, double b)     static double add(double a, int b)
{                                       {
      return a + b;                           return a + b;
}                                       }
```

Which, if any, of the following invocations fail to compile? Give reasons.

i. add(1,2)
ii. add(1.0,2.0)
iii. add(1.0, 2)
iv. add(2.0,2)

b. Method sub(...) is overloaded as follows:

```
int sub( int a, int b)          double add(double a, double b)
{                               {
      return a - b;                   return a - b;
}                               }
```

Which, if any, of the following invocations fail to compile? Give reasons.

i. sub(1,2)
ii. sub(1.0,2.0)
iii. sub(1.0, 2)
iv. sub(2.0,2)

c. What is the problem with the following overloaded method that returns a product as either an int or a long?

```
int mul(int a, int b)           long mul(int a, int b)
{                               {
      return a * b;                   return a * b;
}                               }
```

5. **Pass By Value**

Harry Hacker has written the following method that is supposed to swap the contents of two variables:

```
static void swap(int a, int b)
{
    int temp = a;
    a = b;
    b = temp;
}
```

However, the statements

```
int a = 5;
int b = 6;
swap(a,b);
System.out.println("a = " + a + " and b = " + b);
```

produce the output

```
a = 5 and b = 6.
```

Explain why Harry's method does not work as intended.

PROGRAMMING EXERCISES

1. **Min and Max**
   Write two methods

   ```
   int myMax(int x, int y) and
   int myMin(int x, int y),
   ```

   each of which accepts two integers x and y, and outputs the larger/smaller of the two, respectively. The main method of your program should prompt for two numbers, pass these numbers to myMax(...) and myMin(...), and then print the results with appropriate explanatory text.

2. **Celsius to Fahrenheit**
   Write a method

   ```
   int cToF(int x)
   ```

   that converts a Celsius temperature to a Fahrenheit temperature. The conversion formula is:

   $$F = (9.0/5.0)C + 32.$$

   The returned value should be rounded to the nearest degree. Test your method by displaying a table of Celsius temperatures from -40 to 100, in increments of five degrees, with the Fahrenheit equivalents.

3. **Random Numbers**
   Write a method

   ```
   int randomInt(int x, int y)
   ```

   that returns a random integer between x and y, inclusive. Note that x and y can be positive or negative.

4. **Average**
   Write a method

   ```
   double average(int n)
   ```

that reads n numbers of type double and returns the average of those numbers. Include this method in a program that requests a value for n and displays the average of n numbers supplied by a user.

5. **Consumer Price Index**
   The Consumer Price Index (CPI) represents the change in the prices paid by urban consumers for a representative basket of goods and services. It is a percentage value rounded to the nearest tenth, for example, 9.2 or −0.7. Write a method

   ```
   double getCPI()
   ```

   that asks a user to enter a number between −20 and 20 with one digit after the decimal point. If the user supplies an unacceptable number, the method should display an appropriate error message ("number too high," "number too low," or "number has wrong precision") and prompt the user for another value. When the user succeeds, the method should return that number.

   Test your method by continually prompting a user for a value and displaying the value. When you are confident that the method is correct, write a second method

   ```
   double inflation( double cpi, double expenses)
   ```

   that accepts the CPI and last year's annual expenses. Method inflation(...) returns what you might expect to pay for the same goods in the coming year. Write a main(...) method that calls both getCPI() and inflation(...).

6. **Price Adjustment**
   Write a method

   ```
   int bumpMe(int price, int increase, boolean updown)
   ```

   that accepts a price in dollars and returns a new price rounded to the nearest dollar, after increasing/decreasing price by increase percent. If updown is true then you should increase the price; otherwise, decrease the price. Write an appropriate main(...) method to test bumpMe(...).

7. **Simulations**
   Simulation is one way that casinos analyze games; simulation is less expensive than hiring a mathematician. The "over-under" bet is described in Example 6.3. Write three methods, each of which simulates 10,000 plays of a \$1/bet game and returns the amount of money that is won or lost over 10,000 games. A negative number denotes a loss. The three methods operate as follows:

   - Method 1 chooses the bet ("over 7," "under 7," or "exact") at random.
   - Method 2 always chooses the "over 7" bet.
   - Method 3 chooses the "over 7" bet 4000 times, the "under 7" bet 4000 times, and the "exact" bet 2000 times.

   Test these methods in a program. Write, test, and debug the methods one at a time, that is, get Method 1 working perfectly before including Method 2 in your program.

8. **Hello World Revisited**
   Write a program that prompts a user for a positive integer *n* and prints "Hello There" *n* times. Of course, a value of *n* that is less than or equal to 0 is illegal. To ensure valid input, include a method

   ```
   int getPos()
   ```

   that prompts for a positive integer. If the value of that integer is less than or equal to 0, the method should print an appropriate message and request a positive number. When the user supplies a valid number, the method returns that number.

9. **Carnival Game Simulation**
The rules of a certain carnival game stipulate that a player throws one standard 6-sided die, one 20-sided die, one 8-sided die, one 4-sided die, and one 12-sided die. The player wins if the total on the five dice is greater than 35 or less than 20. Write a program that simulates the carnival game 100 times and reports the number of times a player wins. Your program should include a method

```
int dieRoll(int x)
```

that returns a random number between 1 and x.

10. **Present Value of an Investment**
The present value on an investment of A dollars for Y years at an annual rate of R percent compounded C times yearly is

$$\text{Present Value} = A(1 + R/C)^{YC} \tag{1}$$

Of course, if interest is compounded yearly, then $C = 1$ and (1) simplifies to:

$$\text{Present Value} = A(1 + R)^{Y}. \tag{2}$$

Overload a method presentValue(...) so that presentValue(...) implements formulas (1) and (2). Write a main(...) method that tests both versions of presentValue(...).

11. **Craps Simulation**
When playing craps, a player rolls two dice repeatedly until she wins or loses. The first roll of the dice is called the *come-out* roll. If the player rolls a 7 or an 11 on the come-out roll, then she wins immediately; a 2, 3, or 12 on the come-out roll results in an immediate loss. If she rolls a 4, 5, 6, 8, 9, or 10 on the come-out roll, then that number becomes her *point* and she continues rolling until she rolls either her point or a 7. If she rolls her point, she wins, but if she rolls a 7 before rolling her point, she loses. Once a player has established her point, no other numbers (including 2, 3, 11, or 12) affect her winning or losing.
Write a method

```
boolean craps()
```

that simulates one game of craps and returns *true* if and only if the player wins. Test your method by printing the values of each roll of the dice. When you are convinced that your simulation is correct, include this method in a program that executes craps() 1000 times and reports the percentage of wins.

12. **Mean Versus Median**
Implement two methods:

    1. int median(int x, int y, int z) that calculates the median of three integers.
    2. int mean(int x, int y, int z) that calculates the average of three integers, rounding the result to the nearest integer.

Devise a main(...) method that accepts three integers and states whether the median of the three is larger than the mean, smaller than the mean, or equal to the mean.

13. **Zeno's Paradox**
A famous paradox devised by Zeno, an Eleatic philosopher (b. 488 BCE), asserts that to run from point A to point B, a runner must first traverse half the distance between A and B. Before he can do that, he must traverse a "half of the half," and so on ad infinitum. He must, therefore, pass through an infinite number of points, and that is impossible in a finite time. Design and implement a method

```
double zeno(int n)
```

that calculates the sum $1/2 + 1/4 + 1/8 + \ldots + 1/2^n$. The method should call an auxiliary method

```
int powerTwo(int n)
```

that returns 2^n. Test both methods in a complete program. *Hint:* Implement and test the two methods one at a time. First write, compile, and test powerTwo(...). Once that method is working correctly, add zeno(...) to your program.

14. **Date Calculations**
Implement an application that prompts for two dates each comprised of three integers: a month, a day, and a year between 1900 and 2100, inclusive. If both dates are valid, your program should display the number of days between the two dates; otherwise, your program should issue an error message. Include a method

```
boolean validDate(int month, int day, int year)
```

that returns true if and only if a date is valid. For example (12, 29, 1980) is valid but (29, 12, 1980), (13, 11, 2007), and (1, 1, 1899) are not. You should also design a method

```
int dateDifference(int day1, int month1, int year1, int day2, int month2, int year2)
```

that returns the number of days between the dates (month1, day1, year1) and (month2, day2, year2), provided these dates are valid. Don't forget to take leap years into account, and recall that 1900 and 2100 are *not* leap years.

15. **Geometric Mean**
A home purchased for 300,000 dollars increases in value by 10% after one year and by another 20% after a second year. Thus, a year after purchasing the house, its value is **1.10** × 300,000 dollars and after two years **1.20** × 1.10 × 300,000 dollars. A third year *decrease* of 6% drops the value to 94% of the previous value. **0.94** × 1.20 × 1.10 × 300000 = 372240 dollars. Notice that the multiplier is 1 − 0.06 = 0.94. The *average* annual increase over the three-year period is the *geometric mean* of 1.10, 1.20 and 0.94.
In general, the *geometric mean* of n numbers is the nth root of their product. Thus, the geometric mean of 1.10, 1.20, and .94 is $(1.10 \times 1.20 \times .94)^{1/3} =$ 1.074568 and the product 1.074568 × 1.074568 × 1.074568 × 300000 equals 372240, as does the original product, .94 × 1.20 × 1.10 × 300000. In other words, the home's value after three annual changes of 10%, 20%, and −6% is the same as if, each year, the home's value increased by 7.4568%.
Write a program that calculates the average increase or decrease on an investment held from one to six years. Your program should first prompt for the length of time of the investment (an integer between 1 and 6, inclusive) and then the percent increase or decrease for each year. A negative number indicates a decrease. The program should display the average annual increase or decrease. For example, if a home, over a six-year period, has changed in value by 10%, 20%, 6%, −8%, −12%, and 3%, then to compute the average annual increase (or decrease), you would calculate the geometric mean of 1.1, 1.2, 1.06, 0.92, 0.88, and 1.03.
Hints: Overload a method, geometricMean(...). Make five versions that have two, three, four, five, and six parameters of type double. Use Math.pow(x,y).

16. **Harmonic Mean**
If it takes one hose 12 hours to fill a pool, and another hose 4 hours, then together they fill the pool in (2 × 4 × 12) / (4 + 12) = 6 hours. The *harmonic mean* of two positive numbers a and b is $2ab/(a + b)$. Write a method

```
double harmonicMean(int x, int y)
```

that returns the harmonic mean of $a > 0$ and $b > 0$. Write another method that returns the arithmetic mean of a and b, that is, the average of a and b. Finally, include a third method that returns the geometric mean of a and b, that is, the square root of $a \times b$ (see Exercise 15).

Test your methods in a program that reads two positive integers and displays their harmonic mean, arithmetic mean, and geometric mean. For example, if a and b have values 12 and 4, the harmonic mean is 6.0, the arithmetic mean is 8.0, and the geometric mean is $\sqrt{48} \approx 6.928$. Did you notice that the harmonic mean times the arithmetic mean equals the square of the geometric mean? This identity might be helpful to you when you design your methods.

17. **Median of Five**

A teacher wishes to use the median (middle value) of five grades as the final grade for each of n students. Write a method that returns the median of five integers. For example, the median of 10, 50, 48, 35, and 22 is 35. Test your method in a program that accepts the number of students, followed by five grades per student, and prints the final grade for each student. Do *not* assume that the grades are ordered.

18. **Lottery Games**

Most states sell lottery tickets of one of the following two types:

a. A player picks k distinct numbers between 1 and n, inclusive. For example, to play Massachusetts' Megabucks game, a player picks six numbers between 1 and 42. In this case, the number of possible lottery tickets is:

$$\frac{42 \times 41 \times 40 \times 39 \times 38 \times 37}{6 \times 5 \times 4 \times 3 \times 2 \times 1} = 5{,}245{,}786$$

(Notice that six numbers must be selected and there are six factors in the numerator, counting down from 42.) Thus, a player who buys a single ticket has one chance in 5,245,786 of attaining an instant fortune. In general, if a player must choose k numbers between 1 and n, the number of possible tickets is:

$$\frac{n \times (n-1) \times (n-2) \times \ldots \times (n-k+1)}{k \times (k-1) \times (k-2) \times \ldots \times 3 \times 2 \times 1}$$

b. The second type of game requires that a player pick k numbers between 1 and n as well as one additional number between 1 and m. For example, to play California's Super Lotto game, a player picks five numbers between 1 and 47, inclusive, and one additional number between 1 and 27, inclusive. In this case the number of possible tickets is:

$$\frac{47 \times 46 \times 45 \times 44 \times 43}{5 \times 4 \times 3 \times 2 \times 1} \times 27 = 41{,}416{,}353$$

In general, the number of possibilities is:

$$\frac{n \times (n-1) \times (n-2) \times \ldots \times (n-k+1)}{k \times (k-1) \times (k-2) \times \ldots \times 3 \times 2 \times 1} \times m$$

Write an application that calculates the number of possible lottery tickets for each type of game, (a) and (b). Overload numberOfTickets(...) as

```
int numberOfTickets(int n, int k) // choose k numbers from 1 to n
```

and

```
int numberOfTickets( int n, int m, int k)    // choose k numbers from 1 to n
                                             // and an additional number from 1 to m.
```

These methods return the number of possibilities described in (a) and (b) above, respectively.

To play New York's Lotto game, a player picks six numbers between 1 and 59; and to play the state's Mega Millions game, a player picks five numbers between 1 and 56 and an additional number between 1 and 46. Write a main(...) method that determines which of the two games gives the better chance of an instant fortune.

THE BIGGER PICTURE

1. TIME COMPLEXITY

The amount of time it takes to run a program is the most important measure of program performance. A clock can be used to measure the real running time of a program, but results can be misleading if programs are run on different computers. Some computers are faster than others, and a fast computer might conceivably run a poorly designed program in less time than a slow computer runs a well-designed one.

A better measure of performance treats the program as an abstract *algorithm*—that is, a step-by-step method for solving a problem—and calculates the number of steps that the algorithm requires as a function of input size. This focus on the algorithm cuts out the disparity in hardware and allows an even-handed comparison.

For example, consider the following algorithm that computes the average of n integers:

```
sum = first integer;
for each of the remaining n − 1 integers
{
    sum = sum + next integer;
}
average = sum/n;
```

This algorithm takes approximately n steps to accomplish its task, where each step is a single addition or division. The *time complexity* of the algorithm is n. A Java implementation would accomplish the task using a loop.

Following are two algorithms, written in Java-like pseudocode, that calculate the *greatest common divisor* (*gcd*) of two numbers a and b, where $a > b$. The greatest common divisor of a and b is the largest positive integer that evenly divides both a and b. For example, the greatest common divisor of 36 and 27 is 9, and the greatest common divisor of 101 and 68 is 1.

Algorithm I:

```
// This is a brute force algorithm that starts with the smaller number (b) and finds
// the first number less than or equal to b that divides evenly into both a and b.
// Assume a > b.

for k = b downto 1                          // for each possible divisor, k
    if ( (b % k == 0) && (a % k == 0) )     // if k evenly divides both b and a
        return k;
```

Algorithm II:

// This is a clever, sophisticated algorithm called Euclid's algorithm.

```
while (b != 0)
{
    int temp = a % b;
    a = b;
    b = temp;
}
return a;
```

It should be clear why Algorithm I works, but perhaps it is not so obvious why Algorithm II accomplishes the same task. Algorithm II is based on a theorem of Euclid (300 BCE) that states that given two positive integers a and b, where $a > b$,

> the greatest common divisor of a and b is the same as the greatest common divisor of b and a % b, that is, $\gcd(a,b) = \gcd(b, a \% b)$.

For Algorithm I, the worst-case scenario is that the loop iterates from b down to 1. So, at worst, Algorithm I takes b steps. For example, to calculate the greatest common divisor of 101 and 37, Algorithm II requires 37 steps.

For Algorithm II, the number of steps, that is, the time complexity, is not obvious. However, 19th century mathematician Gabriel Lamé proved that Euclid's algorithm requires at most $5k$ steps, where k is the *number of digits* in b.[1] For example, Euclid's algorithm takes at most $5 \times 2 = 10$ steps to find the greatest common divisor of $a = 472$ and $b = 36$, since 36 has two digits.

Compare $5k$ with the time complexity of Algorithm I, which requires at most b steps. The difference is astronomical. For example, if $b = 10^{10} = 10{,}000{,}000{,}000$, then Algorithm I may take 10^{10} steps, but Euclid's algorithm takes at most $2 \times 11 = 22$ steps! Because a number with n digits is roughly 10^n, the difference between the two algorithms is akin to the difference between 10^n and n.

Exercises

1. Estimate the number of steps used by Algorithm I and Algorithm II when $a = 298765$ and $b = 89765$.
2. Implement methods for Algorithm I and Algorithm II. Include your implementations in a program.
3. Write a program that compares the running times of Algorithm I and Algorithm II. Use the data: $a = 12000111$, $b = 9899111$. To calculate the running time of each method, invoke System.currentTimeMillis(), which returns the current time (long) to the nearest millisecond:

```
long startTime = System.currentTimeMillis();
myMethod(); // call your method here
```

[1]Lamé used the *Fibonacci sequence* to prove his result. The Fibonacci sequence is a sequence of positive integers such that the first two terms of the sequence are both 1 and each succeeding term is the sum of the previous two numbers. The first 10 terms of the Fibonacci sequence are 1, 1, 2, 3, 5, 8, 13, 21, 34, and 55. Lamé proved that if $a > b \geq 0$ and b is less than the $(n + 1)^{st}$ term of the Fibonacci sequence, then the number of steps required by Euclid's algorithm is at most n. For example, if b is 100, then the number of steps required by Euclid's algorithm is at most 11 because 100 is less than the 12th term of the Fibonacci sequence: (1 1 2 3 5 8 13 21 34 55 89 **144**). Lamé's theorem implies that the number of steps required by Euclid's algorithm is no more than 5 times the number of digits in b.

```
long endTime = System.currentTimeMillis();
long totalTime = endTime − startTime;
```

How do the two algorithms (I and II) compare?

4. To each method of Exercise 2, add a counter that keeps track of the number of loop iterations, that is, the number of steps performed by each algorithm. Compare the number of steps required by Algorithm I and Algorithm II when $a = 12000111$ and $b = 989111$. Are your results consistent with the theory? Run the program with numbers of your own choice.

2. RECURSION, A PREVIEW

You have seen that a method can invoke another method. Well, you may be surprised to learn that a method can call *itself*. A method that includes a call to itself is called a *recursive* method. You might surmise that a method that calls itself would create an infinite loop. And, indeed, that may happen. Trace through the following method that forever begs you to end its misery!

```
Public static void runMeForever()
{
   System.out.println("Stop me. This hurts!");
   runMeForever();
}
```

The method runMeForever() produces the following, rather redundant, cry for help:

```
Stop me. This hurts!
Stop me. This hurts!
Stop me. This hurts!
Stop me. This hurts!
Stop me. This hurts!
Stop me. This hurts!
Stop me. This hurts!
...
```

Yes, the runMeForever() invokes runMeForever() which invokes runMeForever() which invokes runMeForever(), well, forever. However, you can rewrite this method so that it prints the message just *n* times and then stops. As a boolean condition terminates a while loop, we can use a boolean condition to put a stop to the infinite chain of recursive method calls.

```
public static void runMeAwhile(int n)
{
      if (n != 0) // stops the chain of method calls to itself when n=0
      {
            System.out.println("Stop me. This hurts!");
            runMeAwhile(n – 1 );
      }
}
```

The following class invokes the method runMeAwhile(...) with the argument n = 3.

```
public class Test
{
   public static void runMeAwhile(int n)
   {
```

THE BIGGER PICTURE

```
        if (n != 0)
        {
            System.out.println("Stop me. This hurts!");
            runMeAwhile(n - 1 );
        }
    }
    public static void main(String[] Args)
    {
        runMeAwhile(3); // invokes method for the first time
    }
}
```

The main(...) method of Test calls runMeAwhile(3) which displays "Stop me. This hurts!" and calls runMeAwhile(2), which prints "Stop me. This hurts!" and calls runMeAwhile(1), which prints "Stop me. This hurts!", and calls runMeAwhile(0), which does nothing because n == 0. The following diagram depicts the actions of Test:

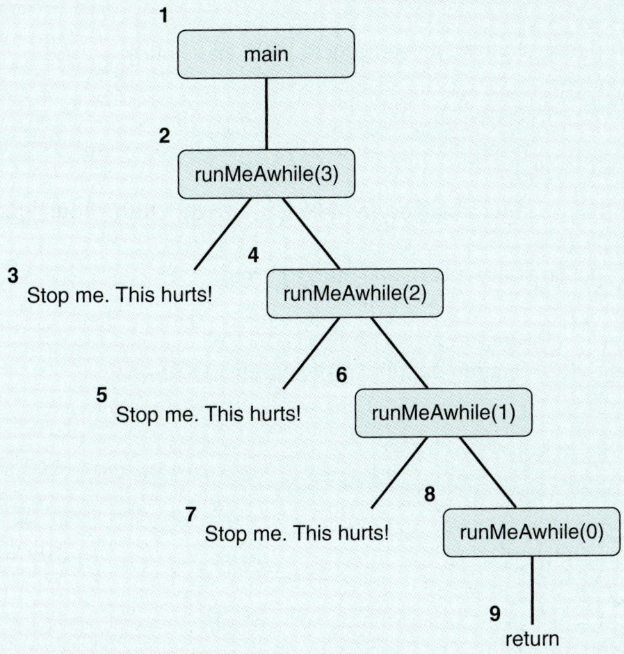

In theory, recursion and iteration are equivalent; anything that you can accomplish with one you can do with the other. Java provides both recursion and iteration for the same reason that it provides three different loops (do-while, while, and for): different problems are solved more naturally with different tools.

Recursion, however, is a powerful way of thinking and problem solving that extends well beyond the notion of loops. Recursion is one of the major techniques employed in the development of powerful computer algorithms. A more thorough discussion of recursion follows in Chapter 8.

Exercises

1. Write a recursive method int getPos() that requests a positive integer supplied by a user. On input less than or equal to 0, the method displays an appropriate error message and asks again for a positive integer via a recursive call to itself. If the number is legal, the method returns the number.

2. Write a recursive method int addUp(int n) that returns the sum of the numbers from 1 through *n*. *Hint*: addUp(n – 1) will return the sum of the numbers from 1 through *n* – 1. All you need to do is add *n* to this sum and return.

3. Test the methods of Exercises 1 and 2 in a program that includes the following main(...) method:

```
public static void main(String[] args)
{
    System.out.println("Enter a positive integer: ");
    int n = getPos();
    System.out.println("The sum 1 through n is "+ addUp(n));
}
```

4. Determine the output of the following program. If you trace through the method calls carefully, you will discern a pattern.

```
public class Recursion
{
    public static int mystery(int a, int b, int c, int d)
    {
        if (a == b)
            return c;
        else
            return mystery(a, b + 1, d, c + d);
    }
    public static void main (String[] args)
    {
        for(int i = 1; i < 10; i++)
            System.out.println(mystery(i,1,1,1));
    }
}
```

CHAPTER 7

Arrays and Lists: One Name for Many Data

"Hi, I'm Larry, this is my brother Darryl, and this is my other brother Darryl"
—from the TV comedy *Newhart*

Objectives

The objectives of Chapter 7 include an understanding of

- array declaration, instantiation, initialization, and use,
- reference variables,
- how arrays are passed to methods and used in methods,
- basic sorting,
- linear and binary search, and
- multi-dimensional arrays.

7.1 INTRODUCTION

Lists are certainly part of our culture. There's David Letterman's daily top 10 list, the American Film Institute's list of the best 100 films of all time, the best-dressed list, the worst-dressed list, Forbes list of the richest people in America, Billboard's Top 40 list, your grocery list, and even Santa's list of who is naughty and who is nice—to list a few. Everyone makes lists. Everyone reads lists. Everyone uses lists.

In this chapter we explain how an application can create, maintain, update, sort, and search a list of data using an *array*.

> An *array* is a named sequence of contiguous memory locations capable of holding a collection of data of the same type.

Unlike the variables of previous programs, an array can store more than one value. An array can store a list of thousands or even millions of data. Figure 7.1 contrasts a simple variable with an array.

In this chapter, you will learn the basics of programming with arrays. Do you need to search a list of 1000 ID numbers? One million numbers? It's not a problem.

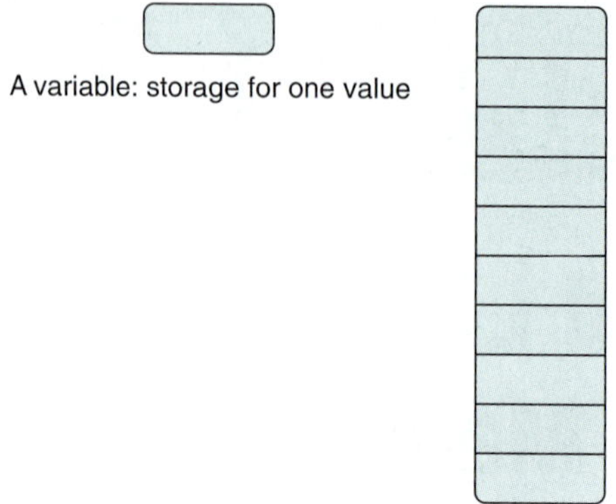
A variable: storage for one value
An array: contiguous memory storage for many values.

FIGURE 7.1 A variable in contrast to an array

7.2 ARRAY FUNDAMENTALS: DECLARATION AND INSTANTIATION

Using an array requires two preliminary steps:

- declaration
- instantiation

7.2.1 Array Declaration

Java's syntax allows two forms of array declaration:

- type[] name
- type name[],

where *type* is a data type such as int, char, double, or boolean and *name* is a valid Java identifier that provides a name for an array.

The following declarations illustrate both styles of declaration, and although either type of declaration is permissible, most Java programmers opt for the first version.

- int[] myArray
- double yourArray[]

The variables myArray and yourArray are different than the variables of previous programs. These variables are *reference* variables. A reference variable does not hold an integer, a floating-point number, a character, or a boolean value.

> A reference variable holds a memory address.

Indeed, Java provides just two types of variables, *primitive* and *reference*.

- A *primitive variable* stores a single value of type byte, short, int, long, float, double, boolean, or char.
- A *reference variable* holds a memory address or reference.

There is no other kind of variable. Soon, you will see that references are major players in almost every Java program.

Each of the two variables myArray and yourArray, *when assigned a value*, holds a memory address, the address of the first cell of a block of storage locations. See Figure 7.1. Although references can be compared and also used in assignment statements, unlike integer or floating-point numbers, references cannot be part of an arithmetical expression. Array references are used by the system to access the first storage cell of an array.

7.2.2 Array Instantiation

The references myArray and yourArray are uninitialized; a declaration does not create an array. Once an array reference is declared, memory for the array must be allocated. An array is created or *instantiated* via the *new* operator:

- *type* [] name; // declaration
  name = new *type[size]*; // array instantiation

or

- ***type*[] name = new *type[size]* // declaration and instantiation**

where *type* is a data type and *size* is a positive number and of type int or an expression that evaluates, or is automatically converted, to a positive number of type int. The integer *size* indicates the *length* of the array, that is, the number of cells in the array. The array in Figure 7.1 has 10 cells and can thus store 10 items such as 10 integers or 10 characters.

The values held in an array must all be the same data type.

For example, you cannot store both double and boolean values in the same array. It's one or the other.

When an array is created, each cell is automatically given a unique name. For example, the segments

```
int myArray = new int[5];
```

and

```
double yourArray = new double[10];
```

declare and instantiate two arrays. The names of the cells of the array are myArray[0], myArray[1], myArray[2], myArray[3], and myArray[4]. In this case, the array is *indexed* from 0 to 4. The cells of yourArray are named yourArray[0], yourArray[1], yourArray[2]...yourArray[9]. Here the array is indexed from 0 to 9.

The first index of every array is 0.

Figure 7.2 shows these two arrays. The reference variables myArray and yourArray hold the addresses of myArray[0] and yourArray[0], respectively.

Finally, when an array is instantiated, each memory cell is initialized with the "zero value" of its data type. Thus every cell of an array of int or char data is initialized to 0, and all cells of an array of doubles are set to 0.0. Each cell of a boolean array is initialized to false. The code snippets of Figure 7.3 are examples of array instantiation.

Once an array is created, its length is fixed. The length of an array cannot be altered. Conveniently, if variable x refers to an array, then x.length gives the number of memory cells allocated to the array. For example, referring to Figure 7.3, numberList.length has the value 5 and letters.length has the value 6.

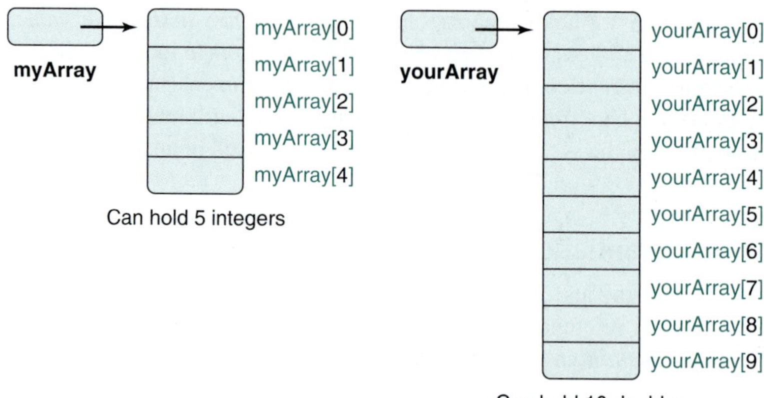

FIGURE 7.2 Two arrays *myArray* and *yourArray*

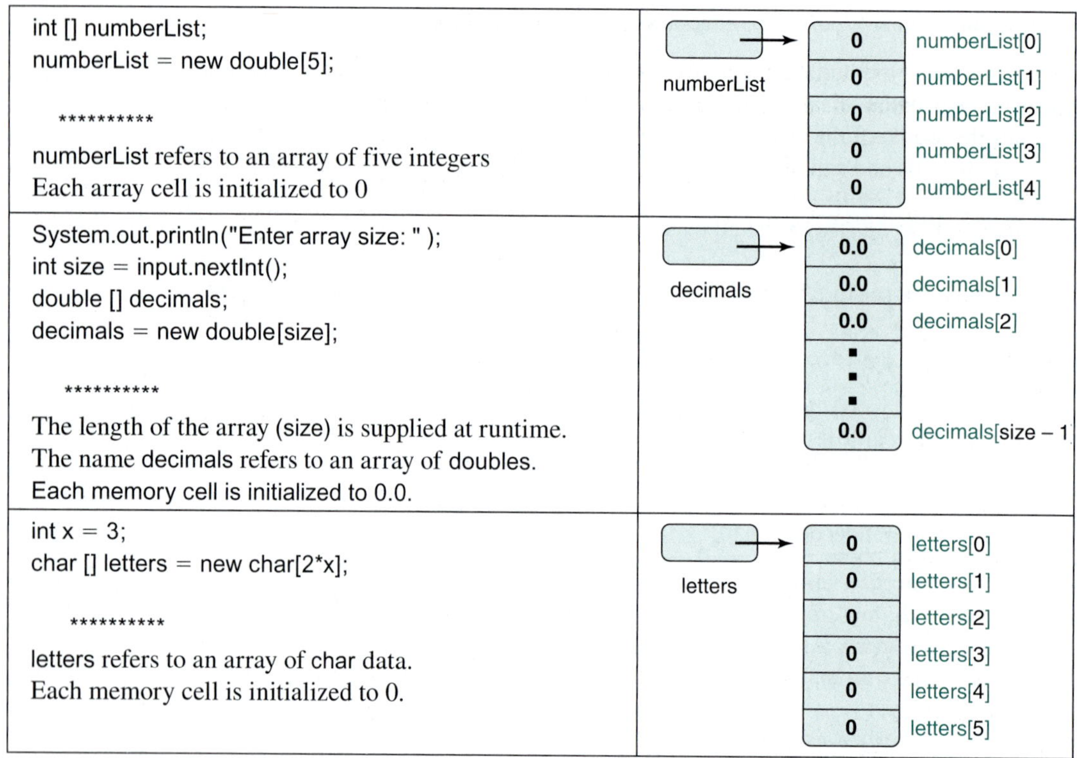

FIGURE 7.3 Examples of array instantiation

7.3 USING AN ARRAY

Using a cell of an array is no different than using a simple variable.

> You can use array variables in assignment statements or any expression.

For example, the statement

```
int[] numbers = new int[5]
```

declares and instantiates an array named numbers such that:

- numbers is indexed from 0 to 4,
- numbers is capable of storing 5 integers in locations numbers[0], numbers[1], numbers[2], numbers[3], and numbers[4],
- numbers.length has the value 5, and
- the initial value stored in each cell of numbers is 0.

See Figure 7.4.

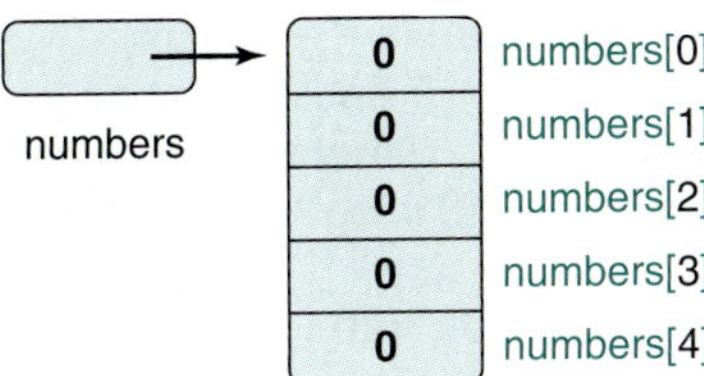

FIGURE 7.4 The array *numbers*

Once the array numbers has been instantiated, you can use individual memory cells of the array in any place that you might use a variable of type int. Indeed, each memory cell is a variable. For example, the statements

```
numbers[0] = input.nextInt();           // reads a value into numbers[0]
numbers[1] = 2 + numbers[0];            // assign 2 + numbers[0] to numbers[1]
System.out.println(5 * numbers[1] + 3 * numbers[0]);
```

are all valid and meaningful.

If an array has length n, an application can access locations indexed 0, 1, 2, 3, …, $n-1$. Any other index value causes an "array out of bounds" error. For example, the statement

```
int[] x = new int[4];    // x is indexed 0 to 3
```

declares and instantiates an array of length 4, so the assignment

```
x[4] = 23;    // ERROR! Index out of range.
```

causes an "array out of bounds" error. Similarly, the loop

```
for (int i = 0; i <= 4; i++)
        x[i] = i;
```

also causes an error. In both cases, an attempt to access x[4] creates the problem. The array location x[4] does not exist because the range of the index values is 0 through 3, that is, the cells of the array are designated x[0], x[1], x[2], and x[3].

Example 7.1 illustrates a few fundamental concepts of array processing. The example demonstrates how to create an array and how to iterate through an array.

EXAMPLE 7.1

Program Statement Write a program that prompts for 10 integers and displays those same numbers in reverse order. For example, if you enter the numbers:

0 11 2 33 4 55 6 77 8 99

the program's output is:

99 8 77 6 55 4 33 2 11 0

Java Solution The following application stores 10 integers in an array named list. The array consists of 10 memory cells that are named list[0], list[1]...list[9]. The user supplies 10 numbers. The numbers are stored in these 10 cells and finally, the numbers are displayed in reverse order.

```
1. import java.util.*;
2. public class ReverseList
3. {
4.     public static void main(String[] args)
5.     {
6.         Scanner input = new Scanner(System.in);
7.         int [] list;              // declare list an array variable
8.         list = new int[10];       // instantiate or create an array named list
9.         System.out.print("Enter 10 integers: ");

10.        // read values into list[0], list[1],..,list[9]
11.        for (int i = 0; i < 10; i++)
12.            list[i] = input.nextInt();

13.        System.out.print("List in reverse : ");
14.        // print values stored in list[9], list[8], ... , list[0]
15.        for (int i = 9; i >= 0; i--)
16.            System.out.print(list[i] + " ");

17.        System.out.println();
18.    }
19. }
```

Output

Enter 10 integers: **0 11 2 33 4 55 6 77 8 99**
List in reverse: 99 8 77 6 55 4 33 2 11 0

Discussion The program prompts for 10 integers. After the data is entered (lines 11–12), you might visualize the array as in Figure 7.5.

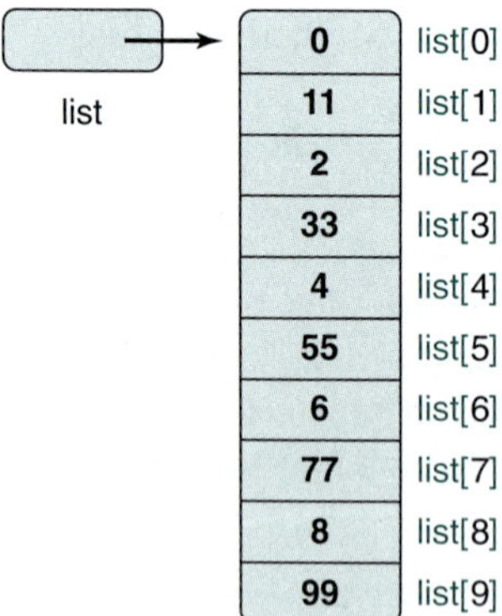

FIGURE 7.5 The array *list* holds 10 integers. The individual memory cells are designated *list*[0], *list*[1], *list*[2], . . . , *list*[8], and *list*[9].

We begin our discussion with line 7.

Line 7: int [] list;

Line 7 is an *array declaration* as indicated by the square brackets []. Like any variable, list must be declared before its use. And also, like the variables of previous programs, list can hold but a single value. However, as previously noted, the similarity stops there. A value stored in list is neither an int, nor a float, nor a double, boolean, or char; it's a *reference,* a memory address, useful to the system but not to the programmer.

The statement on line 7 *declares* that list is a reference variable. That's all. The declaration does not assign a value to list. No memory has been allocated yet; no array exists yet; list has not been initialized with any reference/address. That's the next step.

Line 8: list = new int[10];

The segment new int[10]

- allocates a block of memory large enough to store 10 integers, and
- returns the starting address of this memory chunk.

The new operator creates or instantiates a new array. The operator reserves a consecutive block of storage locations in memory and returns the starting address of the block.

The memory address (reference) returned by the new operator is subsequently assigned to the reference variable list (list = new int [10]). Unlike a primitive variable, a program cannot use list in an arithmetic expression.

Now, storage is available for 10 integers. The reference variable list holds the address of the first storage cell. Moreover, each memory cell is initialized to 0. The arrow in Figure 7.6 indicates that list holds an address or reference.

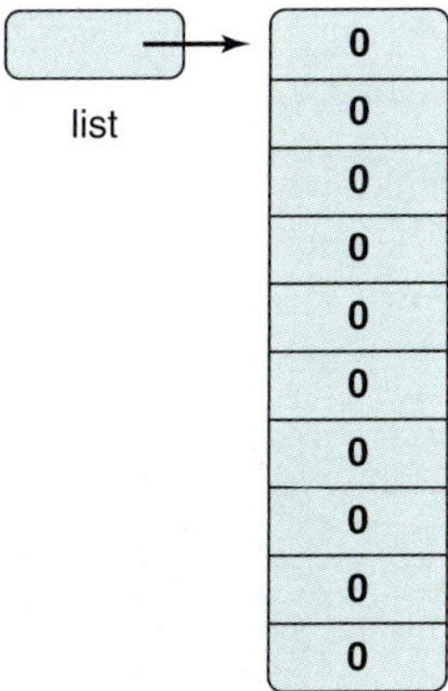

FIGURE 7.6 Array instantiation; *list* is a reference; *list* holds an address. Initially each cell has a value of 0.

Lines 11 and 12: for (int i = 0; i < 10; i++) list[i] = input.nextInt();

Lines 11 and 12 comprise a for loop that accepts interactive input and stores the values in the array, list. The array consists of 10 cells or variables with the similar, if rather unimaginative, names list[0], list[1], list[2], list[3], list[4], list[5], list[6], list[7], list[8], and list[9]. Alternatively, we say that the array is *indexed* from 0 to 9.

The numbers stored in this array (0, 11, 2, 33, 4, 55, 6, 77, 8, 99) represent arbitrary input. See Figure 7.7.

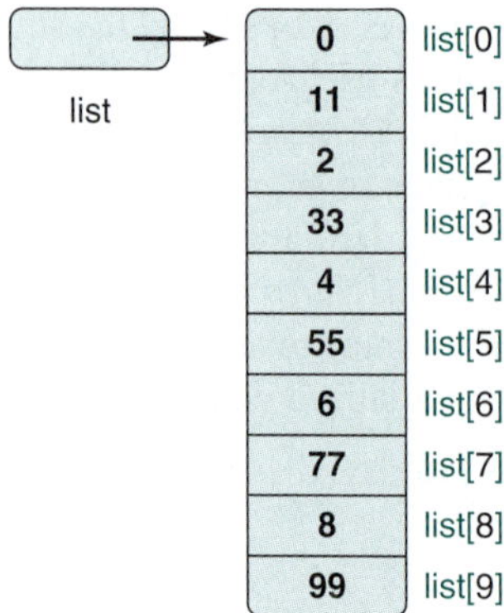

FIGURE 7.7 The array *list* holds 10 numbers

Lines 15 and 16: for (int i = 9; i >= 0; i--) System.out.print(list[i] + " ");

The for loop prints the array items in reverse. The loop counter begins with 9 and ends with 0. Thus, the program displays the values stored in list[9], list[8], . . ., and list[0]. Again, notice that an array of 10 values is indexed from 0 to 9. Similarly, an array of 1000 values is indexed 0 … 999.

Example 7.2 declares, creates, and uses an array of size 38 to test the randomness of a random number generator.

EXAMPLE 7.2 In casino roulette, the croupier spins a wheel that stops on one of 38 numbers—a number in the range 1 to 36 as well as two special numbers, 0 and 00. Figure 7.8 shows a typical roulette board.

FIGURE 7.8 A roulette board has numbers 1 through 36 as well as 0 and 00

Slippery Sam, programmer by day and gambler by night, has written a program that plays "video roulette." Sam's program uses Java's random number generator Math.random(). However, Sam is not quite convinced that Math.random() is really random. So he decides to run a few tests on Math.random().

Problem Statement To test the randomness of Math.random(), write a program that generates 1,000,000 random integers ranging from 0 to 37 (37 represents 00). If Math.random() works correctly, then each number, 0 through 37, should appear approximately 1/38th or about 2.632% of the time.

Java Solution Using the expression

```
(int)(38*Math.random()),   // a random integer in the range 0..37
```

the following application generates a sequence of 1,000,000 random integers between 0 and 37, inclusive. These numbers model 1,000,000 spins of the roulette wheel.

An array, numbers, indexed 0 to 37, keeps count of the number of times that each value, 0 through 37, appears. For example, if 23 is generated 20,234 times, then numbers[23] eventually has the value 20,234. Each cell of numbers is used as a counter. If number[i] is the number of times that i appears, then

```
100* (number[i] / 1000000.0) // notice that the denominator is type double
```

gives the *percentage* of times that i appears.

To emphasize that numbers is used for counting, the program initializes each cell number[i] to 0, but the initialization is redundant because array instantiation performs this task automatically.

```
public class Roulette

{
    // generates 1,000,000 random integers (range: 0..37)
    // number[i] is the number of times i is generated
    // program displays the percentage of times each value is generated

    public static void main(String[] args)
    {
        int spin;                  // holds a random integer in the range 0..37; 37 denotes 00
        int [] numbers;            // array declaration
        numbers = new int[38];     // array instantiation, 38 numbers on the board

        //initialize each storage location numbers [i] to 0 ( actually done when array is created)

        for (int i = 0; i < 38; i++)
            numbers[i] = 0;

        for (int i = 0; i <= 1000000; i++)
        {
            spin = (int)(38 * Math.random());   // a random int 0..37
            numbers[spin]++;                    // e.g., if spin is 23 then increment numbers[23]
        }

        // 37 represents the roulette value "double zero"
        System.out.println("Number Percent");
        System.out.println("00    "+ 100 * (numbers[37] / 1000000.0) ); // convert to percent

        for (int i = 0; i < 37; i++) // 0 to 36
            System.out.println(i + "    "+ 100 * ( numbers[i] / 1000000.0)); // convert to percent
        System.out.println();
    }
}
```

Even a cursory glance at the following output should convince doubting Sam that Java's Math.random() function works pretty well.

Output

Number	Percent
00	2.6341
0	2.6586
1	2.6281
2	2.6418
3	2.6275
4	2.6333
5	2.622
6	2.646
7	2.6187
8	2.6177
9	2.646
10	2.6352
11	2.6234
12	2.6433
13	2.6044
14	2.6303
15	2.6116
16	2.6385
17	2.665
18	2.6389
19	2.6328
20	2.6136
21	2.6323
22	2.6704
23	2.6318
24	2.6247
25	2.6108
26	2.6288
27	2.6227
28	2.6165
29	2.6231
30	2.6313
31	2.6492
32	2.6249
33	2.6556
34	2.6308
35	2.6065
36	2.6299

Discussion The program uses the indexed array locations numbers[0], numbers[1], and so on, no differently than a program might use ordinary variables. For instance, on line 14, numbers[i] appears in an assignment statement; on line 18 the increment operator is applied to numbers[spin]; and on lines 22 and 24 numbers[i] is part of a simple arithmetic expression. The array numbers provides 38 easily accessible and very convenient variables.

Of course, you *could* write a rather cumbersome program to accomplish the same task without using an array. But such a program would not be very pretty. Indeed, you might first declare *38 different variables* (!) to serve as counters:

```
numZero = 0; numOne = 0; numTwo = 0; numThree = 0; numFour = 0; . . .;
numThirtyEight = 0;
```

Then, perhaps, you would include a rather extensive and tedious if-else or a switch statement:

```
if (spin == 0)
        numZero++
else if (spin == 1)
        numOne++;
else if (spin == 2)
        numTwo++;
else if (spin == 3)
        numThree++;
etc.
```

These code segments should be enough to convince you that an array is really a "necessary convenience."

7.4 ARRAY INITIALIZATION

As previously stated, when an array is instantiated, all the storage locations are automatically initialized to the "zero value" of the declared data type. For example, the code segment

```
double x[] = new double[3];
for int(i = 0; i < 3; i++)
        System.out.println(x[i]);
```

displays

```
0.0
0.0
0.0
```

as output. Of course, these initial values are usually just "placeholders" for values that an application ultimately stores in an array.

Java provides a second convenient form of array initialization. The following code segment declares and explicitly initializes an array of characters.

```
char letters[] = {'a', 'b', 'c'};
```

Instantiation is implicit here; the new operator is not explicitly used. The preceding declaration and initialization of letters is equivalent to:

```
char letters[] ;
letters = new char[3];
letters[0] = 'a';
letters[1] = 'b';
letters[2] = 'c';
```

Similarly, the following declaration/instantiation/initialization

```
int squares = {0, 1, 4, 9, 16, 25, 36, 49, 64, 81, 100};
```

is shorthand for

```
int squares = new int[10];
for (int i = 0; i < 11; i++ )
        squares[i] = i*i;
```

Clearly, this explicit method of array initialization is convenient only when the size of the array is not particularly large. In most circumstances, initialization is performed using a loop.

7.5 A CAVEAT: USING THE = AND THE == OPERATORS

7.5.1 The = Operator

The assignment operator (=) can be used with array references, but such use can lead to some unexpected results and subtle bugs.

The code segment

```
int a = 5;
int b = 0;
b = a;
a = 100;
System.out.println(" a is " + a + " and b is " + b);
```

produces the output

```
a is 100 and b is 5.
```

There is no surprise here. Now, look at a similar segment that makes assignments to array variables.

```
1. int [] a = {5, 4, 3, 2, 1};
2. int [] b = new int[5]; // initialized to 0's
3. b = a;
4. a[0] = 100;
5. System.out.println(" a[0] is " + a[0] + " and b[0] is " + b[0]);
```

Can you determine the output? In this case, the segment displays

```
a[0] is 100 and b[0] is 100
```

That's right; *both* a[0] and b[0] are 100. Let's see why this happens.

Recall that a and b are both *references*, that is, a and b each holds a single address. Figure 7.9 shows the effect of lines 1 and 2.

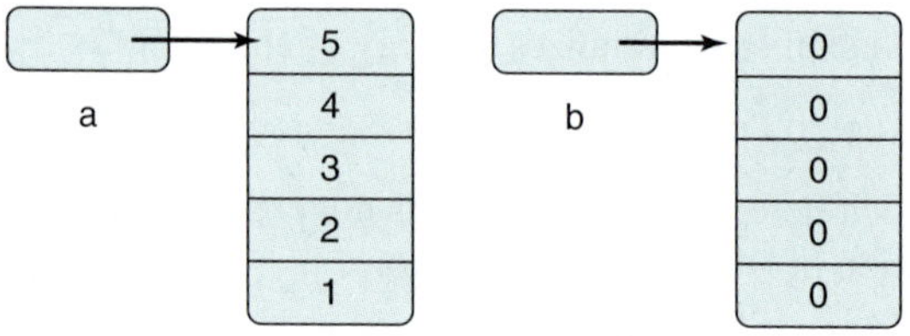

FIGURE 7.9 The arrays *a* and *b* are instantiated and initialized

The assignment on line 3 (b = a) assigns the *reference* a to b. So, after line 3 executes, a and b refer to the same block of memory and, moreover, the memory originally referenced by b is no longer accessible. See Figure 7.10.

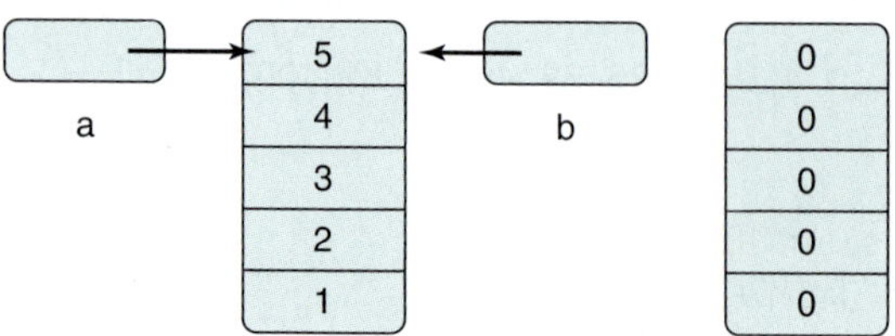

FIGURE 7.10 After the assignment *b* = *a*

Consequently, as seen in Figure 7.11, the assignment on line 5 (a[0] = 100) affects not only a[0] but also b[0], since a and b both reference the same memory.

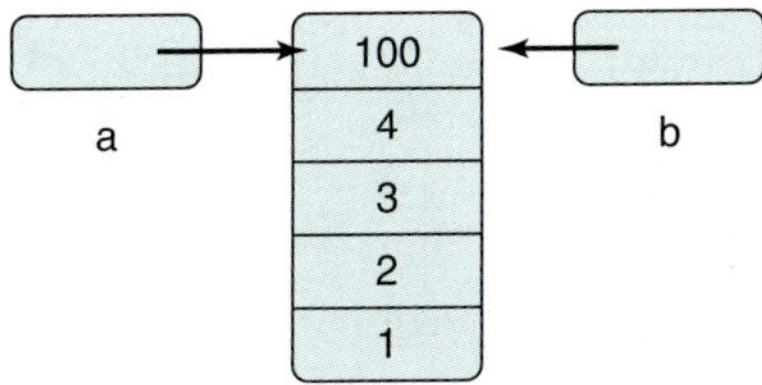

FIGURE 7.11 After executing *a*[0] = 100

After the segment executes the assignment b = a, the references a and b both refer to the same memory, and any changes to a[i] affect b[i]. There are two references to the data but just one copy of the data. Two names refer to the same block.

How do we copy the values in one array to another? To copy one array to another, use a loop:

```
int[] a ={5, 4, 3, 2, 1};
int[] b = new int[a.length]   // be sure to instantiate b

for (int i = 0; i < a.length; i++) // copy each a[i] to b[i]
        b[i] = a[i];

a[0] = 100;
System.out.println(" a[0] is "+ a[0]+ " and b[0] is "+ b[0]);
```

The output of this segment is

```
a[0] is 100 and b[0] is 5.
```

Figure 7.12 shows the effect of this code segment.

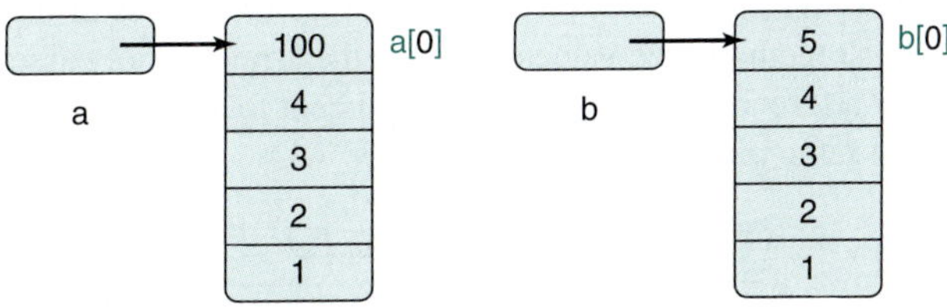

FIGURE 7.12 Copying an array using a loop

7.5.2 The == Operator

Like the assignment operator, the == operator can also be applied to arrays. As you might suspect, a == b returns true if and only if the *references* stored in a and b are identical.

> The == operator does not compare the *contents* of the arrays; the == operator compares references.

For example, consider the following statements:

```
int[] a = {5, 4 ,3, 2, 1};
int[] b = {5, 4, 3, 2, 1};
int[] c = a;
```

Although the *values* of a[i], b[i], and c[i] are the same for each index i, the expression a == b is false because a and b hold different *references*; on the other hand, a == c evaluates to true. See Figure 7.13.

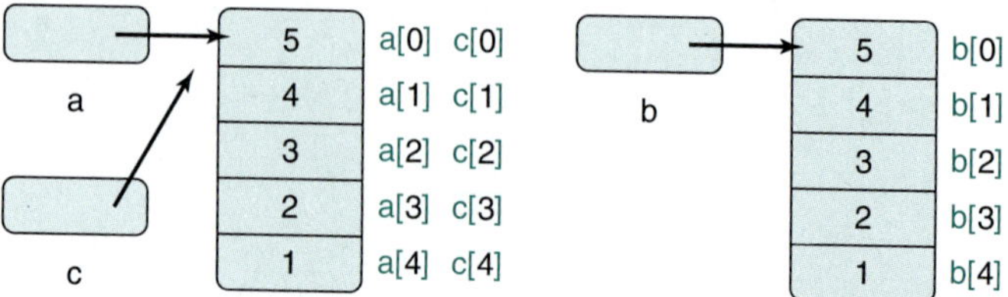

FIGURE 7.13 Comparing array references

To compare two equal-length arrays, a and b, for equality of contents, use a loop:

```
boolean sameData = true;    // sameData is set to false if a[i] != b[i] for any index i
for (int i = 0; i < a.length); i++)
    if (b[i] != a[i])
    {
        sameData = false ;    // arrays differ at index i
        break;
    }
```

7.6 ARRAYS AND METHODS

Not surprisingly, an array can be passed as a parameter to a method. Or, more precisely, it is the array reference that is passed, not the values.

An array *reference* can be passed as a parameter to a method.

When an array is passed to a method, only the reference or address of the array is copied to the parameter of the method. The values stored in the array are not passed or copied. For example, if an array reference x is passed as an argument to a parameter data, then both x and data refer to the same memory block. See Figure 7.14.

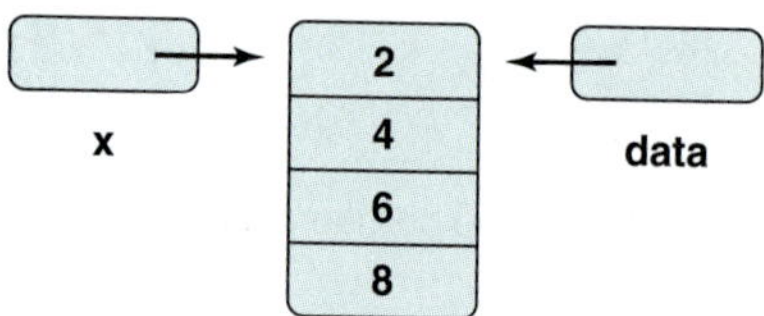

FIGURE 7.14 Both argument *x* and parameter *data* refer to the same array

Because the array of Figure 7.14 is referenced by both x and data, an assignment such as data[0] = 200 has the same effect as x[0] = 200. For example, consider the following segment:

```
public static void changeMe(int[] data)
{
    data[0] = 200;
    data[1] = 400;
}
public static void main(String [] arga)
```

```
{
    int x[] = {2, 4, 6, 8};
    changeMe(x);
    System.out.print("x now has values "+ x[0] + "   " + x[1] + "   "+ x[2]+ "   " + x[3]);
}
```

Initially, x refers to an array as shown in Figure 7.14. When x is passed as an argument to changeMe(int[] data)

- the *address* that is stored in x is passed to data;
- data and x refer to the same block of memory;
- the method changeMe(...) assigns new values (200 and 400) to data[0] and data[1] and consequently to x[0] and x[1];
- when the changeMe(...) returns, the final print(..) statement displays:

    x now has values 200 400 6 8

This technique of passing an array reference allows a method to alter the contents of an array. Example 7.3 demonstrates a method that swaps or interchanges two values in an array.

EXAMPLE 7.3

Problem Statement Write a method

    void swap(int [] x, int i, int j)

that accepts three parameters:

- an array reference x, and
- two array indices i and j

and interchanges the contents of x[i] and x[j]. Embed the method in a program.

Java Solution

```
public class Swap
{
    public static void swap( int[] x, int i, int j)
    {
        // swaps x[i] and x[j]
        int temp = x[i];
        x[i] = x[j];
        x[j] = temp;
    }
    public static void main(String[] args)
    {
        int []list = {1, 3, 5, 7, 9}; // array declaration and initialization
        System.out.print("Before: ");
        for (int i = 0; i < list.length; i++)
            System.out.print(list[i] + "   ");

        swap(list, 2, 4); // swap list[2] and list[4]

        System.out.println();
        System.out.print("After: ");
        for (int i = 0; i < list.length; i++)
            System.out.print(list[i] + "   ");
    }
}
```

Output

Before: 1 3 **5** 7 **9**
After: 1 3 **9** 7 **5**

Discussion The method call on line 16

```
swap(list, 2, 4)
```

passes the *reference* list to the parameter x. Thus list and x refer to the same array.

Let's take a closer look at the program to understand how the method handles an array. We begin with line 12.

Line 12: int[] list = {1, 3, 5, 7, 9}
Array variable list is declared, instantiated, and initialized. See Figure 7.15.

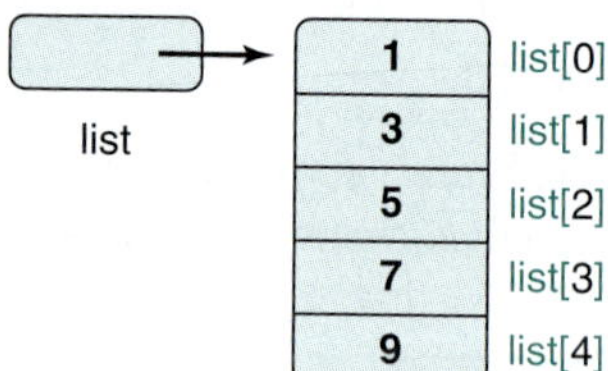

FIGURE 7.15 The array referenced by *list*

Line 16: swap(list, 2, 4)
Method swap(...) is invoked with three arguments. The argument list, a reference, is passed to parameter x so that list and x hold the same address. Also, the values 2 and 4 are passed to parameters i and j. Figure 7.16 shows that just one copy of the array exists, but two different variables (list and x) refer to the array. In main(...), the array is referenced by list and in swap(...), it is referenced by x.

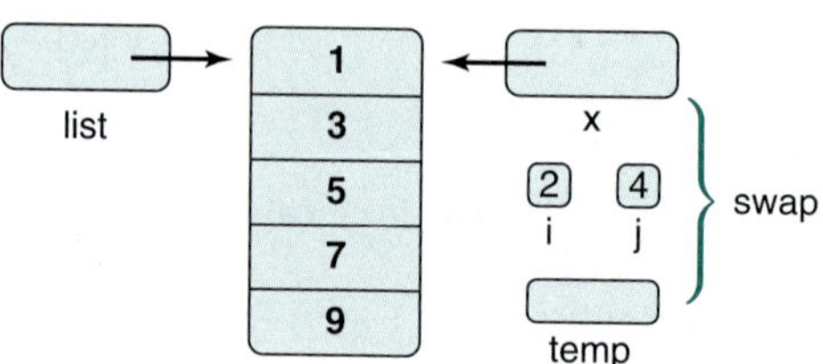

FIGURE 7.16 One array is referenced by *list* and *x*

Program control now passes to swap(...).

Line 6: temp = x[i]
The assignment temp = x[i] stores the value of x[2] (it is 5) in variable temp. See Figure 7.17.

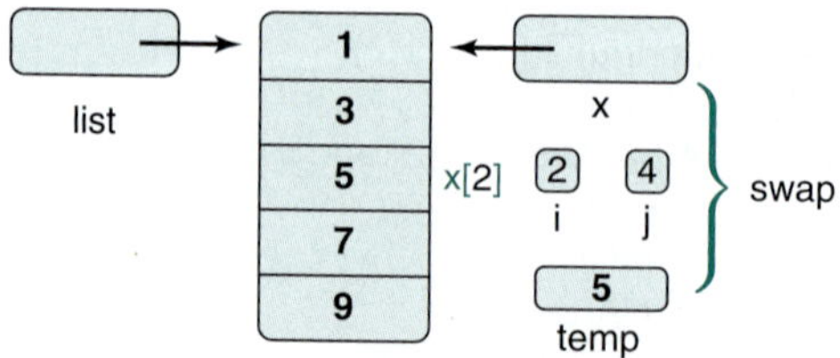

FIGURE 7.17 temp = x[i]

Line 7: x.[i] = x[j]
Since i has the value 2, and j has the value 4, line 7 can be read as x[2] = x[4]. See Figure 7.18.

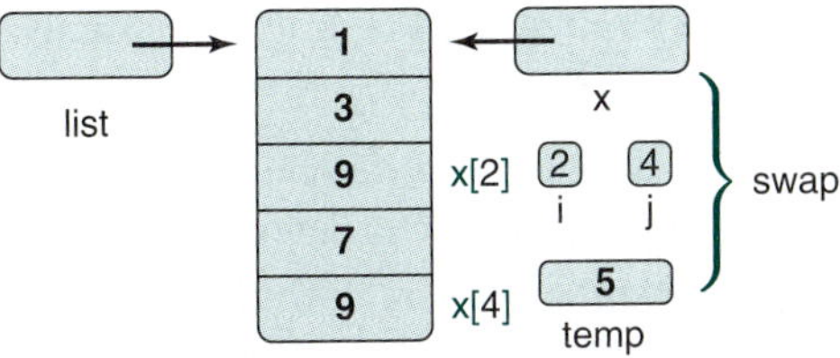

FIGURE 7.18 x[i] = x[j]

Line 7: x[j] = temp

Because j equals 4, this assignment statement places the value of temp into x[4]. See Figure 7.19.

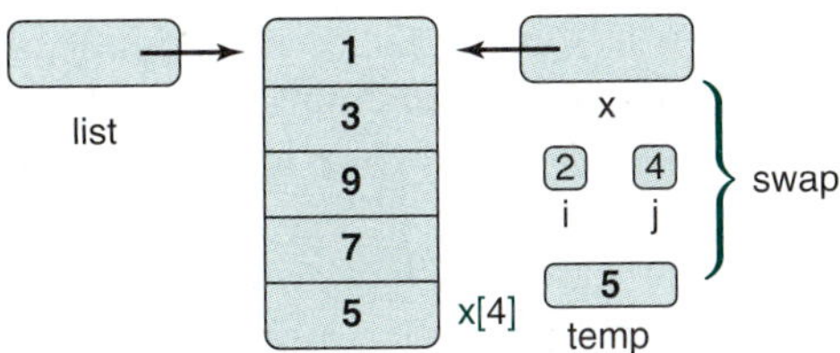

FIGURE 7.19 x[j] = temp

The method exits, and program control passes back to the caller at line 17.

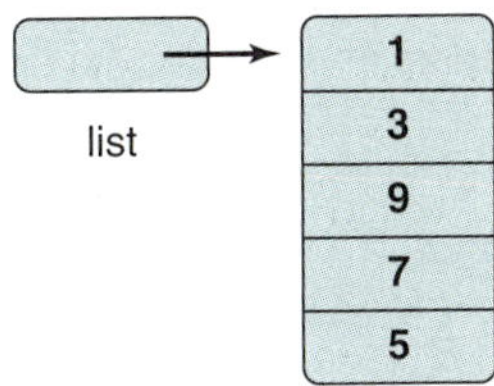

FIGURE 7.20 After the call to *swap*

Figure 7.20 shows the array rearranged as [1 3 9 7 5]. The swap(...) method changed the *contents* of the array but not the *reference* to the array.

7.7 SORTING AN ARRAY WITH INSERTION SORT

Sorting a list is a problem that is fundamental to computer science—indeed, sorting algorithms abound. From dozens of sorting algorithms, we choose *insertion sort* as a first example because it is simple, easy to program, and easy to understand. Insertion sort works the way most people arrange a hand of playing cards. The cards are examined from left to right. A sorted group of all the cards already examined is kept on the left, and a new card is inserted into the sorted group at its correct position within the group.

7.7.1 The Insertion Method

The heart of this sort is the insertion process, which we now describe. Rather than a hand of cards, consider an array of integers:

[2 3 5 9 4]

Assume that this particular arrangement occurs after the first four elements have already been examined. Notice that the first four values in the array are ordered lowest to highest.

Now, the last element must be inserted into the sorted group at its correct position. To place this number (4) into its proper position:

- Copy the value in the last position (4) to a temporary variable, temp, so that the value is "safe." That is, the value is put aside for safekeeping.
- Compare 4 to 9, the element in the last position of the sorted sub-array. Since 9 is larger, 4 precedes 9 in the sorted array, so shift (copy) 9 one position to the right:

  [2 3 5 9 4]→ [2 3 5 9 **9**]. We did not "lose" the 4; it is stored in temp.

- Compare 4 to 5. Since 5 is the larger number, shift 5 one position to the right:

  [2 3 5 9 9]→ [2 3 5 **5** 9]

- Compare 4 to 3. Since 3 is less than 4, the correct position of 4 has been found. Now, place 4, which has been saved in temp, in the position immediately following 3 and stop. The value 4 now sits in its correct place following 3 and preceding 5:

  [2 3 5 5 9]→ [2 3 **4** 5 9]

This process is illustrated in Figure 7.21.

temp [4]	Copy 4 into a temporary variable.		
2 3 5 9 4 (↑ at 9)	9 > 4? x[3] > temp?	Yes. Yes.	Shift 9 to the right. x[4] = x [3]
2 3 5 9 9 (↑ at 5)	5 > 4? x[2] > temp?	Yes. Yes.	Shift 5 to the right. x[3] = x [2]
2 3 5 5 9 (↑ at 3)	3 > 4? x[1] > temp? Stop.	No. No.	Place **4** in the position following 3. x[2] = temp
2 3 4 5 9			

FIGURE 7.21 Insert a number into its correct position within a sorted list

This insertion process can be implemented as a void method

void insert(int[] x, int i)

that places the ith value of x into its proper position among the *sorted* values x[0], x[1], . . . x[i−1], shifting numbers to the right if necessary. The method operates as follows:

```
copy x[i] into a temporary variable, temp.
initialize a counter j to i – 1, the largest index of the sorted sub-array.
        while (j >= 0 and temp < x[j])
         copy x[j] to x[j + 1] and decrement j // shift.
copy temp to x[j + 1].
```

7.7.2 Putting the Insertion Method to Work

To sort an array of n elements, insertion sort invokes the insert(...) method $n - 1$ times, incrementally building sorted sub-arrays (x[0] x[1]) , then (x[0] x[1] x[2]), then (x[0] x[1] x[2] x[3])... and finally (x[0] x[1] x[2] x[3] ... x[n – 1]). Figure 7.22 shows an array of five elements after four successive calls to insert(...).

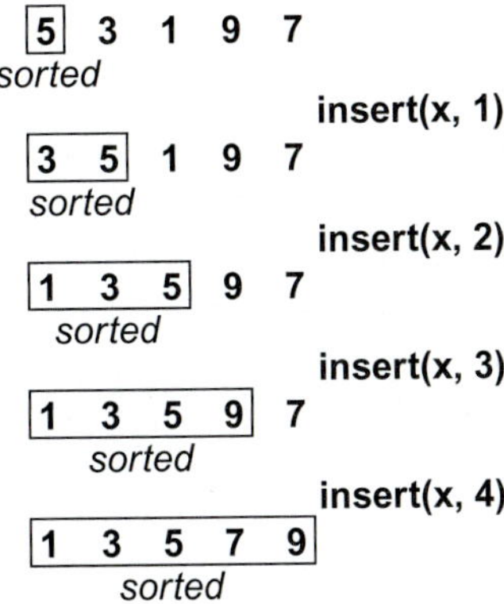

FIGURE 7.22 Insertion sort calls *insert* $n - 1$ times

EXAMPLE 7.4

Problem Statement Implement insertion sort. Include a main(...) method that queries a user for the number of data followed by the data elements.

Java Solution The following implementation of insertion sort includes two methods:

void insert(int x[], int i),

which places element x[i] in its correct position among the sorted elements x[0]...x[i−1], and

void insertionsort(int []x, int n),

which invokes insert(...) $n - 1$ times, where n is the number of elements stored in array x. Notice that x can hold up to 1000 integers. That is, the array may be partially filled.

```
import java.util.*;
public class Insertionsort
{
    public static void insert(int[] x, int i)
    {
    // place x[i] in its proper place among sorted values x[0], x[1]...x[i–1]
            int temp = x[i];              // save the value
            int j = i – 1;
            while ( j >= 0 && temp <x[j]) // determine where to place temp
            {
                x[j + 1] = x[j];          // shift right
                j––;
            }
            x[j + 1]= temp;               // place temp (x[i]) in its correct position
    }

    public static void insertionsort(int[] x, int n)
    {                                     // n is the number of data stored in array x
         for (int i = 1; i < n; i++)
                insert(x, i);
    }

    public static void main(String[] args)
    {
       Scanner input = new Scanner(System.in);
       int []numbers = new int[1000];     // array can hold up to 1000 integers
       int size;                          // number of integers that are actually stored
       System.out.print("Enter the number of data: ");
       size = input.nextInt();
       System.out.print("Enter " + size + " integers: ");
```

```
        // Read the data
        for (int i = 0; i < size; i++)
            numbers[i] = input.nextInt();
        System.out.println();

        insertionsort(numbers,size);

        System.out.print("Sorted: ");
        for (int i = 0; i < size; i++)
            System.out.print(numbers[i] + "  ");
        System.out.println();
    }
}
```

Output (from Two Executions)

Enter the number of data: **9**
Enter 9 integers: **1 4 3 7 2 8 6 9 5**
Sorted: 1 2 3 4 5 6 7 8 9

Enter the number of data: **5**
Enter 9 integers: **1 4 3 2 5**
Sorted: 1 2 3 4 5

Discussion Although the array was dimensioned to hold 1000 integers, just nine locations are used in the first execution and five in the second. In each case the array is partially filled. The number of elements that must be sorted is size, and not x.length.

Dozens of sorting algorithms exist, but not every sort is created equal. An assessment of a sorting routine is often based on the number of comparisons that the procedure performs. The number of comparisons, of course, depends on the number of data. For a data set of size n, insertion sort performs at most $\frac{1}{2}(n^2 - n)$ comparisons. On the other hand, if the data are already sorted, insertion sort makes just $n - 1$ comparisons. That's a nice feature but not nice enough to make up for some very slow sorting in other cases. Let's look at some worst-case figures for insertion sort:

n	**Number of comparisons**
100	4,950
200	19,900
400	79,800
800	319,600
1600	1,279,200

Notice that as the size of the data doubles, the number of comparisons approximately quadruples. Although insertion sort is easy to code and performs satisfactorily for small data sets, other methods are much more efficient for large amounts of data. Quicksort, heapsort, and merge sort are just a few of the sorting algorithms that, while a bit more complicated, perform much more efficiently.

7.8 SEARCHING AN ARRAY

Along with sorting data, searching data for a particular item is another fundamental operation. The item of interest, be it a social security number, a name, or a film title, is called the *key*.

7.8.1 Linear Search

The obvious method of searching an array, x, is the *linear search*. Beginning with x[0], a linear search successively compares key to each item in the array:

Does key == x[0]?
Does key == x[1]?
Does key == x[2]? etc.

If key matches x[i] for some index i, the search terminates and returns array index i, the index of the cell of the array where key resides. If key is not found in the array, the search returns −1 or some other value indicating a failure to locate key. Example 7.5 implements and uses a linear search.

EXAMPLE 7.5

Problem Statement Write a program that exercises and improves your memory. Your program should display an unsorted list of as many as 25 numbers in the range 1 through 1000. After carefully studying the numbers and when you believe that you have them memorized, type 1. This action should make the list scroll off the screen and out of view. Next, enter all the numbers that you can recall, not necessarily in any order. The program scores your response and tells you exactly how many numbers you correctly remembered. The program should prompt for the size of the list.

Java Solution

```
import java.util.*;
public class MemoryExerciser
{
    // Linear Search
    public static int search(int[] x, int n, int key)
    {
        // returns the position of key in x
        // if key is not found returns −1
        // the array x may be partially filled; n is the number of data in x

        for ( int i = 0; i < n; i++)
            if (key == x[i])                        // key is found
                return i;                           // return the index
        return −1;                                  // key is not found
    }

    public static void makeList(int [] list, int size)
    {
            // inserts size unique random numbers into the array, list
        int count = 0;
        while (count < size)
        {
            int number = (int)(1000*Math.random() + 1);
            if ( search(list, count, number) == −1)  // if number is not already on the list
            {
                list[count] = number;                // add number to the list
                count++;
            }
```

```
        }
    }
    public static int checkAnswers(int[] numbers, int size)
    {
        // returns the number of correct answers

        Scanner input = new Scanner(System.in);
        int numCorrect = 0;
        System.out.println("Enter "+ size + " numbers in the range 1–1000");

        for (int i = 1; i <= size; i++)                 // read and check answers
        {
            int answer = input.nextInt();
            if (search(numbers,size,answer) != –1 )     // if answer is on the list
                numCorrect++;
        }
        return numCorrect;
    }

    public static void main(String[] args)
    {
        Scanner input = new Scanner(System.in);
        int []numbers = new int[25];                    // array holds up to 25 integers
        int size;                                       // number of integers on the list

        System.out.print("How many numbers (up to 25) would you like to see? ");
        size = input.nextInt();
        if (size > 25)
            size = 25;                                  // 25 is the maximum number

        makeList(numbers, size);                        // construct list of random numbers

        for (int i = 0; i < size; i++)                  // display the contents of numbers
            System.out.println(numbers[i]);

        System.out.print("Now, type 1 to hide the numbers ");
        int resume = input.nextInt();        // pause until user types 1
        for (int i = 1; i < 100; i++)
            System.out.println();            // scroll the numbers off the screen
        System.out.print("Score: " + checkAnswers(numbers, size) + " correct answers");
    }
}
```

Output

How many numbers (up to 25) would you like to see? **10**
915
359
774
166
448
427
663
81
99
998
Now, type 1 to hide the numbers **1**

(The preceding numbers have scrolled out of view.)

Enter 10 numbers in the range 1–1000
345
774

81
678
448
99
127
359
568
366
You correctly identified 5 numbers on the list

Discussion The program uses a linear search in two places:

- When creating the list of random numbers, each time that a random number is generated, a search is performed on the list to ensure that the number is not already present in the list (lines 22–26). If that is the case, the number is added to the list.
- The list is searched for each number entered by the user (lines 35–40).

The linear search method (lines 5 through 14) is very simple. If key is found in the array, the method exits and returns the index of key. If the for loop runs to completion, then key is not on the list and the method returns –1.

A linear search is easy to implement and easy to understand. However, a linear search is not particularly efficient. To determine that a key is *not* in an array, a linear search examines *every* location. Well, if the size of an array is 1,000,000, or worse 10,000,000, that's quite a lot of work. Indeed, on average, a successful linear search checks *n*/2 locations, where *n* is the size of the array.

7.8.2 Binary Search

A search routine that performs much better than linear search is *binary search*. However, there is one very important prerequisite.

Binary search requires that the array be sorted.

To search an array x for key, binary search first compares key to the item situated in the middle of the array, say x[mid].

- If key equals x[mid], the search ends successfully.
- If key < x[mid], then x[mid] and all elements greater than x[mid] are eliminated from the search.
- If key > x[mid], then x[mid] and all items less than x[mid] can be eliminated.

Thus after examining a single location, half of the data in the array can be eliminated from the search.

Binary search repeats this process on the part of the array that has not yet been eliminated until the key is located or there are no more items to examine.

Let's consider a numerical example. Consider a search for the key 27 in the sorted array

[3 5 6 9 11 23 25 26 27 29 33 35 36 37 39 42 45 46 48 58 62 67 70].

Binary search first compares 27 to the middle item of the array, which is 35. Because 27 is less than 35 *and the array is sorted*, the "sub-array" [35 36 37 39 42 45 46 48 58 62 67 70] can be eliminated from any further searching. If 27 is indeed on the list, then 27 must be situated in the sub-array [3 5 6 9 11 23 25 26 27 29 33]. See Figure 7.23.

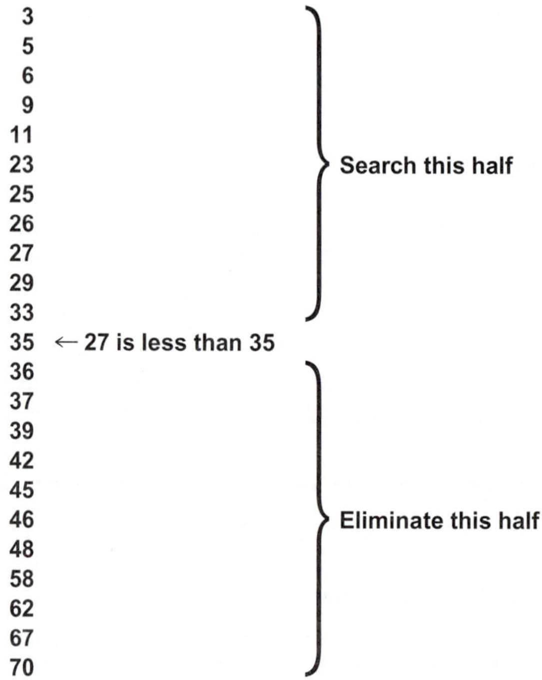

FIGURE 7.23 After one comparison, half the array is eliminated

Next, as Figure 7.24 indicates, binary search compares the key (27) to the middle element of this sub-array:

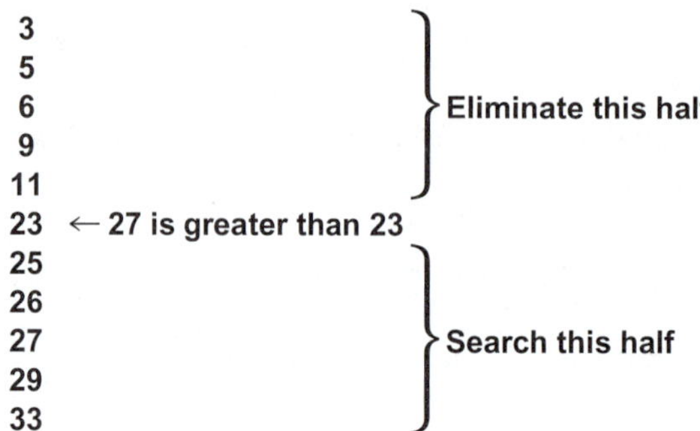

FIGURE 7.24 Binary search after two comparisons

Since 27 is greater than the middle element (23), binary search now searches those values greater than 23. See Figure 7.25.

25
26
27 ← 27 is found
29
33

FIGURE 7.25 The key is found

The key value 27 is located after examining just three locations. A linear search examines eight locations, almost three times as many.

The following Java method implements binary search. The local variables lo and hi hold the lowest and highest indices of the sub-array currently under consideration; mid is the index of the item halfway between x[lo] and x[hi]. Initially, for an array of size n, lo = 0 and hi = $n - 1$.

```
1.  public static int search(int[] x , int n, int key)

2.  // x is a sorted array of n integers; key has an integer value
3.  // x is sorted in ascending order;

4.  {
5.     int lo = 0;                  // lowest index of the array
6.     int hi = n–1;                // highest index
7.     int mid;                     // middle index

8.     while (hi >= lo)
9.     {
10.       mid = (hi + lo) / 2;      // get the middle index
11.       if (key == x[mid])
12.          return mid;            // key found --exit
13.       if (key < x[mid])
14.          hi = mid – 1;          // eliminate x[mid] thru x[hi]
15.       else
16.          lo = mid + 1;          // eliminate x[lo] thru x[mid]
17.    }
18.    return –1;                   // key not found
19. }
```

Using the previous array of 23 integers and the key 27, the loop of the binary search (lines 8–17) executes three times before the key is located. On each iteration, if the key is not found, either hi or lo is adjusted. Figure 7.26 shows each iteration.

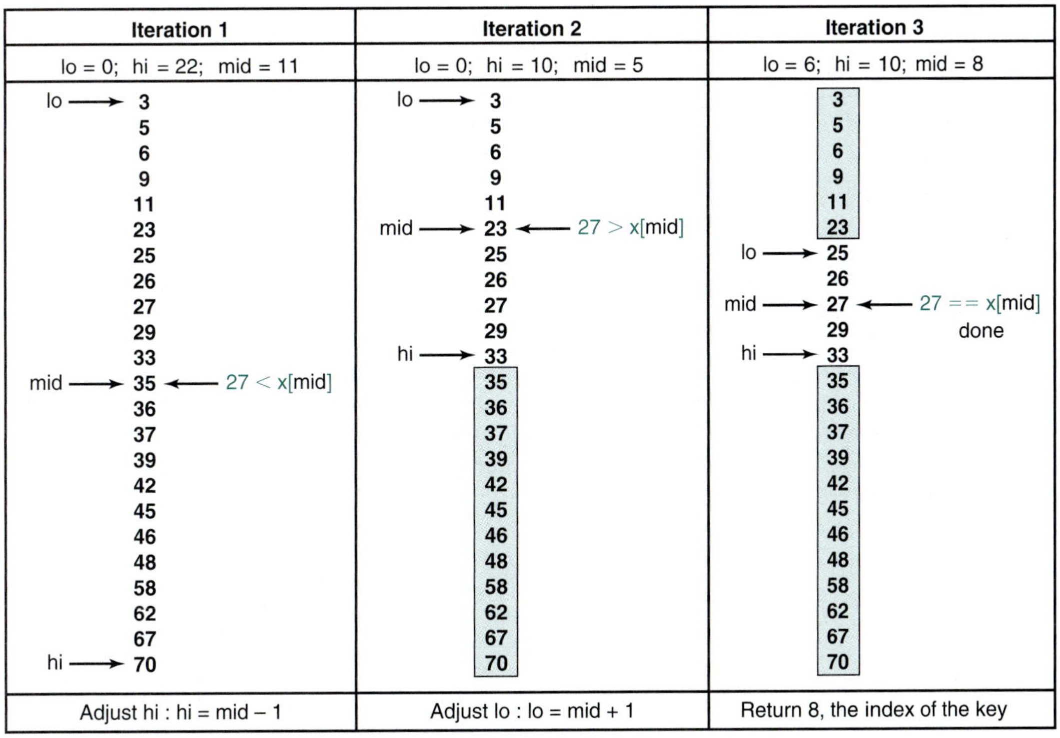

Iteration 1	Iteration 2	Iteration 3
lo = 0; hi = 22; mid = 11	lo = 0; hi = 10; mid = 5	lo = 6; hi = 10; mid = 8
lo → **3**	lo → **3**	**3**
5	**5**	**5**
6	**6**	**6**
9	**9**	**9**
11	**11**	**11**
23	mid → **23** ← 27 > x[mid]	**23**
25	**25**	lo → **25**
26	**26**	**26**
27	**27**	mid → **27** ← 27 == x[mid] done
29	**29**	**29**
33	hi → **33**	hi → **33**
mid → **35** ← 27 < x[mid]	**35**	**35**
36	**36**	**36**
37	**37**	**37**
39	**39**	**39**
42	**42**	**42**
45	**45**	**45**
46	**46**	**46**
48	**48**	**48**
58	**58**	**58**
62	**62**	**62**
67	**67**	**67**
hi → **70**	**70**	**70**
Adjust hi : hi = mid – 1	Adjust lo : lo = mid + 1	Return 8, the index of the key

FIGURE 7.26 Binary search in action. Highlighted block are eliminated from the search

In the event of an unsuccessful search, the condition of the while loop (line 8) eventually evaluates to false and the method returns −1 (line 18). As an exercise, you should trace through a few unsuccessful searches to convince yourself that the boolean condition on line 8 does, in fact, eventually return false and that no infinite loop can occur.

We've already mentioned that for a list of *n* items, linear search, on average, examines *n/*2 locations. In contrast, binary search checks only about $log_2 n - 1$ locations. That's quite a difference as the following data demonstrate:

n	***n*/2 (linear search)**	**$\log_2 n - 1$ (binary search)**
$2^{10} = 1024$	512	9
$2^{15} = 32768$	16384	14
$2^{20} = 1048576$	524288	19
$2^{25} = 33554432$	16777216	24

The statistics are quite impressive. From a directory of more than 1,000,000 names, binary search can find a specific name, on average, by examining just 19 entries. Compare this to the 500,000 entries that linear search is expected to examine.

7.9 TWO-DIMENSIONAL ARRAYS

To this point, we have used arrays to store one-dimensional lists. A *two-dimensional array* holds tabular data. For example, the following table, which shows the growth of a single dollar investment after several years and at various interest rates, can be stored in a two-dimensional array.

	1%	**2%**	**3%**	**4%**	**5%**	**6%**
10 years	1.10	1.22	1.34	1.48	1.63	1.79
15 years	1.16	1.35	1.56	1.80	2.08	2.40
20 years	1.22	1.49	1.81	2.19	2.65	3.21
25 years	1.28	1.64	2.09	2.67	3.39	4.29
30 years	1.35	1.81	2.43	3.24	4.32	5.74

Similarly, you might use a two-dimensional array to store a tic-tac-toe board, a chess configuration, or a Sudoku puzzle.

The values stored in a two-dimensional array, like its one-dimensional cousin, must all be of the same data type.

You can conceptualize a two-dimensional array as a table or grid. Each storage cell in the table is uniquely identified by its row and by its column. The rows and columns of a two-dimensional array are indexed starting at 0. The 4 × 3 (read 4 by 3) array in Figure 7.27 has 4 rows and 3 columns. The rows are numbered 0, 1, 2, 3 and the columns 0, 1, 2. The cell marked "X" resides in row 3, column 1:

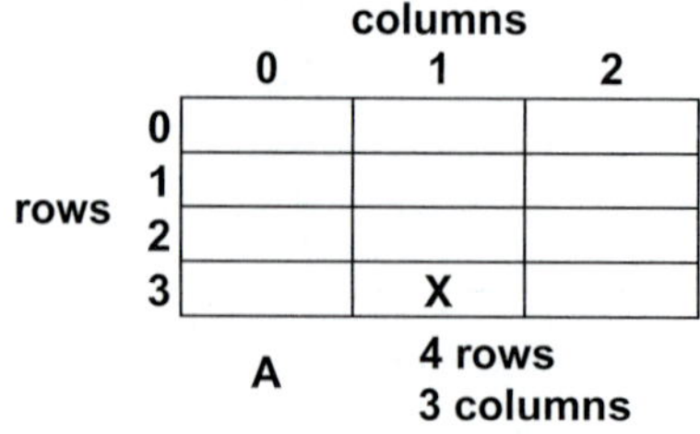

FIGURE 7.27 A two-dimensional array

Similarly, Figure 7.28 shows a 2 × 2 array B with rows and columns indexed 0 and 1 and a 3 × 2 array C.

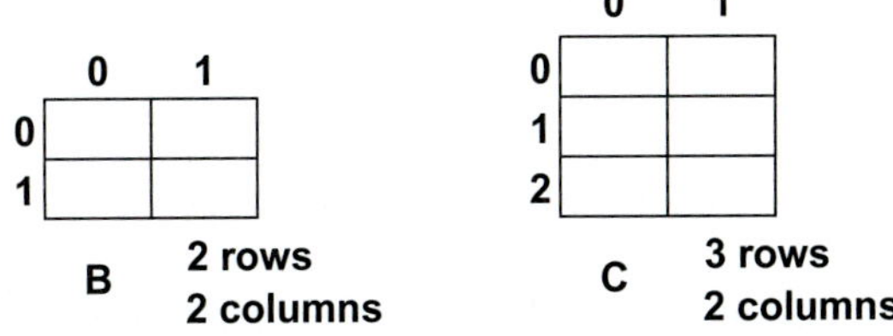

FIGURE 7.28 A 2 × 2 array and a 3 × 2 array

Each cell in a two-dimensional array can be accessed using its row and column number. If A is a two-dimensional array, then cell A[i][j] is the cell of row i and column j. For example, A[1][2] is the cell of row 1 and column 2 and *A*[0][0] is the cell in the upper left corner of the array. Figure 7.29 names each cell of array A.

columns

rows	0	1	2
0	A[0][0]	A[0][1]	A[0][2]
1	A[1][0]	A[1][1]	A[1][2]
2	A[2][0]	A[2][1]	A[2][2]
3	A[3][0]	A[3][1]	A[3][2]

A

FIGURE 7.29 Each cell can be accessed with two indices

7.9.1 Declaring and Instantiating Two-Dimensional Arrays

A two-dimensional array declaration is similar to its one-dimensional counterpart. In both cases, the array name denotes a reference variable. The statement

```
int[][] table;   // or equivalently int table[][];
```

declares table as a reference to a two-dimensional array of integers.

Instantiation is also similar to one-dimensional instantiation. Two-dimensional instantiation includes the number of rows as well as the number of columns, in that order:

```
table = new int[2][3];   // table has 2 rows and 3 columns
```

As you might expect, declaration and instantiation can be done with a single statement:

```
int table = new int[2][3];
```

The new operator creates a 2 × 3 two-dimensional array with all cell values initialized to 0. See Figure 7.30.

	0	1	2
0	0	0	0
1	0	0	0

table

FIGURE 7.30 int[] table = new int[2][3];

Although it is intuitive to view a two-dimensional array as a simple table, the underlying structure is more complex.

> A two-dimensional array is actually an "array of arrays."

For example, the array table is implemented as shown in Figure 7.31.

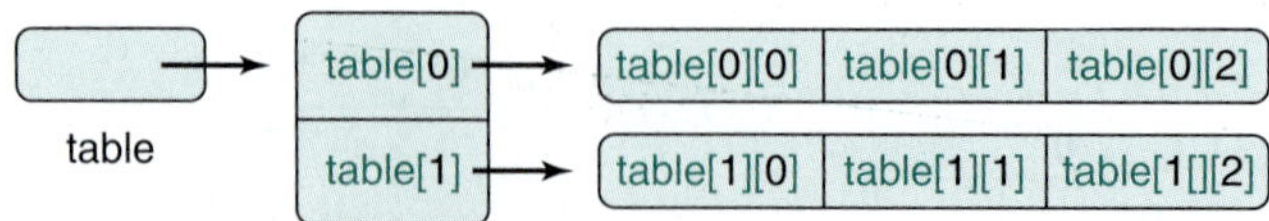

FIGURE 7.31 An array of arrays

As Figure 7.31 indicates, table, table[0], and table[1] are references. In fact, the declaration

```
int[][] table = new int[2][3];
```

is just a shortcut for

```
int[][] table = new int[2][];
table[0] = new int[3];
table[1] = new int[3];
```

Furthermore, because table, table[0], and table[1] refer to arrays,

- table.length has the value 2 (the number of rows), and
- both table[0].length and table[1].length are 3 (the number of columns).

Although a two-dimensional array is, in fact, an array of arrays, it is nonetheless helpful to conceptualize a two-dimensional array as a simple table or grid as pictured in Figure 7.32.

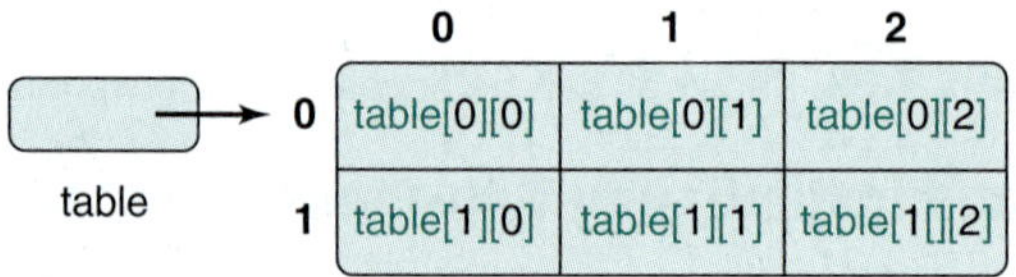

FIGURE 7.32 A two-dimensional array pictured as a table or grid

7.9.2 Processing a Two-Dimensional Array

With two indices, a two-dimensional array is usually initialized and/or processed with a nested loop. The following code snippet initializes each cell of an array with the product of its row and column numbers:

```
int A[][] = new int[3][4]; // declares and instantiates a 3 × 4 array

for (int row = 0; row < 3; row++)  // for each row
   for (int col = 0; col < 4; col++) // for each column
      A[row] [col] = row*col;
```

The loops work as follows:

row = 0	col = 0	A[0][0] = 0
	col = 1	A[0][1] = 0
	col = 2	A[0][2] = 0
	col = 3	A[0][3] = 0
row = 1	col = 0	A[1][0] = 0
	col = 1	A[1][1] = 1
	col = 2	A[1][2] = 2
	col = 3	A[1][3] = 3

```
row = 2     col = 0     A[2][0] = 0
            col = 1     A[2][1] = 2
            col = 2     A[2][2] = 4
            col = 3     A[2][3] = 6
```

The initialized array is shown in Figure 7.33.

0	0	0	0
0	1	2	3
0	2	4	6

FIGURE 7.33 Array initialized with nested loops

Not surprisingly, a two-dimensional array can be explicitly initialized in a declaration by listing the values of each row enclosed by curly braces and separated by commas:

```
int[][] table = { {2, 4, 6} {8, 10, 12} };
```

The declaration of table creates and initializes the 2×3 array of Figure 7.34. The number of rows and the number columns are implicit in the declaration/initialization statement.

	0	**1**	**2**
0	**2**	**4**	**6**
1	**8**	**10**	**12**

table

FIGURE 7.34 An array explicitly initialized in its declaration

Finally, we mention that Java allows arrays of dimension higher than two. For example, the following segment declares and instantiates a three-dimensional array:

```
int[][][] threeD;
threeD new int[3][4][5];
for (int i = 0; i < 3; i++)
  for (int j = 0; j < 4; j++)
    for (int k = 0; k < 5; k++)
      threeD[i][j][k] = i * j * k;
```

Can you visualize this array?

As you might expect, a three-dimensional array is an array of two-dimensional arrays, and an n-dimensional array is an array of $(n - 1)$-dimensional arrays.

EXAMPLE 7.6

A *contingency table* is a two-dimensional grid often used as an aid for analyzing the relationship between two variables. For example, a researcher interested in whether or not a relationship exists between gender and music preference surveyed 1000 people with the following results:

Preferred Style of Music

	Rock	**Heavy Metal**	**Folk**	**Jazz**	**R&B**	**Pop**	**Country**	**Other**	**Total**
Males	123	145	33	34	16	71	18	42	**482**
Females	138	112	50	27	93	75	10	13	**518**
Total	**261**	**257**	**83**	**61**	**109**	**146**	**28**	**55**	**1000**

The numbers in the last column and last row are not part of the collected data. These are the row totals and the column totals. The number in the bottom right corner is the grand total, the sum of all data.

Problem Statement Write an application that

- queries a user for the number of rows and columns of a contingency table,
- reads the data, row by row, and
- displays the data in tabular form along with the row totals, column totals, and grand total.

For example, if the six data of a 2 × 3 table are

1, 3, 6, 7, 9, and 8,

the program displays these six numbers together with the appropriate totals as:

```
1  3   6  |  10
7  9   8  |  24
8  12  14 |  34
```

Here, 10 and 24 are row totals, 8, 12, and 14 the column totals, and 34 the grand total. The "|" character is used to separate the data from the row totals.

Java Solution Besides a main(...) method that queries the user for the number of rows and columns in the table, the solution utilizes three methods:

- readData(...) fills a two-dimensional array with data supplied by the user. The data is entered row by row.
- display(...) prints the table along with the row, column, and grand totals.
- getTotals(...) calculates the row totals and the column totals.

```
import java.util.*;

public class ContingencyTable
{
   public static void readData( int[][] table, int numRows, int numCols)
   {

      // reads the data for a table row by row
      // the table has rows rows and cols columns

      System.out.println("Enter data, row by row: ");
      Scanner input = new Scanner(System.in);

      // read data , row by row
      for (int row = 0; row < numRows; row++)
         for (int col = 0; col < numCols; col++)
            table[row][col] = input.nextInt();

   }

   public static void display(int table[][], int numRows, int numCols,
                                                int[] rowSums, int[] colSums)
   {
        // displays the contingency table
        // displays row and column totals and grand total

      System.out.println();
```

```
        System.out.println();
        System.out.println("Data including row and column totals: ");
        System.out.println();

        // print the table row by row
        // after printing a row, print the row total
        for(int row = 0; row < numRows; row++)              // for each row
        {
            for (int col = 0; col < numCols; col++)         // for each column
                System.out.print("    " + table[row][col] + "\t");

            System.out.println("| " + rowSums[row]);        // print the row total
        }

        System.out.println();

        int grandTotal = 0;

            // calculate the grand total from the column sums
            // print the column sums then the grand total
        for (int col = 0; col < numCols; col++)        // for each column
        {
            grandTotal += colSums[col];                 // add column sum to grandTotal
            System.out.print("    " + colSums[col] + "\t"); // print column sum
        }
        System.out.println("| " + grandTotal);
    }

    public static void getTotals(int[][] table, int numRows, int numCols,
                                    int[] rowSums, int [] colSums)
    {
        // calculates the row sums and column sums
        // get row sums
        for (int row = 0; row < numRows; row++) // for each row
            for (int col = 0; col < numCols; col++) // for each column
                rowSums[row] += table[row][col]; // add the table entry to the row sum
        // get column sums
        for (int col = 0; col < numCols; col++)     // for each column
            for (int row = 0; row < numRows; row++) // for each row
                colSums[col] += table[row][col];    // add the table entry to the column sum
    }

    public static void main(String[] args)
    {
        Scanner input = new Scanner(System.in);
        int rows, cols;             // dimensions of the table
        int[][] table;              // contingency table
        int[] rowSums;              // holds the row totals
        int colSums[];              // holds the column totals
        System.out.print("Number of rows: " );
        rows = input.nextInt();
        System.out.print("Number of columns: ");
        cols= input.nextInt();
        table = new int[rows][cols];
        rowSums = new int[rows];
        colSums = new int[cols];
        readData(table, rows, cols);
        getTotals(table, rows, cols, rowSums, colSums); // calculate the sums
        display(table, rows, cols, rowSums, colSums);
    }
}
```

Output

Number of rows: 2
Number of columns: 8
Enter data, row by row:
123 145 33 34 16 71 18 42 138 112 50 27 93 75 10 13

Data including row and column totals:

```
123  145  33  34  16   71   18  42  | 482
138  112  50  27  93   75   10  13  | 518


261  257  83  61  109  146  28  55  | 1000
```

Discussion The work of the application is done via three method calls:

- line 68: readData(table, rows, cols);
- line 69: getTotals(table, rows, cols, rowSums, colSums);
- line 70: display(table, rows, cols, rowSums, colSums);

Lines 4–14: void readData(int[][] table, int numRows, int numCols)
The nested loop on lines 11–13 iterates through the table row by row. For example, if the table has 2 rows and 3 columns, the nested loop runs through the indices of the array in the following order:

```
[0,0]  [0,1]  [0,2]  //  row = 0, col = 0,1,2
[1,0]  [1,1]  [1,2]  //  row = 1, col = 0,1,2
```

Lines 15–41: display (int table[][], int numRows, int numCols, int[] rowSums, int[] colSums)

- The nested loop on lines 25–30 iterates through the table row by row. Before incrementing the loop counter row, the method prints a separator character ('l') followed by the row total. The effect is that the data of each row is printed, followed by the separator, followed by the row total. If the table consists of two rows and three columns, printing proceeds:

  ```
  [0,0]  [0,1]  [0,2]  rowSum[0]  // row = 0, col  =  0,1,2
  [1,0]  [1,1]  [1,2]  rowSum[1]  // row = 1, col  =  0,1,2
  ```

- The single loop on lines 35–39, which iterates through the columns,
  - adds each column sum to the grand total (line 37), and
  - prints each column sum (line 38).

- The statement on line 40 prints the separator and the grand total.

Lines 42–53: void getTotals(int[][] table, int numRows, int numCols, int[] rowSums, int[] colSums)
This method calculates values stored in the two one-dimensional arrays, rowSums and colSums.

- The nested loop on lines 46–48 iterates through the table, row by row. For each row, the corresponding column value is added to the row total. If table is a 2×3 array the calculation proceeds as follows:

  Initially rowSum[0] and rowSum[1] have value 0

```
row = 0 col = 0 rowSum[0] += table[0][0]
        col = 1 rowSum[0] += table[0][1]
        col = 2 rowSum[0] += table[0][2]

row = 1 col = 0 rowSum[1] += table[1][0]
        col = 1 rowSum[1] += table[1][1]
        col = 2 rowSum[1] += table[1][2]
```

- The nested loop on lines 50–52 iterates through the table, column by column. For each column, the corresponding row value is added to the column sum. This is similar to the nested loop of lines 46–48 with row and column switching roles.

7.10 A CASE STUDY—PUTTING IT ALL TOGETHER

Our final program not only utilizes most of the concepts from Part I but also provides the legend and lore of a famous and, indeed, infamous game.

The Fifteen Puzzle, credited to master puzzle maker Sam Loyd[1], has been confounding and intriguing puzzle enthusiasts for more than one hundred years. Even today, a plastic version of the puzzle is available in most novelty shops. Figure 7.35 shows a commercial version of the game.

FIGURE 7.35 A commercial version of the 15 puzzle for ages 8 to adult

13	6	11	4
5	2	7	8
12	10	3	9
1	15	14	

FIGURE 7.36
The Fifteen Puzzle

1	2	3	4
5	6	7	8
9	10	11	12
13	14	15	

FIGURE 7.37
A solved puzzle

1	2	3	4
5	6	7	8
9	10	11	12
13	15	14	

FIGURE 7.38
Loyd's puzzle. Only 15 and 14 are initially interchanged.

The Fifteen Puzzle consists of tiles numbered 1 to 15 that are placed randomly in a frame or box as shown in Figure 7.36.

There is one empty place or blank space in the frame. Using the empty position, a player slides tiles around the frame. The object of the game is to rearrange the tiles so that the numbers are ordered as in Figure 7.37.

In 1878, Sam Loyd offered $1000 to the first person who could solve the "14–15" puzzle. In this version of the puzzle, all numbers are already in order except 14 and 15. Figure 7.38 shows Loyd's puzzle.

Sound easy? Try it.

[1]Recently, Jerry Slocum and Dic Sonneveld in their book *The 15 Puzzle* (published by Slocum Puzzle Foundation, 2006), uncovered that Sam Loyd was not the inventor of the 15 puzzle. Loyd, it turns out, stole the puzzle from Noyes Chapman, the Postmaster of Canastota, New York. Loyd was a master PR-man as well as a master puzzle maker.

Hordes of people, hungry for the prize money, became fascinated with the game. The game was as popular at the end of the 19th century as Rubik's Cube was at the end of the 20th. However, Loyd's money was safe: although some starting configurations of the Fifteen Puzzle are solvable, the "14–15" puzzle is impossible to solve—and Loyd knew it.

In spite of Loyd's little prank, there are many configurations that *are* solvable. How can you determine whether or not a solution exists for a particular configuration of the Fifteen Puzzle? Here is a method. *We assume that the blank always appears in the lower right corner.*

- Make a list of the numbers starting at the top left corner of the frame moving left to right and row by row.
- For each number on the list, count the number of *inversions*. This means, for each number *n*, count how many numbers *preceding n* are larger than *n*.
- Add up the total number of inversions.
- If the total number of inversions is even, the puzzle is solvable; otherwise it is not.

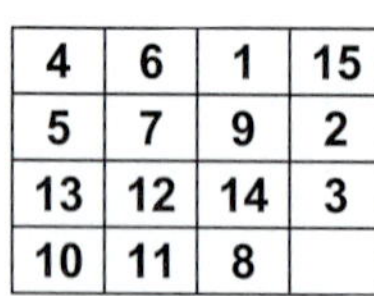

4	6	1	15
5	7	9	2
13	12	14	3
10	11	8	

FIGURE 7.39
A solvable puzzle

For example, the list formed from Loyd's "14–15" puzzle is:

1 2 3 4 5 6 7 8 9 10 11 12 13 **15** **14**

There is only one inversion (15 14). Since the total number of inversions is odd, the puzzle is unsolvable.

Now consider the puzzle with an initial configuration as in Figure 7.39. Writing the numbers, top to bottom, left to right produces the following list:

4 6 1 15 5 7 9 2 13 12 14 3 10 11 8

From this list, we count the number of inversions.

Tile Number	Number of Inversions	
4	0	
6	0	
1	2	$6 > 1, 4 > 1$
15	0	
5	2	$15 > 5, 6 > 5$
7	1	$15 > 7$
9	1	$15 > 9$
2	6	$9 > 2, 7 > 2, 5 > 2, 15 > 2, 6 > 2, 4 > 2$
13	1	$15 > 13$
12	2	$13 > 12, 15 > 12$
14	1	$15 > 14$
3	9	$14 > 3, 12 > 3, 13 > 3, 9 > 3, 7 > 3, 5 > 3, 15 > 3, 6 > 3, 4 > 3$
10	4	$14 > 10, 12 > 10, 13 > 10, 15 > 10$
11	4	$14 > 11, 12 > 11, 13 > 11, 15 > 11$
8	7	$11 > 8, 10 > 8, 14 > 8, 12 > 8, 13 > 8, 9 > 8, 15 > 8$
Total	40	

Since 40 is even, the puzzle is solvable.

Problem Statement Write an application that

- generates a random *solvable* puzzle, and
- allows a user to interactively solve the puzzle.

Java Solution A general algorithm for a "fifteen puzzle program" can be expressed as:

1. Generate a random *solvable* puzzle.
2. Play the game.
3. Determine whether or not the puzzle has been solved.

Of course, this algorithm is very broad and needs a bit of refinement.

1. **Generate a random solvable puzzle.**

   Do

   > Place 0 in the lower right corner of a 4 × 4 array and randomly place the numbers 1 through 15 in the other locations. The number 0 designates the empty space.

   While the number of inversions is odd, that is, until a solvable puzzle is generated.

   Print the board.

2. **Play the game.**

   Do

   > Accept a move from the player.
   >
   > if the move is valid
   >
   > > Update the board and print the board.
   >
   > else
   >
   > > Issue a message indicating that the move is invalid.

   While player wishes to continue play.

3. **Determine whether or not the puzzle has been solved.**

   Traverse the board row by row and determine whether or not the tiles are in order.

The following program implements the preceding algorithm via several methods, each of which executes a single task. For example, one method displays the board and another generates a solvable game. Other methods count the number of inversions, play the game, and check whether or not a player's move is valid. To move a tile, a player supplies the coordinates (row and column) of the square that he/she would like to slide into the empty position. The empty position contains the digit 0.

This application is larger and more complicated than any of the previous programs that we have discussed. A quick pass over the code may leave you confused. To understand the logic of the program, we recommend that you read the discussion in parallel with the code.

```
import java.util.*;
public class SamLoydPuzzle
{
   public static void printPuzzle(int[][] puzzle)  // prints a two-dimensional array
   {
      for (int i = 0; i < 4; i++)                  // for each row
      {
         for (int j = 0; j < 4; j++)               // for each column
            System.out.print(puzzle[i][j] + "\t");
         System.out.println();                     // print a new line after each row
      }
   }

   public static void swap(int[][] p, int i, int j, int r, int s)
   {
      // swap [i][j] with p[r][s]
      int temp = p[r][s];
      p[r][s] = p[i][j];
```

```
        p[i][j] = temp;
    }

    public static int[] makeList(int[][] p)
    {
        // writes the puzzle numbers into a one-dimensional array
        // left to right, top to bottom

        int index = 0;
        int[] list = new int[16];
        for (int row = 0; row < 4; row++)          // for each row
            for (int col = 0; col < 4; col++)      // for each column
                if (p[row][col] != 0)              // 0 is the empty space
                {
                    list[index] = p[row][col];     // add p[i][j] to the list
                    index++;
                }
        return list;
    }

    public static int countInversions(int [][] p) // returns the number of inversions
    {
        int count = 0;                 // total number of inversions
        int [] s = makeList(p);        // make a list of the numbers row by row
        for (int i = 0; i < 16; i++)   // for each number on the list
        {
            int num = 0;               // counts values that precede i that are greater
            for (int j = 0; j < i; j++)   // for each j that precedes i
                if (s[j] > s[i])          // is there an inversion?
                    num++;
            count = count + num;
        }
        return count;
    }

    public static void createSolvablePuzzle(int[][] p) // makes a new puzzle
    {
        int totalInversions;
        do // repeat until a solvable board is generated
        {
            // for each position on the board generate a random
            // position and make a swap but leave 0 in the lower right corner
            for (int row = 0; row < 4; row++)        // for each row
                for (int col = 0; col < 4; col++)    // for each column
                {
                    int a = (int)(4 * Math.random()); // a random row : 0 to 3
                    int b = (int)(4 * Math.random()); // a random column: 0 to 3
                    if (p[row][col] ! = 0 && p[a][b] ! = 0)
                        swap(p, row, col, a, b);
                }
            totalInversions = countInversions(p);   // how many inversions?
        } while (totalInversions % 2 != 0);          // while the configuration is unsolvable
    }

    public static boolean checkWin(int[][] p)
    {
        // traverses the board row by row and
        // determines whether or not the tiles
        // are in numerical order
        int num = 1;
        for (int row = 0; row < 4; row++)        // for each row
```

```
            for (int col = 0; col < 4; col++)          // for each column
            {
               if (p[row][row] !=0)                    // if the space is not empty
               {
                  if (p[row][col] != num)              // is a number out of place?
                     return false;
                  num++;
               }
            }
            return true;
        }

    public static boolean validMove(int row, int col, int blankRow, int blankCol)
    {
        // checks to see whether the player's move is either next to the empty space or
        // above/below the empty space
        return
           (row >= 0) && (row <= 3) && (col >= 0) && (col <= 3) && // must be on the puzzle
           (row == blankRow && (col + 1 == blankCol || col - 1 == blankCol)) // same row, or
           || (col == blankCol && (row + 1 == blankRow || row - 1== blankRow)); // same column
    }

    public static void play(int[][] p)
    {
        Scanner input = new Scanner(System.in);
        int row, col;                               // for the player's move
        int blankRow = 0, blankCol = 0;             // position of the empty space
        int more;                                   // to continue the game
        // find the blank space on the board
        for (int r = 0; r < 4; r++)                 // for each row
           for (int c = 0; c < 4; c++)              // for each column
              if (p[r][c] == 0)                     // if the position is empty
              {
                 blankRow = r;                      // row of the blank
                 blankCol = c;                      // column of the blank
                 break;                             // because the blank has been found
              }
        do // as long as player wishes to play
        {
           // get a tile position from the player
           System.out.print("Enter row ");
           row = input.nextInt();
           System.out.print("Enter column ");
           col = input.nextInt();
           // if the move is valid, slide tile into the empty space
           // and adjust the row and column of the empty space
           if (validMove(row, col, blankRow, blankCol))
           {
                 swap(p, row, col, blankRow, blankCol);   // swap the blank and player's choice
                 blankRow = row;                          // blank's new row
                 blankCol = col;                          // blank's new column
                 printPuzzle(p); // puzzle after the move
           }
           else
                 System.out.println("Invalid move");
           // Continue to play?
           System.out.print("Continue? 1 for yes: "); // and any digit for "no"
           more = input.nextInt();
           System.out.println();
        } while (more == 1);
    }
```

```
131.        public static void main(String[] args) throws Exception
132.        {
133.           // initialize puzzle
134.           int[][]puzzle = {{1, 2, 3, 4}, {5, 6, 7, 8}, {9, 10, 11, 12}, {13, 14, 15, 0}};
135.           // get a random, solvable puzzle
136.           createSolvablePuzzle(puzzle);
137.           printPuzzle(puzzle);
138.           System.out.println();
139.           play(puzzle);
140.           if (checkWin(puzzle))
141.              System.out.println("You have solved the puzzle");
142.           else
143.              System.out.println("You have failed to solve the puzzle");
144.        }
145. }
```

Output Here is output produced by the program after two moves. Remember that rows and columns are indexed from 0. On the first move, the player slides the 15-tile, and on the next move he/she moves the 1-tile. The player then chooses to stop and, as the message indicates, the puzzle is not solved.

```
2     15    1     13
6     12    4     9
11    3     14    8
7     5     10    0

Enter row 3
Enter column 2

2     15    1     13
6     12    4     9
11    3     14    8
7     5     0     10
Continue? 1 for yes: 1

Enter row 3
Enter column 1

2     15    1     13
6     12    4     9
11    3     14    8
7     0     5     10
Continue? 1 for yes: 0

You have failed to solve the puzzle.
```

1	2	3	4
5	6	7	8
9	10	11	12
13	14	15	0

FIGURE 7.40
The board with tiles in order

Discussion Initially, the program instantiates a two-dimensional array (Figure 7.40) with the tiles in numerical order, and a zero representing the blank tile (line 134).

This array represents the game board. Next, main(...) invokes those methods that accomplish the steps outlined in the general algorithm:

1. Generate a random solvable puzzle (line 136).
2. Play the game (line 139).
3. Determine whether or not the puzzle has been solved (line 140).

We now look at each of these procedures and how each achieves its purpose.

1. **Generate a random solvable puzzle**

   On line 136, main(...) passes the array puzzle to the method createSolvablePuzzle(...). This method repeats the following actions until a solvable puzzle is generated:

   - createSolvablePuzzle(...) swaps each number in the original ordered puzzle with the number that resides at some randomly generated position (lines 56–63). This action scrambles the numbers/tiles. Why not use Math.random() to simply generate 15 random integers in the range 1 through 15? Why all the swapping? Answer: To avoid duplicate numbers.
   - Having randomized the board, createSolvablePuzzle(...) passes the two-dimensional array p (the puzzle) to countInversions(...) (line 64), which returns the number of inversions (lines 35–48) in the current puzzle configuration. The method countInversions(...) invokes makeList(...) (line 38), which places the puzzle numbers into a one-dimensional array to facilitate processing.
   - If the number of inversions is even, createSolvablePuzzle(...) exits; otherwise the process repeats (line 64).

2. **Play the game**

   Once the program generates a solvable puzzle, main(...) invokes play(...) with the argument puzzle (line 139). The play(...) method executes as follows:

   - play(...) scans the puzzle configuration to find the empty space, storing the row and column of the empty space in blankRow and blankCol (lines 99–106).
   - play(...) accepts the row and column of the tile that the player wishes to slide into the empty space (lines 109–113).
   - If the player's move is valid, that is, the selected tile is adjacent to the empty space (line 116), then the selected tile and the empty space are swapped; otherwise an error message is issued.
   - If the player chooses to continue the game, he/she enters "1" and the process repeats, otherwise play(...) exits (lines 126–129).

3. **Determine whether or not the puzzle has been solved**

   When play(...) returns, the altered puzzle is passed to the boolean method checkWin(...) (line 140), which determines whether or not the tiles are in order (lines 67–84).

   The game terminates with a message indicating whether or not the puzzle has been solved.

You probably noticed that the method printPuzzle(...) (lines 4–11) is invoked several times in the program. Displaying a two-dimensional array requires a nested loop. However, so that each row appears on a separate line, a println() executes each time the inner loop terminates. And, using a tab (\t) on line 9 ensures that the columns of the table are aligned.

Finally, notice that when a two-dimensional array is a formal parameter, two sets of square brackets are required in the array heading (lines 4, 13, 20, 49, 67, and 92).

Figure 7.41 shows the structure and relationships of the methods used in the program.

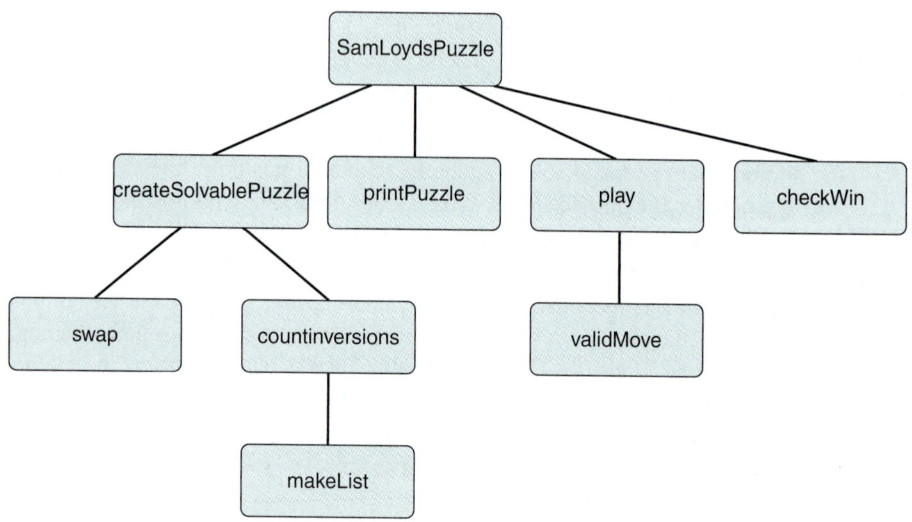

FIGURE 7.41 Method structure in the Java solution of the Sam Loyd Puzzle

7.11 IN CONCLUSION

Computers can easily handle large sets of data that number in the millions. One-dimensional and two-dimensional arrays are fundamental tools that facilitate the maintenance of such data sets. Normally, a data set with thousands of entries is not interactively entered into an array but read into an array from a file. In Part II, we demonstrate how large amounts of data can be stored in an array, not by prompting the proverbial weariless user, but via a "file object."

Just the Facts

- An array is a structure that gives a single name to an ordered collection of variables all of the same type.
- You can create an array of any type, including an array of arrays (called a two-dimensional array).
- You declare an array by specifying its name and data type, e.g., double[] x.
- An array variable is a reference variable that holds the address of a memory location. The declaration

  ```
  int[] x;
  ```

  declares x as a reference but does not initialize x.
- No memory is allocated to an array until the array has been instantiated.
- You create (or instantiate) an array with the **new** operator. The syntax is

  x = **new** *dataType*[*n*]

  where x is an array reference, *dataType* is the data type of the array elements, and *n* is the size of the array. For example,

  ```
  double[] x;
  x = new int [50];
  ```

declares that x refers to an array of type double and allocates 50 memory cells to the array.

- Declaration and instantiation can be done in a single statement:

```
double[] x = new int [50];
```

- The length or maximum capacity of an array x is available as x.length.
- All arrays are indexed from 0. The first cell of an array is designated x[0] and the last cell x[x.length – 1].
- Array instantiation initializes all cells to the zero-element of the array's data type.
- You can explicitly initialize an array in a declaration. The statement

```
int[] x = {1, 3, 5, 7, 9}
```

declares, instantiates, and initializes x. The number of items in the initialization list implicitly determines the length of the array (5 in this case).

- An array reference can be passed to a method as a parameter.
- A method can change the *contents* of an array but not the variable that references an array.
- The assignment operator (=) copies array *references*. The assignment operator does not copy the contents of one array to another.
- A two-dimensional array is declared and instantiated as:

```
dataType [] [] x;
x = new dataType[rows][columns];
```

where x is the name of the array, *dataType* is the data type of the array elements, rows is the number of rows of the array, and *columns* is the number of columns of the array. For example, the statements:

```
int[][] numbers;
numbers = new int[4][5];
```

declare and instantiate a two-dimensional array of integers. The array numbers has 4 rows and 5 columns.

- A two-dimensional array is an array of one-dimensional arrays—an array of arrays.
- The element stored in row i and column j of a two-dimensional array x is x[i][j].
- Processing a two-dimensional array usually requires a nested loop.

Bug Extermination

No programmer has eluded the infamous "array index out of bounds" error. Remember that an array x of length n is indexed from 0 to $n - 1$. Consequently, an attempt to access x[n] or x[x.length] results in a runtime error, that is, one that occurs during the run of the program and terminates the program. When using a for loop to process x, the correct form is

```
for (int i = 0; i < x.length; i++)
```

and not

```
for (int i = 0; i <= x.length; i++)
```

The "off by one" looping error often results in an "array index out of bounds" error. Other common array-based errors are:

- Failing to create or instantiate an array. A declaration creates an array reference but allocates no memory for an array. Unless you initialize an array explicitly with a list, you must use the new operator to instantiate an array.
- Accessing cell x[x.length – 1] when array x is partially filled. It is common practice to allocate enough memory for an array to accommodate lists of various sizes; in other words, "over-dimension" an array. In such cases, it is important to keep track of how many valid data elements are, in fact, stored in the array. If a partially filled array x contains a list of *n* ID numbers, the last element is x[n – 1] not x[x.length – 1]. Because every array is initialized with 0 values, a program may run to completion. But if those initial 0's are not part of your data, your results may be surprising.
- Using an index of a data type other than int (or a data type that can be automatically cast to int). You cannot *index* an array with a value of type long, boolean, or double, or float.
- Misusing the assignment operator with arrays. Array assignment such as a = b is perfectly legal in Java. However, the consequences may not be what you had intended. Remember a and b are *references*, and the result of the assignment a = b is that both a and b refer to the same memory location, that is, the same array. The assignment operator does *not* copy the contents of one array to another. To do that, use a method with an appropriate loop.

EXERCISES

LEARN THE LINGO

Test your knowledge of the chapter's vocabulary by completing the following crossword puzzle.

Across

4 An array is a convenient structure used for _____ storage.

7 int[] x = {1, 2, 3} declares and _____ an array.

8 All arrays are indexed from _______.

10 A reference is a(n) _______.

11 The i of a[i][j]

12 Processing a two-dimensional array usually requires a _____ loop.

19 Operator that creates an array

20 An array reference is _____ before the array is created.

21 A two-dimensional array is an array of _______.

23 Searched item is called the _______.

24 Search that examines each array cell in order

25 All array data must be of the same _______.

26 When an array reference is passed to a parameter, both references refer to the _____ array.

27 Doubling the array size _____ the number of comparisons performed by insertion sort.

Down

1 The == operator compares _______.

2 x[x.length] results in an _____ (three words) error.

3 A method can _____ the contents of an array.

5 Array creation

6 Search from the middle of an array

9 An array is stored as a _______ block of memory.

13 An array of length 10 is similar to having 10 different _______.

14 Data type of a in the declaration int[] a

15 Size of an array

16 Data type of every array index

17 j in a[i][j]

18 temp = a, a = b; b = temp

22 Fifteen puzzle exploiter

SHORT EXERCISES

1. **True or False**
   If false, give an explanation.
   a. The values stored in an array must all be of the same type.
   b. All Java arrays are indexed from 1.
   c. Java arrays can hold at most 65,535 items.
   d. A two-dimensional array is an array of arrays.
   e. When an array is passed to a method, the values in the *argument* array are copied to the *parameter* array.
   f. Once declared, you cannot change the value of an array reference.
   g. Once declared, you cannot change the value of an array entry.
   h. Once declared, you cannot change the dimensions of an array.
   i. Java prohibits three-dimensional arrays.
   j. The index value of a Java array must be an integer.

2. **Explain the Error**
   Explain why the statement swap(a[0], a[1]) does *not* swap the values stored in a[0] and a[1].

```
public static swap(int x, int y)
{
   int temp = x;
   x = y;
   y = temp;
}
```

3. **Tracing**
   What are the values stored in the array a after the following code executes?

```
int[] a = new int[10];
for (int i = 0; i < a.length; i++)
   a[i] = 2 * i - 1;
```

4. **Tracing**
   What are the values stored in the array a after the following code executes?

```
int[] a = new int[10];
a[0] = 1;
for (int i = 1; i < a.length; i++)
   a[i] = 2 * a[i - 1] - 1;
```

5. **Tracing**
   What are the values stored in the array a after the following code executes?

```
int[] a = new int[10];
a[0] = 0;
a[1] = 1;
for (int i = 2; i < a.length; i++)
   a[i] = 2 * a[i - 1] - a[i - 2];
```

6. **Tracing**
   Determine the values stored in the arrays a and b after each of lines iii, iv, v, vi, and vii executes.

```
i.    int[] a = new int[10];
ii.   int[] b = new int[10];
iii.  for (int i = 0; i < a.length; i++)
          a[i] = 2 * i - 1;
```

iv.
```
for (int i = 0; i < b.length; i++)
    b[i] = 2 * i + 1;
```
v.
```
for (int i = 0; i < a.length; i++)
    a[i] = b[i] - 1;
```
vi.
```
a = b;
```
vii.
```
b = a;
```

7. **Playing Compiler**
Find the error(s) in each of the following code segments.

a.
```
char[] a = new char[10];
a[10] = 's';
a[9] = 76;
```

b.
```
char[] a = new char[10];
char[9] = 's';
```

c.
```
char[] a = new int[10];
a[0] = 's';
a[1] = 80;
```

d.
```
int[] a;
a = new int[255];
a[0] = 's';
a[a[0]] = 35;
a[35] = 12345654321;
```

e.
```
int[] a;
a = new int[255];
a[0] = a.length;
a[0]--; a.length--;
a[a[0]] = 2;
```

f.
```
int[] b = new int[9];
int[][] a;
a = new int[255][];
a[0] = b;
a[0][3] = 9;
a[3][0] = 9;
```

8. **Algorithm Analysis**
In the worst case, how many comparisons must linear search perform to locate a value in an array of size 50,000? Answer the same question for binary search.

9. **Algorithm Analysis**
Why does insertion sort make no more than $½(n^2 - n)$ comparisons? *Hint:* $1 + 2 + 3 + \ldots + k = (1/2)(k)(k + 1)$

10. **Algorithm Analysis**
Give an example of an array that contains five elements such that insertion sort makes 10 comparisons. Explain your answer.

11. **The Fifteen Puzzle**
Does the board configuration of the Fifteen Puzzle shown in Figure 7.36 have a solution? (*Hint*: count the number of inversions.)

12. **What's the Output?**
The following program presents a more sophisticated method for calculating the solvability of a starting configuration for the Fifteen Puzzle of Section 7.10. Trace through the program by hand, and count how many times the statements `length++` and `numSwaps += length` execute. What is the output?

```
public class SolvableGame
{ // counts number of swaps necessary to restore the values in a[1]..a[15] to 1,2,...,15
  public static void main(String[] args)
  {
    int numSwaps = 0;
  // the board is stored in a[1]..a[15]; a[0] is not considered, -1 is a dummy value
    int[] a = {-1, 5, 6, 3, 12, 2, 1, 7, 4, 9, 8, 15, 13, 10, 11, 14};
    for (int i = 1; i < a.length; i++)
    if (a[i] != 0)
    {
      int j = a[i];
      a[i] = 0;
      int length = 0;
       while (j != i)
      {
        int temp = j;
        j = a[j];
        a[temp] = 0;
        length++;
      }
      numSwaps += length;
      }
      System.out.println(numSwaps);
      if (numSwaps % 2 == 0) System.out.print("Solvable");
      else System.out.print("Unsolvable");
  }
}
```

Repeat the problem again after changing the line:
int[] a = {−1, 5, 6, 3, 12, 2, 1, 7, 4, 9, 8, 15, 13, 10, 11, 14} to:

i. int[ ] a = {−1, 1, 2, 3, 4, 5, 6, 7, 8, 9, 10, 11, 12, 13, 14, 15}
ii. int[ ] a = {−1, 1, 2, 3, 4, 5, 6, 7, 8, 9, 10, 11, 12, 13, 15, 14}

Using the data of (i) and (ii), compare the number of steps taken by this method with the more intuitive countInversions(...) method used in the case study of Section 7.10. The number of steps required by countInversions(...) is the number of times the if statement on lines 43–44 executes plus the number of times line 45 executes.

PROGRAMMING EXERCISES

1. **Array Data**
   Write two methods that read data from the console and store the data in an array:
   a. The method
      int readData(int [] x)
      reads a list of at most 100 integers into the array x. A sentinel −999 terminates the list. The method returns the size of the list.

   b. The method
      int[] readData()
      reads and returns a list of integers. The list is preceded by the number of items in the list. For example, the data 6 9 7 5 3 1 2 indicates that there are six items in the list. The leading 6 is not included in the list.

   Test both of these methods within a single program that includes a method
   void printList([] x, int n)
   that displays x[0] through x[n − 1].

2. **Vote Tally**
Ten candidates, designated 0 to 9, are competing in a preliminary election for mayor. Write a program that counts the votes for each candidate. The input to your program is a list of numbers in the range 0–9 such that a value of *i* signifies a vote for candidate *i*. Terminate the data with a flag. Use an array to keep a tally of the votes. Do not use 10 different variables. Discard all invalid votes. Output from your program should be 10 pairs (one pair per line) of the form:

(candidate number, number of votes)

Typical input might be:

1 1 3 3 3 4 1 2 6 7 9 0 2 3 1 4 5 4 4 7 8 9 0 3 4 5 3 1 2 3 4 1 2 3 1 1 1 2 3 −999

3. **Dice Roll Simulation**
Write a program that simulates rolling two dice 100,000 times and displays the number of occurrences of each sum from 2 to 12.

4. **Zero Sum**
Write a program that accepts two lists of integers, each terminated by the sentinel −999, and reports whether or not there are two values, one from each list, with sum equal to zero. Your program should utilize two methods: one that reads a list of integers into an array (see Exercise 1a) and another that returns true if and only if there are two values, one from each array, with sum equal to zero. For example, the two arrays [2, −3, 1, 7, 9] and [6, 7, −5, −3, 4, −2] satisfy the "zero sum" criterion because the first array contains 2 and the second −2.

5. **Intersection**
Write a program that includes two methods: one that reads a list of integers into an array and another that accepts two integer arrays, x and y, and displays the intersection of the two lists, that is, all the values that x and y have in common. The data for each list are preceded by the number of items in the list (see Programming Exercise 1b).

6. **Duplicate Detection**
Write a method that returns true if and only if an integer array contains duplicate items. Test this method in a program. Include a method that reads a list of numbers, terminated by −999, into an array (see Programming Exercise 1a).

7. **Second Largest**
Design and implement a method that returns the *second*-largest value stored in an array of type int. Include this method in a program that displays the second-largest value as well as a method that reads a list of numbers, terminated by −999, into an array (see Programming Exercise 1a).

8. **Longest Increasing Contiguous Subsequence**
Write a program that displays the longest *increasing* contiguous subsequence in an integer array. For example, the longest increasing contiguous subsequence of

4, 5, 7, 3, 12, 2, 5, 6, 19, 21, 14 is
2, 5, 6, 19, 21.

9. **Largest and Smallest**
Design a method that determines the largest and smallest values stored in an integer array, x. Your method should return these values in an array of length two. Use the following algorithm:

Initialize variables currentBig and currentSmall to the larger and smaller values of x[0] and x[1]. Process the rest of the list, two elements at a time. Compare the larger of the two elements to currentBig, and replace currentBig if necessary.

Compare the smaller of the two elements to currentSmall, and replace currentSmall if necessary.

Test your method in a program and include a method that reads a list, terminated by −999, into an array (see Programming Exercise 1a).

10. **Coin Flip Simulation**
Write a program that simulates flipping a coin 100,000 times and reports the number "runs of heads" of length *i*, where *i* ranges from one to the length of the longest consecutive sequence of heads. For example, the longest run of heads in the sequence HHTHTHTHHT**HHHH**TH is of length 4. Consequently, the program would display the following output:

Length	Number of runs of heads
1	3
2	2
3	0
4	1

11. **Merging**
Write a method that accepts two *sorted* integer arrays, a and b, and returns a *sorted* array containing the values stored in both a and b. In other words, your method should *merge* arrays a and b into a third array. You can merge two sorted arrays as follows:

    Declare a new array c that is large enough to hold the contents of both a and b; also declare two integer variables, i and j. Initialize i and j to 0.

    Compare a[i] and b[j] and copy the smaller value into c.
    Increment i if a contains the smaller value, otherwise increment j.
    Repeat this procedure until either i or j exceeds, the highest index of a or b, respectively.

    Copy the remainder of either a or b to c.
    Return c.

    Include this method in a program that:

    a. Interactively reads two lists of integers into two arrays. Each list ends with the sentinel −999. (See Exercise 1a.)
    b. Sorts the arrays;
    c. Merges the arrays; and
    d. Displays the merged array.

    The two lists might not be the same size. Make sure that your program keeps track of how many data are in each list.

    Use a method for each task. Design, implement, and test one method before including the next.

12. **A Checking Account**
Write a program that processes checking account transactions. A positive entry signifies a deposit, a negative number denotes a withdrawal, and zero signals the end of data. Your program should display a checkbook ledger. Assume an initial balance of zero. For example, if input to the program is 10.52, 1900.78, −234.78, 0, then the

program displays:

Transaction	**Balance**
Deposit 10.52	10.52
Deposit 1900.78	1911.30
Withdrawal 234.78	1676.52

13. **Simplified Counting Sort**
Write a program that sorts a collection of 30 test scores each in the range 0 to 100. Use the following algorithm:
Initialize each member of an integer array, score (length 101), to zero.
    For each test score x, increment score[x].
    For each i from 0 to 100, print i as many times as the array entry score[i] indicates.

    This sorting routine is useful when the range of the data is limited. The procedure is a simplified version of what is appropriately called *counting sort*.

14. **Max Sort**
Implement a method

```
void maxSort(int[ ] x, int size) // (size <= x.length)
```

that sorts the partially filled array x. The method maxSort(...) first determines the largest value in x and swaps that value with x[size – 1] ; then maxSort(...) finds the next largest value and swaps that value with x[size – 2], and so on. Include an auxiliary method

```
int max(int[ ] x, int i)
```

that returns the index of the largest element between x[0] and x[i], inclusive. Test your methods in a program.

15. **Selection Sort**
Implement a method

```
void selectionSort(int[] x, int size)      // (size <= x.length)
```

that sorts the partially filled array x. The method selectionSort(...) first determines the smallest value in x and swaps that value with x[0]; then selectionSort(...) finds the next smallest value and swaps that value with x[1], and so on. Include an auxiliary method

```
int min(int[] x, int i)
```

that returns the index of the smallest element between x[i] and x[size – 1], inclusive. Test your methods in a program.

16. **Partitioning an Array**
Suppose that x is an integer array of size n and that a = x[0] is the first element of x. Write a method that reorders the values stored in x so that in the rearranged array:
    i. a is in position k,
    ii. the numbers stored in cells x[0] though x[k–1] are all less than or equal to a, and
    iii. the numbers stored in cells x[k+1] through x[n–1] are all greater than or equal to a.

    For example, if x is initially

    9, 6, 3, 22, 16, 2, 19, (x[0] is 9)

you might reorder x as

6, 3, 2, **9**, 22, 16, 18. or
6, 2, 3, **9**, 16, 22, 19 or possibly
3, 2, 6, **9**, 19, 22, 16.

This operation is called *partitioning* the array. Your method should accomplish this task without using any additional arrays.

Test your method in a program. Data for your program is a list of integers such that the first datum specifies the size of the list and is not a member of the list.

17. **Sieve of Eratosthenes**
A prime number is an integer greater than 1 and divisible only by itself and 1. For example, 2, 3, 5, 7, 11, and 101 are prime numbers but 4, 6, 9, 12, and 100,000 are not.

There are many algorithms that identify prime numbers, and the *Sieve of Eratosthenes* is among the simplest. Using this method, we show how to find all prime numbers less than or equal to 50.
First, list all numbers between 2 and 50:

	2	3	4	5	6	7	8	9	10
11	12	13	14	15	16	17	18	19	20
21	22	23	24	25	26	27	28	29	30
31	32	33	34	35	36	37	38	39	40
41	42	43	44	45	46	47	48	49	50

Begin with 2 and "cross out," mark, or eliminate all numbers greater than 2 that are multiples of 2 that is, any number divisible by 2:

	2	3	X	5	X	7	X	9	X
11	X	13	X	15	X	17	X	19	X
21	X	23	X	25	X	27	X	29	X
31	X	33	X	35	X	37	X	39	X
41	X	43	X	45	X	47	X	49	X

Then, find the next *unmarked* number (it's 3) and cross out all unmarked numbers greater than 3 that are multiples of 3:

	2	3	X	5	X	7	X	X	X
11	X	13	X	X	X	17	X	19	X
X	X	23	X	25	X	X	X	29	X
31	X	X	X	35	X	37	X	X	X
41	X	43	X	X	X	47	X	49	X

Now, find the next unmarked number (it's 5) and likewise cross out all multiples (of 5) that have not already been marked:

	2	3	X	5	X	7	X	X	X
11	X	13	X	X	X	17	X	19	X
X	X	23	X	X	X	X	X	29	X
31	X	X	X	X	X	37	X	X	X
41	X	43	X	X	X	47	X	49	X

Continue the process. When you are finished, the unmarked numbers are the primes. These are : 2 3 5 7 11 13 17 19 23 29 31 37 41 43 47.

Write a program that accepts a positive integer, n, ($2 < n < 500$) and uses the Sieve of Eratosthenes to determine all prime numbers less than or equal to n.

18. **Matrix Arithmetic**
An $m \times n$ matrix is a two-dimensional array of numbers with n rows and m columns. If X is an $m \times n$ matrix, then x_{ij} signifies the number in row i and column j. For example,

$$X = \begin{bmatrix} 2 & 3 \\ 5 & 8 \\ 1 & 9 \end{bmatrix}$$

is a 3×2 matrix such that $x_{11} = 2$, $x_{12} = 3$, $x_{21} = 5$, etc.

Let A and B be $m \times n$ matrices. The *sum* of A and B is an $m \times n$ matrix C such that $c_{ij} = a_{ij} + b_{ij}$. For example,

$$\underset{A}{\begin{bmatrix} 2 & 3 \\ 5 & 8 \\ 1 & 9 \end{bmatrix}} + \underset{B}{\begin{bmatrix} 6 & 2 \\ 2 & 1 \\ 3 & 2 \end{bmatrix}} = \underset{C}{\begin{bmatrix} 8 & 5 \\ 7 & 9 \\ 4 & 11 \end{bmatrix}}$$

In contrast, the *product* AB of two matrices is defined if and only if the number of columns of A is equal to the number of rows of B. If A and B are $m \times n$ and $n \times p$ matrices, the product of A and B is the $m \times p$ matrix C such that $c_{ij} = (a_{i1}b_{1k} + a_{i2}b_{2k} + \ldots + a_{in}b_{nk})$. For example,

$$\underset{A}{\begin{bmatrix} 3 & 4 & 2 \\ 5 & 1 & 6 \end{bmatrix}} \underset{B}{\begin{bmatrix} 2 & 3 \\ 5 & 8 \\ 4 & 9 \end{bmatrix}} = \begin{bmatrix} 3 \times 2 + 4 \times 5 + 2 \times 4 & 3 \times 3 + 4 \times 8 + 2 \times 9 \\ 5 \times 2 + 1 \times 5 + 6 \times 4 & 5 \times 3 + 1 \times 8 + 6 \times 9 \end{bmatrix} = \underset{C}{\begin{bmatrix} 34 & 59 \\ 39 & 77 \end{bmatrix}}$$

Matrix addition and multiplication provide convenient devices for processing data. For example, suppose that A is a 5×2 matrix that holds the number of hot dogs and the number of hamburgers eaten by the starting five players after a Sunday night Quidditch game.

	Hot Dogs	**Hamburgers**
Ron	1	3
Hermione	1	1
Harry	0	4
Fred	2	2
Shaquille	6	4

Likewise, suppose that B is a 5×2 matrix that holds the number of hot dogs and the number of hamburgers eaten by the starting five players after a Monday night Quidditch game.

	Hot Dogs	**Hamburgers**
Ron	1	2
Hermione	2	0
Harry	1	4
Fred	5	1
Shaquille	6	2

Then the sum A + B represents the total hot dogs and hamburgers eaten by the players over two days.

	Hot Dogs	**Hamburgers**
Ron	2	5
Hermione	3	1
Harry	1	8
Fred	7	3
Shaquille	12	6

Furthermore, suppose that C is a 2 × 3 matrix that holds the number of calories, grams of fat, and grams of protein contained in a hot dog and a hamburger.

	Calories	**Grams Fat**	**Grams Protein**
Hot dog	275	15	9
Hamburger	310	13	17

Then the product BC represents the total calories, grams of fat, and grams of protein consumed by the five players on Monday night.

	Calories	**Grams Fat**	**Grams Protein**
Ron	895	41	43
Hermione	550	30	18
Harry	1515	67	77
Fred	1685	88	62
Shaquille	2270	116	88

Design methods using the following headings:

```
int[][] add(int[][] x, int[][] y)
int[][] multiply(int[][] x, int[][] y)
```

that add and multiply two matrices and return references to the sum and product matrices.

If the dimensions of x and y are not compatible with addition (multiplication), then the method should issue an appropriate error message and exit. Test your methods in a program. Include two additional methods that

- print the contents of a two-dimensional array, and
- read data, row by row, into a two-dimensional array.

Assume that the data are preceded by two positive integers indicating the dimensions of the array. For example, the data

3 2 2 3 8 5 8 1 9

specify the 3 x 2 array:

$$\begin{bmatrix} 2 & 3 \\ 5 & 8 \\ 1 & 9 \end{bmatrix}$$

19. **Markov Matrices**

An $n \times n$ matrix (as defined in programming problem 18) is called a *positive Markov matrix*, if and only if each entry is positive and the sum of the entries of each column is 1. For example, the following matrix is a positive Markov matrix:

	NewYork	Philadelphia	Newark
New York	.9	.35	.3
Philadelphia	.08	.6	.2
Newark	.02	.05	.5

The preceding matrix contains data collected by a rental car company. The first column indicates that a car rented in New York is returned to

- New York 90% of time,
- Philadelphia 8% of the time, and
- Newark 2% of the time.

The second column shows that a car rented in Philadelphia is returned to

- New York 35% of time,
- Philadelphia 60% of the time, and
- Newark 5% of the time.

And finally, from the third column you can see that a car rented in Newark is returned to

- New York 30% of time,
- Philadelphia 20% of the time, and
- Newark 50% of the time.

If M is a positive Markov matrix, the powers M, $M^2 = M \times M$, $M^3 = M^2 \times M$, $M^4 = M^3 \times M$… approach a matrix P with the properties that P is also a positive Markov matrix and the columns of P are identical. For example, multiplying the car rental matrix by itself 50 times produces the matrix P:

	NewYork	Philadelphia	Newark
New York	.772	.772	.772
Philadelphia	.179	.179	.179
Newark	.049	.049	.049

The columns of P represent the *steady-state vector*, (.772, .179, .049). The steady-state vector gives the eventual distribution of cars that results from the behavior implied in the original matrix. In other words, if the rental car company has 1000 cars, then the company knows to keep 772 parking spaces in New York, 179 in Philadelphia, and 49 in Newark.

Write a program that reads a positive Markov matrix, M, and displays the steady-state vector for M. You can safely approximate the steady-state vector with the columns of M^{50}. With regard to your input, assume that the number of rows and the number of columns of M precede the data for M.

20. **Ragged Arrays**
The following code defines a *ragged* two-dimensional array. The term *ragged* indicates that the rows are not all the same length.

```
int[][] triangle = new int[5][]; // allocate array of rows
for (int i = 0; i < triangle.length; i++)
   triangle[i] = new int[r + 1];
```

a. Draw a picture of the ragged array created by this code fragment.
b. Write a method

```
int [][] buildRagged(int n)
```

that returns a (possibly) ragged array with n rows. The method reads $n + 1$ lines of data from the console. The first line contains the number of rows of a ragged array. Each succeeding line specifies one row of a ragged array. The first entry of each line gives the number of items in that row. For example, the input

```
3
3 1 5 7
6 5 6 8 9 3 2
2 5 8
```

indicates that there are 3 rows and that the first row of the ragged array has 3 entries (1, 5, and 7), the second row 6 entries (5, 6, 8, 9, 3, and 2), and the third row 2 entries (5 and 8).

c. Write a method

```
void printArray(int [][] x)
```

that displays a (possibly) ragged array.

d. Test your methods in a program using the main(...) method:

```
public static void main( String[] args)
{
   Scanner input = new Scanner(System.in);
   System.out.print("Enter the data for the array, begin with the number of rows: ");
   int rows = nextInt();
   int[][] array = build(rows);
   printArray(array);
}
```

21. **Column Sorting**
Write a method

```
void columnSort(int[][] x)
```

that sorts each column of a 5 x n array of integers. For example, if x is the 5 by 9 array:

12	6	7	17	18	19	8	29	2
0	14	8	15	5	3	2	1	18
8	2	1	6	9	18	21	2	8
1	5	9	3	7	11	2	7	10
89	12	6	1	0	19	27	21	5

The method columnSort(...) rearranges x as:

0	2	1	1	0	3	2	1	2
1	2	6	3	5	3	2	2	5
7	6	7	6	7	18	8	7	8
12	12	8	15	9	19	21	21	10
89	14	9	17	18	19	27	29	18

Test columnSort(...) in a program and include another method

```
int[][]readArray(int n)
```

that interactively reads and returns a 5 x n array. Your program should prompt for the value of n.

22. **Sudoku**
A Sudoku puzzle is a 9 × 9 grid partially filled with the digits from 1 to 9, inclusive. Figure 7.42 shows a typical puzzle.

		9	8					7
5	1	6			2			8
7				5				1
					4	8		9
		5		8		1		
8		1	7					
1				6				2
9			5			7	1	6
2					1	3		

FIGURE 7.42 A Sudoku puzzle

To solve the puzzle, a player must fill the empty squares of the grid so that each row, each column, and each of the nine 3 × 3 boxes (as shown in Figure 7.42) contains every digit from 1 to 9. That is, no row, column, or box contains a duplicate digit. Figure 7.43 gives a solution for the puzzle of Figure 7.42.

4	2	9	8	1	3	5	6	7
5	1	6	4	7	2	9	3	8
7	8	3	6	5	9	2	4	1
6	7	2	1	3	4	8	5	9
3	9	5	2	8	6	1	7	4
8	4	1	7	9	5	6	2	3
1	5	8	3	6	7	4	9	2
9	3	4	5	2	8	7	1	6
2	6	7	9	4	1	3	8	5

FIGURE 7.43 A solution to the puzzle of Figure 7.42

Write a program that reads a 9 × 9 grid of digits and determines whether or not the grid is a solution to a Sudoku puzzle.

23. **Connect Four**
Connect Four© is a game in which two players, Black and Green, alternate placing chips in one of seven columns. Each column can contain up to six chips. The chips, inserted at the top of a column, slide down the column and come to rest above the last chip placed in that column. A player wins the game when there are four chips in a row vertically, horizontally, or diagonally, of his color.

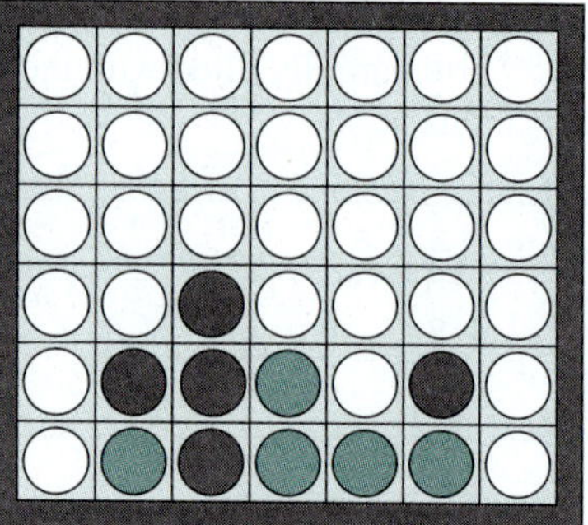

FIGURE 7.44 Connect Four

a. A configuration of the game is a 6 × 7 integer array, board, such that

   i. board[i][j] == 1 indicates that a green chip occupies position (*i,j*);
   ii. board[i][j] == 2 indicate that a black chip occupies position (*i,j*); and
   iii. board[i][j] == 0 indicates that position(*i,j*) is empty.

   The configuration that models the picture of Figure 7.44 is

```
0 0 0 0 0 0 0
0 0 0 0 0 0 0
0 0 0 0 0 0 0
0 0 2 0 0 0 0
0 2 2 1 0 2 0
0 1 2 1 1 1 0
```

   Write a method that accepts a game configuration and determines whether or not a player has won, returning 'G' for green, 'B' for black, or 'N' for neither. Test your method in a program that reads a board configuration and reports the winner, if there is one.

b. Write a method

```
int makeMove(int[][] configuration, int column, char color)
```

   such that configuration is a board configuration, column is an integer in the range 0 to 6, and color is either 'G' or 'B'. The method makeMove(...) updates the board configuration by placing a chip of the specified color in the appropriate column. If a column is full, then the method simply returns 0, otherwise the method performs the update and returns 1, indicating a successful move.

c. Write a method that plays the game interactively against the computer. Your method must check for illegal moves and report when the game is over. The computer can play by choosing a random column and retrying if the move is illegal. However, to make the game more interesting, you might devise a "strategy" for the computer's move. You need to check if the game ends in a tie. Include your methods in a program that plays the game.

THE BIGGER PICTURE

1. ARRAY IMPLEMENTATION

An array holds values of the same data type. Why is that? The answer relates to array storage and array access. Let's look at an example.

The statement

```
int [] myArray = new int[50];
```

- creates an array of 50 consecutive memory cells each capable of storing one integer, and
- assigns the address of the first element of the array (myArray[0]) to the reference variable myArray.

Because an integer requires four bytes of storage, an array of 50 integers uses 200 consecutive bytes. The reference variable myArray holds the address myArray[0], the first of these bytes.

For any valid array index i, the computer locates the value of myArray[i] by calculating the address **4** × i + myArray. This computation only works when every element in the array is *four* bytes long. See Figure 7.45.

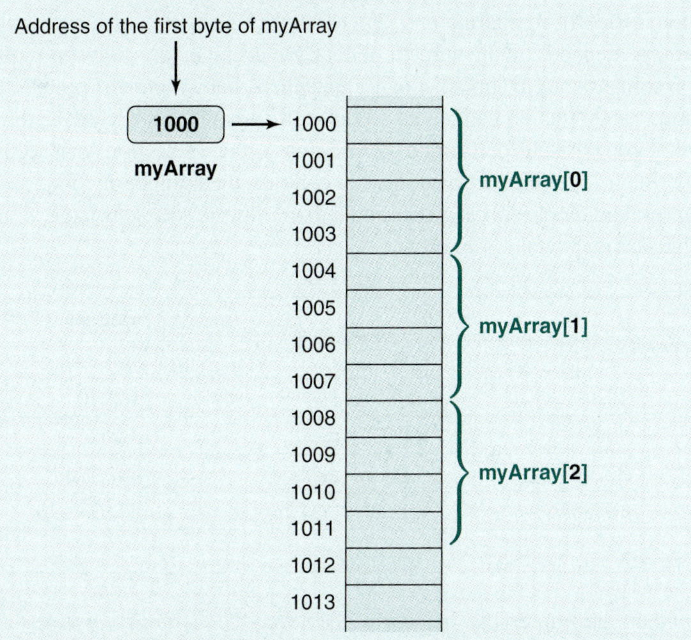

FIGURE 7.45 The address of myArray[2] is 1008

Exercises

1. Given the declaration

   ```
   short[] a = new short[20],
   ```

   if the reference a has the value 1300, what is the address of a[10]?

2. Recall that a two-dimensional array is an array of arrays. How does Java calculate the address of a[3][7], given the declaration

```
int[][] a = new int[10][10]?
```

3. How many bytes are allocated for an array declared and instantiated as

```
double[][] a = new double[10][10]?
```

2. SORTING

Sorting is so common an operation that it is rightly emphasized in any introductory programming book. In this chapter, you can find four different sorting algorithms—insertion sort, selection sort, max sort, and counting sort. And these are just a few of the possibilities. There is also bucket sort, radix sort, Shell's sort, heapsort, merge sort, quicksort, and dozens more. Why not just study the best procedure and be done with it? Because there is no *best* sorting algorithm—what is *best* depends on a number of considerations. Indeed, there are many ways to measure the effectiveness of a sorting algorithm:

- How fast can an algorithm sort?

  When analyzing the efficiency of an algorithm, we usually count the number of times the algorithm performs some fundamental operation. For a sorting algorithm, that operation is usually comparing one item to another. And, of course the number of comparisons depends on the number of data. On average, insertion sort requires about 500,000 comparisons to sort a list of 1000 integers, but a more efficient sort, such as quicksort, can do the job with about 14,000 comparisons. To sort n data, the maximum number of comparisons performed by insertion sort and selection sort (see Programming Problem 15) is proportional to n^2. In contrast, the number of comparisons done by heapsort and merge sort is proportional to $n \times \log_2 n$. As n gets large, n^2 increases at a much faster rate than $n \times \log_2 n$:

n	n^2	$n\log_2 n$
32	1,024	160
1024	1048576	10,240
4096	16,777,216	5,952
32768	1,073,741,824	491,520
1048576	1,099,511,627,776	20,971,520

  The numbers are impressive. In practice, however, the *theoretically* fastest algorithm doesn't always correlate to the fastest algorithm. For one thing, theoretical calculations often assume the worst-case scenario for every algorithm, but sometimes an algorithm gets lucky. For example, insertion sort performs only $n - 1$ comparisons if, by chance, the data is already sorted. This is the best case for insertion sort. Every algorithm has a best case, average case, and a worst case. Practically speaking, the worst case may not happen very often.

  Computer science is distinguished as a field that combines the best of mathematical analysis with clever engineering. And the question of which is the fastest algorithm is always met with a dual attack of theoretical results and experimental analysis.

- Does a sorting algorithm require extra memory?

  A sorting algorithm frequently requires extra memory. For example, to sort an array of size *n*, merge sort requires a second array of the same size to accomplish its task. Insertion sort, on the other hand, requires just one extra variable (temp) regardless of the number of data, 10 or 10,000. To sort an array of size *n*, many algorithms, such as insertion sort, use a fixed amount of extra space, but other algorithms, such as merge sort, require an amount of extra space that is proportional to *n*; so as the length of the list grows, so does the additional space.

  Algorithms that use a fixed amount of extra space are called *in-place*. When sorting very large lists, space considerations are sometimes more important than time considerations.

- Does the algorithm change the order of equal elements?

  Sometimes a list has duplicate copies of the same value. A sorting algorithm that preserves the order of equal elements is called *stable*.

- Does the algorithm perform well on any particular type of data?

  Sometimes a sorting algorithm exhibits its best behavior on certain kinds of data. For example, some sorting algorithms perform better than others on

  - lists that start out almost sorted,
  - very small lists,
  - very large lists, or
  - lists with a restricted range of values.

  In general, empirical testing of actual data is recommended before choosing a sorting algorithm.

Exercises

1. For insertion sort (Example 7.4), selection sort (Programming Exercise 15), and counting sort (Programming Exercise 13), determine:

   a. How many comparisons, in terms of the input size *n*, does each sort make in the worst case?

   b. How many comparisons, in terms of the input size *n*, does each sort make in the best case?

   c. How much extra space does the sort use? Is it an *in-place* sort?

   d. Is the sort stable? Does this question make sense for counting sort? Explain.

2. Of the sorting methods: insertion sort, selection sort, and counting sort, which works best with

   - small lists,
   - large lists,
   - lists that are almost sorted, and
   - lists with a restricted range of values? Justify your answers.

3. Add a counter to each of the four sorting methods that keeps track of the number of comparisons performed by the algorithm. Initialize an array with 5000 random integers in the range 1 to 1000. Run all four sorts on the same array. How do the sorts compare?

CHAPTER 8

Recursion

And then Little Cat A took the hat off HIS head.
"It is good that I have some one
To help ME," he said.
"This is Little Cat B.
And I keep him about,
And when I need help
Then I let him come out."
—from Dr. Seuss's *The Cat in the Hat Comes Back*

Objectives

The objectives of Chapter 8 include an understanding of

- recursion as a method of program control,
- problem solving via recursive thinking,
- Java's implementation of recursive algorithms,
- tracing and debugging a recursive method,
- the connection between tail recursion and iteration, and
- the factors that affect the efficiency of recursive programs.

Recursion is a fundamental problem-solving tool that is part of the control structure of most programming languages, object-oriented or not. There is nothing particularly object-oriented about recursion. Whether you study recursion here, or delay until after Part II, wrapping up recursion with object-oriented methodology is a distraction for students new to both ideas.

8.1 INTRODUCTION

You know that methods can call other methods. You may be surprised to learn that a method can call itself. Such a method is called *recursive*, and using recursive methods to solve a problem is called *recursion*. In the Dr. Seuss classic *The Cat in the Hat Comes Back*, the Cat in the Hat finds that cleaning up his mess is too tough a job to do alone. So he pulls Little Cat A out of his hat to help, but Little Cat A also needs help, so Little Cat A pulls out Little Cat B, and so on. After a while there are enough cats to get the job done, and the cats start to jump back into the hats. When the cats have finished climbing back, the Cat in the Hat packs up and says that his job is done. Recursion is a lot like that. The Cat in the Hat is the method, and when a cat pulls out another cat to help him, that's a method calling itself. That's recursion.

8.2 A SIMPLE RECURSIVE METHOD

We begin by repeating ourselves. See if you can trace through the execution of this never-ending electronic Hallmark card:

```
public static void forgetMeNot()
{
   System.out.println("I Miss You");
   forgetMeNot(); // a recursive call
}
```

The method prints "I Miss You" and then calls itself, which prints "I Miss You" and then calls itself, which prints "I Miss You" and then calls itself, and so on.

```
I Miss You
I Miss You
I Miss You
...
```

Unless your intention is to annoy, amuse, or disturb the recipient, this electronic greeting card should be rewritten with a little more restraint. This infinite e-card can be fixed so that it prints "I Miss You" only three times and then prints a closing "Love, Me". This revised method requires a parameter that counts how many times the message is printed. The program of Example 8.1 does precisely that.

EXAMPLE 8.1

Problem Statement Write a recursive method that prints "I Miss You" *n* times and signs off "Love, Me".

Java Solution

```
public class GreetingCard
{
   public static void forgetMeNot(int n) // n is the number of times the message is printed.
   {
      if (n != 0)
      {
         System.out.println("I Miss You");
         forgetMeNot(n – 1); // the recursive call
      }
   }

   public static void main(String[] args)
   {
      forgetMeNot(3); // invokes method for the first time
      System.out.println();
      System.out.println("Love, Me");
   }
}
```

Output

```
I Miss You
I Miss You
I Miss You
Love, Me
```

Discussion The recursive method forgetMeNot(...) is called by main(...) and passed the argument 3. In order to discern what this method does, it is helpful to trace through it.

Tracing a recursive method is harder than tracing an iterative method, because, as you will see, there might be many different instances of the method running simultaneously—one active and the rest suspended and waiting to become active. In the GreetingCard class, the main(...) method begins with the call forgetMeNot(3), which prints "I Miss you" and then calls forgetMeNot(2), which prints "I Miss You" and then calls forgetMeNot(1), which prints "I Miss You" and finally calls forgetMeNot(0), which does nothing because n!=0 evaluates to false. forgetMeNot(0) returns (i.e., exits) and the previous call, forgetMeNot(1), picks up where it left off, but forgetMeNot(1) has nothing more to do, so it just exits and program control returns to the suspended forgetMeNot(2), which exits and control returns to forgetMeNot(3), which also exits, passing control back to main(...), which finally prints "Love, Me". Figure 8.1 shows a *trace* of the calling sequence.

```
1.   main
2.           forgetMeNot(3)
3.           "I Miss You"
4.                   forgetMeNot(2)
5.                   "I Miss You"
6.                           forgetMeNot(1)
7.                           "I Miss You"
8.                                   forgetMeNot(0)
9.                                   return
10.                          return
11.                  return
12.          return
13.  "Love, Me"
```

FIGURE 8.1 A trace of *forgetMeNot*(3)

Traces such as the one in Figure 8.1 occur throughout this chapter, and learning to read them is important. The trace is read from top to bottom as the program executes.

- Indentations are made every time a recursive call is made.
- When a method returns, the indentation goes back to the previous level.
- Execution continues at the statement following the recursive call.

This is a convenient way to represent the execution of a recursive program because you can tell at any time:

1. which instance of a method is currently active,
2. which are suspended and waiting, and
3. which are finished running.

For example, look at line 11 of Figure 8.1. The method calls forgetMeNot(0) and forgetMeNot(1) are finished, forgetMeNot(2) is running and near completion, and forgetMeNot(3) is suspended and waiting for forgetMeNot(2) to return.

This electronic greeting card is a very simple example, but it illustrates a very important principle of recursion.

Every recursive method must have a way out, that is, a terminating case. In other words, every recursive method must have a nonrecursive option.

This terminating case is sometimes called the *base case*. Without a base case, a recursive method runs forever. Just having a base case is not enough. The sequence of recursive calls must eventually reach the base case or the method will fall into an infinite recursion. In the program of Example 8.1, the base case is the condition on line 5, if n! = 0. This base case eventually evaluates to false, preventing the method from falling into an infinite recursion.

8.2.1 Tail (Loop) Recursion

The forgetMeNot(...) method is easy to trace because the recursion occurs at the very end of the method, and nothing remains for the method to execute when the recursive call returns. You can see this behavior in Figure 8.1: all the returns are stacked diagonally, and no statements are left to execute after each recursive call returns. This kind of recursion is called *tail recursion* or *loop recursion*, and the recursive method executes very much like a loop.

> A tail recursive method makes just one recursive call and exits immediately after the recursive call returns.

Indeed, tracing tail recursion may remind you of a simple loop.

What if forgetMeNot(...) included a few additional statements following the recursive call? You can imagine a much more complicated trace. The tracing of a recursive method can quickly become a maze of calls and returns, all intertwined at different levels. How does a programmer keep track? Or more importantly, how does a programmer *design* a recursive program?

The good news is that the computer keeps track of this potential maze of method calls. The programmer does not need to think about this at all. Indeed, the programmer *should not* think about this at all. Solving problems recursively requires a new way of thinking that, unlike iterative programs, does not involve tracing through the execution of the program. Beginners sometimes find this both unnatural and challenging. The next section introduces you to the process of recursive thinking.

8.3 RECURSIVE THINKING

Recursion is a powerful mechanism that can control the flow of a program. Any loop can be reprogrammed using tail recursion, but recursion is not just an alternative way of implementing loops. Recursion provides an elegant method for describing complicated program flow and solving very difficult problems. To program with recursion, one must learn to *solve problems* recursively. The first and most important step in writing recursive programs is to *think recursively*—like The Cat in the Hat.

> To think recursively, assume that you have a best friend who is willing and able to solve the *same kind of problem* that you are trying to solve. *Recursive thinking is the process of using your friend to help you solve your problem.*

This two-line algorithm is an example of recursive thinking. To sort a list of n numbers:

1. Ask your friend to sort the first $n - 1$ numbers.
2. Insert the last number into the appropriate spot in the sorted list of $n - 1$ numbers.

The logic of this little algorithm is elegant. Once the first $n - 1$ numbers are sorted, the only thing left to do is insert the last value into the list where it belongs. The correctness of the algorithm is based on the assumption that your friend did her job correctly in step 1. Step 1 may seem like magic, and in a way it is. When first solving a problem recursively, it is natural to think hard about what your friend should do and how your friend calls another friend, and so on, but, in fact, you do *not* need to know or care about how your friend does her job. Rest assured that she always comes through. For now, don't worry about how it all works, you will see soon enough. To think recursively, trust that your friend will do her job correctly, and concentrate on using your friend's effort in the right way.

Here is a simple example of recursive thinking. Suppose that you are at an ATM and that you must enter a dollar value between 20 and 200. The machine continues requesting an amount until you supply a valid value. A computer program typically would use a loop to do this type of input checking, but it is quite natural to use tail recursion.

Recursive Solution:
To **"Accept a deposit between 20 and 200"**

a. Accept a value.
b. If the value is between 20 and 200 then accept it and stop, otherwise go on to step c.
c. Have your friend **"Accept a deposit between 20 and 200"**.

Note that step c is a request to your friend to solve the same kind of problem you are trying to solve. At this point, you might wonder:

- How does step c work? How does my friend know what to do?
  Answer: Your friend follows the same instructions that you follow.
- Isn't this logic circular? Won't my friend just have to ask another friend for help?
  Answer: Yes, your friend will call his friend, and his friend will call another friend, and so on. But this is not circular, because at some point a friend is no longer needed. This happens at the *base* case (step b), when the input value is between 20 and 200.

Of course this task can also be accomplished with a loop. Contrast the following iterative algorithm with the recursive algorithm. The loop version explicitly checks values until a valid amount is entered.

Loop Solution:
To **"Accept a deposit between 20 and 200"**

a. Accept a value;
b. While the value is not between 20 and 200
c.   Accept a value;

8.3.1 From Recursive Thinking to a Java Method

Once you have a recursive algorithm, translating your algorithm into a Java method is a mechanical process. Every request of your friend becomes a recursive call. In Example 8.2, we transform the previous algorithm into a recursive method.

EXAMPLE 8.2

Problem Statement Write a program using a recursive method that accepts an ATM deposit between 20 and 200 dollars.

Recursive Solution In the following program, main(...) requests and prints the value returned by getDeposit(). You should have no problem understanding this. The recursive method getDeposit() on lines 4–14 of the Java solution mimics the following algorithm:

To **"Accept a deposit between 20 and 200"**

a. Accept any value. (Lines 8–9)
b. If the value is between 20 and 200, then return it, otherwise go on to step c. (Lines 10–13)
c. Have your friend **"Accept a deposit between 20 and 200".** (Line 13)

Java Solution

```
1.  import java.util.*;
2.  public class Deposit
3.  {

4.     public static int getDeposit()
5.     {
6.        int value;
7.        System.out.println("Please input a value between 20 and 200");
8.        Scanner input = new Scanner(System.in);
9.        value = input.nextInt();
10.       if ((value > 20) && (value < 200))
11.          return value;
12.       else
13.          return getDeposit();                // a recursive call
14.    }

15.    public static void main(String[] args)
16.    {
17.       int x = getDeposit();
18.       System.out.println("Your deposit was " + x + " dollars");
19.    }

20. }
```

Output The output of this program is shown below with the input 130.

Please input a value between 20 and 200 **130**
Your deposit was 130 dollars

The output is shown again for the input: 298, 12, 109.

Please input a value between 20 and 200 **298**
Please input a value between 20 and 200 **12**
Please input a value between 20 and 200 **109**
Your deposit was 109 dollars

Discussion Like the greeting card method, getDeposit(), is tail recursive because no actions occur in getDeposit() after the recursive call. The last statement executed in the method is the recursive call. Figure 8.2 shows a trace.

```
main
        getDeposit()
        "Please input a value between 20 and 200"
        298
                getDeposit()
                "Please input a value between 20 and 200"
                12
                        getDeposit()
                        109
                        return 109
                return 109
        return 109
"Your deposit was 109 dollars"
```

FIGURE 8.2 Trace of *getDeposit*()

One difference between the recursive methods of Example 8.2 and Example 8.1 is that getDeposit() returns a value. That is, getDeposit() is not a void method. In the previous example, getDeposit() is called three times. Observe how **109** is returned by the third call of getDeposit() to the second call of getDeposit(), which returns it to the first call of getDeposit(), and finally to main(...), which prints "Your deposit was **109** dollars."

A recursive method can and often does return a value.

If a recursive method returns a value, do not ignore that value. Ignoring a returned value usually indicates a logical error. In Example 8.2, getDeposit() includes two return statements, one on line 11 and the other on line 13. Each statement returns an integer. The number returned via the statement on line 13 is used; it is itself returned. If we change the statement on line 13 from

```
return getDeposit();
```

to

```
getDeposit();
```

then, when the recursive call on line 13 terminates, the returned value "hangs." In this case, the compiler catches the error and reports

```
missing return value
```

but not every such error is caught by the compiler.

8.3.2 Designing Recursive Methods with Parameters

Like nonrecursive methods, recursive methods can have parameters.

The next example, like Example 8.1, illustrates a recursive method that accepts a parameter.

EXAMPLE 8.3

Suppose that you keep a record of your checkbook transactions such that positive numbers indicate deposits and negative numbers withdrawals. One day, you discover that your account is overdrawn, a check has bounced, and to add insult to injury you are being assessed a penalty of $25. You are certain that you had deposited enough money to cover your checks, so you reexamine your last 30 to 40 transactions, recalculate your transactions, and hope that the bank has made an error. It could happen!

Problem Statement Write a program that calculates the sum of all deposits among the first n transactions of a checkbook register.

Recursive Solution To **sum the deposits among the first n transactions of your checkbook**:

a. If n equals 1, then handle the task yourself and don't bother your friend. Return the single value if it is positive, otherwise return 0 (lines 8–12 in the solution that follows). If n is greater than 1, go to steps b and c (lines 13–17).
b. Ask your friend to **sum the deposits among the first $n - 1$ transactions in your checkbook**, and tell you the answer (line 13).
c. If the nth transaction is positive then add that number to what your friend tells you and return the sum, otherwise just return what he tells you (lines 14–17).

A Caveat: Your friend is tireless and trustworthy, but you must not overwork him. When you ask your friend for help, make sure that you give him a job slightly smaller than the original task. If your original job requires n transactions, give your friend $n - 1$ transactions. If you start with only one transaction, do it yourself. This ensures that your method does not fall into an infinite succession of recursive calls!

Java Solution Here is the Java version of the recursive method that adds the deposits in a list of transactions. The transactions, positive values for deposits and negative values for withdrawals, are stored in an integer array of size n.

```
1.  import java.util.*;
2.  public class AddDeposits
3.  {
4.      public static int addDeposit(int[] checkbook, int numEntries)
5.      {
6.          if (numEntries <= 0) // Just in case the user enters 0 or fewer transactions
7.              return 0;           // Normally, this should not occur.
8.          if (numEntries == 1) // The actual base case in a normal execution
9.              if (checkbook[0] > 0)
10.                 return checkbook[0];
11.             else
12.                 return 0;

13.         int sum = addDeposit (checkbook, numEntries - 1); // Here is the recursion (step b)
14.         if (checkbook[numEntries - 1] > 0)
15.             return (sum + checkbook[numEntries - 1]);
16.         else
17.             return (sum); // (step c)
18.     }

19.     public static void main(String[] args)     // The main method asks how many transactions
20.                                                // to expect, and accepts that many into an array.
21.     {                                          // Transactions are negative integers for withdrawals
```

```
22.       Scanner input = new Scanner(System.in);      // and positive integers for deposits.
23.       System.out.println("How many transactions?");
24.       int size = input.nextInt();
25.       int checkbook[] = new int[size] ;
26.       for (int i = 0; i < size ; i++)
27.       {
28.          System.out.println("Input next transaction:");
29.          checkbook[i] = input.nextInt();
30.       }
31.       System.out.println("Your deposits add up to " + addDeposit(checkbook, size) + " dollars.");
32.    }

33. }
```

Output

```
How many transactions? 5
Input next transaction:    10
Input next transaction:    20
Input next transaction:    −15
Input next transaction:    30
Input next transaction:    −10
Your deposits add up to 60 dollars.
```

Discussion Notice the direct correspondence between the Java method and the recursive algorithm. The main method on lines 19–33 fills an array with a list of integers that represent banking transactions. The recursive method addDeposit(...) on lines 4–18 implements the recursive computation that adds the deposits.

Unlike the previous recursive algorithms, this algorithm is *not* tail recursive. We trace the algorithm in Figure 8.3. The difference between this algorithm and the previous ones is that here, additional statements execute when a recursive call returns. The next number in the array, if it is positive, is added to the sum returned by the previous recursive call.

```
addDeposit(arr, 5)
        addDeposit(arr, 4)
                addDeposit(arr, 3)
                        addDeposit(arr, 2)
                                addDeposit(arr, 1)
                                return 10
                        sum = 10
                        return (10 + arr[2]) // return 30
                sum = 30
                return 30
        sum = 30
        return (30 + arr[4]) // return 60
sum = 60
return 60
```

FIGURE 8.3 Trace of *addDeposit(arr, 5)*

Following is an iterative solution that accomplishes the same task as the recursive method addDeposit(...). This version uses a for loop to sum n transactions that are stored in an integer array transaction indexed from 0 through $n - 1$ inclusive.

Loop Solution

```
sum = 0
for i = 0 to n - 1
   if (transaction[i] > 0) then sum = sum + transaction[i]
return (sum)
```

You should have no trouble translating this algorithm into a Java method.

Here is another example of a method that is non–tail recursive.

EXAMPLE 8.4

Problem Statement Your school runs a housing lottery for dormitory rooms. Each student is assigned a random number, and the student given the lowest number chooses a room first, followed by the student with the next lowest number, and so on. These numbers are all stored in an array, and they are announced one by one in order from lowest to highest. When a student's number is announced, he/she steps up to choose a room. Design and implement a method that returns the lowest integer stored in an array.

Recursive Solution **To find the lowest value in an array:**

a. If the array has just one value, return that value.

b. Otherwise, ask your friend to consider an array identical to yours but with the last value excluded, and **find the lowest value in this smaller array** (line 9 in the solution that follows).

c. Return either the last value in the array or the value your friend returned to you, whichever is smaller (lines 10–12).

Java Solution Let's turn these steps into a Java method that is embedded in a complete application.

The recursive method occurs on lines 4–13.

```
1.  import java.util.*;
2.  public class Lottery
3.  {

4.     public static int findLowest (int arr[], int size)
5.           // Finds the lowest integer in arr[]from index start to end
6.     {
7.        if (size == 1)
8.           return arr[0];                          // Step (a) above
9.        int temp = findLowest(arr, size - 1);      // Step (b) above
10.       if (temp < arr[size - 1])
11.          return (temp);
12.       else return arr[size - 1];                 // Step (c) above
13.    }

14.    public static void main(String[] args)    // The main method asks for the number of students
15.    {
16.       Scanner input = new Scanner(System.in);   // and requests the lottery number for each.
17.       System.out.println("How many students?");
18.       int size = input.nextInt();
19.       int a[] = new int[size] ;
20.       for (int i = 0; i < size ; i++)
21.       {
22.             System.out.println("Input lottery number:");
```

```
23.         a[i] = input.nextInt();
24.     }
25.     System.out.println("The lowest lottery number is: " + findLowest(a, size));
26.   }
27. }
```

Output

```
How many students?
3
Input lottery number:
28
Input lottery number:
32
Input lottery number:
20
The lowest lottery number is: 20
```

Discussion

Lines 15–24: The statements that occur on these lines request the number of students and fill the array with student housing numbers. You should have no trouble understanding these lines.

Line 25: The call findLowest(a, size) returns the lowest value in the array.

Lines 4–13: This is the recursive method, findLowest(int [] arr, int size). Let's trace the method using an array that has three integers, 28, 32, and 20. The trace is shown in Figure 8.4.

```
findLowest(a, 3)
        findLowest(a, 2)
                findLowest(a, 1)
                return 28
        temp = 28;
        if (28 < arr[2 – 1]) return 28 else return arr[1]
        Since arr[1] = 32, 28 is returned
        return 28
temp = 28;
if(28 < arr[3 – 1]) return 28 else return arr[2]
Since arr[2] = 20, 20 is returned
return 20
```

FIGURE 8.4 Trace of *findLowest(a, 3)*

Notice that the variable size has a different value depending on which instance of findLowest(...) is executing. Indeed, Java keeps track of the values of all parameters and local variables in a recursive method in this way. For example, findLowest(a, 3) is first called with size = 3. This is seen in the first line of the trace. The call findLowest(a, 2) has its own variable size with value 2. The value of size (3) from the first call is stored until the call findLowest(a, 2) returns. Then, findLowest(a, 3) resumes execution from where it had paused. Indeed, the value of size (3) is used when the line:

```
if (temp < arr[size – 1])
   return (temp);
else
   return arr[size];
```

executes. You can see this on the third line from the bottom of the trace.

The recursive method findLowest(...) has two parameters. The next example also uses multiple parameters and illustrates that a recursive method may include more than one recursive call.

8.3.3 Methods with More than One Recursive Call

The previous examples demonstrate how to think recursively and how to incorporate recursive thinking into a Java program. We emphasize that you do not need to know how to trace a recursive method in order to write a recursive method. If you have faith in your "friend," your recursive methods will work.

Nevertheless, tracing a method can be useful if you make an error and need to debug a program. Moreover, understanding how to trace a recursive program might also improve your ability to think recursively. In the next example, we consider a problem that requires one of two possible recursive method calls.

The application of Example 5.12 is a simple guessing game. To play, the computer chooses a random number between 1 and 100 and the player attempts to discover the number with as few guesses as possible. With each guess, the program responds "too high" or "too low." Consequently, with each subsequent guess, the player narrows the range of possibilities until the secret number is discovered. For example, if 26 is the mystery number, the game might proceed as follows:

Player's Guess	Computer's Response
30	too high
10	too low
20	too low
23	too low
24	too low
29	too high
28	too high
27	too high
26	that's it!

This player was not so clever. A clever player can guess any number between 1 and 100 in at most seven guesses. Can you see the recursive idea? With each guess the player can cut the range of possibilities in half, by guessing the middle number in the range. After receiving a response from the computer, the player can call on his or her "friend" to guess the number in the reduced range. That's right, recursion! Using this method, the correct sequence of guesses is:

50	too high	(The new range is 1–49.)
25	too low	(The new range is 26–49.)
37	too high	(The new range is 26–36.)
31	too high	(The new range is 26–30.)
28	too high	(The new range is 26–27.)
26	that's it!	

This simple game is at the heart of the *binary search* algorithm presented in Chapter 7. Binary search is used by all computer programs that accomplish fast searches—programs such as the ones used on eBay, Amazon, or Expedia—the workhorses of e-commerce. Example 8.5 presents another slant on binary search, a recursive version.

To search for a value, *x*, in a *sorted* array, first examine the value in the middle position, and depending on whether that middle value is greater than *x* or less than *x*, ask your friend to search another array, half the size. The base case occurs when the middle value is equal to *x*; then you have succeeded in finding it, and you do not make a recursive call.

EXAMPLE 8.5 **Problem Statement** Write a program that searches for a key in an array of characters using a recursive binary search algorithm.

Java Solution

```
1.  import java.util.*;
2.  public class BinarySearch
3.  {
4.     public static int binSearch(char[] x, int start, int finish, char key)

5.        // x is an ascending sorted array of characters
6.        // key is the character for which we are searching
7.        // start and finish are the indices that mark the subarray of the array being searched
8.        // returns the index of the cell that contains key, or (−1) if the key is not found.

9.     {
10.       if (start > finish) return −1;          // key is not found, the range has collapsed
11.       int mid = (start + finish)/2;          // mid is halfway between the two endpoints
12.          if (x[mid] == key)                  // key is found
13.             return mid;
14.          else
15.             if (x[mid] < key)                // search the upper half
16.                return binSearch(x, mid + 1, finish, key);
17.             else
18.                return binSearch(x, start, mid − 1, key); // search lower half
19.    }
20.    public static void main(String[] args)    //This tests the binSearch method by filling an array
21.    {                                          // with the characters 'A' through 'Z'
22.       char[] a = new char[26] ;
23.       for (int i = 0; i < 26 ; i++)           // fill the array 'A' − 'Z'
24.          a[i] = (char)(i + 65) ;              // 65 represents 'A'
25.       System.out.println( "F is in location " + binSearch(a, 0, 25, 'F') + " of the array");
26.       System.out.println("S is in location " + binSearch(a, 0, 25, 'S') + " of the array");
27.       System.out.println("Z is in location " + binSearch(a, 0, 25, 'Z') + " of the array");
28.       if (binSearch(a, 0, 25, '!') == −1)
29.          System.out.println("! is not located in the array");
30.    }

31. }
```

Output

```
F is in location 5 of the array
S is in location 18 of the array
Z is in location 25 of the array
! is not located in the array
```

Discussion The main(...) method (lines 20–30) creates a sorted character array with the characters 'A' through 'Z' and tests the binSearch(...) method with a number of different data. We trace through the execution of the recursive call on line 26,

binSearch(a, 0, 25, 'S').

The trace in Figure 8.5 goes five levels deep.

```
binSearch(a, 0, 25, 'S')
        mid = (0 + 25)/2 = 12;
        a[12] == 'S' is false; a[12] < 'S')
        return binSearch(a, 13, 25, 'S')
                mid = (13 + 25)/2 = 19;
                a[19] == 'S' is false; a[19] > 'S'
                return binSearch(a, 13, 18, 'S');
                        mid = (13 + 18)/2 = 15;
                        a[15] =='S' is false; a[15] < 'S'
                        return binSearch(a, 16, 18, 'S');
                                mid = (16 + 18)/2 = 17;
                                a[17] == 'S' is false; a[17] < 'S'
                                return binSearch(a, 18, 18, 'S');
                                        mid = (18 + 18)/2 = 18; a[18] =='S' is true
                                        return 18
                                return 18
                        return 18
                return 18
        return 18
return 18
```

FIGURE 8.5 Trace of *binSearch(a, 0, 25, 'S')*

Unlike the methods of previous examples, binary search includes two recursive calls. The recursion increases to five levels choosing one of the two possible recursive calls each time. Is binary search tail recursive? You bet it is.

> A recursive method is tail recursive when the method exits after the return of the recursive call.

Although there are two *possible* recursive calls in binSearch(...), each one is the last statement executed in the method, and only one of them is called with each invocation of binSearch(...).

> More than one recursive call can appear in a recursive method. The number of different method calls and the number of parameters in each call are independent of whether or not the method is tail recursive.

8.4 THE RUNTIME STACK: TAIL RECURSION VERSUS CLASSIC RECURSION

Any method, recursive or not, may have parameters and local variables.

> When a method is called, the JVM *allocates* or reserves memory for the parameters and local variables of the method.

This section of the computer's memory allocated to parameters and local variables is called the *runtime stack* or simply the *stack*. Other data are stored on the stack, but that does not concern us now. When a method exits, the memory allocated to its parameters and variables is freed or deallocated for other use. For example, consider the following class with a (nonrecursive) method that returns the sum of two integers.

```
1.  public class AddEmUp
2.  {
3.     public static int add(int first, int second)
4.     {
5.        int sum;
6.        sum = first + second;
7.        return sum;
8.     }

9.     public static void main(String [] args)
10.    {
11.       int num1 = 5;
12.       int num2 = 6;
13.       int sum = add(num1, num2);
14.       System.out.println("The sum is " + sum);
15.    }
16. }
```

Figure 8.6 shows the stack

- before line 13 executes,
- when add(...) begins execution on line 5,
- before line 7 executes,
- and again at line 14.

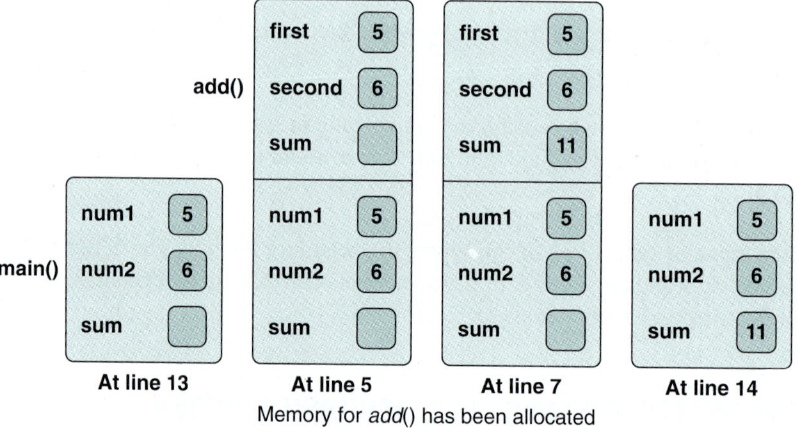

FIGURE 8.6 Memory is allocated for a method.

A recursive method may call itself many times, and each time a method calls itself, new memory is allocated for that particular invocation. Consider the following class, Recur, with one recursive method:

```
public class Recur
{
```

```
3.  public static void recur(int n)
4.  {
5.    if (n <= 1) // the base case, stops recursion. <= is safer style but == is okay.
6.      System.out.println(n + n);
7.    else
8.    {
9.      int sum = n + n;
10.     recur(n - 1); // a recursive call
11.     System.out.println(sum); //executes this upon return
12.   }
13. }

14.   public static void main(String[] args)
15.   {
16.     int number = 3;
17.     recur(number);
18.     System.out.println("All Done!");
19.   }

20. }
```

The program begins in main(...) and proceeds as follows:

- main(...) invokes recur(3) at line 17; main(...) has not finished executing at this point.
- recur(3) begins execution and at line 10 calls recur(2); recur(3) has not finished its work.
- recur(2) begins execution and at line 10 calls recur (1); recur(2) has not finished.
- recur(1) starts execution, prints 2, and exits (lines 5 and 6); recur(1) is complete, and returns.
- recur(2) resumes execution at line 11, prints 4 and exits.
- recur(3) is awakened, prints 6 and exits.
- Control passes back to main() (line 18), which prints "All Done!" and exits.

Each time recur(…) is called, memory for its single parameter and local variable is allocated. So, in theory, the stack can grow rather large and require quite a bit of memory. Each time a recursive call returns to the calling method, which then resumes execution, the values of the calling method's variables and parameters are ready, waiting, and saved on the stack. Figure 8.7 shows how the stack grows and shrinks during the execution of the application Recur.

Unlike the recur(int n) method, which prints the value of sum upon return, a tail recursive method performs no actions after the recursive call returns. Thus, upon return of a tail recursive method, no values that have been saved on the stack are accessed.

At compile time, the compiler *can* tell whether or not a method is tail recursive. If the last statement executed by a method is a recursive call, then the method is tail recursive. On the other hand, if any instruction occurs after the recursive call, whether it be arithmetic, an if statement, or output, then the method is not tail recursive.

Why should we care whether or not a method is tail recursive? Because if a method is tail recursive, then there is no need to stack the local variables and parameters for each recursive call. These values are not needed upon return. And consequently, the method can be executed like a loop, running faster and using less memory.

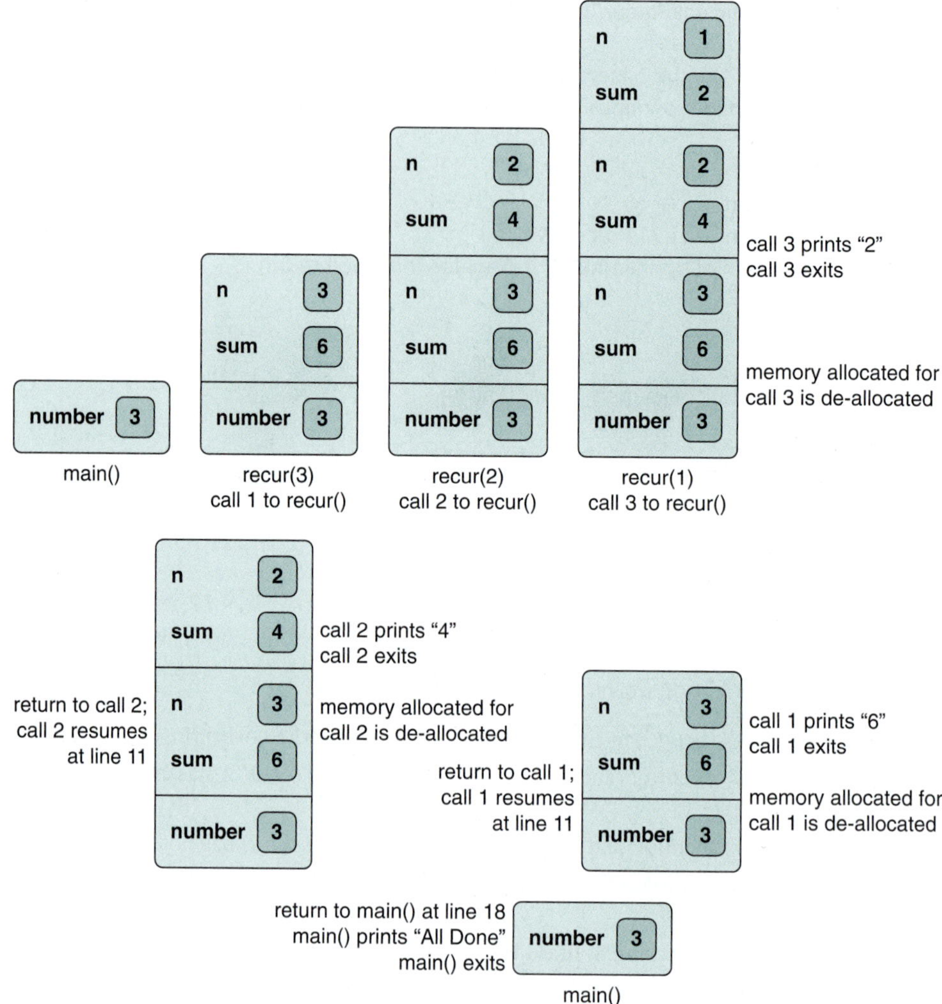

FIGURE 8.7 A trace of *recur*(3). The stack grows and shrinks.

8.4.1 Java and Tail Recursion

Some language compilers automatically translate tail recursion into a loop structure.

> Unfortunately, the Java compiler does *not* transform tail recursion into stack-efficient execution.

The Java compiler handles every recursive method identically, tail recursive or not. Therefore, recursive Java methods that execute too many recursive calls may run out of space, and trigger a *stack-overflow* error. This catastrophe would be commonplace if recursion were used, for example, in a method that waits for a user to click a mouse. The method might check the mouse millions of times a second before the user actually clicks, with the stack growing with each successive recursive call until the stack uses all available memory and *overflows*.

As of 2008, the JVM does not handle tail recursion efficiently. Partly because of this, Java has a well-deserved reputation for being slow and using lots of memory. Therefore, the careful Java programmer should stick to iteration whenever possible, using recursion only when it is really necessary.

Java's well-deserved bad reputation is unfortunate, but note well that it is due to Java's limitations and not to recursion. Any tail recursive method *could* be automatically translated by the compiler into a loop structure, and thereby perform as quickly and with the same memory usage as its iterative counterpart. Compilers for programming languages that rely heavily on recursion do exactly this.

8.4.2 Classic Recursive Algorithms

The careful Java programmer should favor iteration over tail recursion. However, it would be foolish to avoid recursion altogether. A simple and straightforward implementation of an algorithm is not always possible without recursion.

Some algorithms intrinsically need to maintain the stack of values. These are so-called *classic* recursive algorithms. Recursion shows its full power in these algorithms. The following *quicksort* routine is one such classic recursive algorithm.

8.5 QUICKSORT—A CLASSIC RECURSIVE ALGORITHM

The algorithms of Examples 8.1, 8.2, and 8.5 use tail recursion, while those of Examples 8.3 and 8.4 do not. Yet none of these algorithms are classic recursive algorithms. Indeed, these algorithms could easily be implemented using either tail recursion or loops. There are algorithms, however, that cannot be implemented using loops or tail recursion. Such algorithms require the full power of the runtime stack.

> It is not always possible to implement an algorithm with tail recursion.

We next look at a classic recursive sorting algorithm. It is very difficult comprehend this algorithm in terms of iteration. Understanding this algorithm requires that you think recursively. Look ma, no loops!

Sorting routines are perhaps the most common of all algorithms. If searching is the workhorse of e-commerce, then sorting is its twin brother. Consider the following recursive algorithms: one is a famous classic recursive algorithm and the other is a recursive version of a well-known algorithm usually implemented iteratively.

Algorithm A

To sort a list of n numbers:

a. Ask your friend to sort the first $n - 1$ numbers recursively.
b. Insert the last number into the appropriate spot in the sorted list of $n - 1$ numbers.

For example:

To sort the list of numbers:	7, 5, 13, 1, 16, **9**.
After step 1 the list looks like this:	1, 5, 7, 13, 16, **9**.
After step 2 the list is sorted:	1, 5, 7, **9**, 13, 16.

Algorithm B

To sort a list of n numbers:

a. Look at the last number in the list and remember it. Call it *pivot*.
b. *Partition* the list around *pivot*. That is, reorder the list so that all the numbers smaller than *pivot* come first, followed by *pivot*, followed by all the numbers greater than *pivot*. Note that partitioning the list does *not* in itself sort the list.

c. Ask your friend to sort the list of numbers smaller than *pivot*, and then sort the list of numbers greater than *pivot*.

For example:
To sort the list of numbers: 7, 5, 13, 1, 16, **9**.
The pivot is **9**.
After Step 2: 7, 5, 1, **9**, 16, 13.
Note that the list is not sorted yet. It is just partitioned around **9**.
After step 3 the list is sorted: 1, 5, 7, **9**, 13, 16.

Notice how elegant and simple these algorithms are compared to iterative sorting algorithms. The details are left to the compiler, and we are free to think at a higher level. Recursive thinking is a beautiful thing.

Do you recognize one of these algorithms? Indeed, Algorithm A is the recursive version of insertion sort, which was presented in Chapter 7. Algorithm B is a classic recursive algorithm called *quicksort.* Quicksort is no misnomer! Quicksort got its name because, in practice, with careful pivot selection, it is the fastest of all key-comparison sorting algorithms. Its use is so common that it may be the world's most frequently executed algorithm. Yes, that's right—a recursive algorithm underlies almost every single e-commerce application!

We leave the recursive Java implementation of insertion sort (Algorithm A) as an exercise and discuss the implementation of quicksort (Algorithm B) in Example 8.6.

EXAMPLE 8.6 **Problem Statement** Write a program that sorts an array of integers using the quicksort algorithm.

In the following implementation of quicksort, the method

`int partition(int [] a, int low, int high)`

rearranges the array elements around pivot = a[high]. That is, it reorders the array so that all the values in the array less than *pivot* appear to the left of *pivot*, and all the values greater than *pivot* appear to its right. The partition algorithm is not recursive but it is a bit complex. A detailed discussion would be a distraction, so we leave a more detailed analysis as an exercise (see Programming Exercise 17).

Be aware that partition(...) does not itself sort the array. For example, if

$$x = [9, 5, 7, 2, 0, 3, 8, 4, 1, \mathbf{6}]$$

a call to partition(x, 0, 9) rearranges the numbers in x as

[5, 2, 0, 3, 4, 1, **6,** 7, 9, 8].

Here *pivot* is 6. All values to the left of 6 are less than 6, and all values to the right of 6 are greater than 6. In other words, 6 is in its final position within the soon-to-be sorted array, but the other elements have yet to be sorted. Once 6 has been placed, two smaller sorting problems remain:

sort [5, 2, 0, 3, 4, 1] and sort [7, 9, 8].

Java Solution In the following implementation of quicksort, assume that partition(...) behaves as previously described. That is,

`partition(int [] a, int low, int high)`

is a black box that places pivot = a[high] into its final position so that all values to the "left" of pivot are less than or equal to "pivot" and all values to the "right" of "pivot" are greater than "pivot".

```
public class QuickSort
{
```

```
3.   public static int partition (int[] a, int low, int high) // places pivot = a[high] in its final position
4.   {                                                        // returns final position of pivot
5.      int left = low - 1; int temp;
6.      int pivot = a[high];

7.      for (int right = low; right < high; right++)
8.      {
9.         if (a[right] <= pivot)
10.        {
11.           left++;
12.           temp = a[left]; // swap a[left] and a[right]
13.           a[left] = a[right];
14.           a[right] = temp;
15.        }
16.     }
17.     temp = a[left + 1] ; // swap pivot = a[high] with a[left+1]
18.     a[left + 1] = a[high];
19.     a[high] = temp;
20.     return left + 1;      // pivot's new position in the array
21.  }

22.  public static void quickSort (int[] a, int low, int high)
23.  {
24.     if (low < high)                                   // if the array has more than one item
25.     {
26.        int pivotPlace = partition(a, low, high);      // place pivot into its final position
27.        quickSort(a, low, pivotPlace - 1);             // sort the values left of the pivot
28.        quickSort(a, pivotPlace + 1, high);            // sort the values right of the pivot
29.     }
30.  }
31. }

32. public class QuickSortDemo
33. {
34.  public static void main(String[] args)
35.  {
36.     int a[] = {9, 5, 7, 2, 0, 3, 8, 4, 1, 6} ; // some sample data
37.     QuickSort.quickSort(a, 0, 9);
38.     System.out.print("The sorted data : ");
39.     for (int i = 0; i < 10; i++)
40.        System.out.print(a[i] + " ");
41.  }

42. }
```

Output

```
The sorted data : 0 1 2 3 4 5 6 7 8 9
```

Discussion The main(...) method of QuickSortDemo (lines 34–41) initializes an array with 10 integers and passes the array to the quickSort(...) method (line 37). When quickSort() returns, the sorted data are displayed.

The QuickSort class (lines 1–31) consists of two static methods. As you know, partition(...), lines 3–21, rearranges the array so that the pivot element (the last item of the array) is placed in its proper position. All data to the left of pivot are less than or equal to pivot, and those to the right are greater than pivot. The partition(...) method returns the index of the pivot element after the array has been rearranged.

The second method of QuickSort is quickSort(...) itself. Compared to partition(...), quickSort(...) is rather simple. The arguments supplied to quickSort(...) are an array a[] and two integers, low and high, delineating a section of the array.

For example, if

a[] = {5, 2, 0, 3, 4, 1, **6,** 7, 9, 8}, low = 0, and high = 5,

then the call quickSort(a, low, high) sorts the subarray a[0 .. 5] = [5, 2, 0, 3, 4, 1]. Similarly, quickSort(a, 7, 9) performs its magic on a[7 .. 9] = [7, 9, 8].

Line 24 (if low < high) guarantees that the array has more than one element. If this is not the case, no sorting is necessary. This condition, the base case, stops the recursion.

Figure 8.8 traces quickSort(a, 0, 5) using the array a[] = {7, 5, 16, 1, 13, 9}. This trace is harder to follow than a tail recursive trace. To help understand the trace, use the indentations to keep track of which invocation of quickSort(...) is active. We show the array after each call to partition(...) with the pivot value shown in bold in its final position and the active subsection of the array underlined.

quickSort(a, 0, 5)
partition(...) rearranges the array around pivot element 9: [7, 5, 1, **9,** 16, 13]
Then, the first of two recursive calls is made, this one on the subarray [7, 5, 1].

  quickSort(a, 0, 2)
  partition(...) rearranges the subarray [7, 5, 1] around pivot element 1: [**1,** 5, 7, 9, 16, 13]

    quickSort(a, 0, −1)
        0 is not less than −1 so the method returns
    return

    quickSort(a, 1, 2)
    partition(...) rearranges the subarray [5, 7] around pivot element 7: [1, 5, **7,** 9, 16, 13]
    Two recursive calls are made both of which return immediately.

      quickSort(a, 1, 1)
          1 is not less than 1 so this returns
      return

      quickSort(a, 3, 2)
          3 is not less than 2 so this returns
      return
    return
  return

Finally, the second recursive call generated by quickSort(a, 0, 5) is made. This one, quickSort(a, 4, 5), sorts the subarray [16, 13].

  quickSort(a, 4, 5)
  partition(...) rearranges the subarray [16, 13] around 13: [1, 5, 7, 9, **13,** 16]
  As before, two recursive calls are made both of which return immediately.

    quickSort(a, 4, 3)
        4 is not less than 3 so this returns
    return
    quickSort(a, 5, 5)
        5 is not less than 5 so this returns
    return
  return
return

FIGURE 8.8 A trace of *quickSort(...)* on the array [7, 5, 16, 1, 13, 9]

Figure 8.9 gives another view of the actions of quickSort(...).

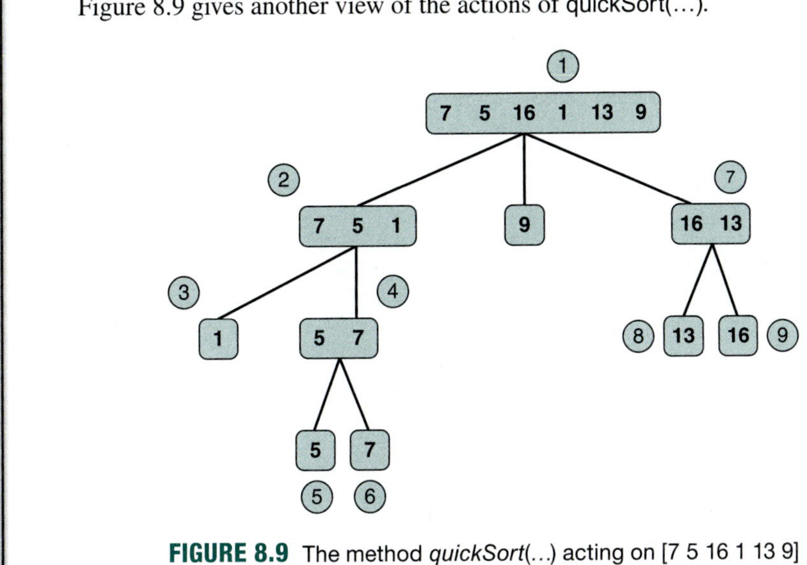

FIGURE 8.9 The method *quickSort(...)* acting on [7 5 16 1 13 9]

Tracing a classic recursive algorithm can be a daunting task. But remember, if you can think recursively, then a trace is not necessary, or even useful, when designing a recursive algorithm. Why bother tracing a recursive algorithm at all? A trace can help you understand what goes on behind the scenes.

> Recursive thinking does not require tracing through the details; it requires only that you make correct use of the recursive call. However, a trace can help you debug a poorly designed algorithm.

In the next section we design a real-life *classic* recursive algorithm. We purposely make a mistake in the design and use a trace to uncover the mistake. Then, we redesign the algorithm correctly and conclude with a Java implementation.

8.6 A CASE STUDY—DESIGNING AN ANAGRAM GENERATOR

Millions of Scrabble© sets have been sold since Alfred Mosher Butts invented the word game during the Great Depression. Each Scrabble player has a rack of seven tiles each displaying a letter, from which he/she tries to make words and subsequently accumulate points. A player gets a 50 point "bingo" bonus for using all seven of his/her tiles in one turn. Scrabble requires a great deal of skill, and a "serious" Scrabble game is much more complex than a casual game among friends. A world-class tournament Scrabble player must be skilled at *anagramming*. Anagramming is the ability to look at a set of letters and visualize possible bingos.

Computers play world-class Scrabble by brute force. To find a seven-letter bingo, a computer simply enumerates all the arrangements or permutations of those letters, checking the validity of each permutation in a dictionary. There are 5040 possible permutations of seven letters, too many for a human to check one by one. But a computer can examine the 5040 possibilities in what seems like no time at all.

In this case study, we design a classic recursive algorithm that generates all the permutations of a given word. In previous examples, we immediately presented a correct recursive solution for the problem, but here, we move more slowly: trying an idea that doesn't quite work, debugging the solution, and refining the idea until it works. This is more akin to the process that you actually engage in as a programmer, especially when designing a difficult recursive algorithm.

8.6.1 A First Attempt

How might we generate and print all permutations of a given word? Is there a way for our *friend* to help? In other words, can we print permutations of a word by printing permutations of smaller words? Does recursive thinking help? Absolutely.

A permutation of a word can begin with any letter of the word, and continues with any other letter, and so on. Indeed,

> a permutation of a word begins with any letter of the word followed by any permutation of the remaining letters.

Hence, to print all the permutations of a particular word, we can rely on our friend to print the permutations of the remaining letters.

Here's a first attempt in pseudocode:

```
permute(word)        // prints all the permutations of a word

    if (word has no characters) // an empty word has no permutations
        return
    else
                              // print each letter followed by all the permutations
                              // of the remaining letters.
    for each letter L in word
    {
        print L;
        permute(word – L);    // (word – L means word with L deleted)
        printnewline;
    }
```

The algorithm looks good, but unfortunately this is wishful thinking. Can you see why this algorithm does not work? Recursion can be subtle, and this recursive algorithm has a flaw. It may be difficult to find the flaw or even notice that there is one, so implement the algorithm, run it, and see what happens.

```
public class PermuteAlt
{

public static void permute(char[] array)
{
 if(array.length != 0)
    for (int j = 0; j < array.length; j++)
    {
      // build a new array from array but without the jth character
      char newWord[] = new char[array.length – 1];
      for (int k = 0; k < j ; k++)                 // copy array[0 .. j – 1] to newWord
          newWord[k] = array[k];

      for (int k = j; k < array.length – 1; k++)   // copy array[j + 1 .. length – 1] to newWord
        newWord[k] = array[k + 1];

      // print the jth character of array
      System.out.print(array[j]);
      // recursively call permute on newWord, i.e., array without the jth character
      permute(newWord);
```

```
            System.out.println();
        }
    }

    public static void main(String[] args)
    {
        char letters[] = {'a', 'b', 'c'};
        permute(letters);
    }

}
```

Using the word abc, the application displays the following words interspersed with various blank lines:

```
abc

cb


bac

ca


cab

ba

```

That's not quite what we expected. We were hoping for:

```
abc
acb
bac
bca
cab
cba
```

A bad recursive idea often gives surprising results. Figure 8.10 displays a trace. Try to find the flaw.

You can check the output from Figure 8.10 and see that it is indeed:

```
abc
newline
cb
newline
newline
bac
newline
ca
newline
newline
cab
newline
ba
newline
newline
```

```
permute({'a', 'b', 'c'})
          print 'a'
          permute({'b', 'c'})
                    print 'b'
                    permute({'c'})
                              print 'c'
                              permute({})
                                        return
                              printnewline
                              return
                    printnewline
                    print 'c'
                    permute({'b'})
                              print 'b'
                              permute ({})
                                        return
                              printnewline
                              return
                    printnewline
                    return
          printnewline
          print 'b'
          permute({'a', 'c'})
                    print 'a'
                    permute({'c'})
                              print 'c'
                              permute({})
                                        return
                              printnewline
                              return
                    printnewline
                    print 'c'
                    permute({'a'})
                              print 'a'
                              permute ({})
                                        return
                              printnewline
                              return
                    printnewline
                    return
          printnewline
          print 'c'
          permute({'a', 'b'})
                    print 'a'
                    permute({'b'})
                              print 'b'
                              permute({})
                                        return
                              printnewline
                              return
                    printnewline
                    print 'b'
                    permute({'a'})
                              print 'a'
                              permute ({})
                                        return
                              printnewline
                              return
                    printnewline
                    return
          printnewline
return
```

FIGURE 8.10 A flawed recursive method

The trace in Figure 8.10 makes a pretty design, but the output is a mess. The letter a is missing from what should be acb on the third line; the letter b is similarly missing from the front of ca on the eighth line; the letter c should appear before ba on the third to last line; and, then there are all the blank lines! What went wrong? How do we fix it? One thing is certain: we *don't* start by randomly patching up the program.

> Do not attempt to fix a program by changing some detail that causes an effect you cannot predict!

This warning is particularly important for a recursive algorithm in which the effects of small changes in code are hard to predict. So don't rush. First determine what is wrong with your algorithm. Then redesign it to fix the problem.

8.6.2 A Better Plan

The missing letters in the output lead us to the problem. The problem with the algorithm of the previous section is the loop:

```
for each letter L in word
{
        print L;
        permute(word – L);
        printnewline;
}
```

This idea is not correct. In this loop, each letter of word is printed *just once* (print L) before the recursive call that is supposed to print all the subsequent permutations, (permute(word − L)). In fact, the letter L should appear *in front of each one* of the permutations of word − L, and not just once in front of the entire list of permutations. Read that last sentence again, and make sure you see why our original idea was flawed. We might have found this flaw just by thinking about it, but a careful trace points us in the right direction.

To fix this problem send each letter to permute(...) as an argument, so that permute(...) prints the letter in front of each permutation that it recursively generates. This suggests a new version of the method permute():

permute(word, precede),

with two parameters:

1. word—the original word, and
2. precede—a letter (or letters) to be printed before each permutation.

We reformulate a recursive idea in terms of this new method:

To **print *precede* before each one of the permutations of *word*,** do the following:

> for each letter *L* in *word*, (reading left to right)
> delete *L* from *word*,
> concatenate *L* to the right end of *precede*, and
> **print *precede* before each of the permutations of the new *word*.** // Recursion!

For example, the method call

permute (**abc, d**)

generates three recursive calls, in order:

permute(**bc, da**),
permute(**ac, db**), and
permute(**ab, dc**).

Here is the pseudocode that describes the algorithm:

```
permute (word, precede)

if (word is empty) then // there are no permutations of word, so just print precede
      print precede followed by newline;

else
      for each letter L in word
            permute(word − L, precede + L)
                  // to print precede in front of all the permutations of word
                  // print precede + L in front of all the permutations of word − L
                  // word − L is word with L deleted
                  // precede + L is precede with L appended to the right end of precede
```

To print the permutations of word, we call permute(word, { }). That is, we print nothing ({ }) in front each of the permutations of word.

Figures 8.11 and 8.12 trace the pseudocode algorithm for the word **abc**.

```
permute(abc, {} )
      permute(bc,a)
            permute(c, ab)
                  permute({}, abc)
                  print "abc" newline
                  return
            permute(b, ac)
                  permute({}, acb)
                  print "acb" newline
                  return
      return
      permute(ac, b)
            permute(c, ba)
                  permute({}, bac)
                  print "bac" newline
                  return
            permute(a, bc)
                  permute({}, bca)
                  print "bca" newline
                  return
      return
      permute(ab, c)
            permute(b, ca)
                  permute({}, cab)
                  print "cab" newline
                  return
            permute(a, cb)
                  permute({}, cba)
                  print "cba" newline
                  return
      return
return
```

FIGURE 8.11 A trace of the pseudocode, *permute(abc, {})*

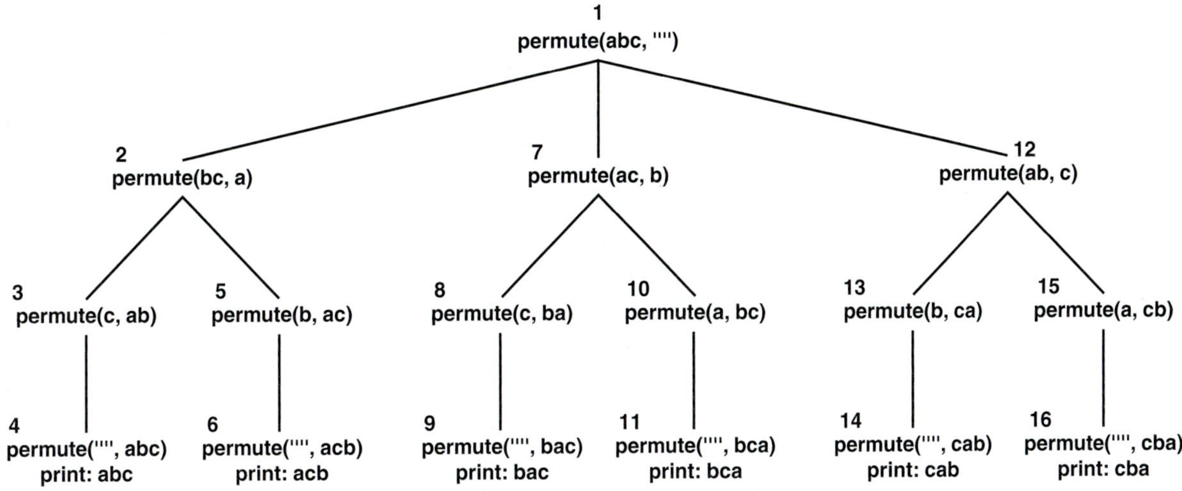

FIGURE 8.12 A graphical trace of the pseudocode, *permute(abc, {})*

The algorithm produces the following output:

```
abc
acb
bac
bca
cab
cba
```

EXAMPLE 8.7

Problem Statement Write a recursive method to generate all permutations of *n* characters.

Java Solution The following class includes the new two-parameter version of permute(...) as well as a main(...) method that demonstrates the action of permute({'e', 'a', 't'}, {}). That is, the permutations of the word **eat** are displayed. We use two char arrays for word and precede.

```
public class Permute
{

public static void permute(char[] word, char[] precede)
{
   if (word.length == 0) // word is empty so just print precede
   {
      for (int k = 0; k < precede.length; k++)
           System.out.print(precede[k]);
      System.out.println();
   }
   else
      for (int j = 0; j < word.length; j++)
         {
            // create newWord from word but with with the jth character deleted
               char newWord[] = new char[word.length - 1];
```

```
            for (int k = 0; k < j ; k++)
               newWord[k] = word[k];
            for (int k = j; k < word.length − 1; k++)
               newWord[k] = word[k + 1];

         // creates newPre from precede with jth character added at end
            char newPre[] = new char[precede.length + 1];
            for (int k = 0; k < precede.length; k++)
               newPre[k] = precede[k];
            newPre[newPre.length − 1] = word[j];

         permute(newWord, newPre);
      }
   }

   public static void main(String[] args)
   {
      char word[] = {'e', 'a', 't'};
      char precede[] = {};
      permute(word, precede);
   }

}
```

Output A call to permute({'e', 'a', 't'}, {}) produces the following set of permutations:

```
eat
eta
aet
ate
tea
tae
```

The permutations of **eat** produce four valid words: eat, eta, ate, and tea... well, five if you include TAE (Telekommunikations-Anschluss-Einheit), the German standard for telephone plugs.

Discussion This final algorithm is not the algorithm that we had initially conceived, but the idea is closely related to our original flawed plan. To begin with an idea, right or wrong, and to refine it and test it until it eventually evolves into a correct solution is a natural and productive process.

8.7 IN CONCLUSION

Recursion is an important tool for problem solving and algorithm design. It is a fundamental method of program control included in virtually every modern programming language. Recursive thinking means having faith that your friend (or cat) will do the job that you ask of him or her. Recursive thinking does *not* require you to imagine a lengthy sequence of recursive calls with corresponding details of the stack.

Recursion provides a simple and elegant tool for problem solving. Programs written recursively are usually easier to understand than other programs. Recursion carries with it a small price, and that is the necessity of maintaining a potentially large stack of values for local variables and parameters. The maintenance of the stack may slow down a program, but often the extra time is negligible.

Tracing a recursive program can be tricky, but it is a good way to observe the amount of work that is done for you behind the scenes. Tracing through the execution of a program step by step is unnecessary when designing a recursive algorithm, but a trace can help when you make a mistake in your design and you need to debug and/or redesign.

Just the Facts

- A recursive method is a method that calls itself.
- Recursion is a powerful method for problem solving.
- When designing a recursive algorithm, assume that you have a friend who is willing and able to solve the same kind of problem that you are trying to solve.
- Recursive thinking does not require you to imagine a lengthy sequence of recursive calls with corresponding details of the stack, but instead insists on "faith in your friend."
- Every recursive method needs a base case that stops the recursion. Recursive calls must eventually reach the base case.
- Tracing a recursive method is useful for debugging, and it forces you to step through the details of the recursive calls and stack values.
- A recursive method can contain several recursive calls.
- A recursive algorithm is often easier to describe and understand than an iterative algorithm.
- Recursion allows you to think at a higher level of abstraction and leave the driving to the compiler.
- Like any method, a recursive method can have any number of parameters.
- Tracing a recursive method is harder than tracing an iterative method because several different instances of the method may be active, one executing and the others suspended and waiting to resume.
- Local variables and parameters for all recursive calls are saved on the stack.
- Recursion, due to the overhead necessary in maintaining the stack, can slow down the execution of a program.
- A tail recursive method is a special kind of recursive method in which the last statement executed is always a recursive call. In other words, the method executes no statements after a recursive call resumes.
- Any loop can be implemented with tail recursion.
- A tail recursive method can always be rewritten as a loop.
- Java does not rewrite tail recursive methods as loops. As a result, the runtime stack can grow very large when executing a tail recursive method.
- Some recursive methods cannot be implemented iteratively as loops. These *classic* recursive algorithms require the full power a stack.

Bug Extermination

- Make sure to include a condition that stops the recursion, and check that the sequence of recursive calls eventually activates this condition. Otherwise, a program falls into infinite recursion.
- When a recursive method returns a value, use the returned value. Letting a returned value "hang" is either a logical error or a sure sign that you shouldn't be returning a value in the first place.
- When you are using recursion, use tail recursion whenever possible.
- A loop is preferable to recursion when the time/space needs of the runtime stack noticeably affect the speed of the program as can sometimes be the case with Java.
- Recursion is preferable to a loop whenever a recursive solution makes the program easier to understand. This is often the case with *classic* recursive algorithms.
- Recursive methods sometimes exhibit great differences in performance on different size data. Be vigilant about testing your recursive methods on realistic data.

EXERCISES

LEARN THE LINGO

Test your knowledge of the chapter's vocabulary by completing the following crossword puzzle.

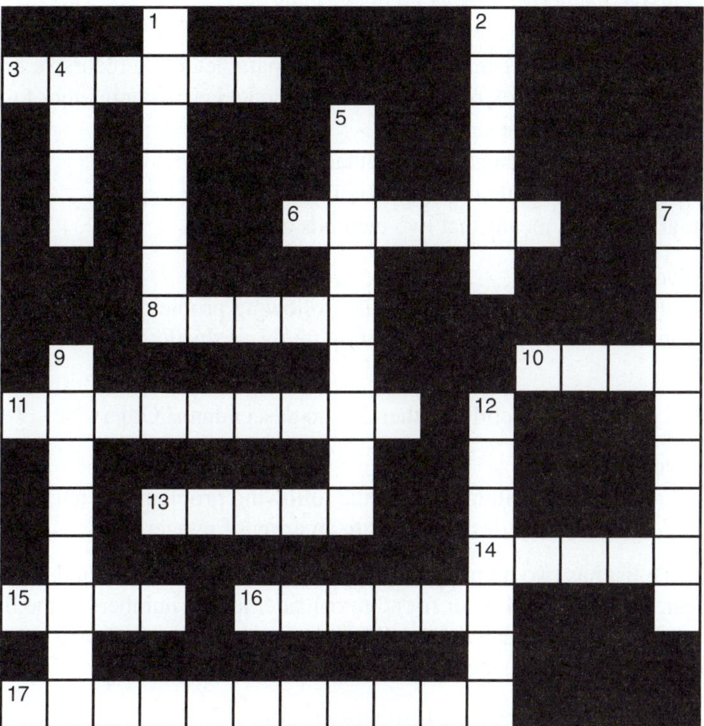

Across

3 A recursive method calls ________

6 Recursive search algorithm

8 The JVM allocates memory for parameters and variables on the ________

10 Tail recursion can be implemented as a ________

11 Helper, nonrecursive method of quicksort

13 The partition method of quicksort rearranges the elements of an array around the ________

14 Debugging method

15 A sequence of recursive calls must eventually reach the ________

16 Binary search first examines this value

17 A rearrangement

Down

1 When a tail recursive call resumes, it immediately ________

2 Infinite recursion will cause a program to run out of ________

4 Last call of a method is a recursive call

5 A sort routine with two recursive calls

7 If method(n) calls method(n − 1), method(n − 1) begins and method(n) is ________

9 Ensures that the recursion stops

12
```
int guess(int n)
{
  if (n ==1) return 1;
  else return n + guess(n – 1);
}.
guess(5) returns (word)
```

SHORT EXERCISES

1. **True or False**
   If false, give an explanation.
   a. Every recursive method must return an integer.
   b. Every recursive method must have at least one parameter.
   c. Any loop can be rewritten as a recursive method.
   d. A recursive method can make recursive calls.
   e. Tail recursion is recursion with a story.
   f. An object or an array cannot be passed as a parameter to a recursive method.
   g. Java always keeps track of each local variable and each parameter of a recursive method on the runtime stack.
   h. Recursion in Java is usually slower than iteration.
   i. Any tail recursive method can be accomplished using loops.
   j. Mutual recursion means that two methods are in love.

2. **Recursive Design**
   Design a recursive algorithm to solve the following problem. Do not write any code. You are given a diagram showing a family tree. List the descendents of any given person.

   Hint: If a person has no children then list no descendants. Otherwise…?

3. **Recursive Design**
   Design a recursive algorithm to solve the following problem. Do not write any code. Find the *largest* and *smallest* numbers in an array of integers.

   Hint: If the list has two numbers then the *smallest* is the smaller and the *largest* is the larger. Otherwise, ask your friend to consider all the numbers in the list except the first two, and determine the *smallest* and *largest* in the shortened list. You take it from there using three if statements.

4. **Testing Java's Tail Recursion Implementation**
   Recall that recognizing tail recursion and transforming the code into a loop is something that the standard Java compiler does not do. Indeed, there are a few (nonstandard) Java compilers that do convert tail recursion. The following code can be used to test whether or not your Java compiler recognizes and converts tail recursion:

```
public class TailRecursionTest
{

  private static int loop(int i)
  {
    return loop(i);
  }

  public static void main(String[] args)
  {
    loop(0);
  }
}
```

   When the JVM executes this code, what do you expect to happen if the compiler recognizes tail recursion and converts the program into a loop, and what do you expect to happen if the compiler does not? Feel free to experiment, but make sure to explain your answer.

5. **Recursive Thinking—Secret Santa**
You live in a village that has an annual Holiday of Gifts when each person in the village gives another person a gift. The tradition is that children do not give gifts, and seniors do not receive gifts. Everyone else gives one gift and receives one gift. It is public knowledge who is responsible for whose gift. Starting with every senior there is a chain of giftgivers terminating with a child. Assume that you are neither a senior nor a child. Design a recursive algorithm to determine the length of the chain from a senior to you, and another recursive algorithm to calculate the length of the chain from you to a child.

6. **Recursive Thinking—*K*th Smallest**
Design a recursive algorithm to solve the following problem. Do not write any code. Find the *k*th smallest value in an array t of numbers.

   Hint: If *k* equals the size of t, then return the largest value in t. Otherwise, create two new arrays, one containing the values less than t[0] and one with the values larger than or equal to t[0]. (If *all* the values are larger than or equal to t[0], then move t[0] to the empty first array.) Keep track of how many elements are in each new array. Now what?

7. **Recursive Thinking—Trees**
You live in B-land where the King is named B. The King has two advisers. Each of these advisers has two other advisers and so on. Everyone in the village has two advisers except the peasants. Everyone in the village advises exactly one person, except the King who advises nobody. The peasants have no advisers (but each advises one other person). The name of a person's two advisers is public knowledge.
   Design recursive algorithms to:
   - count the number of peasants in B-land.
   - count the total number of people in B-land.
   - list the names of everyone in B-land.

   Hint: Start with the King.

8. **Tracing**
Trace the following program. Show the trace and the final output. What do you think the method does?

```
public class Testmys
{
    public static void main(String[] args)
    {
        int a[] = {1, 0, 0, 1, 0};
        System.out.println(mystery(a, 5));
    }

    public static int mystery(int a[], int size)
    {
        if (size == 0)
            return 0;
        else if (a[size – 1] == 0)
            return 2 * mystery(a, size – 1);
        else return 2 * mystery(a, size – 1) + 1;
    }
}
```

9. **Tracing**
Trace the following program. Show the trace and the final output. What do you think the method does?

```
public class Testmys
{
    public static void main(String[] args)
    {
        int a[] = {24, 35, 67, 89, 102, 134, 167, 189, 209, 289, 354, 396, 425};
        System.out.println(mystery(a, 13));
        int b[] = {35, 67, 89, 105, 135, 179};
        System.out.println(mystery(b, 6));
    }

    public static int mystery(int a[], int size)
    {
        if (size == 1)
            return a[0];
        if (size == 2)
            return (a[0] + a[1]) / 2;
        int helper[] = new int[a.length - 2];
        int k = 0;
        for (int j = 1; j < size - 1; j++)
        {
            helper[k] = a[j];
            k++;
        }
        return mystery(helper, size - 2);
    }
}
```

10. **Find and Fix the Errors**
The following recursive method addeven(...) is supposed to add the even indexed values of an array, i.e., $a[0] + a[2] + a[4] + \ldots$ There are bugs in the method. Trace the method using test data, find the bugs, and correct them. Be thorough. The method may work on some data sets.

```
public static int addeven(int a[], int size)
{
  if (size == 2)
    return a[1];
  return a[size - 1] + addeven(a, size - 2) ;
}
```

11. **Analyzing Partition**
Examine the partition(...) method of Example 8.6, and give a brief description of the algorithm underlying the code. Explain why it works. Use an example or diagrams to help you if necessary.

   a. If x[] is the array [13, 4, 62, 26, 83, 6, 12, 55, 23, 81, 35], what value is returned by partition(x, 0, 10)? What are the contents of x[] after the call partition(x, 0, 10)?
   b. If y[] is the array [3, 6, 8, 7, 9, 10, 13, 18, 36, 11], what value is returned by partition(y, 5, 9)? What are the contents of y[] after the call partition(y, 5, 9)?

12. **Find and Fix the Errors**

To find the greatest common divisor of a pair of two non-negative integers:

- Continually form a "new pair" of integers by replacing the larger number with the positive difference of the two, until the smaller number is zero.
- The larger number of the final pair is the greatest common divisor of the original numbers. Return that number.

The following chart shows the calculation of the greatest common divisor of 100 and 38. On the last line of the chart, the smaller number is 0, therefore the greatest common divisor of 100 and 38 is 2.

Pair	Difference	New Pair
100, 38	$100 - 38 = 62$	**62**, 38
62, 38	$62 - 38 = 24$	38, **24**
38, 24	$38 - 24 = 14$	24, **14**
24, 14	$24 - 14 = 10$	14, **10**
14, 10	$14 - 10 = 4$	10, **4**
10, 4	$10 - 4 = 6$	**6**, 4
6, 4	$6 - 4 = 2$	4, **2**
4, 2	$4 - 2 = 2$	**2**, 2
2, 2	$2 - 2 = 0$	**2**, 0

The following recursive method is a buggy attempt to implement this algorithm. Find the bug and fix it. Make sure to thoroughly test the method. The method may work correctly under some circumstances.

```
public static int gcd(int small, int large)
{
    if (small == 0)
            return large;
    return gcd (small, large – small);
}
```

PROGRAMMING EXERCISES

1. **Factorial**

Write and test a recursive method to compute $n!$, the product of the first n positive integers. Given an integer parameter n, your method should return $n!$. For example $3! = 1 \times 2 \times 3 = 6$. Optional: Write a tail recursive version.

2. **Triangle Numbers**

Write and test a recursive method to compute $1 + 2 + \ldots + n$, the nth *triangle* number. Given an integer parameter n, your method should return the nth triangle number. Optional: Write a tail recursive version.

3. **Multiples of Ten**

Write and test a recursive method to check whether or not all the numbers in an array are multiples of 10.

4. **Input Loop**

Write and test a recursive method that accepts and returns an integer in the range 20 through 80, inclusive. If the user enters an invalid number, the method should issue an error message and prompt again.

5. **Guessing Game**
   Write and test a recursive method that plays a high/low guessing game. In the game, the method randomly chooses an integer between 0 and 100. A player tries to discover the number with a series of guesses. After each guess, the player is told whether his/her guess is too high or too low.

6. **Numerical Palindromes**
   Write and test a recursive method that determines whether or not an integer is a numerical palindrome. A number is a palindrome if it reads the same forward and backwards. For example, 23432 and 1010101 are palindromes. Your method should return `true` or `false`.

7. **Simultaneous Largest and Smallest**
   Write and test a recursive method that simultaneously finds the largest and second-largest values in an integer array `b[]`.

   Hint: Your friend finds the largest and second-largest of the first `b.length` − 2 values. Then use just three `if` statements to determine the overall largest and second largest. Note that this method must return two integers. Because a method can return just one value, you will need to "wrap up" the two integers in an array of size two.

8. **Exponentiation**
   Write and test two recursive methods to calculate a^b for positive integers a and b.
   Method 1: If $b = 0$ then return 1 else return $a \times (a^{b-1})$.
   Method 2: If $b = 0$ then return 1 else if b is even return $(a^{b/2})^2$ else return $a \times (a^{b-1})$.
   Time both methods. Which is faster?

9. **Positive Numbers**
   Write and test a recursive method to determine whether or not all the values stored in an integer array are greater than zero.

10. **Print an Array**
    Write and test a recursive method that prints all the values in an array.

11. **Reverse an Array**
    Write and test a recursive method that reverses the elements in an array. *Hint*: Swap the first element with the last and "recurse" on the inner portion of the array.

12. **Recursive Max Sort**
    To recursively sort an array, find the largest element in the array and swap it with the last element. Then recursively sort the array from the start to the next-to-the-last element. Write and test a method that recursively sorts an array in this manner.

13. **Intersection**
    Write and test a recursive method that computes the intersection of two sets—that is, the elements that the two sets have in common. You may assume that a set is implemented as an array of integers and contains no duplicate elements. For example, the intersection of $\{6, 3, 8, 1\}$ and $\{1, 9, 2, 16, 8, 19, 32, 11\}$ is $\{8, 1\}$. Your method should return an array.

14. **Union**
    Write and test a recursive method that computes the union of two sets. The union of two sets consists of the elements that are in one set or both of the sets. For example, the union of $\{6, 3, 8, 1\}$ and $\{1, 9, 2, 18, 8, 19, 32, 11\}$ is $\{6, 3, 8, 1, 9, 2, 18, 19, 32, 11\}$. You may assume that the sets are implemented as integer arrays with no duplicates.

15. **Insertion Sort**
Write and test a recursive version of the insertion sort described in Algorithm A, Section 8.5.

To recursively perform insertion sort on a list of n numbers:
a. Sort the first n − 1 numbers recursively.
b. Insert the last number into the appropriate spot in the sorted list of n − 1 numbers.

The method of part (b) should also be written recursively. Your solution, therefore, will have a recursive method that calls another recursive method.

Hints: To insert element into a sorted (ascending) list of n − 1 numbers:
a. Compare element with the last number in the list.
b. If element is greater than the last number, then return a sorted array consisting of the sorted list of n − 1 numbers followed by element.
c. Otherwise, remove and store the last number in the list. Call this last. Recursively insert element into the sorted list of the remaining n − 2 numbers; call the result x[]. The result x[] is a sorted list of n − 1 numbers. Return a sorted array of n numbers consisting of x[] followed by last.

16. **Towers of Hanoi**
The Towers of Hanoi is a famous puzzle, invented in 1883 by mathematician Edouard Lucas, used today primarily for teaching recursion. The most natural solution exhibits a classic recursive algorithm. An iterative solution is not at all obvious. The puzzle consists of three pegs with *n* disks, of decreasing size, stacked upon one of them. To solve the puzzle, move all of the disks to one of the other pegs one at a time without ever placing any disk on top of a smaller one. See Figure 8.13.

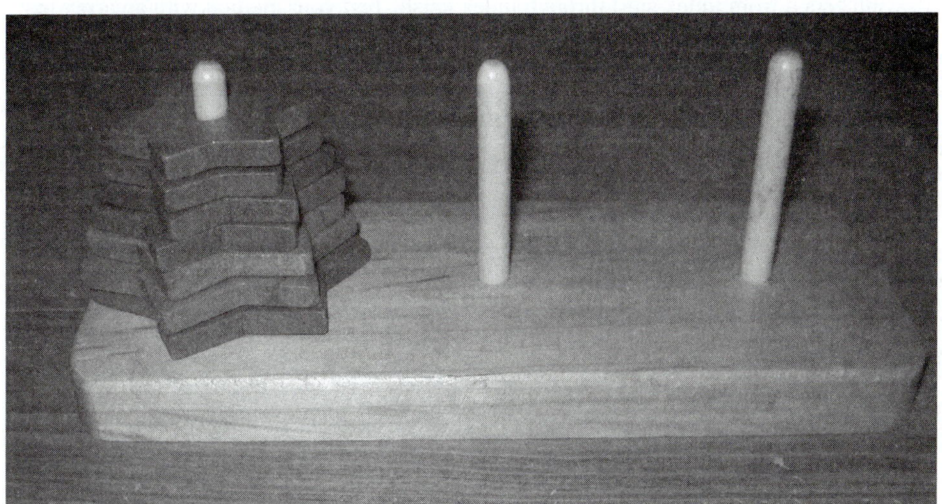

FIGURE 8.13 Towers of Hanoi with star-shaped disks

Write and test a recursive method that solves the Towers of Hanoi puzzle. Your method hanoi(...) should have four parameters: int n, char start, char finish, char using. Your test call should be

```
hanoi(5, 'A', 'B', 'C');
```

where the pegs are called 'A', 'B', and 'C', and you are trying to move five disks from 'A' to 'B', using 'C'.

For example, hanoi (2, 'A', 'B', 'C') will output:

```
Move a disk from A to C
Move a disk from A to B
Move a disk from C to B
```

Hint: hanoi(5, 'A', 'B', 'C') can be done in three steps:

```
hanoi(4, 'A', 'C', 'B');
Move a disk from A to B;
hanoi(4, 'C', 'B', 'A');
```

17. **Partition Revisited**
A certain partition algorithm (not recursive) reorders an array, a, around the first element, pivot = a[0], so that all the values in *a* that are less than or equal to pivot precede pivot, and all the values greater than pivot appear after pivot. The algorithm uses an extra "helper" array and works like this:
   - Compare all the elements in the array one at a time to pivot.
   - The values less than pivot are inserted into the new array on the left side, that is, beginning with position 0, and the larger values are inserted on the right side.
   - Finally, pivot is placed in the one remaining slot of the new array between the smaller group and the larger group.

   Using this algorithm, rewrite partition(…) of Example 8.6. Sort a large array of 10,000 random integers using quickSort(…) with this new version of partition(…), and then again with the version of Example 8.6. Time the two programs, and compare the results.

18. **Merge Sort**
Write a recursive method mergeSort(int[] a, int start, int finish) that sorts an array of integers a from index start through index finish. Test your method with an array test of 100 random numbers.
   The algorithm works as follows:
   - Sort the first half of the array recursively.
   - Sort the last half recursively.
   - Merge the two sorted halves together.

   Merging is accomplished via a method

   ```
   int[] merge(a, start, finish),
   ```

   which returns an array with the two sorted halves of a merged into a single sorted array.

   This new array must be copied back to a.

   ```
   Hint: To merge the two halves:
   Create a new temporary array b
      leftpointer = start;            // leftpointer traverses the left half of the array.
      halfway = (start+finish)/2 ;
      rightpointer = halfway,         // rightpointer traverses the right half, and
      bpointer = 0;                   // bpointer traverses the new array b[].

   while ( leftpointer <= halfway )and (rightpointer <= finish)
        if ( a[leftpointer] < a[rightpointer] )
      {
        b[bpointer] = a[leftpointer] ;
        leftpointer++;
      }
   ```

```
else
{
    b[bpointer] = a[rightpointer];
    rightpointer++;
}
bpointer++;

if (leftpointer > halfway)
        copy the remainder of the right half of a to b
if (rightpointer > finish)
        copy the remainder of the left half of a to b
return(b)
```

19. **(Challenging) The Josephus Puzzle**
Josephus Flavius was a famous Jewish historian of the first century. During the Jewish-Roman war he was trapped in a cave with a group of 40 Jewish rebels, surrounded by Romans. As legend has it, preferring suicide to capture, the Jews decided to form a circle and moving clockwise, one at a time, every other person would commit suicide until no one was left. Thus, the first person to die was seated in position 2, the next in 4, the third in 6, and so on. Josephus, not keen to die, quickly found the place in the circle where he would be the last one to commit suicide, the 17th position. But at the end, instead of killing himself, he joined the Romans. The soldiers committed suicide in the following order: 2, 4, 6, 8, 10, 12, 14, 16, 18, 20, 22, 24, 26, 28, 30, 32, 34, 36, 38, 40, 3, 7, 11, 15, 19, 23, 27, 31, 35, 39, 5, 13, 21, 29, 37, 9, 25, 1, 33, 17.
Write and test a recursive method that determines the last soldier to die when there are *n* soldiers in a circle.
Hint: Ask a friend to solve the problem with half the number of soldiers and try to use that information. It makes a difference if there is an odd or an even number of soldiers.

THE BIGGER PICTURE

THE COMPLEXITY OF RECURSIVE ALGORITHMS

The complexity of an algorithm is synonymous with the speed of an algorithm. Does the algorithm run efficiently, that is, quickly, or not? The faster a program runs, the better; and behind every fast program there is an efficient algorithm. When designing a recursive algorithm, it is not only correctness that is important, but efficiency. Let's look at an example.

The Fibonacci numbers comprise the infinite sequence: 1, 1, 2, 3, 5, 8, 13, 21, 34, 55, 89, and so on, in which each number (except the first two) is the sum of the previous two numbers. In computer science, Fibonacci numbers have many applications ranging from data structures (Fibonacci heaps) to pseudo-random number generators (lagged Fibonacci generators). Fibonacci numbers also manifest themselves in leaf arrangements, seashells, pine cones, and sunflower seeds. The sunflower in Figure 8.14, for example, has 21 and 34 spirals of seeds, one set curving right and one set curving left. Note that 21 and 34 are the 10th and 11th Fibonacci numbers.

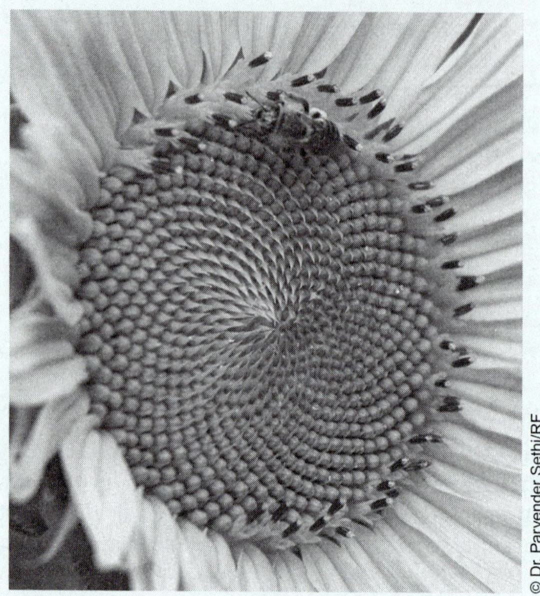
© Dr. Parvender Sethi/RF

FIGURE 8.14 A sunflower with hidden Fibonacci numbers.

Three Methods that Calculate the *n*th Fibonacci number, Fibonacci(*n*)

There are several algorithms that compute the *n*th Fibonacci number. In the following section we present three such methods.

Method 1

The simplest algorithm is an iterative one. Keep track of the last two Fibonacci numbers, the highest and next highest, and compute the next Fibonacci number by adding these last two together. The following method returns the *n*th Fibonacci number:

```
public static long fib1(int n)
{
        // Computes the nth Fibonacci number by keeping track
        // of the current two highest Fibonacci numbers
        if (n <= 2)
                  return 1;
        long temp;
        long nexthighest = 1;
        long highest = 1;
        for (int count = 3; count <= n ; count++)
        {
          temp = nexthighest + highest;
          nexthighest = highest;
          highest = temp;
          // computes the next Fibonacci number which becomes the highest
          // and the next highest becomes the previous highest
        }
        return highest;
}
```

THE BIGGER PICTURE

Method 2

Here is a simple but inefficient recursive version. The code is self-explanatory. The next Fibonacci number is simply the sum of the previous two, exactly as the definition says.

```
public static long fib2(int n)
{
    if (n <= 2)
        return 1;
    return (fib2(n – 1) + fib2(n – 2));
}
```

To understand just how poorly fib2(...) performs when compared to fib1(...), we ran both methods for several values of n. Both methods fib1(10) and fib2(10) returned the correct answer of 55, without any noticeable delay. However, fib1(50) ran instantaneously, returning the correct value of 12,586,269,025, while fib2(50), after 20 minutes, did not finish. (We stopped the program to prevent the computer from overheating.)

Why does fib2(...) run so slowly? Why is it so inefficient? It is *not* because one algorithm is recursive and the other is iterative! Indeed the algorithm underlying fib1(...) can be implemented recursively, and the algorithm underlying fib2(...) can be implemented without explicit recursion. It is not an issue of iteration versus recursion but an issue of efficient algorithm design versus inefficient algorithm design. Sure, there is overhead due to the runtime stack, but that is *not* why this recursive algorithm is a disaster.

Before we show you why the algorithm underlying fib2(...) is so bad, let's first construct a recursive algorithm fib3(...) that is just as good as fib1(...). The method fib3(...) is an efficient tail recursion version based directly on the iterative version of fib1(...). Indeed, if you study the relationship between the two methods, you will learn how to take any iterative algorithm and implement it efficiently using tail recursion.

Turning Loops into Tail Recursion

The trick to rewriting a loop using tail recursion is to wrap all the local variables into the parameter list. In particular, we wrap the local variables of fib1(...) into the parameter list of fib3(...) so that fib3(...) itself has no local variables. Then, design fib3(...) to be tail recursive.

Method 3

```
public static long fib3(int n, int count, long nexthighest, long highest)
{
        if (n <= 2)
          return 1;
        if (count > n)
          return highest;
        return fib3(n, count + 1, highest, highest + nexthighest);
}
```

To use fib3(...), set count to 3, and nexthighest and highest to 1, just as they are initialized in fib1(...). To calculate the sixth Fibonacci number, call fib3(6, 3, 1, 1), and the *n*th is calculated with fib3(n, 3, 1, 1).

Figure 8.15 traces the calls fib3(6, 3, 1, 1) and fib1(6). Notice the similarity between the two. The values of the local variables count, nexthighest, and highest in fib1(6) are exactly the same as the values of the parameters with the same names in fib3(6, 3, 1, 1). In fact, fib1(75) and fib3(75, 3, 1, 1) both calculate the correct value 2,111,485,077,978,050 in the same seemingly instantaneous time.

```
fib3(6, 3, 1, 1)
    fib3(6, 4, 1, 2)
        fib3(6, 5, 2, 3)
            fib3(6, 6, 3, 5)
                fib3(6, 7, 5, 8)
                return 8
            return 8
        return 8
    return 8
return 8
```

Compare this to fib1(6).

count	nexthighest	highest
3	1	1
4	1	2
5	2	3
6	3	5
7	5	8

return 8

FIGURE 8.15 Comparing the traces of *fib*3(6, 3, 1, 1) and *fib*1(6)

Both fib1(6) and fib3(6, 3, 1, 1) each took eight additions to calculate the sixth Fibonacci number, half of these were performed incrementing count. In general, it takes each method $2(n - 2)$ steps to calculate the nth Fibonacci number, $n - 2$ increments of count and $n - 2$ actual Fibonacci additions. That's why fib1(75) and fib3(75, 3, 1, 1) calculate 2,111,485,077,978,050 so quickly. Each is doing only $2(75 - 2) = 146$ additions—peanuts and microseconds for a computer. The methods fib1(...) and fib3(...), one iterative and one recursive, are both equally fast Fibonacci calculators.

If the inefficiency of fib2(...) is not a recursion versus iteration issue, then what is it? It is an algorithm *design* issue. The algorithm behind fib2(...) is inefficient, whether implemented recursively or iteratively. When $n = 6$, the algorithm performs as in Figure 8.16.

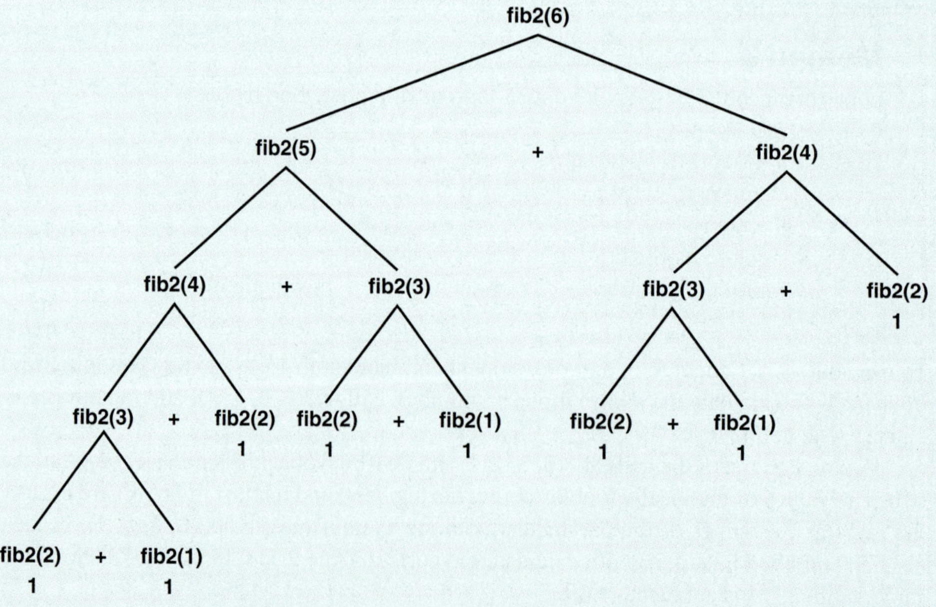

FIGURE 8.16 A trace of *fib2*(6), which returns 8

A glaring inefficiency that you should notice is the great many times that fib2(...) is called with the same parameters! That can't be good. Why should we ever call the same method with the same parameters more than once?

How bad is this wasted effort? If you look carefully and count the plus signs in Figure 8.16, you will see that fib2(6) makes seven additions to calculate the sixth Fibonacci number, 8. This is actually *less* than fib1(6) and fib3(6, 3, 1, 1), each of which requires eight additions. That doesn't seem so bad. Because fib2(6) does not update the variable such as count, the method uses fewer additions than fib1(6) and fib3(6, 3, 1, 1), despite the duplicate method calls. But look what happens for larger values of *n*. The wasted method calls vastly overwhelm any savings gained by not explicitly incrementing count.

To calculate the *n*th Fibonacci number, fib2(n) requires fib2(n) – 1 additions, while fib1(n) and fib3(n, 3, 1, 1) can complete the same task with just 2(*n* – 2) additions. Figure 8.17 contrasts the number of additions performed by fib1(n), fib2(n), and fib3(n, 3, 1, 1) for several values of n. The difference is astounding and explains why it took more than 20 minutes to calculate fib2(50). The algorithm was busy performing 12,586,269,024 additions instead of just 96. And even for the fastest computers, 12,586,269,024 additions isn't easy. In fact, there is currently no computer in the world that could calculate fib2(75) in under a month of computing time. And, computing fib2(100) would take more than a lifetime!

n	*n*th Fibonacci Number	Number of Additions fib1(n) and fib3(n, 3, 1, 1)	Number of Additions fib2(n)
10	55	16	54
20	6,765	36	6,764
30	832,040	56	832,039
40	102,334,155	76	102,334,152
50	12,586,269,025	96	12,586,269,024
75	2,111,485,077,978,050	146	2,111,485,077,978,049
100	354,224,848,179,263,100,000	196	354,224,848,179,263,099,999

FIGURE 8.17 The number of additions performed by *fib1(n)*, *fib2(n)*, and *fib3(n, 3, 1, 1)*

Use the following class to experiment for yourself by changing the value of the parameter *n*. The method System.currentTimeMillis() returns the system time in milliseconds, giving a crude but reasonable way to distinguish the running time for each method. Note that for small values of *n,* the time for all three methods will likely be indistinguishable.

```
public class FibTester
{
   public static long fib1(int n)
   {
      // Computes the nth Fibonacci number by keeping track
      // of the current two highest Fibonacci numbers
      if (n <= 2)
         return 1;
      long temp;
      long nexthighest = 1;
      long highest = 1;
```

```
        for (int count = 3; count <= n ; count++)
        {
            temp = nexthighest + highest;
            nexthighest = highest;
            highest = temp;
            // the next Fibonacci number is assigned to highest
            // the previous value of highest is assigned to nexthighest
        }
        return highest;
    }

    public static long fib2(int n)
    {
        if (n <= 2)
            return 1;
        return (fib2(n - 1) + fib2(n - 2));
    }

    public static long fib3(int n, int count, long nexthighest, long highest)
    {
        if (n <= 2)
            return 1;
        if (count > n)
            return highest;
        return fib3(n, count + 1, highest, highest + nexthighest);
    }

    public static void main(String [] args)
    {
        int n = 50;
        System.out.println(System.currentTimeMillis()); // for looking at time
        System.out.println(fib1(n));
        System.out.println(System.currentTimeMillis());
        System.out.println(fib3(n, 3, 1, 1));
        System.out.println(System.currentTimeMillis());
        System.out.println(fib2(n));
        System.out.println(System.currentTimeMillis());
    }
}
```

Conclusion

The design of efficient algorithms is in many ways the central theme in all of computer science. Recursion is one of the major techniques used to design algorithms. Recursive algorithms are sometimes efficient and sometimes inefficient. The crux is not whether to use recursion or iteration but how to design the algorithm in the first place. Some algorithms are efficient and some are not.

Exercises

1. Write a tail recursive method that computes $n!$ Model your method on an iterative method as we did for the Fibonacci numbers. You will need two parameters for a tail recursive factorial. Note that the standard recursive method with one parameter:

```
int factorial (int n)
{       if (n == 0) return 1;
        return n * factorial(n − 1);
}
```

is *not* tail recursive, because the multiplication by *n* takes place *after* the recursive call.

2. Pascal's triangle is a tower of numbers the top part of which is shown in Figure 8.18. The triangle continues downward forever. Pascal's triangle is useful in hundreds of applications, one of which is calculating poker hand probabilities.

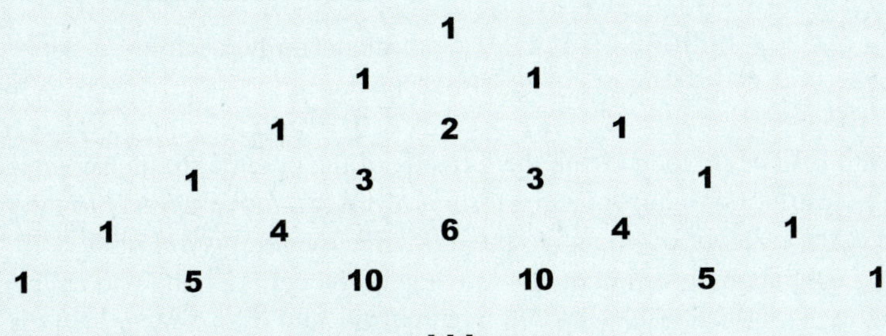

FIGURE 8.18 Pascal's triangle

The rows of Pascal's triangle are numbered 0, 1, 2, 3..., and the entries in row *n* are numbered 0, 1, 2, 3,..., *n*. The notation Pascal(*i, j*) designates the *j*th entry in row *i*. Thus Pascal(5, 3) is 10, Pascal(4, 4) is 1, and Pascal(2, 1) is 2.

The numbers of the triangle can be calculated as:

Pascal(n, 0) = Pascal(n, n) = 1, for $n = 0, 1, 2 \ldots$
Pascal(n, k) = Pascal($n - 1$, $k - 1$) + Pascal($n - 1$, k), for $k = 1$ to $n - 1$.

For example,

Pascal(6, 2) = Pascal(5, 1) + Pascal(5, 2) = 5 + 10 = 15, and
Pascal(6, 4) = Pascal(5, 3) + Pascal(5, 4) = 10 + 5 = 15.

a. Write and test an iterative method

```
int pascalIter(int i, int j)
```

that returns the jth number in the ith row of Pascal's triangle.

b. Write and test a recursive method

```
int pascalRecur(int i, int j)
```

that performs the same function as pascalIter().

c. Run and time both methods when:
- i = 8 and j = 4,
- i = 20 and j = 10, and
- i = 40 and j = 20.

Discuss your findings.

THE BIGGER PICTURE

d. Trace the recursive program by hand for the value *Pascal*(6, 3) and explain your results.

3. Consider a two-dimensional array of integers rolled into a cylinder, so that the top and bottom rows are glued together. See Figure 8.19.

FIGURE 8.19 A two-dimensional array rolled into a cylinder

A path is to be threaded from the left side of the cylinder to the right side, subject to the restriction that from a given square you can move directly to the right, up and to the right, or down and to the right. See the arrows in Figure 8.19. A path may begin at any position on the left side of the cylinder and end at any position on the right side. The cost of a path is the sum of the integers in the squares through which it passes.

For example, consider the 5 by 8 array shown in Figure 8.20. The numbers in bold represent a path through the cylinder with cost equal to $-10 + 8 - 3 - 7 - 5 + 7 + 7 - 9 = -12$. This is a good path with low cost, but it is not the path of least cost.

12	9	15	**−7**	**−5**	28	−24	17
27	−19	16	−2	3	**7**	19	1
−1	12	23	14	10	45	**7**	−5
−10	**8**	12	71	−23	34	12	**−9**
26	17	**−3**	24	42	56	18	2

FIGURE 8.20 Bold numbers show a path through the cylinder

a. Design two algorithms, one recursive and one iterative, to find the minimum cost path through this cylinder.
b. Run and time both algorithms using the 5 by 8 array (Figure 8.20).
c. What are your observations?
d. Explain your observations by showing what happens when you trace the recursive version.

4. In the United States, every presidential election is decided by the Electoral College. Every state has a certain number of electoral votes, and that state decides how to distribute its votes among the candidates. Traditionally, each state gives all or none of its votes to a single candidate.

There are 50 states and the District of Columbia, each with some number of electoral votes. The total number of electoral votes is 538 (as of 2008). A tie occurs if some subset of the 51 electoral numbers equals 269 (538/2). Can a presidential election result in a tie?

To answer this question, we formulate a more general problem called *Subset Sum* and solve it recursively. Given an array of integers a and a value k, let subsetSum(n, k) = true whenever a subset of the first n integers in the array sums to k. Then

subsetSum(n,k) = subsetSum(n – 1, k – a[n – 1]) || subsetSum(n – 1, k).

This relationship holds because either the *n*th number, a[n – 1], contributes to the sum or it doesn't. If it does, then the remaining sum, k – a[n – 1], must be constructed from a subset of the first n – 1 numbers. If a[n – 1] doesn't contribute to the sum, then the all of k must be obtained from a subset of the first n – 1 numbers.

a. Using the preceding formula, derive a recursive algorithm to determine whether or not a subset of the first n numbers in a sums to k. Create the appropriate base cases: if (k == 0) return true; if (k < 0) return false; and, if (n == 0) return false;
b. Implement your algorithm iteratively and recursively.
c. Test and time both methods by determining whether or not the presidential election in the USA can end in a tie. You will need to calculate subsetSum(51, 269). Here is the list of numbers for the 538 electoral college votes:

   3, 3, 3, 3, 3, 3, 3, 3, 4, 4, 4, 4, 4, 5, 5, 5, 5, 5, 6, 6, 6, 7, 7, 7, 7, 8, 8, 9, 9, 9, 10, 10, 10, 10, 11, 11, 11, 11, 12, 13, 15, 15, 15, 17, 20, 21, 21, 27, 31, 34, 55.
d. Report the results of your test. Which implementation runs faster?

PART 2

Principles of Object-Oriented Programming

CHAPTER 9

Objects and Classes I: Encapsulation, Strings, and Things

"Intelligence is the faculty of making artificial objects, especially tools to make tools."
—Henri Bergson (1859–1941)

Objectives

The objectives of this chapter include an understanding of

- objects and classes
- encapsulation, and
- some Java classes:
  - The Random class
  - The String class
  - The StringBuilder class
  - The File class
  - The DecimalFormat class

9.1 INTRODUCTION

This chapter begins our study of object-oriented programming (OOP). What is OOP? One popular definition describes OOP as a methodology that organizes a program into a collection of interacting objects. A more technical definition asserts that OOP is a programming paradigm that incorporates the principles of *encapsulation*, *inheritance*, and *polymorphism.* If these characterizations mean little or nothing to you, don't be dismayed. OOP is not a concept that can be easily described or explained in a single sentence or even a single paragraph. In fact, the foundations of OOP—encapsulation, inheritance, and polymorphism—comprise the topics of the next four chapters. With a bit of time and practice, OOP will become quite natural to you. For the present, however, let's just say that OOP is all about *objects*.

In this chapter you will learn about objects—what they are and how to use them. Once you understand objects, then encapsulation, inheritance, polymorphism, and all the nuances and advantages of OOP easily follow.

9.2 OBJECTS

In the context of a computer program, an *object* is a representation or an abstraction of some entity such as a car, a soda machine, an ATM machine, a slot machine, a dog, a flea, an elephant, a person, a house, a string of twine, a string of characters, a bank account, a pair of dice, a deck of cards, a point in the plane, a TV, a DVD player, an iPod, a rocket, an elevator, a square, a rectangle, a circle, a camera, a movie star, a shooting star, a computer mouse, a live mouse, a phone, an airplane, a song, a city, a state, a country, a planet, a glass window, or a computer window. Just about anything is an object. An object may be physical, like a radio, or intangible, like a song. Just as a noun is a person, place, or thing, so is an object. And, just as people, places, and things are defined through their attributes and behaviors, so are objects.

> An object has characteristics or *attributes*; an object has actions or *behaviors*. Specifically, an object is an entity that consists of:
>
> - data (the attributes), and
> - methods that use or manipulate the data (the behaviors).

The remote control unit of Figure 9.1 provides a good example. With this rather bare-bones remote, an armchair viewer can turn a TV on or off, raise or lower the volume, or change the channel.

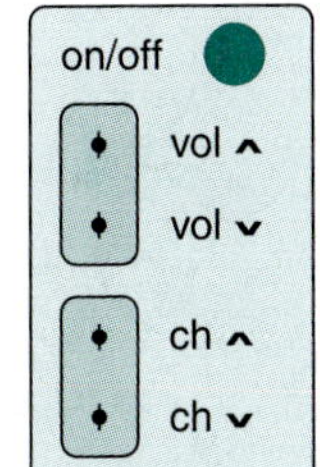

FIGURE 9.1 A bare-bones remote control unit

Accordingly, a remote control *object* has three *attributes*:

1. the current channel, an integer,
2. the volume level, an integer, and
3. the current state of the TV, on or off, true or false,

along with five *behaviors* or methods:

1. raise the volume by one unit,
2. lower the volume by one unit,
3. increase the channel number by one,
4. decrease the channel number by one, and
5. switch the TV on or off.

Figure 9.2 shows three different remote objects, each with unique attribute values (data) but all sharing the same methods or behaviors.

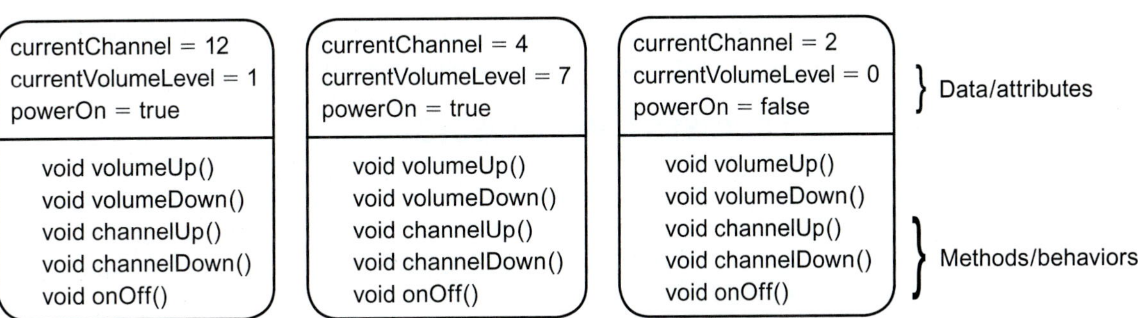

FIGURE 9.2 Three remote control objects

The remote control unit exemplifies *encapsulation*, one of the three major tenets of OOP. (The other two are inheritance and polymorphism.)

> *Encapsulation* is defined as the language feature that packages attributes and behaviors into a single unit. That is, data and methods comprise a single entity.

Accordingly, each remote control object encapsulates data and methods, attributes and behaviors. An individual remote unit, an object, stores its own attributes—channel number, volume level, power state—and has the functionality to change those attributes. It's all in a single package.

A rectangle is also an object. The attributes of a rectangle might be length and width, two floating-point numbers; the methods compute and return area and perimeter. Figure 9.3 shows three different rectangle objects. Again notice that data and methods come bundled together; data and methods are encapsulated in one object. Each rectangle has its own set of attributes; all share the same behaviors.

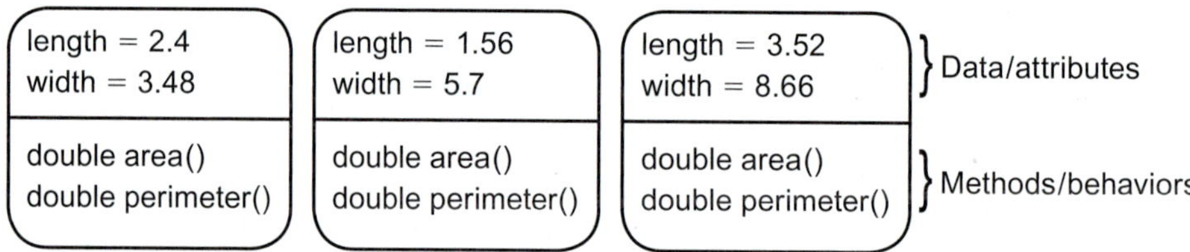

FIGURE 9.3 Three different *Rectangle* objects

A character string is also an object that encapsulates data and methods. The string data consists of an ordered sequence of characters and two (of many) methods, including a method that returns the number of characters in the string and one that returns the ith character. See Figure 9.4.

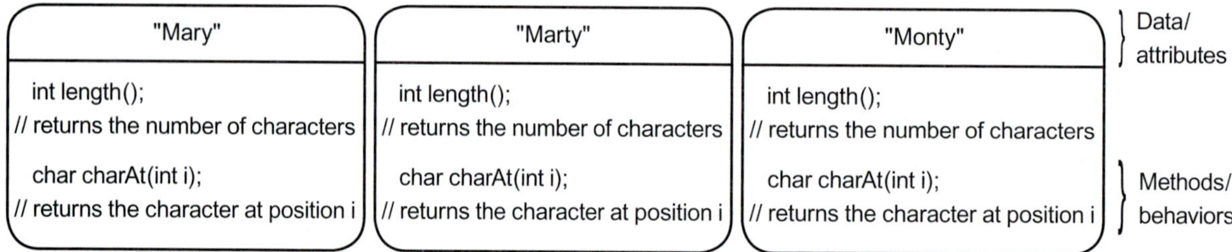

FIGURE 9.4 Three *String* objects, each with its own data, all with the same methods

Figures 9.2, 9.3, and 9.4 underscore the concept that objects are data and methods boxed as a single package or module. In other words, objects encapsulate.

9.3 FROM CLASSES COME OBJECTS

As you know, every primitive variable is tied to a data type such as int, char, double, or boolean. Likewise, every object is a member of a *class*. The three rectangle objects of Figure 9.3 belong to a "Rectangle" class just as the three objects depicted in Figure 9.4 are members of a "String" class.

> A class is a template, or blueprint, from which objects are created.

As a builder creates houses from the specifications of a blueprint, a program creates *objects* from the specifications of a class. From one blueprint, a builder can build many individual houses; and from one class, a program can create many objects. Every object is manufactured or *instantiated* according to its class specifications. More precisely, a class defines the variables and methods that comprise each of its objects. A class describes how data and methods are encapsulated as a single object. Every object is an *instance* of some class.

For example, a Rectangle class might specify that every Rectangle object consists of two variables of type double,

- double length, and
- double width,

and also every Rectangle object comes equipped with two methods,

- double area(), and // returns the area, length x width,
- double perimeter(), // returns the perimeter, 2(length + width).

Individual Rectangle objects may differ in dimension, but *all* Rectangle objects share the same methods; that is, all Rectangle objects have the same behaviors. Accordingly, each of the three Rectangle objects of Figure 9.3 has its own length and width, but all three share the same two methods, area() and perimeter(). Figure 9.5 illustrates four Rectangle objects constructed according to the specifications of the Rectangle class.

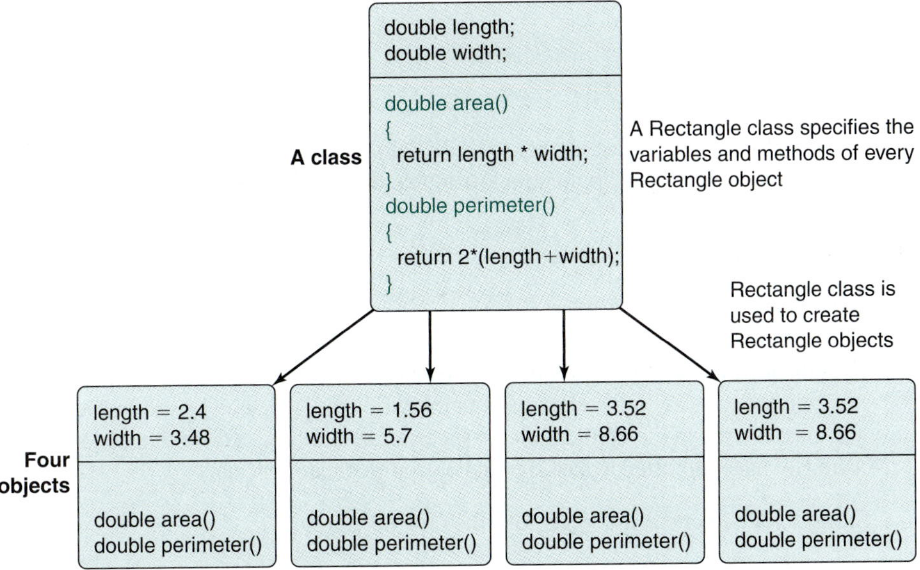

FIGURE 9.5 A *Rectangle* class and four *Rectangle* objects. Each object has unique attributes. The class is a blueprint for all objects.

One class that we have already utilized is Scanner. The Scanner class, which is a member of the java.util package, comprises a host of methods, including nextInt() and nextDouble(). The now familiar statement

```
Scanner input = new Scanner(System.in);
```

instantiates or creates a new Scanner object from a blueprint in java.util. The variable input is a reference that holds the address of the newly created Scanner object. All methods are accessed via input: for example, input.nextInt(), input.nextDouble().

Every Scanner object shares the same methods, but you will soon see that some Scanner objects use these methods to read data from the keyboard and others use these same methods to read data from a file. Every Scanner object has its own attributes, but all share the same behaviors.

At this point, you probably have a very general, albeit sketchy, understanding of objects and classes. Deeper understanding comes with practice. In this chapter, we show you how to *create* objects using a few classes that Java supplies. Scanner is one such class. In Chapter 10, you will learn how to design your own classes as well as create and use objects built from *your* classes. Gradually, the concept of classes and objects will become perfectly natural to you, as will the notions of encapsulation, inheritance, and polymorphism.

9.4 JAVA LIBRARIES AND PACKAGES

Java provides a rather large library containing hundreds of predefined classes that can be used as blueprints to create objects. Related classes are organized or grouped into *packages*. For example, the Abstract Window Toolkit package (java.awt) contains dozens of classes that are useful for graphics programming. The java.text package provides classes that simplify text formatting, and the java.util package contains, among other classes, the familiar Scanner class.

> To include a Java class in an application, use an import statement in either of two forms:
>
> import java.*packagename.classname;* or
> import java.*packagename*.*;

All import statements must appear in a file before any class definitions. For example, to use the Scanner class in an application, include either of the following import statements at the start of the file:

```
import java.util.Scanner; or
import java.util.*;
```

The first statement imports just the Scanner class, while the second imports all of the classes of the java.util package, including the Scanner class.[1] Importing the entire package does not increase the size of the class (executable) file that is created by the Java compiler. Only the classes used in the application are incorporated into the executable code.

Once you have imported a class, it can be used to create objects.

> To instantiate or create an object, use the new operator.

For example, to create an object belonging to the Scanner class we use the statement

```
Scanner myScanner = new Scanner(System.in);
```

[1] As a folder in a file system can contain subfolders and those folders can contain subfolders, a Java package can contain sub-packages. For example, java.util contains a sub-package named java.util.**zip**, which contains a number of predefined classes that facilitate reading and writing compressed (zip) files. The statement

```
import java.util.*;
```

imports the classes of java.util, including java.util.Scanner, but *not* the classes of java.util.zip, which includes java.util.zip.ZipFile, java.util.zip.ZipEntry, and many others. To import the classes of java.util.zip, you must explicitly import the sub-package, using:

```
import java.util.zip.*;
```

or equivalently, the two-statement combination

```
Scanner myScanner;
myScanner = new Scanner(System.in);
```

In addition to Scanner, java.util contains another class that is particularly useful for applications that generate random integers.

> The Random class provides methods that are more convenient and flexible than Math.random().

9.4.1 *Random*—Another Class of *java.util*

The methods available to a Random object can generate random numbers, both integer and floating point. The following statement instantiates a Random object and assigns its address to the reference variable random

```
Random random = new Random();
```

The Random class comes equipped with a number of methods that generate random numbers, but two are particularly useful:

- int nextInt(int n)

  returns an integer greater than or equal to 0 and less than *n*.

- double nextDouble()

  returns a double value greater than or equal to 0.0 and less than 1.0.

For example, the following code segment instantiates a Random object and generates two random numbers between 1 and 6 inclusive that might simulate rolling a pair of dice:

```
Random die = new Random();
int dice = (die.nextInt(6) + 1) + (die.nextInt(6) + 1);
```

Because die.nextInt(6) returns an integer between 0 and 5 inclusive, die.nextInt(6) + 1 returns an integer between 1 and 6.

The next segment utilizes a random integer, 0 for heads and 1 for tails, to simulate flipping a coin 100 times:

```
Random coin = new Random(); // instantiate a Random object
int heads = 0, tails = 0;          // counters
for (int i = 1; i <= 100; i++)
{
        if (coin.nextInt(2) == 0)  // a random number 0 or 1
           heads++;                // 0 signifies heads
        else
           tails++;
}
System.out.println("Heads:" + heads + " Tails: " + tails);
```

Programs must be tested, debugged, retested, debugged again, and eventually fixed. Debugging applications that involve random numbers can be especially tricky if each time that a program executes, a different sequence of random numbers is used. Conveniently, you can instantiate a Random object so that it always produces the same sequence of "random" numbers. This is done by passing Random(...) a "seed," that is, an integer of type long. For example, the following Random object always produces the same sequence of random numbers:

```
Random rand = new Random(12345678); // 123456768 is the seed
                                    // the seed can be any long integer
```

When embedded in a program, the segment

```
for (int i = 1; i <= 10; i++)
        System.out.print (rand.nextInt(100) + " ");
```

produces the sequence

```
63 2 85 71 45 11 16 85 35 40
```

each time that the program runs.

The seed that is passed to Random(...) can be any integer. Different seeds produce different sequences.

9.4.2 The *java.lang* Package

One special package,

```
java.lang
```

is automatically imported into every application, so an import statement is both redundant and unnecessary. The java.lang package contains many useful classes, including the Math class and one of Java's most fundamental and widely used classes, the String class.

9.5 STRINGS ARE OBJECTS

Except for labeled output, none of our previous programs has the capability of manipulating strings. We can write applications that sort a list of house *numbers* but not a list of home addresses. We can implement a program that searches for an ID *number*, but not a name. Except in the simplest cases, strings have not been part of our programming toolbox. From spell checking to Internet searching to bioinformatics, string processing is an important and common application.

Java's String class includes dozens of methods that facilitate string processing.

> The String class is contained in the java.lang package, which is imported automatically into every application.

As with all objects, the instantiation of a String object is accomplished with the new operator. For example,

```
String myDog = new String("Fido");
```

The variable myDog is *not* a String object but a *reference* to a String object. That is, myDog holds the address of a String object. See Figure 9.6.

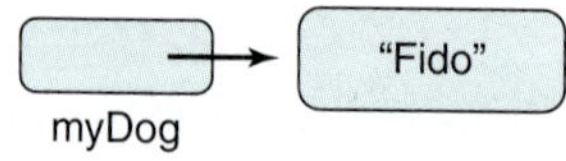

FIGURE 9.6 The variable *myDog* is a reference

Because String objects are so common, Java provides a shorter form of String instantiation. The more compact statement

```
String myDog = "Fido"
```

assigns the address of the String literal "Fido" to the reference myDog.

Java's String class provides the blueprint for all String objects. Each String object encapsulates a character sequence together with a host of methods, such as

int length(),

which returns the number of characters in a String, and

char charAt(int i),

which returns the character at position i.

The dot operator is used to invoke the methods of a String object.

For example,

myDog.length() returns 4 since "Fido" consists of four characters;

myDog.charAt(0) returns the character 'F' because, like arrays, strings are indexed from 0; and

myDog.charAt(2) returns 'd'.

Example 9.1 illustrates String instantiation and utilizes the length() and charAt(...) methods. The program also includes a new Scanner method,

String next() // returns a reference to the next input string

which facilitates string input.

EXAMPLE 9.1

Problem Statement Anyone who has seen the film *Mary Poppins* has, no doubt, heard Julie Andrews pronounce "supercalifragilisticexpialidocious" backwards. Well, Julie is no match for Java. The following program interactively accepts an arbitrary character string and displays the string in reverse.

Java Solution

```
// Reads a character string and prints it in reverse
import java.util.*;
public class Reverse
{
   public static void main(String[] args)
   {
      Scanner input = new Scanner(System.in);

      System.out.print("Enter a word: ");
      String word = input.next();                    // returns a String (reference)

      System.out.print(word + " in reverse is ");
      for(int i = word.length() - 1; i >= 0; i--)
         System.out.print(word.charAt(i));
      System.out.println();
   }
}
```

Output 1

Enter a word: **supercalifragilisticexpialidocious**
supercalifragilisticexpialidocious in reverse is suoicodilaipxecitsiligarfilacrepus

Output 2

Enter a word: **racecar**
racecar in reverse is racecar

Discussion We begin with line 9.

Line 9: String word = input.next();

Initially, word is declared as a reference variable. The variable word is not a String *object*; word is a reference that can hold the address of a String object.

The next action is the call input.next(). The method input.next() is similar to other Scanner methods such as input.nextInt() or input.nextDouble(). Just as input.nextInt() skips all whitespace and returns the "next integer" that is entered at the console, input.next() skips whitespace and returns the next string entered at the keyboard. More precisely, the method returns a *reference* to a String object. The next() method consumes characters until a whitespace character is encountered. Thus, a string returned by next() contains no spaces, tabs, or newline characters.

Finally, the address of this String object is assigned to the reference variable, word. Figure 9.7 shows a String reference and a String object that holds a character sequence that is a bit simpler than "supercalifragilisticexpialidocious".

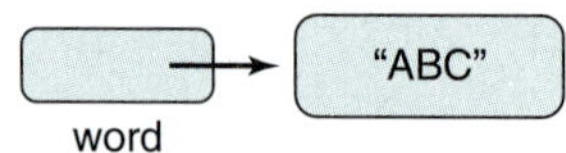

FIGURE 9.7 *word* is a *String* reference, not a *String* object

Lines 11–12:
```
for(int i = word.length() – 1; i >= 0; i--)
        System.out.print(word.charAt(i));
```

Because "ABC" contains three characters, the method word.length() returns 3. Consequently, the loop iterates from 2 down to 0. On each iteration, word.charAt(i) returns the character at position i:

i = 2; charAt(2) returns 'C'
i = 1; charAt(1) returns 'B'
i = 0; charAt(0) returns 'A'.

These three characters are displayed as output. Thus the output is the string "CBA".

9.5.1 String Concatenation

Routinely, our programs have used string concatenation within the print() and println() statements. For example, the statement

```
System.out.println("Frankenstein" + " meets " + "Dracula");
```

effects the concatenation of three strings: "Frankenstein"," meets ", and "Dracula".

Concatenation is the process of joining, connecting, or linking Strings together.

Strings can be joined or concatenated using the + operator or the more compact += operator. The segments of Figure 9.8 illustrate both operators.

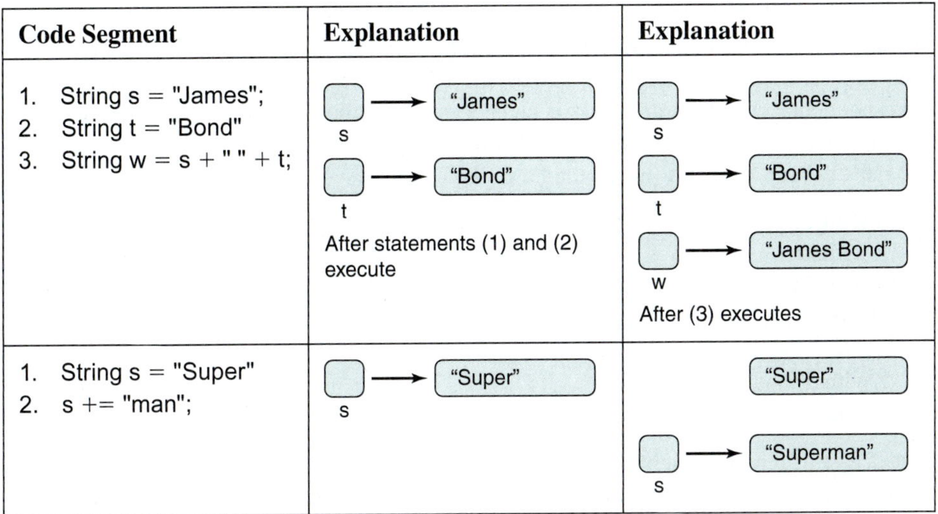

Code Segment
Explanation
Explanation
1. String s = "James";
2. String t = "Bond"
3. String w = s + " " + t;
"James"
s
"Bond"
t
After statements (1) and (2) execute
"James"
s
"Bond"
t
"James Bond"
w
After (3) executes
1. String s = "Super"
2. s += "man";
"Super"
s
"Super"
"Superman"
s

FIGURE 9.8 *String* concatenation using + and +=

Figure 9.8 also illustrates an important feature of concatenation.

> Concatenation results in the creation of a new String object.

The next example utilizes the + operator to accomplish concatenation and introduces two new methods of the String and Scanner classes. The String method

```
String toUpperCase()
```

creates a new string by converting all characters in the invoking object to uppercase. That is, if s is a String reference, then

```
s.toUpper()
```

returns a reference to a new string such that all the lowercase characters of s have been converted to uppercase. For example, the segment

```
String lower = "skyscraper";
String upper = lower.toUpperCase();
System.out.print(lower + " " + upper);
```

displays

```
skyscraper SKYSCRAPER
```

Notice that the characters of lower are not capitalized. A *new* String object with uppercase letters is created.

The Scanner method

```
String nextLine(),
```

is used to read an entire line of text, including whitespace. The Scanner method next() is inconvenient when reading strings that contain spaces or other whitespace. Example 9.2 uses nextLine() to read an entire line of text, including whitespace.

EXAMPLE 9.2 Message encryption predates the Internet, online banking, and electronic commerce by a few thousand years. History reports that Julius Caesar regularly encrypted his military correspondence. The *Caesar cipher* is an encryption method that replaces each letter of some text by another letter that is a fixed number of positions farther down in the alphabet. For example, a *2-shift* (also called a *C-shift*) replaces

A with *C*,
B with *D*,
C with *E*,
D with *F*
. . .
Y with *A*, and finally,
Z with *B*.

Thus a 2-shift replaces each letter with the letter two positions farther down the alphabet, cycling back to the beginning of the alphabet for *Y* and *Z*. Accordingly, the message "DIZZY" encrypts as "FKBBA". Similarly, a 17-shift or *R*-shift replaces

A with *R*,
B with *S*,
C with *T*,
. . . .
J with *A*, (cycling back), and
K with *B*.

In this case, each letter is "shifted" 17 positions so that an *R*-shift encodes "DIZZY" as "UZQQP".

The Caesar cipher is a very simple scheme, and a codebreaker would need to try at most 25 possible shifts in order to break the code.

Problem Statement Write an application that encrypts a message using a Caesar cipher. The program should accept one line of text as well as an integer representing a character shift. The original message may consist of alphabetical characters, whitespace, and punctuation. The encrypted message is comprised of uppercase letters with no punctuation or whitespace.

Java Solution The following application exploits character arithmetic when encoding each character of a message. Because Java stores a character using its ASCII value, which is an integer, arithmetical operations such as addition and subtraction of characters amount to addition and subtraction of integers. For example, Java computes the difference 'B' − 'A' as

$$\begin{aligned} \text{'B'} - \text{'A'} &= \\ \text{ASCII('B')} - \text{ASCII('A')} &= \\ 66 - 65 &= 1 \end{aligned}$$

The program also utilizes an *empty string*. An empty string is a string with no characters; it is a string of length 0.

```
// encrypts a message using a Caesar cipher
import java.util.*;

public class CaesarCipher
{
   public static String encrypt(String msg, int shift)
```

```
6.       {
7.       // returns message after performing a shift encryption
8.       String encryptedMessage = new String();     // creates an empty string (length 0)
9.       msg = msg.toUpperCase();                    // change all letters to uppercase
10.      for (int i = 0; I < msg.length(); i++)      // for each letter of the message
11.      {
12.         char ch = msg.charAt(i);
13.         if ( ch >= 'A' && ch <= 'Z')             // do not include punctuation or whitespace
14.         {
15.            int oldPositionInAlphabet = ch – 'A';   // if ch is 'B' then ch – 'A' = 66 – 65 = 1
16.            int newPositionInAlphabet = (oldPositionInAlphabet + shift) % 26;
17.            encryptedMessage = encryptedMessage + (char)(newPositionInAlphabet + 'A');
18.         }
19.      }
20.      return encryptedMessage;
21.      }
22.   public static void main (String[] args)
23.   {
24.      Scanner input = new Scanner(System.in);
25.      System.out.print("Enter a message on one line: ");
26.      String message = input.nextLine();
27.      System.out.print("Enter an integer in the range 0–25: ");
28.      int shift = input.nextInt() ;
29.      System.out.println("The encrypted message is " + encrypt(message, shift));
30.   }
31. }
```

Output 1

Enter a message on one line: **Veni, Vidi, Vici**
Enter an integer in the range 0–25: **5**
The encrypted message is AJSNANINANHN

Output 2

Enter a message on one line: **All Gaul is divided into three parts**
Enter an integer in the range 0–25: **18**
The encrypted message is SDDYSMDAKVANAVWVAFLGLZJWWHSJLK

Output 3

Enter a message on one line: **Tonight is karaoke night at the Coliseum**
Enter an integer in the range 0–25: **13**
The encrypted message is GBAVTUGVFXNENBXRAVTUGNGGURPBYVFRHZ

Discussion

Line 26: String message = input.nextLine();

The reference variable, message, can store the address of a String object. The next action is the Scanner call

input.nextLine().

> The nextLine() method advances the Scanner to the beginning of the next line of input and returns a reference to a String object comprised of all the characters that were skipped in the process, including whitespace but excluding the newline character.

Thus, if input consists of a single line of text, nextLine() returns a reference to a String comprised of the entire line, *including spaces and tabs*.

For input, we use the name of one of Caesar's many adversaries, "Cato". See Figure 9.9.

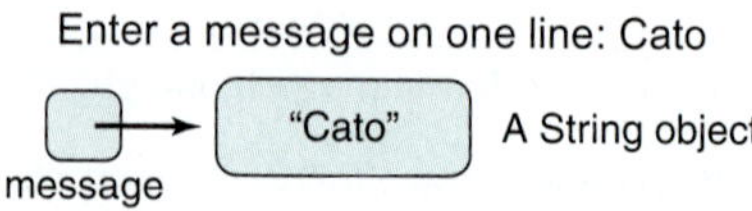

FIGURE 9.9 *message* is a reference to a *String* object

Lines 27–28: System.out.print("Enter an integer in the range 0–25: ");
int shift = input.nextInt();

The variable shift determines the shift value of the encryption process. See Figure 9.10.

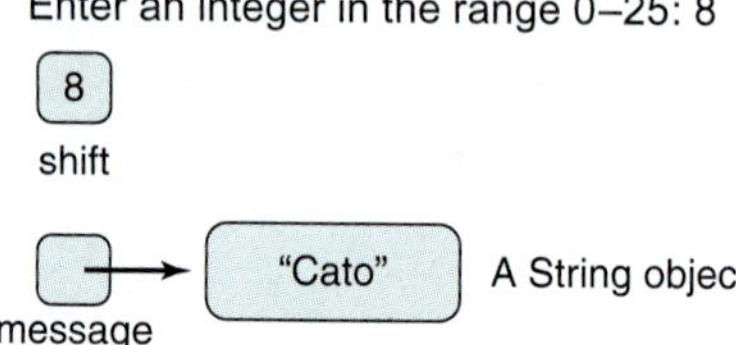

FIGURE 9.10 The integer variable *shift* determines the character shift

Line 29: System.out.println("The encrypted message is " + encrypt(message, shift));

Line 29 exhibits a call to encrypt(...), passing the reference variable message and the integer *s*hift as arguments to the formal parameters msg and shift. Notice that message and msg both refer to the same String object. Only one String object exists. See Figure 9.11.

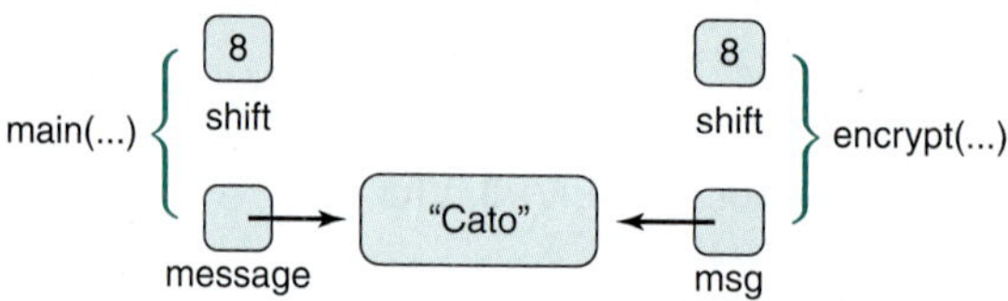

FIGURE 9.11 One *String* object but two references

Control passes to encrypt(...).

Line 8: String encryptedMessage = new String();

Here, a new reference variable encryptedMessage is declared. This reference stores the address of the empty string, that is, a String object with no characters. The empty String, created on line 8 using the new operator, can also be instantiated as

```
String encryptedMessage = ""; // no spaces between the quotes
```

See Figure 9.12.

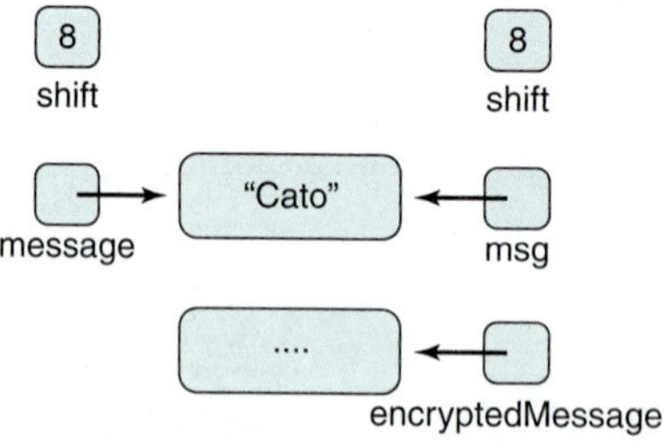

FIGURE 9.12 *encryptedMessage* refers to the empty string.

Line 9: msg = msg.toUpperCase()

The method toUpperCase() creates a *new* String object and returns a reference to that object. This newly created String object contains the uppercase equivalents of all the letters of msg. The call

```
msg.toUpperCase()
```

does not alter the characters of the original String object. However, the reference msg is assigned the address of the newly created String object, "CATO", and no longer refers to "Cato". See Figure 9.13.

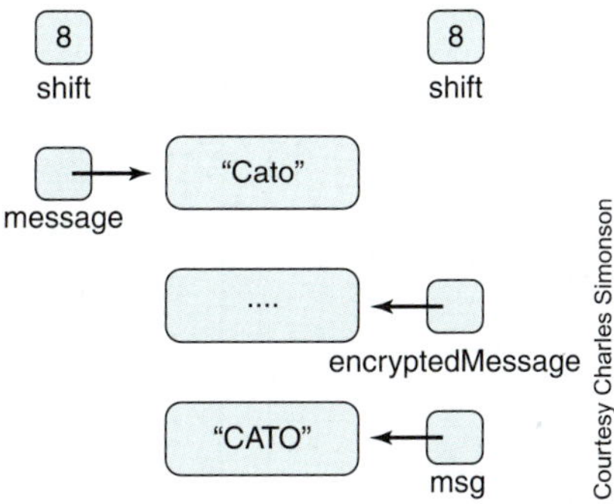

FIGURE 9.13 *msg* now refers to "CATO" and not "Cato"; *message* still refers to "Cato"

Lines 10–19:
```
for (int i = 0; i < msg.length(); i++)      // for each character of the message
{
   char ch = msg.charAt(i);
   if (ch >= 'A' && ch <= 'Z')        // do not include punctuation or whitespace
   {
      Int oldPositionInAlphabet = ch – 'A';
      int newPositionInAlphabet = (oldPositionInAlphabet + shift) % 26;
      encryptedMessage = encryptedMessage + (char)(newPositionInAlphabet + 'A');
   }
}
```

The call on line 10, msg.length(), returns the length of the String referenced by msg. That string is "CATO", so msg.length() returns 4. Thus, the loop executes four times, once for each letter of the message "CATO".

For each letter, ch, of "CATO",

- The alphabetical position of ch (oldPositionInAlphabet) is computed as ch – 'A'. For example, 'C' – 'A' =

  67 – 65 = 2, the alphabetical position of 'C', and

  'T' – 'A' =
  84 – 65 = 19, the place of 'T' in the alphabet.

- Each character must be replaced by the letter eight places forward in the alphabet. The replacement letter is the one at position

  (oldPositionInAlphabet + shift) % 26.

  Addition mod 26 ensures that letters wrap around to the beginning of the alphabet. For example, with shift equal to 8, 'T' is replaced by the letter that is eight places forward in the alphabet, that is, 'T' is replaced by the letter in position

  (19 + 8) % 26 = 1.

  Thus, 'T' is encrypted as 'B'. Similarly, 'C' is replaced by the letter at position

  (2 + 8) % 26 = 10. That letter is 'K'.

- The ASCII value of the encrypted letter is computed as:

  newPositionInAlphabet + 'A'.

  For example, because 'T' is encrypted as 'B'

  newPositionInAlphabet + 'A' =
  1 + 65 = 66, the ASCII value of 'B'.

On each iteration, a new String object is created by appending the encrypted letter (a character) to the String referenced by encryptedMessage. This is achieved using the + operator. The address of the new String object is assigned to encryptedMessage. Figure 9.14 traces the execution of the loop.

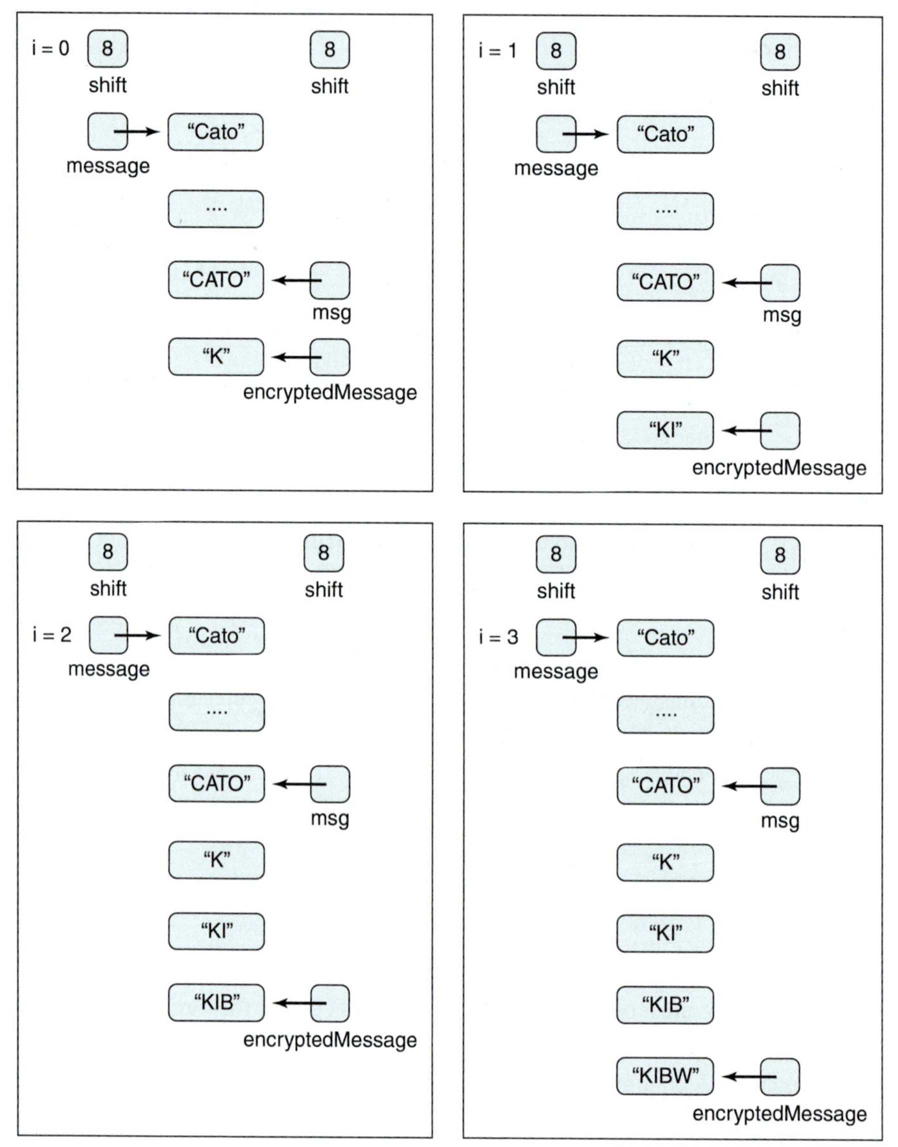

FIGURE 9.14 Each concatenation operation creates a new *String* object

Line 20: return encryptedMessage

The reference encryptedMessage is returned to the caller (Line 28).

Line 29: System.out.println("The encrypted message is " + encrypt(message, shift));

The output

The encrypted message is KIBW

is displayed. Notice that even though encrypt(message, shift) returns a reference, the characters of the corresponding String object, not the reference, are displayed.

9.5.2 Passing References to Methods

The method

```
String encrypt(String msg, int shift)
```

of Example 9.2 accepts two parameters; a String reference and an integer. This method is invoked on line 29 as

```
encrypt(message, shift).
```

As you know, when passing arguments to a method the *values* of the arguments are copied to the parameters. Consequently, the value of the integer argument shift is copied to the parameter shift, and the *reference* message is copied to the parameter msg. The String object referenced by message is not passed to encrypt(...), only its address is passed. The String object is not copied.

References, not objects, are passed as arguments to methods.

9.5.3 The *nextLine*() Method

The Scanner method

```
String nextLine(),
```

introduced in Example 9.2 has some subtle features that can cause errors if the method is used carelessly. The Java documentation states that the nextLine() method advances the Scanner past the current line and returns the input that was skipped. The method returns the rest of the current line, excluding any line separator at the end. The Scanner position is set to the beginning of the next line. Careless application of this method can cause surprising results.

On one hand, consider the following segment from Example 9.2:

```
System.out.print("Enter a message on one line: ");
String message = input.nextLine();

System.out.print("Enter an integer in the range 0-25: ");
int shift = input.nextInt() ;
```

If the input is

```
Cato
8
```

then message refers to "Cato" and shift gets the value 8.

On the other hand, suppose that the code in the segment is reversed and begins with a request for shift:

```
System.out.print("Enter an integer in the range 0-25 : ");
int shift = input.nextInt() ;

System.out.print("Enter a message on one line: ");
String message = input.nextLine();
```

With valid input

```
8
Cato
```

the results may surprise you. As expected, shift gets the value 8. After reading the 8, the Scanner is positioned before the (invisible) newline character following 8. The call to nextLine() advances the Scanner to the beginning of the next line and returns the input that was skipped, that is, the empty string! Thus message refers to the empty string and not "Cato".

> Using nextLine() for reading strings line by line causes no problems. However, care must be taken when mixing calls to nextLine() with other Scanner calls such as next(), nextInt(), or nextDouble().

9.5.4 Strings Are Immutable

Examples 9.1 and 9.2 demonstrate some of the basics of the Java String class. Implicit in these examples is a very important property of String objects:

> Java String objects are *immutable*. Strings are read-only.

Although a String *reference* may be reassigned, once a String *object* is created, that object cannot be altered. For example, consider the following code segment:

```
1. String s = "E.T.";
2. s = s.toLowerCase();
```

The assignment statement on line 1 instantiates a new String object referenced by s (see Figure 9.15).

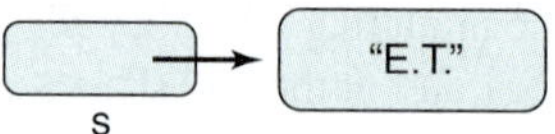

FIGURE 9.15 The variable s references the *String* "E.T."

The method call on line 2 creates a *new* object (with lowercase letters). The address of this new object is assigned to s as Figure 9.16 illustrates.

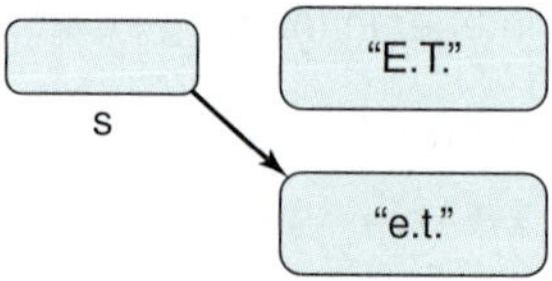

FIGURE 9.16 The variable s references a new *String*; "E.T." is no longer accessible

The original String object ("E.T.") has not been changed. Instead, a new String is created. Moreover, the original String object ("E.T.") is now inaccessible because no reference holds its address; see Figure 9.16. In Chapter 10, we discuss the fate of this "abandoned" memory.

9.5.5 More String Methods

Examples 9.1 and 9.2 illustrate just a few methods of Java's String class. There are many more. Figure 9.17 lists, some additional methods. A String object is much more than a sequence of characters. Every String object encapsulates data and a host of methods into a single unit. Methods that return String, of course, return not a String object but a *reference* to a String object.

Method	Explanation	Example
char charAt(int index)	s.charAt(i) returns the character at index i. All Strings are indexed from 0.	String s = "Titanic"; s.charAt(3) returns 'a'
int compareTo(String t)	compares two Strings, character by character, using the ASCII values of the characters.s.compareTo(t) returns a negative integer/ 0/positive integer if the string s lexicographically precedes/equals/ follows the string t.	String s = "Shrek"; String t = "Star Wars"; String u = "Shrek"; s.compareTo(t) returns a negative number. s.compareTo(u) returns 0. t.compareTo(s) returns a positive number.
int compareToIgnoreCase(String t)	similar to compareTo(...) but ignores differences in case.	String s = "E.T."; String t = "e.t."; s.compareToIgnorecase(t) returns 0.
String concat(String t)	s.concat(t) returns s with t appended.	String s = "Spider"; s.concat("-Man") returns "Spider-Man".
boolean endsWith(String suffix)	s.endsWith(t) returns true if t is a suffix of s.	String s = "Forrest Gump"; s.endsWith("ump") returns true
boolean startsWith(String prefix)	s.startsWith(t) returns true if t is a prefix of s.	String s = "Jurassic Park"; s.startsWith("Jur") returns true s.startsWith("jur") returns false
boolean equals(Object t) (The strange parameter will make sense later. For now, think of the parameter as String.)	s.equals(t) returns true if s and t are identical.	String s = "FINDING NEMO"; String t = "Finding Nemo"; s.equals(t) returns false s.equals("FINDING NEMO") returns true
boolean equalsIgnoreCase(String t)	s.equalsIgnoreCase(t) returns true if s and t are identical, ignoring case.	String s = "FINDING NEMO"; String t = "Finding Nemo"; s.equalsIgnorecase(t) returns true
int indexOf(String t)	s.indexOf(t) returns the index in s of the first occurrence of t and returns –1 if t is not a substring of s.	String s = "**The** Lord Of The Rings"; s.indexOf("The") returns 0; s.indexOf("Bilbo") returns –1.
int indexOf(String t, int from)	s.indexOf(t, from) returns the index in s of the first occurrence of t beginning at index from; an unsuccessful search returns −1.	String s = "The Lord Of **The** Rings"; s.indexOf("The", 6) returns 12;
int length()	s.length() returns the number of characters in s.	String s = "Jaws"; s.length() returns 4
String replace(char oldChar, char newChar)	s.replace(oldCh, newCh) returns a String obtained by replacing every occurrance of oldCh with newCh.	String s = "Harry Potter"; s.replace ('r','m') returns "Hammy Pottem"
String substring(int index)	s.substring(index) returns the substring of s consisting of all characters with index greater than or equal to index.	String s = "The Sixth Sense"; s.substring(7) returns "th Sense"
String substring(int start, int end)	s.substring(start, end) returns the substring of s consisting of all characters with index greater than or equal to start and strictly less than end.	String s = "The Sixth Sense"; s.substring(7, 12) returns "th Se"
String toLowerCase()	s.toLowerCase() returns a String formed from s by replacing all uppercase characters with lowercase characters.	String s = "The Lion King"; s.toLowerCase() returns "the lion king"

(continued)

String toUpperCase()	s.toUpperCase() returns a String formed from s by replacing all lowercase characters with uppercase characters.	String s = "The Lion King"; s. toUpperCase() returns "THE LION KING"
String trim()	s.trim() returns the String with all leading and trailing white space removed.	String s = "Attack of the Killer Tomatoes "; s.trim() returns "Attack of the Killer Tomatoes"

FIGURE 9.17 Some *String* methods

9.5.6 *equals*(...) and ==

When utilizing the String class, be wary of comparisons using the == operator. The == operator compares references, not characters.

> To determine whether or not the character sequences of two String objects are identical, use the equals(...) method.

For example, the expression s == t, shown in the segment of Figure 9.18a, returns false because the two *references*, s and t, are different, while s.equals(t) returns true because the two String objects hold identical character sequences. The expressions s == t and s.equals(t) of Figure 9.18b both return true because the references as well as the character sequences are equal.

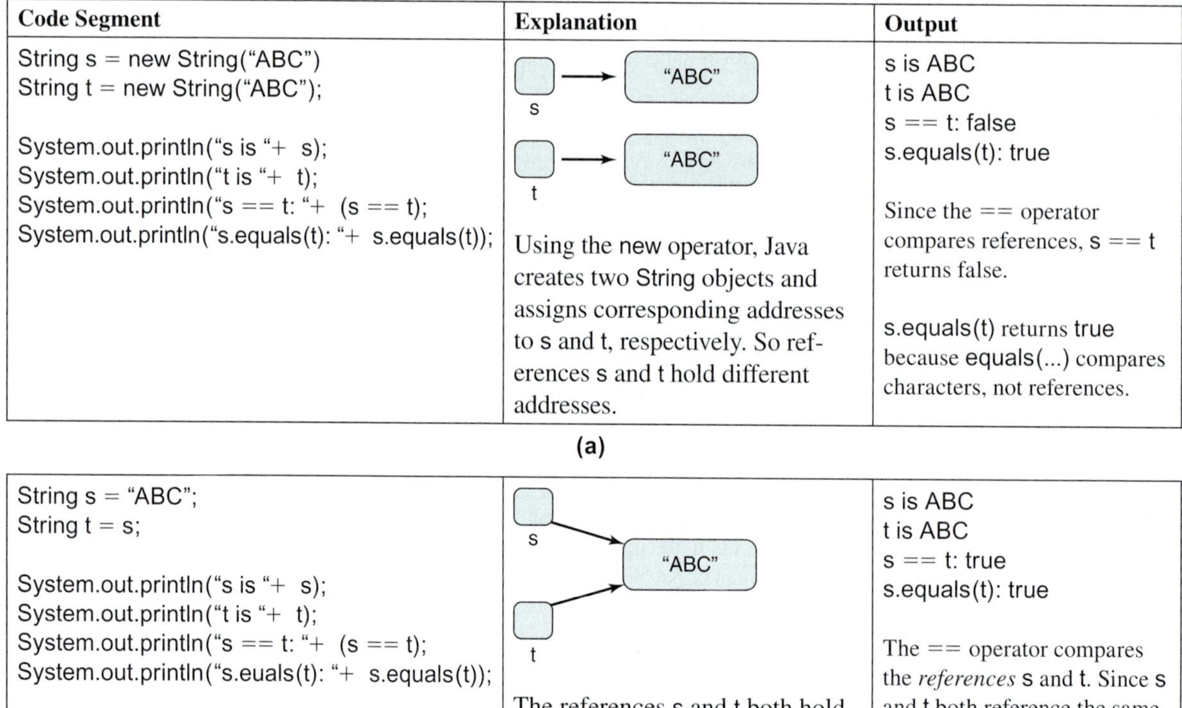

Code Segment	Explanation	Output
String s = new String("ABC") String t = new String("ABC"); System.out.println("s is "+ s); System.out.println("t is "+ t); System.out.println("s == t: "+ (s == t); System.out.println("s.equals(t): "+ s.equals(t));	s → "ABC" t → "ABC" Using the new operator, Java creates two String objects and assigns corresponding addresses to s and t, respectively. So references s and t hold different addresses.	s is ABC t is ABC s == t: false s.equals(t): true Since the == operator compares references, s == t returns false. s.equals(t) returns true because equals(...) compares characters, not references.

(a)

String s = "ABC"; String t = s; System.out.println("s is "+ s); System.out.println("t is "+ t); System.out.println("s == t: "+ (s == t); System.out.println("s.euals(t): "+ s.equals(t));	s → "ABC" ← t The references s and t both hold the address of this object.	s is ABC t is ABC s == t: true s.equals(t): true The == operator compares the *references* s and t. Since s and t both reference the same object, s == t returns true.

(b)

FIGURE 9.18 *equals*() and == are not the same

In the final example of this section, we use the Random class together with the String class to tackle a bit of Shakespeare.

EXAMPLE 9.3

It has been hypothesized that an infinite number of monkeys, typing for an infinite amount of time, would eventually produce the complete works of William Shakespeare. Since monkeys are expensive and time is precious, we scale down the experiment to a single monkey and *King Lear*—well, not the whole play.

Problem Statement Write a program that iteratively produces random letters until either the word "LEAR" appears or two million characters have been generated.

Java Solution We first describe the solution as an algorithm:

```
Create a String, letters, consisting of four randomly generated uppercase letters.
Initialize count to 4   // count enumerates the number of random letters generated
while letters is not equal to "LEAR" and count <= 2,000,00
{
    remove the first character from letters;
    append a new random letter to letters so the length of letters remains four;
    increment count;
}
if "LEAR" was generated,
        output success along with the character count
else
        output failure
```

The following program implements the previous algorithm. The program uses Java's Random class to produce random integers between 0 and 25 inclusive. Each random integer represents a random letter: 0 for 'A', 1 for 'B', and so on.

The program follows:

```
import java.util.*; // for the Random class

public class MonkeyBusiness
{
// Generates random letters until the program produces the name "LEAR"
   public static void main(String[] args)
   {
      final int MAXIMUM = 2000000;  // stop at 2,000, 000 characters
      final String GOAL = "LEAR";    // the match "LEAR"
      String letters = "";           // The empty String—the String with no characters
      Random num = new Random();    // instantiate a Random object
      // build an initial String of 4 random characters
      for (int i = 1; i <= GOAL.length(); i++)          // for i = 1 to 4
      {
         int x = num.nextInt(26);          // x denotes a random alphabet position (0 to 25)
         letters = letters + (char)(x + 'A');// the ASCII code for 'A' is 65
      }

      int count = GOAL.length();         // count is initially set to 4

      while (!letters.equals(GOAL) && count <= MAXIMUM)
```

```
19.      {
20.         letters = letters.substring(1);   // form a new String by eliminating the first character
21.         int x = num.nextInt(26);          // x denotes a random alphabet position(0 to 25)
22.         letters = letters + (char)(x + 'A'); // add a new random character to the end of letters
23.         count++;
24.      }
25.      if (letters.equals(GOAL))
26.         System.out.println("It took " + count + " letters to generate LEAR");
27.      else
28.         System.out.println("Whew! I gave up!");
29.      }
30. }
```

Running the program three times produced the following output.

Output 1

```
It took 794188 letters to generate LEAR
```

Output 2

```
It took 594913 letters to generate LEAR
```

Output 3

```
It took 872108 letters to generate LEAR
```

Discussion

Line 9: Here, letters is initialized to the empty string. Had letters not been initialized, concatenation would have resulted in a syntax error. For example, the code

```
String s;          // no initialization here, s is not the empty string
s = s + 'a';
```

generates the compiler error:

```
variable s might not have been initialized
s = s + 'a';
```

Be sure to initialize String references.

Line 10: A Random object is instantiated and referenced by num.

Lines 12–16: A new String object comprised of four random characters is created within the for loop. The loop includes a method call

num.nextInt(26),

which returns a random integer in the range 0 to 25, inclusive. This value, assigned to x, designates an alphabetical character, 0 for 'A', 1 for 'B', and so on.

The expression

```
(x + 'A')
```

computes the ASCII value of the character at position x; and finally, the cast

```
(char)(x + 'A')
```

produces the uppercase letter at alphabetical position x.

For example, if x has the value 2, then

```
(x + 'A') =            // 2 is the position of 'C'
2 + 65 = 67            // 67 is the ASCII code for 'C'
```

and (char)(67) is 'C'—the uppercase letter at alphabetical position 2. (Recall that the first position is numbered 0.)

Line 17: Initialize count to 4; count keeps track of the total number of random letters that are generated.

Line 18–24: While letters is not equal to "LEAR" *and* count does not exceed MAXIMUM

> **Line 20**: letters.substring(1) returns a new String consisting of the last three characters of letters. This new String object is referenced by letters.
>
> **Line 21**: Variable x is assigned a random number in the range 0 to 25. This number represents the alphabetical position of a random letter.
>
> **Line 22**: The uppercase character at position x is appended to letters forming a new String of 4 characters.
>
> **Line 23**: Increment count.

Lines 25–28: If "LEAR" appears, then report the number of random characters otherwise report failure.

9.6 THE *StringBuilder* CLASS

You may have noticed that the String class includes the method

```
boolean endsWith(String s)
```

For example, the segment

```
String s = "ASDFGHJHGFDSLEAR"
s.endsWith("LEAR")
```

returns true.

You might guess that, by using endsWith(...), the code of Example 9.3 could be streamlined as shown in Figure 9.19.

```
String letters = "";
int count = 0;
while (!letters.endsWith("LEAR") && count <= MAXIMUM)
{
        int x = num.nextInt(26);
        letters = letters + (char)(x + 'A');
        count++;
}
if (letters.endsWith("LEAR")) .....
```

FIGURE 9.19 Is this better?

The code of Figure 9.19 may appear simpler and more compact than the version of Example 9.3. However, if you embed this segment into a program and execute it, you may have a long wait before you see any results.

Remember, String objects are constant, immutable, and read-only. Consequently, String concatenation always produces a brand new String object. For each of the three sample runs of Example 9.3, on average, about 750,000 new String objects of length 4 are created—one new object of length 4 for each random letter generated. The loop of Figure 9.19 also creates a new String object with each iteration. If the loop executes 750,000 times, then the first String has just one character, the second has two characters, the third three characters, . . . the 749,997th new String has 749,997 characters, and the 749,998th has 749,998 characters, and so on. Each time a new String is created, all the characters of the "old" String are copied to new memory locations. Copying 749,998 characters is certainly a bit more work than copying just four! Figure 9.20 compares the two implementations.

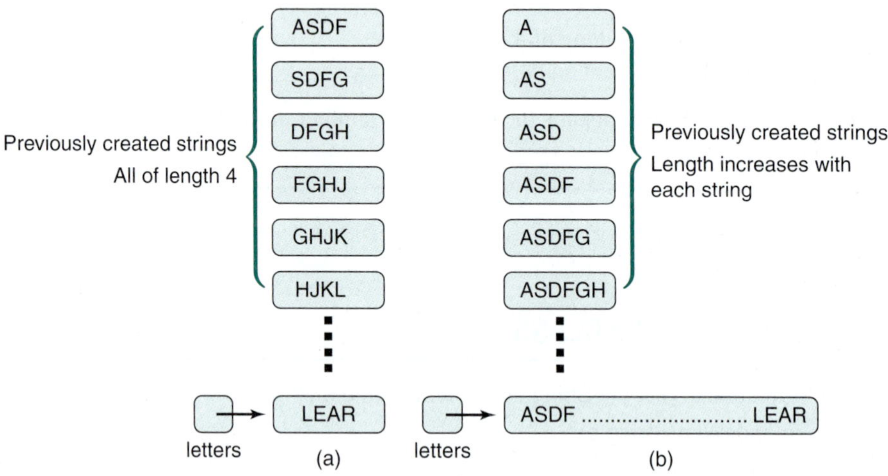

FIGURE 9.20 (a) Strings created with the program of Example 9.3
(b) Strings created using the *endsWith*() method

A String object is immutable; once created, a String object cannot change. On the other hand, a StringBuilder object *can* be changed. You can add or delete characters to or from a StringBuilder object, *without creating a new StringBuilder object*. To accomplish this, the capacity of a StringBuilder object automatically expands as needed. You can also change individual characters of a StringBuilder object without creating a new object.

For programs that are heavy with string concatenation, or any operation that alters the characters of a string, Java provides the StringBuilder class with methods that do not create a new object each time a String is altered.

Let's look behind the scenes for a minute. Suppose that word references the String "computer". To append the "s" to word, each letter of "computer" is copied and "s" is appended to this new copy of "computer". See Figure 9.21a. However, if wordBuilder references a StringBuilder object, in contrast to a String object, no copying occurs. See Figure 9.21b.

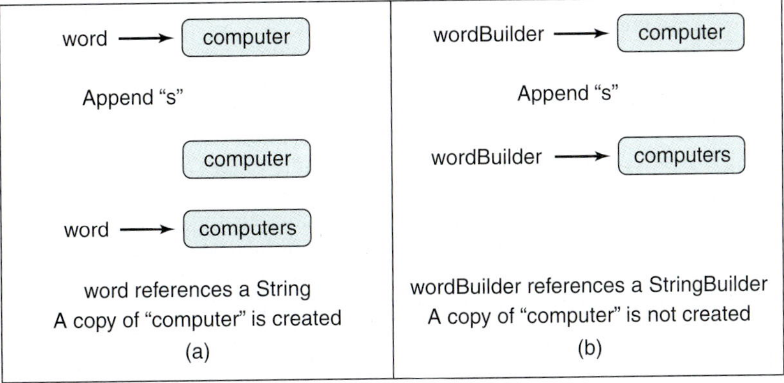

FIGURE 9.21 Appending to a *String* versus appending to a *StringBuilder*

For programs with excessive String modification or concatenation, the StringBuilder class may improve performance. For *read-only* strings, the String class is preferable, more efficient, and provides more functionality.

To instantiate a StringBuilder object, use the new operator:

```
StringBuilder s = new StringBuilder();          // initial capacity 16 characters
StringBuilder s = new StringBuilder(50);        // initial capacity 50
StringBuilder s = new StringBuilder ("Hello");  // initializes s to "Hello"
```

The capacity of a StringBuilder object automatically expands as needed.

Figure 9.22 gives a few of the more common methods of the StringBuilder class.

Method	Explanation (sb refers to a StringBuilder)	Example
StringBuilder append(String s) StringBuilder append(char c) StringBuilder append(StringBuilder s)	sb.append(x) appends x to the end of sb and returns a reference to the *altered* StringBuilder object.	StringBuilder s = new StringBuilder("New"); s.append("York"); returns StringBuilder("New York") *and* alters s
char charAt(int i)	sb.charAt(i) returns the character at position i. StringBuilder character sequences are indexed from 0.	StringBuilder s = new StringBuilder("Iowa"); char ch = sb.charAt(3); ch has the value 'a'
StringBuilder delete(int start, int end)	sb.delete(start, end) removes the characters from position start to position end −1 and returns a reference to the altered StringBuilder object.	StringBuilder s = new StringBuilder("Delaware"); s.delete(2,6); returns StringBuilder("Dere") and alters s
StringBuilder deleteCharAt(int i)	sb.deleteCharAt(i) removes the character at index i and returns a reference to the altered StringBuilder object.	StringBuilder s = new StringBuilder("Maine"); s.deleteCharAt(1); returns StringBuilder("Mine") and alters s

(continued)

Method	Explanation (sb refers to a StringBuilder)	Example
int indexOf(String s)	sb.indexOf(s) returns the index of the first occurrence of s in sb. If s is not a substring of sb, returns −1.	StringBuilder s = new StringBuilder("Florida"); int x = s.indexOf("or"); x has the value 2
int indexOf(String s, int from)	sb.indexOf(s, from) returns the index of the first occurrence of s in sb starting at index from. If s is not a substring of sb, returns −1.	StringBuilder s = new StringBuilder("Mississippi"); int x = s.indexOf("is",2); x has the value 4
StringBuilder insert(int index, String s) StringBuilder insert(int index, char ch)	sb.insert(index, s) inserts s into sb at position index.	StringBuilder s = new StringBuilder("Oo"); s.insert(1, "hi); returns StringBuilder("Ohio") and alters s
int length()	sb.length() returns the number of characters in sb.	StringBuilder s = new StringBuilder("Vermont"); s.length() returns 7
StringBuilder replace(int start, int end, String s)	sb.replace(start, end, s) replaces all characters from start to end − 1 with s and returns a reference to the altered StringBuilder object.	StringBuilder s = new StringBuilder("Texas"); s.replace(1,4,"axe") returns "Taxes" and alters s
StringBuilder reverse()	sb.reverse() reverses the order of the characters of sb and returns a reference to the altered StringBuilder object.	StringBuilder s = new StringBuilder("Utah"); s.reverse() returns StringBuilder("hatU") and alters s
String substring(int index)	s.substring(index) returns the substring of s consisting of all characters with index greater than or equal to index. Notice that the method returns a String reference.	StringBuilder sb = new StringBuilder("New Jersey"); sb.substring(4) returns "Jersey"
String substring(int start, int end)	s.substring(start, end) returns the substring of s consisting of all characters with index greater than or equal to start and strictly less than end. Notice that the method returns a String reference.	StringBuilder sb = new StringBuilder("New Jersey"); sb.substring(0,3) returns "New"
String toString()	sb.toString() returns a String representation of the characters of sb.	StringBuilder s = new StringBuilder("Illinois"); String str = s.toString(); str refers to the String object "Illinois"

FIGURE 9.22 Some *StringBuilder* methods

In contrast to the String class, the equals(...) method of StringBuilder compares *references* and not the contents of a StringBuilder object.

For example,

```
String s = new String(" Monkey Business");
String t = new String ("Monkey Business");                (1)
System.out.println(s.equals(t));
```

displays true, but the segment

```
StringBuilder s = new StringBuilder(" Monkey Business");
StringBuilder t = new StringBuilder ("Monkey Business");   (2)
System.out.println( s.equals(t));
```

displays false.

Segment (1) compares characters, but segment (2) compares references. To compare the contents of two StringBuilder objects a and b, use

```
a.toString().equals(b.toString()).
```

Using the StringBuilder class, we rewrite the segment of Figure 9.19 in Example 9.4.

EXAMPLE 9.4

Problem Statement Using the StringBuilder class, write a program that iteratively produces random letters until either the word "LEAR" appears or two million characters have been generated.

Java Solution The fragment of Figure 9.19 uses the String method endsWith(...) to determine whether or not the word "LEAR" has been randomly generated. The StringBuilder class does not come packaged with an endsWith(...) method. However, the method

```
int indexOf(String s, int from)
```

serves the same purpose. For example, consider the declaration and instantiation

```
StringBuilder s = new StringBuilder('SHFJDKLEAR') // "SHFJDKLEAR" has 10 characters
```

The call s.indexOf("LEAR", 6) examines the last four characters of s, finds a match, and returns 6, the index of 'L'.

Similarly, if s references a StringBuilder object initialized with "ASWTHAMLET", then indexOf("LEAR", 6) returns -1 because "LEAR" does not appear as the last four characters of "ASWTHAMLET".

In general,

```
int indexOf("LEAR" , s.length()-4)
```

returns a non-negative number if s ends with "LEAR" and -1 otherwise. The following program uses the logic of Figure 9.19 but with a StringBuilder object.

```
// Generates random letters until the word "LEAR" appears
// Generates a maximum of 2 million letters
import java.util.*;

public class MoreMonkeyBusiness
{
   public static void main(String[] args)
```

```
7.  {
8.    final int MAXIMUM = 2000000;
9.    final String GOAL = "LEAR";
10.   StringBuilder letters = new StringBuilder();
11.   Random random = new Random();

12.   while ( letters.indexOf(GOAL, letters.length()-4) < 0 && letters.length() <= MAXIMUM)
13.   {
14.     int position = random.nextInt(26);           // a random alphabet position
15.     char nextLetter = (char)(position + 'A');    // position+'A' is the ASCII code of the next letter
16.     letters.append(nextLetter);                  // append the new letter
17.   }

18.   if(letters.indexOf(GOAL, letters.length()-4) >= 0)   // if letters ends with "LEAR"
19.     System.out.println("It took " + letters.length() + " characters to generate LEAR");
20.   else
21.     System.out.println("Whew! I gave up");
22.   }
23. }
```

Output 1

It took 93444 characters to generate LEAR

Output 2

It took 139345 characters to generate LEAR

Output 3

It took 783586 characters to generate LEAR

Discussion Lines 12–17 do all the work. The loop condition determines whether the current StringBuilder object ends with "LEAR" or whether the maximum number of random letters has been generated. If the StringBuilder object ends with "LEAR", then letters.indexOf(GOAL, letters.length()-4) returns the position of "LEAR", a positive number. Within the loop:

- a new random integer in the range 0 to 25 is generated corresponding to an alphabetical character between 'A' and 'Z' inclusive,
- the random number is converted to the corresponding alphabetical character, and
- the character is appended to the StringBuilder object, letters.

The function call letters.length() gives the total number of characters that have been generated.

9.7 THE MYSTERIOUS *String[] args*

Every application that you have implemented includes the heading

```
public static void main(String[] args);
```

What does all this Java-speak mean? Is it all necessary? In Chapter 10, we explain the meaning of the words public and static. Now, however, you probably recognize

```
String[] args
```

as an array of String. The following short program uses this mysterious array args:

```
public class Tester
{
```

```
        public static void main(String[] args)
        {
                System.out.println("Hello " + args[0]);
                System.out.println("Hello " + args[1]);
        }
}
```

Array elements args[0] and args[1] are String references that are passed to main(...) via the command line.

If you execute this program with the command

```
> java Tester Newman Jerry
```

or

```
> java Tester "Newman" "Jerry"
```

the two Strings ("Newman" and "Jerry") entered at the command line are passed to the program, and references to these strings are stored in the array args. Consequently, args[0] holds a reference to the String "Newman" and args[1] holds a reference to the String "Jerry". The output of the program is:

```
Hello Newman
Hello Jerry
```

You can pass any number of arguments to a program via the command line. Moreover, the number of arguments passed is available as args.length. The following fragment accepts and prints an arbitrary number of command line arguments.

```
Public static void main(String[] args)
{
        for (int i = 0; i < args.length; i++)
                System.out.println("Hello " + args[i]);
}
```

9.8 CLASSES FOR HANDLING FILES

To this point, all of our programs have been interactive. However, applications that require a large amount of data often take input from (or place output to) disk files that do not disappear when you turn off your computer. A word processing program saves your document as a file, as do spreadsheets and database programs. Permanent data reside in files. Most programs use and/or create data in files that exist before and persist after the program executes.

A file is a collection of data saved under a single name. There are many different types of files, but for the present, we concentrate on text files, a type of file that consists of ordinary ASCII characters. A text file is a file that you can create or read with an ordinary text editor such as Notepad (Windows), TextEdit (Mac OS X), or Emacs (Linux/Unix).

> To use a file, you must first instantiate a File object.

A File object is a proxy that represents a physical disk file within a program. Once instantiated, a File object is passed to another object that is capable of reading data from the file or writing data to the file. Reading is accomplished with a Scanner object and writing with a PrintWriter object. The program of Example 9.5 uses the File class along with some new methods of the Scanner class to read data from a text file.

EXAMPLE 9.5 **Problem Statement** Read the contents of a text file and display the file's contents on the screen.

Java Solution To accomplish this task, the following program uses two Java classes: the File class and the Scanner class. Because the File class resides in the java.io package, the program must include the statement: import java.io.*. Also, notice the clause

throws IOException

in the heading of main(...). For now, whenever a method, myMethod(...), uses the File class for Scanner I/O, include throws IOException in myMethod(...)'s heading as well as in the heading of any other method that calls myMethod(...). We discuss the "throws clause" in detail in a subsequent chapter.

The name of the disk file is quotations.txt and it contains several quotations attributed to comedian and satirist Groucho Marx (1890–1977). The program reads from quotations.txt and displays the contents of quotations.txt on the screen.

The files that we use in this section are all *sequential* files. Data in a sequential file must be accessed sequentially, that is, in order from the beginning of the file to the end. To read the tenth line of the file, a program must read the previous nine lines first.

The program and a line-by-line discussion follow.

```
// displays the contents of the file quotations.txt on the screen
import java.util.*;
import java.io.*;

public class File1
{
   public static void main (String[] args) throws IOException
   {
      File inputFile = new File("quotations.txt");
      if( !inputFile.exists())
      {
         System.out.println("File quotations.txt not found ");
         System.exit(0);
      }
      Scanner input = new Scanner(inputFile);
      String line;                  // to hold one full line from the file

      while (input.hasNext())       // while there is more data
      {
         line = input.nextLine();   // advance to next line, returns all "skipped" data
         System.out.println(line);
      }
      input.close();
   }
}
```

Output

Quotations of Groucho Marx (1890–1977)

A child of five would understand this.
Send someone to fetch a child of five.

Age is not a particularly interesting subject.
Anyone can get old. All you have to do is live long enough.

Either this man is dead or my watch has stopped.

I could dance with you until the cows come home.
On second thought I'd rather dance with the cows until you come home.

I find television very educating.
Every time somebody turns on the set, I go into the other room and read a book.

I sent the club a wire stating,
PLEASE ACCEPT MY RESIGNATION.
I DON'T WANT TO BELONG TO ANY CLUB THAT WILL ACCEPT ME AS A MEMBER.

I've had a perfectly wonderful evening. But this wasn't it.

Those are my principles,
and if you don't like them... well, I have others.

I don't have a photograph, but you can have my footprints.
They're upstairs in my socks.

Discussion The program displays the contents of the file quotations.txt. The file might have been created with a text editor such as Notepad or Emacs, or even with Word (*if saved as a text file*). Let's look at the program, line by line.

Lines 2–3: These import statements are necessary when using the File class and the Scanner class.

Line 8: The variable inputFile is declared as a reference to a File object. Like other objects, a File object is created via the new operator. The object is initialized with the string "quotations.txt". If the disk file does not reside in the same directory as the class file that is created by the compiler, use a qualified filename such as "c:\\myfiles\\quotations.txt". (Because a slash \ is used within a string to signify an escape character such as \n or \t, a double slash is necessary to denote an actual quoted slash.) The File object is the program's representation of the physical disk file quotations.txt.

Lines 9–12: In the event that the file quotations.txt cannot be found, the program takes action. The exists() method of the File class returns true if the file exists and false otherwise. If the named file cannot be found, the program displays a message to that effect, and the call

```
System.exit(0)
```

aborts the program.

Line 14: A new Scanner object is instantiated with parameter inputFile (rather than the usual System.in), indicating that the Scanner reads data from the file quotations.txt rather than the keyboard.

Line 15: The hasNext() method of the Scanner class returns true if input remains and false otherwise. Thus, if all data has been read from the file, the loop terminates because input.hasNext() returns false.

Line 18: Each call

```
input.nextLine()
```

returns one line of the file quotations.txt.

Line 19: Each line of the file is displayed on the screen.

Line 21: The close() method of the Scanner class closes the Scanner object, that is, disassociates the file object from the Scanner. In this small program, there was no gain in closing the Scanner. However, in larger programs that read from many files, closing the Scanner can free up system resources and make a difference in program performance.

From Example 9.5 we can extrapolate a methodology for reading data from a text file.

1. Instantiate a File object using the filename:

   File inputFile = new File(*filename*); // the name *inputFile* is arbitrary

2. Instantiate a Scanner object passing the File object to the Scanner:

   Scanner input = new Scanner(inputFile); // the name *input* is arbitrary

3. Use the methods of the Scanner class to read data from the file.

   All of the familiar methods such as nextInt(), nextDouble, and next() can be used in addition to nextLine().
   The method hasNext() returns false when all data has been read.

4. Close the Scanner.

   input.close()

Do not forget to include the clause

```
throws IOException
```

as part of the heading of a method that uses the File class. In fact, if the heading of method A() includes a throws clause and method B() invokes A(), then the heading of B() should also include a throws clause. In Chapter 14, you will see that there are exceptions to this rule.

The filename of Example 9.5 was hard-wired into the program. More conveniently, the name of the file can be supplied at runtime. In this case, a program instantiates two Scanner objects, one that reads from the keyboard and the other that reads from a file.

```
Scanner keyboard = new Scanner(System.in);    // read from keyboard
System.out.print("Enter the file name: ");    // prompt user for filename
String filename = keyboard.next();            // read filename from keyboard

File inputFile = new File(filename);          // instantiate a File object
Scanner input = new Scanner(inputFile);       // read from the file
```

The next example not only reads from a file but sends output to another file.

To write data to a file, use the PrintWriter class and the following procedure:

1. Instantiate a File object with the name of the output file.
2. Instantiate a PrintWriter object, passing the newly created File object as an argument. If the specified output file already exists, its contents are erased; otherwise a new file is created.

The PrintWriter class implements the familiar methods print() and println().

EXAMPLE 9.6 During World War II, the British waged a war behind the war trying to intercept and decode German transmissions. The Germans, however, used methods a bit more clever than the Caesar cipher of Example 9.2. Rather than a single letter shift, the Germans used a *codeword* shift such that each letter of some secret codeword represents a different shift. For example, assume that the codeword is "CAT" and the message is "LEOPARD". If we agree that A occupies position 0 in the alphabet, B holds position 1, C is in position 2, and so on, then the letters of the codeword "CAT" occupy alphabet positions 2(C), 0(A), and 19(T) and consequently represent successive alphabet shifts of 2, 0, and 19 places when encrypting the message. Thus, to encode "LEOPARD" replace:

L with N: a 2-place shift (C)
E with E: a 0-place shift (A)
O with H: a 19-place shift (T)

P with R: a 2-place shift (C)
A with A: a 0-place shift (A)
R with K: a 19-place shift (T)

D with F: a 2-place shift (C)

By repeatedly cycling the codeword "CAT", this method transforms "LEOPARD" into "NEHRAKF". If the codeword is "MOUSE" then "LEOPARD" encrypts as "XSIHEDR". For a code word with 13 letters, such as "DETERMINATION", a code breaker would be faced with 26^{13} or 2,481,152,873,203,736,576 possible encodings.

Problem Statement Write a program that, given a file of English text, encrypts the passage using a codeword shift. The codeword and the names of the input and output files are supplied interactively. For simplicity, encode the file, line by line. That is, consider each line of the file to be a "new message." Assume that the input file contains only alphabetical characters and no whitespace.

Java Solution The program requires two Scanner objects: one object that accepts the filenames and codeword interactively and the other that reads text from the input file. In addition, the program instantiates a PrintWriter object that writes encrypted text to an output file. The method

String Encrypt(String msg, String cw)

is almost identical to the method of Example 9.2. However, instead of using the same shift for each letter, the program of Example 9.6 uses a codeword shift. The method accepts one line of text and returns an encrypted version of that text. The program encrypts the text, line by line.

```
import java.util.*;
import java.io.*;

public class EncryptFile
{
  // returns one line of encrypted text
  public static String encrypt(String msg, String cw)
  {
    String encryptedMessage = new String();
    msg = msg.toUpperCase();
    cw = cw.toUpperCase();
    for (int i = 0; i < msg.length(); i++)
    {
      char ch = msg.charAt(i);
      int shift = (cw.charAt(i % cw.length()) – 'A');
      int oldPositionInAlphabet = ch – 'A';
      int newPositionInAlphabet = (oldPositionInAlphabet + shift) % 26;
      encryptedMessage = encryptedMessage + (char)(newPositionInAlphabet + 'A');
    }
```

```
19.       return encryptedMessage;
20.    }
21.    public static void main (String[] args) throws IOException
22.    {
23.       // Instantiate a Scanner object for keyboard input
24.       Scanner keyboard = new Scanner(System.in);
25.       System.out.print("Unencrypted file: ");
26.       String unencryptedFile = keyboard.next();
27.       File inputFile = new File(unencryptedFile);
28.       Scanner input = new Scanner(inputFile);
29.       if (!inputFile.exists())
30.       {
31.          System.out.println("Error:" + unencryptedFile + " not found");
32.          System.exit(0);
33.       }
34.       // Open a new file for output
35.       System.out.print("Encrypted file: ");
36.       String encryptedFile = keyboard.next();
37.       File outputFile = new File(encryptedFile);
38.       PrintWriter output = new PrintWriter(outputFile);
39.       if (!outputFile.exists())
40.       {
41.          System.out.println("Error: cannot open " + encryptedFile);
42.          System.exit(0);
43.       }
44.       System.out.print("Codeword: ");
45.       String codeword = keyboard.next();
46.       while( input.hasNext()) // encrypt the file line by line
47.       {
48.          String line = input.nextLine();
49.          String encryptedLine = encrypt(line, codeword);
50.          output.println(encryptedLine);
51.       }
52.       input.close();
53.       output.close();
54.    }
55. }
```

Output

Unencrypted file: **Caesar.txt**
Encrypted file: **CaesarCoded.txt**
Codeword: **MarcAntony**

The two files used in the program are:

Caesar.txt	CaesarCoded.txt
FriendsRomansCountrymenLendMeYourEars	RRZGNQLFBKMNJEOHGHEWYEENEAWARWAUIGAEL
IComeToBuryCaesarNotToPraiseHim	UCFOEGHPHPKCRGSNKBBRFOGTAVLSUGY
TheEvilThatMenDoLivesAfterThem	FHVGVVEHUYFMVPDBEWICEAWVEEMVRK
TheGoodIsOftInterredWithTheirBones	FHVIOBWWFMRTZPTRKFRBIIKJTUXWEZANVU

Discussion

Lines 23–33: A Scanner object for interactive input is instantiated and a user supplies the name of the unencrypted file ("Caesar.txt"). Next, a File object is created along with a second Scanner object that reads from an unencrypted file. Thus the program uses two Scanner objects. The first Scanner, keyboard, takes input from the console; the second, input, takes input from a File object. Both Scanners share the same methods. See Figure 9.23.

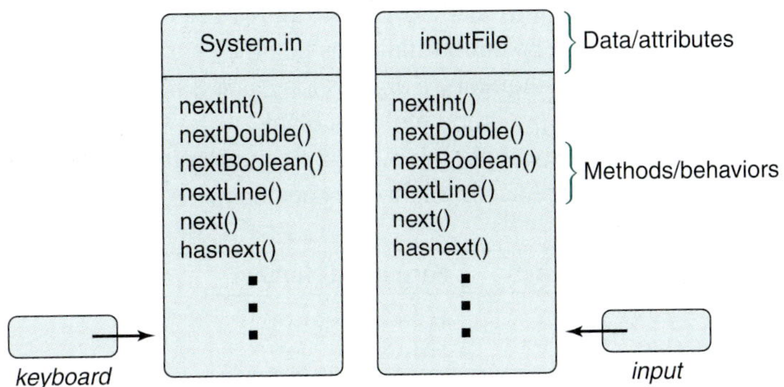

FIGURE 9.23 Two different *Scanner* objects instantiated from the *Scanner* class

Lines 34–38: The user supplies the name of the output file ("CaesarCoded.txt"). A File object (outputFile) is created along with a PrintWriter object (output) that writes to the specified output file. If the output file already exists, all data is erased; otherwise, a new file is created.

Lines 39–43: If, for example, the disk is full, it may be impossible to create the output file. In this case, an error message is displayed on the screen and the program aborts.

Lines 44–45: The user supplies a codeword ("MarcAntony") for the encryption.

Lines 46–51: The while loop operates as follows:

For each line of the original file:

Read one line of text.
Invoke encrypt(...), which encrypts the line of text.
Write the encrypted line to the output file using Printwriter's println() method.

Lines 52–53: The input Scanner and the PrintWriter are closed.

As we noted, the method

```
String encryptMessage(String msg, String cw)
```

is almost identical to the method of Example 9.2. This version, however, accepts a codeword as a parameter rather than an integer that denotes a shift. Each letter is encrypted with a different shift as determined by the codeword. This is accomplished by the statement on line 14:

```
int shift = (cw.charAt(i % cw.length()) - 'A').
```

9.9 THE *DecimalFormat* CLASS

We conclude this chapter with one more Java class that provides some control over the output of floating-point numbers.

The DecimalFormat class allows you to format a floating-point number using a "pattern string" that specifies exactly how a number should be displayed.

One form of a pattern string includes a decimal point and any number of '#' and '0' characters. A '0' in position *i* indicates that a digit is required in position *i*, even if the digit is a leading or trailing 0. A '#' in position *i* indicates that the character in position *i* may be a digit or a blank. The character should be a digit as long as it is not a leading or trailing zero, in which case the character in position *i* will be a blank.

Figure 9.24 gives a few examples showing a floating-point number, a pattern string, and the same number formatted according to the specifications of the pattern.

Number	Pattern String	Formatted Number
123.123456	0.### 0.	123.123 123.
8.125	00.## ##.0000	08.13 (rounds) 8.1250
.123	###.# 0000.#########	0.1 (Yes **one** zero will appear before the decimal) 0000.123

FIGURE 9.24 Using a pattern string

A DecimalFormat object is instantiated using the new operator as follows:

```
DecimalFormat formatter = new DecimaFormat(String pattern)
```

Two particularly useful methods are

```
String format(double x)
```

which returns a String version of x, formatted according to the specifications of the pattern string, and

```
void applyPattern(String pattern),
```

which supplies a new pattern string to a DecimalFormat object

The following code snippet illustrates the use of the methods of the DecimalFormat class

```
DecimalFormat formatter = new DecimalFormat("0.##");
double x = 123.123456789;
double y = .987654321;
System.out.println( formatter.format(x));          // 123.12
System.out.println( formatter.format(y));          // 0.99 – rounding occurs
formatter.applyPattern("##.###");                  // change the pattern
System.out.println( formatter.format(x));          // 123.123
System.out.println( formatter.format(y));          // 0.988 – rounding again
```

To use the DecimalFormat class, import the java.text package.

The chapter's final example uses the String class, the DecimalFormat class, and the File class to process a list of averages.

EXAMPLE 9.7 Sara Starstruck is president of The Curious Cult Film Club. Whenever a member views a new film, he/she assigns it a rating from 0 to 5 stars and passes that information to Sara. Sara maintains a file of films together with members' ratings. Each line of the file consists of the title of a film followed by an arbitrary number of ratings. The title and the ratings are separated by the # symbol. The following line is a typical entry in Sara's file:

Frankenstein Meets the Space Monster # 2 3 1 1 4 0 2

Here, whitespace separates the title and ratings from the # symbol.

Problem Statement Write a program that reads Sara's file (films.txt) and produces a second file (ratings.txt) that lists the title of each film followed by the film's average rating. Ratings should be rounded to one decimal place.

Java Solution The following program uses a DecimalFormat object with pattern string "#.0" to ensure that the average ratings are printed with one decimal place.

```
// find the average rating of a film
// input file: films.txt
// output file: ratings.txt

import java.util.*;
import java.io.*;
import java.text.*;

public class RateFilms
{
   public static void main (String[] args) throws IOException
   {
      // Open input file and attach it to a Scanner
      File filmFile = new File("films.txt");
      Scanner input = new Scanner(filmFile);
      if (!filmFile.exists())
      {
         System.out.println("Error: films.txt is not found");
         System.exit(0);
      }
      // Open a new file for output and attach to a Printwriter
      File ratingFile = new File("ratings.txt");
      PrintWriter output = new PrintWriter(ratingFile);

      if (!ratingFile.exists())
      {
         System.out.println("Error: cannot open ratings.txt");
         System.exit(0);
      }

      // Floating point numbers have one decimal place
      DecimalFormat formatter = new DecimalFormat("#.0");

      final String SEPARATOR = "#"; // # symbol separates title from ratings

      while( input.hasNext()) // while input remains
      {
         // read and print the title
         String title = input.next(); // read and print first word of the title
```

```
33.             while (!title.equals(SEPARATOR)) // read and print the remainder of the title
34.             {
35.                 output.print(title + " ");
36.                 title = input.next();
37.             }

38.             int sum = 0; // for each film
39.             int count = 0; // the number of ratings

40.             while (input.hasNextInt()) // read each rating and add to sum
41.             {
42.                 sum += input.nextInt();
43.                 count++;
44.             }

45.             // Calculate the average of the ratings with one decimal place
46.             output.println("--" + formatter.format (((double)sum)/ count));
47.         }

48.         input.close();
49.         output.close();
50.     }
51. }
```

Output

films.txt (input file)	**ratings.txt** (output file)
Frankenstein Meets the Space Monster # 2 3 1 1 4 0 2 Hercules in New York # 1 3 5 5 5 2 1 1 3 2 4 1 3 2 1 1 Theater of Blood # 3 2 4 5 3 4 5 1 3 2 4 5 2 3 4 5 3 The Tingler # 2 3 2 1 3 4 5 4 3 2 3 4 2 The Body Snatchers # 5 4 5 4 5 5 5 3 4 4 2 2 3 4 4	Frankenstein Meets the Space Monster -- 1.9 Hercules in New York -- 2.5 Theater of Blood -- 3.4 The Tingler -- 2.9 The Body Snatchers -- 3.9

Discussion

Lines 11–26: These statements should be familiar by now. They open files for input and output as well as instantiate Scanner and PrintWriter objects.

Line 28: **DecimalFormat formatter = new DecimalFormat("#.0")**
A DecimalFormat object is instantiated with pattern string "#.0", ensuring that floating-point numbers are printed with a single digit to the right of the decimal.

Lines 30–47: The nested loops of these lines operate as follows:

```
while input remains (for each film)
{
   Read and print the title, i.e., read and print strings until '#' appears in the input.
   Set sum and count to 0.
   For each rating: add the rating to the current sum, and increment count.
   Calculate and print the average of the ratings using the formatter object.
}
```

9.10 IN CONCLUSION

Object-oriented programming is a programming paradigm that incorporates the principles of encapsulation, inheritance, and polymorphism. In this chapter, you have been introduced to objects and classes—the features of Java that enable encapsulation. You have seen how to create objects from classes such as String, StringBuilder, and DecimalFormatter—classes that come packaged with Java.

In the next chapters, you will learn how to design and construct your own classes, understand more about the underlying principles of object-oriented programming, and implement programs that are truly object-oriented. The Scanner class, the String class, the StringBuilder class, the File class, the PrintWriter class, the Random class, and the DecimalFormat class are just the beginning. Objects come in all shapes and sizes.

Just the Facts

- OOP is a programming paradigm that incorporates the principles of *encapsulation*, *inheritance*, and *polymorphism*.
- Understanding the principles of OOP requires time and experience. A single sentence or even a single page is not enough to convey the idea accurately.
- An object is an entity consisting of attributes and behaviors, that is, data and methods.
- A class is a blueprint used to create objects.
- Each object has its own data but shares methods with other objects of the same class.
- The bundling of data and methods into objects is known as *encapsulation*.
- Java provides huge libraries with many built-in classes that can be accessed using import statements.
- Java's String class encapsulates a character sequence with methods that manipulate those characters.
- String objects are *immutable*; they cannot be changed. String objects are read-only.
- StringBuilder objects can be changed and are not immutable.
- For "read-only" strings, the String class is more efficient than the StringBuilder class.
- For programs heavy with concatenation or any string construction, use the StringBuilder class.
- The DecimalFormat class allows a programmer to print formatted floating-point numbers.
- The Random class gives a programmer the capability to define and use random numbers, both integer and floating point.
- The Scanner class provides a mechanism that accepts input from a file, a keyboard, or other source.
- The PrintWriter class allows a programmer to output information to the screen, a file, or other destination.
- A *file* is a collection of data that can exist before and persist after the program manipulates its data.

- A *sequential file* is a file in which data is read and written in order. For example, to read the third line of a sequential file, a program must first read the first and second lines, and to write the third line, a program must first write the first and second lines.
- Use the File class for creating, modifying, or deleting sequential data files.

Bug Extermination

- When using a Java class, don't forget to use the correct import statement.
- All import statements must appear before any class definitions.
- When comparing String objects, the equals(...) method rather than the == operator is usually the correct choice. The == operator compares references; the equals(...) method compares characters. When using StringBuilder objects, the == operator and the equals(...) method are equivalent; both compare references. If you want to compare the contents of two StringBuilder objects a and b, use a.toString().equals(b.toString();
- Do not confuse class methods with data fields. A method call requires parentheses. For example, String x = "hello"; x.length() returns 5, but x.length generates an error. For arrays, length is a data field rather than a method, so that if a[] = {1, 2, 3} then a.length has the value 3, and a.length() generates an error.
- Be sure to initialize all String references before you use them. String x; x += "a"; generates an error. Instead, first initialize a String reference to the empty String: String x = ""; x += "a";
- Be careful when mixing the Scanner method nextLine() with other Scanner calls such as next(), nextInt(), or nextDouble(). After a call to nextInt() or nextDouble(), if no other data remain on the same line, a call to nextLine() returns the empty String and not the data on the "next line."
- Strings are immutable. Be aware that excessive reassignment of String references may create quite a bit of *garbage* and may slow down program execution. Use StringBuilder objects for these kinds of applications.
- The methods nextInt(int n) and nextDouble() of the Random class return values between 0 and $n - 1$, and 0.0 up to 1.0, respectively. That is, the ranges *include* 0 at the low end, but do not include n and 1.0, respectively, at the high end. So, to generate a random integer between 1 and n inclusive, use nextInt(n) + 1.
- Before a Scanner object reads from a file, check to see whether or not the file exists. This allows your program to handle errors gracefully.
- Do not forget to include the clause throws IOException in the heading of a method A() that uses the File class for Scanner I/O. Also, include the throws IOException clause in the heading of any method, B(), that invokes A().

EXERCISES

LEARN THE LINGO

Test your knowledge of the chapter's vocabulary by completing the following crossword puzzle.

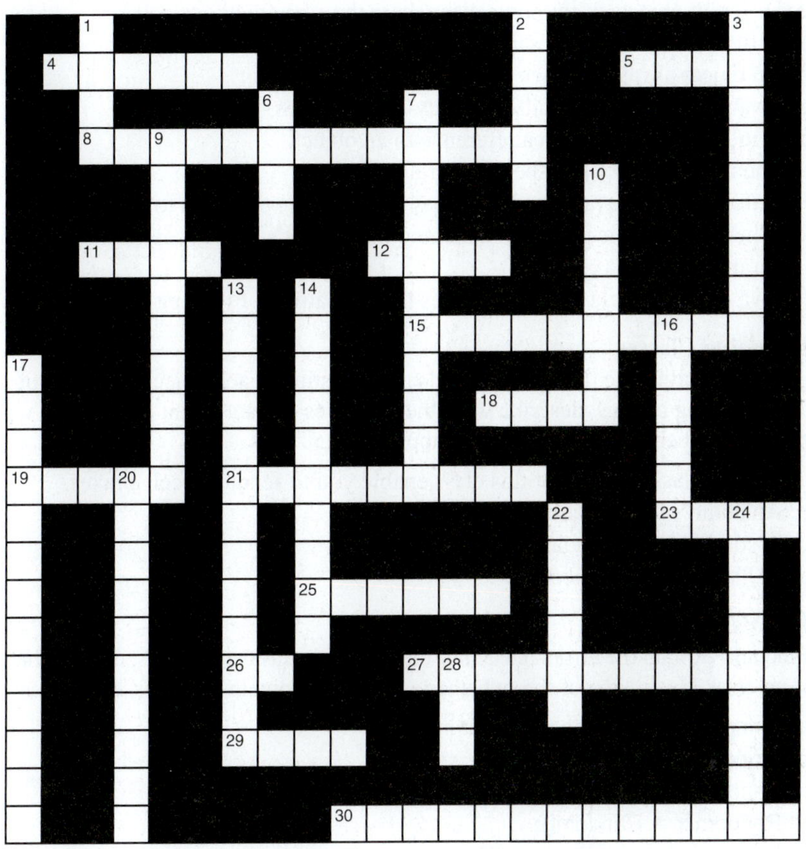

Across

4 Returns the number of characters of String
5 A collection of data stored on a disk
8 Class used to format output
11 "hello".compareTo("hello") returns ______.
12 Package containing Random
15 The == operator compares ______.
18 Package containing DecimalFormat
19 Every object belongs to a ______.
21 Returns part of a string
23 Returns a string without leading or trailing whitespace
25 StringBuilder method compares references
26 Package containing File
27 Create a new object.
29 Scanner method returns a String.
30 Alternative to the String class

Down

1 To produce the same sequence of random numbers, pass a ______ to Random().
2 String with no characters
3 Methods of a class are the class ______.
6 Package containing String
7 Class that is used to write data to a file
9 The equals method of String compares ______.
10 Returns true if input remains
13 Methods and data bundled together
14 Data of a class are the ______.
16 Returns one character of a String
17 Joining two strings
20 Type of file read in order from beginning to end
22 DecimalFormatter object requires a ______ string.
24 String objects are read-only or ______.
28 Operator that instantiates an object

SHORT EXERCISES

1. **True or False**
   If false, give an explanation.
   a. A class describes how data and methods are encapsulated into a single object.
   b. From one object you can build many classes.
   c. Every object belongs to some class.
   d. Different objects of the same class share the same methods.
   e. Different objects of the same class always share the same data.
   f. An object always belongs to more than one class.
   g. Java provides many "built-in" ready-to-go classes.
   h. A method cannot return a reference to an object.
   i. The name of an object specifies a reference.
   j. Unfortunately, Java provides no way to read and write data to files.
   k. When an object is passed to a method, the object's data is copied into a method parameter.
   l. Java provides a class that facilitates the formatting of floating-point numbers.

2. **Designing Classes**
   A class specifies the data and methods that constitute each object. For each of the following classes, describe what the attributes or data might be and also what methods or behaviors you think are appropriate.
   a. A FAX class. Objects of this class enable you to send or receive faxes.
   b. An audio speaker class.
   c. A computer mouse class.
   d. A TV remote control class.

3. **What's the Error?**
   Find and explain the errors in each of the following Java statements, or state that there is no error. If you are not sure whether a statement contains an error, experiment.
   a. String howAboutThat = new String('a');
   b. String String = "String";
   c. Random randomNum = 3;
   d. Random x = Random();
   e. Random y = new Random(3);
   f. import Java.util;
   g. File myFile.txt = new File();
   h. File MyFile = new File();
   i. File f = new File(myfile.txt);
   j. String text = "myfile.txt"; File myFile = new File(text);
   k. String y = "testme"; y += char(33);
   l. String w = " Why Me? "; int temp = w.trim.length();
   m. StringBuilder z = "How Come This Does Not Work?";
   n. StringBuilder t = new String ("How Come This Does Not Work?");
   o. String Builder u; u = new StringBuilder("I wonder if this will work?");
   p. StringBuilder v = new StringBuilder("Try This"); v += (char) v.length();

4. **What's the Output?**
   Determine the output of each of the following statement groups:
   a. String x = "testme"; x += 33; System.out.println(x);
   b. String y = "testme"; y += (char) 33; System.out.println(y);
   c. String s = "This is too hard!"; System.out.println(s.substring(0,8) + "not");

d. String r = "Check this out"; System.out.println(r.replace(' ', (char) 0).length());
e. String t = "XYZ"; String u = "xyz"; System.out.println(t == u);
System.out.print(t.equals(u));
f. String m = new String ("XYZ"); String n = "XYZ"; System.out.println(m == n);
System.out.println(m.equals(n));
g. StringBuilder p = new StringBuilder("Why Me?");
System.out.println(p.reverse().reverse());
h. String v = new String("Why Not Me?"); v += (char) ('0' + v.length());
System.out.println(v);
i. StringBuilder w = new StringBuilder("One Pond");
System.out.println(w.replace(2,3, " Golden"));
j. String a = "test me"; String b = "me";
System.out.println(a.length() + a.indexOf(b));

5. **Compiler versus Interpreter, and the JVM**
Using the Java compiler, determine the output of the following program:

```
class Str
{
    public static void main(String[] args)
    {
        String p = "XYZ"; String q = "XYZ";
        System.out.println(p == q);
        System.out.println(p.equals(q));
        q = new String("XYZ");
        System.out.println(p == q);
        q = "XYZ";
        System.out.println(p == q);
    }
}
```

The following segment is identical to the Str class (above), but without the class wrapper Str. If you have access to an interactive Java *interpreter* such as Dr. Java (http://drjava.org/), enter:

```
String p = "XYZ"; String q = "XYZ";
System.out.println(p == q); System.out.println(p.equals(q));
q = new String("XYZ");
System.out.println(p == q);
q = "XYZ";
System.out.println(p == q);
```

directly to the interactive interpreter and check the output.

The interpreter probably did not give you the same results as the compiler. An interpreter translates and executes each statement before it sees the next one, and a compiler translates every statement before it executes any. How does this difference affect the output of these two segments?

6. **Fix the Errors**
Find the errors in the following program and correct them so that the program does what it should do. There are both syntax errors and semantic (logical) errors.

```
class WeTryHarder
{       // This program is supposed to read a text file
        // and display a String composed of the first letter
```

```
    // from each line of the file. For example, if the file was
    // composed of the first three lines from the Reel Big Fish
    // song Go Away:

            // She was never what I wanted,
            // I just wanted someone else.
            // Now I'm sittin' here alone,

  // The output would be "SIN".


    void public main(String[] args)
    {
        File inputFile = new ("reelbigfish.txt");
        if (!inputFile.exists())
        {
                System.out.println("File reelbigfish.txt not found");
                System.exit(0);
        }
        Scanner input = Scanner(inputFile);
        String firstLetters = new String();     // to hold the first letters of each line
        String line;                            // to hold a line of input from the file
        while (input.hasNext())
        {
                line = new String(input.nextLine()); // get next line
                firstLetters = firstLetters + line.charAt(0); // concatenates the first
                                                        // character of line to firstLetters
        }
        System.out.println(firstLetters);
        inputFile.close;
    }
}
```

PROGRAMMING EXERCISES

1. **Weird Al's Palindrome**

Weird Al Yankovic's song "Bob" is a satiric homage to Bob Dylan. Here are the first few lines:

```
I, man, am regal - a German am I
Never odd or even
If I had a hi-fi
Madam, I'm Adam
Too hot to hoot
No lemons, no melon
Too bad I hid a boot
Lisa Bonet ate no basil
Warsaw was raw
Was it a car or a cat I saw?
```

If you ignore case and punctuation, you will notice that every line of the song (and the title too) reads the same backwards and forwards. Such lines are called *palindromes*. Write a program that accepts a string and determines whether or not the string is a palindrome. Ignore all whitespace and punctuation, and assume that there is no distinction between upper- and lowercase letters. For example, “a man, a plan, a canal, Panama”, and “a Toyota’s a Toyota” are palindromes, but “Babel” is not.

2. **Uppercase Conversion**
   Write a program that accepts a string and displays another string composed of the characters of the first string but with all lowercase letters capitalized. Any non-alphabetical characters, such as punctuation, should be left unchanged. For example, the string “When Homer blew up the nuclear plant, he yelled “#!#!#!& DOH &&####!!!!” ” should become “WHEN HOMER BLEW UP THE NUCLEAR PLANT, HE YELLED “#!#!#!& DOH &&####!!!!” ”.

3. **Random Strings**
   Write a program that prints 25 random strings of length 4 such that each String is composed of uppercase alphabetical characters.

4. **Substitution Encryption**
   Write a program that prints the following chart that might help children encode secret messages using a single letter shift. Start with the string "abcdefghijklmnopqrtuvwxz" and use a loop; do not code 26 different strings directly into your program!

```
abcdefghijklmnopqrstuvwxyz
bcdefghijklmnopqrstuvwxyza
cdefghijklmnopqrstuvwxyzab
defghijklmnopqrstuvwxyzabc
efghijklmnopqrstuvwxyzabcd
fghijklmnopqrstuvwxyzabcde
ghijklmnopqrstuvwxyzabcdef
hijklmnopqrstuvwxyzabcdefg
ijklmnopqrstuvwxyzabcdefgh
jklmnopqrstuvwxyzabcdefghi
klmnopqrstuvwxyzabcdefghij
lmnopqrstuvwxyzabcdefghijk
mnopqrstuvwxyzabcdefghijkl
nopqrstuvwxyzabcdefghijklm
opqrstuvwxyzabcdefghijklmn
pqrstuvwxyzabcdefghijklmno
rstuvwxyzabcdefghijklmnopq
stuvwxyzabcdefghijklmnopqr
tuvwxyzabcdefghijklmnopqrs
uvwxyzabcdefghijklmnopqrst
vwxyzabcdefghijklmnopqrstu
wxyzabcdefghijklmnopqrstuv
xyzabcdefghijklmnopqrstuvw
yzabcdefghijklmnopqrstuvwx
zabcdefghijklmnopqrstuvwxy
```

5. **More Encyption**
   Write a program that accepts a codeword and displays the substitution lists for that codeword. For example, given the codeword "sauerkraut", the program should display:

```
abcdefghijklmnopqrstuvwxyz
```

```
stuvwxyzabcdefghijklmnopqr
abcdefghijklmnopqrstuvwxyz
uvwxyzabcdefghijklmnopqrst
efghijklmnopqrstuvwxyzabcd
rstuvwxyzabcdefghijklmnopq
klmnopqrstuvwxyzabcdefghij
rstuvwxyzabcdefghijklmnopq
abcdefghijklmnopqrstuvwxyz
uvwxyzabcdefghijklmnopqrst
tuvwxyzabcdefghijklmnopqrs
```

Notice the first substitution list is an *s*-shift, the second an *a*-shift, the third a *u*-shift, and so on. See Example 9.6.

6. **String Rotation**
   Write a program that rotates a given string *n* characters to the right. For example, if the input to your program is

   rotatemeplease 4,

   then the output is

   easerotatemepl

7. **Index of Coincidence**
   If two strings of equal length are superimposed on one another, then some letters may match. For example consider the strings

   `wonderwhowrotethebookonlove` and
   `weallliveinayellowsubmarine`

   Notice that there are three positions that contain the same letter: the 1st (w) , 14th (e), and 27th (e). Of 27 possible positions, matches occur in three positions (11.1%). This percentage is called the *index of coincidence* for two strings, and it is used to decrypt ciphers like those used by the Germans in World War II.

   Write a program that accepts two strings of the same length and determines their index of coincidence. For normal written English, the index of coincidence averages about 6.6%, while for random strings it is 1/26, or around 3.8%.

8. **Counting Words**
   Write a method that accepts a string and returns the number of words in the string. For example, the string "This sentence has too many words in it" has 8 words.

9. **Word Rotation**
   Write an application that accepts a string and an integer *n* as input, prints the string, rotates it *n* words to the right, and prints it again. For example, the input

   here is a good example for this 3,

   results in the output:

   here is a good example for this
   example for this here is a good

10. **Soccer League Standings**
    You manage a kids' soccer league and maintain a file with the results of each game. Each line of your file holds the outcome of a single game: the names of

the two teams together with the scores. For example, the first five lines of the file might be:

Panthers	4	Tigers	3
Sky	2	Panthers	0
Tigers	1	Sky	6
Sky	2	Panthers	1
Tigers	1	Sky	4

Write a program that reads this file and prints a list of the teams and team records. For example, using the file displayed above, the output would be:

Team	Wins	Losses
Panthers	1	2
Tigers	0	3
Sky	4	0

11. **The *JUMBLE***
The *JUMBLE* is a puzzle that rearranges the letters of a word. Your task is to unscramble the letters and discover the original word.
Write a program that accepts a word and produces a "jumbled" version. For example, the letters of the word "TAKEN" might be scrambled as "AKNET". You can scramble the letters of a word by repeatedly exchanging a randomly chosen letter with the first letter. Ten exchanges are more than enough to jumble a five- or six-letter word.

12. **College Transcript**
A text file stores the courses you have taken along with the corresponding grade (A, B, C, D, or F) that you received in each course. The file might look like this:

Introduction to Sociology	A
Physics	B
Experimental Psychology	C
. . .	

Write a program that uses such a file to calculate your grade point average (GPA). A GPA is based on a scale from 0 to 4, where A is 4, B is 3, C is 2, D is 1, and F is 0. You should print the GPA with two decimal places such as 3.62.

13. **Credit Card Transactions**
A text file contains one month's credit card purchases. The file might look like this:

Bicycle	562.90
Groceries	138.43
Hotel	612.00
. . .	

Write a program that reads this file and determines the most expensive purchase. Your program should prompt the user for the filename.

14. **Alphabetized File**
Write a program that reads a list of last names from a file and creates a new file with the names alphabetized.

15. **More File Processing—A Bowling League**
A bowling league maintains a file consisting of the names and bowling averages of its members, one name per line. For example, the file might look this:

Thelma	179
Louise	109
Frankie	132
Zoey	112
Butch	141
Sundance	206
…	

Write a program that reads such a file and creates two new files: one sorted alphabetically by name, and the other sorted by average.

THE BIGGER PICTURE

BIOINFORMATICS

The Human Genome Project (HGP), completed in 2003, was a 13-year project coordinated by the U.S. Department of Energy and the National Institutes of Health to identify all of the approximately 20,000 to 30,000 genes in human DNA and to store the information in databases accessible to researchers throughout the world. Each gene is made up of thousands of DNA *bases*, so the Human Genome Project identified approximately three billion bases (or base-pairs). The analysis of this massive collection of information gave birth to a relatively new discipline called *bioinformatics*.

Bioinformatics is the application of computer technology to the management of biological information. The National Center for Biotechnology Information (NCBI 2001) defines *bioinformatics* as:

"the field of science in which biology, computer science, and information technology merge into a single discipline. There are three important sub-disciplines within bioinformatics:

- the development of new algorithms and statistics with which to assess relationships among members of large data sets,
- the analysis and interpretation of various types of data including nucleotide and amino acid sequences, protein domains, and protein structures, and
- the development and implementation of tools that enable efficient access and management of different types of information."

Bioinformatics helps answer fundamental scientific questions about evolution and the nature of life. Bioinformatics provides scientists with a means to explain normal biological processes and malfunctions in these processes that lead to diseases. A major practical goal of bioinformatics is the discovery of effective drug therapies for these diseases.

The field of bioinformatics has its origins in the mid-20th century, but due in great part to the Human Genome Project, the field has exploded since the 1990s with activity in both computer science and biology labs all over the world.

String algorithms account for many of the computer science techniques used in bioinformatics, especially the techniques used in DNA research. In order to appreciate the connections between string algorithms and DNA, a little biological background is necessary.

PROTEINS

Proteins are the essential building blocks of life. They are responsible for the structure, function, and regulation of the body's tissues and organs. Antibodies, collagen, hormones, and enzymes are all kinds of proteins. Proteins manage reproduction, digestion, the immune system, and cell communication.

Every protein is made up of a sequence of amino acids. There are only 20 *different* amino acids that might appear in sequence for a particular protein. However, the number of amino acids in a sequence for a particular protein ranges from tens to thousands, so of course it is common for many duplicates to occur in a given sequence for a particular protein. For example, a small protein like *insulin* has 51 amino acids, while a big protein like *titin* has more than 28,000.

Each protein is like a large, flexible, floating Tinkertoy that turns, folds, and eventually settles stably into a unique three-dimensional structure that very much determines its function. This structure is called the *native state* of the protein, and it is directly determined by the sequence of amino acids that make up the protein. The sequence of a protein is called its primary structure, and the resulting folding gives rise to secondary and tertiary levels of structure. The three-dimensional structure of a protein is crucial to its function. One of the great challenges in biology is determining the secondary (and tertiary) structures of a protein (and thereby its function), given its primary structure.

To get some perspective on the size of a protein, note that a living cell is about 10,000 times as large as a protein measured linearly from end to end. A cell can be seen with the help of a standard microscope, but a protein cannot. Even though standard microscopes are no help in seeing protein structure, there are other techniques that are used to *derive* a protein's three-dimensional form. Figure 9.25 shows the structure of the protein myoglobin. It looks like a sausage folded up into a globular shape.

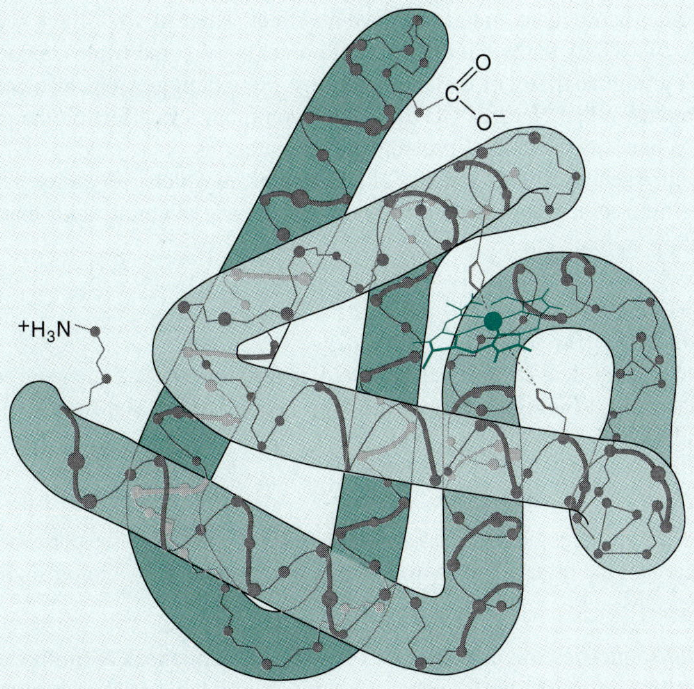

FIGURE 9.25 The three-dimensional structure of a protein molecule

THE BIGGER PICTURE

In biological research, the search for sequence similarity in proteins is extremely important, because *similarity in sequence correlates to similarity in 3-D structure, and similarity in structure correlates to similarity in function*. For instance, a researcher who has discovered a potentially important protein might want to know if a similar sequence has already been identified and characterized by another researcher. This information can provide vital clues as to the role of the sequence in the organism.

CHROMOSOMES, GENES, DNA, AND MUTATIONS

How does the body build proteins? Each of the approximately trillion cells in the human body contains 23 pairs of *chromosomes*. Each chromosome is comprised of between 20,000 and 30,000 *genes*. Every gene determines one protein (there are exceptions to this, but for the most part this is true). Each gene is a sequence of *DNA bases*—the blueprints for building a single protein. The DNA bases are small molecules (much smaller than proteins) called adenine, guanine, cytosine, and thymine represented by the four letters A, G, C, and T. A particular gene might look like this: ATAATCCGGGCAT… continuing on for thousands of letters.

How do the DNA bases in a gene determine a protein? Every three DNA bases encode a particular amino acid from among the 20 possibilities. Hence the sequence of DNA bases in a gene determines a unique sequence of amino acids that define the particular protein created by that gene. The correspondence between three-letter DNA base sequences and amino acids is completely understood by biologists. For example, the triple GGG encodes the amino acid glycine, and the triple GCG encodes the amino acid alanine.

Mutations occur in DNA for various reasons, whereby one base gets exchanged with another. For example, a mutation in GGG in which the middle G is changed to a C would change the amino acid in the protein from glycine to alanine. A change of a single amino acid in a protein, even a protein with a sequence of hundreds of amino acids, may render that protein inactive, so that a single mutation like this can have devastating effects.

On the other hand, many mutations have no effect. There are $4 \times 4 \times 4 = 64$ different triples of the four DNA bases but only 20 amino acids, so some triples encode the same amino acid, muting the effect of certain mutations. For example, GGC also codes for glycine, and a mutation that changes GGG to GGC would have no effect on the protein. This redundancy is one way our bodies protect against mutations.

To sum up, a gene is a long sequence of DNA bases, in which every three bases encodes a particular amino acid. The gene thereby codes a sequence of amino acids that determines a protein unique to that gene.

SEQUENCE RESEARCH

Biologists do a great deal of research on DNA and amino acid sequences. Many of the problems that interest biologists turn out to be related to string algorithms. Here are two examples.

a. Sequence Alignment

Given two sequences of DNA bases, which parts of one sequence correspond to which parts of the other? The answer to this question interests biologists for a number of reasons:

- Similar sequences in DNA, and thereby similar sequences of amino acids, create proteins with similar characteristics, functions, or secondary structures.

For instance, a researcher who has discovered a potentially important DNA or protein sequence might want to know how it folds in order to determine its function. If a protein with a similar sequence of amino acids (primary structure) has already been identified and characterized, then the secondary structure of that characterized protein may shed light on the secondary structure of the discovered protein.

- No two DNA sequences from different individuals are the same; thus sequence alignment helps to determine the common base sequences in all humans. Presumably the base sequences that we all have in common are what make us "human." Determining the common base sequences is exactly what was done in the Human Genome Project.
- A *subsequence* of a string, *s*, is a subset of characters from *s* that appear in the same order they do in *s*. For example, CGGT is a subsequence of A**C**A**G**A**GT**. A *motif* is a short subsequence that occurs frequently in different sequences. Such a phenomenon might mean that the genes containing that motif perform similar functions or evolved one from the other. A motif common to fish and mammals might indicate evolutionary paths. A motif common to diabetes patients who reject a particular drug treatment but not common to patients who respond to the treatment might uncover the responsible gene.

b. Sequence Assembly

Biologists can copy, or *sequence,* DNA in the lab, but the technique is limited to a few hundred bases. In order to sequence a whole gene with thousands of bases, millions of copies of the DNA are cut up randomly into manageable pieces, each piece is sequenced, and then the pieces are put back together by looking for overlapping matches. A maximum overlap is considered a good place to reconnect the pieces.

STRING MATCHING ALGORITHMS

What's all this got to do with strings? Everything! Both DNA and proteins can be represented as strings, the former using an alphabet of 4 letters {A, C, T, G} and the latter using a 20-letter alphabet, one for each amino acid.

Sequence alignment and sequence assembly give rise to five different types of string problems:

1. **String Matching**
Given two strings, search for exact occurrences of one in the other. The classic example of string matching is the "find" utility of any word processor. For DNA sequences, string matching entails looking for one sequence inside another to infer similar functionality of the encoded proteins.

2. **Approximate String Matching**
Mutational events often delete, copy, or insert long sections of DNA so that mismatches or gaps or blanks are particularly common. Two protein sequences are considered similar, that is, they show similar functionality, if their sequences are about 30% similar. Therefore, an exact match is not as important as an approximate match. For example, consider the two DNA sequences

```
AACTGGAAGGGATAG
ACTGGAAGGGC
```

Although the second string is not part of the first, if you modify the second sequence by inserting a blank into the second position and considering it a string of length 12, like this:

```
AACTGGAAGGGATAG
A CTGGAAGGGC
```

then a very close "approximate match" of the two strings occurs. In this case, 10 out of 12 characters in the second string match up with the first string, a significant match.

3. **Weighted Approximate String Matching**
Some mutations are more common than others, so that certain mismatches are less serious than others. Therefore, instead of counting each mismatch equally, assign various weights to the different kinds of mismatches. The best match is the one with the lowest total weight. A perfect match has a weight of zero. For example, assuming that a direct mismatch, like A versus C, has a weight of five, while a mismatch with a blank has a weight of only one, then the two strings:

A**A**C**C**GATAT
A**C**C**G**GATAT

lined up as they are, have two direct mismatches for a total weight of 10. However, by inserting blanks in the right places, no direct mismatches occur and only two mismatches occur on blanks.

```
AACCG ATAT
A CCGGATAT
```

This alignment has a total weight of only two and is considered the better match.

4. **Longest Common Subsequence**
If two DNA sequences have a large subsequence in common they often show similar function regardless of whether there is any exact match. This is the simplest form of sequence similarity—finding the pieces common to both. For example, given the two strings:

```
ACGGTGTCAAGGCTA
CGTTCGATATCGTAT
```

the longest subsequence that appears in both is 10 characters long:

CGTTCAACTA (length 10)
A**CG**G**T**G**TCAA**GG**CTA**
CGTTCG**A**T**A**T**C**G**TA**T

The longest common subsequence problem is equivalent to the special case of weighted approximate string matching in which every match has a positive weight and every mismatch costs 0.

5. **Maximum Overlap**
Given two strings, find the largest overlapping segments. For example, the largest overlapping segment of:

ACCGGTCAATGGCTA, and
CTAGGACCAAACCGG

is ACCGG.

```
          ACCGGTCAATGGCTA
CTAGGACCAAACCGG
```

THE BIGGER PICTURE

Note that CTA, which ends the first string and begins the second, is a shorter overlapping segment.

A more general version of this problem corresponds to a practical sequence assembly problem. The generalization considers many strings, and the problem is to find the best way to "glue" all the strings back together by maximizing the overlaps between all the strings.

THE LONGEST COMMON SUBSEQUENCE—AN EXAMPLE

There are algorithms that tackle each of the five problems in the preceding list. In fact, such algorithms are described in hundreds of research papers. Sometimes, the fastest algorithm is the very same one that a beginner might conceive, but more often the best solution eludes anyone but an expert.

As a start, let's look at the longest common subsequence problem. The following algorithm is not one that a novice is likely to discover, but it is certainly accessible to any motivated student.

An Algorithm for Finding the Length of the Longest Common Subsequence of Two Strings

A surprisingly common technique for creating an algorithm is to generalize the problem to make it easier! Instead of finding the longest common subsequence of two strings, let's consider the more general problem of finding the longest common subsequence of any two *prefixes* of the given strings. In particular,

Let $S(j, k)$ be the length of the longest common subsequence of the first j characters of X and the first k characters of Y, where X and Y are DNA strings. Of course, $S(X.\text{length}(), Y.\text{length}())$ is what really interests us. However, by generalizing the problem we will have an easier time computing the value that we really want.

In order to ultimately compute $S(X.\text{length}(), Y.\text{length}())$, create a two-dimensional array consisting of the values of $S(j, k)$ for $j = 0$ to $X.\text{length}()$ and $k = 0$ to $Y.\text{length}()$. First of all, note that $S(0, k) = S(j, 0) = 0$, for any values of j and k.

> This means that the longest common sequence of a portion of one string and no portion of the other string is zero.

Now assume that j and k are *both* positive.

> If the jth character of X matches the kth character of Y, then
>
> $$S(j, k) = S(j - 1, k - 1) + 1$$
>
> When these characters match, add 1 to the length of the sequence and look at the two smaller substrings formed when these characters are removed.
>
> However, if the jth character of X and the kth character of Y do not match, then
>
> $$S(j, k) = \text{the larger of } S(j, k - 1) \text{ and } S(j - 1, k)$$
>
> When the characters do not match, consider either deleting the kth character of Y or the jth character of X.

With these rules, you can write a program to fill the array S. First set $S(j, 0)$ and $S(0, k)$ to zero for $j = 0$ to $X.\text{length}()$ and $k = 0$ to $Y.\text{length}()$. The other values $S(j, k)$ are computed by examining $S(j-1, k-1)$, $S(j, k-1)$, and $S(j-1, k)$. In other words, each subsequent value in the array is computed by looking at three values: one up and to the left (diagonal), one to the left, and one up. One of these three values determines the value that you are computing.

Here is an example:

X = GTTCG Y = AGCTACCG

X\Y	**-**	A	**G**	C	**T**	A	C	**C**	**G**
-	0	**0**	0	0	0	0	0	0	0
G	0	0	**1**	1	1	1	1	1	1
T	0	0	**1**	**1**	2	2	2	2	2
T	0	0	1	1	**2**	**2**	**2**	2	2
C	0	0	1	2	2	2	3	**3**	3
G	0	0	1	2	2	2	3	3	**4**

FIGURE 9.26 An example of the longest common subsequence algorithm—the array *S*

The number in the bottom right corner indicates the length of the longest common subsequence.

If you want to find an actual subsequence of this length, you need to trace backwards from the bottom right corner. This is done by checking which of the three cells (left, up, left and up) was used to compute the corner cell's value. Call this cell *c*. Continue tracing backwards in this fashion from *c* until you reach the upper left corner. Let's follow this trace in the example.

The bold numbers indicate the sequence of values used to compute $S(5, 8)$. Note that $S(5, 8) = S(4, 7) + 1 = 3 + 1 = 4$, because the fifth character of X matches the eighth character of Y. Similarly, because the fourth character of X matches the seventh character of Y, $S(4, 7) = S(3, 6) + 1 = 2 + 1 = 3$. However, the third character of X is different from the sixth character of Y, so $S(3, 6)$ equals the larger of $S(2, 6)$ and $S(3, 5)$, which both happen to equal 2. We arbitrarily used $S(3, 5)$ rather than $S(2, 6)$. Choosing $S(2, 6)$ would be equally acceptable and would result in the same length longest common subsequence. In this fashion, the calculation can be traced all the way back to $S(0, 1)$.

This trace corresponds to the longest common subsequence **G-T-C-G** shown in bold in each string X and Y, on the left and top sides of the table, respectively. When $S(j, k) = S(j - 1, k - 1) + 1$, that is, a match was counted, then the jth character of X and kth character of Y are marked in bold. Had we chosen $S(2, 6)$ instead of $S(3, 5)$ in the trace, and continued the trace back from there, then in the end the second 'T' in X (rather than the third 'T') would be bold. In either case, the sequence itself **G-T-C-G** remains the same.

REAL-LIFE PALINDROMES AND A PRACTICAL APPLICATION

We end this section with an interesting connection between DNA strings and cancer.

The following item recently appeared on the web page of *Genome Biology*, a bioinformatics journal:

"DNA palindromes appear frequently and are widespread in human cancers, and identifying them could help advance the understanding of genomic instability, according to researchers writing in an advanced online publication of *Nature Genetics* for February 13, 2005."

You may have heard of palindromes, strings that read the same backwards and forwards. But what are DNA palindromes?

You already know that a DNA sequence (or *strand*) can be encoded as a string of letters from the set {A,C,G,T}, but what you may not know is that a DNA molecule is composed of two such strands. Every DNA molecule is twisted into a helical shape resembling a spiral staircase with the two strands twisted in opposite directions, one rotating clockwise, and one counterclockwise; see Figure 9.27. The two strands are joined letter to letter in a double-helix embrace with `A` opposite `T`, and `C` opposite `G`. These letters are called complements. This double helix is the familiar shape on posters in science museums and high school biology labs all over the world.

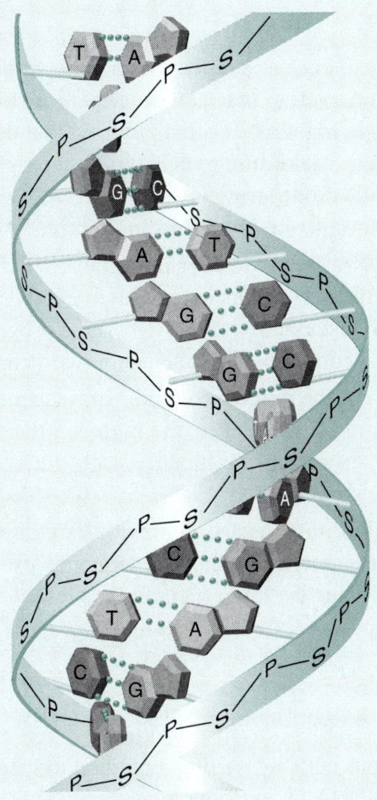

FIGURE 9.27 A DNA molecule showing complementary base pairs in a double helix

Two DNA sequences are called *reverse complements* if you can transform one into the other by reversing one of the sequences and replacing each letter with its complement. For example, CGATTTACCGGATTTAG and CTAAATCCGGTAAATCG are reverse complements. Indeed, in every DNA molecule, the two DNA strands that pair up are reverse complements. To see this, imagine that you pull the two strands apart and realign them with the *same* twist orientation. The reoriented strands line up in reverse order in contrast to how they were originally paired.

A *DNA palindrome* is a sequence that is identical to its reverse complement. For example, ACCTTAAGGT is a DNA palindrome, because its reverse complement is ACCTTAAGGT. Notice that DNA palindromes are not exactly the same as standard palindromes because of the letter substitution, but they are quite similar. If you take a DNA palindrome, pull the two connected strands of DNA apart, and reorient the two strands so that they have the same twist orientation, then the sequences on the two strands are identical. It is fascinating that something as simple as detecting a DNA palindrome might help determine what kinds of cells are cancerous or have potential to become cancerous.

Exercises

1. The bread and butter of bioinformatics is the search for strands of DNA inside other strands. Write a program that accepts two strings and determines whether or not the first string is contained in the second string.

2. Once you find one strand of DNA inside another, you need to know where the match is located. If you were recombining strands, this location would be crucial. Write a program that accepts two strings and displays a list of all the positions in the second string where the first string appears. If the first string does not appear in the second string, then print 0. For example, if one string is AGAA and the other is AGAAGAAGTAGAAACC, then the program should print: 1, 4, 10.
3. When performing sequence assembly with a collection of DNA strands, finding the maximum overlap between every pair of strands helps decide the best way to *glue* them together. Write a program that determines the maximum overlap of two strings. Make sure to check both the right and left sides for overlap. For example, if one string is AAGACCTAGGA and the other is TAGGACTTAGGAAGA, the program should print TAGGA.
4. Exact matches in DNA are not always important. When two DNA strands both contain the same large subsequence, they often exhibit similar functionality. Using the algorithm discussed previously, write a program that calculates the length of the longest common subsequence in two strings X and Y.
5. Knowing the length of the longest common subsequence is interesting because the longer the common subsequence, the more similar the two DNA samples. However, knowing the actual subsequence itself might help us understand how the two samples are similar.

   Challenging: The algorithm discussed previously computes only the length of the longest common subsequence but not the sequence itself. Modify the algorithm so that it also determines the longest common subsequence instead of its length. *Hint:* Use another array to keep track of whether you used

   $S(j-1, k-1) + 1$ or
   the maximum of $S(j, k-1)$ and $S(j-1, k)$

6. Help detect cancerous cells by writing a method to determine whether or not a DNA molecule is a DNA palindrome.

CHAPTER 10

Objects and Classes II: Writing Your Own Classes

"Whatever happened to class?"
—from "Chicago" by John Kander and Fred Ebb

Objectives

The objectives of Chapter 10 include an understanding of

- programmer-defined classes,
- the components of a class: constructors, instance variables, and methods,
- access modifiers,
- encapsulation and information hiding,
- static variables and static methods, and
- garbage collection.

10.1 INTRODUCTION

In Chapter 9, we introduce several of Java's ready-made classes. In fact, Java comes empowered with hundreds of such classes, including classes for graphics, printing, error handling, file processing, set manipulation, and many more applications. You might say that Java is loaded with class. Nonetheless, Java's designers could never anticipate every possible class that a programmer might need. Remember, classes define objects, and an object is practically *anything* that you can imagine. So, we are now ready to design and implement our own home-grown classes. You never know when a movie class, a popcorn class, or a soda machine class will come in handy.

We begin rather simply with a class that models a collection of six-sided dice.

10.2 A *Dice* CLASS

As you now know, an object consists of data and methods or, in the parlance of OOP, attributes and behaviors. Moreover, an object is instantiated or created according to the specifications of a class. As a first example of a programmer-designed class, we consider a Dice class that specifies the attributes and behaviors of a collection of n six-sided dice. Each Dice object has a single attribute: an integer indicating the number of dice in the collection.

The behaviors consist of methods that:

- "roll the dice" and return the total number of spots displayed on the faces of all the dice,
- return the number of dice in the collection, and
- change the number of dice in the collection.

Figure 10.1 shows three Dice objects, each with its unique data, all sharing the same methods.

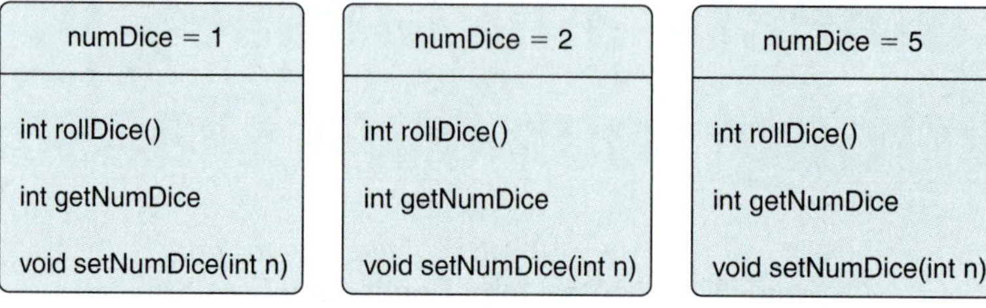

FIGURE 10.1 Three different *Dice* objects. A *Dice* object is an abstraction of a set of *n* dice.

You can use Dice in the same way that you utilize String, Scanner, or Random. Dice is a class with methods that are available to other classes. Just as you can include the statements

```
String s = new String("Hello");
char ch = s.charAt(3);
```

in your applications, you can also use statements such as

```
Dice d = new Dice();
int value = d.rollDice();
```

in any application or class.

Understanding the methods of the Dice class should present no problem. Read the code in Example10.1, along with the subsequent explanation. There are a few new concepts illustrated in the example, but much should be familiar to you.

EXAMPLE 10.1

Problem Statement Design a Dice class that models a collection of n six-sided dice. The class should provide three methods:

1. int rollDice(), which simulates tossing the dice and returns the total number of spots displayed on the dice,
2. int getNumDice(), which returns the number of dice in the set, and
3. void setNumDice(int n), which sets or changes the number of dice.

Java Solution The following class, Dice, contains no main(...) method. Like the String class, Dice is a class that cannot run independently. As you declare a String reference

```
String s = new String();
```

you can also declare a Dice reference

```
Dice d = new Dice();
```

The Dice class contains just a few new features that are explained in the line-by-line discussion. To simulate rolling dice, we use a Random object and the Random method nextInt(int n), which returns an integer in the range 0 to n – 1.

```
1.  import java.util.*;                    // for the Random class

2.  public class Dice
3.  {
4.      private int numDice;
5.      private Random random;

6.      public Dice()                      // default constructor—one die in the set
7.      {
8.          numDice = 1;
9.          random = new Random();
10.     }

11.     public Dice(int n)                 // one argument constructor—n dice in the set
12.     {
13.         numDice = n;
14.         random = new Random();
15.     }

16.     public int rollDice()
17.     // Returns the number of spots shown when tossing numDice dice
18.     {
19.         int sum = 0;
20.
21.         for (int i = 1; i <= numDice; i++)     // for each die in the set
22.             sum += random.nextInt(6) + 1;      // add an integer between 1 and 6 to sum
23.         return sum;
24.     }

25.     public int getNumDice()
26.     {
27.         return numDice;
28.     }

29.     public void setNumDice(int n)
30.     {
31.         numDice = n;
32.     }
33. }
```

Discussion Like every public class, Dice must be saved in a file named Dice.java.

Line 2: public class Dice
The name of the class is Dice.

> Java convention dictates that the name of a class begins with an uppercase letter. All other letters are lowercase, except those that begin new words.

For example, MyDice, MyLuckyDice, and MyVeryLuckyDice all conform to the standard Java naming scheme; myDice and my_dice, although syntactically correct, do not.

The word public is an *access modifier*. If a class is specified as public then the class can be used by any other class. Only one public class can be saved in any file. Classes without an access modifier may be saved in the same file with a public class.

Soon, you will see that there are other, more restrictive access modifiers. If no access modifier is specified then the class has *package access*. This means that only classes in the same *package* have access to the class. For example, you know that the Scanner and Random classes are in the java.util package. Any other class in the java.util package without an access modifier is accessible only to the classes in that package and not to classes that are defined in another package such as java.io.

For the present, the classes that we write are all contained in Java's *default package*. Every class is in some package, and by not specifying a particular package, we allow our classes to be automatically placed in the default package. Consequently, whether we specify the class as public or omit the access modifier, all of the classes that we write are accessible to other classes. Scanner and Random are not members of the default package; they belong to java.util. Consequently, these two classes are not directly accessible to classes of the default package. An import statement is required.

Line 4: private int numDice

The integer variable numDice is an *instance variable* or *field* that specifies the single attribute of the Dice class. Unlike the variables of previous programs, numDice is not local to any one method; numDice is visible to all methods of the class. Consequently, any method defined in Dice has access to this variable. In fact, because numDice is specified as private, only the methods of Dice can access or modify numDice. The field numDice is not visible outside the Dice class. All access to the variable numDice is via the methods of Dice and only through those methods. No other class can access the variable numDice except via the methods of Dice. The methods of Dice specify exactly how the variable can be used and/or modified. For example, the methods defined on lines 25–28 and 29–32 are two such methods that provide access to numDice.

Instance variables are usually assigned private access.

> Public access specifies that the variable is accessible to all code outside the class. Private access dictates that the variable is not visible outside the class. A variable with no access modifier is accessible to classes within its package.

Lines 6–10:

```
public Dice()          // the default constructor — one die
{
    numDice = 1;
}
```

The code on lines 6–10 constitutes the class's *default constructor*. The default constructor is a method, of sorts. Notice, however, that there is no return value, not even void.

> The name of the default constructor is the same as the class name.

The default constructor creates or instantiates a new object of the Dice class, that is, the default constructor transparently allocates memory for each object of a class. The access modifier for the default constructor is usually public. Additionally, the default constructor executes the statements enclosed by the curly braces. In this case, the default constructor assigns the value 1 to the instance variable numDice. The default constructor is called automatically when a dice object is instantiated with a statement such as

```
Dice dice = new Dice();
```

or,

```
Dice dice;
dice = new Dice();
```

In other words, the default constructor

- instantiates a Dice object, and
- initializes a Dice object.

Another name for the default constructor is the *no-argument* constructor.

A program cannot call the default constructor directly; it is invoked via the new operator.

Lines 11–15:
```
public Dice(int n)      // the one-argument constructor
{
   numDice = n;
}
```

This code comprises a *one-argument constructor*. Like the default constructor, the one-argument constructor creates a Dice object and initializes the instance variable numDice. In this case, the statement on line 13 sets numDice to the value of parameter n. The one-argument constructor is invoked as

```
Dice dice = new Dice(2);        // sets numDice to 2
```

or

```
Dice dice;
dice = new Dice(13);            // sets numDice to 13
```

There is no limit to the number of constructors that you can include in a class definition. A two-argument constructor might have the form

```
public Dice( int numBlueDice, int numRedDice)
{
        numDice = numBlueDice + numRedDice;
}
```

If a class defines no constructors at all, Java graciously provides a default constructor that creates and instantiates objects. However, don't assume that Java's version initializes the instance variables the same way that you would. For example, Java's default constructor sets numDice to 0; our default constructor sets numDice to 1. Moreover, if a class provides *any* constructors, Java does *not* provide a default constructor.

It is good practice to always provide a default constructor as part of any class that you design.

Lines 16–24: int rollDice()
The method rollDice() simulates rolling the set of dice according to the following algorithm:

1. Declare a local variable sum.
2. Instantiate a Random object, random.
3. For each die in the set, i.e., for i = 1 to numDice,
   a. generate a random number between 1 and 6, inclusive, and
   b. add the random number to sum.
4. return sum.

Like the Dice class and the instance variable numDice, the method rollDice() has an access modifier. The public access modifier specifies that the method is visible and accessible outside the Dice class.

Lines 25–28: int getNumDice()
The public method getNumDice() returns the value of numDice. Since numDice is private, its value is not visible outside of the class. The method getNumDice() provides access to numDice.

> A method such as getNumDice() that returns the value of some private variable is called a *getter* method.

Lines 29–32: void setNumDice(int n)
Like getNumDice(), the public method setNumDice(int n) provides access to the instance variable numDice via a method. This method sets numDice to the value of parameter n.

> A method that assigns or alters the value of an instance variable is called a *setter* method.

10.2.1 A Test Class for *Dice*

Rarely is a newly designed class free from bugs. Every class must be tested, debugged, then debugged again and, of course, debugged once more. The following class, TestDice, instantiates two Dice objects and invokes each method of the class. Because Dice has no main(...) method, you cannot execute the Dice class. However, TestDice does, in fact, contain a main(...) method and does execute.

```
public class TestDice
{
   public static void main(String[] args) // for testing the Dice class
   {
      Dice d1 = new Dice();
      Dice d2 = new Dice(2);

      System.out.println( "d1: numDice = " + d1.getNumDice());
      System.out.println( "d2: numDice = " + d2.getNumDice())

      for (int i = 1; i <= 10; i++)
         System.out.println(d1.rollDice() + " " + d2.rollDice());

      d1.setNumDice(5);
      System.out.println( "d1: numDice = " + d1.getNumDice());

      for (int i = 1; i <= 10; i++)
         System.out.println(d1.rollDice() );
   }
}
```

10.3 A MORE GENERAL LOOK AT CLASSES

Now that you have seen the implementation of a specific class, we consider the fundamental structure of a class.

For the present, each class that we write has the following structure:

```
[access modifier] class name
{
        instance variables or fields
        constructors
        methods
}
```

See Figure 10.2.

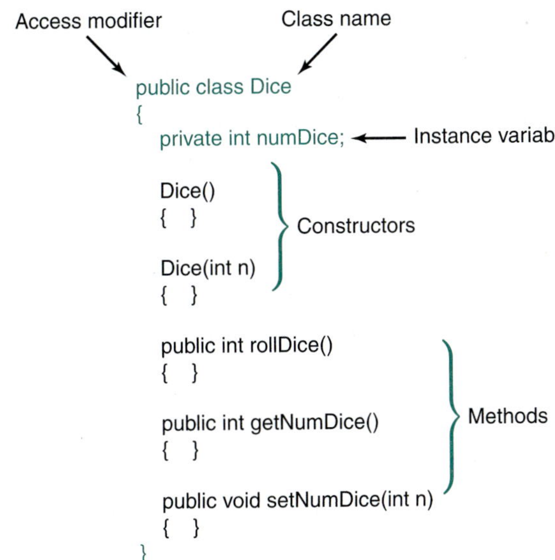

FIGURE 10.2 The *Dice* class

- A class's access modifier is optional. However, for the present, we designate each of our classes as public.

Java specifies that only one public class can be saved in any file, so each class must be saved in a separate file. The name of the file must be *classname*.java.

For example, the Dice class of Example 10.1 is a public class and must be saved as Dice.java.

If no access modifier is specified, then the class has *package access* and is accessible to all other classes in the same package. Since we do not specify a package for our classes, every class that we write is a member of Java's *default package*. Any number of such classes can be saved in one file.

- The name of a class must be a valid Java identifier. Moreover, Java convention dictates that each class name begins with an uppercase letter. All other letters of a class name are lowercase except those that begin new "words." Some other permissible and reasonable names for the Dice class are: MyDice, MyLoadedDice, or SkyMastersonsDice.
- A class can have any number of *instance variables* or *fields*. The instance variables make up the attributes of a class. These variables are accessible to all methods of the class. Each field has an optional access modifier:

  public – The field is visible outside the class.
  private – The field is visible only to the methods of the class.

An instance variable without an access modifier is accessible within its package.

Normally, we specify instance variables as private. That is, private instance variables are accessible only to the methods of the class. Thus, the methods are the guards and gatekeepers for all the fields of a class. The class's methods regulate all access to the instance variables. The Dice class has just one instance variable, numDice, which is private.

- Each class has at least one constructor.

> A constructor is automatically executed each time an object of the class is instantiated.

A constructor initializes instance variables, but it can also perform other computations. The name of a constructor is the same as the class name. A constructor does not have a return value, not even void.

The *default constructor* (*no-argument constructor*) is a constructor with no parameters. The Dice class has two constructors, the default constructor

```
public Dice(),
```

and a *one-argument constructor*

```
public Dice(int n).
```

- If a class does not implement a constructor, Java provides a default, no-argument constructor. An application can create an object with Java's default constructor using a statement such as

  ```
  MyClass myClass = new MyClass() // default constructor provided by Java
  ```

  If a class provides *any* constructors, Java does not provide a default constructor. Thus, if a class has a one-argument or two-argument constructor but no default constructor, a no-argument constructor cannot be used to instantiate an object. Though not required, you should always provide a default constructor for your classes.
- The methods of the class specify the behaviors of the class. Each method may be qualified with an optional access modifier public or private. For the classes that we write, most methods are public. However, occasionally, we write a private method intended for use only within its class. The three methods of the Dice class are all designated public methods.

> The public methods of a class constitute the *interface* of the class.

10.4 USING THE *Dice* CLASS

Now that we have developed a class that models a collection of *n* dice, we use this class in an application. We reiterate: once a class is implemented and debugged, using the class is no different than using one of Java's own classes such as String, Random, File, or Scanner.

EXAMPLE 10.2 The ancient Japanese game Cho-Han is played with a pair of standard dice that are shaken and tossed. A player places a wager on whether the sum of the dice is odd ("cho") or even ("han"). A player wins or loses an amount equal to his/her bet.

Problem Statement Write a class that simulates the game of Cho-Han. The class should:

- ask a player for a bet, an integer,
- play a round of Cho-Han,

- report the result along with the cumulative winnings or losses (a positive or negative integer), and
- inquire whether or not the player wishes to play again and, if so, repeat the game.

When a player decides that he/she would like to quit, the program should report the total winnings or losses for the session.

Java Solution A ChoHan class consists of one instance variable or field, winnings, a default constructor that initializes winnings to 0, and three methods:

1. A void method play() that
   - asks for the wager and whether he/she chooses odd or even,
   - rolls the dice,
   - adjusts the winnings based on the outcome of the bet,
   - inquires whether or not the player wishes to continue playing.

   The play() method uses the Dice class.
2. A boolean method won() that determines whether or not a player has won the game. This method is specified as private because it is intended for use only within the class. No other class has access to this method.
3. A void method reportWinnings() that displays the amount of money won or lost at the conclusion of all play. Like won(), this method is used only in the class.

The following class implements the game.

```
import java.util.*;                          // for the Scanner and Random classes
public class ChoHan
{
   private int winnings;                     // total won or lost (negative)

   public ChoHan()                           // default constructor
   {
      winnings = 0;
   }

   // an auxiliary method, used only in the class
   private boolean win (String choice, int sum)                    // win or lose
   {
      if ( sum%2 == 0 && (choice.equals("e") || choice.equals("E")))  // even and even bet
         return true;
      if ( sum%2 != 0 && (!(choice.equals("e") || choice.equals("E"))))  // odd and odd bet
         return true;
      return false;
   }

   public void play()
   {
      Scanner input = new Scanner(System.in);
      Dice dice = new Dice(2);               // Dice object instantiated; constructor called
      String choice;                         // even or odd
      String answer;                         // play again or not
      int wager;                             // how much
      do
      {
         System.out.print("Enter wager: ");
         wager = input.nextInt();
         System.out.print("Enter 'e' for even anything else for odd: ");
         choice = input.next();
         int sum = dice.rollDice();          // invoke method of Dice class
```

```
            System.out.println("You rolled a " + sum);
            if ( win(choice, sum ))
            {
                winnings += wager;
                System.out.println("You won! Winnings so far: " + winnings);
            }
            else
            {
                winnings -= wager;
                System.out.println("You lost! Winnings so far: " + winnings);
            }

            System.out.print("Play again? 'y' or 'Y' for 'Yes': ");        // anything else for "no"
            answer = input.next();
            System.out.println();

            }while(answer.equals("Y") || answer.equals("y"));
            reportWinnings();
    }

    private void reportWinnings()
    {
        if (winnings > 0)
            System.out.println("You won $" + winnings);
        else if (winnings < 0)
            System.out.println("You lost $" + Math.abs(winnings));
        else
            System.out.println("You broke even ");
        System.out.println("Thanks for playing");
    }
```

The following small class instantiates one ChoHan object and invokes the play() method of that object. The class is saved in a file named PlayChoHan.java. Once compiled, PlayChoHan can be executed and the game played. Notice that PlayChoHan contains a main(...) method. A class without a main(...) method cannot run. The sole purpose of PlayChoHan is to instantiate and play the game.

```
public class PlayChoHan
{
    public static void main(String[] args)
    {
        ChoHan game = new ChoHan();    // create a game
        game.play();                   // start the game
    }
}
```

Output

```
Enter wager: 2
Enter 'e' for even anything else for odd: e
You rolled a 5
You lost! Winnings so far: -2
Play again? 'y' or 'Y' for 'Yes': y

Enter wager: 4
Enter 'e' for even anything else for odd: a
You rolled a 5
```

```
You won! Winnings so far: 2
Play again? 'y' or 'Y' for 'Yes': y

Enter wager: 2
Enter 'e' for even anything else for odd: e
You rolled a 5
You lost! Winnings so far: 0
Play again? 'y' or 'Y' for 'Yes': y

Enter wager: 3
Enter 'e' for even anything else for odd: e
You rolled a 9
You lost! Winnings so far: -3
Play again? 'y' or 'Y' for 'Yes': n

You lost $3
Thanks for playing
```

Discussion Together the classes Dice, ChoHan, and PlayChoHan constitute a single application. PlayChoHan contains a main(...) method, so PlayChoHan is the class that executes.

When PlayChoHan starts execution, the statement

```
ChoHan game = new ChoHan();
```

invokes the default constructor of the ChoHan class. The constructor instantiates a ChoHan object, game, and initializes the instance variable, winnings, to 0. Once a ChoHan object is created, the object's play() method is invoked, and the game is off and running (line 6 of PlayChoHan).

The play() method begins with the instantiation of two objects: a Scanner object, input, and a Dice object, dice. Accordingly, play() invokes two constructors on lines 20 and 21:

```
20. Scanner input = new Scanner(System.in);
21. Dice dice = new Dice(2);            // creates a Dice object with two dice.
```

The remainder of the play() method should be easy to follow.

Finally, notice that ChoHan contains two private methods: win() and reportWinnings(), on lines 10 and 49, respectively. These methods are not accessible outside the class. Indeed, if we include the method call

```
game.reportWinnings()
```

in the PlayChoHan class, the Java compiler issues the following error message:

```
:\JavaPrograms\PlayChoHan.java:10: reportWinnings() has private access in ChoHan
        game.reportWinnings();
```

The methods win() and reportWinnings() are auxiliary or helper methods. They are used to accomplish a task within the class but are not visible outside the class.

10.5 A *TriviaTest* CLASS

Trivia games have become a national pastime. On the Internet, you can find dozens of games and quizzes that challenge your knowledge of baseball trivia, World War II trivia, Star Trek trivia, or Seinfeld trivia. In the next example, we develop a class with methods that generate a trivia quiz, administer the quiz, and score the quiz.

EXAMPLE 10.3 **Problem Statement** Design a class, TriviaTest, with methods that

- read a list of true-false questions and answers from a file,
- interactively administer the test,
- score the test and return the score as a percentage, and
- display the correct answers along with the test-taker's answers.

The first line of the input file contains the number of questions in the file. The second line holds the correct answers (T or F). Answers are separated by whitespace. The remainder of the file consists of the questions, one question per line. Here is a typical input file with some Oz trivia:

```
3
T F T
Tinman wanted a heart.
Lion wanted a mane.
Scarecrow wanted a brain.
```

Java Solution

Figure 10.3 shows the skeletal structure of the TriviaTest class.

```
private String[] correct Answers
private String[] responses[]
private int numQuestions

Scanner input;        // for interactive input
Scanner fileInput     // for file input
-------------------------------------------------------------
public TriviaTest()                   // default construtor
public TriviaTest(String filename)    // one argument Constructor

public void giveTest()
public int scoreTest()
public void showCorrectAnswers()
```

FIGURE 10.3 The *TriviaTest* class

The two arrays correctAnswers and responses hold the correct answers for the test and the test-taker's answers, respectively.

The class contains two constructors. The one-one argument constructor accepts the name of the input file and

- reads the number of questions into numQuestions,
- instantiates the array correctAnswers and reads the correct answers into this array, and
- instantiates the array responses.

The default constructor informs the user that no filename has been supplied and exits.

The methods of the class

- administer the test by displaying each question and soliciting an answer,
- score the test by comparing the answers stored in responses and correctAnswers, and
- display the correct answers along with the test-taker's answers.

The scoreTest() method returns the percentage of correct answers, rounded to the nearest integer.

Following TriviaTest is a small class TriviaTestGiver that uses TriviaTest.

```
import java.util.*;
import java.io.*;                         // for file IO
public class TriviaTest
{

  private String[] correctAnswers;        // Each entry is "T" or "F"
  private String[] responses;             // Test-taker's answers
  private int numQuestions;
  private Scanner input;                  // for interactive input
  private Scanner fileInput;              // for file input

  public TriviaTest()                     // for file usage
  {
    System.out.println("No filename supplied");
    System.exit(0);
  }

  public TriviaTest(String filename) throws IOException
  {
    input = new Scanner (System.in);

    // Open the file with the questions and answers
    File questionFile = new File(filename);
    if (!questionFile.exists())
    {
      System.out.println("Error: " + filename + " not found");
      System.exit(0);
    }
    fileInput = new Scanner(questionFile); // reads from file

    // first read the number of questions in the file
    numQuestions = fileInput.nextInt();

    // Read correct answers from the input file
    correctAnswers = new String[numQuestions];
    for (int i = 0; i < numQuestions; i++)
        correctAnswers[i] = fileInput.next();

    responses = new String[numQuestions];
    fileInput.nextLine();                    // move file pointer to the beginning of the next line
  }

  public void giveTest()
  {
    // Displays each question and records an answer
    System.out.println("Answer each of the following: T or t for True and F or f for False\n");
    for (int i = 0; i < numQuestions; i++)
    {
      System.out.println((i + 1)+ ". " + fileInput.nextLine());
      System.out.print("Answer: ");
      responses[i] = (input.next()).toUpperCase(); // Get user's response, convert to upper case
      System.out.println();
    }

    System.out.println("You scored " + scoreTest() + "% on the test");
    showCorrectAnswers();

    fileInput.close();
  }
```

```
    private int scoreTest()
    {
       // scores the test and returns the per cent of correct answers
       int correct = 0;
       for ( int i = 0; i < numQuestions ; i++)
       if ( responses[i].equals(correctAnswers[i]))
            correct++;
       return Math.round ((100 * correct) / numQuestions);
    }

    private void showCorrectAnswers()
    {
       // Displays the correct answers
       System.out.println("\tCorrect answers:\tYour Answers: ");
       for( int i = 0; i < numQuestions; i++)
          System.out.println((i + 1)+ ".\t" + correctAnswers[i] + "\t\t" + responses[i]);
    }
}
```

--------------TriviaTestGiver.java--------------

```
import java.util.*;
import java.io.*;

public class TriviaTestGiver
{
    public static void main(String[] args) throws IOException
    {
       Scanner input = new Scanner(System.in);
       System.out.print("Enter filename: ");
       String filename = input.nextLine();
       TriviaTest test = new TriviaTest(filename);
       test.giveTest();
    }
}
```

Output The following output shows a Harry Potter trivia test. The test has 10 questions stored in a file HarryPotter.txt.

Enter filename: **HarryPotter.txt**

Answer each of the following: T or t for True and F or f for False

1. Harry's owl is named Hapgood
Answer: **f**

2. Voldemort's name was Tom Marvolo Riddle
Answer: **t**

3. Mr. Weasley's first name is Arthur.
Answer: **t**

4. Ron is frightened by snakes.
Answer: **t**

5. Harry was born on July 29
Answer: **f**

6. There are 9 players on a Quiddich team
Answer: **t**

```
7. There are 7 children in Ron Wesaley's family.
Answer: t

8. The "JK" in JK Rowling's name stands for "Joanne Kathleen"
Answer: t

You scored 75% on the test

         Correct answers:        Your Answers:
1.       F                       F
2.       T                       T
3.       T                       T
4.       F                       T
5.       F                       F
6.       F                       T
7.       T                       T
8.       T                       T
```

Discussion

Lines 10–14: Default constructor

The code on lines 10–14 comprise the default constructor. If a class instantiates a TriviaTest object with a the default constructor, the message

```
No filename supplied
```

is displayed and the application terminates.

Without a default constructor, the statement

```
TriviaTest test = new TriviaTest();          // no filename supplied
```

would have resulted in a syntax error:

```
C:\ TriviaTestGiver.java:13: cannot find symbol
symbol : constructor TriviaTest()
location: class TriviaTest
            TriviaTest test = new TriviaTest();
```

Because TriviaTest provides a one-argument constructor, Java does not automatically provide a default constructor.

Alternatively, rather than issue a message and exit, a default constructor might prompt for a filename and then proceed as the one-argument constructor given on lines 15–34.

Lines 15–34: One-argument constructor

The throws clause on line 15 is essential because the class uses file IO.

The constructor

- instantiates a File object questionFile using the file specified by filename,
- instantiates a Scanner object fileInput that reads from questionFile (lines 19–25),
- reads the number of questions from the file (line 27),
- reads the correct answers into the array correctAnswers (lines 29–31), and
- instantiates the array responses, which stores the user's answers (line 32).

After reading the final answer, T or F, from the file, the file pointer is positioned at the end of the line containing the correct answers:

```
8
F T T F F F T T  ↑
Harry's Owl is . . .
```

The next statement (line 33: fileInput.nextLine()) moves the file pointer to the beginning of the next line before the first question. Thus, a subsequent call to fileInput.nextLine() returns the string

"Harry's Owl is ... ?"

Lines 35–49: giveTest()
This method

- reads and displays each question in the file (line 41),
- accepts an answer from the user (line 43), and
- stores the answer in array responses (line 43).

A user may respond with uppercase or lowercase letters. The call toUpperCase() on line 43 ensures that all answers are stored as uppercase letters.

Lines 50–58: scoreTest()
The scoreTest() private helper method compares the user's answers, stored in the array responses, with the correct answers, stored in correctAnswers, keeping track of the number of correct answers. The method returns the percentage of correct answers, rounded to the nearest integer.

Lines 59–66: showCorrectAnswers()
This method displays, side by side, the correct answers as well as the user's answers. Like scoreTest(), this is a private, helper method.

Lines 69–79: TriviaTestGiver
TriviaTestGiver is a class that uses TriviaTest, that is, TriviaTestGiver is a *client* of TriviaTest.
TriviaTestGiver implements a single main(...) method that

- instantiates a test with a user-supplied filename, and
- calls giveTest() to administer and score the test.

The throws clause on line 71 is required because main(...) invokes the one-argument constructor of TriviaTest, which also includes a throws clause. In Chapter 14, we explain the significance of the throws clause and when it is absolutely required.

10.6 ENCAPSULATION AND INFORMATION HIDING

The TrivaTest and Dice classes, like the String class, provide two more examples of encapsulation; data and methods, attributes and behaviors, are bundled together into a single entity. Another term that is often associated with encapsulation is *information hiding*. Many programmers regard encapsulation and information hiding as synonyms. However, object-oriented purists would define encapsulation as the *technique* that bundles data and methods into one unit and information hiding as the *principle* that hides the implementation of a class. If that seems a bit murky, perhaps a small illustration will clear up the concept of information hiding and demonstrate how information hiding differs from encapsulation.

The ChoHan class of Example 10.2 utilizes the Dice class. As such, ChoHan is a *client* of Dice. As a client of Dice, ChoHan needs to know how to call the methods of Dice, that is, how to *send messages* to a Dice object. To utilize the Dice class, a client need not know the implementation details of Dice. For instance, a client does not need to know that, under the hood, Dice uses the Random method nextInt(...). Nor does a client need to know that Dice stores the current number of dice in numDice. Indeed, the variable numDice has private access and is not even visible to the client ChoHan. The client can access this attribute only through the public methods, that is the interface of the Dice class. Suppose, for example, that dice is a Dice object. If a client must retrieve the number of dice stored in dice, the Dice class provides a getter method, and the client sends the message dice.getNumDice() for that very purpose. To change the number of dice, the client sends a message dice.setNumDice(int n). The client never sees nor accesses numDice directly. The methods of Dice do that. Similarly for clients of the String class, Java provides a set of methods that handle strings. It is with these methods and only these methods that you can manipulate a character string.

Giving an instance variable private access has its advantages. Suppose, for instance, that numDice has public rather than private access. Public access implies that the field numDice is visible to ChoHan and furthermore, that ChoHan can change the value of numDice with a simple assignment statement. How convenient! Thus, line 21 of ChoHan (Example 10.2)

```
21. Dice dice = new Dice(2);
```

can be legitimately rewritten as:

```
21(a). Dice dice = new Dice();
21(b). dice.numDice = 2;        // here, numDice is public and hence accessible
```

with absolutely no complaints from the compiler. After all, numDice is public and ChoHan can use numDice in any legitimate manner.

So what's the problem? Why not declare numDice public? It is a fact of life that software is often rewritten and revised. If, by chance, the implementation of Dice changes so that the instance variable numDice is renamed numberOfDice, then line 21(b) of the client code no longer works. There is no longer a variable named numDice. The client's code must be rewritten to accommodate the newly named numberOfDice attribute. However, by keeping this attribute private and accessible only through methods getNumDice() and setNumDice(int n), whether or not the field is named numDice, numberOfDice, or mickeyMouse, the client code executes correctly.

Information hiding reaches beyond access to instance variables. Suppose, for example, that the Dice method rollDice() is revised using Math.random() rather than a Random object. As long as Dice supplies a rollDice() method, this change in implementation does not affect the ChoHan class. The newly written Dice class is still operable. All implementation details are hidden from the client. It does not matter to the client *how* rollDice() is implemented, just *what* rollDice() *does*. Similarly, a client of String knows what service charAt() or substring() provides but not *how* these methods provide the service. Perhaps the implementors at Sun have rewritten substring() 10 times, or even 100 times. As a client, revisions make no difference to you. The method substring() has its purpose, and how Java chooses to implement that purpose does not affect your classes.

> Information hiding allows classes to be revised without affecting the code of its clients.

In general, information hiding is the principle that hides implementation details from a client class. When implementation details are hidden, all access to the attributes of a class is through its public methods.

As you already know, encapsulation is the mechanism that bundles data and methods into a single entity. Java classes provide encapsulation.

> Classes encapsulate but classes do not necessarily enforce information hiding.
> Restricting access within a class affords information hiding.

Java provides information hiding via access modifiers. The following class is an example of encapsulation *without* information hiding. Notice that both fields are public and hence visible to other classes.

```
class public TwoNumbers
{
   public int one;
   public int two;
   public MyClass() // default constructor
   {
      one = 1;
      two = 2;
   }
   public int sum()
   {
      return one + two;
   }
}
```

Finally, we point out that although we have made a distinction between encapsulation and information hiding, some authors combine both ideas under the single rubric of encapsulation. In any case, encapsulation, with information hiding, is the very first principle of object-oriented programming.

10.7 THE KEYWORD *static*

The keyword static has been part of our programming vocabulary from the very beginning. Well, it's about time we reveal the mystery that lurks within.

10.7.1 *static* Data or Class Variables

Objects consist of attributes and behaviors, data and methods. Each object has storage for its own instance variables. For example, each of the three Dice objects of Figure 10.1 maintains storage for the instance variable numDice. Each object has its own unique data.

In addition to instance variables, a Java class may also define *class variables* or *static variables*. We use the keyword static to denote a class variable.

> A static variable belongs to the class and not to any particular object; a class or static variable is shared by all objects of the class.

Once defined in a class, a static variable exists whether or not any objects have been created; and no matter how many objects exist, only one copy of any static variable can exist. A static variable serves all objects of a class. Static data is not stored in an individual object but in a separate location, and all objects of a class have access to this one location.

Suppose, for example, that each object of an Employee class models an individual employee and that each employee has a unique weekly income. A static variable totalPayroll might hold the grand total of all salaries for the week. Only one copy of totalPayroll is necessary. All objects share totalPayroll. See Figure 10.4.

A static variable is handy if you need to know how many objects of a class exist. The following class is a version of the Dice class with an additional static variable, numDiceObjects, that keeps track of the number of Dice objects that are instantiated.

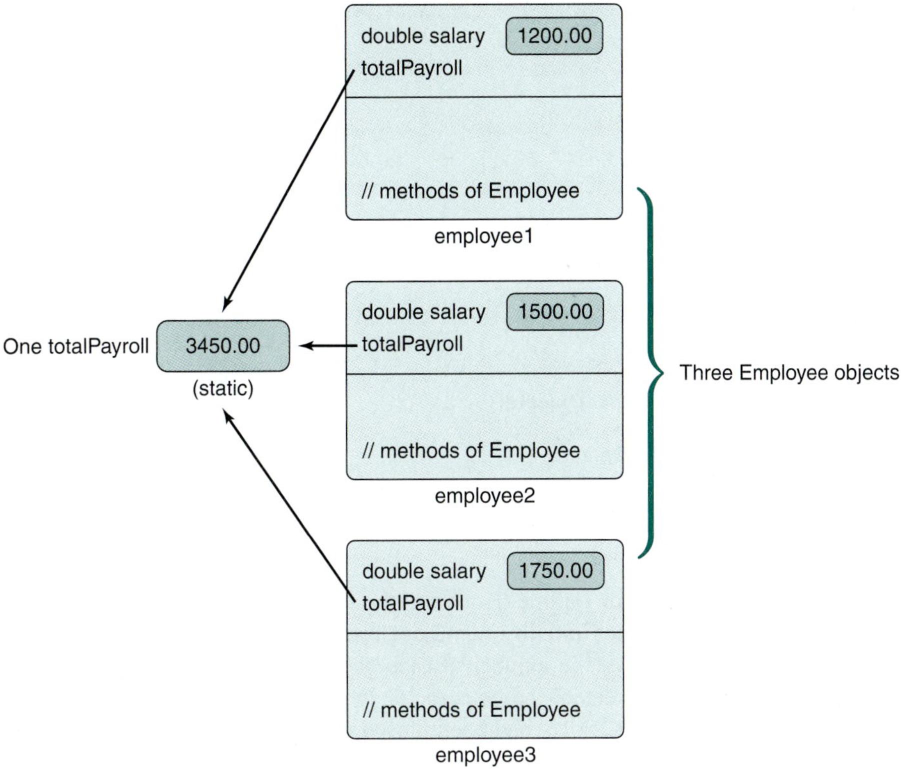

FIGURE 10.4 All *Employee* objects share the same *static* variable, *totalPayroll*

```
import java.util.*;

public class Dice
{
   private int numDice;
   private Random random;
   static private int numDiceObjects 5 0;   // the keyword static denotes a class variable.

   public Dice()                             // default constructor—one die
   {
      numDice = 1;
      random = new Random();
      numDiceObjects++;
   }

   public Dice(int n)                        // one argument constructor—n dice
   {
      numDice = n;
      random = new Random();
      numDiceObjects++;
   }

   public int rollDice()
   // Returns the number of spots shown when tossing numDice dice
   {
      int sum = 0;
      for (int i = 1; i <= numDice; i++) // for each die in the set
```

```
24.         sum += random.nextInt(6) + 1; // sum = an integer between 1 and 6, inclusive
25.       return sum;
26.    }

27.    public int getNumDice()
28.    {
29.       return numDice;
30.    }

31.    public void setNumDice(int n)
32.    {
33.       numDice = n;
34.    }

35.    public int getNumDiceObjects()
36.    {
37.       return numDiceObjects;
38.    }

39. }
```

Notice that the declaration on line 6 includes the static modifier as well as an initialization. The constructors do not initialize numDiceObjects but instead increment this static variable, thus keeping track of the number of Dice objects that have been created. Every time a new Dice object is created, the constructor increases numDiceObjects by one. If the initialization of numDiceObjects had been placed in the constructor, numDiceObjects would be reset to 0 each time a new object was created. The initialization on line 6 is performed just once and not every time a new object is created.

After the following code segment executes, three Dice objects have been created, and the static variable numDiceObjects has the value 3.

```
Dice d1 = new Dice(3);
Dice d2 = new Dice(7);
Dice d3 = new Dice(5);
```

Each time a Dice constructor is invoked, numDiceObjects increases. Figure 10.5 shows that all objects share the static variable numDiceObjects.

Static variables are also convenient if a class declares a constant, that is, a final variable. Because the value of a constant is final and cannot be changed, it makes sense to store a constant just once instead of in each object of the class. The following partial class that models a simple circle contains two static variables: the constant PI and the variable totalArea, which is the sum of the areas of all instantiated Circle objects.

```
public class Circle
{
   public static double totalArea = 0.0;          // class variable
   public final static double PI = 3.14159;       // class variable
   private double radius;

   public Circle()                                // default constructor
   {
     radius = 1;
     totalArea = totalArea + PI * radius * radius;  // adds to the class variable
   }
```

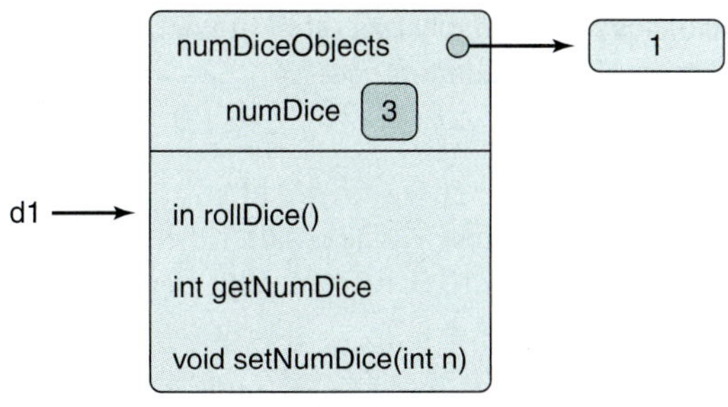

(a) *Dice d1 = new Dice*(3);
static variable *numDiceObjects* has the value 1.

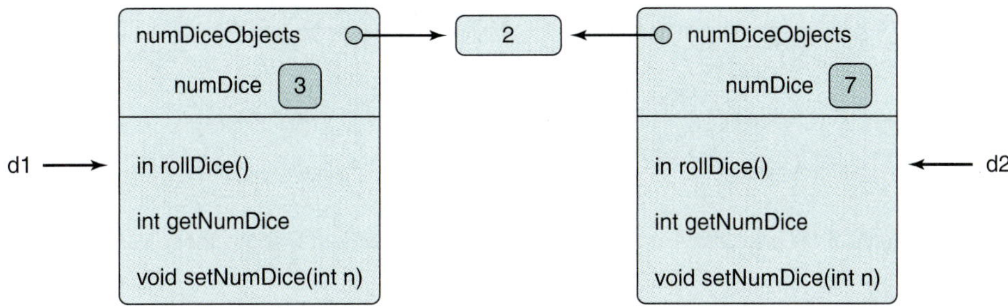

(b) *Dice d2 = new Dice*(7);
static variable *numDiceObjects* has the value 2.

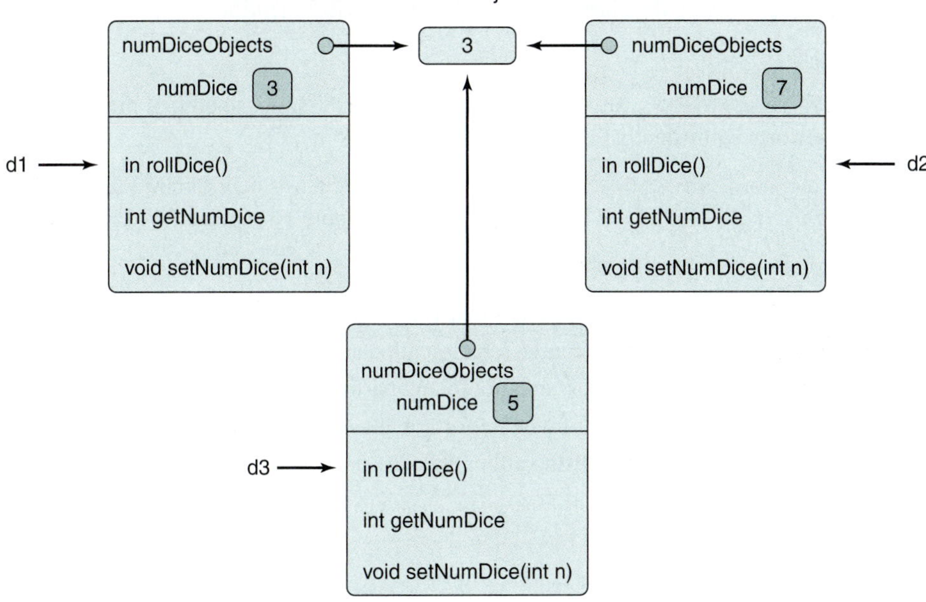

(c) *Dice d3 = new Dice*(5);
static variable *numDiceObjects* has the value 3.

FIGURE 10.5 One *static* variable *numDiceObjects* serves all *Dice* objects

```
public Circle(double r)                    // one argument constructor
{
  radius = r;
  totalArea = totalArea + PI * radius * radius; // adds to the class variable
}
```

```
    // The Circle class presumably has other methods besides constructors,
    // perhaps area() and circumference().
}
```

Figure 10.6 shows the values in all variables after the creation of two Circle objects, circle1 and circle2, with radii 4.0 and 10.0, respectively.

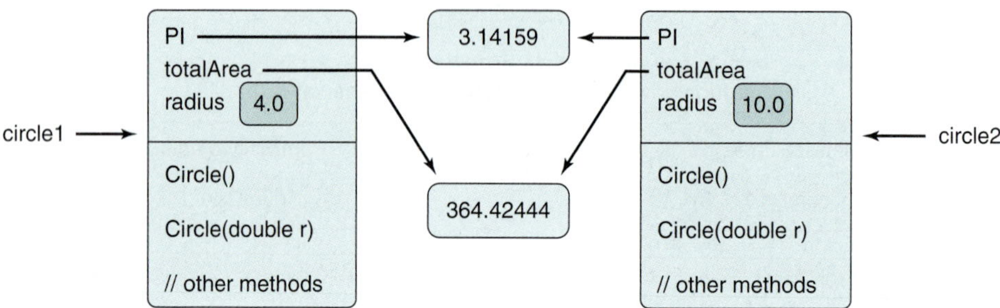

FIGURE 10.6 *PI* and *totalArea* are *static* variables. All objects, share these variables.

Unlike totalArea, PI has public access and is thus visible to other classes. Since PI exists whether or not any Circle object exists, access to PI (or any other accessible static variable) can be achieved by using the class name instead of an object identifier:

```
Circle.PI
```

Nevertheless, access to PI via any Circle object is also permissible, so both of the following segments perform equivalently.

```
Circle c = new Circle(3.5);
double x = c.PI * 15;
```

```
Circle c = new Circle(3.5);
double x = Circle.PI * 15;
```

In general, if a class contains a static variable,

- all objects/instances of the class share that variable;
- there is only one variable or storage location allocated to the whole class;
- the variable belongs to the class and not to any particular object;
- the variable exists regardless of whether or not any objects have been created; and
- the variable may be accessed using either the class name or an object name, if an object has been created.

10.7.2 *static* Methods

Like a static variable, a static method is a class method and exists whether or not any objects exist. A static method, indicated by the keyword static placed before the method's return type, belongs to the defining class. Unlike a non-static or instance method that must be invoked via an object, a static method may be called whether or not an object of the class exists. A static method exists apart from any objects.

The methods Math.random(), Math.sqrt(), and Math.abs() are all static methods. In fact, every method of Java's Math class is static. A static method may be invoked by sending a message to an object, if one exists, or by using the class name, as our use of the methods of the Math class illustrates.

As you know, the main(...) method of an application is static. Why so? Well, suppose that main(...) is not static. Then, some object would have to be created to invoke main(...), that is, an object must be instantiated before main(...) can execute. Now how would that object be created? Every application starts by executing main(...). What method would instantiate such an object? The main(...) method must be static to execute under its own power, so to speak; no object is necessary.

A static method may be called whether or not an object of the class exists, but a static method cannot invoke an instance method except via an object.

In the following class StaticMethods, the main(...) method, which is static, attempts to call notAStaticMethod(), which is not.

```
public class StaticMethods
{
  public void notAStaticMethod()   // an instance method; there is no static modifier
  {
     System.out.println("Hi, I'm not static");
  }

  public static void main(String[] args)
  {
    notAStaticMethod();            // a call to an instance method—not legal
  }
}
```

An attempt to compile this class results in the following error message:

```
C:\JavaPrograms\StaticMethods.java:9: non-static method notAStaticMethod()
cannot be referenced from a static context
```

In order to invoke notAStaticMethod(), a StaticMethods object must be created.

```
public class StaticMethods
{
  public void NotAStaticMethod()
  {
     System.out.println("Hi, I'm not static");
  }

  public static void main(String[] args)
  {
     StaticMethods myObject = new StaticMethods();
     myObject.NotAStaticMethod();
  }
}
```

If a static method A() invokes another method B() without the instantiation of an object, then B() must be static as well.

The previously defined Circle class has two static fields. The following expanded version includes a static method,

```
double getTotalArea(),
```

that returns the value stored in the static variable totalArea. Notice that this method does not access the instance variable radius; that would be illegal.

```
public class Circle
{
   static private double totalArea = 0.0;              // class variable
   public final static double PI = 3.14159;            // class variable
   private double radius;                               // instance variable

   public Circle()                                      //default constructor
   {
      radius = 1;
      totalArea += PI * radius * radius;// adds to the class variable
   }

   public Circle(double r)                 // one argument constructor
   {
      radius= r;
      totalArea += PI * radius * radius;  // adds to the class variable
   }

   public static double getTotalArea()
   {
      return totalArea;
   }
   // Other methods of the Circle class are implemented here
}
```

To invoke the method getTotalArea(), no objects need exist. Of course, if no objects exist, the method call

```
Circle.getTotalArea()
```

returns 0.0, the valued initially assigned to totalArea.

Example 10.4, which is an extension of Example 10.2, uses both static data and static methods.

EXAMPLE 10.4

Gamblin' Gus, Atlantic City's premiere citizen, has decided to design a "casino game" for his son, Gus Jr. What Gus has in mind is a video machine not unlike the video poker or slot machines found in casinos around the world. Gus's machine, however, must be simpler and a bit fairer than a real casino machine. Gus Jr. does not like losing. After a bit of thought, Gus decides to create a "Cho-Han machine." With 50-50 odds and a simple odd-even betting scheme, Gus figures that Cho-Han would be just about perfect for Gus Jr. and his pals.

Gus's Cho-Han machine prompts a player for his/her name and then allows him/her to play Cho-Han (odd-even) until exhaustion, boredom, or bankruptcy. Like a standard slot machine, just one player can operate the Cho-Han machine at any time.

Problem Statement Write a Java application that simulates a Cho-Han machine. For any number of players, the machine should

- prompt for the player's name,
- repeat the game until the player decides to quit,

- report the player's winnings/losses, and
- shut down when a player enters the word "DONE".

Before shutting down, the machine reports how many gamblers played the game as well as the "casino's" gross profits or losses.

Java Solution The problem statement suggests two objects: a ChoHanGame object and a ChoHanMachine object. A ChoHanGame object models a single Cho-Han session for one player and a ChoHanMachine object represents the machine that handles each session. Accordingly, the two objects must communicate with each other.

The following ChoHanGame class is very much like the ChoHan class of Example 10.2. The difference between the classes is the addition of the two static variables, numPlayers and total, which keep track of the number of players and the gross winnings or losses for all players, respectively. Of course, the ChoHanGame class also uses the Dice class of Example 10.1.

The ChoHanMachineClass is very simple. The single method of the class, runMachine(), repeats the following actions until a user enters "DONE":

- prompts for a player's name,
- instantiates a new ChoHanGame object (starts up a new game session for one player), and
- invokes the play() method for the new game.

When all players are finished, the ChoHanMachine object displays the number of players as well as the casino's gross winnings or losses, that is, the contents of the static variables numPlayers and total.

Finally, the following class, with a solitary main(...) method, instantiates a ChoHanMachine object (turns on the machine) and initiates play.

```
public class PlayChoHanMachine
{
      public static void main(String[] args)
      {
            ChoHanMachine machine = new ChoHanMachine();
            machine.runMachine();
      }
}
```

The ChoHanGame and ChoHanMachine classes follow.

```
---------------------ChoHanGame.java---------------------
import java.util.*;              // for the Scanner class

public class ChoHanGame
{
static public int numPlayers = 0;
static public int total = 0;

private int winnings;            // total won or lost (negative)

public ChoHanGame()              // default constructor
{
   winnings = 0;
   numPlayers++;                 // a new object is a new player; count the players
}

// an auxiliary method, used only in the class
```

```
private boolean win (String choice, int sum)// win or lose
{
   if ( sum%2 == 0 && (choice.equals("e") || choice.equals("E")))       // even and even bet
      return true;
   if ( sum%2 != 0 && (!(choice.equals("e") || choice.equals("E"))))    // odd and odd bet
      return true;
   return false;
}
private void reportWinnings()
{
   if (winnings > 0)
      System.out.println("You won $" + winnings);
   else if (winnings < 0)
      System.out.println("You lost $" + Math.abs(winnings));
   else
      System.out.println("You broke even ");
   System.out.println("Thanks for playing\n");
}
public void play()
{
   Scanner input = new Scanner(System.in);
   Dice dice = new Dice(2);
   String choice;                  // even or odd
   String answer;                  // play again or not
   int wager;                      // how much
   do
   {
      System.out.print("Enter wager: ");
      wager = input.nextInt();
      System.out.print("Enter 'e' for even; anything else for odd: ");
      choice = input.next();
      int sum = dice.rollDice();
      System.out.println("You rolled a " + sum);
      if ( win(choice, sum ))
      {
         winnings += wager;
         total -= wager; // a win for the player is a loss for the casino
         System.out.println("You won! Winnings so far: " + winnings);
      }
      else
      {
         winnings -= wager;
         total += wager; // a loss for the player is a gain for the casino
         System.out.println("You lost! Winnings so far: " + winnings );
      }
      System.out.print("\nPlay again? 'y' or 'Y' for 'Yes': ");// anything else for no
      answer = input.next();
      System.out.println();
   } while(answer.equals("Y") || answer.equals("y"));
      reportWinnings();
   }
   public static int getNumPlayers()
   {
      return numPlayers;
   }

   public static int getTotal()
   {
      return total;
   }
}
```

--------------------ChoHanMachine.java--------------------

```
import java.util.*;

public class ChoHanMachine
{

private ChoHanGame game;

public void runMachine()
{
   Scanner input = new Scanner(System.in);
   System.out.print("What is your name ? ");
   String name = input.next();
   while (!name.equals("DONE"))
   {
      System.out.println("Hello " + name + " Goodluck!\n");
      game = new ChoHanGame();
      game.play();
      System.out.print("What is your name? ");
      name = input.next();
   }
   System.out.println("Number of players : " + game.getNumPlayers());
   System.out.println("Casino's winnings/losses : " + game.getTotal());
   }
}
```

Output

What is your name ? **Gus**
Hello Gus Goodluck!

Enter wager: **5**
Enter 'e' for even; anything else for odd: **e**
You rolled a 8
You won! Winnings so far: 5

Play again? 'y' or 'Y' for 'Yes': **y**

Enter wager: **10**
Enter 'e' for even; anything else for odd: **o**
You rolled a 4
You lost! Winnings so far: −5

Play again? 'y' or 'Y' for 'Yes': **y**

Enter wager: **10**
Enter 'e' for even; anything else for odd: **e**
You rolled a 4

You won! Winnings so far: 5

Play again? 'y' or 'Y' for 'Yes': **n**

You won $5
Thanks for playing

What is your name? **Glynda**
Hello Glynda Goodluck!

Enter wager: **1**
Enter 'e' for even; anything else for odd: **e**

You rolled a 5
You lost! Winnings so far: **–1**

Play again? 'y' or 'Y' for 'Yes': **y**

Enter wager: **10**
Enter 'e' for even; anything else for odd: **e**
You rolled a 5
You lost! Winnings so far: –11

Play again? 'y' or 'Y' for 'Yes': n

You lost $11
Thanks for playing

What is your name? **DONE**
Number of players : 2
Casino's winnings/losses : 6

Discussion The main(...) method of the PlayChoHanMachine class first instantiates a ChoHanMachine object and then invokes the runMachine() method of that object. That is, the PlayChoHanMachine object sends a message to the ChoHanMachine object. The runMachine() method consists of a loop that

- prompts for a name,
- instantiates a ChoHanGame object (game), and
- invokes the play() method of the ChoHanGame object.

Figure 10.7a depicts the object after the first iteration of the loop in runMachine(). Notice that the static variable numPlayers has the value 1, and that because the player won $5 and "the casino" lost, the static variable total currently holds –5. Figure 10.7b shows that the second player has lost $11. Notice that the static variable numPlayers is now 2 and total 6 because the casino (machine) is now ahead $6.

Finally, notice that main(...) instantiates a single ChoHanMachine object. Of course main(...) can instantiate several such objects. Consider the following main(...) method:

```
public static void main(String[] args)
{
   ChoHanMachine machine1 = new ChoHanMachine();
   machine1.runMachine();
   ChoHanMachine machine2 = new ChoHanMachine();
   machine2.runMachine();
}
```

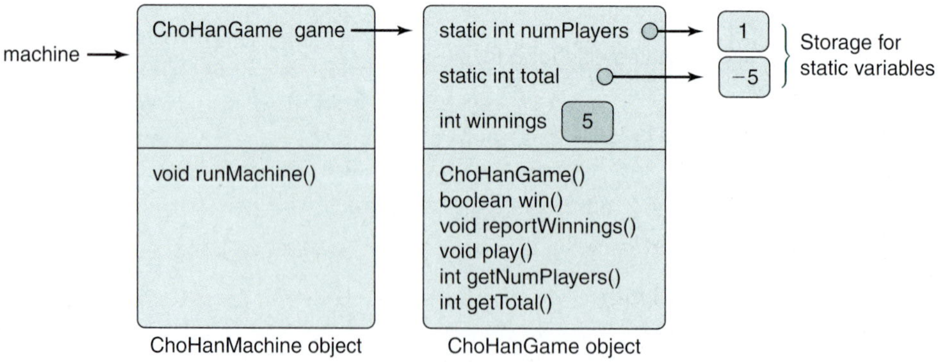

machine →

ChoHanMachine object	ChoHanGame object
ChoHanGame game →	static int numPlayers → 1 static int total → –5 int winnings 5
void runMachine()	ChoHanGame() boolean win() void reportWinnings() void play() int getNumPlayers() int getTotal()

Storage for static variables

FIGURE 10.7 (a) Objects after one session of ChoHan

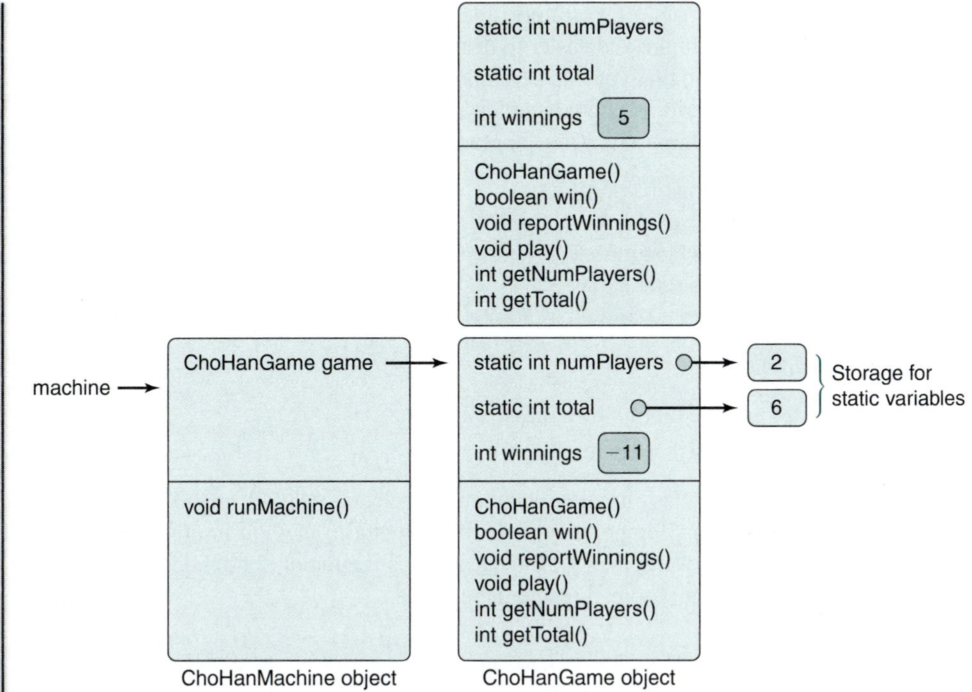

FIGURE 10.7 (b) Objects after two players try their luck

In this case, two ChoHanGame objects are instantiated, each with static class variables numPlayers and total, which give the total number of players and winnings/losses for each machine.

10.8 THE OMNIPRESENT *main(String[] args)* METHOD

Every application begins execution with main(...). In the applications of Part I of this text, most, if not all, functionality resides in main(...). However, the presence of objects changes the programming landscape, and the applications of this chapter look quite a bit different than previous applications. Consider, for example, the main(...) method of PlayChoHanMachine:

```
public static void main(String[] args)
{
   ChoHanMachine machine = new ChoHanMachine();
   machine.runMachine();
}
```

Here, main(...) is simple and uncomplicated. Indeed, the instructions of main(...) merely

- create an instance of the ChoHanMachine class (machine), and
- start the action by calling the runMachine() method, sending a message to machine.

There is no other functionality in main(...). The application consists of three other classes (Dice, ChoHanGame, and ChoHanMachine) and these objects do the work; the objects send messages to one another. Good, clean design assigns functionality to objects that model real entities and make your applications modular. Although it is not always advantageous to keep main(...) so simple, good object-oriented design always makes your programs easier to maintain, and easier to debug.

Finally, we mention that you can certainly include a main(...) method in any class. For example, rather than writing a separate class PlayChoHanMachine, we might include the following main(...) method in the ChoHanMachine class:

```
public static void main(String[] args)
{
        ChoHanMachine machine = new ChoHanMachine();
        machine.runMachine();
}
```

Here, the main method

- instantiates an object of its own class, and
- sends a message to that object.

Usually, only one class in an application includes a main(...) method, and that class "drives" the application. Temporarily including a main(...) method in other classes might be helpful during the development of the class, when the main(...) method serves as a convenient and practical tool for testing and debugging.

> When testing and debugging a class, adding a temporary, functional main(...) method to the class is easy and essential.

10.9 THE KEYWORD *this*

Take another look at the one argument constructor of the Dice class:

```
public Dice(int n)
{
        numDice = n;
        random = new Random();
}
```

and the statement

```
numDice = n;
```

which assigns n to the instance variable numDice.

The name of the parameter n is somewhat nondescript. Can we conjure up a parameter name a bit more revealing than n? Surprisingly, the parameter name can also be numDice, the same name as the instance variable. Doing this, however, requires some way of distinguishing the instance variable numDice from the parameter numDice. If the parameter is also named numDice, the constructor has the form

```
public Dice(int numDice)
{
    numDice = numDice;
    random = new Random();
}
```

and the compiler always assumes that numDice in the statement

```
numDice = numDice;
```

refers to the local variable, that is, the parameter. Thus, the statement reassigns the parameter numDice its own value, and the *instance variable* numDice is not assigned *any* value.

To distinguish between the instance variable and the parameter, Java provides the reference this.

> The reference this refers to the current instance of a class, the object currently being used.

By using this, an object can refer to itself. The following version of the dice constructor uses the reference this to distinguish between the instance variable numDice and the parameter numDice.

```
public Dice( int numDice)
{
        this.numDice = numDice;
        // this.numDice is the instance variable numDice
        random = new Random();
}
```

In the assignment statement, the variable this.numDice refers to the instance variable numDice, that is, the numDice that belongs to *this class*: the object currently being created, and not the parameter numDice.

10.9.1 Using *this* with a Method Call

Distinguishing between instance variables and parameter names is not the only way to make use of this. For example, the following Rectangle class uses this in both the two-argument constructor and the method biggerRectangle().

```
public class Rectangle
{
   private int length, width;
   public Rectangle ()
   {
      int length = width = 0;
   }

   public Rectangle (int length, int width)
   {
      this.length = length;   // this.length – is the instance variable length
      this.width = width;     // this.width – is the instance variable width
   }

   public int area()
   {
      return length * width;
   }

   public Rectangle biggerRectangle (Rectangle r)   // returns the rectangle with larger area
   {
      if ( this.area() > r.area())   // this.area() returns the area of the current (calling) object
                                     // r.area() returns the area of the parameter object
         return this;                // return a reference to "this object" -- the calling object
      else
         return r;
   }

   public static void main(String[] args)
```

```
    {
        Rectangle r1 = new Rectangle (3, 5);
        Rectangle r2 = new Rectangle (1, 4);
        Rectangle r3 = r1.biggerRectangle(r2);          // r1 is the caller; r1 is "this" Rectangle
        System.out.println("The larger area is " + r3.area());
    }
}
```

In the two-argument constructor, this is used to distinguish between instance variables and parameters with the same names, in the same way as the previous Dice example. In contrast, the method

```
Rectangle biggerRectangle(Rectangle r)
```

utilizes this to refer to the calling or current object, and thus to compare the area of the calling object to the area of the parameter object. Without this, there would be no way to refer to the calling object, and no way to make the appropriate comparison.

Notice that the main(...) method includes a call to biggerRectangle():

```
r1.biggerRectangle(r2);
```

The method biggerRectangle(...) returns a reference to the Rectangle with greater area, r1 or r2. When the area of the calling object (r1) is bigger, the statement

```
return this   // a reference to the caller or current object
```

executes, otherwise

```
return r
```

executes. In this illustration, r.1biggerRectangle(r2) returns a reference to r1, the caller. Because this refers to an object, the keyword this cannot be used in a static method because static methods can execute even if no objects have been created; however, this can be used in any non-static method.

10.9.2 A Constructor Can Call Another Constructor Using *this*

Using the keyword this, one constructor can call another constructor.

For example, the following class encapsulates a room.

```
public class Room
{
        private int length;
        private int width;
        private int height;
        private int floorArea;
        private int wallArea;
        private int perimeter;
        private double gallonsOfPaint;   // 1 gallon covers ~ 350 sq. ft. of wall space
        public Room()                    // default constructor
        {
          length = 9;
          width = 12;
          height = 8;
```

```
            floorArea = length * width;
            wallArea = 2 * length * height + 2 * width * height;
            perimeter = 2 * length + 2 * width;
            gallonsOfPaint = wallArea/350.00;
        }
        public Room(int length,int width,int height) // three-argument constructor
        {
            this.length = length;
            this.width = width;
            this.height = height;
            floorArea = length * width;
            wallArea = 2 * length * height + 2 * width * height;
            perimeter = 2 * length + 2 * width;
            gallonsOfPaint = wallArea / 350.00;
        }
        // other methods of Room
}
```

There is much the same about the two constructors. The only difference is the assignment of values to length, width, and height. Conveniently, the default constructor can be rewritten simply as:

```
public Room()
{
        this(9, 12, 8);
}
```

The statement

```
this(9, 12, 8);
```

is a call to the three-argument constructor of the same class. This action accomplishes the same task as the much longer original version of the one-argument constructor Room(). Note that the message to the constructor is sent using this, and *not* by explicitly invoking the constructor name, that is, Room(9, 12, 8), as you might expect. Indeed,

```
public Room()
{
        Room(9, 12, 8); // Error
}
```

results in a compile time error – cannot find symbol.

You should be aware of one additional restriction.

If one constructor calls another constructor, no other statements can precede that call.

For example, the following version of Room() does *not* compile:

```
public Room()
{
        length = 9;      // ILLEGAL FIRST STATEMENT
        this (9,12,8);   // this must be the first statement
}
```

10.10 GARBAGE COLLECTION

Consider the following segment that incrementally builds the string "Happy":

```
1. String s = new String("H");   // s —> "H"
2. s += "a";                     // s —> "Ha"
3. s += "p";                     // s —> "Hap"
4. s += "p";                     // s —> "Happ"
5. s += "y';                     // s —> "Happy"
```

As you know, String objects are immutable, and each concatenation operation causes the instantiation of a new String object. Thus, the preceding segment creates five different String objects. Each time a new object is created, its address is assigned to the reference variable s. As a consequence, after line 5 executes, there are four *unreferenced* String objects in existence. Memory has been allocated, but these objects are inaccessible. No reference variables hold their addresses. See Figure 10.8.

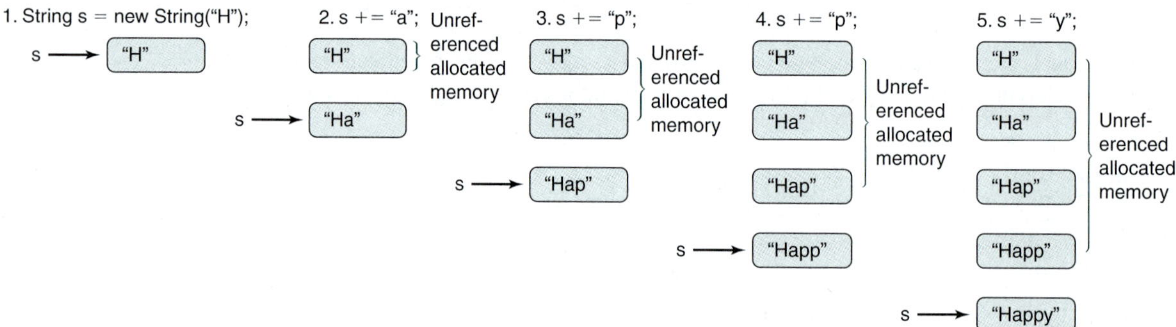

FIGURE 10.8 With the creation of each new *String* object, previously created objects are no longer accessible.

If unreferenced objects accumulate, a gargantuan program with thousands of objects could run out of memory. Even if a program does not run out of memory, if too much memory is allocated, program performance can deteriorate. Fortunately, Java manages memory automatically, and this helps alleviate any potential disaster.

> The Java Virtual Machine automatically reclaims all memory allocated to unreferenced objects for future use. In other words, if an object is no longer referenced and accessible, the memory allocated to that object is freed and made available for the creation of other objects. This clean-up process is called *garbage collection*.

Java's *garbage collection* is more like recycling. Java's garbage collector periodically determines which objects are unreferenced and reclaims the space allocated to those objects. As a program runs, garbage collection occurs transparently in the background. The Java Virtual Machine reclaims unneeded memory quietly without any notice or fanfare. For example, each unreferenced string of Figure 10.8 is certainly garbage, as is the first object of Figure 10.7b. The memory used for these objects is eventually reclaimed and available for use by other objects.

The garbage collector recycles memory allocated to unreferenced objects, but there are limitations. If an object remains referenced but is no longer used in a program, the garbage collector does *not* recycle the memory. For example, consider the following segment that instantiates Square, Triangle, and Circle objects:

```
Square mySquare = new Square (5.0);      // a 5.0 x 5.0 square
double areaSquare = mySquare.area();
```

```
Triangle myTriangle = new Triangle(6.0, 8.0);  // right triangle base = 6.0, height = 8.0
double areaTriangle = myTriangle.area();

Circle myCircle = new Circle(4.0);             // a circle of radius 4.0
double areaCircle = myCirclearea();
. . .
// code that uses these objects
. . .
// more code that does not use the objects created above
. . .
```

Although the Square, Triangle, and Circle objects are no longer used by the program, if the objects remain referenced, that is, if references mySquare, myTriangle, and myCircle continue to hold the addresses of these obsolete objects, the garbage collector will not reclaim the memory for these three objects. Such a scenario causes a *memory leak*.

A *memory leak* occurs when an application maintains references to obsolete objects.

The memory leak caused by the Square-Triangle-Circle fragment can be easily rectified by adding a few lines of code (lines 9–11).

```
1.  Square mySquare = new Square(5.0);          // a 5.0 x 5.0 square
2.  double areaSquare = mySquare.area();

3.  Triangle myTriangle = new Triangle(6.0, 8.0);// right triangle base = 6.0, height = 8.0
4.  double areaTriangle = myTriangle.area();

5.  Circle myCircle = new Circle(4.0);          // a circle of radius 4.0
6.  double areaCircle = myCircle.area()

7.  // code that uses these objects
8.  ...
9.  mySquare = null;
10. myTriangle = null;
11. myCircle = null;
12. // more code that does not use the objects created above
    . . .
```

Figure 10.9a shows the references after line 5 executes. Figure 10.9b shows the same references after line 11 executes. The references mySquare, myTriangle, and myCircle no longer refer to objects; each has the value null.

The Java constant null can be assigned to a reference. A reference with value null refers to no object and holds no address; it is called a *void reference*.

The previous segment no longer causes a memory leak. Variables mySquare, myTriangle, and myCircle are void references: they have the value null and refer to no object. The Square, Triangle, and Circle objects are unreferenced after mySquare, myTriangle, and myCircle are assigned null. Consequently, the garbage collector will reclaim memory for these three unreferenced objects.

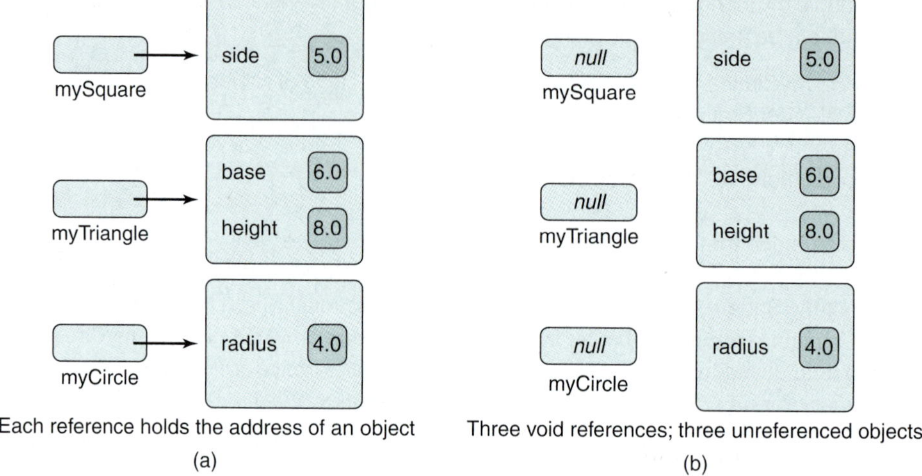

FIGURE 10.9 Referenced and unreferenced objects

Managing memory use is an important part of a programmer's job. The programmer must work in tandem with Java's automatic garbage collection to ensure that there are no memory leaks.

10.11 A CASE STUDY: CLASSY SOUNDS

Our final example combines many of the object-oriented concepts of Chapters 9 and 10, including classes, objects, strings, files, and static methods. In addition, the following application also includes two more classes that come packaged with Java: AudioClip and URL.

EXAMPLE 10.5 Sammy Sound collects audio clips from classic and not-so-classic Hollywood films. Sammy downloads his audio clips from the Internet and stores each clip in a separate file on his computer. For example, Sammy's *Wizard.wav* file holds the famous line from *The Wizard of Oz*, "Toto, I have a feeling we're not in Kansas anymore," and his *NapoleanDynamite.wav* file contains an insightful quotation from Napoleon Dynamite.

For easy listening, Sammy imagines a simplified version of an iPod, which he dubs a *myPod*. Sammy's myPod can play audio files such as wav or midi files, but not MP3 files. A myPod is perfect for playing Sam's film clips or, for that matter, any wav or midi file that Sammy downloads from the Web.

The controls of a myPod are both simple and self-explanatory:

- *down,* advances the selection to the next audio clip.
- *up*, selects the previous audio clip (backs up)
- *play,* play the selected clip.
- *stop*, stop playing the selected clip.
- *loop*, play the selected clip continuously.
- *on/off*, power switch.

A myPod always displays the name of the current selection. See Figure 10.10.

FIGURE 10.10 A MyPod

Problem Statement Write an application that implements a MyPod class. The default constructor should prompt for the name of a text file that lists audio clips. Each clip requires two lines of the file: the display name of the clip and the name of the file that holds the audio clip. Each name appears on a separate line. For example, Sam's file FilmClips.txt contains the lines:

Wizard of Oz
Wizard.wav
Ferris Bueller's Day Off
FerrisBueller.wav
The Godfather
Godfather.wav
Gone With the Wind
GWTW.wav
Napoleon Dynamite
NapoleonDynamite.wav
Psycho
Psycho.wav

After reading the input file, the application displays the name of the current selection (the first clip on the list) and a menu that simulates the buttons on the machine shown in Figure 10.10.

Selected Clip: The Wizard of Oz

Your options:

u. up
d. down
p. play
s. stop
l. loop
e. end

Choice:

The myPod always displays the name of one "selected" clip.

You may assume that the input file is correctly formatted. That is, the file contains entries for no more than 200 clips, and every entry consists of two parts: the name of a sound clip and a file name, each on a separate line.

Java Solution The application consists of two objects that communicate with each other:

- a User Interface (UI) object, and
- a MyPod object.

A more sophisticated program would present you with a *graphical user interface* (GUI) complete with pictures and clickable buttons, perhaps a jazzier version of Figure 10.10. However, we do not yet have a graphics toolset, so we settle for a text-based user interface. Instead of buttons, we give you a menu; and instead of a mouse-click, you indicate your menu choice with a "keyboard-click."

Once you choose a menu item (*play*, *loop*, *next*, etc.) the UI object sends a message to the MyPod object and the MyPod object executes the task. The UI class contains the main(...) method of the application. The only instance variable of the UI class is a reference to a MyPod object. And, in addition to main(...), the methods of the UI class are:

- a default constructor that instantiates a MyPod object using the new operator, and
- a method that displays a menu, accepts a user-supplied choice, and sends a corresponding message to the MyPod object.

The MyPod class is a bit more complex. The instance variables consist of:

- two parallel arrays:

  String[] names, and
  String[] clipFiles,

  that respectively hold the names of the audio clips and the corresponding names of the local audio files where the clips reside,
- two integers:

  numClips that holds the number of audio clips available, and
  selectedClip that holds the array index of the currently selected clip, and

- a reference variable audioClip that references an AudioClip object. AudioClip is a Java class that makes playing audio simple.

The methods of the MyPod class are:

- a default constructor that
  - reads the input file and uses the data of that file to fill the two arrays names and clipFiles, and
  - initializes numClips and selectedClip to 0
- and the methods that implement the functions of a MyPod object:

  playClip(),
  stopClip(),
  loopClip(),
  scrollUp(),
  scrollDown(),
  selectedClip(), and
  off()

Figure 10.11 shows a UI object and a MyPod object.

Notice that the instance variable audioClip holds a reference to an AudioClip object. AudioClip is one of the many classes that are part of Java's extensive library. The AudioClip class resides in the java.applet package, so in order to use this class, the statement

```
import java.applet.*;
```

is required.

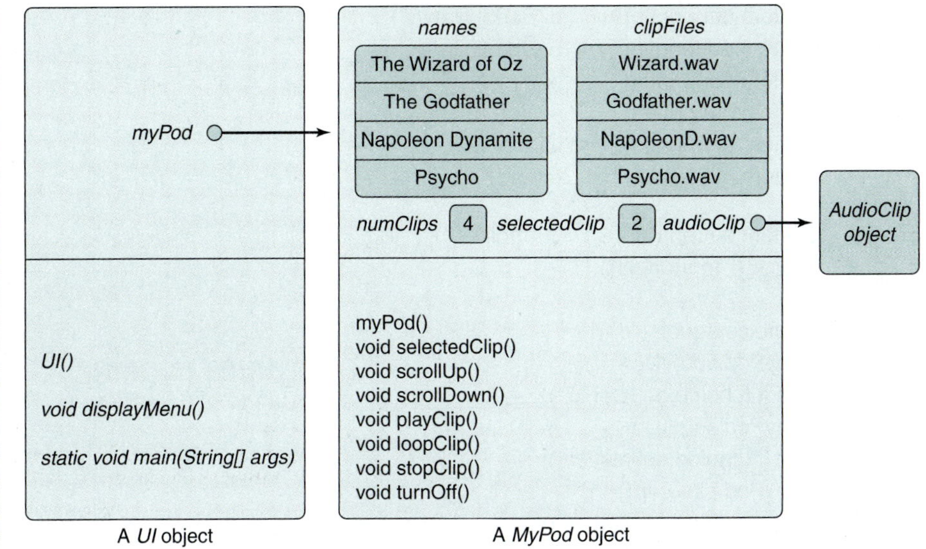

FIGURE 10.11 *UI* and *MyPod* objects

AudioClip supplies three handy methods for playing sound:

void play(),
void stop(), and
void loop().

We initialize an AudioClip object with the location of the file containing the clip. This is explained in greater detail in the discussion that follows.

The two classes that make up the application are:

UI class

```
import java.util.*;
import java.io.*;
public class UI
{
   private MyPod myPod;
   public UI() throws IOException    // since MyPod throws and IOException
   {
      myPod = new MyPod();
   }

   public void displayMenu() throws IOException
   {
      Scanner input = new Scanner(System.in);
      System.out.println();
      String choice = "";
      while(!choice.equals("e"))
      {
         System.out.println();
         System.out.println("      Menu:\n ");
```

```
         System.out.println("       d. Scroll Down");
         System.out.println("       u. Scroll Up");;
         System.out.println("       p. play ");
         System.out.println("       s. stop");
         System.out.println("       l. loop");
         System.out.println("       e. end\n");

         System.out.print("          Choice: ");
         choice = input.next();

         if (choice.equals("d"))
            myPod.scrollDown();
         else if (choice.equals("u"))
            myPod.scrollUp();
         else if (choice.equals("p"))
            myPod.playClip();
         else if (choice.equals("s"))
            myPod.stopClip();
         else if (choice.equals("l"))
            myPod.loopClip();
         else if (choice.equals("e"))
            myPod.turnOff();
         else
               System.out.println("Illegal choice: " + choice);
      }
   }

   public static void main(String[] args) throws IOException
   {
      UI ui = new UI();
      ui.displayMenu();
   }
}
```

MyPod class

```
import java.util.*;
import java.io.*;
import java.applet.*;
public class MyPod
{
   private String[] names;
   private String[] clipFiles;
   private int selectedClip, numClips;
   private AudioClip audioClip;

private final int MAXIMUM_CLIPS = 200;   // MyPod holds at most 200 clips

public MyPod() throws IOException
{
   Scanner console = new Scanner(System.in);
   System.out.print("\n File that lists audio clips: ");
   String filename = console.next();          // file that contains name and location of each clip
   File clipFile = new File(filename);
```

```
    names = new String[MAXIMUM_CLIPS];          // names of each clip
    clipFiles = new String[MAXIMUM_CLIPS];      // location (filename) of each clip

    selectedClip = 0;
    numClips = 0;

      // read the clip name as well as the filename for the clip
      // store the clipname in names
      // store the corresponding filename in clipFiles

    Scanner input = new Scanner(clipFile);

    while (input.hasNext())
    {
      names[numClips] = input.nextLine();
      clipFiles[numClips] = input.nextLine();
      numClips++;
    }
    input.close();
    selectedClip();
  }

  private void selectedClip()
  {
    // Displays name of the selected clip
    System.out.println("Selected Clip: " + names[selectedClip] + "\n");
  }

  public void scrollDown()
  {
    // selects next clip
    if (selectedClip < numClips - 1)
      selectedClip++;
    selectedClip();
  }

  public void scrollUp()
  {
    // selects previous clip
    if (selectedClip > 0) // cannot scroll past first clip
      selectedClip--;
    selectedClip();
  }

  public void playClip()throws IOException
  {
    selectedClip();                 // display name
    if (audioClip != null)          // stops playing current clip
        audioClip.stop();           // prevents two clips from playing simultaneously

    // instantiate a File object for the file where the clip is stored

    File file = new File(clipFiles[selectedClip]);
    // instantiate an AudioClip using the URL of the File object
    audioClip = Applet.newAudioClip(file.toURL());
    audioClip.play();               // method of AudioClip
  }

  public void loopClip()throws IOException
```

```
   {
      selectedClip();
      if (audioClip != null)
         audioClip.stop();
      File file = new File(clipFiles[selectedClip]);
      audioClip = Applet.newAudioClip(file.toURL());
      audioClip.loop();                       // method of AudioClip
   }

   public void stopClip()
   {
      selectedClip();
      if (audioClip != null)
         audioClip.stop();                    // method of AudioClip
   }

   public void turnOff()
   {
      System.out.println("\n\n*****Turning off myPod....Bye*****\n\n");
   }

}
```

The input file, FilmClips.txt, contains the following lines of text:

```
The Wizard of Oz
Wizard.wav
Casablanca
Casablanca.wav
Citizen Kane
CitizenKane.wav
Ferris Bueller's Day Off
FerrisBueller.wav
The Godfather
Godfather.wav
Gone With the Wind
GWTW.wav
Napoleon Dynamite
NapoleonDynamite.wav
Psycho
Psycho.wav
A Streetcar Named Desire
Streetcar.wav
Sunset Blvd.
SunsetBlvd.wav
Tarzan
tarzan.wav
```

Output The output from the program includes sound clips. Due to the rather severe limitations of the printed page, we substitute a textual representation of each selected audio clip.

File that lists audio clips: **FilmClips.txt**

Selected Clip: The Wizard of Oz Menu: d. Scroll Down u. Scroll Up p. play s. stop l. loop e. end Choice: **p** *Toto, I've a feeling we're not in Kansas anymore*	Selected Clip: The Wizard of Oz Menu: d. Scroll Down u. Scroll Up p. play s. stop l. loop e. end Choice: **d**	Selected Clip: Casablanca Menu: d. Scroll Down u. Scroll Up p. play s. stop l. loop e. end Choice: **d**	Selected Clip: Citizen Kane Menu: d. Scroll Down u. Scroll Up p. play s. stop l. loop e. end Choice: **d**	Selected Clip: Ferris Bueller's Day Off Menu: d. Scroll Down u. Scroll Up p. play s. stop l. loop e. end Choice: **p** *I asked for a car, I got a computer. How is that for being born under a bad sign?*	Selected Clip: Ferris Bueller's Day Off Menu: d. Scroll Down u. Scroll Up p. play s. stop l. loop e. end Choice: **e** *****Turning off myPod . . . . Bye*****

Discussion The UI class, which contains the main(...) method of the application, is the interface to the myPod player. The displayMenu() method continually presents a user with options. Each time a user makes a choice, the UI object sends an appropriate message to the MyPod object. For example, if the choice is "p", then UI sends the message myPod.playClip() to the MyPod object. The application terminates when the user enters "e".

The MyPod class is a bit more complex than the UI class.

Lines 1–3:
The package java.util is required for the Scanner class; java.io for the File class; and java.applet for the AudioClip class.

Lines 6–9:
The array names stores the name of each audio clip and the array clipFiles the name of the corresponding audio file. For example, if names[0] holds the string "The Wizard of Oz" then, correspondingly, clipFile[0] gets the filename Wizard.wav. In this sense, the arrays are *parallel*.

The integer variable numClips is the number of clips currently available, and selectedClip is the array index of the "current" clip.

Finally, audioClip is a reference to an AudioClip object. AudioClip is a Java class that is part of the java.applet package.

Because each field is private, only the methods of MyPod can access these variables.

Lines 11–33: The default constructor, MyPod()

Lines 13: A Scanner object is created for interactive input.

Lines 14–15: The user is prompted for the name of a file that contains the name of each film and the filename of each corresponding audio clip. In the sample run, this file is FilmClips.txt.

Line 16: A File object is instantiated using the supplied filename. The local variable clipFile references this File object.

Lines 17–20: The two arrays (names and clipFiles) are instantiated and the two fields numClips and selectedClip are initialized to 0.

Line 24: A Scanner object capable of reading from the input file (clipFile) is instantiated.

Line 25: The loop executes as long as there is still more data to be read from clipFile.

Line 27: Read the name of an audio clip from clipFile, and store the name in names.

Line 28: Read the filename of an audioclip from clipFile, and store the filename in clipFiles.

Line 29: Increment numClips.

Line 31: Close the input file.

Line 32: Display the selected clip (index 0) by invoking the private method selectedClip().

Notice that the heading of the default constructor, MyPod(), contains the phrase throws IOException. This clause is necessary when using a File object. You will learn more about these mysterious "exceptions," where they're "thrown," and what "catches" them in Chapter 14. For now, however, it is necessary to include this clause not only in the heading of MyPod() but also in the heading of any method or constructor in the chain of calls that eventually calls MyPod(). What is this chain of calls? Well, on line 45 of UI, main(...) invokes UI() and then, on line 8, UI() invokes MyPod(). Thus, the chain of calls that eventually invokes MyPod() is main(...) → UI() → MyPod(). Consequently, each of these methods or constructors includes the throws IOException clause in its heading.

If you forget to include a throws clause, the compiler issues an error message to that effect and you can easily remedy the situation.

Lines 34–38: These lines comprise a method that prints the name of the selected audio clip. The name of each clip is stored in the array names. The method has private access and is used only in the class.

Lines 39–52: The scrollDown() and scrollUp() methods increment and decrement the selectedClip field. Calling these methods is akin to pushing the "down" and "up" buttons on a myPod. See Figure 10.10. Both methods ensure that the variable selectedClip is in the range 0 to numClips – 1. Each of these methods invokes the helper method selectedClip() that displays the name of the selected clip.

Lines 53–63: The playClip() method plays the audio clip.

Line 53: Because the method uses a File object (line 61), the clause throws IOException is necessary.

Line 55: The call selectedClip() displays the name of the current clip.

Lines 56–57: If a previous clip is still playing when the user invokes the playClip() method, the message audioClip.stop() terminates that clip. Without this message, the two clips would play simultaneously.

Line 59: A File object is instantiated with the name of the audio file that is stored in clipFiles[selectedClip]. For example, the audio file might be Wizard.wav, Casablanca.wav, or FerrisBueller.wav.

Line 61: The statement on this line is the heart of playClip(). The instance variable audioClip is a reference to an AudioClip object. However, in this case, the AudioClip object is not created using the familiar new operator. Instead, the static method

```
static public AudioClip Applet.newAudioClip(URL url)
```

returns a reference to an audio clip. This method is a member of the Applet class, which is part of the java.applet package. Because the method is static, it can be invoked via the class name, Applet.

The parameter supplied to this method is a URL reference.

As you probably know, a *Uniform Resource Locator* or *URL* is the address of an Internet resource such as a file or a database. For example, http://www.google.com is a valid URL. Another form of a URL is a file URL that specifies the address of a file stored on your computer. For example,

```
file:///C:/MyAudioFiles/Wizard.wav
```

is a file URL.

The parameter passed to Applet.newAudioClip() is a URL *object*. Java has a URL class that encapsulates a URL. Fortunately, instantiating a URL object with a File reference is easy:

If file is a File reference, then the method call

```
file. toURL()
```

converts the pathname of the file to a URL object, no questions asked. Thus, the statement

```
audioClip = Applet.newAudioClip(file.toURL());
```

- calls toURL() which returns a URL object instantiated with file,
- passes the newly created URL object to the static method, Applet.newAudioClip(URL url),
- returns a reference to an AudioClip object, and finally
- assigns the reference to audioClip.

Line 62: The play() method of the AudioClip class is invoked via the audioClip object. The clip (hopefully) plays.

Lines 64–72: The loopClip() method works like playClip(). However, the call audioClip.loop() plays the clip continuously.

Lines 73–78: The stopClip() method invokes the stop() method of AudioClip. The condition on line 76 (if (audioClip != null)) is necessary because if a call to stop() occurs before an audioClip object is created, the JVM issues a runtime error and terminates the program.

Lines 79–82: The turnOff() method display a "good-bye message" on the screen.

Design Tip Encapsulating the user interface and the myPod player into two distinct classes makes the application modular. Later, when you learn how to implement a graphical user interface, you can replace this text-based interface with the graphical interface; and you can accomplish this with absolutely no change to the MyPod class. Sure, we *could* have designed one big class to do all the work, but alterations and upgrades would be bug-prone and would require more overhead, that is, more code rewrites. Modularity provides code reuse, "and that's a good thing."

10.12 IN CONCLUSION

This chapter discusses encapsulation via programmer-defined classes. Although Java provides hundreds of ready-made classes, the need for specialized classes is always present. Classes and objects bundle data and methods together into a single entity. This bundling of attributes and behaviors, that is, encapsulation, is the very foundation of OOP.

The chapter also uncovers a few other Java mysteries: the keywords public and static that we have been using from the very beginning now have meaning. Still, the phrase throws IOException requires a bit of an explanation, and in Chapter 14 we explain exactly what is "thrown" by this statement. In the following chapters, we continue the study of program design using classes and objects, and we examine two more key OOP concepts: inheritance and polymorphism.

Just the Facts

- A constructor is a special kind of method that instantiates and initializes objects.
- Unlike conventional methods, a constructor cannot be called directly. A constructor is invoked automatically whenever a new object is instantiated.
- Unlike ordinary methods, the name of a constructor is the same as the name of the class.
- A constructor may have an access modifier—public, private, or none at all. All constructors that we use are public.
- Unlike a conventional method, a constructor has no return type, not even void.
- A class may have any number of constructors that differ in the number of parameters. A constructor with no parameters is the *no-argument* or *default* constructor.
- It is a good programming practice to provide a default constructor as part of any class that you design.
- If you include no constructors for a class, Java provides a default constructor.
- If a class provides constructors but no default constructor, Java does not provide a default constructor.
- A method that returns the value of some private variables is called a *getter* method.
- A method that assigns or alters the value of one of the instance variables is called a *setter* method.
- A class can have any number of *instance variables* or *fields*. Instance variables are directly accessible to all methods of a class and are not passed as arguments.
- The words public and private are called access modifiers. They are used in front of variables, methods, and classes. If no access modifier is specified for a class, then the class has *package access*.
- Instance variables are *usually* declared as private. private instance variables are not visible outside of a class. public instance variables are accessible to all code outside the class, and a variable with no access modifier is accessible only to classes within its package.
- The public methods of a class constitute the interface of the class. The public methods of a class can provide access to instance variables.
- Most methods are declared public, but it is often useful to write private methods intended for exclusive use by other methods within the class.
- Encapsulation is the mechanism that bundles data and methods into a single entity.
- Information hiding is the principle that hides implementation details from a client class.
- The keyword this used in a method is a reference to the current object, that is, the object currently invoking the method.
- A static variable, as opposed to an instance variable, belongs to the class and not to any particular object. A static variable is shared by all objects of the class.
- A static variable can be accessed with the class name, or via an object of the class, if one exists.
- A static method belongs collectively to the class, rather than individually to the objects of the class. A static method can be invoked using the class name, such as Math.sqrt(), or by an object of the class, if one exists.
- A static method may invoke static methods and use static data. A static method may not invoke a non-static method or manipulate instance variables, except via an object. Thus, if a static method creates an object, then non-static methods and data can be accessed through that object.

- A static method may not use the reference this, which by definition refers to an object.
- The Java Virtual Machine automatically reclaims the memory space of all unreferenced objects. This process is called *garbage collection.*
- A memory leak occurs when an application maintains references to obsolete objects. Even though Java provides automatic garbage collection, careless programming can cause memory leaks.

Bug Extermination

- Do not combine too much functionality in a single method. Assign a single task to each method of a class.
- When designing and implementing a class, work incrementally. Add a method; test the method; add another method; test that method. By working with small pieces, bugs are localized and easier to find.
- Add output statements to your methods, including constructors, to be sure that they are working correctly. When you are convinced of the correctness of a method, remove the output statements.
- Provide getter and setter methods for variables that a client may need to access. Instance variables are usually private, and access is provided via getter and setter methods.
- To avoid a memory leak, set all object references to null when an object is no longer needed.
- It is natural for a constructor to call another constructor. You should use this to accomplish the call, otherwise the compiler generates a "method unknown" error. For example:

```
ClassConstructor(int x)
{
    privateData = x;
}
ClassConstructor()
{
    ClassConstructor(0)
}
```

  generates an error, but

```
ClassConstructor(int x)
{
    privateData = x;
}
ClassConstructor()
{
    this(0)
}
```

  works fine.
- A static method cannot call an instance method, except via an object. In particular, main(...) cannot call an instance method except via an object.
- If you provide any constructors, it is good practice to provide a default constructor.

EXERCISES

LEARN THE LINGO

Test your knowledge of the chapter's vocabulary by completing the following crossword puzzle.

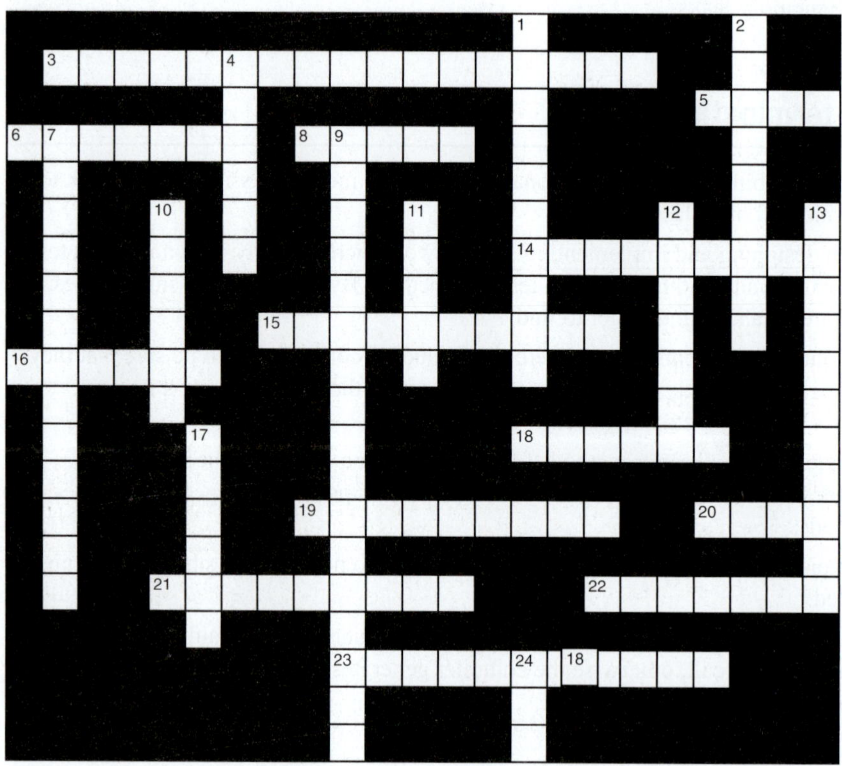

Across

3 How Java automatically reclaims the memory space of all unreferenced objects
5 A public class is saved with this extension.
6 No-argument constructor
8 An instance variable
14 Type of character that usually begins class name
15 An application that maintains references to objects no longer needed causes a ________.
16 Access modifier
18 Method that changes the value of an instance variable
19 Public methods of a class constitute the ________ of the class.
20 To avoid a memory leak, set all references to ________ once an object is no longer needed.
21 Methods
22 Only the methods of a class have access to ________ instance variables.
23 To create a new object

Down

1 Data of an object
2 The name of the constructor is the ________.
4 Method that returns the value of an instance variable
7 Data and methods in a single bundle
9 Principle that hides class information
10 Class method
11 If a class has a static variable, all objects of the class ________ that variable.
12 Normally, instance variables have ________ access.
13 A constructor has no ________.
17 AudioClip class belongs to the package java.________.
24 Operator that creates an object

SHORT EXERCISES

1. **True or False**
   If false, give an explanation.
   a. Java does not allow a programmer to write her own classes.
   b. A private method of a class is accessible to every method of the class.
   c. A public method of a class is accessible to every method of the class.
   d. A public method of a class is accessible to any method external to the class.
   e. A private instance variable is accessible to every method in the class.
   f. A private instance variable is accessible to any method external to the class.
   g. A static variable is the same as an instance variable.
   h. A static variable is shared by all objects of a class.
   i. A static variable x can be accessed by an object p, the same way any instance variable is accessed, namely p.x.
   j. A constructor is a special kind of method with no return type, not even void.
   k. Constructors initialize and instantiate objects.
   l. Only one constructor per class is permitted.
   m. Constructors cannot be overloaded.
   n. If you fail to define a constructor, Java provides a default constructor.
   o. Java can read your mind.
   p. Java's *garbage collection* is more like recycling.
   q. An object is garbage when it is no longer referenced.
   r. The keyword this is a reference to the calling object.
   s. The keyword that allows a method to refer directly to the reference of the called object.
   t. An instance variable must be a built-in Java type, and not a programmer-defined class.

2. **Designing Classes**
   Describe the public methods, instance variables, private methods, static methods, static variables, and/or constructors that you would use to implement the following classes.
   a. A Cell Phone
      - The phone is either on or off, and in-use or not in-use.
      - The phone has its own phone number as well as a list of *n* frequently called numbers.
      - The phone can display its own number as well as the list of frequently called numbers.
      - You can "speed-dial" a frequently called number by providing an integer in the range 1 through *n* that indexes a stored phone number.
      - You can determine whether or not the phone is ringing, and if so, answer the phone.
      - If you make a call or answer a call, the phone is *in-use*.
      - You can make a call only if the phone is not *in-use*.
      - You can hang up the phone, and then it is not *in-use*.
      - You can turn the phone on or off. If you turn it off you also hang up.
      - Your phone remembers all numbers that you dial and stores them.
      - You can view the list of numbers you have dialed.
      - You can redial the most recently called number.
   b. A Computer Speaker
      - A speaker has a green LED that is either on or off.
      - A speaker has a power switch that toggles the power.

- A speaker has a volume switch with 10 settings, 0–9 inclusive.
- A speaker has a color (black, gray, white).
- A speaker has a power rating (high, medium, and low).
- You can bump the volume up or down. Bumping up from 9 or down from 0 has no effect.

3. **Fix the Errors**

Determine and correct the errors in the following Java class.

```
Class TestMe
{
    private int x, y; char y; char z;
    static private useme = 0;
    Testme()
    {
      x = y = 0;
      y = z = '';
      useme++
    }

    void TestMe(int num, char ch)
    {
          x = y = num;
          y = z = ch;
          useme++
    }

    private void method1()
    {
          return (x + y);
    }

    void method2()
    {
          System.out.println(return (method1(x, y)/2);
    }

    public static main(String[] args)
    {
          object1 = new TestMe();
          TestMe object2 = TestMe(3, 'X');
          System.out.println(object1.method1());
          System.out.println(object2.method2);
          System.out.println(Object1.method1());
          System.out.println(TestMe.useme;)
          System.out.println(TestMe.method2(););
    }
}
```

4. **Class Basics**

Answer the following questions regarding the following class.

a. What are the instance variables?
b. Which methods are public and which are private?
c. What is the name of the class?
d. What is the name of an object of this class?

e. Is MyClass.tryMe(); a legal statement?
f. Is MyClass.tryMeToo(); a legal statement?
g. Determine the output.

```
class MyClass
{
private int var1, var2;
private String var3, var4;
static private int count;

    public MyClass()
    {
        count++;
    }

    private void myMethod()
    {
        System.out.println("MyMethod");
    }

    String tryMe(String x)
    {
        System.out.println(++ var1);
        System.out.println (++ var2 + var1);
        System.out.println (var3 + "link" + var4) ; return("tryMe" + x);
    }

    static void tryMeToo()
    {
        for (int j = 0; j < count; j++)
        System.out.println("tryMeToo");
        System.out.println();
    }

    public static void main(String[] args)
    {
        MyClass x = new MyClass();
        System.out.println(x.tryMe(" first try "));
        x.tryMeToo(); MyClass y = new MyClass();
        x.tryMeToo(); y.tryMeToo();
    }

}
```

5. **What's the Output?**
Be very careful. These are difficult and a bit tricky.

a.
```
public class Quine
{
  public static void main(String[] args)
  {
    char c = 34;
    System.out.print(s + c + s + c + ' ; ' + '}');
  }
  static String s1 = "public class Quine{public static void main(String[] args)";
  static String s2 = "{char c = 34;System.out.print(s + c + s + c + ';' + '}');} static String s =";
  static String s = s1 + s2;
}
```

b. public class LinkMeUp

```
{
    private int data;
    private LinkMeUp next;

    LinkMeUp(int num)
    {
        data = num * num; next = null;
    }

    LinkMeUp()
    {
        this(0);
    }

    LinkMeUp add(int num)
    {
        LinkMeUp temp = new LinkMeUp(num);
        temp.next = this;
        return(temp);
    }

    void print()
    {
        LinkMeUp temp = this;
        while (temp != null)
        {
            System.out.println(temp.data);
            temp = temp.next;
        }
    }

    public static void main(String[] args)
    {
        LinkMeUp link = new LinkMeUp();
        for (int k = 1; k < 10; k++)
            link = link.add(k);
        link.print();
    }
}
```

6. **Fix the Errors**

Find all the errors in the following program and correct them so that the program does what it is supposed to do. There are syntax errors and semantic (logical) errors. The easiest way to do this is with your compiler's assistance.

The following program is supposed to create a class ArrayHandler with three methods:

a. A constructor ArrayHandler(int n) that creates an array, arr, of length n containing random elements in the range 0 to $n - 1$.
b. partitionArray(), which partitions the array around the first element a = arr[0] of arr. This means the array is reordered so that:
   - a is repositioned in the array,
   - all elements "to the left" of a are less than or equal to a, and
   - all elements "to the right" of a are greater than or equal to a.

   For example if arr is: [**7**, 2, 15, 9, 13, 26, 36, 1], then one possible partitioning rearranges arr as [2, 1, **7**, 15, 9, 13, 26, 36].

c. PrintArray(), which displays the contents of the array arr.

```
Class ArrayHandler
{
   private int[] arr;

   ArrayHandler(int n)
   {
         for (int j = 0; j < n; j++)
         arr[j] = math.rand(n);
         length = n;
   }

   ArrayHandler() // Default constructor sets up an empty array
   {
         ArrayHandler(0);
   }

   public void partitionArray()
   {
            int temp[] = new int (arr.length);

            // This iterates through the array element by element, from the second element until the end.
            // If an element is smaller than the first element then that element is copied to a new array.
            // After going through the whole array, the first element is then copied to the new array.
            // The original array is once again examined element by element from the second element.
            // If an element is larger than the first element (or equal to it) then that element is copied
            // to the new array.

            int index = 0;
            for (int k = 1; k < arr.length; k++) if arr[k] < arr[0] temp[index] = arr[k]; index++;
            temp[index] = a[0]; index++;
            for (int k = 1; k < arr.length; k++) if arr[k] >= arr[0] temp[index] = arr[k]; index++
   }
}

public void printArray()
{
            for int m = 0; m < length ; m++) System.out.println(arr[m]); System.print(' ');
            // Print a space after each number
            // Skip a line after all the numbers are printed
            System.out.println();
}

public static main(String args)
{
         ArrayHandler t = new ArrayHandler(25);
         t.printArray(); t.partitionArray; t.printArray();}
}
```

PROGRAMMING EXERCISES

1. **A TV Class**

   The attributes of a TV object are the channel, the volume, and a flag (or switch) indicating whether the TV is on or off. The methods perform the following actions:

   - Turn the TV on or off.
   - Set the channel to an integer from 0 to 99 inclusive.

- Raise or lower the volume by one unit. The volume can range from 0 to 20.
- View the value of the volume.
- View the channel.
- Determine whether the TV is on or off.

Write a TV class that implements all relevant functions. A newly created TV object is set to *off* with the channel set to 2 and the volume initially 10. Include a main(...) method that tests the methods of the TV class.

2. **A SuperDie Class**
   Write a class SuperDie that models a single die with an arbitrary number of sides, not just six. A die instantiated with the default constructor has six sides. The methods of this class should be:
   - roll a die and return its value,
   - return the number of sides on a die, and
   - change the number of sides on a die.

   Include a main(...) method that tests all the methods of your class.

3. **The SuperDice Class**
   Write a class called SuperDice that defines a collection of SuperDie objects. (See Exercise 2.)
   The instance variables include a field that holds the number of dice in the collection as well as an array that holds SuperDie objects. The SuperDice class should have methods that
   - change the number of sides on any particular die,
   - return the number of sides on any die,
   - roll all the dice and return the sum of the dice, and
   - return the number of dice in the collection.

   The default constructor creates a single die with six sides. A one-argument constructor accepts an array of n values giving the number of sides on each of n dice. A two-argument constructor with two integer parameters p and q defines p dice each with q sides.
   Test your class by writing a main method that:
   - randomly rolls a collection of five dice (one 6-sided, one 20-sided, one 4-sided, one 8-sided, and one 12-sided) 100 times, and reports the average of the sum of the five dice,
   - randomly rolls a single 6-sided die 100 times, and reports the average,
   - randomly rolls three 6-sided dice 100 times, and reports the average, and
   - randomly rolls three 20-sided dice 100 times, and reports the average.

4. **A Counter Class**
   The single instance variable (counter) of a Counter object holds a non-negative integer. The methods of the Counter class allow a client to add 1 to counter, set the value of counter to zero, and retrieve the current value of counter. The default constructor sets counter to zero, and the one-argument constructor initializes counter to a non-negative integer.
   Implement a Counter class and test your class by writing a main(...) method that
   - instantiates a Counter object,
   - interactively reads a sequence of integers until a zero is entered,
   - and uses the Counter object to determine how many non-zero integers comprise the sequence.

5. **A FancyCounter Class**
   a. A FancyCounter class is similar to the Counter class of Programming Exercise 4, but with an additional method that decrements counter. Consequently, counter can hold a negative number. Implement and test the FancyCounter class.

b. A BalancedString class has two instance variables:
String str, and
FancyCounter counter.

The default constructor of BalancedString initializes str to the empty string and resets counter to zero. The class's one-argument constructor passes a String *s* to str and resets counter to zero. The BalancedString class also provides a boolean method

boolean balanced()

that returns true if a string contains a balanced set of parentheses.

For example: the string "((hello)(goodbye))" has balanced parentheses, but "((a)(b)(())" does not. A string with no parentheses is balanced.

To check whether or not a string contains a balanced set of parentheses:

Scan the string, left to right:
if a character is a left parenthesis, increment the counter, and
if a character is a right parenthesis, decrement the counter.

A string is balanced if
the final counter value equals 0, and
while scanning the string, the value of the counter is never negative.

Implement and test the BalancedString class.

6. **A Door Class**

A computer game usually has many different objects that can be seen and manipulated. One typical object is a door. Whether a player runs through a castle, attacks the forces of an evil empire, or places furniture in a room, a door often comes into play.

Implement a Door class as described below as well as a TestDoor class that instantiates three Door objects labeled "Enter," "Exit," and "Treasure." The "Enter" door should be left unlocked and opened. The "Exit" door should be left closed and locked. The "Treasure" door should be left open but locked.

A Door class

A Door object can
- display an inscription,
- be either open or closed, and
- be either locked or unlocked.

Here are some rules about how Doors work.
- Once the writing on a Door is set, it cannot be changed.
- You may open a Door if and only if it is unlocked and closed.
- You may close a Door if and only if it is open.
- You may lock a Door if and only if it is unlocked, and unlock a Door if and only if it is locked. You should be able to check whether or not a Door is closed, check whether or not it is locked, and look at the writing on the Door if there is any.

The instance variables of a Door class are:
- String inscription,
- boolean locked, and
- boolean closed.

The methods (all public) should be:
- Door(String c); // Constructor - initializes a Door with inscription c, closed and locked.
- isClosed(); // Returns *true* if the Door is closed
- isLocked(); // Returns *true* if a Door is locked.
- open(); // Opens a Door if it is closed and unlocked.
- close(); // Closes a Door if it is open.
- lock(); // Locks a Door if it is unlocked.
- unlock(); // Unlocks a Door if it is locked.

Appropriate error messages should be displayed, if any conditions of the methods are violated.

7. **A Reader Class**

Applications frequently query a user for a string that must be one of a few specific words, such as *yes, no, quit, or start.*

A Reader class implements a method that queries a user for one of the acceptable words and returns the user's response. The one-argument constructor

```
Reader( String[] words)
```

accepts an array that holds the valid or expected words. The default constructor creates a Reader object with a single valid word, *okay*. The single method of Reader repeatedly requests a response from a user until he/she supplies a valid response. The method returns that string with the user's response.

Assume that the Reader class is used in a game where the valid responses from a player are

- *play,*
- *quit,* or
- *instructions.*

If *play* is chosen, then the player is asked whether he/she would like to go first or second. That is, the valid choices are *first* and *second.* Once a player chooses *first* or *second*, the game would commence with the player going first or second as entered. If *instructions* is chosen, then the only valid follow-up is to type *okay* when done reading the game rules and return to the main option of *play, quit, instructions.* If *quit* is chosen, then the program halts.

Write a main(...) method to test your class by setting up a framework for a game program. In your program, there is no actual game, so after the user chooses *first* or *second*, your application should return to the main *play, quit, instructions* option.

8. **A Couple of Interacting Classes and a Game**

Most applications are comprised of several classes that interact by sending messages one to another. Write an application that allows two players to play the game of Nim. The "gameboard" for Nim consists of any number of piles of sticks. Each pile contains an arbitrary number of sticks. Players take turns removing sticks from a single pile. A player can remove any number of sticks at his/her turn, but only from one pile. The player to remove the last stick wins the game.

The application should

- ask each player to enter his/her name,
- choose randomly the player who goes first, and
- play the game.

When a game is over, the application should

- display a message stating which player won, and
- ask the players if they would like to play again.

When all games are complete, the application should

- display the number of games won by each player.

To implement this application, consider using two interacting classes, Game and Player. The design of the classes is up to you. Example 10.3 might provide you with a few ideas.

9. **A MyString Class and a *JUMBLE* Program**

When you play a *JUMBLE*, you are given a scrambled word that you must unscramble. For instance, you may be given *iedmx* and you would be expected to unscramble it to *mixed*.

Write an application that prompts for a list of words and displays four jumbled versions of each word so that you might choose one for creating your own *JUMBLE*. For example:

How many words?

3

Enter the words:

mixed

calendar

then

Output:

Here is a list of possible *JUMBLE*s:

mixed	calendar	then
iedmx	lendarca	hent
dixem	alecdarn	neth
medix	randlace	enth
eximd	recandla	tenh

Hint: Create a class called MyString that stores and manipulates strings. The one-argument constructor should accept a String argument. The methods should include:

```
void printme();     // prints the String.
```

and

```
String MyString permute();
// returns a permuted version of the String.
// This can be done by exchanging random pairs of letters in the String.
// If the length of your string is n, then perform 2n swaps.
```

10. **A StopWatch Class**

A good stopwatch displays elapsed time in hours, minutes, and seconds (to the hundredth).

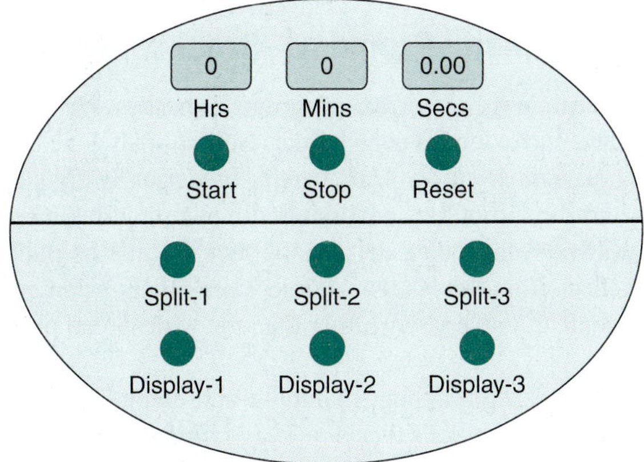

FIGURE 10.12 A stopwatch

Design a StopWatch class that models the stopwatch in Figure 10.12.

You can start the StopWatch, stop the StopWatch, and reset the time to zero. When you stop the StopWatch, the elapsed time remains visible until it is reset to zero. When you start the StopWatch, it continues counting from the current display.

The StopWatch can also remember up to three *split-times* by pressing any one of three split-time buttons. A split-time is the elapsed time from the last time you pressed the same split-time button or from the time that you started the clock if it is the first time you hit that split-time button. Pressing a split-time button does not stop the clock. When you reset the stopwatch, all the split-times return to zero.

Any split-time can be displayed by pressing (and holding down) one of the three Display buttons. If no split-time has been calculated for a particular Display button, then holding the button shows zero. The clock keeps running during the time a Display button is held down, even though the running clock is not displayed. When a Display button is released, the stopwatch time (which continues to run) is once again displayed.

Implement a Stopwatch class as well as a class UseStopwatch that demonstrates the features of a Stopwatch object. Since you have no graphics toolkit yet, for simplicity you should display the time on the clock by printing it only at certain events. The time should be printed when the clock is started, reset, stopped, or any Display button is pressed or released. You will need methods for each of these events.

For simulating the clock, use the System method

```
longSystem.currentTimeMillis(),
```

which returns the current time in milliseconds, that is, the number of milliseconds since January 1, 1970.

THE BIGGER PICTURE

SOFTWARE ENGINEERING

The Software Productivity Problem—Brooks' Mythical Man Month

Writing programs is hard. Writing correct programs is harder. Writing programs that are easy to debug, maintain, and extend is even harder. Getting it all done on schedule is almost impossible. In his book, *The Mythical Man Month*, Frederick Brooks discusses large programming projects and the difficulties encountered when undertaking them. His short but important work is still relevant today, despite the fact that it was published in 1975 and was based on experiences from the 1960s—a time when object-oriented programming was primarily a research topic at universities rather than the widespread programming methodology that it is today.

The study of how to design, debug, maintain, and extend large software systems is called *software engineering*. Brooks's thesis in *The Mythical Man Month* is that large software projects have very different challenges from small ones. In particular, the difficult division of labor in designing large programs makes it extremely difficult to maintain the necessary organization and unity of concept that is critical to the success of the project.

His experience on IBM 360 machines in the 1960s, one of the first massive software efforts, formed the basis of his opinions. Most likely, you have not yet experienced such a large software project. You probably write your programs by yourself, or perhaps in a small team. However, very large software projects can employ hundreds of programmers.

How do we measure the size of a programming project? Although it is somewhat controversial and imperfect, the standard metric for measuring the size of a programming project is "lines of code," or LOC. To gain some perspective, note that a Java course programming assignment might consist of, perhaps, 100 lines of code; a team project might have 1000 to 5000 LOC; a large industry project has well over a million LOC; and a really large project, like the Windows XP operating system, has about 40 million LOC.

Indeed, a programmer's productivity is usually measured by LOC, on the theory that a better programmer, presumably, produces more lines of code per month. The average programmer in the United States creates about 6000 lines of shipped code per year—which means finished, debugged, and sold. This number may surprise you, because if you complete about 40 exercises in this text and perhaps one small project, you might well write over 6000 lines of code in a year! How could a beginner exceed the productivity of a professional? Brooks explains that it is much easier to be a productive programmer on small projects.

Brooks asserts that the programmer time needed to develop larger and larger systems is not linear. That is, doubling a program's size requires more than twice the programming time. Indeed, the industry average for developing a 6000-line program is about one programmer-year, but the average for a program 10 times as large (60,000 lines) is 15 programmer-years, and not 10 years as you might expect. This explains why you might write 6000 lines of code in a semester, while a professional takes a year. Your projects are very small compared to the industry standard. It is much easier to develop thirty 200-line programs than one 6000-line program. You might be able to produce as much, or more, per year than a professional who produces more polished, less-buggy code and works on very large projects.

Brooks's thesis: The productivity rate of programmers in LOC per year goes down with the size of the project.

Solutions to the Software Productivity Problem—Reusable Code

Brooks's thesis gives rise to what is called the *software productivity problem.* The history of software engineering is filled with attempts to solve this problem, and the notion of *reusable code* has been the focus of much effort.

Reusable code is what it sounds like—building applications and systems using code that has already been developed and tested, rather than writing everything from scratch.

The whole style of Java with its massive libraries of built-in classes is a good example of reusable code. Creating larger usable code blocks turns programming into a more efficient practice. The analogies with physical engineering are clear—there are many parts of a design that are not specific to the problem at hand and can be lifted "pre-fab" from a previous design.

There have been many proposals aimed at making code more reusable, and thus increasing productivity, minimizing failure, maximizing efficiency, localizing and minimizing bugs, and solving the software problem discussed by Brooks. The concept of a function (in C or Lisp) or subroutine (in Fortran) was one of the first and simplest forms of code reusability. Functions and subroutines formed the basis of two different programming paradigms, one called *procedural programming* and the other *functional programming,* each with its own adherents.

The current standard paradigm that purports to provide code reusability is *object-oriented programming* (OOP). As you have seen in this chapter, the OOP concepts of encapsulation and information hiding allow the building of classes that can be cleanly lifted and reused. For example, the Dice class is "reused" in the ChoHan class.

There are a number of new ideas "beyond OOP" that promote code reuse. One of these is called *software componentry*. Software componentry pushes the analogy between software components and hardware components. It proposes that software should be developed by "gluing" prefabricated components together just as is done in electrical engineering or mechanical engineering.

A *component* sounds like an object, but unlike objects components do not necessarily model real-world entities. A component is defined by a useful chunk of engineering and not by a conceptual representation of the objects we imagine in our programs. *Component-oriented programming* (COP) may be the new kid on the block in the years to come. Nonetheless, some people consider OOP and COP to be the same paradigm with just two different points of view. In the exercises, we ask you to further investigate COP.

The *software problem* as discussed by Brooks is a fundamental practical problem in the efficient design of large computer systems. Software engineers struggle to find paradigms implemented or supported by new computer languages that will help solve this problem and ultimately bring software engineering onto the same solid ground as more traditional engineering disciplines.

Exercises

1. Explain why lines of code is a good metric for measuring the size of a programming project.
2. What aspects of *large* programs do you think LOC does not measure well?
3. How do you suggest counting LOC? Can you think of variations or controversy about how to count?
4. Is LOC a reasonable way to measure the effectiveness and skill of a programmer? Argue for both sides.
5. "The obsession with reusable code has produced software that, due to the lack of efficiency, was not even usable, not to mention reusable." *Dov Bulka, David Mayhew, Efficient C++: Performance Programming Techniques,* p. 223. What do you think this quote means? Explain why reusability and performance are not necessarily compatible goals.
6. Some claim that the benefits of OOP are lost on a novice who has no experience with the large systems for which the paradigm is intended. What is your experience? Do you feel that classes are providing you with flexibility or are they just getting in your way?
7. The previous paragraphs briefly mentioned component-oriented programming. Investigate component-oriented programming and compare it to object-oriented programming. Do you think they are qualitatively different or just two different views of the same idea?
8. (Research Paper): Investigate the history of programming languages, and list the breakthroughs that were supposed to help solve the *software productivity problem*. In what ways was each breakthrough successful and in what ways did each fail?

CHAPTER 11

Designing with Classes and Objects

"The greatest challenge to any thinker is stating the problem in a way that will allow a solution."

—Bertrand Russell

"Design is a plan for arranging elements in such a way as best to accomplish a particular purpose."

—Charles Eames

"Design is not just what it looks like and feels like. Design is how it works."

—Steve Jobs

"Design is everything. Everything!"

—Paul Rand

Objectives

The main objectives of Chapter 11 include an understanding of

- The basic principles of program design with objects and classes,
- a methodology for determining the classes of a large application,
- a system for determining how those classes should interact with each other, and
- incremental implementation and testing.

11.1 INTRODUCTION

In this chapter our focus shifts away from language features to program design. Here, our concern is not the syntax, semantics, or mechanics of Java but an informal procedure for determining the appropriate classes and objects of an application. The heart of the chapter is problem solving and object-oriented design.

Stylistically, the chapter is a departure from previous chapters: rather than presenting a number of short examples, we develop one large case study. We begin with a problem statement and conclude with a fully implemented video poker game comprised of a collection of interacting objects. On the way, we formulate a design methodology. The classes of our application are not lengthy, and indeed many contain just a few lines. However, each class is a small piece of the solution to a much larger problem.

Sections 11.2 through 11.8 provide an introduction to object-oriented design, and constitute the chapter's most important sections. In these sections, we demonstrate how to choose the classes of a relatively large video poker application and determine how the objects of these classes interact. Section 11.9, which discusses the implementation of the game, is more technical and laden with code. On first reading, you might study Section 11.9 paying attention to the design issues but ignoring or skimming the poker algorithms and their implementations. Indeed, 11.9 can be skipped entirely without loss of continuity. Alternatively, you might read Sections 11.2 through 11.8 and attempt your own implementation of the requisite classes.

Designing with objects is both an art and a science. Mastery comes with practice. So, let's get some practice.

11.2 THE PROBLEM: A VIDEO POKER GAME

Casinos are not lacking in video games and, along with slot machines, video poker games, such as the one shown in Figure 11.1, are among the most popular.

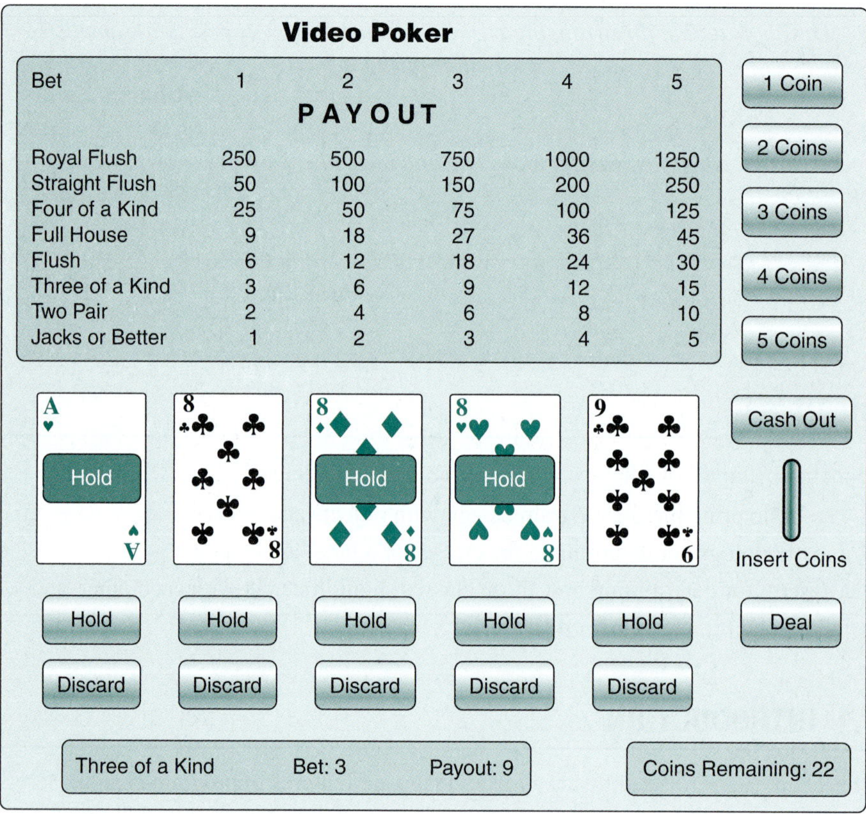

FIGURE 11.1 A video poker machine

11.2.1 Playing the Game

The machine of Figure 11.1 simulates a single hand of five-card stud poker.
To play the video poker game:

- A player deposits an arbitrary number of coins or tokens into the machine. We call this amount the player's *bankroll*.
- The player makes a bet (one to five coins but not more than the bankroll).

- A hand of five cards is dealt from a deck of 52 cards. The deck is reshuffled before each game.
- After viewing his/her hand, the player decides which cards he/she wishes to keep and which he/she would like to replace.
- New cards are dealt for those cards that the player chooses to discard.
- The hand is evaluated and scored.
- If the hand is a winner, a payout amount is added to the bankroll; otherwise, the bet is deducted from the bankroll.
- The player can quit and cash out at any time.
- The player can continue to play as long as the bankroll is not depleted.
- The player can add coins to the bankroll before each game.

Figure 11.1 shows the winning hands and the corresponding payouts for some bets of one to five coins.

11.2.2 Scoring the Game

A standard deck of cards consists of 52 different cards. Each card has a *rank* or *value* as well as a *suit*. The ordered ranks are

Ace, 2, 3, 4, 5, 6, 7, 8, 9, 10, Jack, Queen, King, (Ace).

Note that, in rank, an Ace precedes 2 and also follows King. The suits are hearts, diamonds, spades, and clubs.

The winning hands listed highest to lowest are:

- **Royal Flush**: Ten, Jack, Queen, King, Ace of the same suit. For example,

  10, Jack, Queen, King, and Ace, all clubs.

  Pays 250 to 1. That is, if a player bets one coin and is dealt a royal flush, then he/she wins 250 coins.
- **Straight Flush**: Five cards in rank sequence having the same suit but not a royal flush. For example,

  Ace of Hearts, 2 of Hearts, 3 of Hearts, 4 of Hearts, 5 of Hearts.

  Pays 50 to 1.
- **Four of a Kind**: Four cards of the same rank. For example,

  3 of Hearts, 3 of Diamonds, 3 of Clubs, 3 of Spades, 6 of Hearts.

  Pays 25 to 1.
- **Full House**: Three cards of one rank and two of another. For example,

  4 of Hearts, 4 of Spades, 4 of Clubs, **7 of Clubs, 7 of Spades.**

  Pays 9 to 1.
- **Flush**: All five cards of the same suit but not a straight flush. For example,

  3 of **Hearts**, 6 of **Hearts**, 7 of **Hearts**, 10 of **Hearts**, Jack of **Hearts.**

  Pays 6 to 1.
- **Straight**: Five cards in rank sequence but not a flush. For example,

  Ace of Hearts, **2** of Spades, **3** of Hearts, **4** of Clubs, **5** of Diamonds.

  Pays 4 to 1.
- **Three of a Kind**: Three cards of the same rank and two cards of two other ranks, that is, not a full house or four of a kind. For example,

  5 of Hearts, 5 of Clubs, 5 of Spades, 7 of Clubs, 9 of Diamonds.

  Pays 3 to 1.

- **Two Pair**: Two cards of one rank, two of another, and one card of a third. For example,

  6 of Hearts, 6 of Clubs, 9 of Clubs, 9 of Spades, Ace of Hearts.
  Pays 2 to 1.

- **Jacks or Better**: Exactly one pair of Jacks, Queens, Kings, or Aces and nothing else of interest. For example,

  Jack of Hearts, Jack of Clubs, 2 of Spades, 3 of Clubs, 3 of Hearts.
  Pays 1 to 1.

Figure 11.2 shows several winning hands.

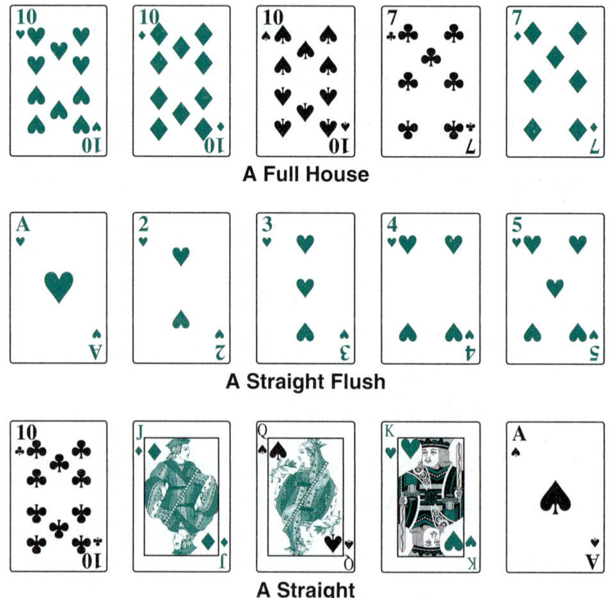

FIGURE 11.2 A few winning poker hands

11.3 PROBLEM STATEMENT

The problem of our case study is the design and implementation of an object-based model for the poker game described in Section 11.2 and pictured in Figure 11.1. This application is, by far, our most elaborate program.

Before attempting an implementation, we make some important design decisions and provide a blueprint for the solution. Specifically, we answer the question:

What are the classes and objects necessary to build the application?

This is the same question you should answer before tackling any complex object-oriented design. Usually, there is no single best set of classes for a particular application, and hence you should not look for the "right answer"; however, some designs are better than others. Moreover, you will probably change and/or refine your classes several times during the design process.

> Program design is not *linear*; it is *iterative*.

Object-oriented design is a topic that fills volumes and is far too complicated for an in-depth discussion here. Nonetheless, we can develop a somewhat simple design process that incorporates the following three steps:

1. Determine the classes.
2. Determine the responsibilities of each class.
3. Determine the interactions and collaborations among the classes.

11.4 DETERMINE THE CLASSES

Classes describe objects and objects are things. In Chapter 9 we state:

> Just as a noun is a person, place, or thing, so is an object.

Accordingly, a common methodology for determining the classes and objects appropriate for an application entails noting and marking the nouns of the problem specification. Although not every noun necessarily gives rise to a class, examining the nouns is a good starting point. Of course, implicit here is the assumption that *the problem is clearly specified*. If the problem is unclear, vaguely stated, or poorly formulated, then you are on soft terrain.

> Before beginning the design process, be sure that you understand the problem.

Here we reiterate the problem specification of Section 11.2 but with the nouns highlighted in boldface.

To play the **video poker game**:

- A **player** deposits an arbitrary number of **coins** into the **machine**. This **amount** is the **bankroll**.
- To play the **game**
  - The player makes a **bet** (one to five coins but not more than the bankroll).
  - A **hand** of five **card**s is dealt from a **deck** of 52 cards to the player.
  - The deck is reshuffled for each game.
  - The player decides which cards he/she wishes to hold.
  - New cards are dealt for those cards that the player wishes to discard.
  - The hand is scored.
  - If the hand is a winner, the winning amount is added to the bankroll. Otherwise, the bet is deducted from the bankroll.
- The player can quit and cash out at any time.
- The player can continue to play as long as the bankroll is not depleted.
- The player can add to the bankroll before any individual game.

The following nouns serve as "class candidates."

- video poker game
- player
- coins
- machine
- amount
- bankroll
- game

- bet
- hand
- card
- deck

Obviously, some words from this list are redundant. For example, *amount* and *bankroll* refer to the same thing. Also, a *coin* probably does not warrant a class of its own. And of course, *video poker game* and *game* are identical.

> Not all nouns will necessarily correspond to classes, and not all classes will always have a corresponding noun.

So, for now, let's settle on seven classes:

- Player
- Bankroll
- Bet
- Hand
- Card
- Deck
- PokerGame

11.5 DETERMINE RESPONSIBILITIES OF EACH CLASS

What service does a class provide?
What is each class's responsibility?
What are the actions and behaviors of each class?

> As the nouns indicate classes, the verbs of the problem statement help determine class responsibilities.

Just as not every noun corresponds to a class, not every verb necessarily designates a class action or responsibility. As we may create classes for which there are no corresponding nouns, we may require actions that do not manifest themselves as verbs. A dose of good common sense is helpful. The process is not mechanical. As with the nouns, we highlight (in boldface) the verbs or actions in the problem statement and use these to determine the actions and responsibilities of each class.

To **play** the video poker game:

- A player **deposits** an arbitrary number of coins into the machine. This amount is the bankroll.
- The player **makes** a bet (one to five coins but not more than the bankroll).
- A hand of five cards is **dealt** from a deck of 52 cards to the player. The deck is **reshuffled** for each game.
- The player **decides** which cards he/she wishes to hold.
- New cards are **dealt** for those cards that the player wishes to discard.

- The hand is **scored.**
- If the hand is a winner, the winning amount is **added** to the bankroll, otherwise the bet is **deducted** from the bankroll.

The player can **quit** and **cash out** at any time. The player can **continue** to play as long as the bankroll is not **depleted**. The player can **add** to the bankroll before any individual game.

We begin with the Player class. What can a poker player do? We compile a list based on the actions noted previously. A player can:

- Deposit coins (add to the bankroll).
- Play the game.
- Make a bet.
- Decide which cards to hold/discard.
- Cash out.
- Quit.
- Play another game.

In fact, the actions of a player correspond to the buttons on the machine of Figure 11.1. Player provides the user interface. The buttons on the machine of Figure 11.1 and the actions of Player are a good match. Each machine action lends itself to a method of the Player class.

Because Player serves as the user interface, we confine all input and output to the Player class. This means that Player is responsible for displaying the cards as well as any other appropriate output.

Bet, Deck, Card, Hand, and Bankroll are less complex than Player, and the actions of these classes follow.

Bet:

- Give (return) its value (a getter method).
- Set a value (a setter method).

Deck:

- Shuffle the cards.
- Deal a card, that is, return one card.

Card:

- Return its suit (a getter method).
- Return its value (a getter method).

Hand:

- Deal and store a new hand.
- Update a hand after the player discards cards.
- Score a hand.
- Return the hand, that is, return the list of cards in the hand.

Bankroll:

- Update the current number of coins in the machine, that is, increase or decrease the number of coins.
- Return the number of coins in the machine (a getter method).
- Change the number of coins in the machine its (a setter method).

One class remains: PokerGame. Every poker game has a dealer who distributes the cards and, for the most part, coordinates play. Similarly, a PokerGame object coordinates the action of our game. Just as the casino dealer provides a hand to a player, the PokerGame object requests a new hand from the Hand object and "deals" that hand to the Player object. PokerGame is the "middleman" between Player and the other classes. Playing the role of game coordinator, the actions of PokerGame might tentatively be listed as:

- Get a new hand from Hand.
- Tell Player to display the hand (all IO is via Player).
- Get the list of discard/hold cards from Player.
- Update the hand, that is, tell Hand which cards to hold and which to displace.
- Score the hand, that is, get the score from Hand.
- Tell Player to display the final results.
- Update Bankroll when the game is finished.

Is PokerGame necessary? Can the Player object work without a coordinator? Can the Player object get the hand, score the hand, and update the bankroll without the assistance of PokerGame? Of course. However, PokerGame, as coordinator, makes each class more independent and less intertwined with other classes. PokerGame provides a cleaner design.

We now have a tentative list of classes and actions. Of course, as we proceed, we may discover new classes and actions. Our design is not necessarily complete, nor is it final.

11.5.1 Design Issues—The Data Model and the View

The list of actions is not exhaustive. There are many alternatives and choices. For example, consider the Hand class. A potential Hand method might display a five-card poker hand. The choice to exclude such an action is intentional: we wish to separate the user interface from the underlying data.

> Good OOP design demands the separation of the user interface, or the *view*, from the underlying representation of the data, or the *data model*.

According to our current design, all output is via the Player object. A Hand does not, and indeed, *should not* know how to print itself. It is the Player class that handles the user interface, or view. The view in this application is text-based, but in Part IV you will learn how to build a visual GUI, a graphical user interface, for this same application. Separating the data model from the view allows us to "plug in" any kind of viewing module without having to redesign the methods of the data model, which is exactly what we do in Part IV.

> The separation of the view from the data model is a flexible design methodology.

11.6 ITERATIVE REFINEMENT

Perhaps some refinement is in order. Can we simplify our design? Can a few Player actions be collapsed into one action? For example, placing a bet initiates play. These two actions, betting and starting the game, are, in fact, the same (assuming the bet cannot be retracted). Once a bet is placed the game begins. Also, "cashing out" implies that a player has decided not to continue play. With a few modifications and guided by Figure 11.1, the responsibilities of Player reduce to the following four actions:

- Deposit coins.
- Make a bet (start the game).

- Decide which cards to hold/discard.
- Quit (cash out).

The responsibility of displaying the cards as well as the number of remaining coins also falls to Player. And, because our application is text based, Player should provide some type of a menu that corresponds to the buttons in Figure 11.1.

The behaviors of the PokerGame fit comfortably into three groups of actions that mimic the progression of a single game:

- Get the initial hand:
  - get a new hand,
  - tell Player to display the hand
- Discard and hold cards:
  - get the discard/hold cards from Player,
  - update the hand, (replace some cards)
  - score a hand,
  - tell Player to display the results
- Update the bankroll

The actions of PokerGame are, in fact, messages or requests sent to other objects. For example, to obtain a new hand, a PokerGame object sends a request to a Hand object, which returns a hand of five cards. Remember, PokerGame is the coordinator, the casino dealer.

The other classes, being somewhat simpler, need no refinement. The classes and actions are given in Figure 11.3.

Player	PokerGame	Bet	Deck
Deposit or accept coins.	Get the initial hand.	Get the bet.	Shuffle the deck.
Make a bet (starts game).	Discard and hold cards.	Set the bet.	Deal a card.
Decide which cards to hold/discard.	Update the bankroll.		
Display a hand.			
Cash out.			
Display a menu.			

Card	Hand	Bankroll
Get the suit.	Score a hand.	Get the bankroll.
Get the rank.	Deal a new hand.	Set the bankroll.
Get the name of a card.	Update a hand.	Change the bankroll.
	Give the hand.	

FIGURE 11.3 Classes and actions for video poker

11.6.1 Determine the Interactions Among the Classes

Objects interact with other objects by sending messages to each other. A message sent by object A to object B is a request for B to provide some service or information to A.

We have mentioned that a PokerGame object sends messages to other objects. PokerGame coordinates. Here we list some possible messages that one object *might* send to another during a video poker session. These messages tell us how the objects interact.

- PokerGame
    - sends a message to Hand requesting a new hand of five cards,
    - sends a message to Player requesting that Player display the hand to the user,
    - sends a message to Player requesting the list of discarded cards,
    - sends a message to Hand requesting an updated hand,
    - sends a message to Player requesting that the new hand be displayed,
    - sends a message to Hand requesting a score for the hand,
    - sends a message to Player requesting that Player display the results, and
    - sends a message to Bankroll updating the current number of coins.
- A Player
    - instantiates an initial Bankroll object,
    - sends a message to the Bankroll object when coins are added,
    - instantiates and initializes a Bet,
    - instantiates a PokerGame,
    - sends a message to the PokerGame requesting the initial hand,
    - sends a message to PokerGame indicating which cards to discard and which to hold, and
    - sends a message to Bankroll requesting the final coin count.
- Hand asks Deck to deal a new hand.
- Deck requests five Card objects.

Figure 11.4 shows how the objects of the application interact. A line between two classes indicates communication between those classes. As we build the application, you may discover that there are other dependencies not reflected in this initial diagram.

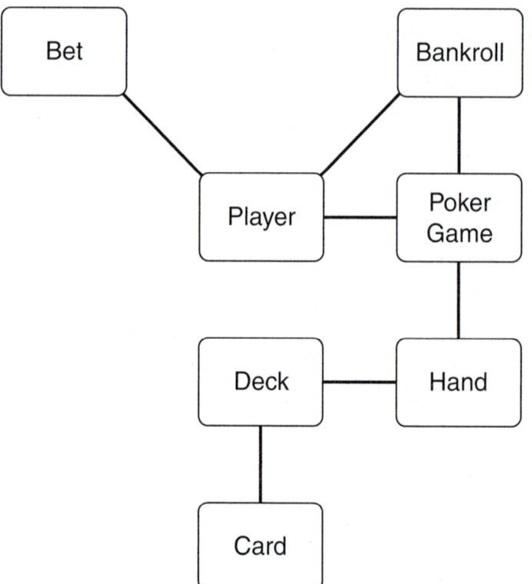

FIGURE 11.4 Interacting objects

Notice that this diagram is very simple. There is, for example, no indication as to which object sends a message to which, that is, the lines have no arrows. Indeed, there are more sophisticated diagrams of this sort that illustrate more features and details of the abstract object model. Such diagrams are part of UML—unified modeling language.

> UML is a general-purpose graphical language used to represent the object structure of an object-oriented program.

UML is a more advanced topic not covered in this text. You will encounter UML again when you study software engineering.

11.7 SOME ATTRIBUTES

Every class consists of both attributes and behaviors. We have (at least tentatively) chosen the behaviors for our classes, but what about the attributes? For example, Bet must store the number of coins inserted into the machine. So, a Bet object should have an instance variable

```
int bet;
```

Bet is uncomplicated and no additional data are necessary. However, Hand cannot function without Deck, so Hand must include a Deck object to get its job done. Similarly a standard deck of cards consists of 52 cards; consequently, Deck requires an array of 52 Card references. And, every Card object should include two integer fields, rank and suit.

PokerGame is a bit more involved. Figure 11.4 shows that PokerGame collaborates with Player, Bankroll, and Hand. Furthermore, to update the bankroll, PokerGame also needs to know the amount of the current bet. (Did we miss this detail in our design?) Thus, the PokerGame class includes the following instance variables:

```
Player player
Bet bet
Bankroll bankroll
Hand hand
```

Figure 11.4 shows that Player collaborates with Bankroll, Bet, and PokerGame. Accordingly, the Player class includes the following instance variables:

```
Bankroll bankroll
Bet bet
PokerGame pg
```

11.8 VIDEO POKER AFTER SOME REFINEMENT

Figure 11.5 displays a summary of the classes, attributes, and behaviors providing one possible design for a video poker application. This plan is not necessarily in final form.

> The design process is iterative. Even as you implement the application, changes inevitably occur.

Furthermore, the lower-level details of the methods still need to be fleshed out. For example, no algorithm for scoring a hand has been discussed. Determining whether or not the hand is a winner presents yet another hurdle, but one at a lower level. What we do have, however, is a first sketch of the application, a model that is fluid and not cast in cement.

Class	Player	PokerGame	Bet	Deck
Attributes	Bankroll bankroll PokerGame pg Bet bet	Player player Bet bet Bankroll bankroll Hand hand	int bet	Card deck[]
Actions	Initialize the bankroll. Add coins. Bet and play. Discard. Display a hand. Quit. Display final results. Present a menu.	View initial hand. Discard or hold cards. Update bankroll.	Get the bet. Set the bet.	Shuffle the deck. Deal a card.

Class	Card	Hand	Bankroll
Attributes	int suit int value	Card [] hand Deck deck	int bankroll
Actions	Get the suit. Get the value, i.e., rank. Get the name of a card.	Evaluate the hand. Deal a new hand. Update a hand. Give the hand.	Get the bankroll. Set the bankroll. Change the bankroll.

FIGURE 11.5 Attributes and behaviors for video poker

As you study the following implementation, look for details that did not appear in this first model. For example, the method that evaluates a hand (in Hand) uses a fair number of private helper functions that are not shown in the model of Figure 11.5. The design process usually involves many iterations with many changes.

11.9 IMPLEMENTING THE VIDEO POKER APPLICATION

With a list of classes as well as the collaborations among classes, we can begin writing the code that implements the application. It is *never* a good idea to write an entire application, push a button, hold your breath, cross your fingers, and hope for the best. Instead, we have a tentative blueprint, and we implement and test each class one at a time.

Any large application should be built and tested incrementally.

For simplicity throughout, we usually assume that user input is correct. Of course, this is unrealistic, and, in the exercises, you are asked to implement methods that check input.

The Bet, Card, and Bankroll classes are certainly the simplest in our design. Moreover, these classes do not interact with other classes. So we choose to implement these classes first.

11.9.1 The *Bet* Class

The Bet class consists of just one integer field, a set of constructors and two methods: a getter method and a setter method. Implementing Bet presents no problems.

```
public class Bet
{
   private int bet;
   public Bet()              // default constructor sets bet to 0
   {
      bet = 0;
   }

   public Bet(int n) // one-argument constructor,  sets bet to n
   {
      bet = n;
   }

   public void setBet(int n) // setter
   {
      bet = n;
   }

   public int getBet() // getter
   {
      return bet;
   }
}
```

It is good practice to test each class before moving on to the next.

This class is not complex; so testing is very simple. To test and subsequently debug the class, we include a main(…) method that tests the methods of Bet. Running and re-running the following main(...) method with various data is one way you might test Bet.

```
public static void main(String[] args)
{
   Scanner input = new Scanner(System.in);
   System.out.print("Enter an integer: ");
   int n = input.nextInt();
   Bet bet1 = new Bet();                      // default constructor
   System.out.println(" Getter " + bet1.getBet());
   bet1.setBet(n);                            // test setter
   System.out.println("After Setter " + bet1.getBet());
   Bet bet2 = new Bet(n);                     // one argument constructor
   System.out.println("Getter; " + bet2.getBet());
   bet2.setBet(n + 10);                       // setter uses an expression
   System.out.println("Getter; " + bet1.getBet());
}
```

There are other scenarios that you might try when testing a class. However, when you are confident that the class is correct, remove the main(...) method and move on to the next class. Of course, you may have to revisit this class at a later stage.

11.9.2 The *Card* Class

The Card class is almost as simple as Bet. The attributes of a Card object are suit and value (rank of a card). These are both integer fields. The methods are the standard getter and setter methods that return and alter suit and value. Because a Card object should return its name, a third method getName() returns the name of a card as a string such as "2 of Spades" or "Queen of Hearts."

The two-argument constructor,

```
public Card (int suit, int value)
```

is normally used to create a new card. However, we also include a default constructor that creates a Card object initialized as the "Ace of Hearts."

```
public class Card
{
   private int suit;   // 1 = Hearts, 2 = Diamonds, 3 = Clubs, 4 = Spades
   private int value;  // 1 = Ace...11 = Jack, 12 = Queen, 13 = King

   public Card() // Ace of Hearts, by default
   {
      suit = 1;
      value = 1;
   }

   public Card(int s, int v)
   {
      suit = s;
      value = v;
   }

   public int getSuit()
   {
      return suit;
   }

   public int getValue()
   {
      return value;
   }

   public void setSuit(int s)
   {
      suit = s;
   }

   public void setValue(int v)
   {
      value = v;
   }

   public String getName() // returns string, e.g., "Ace of Hearts"
   {
      String name = "";
      if (value == 1)
         name = "Ace of ";
```

```
        else if (value == 11)
           name = "Jack of ";
        else if (value == 12)
           name = "Queen of ";
        else if (value == 13)
           name = "King of ";
        else // use the numerical value
           name = value + " of ";

        // Add on the suit

        if (suit == 1)
           name += "Hearts";
        else if (suit == 2)
           name += "Diamonds";
        else if (suit == 3)
           name += "Clubs";
        else
           name += "Spades";
        return name;
     }
  }
```

Again, testing is in order. Testing the getter and setter methods is straightforward. To test the getName() method, include a loop that tests each card :

```
for (int s = 1; s <= 4; s++)                          // 4 suits
        for (int val = 1; val <= 13; val++)           // 13 cards per suit
        {
                Card cd = new Card(s, val);
                System.out.println(s + "," + val + ": " + cd.getName());
        };
```

or, alternatively, a segment that prompts for a suit and rank and displays the name of the corresponding card:

```
System.out.print ("Suit: ");
int s = input.nextInt();
System.out.print("Value: ");
int val = input.nextInt();
Card cd = new Card(s, val);
System.out.println(s + "," + val + ": " + cd.getName());
```

11.9.3 The *Bankroll* Class

Like Bet and Card, the logic of Bankroll is direct and simple. The class is as follows:

```
public class Bankroll
{
   private int bankroll;

   public Bankroll()            // default constructor
   {
```

```
        bankroll = 0;
    }
    public Bankroll (int n)     // one-argument constructor
    {
        bankroll = n;
    }
    public int getBankroll()
    {
        return bankroll;
    }
    public void setBankroll(int n)
    {
        bankroll = n;
    }

    public void alterBankroll(int n) // n can be negative
    {
        bankroll += n;
    }
}
```

Testing this class is straightforward and much like the other classes.

11.9.4 The *Deck* Class

The only instance variable of the Deck class is an array of 52 Card references. The methods of the class are:

- deal a card, and
- shuffle the deck.

A skeletal version of Deck is:

```
public class Deck
{
        Card[] deck;                // array of  52 Card references
        public Deck()
        {
                // instantiate and populate a deck
        }
        public void shuffle()
        {
                // rearrange deck
        }
        public Card deal()
        {
                // return the "next" card in deck
        }
}
```

We begin with the constructor. Intuitively, the cards of a deck are numbered from 1 to 52, so let's stick with conventional intuition and use an array of size 53, ignoring position 0.

In other words, we utilize deck[1] through deck[52] so that the array index matches the card number. To initialize deck, use a loop:

```
for (int rank = 1; i <= 13; i++)                    // for each rank Ace...King
{          // place cards in order in deck
           deck[rank]      = new Card(1,rank);       // first suit;
           deck[rank+13] = new Card(2,rank);         // second suit;
           deck[rank+26] = new Card(3,rank);         // third suit;
           deck[rank+39] = new Card(4,rank);         // fourth suit
}
```

Notice that the loop iterates over the 13 ranks and on each iteration instantiates the four cards of the current rank. For example, on the tenth iteration the loop instantiates: 10 of Hearts, 10 of Diamonds, 10 of Clubs, and 10 of Spades.

The shuffle() method may not be as obvious as the other methods. A newly instantiated deck is an ordered deck. No doubt, dealing from an ordered deck would remove the elements of surprise and luck from the game. So, we must rearrange deck in some random way. There are a number of shuffle algorithms, and the following simple method works well:

for *card* = 1 to 52
  generate a random integer, *rand*, in the range 1 through 52.
  swap deck[*card*] with deck[*rand*].

Written in Java, the algorithm translates to:

```
public void shuffle()
{
      Random randomNumber = new Random();
      for (int card = 1; card <= 52; card++)
      {         // find a random place in the deck
                int rand = randomNumber.nextInt(52) + 1; // integer between 1 and 52, inclusive

                //swap deck[card] with deck[rand]
                Card temp = deck[card];
                deck[card] = deck[rand];
                deck[rand] = temp;
      }
}
```

Finally, we implement deal(). Here, we run into a problem. When dealing one card, deal() should return the "top" card in the shuffled deck. However, deal() doesn't know which card is the top card. The first card that is dealt should be deck[1], the next card should be deck[2], then deck[3], and so on. Obviously, a Deck object needs to keep track of the number of the top card, that is, the index of the next card to be dealt. However, our design does not take this detail into account. There is no variable that keeps track of the next card to be dealt. To remedy the situation, we include another instance variable

```
int next;
```

that holds the index of the next card. This attribute should be initialized to 1. (Remember, the cards are stored in deck[1] through deck[52].) The variable next must also be reset to 1 whenever the deck is shuffled. So both the constructor and shuffle() must be adjusted.

The entire class follows:

```
public class Deck
{
   private Card deck[];
   private int next;        // holds position of next card to be dealt
   public Deck()
   {
      deck = new Card[53]; // does not use position 0, uses 1...52

      for (int rank = 1; rank <= 13; rank++)
      {  // place cards in order in deck
         deck[rank]    = new Card(1,rank);    // rank of first suit e.g., 3 of hearts
         deck[rank+13] = new Card(2,rank);    // rank of second suit e.g., 3 of diamonds
         deck[rank+26] = new Card(3,rank);    // rank of third suit e.g., 3 of clubs
         deck[rank+39] = new Card(4,rank);    // rank of fourth suit e.g., 3 of spades
      }
      next = 1;           // first card dealt is deck[next]
   }

   public void shuffle()
   {
      Random randomNumber = new Random();
      for (int card = 1; card <= 52; card++)
      {
         // find a random place in the deck
         int rand = randomNumber.nextInt(52) + 1;
         //swap deck[card] with deck[rand]
         Card temp = deck[card];
         deck[card] = deck[rand];
         deck[rand] = temp;
      }
      next = 1;           // top card of the deck
   }

   public Card deal()
   {
      if (next > 52)   // if deck is depleted
         shuffle();
      Card c = deck[next];
      next++;
      return c;
   }
}
```

As with the other classes, this class should be tested extensively.

Of the remaining classes (Hand, Player, and PokerGame), only Hand appears to be independent of the other two classes. Thus, we implement Hand next.

11.9.5 The *Hand* Class

Because a poker hand consists of five cards, we choose to model a poker hand with an array of five Card references. Each time that Hand requires a new Card, Hand sends a request to Deck. Therefore, the instance variables of Hand are

```
Card[] hand; // holds 5 Card references
Deck deck;
```

The default constructor is simple and does no more than instantiate the instance variables:

```
public Hand()
{
        hand = new Card[5];     // 5 cards per hand
        deck = new Deck();
}
```

The newHand() method creates and deals a five-card hand. As agreed, the deck is first shuffled.

```
public void newHand()
{
        deck.shuffle();                       // a message to deck
        for (int i = 0; i < 5; i++)
                hand[i] = deck.deal();        // request one card from deck
}
```

Hand should also have a getter method that returns some representation of a hand. Because a hand must be displayed, the following method returns an array of strings, where each string is the name of one card in the hand, for example: "Queen of Hearts", or "6 of Clubs".

```
public String[] getHand()
 {
   String[] cardsInHand = new String[5];

   for (int i = 0; i < 5; i++)
      cardsInHand[i] = cards[i].getName();

   return cardsInHand;
 }
```

Notice that Hand does more than store an array of Card references. Hand sends a message (getName()) to Card. Figure 11.4 does not show this new detail.

To test getHand(), we add temporary code that creates a hand interactively and displays the name of the hand:

```
public String[] getHand()
{
  ///// TEMPORARY /////
  Scanner input = new Scanner(System.in);
  for (int i = 0; i < 5; i++)
  {
        System.out.println("Rank: ");
        int rank = input.nextInt();
        System.out.println("Suit: ");
        int suit = input.nextInt();
        cards[i] = new Card(suit,rank);
}
  ///// END TEMPORARY /////

 String[] cardsInHand = new String[5];
   for (int i = 0; i < 5; i++)
      cardsInHand[i] = cards[i].getName();
   return cardsInHand;
}
```

We include the following main() method in Hand:

```
public static void main(String[] args)
{
    Hand hand = new Hand();
    String[] s = hand.getHand();
    for(int i = 0; i < 5; i++)
        System.out.println(s[i]);
}
```

Compiling and running the class produces the following output:

Rank: **1**
Suit: **1**
Rank: **2**
Suit: **2**
Rank: **11**
Suit: **3**
Rank: **13**
Suit: **4**
Rank: **6**
Suit: **1**
Ace of Hearts
2 of Diamonds
Jack of Clubs
King of Spades
6 of Hearts

This is only one set of input, and of course, you must test your code with more than one case. However, don't attempt a loop that generates every possible hand—there are 2,598,960 possibilities! A few more sample cases are probably enough to convince you that the code is correct. When you are certain that the class has been implemented correctly, you can remove the temporary statements.

Thorough testing is important, but it is often not practical to test every conceivable case.

The next method that we consider is updateHand(...). To update or revise a poker hand, a Hand object must know those cards that the player wishes to discard and replace. As our original design dictates, PokerGame, in the role of game coordinator, queries Player for the discards and communicates this information to Hand. We choose to send this data from PokerGame to Hand as a boolean array parameter

boolean[] keep

such that if keep[i] == false, the ith card of the hand must be replaced. See Figure 11.6.

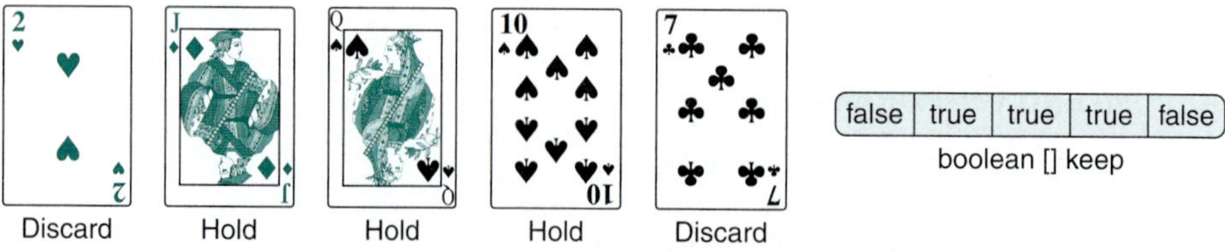

FIGURE 11.6 A player chooses to replace two cards and hold three. This information is passed to *UpdateHand*() in the *boolean* array *keep*[]

The code for updateHand() follows:

```
public void updateHand(boolean keep[])
{
        for(int i = 0; i < 5; i++)
            if (!keep[i])
              hand[i] = deck.deal();
}
```

The code is simple, but how do we test this method without having implemented the Player and PokerGame classes? One way to accomplish this is to include a temporary main(...) method that includes a boolean array and to fill the array interactively. The following method does just that.

```
public static void main(String[] args)
{
   Scanner input = new Scanner(System.in);
   Hand hand = new Hand();
   hand.newHand();

   // for testing only
   boolean[] holdCards = { false, false, false, false, false};
   String[] h = hand.getHand();
   for (int i = 0; i < 5; i++)
   {
      System.out.print(h[i]); // print a card
      System.out.print(": Discard:0 or  keep:1 -->");
      int ans = input.nextInt();
      if (ans = 1) // keep card
         holdCards[i] 5 true;
   }
   hand.updateHand(discards);
   h = hand.getHand();
   System.out.println("*****New Hand ********");  // print new hand
   for (int i = 0; i < 5; i++)
      System.out.println(h[i]);
}
```

Executing main(...) produces the following output. Notice that the decision whether to keep or discard a particular card is entered as 0 or 1.

```
Queen of Diamonds: Discard:0 or  keep:1 -->1
9 of Clubs: Discard:0 or  keep:1 -->0
10 of Hearts: Discard:0 or  keep:1 -->0
3 of Clubs: Discard:0 or  keep:1 -->1
3 of Hearts: Discard:0 or  keep:1 -->0
*****New Hand ********
Queen of Diamonds
4 of Diamonds
4 of Spades
3 of Clubs
9 of Diamonds
```

Certainly, there are other ways to test the updateHand(...) method. For example, you might write a skeletal PokerGame class that sends a message to the Hand class. However, regardless of *how* you test a method, you should test incrementally, that is, test each method before moving to the next.

> A bug restricted to 40 lines of code is easier to detect than a bug hiding somewhere in 400 or 4000 lines.

The final method of the Hand class is evaluateHand(), which determines whether or not a particular hand is a winner. This method takes a bit of thought and careful planning.

When a player is dealt a hand of cards, he/she usually arranges or sorts the cards. Seeing the cards arranged in order makes it easier to recognize a winning hand. We subscribe to that line of reasoning, so we include a sort() method that orders a hand based on rank.

One type of winning hand is a flush. A flush is a hand in which all five cards have the same suit. We number the suits 1 to 4 and arbitrarily assign 1 to hearts, 2 to diamonds, 3 to clubs, and 4 to spades. Accordingly, we can keep track of the number of hearts, diamonds, clubs, and spades with an array suits[] such that

suits[1] holds the number of hearts,
suits[2] holds the number of diamonds,
suits[3] holds the number of clubs, and
suits[4] holds the number of spades.

Since we have numbered the suits 1 to 4, we do not use suits[0].

If for any i, suits[i] has the value 5, the hand is a flush. Figure 11.7 illustrates the suits array.

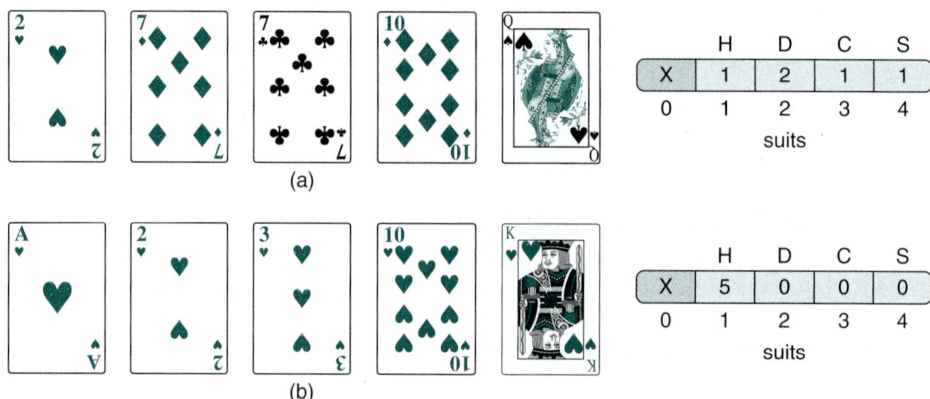

FIGURE 11.7 (a) The *suits*[] array: 1 heart, 2 diamonds, 1 club, and 1 spade. (b) A flush: *suits*[*1*] == 5

Several winning hands are comprised of two, three, or four cards of the same value or rank. Consequently, we use an integer array values[] such that values[i] holds the number of cards dealt with rank i. For example,

values[1] holds the number of Aces,
values[2] holds the number of 2's,
values[3] holds the number of 3's,
...
values[11] holds the number of Jacks,
values[12] holds the number of Queens, and
values[13] holds the number of Kings.

We do not use values[0] since no card has value 0. See Figure 11.8.

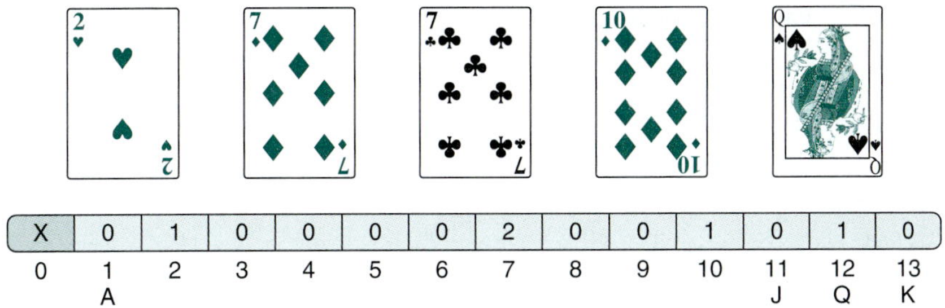

FIGURE 11.8 The array *values*[] shows 1 two, 2 sevens, 1 ten, and 1 queen

Using values[], it is easy to discern whether or not a hand holds two pair, four of a kind, or a full house. For example, if values[2] = 3 and values[7] = 2, then the hand is a full house consisting of 3 twos and 2 sevens.

In summary, to implement evaluateHand() we need:

- A helper function

  void sort()

  that sorts a hand based on the ranks of the cards, and
- two instance variables

  int[] suits and int[] values

  that store information about a hand.

The following revised implementation of Hand includes these arrays and also a sort() method. Of course, the methods of Hand must also be adjusted to update values[] and suits[]. Additions to Hand appear in boldface.

```
class Hand
{
   private Card[] cards;
   private Deck deck;
   private int suits[];    // holds the number of each suit in a hand
   private int values[];   // holds the number of each type card (A,2,3,4,...,K)

   public Hand()
   {
      cards = new Card[5];
      suits = new int[5];      // uses indices 1..4
      values = new int[14];    // uses indices 1..13
      deck = new Deck();
   }

   public void newHand()
   {
      deck.shuffle();
      for (int i = 0; i < 5; i++)
      {
         cards[i] = deck.deal();
         suits[cards[i].getSuit()]++ ;
```

```
            values[cards[i].getValue()]++;
        }
        sort();
    }

    public void  updateHand(boolean[] x)
    {
        for (int i = 0; i < 5; i++)
        if (!x[i])
        {
            // remove card data for card i
            suits[cards[i].getSuit()]--;
            values[cards[i].getValue()]--;

            // get a new card
            cards[i] = deck.deal();

            // update data for card i
            suits[cards[i].getSuit()]++ ;
            values[cards[i].getValue()]++;
        }
        sort();
    }

    public String[] getHand()
    {
        String[] cardsInHand = new String[5];
        for (int i = 0; i < 5; i++)
            cardsInHand[i] = cards[i].getName();
        return cardsInHand;
    }

    private void sort()     // orders cards by value field; a helper function
    {
        int max; // holds the position of the highest valued card
        for (int place = 4; place > 0; place--)
        {
            max = 0;
            // find the position of the highest valued card between 0 and place
            // the position of the high card is stored in max
            for (int i = 1; i <= place; i++)
                if (cards[i].getValue() > cards[max].getValue())
                    max = i;
            // swap the highest valued card with the card in position place
            Card temp = cards[place];
            cards[place] = cards[max];
            cards[max] = temp;
        }
    }
}
```

The additions to the previous Hand class are:

- Lines 5 and 6 contain declarations for the instance variable suits[] and values[].
- Lines 10 and 11 (in the constructor) instantiate suits[] and values[].
- Lines 20 and 21 update the arrays for each card dealt to a new hand.
- Lines 31 and 32 update the arrays when a card is discarded.
- Lines 36 and 37 update the arrays when a discarded card is replaced.
- Lines 48 through 64 implement a standard sort method called selection sort. The method arranges the array hand[] according to rank (retrieved by the getValue() method on line 57). The sort() method is a helper method that has private access. Thus, sort() is not visible outside the Hand class; only the methods of Hand can invoke sort().

With these alterations in place, we are now ready to tackle evaluateHand(), which is the most complex method of the application.

Rather than create one gigantic method that checks each winning hand, we implement nine smaller boolean methods:

- boolean royalFlush(); // returns true if a hand is a royal flush
- boolean straightFlush(); // returns true if a hand is a straight flush
- boolean fourOfAKind(); // returns true if a hand is four of a kind
- etc.

Each method checks for one particular type of hand, so evaluateHand() has the following structure:

```
TypeOfHand evaluateHand()
{
   if (royalFlush())                        // if the hand is a  royal flush
      return Royal Flush;
   else if (straightFlush())                // else if the hand is a  straight flush
      return Straight Flush;
   else if (fourOfAKind())                  // else if the hand is  four of a kind
      return Four of A Kind;
   else if (fullHouse())                    // else if the hand is a  full house
      return Full House;
   else if (flush())                        // else if the hand is a  flush
      return Flush;
   else if (straight())                     // else if the hand is a straight
      return Straight;
   else if (threeOfAKind())                 // else if the hand is three of a kind
      return Three of a Kind
   else if (twoPair())                      // else if the hand is two pair
      return Two Pair;
   else if (pair())                         // else if the hand is a  pair of Jacks or better
      return Pair of Jacks or Better;
   return  Losing Hand;                     // otherwise, a losing hand
}
```

The return type of the previous algorithm is TypeOfHand, which is not a defined type. An implementation might define TypeOfHand to be a String such as "flush" or "straight," or an integer in the range 0 through 9, where 9 indicates a royal flush and 0 indicates a losing hand. Although these are viable alternatives, we choose to return the payout associated with each hand. For example, if a hand is a royal flush, evaluateHand() returns 250, since a royal flush pays 250 to 1; if a hand is a straight flush, evaluateHand() returns 50, and so on. A losing hand returns −1. We choose this option because the payout uniquely identifies the hand *and* can also be used to calculate a player's winnings. Consequently, evaluateHand() is implemented as:

```
public int evaluateHand()              // returns the payout for each hand
{
   if (royalFlush())                   // royal flush pays 250 to1
      return 250;
   else if (straightFlush())           // straight flush pays 50 to1
      return 50;
   else if (fourOfAKind())             // four of a kind plays 25 to 1
      return 25;
   else if (fullHouse())               // full house pays 9 to 1
      return 9;
   else if (flush())                   // flush pays 6 to 1
      return 6;
   else if (straight())                // straight pays 4 to 1
      return 4;
   else if (threeOfAKind())            // three of a kind pays 3 to 1
      return 3;
   else if (twoPair())                 // two pair pays 2 to 1
      return 2;
   else if (pair())                    // pair of Jacks or better pays 1 to 1
      return 1;
   return -1;                          // losing hand
}
```

Because winning hands are evaluated highest to lowest, the else-if construction ensures that evaluateHand() returns the highest possible payout. For example, if a hand holds four of a kind, the method returns 25 and does not check for three of a kind or a pair. The method returns the payout of the best hand that a player holds and no lesser hand.

As we have done with the other methods of this class, we implement and test one method before attempting the next. We begin with royalFlush(). So that the else-if statement might be complete and functional, we provide dummy methods for flush(), straightFlush(), and so on. Each of these methods checks nothing and returns false.

These dummy methods are called *stubs*. Stubs are used for testing a method that is dependent on other methods that have not yet been fully implemented or tested. A stub is a temporary stand-in for the unimplemented or untested methods.

A *stub* is a skeletal method that will eventually be replaced by a fully implemented, functional method. Stubs are used for incremental testing.

The following segment implements royalFlush().

```
private boolean royalFlush()
{
   // 10,J,Q,K,A of the same suit
   boolean sameSuit = false;                   // true if all same suit
   boolean isRoyalty = false;                  // true if cards are 10,J,K,Q,A

   for(int i = 1; i <= 4; i++)
      if (suits[i] == 5)                       // all five cards of one suit?
         sameSuit = true;
```

```
        isRoyalty = (values[1] == 1 &&          // one Ace       &&
                     values[10] ==1 &&          // one Ten       &&
                     values[11] ==1 &&          // one Jack      &&
                     values[12] == 1 &&         // one Queen     &&
                     values[13] == 1);          // one King
    return (sameSuit && isRoyalty);             // true,  if both conditions are true
}

//
// the stubs—not yet implemented and all return false
//
   private boolean straightFlush()
   {   return false; }

   private boolean fourOfAKind()
   {   return false; }

   private boolean fullHouse()
   {   return false; }

   private boolean flush()
   {   return false; }

   private boolean straight()
   {   return false; }

   private boolean threeOfAKind()
   {   return false; }

   private boolean twoPair()
   {   return false; }

   private boolean pair()
   {   return false; }
```

The logic of royalFlush() is direct. The method returns true if there are five cards of a single suit, that is, if suits[i] = 5 for some i, and the cards happen to be A, 10, J, Q, and K. See Figure 11.9.

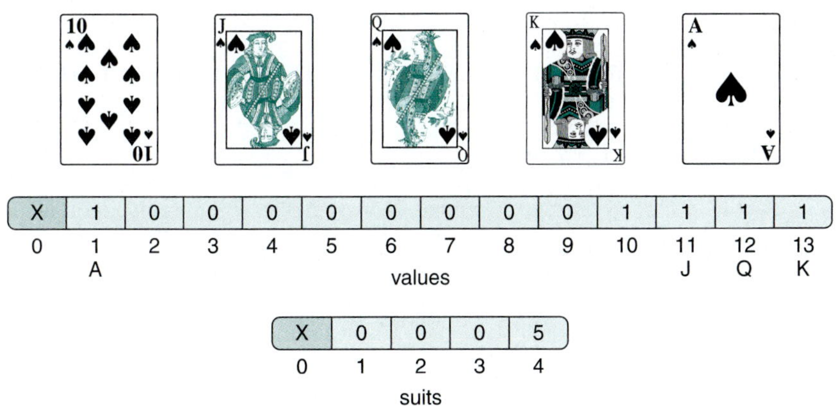

FIGURE 11.9 A royal flush

Before continuing with the next method, straightFlush(), we test royalFlush().

Of the 2,598,960 possible poker hands, just four qualify as a royal flush. So testing royalFlush() with randomly dealt hands may be somewhat tedious, if not time consuming. Rather than rely on chance to deal a royal flush, we create a "test hand" interactively. We implement a method

```
void makeHand()
```

that creates a poker hand interactively rather than by dealing a random hand. However, makeHand() does more than just build a hand; makeHand() adjusts the arrays suits[] and values[] and also invokes sort() so that the type of hand can be determined. In fact, makeHand() operates like newHand() but without the element of randomness. The cards are supplied interactively.

```
public void makeHand()
{
   Scanner input = new Scanner(System.in);
   for (int i = 0; i < 5; i++)
   {
      // get the hand interactively and not randomly
      System.out.println("Rank: ");
      int rank = input.nextInt();
      System.out.println("Suit: ");
      int suit = input.nextInt();
      cards[i] = new Card(suit,rank);
      suits[cards[i].getSuit()]++ ;
      values[cards[i].getValue()]++;
   }
   sort();
}
```

The following main method tests royalFlush().

```
public static void main(String[] args)
{
   Hand hand = new Hand();
   hand.makeHand(); // make a hand with the five cards
   // print the code number for the hand
   System.out.println("Payout for this hand is " + hand.evaluateHand());
}
```

Running some test data provides the following output. The test hand is 10H, JH, QH, KH, and AH.

```
Rank: 10
Suit: 1
Rank: 12
Suit: 1
Rank: 1
Suit: 1
Rank: 11
Suit: 1
Rank: 13
Suit: 1
Payout for this hand is 250
```

A second test with the hand AH, 3D, 5S, JD, and QC produces the following output:

Rank: **1**
Suit: **1**
Rank: **3**
Suit: **2**
Rank: **5**
Suit: **4**
Rank: **11**
Suit: **2**
Rank: **12**
Suit: **3**
Payout for this hand is −1

When you are convinced that royalFlush() works correctly, continue on to straightFlush() and subsequently to each of the other helper methods. When you are satisfied with all nine methods, remove main(...) and makeHand().

The code for the other helper methods follows:

```
private boolean straightFlush()
{
   boolean sameSuit = false;
   boolean ranksInOrder = false;
   for (int i = 1; i <= 4; i++)  // same suit
        if (suits[i] == 5)
             sameSuit = true;
   // cards in sequence? Ace is assumed to be low here since a Royal Flush was checked first
   ranksInOrder =
      cards[1].getValue() == (cards[0].getValue() + 1) &&
      cards[2].getValue() == (cards[0].getValue() + 2) &&
      cards[3].getValue() == (cards[0].getValue() + 3) &&
      cards[4].getValue() == (cards[0].getValue() + 4);
   return (sameSuit && ranksInOrder);
}
```

```
private boolean flush()
{
   for(int i = 1; i <= 4; i++)
      if (suits[i] == 5)  // all the same suit?
         return true;
   return false;
}
```

```
private boolean fourOfAKind()
{
   for (int i = 1 ; i <= 13; i++)
      if (values[i] == 4)
         return true;
   return false;
}
```

```
private boolean fullHouse()
{
   boolean three = false;
   boolean two = false;
   for (int i = 1 ; i <= 13; i++)
      if (values[i] == 3)          // three of one kind
         three = true;
      else if (values[i] == 2)  // two of another kind
```

```
            two = true;
        return  two && three;            // both conditions
}
```

```
private boolean straight()
{
    // cards in sequence?
    return
        // Ace precedes 2
        (cards[1].getValue() == (cards[0].getValue() + 1) &&
        cards[2].getValue() == (cards[0].getValue() + 2) &&
        cards[3].getValue() == (cards[0].getValue() + 3) &&
        cards[4].getValue() == (cards[0].getValue() + 4)) ||
        // Ace follows King
        (values[1] == 1 &&     // Ace
        values[10] == 1 &&     // Ten
        values[11] == 1 &&     // Jack
        values[12] == 1 &&     // Queen
        values[13] == 1);      // King
}
```

```
private boolean threeOfAKind()
{
    for (int i = 1 ; i <= 13; i++)
        if (values[i] == 3)
            return true;
        return false;
}
```

```
private boolean twoPair()
{
    int count = 0;
    for (int i = 1; i <= 13; i++)
    if (values[i] == 2)              // count the number of pairs
        count++;
    return (count == 2);
}
```

```
private boolean pair()               // Jacks or higher
{
    if (values[1] == 2)              // pair of aces
        return true;
    for (int i = 11; i <= 13; i++)   // pair of Jacks or higher
        if (values[i] == 2)
            return true;
    return false;
}
```

Figure 11.10 shows the contents of values[] and suits[] for a few winning hands.

Two classes remain: Player and PokerGame. A Player object sends messages to a PokerGame object and reciprocally a PokerGame object sends messages to a Player object. Thus, a PokerGame reference is an attribute of Player, and a Player reference is an attribute of PokerGame. Must we implement both classes to test either class? We could certainly proceed along that path, but instead we choose to concentrate first on PokerGame. To test the PokerGame class, we implement just enough of Player to run test scenarios. And, once again, we use stubs.

> Stubs are useful when testing one class that is dependent on another class that has not yet been fully implemented or tested.

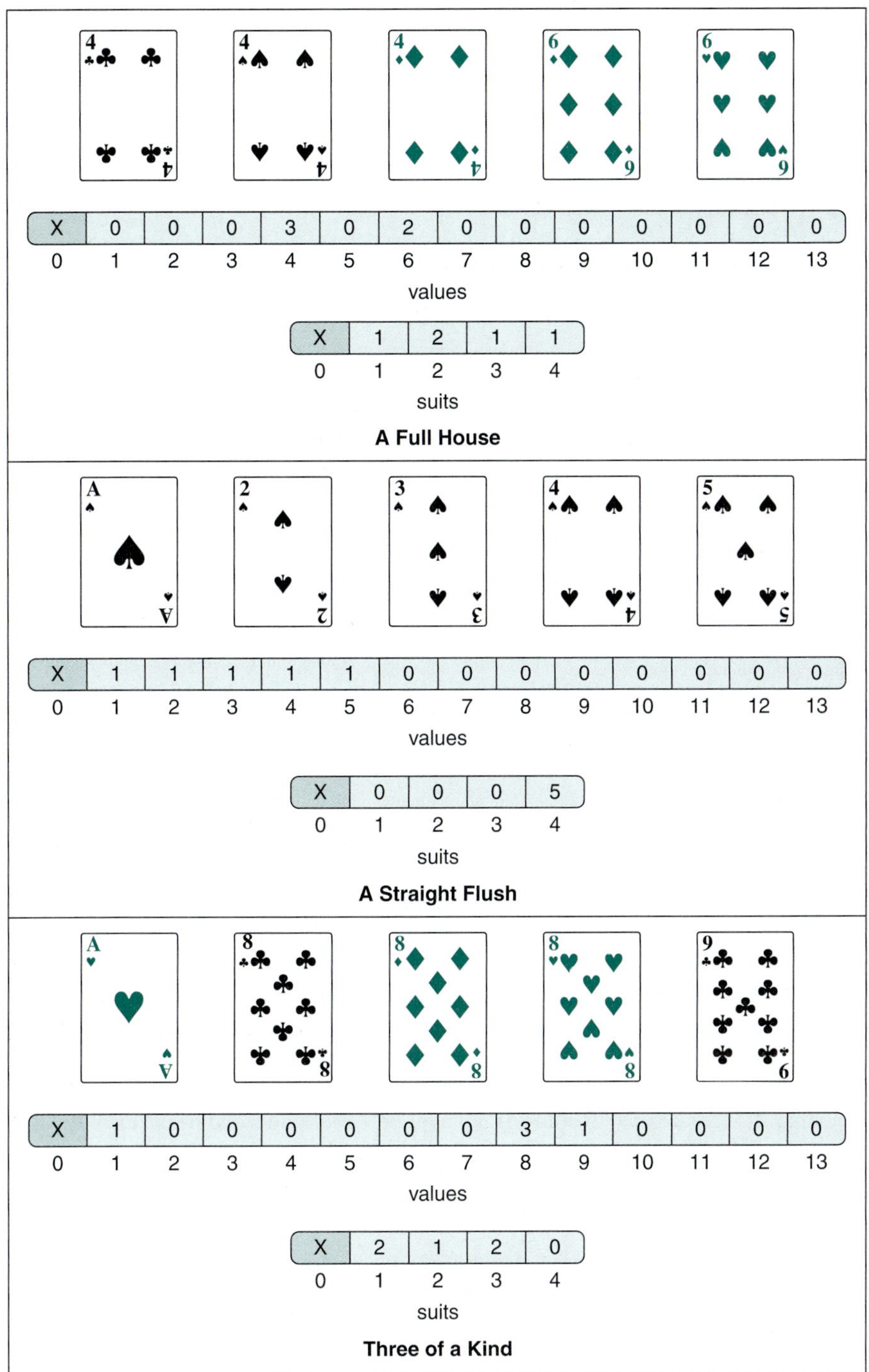

FIGURE 11.10 Three winning hands along with the corresponding *values*[] and *suits*[] arrays

11.9.6 The *PokerGame* Class

As shown in Figure 11.5, the attributes of PokerGame are references to Bankroll, Bet, Hand, and Player. Because PokerGame passes the list of discarded cards to Hand, PokerGame also maintains a boolean array indicating those cards that are to be discarded and those retained. Following is a first iteration of PokerGame that includes declarations and a constructor.

```
public class PokerGame
{
    private Bankroll bankroll;
    private Bet bet;
    private Hand hand;
    private Player player;
    private boolean[] holdCards;

    public PokerGame(Bet coinsBet, Bankroll br, Player pl)
    {
        bankroll = br;
        bet = coinsBet;
        player = pl;
        hand = new Hand();
        holdCards = new boolean[5];
    }

    public int updateBankroll(int payout)
    {
        // alters the bankroll and returns the total winnings
    }

    public void viewInitialHand()
    {
        // deals the first hand
    }

    public void discardOrHoldCards()
    {
            // gets discards and a new hand
    }
```

The updateBankroll(...) method is short and simple, so we implement it first. The method adds or subtracts some number of coins to or from the player's current bankroll. That number depends on the game's payout, which must be passed to updateBankroll(...). For example, if a player bets three coins and wins with a full house, the payout is 25 to 1, so the bankroll increases by 75 coins. If a player bets four coins and loses, the payout is –1 and the bankroll is decreased by four. The code follows:

```
int updateBankroll(int payout)
{
    int winnings = payout * (bet.getBet());   // negative for a loss
    bankroll.alterBankroll(winnings);
    return winnings;
}
```

Next, we implement viewInitialHand() and discardOrHoldCards(). As already noted, these methods are comprised of messages sent to other objects.

```
public void viewInitialHand()
{
    hand.newHand();                          // send a message to hand, instantiate a hand
    player.displayHand(hand.getHand());      // tell player to display the new hand
}
```

```
public void discardOrHoldCards()
{
   player.getDiscard(holdCards);              // ask player for the discard list
   hand.updateHand(holdCards);                // passes discards to hand and hand updates itself
   player.displayHand(hand.getHand());        // tell player to show the (revised) hand
   int payout = hand.evaluateHand();          // tell hand to evaluate itself and return the payout
   int winnings = updateBankroll(payout);     // update the bankroll, a PokerGame method
   player.displayResults(payout, winnings);   // tell player to display outcome of the game
}
```

Because a PokerGame object sends messages to a Player object, before we can test (or even compile) the methods of PokerGame, we write a skeletal implementation of Player.

```
public class Player
{
   private Hand hand;
   public void displayHand(String[] handString)              // print one hand
   {
     // the five card hand is passed as a String[5] array
     for (int i = 0; i < 5; i++)
        System.out.println((I + 1) + ".    " + handString[i]);
     System.out.println();
   }

   public void getDiscard(boolean[] x)                       // ask for discards
   {
      String ans;
      Scanner input = new Scanner(System.in);
      System.out.println("Hold or discard? ");
      for (int i = 0; i < 5; i++)
      {
         System.out.print("Hold (h) or Discard (d) card number " + (I + 1) + ":");
         ans = input.next();
         if (ans.equals("h") )
            x[i] = true;                  // hold
         else if (ans.equals("h") )
            x[i] = false;                 // discard
      }
   }

   public void displayResults(int payout, int winnings) // print payoff and total winnings
   {         // a dummy method for testing
      System.out.println("Payout: " + payout + " Winnings: " + winnings);
   }
}
```

We leave the testing of the PokerGame class methods as an exercise. As with the other classes, you will need to include a temporary main(...) method.

11.9.7 The *Player* Class

With all the other classes fully implemented and tested, we now implement the Player class. The Player class is our user interface, our view. All input and output is done via Player. The attributes and methods of the Player class are specified in Figure 11.5. Each method consists of just a few statements, and you should have no trouble following the logic. The implementation follows:

```
public class Player
{
    private Scanner  input;
    Bankroll bankroll;
    PokerGame pokerGame;
    Bet bet;
    Hand hand;

    Player()
    {
        input = new Scanner(System.in);
        bankroll = new Bankroll();
        bet = new Bet();
    }

    void getInitialBankroll()                  // queries the user for the initial bankroll
    {
        int numCoins;
        do
        {
            System.out.print("How many coins do you wish to insert into the machine: ");
            numCoins = input.nextInt();
        }while (numCoins <= 0);

        System.out.println();
        bankroll,setBankroll(numCoins);
    }

    void addCoins()                            // adds more coins to the machine
    {
        int numCoins;
        do
        {
            System.out.print("How many coins do you wish to insert into the machine: ");
            numCoins = input.nextInt();
        } while (numCoins <= 0);

        bankroll.alterBankroll(numCoins);
        System.out.println("Currently you have " + bankroll.getBankroll() + " coins");
        System.out.println();
    }

    public void betAndPlay()                   // get the bet and play the game
    {
        int coins;
        do
        {
            System.out.print("Enter a bet: 1 to 5 coins: ");
            coins = input.nextInt();
        } while (coins <=0 || coins > 5 || coins > bankroll.getBankroll());

        bet.setBet(coins);
        pokerGame = new PokerGame(bet, bankroll, this);
        pokerGame.viewInitialHand();
        pokerGame.discardOrHoldCards();
```

```
}
public void displayHand(String[] handString)
{
    // five card hand is passed as a String[5] array
    System.out.println("********** Your Hand`1 **********");
    for(int i = 0; i < 5; i++)
        System.out.println((I + 1) + ".     " + handString[i]);
    System.out.println("*********************************");
    System.out.println();
}

public void getDiscard(boolean[] x)
{
    String ans;
    System.out.println("Hold or discard? ");
    for (int i = 0; i < 5; i++)
    {
        do
        {
            System.out.print("Hold (h) or Discard (d) card number " + (I + 1) + ": ");
            ans = input.next();
            if (ans.equals("h") )
                x[i] = true; // hold
            else if (ans.equals("h") )
                x[i] = false; // discard
        } while (!(ans.equals("h") || ans.equals("d")));
    }
    System.out.println();
}

public void displayResults(int payout, int winnings)
{
    String nameOfHand = "Lose";
    if (payout == 250)
        nameOfHand = "Royal Flush";
    else if (payout == 50)
        nameOfHand = "Straight Flush";
    else if (payout == 25)
        nameOfHand = "Four of a Kind";
    else if (payout == 9)
        nameOfHand = "Full House";
    else if (payout == 6)
        nameOfHand = " Flush";
    else if (payout == 4)
        nameOfHand = "Straight ";
    else if (payout == 3)
        nameOfHand = "Three of a Kind";
    else if (payout == 2)
        nameOfHand = "Two Pair";
    else if (payout == 1)
        nameOfHand = " Pair of Jacks or Better";
    if (winnings > 0 )
    {
        System.out.println("Winner: " + nameOfHand);
        System.out.println("Payout is " + winnings + " coins.");
    }
```

```
        else
            System.out.println("You lost your bet of " + bet.getBet());
            System.out.println("Current Bankroll is " + bankroll.getBankroll());
            System.out.println();
    }

    public void quit()
    {
        int br = bankroll.getBankroll();
        System.out.println("\n******Game Over****** \n");
        if (br > 0)
            System.out.println("Returned: " + br + " coin(s)");
        else
            System.out.println("No coins remain");
        System.out.println("\n**********************");
    }

    public void menu()
    {
        String choice;
        do
        {
            System.out.println("Choose");
            System.out.println("1: Make a bet and play poker");
            System.out.println("2: Add coins to the machine ");
            System.out.println("3: Cash out and quit");
            System.out.print("Your choice: ");
            choice = input.next();
            if (choice.equals("1"))
                betAndPlay();
            else if (choice.equals("2"))
                addCoins();
        }while ((!(choice.equals("3") ) && bankroll.getBankroll() > 0));
    }

    public static void main(String[] args)
    {
        Player player = new Player();
        player.getInitialBankroll();
        player.menu();
        player.quit();
    }
}
```

Because the application has been broken up, dissected, and discussed over many paragraphs and pages, the complete implementation of the video poker application appears in Section 11.11.

11.9.8 Output: Playing Poker

Following is typical output displayed by the application.

```
How many coins do you wish to insert into the machine: 10

Choose
1: Make a bet and play poker
2: Add coins to the machine
```

```
3: Cash out and quit
Your choice: 1
Enter a bet: 1 to 5 coins: 2
********** Your Hand **********
1. Ace of Clubs
2. 4 of Diamonds
3. 8 of Clubs
4. Jack of Diamonds
5. Jack of Spades
*******************************

Hold or discard?
Hold (h) or Discard (d) card number 1: h
Hold (h) or Discard (d) card number 2: d
Hold (h) or Discard (d) card number 3: d
Hold (h) or Discard (d) card number 4: h
Hold (h) or Discard (d) card number 5: h

********** Your Hand **********
1. Ace of Spades
2. Ace of Clubs
3. 3 of Clubs
4. Jack of Spades
5. Jack of Diamonds
*******************************

Winner: Two Pair
Payout is 4 coins.
Current Bankroll is 14

Choose
1: Make a bet and play poker
2: Add coins to the machine
3: Cash out and quit
Your choice: 1
Enter a bet: 1 to 5 coins: 5
********** Your Hand **********
1. 4 of Diamonds
2. 5 of Hearts
3. 6 of Clubs
4. 9 of Hearts
5. Jack of Hearts
*******************************

Hold or discard?
Hold (h) or Discard (d) card number 1: h
Hold (h) or Discard (d) card number 2: h
Hold (h) or Discard (d) card number 3: h
Hold (h) or Discard (d) card number 4: d
Hold (h) or Discard (d) card number 5: d
```

```
********** Your Hand **********
1. 2 of Hearts
2. 3 of Hearts
3. 4 of Diamonds
4. 5 of Hearts
5. 6 of Clubs
******************************

Winner: Straight
Payout is 20 coins.
Current Bankroll is 34

Choose
1: Make a bet and play poker
2: Add coins to the machine
3: Cash out and quit
Your choice: 2
How many coins do you wish to insert into the machine: 5
Currently you have 39 coins

Choose
1: Make a bet and play poker
2: Add coins to the machine
3: Cash out and quit
Your choice: 1
Enter a bet: 1 to 5 coins: 5
********** Your Hand **********
1. 2 of Spades
2. 8 of Clubs
3. 9 of Spades
4. Jack of Diamonds
5. Queen of Spades
******************************

Hold or discard?
Hold (h) or Discard (d) card number 1: d
Hold (h) or Discard (d) card number 2: d
Hold (h) or Discard (d) card number 3: d
Hold (h) or Discard (d) card number 4: h
Hold (h) or Discard (d) card number 5: h

********** Your Hand **********
1. 2 of Diamonds
2. 3 of Hearts
3. 10 of Clubs
4. Jack of Diamonds
5. Queen of Spades
******************************

You lost your bet of  5
Current Bankroll is 34
```

```
Choose
1: Make a bet and play poker
2: Add coins to the machine
3: Cash out and quit
Your choice: 3

******Game Over******

Returned: 34 coin(s)

********************
```

11.10 IN CONCLUSION

Choosing the classes that comprise an application takes practice, and no single design is the "best" design. This chapter provides a simple rubric for choosing and designing the classes of an application. No matter how meticulous you are with your initial design, revision is inevitable. As presented in a textbook, building an application seems like a smooth process: choose the classes, identify the methods, implement the classes, and test the classes. It all works. It all fits together nicely. However, in reality, the design process involves trial, error, and even frustration. Design is iterative.

With the poker application, we implement one class at a time, method by method. We test and test again before moving to the next class or method. Incremental testing can save hours of bug detection later on. Choose your classes, determine the actions and interactions, revise, implement and test, test, test … and revise again. No large application is perfect on the first iteration.

The entire application appears in the following appendix. Run it and try your luck and skill at a few hands of poker.

In Chapter 20, we return to the poker application and replace the text-based interface with a graphical interface complete with pictures and buttons. You may be surprised at the ease with which this can be accomplished. Because we confine all IO to one class, Player, only Player needs to be designed.

11.11 APPENDIX: THE COMPLETE APPLICATION

```
////////////////// Bet.java //////////////////

import java.util.*;
public class Bet
{
   private int bet;
   public Bet()                  // default constructor sets bet to 0
   {
      bet = 0;
   }

   public Bet(int n)             // one-argument constructor, sets bet to n
   {
      bet = n;
   }
```

```
    public void setBet(int n)            // setter
    {
        bet = n;
    }

    public int getBet()                  // getter
    {
        return bet;
    }
}

/////////////////// Bankroll.java ///////////////////

public class Bankroll
{
    private int bankroll;

    public Bankroll()                    // default constructor
    {
        bankroll = 0;
    }

    public Bankroll (int n)              // one-argument constructor
    {
        bankroll = n;
    }

    public int getBankroll()
    {
        return bankroll;
    }
    public void alterBankroll(int n)     // n can be negative
    {
        bankroll += n;
    }
}

/////////////////// Card.java ///////////////////

public class Card
{
    private int suit;                    // 1 = Hearts, 2 = Diamonds, 3 = Clubs, 4 = Spades
    private int value;                   // 1 = Ace...11 = Jack, 12 = Queen, 13 = King

    public Card()                        // Ace of Hearts, by default
    {
        suit = 1;
        value = 1;
    }

    public Card(int s, int v)
    {
        suit = s;
        value = v;
    }
```

```
    public int getSuit()
    {
        return suit;
    }

    public int getValue()
    {
        return value;
    }

    public void setSuit(int s)
    {
        suit = s;
    }

    public void setValue(int v)
    {
        value = v;
    }

    public String getName()                 // returns string, e.g., "Ace of Hearts"
    {
        String name = "";
        if (value == 1)
            name = "Ace of ";
        else if (value == 11)
            name = "Jack of ";
        else if (value == 12)
            name = "Queen of ";
        else if (value == 13)
            name = "King of ";
        else                                // use the numerical value
            name = value + " of ";

        // Add the suit onto the name

        if (suit == 1)
            name += "Hearts";
        else if (suit == 2)
            name += "Diamonds";
        else if (suit == 3)
            name += "Clubs";
        else
            name += "Spades";
        return name;
    }
}

////////////////// Deck.java //////////////////

import java.util.*;                         // for Random
public class Deck
{
    private Card deck[];
    private int next;                       // holds position of next card to be dealt
    public Deck()
```

```
    {
       deck = new Card[53];                       // does not use position 0, uses 1..52

       for (int rank = 1; rank <= 13; rank++)
       {
          // place cards in order in deck
          deck[rank]    = new Card(1, rank);      // rank of first suit e.g., 3 of hearts
          deck[rank+13] = new Card(2, rank);      // rank of second suit e.g., 3 of diamonds
          deck[rank+26] = new Card(3, rank);      // rank of third suit e.g., 3 of clubs
          deck[rank+39] = new Card(4, rank);      // rank of fourth suit e.g., 3 of spades
       }
       next = 1;
    }

    public void shuffle()
    {
       Random randomNumber = new Random();
       for (int card = 1; card <= 52; card++)
       {
          // find a random place in the deck
          int rand = randomNumber.nextInt(52) + 1;
          // swap deck[i] with deck[m]
          Card temp = deck[card];
          deck[card] = deck[rand];
          deck[rand] = temp;
       }
       next = 1;                                  // top card of the deck
    }

    public Card deal()
    {
       if (next > 52)                             // if deck is depleted
          shuffle();
       Card c = deck[next];
       next++;
       return c;
    }
 }
```

```
////////////////// Hand.java //////////////////

public class Hand
{
   private Card[] cards;
   private Deck deck;
   private int suits[];                // holds the number of each suit in a hand
   private int values[];               // holds the number of each type card (A,2,3,4,...K)

   public Hand()
   {
      cards = new Card[5];
      suits = new int[5];              // uses indices 1..4
      values = new int[14];            // uses indices 1..13
      deck = new Deck();
   }
```

```
public void newHand()
{
    deck.shuffle();
    for (int i = 0; i < 5; i++)
    {
        cards[i] = deck.deal();
        suits[cards[i].getSuit()]++ ;
        values[cards[i].getValue()]++;
        }
        sort();
}

public void  updateHand(boolean[] x)
{
    for (int i = 0; i < 5; i++)
    if (!x[i])
    {
        // remove card data for card i
        suits[cards[i].getSuit()]--;
        values[cards[i].getValue()]--;
        // get a new card
        cards[i] = deck.deal();
        // update data for card i
        suits[cards[i].getSuit()]++ ;
        values[cards[i].getValue()]++;
    }
    sort();
}

public String[] getHand()
{

    String[] cardsInHand = new String[5];
    for (int i = 0; i < 5; i++)
        cardsInHand[i] = cards[i].getName();
    return cardsInHand;
}

private void sort()                    // orders cards by value field; a helper function
{
    int max;                           // holds the position of the highest valued card
    for (int place = 4; place > 0; place--)
    {
        max = 0;
        // find the position of the highest valued card between 0 and place
        // the position of the high card is stored in max
        for (int i = 1; i <= place; i++)
        if (cards[i].getValue() > cards[max].getValue())
            max = i;
        // swap the highest valued card with the card in position place
        Card temp = cards[place];
        cards[place] = cards[max];
        cards[max] = temp;
    }
}
```

```
public int  evaluateHand()
{
    if (royalFlush())                          // royal flush pays 250:1
        return 250;
    else if (straightFlush())                  // straight flush pays 50:1
        return 50;
    else if (fourOfAKind())                    // four of a kind
        return 25;                             // four of a kind pays 25:1
    else if (fullHouse())                      // full house
        return 9;
    else if (flush())
        return 6;
    else if (straight())
        return 4;
    else if (threeOfAKind())                   // three of a kind
        return 3;
    else if (twoPair())
        return 2;
    else if (pair())                           // Jacks or better
        return 1;
    return -1;                                 // losing hand
}

private boolean royalFlush()
{
    //10, J,Q,K,A of the same suit
    boolean sameSuit = false;                  // true if all same suit
    boolean isRoyalty = false;                 // true if cards are 10,J,K,Q,A
    for (int i = 1; i <= 4; i++)
        if (suits[i] == 5)                     // all five cards of one suit?
            sameSuit = true;
    isRoyalty = (values[1] == 1 &&
                 values[10] ==1 &&
                 values[11] ==1 &&
                 values[12] == 1 &&
                 values[13] == 1);             // one Ace && one 10 && one J &&one Q&&one K
    return (sameSuit && isRoyalty);            // true if both conditions are true
}

private boolean straightFlush()
{
    boolean sameSuit = false;
    boolean ranksInOrder = false;
    for (int i = 1; i <= 4; i++)               // same suit
        if (suits[i] == 5)
            sameSuit = true;
    // cards in sequence?
    ranksInOrder =
    cards[1].getValue() == (cards[0].getValue() + 1) &&
    cards[2].getValue() == (cards[0].getValue() + 2) &&
    cards[3].getValue() == (cards[0].getValue() + 3) &&
    cards[4].getValue() == (cards[0].getValue() + 4);
    return (sameSuit && ranksInOrder);
}

private boolean flush()
```

```
    {
        for (int i = 1; i <= 4; i++)
            if (suits[i] == 5)                  // all the same suit?
                return true;
        return false;
    }

    private boolean fourOfAKind()
    {
        for (int i = 1 ; i <= 13; i++)
            if (values[i] == 4)
                return true;
        return false;
    }

    private boolean fullHouse()
    {
        boolean three = false;
        boolean two = false;
        for (int i = 1 ; i <= 13; i++)
            if (values[i] == 3)                 // three of one kind
                three = true;
            else if (values[i] == 2)            // two of another kind
                two = true;
        return  two && three;                   // both conditions
    }

    private boolean straight()
    {
        // cards in sequence?
        return
        // Ace precedes 2
         (cards[1].getValue() == (cards[0].getValue() + 1) &&
        cards[2].getValue() == (cards[0].getValue() + 2) &&
        cards[3].getValue() == (cards[0].getValue() + 3) &&
        cards[4].getValue() == (cards[0].getValue() + 4)) ||
        //Ace follows King
         (values[1] == 1 &&                     // Ace
        values[10] ==1 &&                       // Ten
        values[11]==1 &&                        // Jack
        values[12] == 1 &&                      // Queen
        values[13] == 1);                       // King
    }

    private boolean threeOfAKind()
    {
        for (int i = 1 ; i <= 13; i++)
            if (values[i] == 3)
                return true;
        return false;
    }

    private boolean twoPair()
    {
        int count = 0;
        for (int i = 1; i <= 13; i++)
```

```
            if (values[i] == 2)                    // count the number of pairs
                count++;
        return (count == 2);
    }

    private boolean pair()                         // Jacks or Higher
    {
        if (values[1] == 2)                        // pair of aces
            return true;
        for (int i = 11; i <= 13; i++)             // pair of Jacks or higher
            if (values[i] == 2)
                return true;
        return false;
        }
    }
```

```
///////////////// PokerGame.java //////////////////

public class PokerGame
{
    private Bankroll bankroll;
    private Bet bet;
    private Hand hand;
    private Player player;
    private boolean[] holdCards;

    public PokerGame(Bet coinsBet, Bankroll br, Player pl)
    {
        bankroll = br;
        bet = coinsBet;
        player = pl;
        hand = new Hand();
        holdCards = new boolean[5];
    }

    int updateBankroll(int payoff)
    {
        int winnings = payoff * (bet.getBet());   // negative for a loss
        bankroll.alterBankroll(winnings);
        return winnings;
    }

    public void viewInitialHand()
    {
        hand.newHand();
        player.displayHand(hand.getHand());
    }

    public void discardOrHoldCards()
    {
        player.getDiscard(holdCards);
        hand.updateHand(holdCards);
        player.displayHand(hand.getHand());
        int payoff = hand.evaluateHand();
        int winnings = updateBankroll(payoff);
```

```
        player.displayResults(payoff, winnings); // the hand & the number of coins won(lost)
    }
}

////////////////// Player.java //////////////////

import java.util.*;
public class Player
{
    private Scanner  input;
    Bankroll bankroll;
    PokerGame pokerGame;
    Bet bet;
    Hand hand;

    Player()
    {
        input = new Scanner(System.in);
    }

    void getInitialBankroll()
    {
        int numCoins;
        do
        {
            System.out.print("How many coins do you wish to insert into the machine: ");
            numCoins = input.nextInt();
        }while (numCoins <= 0);
        System.out.println();
        bankroll = new Bankroll(numCoins);
    }

    void addCoins()
    {
        int numCoins;
        do
        {
            System.out.print("How many coins do you wish to insert into the machine: ");
            numCoins = input.nextInt();
        } while (numCoins <= 0);

        bankroll.alterBankroll(numCoins);
        System.out.println("Currently you have " + bankroll.getBankroll() + " coins");
        System.out.println();
    }

    public void betAndPlay()
    {
        int coins;
        do
        {
            System.out.print("Enter a bet: 1 to 5 coins: ");
            coins = input.nextInt();
        } while (coins <=0 || coins > 5 || coins > bankroll.getBankroll());
```

```
        bet = new Bet(coins);
        pokerGame = new PokerGame(bet, bankroll, this);
        pokerGame.viewInitialHand();
        pokerGame.discardOrHoldCards();
    }
    public void displayHand(String[] handString)
    {
        System.out.println("********** Your Hand **********");
        for (int i = 0; i < 5; i++)
            System.out.println((I + 1) + ".    " + handString[i]);
        System.out.println("*******************************");
        System.out.println();
    }

    public void getDiscard(boolean[] x)
    {
        String ans;
        System.out.println("Hold or discard? ");
        for (int i = 0; i < 5; i++)
        {
            do
            {
                System.out.print("Hold (h) or Discard (d) card number " + (I + 1) + ": ");
                ans = input.next();
                if (ans.equals("h") )
                    x[i] = true; // hold
                else if (ans.equals("h") )
                    x[i] = false; // discard
            }while (!(ans.equals("h") || ans.equals("d")));
        }
        System.out.println();
    }

    public void displayResults(int payoff, int winnings)
    {
        String nameOfHand = "Lose";
        if (payoff == 250)
            nameOfHand = "Royal Flush";
        else if (payoff == 50)
            nameOfHand = "Straight Flush";
        else if (payoff == 25)
            nameOfHand = "Four of a Kind";
        else if (payoff == 9)
            nameOfHand = "Full House";
        else if (payoff == 6)
            nameOfHand = " Flush";
        else if (payoff == 4)
            nameOfHand = "Straight ";
        else if (payoff == 3)
            nameOfHand = "Three of a Kind";
        else if (payoff == 2)
            nameOfHand = "Two Pair";
        else if (payoff == 1)
            nameOfHand = " Pair of Jacks or Better";
```

```
        if (winnings >0 )
        {
            System.out.println("Winner: " + nameOfHand);
            System.out.println("Payoff is " + winnings + " coins.");
        }
        else
            System.out.println("You lost your bet of " + bet.getBet());
            System.out.println("Current Bankroll is " + bankroll.getBankroll());
            System.out.println();
    }

    public void quit()
    {
        int br = bankroll.getBankroll();
        System.out.println("\n******Game Over****** \n");
        if (br > 0)
            System.out.println("Returned: " + br +" coin(s)");
        else
            System.out.println("No coins remain");
        System.out.println("\n**********************");
    }

    public void menu()
    {
        String choice;
        do
        {
            System.out.println("Choose");
            System.out.println("1: Make a bet and play poker");
            System.out.println("2: Add coins to the machine ");
            System.out.println("3: Cash out and quit");
            System.out.print("Your choice: ");
            choice = input.next();
            if (choice.equals("1"))
                betAndPlay();
            else if (choice.equals("2"))
                addCoins();
        }while ((!(choice.equals("3") ) && bankroll.getBankroll() >0));
    }

    public static void main(String[] args)
    {
        Player player = new Player();
        player.getInitialBankroll();
        player.menu();
        player.quit();
    }
}
```

Just the Facts

- Any large application should be built incrementally.
- The design process involves many iterations with many changes.
- OOP design starts with a problem description.
- The classes in the design correspond roughly to the nouns of the problem description.
- The responsibilities of each class correspond roughly to the methods of the class and to the verbs of the problem description.
- The *data model* is the abstract representation of the information processed by that program.
- The *view* of a program is the code that implements the user interface.
- Separating the data model from the view is a flexible OOP design methodology.
- Every method should be tested before moving to the next one.
- A stub is a skeletal method that will eventually be replaced by a fully implemented, functional method. Stubs are used for testing a method that is dependent on other methods that have not yet been fully implemented or tested.
- Find bugs early. A bug restricted to 40 lines of code is easier to detect than a bug hiding somewhere in 400 or 4000 lines!

Bug Extermination

- Bugs are always present. Even the most meticulous programmer cannot avoid bugs.
- Incremental testing is a painless methodology for detecting programming bugs.
- It is not always possible to test every possible input pattern. Most of the time you must be satisfied with testing a few representative samples.
- Do not write a large application, cross your fingers, and hope for the best. Write small segments and test those segments before continuing.
- When necessary, use stubs for testing.
- When you debug, use both typical and atypical data. Be thorough.
- Test early and frequently in the development process. The minutes of early testing will save hours of tedious debugging.

EXERCISES

SHORT EXERCISES

1. **OOP Modeling**
   Make a labeled rectangle for each class of the Poker case study, and draw an arrow from box A to B if an object belonging to A sends a message to an object belonging to B.
2. **OOP Implementation**
   Review the order in which we build and test the classes in the case study. Why is this order used? Can you suggest a different sequence?
3. **Stubs**
   What is a stub and what is its purpose?
4. **Nouns**
   Why are the nouns of a problem description a good place to look for the class names?
5. **Verbs**
   What do the verbs in a problem description help us determine? Why?
6. **Iterative Refinement**
   What is meant by *iterative refinement*?
7. **Testing**
   Why is testing each class and each method, one at a time, a good idea?
8. **Data Model and View**
   What is the difference between the *data model* and the *view* components of a program?
9. **Separation of Data Model and View**
   Why is it good design to separate the classes that maintain the data model from those that implement the view?
10. **OOP Design—Your Opinion**
    Do you feel that object-oriented program design is a natural way to design programs? Why or why not?

PROGRAMMING AND DESIGN EXERCISES

1. **A Better Poker Machine**
   A fancier version of the poker machine described in the case study displays the "current best hand" that a player has achieved in a session as well as its evaluation and payout. For example, if a player's best hand has been 6C 6H 6D 6S 3C, and the bet was five coins, the machine displays the following information:

   Best Hand: Four of a Kind: 6C 6H 6D 6S 3C, Bet = 5, Payout: 125.
   Modify the case study to include this feature.

2. **Modifications for Debugging**
   It is questionable style to have a displayHand() method inside the Hand class. To separate the data model from the view, we place the displayHand() method in the Player class. Nevertheless, for early debugging purposes, before the Player class is even built, it may be handy to have a displayHand() method in Hand. Add a temporary displayHand() method to the Hand class, and use it to "retest" the Hand class.

3. **Testing and Debugging**
   Design and implement a technique that tests the PokerGame class. Create a temporary main(...) method to help you.

4. **Testing and Debugging**
   In the design of the poker application, the last class that we implement is the Player class. Suppose that we implement the Player class first—how would we test the class? What stubs are necessary? Do you think leaving the implementation of the Player class for last is a good idea?

5. **A Two-Player Poker Machine**
   Consider a poker machine exactly like the one in the case study except that two people are allowed to play simultaneously. The game treats both players no differently than single players, that is, bets are taken and payouts are made. However, this machine offers each player an additional option to play against the other player. Both players must agree to an amount, which is an additional bet of one to five coins. The winning player receives all the money. The losing player loses his/her bet. If there is a tie, no money changes hands. *Note:* Hands are compared on the poker machine's scale. For example, if both players get a full house, it is a tie, regardless of the cards they hold. There is no distinction between hands at the same level. Implement the two-player machine.

6. **Strictly for Poker Players**
   This problem is similar to problem 5, except that hands are evaluated according to the complete rules of poker. For example, a full house of Queens over Kings beats a full house of Tens over Aces. A flush to the Ace beats a flush to the King. Ties can still occur (e.g., two straights of the same denomination), but there will be fewer ties with this machine than with the one of problem 5.

7. **User Interface Redesign**
   Modify the code of the case study so that the hold or discard menu, instead of expecting 'h'or 'd' for each card, allows a player to enter the cards that he/she wants to hold. Card input consists of a two-character string; the first character represents the value (A, 2, 3, 4, 5, 6, 7, 8, 9, T, J, Q, K) and the second character represents the suit (C, D, H, S). For example, "JC" is the Jack of Clubs, "AH" is the Ace of Hearts, and "TD" is the Ten of Diamonds. Do you think this method is better or worse than the one used in the case study?

8. **Realistic User Input Checking**
Generally, it is not wise to assume that user input is correct—indeed, input errors are very common. Revise the case study and add a method that accepts the player's reply if and only if it is a valid response.

9. **A Simulated Chat Room**
A chat room serves many simultaneous visitors. Any visitor can post a message simultaneously on every visitor's screen, or direct his/her message to a particular person.

   In lieu of screens, cell phones, terminals, or other devices, let's assume that everyone in a chat room types his/her messages one at a time into one program and that the messages are displayed with a header indicating to whom they are directed. Each chat room visitor has a name and a status: logged in or logged out. Each logged-in visitor can send a message to the whole room or to an individual in the room. Each visitor can see a list of people currently in the room. Each visitor may log in and log out. When a person logs in or out, a message is sent to all others in the chat room.

   Write an application that simulates a chat room. Make sure to clearly separate the data model from the view.

   a. Write a detailed problem description and identify the nouns and verbs of the problem.
   b. Determine the classes that your program will use.
   c. Determine the methods for each class.
   d. Determine the attributes of each class by observing which classes need to send messages to which.
   e. Refine your design. Write headers for all methods, but do not implement the methods.
   f. Complete the implementation using a text-based user interface.

10. **Extending the Chat Room Simulation**
A more realistic scenario for Programming Exercise 9 implements many chat rooms simultaneously. Each room has its own set of members—the people visiting that room. Each person, on the other hand, can join (log in) or leave (log out) any number of rooms as often as he or she pleases. A person should be able to see a list of the chat rooms which he or she is currently visiting. Furthermore, any user should be able to see a list of currently open rooms and its members. If a user joins more than one room, then he or she receives the messages from all those rooms. Any user may open a new chat room, which must be given a name different from the other currently open chat rooms. Only that user is allowed to close the chat room, and when that occurs, all the current members are immediately removed.

   a. Extend the design of Programming Exercise 9 to handle this generalization.
   b. Complete the implementation using a text-based user interface.

   As in Programming Exercise 9, assume that all the users take turns typing commands and messages into one program on a single keyboard.

11 **Tic-Tac-Toe Versus Computer**
Create a high-level design for a program that allows a person to play Tic-tac-toe against the computer. After each game, give the player the option to quit or play again. The computer can play its moves randomly. The computer keeps track of who has won and how many games have been played. When requested by the player, the application displays a summary of wins, losses, and ties. Make the user interface independent of the game logic.

   a. Write a detailed problem description and identify the nouns and verbs of the problem.
   b. Determine the classes that your program will use.

c. Determine the methods for each class.

d. Determine the attributes of each class by observing which classes need to send messages to which.

e. Refine your design. Write headers for all methods, but do not yet implement the methods.

f. Complete the implementation using a text-based user interface.

12. **Two Player Tic-Tac-Toe**
Redesign the program in problem 11 to allow play against another human player rather than against the computer.

13. **Tic-Tac-Toe with Perfect Computer Play**
Redesign the program in problem 11 so that the computer plays perfectly (i.e., never loses).

14. **A Calendar-Making Program**
Write an application that accepts a year and displays a 12-month planning calendar. Each month should be printed separately, one below the next. For example, for 2007,

January 2007

Sun	Mon	Tues	Wed	Thurs	Fri	Sat
	1	2	3	4	5	6
7	8	9	10	11	12	13
14	15	16	17	18	19	20
21	22	23	24	25	26	27
28	29	30	31			

February 2007

Sun	Mon	Tues	Wed	Thurs	Fri	Sat
				1	2	3
4	5	6	7	8	9	10
11	12	13	14	15	16	17
18	19	20	21	22	23	24
25	26	27	28			

etc.

...

Allow a user to specify any number of dates to be noted underneath the month (birthdays, anniversaries, and so on). For example, a user should be able to request that January 8 be printed with the note: "Elvis's Birthday," or February 18, "Take Dog to Groomer," or December 25, "Christmas." A list of annotated dates should appear following that month's calendar. For example, the first month of the annotated calendar might look like this:

January 2007

Sun	Mon	Tues	Wed	Thurs	Fri	Sat
	1	2	3	4	5	6
7	8	9	10	11	12	13
14	15	16	17	18	19	20
21	22	23	24	25	26	27
28	29	30	31			

January 1: New Year's Day
January 8: Elvis' Birthday; visit Graceland
January 23: Get Fifi a trim at the Pet Central
January 31: Phantom of the Opera
Hint: In Chapter 3, we give a method for determining the day of the week of January 1, given a particular year.

a. Write a detailed problem description and identify the nouns and verbs of the problem.
b. Determine the classes that your program will use.
c. Determine the methods for each class.
d. Determine the attributes of each class by observing which classes need to send messages to which.
e. Refine your design. Write headers for all methods, but do not implement the methods.
f. Complete the implementation using a text-based user interface.

15. **Go Fish**

Every kid plays *Go Fish*. But just in case you missed this one, two players, say Bette and Bob, are each dealt seven cards from a standard deck. Each player in turn may ask the other player if he or she has any cards of a particular rank, for example, "got any kings?" A player cannot request a certain type of card unless he or she holds at least one of that type.

For example, Bette cannot ask for kings unless she holds at least one king. If Bob has any kings then he must relinquish all of them to Bette. Bette continues requesting cards from Bob as long as Bob can fulfill her requests. When Bob can no longer hand over cards to Bette, he tells her to "go fish" and Bette is dealt one more card from the deck. If it happens to be the card she had just unsuccessfully requested, she continues querying Bob for cards; otherwise Bob gets to query Bette. When either player collects all four cards of a particular denomination, he or she immediately removes them from his or her hand and places the "set" off to the side. The game is over when all the cards are made into sets. The player with the most sets wins.

Write an application that implements *Go Fish* so that a human can play against the computer. After each game a player may quit or play again. When a player quits, the program should print summary win/loss statistics.

a. Write a detailed problem description and identify the nouns and verbs of the problem.
b. Determine the classes that your program will use.
c. Determine the methods for each class.
d. Determine the attributes of each class by observing which classes need to send messages to which.
e. Refine your design. Write headers for all methods, but do not yet implement the methods.
f. Complete the implementation using a text-based user interface.

16. **Go Fish with Multiple Players**

Redesign the program of Programming Exercise 15 so that multiple players (3 to 6) may play. In this version, each player is originally dealt five cards, rather than seven. Each player's hand is displayed only during his/her turn. When a player requests cards, he/she must specify not the just the kind of card, but the player to whom the request applies. The computer automatically hands over the appropriate cards from the player queried, if possible.

Obviously, playing the game on a single computer requires that each player not look at the screen during another player's turn. That is, no player should ever see another player's hand.

17. **A Music Collection**

    You have a large music collection that is continually expanding. You keep track of each song with an index number, song name, artist, style (pop, rock, classical, jazz, etc.), length (in minutes and seconds), and year recorded. The collection is stored in a text file. Design a program that allows you to add a song to your collection, delete a song from your collection, modify information about a song in your collection, print the data for all the songs of a particular artist, and print the data for all songs of a particular style. Your program should read from the file, and upon termination, write to another file.

    Finally, your program should allow you to choose a collection of songs that you can take with you on a vacation. These songs are chosen by index number one at a time. To remove a song from your vacation list, just select the song again. After any modification to the vacation list, the program should print the combined total playing time of all songs currently selected.

    a. Write a detailed problem description and identify the nouns and verbs of the problem.
    b. Determine the classes that your program will use.
    c. Determine the methods for each class.
    d. Determine the attributes of each class by observing which classes need to send messages to which.
    e. Refine your design. Write headers for all methods, but do not yet implement the methods.
    f. Complete the implementation using a text-based user interface.

18. **A Daily Planner**

    To manage your schedule, you need to keep track of day-to-day events. An event might be an appointment, an errand, a reminder, or whatever you need to remember.

    Write a planner application to manage your daily events. Your application should accept an event entered on two lines:

    Line 1: Date/time—month (1–12), day, year, hour (0–23, military style), and
    Line 2: Event description (text).

    The time is optional if the event has no specific time on that day.

    For example, an event might look like this:

    ```
    11    16    1959
    Sister's Birthday
    ```

    or this:

    ```
    12    25    2008    15
    Christmas Dinner at Grandma's
    ```

    When you enter an event, the application should check that the time of the event does not conflict with another event. The planner, if queried, should be able to list all events for a particular date or range of dates. The planner should read events from a file when the program starts and write the new list of events to a new file when the program ends.

    a. Write a detailed problem description and identify the nouns and verbs of the problem.
    b. Determine the classes that your program will use.
    c. Determine the methods for each class.
    e. Determine the attributes of each class by observing which classes need to send messages to which.

d. Refine your design. Write headers for all methods, but do not yet implement the methods.
f. Complete the implementation using a text-based user interface.

19. **Testing Variations of *Craps*—with Suggested Design**
Craps is a casino game played with two dice. In the basic version, a player bets a certain amount of money, and the house pays back the amount of the bet if the player wins.

Here are the rules of the game. You roll a pair of six-sided dice.
If the dice show 7 or 11, that's a *natural*! You win.
If the dice show 2, 3, or 12, that's *craps*. You lose.

If the dice show any other number (4, 5, 6, 8, 9, or 10), that number is your *point* and the game is not over yet. In this case, continue rolling the dice until you roll your *point* or a 7. If you roll your *point* before a 7, you win. If you roll a 7 before your *point*, you lose. In this case, seven is called the *pointbreaker*. No other rolls matter except for the point and pointbreaker.

Casinos offer games with odds that favor the house. They are, after all, in the business of making money. To be convinced that a game favors the house, a casino may hire a mathematician to analyze the game or a programmer to simulate it. Depending on the game, one of these options may be more successful than the other. Neither way is always the best way. Here we take the programmer's route.

Write an application that simulates 1000 games of craps and reports the number of games won by the player and the number won by the house. Then change the rules slightly and repeat the simulation. For example, move 3 from the *craps* row to the *point* row. That is, when a 3 is rolled on the first roll, you do not lose immediately. Instead, the 3 becomes your *point* just as if the roll had been 4, 5, 6, 8, 9, or 10. Many other variations of the game could be tested in this way. For example, in Las Vegas, a value of 12 on the first roll ends the game in a tie.

Rather than ask you to design this one, here is a reasonable list of classes that your application might use.

1. **Dice**—This class lets you roll the dice. Methods include roll(), which returns the sum of two random integers in the range 1–6. A Player sends a message to a Dice object.

2. **Rules**—This class stores the rules of your particular version of the game and allows changes to those rules. Instance variables include an array to keep track of which rolls from 2 through 12 are *natural*, *craps*, and *points*, and also an integer between 2 and 12 inclusive that represents the *pointbreaker*. For example the array {'c', 'c', 'p', 'p', 'p', 'n', 'p', 'p', 'p', 'n', 'c'} along with the integer 7 represent standard craps rules.

   Methods include:

   Constructor methods:
   The default constructor should use standard craps rules.

   Getter methods:
   getStatus(int x) // returns 'n', 'p', or 'c', given a roll x.
   getPointbreaker() // returns value of the *pointbreaker*.

   Mutator methods:
   boolean moveCrapsToPoint(int x) // moves x from the *craps* list to the *point* list.
   boolean moveNaturalToPoint(int x) // moves x from the *natural* list to the *point* list.
   boolean movePointToCraps(int x) // moves x from the *point* list to the *craps* list.
   boolean moveNaturalToCraps(int x) // moves x from the *natural* list to the *craps* list.
   boolean moveCrapsToNatural(int x) // moves x from the *craps* list to the *natural* list.
   boolean movePointToNatural(int x) // moves x from the *point* list to the *natural* list.
   setPointbreaker(int x) // sets x to be the *pointbreaker*.

The parameter x of moveCrapsToPoint(int x) and moveNaturalToPoint(int x) cannot be the *pointbreaker*. Likewise, parameter x of setPointbreaker(int x), cannot be a point.

All mutator methods return true if successful or false if an incorrect change is attempted. For example, having the *pointbreaker* become one of the *points*, or an illegal attempt to move a number from one list to another, returns false.

3. **Player**—A Player has a name and a number of chips. The methods include

   boolean play (int bet, Rules rules)

   and returns true or false, depending on whether the player wins according to Rules.

A test class should do the following:

- Create an instance of Rules using the default craps rules.
- Create a player with your first name and 1000 chips.
- Simulate 1000 games and keep track of the results, which are printed when the application ends. (Each game costs one chip to play and pays out even odds.)
- Modify the rules, using the moveCrapstoPoint(3), so that the roll 3 is a *point* rather than *craps*.
- Run another simulation (1000 games) and report the results.

THE BIGGER PICTURE

SOFTWARE DESIGN AND THE MODEL-VIEW-CONTROLLER PARADIGM

A practical, albeit simplistic, way to measure the size of a software project is lines of code. It should come as no surprise that, generally speaking, larger programs are harder to write than smaller ones. Of course there are some very small complex methods and some very large simple ones, but we are speaking of overall complexity that comes from having multiple classes and lots of communication among them.

A single programmer's productivity can be measured in lines of code written per week. A programmer's productivity on a large project is likely to be less than his/her productivity on a small project. For example, it would probably take the average programmer less than a month to write 5000 lines of code comprised of 50 short, independent 100-line programs, like the programming examples in this text. On the other hand, it might take almost a year to write a 5000-line section of code to be shipped as part of a huge 500,000-line project (e.g., Microsoft Word, or Internet Explorer). Such programs are built by dozens of programmers whose code must all merge together in a symphony of planning and testing.

This phenomenon of *scale* is not specific to programming; it is inherent in any creative work. A good writer can pump out a few clear sentences in seconds, but a full-fledged story with a few hundred sentences takes far more time than a few hundred seconds! And a novel with a few thousand sentences can take years.

One way to manage programmer productivity is to invent software design methodologies or "software architectures" that act as guidelines for programmers who work with specific types of large systems. One such architecture, built for the large number of modern software systems with graphical user interfaces or GUIs, is the model-view-controller architecture, or MVC.

The Model-View-Controller Software Architecture (MVC)

The MVC software architecture is based on three major modules: the (data) model, the view, and the controller. The *(data) model* is an abstract representation of the information processed by the program. The *view* deals with the user interface. The *controller* handles input (often called input events or simply events) and directs results to where they need to go. A simplistic but good first understanding of MVC is that the *controller* handles input, the *model* handles processing, and the *view* handles output.

For example, in our Poker program, the arrays representing hands and cards, and the decisions about how much a hand should pay off, are part of the (data) model. The way the program looks to the user, and the way information is entered and displayed, is part of the view. Finally, the processing of input as it may effect both *view* and *model* is handled by the controller.

With this in mind, notice that the controller must send messages to both the view and the model. In this way, the controller can ask the view and model to update themselves depending on the input event that occurred. The controller may also ask the view or model to perform a relevant calculation.

The view also sends general messages to the model in order to request information and order calculations. The view may ask the model for information so that the view can display the appropriate features. Any message is fair game. Finally, the view is in charge of sending user input events (mouse clicks, typed text, etc.) to the controller for processing. The model, on the other hand, sends updates to the view whenever the data in the model (the *state* of the model) changes.

Figure 11.11 represents the relationships between the model, view, and controller in the MVC model. Solid lines are method invocations and dotted lines are event notifications. The solid lines are accomplished via message passing from one object to another like those that you have seen in the case study. The dashed lines represent a more passive relationship. In particular, the model has no direct knowledge of the view. Rather, the model indirectly notifies the view of changes in the model's state, and the view reacts appropriately. This indirect notification *can* also be accomplished via direct message passing, but some systems have different mechanisms for accomplishing this passive information passing without allowing the full control of message passing. The same indirect relationship exists between the view and the controller.

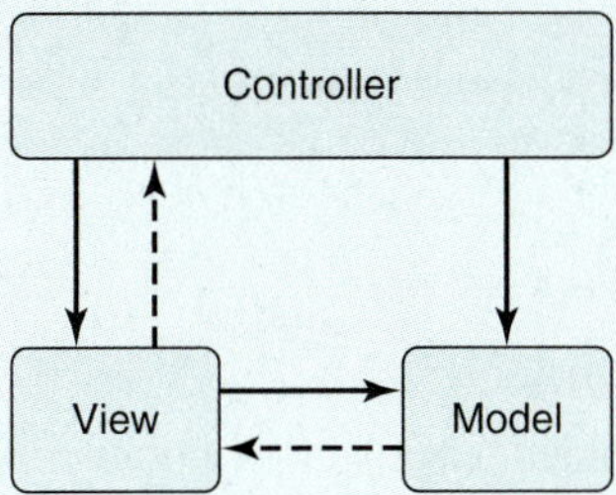

FIGURE 11.11 The Model-View-Controller paradigm

The poker application in this chapter is too simple and short to benefit greatly from a software paradigm as far-reaching and general as MVC. Nevertheless, the program does follow the general guidelines of MVC. It carefully separates the model from the view, and to a lesser extent, the view from the controller.

Exercises

1. Argue for or against the thesis that the Poker program in this chapter follows the MVC architecture.
2. What classes in the Poker program are clearly part of the model module? Explain.

3. What classes in the Poker program are clearly part of the view? Explain.
4. What classes in the Poker program are clearly part of the controller? Explain.
5. Using the Poker program of this chapter, find examples of methods and events represented by each solid and dotted line in Figure 11.11. For example: what methods in the Poker program are part of the view that send messages to the model? What "events" detected by the view are forwarded to the controller for processing?
6. How might you redesign the case study to make it more in tune with the MVC architecture?

CHAPTER 12

Inheritance

"I inherited a painting and a violin which turned out to be a Rembrandt and a Stradivarius. Unfortunately, Rembrandt made lousy violins and Stradivarius was a terrible painter."

—Tommy Cooper, comedian

Objectives

The objectives of Chapter 12 include an understanding of

- inheritance and its benefits and pitfalls,
- the *is-a* relationship between a *derived* class and a *base* class,
- *abstract* classes designed for inheritance,
- upcasting and downcasting,
- the instanceof operator,
- inheriting from Object,
- overriding toString() and equals(Object o),
- interfaces, and
- the Comparable interface and a generic sort routine.

12.1 INTRODUCTION

Object-oriented programming is built upon the principles of encapsulation, inheritance, and polymorphism. The previous three chapters deal with classes and objects, the cornerstone of encapsulation. This chapter provides an introduction to inheritance.

> Inheritance makes it possible to build new classes from existing classes, thus facilitating the reuse of methods and data from one class in another. Moreover, inheritance allows data of one type to be treated as data of a more general type.

Example 12.1 provides one more illustration of encapsulation. Using this application as a starting point, we move on to inheritance.

12.2 A BASIC REMOTE CONTROL UNIT

EXAMPLE 12.1

Figure 12.1 shows a rather basic remote control unit that can be used to turn a TV on or off, raise and lower the volume, or change the channel. Volume levels range from 0 to 20 and channel numbers from 1 to 199. Pressing a volume (channel) button increases or decreases the volume (channel) by one unit. For example, if the current channel is 5, pressing the "channel up" button twice sets the channel to 7.

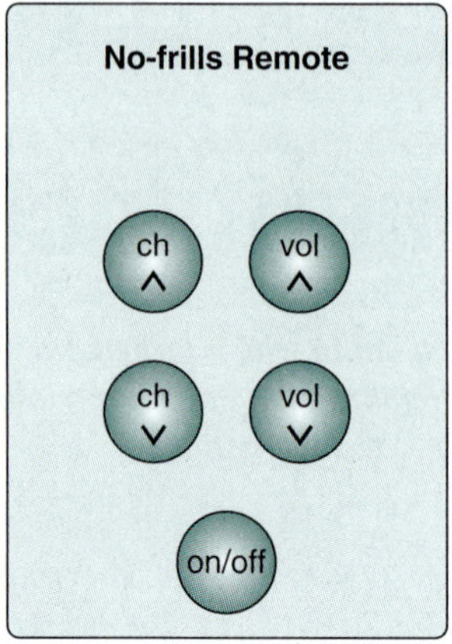

FIGURE 12.1 A no-frills remote control unit

Problem Statement Implement a Remote class that models the remote control unit of Figure 12.1. When the TV is initially switched on, the default channel is 2 and the default volume is 5.

Java Solution The Remote class has two attributes:

- volume, an integer in the range 0 through 20, and
- channel, an integer in the range 1 through 199.

The methods simulate the functions of the buttons in Figure 12.1. These methods are

- channelUp() and channelDown(), which respectively increase and decrease channel by one, and
- volumeUp() and volumeDown(), which increase or decrease volume.

The Remote class has no fancy code or complicated methods. In addition to the methods channelUp(), channelDown(), volumeUp(), and volumeDown(), the Remote class implements two additional methods:

- display(), which displays the current volume and channel, and
- menu(), which presents a list of options to a user.

Each time a user "presses any button," display() shows the current channel and the volume.

You may notice that the instance variables of the following class are declared as protected. For the present, ignore this access modifier. We explain its meaning in Example 12.2.

```
import java.util.*;
public class Remote

{
    protected int volume; // notice the protected access modifier
    protected int channel;

    protected final int MAXIMUM_VOLUME = 20;        // highest volume setting
    protected final int MAXIMUM_CHANNEL = 199;      // highest channel number
```

```
    protected final int DEFAULT_CHANNEL = 2;        // default channel number
    protected final int DEFAULT_VOLUME = 5;         // default volume setting
    protected final int MINIMUM_VOLUME = 0;         // minimum volume, no sound
    protected final int MINIMUM_CHANNEL = 1;        // lowest channel number

    public Remote()                                 // default constructor
    {
       channel = DEFAULT_CHANNEL;
       volume = DEFAULT_VOLUME;
    }

    public Remote(int ch, int  vol )                //  two argument constructor
    {                                               //  assumes valid data
       channel = ch;
       volume = vol;
    }

    public void volumeUp()                          // increase volume by one unit
    {
       if (volume <  MAXIMUM_VOLUME)                // cannot exceed MAXIMUM_VOLUME
       volume++;
    }

    public void volumeDown()                        // decrease volume by one unit
    {
       if (volume > MINIMUM_VOLUME)                 // cannot go lower than MINIMUM_VOLUME
          volume--;
    }

    public void channelUp()                         // increase channel number by 1
    {
       if (channel < MAXIMUM_CHANNEL )              // cannot exceed MAXIMUM_CHANNEL
          channel++;
    }

    public void channelDown()                       // decrease channel number by 1
    {
       if (channel > MINIMUM_CHANNEL)               // cannot go lower than MINIMUM_CHANNEL
          channel--;
    }

    public void display()                           // show the volume and the channel
    {
       System.out.println("\n----------------------");
       System.out.println("Channel: " + channel);
       System.out.println("Volume:  " + volume);
       System.out.println("----------------------\n");
    }

    public void menu() // presents user with the choices of Figure 12.2
    {
       Scanner input = new Scanner(System.in);
       String choice;
       System.out.println("POWER ON");
       display();
       do
       {
          System.out.println("Channel up:     +");
          System.out.println("Channel down:   -");
          System.out.println("Volume up:      ++");
```

```
            System.out.println("Volume down:   --");
            System.out.println("Power off:       o");
            System.out.print("Choose: ");
            choice = input.next();
            if (choice.equals("+"))
                channelUp();
            else if (choice.equals("-"))
                channelDown();
            else if (choice.equals("++"))
                volumeUp();
            else if (choice.equals("--"))
                volumeDown();
            display();
        } while (! choice.equals("o"));
        System.out.println("POWER OFF");
    }

    public static void main(String[] args)
    {
        Remote remote = new Remote();
        remote.menu();
    }
}
```

Output

```
POWER ON

----------------------
Channel: 2
Volume:  5
----------------------

Channel up:     +
Channel down:   -
Volume up:      ++
Volume down:    --
Power off:      o
Choose: +

----------------------
Channel: 3
Volume:  5
----------------------

Channel up:     +
Channel down:   -
Volume up:      ++
Volume down:    --
Power off:      o
Choose: ++

----------------------
Channel: 3
Volume:  6
----------------------
```

```
Channel up:      +
Channel down:    –
Volume up:       ++
Volume down:     ––
Power off:       o
Choose: o

----------------------
Channel: 3
Volume:  6
----------------------

POWER OFF
```

Discussion Except for the keyword protected, the Remote class is not much different from any of the other classes that you have seen, and understanding it should present no difficulty. The Remote class supplies the functions illustrated in Figure 12.1. Each menu option corresponds to a button on the remote unit, and each button is simulated by a method. Remote is yet another example of encapsulation—methods and data tied together in a single entity.

Example 12.2 illustrates the second principle of object-oriented programming: *inheritance*.

> *Inheritance* is the mechanism that allows us to reuse the attributes and methods of one class in the implementation of another class.

In Example 12.2, you will see how to "extend" the Remote class so that the attributes and methods of Remote can be used (or *re*used) to build a new class with all of the features of Remote and then some. This is where inheritance takes center stage.

EXAMPLE 12.2

The "up and down" buttons of the no-frills remote of Example 12.1 may satisfy the needs of a sedentary channel surfer, but a better design would allow a viewer to access channels directly by punching in a channel number. Figure 12.2 shows an upgraded version of the no-frills remote. The *last* button on the new remote switches the channel back to the previously viewed channel. The direct access remote is a no-frills remote with additional functionality.

Problem Statement Implement a class, DirectRemote, that simulates the remote control unit of Figure 12.2.

Java Solution DirectRemote is not much different than Remote. In fact, the attributes and methods of Remote, such as volumeUp() and volumeDown(), can be used (or reused) in the implementation of DirectRemote. DirectRemote need not be built from scratch. Remote can give its attributes and methods to DirectRemote, or stated differently, DirectRemote can *inherit* the attributes and methods of Remote.

How is this magic performed? The clause extends Remote in the class heading

public class DirectRemote **extends** Remote (line 2)

declares that DirectRemote inherits from Remote. That is, DirectRemote has the features and functionality of Remote . . . and possibly more.

FIGURE 12.2 A direct access remote

The following implementation of DirectRemote does not explicitly declare the instance variables channel and volume; they are inherited from Remote. Likewise, DirectRemote does not implement volumeUp() or display(); they come to DirectRemote via inheritance. On the other hand, DirectRemote has the option of declaring its own additional variables and providing its own implementation of any method, new or inherited. In particular, DirectRemote implements new methods that handle direct channel access and last channel access, and it provides its own modified versions of channelUp() and channelDown().

The implementation of DirectRemote is easy to comprehend if you keep in mind that DirectRemote inherits the variables, constants, and methods of Remote. Although none is explicitly declared, each variable, constant, and method is present and available because DirectRemote inherits it from Remote. Remote is called a *base class,* a *superclass,* or a *parent class* and DirectRemote a *derived class*, a *subclass,* or a *child class.*

Besides the new keyword, extends, the following implementation of DirectRemote includes two additional new keywords: protected and super, which are explained in the subsequent discussion section.

DirectRemote, a subclass of Remote

```
import java.util.*;
public class DirectRemote extends Remote                // Remote is the base class; DirectRemote a subclass
{
   protected int lastChannel;                           // to reset to the previous channel

   public DirectRemote()                                // default constructor
   {
      super();                                          // call the default constructor of remote
      lastChannel = DEFAULT_CHANNEL;                    // DEFAULT_CHANNEL inherited from Remote
   }

   public DirectRemote(int ch, int vol, int last)       // three-argument constructor
   {
      super(ch, vol);                                   // a call to the two-argument constructor of Remote
      lastChannel = last;
   }

   public void channelUp()                              // overrides the channelUp() method of Remote
   {
      lastChannel = channel;
```

```
      super.channelUp();                       // a call to the channelUp() method of Remote
   }

   public void channelDown()                   // overrides the channelDown() method of Remote
   {
      lastChannel = channel;
      super.channelDown();                     // a call to the channelDown() method of Remote
   }

   public void setChannel(int ch)
   {
      lastChannel = channel;
      channel = ch;
   }

   public void last()                          // sets channel to previously viewed channel
   {
      int temp = channel;
      channel = lastChannel;
      lastChannel = temp;
   }

   public void menu()                          // the user interface
   {
      Scanner input = new Scanner(System.in);
      String choice;
      System.out.println("POWER ON");
      display(); // method inherited from Remote
      do
      {
            System.out.println("Channel up:        +");
            System.out.println("Channel down:      -");
            System.out.println("Volume up:         ++");
            System.out.println("Volume down:       --");
            System.out.println("Last channel:      <<");
            System.out.println("Enter channel number: ");
            System.out.println("Power off          o");
            System.out.print("Choose: ");
            choice = input.next();
            if (choice.equals("+"))
               channelUp();                    // overrides the Remote methode
            else if (choice.equals("-"))
               channelDown();                  // overrides the Remote method
            else if (choice.equals("++"))
               volumeUp();                     // inherited from Remote
            else if (choice.equals("--"))
               volumeDown(); // inherited from Remote
            else if (choice.equals("<<"))
               last();                         // resets channel to previously viewed channel
            else  if ( !choice.equals("o"))    // choice is a number or invalid
            {
               int ch = getChannel(choice);
               if (ch >= 1 && ch <= 200)       // if valid channel
                  setChannel(ch);
            }
            display();
         } while (! choice.equals("o"));
         System.out.println("POWER OFF");
   }

   private int getChannel(String ch)           // a helper method
```

```
            // converts a string of digits to an integer
            // if a character of ch is not a digit returns 0
   {
      int number = 0;
      for (int i = 0; i < ch.length(); i++)
      {
         char digit = ch.charAt(i);
         if ( digit > '9' || digit < '0')
            return 0;
         number = 10 * number + (digit - '0');
      }
      return number;
   }

   public static void main(String[] args)
   {
      DirectRemote remote = new DirectRemote();
      remote.menu();
   }
}
```

Output

Instantiation of a DirectRemote object produces the following output:

```
POWER ON

----------------------
Channel: 2
Volume:  5

----------------------
Channel up:        +
Channel down:       -
Volume up:         ++
Volume down:        --
Last channel:      <<
Enter channel number:
Power off      o
Choose: 16

----------------------
Channel: 16
Volume:  5
----------------------

Channel up:        +
Channel down:       -
Volume up:         ++
Volume down:        --
Last channel:      <<
Enter channel number:
Power off      o
Choose: 12

----------------------
Channel: 12
Volume:  5
----------------------
```

```
Channel up:          +
Channel down:         -
Volume up:          ++
Volume down:         --
Last channel:       <<
Enter channel number:
Power off       o
Choose: <<

----------------------
Channel: 16
Volume:  5
----------------------

Channel up:          +
Channel down:         -
Volume up:          ++
Volume down:         --
Last channel:       <<
Enter channel number:
Power off       o
Choose: ++

----------------------
Channel: 16
Volume:  6
----------------------

Channel up:          +
Channel down:         -
Volume up:          ++
Volume down:         --
Last channel:       <<
Enter channel number:
Power off       o
Choose: o

----------------------
Channel: 16
Volume:  6
----------------------

POWER OFF
```

Discussion At last, we explain the keyword protected.

The access modifier protected falls between public and private.

- A private variable or method is visible only to its defining class.
- A public variable or method is visible to any class.
- A protected variable or method is visible to its defining class and all its subclasses, as well as any other classes in the same package.

Because the instance variables, channel and volume, of the base class Remote are protected, they are visible to the derived class DirectRemote. DirectRemote inherits these attributes from parent Remote and has access to channel and volume. If volume and channel were declared private in Remote, they would not be visible to DirectRemote, and DirectRemote would not be able to alter these variables except via getter and setter methods.

The public methods of Remote are also inherited by DirectRemote—well, mostly. Notice that both Remote and DirectRemote implement channelUp(), channelDown(), and menu(). DirectRemote *overrides* Remote's version of these methods. That is, DirectRemote has its own versions of these methods that are different from Remote's version.

A subclass inherits all public and protected methods of a base class unless the subclass overrides a method, thus providing its own implementation.

There is one notable exception to the inheritance rule for methods.

A subclass does not inherit the constructors of the base class.

The constructors of a base class are not considered constructors of a subclass. This is explained in more detail in the following line-by-line discussion.

Line 2: The phrase DirectRemote extends Remote indicates that Remote is the base class and DirectRemote a subclass. DirectRemote inherits from Remote.

Line 4: DirectRemote declares an additional instance variable, lastChannel with protected access. Thus, any class that extends DirectRemote inherits lastChannel. The variable lastChannel is declared in DirectRemote and is not an attribute of Remote, the parent class. A Remote object knows nothing of lastChannel.

Lines 5–14: The statements contained on lines 5–14 define a default constructor and a two-argument constructor for DirectRemote. As mentioned previously, a child class does not inherit the constructors of the parent. However, a child class may invoke a parent constructor using the keyword super as shown on lines 7 and 12:

super() calls the default constructor of Remote (line 7), and
super(ch, vol) calls the two-argument constructor of Remote (line 12).

If super is used, then it must be the first statement of a constructor.

Finally, we note that if a base class constructor is not explicitly called using super, the default constructor of the base class is automatically invoked. In this case, if the default constructor of the base class does not exist, a compilation error results.

Lines 15–19: Because lastChannel (defined in DirectRemote) must be reset each time the channel is changed, the channelUp() method inherited from Remote is not suitable. A new channelUp() method overrides the channelUp() method of Remote. This version of channelUp() first stores the value of the current channel (channel) in the instance variable lastChannel and then invokes the channelUp() method of the base class with the keyword super

super.channelUp(),

which increments channel, provided channel is currently less than MAX_CHANNEL.

You may wonder why not increment channel directly. Why bother calling the channelUp() method of Remote? A call to channelUp() of Remote is safer and more robust than directly accessing the data of Remote. If the implementation of Remote changes, as long as Remote supplies a channelUp() method, no change to channelUp() of DirectRemote is necessary. This is discussed in more detail in Section 12.3.

Lines 20–24: As with channelUp(), this method overrides the corresponding channelDown() method of Remote. Notice the call to channelDown() of the parent class: super.channelDown().

Lines 25–29: These lines define a setter method that sets channel.

Lines 30–35: The last() method swaps channel with lastChannel, making the current channel the previously viewed channel.

Lines 36–72: The menu() method presents the user with a menu of options that correspond to the buttons on the remote unit of Figure 12.2. When the user makes a choice, the corresponding button is "pressed." Notice that after every choice, display() shows the current values of the instance variables channel and volume. DirectRemote inherits display() from Remote.

Lines 73–86: The method

```
int getChannel(String ch)
```

is a helper method with private access. Thus, the method is not accessible outside of the class. This method accepts a string version of the channel number and returns the channel number as an integer. If the string ch contains characters that do not represent digits, the method returns the invalid channel, 0.

Figure 12.3 shows the attributes and methods of both classes.

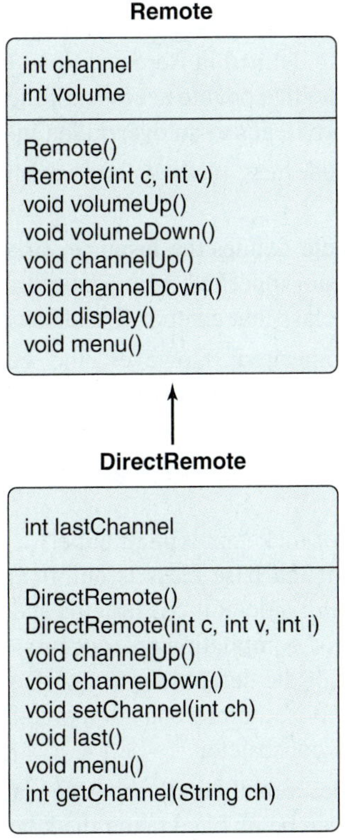

FIGURE 12.3 *DirectRemote* extends *Remote*

Examples 12.1 and 12.2 illustrate many of the concepts of inheritance. We summarize the key points:

- The keyword extends signifies an inheritance relationship.

  For example, DirectRemote extends Remote means that DirectRemote inherits from Remote and that Remote is a parent class of DirectRemote. The Remote class is called the *base class*, *superclass*, or *parent class*, and DirectRemote is the *derived class*, *subclass*, or *child class*.

- The access modifier protected is used in a base class. A protected variable or method is visible to any subclass or any class in the same package. A private variable or method of a base class is not visible to a subclass. However, if the base class provides getter and setter methods for private variables, a subclass can access private variables defined in the base class via these methods.

  For example, if Remote assigns private access to channel, DirectRemote can, nonetheless, access channel, provided Remote includes methods such as

```
public int getChannel()          and          public void setChannel(int ch)
{                                             {
   return channel;                               channel = ch;
}                                             }
```

- A derived class inherits the data and methods of the base class that are not private. Additionally, a derived class can *override* or redefine an inherited base class method.

  For example, DirectRemote can override a Remote method and provide its own implementation. In particular, DirectRemote overrides menu(), channelUp(), and channelDown(), which are defined in Remote. Note, however, that a subclass may not override a public method with a private access modifier. In general, you may not assign more restrictive access privileges to an overridden method.

- A derived class can include new methods and variables that are not part of the base class.

  For example, DirectRemote defines the instance variable lastChannel and the method setChannel(), which are not inherited from Remote. Notice that lastChannel has protected access. Thus, any class that extends DirectRemote inherits lastChannel.

- Constructors are not inherited. However, the constructors of a derived class can invoke the constructors of the parent class with the keyword super, that is, super() or super(...). If a derived class calls a base class constructor with the keyword super, the call must occur before any other code is executed in the base class constructor.

- If a derived class does not make an explicit super(...) call to a base class constructor, the default constructor of the base class is automatically invoked. If the base class defines constructors but *not* a default constructor and the derived class does not make an explicit super(...) call, a compilation error occurs. The derived class cannot rely on the automatic invocation of the default constructor bescause the default constructor of the parent does not exist. It is, therefore, a good practice to define a default constructor whenever you define any constructor.

- If a derived class overrides a method x(), the base class version of x() is still available to the derived class and can be invoked using the keyword super:

```
super.x().
```

For example, both Remote and DirectRemote implement channelUp(). The call

```
super.channelUp()
```

in DirectRemote invokes the channelUp() method of Remote.

12.3 INHERITANCE AND ENCAPSULATION

Inheritance brings certain risks. In a very real way, inheritance violates encapsulation and information hiding: the DirectRemote class depends on the implementation of Remote. If Remote's instance variable channel is renamed, altered, or eliminated, the DirectRemote method setChannel() fails because setChannel() accesses channel directly. On the other hand, channelDown() of DirectRemote functions correctly as long as the *interface* of Remote remains unchanged. The channelDown() (or channelUp()) method of DirectRemote does not directly manipulate the variable channel but instead uses a method call:

```
super.channelDown().
```

Indeed, had Remote provided a setter method for channel, the DirectRemote method setChannel() would be more secure.

> If a base class changes some implementation, a subclass that works today may break tomorrow.

Careful design minimizes these potential dangers, but the possibility for disaster always exists. This does not mean that you should avoid inheritance. Inheritance is a powerful and useful concept. However, you should be aware that inheritance has its dangers and pitfalls.

12.4 THE *IS-A* RELATIONSHIP: A *DirectRemote IS-A Remote*

Inheritance allows the creation of a more specialized class from a base class. A derived class extends the attributes and/or functionality of the base class. A derived class has everything that the base class has, and more. Well, not everything—constructors are not inherited. Inheritance enables code reuse.

> The relationship between the base class and a derived class is termed an *is-a* relationship because every derived class *is-a* (kind of) superclass.

For example, a DirectRemote *is-a* Remote in the sense that a DirectRemote object can do everything that a Remote object can do. A DirectRemote object has all the attributes and functionality of a Remote object, and more.

> When deciding whether or not to extend a class, you should determine whether or not an *is-a* relationship exists. If not, inheritance is probably inappropriate.

12.5 INHERITANCE VIA FACTORING: MOVIES AND PLAYS

We now move from TV to film and theater. Consider a Film class with attributes:

- title,
- director,
- screenwriter, and
- total box office gross, in millions of dollars adjusted for inflation.

The methods of a Film class might include

- constructors,
- getters and setters, and
- a method that displays the values of each attribute.

Like a Film object, a Play object has

- a title,
- a director, and
- a writer or playwright.

Additionally, a Play object also holds the number of performances of a play. The Play methods are

- getter and setter methods, and
- a method that displays the values of each attribute.

Figure 12.4 shows the attributes and methods of both classes.

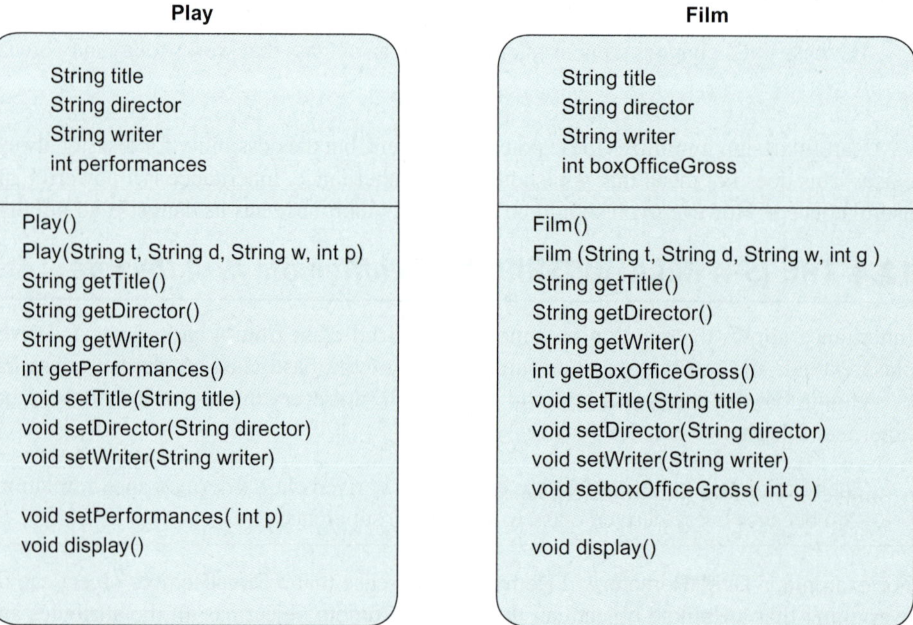

FIGURE 12.4 A *Play* class and a *Film* class

The Play class and the Film class are very similar and share many of the same attributes and methods. In fact, they are more the same than different. Should one class extend the other? On one hand, a Play *is-not-a* Film and a Film *is-not-a* Play. On the other hand, Play and Film share many of the same attributes. Couldn't these attributes and methods be passed from one class to the other?

To exploit code reuse, we *factor out* what is common to Film and Play and design a new class, Production, so that Production has all the attributes and methods common to both Film and Play. Moreover, a Film *is-a* Production and similarly a Play *is-a* Production. Production is a base class designed for inheritance and not instantiation. Film extends Production, and Play extends Production. The raison d'etre for Production is inheritance, not instantiation. Figure 12.5 shows the Production *hierarchy* and Example 12.3 gives an implementation.

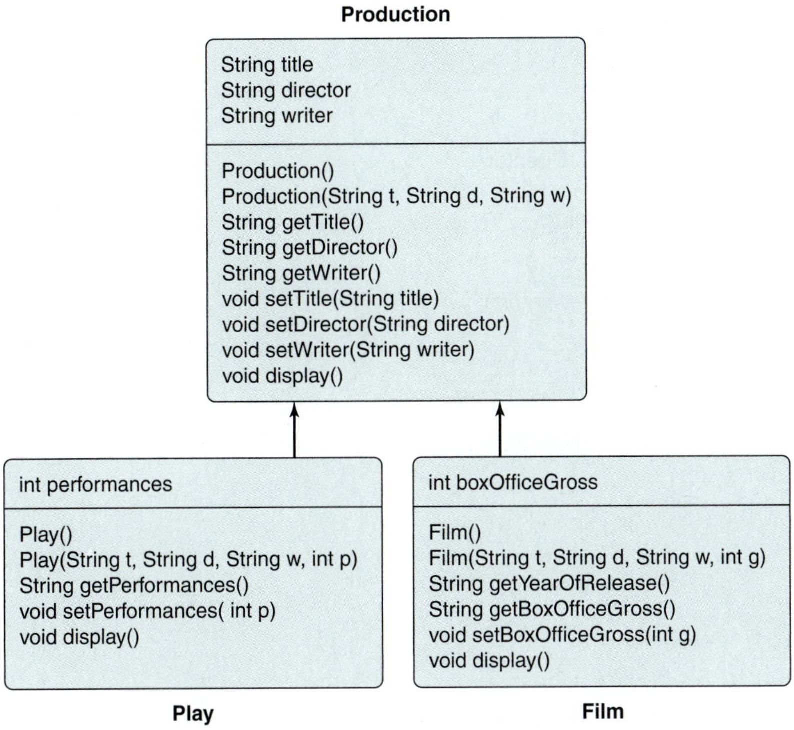

Production

String title
String director
String writer

Production()
Production(String t, String d, String w)
String getTitle()
String getDirector()
String getWriter()
void setTitle(String title)
void setDirector(String director)
void setWriter(String writer)
void display()

int performances

Play()
Play(String t, String d, String w, int p)
String getPerformances()
void setPerformances(int p)
void display()

Play

int boxOfficeGross

Film()
Film(String t, String d, String w, int g)
String getYearOfRelease()
String getBoxOfficeGross()
void setBoxOfficeGross(int g)
void display()

Film

FIGURE 12.5 *Play* extends *Production*; *Film* extends *Production*

EXAMPLE 12.3

Problem Statement Implement Production as well as subclasses Play and Film as shown in Figure 12.5

Java Solution The following Production class serves as a parent or base class. Production defines the attributes and methods common to Film and Play. Following the implementation of Production are the two subclasses Film and Play. The methods are simple and should require no explanation.

```
public class Production
{
   protected String title;
   protected String director;
   protected String writer;
   public Production()    // default constructor
   {
      title = "";
      director = "";
      writer = "";
   }

   public Production(String t, String d, String w) // three argument constructor
   {
      title = t;
      director = d;
      writer = w;
   }
```

```
    public String getTitle()
    {
       return title;
    }

    public String getDirector()
    {
       return  director;
    }

    public String getWriter()
    {
       return writer;
    }

    public void setTitle(String t)
    {
       title = t;
    }

    public void setDirector(String d)
    {
       director = d;
    }

    public void setWriter(String w)
    {
       writer = w;
    }

    public void display()
    {
       System.out.println("Production class");
    }
}

public class Play extends Production
{
    protected int performances;
    public Play()
    {
       super();                   // call Production default constructor
       performances = 0;
    }

    public Play(String t, String d, String w, int p)
    {
       super(t, d, w);            // call Production  constructor
       performances = p;
    }

    public int getPerformances()
    {
       return performances;
    }

    public void setPerformances(int p)
```

```
    {
        performances = p;
    }

    public void display()
    {
        System.out.println("Title:        " + title);
        System.out.println("Director:     " + director);
        System.out.println("Playwright: " + writer);
        System.out.println("Performances: " +    performances);
    }
}

public class Film extends Production
{
    protected int boxOfficeGross;
    public Film()
    {
        super();                    // call Production default constructor
        boxOfficeGross = 0;
    }

    public Film(String t, String d, String w, int g)
    {
        super(t, d, w);             // call Production constructor
        boxOfficeGross = g;
    }

    public int getBoxOfficeGross()
    {
        return boxOfficeGross;
    }

    public void setBoxOfficeGross(int g)
    {
        boxOfficeGross = g;
    }

    public void display ()
    {
        System.out.println("Title:        " + title);
        System.out.println("Director:     " + director);
        System.out.println("Screenwriter: " + writer);
        System.out.println("Total gross: $" +  boxOfficeGross + " million");
    }
}
```

Output The demonstration class

```
public class ThatsEntertainment
{
    public static void main(String[] args)
    {
        Film film = new Film("Titanic", "James Cameron",
                                        "James Cameron", 2245);
```

```
        Play play = new Play("Bus Stop", "Harold Clurman", "William Inge", 478);
        film.display();
        System.out.println();
        play.display();
    }
}
```

produces the following output.

```
Title:          Titanic
Director:       James Cameron
Screenwriter:   James Cameron
Total gross:    $2245 million

Title:          Bus Stop
Director:       Harold Clurman
Playwright:     William Inge
Performances:   478
```

Discussion Subclasses Film and Play inherit the data and methods of the base class Production. Indeed, Film *is-a* Production and Play *is-a* Production. Both Play and Film *extend* Production. Each overrides display(), and each has an additional instance variable. Because Production is designed for inheritance and not for implementation, the display() method of Production does no more than print the name of the class, "Production class". The method is not strictly necessary; it is there to be overridden.

12.6 INHERITANCE VIA *Abstract* CLASSES

The Production class is a base class designed for inheritance and not instantiation. A Film *is-a* Production and a Play *is-a* Production. We might instantiate Play and Film and thus create Film and Play objects, but we do not create Production objects. A Production is abstract, a Play or Film is concrete.

Java's notion of an *abstract* class is very precise:

> An abstract class is a class that cannot be instantiated. However, an abstract class can be inherited.

In general, an abstract class has the following properties:

- The keyword abstract denotes an abstract class. For example,

  ```
  public abstract class Production
  ```

  specifies that Production is an abstract class.
- An abstract class *cannot* be instantiated. You cannot create an object of an abstract class.
- An abstract class can be inherited by other classes. Indeed, an abstract class is designed for inheritance, not instantiation.
- An abstract class *may* contain abstract methods. An abstract method is a method with no implementation. For example, the method

  ```
  public abstract void display(); // method has no body
  ```

  is an abstract method. Notice the keyword abstract and the terminal semicolon.

- If an abstract class contains abstract methods, those methods *must* be overridden in any non-abstract subclass; otherwise the subclass is also abstract.
- All abstract classes and methods are public.
- To be of any use, an abstract class must be extended.

The Production class of Example 12.3 is an excellent candidate for an abstract class. Production is designed for inheritance and not instantiation. As an abstract class, Production has the following form:

```
public abstract class Production
{
   // all attributes and methods, except display(), as in Example 12.3

      public abstract void display(); // Look! No implementation
}
```

The keyword abstract in the heading indicates that Production cannot be instantiated; Production is designed solely as a base class. Also, display() is tagged an abstract method: display() has no implementation. Contrast this with the display() method used in the non-abstract version of the Production class.

```
public void display()
{
     System.out.println("Production class");
}
```

This "dummy" method is no longer necessary.

Every non-abstract or concrete subclass that extends Production must implement the abstract method display(). Thus, any non-abstract subclass of Production is guaranteed to have a display() method. That's the contract. A subclass that does not implement every abstract method of its parent class is also abstract and cannot be instantiated. Adhering to this rule, both Play and Film, being non-abstract subclasses of Production, implement display().

12.7 EXTENDING THE HIERARCHY

A Musical *is-a* Play with songs. A Musical object has all the attributes of a Play object as well as a composer and a lyricist. Example 12.4 demonstrates how easily a Musical class can be implemented by extending Play and reusing the methods of Play.

EXAMPLE 12.4

Problem Statement Implement Musical as a subclass of Play. Include new attributes

```
String composer, and
String lyricist
```

along with getter and setter methods. Override display() to include all attributes of a Musical object.

Java Solution Most of the work has been done. Musical inherits the attributes and methods of Play and adds just a few of its own.

```
1.   class Musical extends Play
2.   {
```

```
3.      protected String composer;
4.      protected String lyricist;

5.      public Musical()                    // default constructor
6.      {
7.         super();                         // invokes the default constructor of Play
8.         composer = "";
9.         lyricist = "";
10.     }

11.     public Musical(String t, String d, String w, String c, String l, int p)
12.      // t(itle), d(irector), w(riter), c(omposer), l(yricist), p(erformances)
13.     {
14.        super(t, d, w, p);            // invokes the 4-argument constructor of Play
15.        composer = c;
16.        lyricist = l;
17.     }

18.     public String getComposer()
19.     {
20.        return composer;
21.     }

22.     public void setComposer(String c)
23.     {
24.        composer = c;
25.     }

26.     public String getLyricist()
27.     {
28.        return lyricist;
29.     }

30.     public void setLyricist(String l)
31.     {
32.        lyricist = l;
33.     }

34.     public void display()            // overrides the display() method of Play
35.     {
36.        System.out.println("Title:       " + title);
37.        System.out.println("Director:    " + director);
38.        System.out.println("Playwright: " + writer);
39.        System.out.println("Composer: " + composer);
40.        System.out.println("Lyricist: " + lyricist);
41.        System.out.println("Performances: " + performances);
42.     }
43. }
```

Discussion With no trouble at all, Musical has joined the Production hierarchy. Remember, Musical does *not* inherit Play's constructors or any other constructors. Access to Play's constructors is accomplished via the super keyword. The calls to super() on lines 7 and 14 invoke the constructors of Play.

The Production hierarchy is pictured in Figure 12.6.

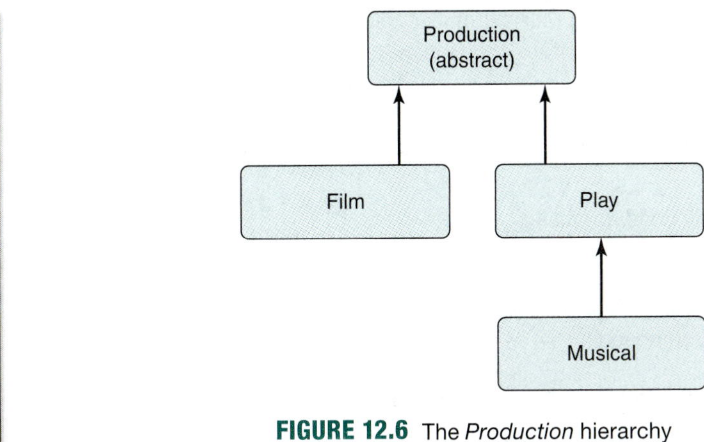

FIGURE 12.6 The *Production* hierarchy

12.8 UPCASTING AND DOWNCASTING

A Musical *is-a* Play and, as such, Java considers a Musical object a Play object. Accordingly, the following assignments are valid:

```
Play play = new Musical("Sweeny Todd", "Harold Prince", "Hugh Wheeler",
                        "Stephen Sondheim", " Stephen Sondheim", 557);
```

or

```
Play play;
Musical musical = new Musical("South Pacific", "Joshua Logan", "Oscar Hammerstein",
                              "Richard Rodgers", " Oscar Hammerstein", 1925);
play = musical;
```

In both cases, a Play reference refers to a Musical object. This type of assignment is called *upcasting.*

Upcasting is a language feature that allows a base-type reference to refer to an object of a derived type.

Thus any object of a class derived from Play (e.g., Musical) is also considered a Play object.

Objects of a derived type may be considered objects of the base type.

And, even though Production is an abstract class that cannot be instantiated, any type derived from Production may be upcast to Production. For example,

```
Production p = new Film(),
Production q = new Play(), and
Production r = new Musical()
```

are all valid assignments, but Production s = new Production() is not. A Film *is-a* Production; a Play *is-a* Production; and a Musical *is-a* Production, but Production is an abstract class and cannot *directly* be instantiated.

In contrast to upcasting, the following segment generates a compiler error.

```
Play play = new Play();
Musical musical = play;
```

The reference musical refers to a Musical object and a Play object does not qualify as a Musical object. Every Play is *not* a Musical. However, under certain conditions, an explicit *downcast* is permissible.

Downcasting means casting an object to a derived or more specialized type.

Consider the following code fragment:

```
1. Play play = new Musical();
2. Musical musical = (Musical)play;
3. musical.getComposer();
```

We examine the code line by line:

Line 1: The variable play is a Play reference. A Musical *is-a* Play. There is no problem here; the assignment is legal. This is an example of upcasting. Note that a Musical object has been instantiated.

Line 2: The variable musical is a Musical reference. The reference play is a Play reference which, in this case, refers to a Musical object. *The assignment is legal with an explicit downcast*. As a Play reference, play is unaware of its status as a Musical unless explicitly downcast to Musical. The statement

```
Musical musical = play;
```

without the explicit downcast generates an error. The downcast informs the compiler that play actually refers to a Musical object.

Line 3: The variable musical is a Musical reference and getComposer() is a Musical method. There is no problem here.

What do you think happens when the following segment is compiled?

```
1. Play play = new Musical(...);
2. String name = play.getComposer() ;
```

Again, line 1 is a valid upcast. However, the compiler complains about the method call on line 2. To the compiler, play is a Play reference and Play has no getComposer() method. So the compiler generates an error:

```
cannot find symbol
symbol : method getComposer()
location: class Play
  String name = play.getComposer();
```

Yet, because a Musical object is instantiated (line 1), an explicit downcast informs the compiler that play refers to a Musical object and fixes the problem:

```
Play play = new Musical(...);
String name = ((Musical)play).getComposer() ;
```

Here is another illustration using an array of Production references.

```
Production productions[] = new Production[3]; // holds 3 Production references
productions[0] = new Film (...);
productions[1] = new Play(...);
productions[2] = new Musical(...);
```

Each of these assignments is legal: Film *is-a* Production, Play *is-a* Production, and Musical *is-a* Production.

On the other hand, the method calls

```
productions[0].getBoxOfficeGross() and
productions[2].getComposer()
```

generate errors. The references productions[0] and productions[2] know nothing of the methods getBoxOfficeGross() and getComposer(). Nonetheless, a downcast fixes these errors and produces the desired results:

```
((Film)productions[0]).getBoxOfficeGross()
((Musical)productions[2]).getComposer()
```

To invoke a derived class method using a base class reference, a downcast is necessary.

Finally, note that Java does not allow the downcast

```
((Film)productions[2]).getBoxOfficeGross()
```

since productions[2] refers to a Musical object, which is not a descendent of Film.

12.8.1 A Feature of Upcasting and Downcasting

The relationship between the base class and its derived classes is a very powerful feature of inheritance. Yes, it is dandy that you can add new attributes and methods to the Play class, but it is even dandier that an object of type Musical can be considered an object of type Play. If you can't yet appreciate this programming muscle, with a few more tools, you will see the real power behind this concept. Indeed, because objects of a derived type can be considered objects of a base type, a single sorting or searching method can work with many different types. That is, a single method can handle many different types of objects. We will discuss this feature in detail shortly.

12.8.2 The *instanceof* operator

Like && and ||, instanceof is a boolean operator that requires two operands. The form of the instanceof operator is

object **instanceof** *class*

where *object* is any object and *class* is any class name.

If *object* belongs to or is derived from *class*, then instanceof returns true, otherwise instanceof returns false. For example, consider the following declarations:

```
Play play = new Play();
Musical musical = new Musical();
Film film = new Film();
```

Then

film instanceof Film returns true,
film instanceof Production returns true,
musical instanceof Play returns true,

musical instanceof Film returns false, and
musical instanceof Production returns true.

The instanceof operator can help a programmer to avoid casting errors.

The following code fragment uses the instanceof operator to check whether or not an object belongs to the Musical class before invoking the getComposer() method:

```
if (productions[2] instanceof Musical)
        string name = ((Musical)productions[2]).getComposer();
else...
```

The following example illustrates the instanceof operator within the context of a class.

EXAMPLE 12.5

Problem Statement Some films gross hundreds of millions of dollars and some plays seem to run forever. Write a single method,

```
int getData(Production p)
```

that returns the box office gross for a Film, or the number of performances for a Play. If an object p is neither a Film nor a Play, then getData(p) returns –1.

Java Solution The reference, p, passed to getData(...) refers to a Production object, which can be either a Film object or a Play object. Consequently, getData(...) accepts a Film reference, a Play reference, or even a Musical reference, because each of these *is-a* Production. The getData(...) method determines whether its parameter refers to a Film or a Play by utilizing the instanceof operator.

The following class includes getData(...) along with a main(...) method that invokes getData(...).

```
public class InstanceOfDemo
{
   public static int getData(Production p)  // Parameter is Production reference
   {
      if (p instanceof Film)
         return ((Film)p).getBoxOfficeGross();      // note the downcast
      else if (p instanceof Play)
            return ((Play)p).getPerformances();  // note the downcast
      else
         return –1;
   }

   public static void main(String[] args)
   {
      Production productions[] = new Production[3];
      productions[0] = new Film("Titanic", "James Cameron", "James Cameron", 2245);
      productions[1] = new Play("Rumors", "Gene Saks", "Neil Simon", 535);
      productions[2] = new Musical("Pippin", "Bob Fosse", "Roger O.  Hirson",
                                    "Stephen Schwartz", "Stephen Schwartz", 1944);
      for (int i = 0; i < 3; i++)
      {
         System.out.print(productions[i].getTitle() + ": " + getData(productions[i]));
         if (productions[i] instanceof Play)
            System.out.println(" performances");
         else
```

```
24.                System.out.println(" million dollars");
25.          }
26.     }
27. }
```

A main(...) method is included for illustrative purposes. The class produces the following output:

Output

```
Titanic: 2245 million dollars
Rumors: 535 performances
Pippin: 1944 performances
```

Discussion We examine the code, line by line.

Line 3: The argument passed to getData(...) is a Production reference. A Film reference, a Play reference, and a Musical reference are all Production references. Upcasting is always permissible.

Lines 5–6: If the instanceof operator returns true, then the object belongs to the Film class and consequently can invoke getBoxOfficeGross(). However, the object must be specifically downcast to Film because Production knows nothing of money.

Lines 7–8: These lines are similar to lines 5 and 6, but they use Play rather than Film.

12.9 EVERYTHING INHERITS: THE *Object* CLASS

The package java.lang, which is automatically imported into every application, contains Java's Object class. That's Object with an uppercase O.

> Every class is a subclass of Object. Every class is derived from Object.

Every class extends Object. Math, String, and Scanner all extend Object. Play, Film, Musical, Remote, and DirectRemote also extend Object. Film *is-an* Object; Play *is-an* Object. There is no escape; everything *is-an* Object. Object is the mother of all classes.

Being a descendent of Object brings several familial privileges.

- Every class inherits methods

  ```
  public boolean equals(Object object), and
  public String toString()
  ```

  from Object.
- Because every class extends Object, every class can be upcast to Object.

For example,

```
Object remote = new Remote();
Object film = new Film();
```

are both legal assignments: Remote *is-an* Object and Film *is-an* Object.

Example 12.6 shows that a single method can handle objects whose only common ancestor is Object.

EXAMPLE 12.6 The following Rectangle and Cube classes encapsulate the properties of a rectangle and a cube. They share no ancestor other than Object.

```
public class Rectangle
{
    protected int length;
    protected int width;
    public Rectangle()
    {
        length = 0;
        width = 0;
    }

    public Rectangle (int x, int y)
    {
        length = x;
        width = y;
    }

    public int area()
    {
        return length * width;
    }
}
```

```
public class Cube
{
    protected int length;
    protected int width;
    private int height;
    public Cube()
    {
        length = 0;
        width = 0;
        height = 0;
    }

    public Cube(int x, int y, int z)
    {
        length = x;
        width = y;
        height = z;
    }

    public int volume()
    {
        return length * width * height;
    }
}
```

Problem Statement Design a method, size(Object z), that accepts a single reference argument, z. If z refers to a Rectangle then size(z) returns its area, and if z is a reference to a Cube then size(z) returns its volume. If z refers to an object of any other class, then size(z) returns −1.

Java Solution Because both Rectangle and Cube extend Object, the method

```
int size(Object z)
```

can accept a Rectangle reference or a Cube reference. In fact, size(...) can accept *any* reference: Rectangle, Cube, Dodecahedron, or FlyingMonkey. *Every* class extends Object; every reference can be upcast to Object.

The following class includes a static method size(...) that accepts a reference to *any* object.

```
public class Size
{

    public static int size(Object z)          // notice that z refers to Object
    {
        if (z instanceof Rectangle)
            return ((Rectangle)z).area();     // downcast is necessary
        else if (z instance of Cube)
            return ((Cube)z).volume();        // downcast is necessary
        else
            return -1;
    }
```

```
12.     public static void main( String[] args)
13.     {
14.        Cube cube = new Cube(3, 4, 5);
15.        Rectangle rectangle = new Rectangle(3, 4);
16.        System.out.println("Rectangle has size " + size(rectangle));
17.        System.out.println("Cube has size " + size(cube));
18.     }
19. }
```

Output

```
Rectangle has size 12
Cube has size 60
```

Discussion The argument z of size(z) refers to an Object. Because every object (lowercase "o") *is-an* Object (uppercase "O"), *any* reference can be passed to size(...). That is, any object reference can be upcast to Object.

The size(...) method uses the instanceof operator to determine whether or not z refers to a Rectangle object or a Cube object (lines 5 and 7). In each case, to call the appropriate method, a downcast is necessary (lines 6 and 8).

12.9.1 Inheriting from *Object:* The *equals*(*Object p*) Method

Every class inherits

```
boolean equals(Object p)
```

from Object. The equals(...) method accepts an Object reference p and returns true or false.

Like the == operator, the equals(...) method tests whether or not two *references* are the same. The following code segment utilizes the Rectangle class of Example 12.6 in conjunction with the equals(...) method inherited from Object:

```
Rectangle x = new Rectangle(3, 4);
Rectangle y = new Rectangle(3, 4);
Rectangle z = x;                  // z and x refer to the same Rectangle object
System.out.println("x equals y: " + x.equals(y));
System.out.println("x equals z: " + x.equals(z));
```

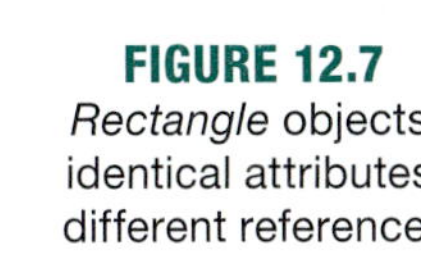

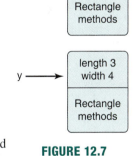

FIGURE 12.7
Rectangle objects: identical attributes, different references

Figure 12.7 shows each reference.

The segment produces the following output:

```
x equals y: false
x equals z: true
```

Although references x and y refer to objects with identical attributes, the addresses stored in x and y are different. Consequently, x.equals(y) returns false. In contrast, x and z refer to the same object.

Every class inherits equals(...) from Object, but each class also has the option of overriding the inherited equals(...). For instance, String inherits equals(...) from Object and conveniently overrides the inherited method.

> String overrides the equals(...) method with a version that compares *characters*, not references.

That is, two Strings are equal if and only if both Strings are composed of the same character sequence. The following fragment contrasts the equals(...) method with the == operator when applied to members of String.

```
1. String s = new String("Bingo!");
2. String t = new String("Bingo!");
3. System.out.println(s.equals(t)); // returns true
4. System.out.println(s == t);      // returns false
```

The output that is displayed by this fragment is:

```
true
false
```

On line 3, the equals(...) method returns true because both strings hold identical data, "Bingo!". The output from line 4 is false because the == operator checks references, and s and t refer to different objects. See Figure 12.8.

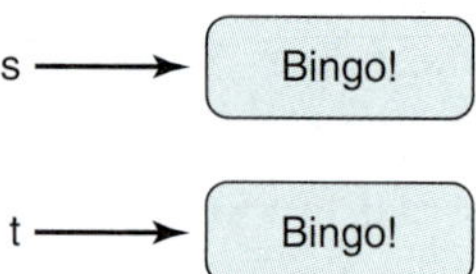

FIGURE 12.8 Strings: *s.equals(t)* returns *true*; *s == t* returns *false*

> As a general rule, to determine whether or not two objects of a class are equal based on some criteria other than references, a class should override
> boolean equals(Object o), which is inherited from Object.

In Example 12.7, the Rectangle class overrides the equals(...) method with a version that declares two Rectangle objects equal if and only if they have the same length and width.

EXAMPLE 12.7

Problem Statement Implement a class AnotherRectangle that extends the Rectangle class of Example 12.6 and overrides the equals(...) method that is inherited from Object. Implement equals(...) so that two objects belonging to AnotherRectangle are equal if they agree in both length and width.

Java Solution AnotherRectangle inherits attributes length and width from Rectangle as well as the area() method.

```
public class AnotherRectangle extends Rectangle
{
    public AnotherRectangle ()
    {
        super();        // call default constructor of Rectangle
    }

    public AnotherRectangle (int x, int y)
    {
        super(x, y); // call the two argument constructor of Rectangle
    }

    public boolean equals(Object p) // override equals(..) inherited from Object
    {
```

```
13.         if ( ! (p instanceof AnotherRectangle)) // p must belong to AnotherRectangle
14.         {
15.            System.out.println("Error: Object p must belong to AnotherRectangle");
16.            System.exit(0);                        // terminate the application
17.         }
18.         return                                   // if p is an AnotherRectangle object
19.               length == ((AnotherRectangle)p).length &&
20.                width == ((AnotherRectangle)p).width;
21.      }
22.      public static void main(String[] args)
23.      {
24.         AnotherRectangle r1 = new AnotherRectangle (3, 4);
25.         AnotherRectangle r2 = new AnotherRectangle (3, 4);
26.         AnotherRectangle r3 = new AnotherRectangle (5, 6);
27.         System.out.println("r1.equals(r2): " + r1.equals(r2));
28.         System.out.println("r1.equals(r3): " + r1.equals(r3));
29.         System.out.println("r1 == r2:      " + (r1 == r2));
30.      }
31. }
```

Output

```
r1.equals(r2): true
r1.equals(r3): false
r1 == r2:      false
```

Discussion

Lines 11–17: The equals(...) method inherited from Object has an Object parameter. However, in this case, Object p must also belong to the AnotherRectangle class. Otherwise, an error message is displayed and the application exits.

Lines 19–20: The compiler knows that o belongs to the Object class. As such, p does not have length and width attributes. Thus, a downcast to AnotherRectangle is required.

Line 27: Using the overridden equals(...) method, r1 and r2 are compared. The comparison is based on the attributes length and width. Both Rectangle objects have length 3 and width 4, so the two objects are considered equal.

Line 28: Using equals(...), r1 and r3 are compared. Once again, the comparison uses the attributes length and width. In this case, the Rectangle referenced by r1 has length 3 and width 4 and the Rectangle referenced by r3 has length 5 and width 6, so the two objects are not considered equal.

Line 29: Finally, *references* r1 and r2 are compared using the == operator. Although r1 and r2 reference Rectangle objects that have the same length and width, r1 and r2 refer to distinct objects and hold different addresses. Consequently, == returns false.

You may be wondering, why not write an equals(...) method for AnotherRectangle as

boolean equals(**AnotherRectangle x**) ?

Isn't this simpler? Why bother overriding the inherited equals(...) method:

boolean equals(**Object** 0) ?

Unlike the method of Example 12.7, a method such as

boolean equals(**AnotherRectangle x**)

requires no downcast. It is simpler and even more lucid.

Yes, such a version of equals(...) does the job. And yes, this implementation appears simpler. However, you will shortly see the real benefit in overriding the equals(...) method inherited from Object. Just wait a bit more.

12.9.2 Inheriting from *Object:* The *toString*() Method

Like equals(...), every object inherits the method

```
String toString()
```

from mother Object. Unfortunately, the inherited version of toString() is not particularly useful. As passed down from Object, toString() returns the class name of the calling object along with a "system number." The following main(...) method includes a call to toString() that is inherited by Film:

```
public static void main(String[] args)
{
   Film film = new Film("Star Wars", "George Lucas", "George Lucas", 1172);
   System.out.println(film.toString());
}
```

The output produced by this segment is:

```
Film@82ba41
```

Obviously, only the best of hackers find such output enlightening, informative, or amusing. Overriding toString() makes good sense. The following example overrides toString() so that the string representation of a Film object gives information more useful than "Film@82ba41".

EXAMPLE 12.8 **Problem Statement** Override the toString() method inherited by Production so that the method returns the title attribute of an object in the Production hierarchy.

Java Solution To override the toString() method that Production inherits from Object, include the following method in the Production class:

```
public String toString()
{
    return title ;
}
```

That's all there is to it.

Output The following main(...) method invokes the new version of toString():

```
public static void main(String[] args)
{
   Production film = new Film("Star Wars", "George Lucas", "George Lucas", 1172);
   System.out.println(film.toString());
}
```

and displays the following line of text:

```
Star Wars
```

Discussion The new toString() method returns a String containing the title attribute of a Production object. Naturally, all subclasses of Production inherit this method.

The toString() method is automatically called when a reference is passed to println().

This means the statements

```
System.out.println(film.toString());
```

and

```
System.out.println(film);
```

produce the same output. That's just one more nice convenience provided compliments of Java.

Finally, if you override toString() so that the method returns the current values of a few critical instance variables, then some well-placed print() statements can simplify and expedite debugging.

12.10 INTERFACES

The English word *interface* can mean anything from the buttons on a TV to the public methods of a class. However, in Java, the term *interface* has a very specific meaning.

An *interface* is a named collection of static constants and abstract methods. An interface specifies certain actions or behaviors of a class but not their implementations.

For example, the following interface, Geometry, consists of one static constant and two abstract methods.

```
public interface Geometry
{
    public static final double PI = 3.14159;
    public abstract double area();
    public abstract double perimeter();
}
```

Unlike a class,

- all methods of an interface are public,
- all methods of an interface are abstract, that is, there are no implementations at all, and
- an interface has no instance variables.

Like an abstract class, an interface cannot be instantiated. In contrast to an abstract class, a class *does not extend* an interface. Instead, a class *implements* an interface.

Example 12.9 includes three simple classes that implement the Geometry interface.

EXAMPLE 12.9

Problem Statement Define Circle, Square, and Triangle classes each of which implements the Geometry interface.

Java Solution Because the following classes implement Geometry, each class is required to implement the area() and perimeter() methods. For simplicity, the usual getter and setter methods are not included.

```
public class Circle implements Geometry
{
   private double radius;

   public Circle()
   {
      radius = 0.0;
   }

   public Circle (double r)
   {
      radius = r;
   }

   public double perimeter()
   {
      return 2 * PI * radius;
   }

   public double area()
   {
      return PI * radius * radius;
   }
}
```

```
public class Square implements Geometry
{
   private double side;

   public Square()
   {
      side = 0.0;
   }

   public Square (double s)
   {
      side = s;
   }

   public double perimeter()
   {
      return 4 * side;
   }

   public double area()
   {
      return side * side;
   }
}
```

```
public class Triangle implements Geometry
{
   // three sides a, b, c
   private double a, b, c;

   public Triangle()
   {
      a = b = c = 0.0;
   }

   public Triangle (double a1, double b1, double c1)
   {
      a = a1;
      b = b1;
      c = c1;
   }

   public double perimeter()
   {
      return a + b + c;
   }

   public double area()
   {
     double s = (a + b + c)/2.0;
     return Math.sqrt(s * (s - a) * (s - b) * (s - c));
   }
}
```

Discussion The three classes do not *extend* Geometry; each *implements* Geometry. Geometry is not a class; Geometry is an interface and a class *implements* an interface. Because each class implements Geometry, each class must implement both of Geometry's methods, area() and perimeter(). The constant PI used in Circle is defined in the Geometry interface.

12.10.1 An Interface Is a Contract

An interface is a contract. An interface specifies a set of responsibilities, actions, or behaviors for any class that implements it.

> A class that implements an interface must implement all the methods of the interface, or be tagged as abstract.

Because Circle of Example 12.9 implements Geometry, Circle must implement the perimeter() and area() methods that are declared in the interface. Moreover, because Circle implements Geometry, any client of Circle is guaranteed area() and perimeter() methods. It's in the contract. That's the deal.

12.10.2 The Difference Between an Interface and an *abstract* Class

But isn't this idea of a *contract* true of an abstract class? Doesn't every (non-abstract) class that extends an abstract class have an obligation to implement the abstract methods? Why confuse the issue with interfaces? Why not simply define an abstract class in which every method is abstract? Wouldn't such a class accomplish the same thing as an interface?

As we have stated, an *is-a* relationship should hold between an abstract class and any subclass. However, the *is-a* relationship between a parent and child class need not hold between an interface and an implementing class. For example, a class, SwimmingPool, that implements the Geometry interface has a contract to implement area() and perimeter(), yet there is no implication that a SwimmingPool *is-a* Geometry.

> There is not necessarily any commonality among classes that implement a particular interface other than a shared collection of methods that each class must implement. On the other hand, classes that extend a particular abstract class usually share some instance variables and method implementations.

In the next two sections, we discuss some very real but not-so-apparent benefits of interfaces.

12.10.3 Multiple Inheritance and Interfaces

Some object-oriented languages such as C++ allow *multiple inheritance.* Multiple inheritance means that a subclass can inherit from more than one base class. The unrestricted use of multiple inheritance is a controversial feature with many complexities and pitfalls. For example, suppose that class A implements a display() method and class B implements a different display() method. If class C extends both A and B but does not override display(), which display() method does C inherit? There is no clear answer.

Nonetheless, there are many advantages and conveniences that multiple inheritance provides. By providing interfaces, Java avoids the complexities of multiple inheritance but retains some of its conveniences. On one hand, Java does not allow multiple inheritance.

> A subclass cannot inherit from two different base classes.

On the other hand, a class may implement any number of interfaces.

> A class may extend one class as well as implement any number of interfaces.

Suppose, for example, interface A and interface B both declare a display() method. If class C implements both A and B, by contract, C *must* implement display(). Consequently, C knows just one version of display(). No ambiguity exists.

In The Bigger Picture section at the end of the chapter, we delve into the problems of multiple inheritance in more detail. Needless to say, the issues are more subtle and complex than this brief discussion implies.

12.10.4 Upcasting to an Interface

Multiple inheritance aside, you may still be asking: what is so special about an interface? Why bother? Can't you just include the specified methods in a class without the extra burden of an interface?

That is certainly possible. But the real power of an interface lies in upcasting.

> A derived class can be upcast to any one of its interfaces.

In particular, the Circle, Square, and Triangle objects of Example 12.9 can be upcast to Geometry. So, for example, a single array can store *any* object that implements Geometry, as the following segment demonstrates:

```
Geometry[] shapes = new Geometry[3]; // Geometry is an interface
shapes[0] = new Circle(2.0);
shapes [1] = new Square(5.0);
shapes [2] = new Triangle(8.0, 5.0, 5.0);
```

12.10.5 The *Comparable* Interface

As Java provides a plethora of ready-made classes, Java also provides a large number of ready-made interfaces. Among one of the most useful Java-supplied interfaces is the Comparable interface. Comparable is an interface with just one method, compareTo(...):

```
public interface Comparable
{
   int compareTo(Object o);
}
```

Notice that compareTo(...) returns an integer and accepts any Object reference as an argument. A class that implements the Comparable interface implements compareTo(...) so that

a.CompareTo(b) returns a negative integer, if a is "less than" b,
a.CompareTo(b) returns 0, if a "equals" b, and
a.CompareTo(b) returns a positive integer, if a is "greater than" b.

In practice, compareTo(...) is *usually* implemented so that

a.CompareTo(b) = −1 if a is less than b,
a.CompareTo(b) = 0 if a equals b, and
a.CompareTo(b) = 1 if a is greater than b.

A class that implements Comparable is advertising to its clients that its objects can be "compared."

In Example 12.10, Film implements Comparable, as does Play. In Hollywood, money talks. Consequently, Film objects are compared based upon financial gross, and plays are compared using the number of performances.

EXAMPLE 12.10 **Problem Statement** Redefine the Production hierarchy so that Film and Play implement the Comparable interface. Compare two Film objects based on the value of boxOfficeGross and two Play objects according to the number of performances.

Java Solution Because Play implements Comparable, Play must implement compareTo(...). This is done on lines 4–11.

```
1.  public class Play extends Production  implements Comparable
2.  {
3.     // exactly as before (Play) with the addition of compareTo()

4.     public int compareTo(Object p) // from the Comparable interface
5.     {
6.        if ( !(p instanceof Play) )       // p must belong to Play
7.        {
8.           System.out.println("Error: Object does not belong to Play");
9.           System.exit(0);
```

```
10.        }
11.        if (performances < ((Play)p).performances)  // p must be downcast to Play
12.           return -1;
13.        if (performances > ((Play)p).performances)
14.           return 1;
15.        return 0;
16.     }
17. }
```

The Film class also implements Comparable and is outfitted with its own compareTo() method.

```
1.  public class Film extends Production implements Comparable
2.  {
3.     // exactly as before with the addition of compareTo()

4.     public int compareTo(Object p)      // from the Comparable interface
5.     {
6.        if ( !(p instanceof Film))        // p must belong to Film
7.        {
8.           System.out.println("Error: object must belong to Film");
9.           System.exit(0);
10.       }
11.       if (boxOfficeGross < ((Film)p).boxOfficeGross)    // note downcast
12.          return –1;
13.       if (boxOfficeGross > ((Film)p).boxOfficeGross)    // note downcast
14.          return 1;
15.       return 0;
16.    }
17. }
```

Discussion The compareTo(...) method accepts a single argument belonging to the Object class. Because Object does not declare instance variables, performances, or boxOfficeGross, a downcast is required on lines 11 and 13.

Also, because Play and Film implement Comparable, a Play or Film reference can be upcast to Comparable. For example, the statement

```
Comparable play = new Play();
```

is legal.

Finally, the implementation of the Comparable interface highlights the distinction between interfaces and abstract classes:

> Classes that extend the same abstract class share instance variables and perhaps also some code, but classes that implement the same interface do not necessarily have anything in common except a collection of methods that each class must implement.

A Play class can implement Comparable—so can a Car class, a Person class, a Llama class, or a Vampire class. Indeed, those classes that implement Comparable are not necessarily related in any way except that each one promises that objects can be compared. However, because an abstract class may contain some implementations, all derived classes share these implementations and are thereby *logically* linked through them.

12.11 A GENERIC SORT

Classes that implement the Comparable interface can utilize a general sort routine that orders objects based on the implementation of compareTo(...). That is, if a class A agrees to abide by the contract of the Comparable interface, then the sort(...) method of Example 12.11 can sort objects belonging to A.

EXAMPLE 12.11

Problem Statement Devise a generic sort method that can be used to sort objects of *any* class that implements the Comparable interface.

Java Solution In this example, we implement *selection sort,* also called *max sort.* First, sort(...) determines the largest value (max) that is stored in array x and swaps max with x[size−1]; then sort(...) finds the next-largest value and swaps that value with x[size−2], and so on. In other words, selection sort places the largest value in its proper place, then the second-largest value in its place, then the third-largest value, continuing until the array is sorted.

The following version of selection sort accepts and sorts an array of objects belonging to *any* class that implements the Comparable interface.

```
public class SelectionSort
{
   public static void sort(Comparable[] x, int size)   // accepts an array of Comparable objects
   {
     Comparable max;                    // max belongs to a class that implements Comparable
     int maxIndex;
     for (int i = size – 1; i >= 1; i--)
     {
                                        // Find the maximum in the x[0..i]
        max = x[i];                     // the "current" maximum is x[i]
        maxIndex = i;                   // the index of the "current" maximum

        for (int j = i – 1; j >= 0; j--)   // compare other values to "current" maximum
        {
          if (max.compareTo(x[j]) < 0)   // if max is "less than" x[i]
          {
             max = x[j];                // a "new" maximum
             maxIndex = j;
          }
        }
        if (maxIndex != i)              // place the maximum in its proper position
        {
          x[maxIndex] = x[i];
          x[i] = max;
        }
     }
   }
}
```

Discussion Notice that the reference passed to sort(...) has type Comparable. Object references of any class that implements the Comparable interface can be upcast to Comparable. And Comparable objects can be sorted with this method.

Let's look at a few details.

Line 3: The SelectionSort class contains a single static method,

public static void sort(Comparable[] x, int size).

As with Java's Math class, a call to the sort(...) method of SelectionSort uses the class name:

SelectionSort.sort(x, size).

No object need be instantiated. No object is required.

Because references of any class that implements Comparable can be upcast to Comparable,

sort(Comparable[] x, int size)

can accept an array of references to objects of any class that implements the Comparable interface.

Line 5: The local variable max holds the a reference to the "current" maximum object. Notice that the data type is Comparable. One size fits all.

Line 14: Two objects are compared using the compareTo(...) method.

The following class demonstrates the use of SelectionSort in conjunction with an array of Film references.

EXAMPLE 12.12

Problem Statement A text file movies.txt contains the data of at most 200 Film objects. The data for each film consist of four lines:

String title
String director
String writer
int adjusted-box-office-gross-in-millions

Devise a class with a main(...) method that reads the data from movies.txt into an array and displays the five highest-grossing films. We assume that movies.txt is correctly formatted, that is, the file contains data for no more than 200 films and that each film consists of exactly four entries on separate lines.

Java Solution Because the data comes via a text file, it is necessary to import the java.io package. The following class

- declares and opens the file, movies.txt, for input,
- reads the data into an array,
- passes the array to SelectionSort.sort(...), and
- displays the five highest-grossing films.

Recall that Film implements compareTo(...) using a film's gross as the criterion of comparison.

```
import java.util.*;
import java.io.*;
public class SortFilms
{
```

```
5.  public static void main(String[] args) throws IOException
6.     {
7.          Film [] films = new Film [200];
8.          File inputFile = new File("movies.txt");
9.          if (!inputFile.exists())
10.         {
11.            System.out.println("File movies.txt not found ");
12.            System.exit(0);
13.         }
14.         Scanner input = new Scanner(inputFile);
15.         int filmNumber = 0;
16.         while (input.hasNext())       // while there is more data
17.         {
18.            String title =  input.nextLine();
19.            String director = input.nextLine();
20.            String writer = input.nextLine();
21.            int gross = input.nextInt();
22.            films[filmNumber] = new Film (title, director, writer, gross);
23.            filmNumber++;
24.            if (input.hasNext())       // move to next line, if there is one
25.                 input.nextLine();
26.         }
27.         input.close();
28.         SelectionSort.sort(films, filmNumber);
29.         System.out.println("The five top-grossing films, adjusted for inflation, are ");
30.         for (int i = 1; i <= 5; i++)  // the last 5 are the top grossing films
31.         {
32.            System.out.print((i) + ". " + films[filmNumber - i] + ": ");
33.            System.out.println("$" + films[filmNumber - i].getBoxOfficeGross() + " million");
34.         }
35.     }
36. }
```

Output Input from the file movies.txt produces the following output:

The five top-grossing films, adjusted for inflation, are

1. Gone With The Wind: $2699 million
2. Snow White and the Seven Dwarfs: $2425 million
3. Titanic: $2245 million
4. Star Wars: Episode IV: A New Hope: $1436 million
5. Jurassic Park: $1236 million

Discussion

Line 5: Because the application uses the File class for I/O, the throws IOException clause is required.

Line 7: The array films is capable of holding up to 200 Film references.

Lines 8–13: Instantiate a File object, inputFile, with the text file movies.txt.

Line 14: Instantiate a Scanner object with argument inputFile. Consequently, input reads data from inputFile and not from System.in.

Lines 15–25: Read data and build an array of Film references. The variable filmNumber keeps track of the number of Film references stored in the array films.

Line 28: Pass the array films as well as the number of objects instantiated to SelectionSort.sort(...).

Lines 30–34: The array is sorted lowest to highest. Therefore, the five highest-grossing films hold the last five places in the array. Print the name of each film and its box office gross.

The Comparable interface provides the capability to upcast to Comparable. Because Play and Film both implement Comparable, we can use the generic sort for both Play object and Film objects. There is no need to downcast, and no need for distinct sort methods. We can use a single sort method for *any* Comparable collection.

An interface provides a contract as well as a large dose of flexibility.

12.12 COMPOSITION AND THE *has-a* RELATIONSHIP

Inheritance, as you know, is characterized by an *is-a* relationship:

a Square *is-a* Shape,
a RightTriangle *is-a* Shape,
a Film *is-a* Production,
a Dog *is-an* Animal, and
a Bloodhound *is-a* Dog.

Oftentimes, classes are related, but not via an *is-a* relationship. In these cases, upcasting is not of any apparent value. Consider for example the two (partial) classes Person and BankAccount:

```
public class Person
{
   private String name:
   private String address;
   // etc.
}
```

```
public class BankAccount
{
   private String accountNumber;
   private double balance;
   . . .
   public double balance()
   // etc.
}
```

It may be *possible* to derive BankAccount from Person or Person from BankAccount, but the relationship is not natural. A person is *not* a BankAccount and a BankAccount is *not* a Person. There is no apparent or logical reason to consider a Person a type of BankAccount or vice versa. Inheritance is not a good fit.

Suppose, however, that every Person possesses a BankAccount. You have already seen that one object may contain objects of another class. Indeed, String objects have been included in many of our previous classes, as have File and Scanner objects. Thus, a BankAccount reference can be declared an instance variable of the Person class. In such a case, the relationship between the Person and the BankAccount classes is a *has-a* relationship. A Person *has-a* BankAccount. And a Person class can be defined with a BankAccount attribute.

```
public class Person
{
   private String name:
   private String address;
   private BankAccount account;
   // etc.
}
```

The relationship between Person and BankAccount is an example of *composition*—a relationship in which one object is composed of other objects.

> As an *is-a* relationship indicates inheritance, a *has-a* relationship signals composition.

Inheritance implies an extension of functionality and the ability to upcast; composition indicates ownership. Inheritance and composition are very different concepts; the two should not be confused.

12.13 IN CONCLUSION

If inheritance merely provided new functionality for existing classes, it would still be a useful technique. However, the real muscle in inheritance lies in upcasting: a reference of a derived type can be considered a reference of a base type. Upcasting works with interfaces, too. A reference to an object of a class that implements an interface, X, can be upcast to X. Upcasting ensures, for example, that the sort(...) method of Example 12.10 can be used to sort any array of objects belonging to any class that implements Comparable.

Inheritance, however, breaks encapsulation. Changes in a base class can affect a derived class and infest a derived class with bugs. Inheritance is powerful, but inheritance has its downside.

Finally, if two classes are related via an *is-a* relationship, inheritance is usually the right choice. A *has-a* relationship generally implies composition. And sometimes, neither inheritance nor composition is a good match.

Just the Facts

- Inheritance is an *is-a* relationship. If X inherits from Y then X *is-a* kind of Y.
- The access modifier protected falls between private and public. Protected variables and methods are visible and accessible to a class's subclasses and to other classes in the same package, but not to classes outside the class's package.
- A subclass inherits each public and protected method of a superclass *unless* the subclass provides its own implementation.
- A subclass does *not* inherit the constructors of the base class. To invoke the constructors of the base class, a subclass uses the keyword super.
- If a constructor of a derived class calls a superclass constructor, the call must be made before any other code is executed in the constructor of the derived class.

- If an explicit call to super() is not made in a constructor of a derived class, then an implicit call is made to the default constructor of the parent class. Hence, it is always good practice to define a default constructor in any base class.
- X extends Y means that X inherits from Y, Y is the parent or base class of X, and X is the derived class.
- Objects of a derived class are also objects of the base class.
- Upcasting means casting an object to a parent or more general type.
- Downcasting means casting an object to a derived or more specialized type.
- Every class is derived from Object. The Object class is the mother of all classes.
- instanceof is a boolean operator such that x instanceof ObjectType returns true if x belongs to ObjectType.
- An abstract class is a class that cannot be instantiated. A class is declared abstract using the keyword; abstract; for example, public abstract class X.
- An abstract class may contain abstract methods. An abstract method is declared as

  ```
  public abstract return-type methodName();
  ```

  and has no implementation.
- An abstract class may be inherited, and any class that inherits from an abstract class is required to override and implement all the abstract class's methods, otherwise the inherited class is also abstract.
- To test the equality of objects based on a criterion other than references, the equals(Object o) method inherited from the Object class should be overridden.
- It is good style to override the toString() method inherited from Object. The default implementation returns the class name followed by a system number, and that is not usually useful.
- The toString() method is automatically called when a reference is passed to println(). Thus, System.out.println(x.toString()) produces the same output as System.out.println(x).
- Overriding toString() to return the values of instance variables can simplify and expedite debugging.
- An interface is a named collection of static constants and abstract methods. An interface specifies certain actions or behaviors of a class but not their implementations.
- An interface is similar to an abstract class in that an interface cannot be instantiated.
- An interface is different from an abstract class in that no interface methods have implementations, and an interface has no instance variables.
- A class does not extend an interface; instead, a class implements an interface.
- If a class implements an interface, the class is required to implement all of the methods of the interface or be tagged abstract.
- A class can implement many interfaces but extend only one class.
- Classes that extend the same abstract class share instance variables and perhaps also some code, but classes that implement the same interface do not necessarily have anything in common except a collection of methods that each class must implement.
- If aClass implements anInterface, then a reference to an object belonging to aClass can be upcast to anInterface, and the statement

  ```
  anInterface x = new aClass();
  ```

  is legal.

- A class that contains an object of another class exploits *composition*.
- A *has-a* relationship signifies composition.

Bug Extermination

- Every public class in an inheritance hierarchy must be stored in a separate file.
- Do not attempt to call a parent constructor directly from a derived class. Instead, use super(). If a constructor invokes super(), the call must precede all other statements.
- Do not neglect to define default constructors at all levels of an inheritance hierarchy. If a subclass does not explicitly invoke a base class constructor using super, the default constructor of the base class is automatically invoked, provided the base class has a default constructor.
- Distinguish carefully between *has-a* (composition) and *is-a* (inheritance) relationships. Use inheritance only when it is appropriate.
- A class can extend only one other class but can implement many interfaces. Use interfaces to add different kinds of functionality to a class without having to pigeonhole the class into an artificial hierarchy.
- Use protected variables when you intend to extend a class; private variables are inaccessible to subclasses except via getter and setter methods.
- When inheriting from an abstract class, do not neglect to implement all abstract methods of the abstract class; otherwise, your class will be abstract as well. You do *not* need to override any of the non-abstract methods.
- Do not confuse *overriding* with *overloading*. If a derived class *overrides* a method, it must use the same signature as the parent class—that is, the same name, number of arguments, and argument types. Method *overloading* requires *different* signatures for methods *within* a class.
- You may not override a public method with a private method. In general you may not assign more restrictive access privileges to an overridden method or instance variable.
- The instanceof operator is not a method. The syntax is

  object instanceof Production, and *not*
  object.instanceof(Production).

- When overriding the equals(...) method inherited from Object, be sure that the parameter belongs to Object. That is, equals(Object o) is usually preferable to equals(MyClass o).
- In general, changes in the base class of an inheritance relationship can infest the derived class with bugs. Design your subclass methods with care.

EXERCISES

LEARN THE LINGO

Test your knowledge of the chapter's vocabulary by completing the following crossword puzzle.

Across

3 A class ______ an interface.
5 Every class extends ______.
6 Access modifier that specifies that an instance variable can be inherited
10 equals(Object o) tests whether or not two ______ are the same.
13 Inheritance relationship
15 A class may extend ______ base class.
16 boolean operator that tests whether or not an object belongs to a particular class
18 If a specific call to a parent constructor is not made, then the ______ constructor is called.
20 Used to call a base class constructor
21 Casting an object to a base or more general type
23 Casting an object to a derived or more specialized type
24 Inheritance facilitates code ______.

Down

1 A subclass does not inherit ______ from the base class.
2 Another term for subclass
4 In a sense, inheritance breaks ______.
7 A subclass can redefine or ______ a method of the base class.
8 Inheritance allows data of one type to be treated as data of a more ______type.
9 Inherited from Object. Returns the class name and a system number.
11 Interface with compareTo()
12 *has-a* indicates ______.
14 Named collection of static constants and abstract methods
17 An ______ class cannot be instantiated.
19 Keyword that signifies an inheritance relationship
22 Parent class

SHORT EXERCISES

1. **True or False**

   If the answer is false, give an explanation.

   a. A private instance variable is no different than a protected instance variable.
   b. A subclass inherits all the methods from the base class except for the constructors.
   c. X extends Y means that Y inherits from X.
   d. Every class extends Object.
   e. The main advantage of inheritance is to save the programmer the trouble of retyping sections of class definitions.
   f. X inherits from Y implies X *is-a* Y.
   g. Y inherits from X implies X *has-a* Y.
   h. X is in love with Y implies X *wants-a* Y.
   i. It is illegal for a class to extend two classes.
   j. It is legal for more than one class to extend the same class.
   k. It is illegal for a class to implement more than one interface.
   l. There is no difference between an abstract class and an interface.
   m. An interface can have only private instance variables.
   n. An interface never implements its methods.
   o. An interface can be instantiated if it has no static constants.
   p. An interface has no instance variables.
   q. If X extends Y then X *has-a* Y.
   r. If X extends Y then X *is-a* Y.
   s. It is illegal for a class to have two attributes with the same name.
   t. It is illegal for a subclass to have an attribute with the same name as an attribute in its superclass.

2. **Composition, Inheritance, or Neither?**

   For each of the following pairs of classes, state whether one class might inherit from the other, contain the other, or neither. Explain your answers.

   a. RetailStore and Manager
   b. CashRegister and RetailStore
   c. BookStore and RetailStore
   d. Book and Bookstore
   e. Employee and Manager
   f. Manager and Bookstore
   g. Shelf and Book
   h. Shelf and BookStore
   i. Customer and Bookstore
   j. Manager and Cashier
   k. Cashier and RetailStore
   l. Salary and Employee
   m. Cashier and Salary
   n. Abbott and Costello
   o. Singer and MichaelJackson
   p. Square and Cube (tricky!)
   q. Game and Dice
   r. Game and Monopoly
   s. Opera and Musical (tricky!)
   t. Musical and MusicalComedy
   u. Beer and Drinks

v. Telephone and Buttons
w. Wardrobe and Pants
x. ProgrammingExercises and ProgrammingBook
y. Editor and Author
z. Circle and Cylinder (controversial!)

3. **Playing Compiler—Constructors**
Explain why the following classes do not compile.

```
public class Papa
{
  protected int x;
  public Papa(int y)
  {
    x = y;
  }
}

public class Son extends Papa
{
  public Son()
  {}

  public static void main(String[] args)
  {}

}
```

4. **Playing Compiler—Constructors**
Explain why the following classes do not compile.

```
public class Mama
{
  protected int x;
  public Mama()
  {
    x = 0;
  }
  public Mama(int y)
  {
    x = y;
  }
}

public class Son extends Mama
{
  public Son()
  {}
  public static void main(String[] args)
  {
    Son s = new Son(2);
  }
}
```

5. **Playing Compiler—Upcasting and Downcasting**
Explain why the following classes do not compile.

```
public class Papa
{
  protected int x;
  public Papa()
  {
    x = 0;
  }
  public Papa(int y)
  {
    x = y;
  }
}

public class Daughter extends Papa
{
  public Daughter()
  {}
  public static void main(String[] args)
  {
    Daughter d = new Papa(2);
  }
}
```

6. **What's the Output?**
What is the output of the following code? Give an explanation.

```
public class Mama
{
  protected int x;
  public Mama()
  {
      x = 0;
  }
  public Mama(int y)
  {
      x = y;
  }
}

public class Daughter extends Mama
{
  public Daughter()
  {}

  public Daughter(int x)
  {
      super(x);
  }

public static void main(String[] args)
{
```

```
        Daughter d = new Daughter();
        System.out.println(d.x);
        Mama t = new Daughter(2);
        System.out.println(t.x);
    }
}
```

7. **What's the Output?**
What is the output of the following code? Give an explanation.

```
public class Papa
{
    protected int x;

    public Papa()
    {
        x = 0;
    }

    public Papa(int y)
    {
        x = y;
    }
}

public class Son extends Papa
{
    public Son()
    {}
    public Son(int x)
    {}
    public static void main(String[] args)
    {
        Son s = new Son();
        System.out.println(s.x);
        Papa t = new Son(2);
        System.out.println(t.x);
    }
}
```

8. **What's the Output?**
What is the output of the following code? Give an explanation.

```
public class Mama
{
    protected int x;
    public Mama()
    {
        x = 0;
    }
    public Mama(int y)
    {
        x = y;
    }
}
```

```
public class Son extends Mama
{
  public Son()
   {}
  public Son(int x)
  {
    super(x);
  }
  public static void main(String[] args)
  {
    Son s = new Son();
    System.out.println(s.x);
    Son t = new Son(2);
    System.out.println(t.x);
  }
}
```

9. **Playing Compiler—Access Issues**
Explain why the following code does not compile.

```
public class Papa
{
  private int x;
  public Papa()
  {
    x = 0;
  }
  public Papa(int y)
  {
    x = y;
  }
}

public class Son extends Papa
{
  public Son()
  {}

  public Son(int x)
  {
    super(x);
  }

  public static void main(String[] args)
  {
    Son s = new Son();
    System.out.println(s.x);
    Papa t = new Son(2);
    System.out.println(t.x);
  }
}
```

10. **Fix the Errors**
Examine the classes and answer the following questions.

a. Find the two System.out.println() statements that generate compilation errors. What is (are) the error(s)?

b. If these two lines are deleted, the code compiles. What do the other System.out.println() statements display?

```
public class X
{
  private int x;
  protected int y;
  public X()
  {
    x = 0;
    y = 0;
  }
  private int helper(int x)
  {
    return x * x;
  }
  public int access()
  {
    return (helper(x));
  }
}


public class Y extends X
{
  int x;
  public Y()
  {
    super(); x = 2;
  }


  public static void main(String[] args)
  {
    X temp = new X();
    Y tempo = new Y();
    System.out.println(temp.access());
    System.out.println(tempo.access());
    System.out.println(tempo.x);
    System.out.println(temp.x);
    temp = tempo;
    System.out.println(temp.access());
    System.out.println(tempo.access());
    System.out.println(tempo.x);
    System.out.println(temp.x);
  }
}
```

11. **Playing Compiler**
Identify the errors in the following classes.

```
public class Huh
{
  private int x;
  int y;
  protected int z;
  public Huh()
  {
    x = y = z = 0;
  }

  public Huh(int x)
  {
    x = y = z = x;
  }

  public void iLikeIt(int x)
  {
    System.out.println(x * x * x);
  }

  public void iHateit()
  {
    System.out.println(y * y);
  }
}

public class Hoo extends Huh
{
  int w;
  public Hoo()
  {
    w = 0; super();
  }

  public Hoo(int x)
  {
    super(x); w = x;
  }

  public int myOwn()
  {
    System.out.println(w);
  }

  public void iLikeIt(int x)
  {
    System.out.println(x * x);
  }
```

```
  private void iHateit(()
  {
    System.out.println(w * w);
  }
}
```

12. **What's the Output?**
Examine the following code and determine the output.

```
public abstract class Test
{
  protected int value1;
  int value2;
  Test()
  {
    value1 = 0;
    value2 = 0;
  }

  Test(int value1)
  {
    this.value1 = value1;
    value2 = value1;
  }

  public void implementEd()
  {
    for (int j = 0; j < value1 ; j++)
    System.out.println("All done");
  }
  public abstract void notImplemented(int x);
}

public class TestTest extends Test
{
  int myvariable;

  TestTest()
  {
    super();
    myvariable = 3;
  }

  TestTest(int x)
  {
    super(x);
    myvariable = x + 3;
  }

  public void notImplemented(int x)
  {
    value2 = value2 + x;
```

```
        value1 = value1 * x;
        System.out.println("This was called with the value " + x);
        System.out.println("My variable is " + myvariable);
    }
    public static void main(String[] args)
    {
        TestTest h = new TestTest();
        TestTest j = new TestTest(4);
        h.implementEd(); h.notImplemented(5); h.implementEd();
        System.out.println(h.value2);System.out.println(h.value1);
        j.implementEd(); j.notImplemented(5); j.implementEd();
        System.out.println(j.value1); System.out.println(j.value2);
    }
}
```

13. **A Video Arcade Car Racing Game**

You are writing software that controls a car racing game. At the start of the game, the drivers choose their cars, and each car races down a simulated course through either a city or country landscape. Each car has a brake, accelerator, gears, and a steering wheel. Methods for all cars include:

void accelerate(int x)
void brake(int x)
    where x is a number from 1 to 10 indicating how far down the accelerator/brake pedal is pressed
void turn(int x)
    where x is an angle ranging from −180 to 180.
void gear(int x)
    where x is a gear from 0 to 4, 0 meaning reverse.

Different cars respond differently to these methods. For example, a large, heavy car does not accelerate or brake as quickly as a light car. A really fast car has a higher maximum speed than a slower car. Cars become damaged in the race, and damaged cars respond differently when accelerating, braking, and turning.

A driver can choose from hundreds of different cars. Every car has a color, a length, a maximum speed, a damage value, and a weight. Some cars have extra features such as guns, oil sprayers, or tire cutters—and methods are required to manipulate these features.

You would like to add cars to the game with minimum change in software. Design a hierarchy that enables the easy addition of new types of cars. The hierarchy should use Car at the top level, with SUV (big, strong, relatively slow), Formula1Racer (light and fast, fragile), StockCar (all around performer), and FunnyCar (very fast, not easily controlled, very fragile) extending Car. Indicate all classes, methods, attributes, and method signatures of each class. Be sure to indicate which classes are abstract and which methods in these classes are abstract.

14. **Extending the Production Hierarchy**

Extend the Production class to include a class TVShows. Then extend TVShows to TVSitcoms and TVRealityShows. Determine what new methods or instance variables, if any, are necessary, and whether any abstract methods of Production should be overridden.

15. **Abstract Classes, Upcasting, Downcasting—The Production Hierarchy**
Determine which of the following lines generates an error. Use the Production hierarchy of this chapter. In each case, explain the cause of the error.
   a. Production p = new Musical("Sweeny Todd", "Harold Prince", "Hugh Wheeler", "Stephen Sondheim", " Stephen Sondheim", 557);
   b. Production p = new Production();
   c. Musical m = new Film();
   d. Musical m = new Musical();
   e. Play p = new Musical(); p.getDirector(); (Musical) p.getComposer();
   f. Film play = new Musical();
   g. Production p = new Musical(); p.getDirector(); (Play) p.getDirector(); (Play) p.getComposer();
   h. Comparable c = new Musical(); Film f = new Musical(); c.compareTo(f);

16. **Inheritance vs Interface**
The following text is from Roedy Green's *Java Glossary* on the Web.

> On the surface, interfaces and abstract classes seem to provide almost the same capability. How do you decide which to use?
>
> ***When to Use Interfaces***
> An interface allows somebody to start from scratch to implement your interface or implement your interface in some other code whose original or primary purpose was quite different from your interface. To them, your interface is only incidental, something that they have to add on to their code to be able to use your package.
>
> ***When to Use Abstract Classes***
> An abstract class, in contrast, provides more structure. It usually defines some default implementations and provides some tools useful for a full implementation. The catch is, code using it must use your class as the base. That may be highly inconvenient if the other programmers wanting to use your package have already developed their own class hierarchy independently.

Explain these ideas in your own words. Give an example of an application where an interface is more natural and one where inheritance of an abstract class is more natural.

17. ***Is-a, Has-a,* and Notions of Inheritance**
Sometimes *is-a* doesn't help to determine when inheritance is the right idea. In English, *is-a* can mean specificity in the sense of more detail (inheritance) or it can mean specificity in terms of less detail (a special case).
    For example, when we say a manager is a kind of employee, we mean that a manager has everything an employee has and more. In this sense, a manager extends or generalizes the notion of an employee, even though it is a special case of an employee. But when we say that every integer is a fraction, we do not mean that an integer extends or generalizes the concept of a fraction. We mean that an integer is a special case of a fraction and, if anything, a fraction has everything an integer has and more. Manager naturally extends employee, but integer does not naturally extend fraction.
   a. In general, if A *is-a* B, then which class is more specific and which is more general?
   b. When a class is more specific, does it have more instance variables and methods, or fewer? Explain.
   c. Is a square a kind of cube, vice versa, or neither? Is a square a kind of rectangle, vice versa, or neither? Among the classes Cube, Square, and Rectangle, which might inherit from which and why? Explain your reasoning in light of (a) and (b).

That is, what extra instance variables or methods would apply to your more specific classes in any inheritance hierarchy you propose?

d. Is a point a kind of circle, vice versa, or neither? Is a circle a kind of cylinder, vice versa, or neither? Among the classes Point, Circle, and Cylinder, which might inherit from which and why? Explain your reasoning in light of (a) and (b). That is, what extra instance variables or methods would apply to your more specific classes in any inheritance hierarchy you propose?

e. "Favor composition over inheritance" is a maxim of object-oriented design. Go back to problems (c) and (d) and discuss whether any of those classes might be built naturally out of the others via composition rather than inheritance. Give details.

18. **Subsets vs Inheritance**

A set is a collection of things. A set can be a collection of numbers, colors, socks, or anything. *B* is a subset of *C* if all the elements of *B* are contained in *C*. For example, the set of prime numbers is a subset of the set of integers. The set of all sweatpants is a subset of the set of all gym clothes.

You are already familiar with classes and inheritance. B extends C, or B inherits from C, when every object of B *is-a* kind of C. For example, the class Manager extends Employee, and Film extends Production.

a. In what ways are the notions of sets and classes the same?

b. In what ways are the notions of sets and classes different?

c. Give an example of two classes A and B, where B naturally extends A, and B is a subset of A.

d. Give an example of two classes A and B, where B is a subset of A, but B does *not* naturally extend A.

PROGRAMMING EXERCISES

1. **Publishing—Using Inheritance and Composition**

A Publication has a publisher, number of pages, a price, an owner, and a title. When a Publication object is created using a constructor, the number of pages, price, and the title must be supplied. A default constructor uses blank and zero values. When a Publication is created, it has no owner. An owner can be set, and the publication explicitly sold, using the

```
double sell(String owner, double amount)
```

method. The method call

```
p.sell(String owner, double amount)
```

sells publication p to owner and returns the change, from amount if there is any. For example, if the price of publication p is \$5.89, then p.sell("Shai", 6.0); sets "Shai" as the owner of publication p and returns 0.11. The sell(...) method can be called numerous times, as the publication is sold and resold.

A Magazine is a publication that has a publication unit (monthly, weekly, biweekly), and number of issues left on the subscription. You should be able to decrement the number of issues left on the subscription. If you own a magazine, you own a subscription to it. You should be able to print the title of a magazine and subscribe for an additional year. When you purchase a subscription you must provide a dollar amount for the purchase. If the dollar amount is not enough then the ownership should not change.

A Book is a Publication that has an author. The author automatically owns the book at no cost.

A KidsMagazine is a Magazine that has a recommended age range. When you subscribe to a kid's magazine, you must provide the age of the subscriber. The subscription is accepted only if the age is in the proper range.

Define a Publication hierarchy.

Write a test class that creates a $14.00 book about Java by Java Javison, a magazine called *Bicycling* that is published monthly for $4 an issue, and a kid's magazine called *Ranger Rick* for ages 6–11 that is published weekly and costs $2.00 an issue. Simulate the following transactions with the appropriate method calls.

- Shai subscribes to *Bicycling* magazine and pays $45.
- Java Javison owns his own book and then sells it to Ralph for $35.
- Another copy of Java Javison's book is created and owned by the author.
- Emily, an 11-year-old girl, subscribes to *Ranger Rick* and receives four issues.
- Emily adds an extra two years to her subscription and then sells it to Charlie, who is 10 years old, who pays $250.
- Charlie receives 10 issues and tries to sell it for $200 to Java Javison, who is 27 years old.

2. **A Simple Inheritance Hierarchy**

Implement a class Employee such that a member of Employee has a name, an ID number, an age, a salary, a title, and a department name. An Employee can:

a. Print a confidential employee record with all the above information.
b. Change a salary (takes an int or a double argument). If the argument is int, then the salary is increased by that amount (a bonus addition, not a percent increase). If the parameter is double, then the salary is multiplied by the value of the argument and may increase or decrease depending on whether the double value is greater than or less than 1.0.
c. getSalary().

Implement a subclass of Employee, called Manager. A manager is an employee who supervises other employees. A manager has a group of employees that he/she supervises. The confidential record of a manager includes all the information included in a regular employee's confidential record plus a list of ID numbers of the employees that he/she supervises.

Executive extends Manager. An executive is a manager who gets a bonus at the end of each year equal to a percentage of company profits. Implement Executive. You should redefine getSalary() to include the bonus. You should also add a method to change the percentage of the executive's bonus.

3. **Investments—Practice with Inheritance**

There are many different kinds of investments, including stocks, mutual funds, real estate, and bank accounts. There are two kinds of bank accounts: checking and savings.

Design an abstract Investment class that includes a name attribute, a value attribute (double), and a getter method, getValue(). The Investment class, being abstract, cannot be instantiated.

Design subclasses: Stocks, MutualFunds, RealEstate, and BankAccount.

- The attributes of Stocks are name, pricePerShare, numberOfSharesOwned, and dividend (a percent of the investment paid annually).
- The attributes of MutualFunds are: name, pricePerShare, and numberOfSharesOwned.
- The attributes of RealEstate are: name, addressOf Property, purchasePrice, and currentAssessedValue.
- BankAccount is an abstract class that extends Investment. The name field holds the bank's name. An additional attribute accountNumber (String) represents an account number.

- BankAccount has two subclasses: SavingsAccount and CheckingAccount.
- A SavingsAccount object has an annual interest rate paid quarterly. SavingsAccount has a method addInterest() that adjusts the balance of the account.
- A CheckingAccount *is-a* BankAccount with a minimum balance, a penalty if the balance goes below the minimum in any month, and an annual interest rate (paid monthly) on the money in excess of the minimum balance. Include method addInterest(), which adds one month's interest to the balance, and a method checkBalance(), which adjusts the balance if the balance falls below the minimum.

The classes are simple. Each class has a default constructor that sets each instance variable to the empty string or zero, whichever is appropriate, and a second constructor that sets the class attributes, including value. Each class that is not abstract should also include a method displayData() that prints all the information of a particular investment, properly labeled. The Investment hierarchy is shown in Figure 12.9

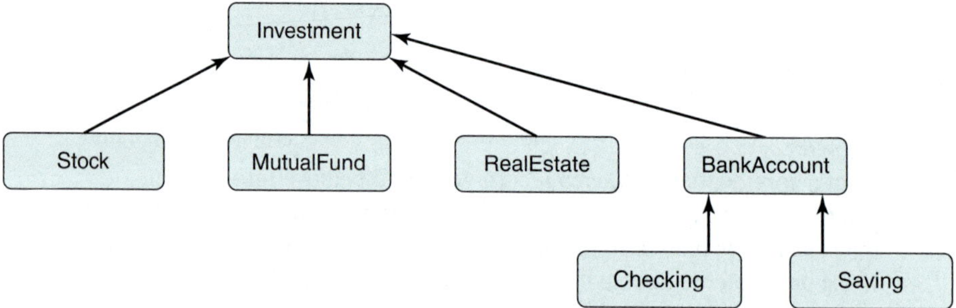

FIGURE 12.9 The *Investment* hierarchy

A portfolio is an array of Investment references. Implement a Portfolio class that also includes a getNetValue() method. This method returns the sum of the values of all investments referenced by portfolio. Interactively, create a portfolio with at least six investments, including stocks, mutual funds, real estate, and a bank account. Display the data for each investment along with the net value of all investments.

4. **A Grocery Store**

A grocery store sells many different items. Construct an abstract class Item with attributes

- String name ("apples" "soup" "candy bar")
- double unitPrice.

The methods of Item are getters and setters along with the requisite constructors.

UnitItem and WeightItem are concrete classes that extend Item. An object belonging to UnitItem encapsulates a grocery item that is sold by the unit, such as a can of soup or a gallon of milk. The instance variable unitPrice (inherited from Item) stores the price of one item. UnitItem has an additional instance variable, amount, that holds the number of units of a particular item. UnitItem implements a method

```
double cost()
```

that returns the cost of amount units of an item.

WeightItem represents an item sold by weight, such as nuts, fruits, or vegetables. In this case, unitPrice represents the price per pound of an item. WeightItem has an additional instance variable, weight, that holds the number of pounds of some item. WeightItem also implements a method

```
double cost()
```

WeightItem's implementation of cost() returns the total cost of weight pounds of the item. The weight of an item is set by placing the item on a scale. To simulate a scale, include a private helper method

```
private double scale()
```

that "weighs" the item and sets the weight field. This is done by generating a random number, with two decimal places, between 0.01 and 4.00. The constructor uses this virtual "scale" to set the weight field.

Both classes should include the appropriate constructors as well as getter and setter methods.

a. Design and implement Item, WeightItem, and UnitItem. Test your methods.
b. A ShoppingCart class has an array of Item such that each array entry is a UnitItem or a WeightItem reference. Additionally, ShoppingCart implements a method

```
void checkout()
```

that determines the total cost all items in the "cart," that is the array. A typical call to checkout() might produce the following interactive output:

Enter U or W or Return to end: **U**
Enter name: **Soup**
Number of Units: **2**
Enter price per unit: **2.39**
Cost is 4.78

Enter U or W: **W**
Enter name: **Apples**
Enter price per pound: **1.29**
Weight is 2.8
Cost is 3.61

Enter U or W: **W**
Enter name: **Green Beans**
Enter price per pound: **1.19**
Weight is 3.53
Cost is 4.2

Enter U or W: **U**
Enter name: **Muffins**
Number of Units: **6**
Enter price per unit: **.79**
Cost is 4.74

Enter U or W:
Total cost: 17.33

Implement the ShoppingCart class. Include a main(...) method that instantiates a ShoppingCart object and calls checkout().

5. **Sorting Boxes Using the Comparable Interface**
A Box has three integer dimensions: length, width, and depth, and two methods: surfaceArea() and volume(). Box implements the Comparable interface and defines compareTo() based on surface area. Implement and test the Box class.

Write a second class TestSort with a method that sorts *n* boxes in ascending order by surface area. Redefine the compareTo(…) method, and run the sort of TestSort again, this time sorting the boxes in ascending order by volume.

6. **An abstract Box Class with a Comparable Interface**
   Write an abstract Box class that has three integer dimensions: length, width, and depth, and two methods: surfaceArea() and volume(). Box should implement the Comparable interface, but leave compareTo(...) undefined. That is, compareTo(…) is an abstract method.
   Create two subclasses of Box: BoxArea and BoxVolume. Each of these subclasses extends Box and does nothing extra except implements the abstract method compareTo(...). Note that since Box implements Comparable, the derived classes BoxArea and BoxVolume do *not* also need to explicitly implement Comparable, but they do need to implement compareTo(…).
   - BoxArea defines compareTo(...) by comparing surface areas.
   - BoxVolume defines compareTo(...) by comparing volumes.

   Write a class with a single static method

   ```
   public static boolean orderedUp(Comparable[] x, int size)
   ```

   that determines whether or not the elements of Comparable array x are in strict ascending order.
   Write a test class with a main() method that asks the user to enter three dimensions for each of five different boxes. Create two arrays of BoxArea and BoxVolume, each containing the data for these five boxes. Your test class should print a message indicating whether or not the boxes in each array are in strict ascending order according to the appropriate compareTo(…) methods.

7. **A Dump Interface**
   Even if a class overrides toString(), it may be convenient, for debugging, to implement another method that displays or "dumps" many or all of the values stored in an object.

   Define a Dump interface with one method dumpMe(). The method dumpMe() should *dump* the values of an object belonging to a class that implements Dump. For example, suppose that Rectangle is a class with attributes length and width. If rectangle belongs to Rectangle, then rectangle.dumpMe() might display the values of length and width, appropriately labeled.
   Modify the Play and Film classes of this chapter so that they both implement the Dump interface.

8. **A Mergeable Interface**
   Some objects can be combined with other objects of the same type to create larger objects of the same type. This is not the case with Remote or Film objects, but it is the case with Strings, MusicCollections, or ClassLists.

   a. Define a Mergeable interface with one method

   ```
   Object merge(Object x).
   ```

   b. Design a class IntegerSet that implements Mergeable. IntegerSet stores a set of integers. Methods of IntegerSet should include:

   ```
   void printElements();
   int size();
   boolean elementOf(int x);
   ```

c. Define merge(Object x) so that if x and y belong to IntegerSet then x.merge(y) returns a reference to an IntegerSet, z, containing the integers in x and/or y. Set z contains no duplicates. For example, if x = {1, 2, 3, 4, 5} and y = {3, 4, 5, 6, 7, 8} then z = {1, 2, 3, 4, 5, 6, 7, 8}.

d. A particular lottery allows people to play any set of numbers from 1 through 1,000,000. Each number played costs $1. There is one winning number chosen each week. A group of friends play the lottery, and each one has some set of favorite numbers. Possibly, some of the friends have chosen the same numbers. They decide to pool their numbers and split the winnings if any one of their numbers wins.

Write a test class that creates three IntegerSet objects containing the lottery numbers played by three different friends. Your test class should create a merged set from the three sets and print out all the numbers in it and how much it will cost to play these numbers (i.e., how many numbers).

9. **Lattice Points and Complex Numbers**

A *lattice point* on a graph is a pair of coordinates, (x, y) such that x and y are two integers. For example, (2, 3), (−1, −2), and (4, 0) are lattice points. The point (0, 0) is called *the origin*. These points are illustrated as follows:

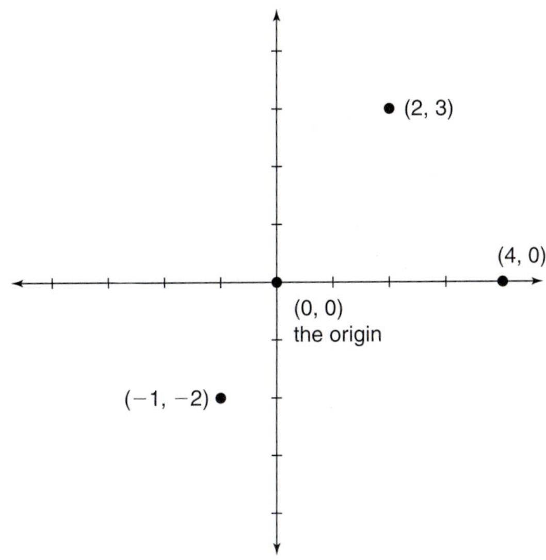

a. Create a LatticePoint class such that each point consists of a pair of integers (x, y). Include constructors, getter and setter methods, and an addition method,

```
LatticePoint add(LatticePoint p);
```

defined by the rule $(a, b) + (c, d) = (a + c, b + d)$.
Implement a method that returns the distance between two points:

```
double distance(LatticePoint p);
```

such that the distance between (a, b) and (c, d) is defined as $\sqrt{(a - c)^2 + (b - d)^2}$.
Overload the distance method, so that the call

```
p.double distance()
```

returns the distance from (0, 0) to p.

Complex Numbers

In the real number system, the square root of a negative number is undefined. However, there is a number system, the *complex numbers*, where $\sqrt{-1}$ makes perfect sense. Indeed, in the complex number system, the symbol i signifies $\sqrt{-1}$, and consequently $i \times i = (\sqrt{-1})^2 = -1$.

Complex numbers are written in the form $x + yi$ where x and y are real numbers and $i = \sqrt{-1}$. The number x is called the *real part* of $x + yi$, and y is called the *imaginary part* of $x + yi$. For example, $3 + 4i$, $9 - 2i$, and $7 - 0i$ are complex numbers.

Addition and multiplication of complex numbers is defined as:

$$(a + bi) + (c + di) = (a + c) + (b + d)\,i$$
$$(a + bi) \times (c + di) = (ac - bd) + (bc + ad)\,i$$

The distance between complex numbers $a + bi$ and $c + di$ is defined as

$$\sqrt{(a - c)^2 + (b - d)^2}.$$

A complex number $x + yi$ is often expressed as a pair of two coordinates, (x, y). For example, (2, 4), (–1, –2), and (4, 0) denote complex numbers $2 + 4i$, $-1 - 2i$, and $4 - 0i$, respectively. Thus, every complex number can be plotted as a point in an x-y coordinate system.

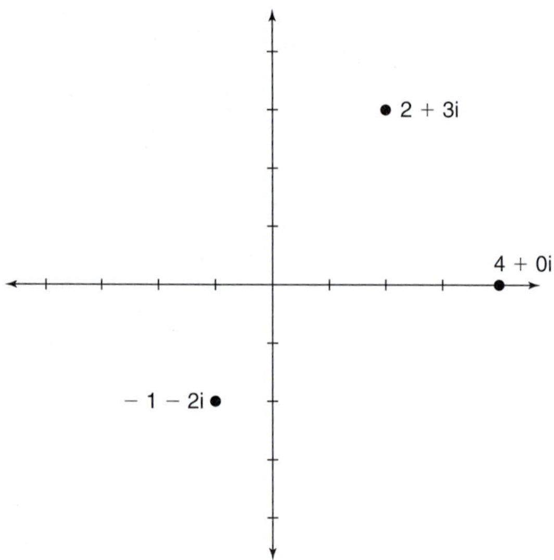

b. Design a class IntegerComplex that extends LatticePoint. Each IntergerComplex object represents a complex number with two integer coordinates. IntegerComplex inherits the addition and distance methods from LatticePoint. However, you must add a multiplication method.

c. Write a test class with a main(...) method that prompts for the real and imaginary parts of an integer complex number. Your method should multiply the number by itself, and then multiply the result by itself again, and so on, up to five times or until the result is more than a distance of 10 units from the origin, (0, 0). Report either the number of multiplications performed or that the result did not exceed a distance of 10 units from the origin.

THE BIGGER PICTURE

MULTIPLE INHERITANCE

Java specifies that a class can extend just one class but can implement any number of interfaces. This restriction is one of the many purposeful decisions made by the architects of Java. There are some very popular languages such as C++ that support *multiple inheritance*, the language feature that allows a class to extend two or more classes. The Java's designers, whose goals were to build a simple, object-oriented, and familiar language, believe that multiple inheritance causes confusion and creates problems. Let's look at some implications of multiple inheritance and you can judge for yourself whether or not the possible advantages outweigh the potential for error and confusion.

The Diamond Problem

Imagine a university at which every student has a work-study job to help defray tuition expenses. That is, every student *is-an* employee of the university. Furthermore, any faculty member may take courses for free, so some employees (we'll call them StuFac's) are both students and faculty members. As shown in the code that follows, Student and Faculty both inherit from Employee, and a StuFac inherits from both Student and Faculty. Of course, *Java does not allow such an inheritance hierarchy.*

```
abstract class Employee
{
  public int idNumber;
  abstract void talk();
  ...
}

class Student extends Employee
{
  void talk()
  {
    System.out.println("I am a student on work-study");
  }
  ...
}

class Faculty extends Employee
{
  void talk()
  {
    System.out.println("I am a professor");}
  }
  ...
}
// THIS NEXT CLASS DOES NOT COMPILE
// YOU CANNOT EXTEND MULTIPLE CLASSES

class StuFac extends Student, Faculty
{
    ...
}
```

This inheritance scheme, shown in Figure 12.10, resembles a diamond, hence the name "the diamond problem."

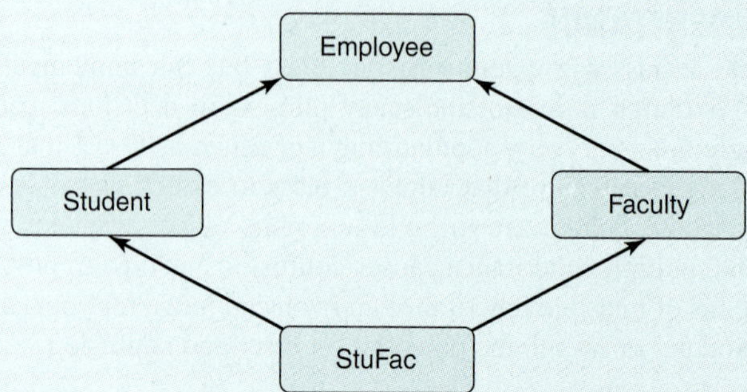

FIGURE 12.10 The diamond problem

There are two kinds of problems with diamond multiple inheritance. One problem occurs when a StuFac object, upcast to Employee, invokes the talk() method as illustrated by the following code segment:

```
Employee employee = new StuFac();
employee.talk();
```

At runtime, the system does not know which talk() method to choose, the one for Student or the one for Faculty. The attribute idNumber, defined in Employee, gives rise to a second problem. Which idNumber does StuFac inherit? Is it the one inherited by Student, or the one inherited by Faculty, or is there just one "unified" idNumber in StuFac?

There are no right answers to these questions. Indeed, it is possible that no answers are satisfactory. Multiple inheritance implies ambiguities, and these are issues that must be addressed when designing a programming language.

Some programmers claim that multiple inheritance is convenient and useful, and problems stemming from the diamond problem are rare and avoidable. Other programmers claim that the use of multiple inheritance is inherently bad design, and that the features achieved by multiple inheritance can be implemented in other ways.

Multiple Inheritance and Java

How does Java handle multiple inheritance? The short answer is that Java forbids multiple inheritance. Java stipulates that variables and method implementations can be inherited from a single class. As a result, there is no confusion about which inherited instance variable or method implementation is applicable. However, Java provides interfaces that can be used to achieve the features of multiple inheritance without the potential ambiguities and problems. That's the bigger picture.

Java specifies that a class may implement many interfaces and consequently "inherit" all the *method names* from those interfaces. This is a different kind of "inheritance" in that no implementations of these methods are inherited but only the method signatures (that is, the name of the method as well as the number and types of parameters in a specified order). This kind of inheritance is sometimes called *inheritance of interface*. Java uses inheritance of interface to avoid the ambiguities of the diamond problem.

As you know, a concrete (non-abstract) class that implements an interface is required to define each method of the interface. The StuFac class, rather than inheriting from both the Student and Faculty classes, can implement a Student interface and a Faculty interface.

The StuFac class would then be obligated to implement all the methods from each interface, without actually inheriting any actual method implementations.

For example,

```
public interface Student
{
  void talk();
  ...
}
public interface Faculty
{
  void talk();
  ...
}
class StuFac implements Student, Faculty
{
  public void talk()
  {
    System.out.println("I am a professor taking courses");
  }
}
```

StuFac implements two interfaces, Student and Faculty, each of which declares a talk() method. There is no ambiguity here: neither Faculty nor Student implements talk(). StuFac must supply its own implementation of talk(). The talk() methods of Student and Faculty have identical signatures (number and/or type of parameters), so StuFac implements only one version of talk(). On the other hand, if the interfaces have different signatures such as:

```
public interface Student
{
    public void talk(int x); // notice the parameter
}
```

and

```
public interface Faculty
{
    public void talk();
}
```

then StuFac is obligated to implement two distinct talk(…) methods, one for each interface, or be tagged abstract.

Exercise

1. Following are two interfaces, Student and Faculty, such that each declares talk(). The signatures are identical, but the return types differ.

```
public interface Student
{
  public void talk();
}

public interface Faculty
{
  public int talk();
}
```

Suppose that StuFac implements both Student and Faculty. With the help of the Java compiler, determine the problems that arise in this situation. How might you fix the problem?

Two Interfaces and a Name Clash—A Complex Example

Java's response to multiple inheritance is good but not perfect. The problem in Exercise 1 is a no-win situation. Although the return types differ, you cannot implement two versions of talk() because the signatures are identical. On the other hand, an implementation of StuFac with just one version of talk() generates a compilation error. But this kind of problem is not the only one you may encounter.

This section describes a more subtle problem that Java interfaces cannot easily handle. The problem arises when two interfaces use the same signature and return type for a method, but a single implementation of that method does *not* fit the needs of the class implementing the two interfaces.

Interface designers do not huddle together when choosing method names. Suppose that two interfaces declare identical method signatures and a concrete class implements both interfaces. If one implementation of the method works for both interfaces, there is no problem, but what happens if a single implementation does not suffice for both?

In this example, a Box class implements two interfaces, Comparable and PartialOrder. Each interface has a method int compareTo(...) with the same signature and return type, but Box is logically unable to use a single implementation for both. A Box class has integer attributes signifying the dimensions of the box—length, width, and depth—and overrides boolean equals(object O) such that two Box objects are equal if they have the same dimensions. Box also includes methods that

- compare boxes by comparing their volumes, and
- compare boxes by checking whether one box fits inside the other.

The Box class implement the Comparable interface and overrides compareTo(...) using volume as a basis for comparison.

The Comparable interface is appropriate when you wish to impose a *total ordering* on a class. That is, if a and b are two objects, then either a is less than b, a is greater than b, or a equals b. Objects of a totally ordered class can be sorted in ascending order. If Box implements compareTo(…) based on volume, then the objects of Box are totally ordered and, consequently, boxes can be sorted in ascending order.

However, not every method of comparison imposes a total ordering on the objects of a class. For example, if you compare boxes according to the criterion "box a is less than box b if a fits inside b," then it is not always the case that boxes can be sorted in order. It is possible that, for two distinct boxes a and b, neither fits inside the other. This means that one box is neither greater than, less than, nor equal to the other! The two boxes cannot be compared based on the nesting criterion, and the Comparable interface is not appropriate. The following exercise investigates this further.

Exercise

2. Assume you *inappropriately* implement the compareTo(…) method of Comparable using box nesting rather than volume. That is,

   a.compareTo(b) = − 1 if a fits inside of b,
   a.compareTo(b) = 1 if b fits inside of a, and
   a.compareTo(b) = 0 otherwise. In this case, the two boxes are incomparable.

THE BIGGER PICTURE

a. Give an example of two boxes a and b such that a.compare(b) = 0, but a and b do not have the same dimensions.

b. You execute the generic sort method of Section 12.11 on an array holding three boxes with dimensions (2, 3, 4), (1, 5, 6), and (7, 8, 9). Describe what happens.

c. An array holding three boxes with dimensions (7, 8, 9), (1, 2, 3), and (4, 5, 6) is sorted using the generic sort of Example 12.11. How are these boxes ordered?

d. The box-nesting implementation of compareTo(…) is inappropriate for Comparable objects because it does not impose a total ordering on the boxes. Using (b) and (c), describe when the generic sort fails and how this failure relates to the inappropriate implementation of compareTo(…).

Box-nesting imposes a *partial order* on the boxes but not a total order. A partial order specifies that if a is greater than b, then b is not greater than a, and vice versa. To handle box nesting, we can implement a PartialOrder interface, rather than a Comparable interface. PartialOrder declares a single method compareTo(...) with the same signature and return type as the compareTo(...) method of Comparable.

```
int compareTo(Object p)
    // returns positive if this object is greater than p (usually returns 1)
    // returns 0, otherwise
```

For example, if Box implements PartialOrder, then the method call a.compareTo(b) returns 1 if box b fits inside box a, and 0 otherwise. Note that if box b fits inside a, then a does not fit inside b, and vice versa.

Although the two methods have the same signature and return type, semantically, compareTo(...) of PartialOrder differs from compareTo(...) of Comparable. For PartialOrder, it is feasible that both c.compareTo(b) and b.compareTo(c) return 0 even when b and c are not equal. That is, neither box fits inside the other, and the boxes are not equal. For Comparable, if b and c are not equal, then one of the two method calls, c.compareTo(b) and b.compareTo(c), *must* return 1. Thus, a single implementation of compareTo(…) cannot suffice for both interfaces.

Suppose that Box implements both Comparable and PartialOrder. Box must implement two different methods: compareTo(...) of Comparable and compareTo(...) of PartialOrder. Unfortunately, both compareTo(...) methods have the same signature, so Box can implement just one version of compareTo(…). And, since the methods clash semantically, one implementation cannot work correctly for both interfaces.

In the following exercises, we ask you to resolve this problem by changing the name of the compareTo(...) method in one of the interfaces. Of course, this solution assumes that you have access to the interface source code. Unfortunately, in the real world you may not have write-access to these interfaces. Perhaps the interfaces have been written by two programmers who maintain their own code, and who no doubt did *not* consult with each other on method names. In this case, the *name clash* has killed your program.

Exercises

3. Define a Box class with integer instance variables length, width, and depth. Write constructors. The default constructor should instantiate a box with all three dimensions equal to zero. The dimensions should be specified in inches.
4. Define a PartialOrder interface with one method greaterThan(...).
5. Box should implement the standard Java interface Comparable so that compareTo(...) compares boxes based on volume. The shipping cost of a box is

proportional to its volume. Write a main(...) method that interactively accepts two boxes and determines which box costs more to ship.

6. Box should also implement the PartialOrder interface. Define the greaterThan(..) method so that b.greaterThan(c) returns 1 whenever Box c fits inside Box b. Note that c fits inside b if there is a way to arrange the dimensions of each box so that the corresponding dimensions of b are each larger than those of c. Write a main(...) method that determines whether or not three boxes can be stacked one inside the other.

Conclusion

An interface allows you to simulate the features of multiple inheritance without the associated ambiguities and problems. Despite Java's attempt to avoid the difficulties of multiple inheritance, problems with interfaces still exist. You will see more of the power of interfaces when you study polymorphism in Chapter 13. Simulating multiple inheritance is not the only function of interfaces, but just one of several.

CHAPTER 13

Polymorphism

"Must a name mean something?" Alice asked doubtfully.
"Of course it must," Humpty Dumpty said: "my name means the shape I am—and a good handsome shape it is, too. With a name like yours, you might be any shape, almost."
—Lewis Carroll, *Through the Looking Glass*

Objectives

The objectives of Chapter 13 include an understanding of

- the types of polymorphism,
- polymorphism and dynamic binding,
- polymorphism and class extensibility,
- polymorphism and interfaces, and
- polymorphism behind the scenes.

13.1 INTRODUCTION

The previous chapters describe encapsulation and inheritance, two foundational ideas underlying object-oriented programming. *Polymorphism* is the third fundamental concept of OOP. In Chapter 12, you saw that, by exploiting *similarity* among classes, inheritance makes it possible to build new classes from existing classes.

In contrast to inheritance, polymorphism underscores the *differences* of class behavior in an inheritance hierarchy.

The word *polymorphism*, derived from the Greek words *polus* and *morphe*, means "many shapes" or "many forms." Method overloading, which allows several methods to share the same name, is a simple type of polymorphism that we have already encountered. However, the real muscle of polymorphism derives from method overriding and the concept of late binding, which is the major topic of this chapter.

13.2 TWO SIMPLE FORMS OF POLYMORPHISM

13.2.1 Ad-hoc Polymorphism—Method Overloading

The following short examples illustrate two simple types of polymorphism. The first code segment overloads the constructor of a Song class. The constructor is polymorphic; the constructor has three forms.

```
public class Song
{
    private String composer;
    private String lyricist;

    public Song ()                    // default constructor
    {
        composer = "" ;
        lyricist = "";
    }
    public Song(String name) // same person wrote words and music
    {
        composer = name ;
        lyricist = name;
    }
    public Song (String name1, String name2) // two songwriters
    {
        composer = name1;
        lyricist = name2;
    }
    // other Song methods go here.......
}
```

Method overloading, a form of polymorphism, is also known as *ad-hoc polymorphism*.

13.2.2 Upcasting

A second form of polymorphism comes in the guise of upcasting. Recall that upcasting in an inheritance hierarchy allows an object of a derived type to be considered an object of a base type. For example, consider the following hierarchy and code fragment.

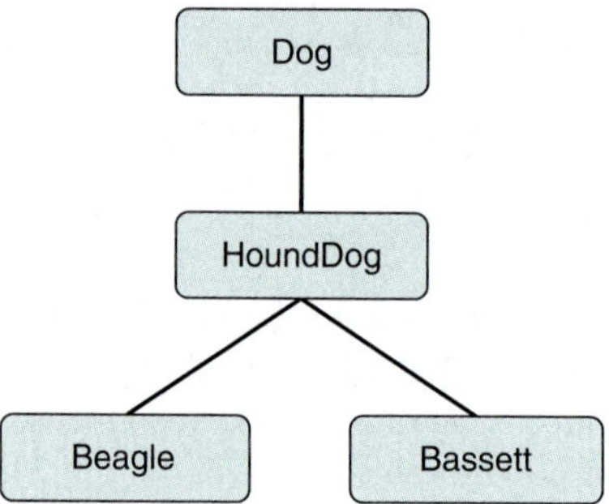


```
1. Dog elvis;
2. elvis = new HoundDog();
3. elvis = new Beagle();
4. elvis = new Bassett();
```

Because a HoundDog *is-a* Dog, a HoundDog reference can be upcast to Dog (line 2). Similarly, a Beagle reference and a Bassett reference can also be considered Dog references (lines 3 and 4). The reference elvis is *polymorphic*, that is, elvis has "many forms" and elvis can refer to a Dog object, a HoundDog object, a Beagle object, or a Bassett object.

13.3 DYNAMIC (OR LATE) BINDING

Method overloading and upcasting are two simple forms of polymorphism.

A third form of polymorphism, *dynamic or late binding,* accentuates the *behavioral differences* among objects of different classes in a hierarchy.

This is in contrast to inheritance, which exploits the similarities of classes. And, although method overloading and upcasting both exhibit polymorphic behavior, object-oriented purists would insist that true polymorphism should be defined strictly in terms of late binding.

To illustrate and explain dynamic binding we devise a new hierarchy of classes, the Shape hierarchy, which provides a poor man's version of a graphics program. Indeed, modern graphics programs usually provide tools for drawing different shapes such as rectangles, circles, or triangles. A would-be artist selects a drawing pen, a color, and a possible shape, and uses the mouse as a paintbrush and the screen as an easel.

We are not quite ready to implement such an application. That's coming later. So, we downsize our expectations. Example 13.1 provides classes with methods that draw rectangles and triangles using standard keyboard characters. Each class encapsulates a different geometric shape. Some typical shapes are shown in Figure 13.1.

```
*****   %           #
*****   %%         # #
*****   %%%       # # #
*****   %%%%     # # # #
*****   %%%%%   # # # # #
Square  RightTriangle  Triangle
```

FIGURE 13.1 Three shapes—each uses a different drawing character

EXAMPLE 13.1

Problem Statement Design classes Square, RightTriangle, and Triangle that encapsulate three geometric shapes. Each class should implement a method

```
void draw (int x, int y)
```

that "draws" a square, a right triangle, or an equilateral triangle (a triangle with three equal sides), respectively. See Figure 13.1. The parameters x and y specify the relative position of the figure: y lines down and x spaces across from the current position of the screen cursor.

The instance variables of each class are:

int rows, the number of rows that comprise the figure,

and

char character, the keyboard character used for drawing the figure.

Each shape of Figure 13.1 consists of five rows. The drawing characters are '*' for the square, '%' for the right triangle, and '#' for the equilateral triangle.

Java Solution There is much the same about the three classes: the attributes are the same, and except for the draw(...) method, the getter and setter methods are the same. In fact, the classes are more similar than different. Consequently, we factor out the commonality of the classes into one (abstract) superclass, Shape, which serves as a base class in an inheritance hierarchy that includes Square, RightTriangle, and Triangle. See Figure 13.2.

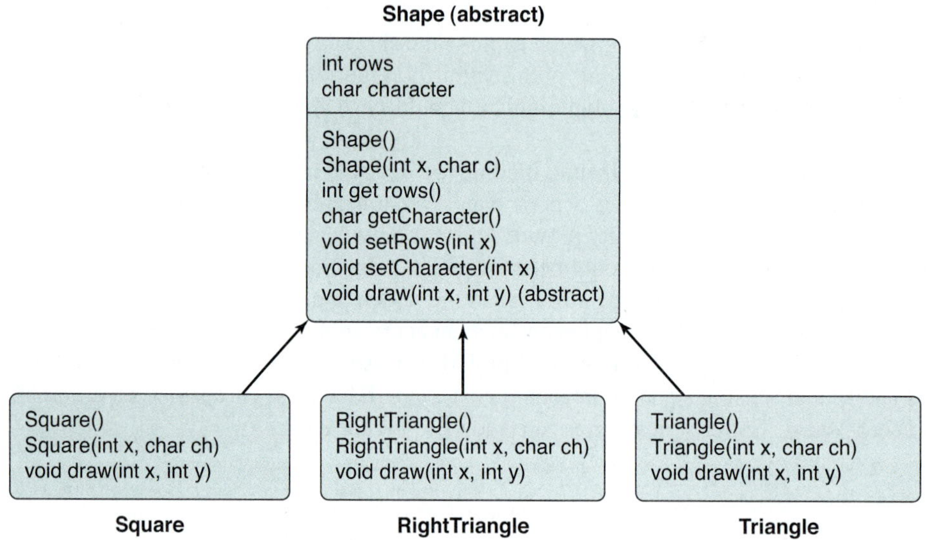

FIGURE 13.2 The *Shape* hierarchy

The abstract class Shape has the following form:

```
public abstract class Shape
{
   protected int rows;                  // figure drawn on rows rows
   protected char character;            // the drawing character

   public Shape()
   {
      rows = 0;
      char character = ' ';
   }

   public Shape(int x, char ch)
   {
      rows = x;
      character = ch;
   }

   public int getRows()
   {
      return rows;
   }

   public char getCharacter()
   {
      return character;
   }

   public void setRows(int y)
   {
      rows = y;
```

```
    }

    public void setCharacter(char ch)
    {
       character = ch;
    }

    public abstract void   draw(int x, int y);   // must be implemented in concrete subclasses

}
```

The three classes derived from Shape follow. Each implements constructors and a unique draw(...) method.

```
public class Square extends Shape
{
public Square()
{
    // call Shape default constructor
    super();
}

public Square(int x, char ch)
{
   // call Shape 2 argument constr.
   super(x, ch);
}

public void draw(int x, int y)
{
   // move down y lines
   for ( int i = 1; i <= y; i++)
      System.out.println();

   // for each row
   for (int len = 1; len <= rows; len++)
    {
      // indent x spaces
      for (int i = 1; i <= x; i++)
         System.out.print(' ');
      for(int j = 1; j <= rows; j++)
         System.out.print(character);
      System.out.println();
    }
}
}
```

```
public class RightTriangle extends Shape
{
public RightTriangle()
{
   // call Shape default constructor
   super();
}

public RightTriangle(int x, char ch)
{
   // call Shape 2 argument constr.
   super(x, ch);
}

public void draw(int x, int y)
{
    // move down y lines
   for ( int i = 1; i <= y; i++)
      System.out.println();

   // for each row
   for (int len = 1; len <= rows; len++)
   {
     // indent x spaces
     for (int i = 1; i <= x; i++)
        System.out.print(' ');
     for (int j = 1; j <= len; j++)
        System.out.print(character);
     System.out.println();
   }
}
}
```

```
public class Triangle extends Shape
{
public Triangle ()
{
   // call Shape default constructor
   super();
}

public Triangle (int x, char ch)
{
   // call Shape 2 argument constr.
   super(x, ch);
}

public void draw(int x, int y)
{
   // move down y lines
   for ( int i = 1; i <= y; i++)
      System.out.println();

   // for each row
   for(int len = 1; len <= rows; len++)
   {
      // indent; the vertex is centered
      for(int i = 0; i <= rows - len + x; i++)
         System.out.print(" ");
      for(int i =1; i <= len; i++)
         System.out.print(character + " ");
      System.out.println();
   }
}
}
```

Output An arrow or a tree? Which do you see?

```
      *
     * *
    * * *
   * * * *
  * * * * *
 * * * * * *
* * * * * * *
    *****
    *****
    *****
    *****
    *****
```

Discussion Except for constructors and draw(...), Square, RightTriangle, and Triangle inherit all other methods from Shape. Of course, because Shape is abstract, no Shape objects can exist. The following small class uses two of these draw(...) methods to display an arrow, of sorts, or perhaps a rather primitive tree. Which do you see?

```
public class Arrow
{
    public static void main(String[] args)
    {
        Triangle head = new Triangle(7, '*');
        Square tail = new Square(5, '*');
        head.draw(0, 0);
        tail.draw(5, 0);
    }
}
```

The following example shows a test class that utilizes the Shape hierarchy and gives a first look at polymorphism via dynamic binding.

EXAMPLE 13.2 **Problem Statement** Devise a test class that interactively queries a user for one of three shapes and subsequently draws the requested shape.

Java Solution The main(...) method of the following test class requests input 1, 2, or 3 representing a square, a right triangle, or an equilateral triangle, respectively. Because a Square *is-a* Shape, a RightTriangle *is-a* Shape, and a Triangle *is-a* Shape, all references are upcast to Shape.

```
import java.util.*;
public class TestDraw
{
    public static void main(String[] args)
    {
        Scanner input = new Scanner(System.in);
        Shape shape = null;                  // all references can be upcast to Shape
        int shapeNumber;                     // code number for each type of figure
        System.out.print("Enter 1: Square, 2: RightTriangle, 3: Equilateral Triangle: ");
        shapeNumber = input.nextInt();

        switch (shapeNumber)
        {
            case 1 : shape = new Square(4, '*');          // size 4, draw with *
                     break;
            case 2 : shape = new RightTriangle(5, '#');   // size 5, draw with #
                     break;
            case 3 : shape = new Triangle(6, '+');        // size 6, draw with +
                     break;
            default : System.out.println("Invalid entry"); // shapeNumber is not 1, 2, or 3
                      System.exit(0);                     // bad data, terminate the application
        }
        shape.draw(1, 1);
    }
}
```

Output Running the program twice produces the following output:

```
Enter 1: Square, 2: RightTriangle, 3: Equilateral Triangle: 2
#
##
###
####
#####

Enter 1: Square, 2: RightTriangle, 3: Equilateral Triangle: 1
****
****
****
****
```

Discussion The application runs as you might expect, but only because Java implements polymorphism through *late binding*.

Behind the scenes, there is more going on than you might imagine. Let's take a closer look at line 22:

```
shape.draw(1, 1)
```

On line 22, it *appears* that a Shape object (shape) invokes its draw(…) method. However, Shape is an abstract class, so no Shape object can exist. Furthermore, Shape does not implement draw(...) as part of the Shape class, draw(...) is declared abstract. Well, then, which draw(...) method is invoked?

As you already know, via inheritance and upcasting, the reference variable shape could refer to

- a Square object (line 13),
- a RightTriangle object (line 15), or
- a Triangle object (line 17).

When TestDraw is compiled and translated into bytecode, the Java compiler *cannot* determine which draw(…) method is applicable. The compiler knows that shape refers to a kind of Shape, but it does not know which kind. The appropriate draw(...) method is not discernible until the program runs and the user chooses one of three shapes.

Consequently, the compiled version of the program, that is, the bytecode that executes on the Java Virtual Machine, does not specify which draw(...) method is appropriate. The choice of the correct draw(...) method is postponed until the program executes; that is, the choice is postponed until *runtime*.

> Polymorphism via *dynamic or late binding* refers to choosing the appropriate method not at compile time, but at runtime.

When the TestDraw application *runs*, Java determines which form of draw(...) to execute.

The draw(...) method of Example 13.2 has "many forms" (well, at least three), and Java chooses the appropriate version dynamically, that is, during the run of the program. The notion of late binding is the essence of polymorphism. In fact, late (or dynamic) binding is often given as the definition of polymorphism.

Dynamic binding is a convenience. If Java did not automatically support late binding, we could achieve the same effect explicitly, if less elegantly, using a sequence of if-else statements, instanceof's, and downcasts:

```
if (shape instanceof Square)
        ((Square)shape).draw(1,1);                    // notice the downcasts
else if (shape instanceof RightTriangle)
        ((RightTriangle)shape).draw(1,1);
else if (shape instanceof Triangle)
        ((Triangle)shape).draw(1,1);
```

13.3.1 How Dynamic Binding Works

At the risk of oversimplification, we discuss how the mechanism of dynamic binding works—in particular how the draw(...) method of Example 13.2 is, in fact, chosen.

Notice that the reference variable shape is declared to be of type Shape:

Shape shape (line 7 of Example 13.2).

Shape is the *apparent type* or *declared type of shape*. Of course, a Shape object cannot be instantiated because Shape is an abstract class. On the other hand, variable shape can refer to a Square object or a Triangle object, or an object of any concrete class that extends Shape.

> The *real type* or *actual type* of a reference variable is the type of the object that is created by the new operation.

So, the real type of shape is Square, RightTriangle, or Triangle, depending on user input. See lines 13, 15, and 17 of Example 13.2.

Let's arbitrarily assume that the user, TestDraw, chooses to draw a right triangle. In this case, the real type of shape is RightTriangle (line 15). When the draw(...) method is invoked by shape (see line 22), Java begins searching for a fully implemented draw(...) method. The search begins in the RightTriangle class (the real type of shape). If the RightTriangle class has implemented a draw(...) method then the search ends, and that method is called. If not, then Java searches the parent of RightTriangle. Searching continues all the way up the hierarchy until an implemented draw(...) method is found (or until the Object class is reached).

As another illustration, recall that in the Shape hierarchy, there is a getter method

```
int getRows()
{
    return rows;
}
```

Because the Shape class implements getRows(), the classes Square, RightTriangle, and Triangle inherit getRows().

Now, in Example 13.2, replace line 22 (shape.draw(1,1)) with

```
shape.getRows()
```

If a user again chooses a right triangle, Java begins searching the RightTriangle class (the real type) for a getRows() method. Since RightTriangle does *not* implement a getRows() method, Java continues the search in the parent class (Shape) where such a method does exist. Thus, the getRows() that is implemented in Shape is executed.

How does the compiler handle shape.draw(1,1), which at compile time is ambiguous? It checks the apparent type of shape and works with that. Since Shape declares a draw(...) method, anything below Shape in the hierarchy also has a draw(...) method. Even though the Shape class does not *implement* a draw(...) method, Shape does *declare* a draw method. Consequently the statement

```
shape.draw(1,1)
```

causes no confusion to the compiler. The compiler happily accepts the statement and, during runtime, the appropriate version of draw(...) is selected. Were draw(...) not declared in Shape, a compile time error would be issued:

```
C:\JavaPrograms\TestDraw.java:19: cannot find symbol
symbol : method draw(int,int)
location: class Shape
shape.draw(1,1);
     ^
```

Here is another illustration that utilizes two very simple classes, Parent and (a rather precocious) Child. See Figure 13.3.

```
public class Parent
{
   public void hello()
   {
      System.out.println("Hi");
   }
}
```

```
public class Child extends Parent
{
   public void hello()
   {
      System.out.println("Bonjour");
   }
   public void goodbye()
   {
      System.out.println("Au revoir");
   }
}
```

FIGURE 13.3 A *Parent-Child* hierarchy

The following code segment does *not* compile.

```
Parent x;
x = new Child();
x.goodbye();
```

Here, the apparent type of x is Parent. Notice that Parent has no goodbye() method. Consequently, the method invocation x.goodbye() is *syntactically* incorrect.

A cast fixes the problem:

```
((Child)x).goodbye();
```

The compiler now knows that x is to be treated as a Child object and Child *does* implement a goodbye() method.

On the other hand, in the following fragment, again, the apparent type of x is Parent.

```
Parent x;
x = new Child();
x.hello();
```

In this case, the Parent class contains an implementation of the hello() method, so no syntax error occurs. When the program runs, late binding ensures that the hello() method of Child, rather than Parent, executes. The output is:

```
Bonjour
```

13.3.2 Exceptions to Late Binding

Late binding is the rule, but there are exceptions. Late binding allows the programmer to avoid a tedious sequence of if statements. However, there are situations where late binding does not make sense.

Unlike the draw(…) method of Example 13.2, a final, private, or static method cannot be overridden in a derived class and has only one form. Consequently, a call to a final, private, or static method presents no ambiguity to the compiler. Because such a method has but one version, a method call can be associated with the correct method implementation at compile time, that is, before the program executes. There is no need to wait until runtime to connect the call to the appropriate version of the method.

> Java uses late binding for all method invocations except final, private, and static methods.

13.4 POLYMORPHISM MAKES PROGRAMS EXTENSIBLE

You have seen how polymorphism with late binding can make your code cleaner and more manageable. But wait! Polymorphism gets even better.

> Polymorphism allows you to extend your classes with ease.

In the next example, we add a new Shape to the Square-RightTriangle-Triangle trio.

EXAMPLE 13.3

With most drawing applications, you can create figures that are either filled or unfilled. See Figure 13.4.

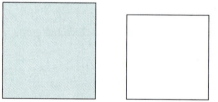

FIGURE 13.4 A filled square and an unfilled square

The "drawings" produced by the methods of the Shape hierarchy are all filled.

Problem Statement Expand the Shape class with a subclass, EmptySquare, that implements a draw method that produces a square that is not filled.

```
*****
*   *
*   *
*   *
*****
```

Java Solution EmptySquare extends Shape and implements draw(x, y) according to the following algorithm:

```
Move the cursor down y lines
For each row
        print x spaces
        for each position within a row
                if the position is on the edge of the square
                        print the drawing character
                else
                        print a space
        move down a row
```

The code for EmptySquare follows:

```
class EmptySquare extends Shape
{
   public EmptySquare()
   {
      super();                  // calls default Shape constructor
   }

   public EmptySquare(int x, char ch)
   {
      super(x, ch);             // call 2-argument Shape constructor
   }

   public void draw(int x, int y)
   {
      // move down y lines
      for ( int i = 1; i <= y; i++)
         System.out.println();

      // for each row
      for (int len = 1; len <= rows; len++)
      {
         // indent x spaces
         for (int i = 1; i <= x; i++)
            System.out.print(' ');

         // print a character on an edge
         // print spaces in the interior

         for (int j = 1; j <= rows; j++)
            if (j == 1 || j == rows || len == rows || len == 1 ) // on edge
               System.out.print(character);
            else
               System.out.print(" ");
         System.out.println();
      }
   }
}
```

Output Enter 1: Square, 2: RightTriangle, 3: Equilateral Triangle, 4: Unfilled Square: **4**

```
******
*    *
*    *
*    *
*    *
******
```

Discussion That's all there is to it. The hierarchy has been easily expanded, and conveniently, the *only* necessary change occurs in the test program (below in bold). Just two lines!

```
import java.util.Scanner;
public class TestDraw
{
   public static void main(String[] args)
   {
      Scanner input = new Scanner(System.in);
      Shape shape = null;
      int shapeNumber;      // code number for each type of figure
      char ch;

      System.out.print("Enter 1: Square, 2: RightTriangle, 3: Equilateral Triangle, 4: Unfilled square: ");
      shapeNumber = input.nextInt();

      switch (shapeNumber)
      {
         case 1 : shape = new Square(4, '*');
                  break;
         case 2 : shape = new RightTriangle(5, '#');
                  break;
         case 3 : shape = new Triangle(6, '+');
                  break;
         case 4 : shape = new EmptySquare(7, '*');
                  break;

      }
      shape.draw(1, 1);
   }
}
```

Nothing in the Shape hierarchy needs alteration. In fact, the previously defined classes (Square, RightTriangle, and Triangle) do not have to be recompiled. A new Shape has been easily added to the hierarchy with its unique version of draw(...). Plug and play. The draw(...) method now has *four* forms, but no significant code was altered. Polymorphism through late binding ensures that the correct form of draw(...) will be chosen at runtime.

13.5 INTERFACES AND POLYMORPHISM

In Chapter 12, you learned that a Java interface allows a programmer some of the flexibility of multiple inheritance without the inherent pitfalls. But interfaces have other advantages. Example 13.4 demonstrates that using an interface can tie classes together into a nice package with the power of polymorphism added to the bundle.

An interface can be used to achieve polymorphism.

EXAMPLE 13.4

Nostalgic Ned collects films and music of yesteryear. Vintage black and white Mickey Mouse cartoons, John Wayne shoot-em-up westerns, or ballads crooned by Frank Sinatra are Ned's pleasure. And, although Ned enjoys the entertainment of the past, he is a bit more modern with his technology. Ned owns a disc changer that holds up to 200 CDs or DVDs. He also has a large MP3 music collection stored on his computer.

Ned has written a program that interacts with his disc changer. His application implements an interface, Playable:

```
public interface Playable
{
        public void play();
}
```

and consists of three classes, DVD, CD, and MP3, each of which implements Playable. The classes shown in Figure 13.5 are written with a single println() statement replacing the code that actually initiates play.

```
public class DVD
        Implements Playable
{
   protected String title;
   public DVD(String t)
   {
      title = t;
   }
   public void play ()
   {
      System.out.println(
      "DVD:playing" + title);
   }
}
```

```
public class CD
        implements Playable
{
   protected String title:
   public CD(String t)
   {
      title = t;
   }
   public void play()
   {
      System.out.println(
      "CD: playing" + title);
   }
}
```

```
public class MP3
        implements Playable
{
   protected String title;
   public MP3(String t)
   {
      title = t;
   }
   public void play()
   {
      System.out.println(
      "MP3: playing " + title);
   }
}
```

FIGURE 13.5 Each of the three classes implements *Playable*

So for example, the segment

```
DVD dvd = new DVD("The Wizard of Oz");
dvd.play();
```

sends Ned down the yellow brick road.

All that is fine, but Ned would like to automate his system a bit so that he can load and play any number of titles, DVD, CD, or MP3. Once Ned selects a collection of music and/or film titles, they play in sequence.

Problem Statement Using the classes of Figure 13.5, implement a more functional class to assist Ned. The application should request the number of items, and for each one the media player (DVD, CD, or MP3) and the music or film title.

Java Solution The constructor of the MediaPlayer class builds an array of at most 30 Playable objects based on user input. Once the array is filled, the play() method is invoked, in turn, by each object. To keep the example simple, we assume that all user input is correct.

```
import java.util.*;
public class MediaPlayer
{
```

```
    Playable[] items;
    final private int MAX_ITEMS = 30; // maximum length of the array, items
    int numItems;
    public MediaPlayer()
    {
        Scanner input = new Scanner(System.in);
        items = new Playable[MAX_ITEMS];
        System.out.print("Number of items : ");
        numItems = input.nextInt();
        for (int i = 0; i < numItems; i++)
        {
            System.out.print("1:DVD, 2:CD, 3:MP3 ---> ");
            int choice = input.nextInt();
            input.nextLine();
            System.out.print("Title: ");
            String title = input.nextLine();
            switch (choice)
            {
                case 1 : items[i] = new DVD(title); break;
                case 2 : items[i] = new CD(title); break;
                case 3 : items[i] = new MP3(title); break;
            }
        }
        System.out.println("All items loaded\n");
    }

    public void playAll()
    {
        for (int i = 0; i < numItems; i++)
            items[i].play();
    }

    public static void main(String [] args)
    {
        MediaPlayer player = new MediaPlayer();
        player.playAll();
    }
}
```

Output

Number of items: **5**
1:DVD, 2:CD, 3:MP3 ---> **1**
Title: **Steamboat Willie**
1:DVD, 2:CD, 3:MP3 ---> **1**
Title: **The Wizard of Oz**
1:DVD, 2:CD, 3:MP3 ---> **2**
Title: **Classic Sinatra**
1:DVD, 2:CD, 3:MP3 ---> **3**
Title: **Marcelle Marceau's Greatest Hits**
1:DVD, 2:CD, 3:MP3 ---> **1**
Title: **The Best of Popeye and Olive Oyl**
All items loaded

DVD playing Steamboat Willie
DVD playing The Wizard of Oz

```
CD playing Classic Sinatra
MP3 playing Marcelle Marceau's Greatest Hits
DVD playing The Best of Popeye and Olive Oyl
```

Discussion Notice that items, declared on line 4, is an array of Playable. Playable is an interface; Playable is not a class.

Each of the three classes DVD, CD, and MP3 implements Playable, and hence the play() method. In that sense, they are similar. Because DVD, CD, and MP3 each implements Playable, a Playable reference can refer to objects of type DVD, CD, or MP3. That is, DVD, CD, and MP3 can each be upcast to Playable. Consequently, the array items can refer to objects that are instantiated from any of these three classes, (lines 22–24), and indeed from any other class that implements Playable.

On one hand, all three classes are similar in that each one implements play() and can be upcast to Playable. On the other hand, polymorphism unwinds the differences among these classes by choosing the appropriate play() method at runtime (line 32). That's right—late binding. We reiterate:

> Inheritance emphasizes similarity among classes—commonality is factored out into the base class.

> Polymorphism accentuates differences among classes in an inheritance hierarchy—at runtime the appropriate and particular method is invoked.

13.5.1 Life Without Polymorphism

Suppose that none of the classes (DVD, CD, or MP3) implements the Playable interface. With such a scenario, we'd certainly have three perfectly good, independent classes, but without the power of polymorphism behind them.

Let's see what happens if we try to accomplish this polymorphic behavior without the Playable interface, through the inheritance structure of mother Object. Instead of the array

```
Playable[] items
```

we might declare an array

```
Object[] items
```

to refer to objects of the various classes DVD, CD, and MP3. Upcasting to Object is no problem. So far, so good.

Now consider the method playAll():

```
1. public void playAll()
2. {
3.     for ( int i = 0; i < numitems; i++)
4.     {
5.         items[i].play()
6.     }
7. }
```

The apparent type of items[i] (line 5) is Object; but the Object class knows nothing about the various play() methods. Consequently, the compiler issues an error message at line 5.

To ensure that the program compiles and runs correctly, we replace line 5 with an else-if construction coupled with several casts:

```
if (items[i] instanceof DVD)
        ((DVD)items[i]).play();
else if (items[i] instanceof CD)
        ((CD)items[i]).play();
else if (items[i] instanceof MP3)
        ((MP3)items[i]).play();
```

Now we have finally succeeded at simulating the polymorphism we achieved naturally with the Playable interface. This rather inelegant solution should be enough to convince you not only of the ease and power of polymorphism and dynamic binding, but also that design with interfaces ultimately simplifies your code and makes life as a programmer just a bit easier.

13.6 POLYMORPHISM AND THE *Object* CLASS

Even without a programmer-defined hierarchy, polymorphism plays a key role in many applications. As you know, every class extends Object; and in this regard every class, if implemented properly, can take advantage of inheritance and polymorphism. In fact, you've probably been exploiting polymorphism without realizing it. Example 13.5 illustrates polymorphism via the Object class.

EXAMPLE 13.5 Horror movies have been popular since the era of silent film. And although some horror flicks trigger goosebumps, their tag lines—catchphrases such as "Frankenstein: A Monster Science Created - But Could Not Destroy!"—more often provoke laughter. As a collector of tag lines from famous and not-so-famous horror flicks, Ms. Holly Wood needs some help organizing her massive collection of slogans.

Problem Statement To help Holly to manage her data, design an application that

- stores Movie objects (a film title and a tag line) in an array, and
- allows Holly to search the array and retrieve a film's tag line, given the title of the film.

Java Solution In addition to the two attributes, title and tagLine, the following Movie class

- implements the standard getter and setter methods,
- overrides the toString() method inherited from Object so that the toString() version of the Movie class returns the title and the tag line as a String,
- overrides the equals(...) method inherited from Object, implementing an equality that is based on the title of a film, so that two Movie objects with the same title are equal, and
- implements the Comparable interface by alphabetically comparing titles so that the array of Movie objects can be sorted by title.

The Movie class is pictured (as a descendent of Object) in Figure 13.6 and is defined below.

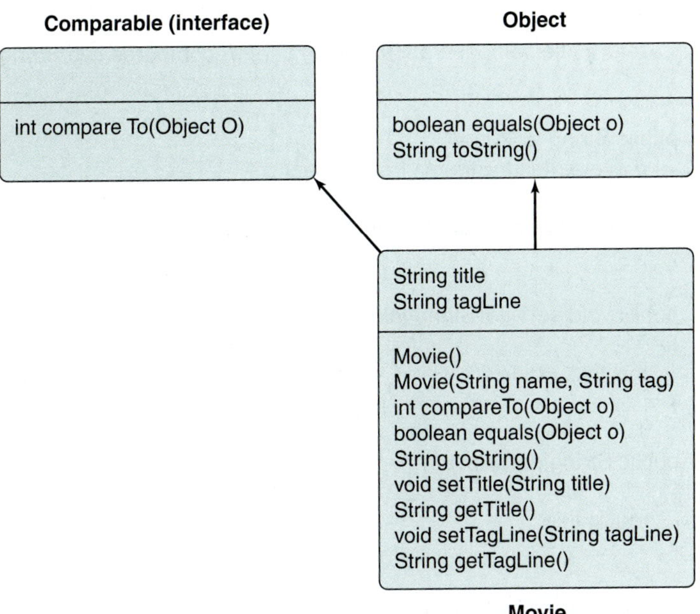

FIGURE 13.6 *Movie* overrides *equals(Object o)* and *toString()*; *Movie* implements *Comparable*

```
public class Movie implements Comparable
{
   private String title;
   private String tagLine;

   public Movie()
   // default constructor, makes an empty Movie object
   {
      title = "";
      tagLine = "";
   }

   public Movie( String name, String tag)
   {
   // two-argument constructor, creates a Movie object with a title and tag line
      title = name;
      tagLine = tag;
   }

   public boolean equals(Object o)
   // override the equals object inherited from Object
   // two Movie objects are equal if they have the same title
   {
      return title.equals(((Movie)o).title); // notice that o must be cast to Movie
   }

   public int compareTo(Object o)
      // implement compareTo from the Comparable interface
      // compareTo compares two titles.       The compareTo from String is invoked
```

```
    {
        return title.compareTo(((Movie)o).title); // compares two Strings
    }

    public String toString()
        // overwrites toString() from Object
    {
        return "Title: " + title + " Tag line: " + tagLine;
    }

    public void setTitle(String title)
    {
        this.title = title;
    }

    public String getTitle()
    {
        return title;
    }

    public void setTagLine(String tagLine)
    {
        this. tagLine = tagLine;
    }

    public String getTagLine ()
    {
        return tagLine;
    }
}
```

To locate a particular movie, the application utilizes the binary search algorithm, introduced in Chapter 7. As you may recall, binary search utilizes a *sorted* array. Because Movie implements the Comparable interface, an array of Movie references can be ordered.

The following implementation of binary search is more general than the version given in Chapter 7 because here, the array parameter x and the key parameter are both declared of type Object. Thus, the method call,

```
search(Object[] x, Object key),
```

can pass arguments *of any class*.

Because Search is a simple utility class that does not depend on the creation of any instance variable, search(...) is declared static. To invoke search(...), use the class name:

```
Search.search(...);
```

```
public class Search
{
    public static int search(Object [] x, Object key, int size)
    {
        // binary search from Chapter 7
        int lo = 0;
        int hi = size - 1;
        int mid = (lo + hi) / 2;
        while ( lo <= hi)
```

```
10.       {
11.          if (key.equals(x[mid]))        // key found
12.             return mid;
13.          else if (((Comparable)key).compareTo(x[mid]) < 0)
14.             hi = mid - 1;
15.          else
16.             lo = mid + 1;
17.             mid = (lo + hi) / 2;
18.       }
19.       return - 1; // key not found
20.    }
21. }
```

The cast on line 13

```
else if (((Comparable)key).compareTo(x[mid]) < 0)
```

is necessary because the parameter key refers to an Object, and Object does not implement Comparable. Without the downcast, the compiler issues a message to the effect that the name compareTo is unknown.

With the Movie and Search classes defined, we implement a class that builds and searches an array of Movie references. Notice that this class invokes the generic sort method (SelectionSort.sort) of Chapter 12. The constructor of the class reads a list of movie titles and corresponding tag lines from a text file, movielines.txt, and creates a Movie object for each title-tagline pair. References to these Movie objects are stored in the array s.

```
import java.util.Scanner;
import java.io.*;

public class MovieSearch
{
   Scanner input = new Scanner(System.in);
   private String title, tagLine;
   private Movie[] movies ;
   private final int MAX_MOVIES = 500;
   private int num;                          // the total number of films in the file

   public MovieSearch() throws IOException
   {
      num = 0;
      movies = new Movie[MAX_MOVIES];
      File inputFile = new File("movielines.txt");
      if( !inputFile.exists())
      {
         System.out.println("File movielines.txt not found ");
         System.exit(0);
      }
      Scanner input = new Scanner(inputFile);
      String line;                           // to hold one full line from the file
      while (input.hasNext())                // while there is more data
      {
         String name = input.nextLine();  // advance to next line, returns all "skipped" data
         String tag = input.nextLine();
         movies[num] = new Movie (name, tag);
         num++;
      }
```

```
        input.close();
        SelectionSort.sort(movies, num);  // the array must be kept sorted to utilize binary search
        System.out.println("\n" + num +" titles entered");
        System.out.println("-------------------\n");
        searchFilm();
    }

    public void searchFilm()
    {
            // Prompt user for a movie title
            // Search the array for the film with that title
            // If the film is in the array, print the title and tagline
            // If the film is not in the array, issue a message

        System.out.println();
        Movie key = new Movie();  // an empty Movie object
        int place;                // a position in the array
        System.out.println("Input a title. Hit Enter to end");
        do
        {              // get title from user
            System.out.print("\nTitle: ");
            title = input.nextLine();
            if (title.equals(""))
                break; // end if user hits 'Enter'
            key.setTitle(title);   // wrap title in a Movie object
            key.setTagLine(""); // the tagline is empty at this point

            // invoke binary search to find a movie object with the title as key
            // if successful, place contains the position in the array; otherwise
            // place contains - 1
            place = Search.search(movies, key, num); // key is a Movie object

            if (place >= 0 && place < num)            // successful search
                System.out.println(movies[place]);    // print the object at place
            else
                System.out.println(title + " not found");
        } while(true);
    }

    public static void main(String[] args) throws IOException
    {
        MovieSearch movieSearch = new MovieSearch();
    }
}
```

Output Running the program with the file movielines.txt produces the following output:

```
234 titles entered
-------------------

Input a title. Hit Enter to exit

Title: Alien
Title: Alien Tagline: In space no one can hear you scream
```

Title: The Thing
Title: The Thing Tagline: Look closely at your neighbors. Don't trust anybody!

Title: Dracula
Dracula not found

Title: Bride of Frankenstein
Title: Bride of Frankenstein Tagline: Beware! The monster demands a mate!

Discussion

The Movie Class:
Line 21 of the Movie class

```
return title.equals(((Movie)x).title);
```

may seem a bit puzzling. Which equals(...) method is being invoked? The equals(...) method invoked on line 21 is called by title, which is a String. Conveniently, the String class overrides equals(Object). So the call

```
title.equals(((Movie)x).title);
```

compares two String objects via String's version of equals(...), that is, by comparing the characters in each String. The cast of x to Movie is necessary because the apparent type of x is Object and Objects do not have title attributes.

Similarly, on line 27, the statement

```
return title.compareTo(((Movie)x).title);
```

invokes the compareTo(...) method of the String class.

The remainder of the Movie class is straightforward and should present no difficulty.

The Search Class
Binary search is introduced in Chapter 7. This version is more generic in that the arguments are of type Object. That certainly makes the search(...) method more flexible, but care must be exercised with this added flexibility.

On line 11 of the Search class,

```
if (key.equals(x[mid]))
```

the key object is compared to x[mid] via equals(...). This is the equals(...) method inherited from Object. If this equals(...) method is not overridden in Movie, then references are compared, and the result is incorrect.

Similarly, on line 13,

```
else if (((Comparable)key).compareTo(x[mid]) < 0)
```

the compareTo(...) method is invoked by key. Accordingly, Movie implements the Comparable interface.

The MovieSearch Class:
The statements on lines 22–28 continually perform the following actions:

- read a title and tagline from the text file, movielines.txt,
- instantiate a Movie object with the two-argument constructor, and
- store a reference to the Movie object in the array movies,

until all data has been read from movielines.txt.

Notice that the constructor contains the clause throws IOException. This clause is necessary for File IO.

The searchFilm() method

- creates an empty Movie object, key (line 42),
- queries a user for the title of a movie,
- sets the title attribute of key appropriately and sets the tagline field to the empty string (lines 51 and 52),
- passes key to search(...), which returns the index of key in the array movies, and
- processes the returned information from search(...), (lines 56–60): if key is not found, search(...) returns −1 and a "title not found" message is issued, otherwise the key and tagline are displayed;

until a user presses Enter without supplying a movie title.

Finally, notice that main(...) includes the clause throws IO Exception. This mysterious *throwing* of exceptions is fully explained in Chapter 14.

13.6.1 A Summary, a Subtlety, and a Warning

Because every class extends Object, all classes share a number of common features. Inheritance emphasizes similarity among classes—commonality is factored out into the base class. Alternatively, polymorphism accentuates differences among classes in an inheritance hierarchy—at runtime the appropriate version of a method is chosen.

The classes of Example 13.5 demonstrate *both* inheritance and polymorphism. They also shed light on a subtle point about equals(Object o). The statement on line 56 of FilmSearch(...) is a call to the static method Search.search(...), which subsequently invokes

```
boolean equals(Object o).
```

See Figure 13.7.

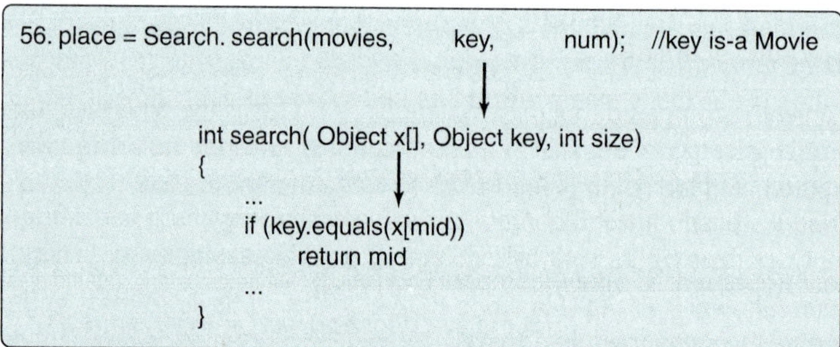

FIGURE 13.7 A call to *search*(...) and then to *equals*(...)

Which equals(...) method is appropriate? There are two: one defined in Object and the other in Movie. At runtime it is known that

- the *apparent* type of key is Object,
- the *real* type of key is Movie, and

because the call, key.equals(x[mid]), is made by key, the Java Virtual Machine begins a search for the appropriate equals(**Object** o) method Movie, the *real* type of key, and successfully finds such a method—polymorphism and dynamic binding in action. See Figure 13.6.

Now, suppose that Movie implements equals(...) not as

```
boolean equals(Object o)                 // parameter type is Object
{
    return title.equals(((Movie)o).title);  // downcast is necessary
}
```

but as

```
boolean equals(Movie o)                  // parameter type is Movie
{
    return title.equals(o.title);         // no downcast is necessary
}
```

The second version of equals(...) may perform correctly under some circumstances but not in the application of Example 13.5. As before, the Java Virtual Machine begins a search for

boolean equals(**Object** o).

in the Movie class. Does Movie have an equals(**Object** o) method? The answer is negative. Movie implements equals(**Movie** o) but *not* equals (**Object** o). So, moving up the inheritance chain, the Java Virtual Machine continues its search for equals(**Object** o) in Object, where such a method exists. See Figure 13.8.

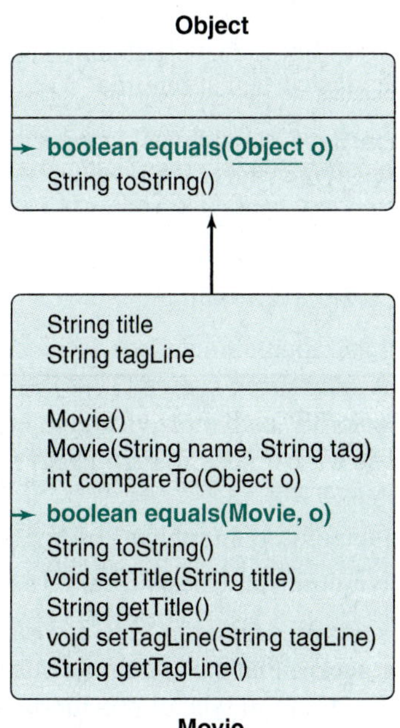

FIGURE 13.8 Begin searching for *equals(Object o)* in *Movie*

Unfortunately, this method does not work! The equals(Object o) method of Object compares *references*, not titles. Consequently, no search ever returns true. The program runs, but not correctly. Polymorphism is broken.

In Chapter 12, we assert that, when implementing equals(...), it is preferable to override

boolean equals(**Object** o)

inherited from Object rather than to define a new method such as

boolean equals(**Movie** o).

Now you can understand why.

When providing an equals(...) method for a class, it is usually preferable to override the equals() method of Object, rather than defining a new equals(...) method. Overriding the equals(...) method from Object allows polymorphism to perform its magic.

13.7 IN CONCLUSION

Encapsulation. Inheritance. Polymorphism. These are the fundamentals of object-oriented programming.

- Encapsulation organizes an application into classes and objects. Objects combine data and actions into one bundle. Indeed, objects model real-world entities.
- Inheritance facilitates code reuse. New classes can be created directly from old ones. Upcasting in an inheritance hierarchy makes it possible for data of one type to be considered data of a more general type.
- A method may have many forms. Polymorphism, through late binding, ensures that the correct form of a method is chosen at runtime.

Chapter 14 introduces two more Java hierarchies: wrapper classes and exception classes. And, yes, we finally explain what gets "thrown" and what "catches" it!

Just the Facts

- Polymorphism means that an entity, such as a method, may have multiple meanings. As inheritance exploits similarity among classes, polymorphism underscores differences among classes of a hierarchy.
- Method overloading is a type of polymorphism (ad-hoc polymorphism).
- Upcasting is a type of polymorphism. Upcasting allows an object of a derived type to be considered an object of a base type.
- Late (or dynamic) binding means that the appropriate method invocation is chosen at runtime. Late binding is the strongest type of polymorphism.
- Late binding is the default for all method calls except calls to final, private, and static methods, which cannot be overridden and have but one form. Early (static or compile time) binding is used for final, private, and static methods.
- The *apparent* type of an object is the declared type of the object; the *real* type of an object is the type of the object as created by the new operator.
- Late binding is implemented as follows: When choosing an appropriate method for a call such as x.myMethod(...), Java first searches the class of the real type of x and then continues up through the ancestors of x until a method with a matching signature is found.

- Polymorphism makes programs extensible. New classes may be added to a hierarchy without recompiling previously existing classes or rewriting code.
- Using an interface is a common and convenient way to effect polymorphism.
- Overriding methods inherited from the Object class makes it possible for classes to exploit polymorphism correctly and safely.

Bug Extermination

- When defining equals(...) for class A, it is preferable to override the equals(Object o) method inherited from Object rather than defining a new equals(A a). Under some circumstances, a program may run, but not correctly. See Section 13.6.1.
- A downcast may be necessary when a parent reference refers to a child object. The segment

```
Parent x;
x = new Child();
x.myMethod();
```

  does not compile if Parent does not declare myMethod(), even if Child does. In such a case, a downcast is appropriate:

```
Parent x;
x = new Child();
((Child)x).myMethod();
```

  However, if Parent has a declaration of myMethod(), no downcast is necessary.

EXERCISES

LEARN THE LINGO

Test your knowledge of the chapter's vocabulary by completing the following crossword puzzle.

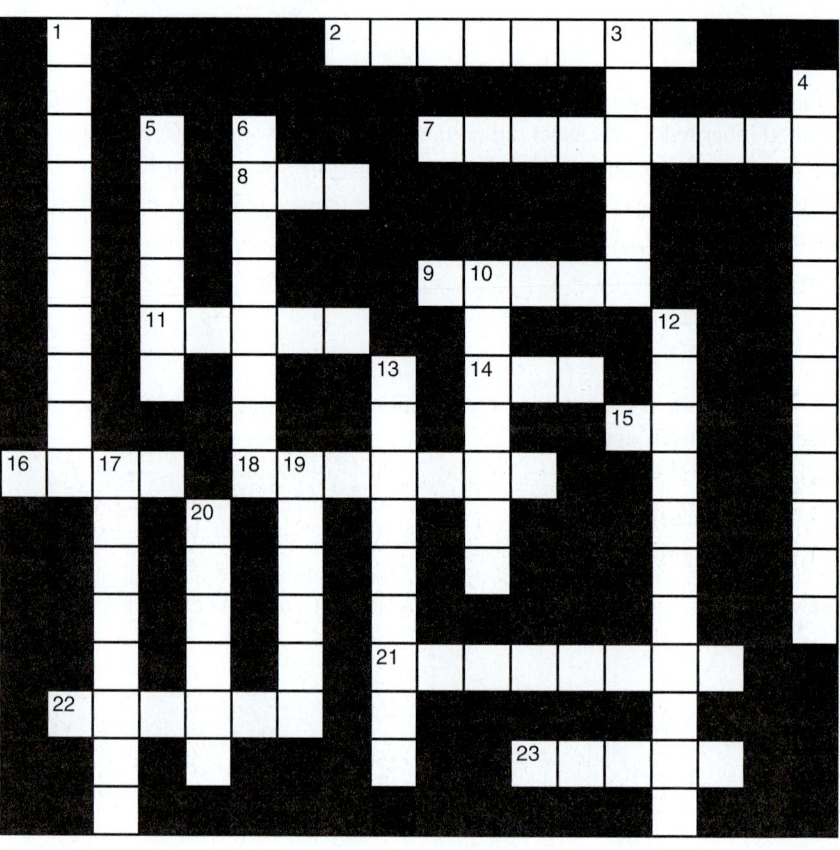

Across

2 A ________ may be necessary when a parent reference refers to a child object.
7 Method of the Comparable interface
8 Encapsulation, inheritance, and polymorphism form the foundation of ________.
9 Overloading is ________ polymorphism.
11 Parent x = new Child(); real type of x
14 Real type is type created by ________.
15 Without polymorphism, a program might use many, many ________ statements.
16 When choosing an appropriate method call for *x*, Java first searches the class of the ________ type of x.
18 Late binding occurs at ________.
21 Declared type
22 Parent x = new Child(); apparent type of x
23 Polymorphism is derived from the ________.

Down

1 Polymorphism makes programs ________.
3 Early binding applies to this type of method.
4 Having many shapes
5 When implementing the equals(...) method for a new class, it is advisable to override the method inherited from ________.
6 Handles early binding
10 Another term for late binding
12 Polymorphism exploits ________ within a hierarchy.
13 Collection of static constants and abstract methods
17 Method without an implementation
19 Object of derived type considered object of the base type
20 Polymorphism means many ________.

SHORT EXERCISES

1. **True or False**

   If false, give an explanation.

   a. The effect of late binding can be accomplished using if-else statements, even if Java had not provided polymorphism.

   b. When the Java compiler scans the statement

   ```
   x.doSomething();
   ```

   the compiler never knows what code will execute at runtime.

   c. When the Java compiler scans the statement

   ```
   x.doSomething();
   ```

   the compiler always knows what code will execute at runtime.

   d. When the Java compiler scans the statement

   ```
   x.doSomething();
   ```

   the compiler sometimes knows what code will execute at runtime.

   e. Method overloading is a form of polymorphism.

   f. The declared type of an object determines which method is chosen at runtime.

   g. Late binding is not applicable to static methods.

   h. Polymorphism helps make code updates smoother and simpler.

2. **Playing Compiler**

   a. Suppose that, in Example 13.4, Playable is implemented as a class rather than an interface:

   ```
   public class Playable
   {
      public void play();
   }
   ```

   and CD, DVD, and MP3 each extends Playable. Will the compiler complain?

   b. Suppose that, in Example 13.4, a new method, source(), is added to each subclass.

   ```
   public class Playable
   {
      public void play();
   }
   ```

```
public class CD implements Playable
{
   // other methods of CD
   public void source()
   {
      System.out.println("CD");
   }
}
```

```
public class DVD implements Playable
{
   // other methods DVD
   public void source()
   {
      System.out.println("DVD");
   }
}
```

```
public class MP3 implements Playable
{
   // other methods of MP3
   public void source()
   {
      System.out.println("MP3");
   }
}
```

The following code, adapted from Example 13.4, causes an error. Is this error a compile time error or a runtime error? Explain your answer.

```
public static printList(Playable[] x)
{
        // accepts an array x of Playable and invokes two methods for each object in x
        for ( int i = 0; i < x.length; i++)
        {
                x[i].play();
                x[i].source();
        }
}
```

3. **Playing Compiler**

   a. Suppose that each of the classes, CD, DVD, and MP3 implements two interfaces, Playable and Source:

```
public interface Playable          public interface Source
{                                  {
   public void play();                public void source();
}                                  }
```

   Is there any problem with the code for the method printList(...) of Short Exercise 2? Explain why or why not.

   b. What errors, if any, occur if we substitute the following code for the shape.draw(1, 1) method call on line 22 of Example 13.2? Explain your answer.

```
if (shape instanceof Square)
        ((Square)shape).draw(1, 1);
else if (shape instanceof RightTriangle)
        ((RightTriangle)shape).draw(1, 1);
else if (shape instanceof Triangle)
        ((Triangle)shape).draw(1, 1);
```

   How about this replacement code? Explain your answer.

```
if (shape instanceof Square)
        shape.draw(1, 1);
else if (shape instanceof RightTriangle)
        shape.draw(1, 1);
else if (shape instanceof Triangle)
        shape.draw(1, 1);
```

4. **What's the Output?**

   a. Determine the output of the following code:

```
public class Point
{
        int x, y;
        public Point ()
        {
                x = y = 0;
        }
        public Point(int a, int b)
        {
```

```
                x = a;
                y = b;
        }
        public boolean equals(Point p) // tests whether or not two Points are equal
        {
                return ( p.x == x && p.y == y);
        }
}

public class Example
{
        public static void main(String[] args)
        {
                Object a;
                Object b;
                a = new Point(3, 4);
                b = new Point (3, 4);
                System.out.println(a.equals(b));
        }
}
```

b. Determine the output of the following code:

```
public class Point
{
        int x, y;
        public Point ()
        {
                x = y = 0;
        }
        public Point(int a, int b)
        {
                x = a;
                y = b;
        }
        public boolean equals(Point p) // tests whether or not two Points are equal
        {
                return ( p.x == x && p.y == y);
        }
}

public class Example
{
        public static void main(String[] args)
        {
                Object a;
                Object b;
                a = new Point(3, 4);
                b = a;
                System.out.println(a.equals(b));
        }
}
```

5. **What's the Output?**
   a. Determine the output of the following code:

```
public class Point
{
        int x, y;
        public Point ()
        {
                x = y = 0;
        }
        public Point(int a, int b)
        {
                x = a;
                y = b;
        }
        public boolean equals(Point p) // tests whether or not two Points are equal
        {
                return ( p.x == x && p.y == y);
        }
}

public class Example
{
        public static void main(String[] args)
        {
                Point a;
                Point b;
                a = new Point(3, 4);
                b = new Point (3, 4);
                System.out.println(a.equals(b));
        }
}
```

   b. Determine the output of the following code:

```
public class A
{
        public void X()
        {
                System.out.println("Class A; method X");
        }
        public static void Y()
        {
                System.out.println("class A; method Y");
        }
}

public class B extends A
{
        public void X()
        {
                System.out.println("class B; method X");
```

```
        }
        public static void Y()
        {
                System.out.println("class B; method Y");
        }
}

public class MethodCalls
{
        public static void main(String[] args)
        {
                A a = new B();
                a.X();
                a.Y();
                B b = new B();
                b.X();
                b.Y();
        }
}
```

6. **Polymorphism Too Limiting?**
   The following is an excerpt from *Sets and Polymorphism* on Wikipedia.

   > *"One of my complaints against polymorphism is that it tends to require that a taxonomy be created such that a given object belong to one and only one sub-type. (I know there are other kinds of polymorphism, but the most common kind requires an explicit or implicit taxonomy.) I find trees too limiting a classification system."*

   Explain the author's point. What does he mean by a *tree*? (If you don't know, you should research the term.) Give an example of something that is not easily modeled with a tree.

7. **Abstract Class vs Interface**
   The following classes are modifications of those in Example 13.4. Here, Playable is an abstract class rather than an interface,

```
public abstract class Playable
{
   public abstract void play();
}
```

   and CD, DVD, and MP3 each extends, rather than implements, Playable.

```
public class CD extends Playable
{
        // methods for CD
}
public class DVD extends Playable
{
        // methods for DVD
}
public class MP3 extends Playable
{
        // methods for MP3
}
```

a. Explain the advantages of designing Playable as an interface rather than as an abstract class.
b. Describe a different example where an interface is clearly preferable to an abstract class.

8. **Polymorphism and OOP Claims**
If you have had experience with another programming paradigm (e.g., procedural programming) you might find the following excerpt, from "OOP Oversold—A Critique of the OO Paradigm" by B. Jacobs, interesting—whether or not you agree with the author.

"One of the reasons for the popularity and management acceptance of Object Oriented Programming is clever little examples that demonstrate the alleged power of OOP. Most experts realize that these examples are not very representative of 'good' real world OO programming. The actual implementation often involves fairly complex arrangements that make real OO messy and more confusing than its competitors. OO fans defend the simple ones as 'just training examples,' but there is rarely a disclaimer of such near the examples. If you are new to OOP, please don't be fooled by simplistic examples. These bait-and-switch examples often take the form of geometric shapes, animal categories, vehicle taxonomies, vehicle parts, employee types, Y2K dates, stacks, device drivers, clothing, or bank account examples.

"These examples often assume the world can usually be divided into clean, never-changing (or hierarchically-changing) categories or 'chunks,' in which groups of features always stay together or change in a lockstep dance within generally non-divisible chunks. The truth is messier, and OO is no better optimized to deal with dynamic feature relationships and changes than competitor paradigms, and in many cases seems to be messier in the end."

a. Support the author's claim by finding an example in this chapter that he might consider a "training example," and explain why.
b. Debate the author's claim by researching and describing an example that demonstrates legitimate practical benefits for polymorphism.

PROGRAMMING EXERCISES

1. **More Shapes**
Add two new classes, LeftTriangle and Diamond, to the Shape hierarchy of Example 13.1. Recall that the subclasses of Shape are Square, RightTriangle, and Triangle. Incorporate the new shapes into the test class TestDraw of Example 13.2. The new shapes should look like this:
• LeftTriangle: A right triangle "facing left."
Below is a LeftTriangle of size 6.

```
     *
    **
   ***
  ****
 *****
******
```

• Diamond: A Square rotated 45 degrees.
Below is Diamond of size 7, that is, there are seven rows.

Here is a Diamond of size 8, that is, eight rows. Notice there are two rows of four "*"s.

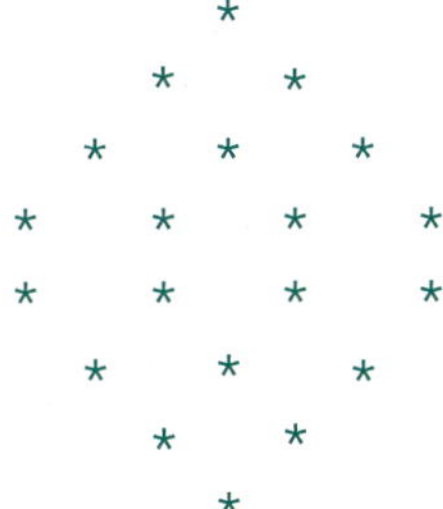

2. **A Second Level of Inheritance—More CDs**
   Add a new class, CDRW, that extends the CD class. A CDRW is a kind of CD. It has the same properties as a CD, but it can also record, erase, and re-record music.
   Create a Recordable interface that CDRW implements.
   Write a Test class that creates an array of Playable objects, plays all of those that are not Recordable, and erases all of those that are Recordable.

3. **A Basic Inheritance Hierarchy with Polymorphism**
   Define an Employee class. An Employee has a name, an ID number, an age, a salary, a title, and a department name. The methods of Employee should:

   a. print an employee record that includes all the above information,
   b. change a salary, changeSalary(...), and
   c. return the salary, getSalary().

   The method changeSalary(...) accepts a parameter, increase, of type int or double. If increase is an int, then the salary should be increased by that amount. If increase is double, then the new salary should be (increase + 1) times the salary. For example, if the increase is 0.10, the salary is multiplied by 1.10, yielding an increase of 10%. The value of the (double) increase should be between 0.0 and 1.0.

   Define a class Manager that extends Employee. A manager is an employee who supervises other employees. A Manager object should include all data of the Employee object plus the list of the employee ID numbers of those employees that he/she supervises. The print method of a Manager should print a list of all those employees under his/her supervision as well as all the other relevant data.

   Define a class Executive that extends Manager. An Executive is a Manager who receives a bonus at the end of each year equal to a percentage of his/her regular salary. Each Executive has his/her own bonus rate. You will need to redefine getSalary() to include the bonus. You will also need to add a setter method, setBonus(...), to set the percentage of the executive's bonus. The default bonus rate should be 10%.

   Implement a test class that demonstrates the facilities of the Employee, Manager, and Executive classes. Your test class should accept employee information for an arbitrary number of employees. Your program should ask whether or not the employee is a manager or an executive, and prompt for all relevant information.

After all data are entered, print an error message if there are any inconsistencies. In particular, a manager cannot manage a nonexistent employee. Also, every employee who is not an executive is supervised by some manager or executive.

Your program should provide the user with the following options:

- Change the salary of an employee.
- Adjust the bonus of an executive.
- Add or delete an employee from a manager's list of employees.
- Print an employee's data.

If any change causes an inconsistency in the data, your program should print an error and not allow the change.

Your program should access an employee via the employee ID number. Use binary search to find an employee's record.

4. **Composition—A Company and the Employee Hierarchy**

This problem builds on programming Programming Exercise 3, exhibiting a classic example of polymorphism for the Employee hierarchy.

A Company has a name, a product, and a list of employees. That is, a Company is *composed* of two String references (name and product), and an array of type Employee.

Design a Company class. Methods should include constructors, getters, and setters, as well as methods that:

- return a reference to an array of all the executives,
- return a reference to an array of all the managers who are not executives,
- return a reference to an array of all the employees who are neither managers nor executives, and
- return the sum of the salaries of all employees.

Include a main(...) method that tests the class. Your application should query the user for the name, product, and employee information. The user should indicate whether each employee is a manager or an executive, and it should include salary and other relevant information. The test class should display:

- the company name,
- company product,
- three lists of names and salaries:
  - executives,
  - managers (who are not executives), and
  - employees (who are neither managers nor executives),
- the sum of the salaries for each list,
- and the sum of all the salaries of all employees.

5. **Inheritance and Polymorphism—Publishing**

Design a class hierarchy consisting of Publication, Magazine, Book, and KidsMagazine classes as follows:

A Publication has a publisher, number of pages, a price, and a title. The class should implement a print method that displays all of this information.

A Magazine is a kind of publication that has a publication unit (monthly, weekly, biweekly). Magazine should override the print method of Publication and display all the new information.

A Book is a kind of publication that has an author. Book should also override the print method of Publication.

A KidsMagazine is a kind of magazine that has a recommended age range. Again, KidsMagazine should override the print method of Publication.

Implement a test class that stores 10 different types of publications: general, magazine, book, or kid's magazine in an array of Publication. Exploit polymorphism and print the information, sorted by title, about each object stored in the array.

6. **A Move Interface for Generating Moves in a Game**
Different games utilize various methods to determine the moves of the players. When playing Candyland, a player picks a card that displays the color of the square to which he/she should move. A Monopoly player rolls two dice; and to play Chutes and Ladders, a player uses a spinner that points to numbers between 1 and 6 inclusive.
To write applications that play these games, you might
• display the move generator (graphics typically)—a picture of rolling dice, or a spinning spinner, or a card being uncovered, and
• indicate the value of the move, for example, the number displayed on the dice or pointed to by the spinner, or the color shown on the uncovered card.
For this project, you should
c. Create a Move interface with two methods:
   • void display()—makes some rough picture (using ASCII characters) of the device used to choose the move, and
   • int getValue()—returns a value representing the move to be made.
d. Implement Die and Spinner classes, which simulate respectively a die and a spinner with n sides/slots, each slot occurring with equal probability.
e. Implement a CandyCard class such that the getValue() method returns a random integer between 1 and 5 inclusive, representing one of the colors: blue, green, yellow, brown, or pink. The getValue() method should display the name of the color as well as return its code number.
In a certain game, a player is allowed to make his/her next move by
• rolling any one of four different dice, 6-sided, 12-sided, 20-sided, or 8-sided, or
• spinning any one of three spinners with 4, 7, or 9 slots, or
• picking a card displaying one of five colors.
Design and implement an application that repeatedly asks the player which method he/she wishes to use and then displays the method (its "picture") as well as the value of the move.

7. **Sorting Containers**
We Pack N Ship 4 U packs and ships items using two kinds of containers: boxes and mailing tubes (cylinders). Rates are determined by the size of the container. The size of a box is the sum of its three dimensions: length, width, and depth, in inches. For a mailing tube, with radius r inches and length l, size is calculated as $2\pi r + l$. The cost of packing and shipping a box is $0.35 times the size of the cube. For a tube, the cost is $0.25 times the size of the container.
Define an abstract class Container with a single instance variable,

    double length,

two abstract methods,

    double getsize() and
    double getCost(),

and one getter method

    double getLength().

Container should also implement Comparable based on cost.

Next, create two subclasses of Container, Box and Tube, that implement getCost() and getSize(), where getCost() returns the cost of packing and shipping and getSize() returns the size of a container, as previously described. Box needs additional instance variables width and depth, and Tube requires radius. Include getter methods for Box and Tube.

Finally, implement a TestContainer class that accepts 10 Container objects and stores them in an array. For each container, TestContainer should ask whether the container is a box or a tube and prompt for the appropriate dimensions.

Sort the 10 containers in ascending order by cost. Print the type of container, the dimensions of the container, and the cost, rounded to two decimal places.
Hint: If x is an object, then x.getClass().getName() returns the name of the class (a String reference) to which x belongs.

8. **Distance in Polymorphictown**
In the bustling metropolis of Polymorphictown, where streets are laid out in a grid-like fashion and each city block is a 0.1 mile square, "distance" is a relative matter. See Figure 13.9.

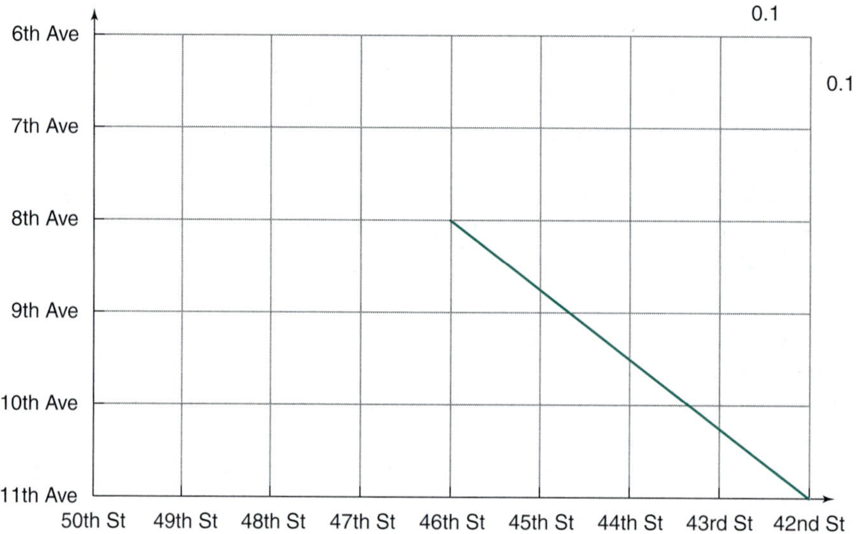

FIGURE 13.9 Polymorphictown street map

For example, straight-line distance ("as the crow flies") from the corner of 42nd St. and 11th Ave. to the corner of 46th St. and 8th Ave. is just five blocks, or half a mile, which is the length of the line segment joining the two corner points. You can easily calculate this distance using the Pythagorean theorem. Such a measure of distance is called the Euclidean distance; see Figure 13.10.

On the other hand, a Polymorphictown taxi driver calculates the "distance" between those same corner points as seven blocks or 0.7 miles. We'll call this measure the *taxi* distance; see Figure 13.11. (Note that more than one route with distance seven blocks is possible.)

Moreover, for Polymorphictown cyclists, "distance" has yet another interpretation. In ecological Polymorphictown, two bicycle paths crisscross every city block along the diagonals. Using Pythagoras's theorem, you can calculate that the length of each bike path is $\sqrt{2}$ blocks or $\sqrt{.02}$ miles; see Figure 13.12.

Cyclists (or skaters or pedestrians) usually travel along adjacent bike paths as far as possible and then continue on city streets. So to a cyclist, the distance between

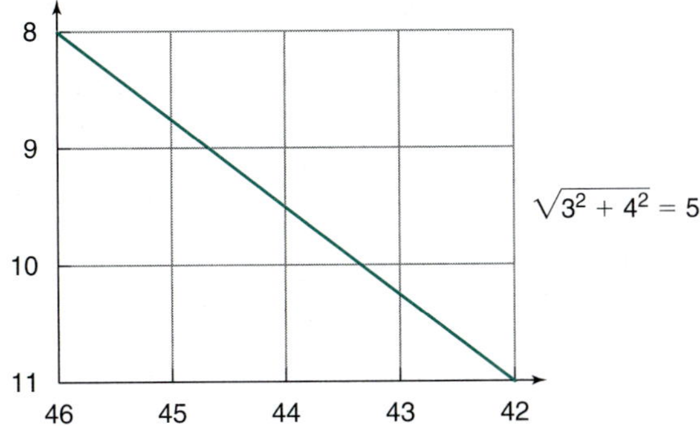

FIGURE 13.10 *Euclidean* distance: five blocks "as the crow flies"

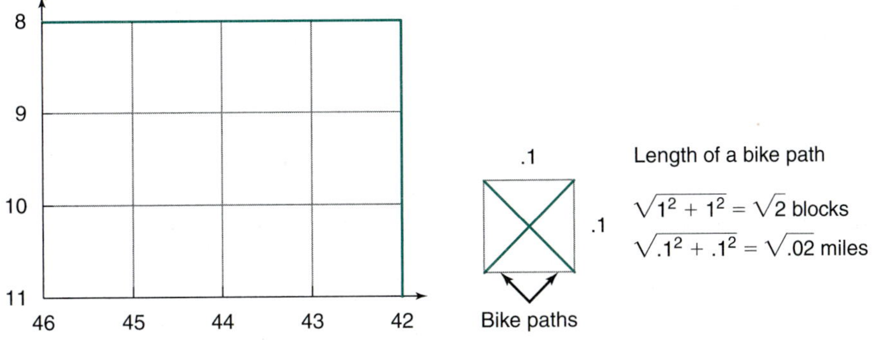

FIGURE 13.11 *Taxi* distance: seven blocks

FIGURE 13.12 Diagonal bike paths

those intersections is $1 + 3\sqrt{2}$ blocks or $1 + 3\sqrt{.02}$ miles. We'll call such a metric the *bicycle* distance; see Figure 13.13.

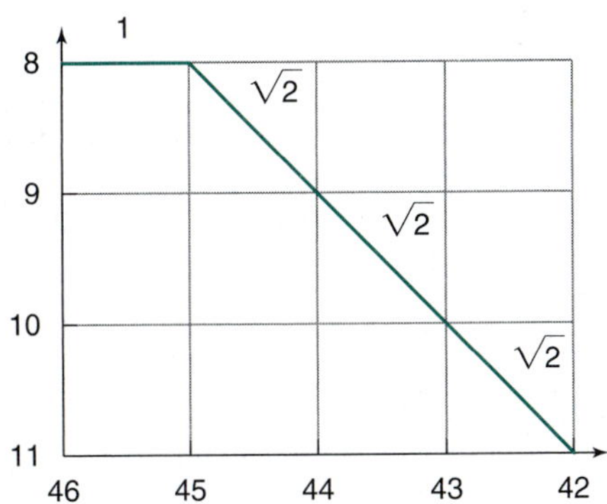

FIGURE 13.13 *Bicycle* distance: $1 + 3\sqrt{2}$ blocks

Write a program that calculates the distance between any two corner locations in Polymorphictown. This distance differs for taxi drivers, cyclists, and soaring pigeons. Your program should also display directions from the starting location to the destination. Following is sample output from the program. Notice how the directions are given. Of course, the directions are not necessarily unique, and any set of directions with minimum distance is fine. Assume streets are numbered from 1 to 100 and avenues from 1 to 12.

Sample Output

Enter T or t for taxi; C or c for cyclists; E or e for Euclidean: **T**
Directions? Y or y for Yes: **Y**

Start location: **42 11**
End location: **46 8**
Distance is 7 blocks or .7 miles
Directions:
42 11
42 10
42 9
42 8
43 8
44 8
45 8
46 8

Again? Y or y for yes: **Y**

Enter T or t for Taxi; C or c for cyclists; E or e for Euclidean: **C**
Directions? Y or y for Yes: **Y**
Start location: **42 11**
End location: **46 8**
Distance is 5.243 blocks or .5243 miles
Directions:
42 11
43 10
44 9
45 8
46 8

Again? Y or y for yes: **Y**

Enter T or t for Taxi; C or c for cyclists; E or e for Euclidean: **e**
Directions? Y or y for Yes: **Y**
Start location: **42 11**
End location: **46 8**
Distance is 5 blocks or .5 miles
Directions:
42 11
46 8

Again? Y or y for yes: **N**

9. **A Polymorphic Video Store**
Your friend Electronic Eddie has decided to open a business that rents movies and games. Unfortunately, Eddie has very little startup money and cannot afford to buy the latest software package to manage his inventory. As a programmer without peer, you have come to Eddie's rescue and have volunteered to write a system for his business.
Your first step is to design a class hierarchy that includes the following classes:

- Item (abstract) with the following attributes:

  a five-digit ID number (String)
  a title (String)
  rental price (double)
  status: true if in stock, false if currently rented (boolean)
  the current renter's name (String).

  The methods of Item might be the standard getter and setter methods as well as an abstract method

  void display()

- Game (extends Item) with the following additional attributes:

  manufacturer: e.g., Nintendo, Gameboy, etc. (String)
  age level: an integer from 3 to 16, 16 signifies 16+ (int)

- Movie (extends Item) with the following additional attributes:

  playing time in minutes (int)
  rating : G, PG, PG13, or R (String)
  format: 'V' for VHS cassette, 'D' for DVD (char)

Each class implements a display method that prints all the data of the invoking object.

Once you have implemented the preceding classes, you should design and implement a class that utilizes the Item hierarchy. Your system should be menu-driven and include the following options:

a. Check out an item.
   Your system should query the user for the ID number of the item and the renter's name. If the item is already checked out, your system should say so.
b. Check in an item.
   Your system should ask for the ID number of the item. If it is already checked in, indicate that.
c. Search for an item by ID number to determine whether it is in stock.
   You should use binary search for this option. Consequently, all rental items are kept sorted by ID number.
d. Search for an item by title.
   Since the rentals are not sorted by title, you might use sequential search here.
e. Display the entire inventory, sorted by ID.
f. Add a new item to the inventory.
g. Delete an item from the inventory (equivalent to selling a used video or game).
   Ask for the ID number of the item to be deleted. If the ID doesn't match one of the items in inventory, a message should be printed.
h. Display the menu.
i. Exit.

When the program begins, the program should obtain data for each item from a file, and store the data in an array sorted by ID number. When the program exits, the current data should be written back to a file.

THE BIGGER PICTURE

PROGRAMMING PARADIGMS AND STYLES

Having studied the three basic tenets of object-oriented programming—

- encapsulation,
- inheritance, and
- polymorphism,

it is time to examine different ways of using these features.

The following discussion is based on "*Understanding Object Oriented Programming*" by J. Bergin and R. Winder.[1] The paper by Bergin and Winder examines a very simple problem and provides four different solutions:

a. The Hacker Solution
b. The Procedural Solution
c. The Naïve Object-Oriented Solution
d. The Sophisticated Object-Oriented Solution

These solutions serve as a hierarchy of poor/fair/better/best uses of encapsulation, inheritance, and polymorphism. Moreover, polymorphism plays a key role in the best design. And, although all the solutions are implemented in Java, only two of the solutions are object oriented.

Using an object-oriented language doesn't automatically make your code object-oriented. It is worth studying each solution to see the differences among the four styles.

The Problem and Four Solutions

The problem posed by Bergin and Winder is simple: Determine the operating system on some computer, display its name, and print an evaluation of it. To help accomplish this, we use a method of Java's System class.

The method

```
String System.getProperty(String property)
```

returns the system property indicated by the parameter property. Specifically,

```
System.getProperty("os.name")
```

returns the name of the operating system running on the computer.

In their article, Bergin and Winder provide four solutions. The PrintOS class in the first three solutions (hacker, procedural, naïve object-oriented) handles four operating systems, two Unix versions (SunOs and Linux), and two Windows versions (Windows 95 and Windows NT). The fourth solution (sophisticated object-oriented) adds a MacBox to the list of operating systems.

The exercises ask you to discuss how each solution would need to be changed to accommodate various modifications. Answering these questions will help you understand how object-oriented programming, and in particular, polymorphism, simplifies program modification.

The first three solutions are fairly self-explanatory.

[1] J. Bergin and R. Winder, "Understanding Object Oriented Programming," *ACM SIGPLAN Notices* 37 (2002): 18–25.

a. The Hacker Solution

```
public class PrintOS
{
   public static void main(final String[] args)
   {
      String osName = System.getProperty("os.name") ;
      if (osName.equals("SunOS") || osName.equals("Linux"))
      {
         System.out.println("This is a UNIX box and therefore good.");
      }
      else if (osName.equals("Windows NT") || osName.equals("Windows 95"))
      {
         System.out.println("This is a Windows box and therefore bad.");
      }
      else {System.out.println("This is not a box.") ;}
      }
}
```

Exercises

1. To add another operating system, such as a Mac, to the list (SunOS, Linux, Windows NT, Windows 95) what modifications are necessary? How about Windows XP?
2. To distinguish between the two UNIX operating systems or the two Windows operating systems (i.e., print different judgments for each), what modifications are necessary?

---

b. The Procedural Solution

```
public class PrintOS
{
   private static String unixBox()
   {
      return "This is a UNIX box and therefore good." ;
   }

   private static String windowsBox()
   {
      return "This is a Windows box and therefore bad." ;
   }

   private static String defaultBox()
   {
      return "This is not a box." ;
   }

   private static String getTheString(final String osName)
   {
      if (osName.equals("SunOS") || osName.equals("Linux"))
      {
```

```
            return unixBox() ;
        }
        else if (osName.equals("Windows NT") ||osName.equals("Windows 95"))
        {
            return windowsBox() ;
        }
        else
        {
            return defaultBox() ;
        }
    }

    public static void main(final String[] args)
    {
        System.out.println(getTheString(System.getProperty("os.name")))
    }
}
```

Exercises

3. To add another operating system, such as a Mac, to the list (SunOS, Linux, Windows NT, Windows 95) what modifications are necessary? What modifications are necessary to add Windows XP?
4. How are these modifications easier than those needed in the hacker solution?
5. Using this solution, is it easier to distinguish between two Windows or two UNIX systems than with the hacker solution? Explain.

c. The Naïve Object-Oriented Solution

This solution comprises a number of files and classes but is otherwise straightforward.

PrintOS.java

```
--------------------

public class PrintOS
{
    public static void main(final String[] args)
    {
        System.out.println(OSDiscriminator.getBoxSpecifier().getStatement());
    }
}
```

OSDiscriminator.java

```
--------------------------------

public class OSDiscriminator
{
    private static BoxSpecifier theBoxSpecifier = null ;
    public static BoxSpecifier getBoxSpecifier()
    {
```

```
        if (theBoxSpecifier == null)
        {
            String osName = System.getProperty("os.name") ;
            if (osName.equals("SunOS") || osName.equals("Linux"))
            {
                theBoxSpecifier = new UNIXBox() ;
            }
            else if(osName.equals("Windows NT") || osName.equals("Windows 95"))
            {
                theBoxSpecifier = new WindowsBox() ;
            }
            else
            {
                theBoxSpecifier = new DefaultBox () ;
            }
        }
        return theBoxSpecifier ;
    }
}
```

BoxSpecifier.java

```
-------------------------
public interface BoxSpecifier
{
    String getStatement() ;
}
```

DefaultBox.java

```
----------------------
public class DefaultBox implements BoxSpecifier
{
    public String getStatement()
    {
        return "This is not a box." ;
    }
}
```

UNIXBox.java

```
--------------------
public class UNIXBox implements BoxSpecifier
{
    public String getStatement()
    {
        return "This is a UNIX box and therefore good." ;
    }
}
```

WindowsBox.java

```
---------------------------
public class WindowsBox implements BoxSpecifier
{
    public String getStatement()
    {
        return "This is a Windows box and therefore bad." ;
    }
}
```

Exercises

6. To add another operating system, such as a Mac, to the list (SunOS, Linux, Windows NT, Windows 95), what modifications are necessary?
7. How are these modifications easier than in the procedural solution?
8. How is ad-hoc polymorphism used in this solution?
9. Suppose that we want to distinguish between two Windows or two UNIX systems. Is this code easier to modify than the procedural solution? Explain.

d. The Sophisticated Object-Oriented Solution

This program adds a MacBox to the list of operating systems, displaying flexibility to easily accommodate modifications. Unlike the first three solutions, the details of this program require a bit of explanation. This program, like the previous one, uses a number of different files and classes. Indeed, PrintOS.java and BoxSpecifier.java are the same as in the naïve object-oriented solution. The details may seem at first mysterious, but with a little diligence, the program's structure should become clear.

The OSDiscriminator class uses a HashMap object to store and retrieve BoxSpecifier objects that handle different operating system names. You don't need to know anything about a HashMap to understand this program except that the operating system names are stored and retrieved by HashMap methods called get(key) and put(key, value) respectively, where key is a String representing the name of the operating system and value is a BoxSpecifier object.

The get(key) method accepts an operating system name (a String) and returns a BoxSpecifier object that handles that name. The put(key, value) stores value, the BoxSpecifier object that handles the operating system named key, into the HashMap, so that value can be retrieved later by a get(key) method call.

PrintOS.java

```
--------------------
public class PrintOS
{
    public static void main(final String[] args)
    {
        System.out.println(OSDiscriminator.getBoxSpecifier().getStatement());
    }
}
```

THE BIGGER PICTURE

OSDiscriminator.java

```
--------------------------------
public class OSDiscriminator
{
    private static java.util.HashMap storage = new java.util.HashMap() ;

    public static BoxSpecifier getBoxSpecifier()
    {
        BoxSpecifier value
            =(BoxSpecifier)storage.get(System.getProperty("os.name"));
        if (value == null)
            return DefaultBox.value ;
        return value ;
    }
    public static void register(final String key,
                                final BoxSpecifier value)
    {
        storage.put(key, value) ; // Should guard against null keys
    }
    static
    {
                WindowsBox.register() ;
                UNIXBox.register() ;
                MacBox.register() ;
    }
}
```

BoxSpecifier.java

```
---------------------------
public interface BoxSpecifier
{
    String getStatement() ;
}
```

DefaultBox.java

```
------------------------
public class DefaultBox implements BoxSpecifier
{
    public static final DefaultBox value = new DefaultBox () ;
    private DefaultBox()
    { }
    public String getStatement()
    {
        return "This is not a box." ;
    }
}
```

UNIXBox.java

```
---------------------
public class UNIXBox implements BoxSpecifier
```

```
{
    public static final UNIXBox value = new UNIXBox() ;
    private UNIXBox() { }
    public String getStatement()
    {
        return "This is a UNIX box and therefore good." ;
    }
    public static final void register()
    {
        OSDiscriminator.register("SunOS", value) ;
        OSDiscriminator.register("Linux", value) ;
    }
}
```

WindowsBox.java

```
--------------------------
public class WindowsBox implements BoxSpecifier
{
    public static final WindowsBox value = new WindowsBox() ;
    private WindowsBox()
    { }
    public String getStatement()
    {
        return "This is a Windows box and therefore bad." ;
    }
    public static final void register()
    {
        OSDiscriminator.register("Windows NT", value) ;
        OSDiscriminator.register("Windows 95", value) ;
    }
}
```

MacBox.java

```
-------------------
public class MacBox implements BoxSpecifier
{
    public static final MacBox value = new MacBox() ;
    private MacBox()
    { }
    public String getStatement()
    {
        return "This is a Macintosh box and therefore far superior." ;
    }
    public static final void register()
    {
        OSDiscriminator.register("Mac OS", value) ;
    }
}
```

Exercises

10. A MacBox is added to the choices of operating systems. In what way is this modification better than your solutions to exercises 1, 3, and 6?
11. How would you modify the code to distinguish between two different MacBox systems? Explain in what way your modification is easier than in the naïve object-oriented solution.
12. Explain how polymorphism is used in the sophisticated object-oriented solution.
13. How does polymorphism help with maintainability and extensibility of the program?

PART 3

More Java Classes

CHAPTER 14

More Java Classes: Wrappers and Exceptions

"It would be a sad situation if the wrapper was better than the meat wrapped inside it"
—Albert Einstein

"There is no exception to the rule that every rule has an exception"
—James Thurber

Objectives

The objectives of Chapter 14 include an understanding of

- Java's wrapper classes
  - The purpose of the wrapper classes
  - The properties of the wrapper classes
  - The methods of the wrapper classes
  - Autoboxing and unboxing
  - Efficiency with wrapper classes
- Java's exception classes
  - The Exception hierarchy
  - The throw-catch mechanism
  - The finally block
  - Checked and unchecked exceptions
  - The throws clause
  - How to create an exception

14.1 INTRODUCTION

The generic sort method

```
public static void sort(Comparable[] x, int size)
```

of SelectionSort (Example 12.11) can order an array of objects belonging to any class that implements the Comparable interface. You can use this method to sort an array of String or an array of Elephant, provided that the Elephant class implements Comparable. Yet, for all its apparent flexibility, this multi-purpose method is not as generic as you might think—SelectionSort.sort (...) cannot handle an array of a primitive type such as int or double. Indeed, the statements

```
int[] x = {3,5,1,7,9,2,4};
SelectionSort.sort(x, x.length);
```

do not compile because int is not a class that implements Comparable. In fact, int is not a class at all.

Similarly, consider the search(...) method of the following LinearSearch class:

```
public class LinearSearch
{
   public static int search(Object[] x, Object key, int size)   // finds the location of key in x
   {
      for (int i = 0; i < size; i++)
         if (x[i].equals(key))
            return i;                        // i is the location of key
      return (-1);                           // return -1 if key not found
   }
}
```

This method willingly accepts *any* array of references but flatly rejects an array of int, char, or double. The statements

```
String[] names = {"Jerry", Elaine", "George", "Kramer"};
int place = LinearSearch.search(names,"Elaine", names.length};
```

cause no problem, but the lines

```
int[] numbers = {22, 33, 44, 55};
int place = LinearSearch.search (numbers, 44, numbers.length);
```

generate a compiler error because the array numbers is not an array of Object references. The integer array numbers is incompatible with the parameter Object[] x.
There is an easy fix to this type incompatibility:

> Java's *wrapper classes* provide genuine classes for each primitive data type.

14.2 THE WRAPPER CLASSES

As you know, a variable can be either

- a reference or
- a primitive (double, float, int, char, boolean, etc.).

Reference variables refer to objects, and being an object has both advantages and disadvantages. On the positive side, all objects inherit the methods equals(Object o) and toString() from the parent class, Object; and every object can be upcast to Object. The downside is that processing objects comes with a bit of overhead. To expedite processing speed, the designers of Java decided that primitives would not be objects.

Nonetheless, many methods, such as LinearSearch.search(…) and SelectionSort.sort(…), require object references as arguments. Combining the best of both worlds, Java provides so-called *wrapper* classes that "wrap" an object around a primitive value. In other words, Java supplies both the *primitive* type int and also the *class* Integer, a *primitive* type double and also the *class* Double, and so on. In fact, Java provides a wrapper class for each one of the primitive data types.

The eight wrapper classes along with their primitive counterparts are listed in Figure 14.1. Notice that the name of each wrapper class begins with an uppercase letter.

Wrapper Class	Primitive Type
Boolean	boolean
Byte	byte
Character	char
Double	double
Float	float
Integer	int
Long	long
Short	short

FIGURE 14.1 The wrapper classes

Like any object, an object belonging to one of the wrapper classes consists of data (in this case, a single field of the corresponding primitive type) along with constructors and other methods that manipulate the data. Figure 14.2 shows a variable x that is a reference to an Integer object with a single data field of type int and value 34. The variable y in Figure 14.2 is a primitive variable with value 34.

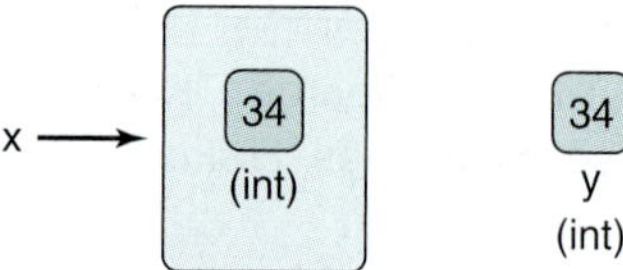

FIGURE 14.2 Reference variable *x* refers to an *Integer* object; *y* is the name of a primitive variable. Both hold the value 34.

14.2.1 Properties of the Wrapper Classes

As you would expect, a wrapper class comes packaged with constructors. Except for the Character class, each wrapper class has two constructors.

- Each numeric class (Integer, Long, Short, Byte, Double, and Float) has a one-argument constructor that accepts an argument of the corresponding primitive type. For example, the one-argument constructor for the Integer class has the form

  ```
  Integer(int value)
  ```

  And, consequently, the statement

  ```
  Integer y = new Integer(5)
  ```

  instantiates an Integer object with value 5. See Figure 14.3.

  The Boolean class has a similar constructor:

  ```
  Boolean( boolean value)
  ```

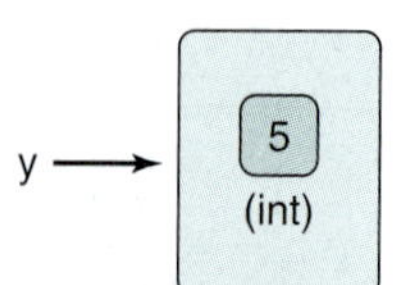

FIGURE 14.3 An *Integer* object with value 5

- Each wrapper class, except Character, has a second constructor that accepts a String argument. The following statements instantiate a Double object with value 234.56, an Integer object with value 12345, and a Boolean object with value true.

  ```
  Double x = new Double ("234.56");
  Integer y = new Integer("12345");
  Boolean z = new Boolean("true");
  ```

The Character class has a single constructor:

```
Character(char ch);
```

Surprisingly, the wrapper classes have no default or 0-argument constructors. So, the statement

```
Integer x = new Integer(); // ILLEGAL – Integer has no default constructor
```

generates a compilation error.

14.2.2 Autoboxing and Unboxing

Since the release of Java 1.5, converting from a primitive type to a reference (wrapper) type or vice versa is automatic, almost invisible. For example, the statement

```
Integer prime = 5;
```

instantiates an Integer object with value 5. That is, this assignment statement is equivalent to

```
Integer prime = new Integer(5);
```

The statements

```
Double pi;
pi = 3.14159;
```

creates a Double object referenced by pi. See Figure 14.4.

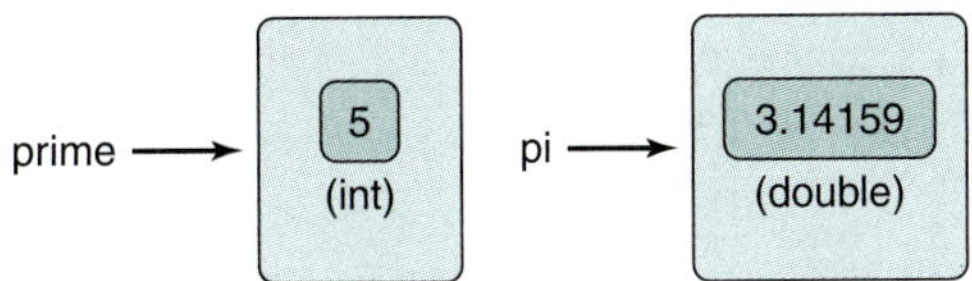

FIGURE 14.4 An *Integer* object and a *Double* object; *prime* and *pi* are references

Similarly, wrapper objects can be automatically converted to primitives. In the following segment an Integer reference, x, is converted to a primitive:

```
Integer x = 5;   // or Integer x = new Integer(5). Note that x is a reference.
int y = x;       // Notice that x is an object reference and y is a primitive.
```

The automatic conversion of a primitive type to its corresponding wrapper (reference) type is called *automatic boxing* or simply *autoboxing*. Similarly, the conversion of a wrapper object to its corresponding primitive type is called *automatic unboxing* or *unboxing*.

Thus, converting from int to Integer is *autoboxing* and from Integer to int, *unboxing*.

14.2.3 Wrappers Inherit and Wrappers Implement

Like every Java class, the wrapper classes inherit the methods of Object. These include:

- boolean equals(Object o) and
- String toString()

The wrapper classes override equals(...) and toString() so that equals(...) compares the *values* inside two wrapper objects, and toString() returns the value of a wrapper object as a String reference.

For example, the code fragment:

```
Integer x = new Integer(5);
Integer y = new Integer(5);
System.out.println(x.equals(y));   // compares values not references
System.out.println(x.toString());
```

displays

```
true
5
```

All wrapper classes, except Boolean, implement the Comparable interface.

Consequently,

x.compareTo(y) returns a negative integer if the value of x is less than the value of y,
x.compareTo(y) returns positive integer if the value of x is greater than the value of y, and
x.compareTo(y) returns 0 if the value of x is the same as the value of y.

When embedded in an application, the code snippet

```
Integer x = 5;
Integer y = 6;
System.out.println( x.compareTo(y));
System.out.println( y.compareTo(x));
System.out.println( x.compareTo(x));
```

displays

```
-1
 1
 0
```

Example 14.1 uses the wrapper class Integer along with SelectionSort.sort(...) of Example 12.11.

EXAMPLE 14.1 **Problem Statement** Construct a test class with a main(...) method that interactively accepts a list of integers and invokes

```
void SelectionSort.sort(Comparable [] x. int size) // Example 12.11
```

to sort the list.

Java Solution As we noted in the introduction to this chapter, the Java compiler complains if the static method

void sort(**Comparable**[] x, int size)

is passed an array of primitives. However, because the Integer class implements Comparable, this generic method can easily handle an array of Integer.

```
import java.util.*; // for Scanner
public class SortDemo
{
    public static void main(String[] args)
```

```
5.     {
6.         Scanner input = new Scanner(System.in);
7.         int number, size;

8.         System.out.print("Enter the number of data items: ");
9.         size = input.nextInt();

10.        Integer [] list = new Integer[size];   // array of Integer references
11.        System.out.println("Enter data: ");
12.        for (int i = 0; i < size; i++)
13.        {
14.           System.out.print(": ");
15.           number = input.nextInt();              // number is type int
16.           list[i] = number; // autoboxing, list[i] is a reference to an Integer
17.        }
18.        SelectionSort.sort(list, size); // list is an array of Integer not an array of int

19.        System.out.println("The sorted data is : ");
20.        for (int i = 0; i < size; i++)
21.            System.out.println(list[i]); // unboxing
22.    }
23. }
```

Output

```
Enter the number of data items: 10
Enter data:
: 3
: 5
: 7
: 9
: 0
: 8
: 6
: 4
: 2
: 1
The sorted data is :
0
1
2
3
4
5
6
7
8
9
```

Discussion The method is simple and direct. However, you should notice the use of wrapper classes on the following lines.

Line 10: The array declared on line 10 (Integer [] list) is an array of Integer references. Because the Integer class implements the Comparable interface, this array can be passed as an argument to sort(Comparable[] x, int size).

Line 15: The method call input.nextInt() returns a primitive (int), not a reference to an Integer object.

Line 16: Here is an example of automatic boxing. The variable list[i] is a reference to an Integer object. The variable number is a primitive. The assignment on line 16 is equivalent to

```
list[i] = new Integer(number);
```

Line 21: The method call println(list[i]) is equivalent to println(list[i].toString()). Because the Integer class overrides toString(), the primitive value stored in list[i] is displayed.

14.2.4 Wrappers and Expressions

Conveniently, references to wrapper objects can be used in arithmetic expressions.

For example, the following segment that mixes primitives and wrappers is perfectly legal and produces the "correct" result:

```
Integer x = 10;        // x, y, and z are references not primitives;
Integer y = 20;
Integer z = x * y;     // Is this multiplication of references?
```

Although x and y are indeed references, the expression x * y is evaluated as follows:

- Variable x is unboxed and its primitive value (10) retrieved.
- Variable y is unboxed and its primitive value (20) retrieved.
- The value 10 * 20 = 200 is calculated.
- A new Integer object with value 200 is instantiated, boxed, and referenced by z.

As you can see from this seemingly innocuous code segment, using wrapper references in an arithmetic expression incurs a bit of processing overhead. The next short example underscores the difference in processing speed when the increment operator (++) is repeatedly applied to a primitive variable and to an Integer reference.

EXAMPLE 14.2 **Problem Statement** Apply the increment operator (++) 10 million times, first to an Integer reference and then to a variable of type int. Compare the running times.

Java Program To compare running times we use the method

```
long System.currentTimeMillis()
```

that returns the current time in milliseconds. For both the Integer reference x and the primitive y, the following method

- records the starting time in milliseconds,
- increments (++) a variable 10,000,000 times,
- records the ending time in milliseconds, and
- displays the elapsed time, *ending time − starting time.*

```
public class CompareTimes
{
```

```
    public static void main(String[] args)
    {
        final int NUM_INCREMENT = 10000000;
        // increment a reference
        long start = System.currentTimeMillis();          // starting time
        Integer x = 1;                                    // x is a reference
        for (int i = 1; i <= NUM_INCREMENT; i++)
            x++;
        long end = System.currentTimeMillis();            // ending time
        System.out.println("Wrapper time: " + (end-start) + " milliseconds");

        // increment a primitive
        start = System.currentTimeMillis();               // starting time
        int y = 1;                                        // y is primitive
        for (int i = 1; i <= NUM_INCREMENT; i++)
            y++;
        end = System.currentTimeMillis();                 // ending time
        System.out.println("Primitive time: " + (end-start) + " milliseconds");
    }
}
```

Output

```
Wrapper time: 172 milliseconds
Primitive time: 16 milliseconds
```

Discussion It is not even close: the "primitive version" wins the race with a processing speed more than 10 times faster than the "wrapper version."

To increment the reference variable x requires several steps:

- The value referenced by x is retrieved, that is, x is unboxed. The unboxing is invisible and automatic.
- The retrieved value is increased by 1.
- The new value is boxed, that is, a new Integer object (referenced by x) is instantiated.

And that is quite a bit of unnecessary work.

Classes are very convenient when a method requires an object, however, when performing basic arithmetic, opt for primitives.

14.2.5 Wrapper Objects Are Immutable

Like String objects, an object belonging to a wrapper class is immutable.

Once a wrapper object has been instantiated, its value cannot be changed. Of course, this does not mean that a *reference* to a wrapper object cannot be reassigned. For example, the loop

```
Integer x = 5;
for (int i = 1; i <= 3; i++)
        x = x + 1;
```

instantiates three new Integer objects. Figure 14.5 shows the objects created by this code segment before the garbage collector reclaims any unreferenced memory. Indeed, the loop of Example 14.2 instantiates ten million Integer objects.

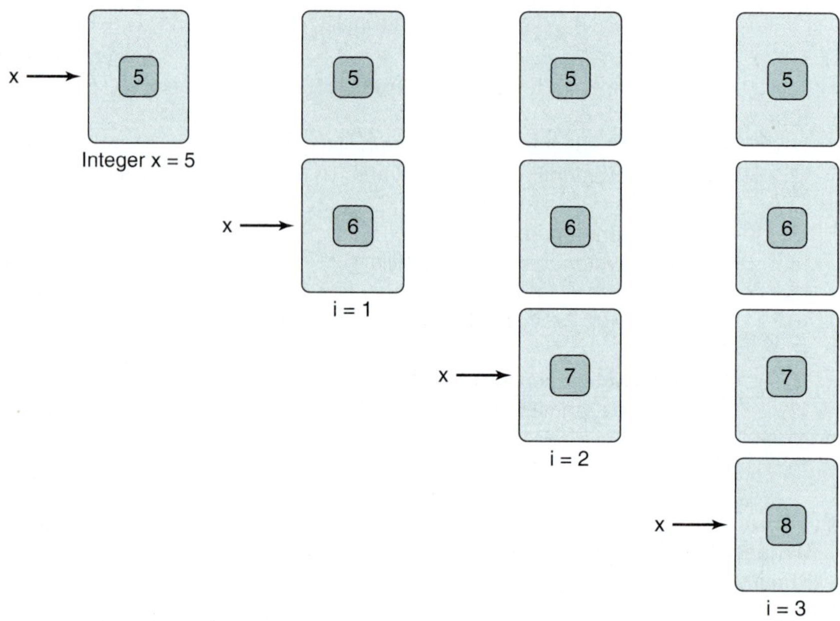

FIGURE 14.5 Wrapper objects are immutable

In Section 14.2.3, we mention that the wrapper classes override the equals(Object o) method inherited from Object so that a.equals(b) compares *values* and not references. In contrast, the == operator compares references. No unboxing takes place. So, for example, the fragment

```
Integer x = new Integer(5);
Integer y = new Integer(5);      // a second object is instantiated
System.out.println( x == y);
```

prints

```
false.
```

However, it may surprise you that the segment

```
Integer x = 5;
Integer y = 5;
System.out.println(x == y);
```

prints

```
true;
```

In the second case, because Integer objects are immutable, Java deems it unnecessary to create two distinct objects with the value 5. So, in fact, the references x and y both refer to the same object. By not creating two separate objects, the compiler saves memory. Java does this for integer values between −128 and 127, inclusive. If we change the value in the two preceding assignment statements to 555 , then x == y evaluates to false. Although autoboxing blurs the line between primitives and wrappers, an Integer is not an int, and an int is not an Integer. Use autoboxing cautiously.

14.2.6 Some Useful Methods

The wrapper classes also implement a number of handy static methods.

Figure 14.6 lists some methods belonging to the Integer and Double classes and Figure 14.7 shows those supplied by Character.

Method	return type	Description	Example
Integer.valueOf(String s)	Integer	Returns reference to an Integer object initialized to the numeric value of s	Integer x = Integer.valueOf("345");
Double.valueOf(String s)	Double	Returns a reference to a Double object initialized to the numeric value of s	Double x = Double.valueOf("3.14159");
Integer.parseInt(String s)	int	Returns the numeric value of s as a primitive	int x = Integer.parseInt("345");
	double	Returns the numeric value of s as a primitive	double x = Double.parseDouble("3.14159");
Integer.toString(int x)	String	Returns the integer x as a String	String s = Integer.toString(123);
Double.toString(double x)	String	Returns the double x as a String	String s = Double.toString(3.14159);

FIGURE 14.6 Some static methods of the *Double* and *Integer* classes. Similar methods are defined for *Byte*, *Long*, and *Float*.

Method	return type	Description	Example
Character.isDigit(char ch)	boolean	Returns true if ch is a digit	Character.isDigit('w') returns false
Character.isLetter(char ch)	boolean	Returns true if ch is a letter	Character.isLetter('w') returns true
Character.isLettorOrDigit(char ch)	boolean	Returns true if ch is a letter or a digit	Character.isDigit('$') returns false
Character.isLowerCase(char ch)	boolean	Returns true if ch is a lower case letter	Character.isLowerCase('w') returns true
Character.isUpperCase(char ch)	boolean	Returns true if ch is an uppercase letter	Character.isUpperCase('w') returns false
Character.isWhitespace(char ch)	boolean	Returns true if ch is a blank, a tab, a form feed, or a line separator	Character.isWhitespace('x') returns false
Character.toLowerCase(char ch)	char	Returns the lowercase version of ch if ch is an alphabetical character, otherwise returns ch	Character.toLowerCase('a') returns 'A' Character.toLowerCase('#') returns '#'
Character.toUpperCase(char ch)	char	Returns the uppercase version of ch if ch is an alphabetical character, otherwise returns ch	Character.toUpperCase('r') returns 'R' Character.toUpperCase('#') returns '#'

FIGURE 14.7 A few static methods of the *Character* class

> In addition to the static methods of the wrapper classes, each wrapper class (except Boolean) defines two static constants, MIN_VALUE and MAX_VALUE, that represent the largest and smallest value of the corresponding primitive type.

For example, Integer.MAX_VALUE is 2147483647, Integer.MIN_VALUE is −2147483648, and Byte.MAX_VALUE is 127.

Example 14.3 uses the static methods of the wrapper classes to validate interactive input and provide error checking.

EXAMPLE 14.3 Murphy's Law ("if anything can go wrong, it will go wrong") certainly applies to programs that require interactive input. When supplying a list of integers to an application, have you ever typed "2w" instead of "23"? Without the proper precautions, such faulty data can cause a program to crash.

Problem Statement Design a class with two static utility methods

int readInt() and
double readDouble()

that can be used for interactive numerical input.

- readInt() returns the next valid integer that is supplied interactively, and
- readDouble() returns the next valid double.

On illegal input, readInt() or readDouble() issues an error message and prompts for correct input, thus providing error checking and preventing a program crash. These methods perform like the Scanner methods nextInt() and nextDouble() but with error checking.

Java Solution To verify integer input we implement the following algorithm.

- Read the input as a string,
- Use the Character.isDigit(char) to validate that each character of the string, except possibly the first character, which may be a minus sign, is a digit.
- If any character is not a digit, prompt the user to reenter the data and return to step 1.
- Use Integer.parseInt(String) to return the integer value of the input string.

We implement a similar algorithm for floating-point numbers.

- Read the input as a string.
- Determine the location of the decimal, if there is a decimal.
- Except for a single decimal point or an initial minus sign, if any character is not a digit, prompt the user to reenter the data and return to step 1.
- Use Double.parseDouble(String) to return the value of the input string.

```
import java.util.*;
public class ReadData
{
   public static int readInt()
   {
      // returns a valid integer that is supplied interactively
      Scanner input = new Scanner(System.in);
      boolean correct;                              // is the input correct?
```

```
      boolean negative = false;                     // is the number negative?
      String number;                                // input string
      do
      {
         correct = true;
         number = input.next();                     // read a string
         if (number.charAt(0) == '-')               // negative number?
         {
            negative = true;
            number = number.substring(1, number.length());
         }

         for ( int i = 0; i < number.length(); i++)
         if (!Character.isDigit(number.charAt(i)))  // input error
         {
            correct = false;
            System.out.print("Input error, reenter: ");
            break;                                  // out of the if-block
         }
      } while(!correct);
      if (negative)
         return - Integer.parseInt(number);
      return Integer.parseInt(number);
   }

   public static double readDouble()
   {
      // returns a valid double that is supplied interactively
      Scanner input = new Scanner(System.in);
      boolean correct;
      boolean negative = false;                     // negative number?
      String number;
      int decimalPlace;                             // index of the decimal point
      do
      {
         correct = true;
         number = input.next();
         if (number.charAt(0) == '-')
         {
            negative = true;
            number = number.substring(1, number.length());
         }
         decimalPlace = number.indexOf(".");        // -1 if no decimal point

         // validate that the characters up to the decimal are digits
         // this loop is skipped if there is
         // no decimal point or the decimal occurs as the first character

         for (int i = 0; i < decimalPlace; i++)     // skipped if decimalPlace == -1
            if (!Character.isDigit(number.charAt(i))) // input error
            {
               correct = false;
               System.out.print("Input error, reenter: ");
               break;                               // out of the if-block
            }
```

```
            // validate that the characters after the decimal are digits
            for (int i = decimalPlace + 1; i < number.length(); i++)
            if (!Character.isDigit(number.charAt(i)))       // input error
            {
               correct = false;
               System.out.print("Input error, reenter: ");
               break;                                        // out of the if-block
            }
         } while (!correct);
         if (negative)
            return - Double.parseDouble(number);
            return Double.parseDouble(number);
   }
}
```

Output The following test class uses the methods of ReadData:

```
public class TestReadData
{
   public static void main(String[] args)
   {
      System.out.println("Enter 4 integers");
      for (int i = 0; i < 4; i++)
      {
         int x =ReadData.readInt();
         System.out.println(" --- " + x);
      }
      System.out.println("\nEnter 4 floating-point numbers");
      for(int i = 0; i < 4; i++)
      {
         double x = ReadData.readDouble();
         System.out.println(" --- " + x);
      }
   }
}
```

Enter 4 integers
2468
--- 2468
246y
Input error, reenter: **−2468**
--- −2468
q357
Input error, reenter: **1357**
--- 1357
asdf
Input error, reenter: **456y**
Input error, reenter: **badData**
Input error, reenter: **1234**
--- 1234

Enter 4 floating-point numbers
3.14159
--- 3.14159
23
--- 23.0

w23
Input error, reenter: **−.23**
--- −0.23
645b
Input error, reenter: 645.
--- 645.0

Discussion If the first character of the string number is a minus sign, the negative flag is set to true and the reference number is reassigned to the substring beginning at position 1. For example, if number is "−12345" then negative gets the value true and number is "12345".

The loop on lines 20–26 of the readInt() method checks each character of the input string number by invoking the static method Character.isDigit(). Only digit characters are valid. If a character fails the test, a flag is set (line 23), a message is displayed (line 24), and input begins again. If all characters are digits, Integer.parseInt(number) returns the integer equivalent of the string number.

The readDouble() method is similar to readInt(). However, readDouble() initially sets the variable decimalPlace equal to the index of the decimal point in the input string number (line 49). If number does not contain a decimal point, then place has the value −1. Subsequently, the loop on lines 53–59 checks the validity of the characters up to the decimal point. If place has the value −1 or 0, this loop does not execute. Next, the loop of lines 61–67 checks the characters that follow the decimal point. As with readInt(), if any character is not a digit, a flag is set, a message is displayed, and the process begins again. If all characters are valid, then the call Double.parseDouble(number) (lines 70 and 71) returns the double equivalent of the string number.

14.3 EXCEPTIONS AND EXCEPTION HANDLING

An abnormal condition that occurs at runtime is called an *exception*.

A file placed in the wrong directory, an array index out of bounds, an illegal argument, or division by zero are a few common exceptions that no programmer has escaped.

Java's Exception class and its subclasses provide an automatic and clean mechanism for handling exceptions.

The subclasses of Exception include

- ClassNotFoundException,
- IOException,
- FileNotFoundException,
- EOFException (End of File Exception),
- ArithmeticException,
- NullPointerException,
- IndexOutOfBoundsException, and
- IllegalArgumentException.

Figure 14.8 gives a partial view of the Exception hierarchy. Figure 14.8 also shows that Exception, along with Error, extends Throwable. The Error class encapsulates internal

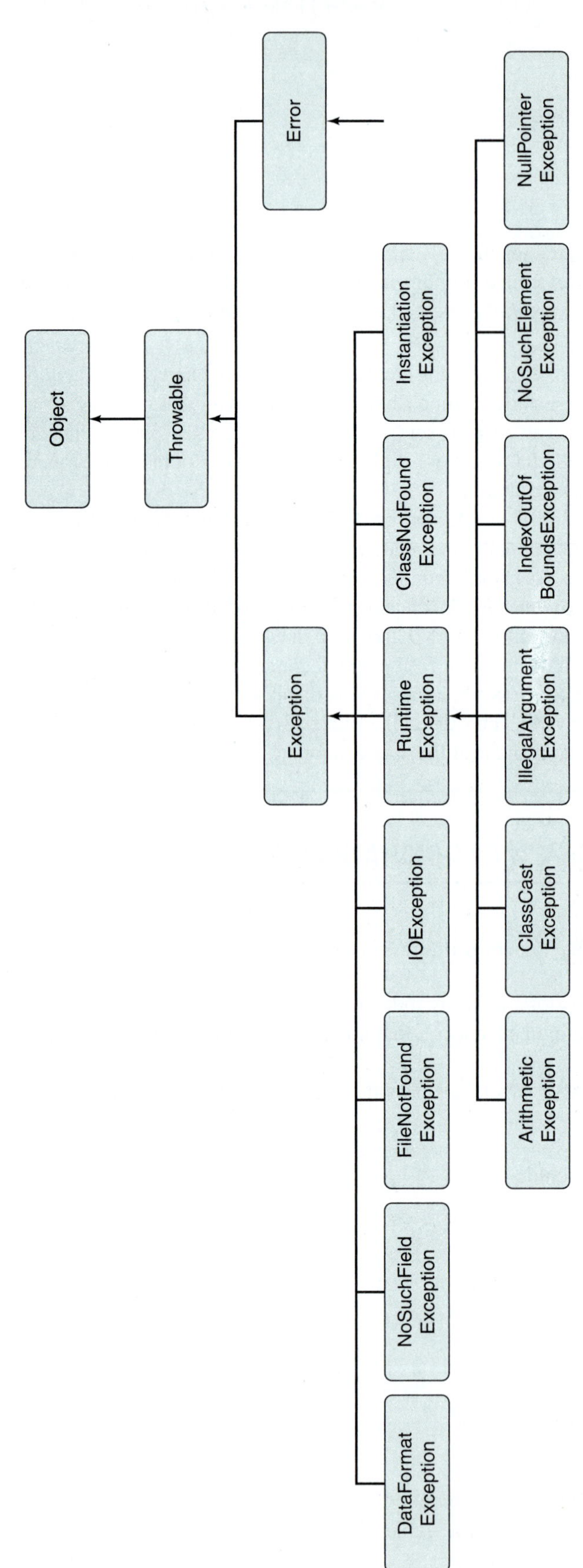

FIGURE 14.8 A partial view of the *Exception* hierarchy

system errors such as the Java Virtual Machine running out of memory. There is not much you can do about system errors so we do not discuss such errors.

In the following sections, we show how to use Java's exception classes to provide a robust handling of abnormal conditions that can trigger runtime errors.

14.3.1 Creating, Throwing, and Catching Exceptions

The following program fragment handles a "division by zero exception" using an if statement and a message sent to standard output.

```
1. int length, area;
2. System.out.println("Enter Length");
3. length = input.nextInt();              // input is a scanner reference
4. System.out.println("Enter the area");
5. area = input.nextInt();
6. if (length == 0)
7.    System.out.println("Error: Division by 0");
8. else
9.    System.out.println("Width is " + (area / length));
```

This code contains a simple fix for a simple exception. When embedded in a program, the if statement on lines 6 and 7 handles a possible runtime error, division by zero. Without handling this exception, division by zero causes a program crash. Handling the exception allows the program to deal with the error more gracefully. Checking for exceptional conditions with if statements is certainly one method for handling exceptions, but Java's built-in mechanism is better.

> To handle exceptions uniformly and efficiently, Java provides the *try-throw-catch* construction.

Generally speaking, when an exception occurs,

- an Exception object that holds information about the exception is instantiated, and
- the Exception object is passed, or *thrown*, to a section of code called a *catch block* that handles the exception.

This scenario implies that, when an exception occurs, program control, along with an Exception object containing information about the exception, is passed, like a parameter, to the catch block, and the catch block takes control or handles the exception. If this description seems a bit abstract, the following simple example, which uses Java's try-throw-catch mechanism to recover from a possible division by zero exception, should make the concept a bit more concrete and show you

- how to create an Exception object,
- how to "throw" an Exception object, and
- how to "catch" an Exception object.

EXAMPLE 14.4

A baseball player is credited with a *plate appearance* (PA) each time he is at bat, unless while at bat, the inning ends for some other reason. A player's *Plate Appearance to Home Run Ratio* (PA:HR) is defined as

(number of plate appearances)/(number of home runs).

For example, if a player has 272 plate appearances and 16 home runs, his PA:HR ratio is

$$272/16 = 17 \text{ (or } 17{:}1)$$

Problem Statement Design an application that calculates and displays a player's PA: HR ratio.

Java Solution The application uses Java's try-throw-catch construction to recover from division by zero in the case that a player has no home runs. A detailed explanation follows.

```
1.  import java.util.*;                                    // for Scanner
2.  public class PAHR
3.  {
4.     public static void main(String[] args)
5.     {
6.        Scanner input = new Scanner(System.in);
7.        System.out.print("Home Runs: ");
8.        int hr = input.nextInt();          // get number of home runs
9.           System.out.print("Plate Appearances: ");
10.          int pa = input.nextInt();       // get number of plate appearances

11.       try
12.       {
13.          if (hr == 0)                    // create and throw an Exception
14.          {
15.             Exception e = new Exception("Division by zero (hr == 0)");
16.             throw e;
17.          }
18.          System.out.println("PA:HR = " + (pa / hr));
19.       }
20.       catch (Exception e)
21.       {
22.          System.out.println(e.getMessage());
23.       }

24.       System.out.println("Done");
25.    }
26. }
```

Output Running the program twice produces the following output:

```
Home Runs: 16
Plate Appearances: 272
PA:HR = 17
Done

Home Runs: 0
Plate Appearances: 158
Division by zero (hr == 0)
Done
```

Discussion The application includes a *try block* (lines 11–19) and a *catch block* (lines 20–23).

Here is how the code works:

If hr, the number of home runs, equals 0 (line 13) then:

1. An object e belonging to Java's Exception class is instantiated and initialized with the string "Division by zero (hr == 0)." The object encapsulates information about the exception (line 15).

2. The object e is *thrown* (passed in the manner of a parameter) to the catch block (line 16).
3. Control passes to the catch block that begins on line 20, and the remainder of the code in the try block (line 18) is skipped.
4. The getMessage() method of Exception returns the string with which e was instantiated. In this case, getMessage() returns "Division by 0 (hr == 0)", which is displayed via the println() method on line 22.
5. The program resumes with the code following the catch block. This is a single statement that prints "Done" (line 24).

If hr is not equal to 0:

1. No Exception object is created.
2. The code in the catch block is skipped.

The idea is simple: if an exception occurs, an object encapsulating information about the exception is created and passed (thrown) to a block of code (the catch block) that handles the exception. The information contained in the Exception object of this example is the string "Division by zero (hr == 0)."

Of course, division by zero is not the only possible exception that can occur. If, for example, a user enters "A1" for the number of home runs, an exception occurs and the program crashes. In this example, the try-throw-catch construction handles just one type of exception. In the next sections, you will see several variations on this theme.

The application of Example 14.4 is a simple illustration of the try-throw-catch construction. In general, the try-throw-catch construction contains the following components:

- **The try block:**

```
try
{
   code
   instantiate an Exception object, e
   throw e  // pass e to the catch block
   code
}
```

When an Exception object is *thrown,* the program branches to the corresponding catch block.

- **The catch block:**

```
catch (Exception e)
{
   code that handles the exception
}
```

The object e, belonging to Java's Exception class, is called the *catch block parameter.* Although the term *parameter* is used in this context, a catch block parameter is not really a parameter, nor is a catch block a method. A catch block is a section of code that executes when an Exception is passed to it.

Every catch block must have an associated try block.

After the code of the catch block executes, the program continues with any statements that follow the catch block.

- **getMessage():**

  The Exception class has two constructors:

  - Exception(String s), which instantiates an Exception object with a message;
  - Exception(), the default constructor, which instantiates an Exception object with a "null message."

  The method

  ```
  String getMessage()
  ```

  returns the string stored in an Exception object or else null.

14.3.2 System-Generated Exceptions

Example 14.4 demonstrates many of the features of exception handling: instantiating an Exception, throwing an Exception, and catching an Exception. The application of Example 14.4 *explicitly* instantiates an Exception object with the new operator and throws the Exception object via the throw statement. More often, it is the case that, when a "standard" exception occurs, the Java Virtual Machine automatically creates and throws the Exception object. No explicit instantiation or throw statement is required. The JVM takes the initiative. For example, when division by zero occurs, the JVM instantiates and throws an ArithmeticException object that holds information about the error; if a program accesses a null reference, a NullPointerException object is automatically instantiated and thrown; or if an application passes an illegal argument to a method, the JVM creates and throws an IllegalArgumentException object.

All exceptions are thrown, but not every exception necessitates an explicit throw statement. If a standard system exception occurs (file not found, array out of bounds, IO exception, arithmetic exception, etc.) the Java system automatically instantiates and throws the exception.

Indeed, the explicit throw statement of Example 14.4 is unnecessary because, even without it, the JVM automatically throws the exception. However, if the Java Virtual Machine throws an exception, no customized message can be attached to the Exception object, although an error message can be printed in the catch block.

For example, consider the following code segment that is part of the main(...) method of a class called FileClass. FileClass also defines a static method void readData(File f) that displays the contents of a file. This code segment causes a FileNotFoundException to be instantiated and thrown *automatically* by the Java Virtual Machine if an invalid filename is supplied by the user:

```
Scanner input = new Scanner(System.in);
System.out.println("Input file: ");
String fileName = input.next();
File inputFile = new File(fileName);    // a bad file name causes a runtime error
                                        // no explicit throw statement necessary
readData(inputFile);
```

If this fragment executes within the main(...) method of a class, the Java Virtual Machine *automatically* creates and throws a FileNotFoundException object if an invalid filename is supplied. Notice that there is no catch block. An Exception object is thrown, but how is it caught?

Although there is no catch block, the exception is nonetheless caught by the Java Virtual Machine, which handles the exception by terminating the program and issuing the following message:

```
Input file: BadFile.txt
Exception in thread "main" java.io.FileNotFoundException: BadFile.txt
(The system cannot find the file specified)
    at java.io.FileInputStream.open(Native Method)
    at java.io.FileInputStream.<init>(Unknown Source)
    at java.util.Scanner.<init>(Unknown Source)
    at FileClass.readData(FileClass.java:7)
    at FileClass.main(FileClass.java:22)
```

Another scenario would have the program explicitly catch and handle this system-generated exception. The following segment has no explicit throw statement, and the Java system automatically creates and throws the exception. This segment, however, catches the exception and handles it.

```
Scanner input = new Scanner(System.in);
System.out.print("Input file: ");
String fileName = input.next();
try                                     // no throw statement necessary
{
   File inputFile = new File(fileName);
   readData(inputFile);
}
catch (FileNotFoundException e)         // exception is explicitly caught
{
   System.out.println("File not found : " + filename);
   System.out.println("Program terminated");
   System.exit(0);      // ends program
}
```

The catch block handles a FileNotFoundException. The try block contains no throw statement. The Exception object is thrown automatically. Embedded in an application, the segment produces the following output:

```
Input file: BadFile.txt
File not found: BadFile.txt
Program terminated.
```

The exception object e in the catch block belongs to the FileNotFoundException class. Because FileNotFoundException *is-an* Exception (see Figure 14.8),

catch (Exception e)

or

catch (IOException e)

can be used in place of

catch (FileNotFoundException e).

However, throwing a FileNotFoundException object is more informative than throwing an IOException object or simply an Exception object. This implies a general rule of thumb when throwing exceptions:

> You should be as specific as possible when throwing an exception.

Example 14.5 illustrates the try-throw-catch construction with a simpler version of ReadData (Example 14.3). Recall that ReadData is a utility class, with methods readInt() and readDouble() that check the validity of interactive input.

EXAMPLE 14.5

Problem Statement Rewrite the ReadData class of Example 14.3 using Java's exception handling facilities. That is, rewrite the methods readInt() and readDouble() so that they exploit exception handling.

Java Solution The methods of ReadDataImproved use exception handling to check the validity of interactive input. As in Example 14.3, input arrives in the form of a string, number, which is passed to parseInt(...) or parseDouble(...). If number does not represent an integer or double (for example, "1234T"), the JVM throws a NumberFormatException exception, which occurs when an application attempts to convert a non-numeric string to a number.

```
import java.util.*;
public class ReadDataImproved
{
   public static int readInt()
   {
      // returns a valid integer that is supplied interactively
      Scanner input = new Scanner(System.in);
      boolean correct = false;                  // is data correct?
      String number;                            // input string
      int value = 0;
      while (! correct)                         // until a correct value is entered
      {
         try
         {
            number = input.next();
            value = Integer.parseInt(number);      // NumberFormatException is possible
            correct = true;                        // parseInt(number) had no problem
         }
         catch (NumberFormatException e)
         {
            System.out.println("Input error; Reenter: ");
         }
      }
      return value;
   }

   public static double readDouble()
   {
      // returns a valid double that is supplied interactively
      Scanner input = new Scanner(System.in);
      boolean correct = false;                  // is data correct?
      String number;                            // input string
      double value = 0.0;
      while (! correct)                         // until a correct value is entered
```

```
34.     {
35.        try
36.        {
37.           number = input.next();
38.           value = Double.parseDouble(number);   // a possible exception
39.           correct = true;
40.        }
41.        catch (NumberFormatException e)
42.        {
43.           System.out.println("Input error; Reenter: ");
44.        }
45.     }
46.     return value;
47.  }
48.}
```

Output The output is identical to that of Example 14.3.

Discussion The method readInt() executes as follows:

The string number is passed to Integer.parseInt(...) (line 16) with two possible outcomes:

1. If number consists entirely of digits with a possible leading minus sign, then parseInt(...) returns the integer value of number, which is assigned to value (line 16). The catch block (lines 19–22) is skipped, and the method returns value (line 24).
2. If number does not represent a valid integer, then the call to parseInt(…) causes the JVM to throw a NumberFormatException object and program control passes to the catch block, which issues an error message (line 21). The process begins again at line 23.

The method readDouble() is similar.

In contrast to the readInt() and readDouble() methods of Example 14.3, these rewritten methods do not explicitly check the validity of input, character by character. If the string passed to parseInt(...) or parseDouble(...) is invalid, an exception is thrown and caught. There is no need for the program to check each character of number.

Again, notice that in this example, the Exception objects are created and thrown by the JVM; no explicit instantiations or throw statements are necessary.

14.3.3 Multiple Catch Blocks

Several catch blocks can be associated with a single try block. For example,

```
try
{
      statements
}
catch ( ArithmeticException e)
{
      statements
}
catch ( NullPointerException e)
{
      statements
```

```
}
catch ( Exception e)
{
        statements
}
```

In this case, the first catch block with parameter matching the type of thrown exception catches the exception. The following fragment prints the square root of a (non-negative) number. Exceptions occur when the user enters a negative number or, possibly, a non-numeric string.

```
try
{
    System.out.print("Enter an integer: ");
    String number = input.next();
    int value = Integer.parseInt(number);    // possible NumberFormatException
     if (y < 0)
        throw new Exception(" Input Error: Negative Number");
    else
        System.out.println("Square root: " + (Math.sqrt(y)));
}
catch (NumberFormatException e)
{
    System.out.println("Illegal number format ");
}
catch (Exception e)
{
    System.out.println(e.getMessage());
}
```

If a user enters *abcd* as input, the Java Virtual Machine throws a NumberFormatException when parseInt(...) is called. The first catch block catches and handles this exception.

On the other hand, if the user input is –54, the statement

```
if (y < 0)
  throw new Exception("Negative Number. Reenter");
```

throws an Exception object. The first catch block does not catch this exception since the parameter of the first catch block is of type **NumberFormatException**. However, the second catch block with parameter type **Exception** does, in fact, catch the exception. Indeed, the final catch block catches *any* exception that is not caught by preceding catch blocks. The final catch block is a "catch all." Notice that the catch blocks are purposely written in order from most specific to least specific. If the "catch(Exception e) block" had come first, then all exceptions would be caught by that block, and the code would not distinguish a NumberFormatException from another type of Exception. The compiler, in fact, forbids this ordering.

Multiple catch blocks should be written in order from most specific to least specific exception.

14.3.4 Checked and Unchecked Exceptions

Java's Exception hierarchy divides exceptions into two categories, *unchecked* exceptions and *checked* exceptions.

RuntimeException exceptions (see Figure 14.8) fall into the category of *unchecked* exceptions. Unchecked exceptions can occur almost anywhere in any method and are the most common types of exceptions. An unchecked exception usually occurs due to some program flaw such as an invalid argument, division by zero, an arithmetic error, or an array out of bounds. Figure 14.9 enumerates some of the more common unchecked exceptions. There are many more that are described on Sun's website.

ArithmeticException	Some arithmetic error, e.g., division by zero.
ArrayIndexOutOfBoundsException	Invalid index value for an array.
ArrayStoreException	Invalid type for an array element.
ClassCastException	Invalid cast.
IllegalArgumentException	Invalid argument when calling a method.
NullPointerException	Attempt to dereference (access) a null pointer.
NumberFormatException	Invalid string in a conversion to a number.
StringIndexOutOfBounds	Invalid index value for a string.

FIGURE 14.9 Some common unchecked *RuntimeException* exceptions

An unchecked exception, such as an out of bounds array index, is one that usually cannot be handled during runtime.

If an unchecked exception occurs, the JVM automatically creates an Exception object and throws the object, but a program need not catch and handle the exception. In fact, a method that generates an unchecked error can usually do nothing productive to recover from the error. Therefore, Java does not insist that a program handle unchecked exceptions.

Catching an unchecked exception is the programmer's choice.

Although a programmer can choose whether or not to handle an unchecked exception, it is not good style to handle too many. Handling every possible unchecked exception could obscure the clarity of the code. Can you imagine using the try-catch construction for all array processing or every time there is the possibility of accessing a null reference? Also, since many unchecked exceptions result from program bugs, neatly handling an exception could possibly disguise and even hide a serious program flaw. Nonetheless, every unchecked exception *is* eventually caught and handled. If the program does not explicitly handle the exception, then it is caught and handled by the Java Virtual Machine. Indeed, this is the more common scenario. For example, when embedded in a program, the following segment generates an unchecked ArrayIndexOutOfBoundsException exception:

```
int[] a = new int[3];
for (int i = 0; i < 30; i++)
        a[i] = 2 * i;
```

When the segment executes, the JVM throws and catches the exception. The JVM handles the exception by terminating the program and issuing the message:

```
Exception in thread "main" java.lang.ArrayIndexOutOfBoundsException: 3
at ArrayException.main(ArrayException.java:7).
```

All of our previous applications ignore unchecked exceptions and leave exception handling to the system.

Of course, there are times when your code might reasonably handle an unchecked exception. Both the readInt() and readDouble() methods of Example 14.5 catch a NumberFormatException, which happens to be an unchecked exception. However, in these cases, the exceptions result from bad user input and recovery is certainly possible.

An exception that is not unchecked is called a *checked exception*. A checked exception is one from which a method *can* reasonably be expected to recover.

All exceptions derived from Exception, except for RuntimeException, are checked exceptions. For example, bad input data such as an invalid file name might generate a FileNotFoundException exception. This is a checked exception.

In contrast to an unchecked exception, a checked exception cannot be ignored. If a checked exception is thrown in a method, the method *must* either handle the exception or pass it back to the caller to handle. In particular, the method must either

- catch the exception with a catch block, or
- pass the exception back to the caller for handling by explicitly listing the exception in a throws clause appended to the method signature.

The latter option is precisely what we have done in previous applications that involved file processing ("throws IOException").

14.3.5 The *throws* Clause

If a method does not explicitly catch and handle a checked exception, the method, by including a throws clause in its heading, passes the exception back to the caller, and it becomes the caller's responsibility to handle or throw the exception.

A throws clause enumerates the type of exceptions that a method might potentially throw. You may recall that a throws clause is required when working with text files:

```
public static void main(String[] args) throws IOException
```

An IOException is a checked exception, and if an IOException object is not caught, a throws clause must be added to the heading of the method that throws the exception. Not catching a checked exception *and* leaving out the throws clause generates a compilation error.

In general, any method that generates a checked exception (or has a checked exception thrown to it) must either catch and handle the exception, or else list the exception in a throws clause.

If a method does not catch a checked exception, the Exception object is passed to the caller, via the throws clause. Checked exceptions can be passed along the chain of method calls right up to the main(...) method and finally to the system, until they are eventually caught and handled.

Example 14.6 illustrates a checked exception handled in three different ways:

1. Using a try-catch construction, the exception is handled directly by the method that generates the exception.
2. The exception is thrown back to the calling method and handled by the caller.
3. The exception is passed (thrown) all the way back through the caller to the Java system and handled by the system.

EXAMPLE 14.6

Problem Statement Construct three versions of a static utility method that displays the contents of a text file on the screen. The first version explicitly handles a FileNotFoundException; in the second the caller handles the exception; and the third uses a throws clause and passes the exception to the system.

Java Solution Version 1: IOException is explicitly handled with a catch block.

```
import java.util.*;
import java.io.*;
public class File1
{
   public static void readData(String fileName)
   {
      try
      {
         File inputFile = new File(fileName);
         Scanner input = new Scanner(inputFile);  // can throw FileNotFoundException
         String line;                             // to hold one full line from the file
         while (input.hasNext())                  // while there is more data
         {
            line = input.nextLine();              // advance to next line, returns all data
            System.out.println(line);
         }
         input.close();
      }
      catch (FileNotFoundException e)
      {
         System.out.println("Error: File not found: " + fileName);
      }
   }

   public static void main(String[] args)
   {
      Scanner input = new Scanner(System.in);
      System.out.print("Input file: ");
      String fileName = input.next();
      readData(fileName);
   }
}
```

Version 2: The FileNotFoundException is thrown to the caller; the caller handles the exception.

```
import java.util.*;
import java.io.*;
public class File2
{
   public static void readData(String fileName) throws FileNotFoundException
   {
      File inputFile = new File(fileName);
      Scanner input = new Scanner(inputFile);  // can throw FileNotFoundException
      String line;                             // to hold one full line from the file
      while (input.hasNext())                  // while there is more data
      {
         line = input.nextLine();              // advance to next line, returns all data
```

```
            System.out.println(line);
        }
        input.close();
    }

    public static void main(String[] args)
    {
        Scanner input = new Scanner(System.in);
        System.out.print("Input file: ");
        String fileName = input.next();
        try
        {
            readData(fileName);
        }
        catch (FileNotFoundException e)
        {
            System.out.println("File not found : " + fileName);
            System.out.println("Program terminated");
        }
    }
}
```

Version 3: Uses two throws clauses

```
import java.util.*;
import java.io.*;
public class File3
{
    public static void readData(String fileName) throws FileNotFoundException    // to caller
    {
        File inputFile = new File(fileName);
        Scanner input = new Scanner(inputFile);   // can throw FileNotFoundException
        String line;                              // to hold one full line from the file
        while (input.hasNext())                   // while there is more data
        {
            line = input.nextLine();              // advance to next line, returns all data
            System.out.println(line);
        }
        input.close();
    }

    public static void main(String[] args) throws FileNotFoundException    // to system
    {
        Scanner input = new Scanner(System.in);
        System.out.print("Input file: ");
        String fileName = input.next();
        readData(fileName);
    }
}
```

Output

Version 1: A "file not found" error is handled via a catch block.

Input file: **badFile.txt**
Error: File not found: badFile.txt

Version 2: The FileNotFoundException object is thrown to the caller.

Input file: **badFile.txt**
File not found : badFile.txt
Program terminated

Notice the throws clause on line 5 of Version 2. The caller, main(...), catches the exception (lines 26–30).

Version 3: Exceptions are passed to the Java System.

Input file: **badFile.txt**

Exception in thread "main" java.io.FileNotFoundException: badFile.txt (The system cannot find the file specified)
at java.io.FileInputStream.open(Native Method)
at java.io.FileInputStream.<init>(FileInputStream.java:106)
at java.util.Scanner.<init>(Scanner.java:621)
at File2.readData(File2.java:8)
at File2.main(File2.java:25)

Discussion Notice that there are two throws clauses in Version 3. This is necessary because neither readData() nor main() catches the FileNotFoundException. A FileNotFoundException can occur in the readData() method. Since there is no catch block to handle the exception, a throws clause is appended to the method header. Consequently, the exception is thrown to the caller (main(...) in this case). Since main(...) does not handle the exception, a throws clause is included in the header of main(...) and the exception is thrown to the Java Virtual Machine. The JVM handles the exception by aborting the program and displaying the rather technical error message shown.

Most of the standard exceptions encountered are unchecked. IOExceptions are the exception, so to speak. If an exception is checked and you fail to catch it or include a throws clause, the Java compiler will persistently remind you.

Notice the difference between throw and throws. The former passes or throws an exception, and the latter indicates that the method does not handle a particular exception, but instead, passes the exception back to the caller. One letter changes the meaning. Be careful.

14.3.6 Catch Can Throw

A system-generated exception includes a system-generated message, which may be a bit cryptic or uninformative. It is possible, however, for a method to catch an exception, create a new exception with a message, and then throw (or rethrow) the new exception to the caller. The following method illustrates the technique.

```
public void myMethod(String filename) throws FileNotFoundException
{
  try
  {
    File file = new File(filename);
    // other code
  }
  catch (FileNotFoundException e)
  {
    String message = "File not found error in MyMethod : " + filename);
    FileNotFoundException e1 = new FileNotFoundException(message);  // add a message
    throw e1;
  }
}
```

Notice that a new FileNotFoundException, instantiated with a customized message, is created and thrown in the catch block. Consequently, a throws clause appears in the heading of the method.

14.3.7 Creating Your Own Exception Classes

You can create your own exception class by extending Exception or any subclass of Exception. For example, many applications require that input data consist of positive integers. The following example creates a class NotPositiveException that extends Exception and thus inherits the getMessage() method from Exception. Such an exception must be explicitly instantiated before it is thrown.

> Any class derived from Exception is checked, unless it is derived from RuntimeException, in which case it is unchecked, (see Figure 14.8).

EXAMPLE 14.7

Problem Statement Devise a class NotPositiveException that extends Exception. Provide a class that demonstrates this new member of the Exception hierarchy.

Java Solution Because NotPositiveException extends Exception, the constructors of Exception are explicitly invoked using the super keyword.

```
public class NotPositiveException extends Exception
{
    // constructors
    public NotPositiveException()
    {
        super("Error: Not a positive number"); // call to one argument constructor of Exception
    }

    public NotPositiveException (String s)
    {
        super(s); // call to one argument constructor of Exception
    }
}
```

The following class utilizes the NotPositiveException class. Note that NotPositiveException is not a system-generated exception, so the NotPositiveExceptionobject must be explicitly created before it is thrown.

```
import java.util.*;
public class NotPositiveTest
{

    public static void main(String[] args)
    {
        int number;
        Scanner input = new Scanner(System.in);
        try
        {
            System.out.print("Enter an integer: ");
            number = input.nextInt();
            if( number <= 0)
                throw new NotPositiveException ("Not positive: " + number);
            else
                System.out.println("Correct data: " + number);
        }
        catch(NotPositiveException e)
        {
            System.out.println(e.getMessage());
```

```
20.        }
21.     }
22. }
```

We demonstrate NotPositiveException with both positive and negative data:

Output

```
Enter an integer: 45
Correct data: 45
Enter an integer: −23
Not positive: −23
```

Discussion Notice the throw statement in main(...) (line 13). A corresponding catch block handles the exception. Without the catch block, it is necessary to append a throws clause to main(...):

```
public static void main(String[] args) throws NotPositive
{
    int number;
    Scanner input = new Scanner(System.in);
    System.out.print("Enter an integer: ");
    number = input.nextInt();
    if( number <= 0)
          throw new NotPositiveException("Not positive: " + number);
    else
          System.out.println("Correct data: " + number);
}
```

Here, the NotPositiveException object is thrown to the Java Virtual Machine, which displays the following output:

```
Enter an integer: −9
Exception in thread "main" NotPositive: Not positive: −9
       at NotPositiveTest.main(NotPositiveTest.java:13)
```

14.3.8 And Finally, *finally*

A *finally block* is a block of code that always executes, regardless of whether or not an exception is thrown. A finally block is paired with either a try-catch pair or a try block.

The syntax of a finally block is:

```
try
{
   code
}
catch ( .....)
{
   code
}
finally
{
   code—always executes
}
```

or

```
try
{
   code
}
finally
{
   code—always executes
}
```

The following example demonstrates a finally block that is used to close files whether or not an exception is thrown.

EXAMPLE 14.8

Problem Statement Merge two sorted text files into a single sorted file. Each text file consists of a list of names, one name per line. For example, if greekWriters.txt contains

Aesop
Euripides
Homer
Plato
Socrates

and romanWriters.txt contains

Cicero
Livy
Ovid
Virgil

the merged file (ancientWriters.txt) contains

Aesop
Cicero
Euripides
Homer
Livy
Ovid
Plato
Socrates
Virgil

Java Solution To merge two sorted files, file1 and file2:

```
Read the first two names (s1 and s2) from file1 and file2, respectively.
Repeat the following until all data has been read from one file
        if (s1 <= s2)
        {
                Write s1 to the output file
                Read the next name from file into s1
        }
        else    // s2 < s1
        {
                Write s2 to the output file
                Read the next name from file2 into s2
        }

if any data in file1 has not been processed
        Write that data to the output file
if any data in file2 has not been processed
        Write that data to the output file
```

The following program, which implements the preceding algorithm, opens three files within a try block. If an exception occurs, a corresponding catch block handles the exception. Whether or not an exception occurs, the finally block closes any open files.

```
import java.util.*;
import java.io.*;

public class Merger
{
   public static void merge(String name1, String name2, String name3)
   {
      File file1 = null, file2 = null, file3 = null;
      Scanner input1 = null, input2 = null;
      PrintWriter output = null;
      try
      {
         file1 = new File(name1);            // input file
         file2 = new File(name2);            // input file
         file3 = new File(name3);            // output file

         input1 = new Scanner(file1);
         input2 = new Scanner(file2);
         output = new PrintWriter(file3);

         String s1 = input1.nextLine();
         String s2 = input2.nextLine();

         while (input1.hasNext() && input2.hasNext())
         {
            if (s1.compareToIgnoreCase(s2) <= 0)      // s1 <= s2
            {
               output.println(s1);
               s1 = input1.nextLine();
            }
            else                                      // s2 < s1
            {
               output.println(s2);
               s2 = input2.nextLine();
            }
         }
                     // compare the last two names that were read
                     // these were not processed in the loop
         if (s1.compareToIgnoreCase(s2) <= 0)
            output.println(s1 + '\n' + s2); // s1 <= s2
         else
            output.println(s2 + '\n' + s1); // s2 < s1

                     // only one of the next two loops can execute
                     // if data remains in file1, this loop executes
         while (input1.hasNext())
            output.println(input1.nextLine());

                     // if data remains in file2 then this loop executes
         while (input2.hasNext()) // file2 has more data
            output.println(input2.nextLine());
      }
      catch (IOException e)
      {
         System.out.println("Error in merge()\n" + e.getMessage());
```

```
50.       }
51.       finally
52.       {
53.          if ( input1 != null)
54.             input1.close();
55.          if (input2 != null)
56.             input2.close();
57.          if (output != null)
58.             output.close();
59.          System.out.println("Finally block completed ");
60.       }
61.    }
62.    public static void main (String[] args)
63.    {
64.       Scanner input = new Scanner(System.in);
65.       String name1, name2, name3;
66.       System.out.print("File 1: ");
67.       name1 = input.next();
68.       System.out.print("File 2: ");
69.       name2 = input.next();
70.       System.out.print("Output File: ");
71.       name3 = input.next();
72.       merge( name1, name2, name3);
73.    }
74. }
```

Output Output with no exceptions:

File 1: **greekWriters.txt**
File 2: **romanWriters.txt**
Output File: **ancientWriters.txt**
Finally block completed.

Output with an invalid file name:

File 1: **geekWriters.txt**
File 2: **romanWriters.txt**
Output File: **ancientWriters.txt**
Error in merge()
geekWriters.txt (The system cannot find the file specified)
Finally block completed.

Notice the error message specifying that the system cannot find the file geekWriters.txt.

Discussion

Lines 7–9: You may wonder why the references on these lines are declared outside the try block. Declarations within the try block are local to that block and not visible in the finally block.

Lines 20–46: These statements implement the merge algorithm described in the problem statement. Notice that, within the while loop, when the final name is read from either file1 or file2, either input1.hasNext() or input2.hasNext() returns false and the loop terminates. Thus, the last two names that are read are not compared inside the loop and consequently, one more comparison is done outside the loop (lines 38–42).

Additionally, when the loop terminates, one of the two files may have unprocessed data. If that file is file1, then the code on lines 46 and 47 executes. If more data remains in file2, then the loop on lines 50 and 51 executes. These loops write the remaining data to the merged file.

Lines 47–50: The catch block displays the message attached to the thrown exception. In this case, the message

```
geekWriters.txt (The system cannot find the file specified)
```

implies that the ancient Greeks were not geeks.

Lines 51–60: The finally block closes all open files. In other words, the finally block takes care of cleanup. The code in this block always executes, whether or not an exception is thrown.

The finally block is used as a cleanup device. Without the finally block in Example 14.8, cleanup would be replicated in both the try and the catch blocks. Moreover, a single try block may have multiple catch blocks, so the replication could even be more cumbersome. A finally block is a cleaner solution.

> Variables declared within a try block are known only within that block and are not visible to the finally block. If the variables of a try block must be accessed in a finally block, declare such variables outside the try block.

Note that references input1, input2, and output of Example 14.8 are declared outside the try block, and they are therefore accessible to the finally block on lines 51–60.

The following class, UsingFinally, presents another example of a finally block. However, unlike the finally block of Example 14.8, this block returns a value. What do you think is the output?

```
import java.io.*;

public class UsingFinally
{
   public int add(int a, int b)
   {
      try
      {
         return (a + b);
      }
      finally
      {
         return 0;
      }
   }

   public static void main(String[] args)
   {
```

```
        UsingFinally x = new UsingFinally();
        System.out.println(x.add(3,4));
    }
}
```

The value that is printed is 0, the value returned by the finally block. When the return in the try block statement is encountered, control immediately passes to the finally block, and the value 0 is returned by the method.

This occurs because the code in the finally block *must* execute. If the statement

```
return(a + b),
```

in method add() executed before the finally block, then the add() method would immediately terminate and the finally block would never execute. Remember, a method returns a single value and then terminates. When control jumps to the finally block, 0 is returned, and the method terminates. Thus, the try block never gets a chance to return 7, the expected value. A return statement in a finally block effectively precludes a return statement in a try block.

In general, a finally block should not be used to return a value.

14.4 IN CONCLUSION

In this chapter we describe a few more Java concepts: the wrapper classes and the Exception hierarchy. The wrappers provide a convenient mechanism for viewing primitive variables as objects, but at the cost of speed. In general, you should not use a wrapper object if a primitive suffices. The designers of Java provide both wrappers and primitives. Use both efficiently and wisely.

Exceptions are Java's mechanism for error handling. Using and extending the Exception class helps avoid program crashes, assists in debugging, and traps errors with more grace than an undecipherable message from the JVM. On the other hand, handling every possible unchecked error can lead to confusing and perplexing code. With practice, you will find the right balance.

Just the Facts

- A Java variable can store either a primitive or a reference.
- The eight primitives are: boolean, byte, char, double, float, int, long, and short.
- Java provides wrapper classes for each primitive: Boolean, Byte, Character, Double, Float, Integer, Long, and Short.
- Like strings, wrapper objects are immutable. That is, once a wrapper object has been instantiated, its value cannot be changed. Of course, a reference to a wrapper object may be reassigned.
- Wrapper classes come with built-in constructors, many useful static methods, and constants.
- Wrapper classes override the inherited equals(Object o) so that the *values* stored in the wrappers are compared.

- Wrapper classes override toString() so that the *value* stored in a wrapper can be converted to a string.
- All wrapper classes, except Boolean, implement the Comparable interface in the natural way, by comparing values stored in the wrappers.
- Converting an object reference from and to a primitive is easy and automatic. The conversions are called autoboxing and unboxing, respectively. For example,

  Integer x = 2; is identical to Integer x = new Integer(2);

  In the other direction, int y = x; assigns the value 2 to the primitive variable y.
- Wrappers in expressions are conveniently and automatically boxed and unboxed as needed. For example,

```
Integer x = 10;      // primitive 10 is boxed and referenced by x
Integer y = 20;      // primitive 20 is boxed and referenced by y
Integer z = x + y;   // x and y are unboxed, added, and the sum (30) is boxed,
                     // and referenced by z
```

- Automatic boxing and unboxing can make computation with wrapper objects slow. Use wrappers only when necessary, such as, when a method expects a reference for a parameter.
- An abnormal condition that occurs at runtime is called an *exception*.
- Java's Exception class encapsulates an abnormal event that occurs during the execution of a program that disrupts the normal flow of the program's instructions. The event may trigger a runtime error, cause unexpected output or behavior, or even crash a program.
- Many exceptions are automatically created and thrown by the Java Virtual Machine.
- A programmer may explicitly create and throw an exception using a throw statement.
- A programmer may extend Exception.
- When an exception is thrown, it is eventually caught and *handled.*
- Java provides the try-throw-catch mechanism to deal with exceptions.
- The try block contains code that may throw an exception. The catch block contains code that handles an exception. The catch block may use whatever information the exception object provides.
- A single try block may have multiple catch blocks, each handling a different exception.
- An unchecked exception is an exception that does not need to be explicitly handled. All instances and descendants of RuntimeException are unchecked. Otherwise, classes derived from Exception are checked.
- If a method throws a checked exception, then that method must include a catch block to handle the exception, or it must list the exception in a throws clause appended to the method signature. That is, the method must handle the exception or pass the exception to the caller.
- The throw keyword throws an exception. The throws keyword declares that a method may throw a particular exception—meaning the method does not catch the exception but throws it back to the calling method.
- A finally block is attached to either a try block alone or to a try-catch pair. The finally block always executes regardless of whether or not an exception is thrown. The finally block is commonly used as a "clean-up" device.

- Handling exceptions can be done in many different ways. Here is a list of the most common.
  - **Acknowledge and Ignore.** Catch the exception and do nothing. This is appropriate when the exception can safely be ignored.
  - **Close the Program.** Catch the exception, print an explanation, and gracefully shut down the program. This is the approach used when the program is unable to continue normally due to the error.
  - **Print Message and Continue.** Catch the exception, print a warning, and let the user choose to end or continue the program at his/her discretion. This is a flexible approach that gives the user control of the situation.
  - **Fix and Continue.** Catch the exception, fix the error, and continue the program. This is the preferred method when it is clear how to fix the problem. For example, automatic conversion of input from mixed upper/lowercase to lowercase.
  - **Pass the Buck.** Do not catch the exception at all, just throw it back to the caller. This is appropriate when the calling method (or one higher up in the sequence of callers) can better handle the exception.
  - **Repackage.** Catch the exception and throw a new exception with different checked/unchecked status, or with more specific detail. This is appropriate when a method had something to say about the exception, but the error requires more attention at the caller's level.

Bug Extermination

- The wrapper classes have no default constructors; the statement `Integer x = new Integer()` generates a compilation error.
- Be careful when using wrapper types in loops containing arithmetic expressions or calculations. The automatic boxing and unboxing from object to primitive and back again can slow down processing.
- You must catch every checked exception (using a `catch` block), *or* pass it back to the calling method (by appending a `throws` clause to the method signature), but don't do both, unless you catch the exception and throw a new checked exception of the same type.
- There is a *big* difference between `throw` and `throws`. The former generates or throws an exception, and the latter indicates that the method does not handle a particular exception, but instead passes the exception back to the calling method. One letter makes a big difference, so be careful.
- It is not necessarily advantageous to catch certain unchecked exceptions such as `NullPointerException`. Such an exception almost always indicates a serious bug that needs fixing.
- Be as specific as you can. Do not throw or catch a general `Exception` or `RuntimeException`. Instead, use subclasses that specify exactly the kind of exception that you are catching.
- A `try` block may have more than one associated `catch` block. List the `catch` blocks in order, from more specific to less specific. Otherwise, the less specific exceptions will not be distinguished.

- It is safer and more convenient to close all files in finally blocks rather than in try blocks.
- Variables declared inside a try block are inaccessible to the finally block. Declare all variables used in a finally block outside the try block.
- Do not return values in a finally block. This may prevent other normal returns from occurring in the try block.

EXERCISES

LEARN THE LINGO

Test your knowledge of the chapter's vocabulary by completing the following crossword puzzle.

Across

1 Block that always executes
3 Numeric wrappers have one constructor that accepts a primitive and another that accepts a ________.
6 Every catch block is paired with a _____ block.
8 All wrapper classes except_____ implement the Comparable interface.
9 An exception from which a program can reasonably be expected to recover
11 If an exception is not specifically handled in the program, the _____ handles it.
12 Wrappers override equals (. . .) and ________.
14 Block of code that handles an exception
17 Class that wraps an int
20 Pass an exception
21 Convert from object to primitive
23 Omitting a required throws clause will be flagged by the ________.
24 Method that returns the integer value of a string
25 An exception that need not be handled
26 Classes that provide object functionality for primitives

Down

2 Common checked exception
4 A checked exception must be handled explicitly or declared in a _____ clause.
5 A Java variable is a reference or a ________.
7 Wrapper classes do not have _____ constructors.
10 Runtime error
13 All exception classes extend________.
15 Unchecked exceptions include _____ exceptions.
16 Values of wrapper objects cannot be changed.
18 With wrappers, == compares ________.
19 Wrapper with a single constructor
22 Convert from primitive to object

SHORT EXERCISES

1. **True or False**
   If false, give an explanation.
   a. Primitive variables must be objects.
   b. Integer x; generates a compile time error.
   c. Integer y = new Integer(); generates a compile time error.
   d. Integer z = new Integer(3); generates a compile time error.
   e. Integer u = new Integer(3.14); generates a compile time error.
   f. Integer v = new Integer("3.2"); generates a compile time error.
   g. Integer w = new Integer("345"); generates a compile time error.
   h. An exception is like a runtime error.
   i. Division by zero causes an ArithmeticException to be thrown.
   j. An array index out of bounds causes an exception.
   k. Too many nested loops is an example of an exception.
   l. An exception is an object.
   m. You must include a finally block with every try block.
   n. You may not define your own exception class.
   o. Exactly one catch block is allowed per try block.

2. **Playing Compiler**
   Determine whether or not each of the following classes compiles, and if not, fix the errors. Each class should compute the square root of 122.0.

   a.
```
public class Test
{
   public static void main(String[] args)
   {
      float x = (float) 122.0;
      float newGuess = (float) 1.0;
      float oldGuess = x;
      // This code computes the square root of x;
      try
      {
         while (oldGuess != newGuess)  {
         oldGuess = newGuess;
         newGuess = (float) (x/oldGuess + oldGuess)/ (float) 2.0;
         System.out.println(oldGuess);
         System.out.println(newGuess);
      }
         // Keep improving the guess until two consecutive guesses are equal
      catch
      {
         System.out.println("Did not work");
      }
   }
}
```

   b.
```
public class Test
{
      public static void main(String[] args) throws ArithmeticException
      {
         float x = (float) 122.0;
         float newGuess = (float) 1.;
```

```
            float oldGuess = x;
            // This code computes the square root of x;
            try
            {
                while (oldGuess != newGuess)   {
                oldGuess = newGuess;
                newGuess = (float) (x/oldGuess + oldGuess)/ (float) 2.0;
                System.out.println(oldGuess);
                System.out.println(newGuess);
            }
                // Keep improving the guess until two consecutive guesses are equal
            finally {}
        }
    }
```

c. public class Test

```
    {
        public static void main(String[] args) throws ArithmeticException
        {
            float x = (float) 122.0;
            float newGuess = (float) 1;
            float oldGuess = x;
            // This code computes the square root of x;
            try
            {
                while (oldGuess != newGuess)
                {
                    oldGuess = newGuess;
                    newGuess = (float) (x/oldGuess + oldGuess)/ (float) 2.0;
                    System.out.println(oldGuess);
                    System.out.println(newGuess);
                }
                  // Keep improving the guess until two consecutive guesses are equal
            }
                catch (Arithmetic Exception e)
                {
                     System.out.println("Bad division in algorithm");
                }
        }
    }
```

3. **Playing Compiler**
   Consider the following class:

```
public class LinearSearch
{
   public static int search(Object[] x, Object key, int size) // finds the location of key in x
   {
      for (int i = 0; i < size; i++)
         if (x[i].equals(key))
            return i;              // i is the location of key
         return -1;                // return -1 if key not found
   }
}
```

Which of the following pairs of instructions compile? Explain.

a. Int[] numbers = {22, 55, 33, 66};
   int place = LinearSearch.search (numbers, 55, numbers.length);
b. int[] numbers = {22, 55, 33, 66};
   int place = LinearSearch.search (numbers, 55, numbers.length);
c. Integer[] numbers = {22, 55, 33, 66};
   int place = LinearSearch.search (numbers, 55, numbers.length);

4. **What's the Output?**
   In the following class, one line causes a compilation error. Which line is it? If you delete the offensive line, what's the output?

```
public class Mystery
{
  public static void main(String[] args)
  {
    int number;
    int [] otherlist = new int[10];       // array of primitives
    Integer [] list = new Integer[10];    // array of references
    for (int i = 0; i < 10; i++)
    {
      list[i] = i * i;
      otherlist[i] = i + i;
    }
    for (int i = 0; i < 10; i++)
    {
      System.out.println(list[i] + " " + otherlist[i] + " " + list[i].compareTo(otherlist[i]));
      System.out.println(list[i] + " " + otherlist[i] + " " + otherlist[i].compareTo(list[i]));
    }
  }
}
```

5. **What's the Output?**
   The product of two 32-bit integers is a 64-bit number. If the 32 most significant bits are zero, then the result is simply the 32 least significant bits. However, if the most significant 32 bits are not zero, then overflow has occurred, but Java does not throw an ArithmeticException. Instead, Java returns the 32 least significant bits of the product. Indeed, the evaluation of the multiplication operator * on integers *never* throws a runtime exception.

   a. What is the output of the following program?

```
public class Testint
{
    public static void main(String[] args)
    {
        Integer x = 2;
        for (int i = 0 ; i < 10 ; i++)
        {
            x = x * x;
            System.out.println(x.equals(0));
        }
    }
}
```

b. What happens if

```
int x = 2;
```

replaces

```
Integer x = 2; ?
```

6. **What's the Output?**

a. What is the output of the following program?

```
class Test
{
    public static void main(String[] args)
    {
        try
        {
            System.out.println("Started the try block");
            int k=0;
            int j = 2/k;
            System.out.println("Finishing the try block");
        }
        // Insert Catch Code Here
        finally
        {
          System.out.println("Executing the finally block");
        }
        System.out.println("Program all done");
    }
}
```

b. What is the output if the comment // Insert Catch Code Here is replaced with the following code?

```
catch (RuntimeException e)
{
    System.out.println(" Am I printed?");
}
```

7. **What's the Output?**

Determine the output of the following program. (Code is from a 1997 *JavaWorld* article by Bill Venners.)

```
public class Ball extends Exception {}

public class Pitcher
{
  private static Ball ball = new Ball();
  static void playBall()
  {
    int i = 0;
    while (true)
    {
      try
      {
        if (i % 4 == 3)
```

```
            {
                throw ball;
            }
            ++i;
            }
            catch (Ball b)
            {
                i = 0;
                System.out.println("Reset");
            }
        }
    }
    public static void main(String[] args)
    {
        Pitcher.playBall();
    }
}
```

8. **Basic Syntax and Semantics of try-catch-finally**
Consider the code structure below and answer the questions that follow.

```
try
   { ... code0 ...}

catch (Exception1 e1)
   { ... code1 ...}

catch (Exception2 e2)
   { ... code2 ...}

finally
   {... code3 ...}

code4 ...
```

a. Which lines (code0, code1, code2, code3, code4) execute if no exception is thrown?
b. Which lines (code0, code1, code2, code3, code4) execute if an exception of type Exception1 is thrown in code0?
c. Which lines (code0, code1, code2, code3, code4) execute if an exception of type Exception2 is thrown in code0?
d. Which lines (code0, code1, code2, code3, code4) execute if an exception is thrown in code0 that belongs to neither Exception1 nor Exception2?

9. **Exception Handling Style**
a. What might be the purpose of the following code structure? Notice that there is a finally block but there are no catch blocks. Give a realistic example in which you might use such a structure.

```
try
   {.. code ...}
finally
   {... code ...}
```

b. Why is the following code structure poorly written?

```
try
  {... code ...}

catch (Exception e)
  {... handler code ...}

catch (IOException)
  {... handler code ...}
```

10. **Guidelines for Exception Handling**
Sourceforge.net publishes guidelines for throwing and catching exceptions. Following are seven examples and seven explanations from Sourceforge.net. Associate each example with its proper explanation.

Examples:

a. public void methodThrowingException() throws Exception {}

b. public class Foo

```
{
 public void bar()
 {
  try
  {
   // do something
  }
  catch (Throwable th)
  {

  }
 }
}
```

c. public class Foo

```
{
   void bar()
   {
     try
     {
       try
       {
       }
       catch (Exception e)
       {
          throw new WrapperException(e);
       }
     }
     catch (WrapperException e)
     {
       // do some more stuff
     }
   }
}
```

d.
```
public class Foo
{
   void bar()
   {
      try
      {
         // do something
      }
      catch (NullPointerException npe)
      {
      }
   }
}
```

e.
```
public class Foo
{
   public void bar() throws Exception
   {
      throw new Exception();
   }
}
```

f.
```
public class Foo
{
   void bar()
   {
      throw new NullPointerException();
   }
}
```

g.
```
public class Foo
{
   void bar()
   {
      try
      {
         // do something

      }
      catch (SomeException se)
      {
         throw se;
      }
   }
}
```

Explanations:

1. Do not catch a NullPointerException. A NullPointerException is a sign of serious bugs in your code. A catch block may obscure the original error, causing other more subtle errors in its wake.
2. Avoid using a method signature that throws Exception. It might be difficult to document and understand the vague interfaces. Use either a class derived from RuntimeException or a checked exception.

3. Avoid catching Throwable exceptions. It casts too wide a net—catching things like OutOfMemoryError.
4. Do not use exception catching as flow control. Using exceptions as flow control leads to GOTOish code and obscures true exceptions when debugging.
5. Avoid rethrowing a caught exception. Catch blocks that merely rethrow a caught exception only add to code size and runtime complexity. There are times when catching an exception and rethrowing a *new* exception is appropriate.
6. Try not to throw "raw" exception types. Rather than throw a raw RuntimeException, Throwable, Exception, or Error, use a subclassed exception or error instead.
7. Avoid throwing a NullPointerException. People will assume that the JVM threw the exception. Consider using an IllegalArgumentException instead; this will be clearly seen as a programmer-initiated exception.

PROGRAMMING EXERCISES

1. **Integer vs int**
   Write a program that creates two arrays, int[] x and Integer[] y, each of size 1,000,000. Initialize each array separately so that x[k] = k and y[k] references an Integer object containing *k*. Time each segment separately and report your results. Do the experiment again but initialize x[k] and y[k] to 1, for all *k*. Explain your results.

2. **Integer vs int**
   Write a program that creates two arrays, int[] x and Integer[] y, each of size 1,000,000. Initialize each array separately so that x[k] = k and y[k] references an Integer object containing *k*. Do not time the initializations. For each value *k*, set x[k] = x[k] + x[k] and y[k] = y[k] + y[k]. Time each segment separately. Report and explain your results. Do the experiment again but initialize x[k] and y[k] to 1, for all *k*. Report and explain your results.

3. **Integer vs int**
   Write a program that creates two arrays, int[] x and Integer[] y, each of size 1,000,000. Initialize each array separately so that that x[k] = k and y[k] references an Integer object containing *k*. Do not time the initialization. For each element x[k] and y[k], set x[k] = x[k] * 2, and y[k] = y[k] * 2. Time each segment separately. Report and explain your results. Do the experiment again but initialize x[k] and y[k] to 1, for all *k*. Report and explain your results.

4. **Strings and Characters**
   Write a program that accepts a String and capitalizes the first letter of each *word* that begins with a letter. A *word* is a sequence of characters surrounded by whitespace. Use the static methods of the Character class.

5. **Character Experiments**
   Write a program that creates an array of char with 1,000,000 elements. Initialize the elements of the array to random characters from the set {'a'..'z', '0'..'9', 'A'..'Z'}. Finally, count the number of digits in the array, checking explicitly whether or not a character lies between '0' and '9'. Repeat the operation using the built-in method Character.isDigit(). Time the loops that do the counting, compare results, and explain.

6. **Integer Extraction**
   A radio station is paying the dollar value of the numerical part of your address, if you can answer a question correctly. For example, if Herman Munster of 1313 Mockingbird Lane, answers a question correctly, he wins $1313. Write a program that accepts a string representing a person's street address, and assigns the numerical

portion of the address to an Integer. Hint: First extract the numerical digits, and then use the built-in parseInt(...) method of Integer. You may assume that the street address has just one number and that number occurs at the start of the address.

7. **Format Exceptions**
   Write a program that accepts a test score, that is, a positive integer in the range 0 through 100 inclusive, and displays an equivalent letter grade: A (90+), B (80–89), C (70–79), D (60–69), F (under 60). Throw an exception if the input is in the wrong format or if it is out of range, print an error message, and halt gracefully.

8. **Format Exceptions**
   Write a class with a static method that accepts characters one at a time, counts the number of characters, and throws an exception if a character is not in the set {'a'..'z', '0'..'9', 'A'..'Z'}. The exception should be thrown but not caught (i.e., no explicit catch block). Write a client program that calls this method and prints "Error in Input" if the method throws an exception.

9. **File Exceptions**
   Write a program that reads an array of String from a file. The class should have a method

   ```
   void getStrings()
   ```

   which reads from the file, and catches in order: FileNotFoundException (handled by printing "Error—file not found"), EOFException (handled by printing "Done reading file"), and IOException (handled by printing "Problem reading file" + e.getmessage).

10. **File Exceptions**
    Write a program that reads characters from a file and echo prints each one. Handle an IOException by printing "Error" along with an explanation, and a FileNotFoundException by printing "File *filename* not Found". Catch these exceptions in the correct order (IOException last). Use a finally block to close the file.

11. **Arithmetic Exceptions**
    For this problem you will design a "safe" class that performs arithmetic on positive integers. The class supports addition and division operations and throws appropriate checked exceptions.

    Recall that the range of type int is

    $$-2{,}147{,}483{,}648 \text{ to } +2{,}147{,}483{,}647 \text{ inclusive.}$$

    You might assume that the addition 2,147,483,647 + 1 causes a runtime (integer overflow) error. This is not so because Java uses a technique called "two's complement" to represent integers; so numbers larger than 2,147,483,647 "wrap around" to negative values, while numbers smaller than −2,147,483,648 "wrap around" the other way to positive values. That is,

    $$2{,}147{,}483{,}647 + 1 = -2{,}147{,}483{,}648, \text{ and}$$
    $$-2{,}147{,}483{,}648 - 1 = 2{,}147{,}483{,}647.$$

    The Bigger Picture section of Chapter 2 explains this in more detail. See Figure 14.10.

    Consequently, integer addition *never* throws a runtime exception. In some situations, however, it might be preferable if integer addition *did* throw overflow and underflow exceptions. Otherwise, a logical bug might go undetected.

    Furthermore, a division by zero throws an unchecked ArithmeticException, but we might prefer that it throw a *checked* exception. This would force a more elegant recovery. After all, division by zero could be caused by something as simple as accidental reversal of dividend and divisor arguments: that is, 0 / 7 is legal while

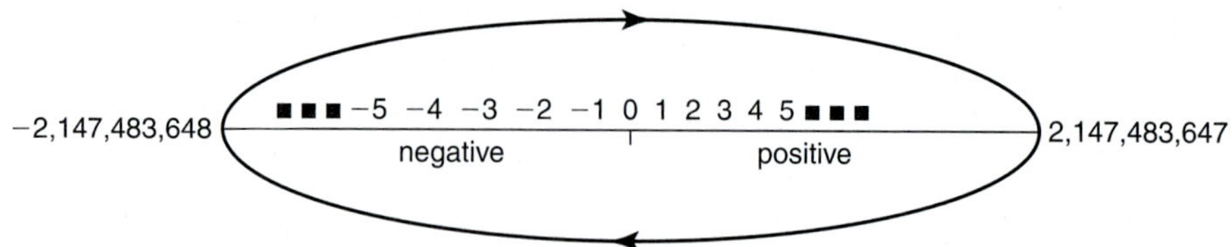

FIGURE 14.10 The integer following 2,147,483,647 is −2,147,483,648

7 / 0 is not. A reasonable recovery plan for catching this exception might be to close the program, report the division by zero, and suggest checking the order of arguments.

Write an Arithmetic class that implements two static methods

```
int divide(int a, int b),   // a > 0, b > 0; returns a / b (integer division)
int add int a, int b),      // a > 0, b > 0; returns a + b
```

These methods should throw *checked* exceptions.

The divide() method should catch the unchecked ArithmeticException and throw its own *checked* DivideByZero exception. The add() methods should throw Overflow and Underflow exceptions. Here are the signatures.

```
public static int divide(int a, int b) throws DivideByZero
public static int add(int x, int y) throws Underflow, Overflow
```

An Overflow or Underflow exception occurs if the sign of the result does not make sense. That is, an Overflow exception is thrown when the sum of two positive integers is negative, and Underflow exception is thrown when the sum of two negative integers is positive. Note that the sum of a positive integer and a negative integer is always legitimate and never results in overflow or underflow.

Define three new exception classes: DivideByZero, Overflow, and Underflow, each derived from Exception. Write a separate class that tests the methods of Arithmetic. Your test class should catch the exceptions that are thrown by the methods of Arithmetic.

THE BIGGER PICTURE

THE BIGGER PICTURE

APIS AND EXCEPTIONS

API stands for Application Programming Interface.

An *API* is a set of routines, tools, and protocols for building software applications.

That is, an API provides building blocks for the programmer. For example, Google Maps is a convenient tool for finding directions, planning a trip, or even conducting market research. Indeed, a programmer might want to borrow some of the features that Google Maps provides.

Suppose, for example, that you are designing a program that generates eye-catching invitations for birthday parties and such. Moreover, you want to give the user the option of including maps and directions with the invitation. Rather than design and program that functionality yourself, you might use the system already built by Google Maps. Unfortunately, you don't have access to the code underneath Google Maps, nor do you have any idea of how the programmers of Google Maps built their system. And even if you did, you would not have the time to rebuild such a powerful tool.

Enter APIs. Google Maps is kind enough to provide an interface (an API) to their system. The interface allows you to use the features of Google Maps through various method calls, following certain standards and protocols. The API is the bridge between your program and their program. You are the client of their system, and the API is the rulebook you must follow to access their system and use their tools.

Still too abstract? To understand the concept of an API, you would not be too far off base using a class as an analogy. A class is like the Google Maps system, and the methods of the class are like the API. Clients can use the public methods of the class without knowledge of the implementation. The interface of a class (its public methods) and an API are in effect the same thing.

It is unlikely that a beginner has seen or used an API. But a professional programmer deals with APIs all the time. APIs come into play when a programmer is ready to hook his or her programs to more powerful tools like graphical user interfaces, operating systems, or Google Maps.

Why discuss APIs when you are likely not to encounter any for a while? Because a very basic understanding of an API helps you appreciate Java's exception handling architecture.

Java's Exception Handling Architecture

As you know, Java allows a programmer to *try* a block of code, and *catch* exceptions that might be *thrown* during the code's execution. An exception is an object belonging to Exception, and a programmer may create his/her own classes that extend Exception.

Furthermore, some of Java's exceptions are *checked*, meaning that the compiler insists that the programmer handle these exceptions by including a catch block or appending a throws clause to the end of the method signature. Making an exception *checked* forces the programmer to consider the possibility of an exception being thrown. An example of a checked exception is IOException, which, as the name suggests, is thrown whenever an input/output operation is abnormally terminated. This kind of exception does not necessarily signify a program bug, but simply an abnormality in the normal expected execution of the program. If a checked exception occurs, the presumption is that the program can take effective action and recover, or at least gracefully print a helpful message and quit. That is the nature of a checked exception.

Unchecked exceptions, such as the subclasses of RuntimeException, are usually the result of programming bugs. Unchecked exceptions need not be caught and handled by the programmer. Indeed, it would be difficult to know exactly how to handle these kinds of exceptions because they encapsulate unexpected behavior that is usually the result of programming errors. Although it is permissible to catch these exceptions, they are best left for the JVM to handle. The JVM provides enough detail to the programmer so that he/she can fix the underlying bug. Contrast this with checked exceptions, which do not represent bugs in the program, but merely unusual circumstances that *can* be handled effectively.

A programmer can create his/her own exceptions either checked or unchecked.

- If a client of your code can reasonably be expected to recover from an exception, then create a checked exception.

- If a client cannot do anything to recover from the exception, make it an unchecked exception.

Exceptions and APIs

The Java compiler forces a method to specify (using the throws keyword) all uncaught checked exceptions that can be thrown within its scope.

> Declaring which exceptions a method might throw is part of the method's API, as much as the number and type of the method's parameters, or the method's return value.

When you write code using a system's API, you are told exactly which exceptions might occur each time you call a particular method. If the method throws a checked exception, then you, the client of the API, must handle it. The API forces the client programmer to write clean, robust code that will not crash. Large programming systems linked through multiple levels of API's would be vulnerable to unforeseen crashes without this enforced handling of checked exceptions.

Exercise

1. APIs only make sense when programmers are offered an interface to a fairly large system of tools. Nevertheless, this exercise is meant to simulate building a tool and an API.

Write a class Invest that provides a static method value(…) that calculates the growth of an investment. The method requires four parameters: initial investment (double) I, interest rate (double) R, number of years (int) Y, and how often the interest is compounded per year (int) C. After Y years the value of the investment is:

$$1\left(1 + \frac{R}{C}\right)^{CY}$$

The method should throw a checked exception if any of the following conditions are violated:

a. The initial investment must be a positive number.
b. The interest rate and number of years must be provided.
c. If C is not provided, then the default value of 1 is used.

Exceptions resulting from violations to rules (a) and (b) should be thrown back to the client with an appropriate message. An exception that results from a violation of (c) should be caught and handled. Each of these exceptions should extend Exception.

Write a short description of an API for your "system." Include the number and types of parameters required by the method, the exceptions thrown, and the kind of output the method provides.

Write a client main(...) that interacts with your class, try some method calls, and handle any exceptions that are thrown by value(…).

Compiler—Friend or Master? The Controversy of Checked Exceptions

Java's exception-handling mechanism provides the following benefits:

- Normal code is separated from error-handling code via try-catch blocks.
- A clean path is created for error propagation. If a method encounters an unmanageable exception, it throws the exception and lets the calling method deal with it.

Without Java's exception-handling mechanism, error codes would have to be explicitly passed back from method to method.

- The compiler ensures that important potential errors (checked exceptions) are anticipated and handled.

Most programmers appreciate the first two benefits. The third benefit is controversial.

Bruce Eckel, in *Thinking in Java*, 3rd edition, advocates the use of RuntimeException as a wrapper class to "turn off" checked exceptions. In this way, he bypasses the strict interpretation of what the compiler says should be checked exceptions. Here is a snippet of a weblog by Tim Bray explaining Eckel's trick:

> "Suppose you're writing code to, as a completely random example, process UTF-8 efficiently in Java. Eventually you'll write something like this:
> b = o.toString().getBytes("UTF8");
> Then when you compile it, Java will whine at you that getBytes can throw a java.io.unsupportedEncodingException. At this point the Java programmer's heart starts to sink, envisioning every other module in the system that calls this sucker having to declare that exception, especially since there's very little likelihood that you can do anything about it except die. I mean what can you do if the system can't read UTF8?
>
> Here's the trick:
>
> ```
> try
> {
>   b = o.toString().getBytes("UTF8");
> }
> catch (java.io.UnsupportedEncodingException e)
> {
>   throw new RuntimeException("UTF8 not supported!?!?");
> }
> ```
>
> The trick, you see, is that RuntimeExceptions don't need to be declared in a throws clause."

Bray is describing a program that reads Unicode (UTF-8). He would rather not declare or handle the checked exception that reading Unicode might throw, because he feels that neither he (nor anyone else) can do anything useful to handle the exception, except quit the program. Rather than declare the exception in a throws clause in this method and in all the other methods that call this method, he hides the exception by catching it at the source, and "rethrowing" his own unchecked exception. This kind of trick is a loophole in Java's enforcement of checked and unchecked exceptions.

Let's read what Gaurav Pal and Sonal Bansal have to say about this practice (*JavaWorld*, 08/18/00):

> "Because the Java programming language does not require methods to catch or to specify unchecked exceptions (RuntimeException, Error, and their subclasses), programmers may be tempted to write code that throws only unchecked exceptions or to make all their exception subclasses inherit from RuntimeException. Both of these shortcuts allow programmers to write code without bothering with compiler errors and without bothering to specify or to catch any exceptions. Although this may seem convenient to the programmer, it sidesteps the intent of the catch or specify requirement and can cause problems for others using your classes. . . . Generally speaking, do not throw a RuntimeException or create a

> subclass of RuntimeException simply because you don't want to be bothered with specifying the exceptions your methods can throw."

Eckel acknowledges this criticism and writes that whenever he uses this trick…

> "it seems right, but I still get the occasional email that warns me that I am violating all that is right and true and probably the USA Patriot Act, as well."

The conflict here is not a simple matter of right and wrong. It is a debate about how much a compiler should control programming style. More experienced programmers feel, perhaps justifiably, that they know when it is okay to break the rules. Beginners rely on the compiler to protect them from themselves. Some believe that all programmers would write better code if they did not decide when and when not to find loopholes in the structure the compiler intends to impose.

Exercise

2. What is your instinct as a programmer? Do you view the compiler as a helper, or as a benevolent dictator? Do you follow the compiler's restrictions, trusting it to know best, or look for ways to bypass the rules when you think they are misguided? Include examples from your own experience.

CHAPTER 15

Stream I/O and Random Access Files

"Once you get into this great stream of history, you can't get out."
—Richard M. Nixon

"Never forget that only dead fish swim with the stream."
—Malcolm Muggeridge

Objectives

The objectives of Chapter 15 include an understanding of

- the Byte Stream and Character Stream classes,
- console I/O using the Byte Stream and Character Stream classes,
- text file I/O using the Byte Stream and Character Stream classes,
- the connections between the Byte Stream hierarchy and the Character Stream hierarchy,
- the difference between a text file and a binary file,
- binary file I/O,
- object serialization, and
- random access files.

15.1 INTRODUCTION

This chapter is an introduction to Java's *stream classes*, the backbone of Java's input/output system. Java provides classes for every imaginable type of input and output ranging from primitive byte I/O to input and output of complex objects that contain objects.

In the following sections, we study I/O with various types of files, take a closer look at some familiar objects such as System.in and System.out, and even learn how to save and retrieve objects. Much of the material in this chapter is of a technical nature, and it may seem in-depth and heavy at times. Still, we barely scratch the surface. We concentrate on just a few of Java's stream classes, and from those classes we select but a handful of methods. A more detailed description of the many facets of Java's stream classes can be found online at Sun's website.

15.2 THE STREAM CLASSES

The Java I/O system is built upon *streams*.

> A *stream* is an abstraction of the flow of data. An *input stream* constitutes the flow of data *to* an application, and an *output stream* represents the flow of data *from* an application.

The data to an application can come from the console, a file, or some other source. Similarly, the data that flow from an application can go to the screen, a file, or some other destination. These flows are all streams. Figure 15.1 shows streams linking a file and an application.

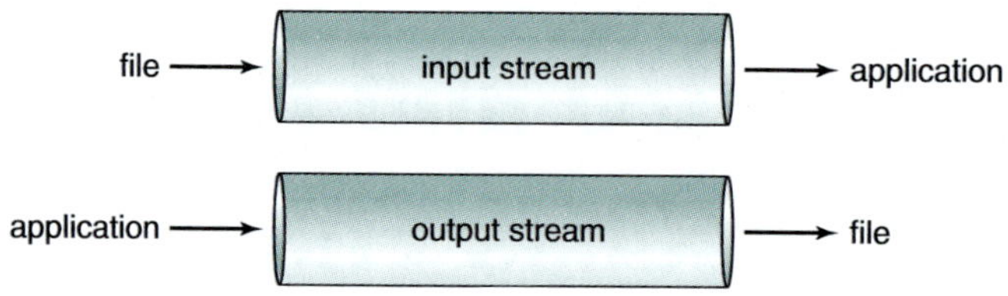

FIGURE 15.1 A *stream* is a flow of data.

15.3 THE BYTE STREAM AND THE CHARACTER STREAM CLASSES

Java's stream classes encapsulate all input and output. Java stores all data, even the most complex object, as a sequence of bytes. All objects are built from bytes. Bytes flow to and from an application via streams. Accordingly, Java provides the *Byte Stream* classes for byte I/O. The Byte Stream classes are the foundation of all Java I/O.

Indeed, the Byte Stream classes can be used independently or as helpers for another hierarchy of I/O classes called the *Character Stream* classes. Character I/O is usually accomplished with the Character Stream classes.

Why does Java provide two separate hierarchies of stream classes? If all character data are composed of bytes, and I/O can be accomplished using the Byte Stream classes, why complicate matters with the Character Stream classes? Recall that Java stores character data using the Unicode encoding scheme, which requires *two* bytes for each character, rather than the one byte used by the ASCII code. Unicode allows Java to handle normal ASCII characters (1 byte each) as well as international character sets such as Chinese, Hebrew, or Arabic. The first release of Java included the Byte Stream classes but not the Character Stream classes. However, it was not long before the developers at Sun realized that the Byte Stream classes did not handle character data as easily and efficiently as they had expected. The Character Stream classes, which appeared with Java 1.1, were introduced to alleviate this problem.

Using the Character Stream classes you can process data independent of a particular character code. These classes are smart enough to automatically and invisibly handle ASCII, Unicode, or any other character code. However, the Character Stream classes are not merely an alternative to the Byte Stream classes. Later, you will see that, in some situations, the Character Stream classes are clients of the Byte Stream classes, and are thereby dependent on them.

The Byte Stream classes and the Character Stream classes have a similar structure.

> Each collection of stream classes is split into a pair of hierarchies, one for input and one for output. For the Byte Stream collection, the root classes of these two hierarchies are InputStream and OutputStream, respectively. The Reader and Writer classes fill this role for the Character Stream classes.

Figures 15.2 and 15.3 emphasize the similarities between the two pairs of hierarchies. These classes reside in the java.io package.

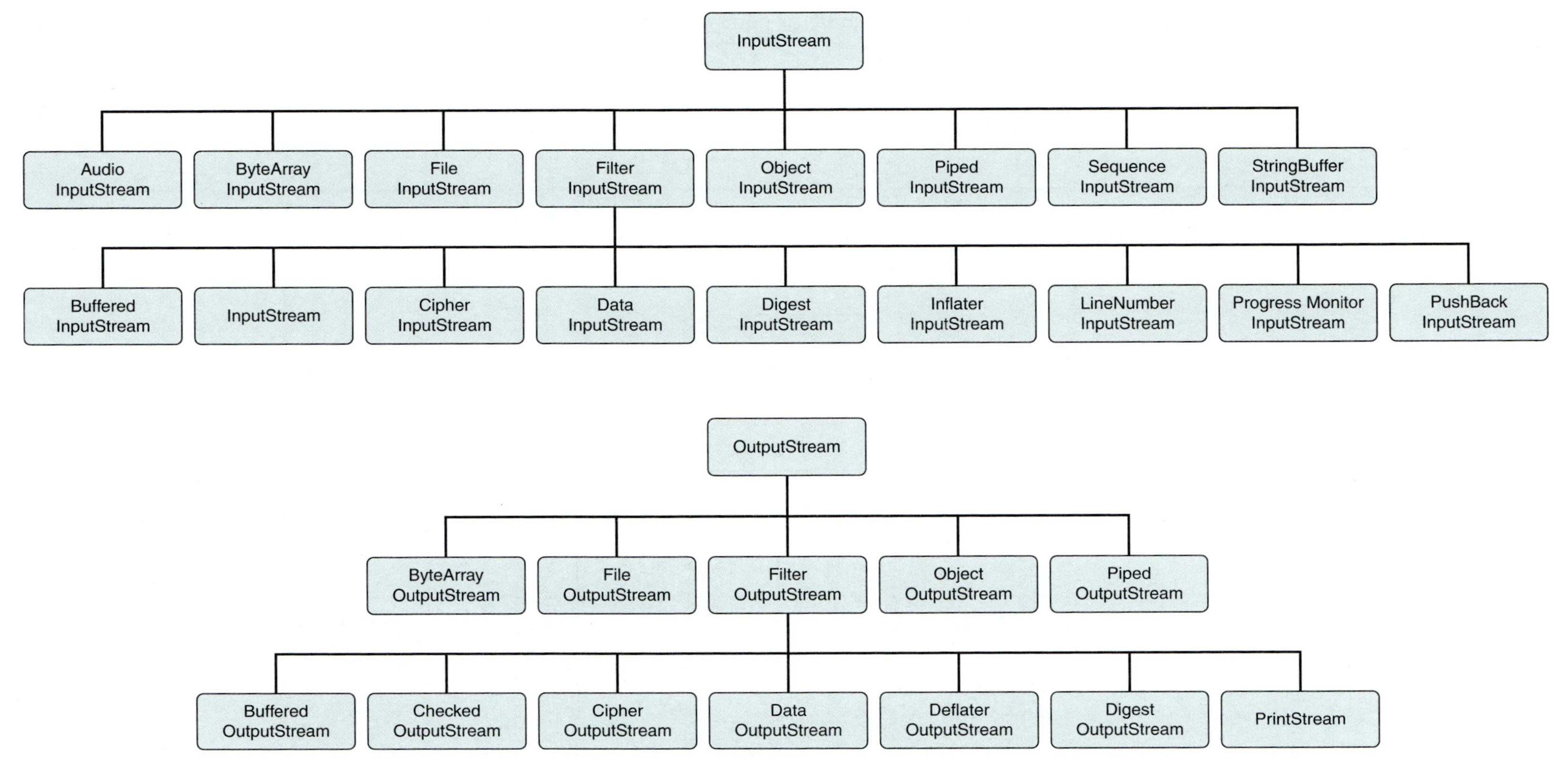

FIGURE 15.2 The *InputStream* and *OutputStream* hierarchies for byte I/O

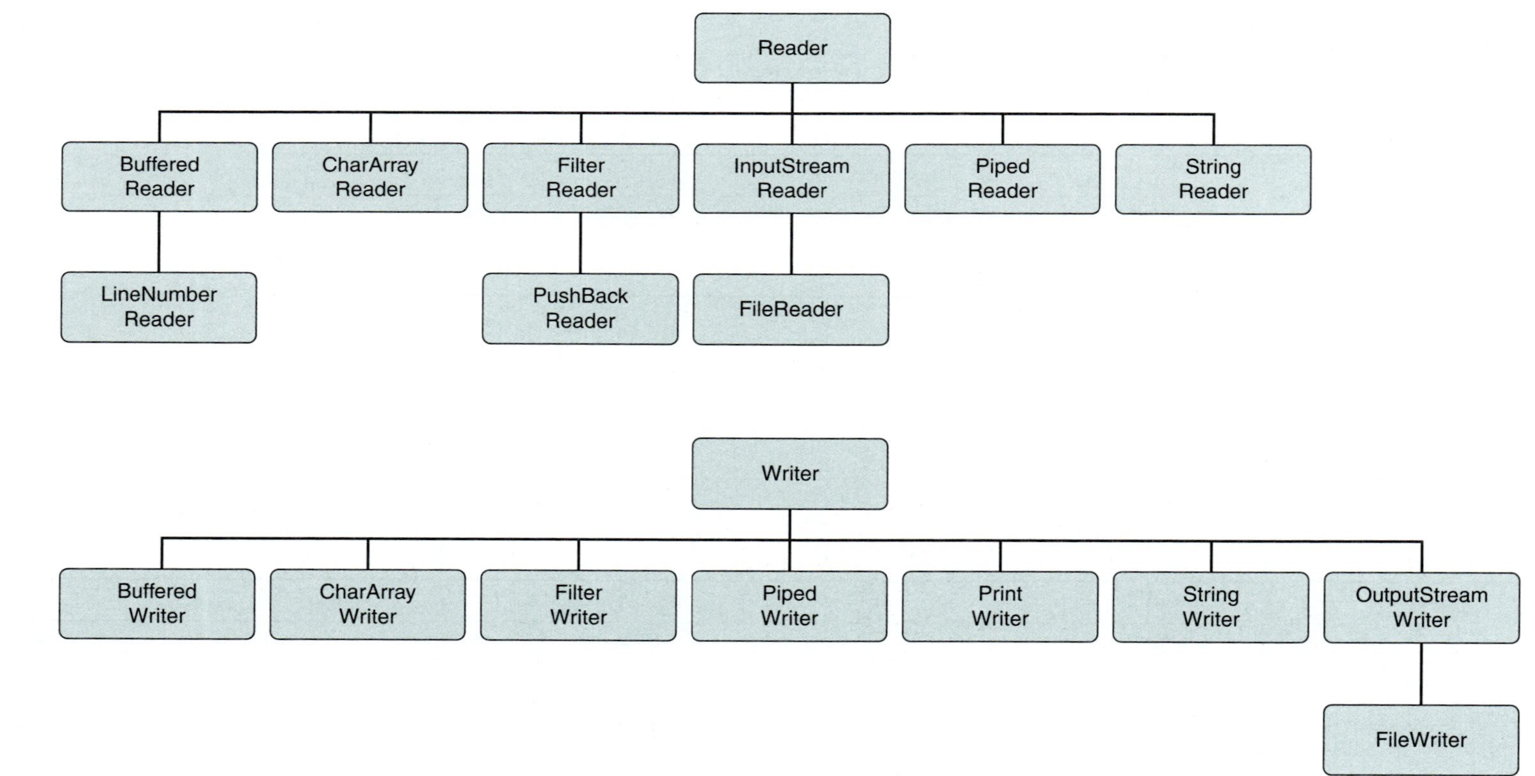

FIGURE 15.3 The *Reader* and *Writer* classes for character I/O

In the next sections we discuss the Byte Stream and Character Stream classes as they apply to

- console I/O,
- text files,
- binary files, and
- random access files.

15.4 CONSOLE INPUT

In this section we describe console input, first via the Byte Stream classes and then via the Character Stream classes. Here, you will see how the Byte Stream and Character Stream hierarchies are interconnected.

15.4.1 Console Input via the Byte Stream Classes

All console input is accomplished using System.in.

For example, a Scanner object that effects console I/O is connected to System.in via the constructor:

```
Scanner input = new Scanner(System.in);
```

System.in is always lingering in the background, doing the work.

So what exactly is System.in? As you know, System is a Java class; and like any class, System has attributes or fields. One such field of the System class is declared as

```
public static final InputStream in;
```

This declaration states that the reference, in, refers to an InputStream object. But InputStream, a member of the Byte Stream classes, is abstract and cannot be instantiated. In fact, in is an instance of the concrete class BufferedInputStream, which extends InputStream. The declaration

```
public static final InputStream in;
```

is one more example of upcasting. Figure 15.2 shows that BufferedInputStream extends InputStream.

Furthermore, because in is static, in can be accessed as System.in, that is, via the class name. Figure 15.4 shows other static fields of the System class.

```
public static final InputStream in;
public static final PrintStream out;
public static final PrintStream err;
---
// static methods of System
```

FIGURE 15.4 The fields of *System*. All are *static*.

And what is BufferedInputStream? The BufferedInputStream class offers the capability to handle I/O efficiently.

A *buffer* is primary memory used to temporarily store data. Using a buffer increases the efficiency and speed of I/O.

With a buffer, data is moved in large blocks (many bytes in each block) between slower devices (like disks) and the faster buffer. A program can retrieve individual bytes more quickly from a buffer. Both the Byte Stream and Character Stream classes provide subclasses with the capability for buffered I/O. The relevant classes are BufferedInputStream and BufferedOutputStream for the Byte Stream classes, and BufferedReader and BufferedWriter for the Character Stream classes. We discuss buffers in more detail later in the context of the Character Stream classes and file I/O, where buffers are most useful. For now, all you need to know is that in is an instance of BufferedInputStream, which extends InputStream.

Some of the methods declared in InputStream, inherited by BufferedInputStream, and thus available to the object System.in, include:

- int read() throws IOException
  returns the next byte in the stream (an int in the range 0..127)
  returns –1 at the end of the stream
- int read(byte[] b) throws IOException
  reads up to b.length bytes
  returns the number of bytes read, or –1 at the end of the stream
- void close() throws IOException
  closes the stream
- int available() throws IOException
  returns the number of bytes that can be read (or skipped over) from this input stream without waiting. If another method tries to read from the input stream, then other methods are *blocked* temporarily and must wait.
- long skip(long n) throws IOException
  skips n bytes in the stream before the next read

To use InputStream and its descendents, import the java.io package.

Example 15.1 demonstrates console I/O via the System.in object.

EXAMPLE 15.1 **Problem Statement** Devise a short application that reads bytes from the console and displays them on the screen. Use a cast to interpret the bytes as characters.

Java Solution Because System.in belongs to InputStream, the application imports java.io.*. Moreover, the read() method can throw an IOException, which, as you know, is checked, and must therefore be caught or declared in a throws clause. System.in.read() returns an integer in the range 0..127, or −1 if the end of the stream is reached.

```
import java.io.*;
public class Console
{
    public static void main(String[] args) throws IOException
    {
        int b;
        int count = 0;
```

```
8.          while ((b = System.in.read()) != -1)
9.          {
10.            count++;
11.            System.out.println(b + " " + (char)b);   // print byte and char value
12.         }
13.         System.out.println("Number of Characters: " + count);
14.    }
15. }
```

Output User input appears in bold. The console is unaware of any typing until the user presses the Enter key or Control-Z. Pressing Enter results in a *newline* character sent to the input stream. On Windows systems,[1] newline is represented by a sequence of two ASCII codes, a carriage return followed by a line feed. The integer 13 is the ASCII code for carriage return, and 10 represents line feed. The Control-Z character signals the end of input.

```
abc
97  a
98  b
99  c
13
10

b
98  b
13
10

hello
104  h
101  e
108  l
108  l
111  o
13
10

^z
Number of Characters: 15
```

Discussion The first three values given to the program are the characters a, b, and c, with character codes 97, 98, and 99, respectively, followed by *newline* represented by character codes 13 and 10. The next input value is the single character b followed again by *newline*. Finally, the characters h, e, l, l, o, *newline*, and Control-z are entered. The program displays the ASCII codes for each letter as well as 13 and 10, the codes for *carriage return* and *line feed* that together represent the *newline* character.

Because read() returns the numerical value of a character (a single byte), the cast **(char)**b on line 11 casts the numerical value of b to a character. This causes the actual characters to be printed except in cases when the characters are unprintable. Characters with code numbers 0 through 31 and 127 are control characters such as the *line feed* and *carriage return*. These are used to control the output device and are considered unprintable.

[1] On Linux/Unix systems, Control-D signifies the end of input, and *newline* is represented by the ASCII value 10 alone. Indeed, the modern style refers to ASCII code 10 as *newline* rather than *line feed*. Output on these systems shows 10 after each sequence of letters and codes, but not 13.

A call to System.in.read() can handle more than a single byte. The following fragment reads an array of four bytes with a single call. Of course, you can read more than four bytes by using a larger array. If the array is larger than the available number of characters in the stream, then the extra bytes in the array remain unused.

```
byte b[] = new byte[4];
int count = 0;
System.out.println("Enter data:");
count = System.in.read(b); // returns the number of bytes read
System.out.println("The following data was read:");
for (int i = 0; i < count; i++)
      System.out.print((char)b[i]);
System.out.println();
System.out.println("Number of characters: " + count);
System.out.println("Number of characters left " + System.in.available());
```

Embedded in a method, this code fragment produces the following output:

```
Enter data:
abcdefghijklmnopqrstuvwxyz
The following data was read:
abcd
Number of characters: 4
Number of characters left 24
```

Notice that the number of characters remaining is 24 (not 22). This count includes the invisible carriage return and line feed characters generated by pressing the Enter key.

We now crossover to the Character Stream classes for a look at a more flexible and efficient version of console input.

15.4.2 Console Input via the Character Stream Classes

> In contrast to the Byte Stream classes, the Character Stream methods are *character* oriented.

A call to read() via a Character Stream object returns a Unicode character code (two bytes). Consequently, the Character Stream classes can read and write many international character sets such as Chinese, Arabic, or Hebrew. Not all programs, however, process characters using two bytes. When you type characters at the terminal, your operating system encodes the characters using just eight bits, a 0 followed by a 7-bit ASCII code, giving 128 possibilities. Moreover, a simple text editor such as Notepad stores and interprets each character using just eight bits. Fortunately and conveniently, the Character Stream classes are smart enough to invisibly adapt to an 8-bit scheme. It's all done under the hood and invisible to you. Indeed, the Character classes are robust enough to handle thousands of different characters from Latin, to Hebrew, to Chinese, but still smart enough to know when the local system uses eight bits with just 128 (or 256) possible characters.[2]

---

[2]*Extended ASCII* assigns all 256 possible 8-bit codes to characters rather than assuming that the first bit is always 0 as in standard ASCII. The extension, however, is not standardized. There are many variations of extended ASCII, the most popular being ISO-8859-1. Unicode is a standardized 16-bit extension to ASCII, consistent with ISO-8859-1.

The BufferedReader class (in the Character Stream classes), similar in purpose to the BufferedInputStream class (in the Byte Stream classes), is used to accomplish efficient character input via the methods:

- int read() throws IOException
  reads a single character and returns its code number, and
- String readLine() throws IOException
  reads a line of text and returns the line as a String.

The convenient readLine() method of the BufferedReader class has no counterpart in BufferedInputStream.

The class constructor is

BufferedReader(Reader in).

As we have mentioned, Character Stream classes do not work independently of the Byte Stream classes.

A BufferedReader object uses System.in, an object from the Byte Stream hierarchy, to accomplish console input.

In fact, System.in is the workhorse of *all* console input. Being an InputStream object, System.in is *byte*—not character—oriented.

Because a BufferedReader uses System.in, you might attempt to pass System.in to the constructor of the BufferedReader class as you do with the Scanner class:

```
new Scanner (System.in)             // No problem here
new BufferedReader(System.in)       // BUT THIS DOES NOT WORK
```

Unfortunately, this does not work. A problem occurs because the BufferedReader constructor is of the form

Character Stream Class

↓

BufferedReader (Reader in)

and System.in is not a Reader object belonging to a Character Stream class but an InputStream object. BufferedReader needs System.in, but System.in cannot be passed directly to BufferedReader. Indeed, System.in belongs to the wrong hierarchy.

To overcome this little difficulty, Java provides a link or bridge between the Character Stream classes and the Byte Stream classes. This bridge is InputStreamReader. As the name suggests, an object belonging to InputStreamReader (a Character Stream class) reads bytes and converts those bytes to characters.

One of the constructors for an InputStreamReader has the form:

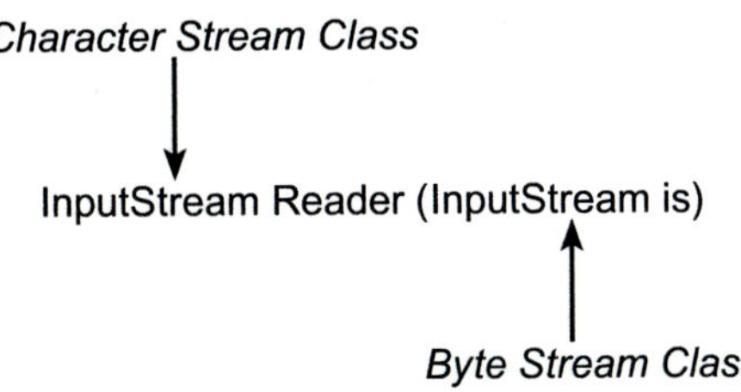

The Character Stream and Byte Stream classes are linked via InputStreamReader.

Consequently, character input is accomplished with a BufferedReader object as:

```
InputStreamReader link = new InputStreamReader(System.in); // link is a Reader object
BufferedReader br = new BufferedReader(link);               // wrap a Reader with BufferedReader
```

or

```
BufferedReader br = new BufferedReader (new InputStreamReader (System.in));
```

We say that the InputStreamReader, link, *wraps* System.in, and the BufferedReader, br, *wraps* link. Wrappers are a common technique in stream I/O and in object-oriented programming in general.

> Wrapping an object means that the functionality of the wrapped object is accessed via the wrapper.

The BufferedReader class supplies a read() method that reads one character, as well as a readLine() method that reads an entire line of text and returns the line (excluding any new line characters) as a String. See Figure 15.5.

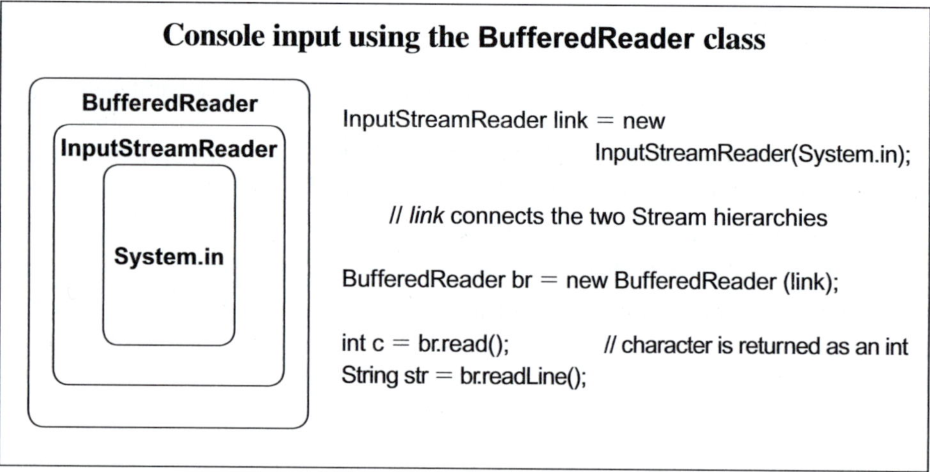

Console input using the BufferedReader class
BufferedReader
InputStreamReader
System.in
InputStreamReader link = new
InputStreamReader(System.in);
// link connects the two Stream hierarchies
BufferedReader br = new BufferedReader (link);
int c = br.read(); // character is returned as an int
String str = br.readLine();

FIGURE 15.5 *System.in* is wrapped in an *InputStreamReader*, which is then wrapped with a *BufferedReader*

The following method reads *characters* via a BufferedReader, br.

```
public void readCharacterData() throws IOException
{
   int c;
   int count = 0;
   InputStreamReader link = new InputStreamReader(System.in);
   BufferedReader br = new BufferedReader(link);
   while ( (c = br.read()) != -1)
   {
      count++;
      System.out.println(c + " " + (char)c);
   }
   System.out.println("Number of Characters: " + count);
}
```

The next method reads *lines of text* until the user enters Control-Z, signaling the end of input.

```
1. public void readLineData() throws IOException
2. {
3.     String str;
4.     InputStreamReader link = new InputStreamReader(System.in);
5.     BufferedReader br = new BufferedReader(link);
6.     System.out.println("Enter lines of text. End with CTRL-Z");

7.     while ( (str = br.readLine()) != null) // str = br,readLine() returns the value assigned to str
8.         System.out.println(str);
9. }
```

The condition on line 7 may seem a bit strange at first glance. Every assignment statement returns a value. The assignment

```
int x = 25;
```

returns the value 25; and the assignment

```
int y = x + 1;   // x = 25
```

returns 26. Likewise, the assignment

```
str = br.readLine(),
```

which is part of the boolean condition on line 7, does more than assign a value to str; it also returns the value assigned to str. When the user signals the end of input, br.readLine() returns a null reference, and consequently the assignment (str = br.readLine())) evaluates to null. Such conditions are often used to terminate a loop.

15.5 CONSOLE OUTPUT

Like console input, console output can be accomplished using methods of the Byte Stream classes as well as those of the Character Stream classes. As before, we begin with the Byte Stream version.

15.5.1 Console Output via Byte Stream Classes

Console output is usually effected with the familiar System.out.print() and System.out.println() methods. Figure 15.4 shows that in addition to in, the System class declares a field out:

```
public static final PrintStream out
```

Thus, System.out refers to an object belonging to the PrintStream class as seen in Figures 15.2 and 15.4.

The methods print() and println() are defined in the PrintStream class. Since we have used these methods for all console output, no further discussion is necessary, but now you finally know what it all means.

Other methods of PrintStream include:

- void write(int b) throws IOException
  writes a byte (an integer in the range 0..127) to the output stream
- void write(byte[] b) throws IOException
  write up to b.length bytes
- void close() throws IOException
  closes the stream

- void flush() throws IOException
  flushes the stream; write out any data remaining in a buffer

The following code fragment uses the write(...) method for output. Notice the cast on line 6.

```
1. int b;
2. int count = 0;
3. while ( (b = System.in.read()) != −1) // System.in.read() returns −1 at the end of the stream
4. {
5.    count++;
6.    System.out.write((char)b);        // write a byte
7. }
8. System.out.println("Number of Characters: " + count);
```

The write() method is rarely used for console output; print() and println() are more flexible.

We now take a look at console output as effected by the Character Stream classes.

15.5.2 Console Output via Character Stream Classes

Console output is usually accomplished with a call to the Byte Stream methods System.out.print() or System.out.println(). However, the Character Stream classes can also be used for character-based output, which is important for internationalization. The PrintWriter class provides an easy mechanism for console output. Like the byte-oriented PrintStream class, PrintWriter methods include print() and println() methods. Two of the PrintWriter constructors have the following form:

```
PrintWriter(OutputStream os);
PrintWriter(OutputStream os, boolean flush);
```

Notice that these constructors accept a parameter belonging to OutputStream, a member of the Byte Stream hierarchy. This is in contrast to BufferedReader, which requires a parameter belonging to Reader, that is, a Character Stream reference. Consequently, PrintWriter *can* accept System.out as an argument. That's one less wrapper!

The second PrintWriter constructor accepts a boolean argument flush. When flush is set to true, automatic line flushing is enabled. This means that the stream is flushed, that is, all characters are sent to the corresponding output device whenever println() is invoked. By default, automatic line flushing is *not* enabled—a call to println(...) does not automatically print a line of text, but sends it to the stream. PrintWriter methods do not throw exceptions. See Figure 15.6.

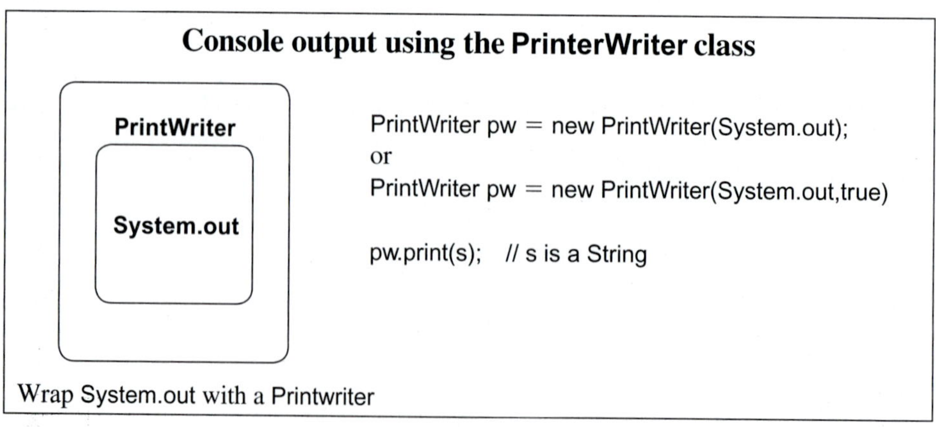

FIGURE 15.6 A *PrintWriter* object

The following code fragment instantiates a PrintWriter object with automatic line flushing and prints a poetic reminder.

```
PrintWriter pw = new PrintWriter(System.out, true);

pw.println("Roses are red, violets are blue");
pw.println("To flush out the buffer");
pw.println("Pass PrintWriter true");
```

Without automatic flushing, the following fragment needs an explicit call to flush() or close() (line 5). Otherwise, no output is produced at all.

```
1. PrintWriter pw = new PrintWriter(System.out); // no automatic flushing

2. pw.println("Blue is a violet; red is a rose");
3. pw.println("If it's not automatic");
4. pw.println("Call flush() or call close()");

5. pw.close();                                   // flushes and closes stream
```

A call to flush() flushes the stream, and a call to close() flushes and then closes the stream. In general, if you want println(...) to automatically print a line of text, use automatic flushing.

15.6 FILES

For our purposes, we define a file as a sequence of bytes and classify a file as either

- a text file or
- a binary file.

A *text file* is a sequence of readable characters, that is, a file that you can create and read with a text editor.

Indeed, an ASCII text file stores each character using eight bits, a 0 followed by a 7-bit ASCII code. The ASCII character set consists of 128 characters of which 33 are non-printable. When you open an ASCII text file with a text editor such as Notepad, the program reads the numeric code for each character and displays the corresponding character on the screen.

A Unicode text file encodes each character with two bytes, thus allowing many more possible character codes. In fact, the Unicode standard character set consists of more than 100,000 characters.

A *binary file* is *any* sequence of binary digits.

In contrast to a text file, each byte in a binary file does not necessarily correspond to a character. An attempt to read a binary file using a text editor produces some very odd-looking symbols. If you have ever tried to read a *class* file, an *exe* file, or an audio file with a text editor, you know exactly what we mean. Specialized programs such as media players, graphics programs, databases, and even word processors process binary files. You might say that text files are readable by humans and binary files are not.

Although binary files cannot be read with a text editor, binary files do have their advantages. Binary files can save space, and they facilitate specialized formatting specific to the needs of a program. For example, binary files are more efficient for both storing and manipulating *numeric* data.

In a text file, the symbols 1234 might be encoded as

00110001 00110010 00110011 00110100

where

- 00110001, the binary equivalent of 49, is the ASCII code for '1';
- 00110010, the binary equivalent of 50, is the ASCII code for '2';
- 00110011, the binary equivalent of 51, is the ASCII code for '3'; and
- 00110100, the binary equivalent of 52, is the ASCII code for '2';

In a binary file, 1234 might be stored as an integer using its 32-bit binary representation of 1234:

00000000 00000000 00000100 11010010

Both representations require four bytes of memory. However, a longer string of symbols such as "1234567890" requires 10 bytes of storage in an ASCII text file but still only four bytes as an integer in binary format. Storing large integers in a binary file rather than a text file saves space.

Saving space is not the only advantage gained by storing numeric data in a binary file; processing time can be reduced. The CPU expects that a number has a 32-bit binary representation. If an integer such as 123456789 is stored as a sequence of nine characters ('1','2','3','4',...,'9'), the character sequence must ultimately be converted to a "real" integer before any arithmetic operations can be performed, and that takes time. Furthermore, if the digits of a number are stored as characters, some type of separator, such as a space, between character sequences is required to distinguish one number from another, and these separators must also be processed.

Text files are efficient when printing and displaying characters, and under certain circumstances, text files are more suitable than binary files for storing numbers. If an application does *not* do arithmetic, it is more practical to store numbers in a text file rather than a binary file. Arithmetic calculations are rarely performed on phone numbers, social security numbers, zip codes, or ID numbers. These "numbers" are, in effect, text.

We have already used text files in a number of previous applications, and in Chapter 9 we introduce Java's File class, which encapsulates the properties of a file. Like any class, File provides constructors and methods. A File object is instantiated as:

```
File name = new File(String filename);
```

where filename is the name of some physical file. If the file does not reside in the same folder as the application, a File object can be created using the complete pathname of the file. The constructor throws a NullPointerException (unchecked) if filename is null.

A few methods supplied by the File class are:

- public boolean exists()
  returns true if the physical file exists; otherwise returns false
- public boolean canRead()
  returns true if the application can, in fact, read from a file; otherwise returns false
- public boolean canWrite()
  returns true if an application has permission to write to a file, otherwise returns false
- public boolean delete()
  attempts to delete a file from the disk and returns true if operation was successful
- public long length()
  returns the size of the file in bytes

If file access is denied for any reason, each of these methods throws a SecurityException, which *is-a* RunTimeException and consequently unchecked.

15.7 TEXT FILE INPUT

We now consider file I/O. As we did for console I/O, we start with the Byte Stream classes and work our way to the Character Stream classes.

15.7.1 Text File Input via the Byte Stream Classes

The FileInputStream class is a member of the Byte Stream hierarchy that facilitates reading bytes from a text file. Two important FileInputStream methods are:

- int read() throws IOException
  returns a single byte
- close() throws IOException
  closes the stream

> To read from a file, an application must connect a FileInputStream object to a File object, that is, wrap a File with a FileInputStream.

To wrap a File with a FileInputStream, use one of the two constructors:

```
FileInputStream(File file);
```

or

```
FileInputStream(String filename);
```

Each constructor throws a FileNotFoundException if the file does not exist. If file access is denied, the constructor throws a SecurityException which *is-a* RuntimeException and hence unchecked.

Figure 15.7 shows a File object wrapped with a FileInputStream.

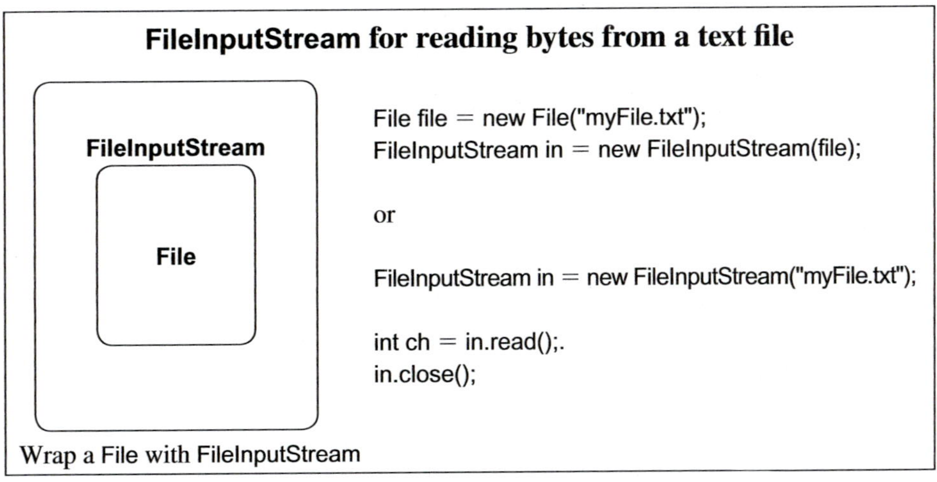
FileInputStream for reading bytes from a text file
FileInputStream
File
File file = new File("myFile.txt");
FileInputStream in = new FileInputStream(file);
or
FileInputStream in = new FileInputStream("myFile.txt");
int ch = in.read();.
in.close();
Wrap a File with FileInputStream

FIGURE 15.7 A *FileInputStream* to read bytes

The following example provides a template that reads from a text file and displays its contents on the console.

EXAMPLE 15.2 **Problem Statement** Implement a class ShowFile with a single static utility method that reads characters from a text file, byte by byte, and displays the contents of the file on the screen. Construct a second class that demonstrates the capability of ShowFile.

Java Solution The method showFile(...) throws an IOException and a FileNotFoundException. These exceptions are thrown to the caller and, in this case, handled by the caller, TestReadOneFile. A standard text file usually stores characters using a single byte for each character.

The ShowFile class

```
import java.io.*;

public class ShowFile
{
    public static void showFile(String filename) throws IOException,
                                                        FileNotFoundException

    {
        int c;
        // Create a File object
        File input = new File(filename);

        // Connect to a stream
        FileInputStream in = new FileInputStream(input);

        // do the reading
        while ( (c = in.read()) != -1)
            System.out.print((char)c); // cast the int to a char, the int is the ASCII code
        System.out.println();

        in.close(); // close the stream
    }
}
```

The TestReadOneFile class

```
import java.util.*;
import java.io.*;

public class TestReadOneFile
{
    public static void main(String [] args)
    {
        Scanner input = new Scanner(System.in);
        System.out.print("File name: ");
        try
        {
            String filename = input.next();
            System.out.println(filename);
            System.out.println();
            ShowFile.showFile(filename);
        }
        catch (FileNotFoundException e)
        {
            System.out.println(e);
        }
```

```
37.         catch (IOException e) // problem with
38.         {
39.             System.out.println(e);
40.         }
41.     }
42. }
```

Output File name: **myfile.txt**

There once was a girl named Elaine
With a microchip lodged in her brain
Her friends were amazed
Bedazzled and dazed,
By the facts that Elaine could retain.

Discussion Notice that showFile(…) throws two types of exceptions. In fact, because a FileNotFoundException *is-an* IOException, declaring an IOException is sufficient but less explanatory. On the other hand, if only a FileNotFoundException is declared, compilation errors occur on lines 12 and 15 because in.read() and in.close() do not throw FileNotFound exceptions. The exceptions are thrown to the caller, TestReadOneFile, which catches them.

Finally, notice that the read() method on line 12 returns a byte, an integer in the range 0 to 127. To display the corresponding character, the cast on line 13 is necessary.

We now consider the Character Stream classes, which not only provide the ability to read international characters but also the convenient readLine() method.

15.7.2 Text File Input via the Character Stream Classes

FileReader, a Character Stream class, includes methods that read characters from a file, one by one—in other words, very slowly. This class needs help. As you know, a *buffer* is an area of primary memory used to temporarily store data. Efficiency improves if an application reads characters from a buffer rather than directly from a disk file.

> BufferedReader provides methods that read and store a group or *block* of characters in a buffer. An application subsequently reads those characters from the buffer.

For example, the read() method of BufferedReader reads a single character from a buffer and not directly from a file. When read() is first invoked, a block of characters is copied from a file to a buffer. Subsequent calls to read() take characters from the buffer. When the characters stored in the buffer are consumed, the next call to read() brings another block of characters into the buffer. By reading a block of characters into a buffer, disk access is minimized and program efficiency improves. For example, using a block size of 100 bytes, an application can read 1000 bytes from a file with just 10 disk accesses. This is much faster than accessing the disk 1000 times and reading data one byte each time.

To use BufferedReader, first connect a FileReader to a File object and then wrap the FileReader with the more efficient BufferedReader. Two constructors of the FileReader class are:

- FileReader (File f) throws FileNotFoundException;
- FileReader(String filename) throws FileNotFoundException;

The methods include:

- int read() throws IOException;
  returns the character code of a single character, and

- void close() throws IOException;
  closes a stream

  A BufferedReader can be instantiated as

  BufferedReader(Reader r);

and implements the Reader methods close() and read() along with the additional method

String readLine() that reads an entire line of text.

Figure 15.8 shows a BufferedReader wrapped around a FileReader.

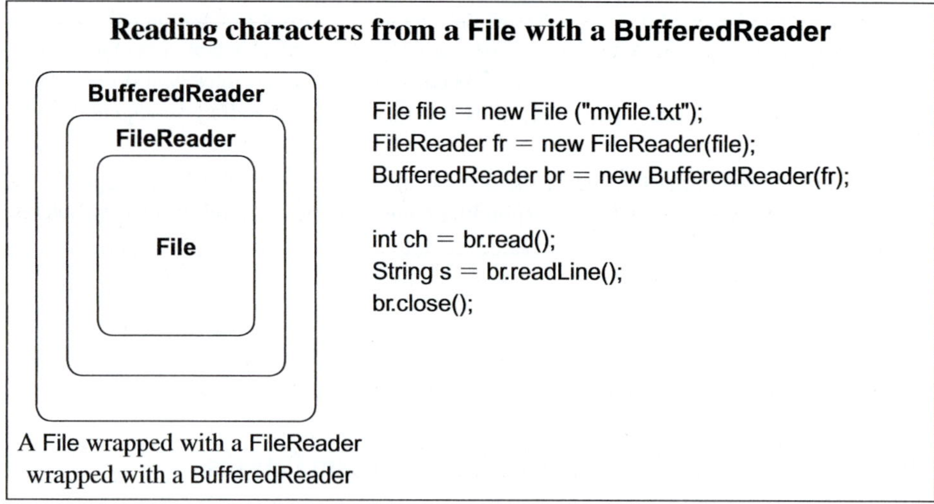

Reading characters from a File with a BufferedReader
BufferedReader
FileReader
File
File file = new File ("myfile.txt");
FileReader fr = new FileReader(file);
BufferedReader br = new BufferedReader(fr);
int ch = br.read();
String s = br.readLine();
br.close();
A File wrapped with a FileReader wrapped with a BufferedReader

FIGURE 15.8 A *BufferedReader* wrapped around a *FileReader*

EXAMPLE 15.3 **Problem Statement** Write a class, NumberLines, that reads lines from a text file, numbers the lines sequentially, and writes the numbered lines to a second file. The class should have two constructors:

- NumberLines(),
  prompts for the names of the input and output files, and
- NumberLines(String inputFile, String outputFile)
  accepts the names of the input and output files.

Include a second class that demonstrates the NumberLines class.

Java Solution The following class uses a BufferedReader object to effect reading and a PrintWriter object for output. FileNotFoundExceptions and IOExceptions are thrown to the caller. It is the caller's responsibility to handle these exceptions with a catch block or a throws clause. The test program uses the try-catch construction.

The NumberLines class

```
import java.util.*;
import java.io.*;

public class NumberLines
{
   private FileReader in;
   private FileWriter out;
   private BufferedReader br;
   private BufferedWriter bw;
   private PrintWriter pw;
   private Scanner scanner = new Scanner(System.in);

   public NumberLines() throws FileNotFoundException, IOException
   {
      String inputFile, outputFile;
      System.out.print("Input File: ");
      inputFile = scanner.next();
      System.out.print("Output File: ");
      outputFile = scanner.next();

      in = new FileReader(inputFile);            // throws FileNotFoundException
      br = new BufferedReader(in);               // wrap a BufferedReader around a FileReader

      out = new FileWriter(outputFile);          // throws an IO Exception
      bw = new BufferedWriter(out);
      pw = new PrintWriter(bw);                  // wrap a PrintWriter around a BufferedWriter
   }

   public NumberLines(String inputFile, String outputFile)
                                    throws FileNotFoundException, IOException

   {
      in = new FileReader(inputFile);            // throws FileNotFoundException
      br = new BufferedReader(in);               // wrap a BufferedReader around the FileReader

      out = new FileWriter(outputFile);          // throws IOException
      bw = new BufferedWriter(out);
      pw = new PrintWriter(bw);                  // wrap a PrintWriter around a BufferedWriter
   }

   public void copy() throws IOException
   {
      String s;
      int linecount = 0;
      while ( (s = br.readLine() ) != null)      // readLine() throws IOException
      {
         linecount++;
         pw.println(linecount + ". " + s);
      }
      pw.close();
   }
}
```

A test application TestNumberLines catches the exceptions that are thrown in NumberLines.

```
import java.io.*;
public class TestNumberLines
{
public static void main(String [] args)
{
    try
    {
            NumberLines numberLines = new NumberLines();
            numberLines.copy();
        }
        catch (FileNotFoundException e)
        {
            System.out.println(e.getMessage());
        }
        catch (IOException e)
        {
            System.out.println(e.getMessage());
        }
    }
}
```

Output 1

Input File: **poems.txt**
Output File: **newpoems.txt**

The input file poems.txt contains the following text:

```
Two Poems by Gellett Burgess (1866 – 1951)

I never saw a Purple Cow,
I never hope to see one;
But I can tell you, anyhow,
I'd rather see than be one.

*********************************

Ah, Yes! I Wrote the "Purple Cow" --
I'm Sorry, now, I Wrote it!
But I can Tell you Anyhow,
I'll Kill you if you Quote it!
```

The output file newpoems.txt contains the numbered lines:

```
1. Two Poems by Gellett Burgess (1866 – 1951)
2.
3. I never saw a Purple Cow,
4. I never hope to see one;
5. But I can tell you, anyhow,
6. I'd rather see than be one.
7.
8. *********************************
```

```
9.
10. Ah, Yes! I Wrote the "Purple Cow" --
11. I'm Sorry, now, I Wrote it!
12. But I can Tell you Anyhow,
13. I'll Kill you if you Quote it!
```

Output 2 Here a FileNotFoundException is thrown and caught:

```
Input File: oldpoem.txt
Output File: newpoem.txt
oldpoem.txt (The system cannot find the file specified)
```

Discussion

Lines 18–19, 26–27: A FileReader is connected to a BufferedReader. The FileReader constructor can throw a FileNotFoundException.

Lines 20–22, 28–30: A FileWriter is wrapped in a BufferedWriter, which in turn is wrapped in a PrintWriter. The FileWriter constructor can throw an IOException.

Line 36: The readLine() method can throw an IOException.

The test application invokes the constructor NumberLines() and calls copy(). Exceptions thrown in NumberLines are passed back to the caller. Because the caller catches these exceptions, no additional throws clause is necessary.

15.8 TEXT FILE OUTPUT

In the following sections we discuss output to text files, first using the Byte Stream classes and then as it is effected using the Character Stream classes.

15.8.1 Text File Output via the Byte Stream Classes

Writing to a text file using one of the Byte Stream classes is no more difficult than reading from a text file. To send output to a file:

- wrap a File with a FileOutputStream, a Byte Stream class,
- use the write() method of FileOutputStream, and
- close the stream.

The constructor FileOutputStream(File file) throws a FileNotFoundException.

The most useful methods of FileOutputStream are:

- void write(int b) throws IOException
  writes a single byte
- void close() throws IOException
  flushes and closes the stream, and
- void flush() throws IOException
  Forces the data in the stream to be written to the appropriate file.
  This method is inherited from the class OutputStream.

See Figure 15.9.

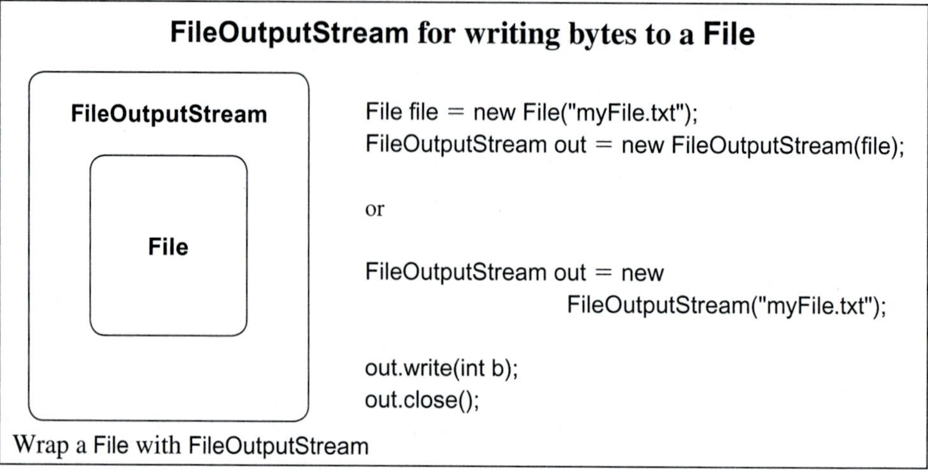
FileOutputStream for writing bytes to a File
FileOutputStream
File
File file = new File("myFile.txt");
FileOutputStream out = new FileOutputStream(file);
or
FileOutputStream out = new
FileOutputStream("myFile.txt");
out.write(int b);
out.close();
Wrap a File with FileOutputStream

FIGURE 15.9 A *FileOutputStream* object

The following fragment reads data from a text file, myinput.txt, and writes that data to another text file, myoutput.txt.

```
int c;
// get a File object
File input = new File("myinput.txt");
File output = new File("myoutput.txt");

// connect to a stream
FileInputStream in = new FileInputStream(input);            // throws FileNotFoundException
FileOutputStream out = new FileOutputStream(output);        // throws FileNotFoundException

while ( (c = in.read()) != –1)                              // throws IOException
   out.write((char)c);                                      // notice the cast to char;
                                                            // throws IOException

in.close();                                                 // throws IOException
out.close();                                                // throws IOException
```

Text file output with the Byte Stream classes can be made more efficient by wrapping a BufferedOutputStream around a FileOutputStream:

```
File output = new File ("myOutput.txt");
FileOutputStream out = new FileOutputStream(output);
BufferedOutputStream brOutput = new BufferedOutputStream(out);
```

In the next section we show that the same trick can be accomplished with the Character Stream classes by wrapping a BufferedFileWriter around a FileWriter.

15.8.2 Text File Output via the Character Stream Classes

The *FileWriter* Class

> The FileWriter class provides several low-level methods for writing character data to a file.

However, because these methods do no buffering, they are rather inefficient. Indeed, these methods write just one character at a time. Therefore, FileWriter methods usually work in conjunction with other classes. So, we begin at the bottom of the food chain with the FileWriter class and work upward.

FileWriter objects are instantiated using the constructors:

- FileWriter(File file); throws IOException;
- FileWriter(String filename); throws IOException;

The FileWriter methods include:

- void write(int ch) throws IOException;
- void write(String s) throws IOException;
- void close() throws IOException;
- void flush() throws IOException;

See Figure 15.10.

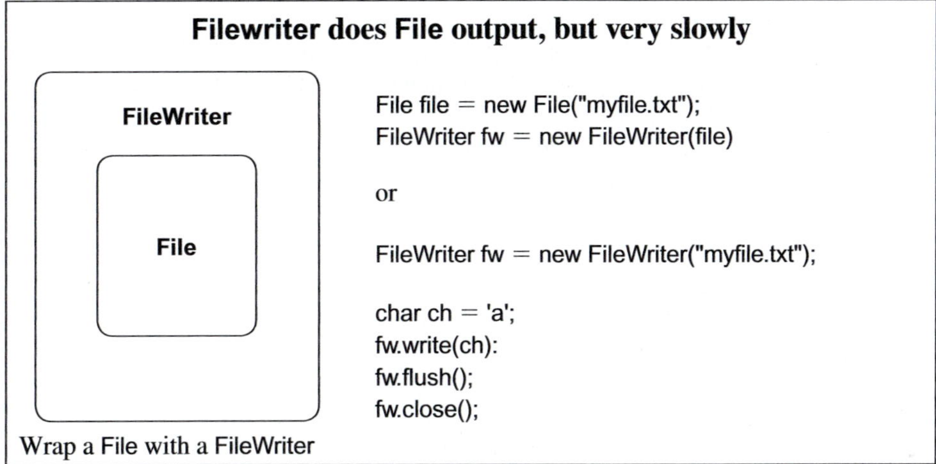

FIGURE 15.10 A *FileWriter* does low-level file output.

The following segment instantiates and uses a FileWriter to print the alphabet to a file alphabet.txt.

```
FileWriter fw = new FileWriter ("alphabet.txt");
for (int i = 0 ; i < 26; i++)
      fw.write(i + 'a'); // i + ASCII('a')
fw.close();
```

The segment writes one character at a time. This is a very inefficient way to write information to a file.

The *BufferedWriter* Class

As you know from Section 15.7.2, it is faster to write characters to a buffer and then write the contents of the buffer to a file, than it is to write each character one at a time to the file.

> Unlike a FileWriter, which writes characters one by one, a BufferedWriter saves characters in a buffer and writes them to a file when the buffer is full.

A BufferedWriter can be instantiated as

```
BufferedWriter(Writer wr);
```

The constructor's argument belongs to Writer. And here specifically, a BufferedWriter wraps a FileWriter.

The methods of the BufferedWriter class include:

- void write (int ch) throws IOException;
- void write (String s) throws IOException;
- void close() throws IOException;
- void flush() throws IOException;

See Figure 15.11.

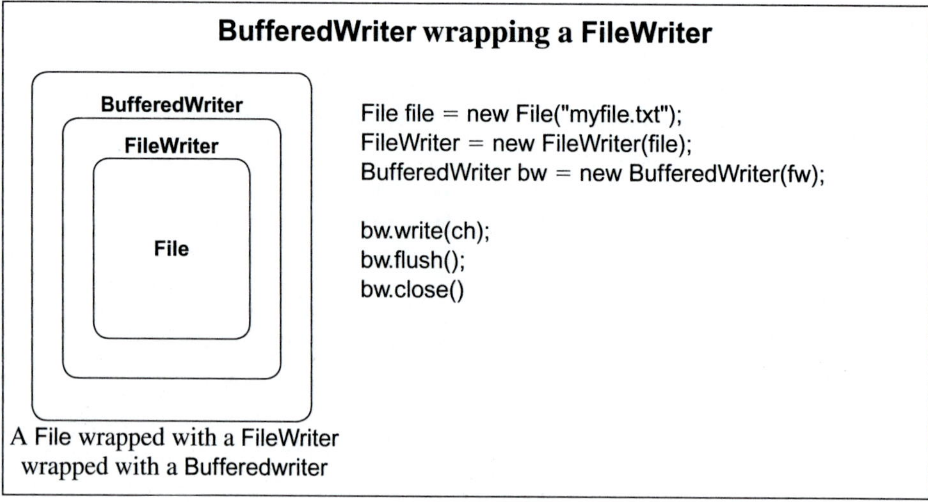
BufferedWriter wrapping a FileWriter
BufferedWriter
FileWriter
File
File file = new File("myfile.txt");
FileWriter = new FileWriter(file);
BufferedWriter bw = new BufferedWriter(fw);
bw.write(ch);
bw.flush();
bw.close()
A File wrapped with a FileWriter wrapped with a Bufferedwriter

FIGURE 15.11 A *BufferedWriter* is more efficient than a *FileWriter.*

The following fragment uses a BufferedWriter to write the alphabet to a file, alphabet.txt.

```
1. FileWriter fw = new FileWriter ("alphabet.txt");
2. BufferedWriter bw = new BufferedWriter(fw); // BufferedWriter wraps a FileWriter
3. for (int i = 0 ; i < 26; i++)
4.         bw.write(i + 'a'); // i + ASCII('a')
5. bw.close();
```

Wrapping a FileWriter with a BufferedWriter makes output more efficient. Example 15.4 underscores the benefits of using BufferedWriter.

EXAMPLE 15.4 **Problem Statement** Write an application that compares the relative speeds in milliseconds of FileWriter and BufferedWriter.

Java Solution To calculate time in milliseconds, we use Java's static method

```
public static long System.currentTimeMillis();
```

The following application writes one million characters to a file, file1.txt, using FileWriter and one million characters to file2.txt, using BufferedWriter. Finally, the program displays the number of milliseconds consumed by each operation.

```
import java.io.*;

public class FileWriterVsBufferedWriter
{
   public static void main(String[] args) throws Exception
   {
      FileWriter fw = new FileWriter("file1.txt");
      BufferedWriter br = new BufferedWriter(new FileWriter("file2.txt"));
      long start = System.currentTimeMillis(); // start time
      for (int i = 1; i <= 1000000; i++)
         fw.write('a');
      fw.close();
      long end = System.currentTimeMillis();
      System.out.println("FileWriter time: " + (end – start) + " milliseconds");

      start = System.currentTimeMillis(); // start time
      for (int i = 1; i <= 1000000; i++)
         br.write('a');
      br.close();
      end = System.currentTimeMillis();
      System.out.println("BufferedWriter time: " + (end – start) + " milliseconds");
   }
}
```

Output

```
FileWriter time: 313 milliseconds
BufferedWriter time: 78 milliseconds
```

Discussion In this case, output to a file using a BufferedWriter wrapped around a FileWriter is about four times faster than output using an "unwrapped" FileWriter. Efficiency depends on the buffer size, among other factors.

The *PrintWriter* Class

The BufferedWriter provides efficiency and the PrintWriter class adds the familiar print() and println() methods, which facilitate *formatted* output. Two PrintWriter constructors are:

- PrintWriter(Writer out);
- PrintWriter(Writer out, boolean flush);

Since a BufferedWriter *is-a* Writer, a BufferedWriter can be passed to PrintWriter. That is, we can wrap a BufferedWriter with a PrintWriter. See Figure 15.12.

Again, the next segment writes the alphabet to a file, this time one letter per line.

```
FileWriter fw = new FileWriter ("alphabet.txt");
BufferedWriter bw = new BufferedWriter(fw);
PrintWriter pw = new PrintWriter(bw)
for (int i = 0 ; i < 26; i++)
         pw.println ((char)(i + 'a'));      // notice the cast
pw.close();
```

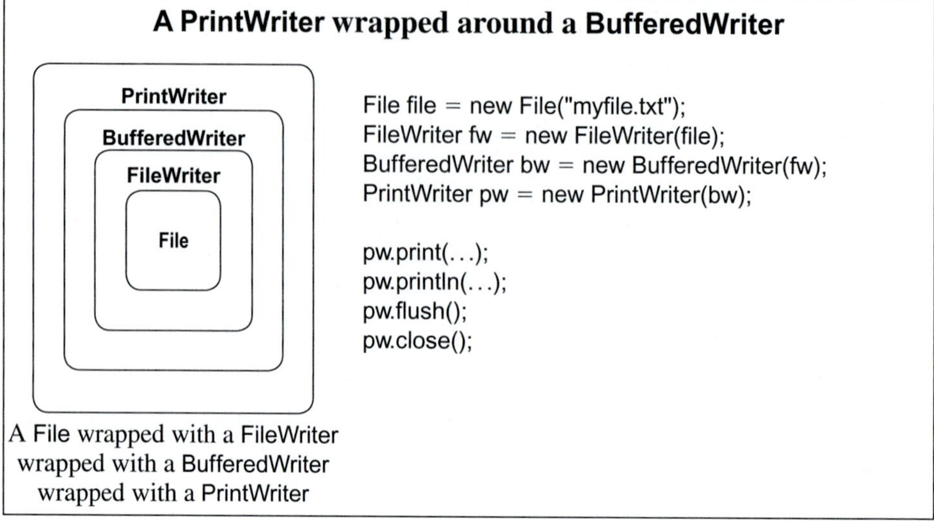
A PrintWriter wrapped around a BufferedWriter
PrintWriter
BufferedWriter
FileWriter
File
File file = new File("myfile.txt");
FileWriter fw = new FileWriter(file);
BufferedWriter bw = new BufferedWriter(fw);
PrintWriter pw = new PrintWriter(bw);
pw.print(...);
pw.println(...);
pw.flush();
pw.close();
A File wrapped with a FileWriter
wrapped with a BufferedWriter
wrapped with a PrintWriter

FIGURE 15.12 The *PrintWriter* class has *print*() and *println*() methods.

15.8.3 Byte Stream or Character Stream?

Unless internationalization is required, I/O can be accomplished with either the Byte Stream or the Character Stream classes. The Character Stream classes are smart enough to adapt to any encoding: ASCII, Unicode, or whatever the local scheme may be. Because of this flexibility and because the Character Stream classes are no more difficult than the Byte Stream classes, you might consider choosing the Character Stream option as the default for typical I/O applications that read from and write to the console or a text file.

We now turn our attention from text files to binary files. Character data is not a relevant issue with binary files. Binary file I/O is achieved using the Byte Stream classes, exclusively.

15.9 BINARY FILES AND DATA STREAMS

> The Byte Stream hierarchy provides two classes for reading and writing binary files: DataInputStream and DataOutputStream.

See Figure 15.2. The Data Stream classes are always wrapped around an OutputStream object. We begin our discussion with output.

15.9.1 Binary File Output via *DataOutputStream*

> A DataOutputStream object is able to write primitive data type values, in binary format, to a file.

Use the DataOutputStream class to create a binary file. The constructor for a DataOutputStream is

```
DataOutputStream(OutputStream out);
```

The parameter OutputStream is an abstract class, so we instantiate a DataOutputStream with a FileOutputStream, which *is-an* OutputStream (upcasting):

```
FileOutputStream fout = new FileOutputStream(new File (String filename));
DataOutputStream out = new DataOutputStream(fout);
```

or

```
FileOutputStream fout = new FileOutputStream(String filename);
DataOutputStream out = new DataOutputStream(fout);
```

If the specified output file does not exist, then one is created; otherwise the output file is cleared of all data. To append data to an existing file, use:

```
FileOutputStream fout = new FileOutputStream(new File (String filename), true)
DataOutputStream out = new DataOutputStream(fout);
```

or

```
FileOutputStream fout = new FileOutputStream(String filename, true)
DataOutputStream out = new DataOutputStream(fout);
```

See Figure 15.13.

DataOutputStream for writing to a file

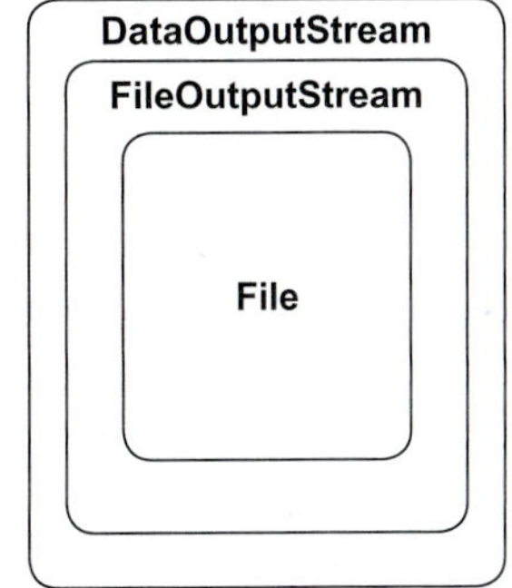

A File wrapped with a FileOutputStream is wrapped with a DataOutputStream

```
File file = new File("myfile.dat");
FileOutputStream fout = new FileOutputStream(file);
DataOutputStream out = new
DataOutputStream(fout);
```

or

```
FileOutputStream fout =
                new FileOutputStream("myfile.dat");
DataOutputStream out = new DataOutputStream(fout);
```

FIGURE 15.13 A *DataOutputStream* object

A few commonly used methods of the DataOutputStream class include:

- void writeByte(byte b) throws IOException;
- void writeShort(short s) throws IOException;
- void writeInt(int i) throws IOException;
- void writeLong(long l) throws IOException;
- void writeFloat(float f) throws IOException;
- void writeDouble(double d) throws IOException;
- void writeChar(char c) throws IOException;
- void writeBoolean(boolean b) throws IOException;
- void writeBytes(String s) throws IOException,
  writes a String as a sequence of bytes

- void writeChars(String s) throws IOException,
  writes a String as a sequence characters (2 bytes)
- int size() throws IOException;
  returns the number of bytes written to the DataOutputStream
- void flush() throws IOException;

Example 15.5 uses the DataOutputStream class to create a binary file.

EXAMPLE 15.5 A prime number is an integer greater than 1 that has no proper divisors. For example, 2, 3, 5, and 7 are prime numbers; 10 is not. Two primes that differ by two are called twin primes. For example, (3, 5), (5, 7), and (11, 13) are each twin primes; (2, 3) is not a pair of twin primes, nor is (19, 23). It has been conjectured, but never proven, that there is an infinite number of twin primes. The last twin prime that was discovered has 58,711 digits.

Problem Statement As a mathematical hobbyist hoping to uncover patterns among twin primes and someday resolve the twin prime conjecture, you maintain a text file, twins.txt, that contains an arbitrary number of eight-digit twin primes. In this file, each twin pair $(p, p + 2)$ is represented by p. For example, the twin pair (10001207,10001209) is stored as 10001207. The first 10 numbers in the file are:

```
10001207
10001399
10001441
10001531
10001567
10001777
10001819
10002017
10002059
10002197
10002257
10002437
```

Stored in an ASCII text file, each number requires eight bytes (64 bits), one byte for each digit, but in a binary file each number can be stored using just four bytes (32 bits). To save disk space for your massive music collection and increase efficiency when perfoming arithmetic, you decide to store this list of twin primes as a *binary* file.

Write a class with a static utility method,

public static void makeBinaryFile(String textFileName, String binaryFileName)

that reads the text file twins.txt and creates a space-saving binary file containing the same numbers.

Java Solution The TextToBinary class with static method makeBinary(...)

```
import java.io.*;
import java.util.*;

public class TextToBinary
{
    public static void makeBinaryFile(String textFile, String binaryFile)
                                                        throws IOException
    {
```

```
7.          Scanner input = new Scanner(new File(textFile));
8.          int number;
9.          FileOutputStream fout = new FileOutputStream(binaryFile);
10.         DataOutputStream out = new DataOutputStream(fout);
11.         while (input.hasNext())
12.         {
13.            number = input.nextInt();
14.            out.writeInt(number);
15.         }
16.         out.close();
17.      }
18. }
```

The TestTextToBinary class that tests makeBinaryFile(...)

```
19. import java.util.*;
20. import java.io.*;

21. public class TestTextToBinary
22. {
23.      public static void main(String[] args) throws IOException
24.      {
25.         Scanner input = new Scanner(System.in);
26.         System.out.print("Text file name: ");
27.         String textFile = input.next();
28.         System.out.print("Binary file name: ");
29.         String binaryFile = input.next();
30.         TextToBinary.makeBinaryFile(textFile, binaryFile);
31.         System.out.println("File " + binaryFile + " created");
32.      }
33. }
```

Output Using the file twins.txt as input:

Text file name: **twins.txt**
Binary file name: **twins.dat**
File twins.dat created

The output of the application is a binary file, twins.dat. The file is not readable or printable using an ordinary text editor. Figure 15.14 shows a picture of the file as displayed in Notepad:

FIGURE 15.14 An attempt to display *twins.dat* with a text editor

Discussion

Line 7: A Scanner object reads integers from the text file, which in this case is twins.txt. The method nextInt() extracts characters from the text file and automatically converts those characters to an integer.

Line 9: A File object is wrapped with a FileOutputStream.

Line 10: The FileOutputStream is wrapped with a DataOutputStream.

Line 13: The next number is read from the text file, twins.txt.

Line 14: The writeInt() method writes integer data to the DataOutputStream.

Line 16: Close the DataOutputStream.

15.9.2 Binary File Input via *DataInputStream*

The DataInputStream class provides methods for reading data from a binary file.

The class constructor is

```
DataInputStream(InputStream in);
```

Because a FileInputStream *is-an* InputStream, you can instantiate a DataInputStream as:

```
File file = new File(String filename);
FileInputStream fin = new FileInputStream(file);
DataInputStream in = new DataInputstream(fin);
```

or

```
FileInputStream fin = new FileInputStream(String filename);
DataInputStream in = new DataInputStream(fin);
```

See Figure 15.15.

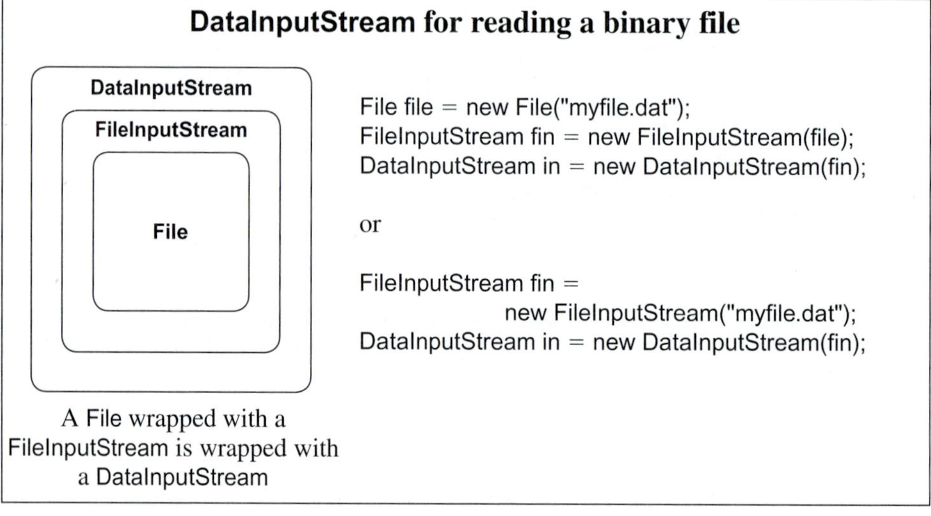
DataInputStream for reading a binary file
DataInputStream
FileInputStream
File
File file = new File("myfile.dat");
FileInputStream fin = new FileInputStream(file);
DataInputStream in = new DataInputStream(fin);
or
FileInputStream fin =
new FileInputStream("myfile.dat");
DataInputStream in = new DataInputStream(fin);
A File wrapped with a
FileInputStream is wrapped with
a DataInputStream

FIGURE 15.15 A *DataInputStream* object

The DataInputStream class provides the following methods:

- int readByte(byte[] b);
  reads bytes from the input stream into the array referenced by b and returns the number of bytes read or −1 to signify the end of file.

- int readByte();
- short readShort();
- int readInt();
- int readLong();
- float readFloat();
- double readDouble();
- char readChar();
- boolean readBoolean();

Each method throws an IOException if any I/O error occurs, and except for readByte(byte[] b), each method also throws an EOFException if a read is attempted beyond the end of the file.

Example 15.6 reads from a binary file and displays the contents on the console.

EXAMPLE 15.6

Problem Statement The binary file twins.dat (see Example 15.5) contains a list of eight-digit twin primes. Display the first 10 twin pairs in the form (a, $a + 2$).

Java Solution

```
import java.io.*;
public class ReadTwinPrimes
{
    public static void main(String[] args)throws IOException
    {
        int prime;
        FileInputStream input = new FileInputStream("twins.dat");
        DataInputStream in = new DataInputStream(input);
        System.out.println("The first 10 twin prime pairs in twins.dat are:\n");
        for (int i = 1; i <= 10; i++)
        {
            prime = in.readInt();
            System.out.println(" (" + prime + "," + (prime + 2) + ")");
        }
    }
}
```

Output The input to the application is stored in the file twins.dat. This is the binary file "pictured" in Figure 15.14. The output is:

```
The first 10 twin prime pairs in twins.dat are:
(10001207,10001209)
(10001399,10001401)
(10001441,10001443)
(10001531,10001533)
(10001567,10001569)
(10001777,10001779)
(10001819,10001821)
(10002017,10002019)
(10002059,10002061)
(10002197,10002199)
```

Discussion

Lines 7–8: Instantiate a DataInputStream object.

Lines 10–14: The code in this loop invokes the readInt() method via the DataInputStream object. Each call to readInt() returns an integer from the file twins.dat.

Notice that the statement on line 13 performs addition. Had we used a *text* file, a number such as 10002197 would be stored as a sequence of ASCII codes, one byte for each digit:

00110001	00110000	00110000	00110000	00110010	00110001	00111001	00110111
49	48	48	48	50	49	57	55
'1'	'0'	'0'	'0'	'2'	'1'	'9'	'7'

Before effecting addition or any arithmetic operation with 10002197, the sequence of ASCII codes would need to be converted to the 32-bit number

00000000100110001001111100010101,

the binary equivalent of 10002197.

But in this application, 10002197 is stored in a *binary* file, no conversion is necessary and, consequently, addition is performed more efficiently.

You may have noticed that the methods readInt(), readShort(), readDouble(), and so on of DataInputStream do *not* return a value of –1 when a read operation is attempted beyond the end of a file. Indeed, –1 might well be a valid value and, consequently, cannot signal an illegal read operation. Instead, each of these methods throws an EOFException when a read operation is attempted beyond the end of a file. The following example capitalizes on this exception.

EXAMPLE 15.7

Problem Statement Write a static utility method that reads a binary file of integers, such as twins.dat, and creates a text file that contains the same numbers.

Java Solution The number of integers in the binary file is arbitrary. The following application uses an EOFException to signal the end of file.

The BinaryToText class

```
import java.io.*;
public class BinaryToText
{
   public static void makeTextFile(String textFile, String binaryFile)
                                                  throws IOException
   {
      FileInputStream infile = null;
      DataInputStream in = null;
      FileOutputStream outfile = null;
      PrintWriter out = null;
      int count = 0;
      try
      {
         infile = new FileInputStream(binaryFile);
         in = new DataInputStream(infile);
         outfile = new FileOutputStream(textFile);
         out = new PrintWriter(outfile);
```

```
17.             while(true) // do until EOFException
18.             {
19.                int number = in.readInt();
20.                count++;
21.                out.println(number);
22.             }
23.          }
24.          catch (FileNotFoundException e)
25.          {
26.             System.out.println(e.getMessage());
27.          }
28.          catch (EOFException e) // when end of file has been reached
29.          {
30.             System.out.println(count + " values read");
31.          }
32.          finally
33.          {
34.             if ( (out != null))
35.                out.close();
36.          }
37.       }
38.  }
```

The TestBinaryToText class, a class that tests makeTextFile(…)

```
39.  import java.util.*;
40.  import java.io.*;
41.  public class TestBinaryToText
42.  {
43.     public static void main(String[] args) throws IOException
44.     {
45.        Scanner input = new Scanner(System.in);
46.        System.out.print("Text file name: ");
47.        String textFile = input.next();
48.        System.out.print("Binary file name: ");
49.        String binaryFile = input.next();
50.        BinaryToText.makeTextFile(textFile, binaryFile);
51.        System.out.println("File " + binaryFile + " created");
52.     }
53.  }
```

Output

Text file name: **twins.txt**
Binary file name: **twins.dat**
24 values read
File twins.txt created

Discussion Once all data has been read, one more call to readInt() (line 19) throws an EOFException. Program control moves to the catch block (lines 28–31). The finally block executes, and the file is closed before the application terminates.

The DataInputStream and DataOutputStream classes facilitate input and output of primitive types. And certainly, the data of any *object* can be saved as a collection of primitives. Nonetheless, Java also provides effective and easy procedures for storing and retrieving an object. This process is called *object serialization.*

15.10 OBJECT SERIALIZATION

Consider the following skeletal class that models a customer account for a video store:

```
public class Customer
{
        private String lastName;
        private String firstName;
        private String[] checkedOutFilms;   // up to five films may be checked out
        private String creditCard;
        // methods go here
}
```

Customer data can be stored in a file, field by field. However, saving the state of a large, complex object with dozens of fields can be tedious, tricky, and error prone.

> *Object serialization* converts an object to a stream of bytes so that the state of an object can be saved in a file with a single statement, and later retrieved.

In short, serialization encodes an object as a byte stream. Serialized objects can be stored in a file and reconstructed later. Serialized objects can also be passed over a network. Note that static fields are not serialized.

Every object is not serializable.

> An object is serializable only if it belongs to a class that implements the Serializable interface.

That's not much of a requirement because the Serializable interface has no methods. Therefore, a class is serializable if the class heading includes the phrase implements Serializable. No other action is necessary. This simple declaration marks the class as serializable.

The Byte Stream hierarchy provides the ObjectInputStream and ObjectOutputStream classes for reading and writing serializable objects. See Figure 15.2. Constructors for these classes include:

- ObjectInputStream(InputStream in), and
- ObjectOutputStream(OutputStream out)

Because a FileInputStream *is-an* InputStream and a FileOutputStream *is-an* OutputStream, the constructors can be invoked as:

```
FileInputStream fin = new FileInputStream(String filename);
ObjectInputStream in = new ObjectInputStream(fin);
```

and

```
FileOutputStream fout = new FileOutputStream(String filename);
ObjectOutputStream out = new ObjectOutputStream(fout);
```

ObjectInputStream and ObjectOutputStream provide numerous methods, but for our purposes the two most useful methods are:

- void readObject(Object o) throws ClassNotFoundException, IOException, and
- void writeObject(Object o) throws IOException.

For readObject(Object o), a ClassNotFoundException is thrown if the class of the serialized object cannot be determined. See Figures 15.16 and 15.17.

ObjectInputStream for reading serialized objects

ObjectInputStream
FileInputStream
File

A File wrapped with FileInputStream wrapped with an ObjectInputStream

Constructor:
ObjectInputStream(InputStream in)

```
FileInputStream fin =
            new FileInputSteam(String filename);
ObjectInputStream in = new ObjectInputStream(fin);

in.readObject(Object o);
```

FIGURE 15.16 An *ObjectInputStream* object

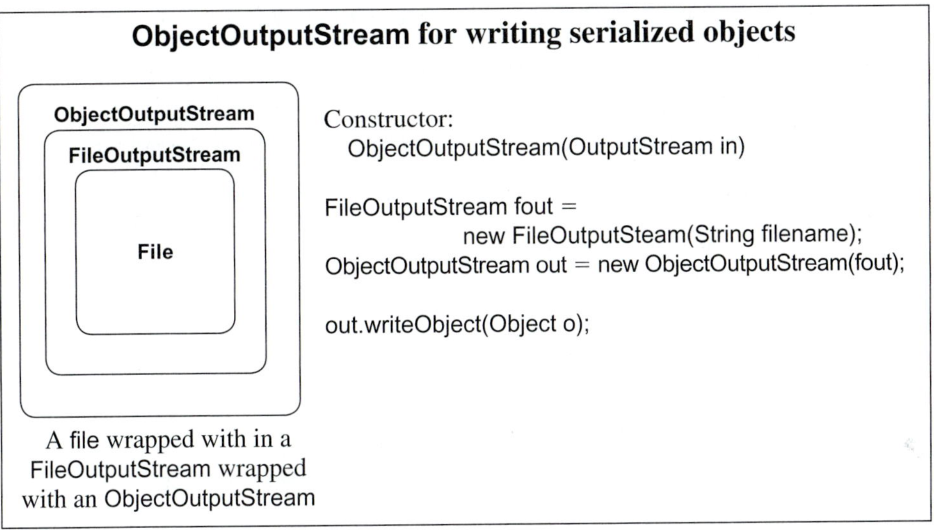
ObjectOutputStream for writing serialized objects
ObjectOutputStream
FileOutputStream
File
A file wrapped with in a FileOutputStream wrapped with an ObjectOutputStream
Constructor:
ObjectOutputStream(OutputStream in)
FileOutputStream fout =
new FileOutputSteam(String filename);
ObjectOutputStream out = new ObjectOutputStream(fout);
out.writeObject(Object o);

FIGURE 15.17 An *ObjectOutputStream* object

EXAMPLE 15.8

The following serializable class VideoCustomer models a customer of a video rental store. The class has several data fields, such as a customer's name and credit card number along with methods to check out a film and return a film. There is nothing unusual about this class except the phrase implements Serializable in the class heading. This phrase indicates that objects of this class can be serialized.

```
import java.io.*;

public class VideoCustomer implements Serializable
{
   private String lastName;
   private String firstName;
   private String[] checkedOutFilms;
   private int numFilms;
   private String creditCard;
```

```
        VideoCustomer() // default constructor
        {
            lastName = "";
            firstName = "";
            numFilms = 0;
            checkedOutFilms = new String[5];
            creditCard = "";
        }

    VideoCustomer(String last, String first, String credit) // three argument constructor
    {
        lastName = last;
        firstName = first;
        numFilms = 0;
        checkedOutFilms = new String[5];
        creditCard = credit;
    }

    public void checkOut(String film)          // supply the title of a film
    {
        if (numFilms == 5)                      // only 5 films may be checked out
        {
            System.out.println("Already have five films");
            return;
        }
        for (int i = 0; i < 5; i++)             // add film to the array of checked out films
        {
            if (checkedOutFilms[i] == null)
            {
                checkedOutFilms[i] = film;
                numFilms++;
                return;
            }
        }
    }

    public void returnFilm(String film)
    {
        for (int i = 0; i < 5; i++)             // find film and take it off the list
            if (checkedOutFilms[i].equals(film))
            {
                checkedOutFilms[i] = null;
                numFilms--;
                return;
            }
        return; // do nothing if someone tries to return a film that he/she did not check out.
    }

    public String toString()
    // returns the customer's name and the titles of all checked out films
    {
        String allFilms = "";
        for (int i = 0; i < 5; i++)
            if (checkedOutFilms[i] != null)
                allFilms += checkedOutFilms[i] + "\n";
        return (lastName + ", " + firstName + "\n\n" + allFilms);
    }
}
```

Problem Statement Write an application that demonstrates the object serialization procedure by storing two VideoCustomer objects in a file and subsequently retrieving the objects.

Java Solution The following test program

- instantiates two VideoCustomer objects using the three-argument constructor,
- allows each customer to check out and/or return a film or two,
- uses the writeObject() method to save the VideoCustomer objects in a file, moviestore.dat,
- retrieves the two saved VideoCustomer objects using the readObject() method, and
- invokes the toString() method for each VideoCustomer object.

```
import java.io.*;
public class TestVideoCustomer
{
   public static void main(String[] args) throws IOException, ClassNotFoundException
   {
      FileOutputStream fout = new FileOutputStream("moviestore.dat");
      ObjectOutputStream out = new ObjectOutputStream(fout);

      VideoCustomer customer1 =
        new VideoCustomer("Filmbuff", "Frannie", "356789012343225");

      VideoCustomer customer2 =
        new VideoCustomer("Celuloid", "Charlie", "545678909843555");

      customer1.checkOut("Psycho");
      customer2.checkOut("The Matrix");
      customer1.checkOut("The Birds");
      customer2.checkOut("The Sixth Sense");
      customer1.returnFilm("Psycho");

      out.writeObject(customer1);
      out.writeObject(customer2);
      out.close();

      FileInputStream fin = new FileInputStream("moviestore.dat");
      ObjectInputStream in = new ObjectInputStream(fin);

      VideoCustomer cust;
      int numObjects = 0;
      try
      {
        while(true)
        {
           cust = (VideoCustomer)(in.readObject());
           System.out.println(cust);
           System.out.println("--------------------------");
           numObjects++;
        }
      }
      catch (EOFException e)
      {
        System.out.println(numObjects + " objects retrieved");
      }
   }
}
```

Output When executed, the application produces the following output:

```
Filmbuff, Frannie

The Birds

--------------------------

Celuloid, Charlie
```

```
The Matrix
The Sixth Sense

--------------------------
2 objects retrieved
```

Discussion

Line 4: The method readObject() (line 28) can throw a ClassNotFoundException. This exception is checked and must be caught or declared in a throws clause. The same is true with the IOException.

Lines 6–7: Instantiate an ObjectOutputStream, out, by wrapping a file first with a FileOutputStream and then with an ObjectOutputStream.

Lines 8–16: Instantiate two VideoCustomer objects. Each VideoCustomer object checks out and/or returns some films.

Lines 17–18: Write each VideoCustomer object to the output stream. Thus, the objects are stored in the file.

Line 19: Close the output stream.

Lines 20–21: Connect the file, movies.dat, to an ObjectInputStream, in.

Lines 24–36: The while loop executes until a readObject() operation is attempted past the end of the file (line 28). When this occurs, an EOFException is thrown and caught by the corresponding catch block. The readObject() method returns an object of the class Object. Thus the cast on line 28 is necessary.

If you do not want a particular field of a class included in a serialized object, use the keyword transient.

For example, if, for security reasons, you do not want to serialize the creditCard field of a VideoCustomer object, then declare the field as:

```
transient String creditCard;
```

In this case, creditCard is set to null by serialization and is not stored in the file. Also, if there is no reason to save a particular field, that field can be marked transient and will not be serialized.

To this point, all file I/O has been *sequential.* To access a particular item in a file, an application starts at the beginning of the file and reads through the file in order, item by item, top to bottom, until the required item is located. However, there are also files that provide *direct access* to any byte. Such files are called *random access files.*

15.11 RANDOM ACCESS FILES

A *random access file* is one that provides *direct* access to any byte in the file.

You might think of a random access file as a sequence of bytes indexed from 0. Access to any byte of a random access file is similar to that of an array: if x is an array, an application can access x[100] without first reading x[0] through x[99]. Access is immediate and direct.

Each byte of a random access file has a *relative address*. The relative address of the first byte of a file is 0, the relative address of the second byte is 1, and so on.

The *file pointer* holds the *relative address* of the next accessible byte in a random access file.

An application accesses a particular byte in a random access file via the file pointer. See Figure 15.18.

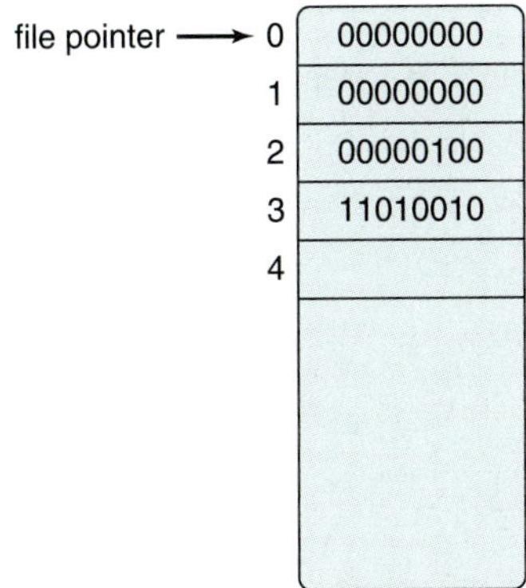

FIGURE 15.18 A random access file. The file pointer references the first byte of the file.

We use Java's RandomAccessFile class to perform I/O on random access files. If the file pointer is positioned at byte 40, then to read byte 100, you simply set the file pointer to 100. There is no need to move through the 60 intermediate locations, one by one.

RandomAccessFile extends Object and implements the interfaces DataInput and DataOutput. RandomAccessFile is *not* a stream class.

The constructors of RandomAccessFile include:

- RandomAccessFile(File file, String accessCode), and
- RandomAccessFile(String filename, String accessCode).

where accessCode is "r" for read only, or "rw" for read/write.

Each constructor throws a FileNotFoundException, as well as an IllegalArgument-Exception, if accessCode is in error, and a SecurityException. The latter two exceptions are unchecked.

A random access file may be opened for *both* reading and writing. See Figure 15.19.

Because RandomAccessFile implements DataInput and DataOutput, RandomAccess-File implements the methods declared in these interfaces:

- int readInt();
- long readLong();
- double readDouble();
- char readChar();

Constructors for a RandomAccessFile


```
File file = new File (String filename);
RandomAccessFile raf =
    new RandomAccessFile(file, "rw");
```

or

```
RandomAccessFile raf =
    new RandomAccessFile( String filename, "rw");
```

FIGURE 15.19 A random access file opened for reading and writing

- void writeInt(int x);
- void writeLong(long x);
- void writeDouble(double x);
- void writeChar(char x);
- void write(int x);
  writes byte x to file.
- void writeBytes(String s);
  writes one byte per character.
- void writeChars(String s);
  writes two bytes per character.

Each method throws an IOException if an I/O error occurs. Additionally, each readX() method throws an EOFException if a read is attempted past the end of the file.

Other methods include:

- int read();
  reads a single byte from a file.
- long length();
  returns the length (in bytes) of a random access file.
- void setLength(long n);
  sets the length of a file to n bytes.
- long getFilePointer();
  returns the offset of the file pointer, in bytes, from the beginning of the file. That is, getFilePointer() returns the current position of the file pointer.
- void seek(long n);
  sets the file pointer to the byte that is n bytes from the beginning of the file. If n exceeds the length of the file, seek() sets the file pointer to the last byte.
- void close();
  closes the file.

Each of the preceding methods throws an IOException if an I/O error occurs.

15.11.1 Fixed-Length Records

Although a file is a sequence of bytes, in practice, data are usually stored in logical units or chunks much larger than a single byte. Such a unit is called a *record*. For example, a "customer record" might consist of three fields:

a name (30 bytes)
an address (50 bytes)
an ID (20 bytes).

Figure 15.20 shows a random access file that holds customer records.

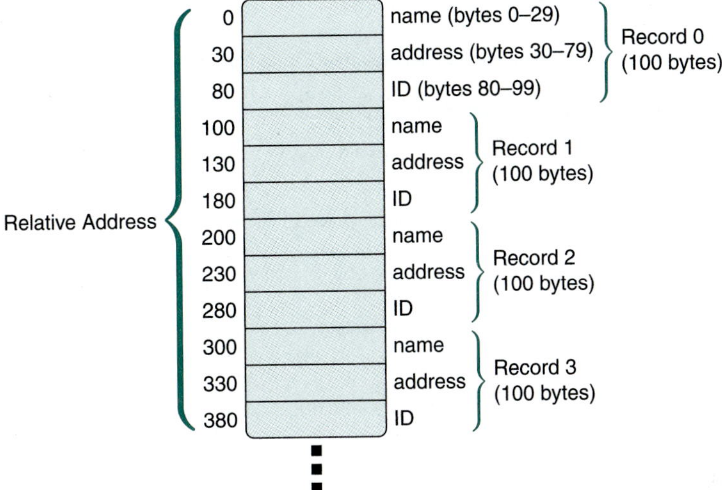

FIGURE 15.20 Each record consists of 100 bytes. Fields are a fixed length.

The records of Figure 15.20 are *fixed length*, that is, the length of each field does not vary from record to record: a customer name is always 30 bytes, an address 50 bytes, and an ID 20 bytes. Every record occupies 100 bytes. Fixed-length records provide easy access to any record. For example, the second record of the file of Figure 15.20 begins at byte 200, the third at byte 300, the 12th record can be found as byte 1200 and the address field in the 34th record is at byte (3400 + 30). Fixed-length records are not mandatory, but they certainly simplify file processing.

In Example 15.9 we create a random access file that contains a number of fixed-length records.

EXAMPLE 15.9

Each year, the Office of Admissions at WeTeach U. creates a random access file containing applicant information. The data for each applicant consists of:

- name (35 characters),
- math SAT score (int),
- verbal SAT score (int),
- writing SAT score (int),
- high school grade point average (double), and
- decision (char: 'A' – accepted; 'R' – rejected; 'W' – waiting list; 'N' – no decision yet).

Problem Statement Write a static utility method that creates a random access file from applicant data. Data are entered interactively.

Java Solution The name field of each record consists of exactly 35 characters. If a student's name contains less than 35 characters, we pad the name with spaces. To keep the example simple, the application does not check for invalid data. Data is entered interactively.

```
import java.io.*;
import java.util.*;

public class CreateRandomAccessFile
{
    public static void makeRandomAccessFile(String filename) throws IOException
    {
        String lName = "", fName = "", name = "", temp = "";
        final int NAME_SIZE = 35;
        int score;
        double gpa;
        int decision;                           // ASCII code number

        // instantiate a random access file object; open the file for reading and writing

        RandomAccessFile out = new RandomAccessFile(filename,"rw");
        out.setLength(0);                                  // make file empty

        Scanner input = new Scanner(System.in);
        System.out.print("Last Name: ");
        lName = input.nextLine();

        while (!lName.equals( ""))
        {
            System.out.print("First Name: ");
            fName = input.nextLine();
            name = lName + " " + fName;

            int size = NAME_SIZE - name.length();       // how many blanks do we need?
            for (int j = 1; j <= size; j++)              // pad the name with blanks
                name = name + " ";
            out.writeChars(name);

            System.out.print("Math: " );                 // Math SAT
            score = input.nextInt();
            out.writeInt(score);

            System.out.print("Verbal: " );               // Verbal SAT
            score = input.nextInt();
            out.writeInt(score);

            System.out.print("Writing: " );              // Writing SAT
            score = input.nextInt();
            out.writeInt(score);

            System.out.print("Grade Point Average: " );  // GPA
            gpa = input.nextDouble();
            out.writeDouble(gpa);
            temp = input.nextLine();

            System.out.print("Decision : ");             // Decision
            decision = System.in.read();
            out.write(decision);
            // move to the next line of input so that the next readLine() is not the null string

            temp = input.nextLine();
```

```
            System.out.print("Last Name: ");
            lName = input.nextLine();
        }
        out.close();
    }
}
```

A small test class follows.

```
import java.util.*;
import java.io.*;
public class TestCreateRandomAccessFile
{
    public static void main(String[] args) throws IOException
    {
        Scanner input = new Scanner(System.in);
        System.out.print("File name: ");
        String filename = input.next();
        CreateRandomAccessFile.makeRandomAccessFile(filename);
    }
}
```

Output The following interactive session creates a random access file, *applicants.dat*, with just three records:

File name: **applicants.dat**
Last Name: **Kent**
First Name: **Clark**
Math: **600**
Verbal: **540**
Writing: **590**
Grade Point Average: **3.3**
Decision : **A**
Last Name: **Parker**
First Name: **Peter**
Math: **500**
Verbal: **450**
Writing: **480**
Grade Point Average: **2.4**
Decision : **R**
Last Name: **Wayne**
First Name: **Bruce**
Math: **500**
Verbal: **510**
Writing: **570**
Grade Point Average: **3.0**
Decision : **W**
Last Name:

Discussion The application prompts the user for each piece of applicant information until the user indicates the end of data by pressing the Enter key when prompted for a last name. The code is easy to follow and uses a number of methods of the RandomAccessFile class.

Each student record contains 91 bytes:

- name—70 bytes, two bytes per character
- math score—4 bytes per integer

- verbal score—4 bytes per integer
- writing score—4 bytes per integer
- gpa—8 bytes per double
- decision—1 byte for 'A', 'R', 'W', or 'N'

The decision is stored as a single byte (ASCII code) because

write(decision) (line 42)

writes one byte to the file. Alternatively, if line 42 were

writeChar(decision),

a two-byte character would have been written to the file and each record would have length 92 bytes.

Note that the CreateRandomAccessFile class does not validate user-supplied data, despite the fact that interactive input is very error prone and data validation is an important part of a "real world" interactive application. Our purpose here is a succinct demonstration of some of the capabilities of RandomAccessFile, so we opt for simplicity.

The next application displays and alters data in the random access file created in Example 15.9.

EXAMPLE 15.10 **Problem Statement** Write an application that accepts the name of an applicant and displays the applicant's admission data. The application should also allow a user to modify the decision status of the applicant. For example, the status of an applicant can change from 'W' (waiting list) to 'A' (accepted).

Java Solution The Applicants class has two methods that manipulate applicant data:

- private long findApplicant(String lastName, String firstName, RandomAccessFile file); and
- public void display(String lastName, String firstName, RandomAccessFile file);

The findApplicants(...) method is a helper method and consequently private. Given an applicant's name, the method locates that applicant's record. If found, the method returns the record number as a long, otherwise the method returns −1. To keep the example simple, we use a linear search.

The display(...) method invokes findApplicants(...) to obtain the record number of a particular applicant, and then displays the applicant's data. The user has the opportunity to change the decision status of the applicant.

The details of these methods follow in the discussion section.

```
import java.io.*;
import java.util.*;

public class Applicants
{
   final int RECORD_LENGTH = 91;                    // bytes
   final int NAME_SIZE = 35;                        // including trailing blanks
```

```
private long findApplicant(String lastName, String firstName, RandomAccessFile file)
                                                           throws IOException

{ // given a name, returns the record number or –1
   String name = "";
   String student = lastName + " " + firstName;
   int size = NAME_SIZE – student.length();                // how many blanks do we need?
   for (int j = 1; j <= size; j++)                          // pad the name with spaces
      student = student + " ";
   long numRecords = file.length()/RECORD_LENGTH; // how many records in the file?
   for (long record = 0; record < numRecords; record++)
   {
      file.seek(RECORD_LENGTH * record);                   // find the next record
      name = "";
      for (int i = 1; i <= NAME_SIZE; i++)
      {
          char ch = file.readChar();
          name = name + ch;
      }
      if (student.equals(name))
          return record;                                    // success, name found
   }
   return –1;                                               // failure, name not found
}

public void display(String lastName, String firstName, RandomAccessFile file)
                                                                     throws IOException

{
   long r = findApplicant(lastName, firstName, file);   // r is the record number
   if (r == –1)
   {
      System.out.println("record for " + lastName + "," + firstName + "not found");
      return;
   }

   file.seek(r * RECORD_LENGTH);            // place file pointer at top of a record
   String name = "";
   char ch;
   for (int i = 1; i <= NAME_SIZE; i++)     // get the name
   {
      ch = file.readChar();
      name = name + ch;
   }
   int math = file.readInt();
   int verbal = file.readInt();
   int writing = file.readInt();
   double gpa = file.readDouble();
   int decision = file.read();
   System.out.println("\n" + name);
   System.out.println(" Math: " + math);
   System.out.println(" Verbal: " + verbal);
   System.out.println(" Writing: " + writing);
   System.out.println(" GPA: " + gpa);
   System.out.println(" Decision : " + ((char)decision));
   System.out.println("To change the decision status enter new decision (A,R,W,N)");
   System.out.println("otherwise press Enter");
   decision = System.in.read();
   if ( (char)decision == 'A' || (char)decision == 'R' ||
       (char)decision == 'W' || (char)decision == 'N' )
   {
```

```
62.       file.seek(r * RECORD_LENGTH + (RECORD_LENGTH - 1)); // the last byte of record r
63.       file.write(decision);
64.       System.out.println ("Decision changed");
65.     }
66.     else
67.       System.out.println("No change in status");
68.   }
69.   public static void main(String[] args) throws IOException
70.   {
71.     Scanner input = new Scanner(System.in);
72.     RandomAccessFile file = new RandomAccessFile("Applicants.dat", "rw");
73.     System.out.print("Last Name: ");
74.     String lName = input.next();
75.     System.out.print("First Name: ");
76.     String fName = input.next();
77.     Applicants aps = new Applicants();
78.     aps.display(lName, fName, file);
79.     file.close();
80.   }
81. }
```

Output

Last Name: **Wayne**
First Name: **Bruce**

Wayne Bruce
 Math: 500
 Verbal: 510
 Writing: 570
 GPA: 3.0
 Decision : W
To change the decision status enter new decision (A, R, W, N)
otherwise press Enter
A
Decision changed

Discussion

Line 5: Each applicant record consists of 91 bytes:

name	(35 Unicode)	70 bytes
math	(1 integer)	4 bytes
verbal	(1 integer)	4 bytes
writing	(1 integer)	4 bytes
gpa	(1 double)	8 bytes
decision	(1 ASCII)	1 byte

Line 6: An applicant's name has exactly 35 characters, including trailing blanks.

Lines 7–28: findApplicant(String lastName, String firstName, RandomAccessFile file)

Lines 12–13: Append spaces to name so that name contains 35 characters.

Line 14: Calculate the number of records in the file. This is straightforward because every record contains the same number of bytes (91).

Lines 13–26: Search the file for the required name.
For each applicant record:

- position the file pointer at the first byte of the record (line 17). Notice that for each record, the statement

```
file.seek(RECORD_LENGTH * record)
```

moves the file pointer to the beginning of that record.

- read the next NAME_SIZE (35) bytes into name.
- if name matches the requested name then return the record number.

Line 27: Return −1 if the search is unsuccessful.

Lines 29–68: display(String lastName, String firstName, RandomAccessFile file)

Line 31: Invoke the helper method, findApplicant(...) that returns the record number, r, of the requested applicant, or −1 if the record is not found.

Lines 32–35: If an applicant's record is not found, print a message and return.

Line 37: Position the file pointer at the first byte of record r.

Lines 38–55: Use the methods of RandomAccessFile to read the data for record r. Display the data on the screen.

Line 58: Accept a new decision value from the user. This is an ASCII code.

Lines 59–65: The last byte of each record in the file stores the character representing the decision about a student. If variable decision is a valid decision ('A', 'R', 'W', or 'N'), reposition the file pointer to the last byte of record r and overwrite this byte with the new decision value.

Lines 69–80: main(...)

Line 72: Instantiate a new RandomAccessFile for both reading and writing.

Lines 73–78: Query the user for the name of an applicant.
Instantiate an Applicants object, aps, which invokes the display(...) method.

Line 79: Close the stream.

15.12 IN CONCLUSION

The Byte Stream, Character Stream, and Random Access classes are not simple, and our coverage provides but an introduction. Even a cursory glance at Sun's documentation should convince you that much more lurks beneath the surface of this chapter. The good news, however, is that the material in this chapter is sufficient for most applications. And, with a bit of practice, using the Stream and Random Access classes will become as natural as programming with loops.

Just the Facts

- A *stream* is an abstraction of the one-way flow of data. Java I/O is built around streams.
- Java provides two categories of stream classes, the Byte Stream classes and the Character Stream classes, each of which is composed of a pair of hierarchies, one for input and one for output.

- The structure of the hierarchies of the Byte Stream and Character Stream classes is similar.
- The root classes of the two hierarchies of the Byte Stream classes are InputStream and OutputStream, and for the Character Stream classes, Reader and Writer. These root classes are abstract, and they declare a variety of methods including read() and print() methods.
- The Character Stream classes, although parallel in structure to the Byte Stream classes, are designed to read and write 2-byte Unicode characters rather than 1-byte ASCII characters.
- The Byte Stream classes can be used independently for byte I/O, but they are more typically used to support the Character Stream classes both for console I/O and file I/O. Indeed, for console I/O, the Character Stream classes use the Byte Stream objects System.in and System.out to perform the physical I/O.
- System.in is an instance of BufferedInputStream, which extends InputStream, and System.out is an instance of PrintStream, which extends OutputStream. These classes belong to the Byte Stream hierarchies. All console I/O is accomplished using System.in and System.out.
- When used with Character Stream classes, System.in, a member of the Byte Stream hierarchy, needs to be double-wrapped: first by an InputStreamReader object and then by a BufferedReader object. InputStreamReader, which extends Reader, serves as a bridge between the BufferedReader object and System.in.
- Wrapping an object means that the functionality of the wrapped object is accessed via the wrapper.
- A *buffer* is memory used to temporarily store output or input. Using a buffer increases the efficiency and speed of I/O. With a buffer, I/O is done mostly to memory and the whole buffer is periodically written to its destination file or read from its source file.
- A file is a sequence of bytes. File access time is slow in comparison to data transfer time. Hence, it is best to use buffers to read/write a block of data from/to a file rather than reading and writing one byte at a time.
- Both the Byte Stream and Character Stream classes provide subclasses with the capability of buffered I/O. The relevant classes are BufferedReader and BufferedWriter for the Character Stream classes, and BufferedInputStream and BufferedOutputStream for the Byte Stream classes.
- Two kinds of files are *text* files and *binary* files. A text file is a special kind of binary file that can be decoded a byte (or two bytes) at a time and displayed as a sequence of characters.
- Each byte of an ASCII text file represents one of 128 characters. Each byte consists of a leading zero followed by a 7-bit ASCII code. A UTF-16 (Unicode) text file encodes each character with two bytes, allowing for many more kinds of characters. Each byte (8 bits) in a binary file can be any one of 256 (2^8) binary patterns and does not necessarily correspond to a displayable character.
- Efficient and convenient output to text files using the Character Stream classes can be complicated. FileWriter objects are simple but slow. Wrapping a File object with a FileWriter object, and then with a BufferedWriter object, ensures efficiency. A final wrapping with a PrintWriter object ensures the convenience of being able to use standard print() and println() methods.
- I/O with binary files is accomplished primarily with the Byte Stream classes, because binary files are not built from characters.

- The DataInputStream and DataOutputStream classes provide many methods for writing and reading primitive data (e.g., integers, float, char, etc.) to and from binary files. Objects of these classes must be wrapped around another Byte Stream object such as a FileInputStream or FileOutputStream object.
- The DataInputStream and DataOutputStream classes are fine for primitive data, but to read and write *objects*, you should use the ObjectInputStream and ObjectOutputStream classes, which provide readObject() and writeObject() methods. These methods can read and write an object only if that object is *serializable*.
- *Serialization* converts an object to a stream of bytes. An object is *serializable* if its class implements the Serializable interface. If you do not want a particular field to be included in the serialization of an object, then declare the field as transient.
- Object I/O with binary files is done by wrapping a File with a FileInputStream or FileOutputStream object and then with an ObjectInputStream or ObjectOutputStream object. Only those objects that implement Serializable can be read or written to binary files.
- A *random access file* provides direct access to any particular byte in the file. Access to a byte is via a *file pointer*. This is in contrast to sequential files, which must be read, in order, from beginning to end.
- The RandomAccessFile class implements the DataInput and DataOutput interfaces and by contract, provides methods to perform I/O with random access files. RandomAccessFile is *not* a stream class.
- The following seven templates can be used to perform most standard I/O tasks. Other options are available, but these should suffice for most common purposes.

1. **Read from the console:**

```
InputStreamReader link = new InputStreamReader(System.in);
BufferedReader br = new BufferedReader(link);
```

   or

```
BufferedReader br = new BufferedReader(new InputStreamReader(System.in));

int ch = br.read();
String s = br.readLine();
```

2. **Write to the console:**

```
System.out.println(String s);
```

3. **Read from a text file:**

```
File file = new File ("myfile.txt");
FileReader fr = new FileReader(file);
BufferedReader br = new BufferedReader(fr);
```

   or

```
BufferedReader br = new BufferedReader(new FileReader("myfile.txt"));

int ch = br.read();
String s = br.readLine();
```

4. **Write to a text file:**

```
File file = new File ("myfile.txt");
FileWriter fw = new FileWriter(file);
BufferedWriter bw = new BufferedWriter(fw);
PrintWriter pw = new PrintWriter (bw);
```

or

```
PrintWriter pw = new PrintWriter (new BufferedWriter(new FileWriter("myfile.txt")));

pw.print(String s);
pw.println(String s);
```

5. **Read from a binary file:**

```
File file = new File ("myfile.dat");
FileInputStream fin = new FileInputStream(file);
DataInputStream in = new DataInputStream(fin);
```

or

```
DataInputStream in = new DataInputStream(new FileInputStream("myfile.dat"));

int readInt();
char read Char();
double readDouble();
```

6. **Write to a binary file:**

```
File file = new File ("myfile.dat");
FileOutputStream fout = new FileOutputStream(fout);
DataOutputStream out = new DataOutputStream(fout);
```

or

```
DataOutputStream out = new DataOutputStream(new
FileOutputStream("myfile.dat"));
out.writeInt(int i);
out.WriteDouble(double d);
out.WriteChar(char ch);
out.writeBytes(String s);
```

7. **Create a random access file:**

```
File file = new File (String filename);
RandomAccessFile raf = new RandomAccessFile(file, “rw”);
```

Bug Extermination

- It is important to check the documentation for any stream class method that you use, especially a constructor, so that you are aware of the checked exceptions that a constructor can throw. Failing to handle a checked exception or to declare a checked exception in a throws clause generates a compiler error.
- When using the stream classes, don't forget the statement import java.io.*;
- Reading from a file one byte at a time means accessing the file 1000 times to read 1000 bytes. This is much slower than accessing the file 10 times, reading 100 bytes each time. A buffer allows your program to access a file fewer times. Use the various Buffered Stream classes to accomplish efficient file I/O.
- To read or write binary data from/to sound files or video files, use the FileInputStream and FileOutputStream classes. However, to read/write text files, use the FileReader and FileWriter classes, typically wrapped with buffered classes.
- FileOutputStream and FileWriter classes normally erase existing files when creating new files, unless you add a boolean append parameter to the constructor with append set to true.

- Before you close a file with f.close(), check that f is not a null reference: if (f != null) {f.close};
- Data Stream, Object Stream, and Buffered Stream objects must always be wrapped around other Byte Stream objects, and *not* directly wrapped around a file.
- Don't forget to implement Serializable if you expect to write the objects to a binary file.
- When using BufferedWriter (Character Stream) or BufferedOutputStream (Byte Stream), make sure that you close the file, otherwise you might lose data remaining in the buffer. The close() method automatically flushes any buffer.
- The DataInputStream class methods do not return –1 when attempting to read past the end of a file. To terminate an input loop, the programmer should check whether an EOFException is thrown. The same technique should be used with the ObjectInputStream class.
- When using the ObjectInputStream class, make sure to downcast the input object to the appropriate class type.

EXERCISES

LEARN THE LINGO

Test your knowledge of the chapter's vocabulary by completing the following crossword puzzle.

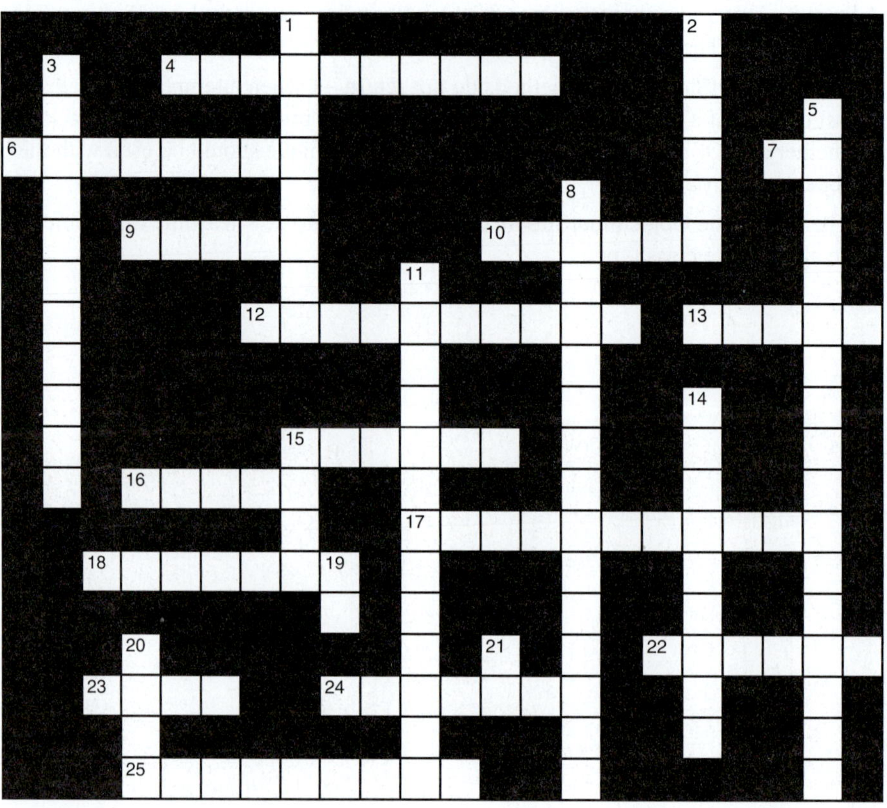

Across

4 To use a BufferedReader object, wrap a File with a _____ and then with BufferedReader.
6 10 is the character code for a _____ (2 words).
7 Console input is done by System _______.
9 Code that uses eight bits for each character
10 Root class of Character Stream hierarchy
12 Files that must be read in order
13 A close operation will also perform a _______.
15 Files that cannot be read with an editor
16 Access to data in a random access file is similar to access to data in a(n) _______.
17 Root class of Byte Stream hierarchy
18 An application accesses a particular byte in a random access file via the file _______.
22 Flow of data
23 Method that sets file pointer
24 A call to read() via a Character Stream object returns a _____ character code.
25 Not serializable

Down

1 Method of BufferedReader that does not have a counterpart in BufferedInputStream
2 Memory used to temporarily store input or output data.
3 Character Stream class for output
5 An object of the _____ class reads bytes and converts those bytes to characters.
8 Class for reading binary files
11 Converts an object to a stream of bytes
14 The _____ Stream classes allow you to write programs that do not depend on any particular character code.
15 It is possible to directly access any particular _____ of a random access file.
19 String that denotes a random access file is open for both reading and writing
20 Files that can be read with an editor
21 Stream classes are in the java._____ package.

SHORT EXERCISES

1. **True or False**
   If false, give an explanation.
   a. All files are random access files.
   b. A text file is composed of binary digits.
   c. A text file is easily displayable and easily read.
   d. A binary file is easily displayable and easily read.
   e. Streams are objects with no methods.
   f. I/O stands for Iodine.
   g. System.in is a member of the InputStream class.
   h. System.out is a descendant of the OutputStream class.
   i. The Byte Stream classes were designed before the Character Stream classes.
   j. Reader and Writer are classes in the Byte Stream hierarchies.
   k. The Byte Stream classes and Character Stream classes are always used independently of each other.
   l. A buffer is used to increase the speed and efficiency of I/O.
   m. A random access file holds records each of which necessarily contains the same number of bytes.

2. **Playing Compiler**
   Explain the error(s) in the segments that follow. If a segment has no errors then say so. Assume all files exist.
   a.
   ```
   import java.io.*;
      File f = new File ("hello.txt");
      BufferedInputStream test = new BufferedInputStream(f);
   ```
   b.
   ```
   import java.io.*;
      File g = new File ("hello.dat");
      FileInputStream test = new FileInputStream(g);
   ```
   c.
   ```
   import java.io.*;
      File h = new File ("goodbye.dat");
      FileInputStream test = new FileInputStream(f);
      FileOutputStream test = new FileOutputStream(f);
   ```
   d.
   ```
   import java.io.*;
      File f = new File ("goodbye.txt");
      DataOutputStream test = new DataOutputStream(f);
   ```
   e.
   ```
   import java.io.*;
      File f = new File ("lastone.dat");
      FileOutputStream test = new FileOutputStream(f);
      DataOutputStream test = new DataOutputStream(f);
   ```

3. **Understanding Stream Hierarchies**
   For each of the following, state whether or not the wrapping is legal. If illegal, explain why.
   a. Wrapping System.in with an InputStreamReader.
   b. Wrapping System.out with an OutputStreamWriter.
   c. Wrapping an InputStreamReader with a BufferedReader.
   d. Wrapping System.in with a FileInputStream.
   e. Wrapping a File with a FileInputStream.
   f. Wrapping a File with a FileReader.
   g. Wrapping a FileReader with a BufferedReader.
   h. Wrapping System.out with a FileWriter.

i. Wrapping a FileWriter with a BufferedWriter.
j. Wrapping a FileOutputStream with a BufferedWriter.
k. Wrapping a File with a FileOutputStream.
l. Wrapping System.out with a PrintWriter.
m. Wrapping System.in with a PrintWriter.
n. Wrapping a File with a BufferedInputStream.
o. Wrapping a BufferedWriter with a PrintWriter.

4. **Playing Compiler**
Determine the problem(s) with each version of the following readCharacterData() methods?

Version I

```
public void readCharacterData()
{
   int c;
   int count = 0;
   InputStreamReader link = new InputStreamReader(System.in);
   BufferedReader br = new BufferedReader(link);
   while ( (c = br.read()) != -1)
   {
      count++;
      System.out.println(c + " " + (char)c);
   }
   System.out.println("Number of Characters: " + count);
}
```

Version II

```
public void readCharacterData() throws IOException
{
   int c;
   int count = 0;
   BufferedReader br = new BufferedReader(System.in);
   while ( (c = br.read()) != -1)
   {
      count++;
      System.out.println(c + " " + (char)c);
   }
   System.out.println("Number of Characters: " + count);
}
```

5. **Stream Concepts**
Associate each type of stream class with its purpose.

Type of Stream Class	Purpose
a. Byte Stream	1. handles binary I/O of primitive data types
b. Character Stream	2. handles I/O from/to the console
c. Buffered Stream	3. optimizes I/O
d. Data Stream	4. handles binary I/O of objects
e. Object Stream	5. handles I/O of raw bytes
f. System.in and System.out	6. handles I/O of 2-byte characters

6. **What's Going On?**
   a. What is the name of the file created by the following program?
   b. Describe the information stored at the beginning of the file (data type, purpose of the data, value of the data).
   c. Describe the information stored in the remainder of the file.

```
import java.io.*;
public class FileWriter
{
    public static void main(String[] args)
    {
        try
        {
            long fillerPos = 0;
            int filler = 1000;
            RandomAccessFile f = new RandomAccessFile("mystery", "rw");
            f.writeLong(0);
            f.writeChars("RalphlikesJava");
            fillerPos = f.getFilePointer();
            f.writeInt(filler);
            f.writeChars("ShailikesCoffee");
            f.seek(0);
            f.writeDouble(fillerPos);
            f.close();
        }

        catch (FileNotFoundException e)
        {
            System.err.println("File not Found " + e);
        }
        catch (IOException e)
        {
            System.err.println("Write Error: " + e);
        }
    }
}
```

7. **Thinking About Streams**
   Figure 15.12 shows a BufferedWriter object wrapped (Character Stream) with a PrintWriter object (Byte Stream).
   a. What was the purpose of wrapping the BufferedWriter object?

   Figure 15.6 shows System.out, an OutputStream object (Byte Stream) wrapped with a PrintWriter object (Byte Stream).
   b. Check Sun's documentation for PrintWriter and explain why it is legal to wrap PrintWriter around objects of two different hierarchies (Byte Stream and Character Stream).
   c. Is it legal to wrap a PrintWriter with a BufferedWriter object? If no, explain why not. If yes, explain a possible rationale for doing so.

8. **Pick the Stream Class(es)**
   For each of the following situations, state which stream class(es) you would use, describe any wrappers involved, and explain your choice.

a. Reading integers from a binary file.
b. Writing characters to a text file.
c. Reading objects from a binary file.
d. Reading characters from a text file.
e. Reading bytes from the console.
f. Reading characters from the console.
g. Writing doubles to the console.
h. Writing doubles to a binary file.
i. Reading strings from a text file.
j. Writing customer records to a file.

PROGRAMMING EXERCISES

1. **Hello World Revisited**
Write an application utilizing System.in and System.out that asks a person to enter his/her first name, and then prints a personalized message saying "hello." For example, your program might print: "Hello Lois", if the user enters the name *Lois*. Do not use a Scanner object.

2. **Text File Output**
Design a program that writes the lowercase letters of the alphabet (a–z) on one line and the uppercase letters (A–Z) on a second (and last) line of a text file called alphabet.txt.

3. **Appending to a Text File**
You can use a FileWriter object to append data to the end of a file:

```
FileWriter writer = new FileWriter (String filename, boolean append);
```

Write a program that opens an existing text file, interactively accepts strings, and writes the strings to the end of the file, one line at a time.

4. **Random Access Files**
The first entry of a random access file is a long value specifying the offset of an integer value somewhere in the middle of the file. Write a program that uses the RandomAccessFile class to display the value of the integer. You will need to create this file to test your program.

5. **Processing Text Files**
Write a program that counts the number of times a particular character occurs in a text file. Your program should prompt for the character.

6. **Text File I/O**
Write a program that reads strings from a text file, data.txt, one string per line, sorts the strings, and writes the sorted strings one per line to a file called sorted.txt.

7. **Character Stream vs Byte Stream**
Write a program that reads 30-byte names from a text file, and a single 30-byte string, name, from the console. The program should print all the names in the file that start with the same first four characters as name. Do this problem first using the Character Stream classes, and then again using only the Byte Stream classes.

8. **Processing Text Files**
Search the Internet for a large text file (say "The Constitution of the USA," but any text file will do, the larger the better). Count and display the number of times each alphabetic character 'a' through 'z' appears in the file. Do not distinguish between uppercase and lowercase characters, and ignore all other characters.

9. **Binary File Output**
Implement an application that interactively accepts double values and writes them to a binary file called data.dat. Write a second application that reads data.dat and reports the number of data as well as the average value of the data.

10. **Binary File I/O**
Write a program that reads double values from a binary file, data.dat, and displays the largest and smallest numbers. If you have not done Programming Exercise 9, you will first need to create a binary file to test your program (see the first half of Programming Exercise 9).

11. **Buffered Versus Non-Buffered Output**
Compare the speed of buffered versus non-buffered output in the Byte Stream classes (as we did in the text for the Character Stream classes). Devise a program that writes 50,000 characters to two different files, once using PrintStream alone and once using PrintStream wrapped with BufferedOutputStream. Compare execution times.

12. **A Serializable Class and a Binary File**
Design and write a class Student with fields that store a name, social security number, number of courses completed, grades for each course, and credits for each course. Include constructors, getter and setter methods, and a method that returns the student's grade point average. Student should implement Serializable. Write a program that accepts data for three students. Store the three Student objects in a binary file called students.dat.
Write a second application that displays the name and gpa field of each Student object stored in the file students.dat.

13. **Binary Search in Random Access Files**
Write a program that creates a random access file that holds a list of *sorted* names. The names are supplied interactively. Pad the names with spaces, if necessary, so that each name consists of the same number of bytes. After the file is created, your program should allow a user to enter a name, and using binary search, determine whether or not the name is in the file. A message confirming or denying the presence of the name should appear on the console.

14. **Storing Objects in Files**
A Tic-Tac-Toe playing program gives a player the option of saving a game so that he/she can continue playing later. A game object stores a 3 by 3 two-dimensional array that holds the x's and the o's currently on the board, and a character "X" or "O" indicating whose turn it is. Write a Game class with methods to save and restore a game object. The default constructor should create an empty board. Include methods that make a move and display the board on the console. Test your class by creating a "game," making a few moves, and saving the "game" in a file using object serialization. Quit the program, restart it, and restore the game. Display the board on the console, along with a message stating whose turn it is.

15. **Putting It All Together—A Short Project Using I/O**
Using an editor or word processor, create a text file movies.txt that contains information about films. Each line of movies.txt holds data for one film:

Title (35 characters)
Year (4 characters)
Director (25 characters)
Star (25 characters)

For example, one line of movies.txt could be

```
The Departed          2006Scorsese, Martin         DiCaprio, Leonardo
```

Movie data is readily available on the Web. The *Internet Movie Database* at *www.imdb.com* is an excellent source. Make the file as large as you like, but have at least 25 entries. The file should not be sorted.

This file serves as input for the following multipart exercise.

a. From movies.txt build a random access file such that each record of the random access file is the same size and of the form:

   Title (35 characters)
   Year (4 characters)
   Director (25 characters)
   Star (25 characters)
   Call the random access file movies.dat.

b. The movies.dat file is unordered, and searches are inefficient. To increase search efficiency, design a *serializable* class, Index. The data consists of:

   - a sorted array (titles) of movie titles,
   - a second parallel array (recordNumber) that holds the record numbers (in movies.dat) of the films, and
   - a field (numFilms) that stores the number of films in movies.dat.

   The following skeleton can be used for Index:

```
public class Index implements Serializable
{
    private String[] titles;
    private long [] recordNumber;          // use long for record number
    private int numFilms;

    // constructors and other methods
    private void sort():                   // a private helper
    public long search(String title);      // binary search
}
```

   Instantiate this class. Build the titles and recordNumber arrays from the data of the random access file: for each record in the random access file, insert the film's title into titles and record number into recordNumber. For example, if movies.dat contains four films, *King Kong*, *Alien, Rodan*, and *Enchanted,* the two arrays are shown in Figure 15.21.
   Sort titles. Each time a title is swapped or moved, a corresponding swap or move should be performed in recordNumber. Figure 15.22 shows the two arrays after titles is sorted.
   Implement a binary search method in your Index class that searches the titles array for a particular title

```
public long search(String title)
```

   Finally, save the Index object to a file called indexfile.dat. This can be done with a single statement because the object is serializable.

c. Write a program that reads the serialized Index object from the file indexfile.dat. You will use this index to perform searches.

   After reading the indexfile.dat and storing the Index object, your program should prompt for the title of a film. Use the binary search of Index to find the title and corresponding record number of that film. If the film is found, access the film's record in the random access file and print the film's data on the screen.

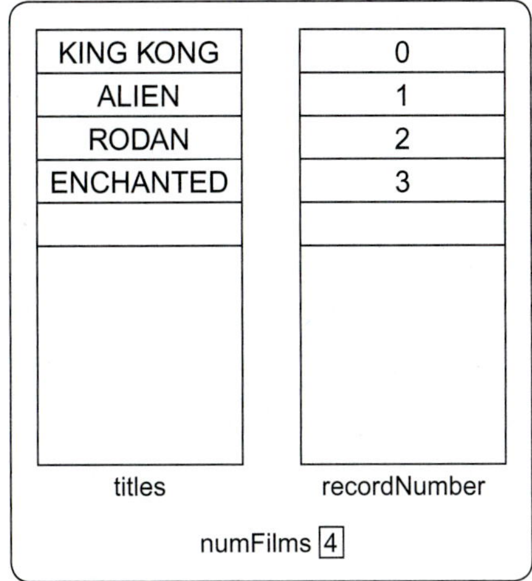

FIGURE 15.21 Parallel arrays

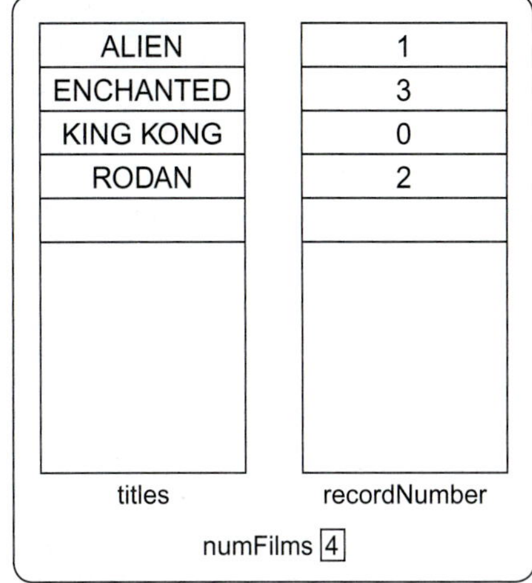

FIGURE 15.22 Two arrays after *titles* is sorted

If the film is not found, print a message. Your program should allow the user to do as many searches as he/she wants.

The user may enter a film title in any form (uppercase, lowercase, or a combination). You must translate the user's title to uppercase characters before searching. Figure 15.23 demonstrates the process.

To find information for **"King Kong"**
1. Search for **"King Kong"** in *titles*
2. Find the corresponding record number in *recordNumber*
3. Retrieve the data from the random access file

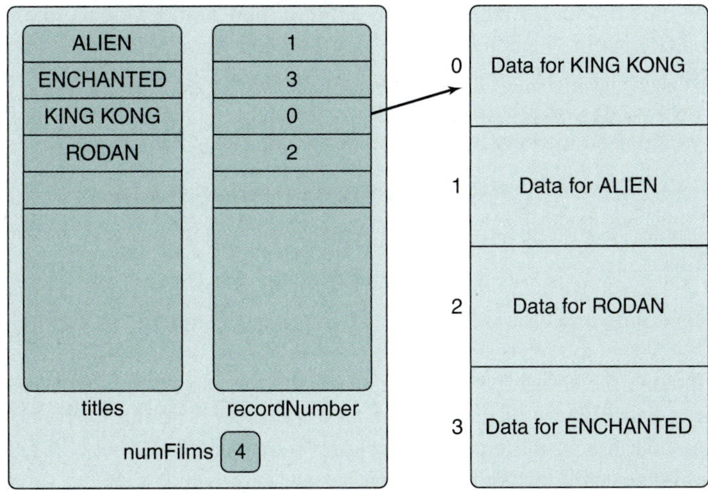

FIGURE 15.23 A random access file to store film data

d. Write a separate application that can alter the information in any record. The program should prompt for the name of the film and use the binary search to find the record number of the film. The program should display the data for the film and ask the user which field he/she would like to change. Finally, the program should prompt for new data and change the appropriate field.

THE BIGGER PICTURE

STREAMS AND NETWORKS

The Client/Server Model

When you run your browser, you are running a *client* program that requests and displays information provided by other programs called *web servers*. In effect, two programs are talking to each other—a client and a server. The same model works for online poker programs, tax-filing programs, and chat rooms. Each user runs a client program, and every client program communicates with a server. The relationship between a client and a server is not symmetric—there are usually many clients for one server, but the reverse is generally not the case.

Sockets

A socket connects a client and a server.

A socket is to a program what a telephone is to a customer service agent—a way to connect. Sockets connect client and server programs via streams over the Internet, while telephones connect people to customer service agents via wires. Just as a telephone number plus an extension connect you to a particular agent at a particular company, so does an IP address and a port number specify a socket that connects to a specific program (or server) running on a particular computer. Just as one company may have many different kinds of customer service agents, so a computer may provide many kinds of services. For example, the same computer can run a web server, a file server, an email server, and a chess-playing server.

The IP address gets you to the right computer, and the port number connects you to the correct server. Every computer has one IP address (or name). Each server program that the computer runs listens for requests on a different port number, hence the need for the client to specify both the machine *and* the port number. Email (SMTP) servers traditionally use port 25, while web servers use port 80. The ports 0 through 1023 are reserved for commonly used servers like these, so if you are writing your own specialized online game server, you would need to choose a port number greater than 1023.

TCP—Communicating Between Sockets Via Streams

Sockets facilitate communication. Both client and server use a socket to effect communication.

Client/server communication is established by creating a stream between the sockets.

Data flows through the stream between the client and server sockets. The server listens for requests from a client. When a client makes a request, the server establishes a connection between the two sockets and answers the request of the client. A stream is created between the two sockets and remains in place until the communication has ended, at which time the stream is closed. Once again, the telephone analogy is apt. You ring someone's phone, she answers, a connection is established, you start to communicate, and each of you hangs up when the call is over.

The stream created between the two sockets is like any other stream that we discuss in this chapter. That is, everything you read in this chapter about file and console I/O works the same way for socket I/O.

Once a stream between sockets is established, it works exactly like a stream between a program and a file.

A stream between sockets of a client and a server program uses a protocol known as TCP—Transfer Control Protocol. It is the first half of the well-known network buzzword TCP/IP. Let's first look at TCP from the client's point of view.

The Java Client Using TCP

If a Java client program wants to create a connection to a server using TCP, the client first creates a Socket object:

```
Socket connectToServer = new Socket("IP address", PortNumber);
```

An IP address consists of four decimal numbers, each between 0 and 255, separated by dots. For example,

```
Socket connectToServer = new Socket("138.212.135.12", 8080);
```

means: create a socket called connectToServer and attempt to connect to the machine with IP address 138.212.135.12 on port 8080.

You can also use the machine's name:

```
Socket connectToServer;
ConnectToServer = new Socket("client.tester.com", 8080);
```

The name client.tester.com is automatically translated to its IP address behind the scenes by another program called a domain name server (DNS), which happens also to be a client/server program.

Because creating a new socket can throw an IOException, a more "exception" friendly way to open the socket is:

```
Socket connectToServer;
try
   {
      connectToServer = new Socket("Machine name", PortNumber);
   }
   catch (IOException e)
   {
      System.out.println(e);
   }
```

Although this is indeed a better way to establish a connection, because the code gets cumbersome and is distracting, we leave out all try-catch blocks in further examples.

The Java Server Using TCP

We have seen how a client connects to a server. Now let's look at the situation from the server's vantage point. To answer the connection requests of clients and establish a stream, the server does two things.

1. Create a ServerSocket object and specify the port on which it listens.
2. Use the ServerSocket object to accept a connection and create a Socket object to connect to clients.

The following segment performs both of these tasks:

```
1. ServerSocket serverSocket = newServerSocket(8080);
   // any port number greater than 1023 is acceptable.
2. Socket connectToClient;                   // declare a Socket to communicate with a client
   connectToClient = serverSocket.accept();  // listen for a request and make the connection
```

THE BIGGER PICTURE

The server waits for a request from a client. This request is processed behind the scenes by the ServerSocket method accept(), which returns a Socket object that the server uses to communicate with the client.

Connecting Two Sockets in Java with a Stream for TCP

When the two Sockets connectToClient and connectToServer are created, a stream between them can be established using the Socket methods getInputStream() and getOutputStream(). See Figure 15.24.

Server	Client
ServerSocket serverSocket = new ServerSocket(*port number*);	Socket connectToServer = new Socket (*IP address, port number*);
Socket connectToClient = serverSocket.accept();	DataInputStream inFromServer; DataOutputStream outToServer;
DataInputStream inFromClient; DataOutputStream outToClient;	inFromServer = new DataInputStream(connectToServer.getInputStream());
inFromClient = new DataInputStream(connectToClient.getInputStream());	outToServer = new DataOutputStream(connectToServer.getOutputStream());
outToClient = new DataOutputStream(connectToClient.getOutputStream());	
// When these streams are established, all input from // *inFromClient* comes from the client, and all output to // *outToClient* goes to the client.	// When these streams are established, all input from // *inFromServer* comes from the server, and all output // to *outToServer* goes to the server.

FIGURE 15.24 Client and server sockets and streams

All the methods of the DataInputStream and DataOutputStream classes are available. For example, the *server* segment

```
int x = inFromClient.readInt();
outToClient..write(x * x);
```

reads an integer x from the client and sends x^2 back to the client.

Of course, you are not limited to using DataInputStream and DataOutputStream. If another subclass of InputStream or OutputStream is more convenient, then by all means use it. For example, the following segment utilizes the BufferedReader and PrintWriter classes:

```
Socket connectToServer = new Socket(host, portnum);

BufferedReader inFromServer = new BufferedReader (
        new InputStreamReader(connectToServer.getInputStream()));
PrintWriter outToServer =
        new PrintWriter(connectToServer.getOutputStream());
```

When the client is finished communicating, it "hangs up the phone," closing the connection with the server, by closing the streams and then closing the socket:

```
inFromServer.close();
outToServer.close();
connectToServer.close();
```

The server hangs up similarly:

```
inFromClient.close();
outToClient.close();
connectToClient.close();
```

A server can communicate simultaneously with multiple clients. Indeed, the server may continue listening to other clients' requests even after it closes a communication with a previous client. In order to completely shut down the server, the listening ServerSocket object must be closed, using:

```
serverSocket.close();
```

This ensures that no new client connection requests are processed.

Multiple Clients

Although our earlier examples illustrate one-client communication, it is commonplace for a server to handle many clients at the same time. How does a server manage this simultaneous processing? Multiple clients are processed by opening a separate socket for each client that requests one. A separate *process* in the server, called a *thread*, is created for each new socket. Each thread runs independently and simultaneously, allowing each client the full attention of the server. Threads have many different uses, but further discussion is beyond the scope of this text.

Summary: How to Establish a Stream Between Sockets for TCP in Java

When programming a client, you must:

1. Open a Socket requesting a connection to a particular server at a particular port.
2. Open a stream to the Socket.
3. Read from and write to the stream to communicate with the server.
4. Clean up.

When programming a server, you must:

1. Open a ServerSocket to listen for client requests on a specific port.
2. Open a Socket to a particular client in response to the client's request.
3. Open a stream to the Socket.
4. Read from and write to the stream to communicate with the client.
5. Clean up.

Exercise

1. Client and Server Classes

How is your monthly payment calculated when you borrow money for the purchase of a new car? How much interest are you paying over the life of your loan? What is the monthly payment on a $200,000, 30-year mortgage at 6% interest?

The formula

$$Payment = \frac{(loan)(r)(1 + r)^n}{(1 + r)^n - 1}$$

gives your monthly payment on a loan such that:

- *loan* is the amount of money borrowed (in dollars),
- r is the annual interest rate divided by 12,
- n is the total number of payments.
  ($n = years * 12$ where *years* is the term of the loan, in years).

For example, if you borrow $50,000 at 6% for 5 years,

loan = 50,000

$r = .06/12 = .005$, and

$n = 5 * 12 = 60$

so

$$Payment = \frac{(50000)(.005)(1.005)^{60}}{(1.005)^{60} - 1} \approx 966.64$$

Implement two classes, a server and a client. The client supplies the server with a loan amount, interest rate, and term in years. The server calculates the monthly payment as well as the total interest over the term of the loan and sends that information back to the client.

If you have access to a network, you might implement these two classes on different computers. The name of the computer that hosts the server can be obtained by executing the following main() method:

```
public static void main(String[] args)
{
    InetAddress host;

    try
    {
      host = InetAddress.getLocalHost();
      System.out.println("Local host is " + host.getHostName());
    }
    catch (UnknownHostException e )
    {
      System.out.println("Unable to get local host name");
    }
}
```

For example, if the name of the host machine is Bingo, then the client might use a constructor

```
Socket connectToServer = new Socket("Bingo", 1776);
```

If you do not have access to a network, you can run both client and server on a single computer. In that case, you can use the string "localhost" in the constructor:

```
Socket connectToServer = Socket("localhost", 1776 );
```

The communication protocol between the client and server is short, simple, and sweet. The server should accept the loan amount, the interest rate, and the term from the client, perform the appropriate calculations, and return the monthly payment and total interest to the client.

The server must be running before the client begins. Use Figure 15.24 as a guide when writing these classes. The server should continually serve the client until the client enters 0 for a loan amount. Once the client enters 0 for a loan amount, the client exits and the server subsequently exits.

Protocols

Client-server communication of the previous example is simple, straightforward, and predictable. In more complex client-server architectures, a more complicated scheme is required to synchronize communication, as you will see in the next exercise.

People speak on a telephone using a combination of intuition and good manners, ensuring that communication is clear and that one person does not interrupt the other. Humans are robust and adaptive, and most people handle this challenge effortlessly. Nonetheless, there are protocols that help us succeed. For example, when we answer a phone call we say "hello." Before ending a call, we say "okay, I gotta go," and then we exchange "goodbyes."

Without these protocols, a simple phone call would become a great challenge. Imagine the confusion you might experience if you called a friend and she did *not* say "hello" when she picked up the phone, but instead remained silent, waiting for you to speak first, as a very young child might do. Would you be annoyed if a person ended a call with no warning after you finished a sentence? Whether we are conscious of it or not, a set of protocols guides us through every conversation. And, if humans need protocols for smooth communication, then all the more so do machines.

How do a client and server communicate smoothly? How can we make sure that one doesn't "hang up" while the other is still communicating? Programs are not as flexible as people, so the protocols for programs need to be more rigid.

> Every client-server pair follows a *protocol*.

A rigid protocol for communication is specified for the client/server pair. The programmers of the client and server must know the protocol and abide by it, guaranteeing smooth communication up to the "goodbye" and the cleanup. The more complicated the communication, the more detailed the protocol needs to be. The protocol is as much a part of client/server programs as the method signatures. In the following exercise, you will see an example of a client-server protocol for an SMTP mail server.

Exercise

2. A Simplified SMTP Client

The SMTP protocol establishes how clients send email to email servers. Every time an email message is sent, a client connects to an SMTP server and initiates a conversation. The standard port for SMTP conversations is port 25.

There are hundreds of thousands of SMTP servers running, ready to accept mail and send it onward. Your job is to write a client program to communicate with an SMTP server.

The SMTP protocol is simple, but for the purposes of this exercise you do not need to look up the formal specification. A study of the following transcript between a server and a client on port 25 provides all that you need.

```
1. Server: 220 mail.example.edu Microsoft ESMTP MAIL Service,
   Version 6.0 Ready at Sun, 1 Mar 2007 10:10:00 -0400
2. Client: HELO location.com
3. Server: 250 mail.example.edu Hello [76.13.135.245]
4. Client: MAIL FROM:user@location.com
5. Server: 250 user@location.com....Sender Ok
6. Client: RCPT TO:person@example.edu
7. Server: 250 person@example.edu
8. Client: DATA
9. Server: 354 Start mail input; end with <CRLF>.<CRLF>
10.Client: Subject: test message
11.Client: From: user@location.com
12.Client: To: person@example.edu
```

```
13.Client:
14.Client: Hello,
15.Client: This is me sending you an email.
16.Client: Goodbye.
17.Client:
18.Server: 250 Ok: Queued mail for delivery
19.Client: QUIT
20.Server: 221 mail.example.edu Service closing transmission
   channel
```

Comments

Line 1: The server starts the conversation by identifying itself. Notice that the line starts with a 3-digit code, 220. This code means everything is fine—talk to me. The rest of the line is information about the server, and the extent of detail varies from server to server. Your client needs only look for the 220 and then continue, otherwise close the connection.

Line 2: The client sends HELO and identifies itself as location.com. The protocol is case sensitive. HELO is mandatory. The identification is optional.

Line 3: The server sends a 250 code meaning "okay go ahead." The rest is the server's name followed by Hello followed by the IP address of location.com looked up by a domain name server (DNS) and translated to an IP address. The client is looking for the 250 code.

Line 4: MAIL FROM: is mandatory, and then any text can follow. In this case, the client is identifying the sender as user@location.com.

Line 5: The server gives an okay code 250, repeats the name of the sender, and says Sender Ok.

Line 6: The client specifies to whom the mail is being sent using RCPT TO: followed by the email address of the intended recipient, in this case person@example.edu.

Line 7: Server replies with 250—the "okay code", followed by the intended recipient of the email.

Line 8: DATA—The client tells the server to get ready for the message.

Line 9: The server replies with a 354 code followed by a reminder to the client to type

CRLF.CRLF

after transmitting the email message (i.e., enter key, a period alone on a single line, enter key).

Lines 10–16: The client sends a message using the standard mail headers.

Line 17: The client finishes with CRLF.CRLF.

Line 18: The server is happy. A 250 "okay" code is sent—message received and queued for delivery.

Line 19: QUIT—bye bye.

Line 20: Code 221—goodbye.

Write a client program to send yourself an email message from yourself through an SMTP server. Due to firewalls, and/or various restrictions of different SMTP servers, you will have more success if you try to connect to the SMTP server that serves your email address. For example, to send email to/from person@myprovider.net, you would open a connection on port 25 to the SMTP server for myprovider.net, which is typically mail.myprovider.net.

As a client, you read server codes and send appropriate commands to the server. There are more server codes than the ones you see in this example (error codes and such), however, you can assume for the purposes of this exercise that the 220, 221, 250, and 354 server codes are the only ones that you will ever see. If you do read another code, assume something went wrong and just close the channel. A more sophisticated client program might also read and store the *non-code* information sent by the server in an attempt to recover if anything goes wrong. Your program doesn't need to do that.

There are additional client commands in the complete SMTP protocol, but you should make do with the subset given here: (HELO, MAIL FROM:, RCPT TO:, DATA, QUIT).

CHAPTER 16

Data Structures and Generics

"The Queue Principle: The longer you wait in line, the greater the likelihood that you are standing in the wrong line."

—Anonymous

Objectives

The objectives of Chapter 16 include an understanding of

- generic classes,
- elementary data structures:
  - ArrayList,
  - stack,
  - queue,
  - linked list, and
- the efficient use of a data structure.

16.1 INTRODUCTION

A *data structure* is a collection of data together with a well-defined set of operations for storing, retrieving, managing, and manipulating the data.

An array is a data structure containing a collection of elements of the same type and with operations for storing and retrieving individual elements. A file is also a data structure.

There are dozens of data structures, and a comprehensive survey of even the most commonly used data structures is well beyond the scope of this book. In this chapter, we study four fundamental data structures including ArrayList, stack, queue, and linked list.

Every data structure entails an *implementation*. An implementation of a data structure consists of an underlying storage structure along with appropriate methods that manipulate the data.

The choice of implementation plays an important role in program efficiency. For example, an array is usually implemented with a contiguous sequence of equal-size memory elements. In line with the principles of encapsulation and information hiding, the implementation details are important for the designer of the data structure, but should be invisible to the client. In the following sections, we examine the implementation of the four data structures: ArrayList, stack, queue, and linked list, and we discuss the advantages and disadvantages of each.

We begin with ArrayList, a data structure that is part of the java.util package.

16.2 THE "OLD" *ArrayList* CLASS

An *array* holds an indexed, contiguous collection of data of a single type.

Arrays are an essential part of our programming toolbox. Arrays facilitate the implementation of many fundamental algorithms, including sorting and searching algorithms; however, arrays have limitations. For instance, once an array is instantiated and its size declared, the size cannot be altered. In situations when the number of data is known in advance, this restriction presents no difficulty. However, for many applications, it is impossible to predict the number of data. Certainly "dynamic arrays," which grow as needed, would offer a convenience not provided by ordinary arrays. Java's ArrayList class, implemented in java.util, provides that very convenience.

An ArrayList object is an indexed list of references that can grow as the number of data increases.

That is, an ArrayList can resize itself, if necessary. An ArrayList is indeed a dynamic array. There are other differences between ArrayLists and standard arrays. Unlike an ordinary array, an ArrayList does not hold primitive values; an ArrayList stores references and only references. However, this is not a serious limitation nor even an inconvenience because Java implements autoboxing and unboxing. Thus, primitive data can be automatically wrapped in objects and subsequently stored using an ArrayList.

Prior to Java 1.5, every ArrayList was a list of Object references. Because all classes extend Object, a single ArrayList might store references to various and sundry objects. That is, a single ArrayList might store references to Strings, Integers, Doubles, and even Dog and Cat objects. Although this generality sounds convenient and enticing, it can lead to runtime problems. So, let's turn back the clock a bit, consider the ArrayList of old, and take a look at its deficiencies as well as Java's solution: *generics*.

The constructors of the original ArrayList class are:

- public ArrayList();
  instantiates an ArrayList that is empty and sets the initial capacity to 10.
- public ArrayList(int initialSize);
  instantiates an ArrayList that is empty and sets the initial capacity to initialSize.

A few methods that manipulate the data of an ArrayList are:

- void add(int index, Object o)
  inserts o into position index. In order to make room for o, the item currently stored at position index is shifted "down" to position index + 1. All items stored in locations greater than index are also shifted down one position.
- boolean add(Object o)
  adds o to the end of the list. The boolean return value is necessary because ArrayList implements Java's Collection interface. For our purposes, we can ignore the return value.
- void clear()
  removes all objects from the list.

- boolean contains (Object o)
  returns true if o is a member of the list.
- Object get(int index)
  returns the Object reference at position index.
- boolean isEmpty()
  returns true if the list has no elements.
- boolean remove (Object o)
  If o is a member of the list, this method removes the first occurrence of o from the list, returns true, and shifts all elements following o "up" one position—that is, an item following o and located in position index is moved "up" one position from index to index − 1.
- Object remove (int index)
  removes and returns a reference to the object o that is currently at position index; shifts all elements following o up one position.
- Object set (int index, Object o)
  replaces the object at position index with o; returns a reference to the object that was replaced.
- int size()
  returns the number of objects currently in the list.
- Object[] toArray()
  returns the objects of a list as an array reference.

The following segment constructs an ArrayList that holds four String references.

```
ArrayList list = new ArrayList(); // initial capacity is 10
list.add("Bart");
list.add("Marge");
list.add("Maggie");
list.add("Homer", 0); // places "Homer" in position 0, shifts other objects
```

Figure 16.1 shows the contents of list after these statements execute.

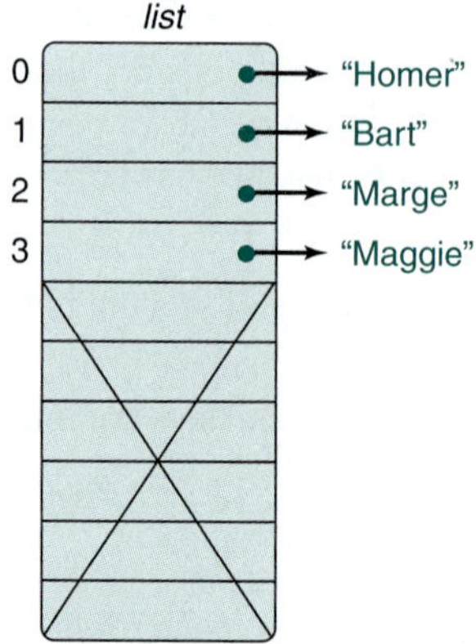

FIGURE 16.1 An *ArrayList* object

Even though the initial capacity of list is 10, a call to get(i) for any i > 3 results in a runtime error. For example, a test such as

```
if (list.get(4) == null)
```

results in a runtime error.

In contrast, the method call

```
list.add(4, o)
```

adds o to the end of the list, while the method calls list.add(5, o), list.add(6, o), and so on, do not succeed unless first preceded by the call, list.add(4, o).

Example 16.1 uses an object belonging to ArrayList to manage a "junior" lottery.

EXAMPLE 16.1

Each year, Sleepy Hollow Elementary School holds a "Principal for a Day" lottery. A student can participate by entering his/her name and ID number into a pool of candidates. The winner is selected randomly from all entries. Each student is allowed one entry.

Problem Statement Implement a class StudentLottery, with methods that

- enter students in the "Principal for a Day" lottery, and
- pick a winner from the entries.

The application should check that no student enters the lottery more than once.

Java Solution The following Student class encapsulates a student. A Student object holds a student's name as well as his/her ID number. The Student class has the usual getter and setter methods. Further, Student overrides the equals(Object o) method inherited from Object so that two students are equal if they have the same name and ID number.

The *Student* class

```
public class Student
{
   private String name;
   private String id;

   public Student()
   {
      name = "";
      id = "";
   }

   public Student (String n, String idNum)
   {
      name = n;
      id = idNum;
   }

   public String getName()
   {
      return name;
   }

   public String getID()
   {
      return id;
   }
```

```
   public void setName(String n)
   {
      name = n;
   }
   public void setID(String idNum)
   {
      id = idNum;
   }
   public boolean equals(Object o) // name and id are the same
   {
      return ( (((Student)o).name).equals(name) &&
      (((Student)o).id).equals(id) );
   }
}
```

The following StudentLottery class uses an ArrayList, entries, to hold Student references. Additionally, the class has methods:

void addStudents()

that enters students in the lottery and

void pickWinner().

The latter uses the Random class to select one winner from among all student entries. The addStudents() method checks that there are no duplicate entries. When all students are entered, the name of the winning student and his/her ID are displayed.

The *StudentLottery* class

```
import java.util.*;

public class SchoolLottery
{
   private ArrayList entries;                    // holds Student references
   public SchoolLottery()
   {
      entries = new ArrayList(250);              // initial capacity is 250
   }

   public void addStudents()
   {
      // prompts for student names and ID numbers
      // adds students to entries list
      // does not allow duplicate entries
      Scanner input = new Scanner(System.in);
      System.out.println("Press Enter to end input");
      System.out.print("Name: ");
      String name = input.nextLine();
      do
      {
         System.out.print("ID: ");
         String id = input.nextLine();
         Student student = new Student(name, id);
         if (!entries.contains(student))         // only one entry per student
         {
            entries.add(student);
            System.out.println(name + " entered in the lottery.");
         }
         else
```

```
65.                System.out.println(name + " not entered.");
66.            System.out.print("\nName: ");
67.            name = input.nextLine();
68.        } while (! name.equals(""));                    // signals end of data
69.        pickWinner();
70.    }
71.    public void pickWinner()
72.    {
73.        // chooses a random entry and displays winners name and ID
74.        int numEntries = entries.size();                // size of ArrayList
75.        Random random = new Random();
76.        Object winner = entries.get(random.nextInt(numEntries));
77.        System.out.print("The winner and Principal for a Day is ");
78.        System.out.println (((Student)winner).getName());  // note the cast to Student
79.        System.out.print("The ID of the winner is ");
80.        System.out.println (((Student)winner).getID());
81.    }
82.    public static void main(String[] args)
83.    {
84.        SchoolLottery lottery = new SchoolLottery();
85.        lottery.addStudents();
86.    }
87. }
```

Output

Press Enter to end input

Name: **Ichabod Crane**
ID: **27512**
Ichabod Crane entered in the lottery.

Name: **Brom Bones**
ID: **34786**
Brom Bones entered in the lottery.

Name: **Katrina Van Tassel**
ID: **978621**
Katrina Van Tassel entered in the lottery.

Name: **Washington Irving**
ID: **23405**
Washington Irving entered in the lottery.

Name:
The winner and Principal for a Day is Katrina Van Tassel
The ID of the winner is 978621

Discussion Notice the casts on lines 78 and 80 in StudentLottery. The reference winner refers to an Object (line 76). The Java compiler does not know that winner is also a Student reference that can invoke getName() and getId(). Consequently, a downcast on line 78 is necessary. Without the cast, the compiler issues the following syntax error:

```
cannot find symbol
symbol : method getName()
location: class java.lang.Object
                    System.out.println ((winner).getName());
```

Likewise, the downcast on line 80 is necessary.

As you know, an ArrayList holds references to objects of *any* class. Consequently, the statements

```
entries.add(new Student( "Ichabod Crane", "34786");   // add a Student
entries.add("Brom Bones");                             // add a String
entries.add(52);                                       // autoboxing here
                                                       // same as entries.add(new Integer(52))
```

place a Student reference, a String reference, and an Integer into the ArrayList entries declared in Example 16.1. There is no problem here; all objects are Objects. The Java compiler is happy. Figure 16.2 shows entries after these lines execute.

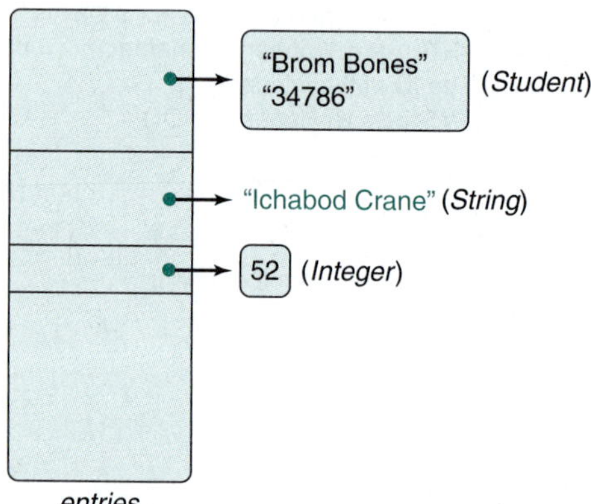

FIGURE 16.2 An *ArrayList* can refer to objects of different classes

This flexibility may seem appealing, but it has drawbacks. When the corresponding class file executes, a *runtime error* occurs, the application halts, and the JVM issues the following message:

The winner and Principal for a Day is Exception in thread "main" java.lang.Class **CastException: java.lang.Integer**

What happened? In this case, the "winner" of the lottery turns out to be the Integer object with value 52. Recall that Integer(52) is stored in entries and can be randomly selected as the winner. The cast on line 78,

```
System.out.println(((Student) winner).getName());
```

causes the runtime error. Because winner is an Integer, winner cannot be cast to Student. The program crashes.

The ArrayList, entries, is not *type safe*. The program performs an operation, a cast, that is inappropriate for a particular data type. The error slips by the compiler because, at compile time, the compiler cannot determine whether or not winner belongs to Student. The error surfaces only when the program runs and an incorrect cast is attempted.

In many applications, an ArrayList is *intended* to hold a single type of reference. In fact, the ability to refer to objects of different classes can be a liability leading to runtime errors, some more serious than an incorrect cast. Java 1.5 introduces *generics*, which ensures type safety and allows the *compiler* to detect type errors *before* an application runs.

16.3 GENERICS AND *ArrayList<E>*

> A *generic* class is one that allows you to specify the data type of one or more fields as a parameter.

For example, the following segment declares and instantiates three different ArrayList objects, each capable of holding references to one and only one type of object.

```
1. ArrayList<Student> students = new ArrayList<Student>();
2. ArrayList<String>strings = new ArrayList<String>(50);
3. ArrayList<Integer>numbers = new ArrayList<Integer>();
```

The ArrayList students is restricted to Student objects; strings to Strings; and numbers to Integer objects. Here we have three lists such that each list holds references to objects of a single, specified type. The statement

```
students.add("Ichabod Crane");        // "Ichabod Crane" is a String not a Student!
```

cannot slip by the compiler. The compiler flags the error and issues the following message:

```
cannot find symbol
symbol : method add(java.lang.String)
location: class java.util.ArrayList<Student>
list.add("Ichabod Crane");
              ^
```

The list students holds Student references, not String references, and the compiler knows this.

The generic version of ArrayList is denoted as

```
ArrayList<E>.
```

where E is a placeholder or *type parameter* for some well-defined reference type such as String, Student, or Integer.

The following segments demonstrate how to instantiate an ArrayList<E> object:

- ```
  ArrayList <Student>students;
            students = new ArrayList<Student>();       // holds Student references
  ```
- ```
  ArrayList <String>strings = new ArrayList<String>();  // holds String references
  ```

Indeed, the statements

```
ArrayList<Student>entries = new ArrayList<Student>();
entries.add(new Integer(52));
entries.getName();
```

do not trigger a runtime error because they are caught first by the compiler. An error is flagged at the compilation stage:

```
add(Student) in ArrayList<Student>cannot be applied to (java.lang.Integer)
                entries.add(new Integer(52));
```

The error message asserts that a reference to an Integer object cannot be placed in a list that is declared to hold references to Student objects. The type mismatch must be fixed *before* the application runs.

Using the ArrayList<E> class, the SchoolLottery class of Example 16.1 can be rewritten as:

```
37.     import java.util.*;

38.     public class GenericSchoolLottery
39.     {
40.        private ArrayList<Student> entries;              // holds Student references
41.        public GenericSchoolLottery()
42.        {
43.           entries = new ArrayList<Student>(250);  // initial capacity is 250
44.        }

45.        public void addStudents()
46.        {
47–69.           // as in Example 16.1
70.        }

71.        public void pickWinner()
72.        {
73.           // chooses a random entry and displays winner's name and ID
74.           int numEntries = entries.size();               // size of ArrayList
75.           Random random = new Random();
76.           Student winner = entries.get(random.nextInt(numEntries));
77.           System.out.print("The winner and Principal for a Day is ");
78.           System.out.println (winner.getName());         // no cast necessary
79.           System.out.print("The ID of the winner is ");
80.           System.out.println (winner.getID());           // no cast necessary
81.        }
82.     }
```

An ArrayList<Student> object is declared and instantiated on lines 40 and 43. In this revised version of Example 16.1, the return type of get() (line 76) is Student, not Object. The compiler knows that entries holds Student references. Also, a cast is no longer needed on lines 78 and 80. Again, the compiler knows that winner is a reference to a Student object. Of course, any subclass of Student is also a Student, so the array entries and the variable winner can also refer to Student subclass objects. The compiler is a gatekeeper: only Student references are allowed.

> The most far-reaching benefit the generic ArrayList<E> class is that the compiler can recognize type mismatches before the program runs and subsequently crashes.

16.3.1 A Few More Facts About Java Generics

In general, a generic class has the form

ClassName $<E_1, E_2, \ldots, E_n>$

where E_i are type parameters. Each E_i is a stand-in or placeholder for some reference type. That is, the arguments supplied in place of each E_i cannot be primitive types.

Restrictions on Generics

Java places some restrictions on the uses of generics. Two of them are:

- Java does not allow generic arrays. The statement

  ```
  E[] myArray = new E[size];              // illegal
  ```

  attempts to create an array called myArray that holds elements of type E. This is illegal; instead, use an explicit cast, such as

  ```
  E[] myArray = (E[]) new Object[size];   // legal
  ```

  Be aware, however, that the Java compiler will issue a warning to the effect that the cast *may* be unsafe. Because of the way that Java implements generics, the compiler has no way of knowing whether or not this type of cast is safe. Consequently, the compiler generates a warning message.

- Java does not permit instantiation of a generic type. For example, the method

  ```
  public illegalMethod (E t)
  {
     E copy = new E(); // illegal
     // other statements
  }
  ```

  generates a compilation error.

Generics, Inheritance, and Polymorphism

The use of inheritance in combination with generics naturally imposes a helpful limitation on the kinds of types allowed. For example, the class declaration

```
public className <T extends P>
```

restricts type parameter T to the class P and its subclasses.

Consider the following small class that contains the method

```
double findAverage().
```

The method is supposed to calculate and return the average value of data in an array, list. The type parameter T is intended to be a numeric type such as Integer, Double, Float, Byte, Short, or Long.

```
public class Average<T > // DOES NOT COMPILE
{
   private T[] list;
   public Average(T[] l)
   {
      list = l;
   }
   public double findAverage()
   {
      double sum = 0.0;
      for (int i = 0; i < list.length; i++)
         sum = sum + list[i].doubleValue();
         return sum/list.length;
   }
}
```

Not surprisingly, the compiler voices the following objection:

```
java:12: cannot find symbol
symbol : method doubleValue()
location: class java.lang.Object
                     sum += list[i].doubleValue();
```

This message makes perfect sense because the compiler does not know the data type of list and in theory, list can be any type. Indeed, to the compiler, the type of list is Object. In practice, however, the method is meant to handle numeric types. Since each numeric type extends the abstract class Number, we rewrite the class declaration as:

```
public class Average<T extends Number>.
```

Now the only permissible types are those that extend Number, and the compiler knows that Number has a doubleValue() method. T is restricted; T is bounded. There is no compiler error related to the doubleValue(). Here we have one more example of polymorphism.

16.3.2 Which Is Better, *ArrayList<E>* or Array?

Is an ArrayList<E> object preferable to an array? Not necessarily. One advantage that ArrayList<E> has is that the ArrayList<E> class supplies simple and convenient insertion and removal methods. A call to add(i, x) makes room for element x and places x into the list at position i. An array has simpler capabilities, and general insertions and deletions must be programmed explicitly. Another advantage, of course, is that an ArrayList<E> object can resize itself, while the size of an array remains fixed. Nonetheless, the advantages of ArrayList<E> come with a cost: longer execution time.

Behind the scenes, Java's implementation of the ArrayList<E> class uses an array for storage. An ArrayList<E> object resizes itself by copying all data into a new, larger array. Obviously, this takes time. Furthermore, with each insertion or deletion, elements may be shifted to make room for the new element or to close the gap left by the removal. If elements are added or removed from or near the end of an ArrayList<E> object, the operations are not so costly, but additions and removals near the beginning require shifting almost every element in the list. Moreover, recall that an ArrayList<E> stores object references, not primitives. Storing and retrieving primitives requires autoboxing and unboxing, which takes time. Storing primitives in an array does not entail this cost.

Therefore, if an application is not time-critical, or if the time payoff is worth the convenience of the automatic insertion/removal methods and resizing capability, then ArrayList<E> is a good choice. On the other hand, many array operations are faster than ArrayList<E> operations. For example, access to elements in an ArrayList<E> requires an method call; array access is direct. If you do not plan to make extensive use of the automatic methods provided by ArrayList<E>, and you are able to avoid resizing the array, then an array is probably a better choice. Resizing can be avoided by instantiating an array large enough to handle the maximum number of elements. That is, you trade memory usage for time, a classic software engineering choice.

In short, the choice of array or ArrayList<E> depends on the application. Each has advantages and drawbacks.

16.4 A STACK

Like an ArrayList, a *stack* is a dynamic ordered list of data. In contrast to an ArrayList, items can be added to and removed from just one end of the list, the *top of the stack*. Thus, access to a stack is more restrictive than access to an ArrayList. Ironically, it is precisely this restriction that makes a stack especially useful.

A well-worn analogy compares a stack to a pile (or stack) of trays in a cafeteria. When you remove a tray from the pile, you take the top tray (well, most people do!); when you return a tray, you again place it on the top of the pile. You remove and add trays to the top of the pile of trays. Similarly, you add (or *push*) and remove (or *pop*) elements from the *top* of the stack. See Figure 16.3.

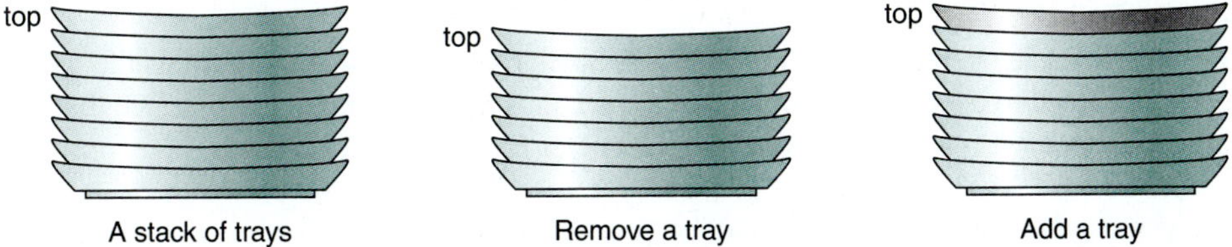

FIGURE 16.3 A stack of trays. Trays are removed from the top and inserted at the top.

The last tray placed on the pile is the first one taken from the pile. For example, if *s* is a stack of strings that is initially empty, the operations

push "Hamlet",
push "Rosencranz", and
push "Guildenstern"

place the three strings on *s*. Because "Guildenstern" is the last string pushed onto *s*, "Guildenstern" occupies the top position. See Figure 16.4a. Two pop operations remove the top two strings from *s*. See Figure 16.4b.

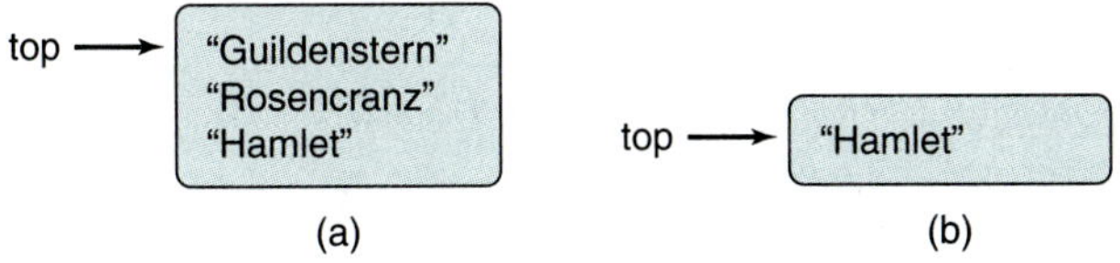

FIGURE 16.4 Stack s after (a) three strings are pushed onto s and (b) two popped

A stack is called a *Last-In First-Out* (*LIFO*) list because the last item pushed onto a stack is always the first item popped from the stack.

Stacks have many natural and useful applications, including:

- determining whether or not the parentheses of an expression are balanced (Example 16.3),
- traversing a graph or network (Example 16.4),
- storing information about nested method calls in a Java application,
- and evaluating numerical or algebraic expressions (Programming Problems 12 and 13).

And, these are just a few of many applications.

In the next sections, we describe and implement a Stack class. We also use the Stack class to check whether or not the parentheses, braces, and brackets of an expression are balanced. You will see that the top-end restrictions of stack access are perfectly suited for solving many different types of problems.

16.4.1 Stack Implementation

The standard stack operations include:

- Push: add an element the stack,
- Pop: remove and return the top element of the stack,
- Peek: view or "peek at" the top of the stack,
- Empty: determine whether or not there are any elements in the stack, and
- Size: get the number of elements stored in the stack.

We bundle these operations into an interface, StackInterface<E>, that declares the methods guaranteed to clients of any class that implements StackInterface<E>. Notice that the StackInterface<E> is generic with type parameter E.

> An interface as well as a class can be generic.

```
public interface StackInterface<E>
{
   public void push(E x);
   // places x on a stack

   public E pop();
   // removes and returns the top item
   // returns null if the stack is empty

   public boolean empty();
   // returns true if no elements are on the stack

   public E peek();
   // returns the top item, does not alter the stack
   // returns null if the stack is empty

   public int size();
   // returns the number of items on the stack
}
```

Example 16.2 gives a complete implementation of a Stack<E> class.

EXAMPLE 16.2 **Problem Statement** Design a Stack<E> class that implements StackInterface<E>. Include a main(...) method that demonstrates the operation of a Stack<E> object.

Java Solution How should the Stack<E> class provide storage for stack elements? Our choices are limited to the structures we have studied—array or ArrayList<E>. A stack is theoretically unlimited in size. Consequently, ArrayList<E> seems appropriate since an ArrayList<E> object can accommodate an arbitrary number of data due to automatic resizing. Although array access is faster, once an array is instantiated, its size is fixed. ArrayList<E> has the disadvantage of slow insertions and deletions, but we can avoid this by identifying the top of the stack with the end of the array. Since insertions and deletions at the end of an ArrayList<E> object are done efficiently, no elements are shifted during push and pop operations. This makes ArrayList<E> an efficient and convenient choice for a Stack<E> implementation.

Figure 16.5 shows an ArrayList<E> implementation of an Integer stack after each of four calls to push(...). Remember that an ArrayList<E> object holds references. You cannot store primitive values in an ArrayList<E> object.

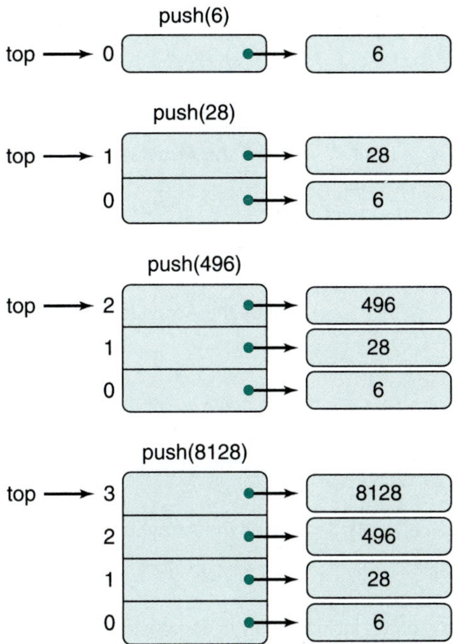

FIGURE 16.5 An *ArrayList* implementation of *Stack<Integer>* after four *push(...)* operations

The implementation of Stack<E> follows.

```
import java.util.*; // for ArrayList<E>
class Stack<E> implements StackInterface<E>
{
   private ArrayList <E>items;

   public Stack()
   // default constructor; creates an empty stack
   {
      items = new ArrayList<E>();      // initial capacity is 10
   }

   public Stack(int initialCapacity)
   // one argument constructor, creates a stack with initial capacity initialCapacity
   {
      items = new ArrayList<E>(initialCapacity);
   }

   public void push(E x)
   {
```

```
      items.add(x);                           // uses the ArrayList method add(E o)
   }

   public E pop()
   {
      if (empty())                            // determine whether or not there is an item to remove
         return null;
      return items.remove(items.size()-1);    // uses the ArrayList method remove(int n)
   }

   public boolean empty()
   {
      return items.isEmpty();                 // uses the ArrayList method isEmpty()
   }

   public int size()
   {
      return items.size();                    // uses the ArrayList method size()
   }

   public E peek()
   {
      if (empty())                            // determine whether or not there is an item on the stack
         return null;
      return items.get(items.size() - 1);     // uses the ArrayList method get(int i)
   }

   // the following main(...) method is included only to demonstrate Stack methods

   public static void main (String[] args)    // for demonstration only
   {
      Stack<Student> s = new Stack<Student>();
      // push five Student references onto s
      s.push(new Student("Spanky", "1245"));
      s.push(new Student("Alfalfa", "1656"));
      s.push(new Student("Darla", " 6525"));
      s.push(new Student("Stimie", "1235"));
      s.push(new Student("Jackie", "3498"));

      System.out.println("The last name pushed was " + s.peek().getName());
      System.out.println();
      System.out.println("The names in reverse order are:");
      while(!s.empty())
         System.out.println(s.pop().getName());
      System.out.println();
      System.out.println("The size of the stack is now " + s.size());
   }
}
```

Output The Stack<E> class contains a main(...) method only to illustrate the properties and methods of the class. Running the application produces the following output:

```
The last name pushed was Jackie
```

```
The names in reverse order are:
Jackie
Stimie
Darla
Alfalfa
Spanky

The size of the stack is now 0.
```

Discussion

Line 2: Stack<E> is a generic class. The type parameter E is a stand-in or placeholder for a reference type E.

Line 4: Stack<E> data are stored in the ArrayList<E> items.

Lines 5–9: By default, the initial capacity of items is 10. Thus, the stack can hold 10 items before the underlying ArrayList<E> object must be resized. Of course, the initial *stack* size is 0. Do not confuse the array capacity with the size of the stack.

Lines 10–14: The one-argument constructor sets the initial capacity of items to initialCapacity. The initial stack size is 0 as it is in the default constructor.

Lines 15–18: The push(E x) method places an element x on the top of the stack. The add(E x) method of ArrayList<E> inserts item x of type E at the end of items. The top of the stack is the element at position items.size() – 1.

Lines 19–24: To remove an item from the stack, first check that the stack is not empty (line 21). If there is at least one item on the stack, the call items.remove(items.size() – 1) removes the last item that was placed into items. That is, the call removes the element that is on top of the stack, and returns that item.

The other methods of Stack are straightforward and require no explanation.

A main(...) method is included to demonstrate the properties of a Stack<E> object. A Stack<E> must be declared and instantiated with a type parameter as illustrated on line 42. Here the type parameter is the class Student. Once a Stack<E> object is instantiated, five student objects are pushed onto the stack and then removed from the stack. Notice that the objects come off the stack in reverse order.

16.4.2 A Stack for Checking Balanced Parentheses, Brackets, and Braces

Have you ever written a Java expression such as

```
x[(a + b) – 5)] = 23;
```

only to have the compiler complain that your expression is missing a parenthesis? (Notice that an opening parenthesis is missing in front of variable a.)

Expressions and statements typically include parentheses, braces, and brackets; syntactically *correct* expressions require *balanced* parentheses, braces, and brackets. For example, the parentheses in the expression ((2 + 3) * 3) are balanced, but those in ((2 + 3) * 3 are not. The parentheses and brackets of myArray[2 * (3 + 4)] are balanced, but the brackets of yourArray[2 * (3 + 4)[are not.

With the aid of a stack, determining whether or not the parentheses, braces, and brackets of an expression are balanced is an easy task that is specified by the following algorithm:

- initialize a stack to empty
- for each character, ch, of an expression
    - if ch is a left parenthesis (, brace {, or bracket [
      push ch onto the stack
    - if ch is a right parenthesis, brace, or bracket

      if a matching left parenthesis, brace, or bracket is on top of the stack
        pop the stack
      else
        report an error and stop

  // No characters remain as input.
- if the stack is empty, the expression is correctly balanced. Otherwise, it is not

Figure 16.6 illustrates the algorithm and Example 16.3 implements the algorithm.

Stack	**Input String**	**Action**
empty	([2 + 3] − (a + b) + 1)	**Push (**
(	[2 + 3] − (a + b) + 1)	**Push [**
([(top)	**2** + 3] − (a + b) + 1)	read 2
([	+3] − (a + b) + 1)	read +
([	**3**] − (a + b) + 1)	read 3
([	] − (a + b) + 1)	read] **Pop the matching left bracket [**
(	− (a + b) + 1)	read −
(	(a + b) + 1)	**Push (**
((	**a** + b) + 1)	read a
((	+b) + 1)	read +
((	**b**) + 1)	read b
((	) + 1	read) **Pop the matching left parenthesis (**
(	+1)	read +
(	**1**)	read 1
(	)	read) **Pop the matching left parenthesis (**
empty	end of string	The expression is balanced.

FIGURE 16.6 Using a stack to check that ([2 + 3] − (a + b) + 1) is balanced

EXAMPLE 16.3 **Problem Statement** Implement a class with a single utility method

public static void boolean expressionChecker(String ex)

that determines whether or not the parentheses, braces, and brackets of ex are balanced. Include a main(...) method that tests expressionChecker(...).

Java Solution The following application implements the previous algorithm using a stack of Character references. Recall that primitive values cannot be stored in a Stack<E> object.

```
import java.util.*;
public class ExpressionChecker
{
    public static boolean checkExpression(String ex)
    {
        Stack<Character> stack = new Stack<Character>();
        for (int i = 0; i < ex.length(); i++)
        {
            char ch = ex.charAt(i);
            // if ch is a left parenthesis, brace, or bracket push ch onto the stack
            if (ch == '(' || ch == '[' || ch == '{')
                stack.push(ch);

            // if ch is a left parenthesis and there is a matching right parenthesis on the stack, pop
            else if (ch == ')' && (!stack.empty()) && stack.peek().equals( '('))
                stack.pop();

            // if ch is a left bracket and there is a matching right bracket on the stack, pop
            else if (ch == ']' && (!stack.empty()) && stack.peek().equals( '['))
                stack.pop();

            // if ch is a left brace and there is a matching right brace on the stack, pop
            else if (ch == '}' && (!stack.empty()) && stack.peek().equals('{'))
                stack.pop();

            // if ch is a left parenthesis, bracket, or brace with no match on the stack,error
            else if (ch == ')' || ch == ']' || ch == '}')
                return false; // expression is incorrect
        }
        if (!stack.empty())
            return false;
        return true;
    }

    public static void main(String [] args)
    {
        Scanner input = new Scanner(System.in);
        System.out.println("Enter an expression; press <ENTER> to exit");
        System.out.print(": ");

        String expression = input.nextLine();
        do
        {
            boolean correct = checkExpression(expression);
            if (correct)
                System.out.println("Expression " + expression + " is correct");
            else
                System.out.println("Expression " + expression + " is incorrect");
            System.out.print("\n: ");
            expression = input.nextLine();
        } while (!expression.equals(""));
    }
}
```

Output

Enter an expression; press <ENTER> to exit
: **(1 + 3) * (3 + 5) * 4**
Expression (1 + 3) * (3 + 5) * 4 is correct

: **(1 + 3) * x [3 − 2] + (a + 5**
Expression (1 + 3) * X [3 − 2] +(a + 5 is incorrect

: **array[3 + (4 + 5]**
Expression array[3 + (4 + 5] is incorrect

Discussion The statement on line 6 instantiates a Stack<**Character**> object. However, the statement on line 12

```
stack.push(ch);
```

pushes a *primitive* value onto the stack. Once again, autoboxing invisibly wraps the value of ch with a Character object. The statement stack.push(ch) is identical to stack.push(new Character(ch)).

Also, notice the check

```
(!stack.empty())
```

on lines 14, 17, and 20. Without first checking whether or not the stack is empty, the notorious NullPointerException could occur in an attempt to evaluate

stack.peek().equals('('),
stack.peek().equals('{'), or
stack.peek().equals('[').

The next example uses a stack to traverse a network of interconnected rooms in a rather peculiar house.

EXAMPLE 16.4 The following is an excerpt from the famous short story "The Lady or the Tiger" written by Frank Stockton in 1884.

> In the very olden time there lived a semi-barbaric king.... When a subject was accused of a crime of sufficient importance to interest the king, public notice was given that on an appointed day the fate of the accused person would be decided in the king's arena.... Directly opposite [the accused subject], were two doors, exactly alike and side-by-side. It was the duty and the privilege of the person on trial to walk directly to these doors and open one of them. He could open either door he pleased.... If he opened the one, there came out of it a hungry tiger, the fiercest and most cruel that could be procured, which immediately sprang upon him and tore him to pieces as a punishment for his guilt.... But, if the accused person opened the other door, there came forth from it a lady, the most suitable to his years and station that his majesty could select among his fair subjects, and to this lady he was immediately married, as a reward of his innocence.... This was the king's semi-barbaric method of administering justice. Its perfect fairness is obvious. The criminal could not know out of which door would come the lady; he opened either he pleased, without having the slightest idea whether, in the next instant, he was to be devoured or married.

If you have not read the story, you will certainly find the ending surprising. We won't spoil it for you here.

In Hollywood's version of Stockton's tale, the semi-barbaric king, now portrayed as fully barbaric, is bored with simple two-door trials. He has bigger ideas. Two doors? Why not twenty-two doors? So, he summons the royal architects and builders (also barbaric) and commissions a soundproof 22-room house built on the lowest level of his arena. The roof of the house is built using a one-way mirror that allows spectators to see into the house. Hey, this is Hollywood! Figure 16.7 is a blueprint of the king's "house of trials." The small rectangles between rooms designate doors.

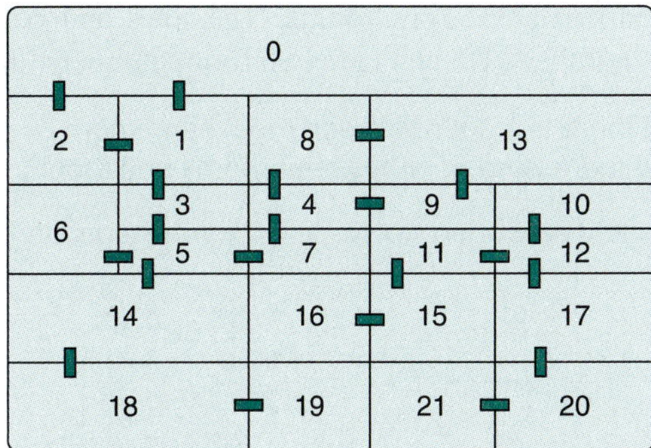

FIGURE 16.7 The king's new *House of Trials*

The network (also called a graph) in Figure 16.8 is a second view of the house. Each numbered circle (vertex) represents a room and each line (edge) that joins two vertices is a door between rooms.

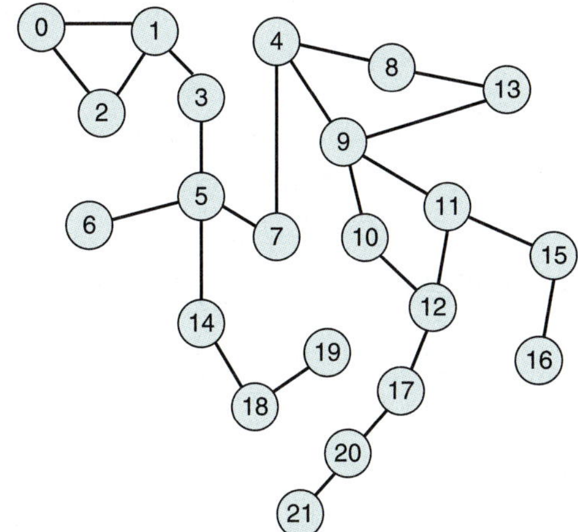

FIGURE 16.8 The *House of Trials* of Figure 16.7, displayed as a network

A blindfolded prisoner is led into the house and abandoned in one of the rooms, where his blindfold is removed. In another room the lady waits, and in a third room the tiger snarls. Unable to hear the cheers and jeers of curious spectators, the prisoner wanders through the house, from room to room to room, until he finds either the lady who leads him to marital bliss or the tiger that . . . well, you know.

If you examine the network in Figure 16.8, you will see that every room is accessible from every other room. So if the prisoner systematically moves through the house, he will eventually come upon either the lady or the tiger.

Problem Statement Write an application that simulates the movements of the prisoner through the rooms of the house. The application should report the rooms that the prisoner visits, in the order that he visits them, as well as the final outcome—the lady or the tiger.

Java Solution Before we can implement an algorithm that moves the prisoner through the house, we must decide on an internal representation of the house. On paper, Figures 16.7 and 16.8 visually capture the important features of the house—the number and location of rooms and the location of each doorway. But these diagrams cannot serve as data for an "eyeless" program. We choose to represent Figures 16.7 and 16.8 as a two-dimensional array, rooms. The rows and columns of rooms are indexed by the room numbers. If i and j are two room numbers, then

rooms(i, j) = 1 if there is a door between room i and room j.
rooms(i, j) = 0 if there is no door between room i and room j.

Figure 16.9 shows a small network of rooms and the corresponding array representation.

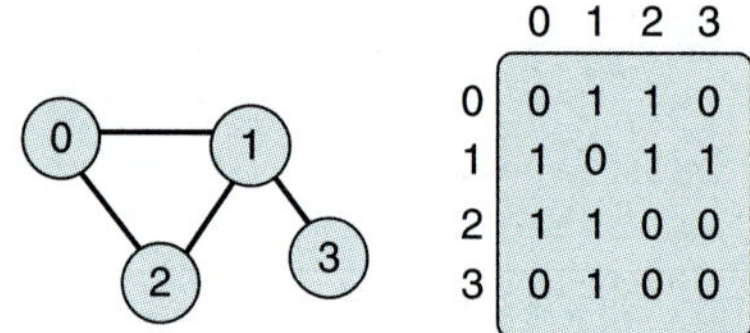

	0	1	2	3
0	0	1	1	0
1	1	0	1	1
2	1	1	0	0
3	0	1	0	0

FIGURE 16.9 A small network and its array representation

The prisoner "visits" rooms until he discovers the lady or the tiger. To ensure that the program eventually terminates, the prisoner never revisits the same room. Here is one method that systematically moves the prisoner through the house until the lady or the tiger is discovered. Notice that he never "visits" a room twice, although he may backtrack through a previously visited room.

```
Mark the initial room as visited.
Push the initial room onto a stack of room numbers.
// the room at the top of the stack is the room currently occupied by the prisoner
// the stack "remembers" previously visited rooms

while both the lady and the tiger are undiscovered
{
   if there is an unvisited room r adjacent to the room on top of the stack (the current room)
        Visit r; mark r as visited.
        if the lady or tiger is in r,
                the search is over
        otherwise
                push r onto the stack, that is, move the prisoner to room r.

   else if there is no unvisited room adjacent to the room on top of the stack
        backtrack to the previous room, that is, pop the stack
        // the most recently visited room is now on top of the stack
}
report the results
```

For example, using Figure 16.8 as a map, assume that the entry room is room 0; the tiger is in 4; and the lady in 14. From room 0, the prisoner might move to room 1, then from 1 to 2. Room 2 is a dead end; he can move to no unvisited rooms from 2 because he has already visited 0 and 1. So, he *backtracks* to room 1. And, from 1 he can move to 3, then to 5, then to 6. Room 6 is a dead end, so he backtracks to 5. From 5, he can go to 7, and to 4, where he meets an unfortunate fate.

We use a stack to implement backtracking. Each time the prisoner enters a room, push the room onto the stack. If the prisoner is ever in a room that is a dead end, then pop the stack, that is, backtrack, and continue from there. The stack keeps track of previous rooms so the prisoner can easily backtrack. Unlike Grimm's Hansel and Gretel, this prisoner has no need to leave a trail of pebbles or breadcrumbs. The stack is better than any trail.

Here is an implementation.

```
import java.util.*;

public class LadyOrTiger
{
   final int numRooms = 22;
   private int[][] rooms = // 2d array representation of the house or network
{
   {0,1,1,0,0,0,0,0,0,0,0,0,0,0,0,0,0,0,0,0,0,0},
   {1,0,1,1,0,0,0,0,0,0,0,0,0,0,0,0,0,0,0,0,0,0},
   {1,1,0,0,0,0,0,0,0,0,0,0,0,0,0,0,0,0,0,0,0,0},
   {0,1,0,0,0,1,0,0,0,0,0,0,0,0,0,0,0,0,0,0,0,0},
   {0,0,0,0,0,0,0,1,1,1,0,0,0,0,0,0,0,0,0,0,0,0},
   {0,0,0,1,0,0,1,1,0,0,0,0,0,1,0,0,0,0,0,0,0,0},
   {0,0,0,0,0,1,0,0,0,0,0,0,0,0,0,0,0,0,0,0,0,0},
   {0,0,0,0,1,1,0,0,0,0,0,0,0,0,0,0,0,0,0,0,0,0},
   {0,0,0,0,1,0,0,0,0,0,0,1,0,0,0,0,0,0,0,0,0,0},
   {0,0,0,0,1,0,0,0,0,0,1,1,0,1,0,0,0,0,0,0,0,0},
   {0,0,0,0,0,0,0,0,0,1,0,0,1,0,0,0,0,0,0,0,0,0},
   {0,0,0,0,0,0,0,0,0,1,0,0,1,0,0,1,0,0,0,0,0,0},
   {0,0,0,0,0,0,0,0,0,0,1,1,0,0,0,0,0,1,0,0,0,0},
   {0,0,0,0,0,0,0,0,1,1,0,0,0,0,0,0,0,0,0,0,0,0},
   {0,0,0,0,0,1,0,0,0,0,0,0,0,0,0,0,0,0,1,0,0,0},
   {0,0,0,0,0,0,0,0,0,0,0,1,0,0,0,0,1,0,0,0,0,0},
   {0,0,0,0,0,0,0,0,0,0,0,0,0,0,0,1,0,0,0,0,0,0},
   {0,0,0,0,0,0,0,0,0,0,0,0,1,0,0,0,0,0,0,0,1,0},
   {0,0,0,0,0,0,0,0,0,0,0,0,0,0,1,0,0,0,0,1,0,0},
   {0,0,0,0,0,0,0,0,0,0,0,0,0,0,0,0,0,0,1,0,0,0},
   {0,0,0,0,0,0,0,0,0,0,0,0,0,0,0,0,0,1,0,0,0,1},
   {0,0,0,0,0,0,0,0,0,0,0,0,0,0,0,0,0,0,0,0,1,0}};

   private boolean[] visited;              //visited[i] = true when a room is visited
   private int currentRoom, lady, tiger;   // room numbers
   private Stack<Integer> roomStack;       // used for backtracking
   public LadyOrTiger()
   {
      Scanner input = new Scanner(System.in);
      System.out.print("What is the starting room?: ");
      currentRoom = input.nextInt();
      System.out.print("Where is the tiger? ");
      tiger = input.nextInt();
      System.out.print("Where is the lady? ");
      lady = input.nextInt();
      visited = new boolean[numRooms];
      // no rooms have been visited yet;
      for (int i = 0; i < numRooms; i++)
         visited[i] = false;
      roomStack = new Stack<Integer>();
   }

   private int nextRoom(int room)          // helper method is private
   {
      // returns the room number of an unvisited room selected at random
      // from the unvisited rooms adjacent to room.
      // If there is no unvisited room adjacent to room returns noRoom (-1)
```

```
      // pick the next room randomly from all unvisited adjacent rooms

      final int noRoom = -1;
      Random rand = new Random();

      // holds a list of unvisited rooms that are adjacent to room
      ArrayList<Integer> unvisitedRooms = new ArrayList<Integer>();
      for (int i = 0; i < numRooms; i++)
         if (rooms[room][i] == 1 && !visited[i]) // get a list of unvisited rooms adjacent to room
            unvisitedRooms.add(i);
      if (unvisitedRooms.size() > 0)           // pick an unvisited room at random
      {
         int roomNumber = rand.nextInt(unvisitedRooms.size());
         return unvisitedRooms.get(roomNumber);
      }
      return noRoom;                            // no unvisited room available
   }

   public void search()
   {
      visited[currentRoom] = true;
      roomStack.push(currentRoom);
      boolean fateDecided = false;
      int room = -1;
      System.out.println("\nStarting in room " + currentRoom + " the prisoner visits rooms:");

      while (!fateDecided)
      {
                  // Is there an unvisited room adjacent to the current room?
         room = nextRoom(roomStack.peek());
         if (room > = 0)                        // if there is an unvisited room, visit that room
         {
            visited[room] = true;
            System.out.println(room);
            if (room == lady || room == tiger)
               fateDecided = true;
            else
               roomStack.push(room);            // the "current room" is now on top of the stack
         }
         else                                   // backtrack
            roomStack.pop();
      }
      if (room == lady)
         System.out.println("He found the lady in room " + room);
      else
         System.out.println("He found the tiger in room " + room);
   }

   public static void main(String[] args)
   {
      LadyOrTiger ladyOrTiger = new LadyOrTiger();
      ladyOrTiger.search();
   }
}
```

Output Running the simulation twice with the same input data produces the following different results. Because the "next room" is selected *randomly*, the outcomes differ.

Output 1	Output 2
What is the starting room?: **0** Where is the tiger? **19** Where is the lady? **21** Starting in room 0 the prisoner visits rooms: 1 3 5 6 14 18 19 He found the tiger in room 19	What is the starting room?: **0** Where is the tiger? **19** Where is the lady? **21** Starting in room 0 the prisoner visits rooms: 1 3 5 6 7 4 8 13 9 11 15 16 12 17 20 21 He found the lady in room 21

Trace	Trace
Here is what happens: 0→1→3→5→6→(***backtrack to 5***)→14→18→19	Here is what happens: 0→2→1→3→5→6→ (***backtrack to 5***)→7→4→8→13→9→11→15→16→(***backtrack to 15***)→(***backtrack to 11***)→12→17→20→21

Discussion

Lines 5–28: Here we have hard-wired the rooms array into the code. Of course this works, but a more flexible version would read the data from a text file.

Lines 47–56: The method

```
int nextMove(int room)
```

accepts a room number and returns the number of an unvisited adjacent room, chosen randomly. The room need not be chosen randomly. For example, the room can be chosen as the adjacent room with the lowest number or the one with the highest number. We choose a random room number to add some non-determinism to the problem. As you can see from the sample output, identical input does not produce identical output.

16.5 A QUEUE

Like a stack, a *queue* is an ordered list of data into which data can be inserted and removed. However, unlike a stack, data is always inserted at one end of a queue, *the rear*, and removed from the other end, *the front*. Figure 16.10 contrasts a queue and a stack.

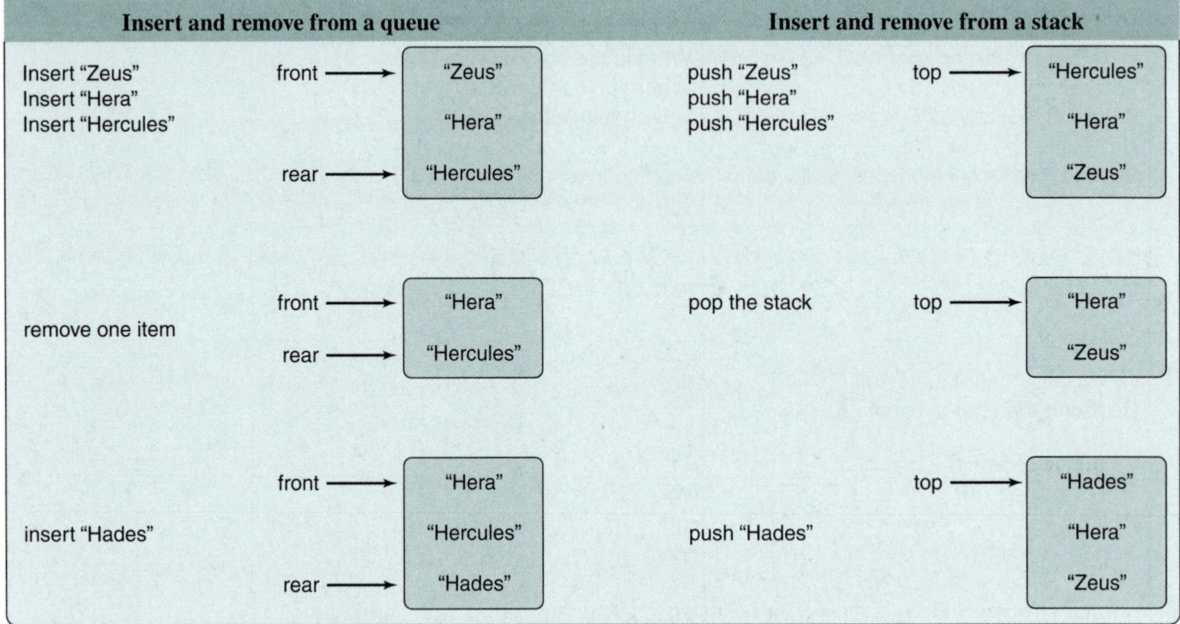

FIGURE 16.10 Contrasting operations: a queue and a stack

You might imagine a queue as a waiting line—the kind that you would find in a bank, a movie theater, or a grocery store. Customers arrive and join the line at the rear, and customers are serviced from the front of the line.

A queue is called a *FIFO* list – *First In, First Out.*

16.5.1 Queue Implementation

Typical queue operations include:

- insert: add an item to the rear of the queue.
- remove: remove and return an item from the front of the queue.
- peek: view or "peek at" the front item.
- empty: determine whether or not there are any elements in the queue.
- size: get the number of elements stored in the queue.

These queue operations are specified in the following generic interface:

```
public interface QueueInterface<E>
{
    public void insert(E x);
    // inserts x at the rear of the queue

    public E remove();
    // removes and returns the front item
    // returns null if the queue is empty

    public boolean empty();
    // returns true if no elements are in the queue
```

```
    public E peek();
    // returns the front item, does not alter the queue
    // returns null if the queue is empty

    public int size();
    // returns the number of items in the queue
}
```

As in the case of a stack, we can implement a queue using an ArrayList<E> for storage. However, this is not the most expedient implementation. Suppose, for example, that items is an ArrayList<E> and that items holds queue elements. The insert() operation can be implemented as:

```
void insert(E x)
{
   items.add(x):
}
```

which places element x at the end of items. The method is easy *and* efficient.

On the other hand, the remove() operation, although easy to implement, is not particularly efficient. If the first queue element is always located at position 0, the remove operation can be implemented as:

```
E remove()
{
      if (empty())
         return null;
      return items.remove(0);
}
```

The method works correctly but at a cost. When the element at position 0 is deleted from an ArrayList<E> object, all other elements in the list are shifted. That is, the element in position 1 is moved to position 0, the element in position 2 is moved to position 1, and so on. So every remove() operation requires that all remaining elements in items be moved. If a queue contains 10,000 elements, a single remove() operation requires 9,999 data shifts. This is not the case with our stack implementation, where the pop() operation removes the element stored at the position with the *highest* index. No shifting occurs.

A queue can be more efficiently implemented using a simple array for storage. The only real limitation with such an implementation is that the size of an array is fixed. However, if you can estimate the maximum size of a queue, an array implementation is a good option.

Figure 16.11 shows a queue that uses an array, items, with maximum capacity 5. The variable front holds the index of the first item in the queue and a second variable rear holds the index of the last item in the queue. Figure 16.11a shows the queue after four insert operations, (b) after two remove operations, and (c) after one more insert operation.

The queue shown in Figure 16.11c contains just three elements, which are stored in items[2], items[3], and items[4]; front has the value 2 and rear has the value 4. Will one more insert() operation throw an ArrayOutOfBoundsException? Well, not necessarily. There are two available cells in the array: items[0] and items[1]. If the next insert operation, insert("Saturn"), places "Saturn" in items[0], then no error occurs. That is, we consider items[0] to be the cell that follows items[4]. In practice, we imagine the array as circular. Figure 16.12 shows that the items in the queue, from front to rear, are stored in locations 2, 3, 4, and 0.

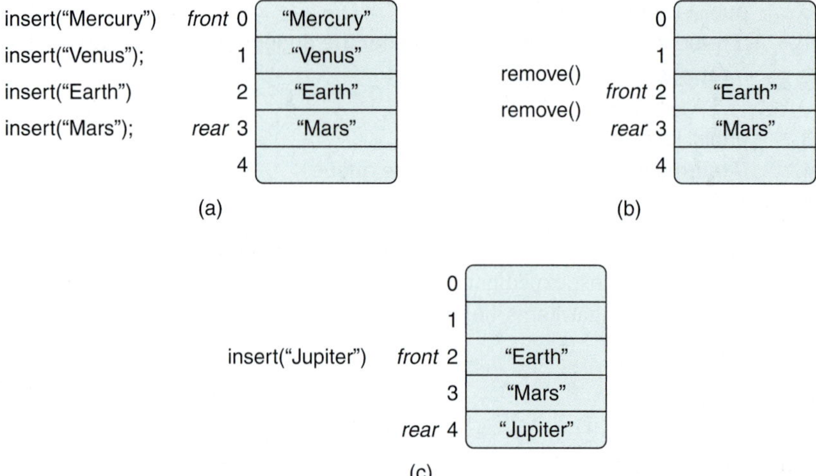

FIGURE 16.11 A queue implemented as an array of size 5

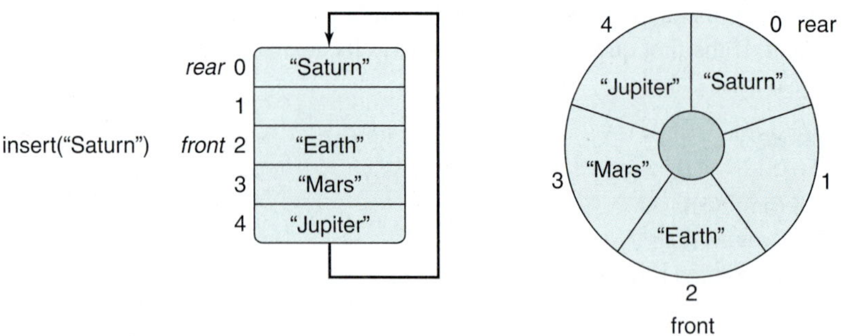

FIGURE 16.12 A circular array used to implement a queue

By using a "circular array," we do not waste any array locations, and the queue can hold as many elements as exist in the underlying array. Nevertheless, overflow errors can still occur once we use *all* the space in the array.

Example 16.5 gives an array implementation of a class Queue<E>.

EXAMPLE 16.5 **Problem Statement** Implement a queue using a circular array for storage. The Queue<E> class should implement QueueInterface<E>.

Java Solution The Queue<E> class uses an array, items for storage. There are also four integer fields:

- front, which holds the index of the first item in the queue,
- rear, which holds the index of the last item in the queue,
- numItems, which stores the number of items in the queue, and
- maxQueue, which stores the maximum capacity of the queue.

The array, items, is considered circular. This means that, if space remains, items[0] is the storage location following items[maxQueue − 1], where maxQueue is items.length.

Because an array has a fixed size, it *is* possible to exceed the capacity of a queue. In this case, the insert() method issues a message and exits. Alternatively, insert() might throw an exception.

The following implementation includes a main(...) method that demonstrates some of the queue operations.

```
import java.util.*;

public class Queue <E>implements QueueInterface<E>
{
   private E[] items;
   private int numItems;                  // number of elements currently in the queue

   int front, rear;                       // holds the indices of the front and rear elements
   int maxQueue;                          // maximum capacity

   public Queue()                         // default constructor, sets maxQueue to 10
   {
      items = (E[]) new Object[10];       // new E[10] is illegal; the cast is necessary
      numItems = 0;
      front = rear = -1;                  // -1 indicates that the queue is empty
      maxQueue = 10;
   }

   public Queue(int max)                  // one argument constructor, accepts maximum capacity
   {
      maxQueue = max;
      items = (E[]) new Object[maxQueue]; // new E[maxQueue] is illegal; the cast is necessary
      numItems = 0;
      front = rear = -1;                  // -1 indicates that the queue is empty
   }

   public void insert(E x)
   // inserts x at the rear of the queue
   // if overflow occurs, issues a message and exits
   {
      if (numItems == maxQueue)           // queue is full
      {
         System.out.println("Queue Overflow");
         System.exit(0);
      }

      rear = (rear + 1) % maxQueue;       // % maxQueue ensures wraparound
      items[rear] = x;
      numItems++;
      if (numItems == 1)                  // if queue was previously empty
         front = rear;
   }

   public E remove()
   // removes and returns the first item in the queue
   // if the queue is empty, returns null
   {
      if (numItems == 0)                  // empty queue
         return null;
      E temp = items[front];              // holds the first item in the queue
      numItems--;
      if (numItems == 0)                  // if the queue is now empty set front and rear to -1
         front = rear = -1;
      else
         front = (front + 1) % maxQueue;  // %maxQueue ensures wraparound
```

```
        return temp;
    }

    public E peek()
    // returns the first item in the queue or null if the queue is empty
    // does not alter the queue
    {
        if (numItems == 0)                          // empty queue
            return null;
        else
            return items[front];
    }

    public boolean empty()
    // returns true if the queue is empty
    {
        return numItems == 0;
    }

    public int size()
    // returns the number of items currently in the queue
    {
        return numItems;
    }

    public static void main(String[] args)
    {
        Queue <String>q = new Queue<String>(5);
        q.insert("Mercury");
        q.insert("Venus");
        q.insert("Earth");
        System.out.println(q.remove() + "removed from queue");
        q.insert("Mars");
        q.insert("Jupiter");
        System.out.println(q.remove() + "removed from queue");
        q.insert("Saturn");
        System.out.println(q.remove() + "removed from queue");
        q.insert("Uranus");
        q.insert("Neptune");
        System.out.println(q.remove() + "removed from queue");
        System.out.println(q.remove() + "removed from queue");
        System.out.println(q.remove() + "removed from queue");
        System.out.println(q.remove() + "removed from queue");
        System.out.println(q.remove() + "removed from queue");
        System.out.println("Number of remaining items" + q.size());
    }
}
```

Output

```
Mercury removed from queue
Venus removed from queue
Earth removed from queue
Mars removed from queue
Jupiter removed from queue
Saturn removed from queue
Uranus removed from queue
Neptune removed from queue
Number of remaining items 0
```

Discussion A few lines in the implementation of Queue<E> may need a bit of clarification.

Lines 10 and 18:

```
items = (E[]) new Object[10];
items = (E[]) new Object[maxQueue];
```

As noted in Section 16.3, Java does not allow generic arrays. The statement

```
items = new E[10];
```

results in a compilation error. To avoid this error, we instantiate an array of Object and cast that to E[].

When the class is compiled, the compiler issues a warning to the effect that the cast on lines 10 and 18 *may* be unsafe. However, no problem occurs here because every item in the queue belongs to the class represented by E.

Lines 31 and 48:

```
rear = (rear + 1)   % maxQueue;
front = (front + 1) % maxQueue;
```

These lines effect wraparound. For example, suppose that that maximum capacity of a queue is 10, and that the queue consists of three items stored at items[7], items[8], and item[9]. Since the value of rear is 9,

```
rear = (rear + 1)% maxQueue = (9 + 1)% 10 = 0.
```

Thus, the next item is stored at items[0]. The array is circular; 0 follows 9.

16.5.2 Queues for Simulation

A queue is an excellent tool for simulations.

From cars lined up at a tollbooth to print jobs waiting for a printer, queues abound in everyday life. The next example uses a queue to model and simulate a customer waiting line at an ATM machine.

EXAMPLE 16.6

During lunch hour, the ATM machine in a large office complex is in heavy demand. Customers complain that the waiting time is much too long. The local bank is considering the addition of a second machine. But first, the bank needs a few statistics to justify the cost.

Problem Statement Simulate a waiting line at the ATM machine for a period of one hour. Make the following assumptions:

- With equal probability, a customer spends:

  one minute,
  two minutes, or
  three minutes

  at the ATM machine.

- During any minute:

  no customers arrive (50% chance),
  one customer arrives (40% chance), or
  two customers arrive (10% chance).

At the end of an hour, display the following summary statistics:

- the number of customers served, that is, the number who accessed the ATM machine,
- the average time that a customer waits in line before being served, and
- the number of customers that remain in the waiting line at the end of the simulation.

Assume that the ATM is available when the simulation begins and that no customers are waiting.

Java Solution Before considering an algorithm that simulates the comings and goings of customers at an ATM machine, we design a class that models an ATM customer.

A customer knows his/her arrival time and how much time he/she spends making an ATM transaction. The following class encapsulates a customer.

```
import java.util.*;

public class Customer
{
   private int arrivalTime;          // 0..60, the minute of the hour when a customer arrives
   private int serviceTime;          // 1, 2, or 3 minutes

   public Customer()                 // default constructor
   {
      arrivalTime = 0;
      serviceTime = 0;
   }

   public Customer(int arrTime)      // one argument constructor
   {
      arrivalTime = arrTime;
      Random rand = new Random();
      serviceTime = rand.nextInt(3) + 1;  // 1, 2, or 3 minutes
   }

   public void setArrivalTime(int arrTime)
   {
      arrivalTime = arrTime;
   }

   public int getArrivalTime()
   {
      return arrivalTime;
   }

   public void setServiceTime(int ser)
   {
      serviceTime = ser;
   }

   public int getServiceTime()
   {
      return serviceTime;
   }
}
```

The algorithm that simulates an ATM waiting line uses a loop that ticks through a 60-minute simulation.

```
For each minute from 0 through 59
{
        Determine the number of new customers arriving: 0, 1, or 2;
        For each new customer
           Place the new customer in the queue;

        If there are customers waiting and the ATM is available
        {
           Remove a customer from the queue;
           Increment the number of customers served;
           Add to the total waiting time the waiting time of the current customer;
           Update the time the ATM is next available;
        }
}
Print the summary statistics;
```

The following class implements this algorithm.

```
import java.util.*;

public class ATMSimulation
{
   Customer customer;
   int ATMisAvailable;              // time the ATM is next available
   int numArrivals;                 // number of arrivals in any minute
   Queue<Customer> queue;

   // statistics
   int totalWaitingTime;            // for all customers
   int numCustomersServed;

   public ATMSimulation()           // default constructor
   {
      ATMisAvailable = 0;           // assume the ATM is available at time 0
      numArrivals = 0;
      totalWaitingTime = 0;
      numCustomersServed = 0;
      queue = new Queue<Customer>(200);
   }

   private int getArrivals()
   // generate a random integer in the range 0..9
   // if the random integer is 0, 1, 2, 3, or 4, then no arrivals (50% chance)
   // if the random integer is 5, 6, 7, or 8, then 1 arrival (40% chance)
   // if the random integer is 9, then 2 arrivals (10% chance)
   {
      Random rand = new Random();
      int randomInteger = rand.nextInt(10);          // 0..9
      if (randomInteger <= 4)                        // 0..4
         return 0;                                   // 50% chance of a single arrival
      if (randomInteger <= 8)                        // 5..8
         return 1;                                   // 40% chance of a single arrival
      return 2;                                      // 10% chance of 2 arrivals
   }

   private void displayStatistics()
   {
      System.out.println("Number of customers served" + numCustomersServed);
      System.out.println("Average wait is about " +
                         totalWaitingTime/numCustomersServed + "minutes");
```

```
70.         System.out.println("Customers left in queue: " + queue.size());
71.     }
72.     public void simulate()
73.     {
74.         for (int time = 0; time < 60; time++)                  // for each minute
75.         {
76.            numArrivals = getArrivals();                        // how many customers arrive?
77.            for (int i = 1; i <= numArrivals; i++)              // place each arrival into the queue
78.                queue.insert(new Customer(time));
79.            if (!queue.empty() && ATMisAvailable <= time)
80.            {
81.                customer = queue.remove();                      // remove the next customer from the waiting line
82.                // Determine the next time that the ATM is available: current time + service time
83.                ATMisAvailable = time + customer.getServiceTime();
84.                // how long did this customer wait?
85.                int timeCustomerWaited = time - customer.getArrivalTime();
86.                totalWaitingTime += timeCustomerWaited;        // add customer's wait to total wait
87.                numCustomersServed++;
88.            }
89.         }
90.         displayStatistics();
91.     }
92.     public static void main(String[] args)
93.     {
94.         ATMSimulation atmSim = new ATMSimulation();
95.         atmSim.simulate();
96.     }
97. }
```

Output Running the application three times produced the following output:

```
Number of customers served 30
Average wait is about 5 minutes
Customers left in queue: 16

Number of customers served 29
Average wait is about 8 minutes
Customers left in queue: 13

Number of customers served 32
Average wait is about 6 minutes
Customers left in queue: 6
```

Discussion The application simulates the waiting line for each minute of an hour. During any minute, customers can arrive as well as gain access to the ATM machine. At the end of the 60-minute interval, a call to the helper method displayStatistics() prints the summary statistics. The loop on lines 74–89 is the heart of the simulation.

The getArrivals() method (lines 51–64) merits some explanation. One of the assumptions of the simulation is that the number of arrivals during any particular minute is 0, 1, or 2 customers with probabilities of 0.50, 0.40, and 0.10, respectively. The method first generates a random integer between 0 and 9 inclusive. The probability that this random integer is 0, 1, 2, 3, or 4 is 0.50. The probability that the random number is 5, 6, 7, or 8 is 0.40. And the probability that the number is 9 is 0.10. Consequently, if the random number is 0, 1, 2, 3, or 4, we assume that there are no arrivals. There is a 50% chance that this happens. If the number is 5, 6, 7, or 8 we assume that there is a single arrival. This happens 40% of the time. And, finally, if the random number is 9, we assume that there are two arrivals.

16.6 A LINKED LIST

A *linked list* is an ordered collection, group, or list of items such that each item holds a reference or "link" to the next item of the collection.

Figure 16.13 shows a linked list consisting of five planets. The first planet on the list is Mercury. The arrow or link from Mercury indicates that the second planet is Venus. And, if you follow the links, you can see that the list of planets (in order) is Mercury, Venus, Earth, Mars, and Jupiter.

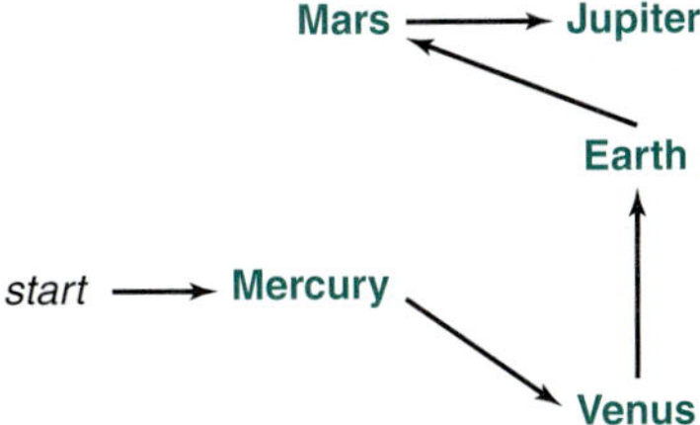

FIGURE 16.13 A linked list: Mercury, Venus, Earth, Mars, and Jupiter

Of course, as a data structure, a linked list is a bit more complex than the picture of Figure 16.13. Nonetheless, Figure 16.13 captures the central idea: each item on the list is linked to the next item. A linked list is ordered in the sense that there is a first item, a second item, a third item, a next item.

In the following sections, we design a class LList<E> that implements a linked list. Our implementation uses objects called *nodes*, which, like the planet names of Figure 16.13, are linked together.

16.6.1 Nodes

A *node* is an object that contains data as well as a reference to another node. Thus, a node has at least two fields, one of which holds the address of another node. The following Node class has exactly two fields, data and next, and two constructors. For convenience, and temporarily, we assume the fields are public and that the type of the data field is String.

```
public class Node
{
      public String data;
      public Node next;            // next is a reference to a Node

      public Node ()               // default constructor
      {
         data = "";                // the empty string
         next = null;
      }
```

```
        public Node(String s)    // one argument constructor
        {
            data = s;
            next = null;
        }
    }
```

Notice that the data type of next is Node. That is, the next field of a Node is itself a reference to a Node object. The next field holds the address of another node. Indeed, Node is a *recursive* data structure.

You can visualize a Node object as

data (String)	next (Node)

The statements

```
Node p = new Node("Mercury"); // the one argument constructor
Node q = new Node ("Venus");
```

instantiate two Node objects, one referenced by p and another referenced by q. These nodes and references are shown in Figure 16.14.

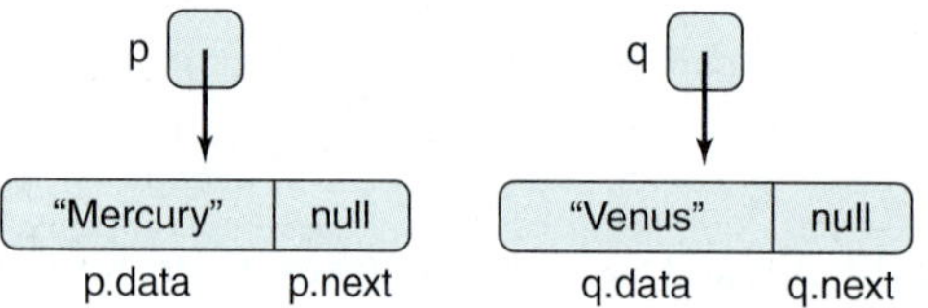

FIGURE 16.14 Two *Node* objects: one referenced by *p*, the other by *q*

Nodes can be linked together to form a "chain of nodes." Figure 16.15 shows the two nodes of Figure 16.14 joined in a rather short chain. The horizontal arrow in Figure 16.15 indicates that the field p.next (in the "Mercury" node) holds the address of the "Venus" node, which also happens to be stored in q.

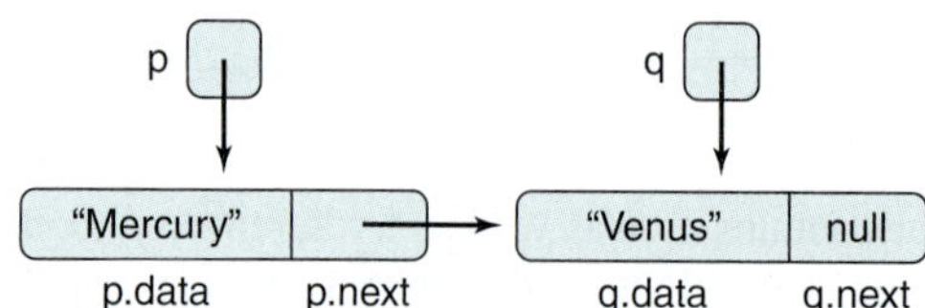

FIGURE 16.15 The statement *p.next* = *q* links two nodes

The linking of these two nodes is accomplished by the statement

```
p.next = q;   // q holds the address of the "Venus" node,
```

which assigns the address of the "Venus" node (q) to the next field of the "Mercury" node (p.next).

Figure 16.16 shows a chain of four linked nodes. The data element in node 0 is the string "Mercury" and, as indicated by the arrow, the reference stored in node 0 is the address of node 1. Node 1 holds the string "Venus" as well as the address of node 2. Node 2 holds "Earth" and a reference to node 3. Finally, node 3 holds "Mars" and its next field is null.

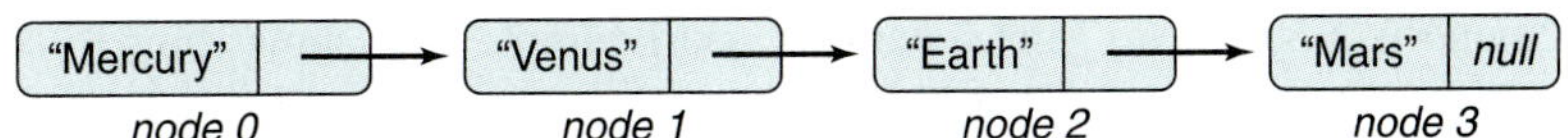

FIGURE 16.16 Three linked nodes

Technically, the data field of each node in Figure 16.16 holds a *reference* to a String rather than the characters of the string.

The code in Figure 16.17 creates the chain of four nodes shown in Figure 16.16.

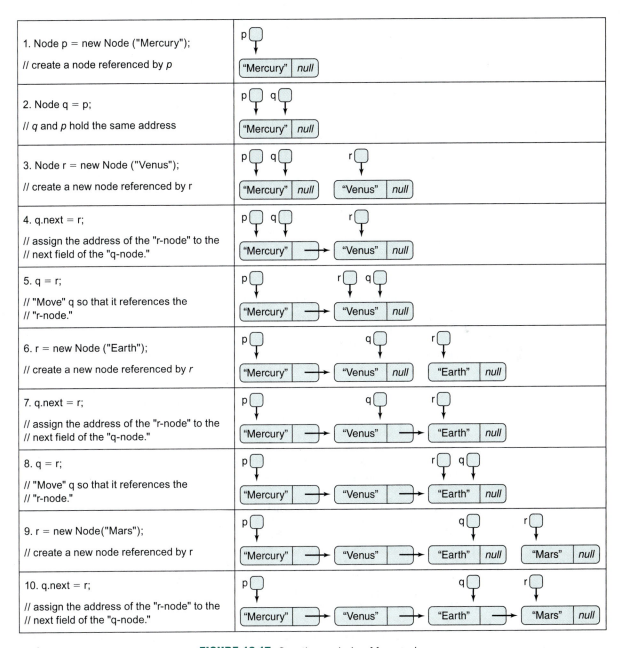

1. Node p = new Node ("Mercury"); // create a node referenced by *p*	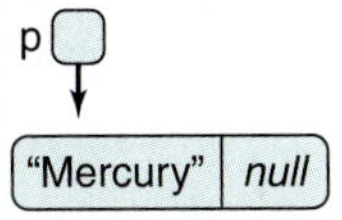 p → [“Mercury” | *null*]
2. Node q = p; // *q* and *p* hold the same address	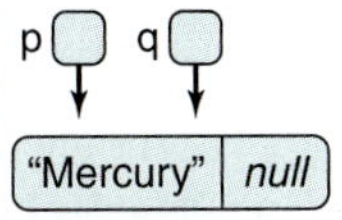 p, q → [“Mercury” | *null*]
3. Node r = new Node ("Venus"); // create a new node referenced by r	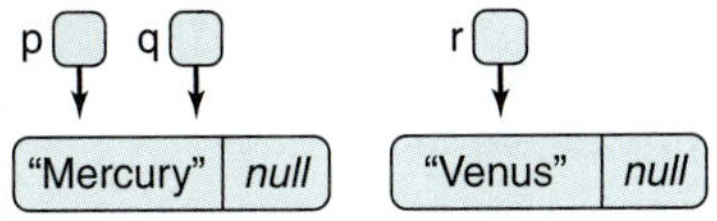 p, q → [“Mercury” | *null*] r → [“Venus” | *null*]

4. q.next = r;
// assign the address of the "r-node" to the
// next field of the "q-node."
	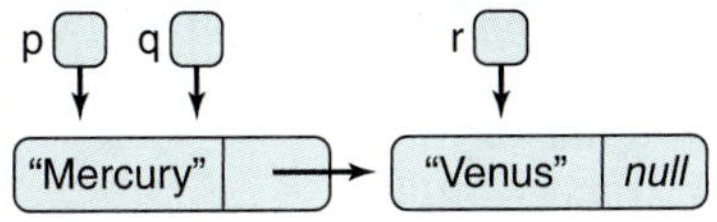 p, q → [“Mercury” | →] → r → [“Venus” | *null*]

5. q = r; // "Move" q so that it references the // "r-node."	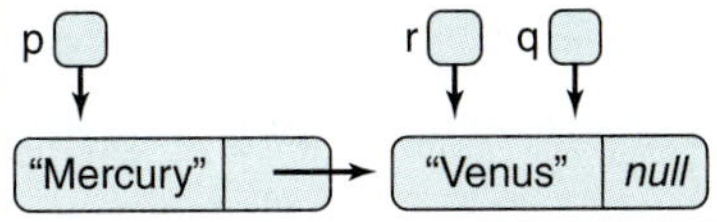 p → [“Mercury” | →] → r, q → [“Venus” | *null*]
6. r = new Node ("Earth"); // create a new node referenced by *r*	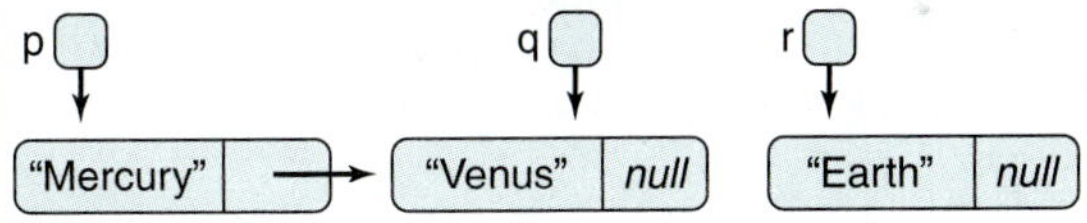 p → [“Mercury” | →] → q → [“Venus” | *null*] r → [“Earth” | *null*]

7. q.next = r;
// assign the address of the "r-node" to the
// next field of the "q-node."
	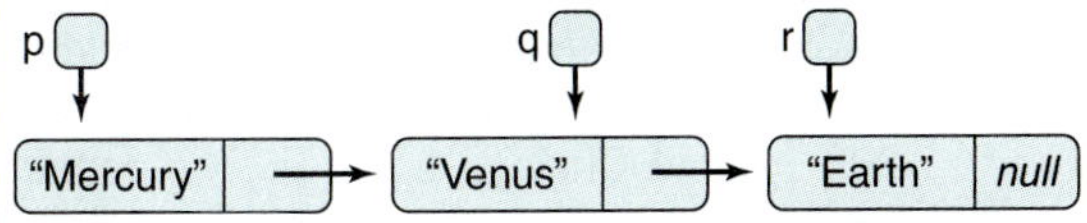 p → [“Mercury” | →] → q → [“Venus” | →] → r → [“Earth” | *null*]

8. q = r; // "Move" q so that it references the // "r-node."	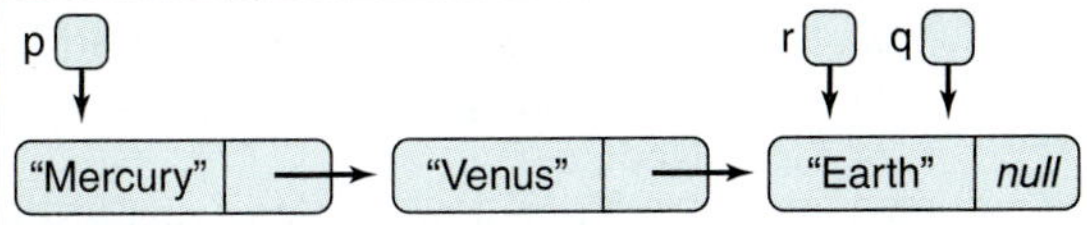 p → [“Mercury” | →] → [“Venus” | →] → r, q → [“Earth” | *null*]
9. r = new Node("Mars"); // create a new node referenced by r	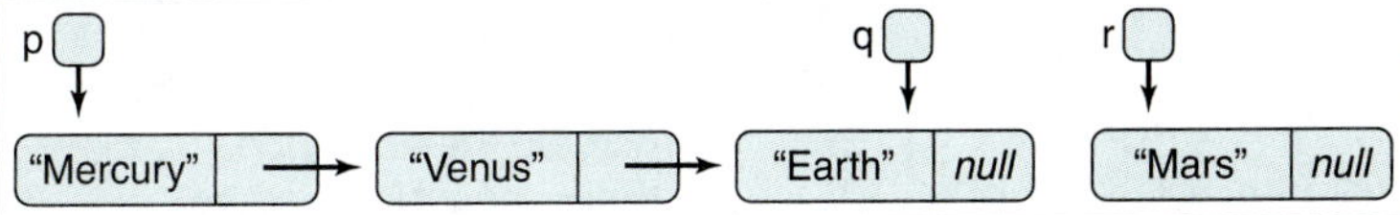 p → [“Mercury” | →] → [“Venus” | →] → q → [“Earth” | *null*] r → [“Mars” | *null*]

10. q.next = r;
// assign the address of the "r-node" to the
// next field of the "q-node."
	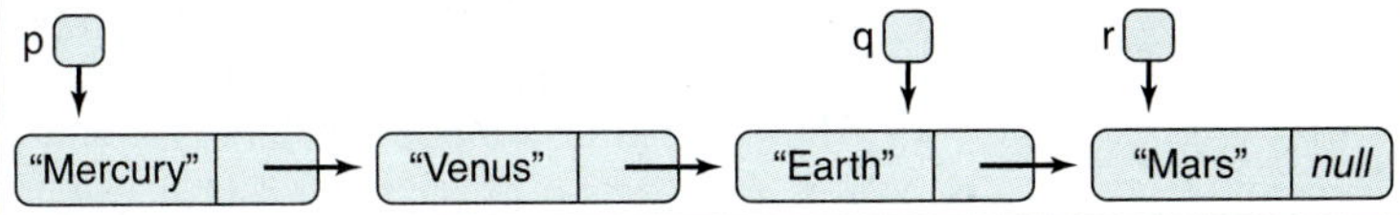 p → [“Mercury” | →] → [“Venus” | →] → q → [“Earth” | →] → r → [“Mars” | *null*]

FIGURE 16.17 Creating a chain of four nodes

The statements of Figure 16.17 are repetitive, and Example 16.7 shows how to create an arbitrary chain of nodes using a loop.

EXAMPLE 16.7 **Problem Statement** Implement a class, Chain, that creates a chain of Node objects such that each Node holds a String entered via the console. Include a method that displays the data stored in the chain.

Java Solution In the following application, note that

- a private Node class is declared within Chain, and
- a reference front holds the address of the first node in the chain. Without such a reference, the data in the chain is inaccessible. The reference front serves as an anchor for the chain of nodes.

```
import java.util.*;

public class Chain
{
    private class Node // a class declared within Chain, an inner class
    {
        private String data;
        private Node next;

        public Node() // default constructor
        {
            data = “”;
            next = null;
        }

        public Node(String s) // one argument constructor
        {
            data = s;
            next = null;
        }
    }

    private Node front;            // holds the address of the first node of the chain

    public Chain()                 // constructor builds a chain
    {
        Scanner input = new Scanner(System.in);
        String name;
        Node q, r;
        System.out.print("Enter name -- Press <Enter>to signal end of data: " );
        name = input. nextLine();

        // create the first node
        front = new Node(name);
        q = front; // front and q both reference the first node
        System.out.print("Enter name: " );
        name = input. nextLine();

        while (!name.equals(""))
        {
```

```
34.         r = new Node(name);        // get a new node
35.         q.next = r;                // link the previous node to the new node
36.         q = r;                     // move q to the "new" node
37.         System.out.print("Enter name: " );
38.         name = input. nextLine();
39.      }
40.   }

41.   public void printChain()
42.   {
43.      Node q = front;               // q references the first node in the chain
44.      System.out.println("\nThe names in the chain of nodes are: ");
45.      while (q!= null)
46.      {
47.         System.out.println(q.data);
48.         q = q.next;                // move q to the next node in the chain
49.      }
50.   }

51.   public static void main(String[] args)
52.   {
53.      Chain chain = new Chain();
54.      chain.printChain();
55.   }
56. }
```

Output

Enter name -- Press <Enter>to signal end of data: **Gandalf**
Enter name: **Frodo**
Enter name: **Bilbo**
Enter name: **Sam**
Enter name: **Gollum**
Enter name:

The names in the chain of nodes are:
Gandalf
Frodo
Bilbo
Sam
Gollum

Discussion

Lines 4–18: Node is declared within Chain; Node is called an *inner* class. Node is defined as a private class within Chain. Node is accessible only to Chain and no other classes.

Lines 32–39: The while loop works in the same way as the code of Figure 16.17 and creates the chain of nodes shown in Figure 16.18.

FIGURE 16.18 A chain created by a *while* loop

Lines 41–50: printChain()

Line 43: Assign to reference variable q the address of the first node in the chain, which is front.

Lines 45–49: While q holds the address of some node, that is, q is not null.

Line 47: Print the data stored in the node referenced by q, that is, print q.data.

Line 48: Assign to q the address of the next node in the chain. That is, "move q down the chain." If q is referencing the last node, then q gets the value null and the loop terminates.

16.6.2 Inner Classes

The declaration of Node in Example 16.7 may seem a bit unconventional, if not peculiar. Node is a private class declared *within* another class, Chain. Node is declared solely for Chain's convenience. Node is called an *inner* class and Chain an *outer* or *surrounding* class. Inner classes are useful when one class has meaning only in the context of another class. For example, on its own, a Node may have no apparent purpose, but as a part of a chain, a Node object has a well-defined function.

The methods of an inner class have direct access to variables and methods of the surrounding outer class. On the other hand, the methods of an outer class can access an inner class field or invoke an inner class method only via an object of the inner class. For example, consider the following class definitions.

```
public class BadOuter
{
    private class Inner
    {
        private String myName;
        // inner class methods
    }

    public void setName(String name)
    {
        myName = name; // illegal
    }
}
```

```
public class Outer
{
    private class Inner
    {
        private String myName;
        // inner class methods
    }

    public void setName(String name)
    {
        Inner inner = new Inner();
        inner.myName = name; // legal
    }
}
```

BadOuter does not compile because the method setName(...) attempts to access the private Inner variable myName directly. Outer, on the other hand, accesses myName via an instance of Inner.

16.6.3 The *LList<E>* Class

Because each node in a chain holds the address of the next node, a chain of nodes suggests a natural storage structure for a linked list class, LList<E>. In addition to the instance variable front, which references the first node of the chain, LList<E> includes a field, rear, which holds the address of last node, and a third reference variable current, which can reference any node in the chain. See Figure 16.19.

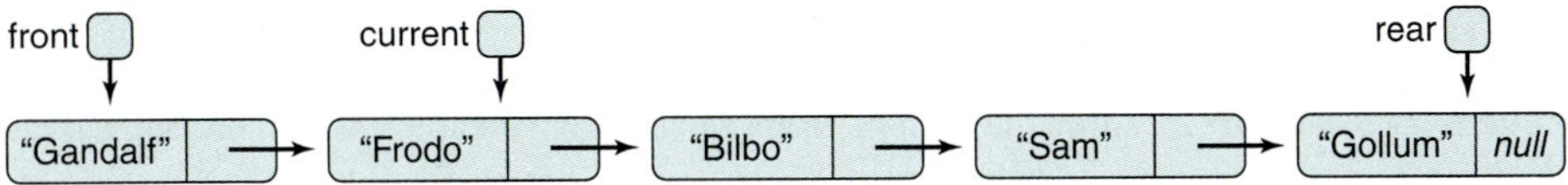

FIGURE 16.19 A linked list: *front* references the first node, *rear* the last, and *current* holds the address of an arbitrary node

The methods of LList<E> include methods for adding, removing, and retrieving data. That is, the methods of LList<E> mirror the methods of ArrayList<E>. These methods, common to ArrayList<E> and LList<E>, are grouped together in the following interface:

```
public interface ListInterface<E>
{
   void add(int index, E x);
   // inserts x into position index

   void add(E x);
   // adds x to the end of the list

   void clear();
   // removes all objects from the list

   boolean contains (E x);
   // returns true if x is a member of the list

   E get(int index);
   // returns the Object at position index

   boolean isEmpty();
   // returns true if the list has no elements

   boolean remove (E x);
   // if x is a member of the list, removes the first occurrence of x from the list, shifts all elements
   // position, and returns true; otherwise returns false.

   E remove (int index);
   // removes and returns the object x at position index;
   // shifts all elements following x down one position

   E set (int index, E x);
      // replaces the object at index index with x; returns the replaced object.

   int size();
      // returns the number of objects currently in the list
}
```

The LList<E> class not only implements ListInterface<E> but also provides three additional methods, not found in ArrayList<E>, that are useful for traversing, or processing the data of a list. These methods are

- void reset(),
  sets current equal to front
- boolean hasNext()
  returns true if current.next is not null, that is, if current is not equal to rear.

- E next().
  if current == null, reports an error and terminates the application; otherwise returns the data of the current node and moves current down the list, that is, sets current equal to current.next.

Figures 16.20 and 16.21 show the actions of three successive calls: reset(), hasNext(), and next().

FIGURE 16.20 A call to *reset*() sets current equal to front and *hasNext*() returns *true*

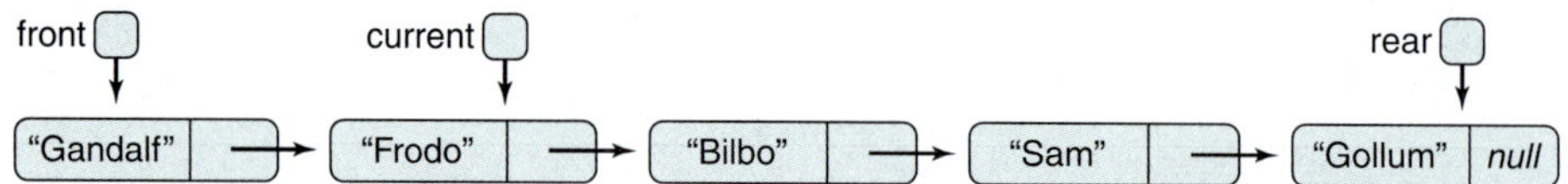

FIGURE 16.21 A call to *next*() returns "Gandalf" and moves *current* down the list

In Example 16.8, we implement LList<E>. LList<E> implements ListInterface<E> and provides the additional methods reset(), hasNext(), and next().

EXAMPLE 16.8 **Problem Statement** Create a linked list class, LList<E>, that implements ListInterface<E>. Include additional methods reset(), hasNext(), and next(). Use a chain of nodes for storage.

Java Solution The LList<E> class contains a private inner class Node. The fields of LList<E> are references front, rear, and current. Each is initially null. In addition to front, rear, and current, LList<E> maintains an instance variable, length, that holds number of data stored in the list. Initially, length is 0.

```
public class LList <E>implements ListInterface<E>
{
   private class Node                // an inner class
   {
      private E data;
      private Node next;

      public Node()                  // default constructor
      {
         data = null;
         next = null;
      }

      public Node(E x)               // two-argument constructor
      {
         data = x;
         next = null;
      }
```

```
} // end Node

private Node front, rear, current;
private int length;                       // the size of the list

public LList() // default constructor
{
    rear = front = current = null;
    length = 0;
}

public void add(E x)                      // adds x to the end of the list
{
    Node p = new Node(x);                 // instantiate a new node referenced by p
    if (rear == null)                     // if list is initially empty
        front = rear = p;                 // the list has just one node
    else
    {
        rear.next = p;                    // places the node referenced by p at the end
        rear = p;
    }
    length++;
}

public void add(int index, E x)           // adds x to list at position index
{
    if (index > length )                  // index out of range
    {
        System.out.println("Out of range in add(int index, E x)");
        System.exit(0);
    }
    Node p = new Node(x);                 // instantiate a new node referenced by p

    // add to the front of the list
    if (index == 0)
    {
        p.next = front;                   // place the address of the first node into the new node

        front = p;                        // front references the new node
        if (rear == null)                 // if list was initially empty
            rear = front;                 // front and rear reference the single node of the list
        length++;
        return;
    }

    // add to the end of the list
    if (index == length)
    {
        add(x);
        return;
    }

    // addition is neither at front nor rear
    Node q = front;
    for (int i = 0; i < index – 1; i++)   // point q to the node at position index
        q = q.next;
    Node r = q.next;                      // r references the node following q (could be null)
    q.next = p;
    p.next = r;
    length++;
}
```

```
public void clear()                            // makes the list empty
{
    front = rear = null;
    length = 0;
}

public boolean contains (E x)                  // returns true if x is a member of the list
{
    Node p = front;
    for (int i = 0; i < length; i++)           // could also use "(while p.next != null)"
    {
        if (x.equals(p.data))
            return true;
        p = p.next;
    }
    return false;                              // search unsuccessful
}

public E get (int index)                       // returns data at position index
{
    if (index >= length)                       // if index is out of bounds
    {
        System.out.println("Error in get (int index)");
        System.exit(0);
    }
    Node p = front;
    for (int i = 0 ; i < index; i++)
        p = p.next;                            // move through the list, node by node
    return p.data;
}

public boolean isEmpty()                       // returns true if list is empty
{
    return length == 0;
}

public boolean remove(E x)                     // removes first occurrence of x;
                                               // returns true if successful
{
    Node p = front;
    Node q = null;
    while (!(p == null) && !x.equals(p.data))          // look for x
    {
        q = p;
        p = p.next;
    }
    if (p == null)                             // not found
        return false;
    if (!(q == null))                          // if x is in the first node q is null
        q.next = p.next;
    if (p == front)
        front = front.next;
    if (p == rear)
        rear = q;
    length--;
    return true;
}
public E remove(int index)                     // removes and returns data at position index
{
```

```
        if (index >= length)            // index out of bounds
        {
            System.out.println("Error in remove (int index)");
            System.exit(0);
        }
        Node p = front;
        Node q = null;
        for (int i = 0; i < index; i++)  // q follows p down the list
        {
            q = p;
            p = p.next;
        }
        if (current == p)               // if removing the current node, move current to the next node
            current = p.next;
        if (!(q == null))               // if not removing the first node
        // q follows p, so q is null when p is the first node.
            q.next = p.next;
        if (p == front)
            front = front.next;
        if (p == rear)
            rear = q;
        length--;
        return p.data;
    }

    public E set (int index, E x)       // sets data at position index to x
    {
        if (index >= length)            // index out of bounds
        {
            System.out.println("Error in get (int index)");
            System.exit(0);
        }
        Node p = front;
        for (int i = 0; i < index; i++)
            p = p.next;
        E temp = p.data;
        p.data = x;
        return temp;
    }

    public int size()                   // returns the number of data on the list
    {
        return length;
    }

    public void reset()                 // makes the first node the current node
    {
        current = front;
    }

    public boolean hasNext()            // returns true if a call to next() will be successful
    {
        if (current == null)
            return false;
        return true;
    }

    public E next()                     // returns data of current node and moves current to the next node
    {
```

```
179.            if (current == null)
180.            {
181.                System.out.println("Error in hasNext() ");
182.                System.exit(0);
183.            }
184.            E temp = current.data;
185.            current = current.next;
186.            return temp;
187.        }
188. }
```

Discussion The following diagrams illustrate the operation of two of the methods of LList<E>. You should trace through each of the other methods to be sure that you understand their implementations.

Lines 25–36: void add(E x)

This method adds a node with data x to the rear of the list.

Suppose that a list consists of three nodes as follows:

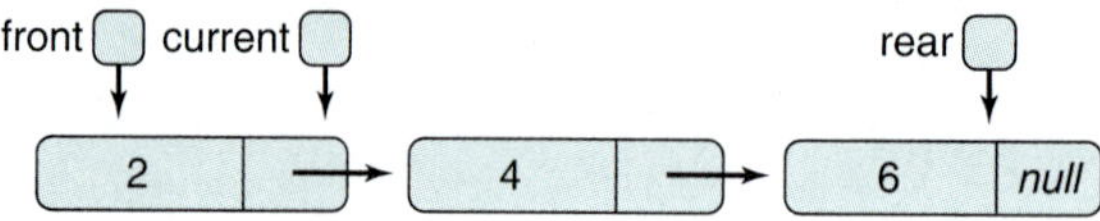

The method call add(8) results in the following actions:

Line 27: Node p = new Node(8);

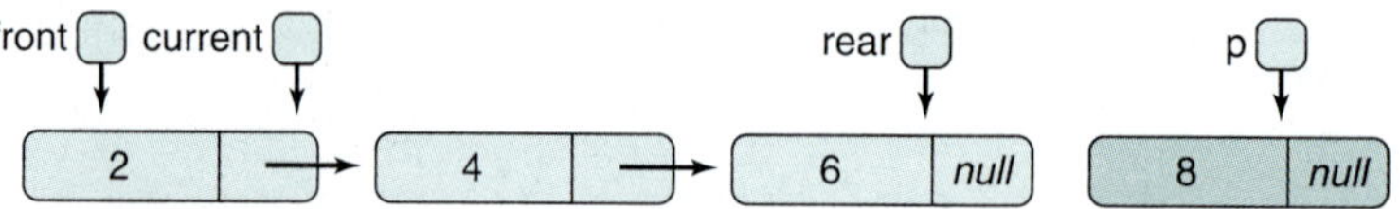

Line 32: rear.next = p;

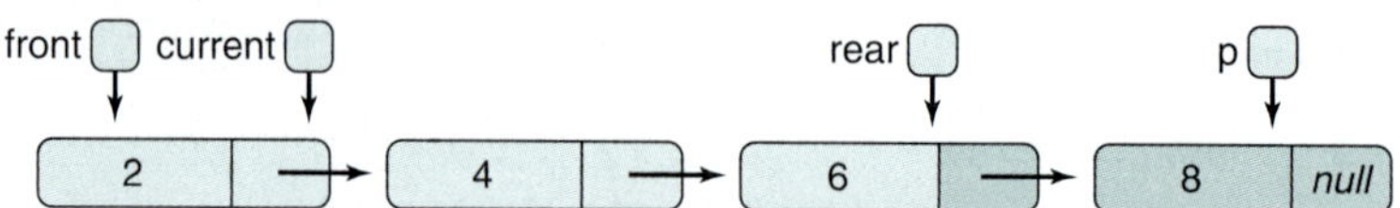

Line 33: rear = p;

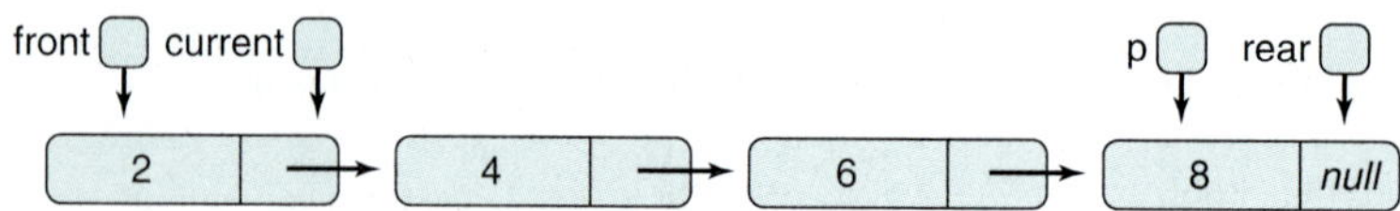

The new node has been added to the end of the list.

We now consider one of the remove(...) operations.

Lines 123–148: E remove(int index)

This method removes the node at a given index. For example, remove(0) removes the first node in the list and remove(2) removes the third node in the list. We trace a call to remove(2).

Unlike an ArrayList, a linked list does not support direct access. To access the third node, the method must traverse the list from the beginning. We assume that, prior to the call remove(2), the list is as follows:

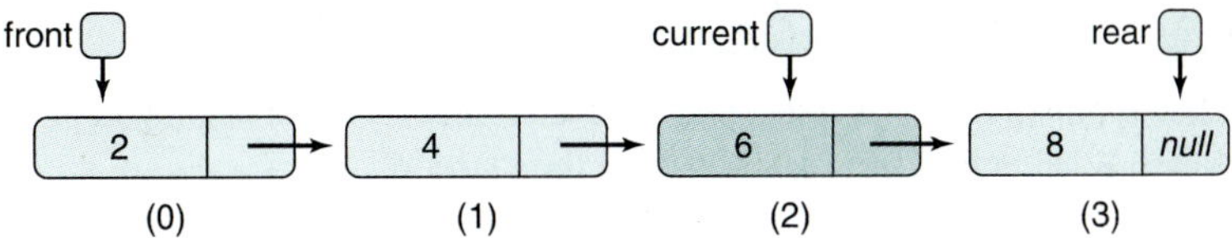

The call to remove(2) removes the node at index 2, which is also, coincidentally, the "current" node.

Lines 130–131: Node p = front; Node q = null;
Reference q follows p down the chain.

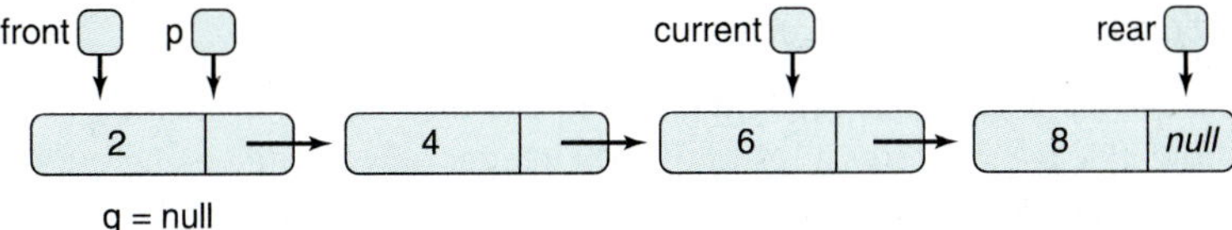

Lines 132–136: for (int i = 0; i < index; i++) {q = p; p = p.next;}
For i = 0 and i = 1,

- set q equal to p, and
- move p down the list.

Notice that q follows p.

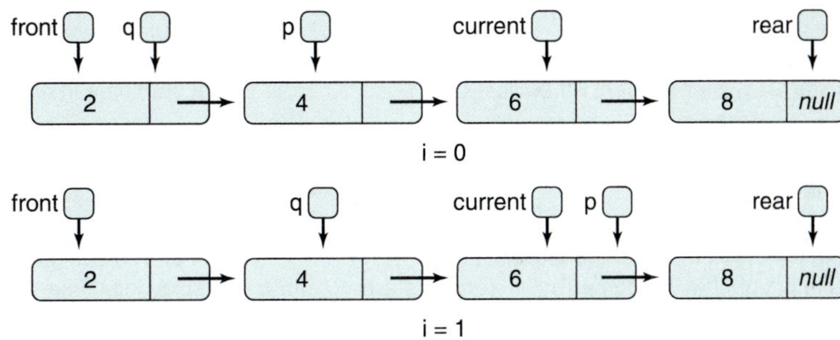

Lines 137–138: if (current == p) current = p.next;
p references the node which is to be removed. If current references the same node as p, move current down the list.

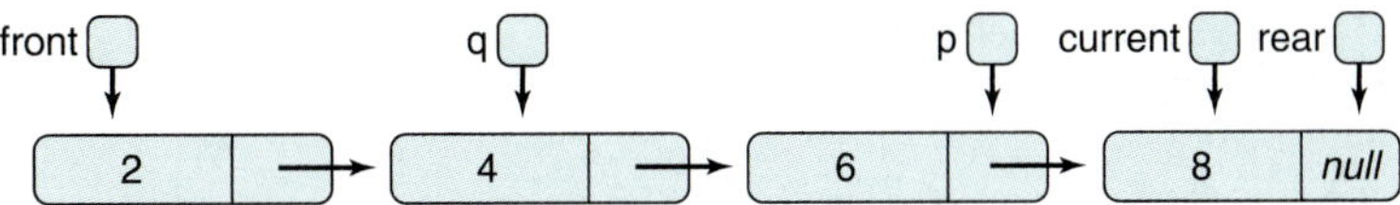

Lines 139–141: if (!(q == null)) q.next = p.next;
If q is null, then the node to be removed is the first node on the list. In this case, q is *not* null. Here, p holds the address of the node that is to be removed and q the address of the preceding node. Change the link in q.next from p to p.next.

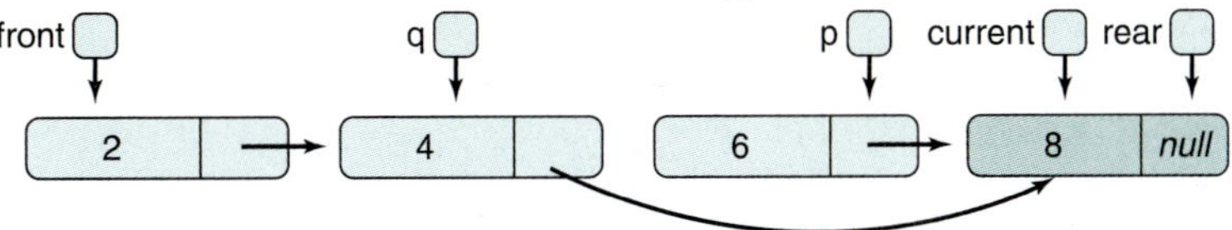

When the method exits, the memory allocated for the deleted node is automatically reclaimed by the garbage collector. (See Chapter 10.)

16.6.4 Why *next*() and *hasNext*()?

A common list application is traversal. That is, each item of a list is displayed or processed in some manner. If list belongs to LList<E> then the for loop

```
for (int i = 0; i < list.size(); i++)
        System.out.println(list.get(i));
```

traverses and displays each element of list. Alternatively, the statements

```
list.reset();
while (list.hasNext())
    System.out.println(list.next());
```

accomplish the same task. Is one method preferable to the other?

The following class traverses a list of 50,000 Integer objects, first using get(i) and then using next(). The results of this comparison should convince you that next() is a method that is both convenient and practical.

```
1.  public class GetVsNext
2.  {
3.     public static void main(String[] args)
4.     {
5.        LList <Integer>list = new LList<Integer>();
6.        final int NUM_DATA = 50000;
7.        for (int i = 0; i < NUM_DATA; i++)
8.           list.add(0,i);
9.        long start = System.currentTimeMillis();                  // get start time in milliseconds

10.       for (int j = 0; j < list.size(); j++)                     // traverse the list
11.          list.get(j);

12.       long end = System.currentTimeMillis();                    // get end time in milliseconds
13.       System.out.println("Using get(i): " + (end – start) + " ms");  // display total time
14.       start = System.currentTimeMillis();
15.       list.reset();

16.       while (list.hasNext())
17.          list.next();

18.       end = System.currentTimeMillis();
19.       System.out.println("Using next(): " + (end – start) + " ms");

20.    }
21. }
```

The program produces the following output:

```
Using get(i): 42431 ms
Using next(): 10 ms
```

Why is there such a considerable difference in time? The traversal on lines 10 and 11,

```
for (int j = 0; j < list.size(); j++)
   get(j);
```

invokes get(j) 50,000 times, once for each node. With *each* invocation of get(j), the statement

```
p = p.next;
```

is executed j times. (See lines 94 and 95 of Example 16.8.) If j ranges from 0 to 49,999 then

```
p = p.next;
```

executes 0 + 1 + 2+ … + 49,999 = 1,249,975,000 times.

On the other hand, each call to next() requires just one step, and 50,000 calls to next() perform just 50,000 operations. That's quite a difference!

16.6.5 *ArrayList<E>* or *LList<E>*: Which Is Better?

Linked lists and ArrayLists are more similar than different. Like an ArrayList, a linked list is a data structure that grows dynamically, as needed. Moreover, the methods of ArrayList<E> are also methods of LList<E>. However, there *are* some striking differences, and these differences can affect the efficiency of a program.

Insertions into and deletions from an ArrayList can slow down execution, especially if these operations occur near the top of the list. A linked list, on the other hand, allows efficient insertions and deletions anywhere in the list. No data are moved by any of the add(…) or remove(…) methods of LList<E>.

In contrast to an ArrayList, a linked list does not support direct access to data via indexing. A linked list provides no efficient method to access the *i*th element in the list. To retrieve the *i*th element, the first $i - 1$ elements must be accessed. A method call such as get(100) must access nodes 0 through 99 to retrieve node 100.

Example 16.9 compares LLlist<E> with ArrayList<E>, first when data are always inserted at the beginning of a list, and then when data are inserted at the end of a list. Can you predict which class provides a more efficient implementation in each case?

EXAMPLE 16.9

Problem Statement Write an application that compares the relative efficiency of ArrayList<E> with LList<E> when Integer data are added

1. to the front of the list (only), and
2. to the rear of the list (only).

Java Solution The main(...) method of the following class inserts Integer data into a LList<Integer> object as well as an ArrayList<Integer> object according to the specifications (1) and (2). Each operation is timed.

```
import java.util.*;

public class TestLists <E>
{

   public static void main(String [] args)
   {
      final int NUM_DATA = 10000;                   // number of data
      LList <Integer>lList = new LList<Integer>();
      ArrayList <Integer>aList = new ArrayList<Integer>();

      //////// Insert at front /////////

      long start = System.currentTimeMillis();      // LList
```

```
        for (int i = 0; i < NUM_DATA; i++)
            lList.add(0,i);
        long elapsed = System.currentTimeMillis() - start;
        System.out.println("LList - add to front: " + elapsed + " ms");

        start = System.currentTimeMillis();            // ArrayList
        for (int i = 0; i < NUM_DATA; i++)
            aList.add(0, i );
        elapsed = System.currentTimeMillis() - start;
        System.out.println("ArrayList - add to front: " + elapsed + " ms");

        //////////// Insert at rear ////////////

        lList.clear();
        aList.clear();
        start = System.currentTimeMillis();            // LList

        for (int i = 0; i < NUM_DATA; i++)
            lList.add(i);
        elapsed = System.currentTimeMillis() - start;
        System.out.println("LList - add to rear: " + elapsed + " ms");

        start = System.currentTimeMillis();            // ArrayList
        for (int i = 0; i < NUM_DATA; i++)
            aList.add(i);
        elapsed = System.currentTimeMillis() - start;
        System.out.println("ArrayList - add to rear: " + elapsed + " ms");
    }
}
```

Output Running the program five times produced the following output:

10000 data LList – add to front: 16 ms ArrayList – add to front: 62 ms LList – add to rear: 0 ms ArrayList – add to rear: 0 ms	20000 data LList – add to front: 32 ms ArrayList – add to front: 218 ms LList – add to rear: 16 ms ArrayList – add to rear: 16 ms	40000 data LList – add to front: 46 ms ArrayList – add to front: 844 ms LList – add to rear: 16 ms ArrayList – add to rear: 15 ms
80000 data LList – add to front: 79 ms ArrayList – add to front: 3821 ms LList – add to rear: 47 ms ArrayList – add to rear: 15 ms	160000 data LList – add to front: 141 ms ArrayList – add to front: 13062 ms LList – add to rear: 63 ms ArrayList – add to rear: 15 ms	

Discussion When adding to the front of a list, LList<E> clearly outperforms ArrayList<E>. This is because the ArrayList<E> method shifts all items in the list to make room for each new item. When inserting 1000 integers into the front of the list, the first insertion requires no shifting, the second insertion 1 shift, the third 2 shifts, the fourth 3 shifts, and so on. Thus, to insert 1000 integers into the front of the list, ArrayList<E> requires $1 + 2 + 3 + 4 + \ldots + 999 = 499{,}500$ shifts. Each time the size of the data is doubled, the execution time is approximately quadrupled.

On the other hand, when inserting data into the front of LList<E>, it makes no difference whether the size of the list is 10 or 10,000. Each insertion requires the same three steps:

```
1. Node p = new Node(x);      // instantiate a new node
2. p.next = front;            // connect p to the front
3. front = p;                 // move the front back to p.
```

For 1000 insertions, LList<E> takes just 3000 steps, in contrast to the half a million performed by ArrayList<E>.

The situation is different when appending to the end of a list. Notice that, in this case, adding data to the rear of an ArrayList is slightly faster than adding data to the rear of a LList. Here, the ArrayList <E>add(...) method shifts no data; nor does the add(...) method of LList<E>. However, the LList <E> add(...) method requires that a new node be instantiated, and that rear be assigned the address of the new node. These actions account for the slightly longer execution times that LList<E> exhibits when inserting items at the rear of a list. However, this difference is not as pronounced as the difference exhibited when inserting at the front of a list.

When adding to the front of a list, LList<E> outperforms ArrayList<E>, and when adding to the rear, the performances of the two are quite close.

Furthermore, if direct access to data is necessary, ArrayList<E> is clearly superior to LList<E>. The LList<E> implementation of get(int index) utilizes a loop:

```
for (int i = 0; i < index; i++)
    p = p.next;
```

and consequently every get(index) operation involves index assignments. In contrast, the get(index) method of ArrayList<E> is accomplished in one step; no loop is necessary.

The choice of data structure depends on the application. No data structure is always "best."

16.7 IN CONCLUSION

Each data structure in this chapter presents a different option for handling a collection of data. If data is always added or removed from the top of a list, a stack is the obvious choice. A queue is appropriate for first-in, first-out situations. A queue is a handy simulation tool. More flexible list manipulation is provided by an array, an ArrayList, or a linked list. The choice of the appropriate data structure depends on the application. Although ArrayList<E> and LList<E> support similar operations, an arbitrary choice of one over the other can result in performance degradation.

Finally, although we implement the Stack<E> class using ArrayList<E> and the Queue<E> class with a circular array, each of these classes can be easily and efficiently implemented using a dynamic chain of nodes. We describe these alternate implementations in the exercises.

In the Chapter 17, we consider Java's Collection classes, a hierarchy of classes that implement numerous data structures. Indeed, the ArrayList<E> class is a member of this hierarchy as is the LinkedList<E> class, which is similar but more flexible than the LList<E> class of this chapter. And, once again, you will see that choosing the right data structure for an application can make all the difference.

Just the Facts

- A *data structure* is a collection of data together with a set of operations for storing, retrieving, managing, and manipulating the data.
- Every data structure must be *implemented* using some underlying storage structure and appropriate set of methods. The choice of implementation is important for efficiency.
- The implementation of a data structure should be invisible to the client.
- Using the right data structure for the right application is a fundamental notion of efficient coding and algorithm design.
- Java's ArrayList class is an indexed list of references that grows as the number of data increases—a dynamic array.
- Java's ArrayList class has many built-in methods, including methods to insert into, remove from, and access an array.
- A generic class is one that allows you to specify the data type of one or more fields as a parameter. This means that a data structure class can be defined generically and instantiated to hold any type of data. For example, ArrayList<E> is a generic class. The type parameter E specifies the type of data stored in an ArrayList<E> object. E cannot be a primitive type.
- A generic class ensures type safety. Generic classes allow the compiler to find type mismatch errors before runtime.
- Interfaces as well as classes can be generic.
- There are a number of restrictions associated with generic classes with regard to arrays and constructors.
- Using inheritance and polymorphism together with generic classes maintains type safety while simultaneously allowing a programmer to write flexible code that the compiler might otherwise flag as a type mismatch.
- A *stack* is an ordered list of data that allows insertions and deletions from one end, the top.
- A stack, despite its very restricted set of methods, is the perfect tool for solving certain kinds of problems, especially those involving backtracking.
- A *queue* is an ordered list of data that allows insertions to its rear and deletions from its front.
- A queue is an excellent tool for simulation.
- A *linked list* is an ordered list of items such that each item holds a link or reference to the next item in the list.
- An advantage that a linked list has over an ArrayList is that a linked list allows efficient insertions and deletions anywhere within the list. On the other hand, a linked list has no efficient method to access the ith element; each of the first $i - 1$ elements must be accessed before processing the ith element.
- Traversing a linked list is more efficiently accomplished by repeatedly calling the next() method rather than the get(...) method.

- When nodes are deleted from a linked list and are no longer accessible, the Java garbage collector automatically reclaims the space allocated for those nodes.
- An *inner* class is a class defined within another class. Inner classes are useful when one class has meaning only in the context of another class.
- The methods of an inner class have direct access to all variables and methods of the surrounding outer class. On the other hand, the methods of an outer class can access an inner class field or invoke an inner class method only via an object of the inner class.

Bug Extermination

- Be careful when invoking the get(...) method of an ArrayList, x. Even though space may be *reserved* for indices greater than x.size() − 1, the call x.get(k) results in a runtime error, if k is greater than x.size() − 1.
- Do not attempt to instantiate an object with a type parameter. The following statement generates a compilation error:

```
E myObject = new E();
```

- Java does not allow generic arrays. The statement

```
E[] list = new E[10];
```

  generates a syntax error. However, it is legal to instantiate an array with a cast such as:

```
E[] list = (E[]) new Object[10];
```

  Nonetheless, the compiler has no way of knowing whether or not this type of cast is safe. Consequently, the compiler generates a warning message that although legal, this *may* be unsafe.
- Always check whether a stack or queue is empty before performing a pop(), peek(), or remove() method.
- If the underlying implementation of a stack or queue does not allow for dynamic and automatic resizing, then overflow might occur. In such cases, check for overflow before invoking a push(...) or an insert(...) method.
- Always implement a data structure with methods that are as efficient as possible.
- Always use the appropriate data structure to solve a problem—neither more nor less powerful than necessary.

EXERCISES

LEARN THE LINGO

Test your knowledge of the chapter's vocabulary by completing the following crossword puzzle.

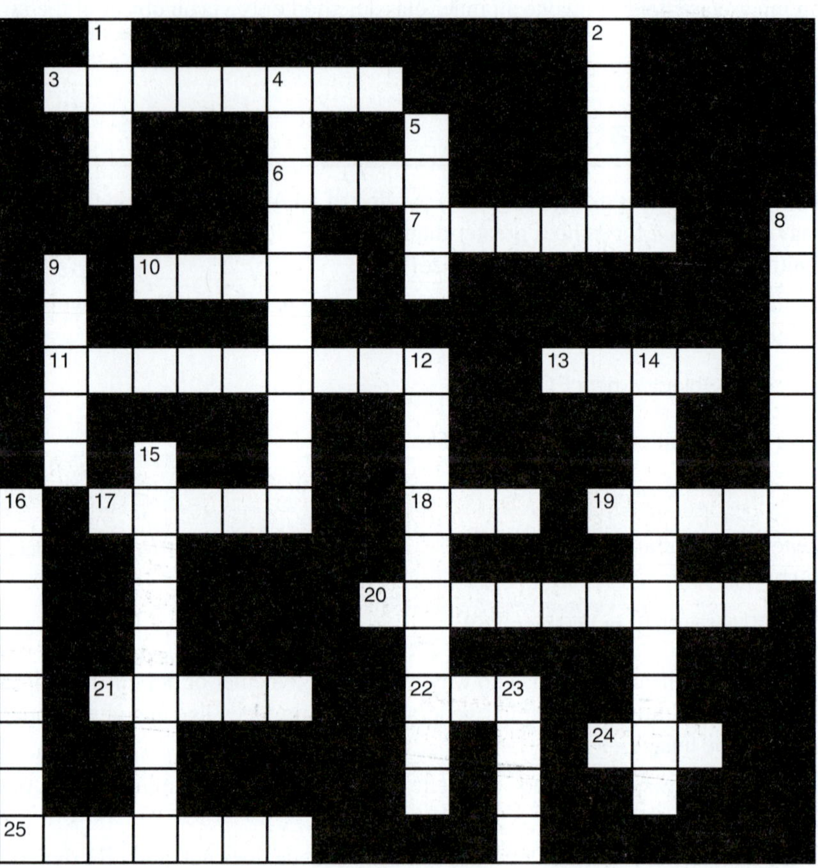

Across

3 Type of array that can be used to implement a queue
6 The "next" field of a node refers to a ________.
7 Java does not allow generic ________.
10 A linked list can be implemented as a chain of ________.
11 Dynamic array
13 Add to a stack
17 Data is removed from the _____ of a queue.
18 Inserting into the _____ of an ArrayList is very efficient.
19 First in, first out
20 When traversing a network, a stack can be used to ________.
21 Last in, first out
22 Data is accessed from the _____ of a stack.
24 Remove from a stack
25 Kind of class with a type parameter

Down

1 The average time that it takes to access an element in a linked list depends on the ________ of the list.
2 Cannot be resized
4 Each item holds a reference to the next.
5 Data is inserted at the _____ of a queue.
8 Type safety ensures that type errors are caught by the ________.
9 Nodes of a linked list form a ________.
12 A generic class ensures ________.
14 A queue is often used for ________.
15 ArrayList cannot store _____ types.
16 Removing the first element in an ArrayList entails _____ all other elements.
23 View but do not remove an element.

SHORT EXERCISES

1. **True or False**
   If false, give an explanation.
   a. A slide at the playground is more like a stack than a queue.
   b. A car with one working door is more like a stack than a queue.
   c. A linked list allows immediate access to any element in the list, independent of the length of the list, as long as the index of the element is known.
   d. An ArrayList, unlike an array, can increase its size dynamically.
   e. The index of a circular array that follows the highest numerical index is zero, and the index that precedes zero is the index with the highest numerical value.
   f. A queue is a good data structure for problems that involve backtracking.
   g. Using a generic class you can define a data structure independent of data type.
   h. A generic class is a class with no brand name.
   i. ArrayList objects handle insertion at the front and rear of a list with equal efficiency.
   j. A *short stack* is a kind of breakfast made with only two pancakes, or a small number of chips at the poker table.

2. **Playing Compiler**
   Find and correct the syntax and logic error(s) in the following class. Board encapsulates a two-person game. Board uses a two-dimensional array that holds pieces of type T. Board also remembers whether it is player 1's turn or player 2's turn.

```
class Board<T>
{
   private ArrayList <T>items;
   int turn;      // which player's turn, 1 or 2

   public Board()
   // default constructor
   {
      items = new <T>bo[8][8];
      turn = 1;
   } // creates an empty 8 by 8 two-dimensional array

   public Board(int initialCapacity, int player )
         // one-argument constructor, creates 2-dim array
         // with initialCapacity rows and columns
   {
      items = new <T>bo[initialCapacity] [initialCapacity];
      turn = player;
   }
   public Board(int initialRowCapacity, int initialColumnCapacity, int player)
          // two-argument constructor, creates 2-dim array with
          // initialCapacity rows and columns
   {
      items = new <T>bo[initialCapacity] [initialCapacity];
      turn = player;
   }

   public T whoseturn()
   // accessor for whose turn it is
   {
```

```
        return (turn);
    }

    public T addtoBoard(T item, int row, int col)
    // lets you put a piece on the board
    {
        bo[row, col] = item;
    }

    public T peek(int row, int col)
    // lets you peek at a piece on the board
    {
        return bo[row][col];
    }

    public void switchturn()
    // lets you switch whose turn it is
    {
        if (turn == 1)
                turn = 2;
        if (turn == 2)
                turn = 1;
    }
}
```

3. **Playing Compiler**
   For each of the following fragments, explain and correct the errors. If the fragment stands correct as it is, then say so.

   a. ```
      ArrayList <Integer> test = new ArrayList <Integer> (20);
      list.add("35");
      list.add(35);
      ```
   b. ```
      ArrayList temp = new ArrayList();
      temp.add("35");
      temp.add(35);
      ```
   c. ```
      Stack <Integer> = new Stack();
      push(1);
      push('a');
      ```
   d. ```
      Stack <ArrayList <Integer>> really = new Stack <ArrayList <Integer>>();
      ```
   e. ```
      LList <Integer> testlist = new testlist <Integer>();
      testlist[3] = 7;
      ```

4. **Which Data Structure?**
   For each problem, describe which data structure(s) you would use and give an explanation for your choice.

   a. Java uses *garbage collection* to find available memory locations and stores such locations in a repository so that allocations for new objects can be made. Whenever the new command is used, memory is allocated to create storage for the new object being instantiated. In what data structure would you store these locations? Why?
   b. A video editor allows a user to create movies by splicing together video clips. The user can add a clip between any two clips and delete or move a clip to a different location. Finally, the spliced clips are played consecutively so that the final video looks right. In what data structure would you store the clips be stored? Why?
      ```

5. **Which Data Structure?**
   For each of the following problems, determine the data structure that you would use to solve the problem in the most efficient way possible. You should use the simplest data structure(s) that allows you to attain that efficiency.
   a. You are writing a browser program for the Web, and your browser must remember all the sites that a user has visited for proper implementation of "back" and "forward" buttons.
   b. You are writing a *web crawling* program that, given a site, finds all the sites to which it links, then find all the sites to which those sites link, and so on, up to 10 levels. Your program lists all the sites and corresponding levels.

6. **Stack Implementations**
   One data structure can sometimes be used to implement another data structure. For example, in this chapter an ArrayList is used to implement a stack. Describe how you would implement a stack using
   a. a linked list.
   b. a queue.

   Does the efficiency of your push(…) and pop() methods depend on the number of elements on the stack?

7. **ArrayList<E> Implementation**
   When an ArrayList<E> object needs more space, it resizes itself by allocating more memory and copying the current object to a larger block of memory.
   How much more space does an ArrayList<E> object allocate when it resizes itself? Consider the following three strategies.
   a. Increase the capacity by 10.
   b. Double the current capacity.
   c. Increase the capacity by 1.

   Assume that
   - an ArrayList <E>is initialized with a capacity of 10 values,
   - new data come one value at a time, and
   - eventually the list will need to accommodate 80 values.

   Calculate the total number of elements that are copied using each of the three strategies for resizing. Which strategy would use you use to implement ArrayList<E> and why?

8. **ArrayList <E> vs LList<E>**
   ArrayList<E> and LList<E> provide many of the same methods. These are enumerated in ListInterface<E>. However, LList<E> provides three methods not provided by ArrayList<E>. These are
   - void reset(),
   - boolean hasNext(), and
   - E next().

   Explain why ArrayList<E> does not implement these methods. Why are these methods included in the implementation of LList<E>?

9. **Using Exceptions with Data Structures**
   a. Rewrite the pop() method of Stack<E> so that pop() throws a NoSuchElementException when the stack is empty. You will also have to alter StackInterface<E>.

b. Rewrite the Queue<E> methods insert(E x) and remove(), so that each throws an appropriate exception rather than returning null or exiting abruptly. Adjust QueueInterface<E> appropriately.

c. Five LList<E> methods terminate abruptly under exceptional conditions. Rewrite these methods so that each throws an appropriate exception.

10. **Find the Flaw**

Suppose that the algorithm used in Example 16.6 was written as:

```
For each minute from 0 through 59
{
   If there are customers waiting and the ATM is available
   {
      Remove a customer from the queue;
      Increment the number of customers served;
      Add to the total waiting time the waiting time of the current customer;
      Update the time the ATM is next available;
   }
   Determine the number of new customers arriving: 0, 1, or 2;
   For each new customer
            Place the new customer in the queue;
}
Print the summary statistics;
```

Find the flaw in this algorithm. Explain how it might generate incorrect output.

PROGRAMMING EXERCISES

Programs marked **(R)** require recursive solutions.

1. **Palindromes**

   A *palindrome* is a sequence of characters that reads the same forwards and backwards such as "mom," "dennis sinned," or "a man a plan a canal panama." Write a program that accepts a string of characters and uses a stack to determine whether or not the string is a palindrome. When deciding whether or not a string is a palindrome, ignore spaces, case, and punctuation. For example, "Madam I'm Adam" is a palindrome.

2. **Recursive Network Traversal**

   (R) Write a recursive version of the algorithm that moves the prisoner through the rooms of a house (described iteratively in Example 16.4). A recursive version uses fewer lines of code and does not explicitly use a stack.

3. **Reversing a List**

   Write and test an iterative method that accepts a reference to a LList<E> and returns a reference to another LList<E> that contains the data of the original list in reverse order.

4. **Recursive Reversal of a List**

   (R) Write and test a **recursive** method that accepts a reference to a LList<E> and returns a reference to another LList<E> that contains the data of the original list in reverse order.

5. **Printing a List**

   (R) Write and test a **recursive** method that accepts a reference to a LList<E> and prints the items in the list.

6. **Another Implementation of LList<E>**
   The implementation of LList<E> given in this chapter includes a private inner class, Node. As such, LList<E> can access the private data of Node. Using an inner class is a convenience but not a necessity. Define a generic class Node<E> as a public independent class and implement LList<E> using Node<E>. Because LList<E> cannot access the private data of Node<E>, your implementation of Node<E> should include setter and getter methods. Devise a third class that instantiates a LList<String> object, interactively stores an arbitrary number of strings, and demonstrates the methods of LList<E>.

7. **Emptying and Printing a Stack**
   Write and test an iterative method that pops and prints all data in a stack.

8. **Recursive Emptying and Printing of a Stack**
   (R) Write and test a **recursive** method that pops and prints all data in a stack.

9. **Insertion Sort Using ArrayList**
   Write a program that reads 50 strings from a file and sorts them by inserting each string into the appropriate place in an ArrayList<String> object. For example, if the strings are:

   Shai
   Ralph
   Hillary
   Tom
   Barbara
   Fred

   Then the ArrayList should grow as follows:

   empty
   Shai
   Ralph Shai
   Hillary Ralph Shai
   Hillary Ralph Shai Tom
   Barbara Hillary Ralph Shai Tom
   Barbara Fred Hillary Ralph Shai Tom

10. **Depth First Search**
    Write a backtracking program similar to Example 16.4 that accepts a network (represented by a two-dimensional array) and visits every "room" in the network. Your search should start with room 0. Rather than visiting adjacent rooms in random order, use ascending order of room numbers. Your program should print the rooms in the order visited. For example, using the network in Figure 16.8, your program should print: 0, 1, 2, 3, 5, 6, 7, 4, 8, 13, 9, 10, 12, 11, 15, 16, 17, 20, 21, 14, 18, 19. This program can be done recursively, or iteratively with the help of a stack.

11. **Connected Components of a Network (Graph)**
    Not all networks are connected. For example, imagine an estate with many buildings, each of which has many rooms. If we model this estate with a network, then the rooms within each building are accessible one to another, but not the rooms between two buildings.

    Write a program that accepts a possibly disconnected network (represented by a two-dimensional array) and prints a list of rooms in each building. Number the buildings beginning with 1. This can be done recursively or iteratively.

For example, if the estate array is:

```
0 1 0 0 1 0 0
1 0 0 0 1 0 0
0 0 0 1 0 1 1
0 0 1 0 0 1 1
1 1 0 0 0 0 0
0 0 1 1 0 0 1
0 0 1 1 0 1 0
```

your output should be:

Building 1: Room numbers 0, 1, 4.
Building 2: Room numbers 2, 3, 6, 5.

Hint: Wrap the solution to the previous problem in a loop.

12. **Postfix Expressions**

Everyone is familiar with arithmetic expressions that place the operator between the operands. Such an expression is called an *infix* expression. For example, 3 + 1, (3 + 2) * 4, and (4 + 6) * (2 + 3) are infix expressions. Infix notation is familiar but inconvenient because an infix expression requires parentheses and operator precedence rules for correct evaluation.

A *postfix* expression is an arithmetic expression in which the operators *follow* their corresponding operands. For example, 32+ is the postfix equivalent of 3 + 2. And, in postfix notation, 325+* means (2 + 5) * 3, while 325*+ means (2 * 5) + 3. No parentheses are necessary to evaluate a postfix expression correctly, and every postfix expression can be evaluated without precedence rules. Compilers and some calculators use postfix expressions. Although postfix may appear tricky to read, with the aid of a stack, the evaluation of a postfix expression is straightforward.

Write a method that accepts a postfix expression (string) and returns its numerical value. For simplicity, assume that all operands are single digits 0 through 9, that there are just two operators '+', and '*', and all postfix expressions are syntactically correct.

The algorithm to evaluate a postfix expression uses the Stack <Integer> class and is given below:

```
While there are still more symbols in the expression:
  a. Read next symbol ch.
  b. If ch is an operand (a digit '0'...'9') then
                push the integer equivalent of ch on the stack.
                   // i.e., ch – '0'
  c. If ch is an operator ('+' or '*')
            pop two values off the stack,
            perform the appropriate operation on them, and
            push the result back on the stack.
Pop the stack and return the value.
```

For example, the postfix string "897*6++" evaluates to: (((9 * 7) + 6) + 8) = 77. Figure 16.22 traces the evaluation of "897*6++".

13. **Infix to Postfix Conversion**

Converting infix expressions to postfix expressions can be accomplished using the following algorithm, due to Edsger W. Dijkstra, called the Shunting Yard Algorithm.

The Shunting Yard Algorithm

```
Input: an infix expression (string)
Output: the equivalent postfix expression (string)
```

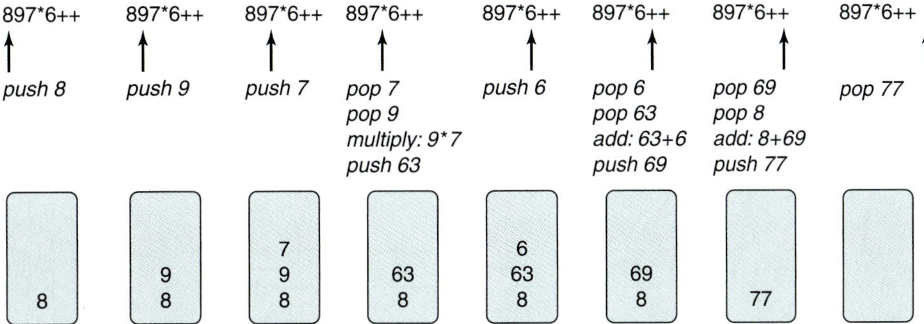

FIGURE 16.22 The stack during the evaluation of the postfix expression 897*6++

```
Initialize the postfix expression to empty.
For each character in the infix expression
{
      1. read a character, ch, from the infix expression
      2. if ch is an operand then append ch to the postfix expression
      3. else if ch is an operator then
                while an operator of greater or equal priority is on the stack
                        pop the stack;
                        append the popped operator to the postfix expression;
                push ch
      4. else if ch is a left parenthesis '('
                push ch onto the stack;
      5. else if ch is a right parenthesis ')'
                while the top of the stack is not a left parenthesis '('
                        pop the stack and append the operator to the postfix expression;
                pop and discard the left parenthesis;
}

While the stack is not empty
    pop the stack and append the popped operators to the postfix expression;
```

Note that the operands always remain in the same order, and only the operators change position. For example, the infix expression 6*7–8/9 converts to a postfix form of 67*89/−. The stack, the infix string, and the postfix string processed are shown in Figure 16.23.

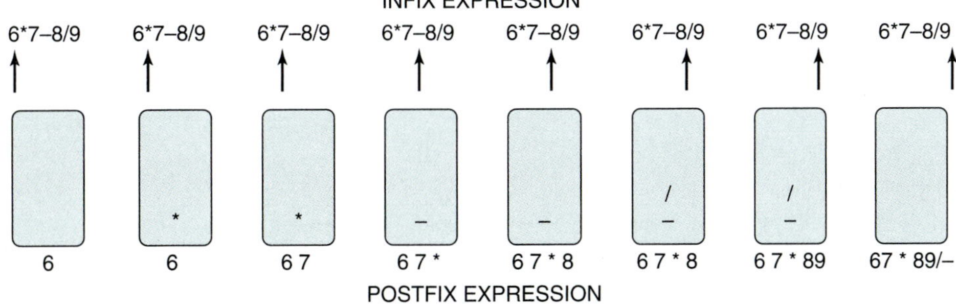

FIGURE 16.23 Conversion of the infix expression 6*7−8/9 to the postfix expression 67*89/–

Implement this algorithm using a stack of char. You may assume that all operands are single digits and operators are from the set { +, –, *, /}. Infix expressions may include parentheses.

14. **Alternate Implementation of Stack<E>**
Use a chain of nodes, rather than an ArrayList, to implement Stack<E>. The time necessary to perform a push() or pop() operation should always be the same, no matter how many elements are on the stack. A single variable, top, should reference the first node of the chain, as shown in Figure 16.24

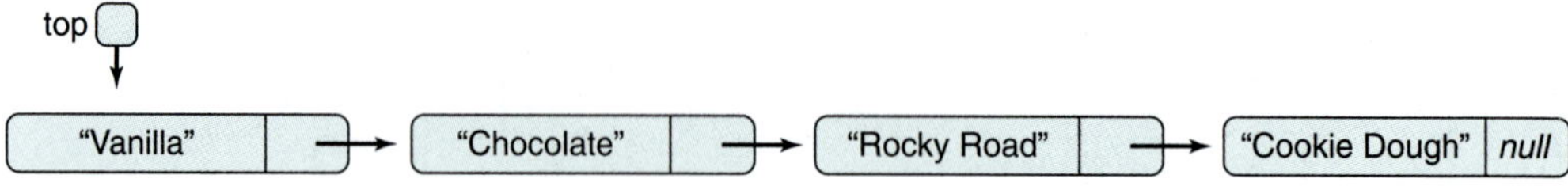

FIGURE 16.24 A linked implementation of a stack

15. **Which Data Structure Is Better for Insertion Sort: ArrayList or LList?**
Write a program that compares the speed of insertion sort (see Chapter 7), first using ArrayList<E>, and then using LList<E>. Report and explain your results. Which data structure appears more suitable for insertion sort? Justify your answer.

16. **A Print Queue**
A print queue is a list of jobs waiting to be printed. Each job is assigned two integers: an *id*, and a *time* that is an estimate of the number of seconds required by the job. Three printers (A, B, and C) serve the same single queue. Whenever a job completes, the next job waiting in the queue is serviced. If two printers finish a job simultaneously, then A has precedence over B, and B has precedence over C.
Write a program that simulates a print queue with 30 print jobs such that *ids* are numbered 1 through 30, and *times* are set to random numbers between 10 and 1000. A new job should be created every 100 seconds. Your program should report
- the total time, in seconds, for each job,
- the number of seconds that each printer was busy and idle throughout the processing of all 30 jobs, and
- how many jobs were processed by each printer.

Total time for each job is counted from the creation of the job until the job is complete.

17. **A Linked Implementation of a Queue**
Use a chain of nodes to implement the Queue <E> class queue. Implement insert(…) and remove() efficiently so that insertions and deletions always take the same amount of time no matter how large the queue. *Hint*: Use two references, front and rear, each a reference to nodes in a chain. See Figure 16.25.

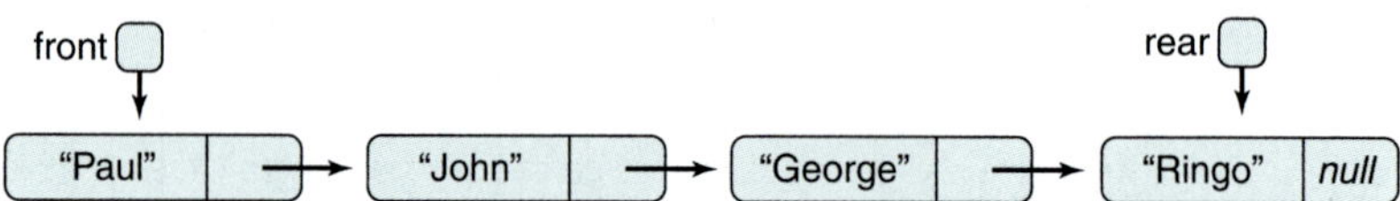

FIGURE 16.25 A linked implementation of a queue

Note that without a reference to the rear of the queue, insertions, which necessarily occur at the rear of the queue, are expensive because accessing the rear of the queue requires a traversal of the entire queue. The time required for this traversal increases with the size of the queue.

18. **Doubly Linked Lists**
A doubly linked list is a chain of nodes, each of which has three components: data, next, and previous. The data component holds a reference to some data, the next component holds the address of the next node in the list, and the previous component holds the address of the previous node in the list. See Figure 16.26.

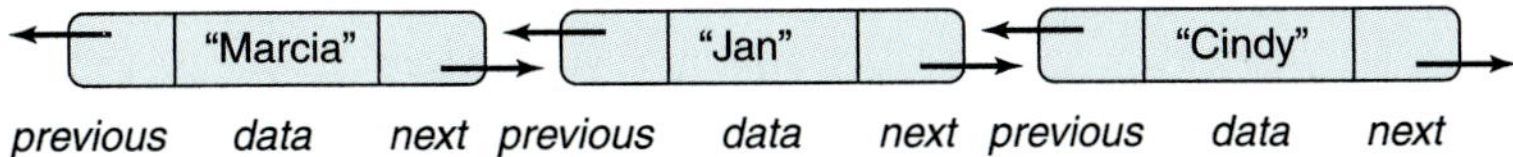

FIGURE 16.26 A doubly linked list

Create a class DList<E> that implements the ListInterface <E> using a doubly linked chain of nodes. Include LList<E> methods
- reset()
- next()
- hasNext()

Include additional methods:
- Eprevious()
  if current == null, reports an error and terminates the application; otherwise returns the data of the current node and sets current equal to current.previous.
- boolean hasPrevious()
  returns true if current.previous is not null.

Use the features of a doubly linked list to improve the efficiency of the methods of LList<E>. In particular, get(int index) can be done 50% faster because the search can start from the right or left end of the list, whichever is closer to the index.

19. **Circularly Linked Lists**
A circularly linked list is a chain of nodes such that the last node refers back to the first. Implement a queue using such a structure. Insertions and deletions should always take the same amount of time, regardless of the size of the queue. Hint: A single reference should hold the address of the rear node, which points, of course, to the front of the queue. See Figure 16.27.

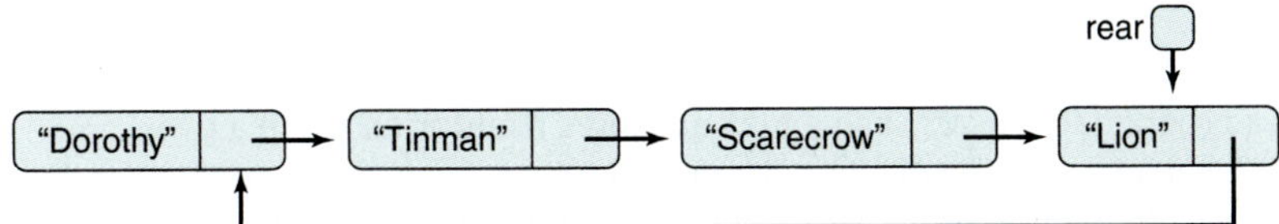

FIGURE 16.27 A queue implemented using a circularly linked list

20. **Breadth First Search of a Family Tree Using a Queue**
A file contains information that describes a family tree. The first line contains an integer n indicating the number of people in the family tree. The next n lines contain strings, each representing a unique name in the family tree. The remainder of the file uses n lines to describe who is the child of whom. The ith line, $1 \leq i \leq n$, contains a list of people who are children of the ith person. People are represented by integers: the mth person in the original list of names is listed as m. If the ith person has no children then the ith line contains the single integer

0. For example:

6
Marie
Ally
Raymond
Robert
Geoffrey
Michael
3 4
0
2 5 6
0
0
0

means that:

There are six people: Marie, Ally, Raymond, Robert, Geoffrey, Michael
Marie has two children: Raymond (3) and Robert (4).
Ally has no children.
Raymond has three children: Ally (2), Geoffrey (5), Michael (6).
Robert has no children.
Geoffrey has no children.
Michael has no children.

See Figure 16.28 for a visual representation.

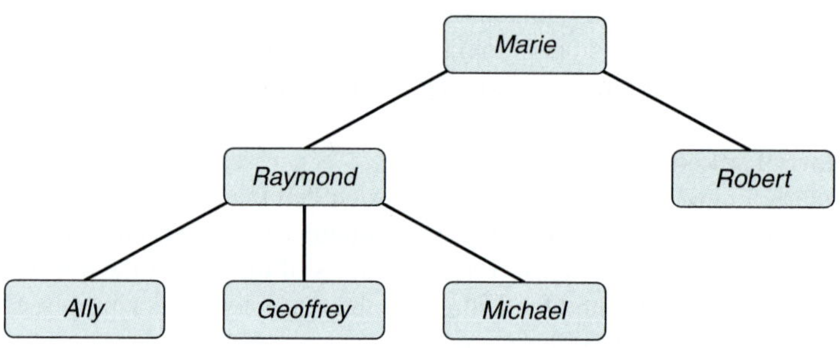

FIGURE 16.28 A visual representation of the family tree

Write a program that reads such a file and stores its information in a two-dimensional array of integers. For example, the two-dimensional array entry that corresponds to the preceding data is shown in Figure 16.29, where entry[i,j] = 1 if i is the parent of j.

Use a queue to print all the names in order of generation. For example, the output for the preceding file is:

Generation 1: Marie
Generation 2: Raymond Robert
Generation 3: Ally Geoffrey Michael

Assume that the first person in the list is the only person in generation 1. Your algorithm should work like this:

```
Define an array, generation, with one entry for each of the names.
Set variable generationNumber = 1;
Print ("Generation " + generationNumber);
```

	Marie	Ally	Raymond	Robert	Geoffrey	Michael
Marie	0	0	1	1	0	0
Ally	0	0	0	0	0	0
Raymond	0	1	0	0	1	1
Robert	0	0	0	0	0	0
Geoffrey	0	0	0	0	0	0
Michael	0	0	0	0	0	0

FIGURE 16.29 A two-dimensional array representation of the family tree

```
Initialize the queue to 1; Set generation[1] = 1;
Until the queue is empty:
{
    Remove an integer x from the queue;
    if generation[x] > generationNumber
    {
        Increment generationNumber;
        Print ("Generation " + generationNumber);
    }
    Print the string S corresponding to the name of x;
    For each of S's children:
    {
        Add the corresponding integer k to the queue;
        Set generation[k] = generation[x] + 1;
    }
}
```

THE BIGGER PICTURE

ABSTRACT DATA TYPES

A Java program consists of interacting classes, and classes consist of data and methods. When designing a class, you should first decide *what* the class should *do*. Look at the "bigger picture," so to speak. Implementation comes later. *What* comes first; then comes *how*.

For example, consider a class that models a deck of cards. Such a class can be specified as:

```
DeckOfCards
{
```

```
        Data:
                deck: an ordered arrangement of 52 Card objects
        Operators:
                dealACard(): returns a single Card chosen from deck
                shuffle(): randomly rearranges the deck
                remainingCards(): returns the number of cards remaining in the deck
}
```

A client of this class knows that it can instantiate a deck, shuffle a deck, deal a card from a deck, and find out how many cards remain in the deck. The client has no idea *how* these tasks get done, just that they do. The client need not know *how* the cards are shuffled, just that they *are* shuffled.

The specification of DeckOfCards is called an abstract data type (ADT).

> An *abstract data type* (*ADT*) consists of data and a set of operators that act on that data. An ADT is defined without regard to its implementation.

The operators of an ADT collectively form its *interface*. An ADT is completely specified by its interface, which is independent of its implementation. The client of an ADT is promised functionality through the interface, but the client need not know anything about the implementation.

The implementation of an ADT may change, but as long as the interface remains unchanged, the correctness of user programs is unaffected. The methods work as advertised. On the other hand, the implementation of an ADT *does* affect the *efficiency* of its methods. And, as you know, some implementations are better than others.

A stack can similarly be specified by an ADT:

```
ADT Stack
{
        Data:
                An ordered collection of elements such that elements are added and
                removed at one end, the top.
        Operators:
                push(Element x): places x in the top position.
                pop(): removes and returns the element in the top position.
                peek(): returns the item in the top position.
                empty(): returns true if there are no elements in the collection.
                size(): returns the number of items currently in the collection.
}
```

The ADT Stack defines the data and the operators but not *how* the operators are implemented and not *how* the data is stored or represented. A Java interface is like an ADT in that it specifies methods but not implementation.

Of course, to be of any use, an ADT requires an implementation. This implementation often involves a data structure.

> A *data structure* consists of a scheme or mechanism that organizes a collection of related data together with a set of algorithms (or methods) that manipulate the data.

If that sounds a bit technical, let's return to the ADT Stack. Example 16.2 provides an implementation of a stack that uses the ArrayList data structure. Another Stack implementation might use an ordinary array, and still another might implement a stack with a chain of nodes. (See Programming Exercise 14.) Every implementation, however, must supply methods push(), pop(), peek(), empty(), and size() as specified by the ADT Stack.

Throughout this chapter, you have seen many examples of data structures. None of these were presented as ADTs, but in fact, many of them, like Stack and Queue, are classic examples of abstract data types. In these cases, the ADT is clearly distinguished from the underlying implementation. Nonetheless, sometimes it is more difficult to distinguish between an ADT and an implementation.

For example, a linked list *could* be implemented somewhat eccentrically using an ArrayList rather than a chain of nodes. Is a linked list an ADT with various possible implementations, or is it defined *intrinsically* as a chain of nodes so that it really has no alternative natural implementation? Similarly, and even more strangely, one can implement an array using a chain of nodes. Is an array an ADT with operations that allow indexed access to equal-sized elements, and thereby allowing different implementations? Or, must an array specifically be implemented with a contiguous section of memory?

The issue of ADT versus data structure can be confusing, but the matter is more about terminology than concepts. The bottom line is that if you intend a particular kind of implementation, then you are *not* talking about an ADT. With arrays and linked lists, most people mean implementations rather than ADTs. However, everyone agrees that dynamic arrays, certain linked list variants, stacks, and queues are all ADTs that can be implemented with a variety of data structures, including arrays and chains of nodes.

We reiterate that a data structure consists of an organized collection of data along with algorithms that manage the data, and an ADT consists of a set of operators that act on data without regard to implementation. Furthermore, not all implementations are created equal. Some are more efficient than others; some are more appropriate to one problem than another. For example, because the ArrayList operation remove(0) shifts all data whenever the first element is removed, an ArrayList implementation of the ADT queue provides a rather inefficient remove() operation. A circular array or a chain of nodes is a more efficient implementation.

In the following section, we look at another ADT, a *deque*, along with several possible implementations. Again, you will see that each implementation has advantages and disadvantages.

Deque: An Abstract Data Type Case Study

A *deque* is an ordered list of elements such that both insertions and removals can take place at either end.

Think of a deque as a deck of cards with a limited set of operations that include inserting, removing, and peeking at cards from both the top and bottom of the deck. Technically, deque stands for **d**ouble **e**nded **que**ue. Part queue and part stack, a deque is handy when neither a queue nor a stack is sufficient, but both are useful.

The following Java interface describes the ADT deque.

Java ADT deque

```
// This generic interface defines the deque ADT.
// A deque is an ordered list with operations
// that operate at either end of a list. You can add an item, remove an item, or
// peek at an item either at the front of the deque or at the back of the deque.

public interface DequeInterface<E>
{
    public void addFront(E item);

    // Inserts item at the front of the deque.
```

THE BIGGER PICTURE

```
    public void addBack(E item);

    // Inserts item at the back of the deque.

    public E removeFront();

    // Removes item from front of the deque and returns item.
    // Returns null if the deque is empty.

    public E removeBack();

    // Removes item from back of the deque and returns item.
    // Returns null if the deque is empty.

    public E peekFront();

    // Returns the item at the front of the deque, leaves deque unchanged.
    // Returns null if the deque is empty.

    public E peekBack();

    // Returns the item at the back of the deque, leaves deque unchanged.
    // Returns null if the deque is empty.

    public int size();

    // Returns the number of elements in the deque.

    public boolean empty();

    // Returns true if the deque has any elements, otherwise false.
}
```

Deque Implementation

Our goal is a dynamic implementation of Deque<E> so that each method executes in constant time. That is, each method always requires the same amount of time regardless of the number of items in the deque. Although such efficiency is not always feasible with every ADT, it is possible with a deque. Therefore, we avoid any implementation that produces methods with execution time that increases as the number of elements in the deque increases.

Several possible implementations of a deque come to mind, but each has its drawbacks. Either the data structure does not provide for dynamic growth, or else one of the operations does not execute efficiently.

- **Circular array.** Using a circular array with two stored indices, as we do for a queue, allows efficient operations, but a circular array cannot grow dynamically. Its size is fixed.

- **ArrayList.** Using an ArrayList is possible, but only insertions and deletions at the back end are efficient. The operations at the front end shift all data in the deque. As the deque grows, so does the execution time for operations at the front.

- **Linked list with one reference variable that holds the address of the first node.** Using a linked list is dynamic, and it allows efficient insertion and deletion at the front end. However, operations at the back end are not efficient because to reach the end of the list every node on the list must be accessed. The time required for this traversal increases as the size of the list increases.

- **Linked list with extra reference variables.** Add two additional reference variables, last and nextToLast, to the previous linked list implementation. This attempt almost works. It has all the benefits of the previous implementation plus it allows fast insertions at the *back end* of the list. For example, inserting a new node at the end of the list can be achieved via:

```
last.next = newnode;
nextToLast = last;
last = newnode;
```

Unfortunately, the extra variables last and nextToLast do *not* allow for fast deletions at the back end of the list. Although last can be shifted back one node, and the last node easily deleted via

```
last = nextToLast;
nextToLast.next = null;
```

the nextToLast reference must also "shift back" one node, and that requires traversing the list from the beginning. A nextToNextToLast node would allow us to avoid the traversal, using

```
nextToLast = NextToNextToLast;
```

but then NextToNextToLast would need to shift back as well, once again requiring a traversal from the start.

Using a linked list to implement a deque is akin to using a bed sheet that just doesn't fit. When you manage to tuck in three corners, the fourth corner pops out. A linked list implementation has limitations.

Thus, none of the data structures listed here provides an efficient implementation of a deque. The following exercises guide you through two alternative deque implementations.

Exercises

1. Devise an implementation of a deque using a circularly linked list. A circularly linked list is a chain of nodes in which the last node points back to the first. See Programming Exercise 19. Determine those deque methods that take constant time and those that take time dependent on the number of elements in the deque. You do not need to compile the code, as this implementation does not meet our criterion of efficiency.

2. A doubly linked list is a chain of nodes, each of which has three components: *data*, *next*, and *previous*. See Programming Exercise 18. The *data* component holds a reference to the data, the *next* component holds the address of the next node in the list, and the *previous* component holds the address of the previous node in the list

   Using a doubly linked list, the methods of a deque *can* be implemented efficiently so that the execution time of each method is independent of the number of data. That is, a doubly linked list implementation allows constant time implementation of every deque method.

   Implement a deque using a doubly linked list such that each method executes in constant time.

3. Most word processors, editors, and games maintain a history of the last 50 or so user actions. An action, keystroke, or move can be undone by clicking the *undo*

THE BIGGER PICTURE

button. The last action performed is, of course, the first one that gets undone ("last in, first out"). On the other hand, after 50 distinct actions, the first action is the one that is deleted from the history ("first in, first out"). Only the most recent 50 actions are stored. The history is a little like a stack and a bit like a queue. A deque seems just right.

Use a deque to simulate the undo feature of a simple video game. This game allows you to repeatedly move a stick in one of eight directions: N, S, E, W, NE, SW, NW, or SE. You can undo up to 10 moves at any time, and then continue moving the stick again. At most 10 directions are stored at any time. For simplicity, your program should repeatedly accept

- integers 1 through 8 for the directions N, S, E, W, NE, SW, NW, and SE;
- 9 for "undo"; and
- 0 to quit.

If "undo" is entered and nothing remains to undo, the program should display a message to that effect. At the end, the current history of directions should be displayed.

4. When you visit the Senate in Washington DC, you may spend considerable time in the waiting line at the visitor's gallery. There are 90 seats in the gallery. Spectators can enter the gallery in groups of 35 but only when a block of 35 seats becomes available. Each person who enters may stay as long as he/she likes. VIPs are allowed to cut to the front of the line rather than wait at the back.

Write a program using a deque to simulate the waiting line for the Senate gallery. Assume that the gallery is initially empty and that 100 people are waiting in line when the day begins. People arrive thereafter at a rate of one person every 20 seconds, with VIPs arriving at a rate of one every 5 minutes. Twenty percent of all spectators remain in the gallery for 5 minutes, 60% stay 10 minutes, and 20% stay 20 minutes.

Calculate the average waiting time for ordinary tourists and for VIPs after an 8-hour simulation.

5. Explain how you might implement a stack using a deque.

6. Explain how you might implement a queue using a deque.

CHAPTER 17

The Java Collections Framework

"I think that I shall never see a graph as lovely as a tree."
—From *Algorhyme* by *Radia Perlman*

Objectives

The objectives of Chapter 17 include an understanding of

- the Java Collections Framework,
- a subset of Java's Collection hierarchy, including:
  - ArrayList,
  - LinkedList,
  - HashSet,
  - TreeSet, and
- efficiency considerations when choosing a collection.

17.1 INTRODUCTION

The data structures of Chapter 16, ArrayList<E>, Stack<E>, Queue<E>, and LList<E>, are generally termed *collection classes.* In this chapter, we continue the study of collection classes with the *Java Collections Framework.*

> The Java Collections Framework is a hierarchy of interfaces and classes used for storing and manipulating *groups* of objects as a single unit, a *collection.*

Each collection comes with a set of methods for managing the collection. Initially, the various collections may seem similar, almost identical, and even redundant. However, choosing the "wrong" collection for an application can result in a working but inefficient program. Choosing the right collection requires at least some general familiarity with implementation details. As we examine each of the collections in the Java Collections Framework, be aware of the underlying implementation, its advantages, and its disadvantages, within the context of a particular application. The Java Collections Framework is contained in the java.util package. The ArrayList<E> class, introduced in Chapter 16, is a member of the Java Collections Framework.

17.2 THE COLLECTION HIERARCHY

The *collection hierarchy* consists entirely of interfaces except at the lowest levels where concrete classes reside.

At the root of the hierarchy is the Collection<E> interface. Figure 17.1 gives a partial view of the collection hierarchy. Figure 17.1 shows just those interfaces and classes that we discuss in the following sections. The complete hierarchy is more extensive.

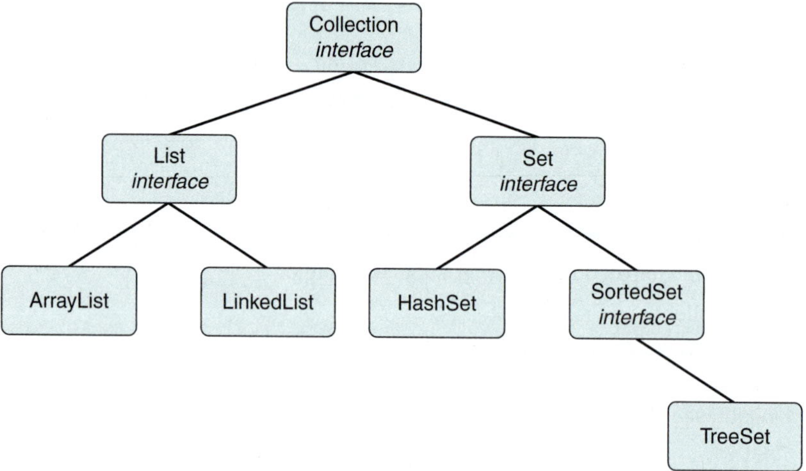

FIGURE 17.1 A partial view of the Collection hierarchy

From Figure 17.1, you can see that the Collection<E> interface splits into Lists and Sets.

List<E> is an interface that extends Collection<E>. ArrayList<E> and LinkedList<E> are classes that implement List<E>. An object belonging to ArrayList<E> or LinkedList<E> is a collection, indexed from 0, that can contain duplicate items.

Notice that ArrayList<E> implements List<E>. As you know, an object belonging to ArrayList<E> can hold duplicate data. For example, if myList belongs to ArrayList<String> then the statements

```
myList.add("Happy");
myList.add("Happy"); and
myList.add("Happy");
```

place three identical strings into the collection.

Like List<E>, Set<E> is an interface that extends Collection<E>. HashSet<E> and TreeSet<E> implement Set<E>. An object belonging to HashSet<E> or TreeSet<E> is a collection that is not indexed and does not contain duplicate items.

The Collection<E> interface defines the following methods. In the descriptions that follow, x refers to an object belonging to a class that implements Collection<E>.

- boolean add(E item)

  x.add(item) adds item to x and returns true, if the contents of x have been changed. If x belongs to a class that implements Set<E> and x already contains item, then x.add(item) returns false because Sets do not hold duplicate elements.
- boolean addAll(Collection<E> c)

  x.addAll(c) appends Collection<E> c to Collection<E> x; x.addAll(c) returns true, if x has been altered, that is, if the call x.addAll(c) adds any additional items to x.
- void clear()

  x.clear() removes all elements from x.
- boolean contains (Object item)

  x.contains(item) returns true if there is a member c of x, such that c.equals(item) is true.
- boolean containsAll(Collection<E> c)

  x.containsAll(c) returns true if every element in c is also in x, that is, if c is a subset of x.
- boolean equals(Object item)

  x.equals(item) returns true if item is equal to x.
- boolean isEmpty()

  x.isEmpty() returns true if x has no elements.
- boolean removeAll(Collection c)

  x.removeAll(c) removes all elements from x that are also in Collection c so that x and c have no common elements; returns true if any element is removed.
- boolean remove(Object item)

  x.remove(item) removes at most one instance of item from x; returns false if nothing is removed from x.
- boolean retainAll(Collection<E> c)

  x.retainAll(c) retains all elements of x that are also in c, that is, x.retainsAll(c) is the intersection of x and c, the collection of elements common to x and c; returns true if any element is removed.
- int size()

  x.size() returns the number of elements in x.
- Object[] toArray()

  x.toArray() returns a reference to an array containing the elements in collection x.
- Iterator iterator()

  Given a collection x, it is often desirable to "loop through x" or "step through x," processing each object in x. In pseudocode:

  ```
  for each object o in x
      process o
  ```

An *iterator* is an object capable of looping through, moving through, or stepping through a collection.

The statement

```
Iterator<E> iter = x.iterator();
```

instantiates an Iterator object. For any Collection x, you can instantiate one or more Iterator objects.

You can think of an Iterator object as containing an albeit imaginary pointer or cursor. Initially, when an iterator for a collection is instantiated, this pointer is positioned just before the first element in a collection.

Once an Iterator is instantiated, the following methods are available:

- E next()

  returns the next item of the collection and advances the pointer.

  The first call to next() returns the first element in the collection and moves the pointer, just "before" the second item in the collection.

  A call to next() throws a NoSuchElementException if there is no "next element" in the collection. For example, if x is a collection of String objects:

  ```
  x = [ "Harpo" "Groucho" "Zeppo" "Chico" ];
  ```

  then the following four lines of code iterate through the collection and produce the output:

  ```
  Harpo
  Groucho
  Zeppo
  ```

  1. `Iterator<String> iter = x.iterator();` // create an iterator for x

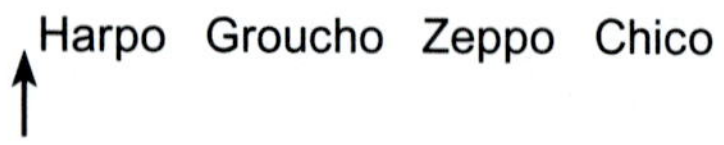

     ```
     ↑Harpo  Groucho  Zeppo  Chico
     ```

  2. `System.out.println(iter.next());` // Print "Harpo" and advance the pointer

     ```
     Harpo ↑Groucho  Zeppo  Chico
     ```

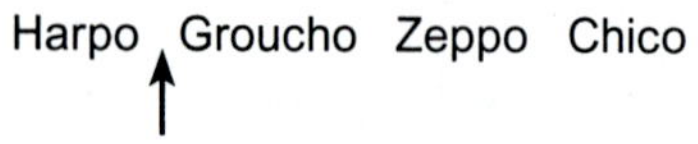

  3. `System.out.println(iter.next());` // Print "Groucho" and advance the pointer

     ```
     Harpo  Groucho ↑Zeppo  Chico
     ```

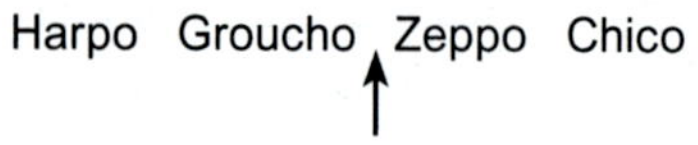

  4. `System.out.println(iter.next());` // Print "Zeppo" and advance the pointer

     ```
     Harpo  Groucho  Zeppo ↑Chico
     ```

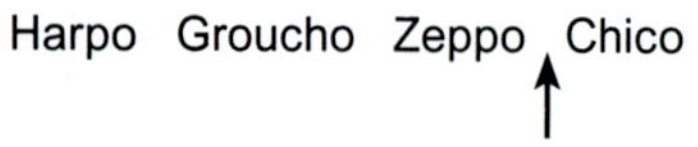

- boolean hasNext()

  returns true if there is a "next element" in the collection.

  For example, if x is the collection ["Harpo" "Groucho" "Zeppo" "Chico"], then the loop:

  ```
  while(iter.hasNext() )
          System.out.println(x.next());
  ```

  produces the output:

  ```
  Harpo
  Groucho
  Zeppo
  Chico
  ```

- void remove()

  removes the last element returned by a call to next(). This method can be called only once for each call to next(), otherwise this method throws an IllegalStateException.

  The following fragment prints the contents of a collection and removes each element in turn. Notice that each call to remove() is preceded by a call to next(). Again, assume that x is the Collection ["Harpo" "Groucho" "Zeppo" "Chico"].

```
Iterator<String> iter = x.iterator();     // position pointer before "Harpo"
while (iter.hasNext())
{
   System.out.println(iter.next());       // print and advance pointer
      iter.remove();                      // remove the last item printed
}
```

17.3 THE *Set<E>* INTERFACE

> The classes that implement Set<E> contain no duplicate objects.

Naturally, the Set<E> interface inherits all the methods of Collection<E>. No new methods are added to the Set<E> interface.

17.3.1 The *HashSet* Class

HashSet<E> is a concrete class that implements Set<E>. See Figure 17.1. To understand HashSet<E>, you must first understand the concept of a *hash function*:

> A *hash function, h,* is a method or mapping that assigns a non-negative integer to a given object x.

That is, *h* pairs x with a non-negative integer. In more mathematical terms, a hash function *maps* x to an integer in the range [0 .. *n*].

For example, suppose that *s* is a nine-character string representing a social security number. A hash function that maps *s* to an integer in the range 0 . . . 999 might pair *s* with the last three digits of the social security number. For example, two such mappings, pairings, or assignments are:

"123456**789**" → 789, and

"323465**156**" → 156

This particular hash function can be expressed as:

```
h(s) = Integer.parseInt(s) % 1000;
```

Again, if *s* is the string "123456**789**" then

```
h(s)                                  =
h("123456789")                        =
Integer.parseInt("123456789") % 1000  =
123456789 % 1000                      =
789
```

The method of Figure 17.2 gives a different hash function, one that maps a string, *s*, to an integer in the range 0 through 10.

```
public static int hash(String s)
{
        int sum = 0;
        for (int i = 0; i < s.length(); i++)
             sum = sum + (int)(s.charAt(i));   // add ASCII codes of the characters
        return sum % 11;
}
```

FIGURE 17.2 A hash function that maps a string to a positive integer

Given a string, s, the method hash(...) of Figure 17.2 first sums the ASCII values of the characters comprising s and returns that sum mod 11. The return value is an integer in the range [0...10]. For example,

hash("Moe") = (77 + 111 + 101) %11 = 289 % 11 = 3
// 'M' has ASCII value 77, 'o' has value 111, and 'e' has value 101.

Similarly,
hash("Larry") = (76 + 97 + 114 + 114 + 121) % 11 = 5
hash("Curly") = (67 + 117 + 114 + 108 + 121) % 11 = 10

Of what use is a hash function?

A hash function can facilitate the placement and retrieval of objects in a table.

A hash function generates table (or array) indices. For example, if o is an object and hash(o) = 15, then a reference to o might be stored at address or location 15. Thus, a hash function calculates a storage location.

In particular, suppose that list is an array of String indexed from 0 to 10 and we wish to store the names (really references) "Moe", Larry", and "Curly" in list so that lookup is efficient. Obviously, we could place the strings, one after the other, into an array. However, lookup would then necessitate a linear search of the array. Of course, linear search on an array of size 3 is not problematic, but a linear search on an array of three million can indeed be slow. Using a hash function, we can do much better than a linear search.

With the hash function of Figure 17.2, we calculate that

hash("Moe") = 3,
hash("Larry") = 5, and
hash("Curly") = 10.

The values calculated via the hash function tell us where to store (and later where to retrieve) each string. That is, store the strings at array locations 3, 5, and 10:

list[3] = "Moe",
list[5] = "Larry", and
list[10] = "Curly".

The table created using a hash function is called a *hash set* or *hash table*.

See Figure 17.3.

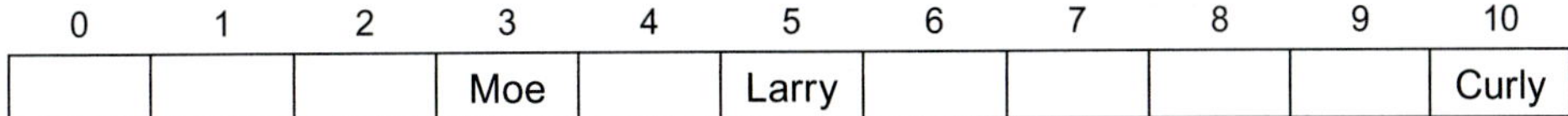

FIGURE 17.3 A hash table with three entries

To find or look up an object, x, that is stored in a hash table, simply use the hash function to calculate the address of the location that holds (or references) x.

Thus to retrieve "Moe", calculate hash("Moe") = 3. "Moe" is stored at list[3]. The hash function computes the address directly. No searching, binary or linear, is required. No matter how many items are stored in the table, lookup takes the same amount of time. That is, one lookup takes one step. In this case, we say that lookup is accomplished in *constant time*.

The idea is simple, and, in the best of all possible worlds, lookups can be achieved with no searching. However, like people, hash functions are seldom perfect. A hash function always maps "equal" objects to the same storage location, so once an object is stored, it can be easily retrieved. Unfortunately, a hash function can generate the same address for different objects. That is, "unequal" objects can be mapped to the same location, as if they were "equal." For example,

hash("Moe") = (77 + 111 + 101) % 11 = 289 % 11 = 3
hash("Shemp") = (83 + 104 + 101 + 109 + 112) % 11 = 509 – %11 = 3

When a hash function assigns two unequal objects the same address, a *collision* occurs.

Obviously, "Moe" and "Shemp" cannot *both* occupy location 3 without poking each other in the eyes! A good hash function produces few collisions, but collisions are often unavoidable.

There are many ways to handle collisions. Collision resolution techniques usually involve some kind of search and consequent slowdown in performance. Even with collisions, however, hashing is one of the most efficient and effective mechanisms for storing and retrieving data.

Java's HashSet<E> class stores objects in a hash table and handles any collisions that may occur.

HashSet<E> has two constructors:

- HashSet<E>(), and
- HashSet<E>(Collection<E> c).

The HashSet<E> methods are those methods of the Collection<E> interface. Notice that the Collection<E> interface provides methods for:

- inserting objects into a HashSet<E>,
- removing objects from a HashSet<E>, and
- checking whether or not an object is contained in a HashSet<E>.

Also note that:

- A HashSet<E> contains no duplicates, no matter how many times an item is added.
- A HashSet<E> has no methods that allow direct retrieval of an object. The only retrieval mechanism is via an iterator, which means stepping through the set.

On the other hand, the HashSet class does provide a method

```
boolean contains(E x)
```

for determining whether or not an object is contained in a HashSet<E>.

- A HashSet<E> is not ordered. Objects contained in a HashSet<E> need not implement the Comparable interface.

HashSet<E> is an appropriate choice when rapid lookup is paramount and ordering is not required, that is, when your main concern is whether or not some object is in a collection.

Example 17.1 demonstrates the construction and utilization of a simple hash table in a somewhat simplistic scenario.

EXAMPLE 17.1

In the city of Springfield, home of the ever-famous Simpson family, whenever a person votes in a city election, his/her name is added to a list of voters. This action is important because several nefarious residents of Springfield, including Mayor Quimby himself, have been known to vote more than once. To curb ballot stuffing, a person's name is validated (the list is checked) before he/she is allowed to cast a vote. If a person has already voted, he/she is barred from voting a second time.

Problem Statement Write an application that adds a name (String) to a list of voters and also performs rapid lookup when a potential voter arrives at the polls.

Java Solution Because Springfield's population is well over one million, very fast lookup minimizes waiting time at the polls. Consequently, HashSet<E> is an excellent choice for the voter list. Storing names in an array is problematic because searching for a name necessitates a linear search, which is slow and inefficient for our purposes. A binary search, though faster than linear search, mandates that the array be kept sorted, which would then make insertion slow and inefficient. HashSet<E> with rapid insertion *and* lookup is ideal for this situation.

The following program implements the Springfield election process.

```
import java.util.*;

public class SpringfieldElection
{
   protected HashSet<String> voters;

   public SpringfieldElection ()
   {
      voters = new HashSet<String>();
   }

   public void validate()
   {
      Scanner input = new Scanner(System.in);
      String name;
      System.out.println("Enter XXX to exit the system");
      System.out.print("Name: ");
      name = input.nextLine();
```

```
16.       while (!name.equals("XXX"))
17.       {
18.          if (voters.contains(name))          // has name voted?
19.             System.out.println(name + " has already voted");
20.          else
21.          {
22.             System.out.println(name + " may vote");
23.             voters.add(name);
24.          }
25.          System.out.print("Name: ");
26.          name = input.nextLine();
27.       } // end while

28.    } // end validate

29.    public static void main(String [] args)
30.    {
31.       SpringfieldElection votingCheck = new SpringfieldElection ();
32.       votingCheck.validate();
33.    }
34. }
```

Output

Enter XXX to exit the system
Name: **Simpson, Homer**
Simpson, Homer may vote
Name: **Simpson, Marge**
Simpson, Marge may vote
Name: **Simpson, Homer**
Simpson, Homer has already voted
Name: **Krusty**
Krusty may vote
Name: **Flanders, Ned**
Flanders, Ned may vote
Name: **Krusty**
Krusty has already voted
Name: **Simpson, Homer**
Simpson, Homer has already voted
Name: **XXX**

Discussion The program is simple and easy to follow. The work is done in the loop on lines 16 through 27. This fragment

- determines if a person has already voted (lines 18–19), and
- if the person has not voted, gives permission to vote and adds the person's name to the list of voters (lines 22–23).

To construct the hash table of Example 17.1, Java uses a method

```
int hashCode()
```

inherited from Object. The hashCode() method maps an object to an integer (positive or negative) and calculates a hash table address using that integer. The value returned by hashCode() is derived from an object's address in memory. Sometimes, it is necessary to override the hashCode() method and provide your own version of hashCode(). Indeed, the String class overrides Object's hashCode(); so that if s is a string of length *n* then

$$\text{s.hashCode()} = \text{s[0]}*31^{(n-1)} + \text{s[1]}*31^{(n-2)} + \text{s[2]}*31^{(n-3)} + \ldots + \text{s[n} - 1]$$

For example, if s = "Moe" then

$$\text{s.hashCode()} = \text{'M'}*31^2 + \text{'o'}*31^1 + \text{'e'} =$$
$$= 77*31^2 + 111*31 + 101 = 77{,}539$$

Note that the ASCII codes for 'M', 'o', and 'e' are 77, 111, and 101, respectively.

The HashSet<E> of Example 17.1 is constructed using the hashCode() method that is implemented in String. Sun's documentation states that:

> If two objects are equal according to the equals(Object) method, then calling the hashCode() method on each of the two objects *must* produce the same integer result.

All this means is that hashCode() cannot change its mind. Given "equal" objects, hashCode() should always compute the same value for each. The hashCode() method of the previous example does not violate Sun's specification. Indeed the loop

```
for (int i = 1; i <= 9; i++)
{
    String name = input.next();
    System.out.println(name + " hash code: " + name.hashCode() );
}
```

when embedded into a program produces the following output (formatting added for readability):

Homer hash code: 69908307
Bart hash code: 2063073
Marge hash code: 74113692
Lisa hash code: 2368683
Homer hash code: 69908307
Bart hash code: 2063073
Marge hash code: 74113692
Lisa hash code: 2368683
Homer hash code: 69908307

and performs as expected. Identical strings have identical hashCode() values.

The HashSet<E> of Example 17.1 consists of String objects, and the String class overrides the hashCode() method inherited from Object. There are no problems here: if two strings are equal they have the same hashCode() value. Suppose, however, that the objects stored in HashSet<E> are not strings but belong to the following Person class:

```
public class Person
{
   private String firstName;
   private String lastName;

   public Person(String first, String last)
   {
      firstName = first;
      lastName = last;
```

```
    }
    public String toString()
    {
        return firstName + " " + lastName;
    }
    public boolean equals(Object o)
    {
        // returns true if first and last names are the same
        return firstName.equals(((Person)o).firstName) && lastName.equals(((Person)o).lastName);
    }
}
```

Notice that Person overrides the equals(Object o) method so that two Person objects are "equal" if and only if first and last names are identical.

Now, consider the program of Example 17.1 modified so that the HashSet<E>, voters, holds Person, rather than String, references.

```
import java.util.*;
public class SpringfieldElection1
{
    protected HashSet<Person> voters;

    public SpringfieldElection1 ()
    {
        voters = new HashSet<Person>();
    }

    public void validate()
    {
        Scanner input = new Scanner(System.in);
        Person person;
        String fName, lName;
        System.out.println("Enter XXX for first name to exit the system");
        System.out.print("First Name: ");
        fName = input.next();
        System.out.print("Last Name: ");
        lName = input.next();

        while (!fName.equals("XXX"))
        {
            person = new Person(fName, lName);
            if (voters.contains(person))
                System.out.println(person + " has already voted");
            else
            {
                System.out.println(person + " may vote");
                voters.add(person);
            }
            System.out.print("First Name: ");
            fName = input.next();
            System.out.print("Last Name: ");
```

```
            lName = input.next();
        } // while
    }     // validate

    public static void main(String [] args)
    {
        SpringfieldElection1 votingCheck = new SpringfieldElection1();
        votingCheck.validate();
    }
}
```

The output of this revised program is:

Enter XXX for first name to exit the system
First Name: **Homer**
Last Name: **Simpson**
Homer Simpson may vote
First Name: **Homer**
Last Name: **Simpson**
Homer Simpson may vote
First Name: **XXX**
Last Name: **XXX**

Homer has voted twice! Has the system gone awry?

Seemingly, two objects that are considered "equal" (same first and last names) generate different hash codes. Yet, equal objects should produce the *same* hash code. This anomaly occurs because the default hashCode() method, which is inherited from Object, returns an integer based on the *address* of the calling object. Each time a name is entered, a new object, with a unique address, is created. Thus, each new Person object with the name "Homer Simpson" has a distinct address and hence a different hash value—even though all "Homer Simpson" objects are considered equal according to the definition of the equals(...) method defined in Person.

A hash code should map "equal" objects to the same value; but in this case, the hash code maps "equal" objects to different values. The solution to this anomaly calls for a hashCode() method that depends on the *name* fields of a Person object and *not* on the address of the object. To avoid this problem, a programmer should adhere to the following guideline:

> Whenever a class overrides equals(Object o) that class should also override hashCode().

The following modification to Person overrides the default hashCode() method. The new hashCode() method is based not on the address of an object but on the characters in the first and last names—the two attribute fields that determine whether or not two objects are equal. Two objects with the same name have the same hashCode() value.

```
public class Person
{
    private String firstName;
    private String lastName;

    public Person(String first, String last)
    {
        firstName = first;
        lastName = last;
    }
```

```
10.     public String toString()
11.     {
12.         return firstName + " " + lastName;
13.     }

14.     public int hashCode()
15.     {
16.         int sum = 0;
17.         String s = firstName + lastName;
18.         for (int i = 0; i < s.length(); i++)      // add the ASCII values of each character
19.             sum += (int)(s.charAt(i));
20.         return (sum % 101);
21.     }

22.     public boolean equals(Object o)
23.     {
24.         return firstName.equals(((Person)o).firstName) &&
                    lastName.equals(((Person)o).lastName);
25.     }
26. }
```

Using this revised version of Person, the SpringfieldElection1 class produces the following output:

```
Enter XXX for first name to exit the system
First Name: Homer
Last Name: Simpson
Homer Simpson may vote
First Name: Homer
Last Name: Simpson
Homer Simpson has already voted
First Name: XXX
Last Name: XXX
```

Lines 14–21 illustrate one possible hashCode() for Person. Another simpler version of hashCode() might take advantage of the fact that String overrides hashCode().

```
public int hashCode()              // for Person
{
        int sum = 0;
        String s = firstName + lastName;
        return s.hashCode() ;      // as implemented in String
}
```

Finally, remember that HashSet<E> maintains no order among objects. In fact, objects belonging to HashSet<E> need not be comparable. If order is required, then another collection class is more appropriate.

> HashSet<E> is an excellent collection choice when rapid lookup is the criterion and there is no implied ordering of elements.

17.3.2 *SortedSet<E>*

SortedSet<E> is an interface that extends Set<E>. Unlike a HashSet<E>, the elements of a class that implements SortedSet<E> are ordered. This, of course, means that the objects belonging to any class that implements SortedSet<E> must be comparable, that is, E must implement the Comparable interface.

The SortedSet<E> interface defines the following methods, and therefore any class that extends SortedSet<E> must implement these methods. In the descriptions that follow, assume that x refers to an object of a class that implements SortedSet<E>.

- E first()

  x.first() returns the first element of x.
- E last()

  x.last() returns the last element of x.
- SortedSet<E> headSet(E a)

  x.headSet(a) returns a reference to a SortedSet containing the elements less than a in x.
- SortedSet<E> tailSet(E z)

  x.tailSet(z) returns a reference to a SortedSet containing the elements greater than or equal to z in x.
- SortedSet<E> subSet(E start, E end)

  x.subSet(start, end) returns a reference to a SortedSet containing those objects of x ranging from start to, but not including, end.

Figure 17.1 shows that TreeSet<E> implements SortedSet<E>.

17.3.3 *TreeSet<E>*

TreeSet<E> is a concrete class that implements SortedSet<E> and consequently Collection<E>. TreeSet<E> is built upon the model of a *binary search tree*.

Although a full development of binary search trees is beyond the scope of our discussion, an intuitive understanding of the concept is very useful for understanding when and when not to use Java's TreeSet<E> class. We begin with the definition of a binary tree.

A *binary tree* is a set, T, of elements (or nodes) such that

- T is either empty, or
- T contains a single element, called the *root,* and all other elements of T are divided into two disjoint sets, each of which is also a binary tree.

If the definition of a binary tree seems a bit circular, it is. That's because the definition of a binary tree is recursive: a binary tree is defined in terms of a binary tree, albeit with a base case so it's not truly circular.

A few pictures should cement the idea for you. Figure 17.4 shows a binary tree consisting of 18 nodes labeled A through R. Like the nodes of a linked list, the nodes of a binary tree can be used to store data.

The *root* of the tree shown in Figure 17.4 is the top node, which we call node-A. According to the definition of a binary tree, the remaining elements of the tree are partitioned into two distinct binary trees. So, if you "erase" node-A, you will notice that the remaining elements form two smaller trees. Figure 17.5 boxes off those two smaller trees. One such tree has node-B as its root and the other has node-C. The first tree is called the *left subtree* of node-A and the second the *right subtree* of node-A.

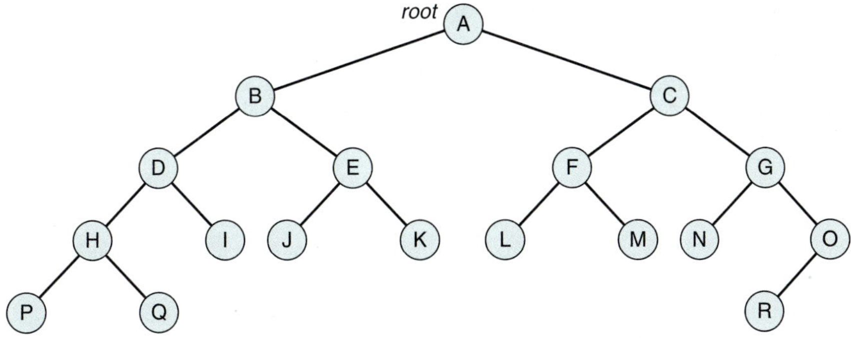

FIGURE 17.4 A binary tree

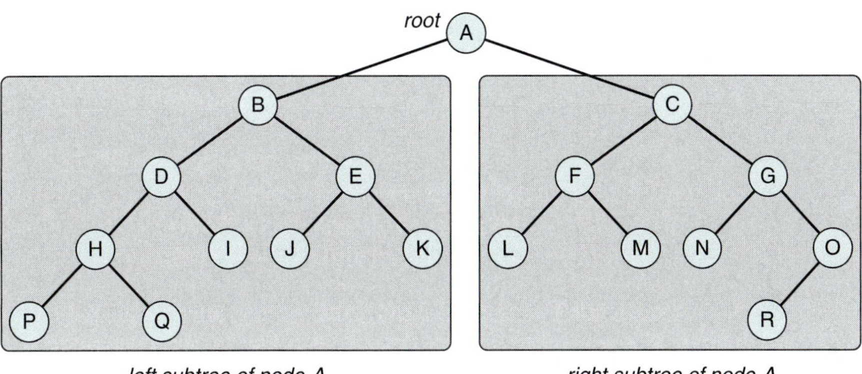

FIGURE 17.5 The left and right subtrees of node-A

Similarly, the left subtree of node-B is the tree rooted at node-D and the right subtree of node-B is the tree rooted at node-E. See Figure 17.6. In fact, every node has a left and right subtree. Of course, as in the case of node-P or node-Q, the left or right subtrees (or both) may be empty trees.

Nodes of a binary tree that have two empty subtrees are called *leaves*.

The leaves of the tree, shown in Figure 17.4, are the nodes labeled P, Q, I, J, K, L, M, N, and R.

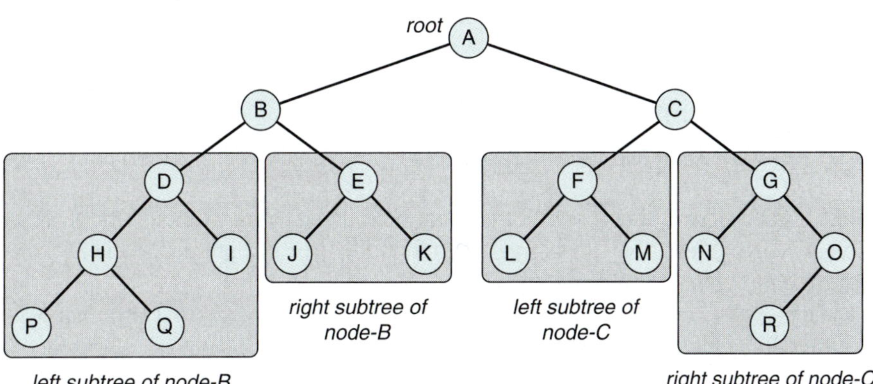

FIGURE 17.6 Left and right subtrees

Our interest here is in a special type of binary tree called a binary *search* tree.

> A *binary search tree* is a binary tree with the following additional property: For any node, *N*, all data contained in the left subtree of *N* are less than the data of *N* and all data contained in the right subtree of *N* are greater than or equal to the data of *N*.

The tree of Figure 17.7a is a binary search tree. The name Jan is the datum in the root. Notice that the data in the left subtree of the root are all alphabetically less than Jan and the data in the right subtree of the root are all alphabetically greater than Jan. This relationship between a node and the data of its left and right subtrees is true for any node in a binary search tree.

The tree of Figure 17.7b is a binary tree but *not* a binary search tree. The value of the root is Alice, but not one of nodes in the left subtree of the root has contents less than Alice.

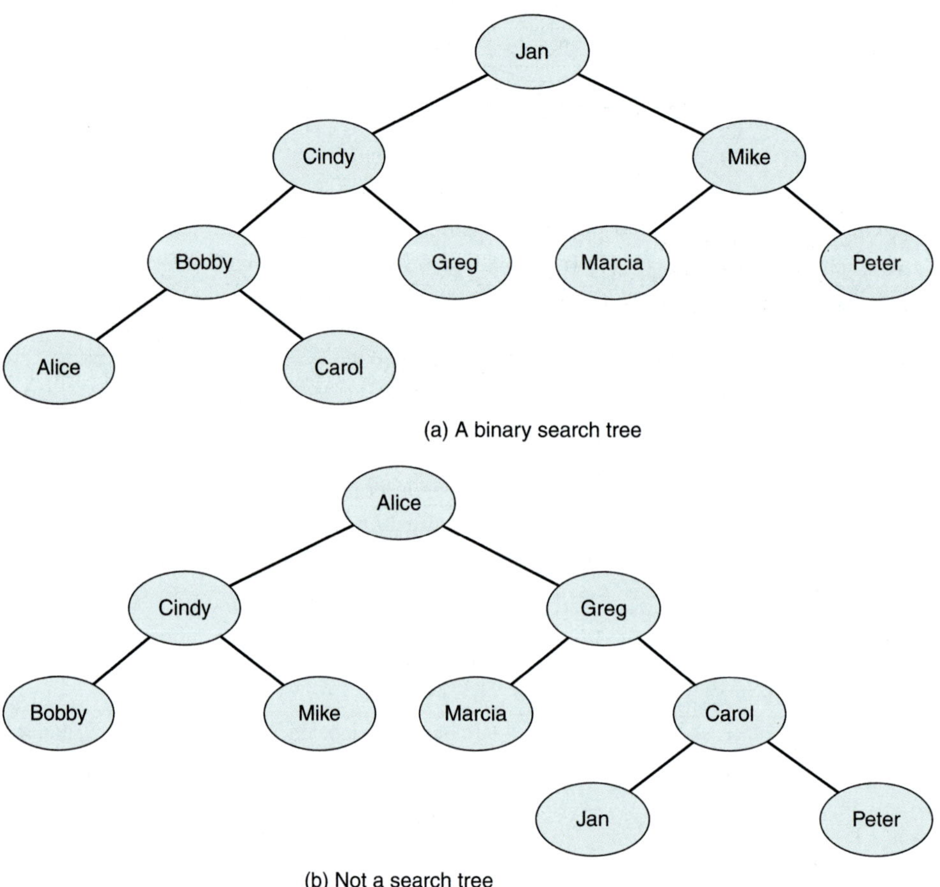

FIGURE 17.7 Two binary trees: (a) is a binary search tree, and (b) is not

Figure 17.8 shows two binary search trees that hold integer data. Although both are bona fide binary search trees, they appear very different: the tree of Figure 17.8a is "balanced" and the tree of Figure 17.8b is not.

Binary search trees provide a straightforward search strategy. Assume that `x` is an object stored in a binary search tree. To locate `x`,

> begin at the root of the tree and proceed along a path down the tree, moving from node to node:

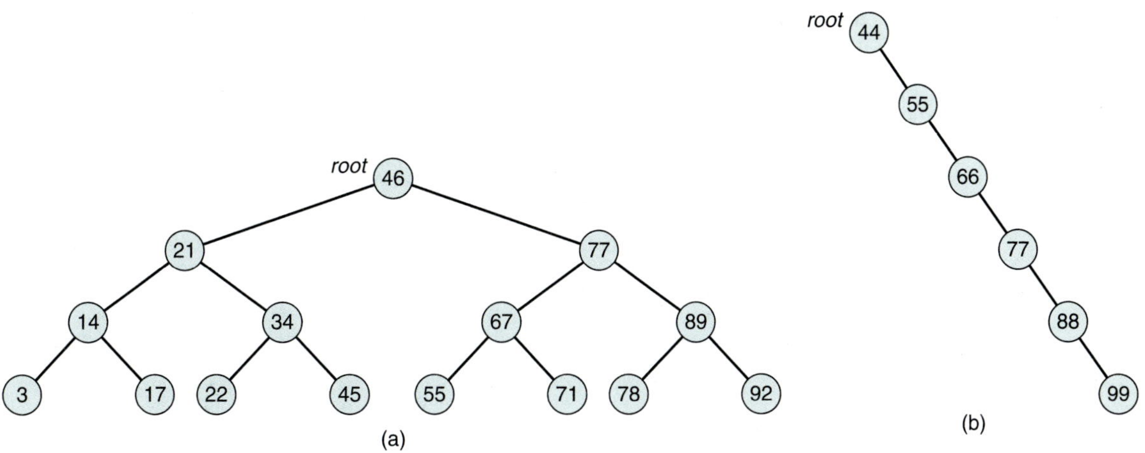

FIGURE 17.8 Two binary search trees: (a) is "balanced" (b) is not

At each node *N* along the path,
if x equals the contents of *N*, stop; x has been located.
if x is less than the contents of *N*, take the left branch,
if x is greater than the contents of *N*, take the right branch.

For example, a search for Carol in the tree of Figure 17.9 is accomplished as follows:

- Compare Carol to the root node, Jan. Carol is less than Jan. Proceed left (Cindy).
- Compare Carol to Cindy. Carol is less than Cindy. Proceed left (Bobby).
- Compare Carol to Bobby. Carol is greater than Bobby. Proceed right (Carol).
- Carol is found. Stop.

Figure 17.9 shows the path that leads to Carol.

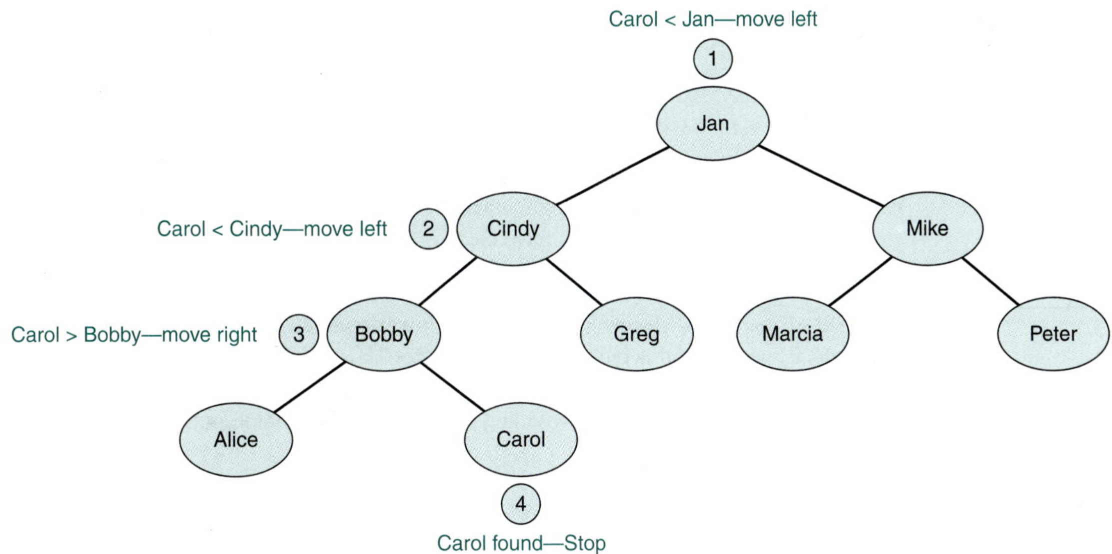

FIGURE 17.9 The search path for Carol

If a binary search tree is "somewhat balanced," the search routine is similar to a binary search: each comparison eliminates about half of the data. If n objects are stored in a balanced or nearly balanced binary search tree, on average, it takes approximately $\log_2(n)$ comparisons to locate an object. So, for example, if $n = 2^{20} = 1{,}048{,}576$, then on average it takes about $\log_2(2^{20}) = 20$ comparisons to find an object stored in a balanced binary search tree.

If a binary search tree is not balanced, however, searching is not so efficient. Searching the tree of Figure 17.8b is, in effect, a linear search. A linear search averages $n/2$ comparisons to locate an element. When $n = 2^{20} = 1{,}048{,}576$, a search that takes 20 comparisons using a balanced tree requires about 524,288 comparisons. That's quite a difference.

> Searching an unbalanced binary search tree is as slow as a linear search. A balanced binary search tree provides a more efficient search.

Java's TreeSet<E> class stores object references in a balanced binary search tree. The constructors of TreeSet<E> are:

```
public TreeSet<E>();
public TreeSet<E>(Collection<E> c);
public TreeSet<E>(SortedSet<E> s);
public TreeSet<E>(Comparator<E> c);   // Comparator? Coming soon . . .
```

The methods are those of the Collection<E> and SortedSet<E> interfaces. Although a binary search tree may contain duplicate elements, a TreeSet<E> object does not.

> If objects must be kept sorted, then a TreeSet<E> is an excellent choice. If objects need not be ordered, a HashSet<E> is probably a better choice.

Using a small test program, we inserted 10,000,000 random numbers into a HashSet<E>. The program required 5938 milliseconds to complete 1,000,000 lookups. Using TreeSet<E>, the same program took 10,535 milliseconds. When lookup is vital and no order is required, HashSet<E> is the clearly the winner.

Example 17.2 brings us back to Springfield and a situation where TreeSet<E> is a handy choice.

EXAMPLE 17.2 At the end the day, Joe Quimby, mayor of Springfield, expects to see an alphabetized list of all of the citizens who have voted. This sorted data must be retrieved just once, but insertion and validation checks are done continuously during the day.

Problem Statement Write an application that does validation checks and produces a sorted list of voters after the polls have closed.

Java Solution The following application utilizes *both* HashSet<E> and TreeSet<E>. HashSet<E> is used during voting hours. However, once the polls close each day, a TreeSet<E> collection is built from the HashSet<E> collection so that a sorted list of voters can be quickly obtained—pleasing Mayor Quimby.

Notice that the new class MoreVoting extends the SpringfieldElection class of Example 17.1.

```
import java.util.*;

public class MoreVoting extends SpringfieldElection
{
```

```
4.     TreeSet <String>tree;

5.     public MoreVoting()
6.     {
7.        super();                   // call the constructor of SpringfieldElection
8.        tree = new TreeSet<String>();
9.     }

10.    public void makeList()
11.    {
12.       int count = 0;
13.       tree.addAll(voters);    // make a TreeSet from the HashSet, voters
14.       System.out.println();
15.       System.out.println();
16.       System.out.println("Today's voters were");
17.             // use an iterator to step through the TreeSet. Values are sorted
18.       Iterator<String> iterator = tree.iterator();
19.       while(iterator.hasNext())
20.          System.out.println((++count) + ". " + iterator.next());
21.    }

22.    public static void main(String [] args)
23.    {
24.       MoreVoting example = new MoreVoting();
25.       example.validate();        // first use the HashSet
26.       example.makeList();       // use a TreeSet when we need an ordered list
27.    }
28. }
```

Output

Enter XXX to exit the system
Name: **Simpson, Homer**
Simpson, Homer may vote
Name: **Simpson, Marge**
Simpson, Marge may vote
Name: **Flanders, Ned**
Flanders, Ned may vote
Name: **Krusty**
Krusty may vote
Name: **XXX**

Today's voters were
1. Flanders, Ned
2. Krusty
3. Simpson, Homer
4. Simpson, Marge

Discussion The MoreVoting class extends SpringfieldElection so MoreVoting inherits the HashSet<E>, voters, which was declared protected in SpringfieldElection.

Line 7: A call to the SpringfieldElection constructor is accomplished with the keyword super.

Line 13: All the voters of the day are added to the TreeSet<E>, tree, via the add(Collection x) method.

Lines 18–20: In order to traverse the tree, an Iterator object must be instantiated. The Iterator invokes hasNext() and next(). Notice that the data is displayed in order.

17.3.4 The *Comparator*<E> Interface

The *natural order* of a class is the order defined by the class's compareTo(...) method.

The natural order of the Integer class is numerical order. The natural order for String is based upon the ASCII value of each character. Thus "ABC" precedes "AXY", that is, "ABC".compareTo("AXY") returns a negative number.

Of course, some classes are not ordered at all, but any class that implements the Comparable interface defines a natural order on its objects. For example, objects of the following Food class are ordered by calories:

```
public class Food implements Comparable
{
   private String name;
   private int calories, gramsOfFat;

   public Food(String n, int cal, int fat)
   {
      name = n;
      calories = cal;
      gramsOfFat = fat;
   }

   public int getFat()
   {
      return gramsOfFat;
   }

   public int getCalories()
   {
      return calories;
   }

   public int compareTo(Object food)
   {
      if (calories < ((Food)food).calories)
         return -1;
      else if (calories == ((Food)food).calories)
         return 0;
      else
         return 1;
   }

   public boolean equals(Object food)  // equals is consistent with compareTo(...)
   {
      return calories == ((Food)food).calories;
   }
}
```

Notice that the compareTo(...) method is consistent with the equals(...) method of Food.

A class's natural order is the order used by TreeSet<E>. For most applications that utilize TreeSet<E>, this natural order is suitable, but sometimes it may be the case that the natural order is inappropriate. For example, an application may require that Food objects be ordered by fat content rather than calories. Conveniently, a TreeSet<E> collection may be constructed using an ordering schema different from the natural order of a class. To do this, define a new class that implements the Comparator<E> interface.

The single method of Comparator (in java.util) is

```
int compare(E object1, E object2)
```

that returns

- a positive integer if object1 is greater than object2,
- 0 if object1 equals object2, and
- a negative integer if object1 is less than object2.

For example, the class

```
import java.util.*;
public class OrderByFatContent implements Comparator<Food>
{
    public int compare(Food food1, Food food2)
    {
        if (food1.getFat() < food2.getFat())
            return -1;
        else if (food1.getFat() == food2.getFat())
            return 0;
        return 1;
    }
}
```

defines another order for the Food class.

A TreeSet<Food> collection can use this alternate order instead of the natural order, if TreeSet<Food> is instantiated as:

```
TreeSet<Food> tree = new TreeSet<Food>(new OrderByFatContent ());
```

Moreover, if a class is defined without a natural order, implementing the Comparator interface can add new functionality to the class.

To avoid subtle bugs, any implementation of compare(...) should be consistent with the equals(...) method of a class. This means that compare(a, b) returns 0 if and only if a.equals(b) also returns 0.

Example 17.3 gives an alternate order for the String class.

EXAMPLE 17.3

Problem Statement Occasionally, Mayor Quimby of Springfield, feeling a bit zany, prefers the voter list printed in reverse alphabetical order. Write an application that displays the list of voters in reverse alphabetical order.

Java Solution Fulfilling the mayor's wishes is a simple task: implement the Comparator<E> interface as follows:

```
import java.util.*;

public class Reverse implements Comparator<String>
{
    public int compare(String x, String y)
    {
        // change the sign of the integer returned by the compareTo(...) method of String
```

```
        return – (x.compareTo(y));
    }
}
```

To construct a TreeSet<String> collection that uses this new ordering scheme, instantiate TreeSet<String> by passing a Reverse object to the TreeSet<String> constructor. TreeSet<String> subsequently uses the order specified by the Reverse class when building a binary search tree. The following class extends the SpringfieldElection class of Example 17.1 and overrides the makeList() method, which displays the voter list.

```
import java.util.*;

public class ReverseVoters extends SpringfieldElection
{
   TreeSet <String>tree;
   public ReverseVoters()
   {
      super();
      tree = new TreeSet<String>(new Reverse()); // use alternative order
   }
   public void makeList()
   {
      int count = 0;
      tree.addAll(voters);
      System.out.println();
      System.out.println();
      System.out.println("Voters in reverse order: ");
      Iterator iterator = tree.iterator();
      while(iterator.hasNext())
         System.out.println((++count) + ". " + iterator.next());
   }

   public static void main(String [] args)
   {
      ReverseVoters reverseVoters = new ReverseVoters();
      reverseVoters.validate();
      reverseVoters.makeList();
   }
}
```

Output

Enter XXX to exit the system
Name: **Simpson, Homer**
Simpson, Homer may vote
Name: **Simpson, Marge**
Simpson, Marge may vote
Name: **Krusty**
Krusty may vote
Name: **Simpson, Homer**
Simpson, Homer has already voted
Name: **Bouvier, Selma**
Bouvier, Selma may vote
Name: **Flanders, Ned**
Flanders, Ned may vote
Name: **Smithers, Waylon**

Smithers, Waylon may vote
Name: **XXX**

Voters in reverse order:
1. Smithers, Waylon
2. Simpson, Marge
3. Simpson, Homer
4. Krusty
5. Flanders, Ned
6. Bouvier, Selma

Discussion

The Reverse class (lines 1–9) implements

```
int compare(String x, String y)
```

using the compareTo(...) method of the String class.

If x and y are strings, then x.**compareTo**(y)

- returns a negative integer if x precedes y alphabetically,
- return 0 if x and y are the same string, and
- returns a positive integer if x follows y alphabetically.

The **compare(String x, String y)** method changes the sign of the value returned by x.compareTo(y). For example,

compare("A", "B") = −("A".compareTo("B")), a positive integer;
compare("B", "A") = −("B".compareTo("A")), a negative integer; and
compare("A", "A") = −("A".compareTo("A")) = 0.

- ReverseVoters extends SpringfieldElection and thus inherits its methods.
- ReverseVoters instantiates tree using the Reverse class (line 17). Thus, tree is ordered according to the order specified by the compare(...) method of Reverse.

17.4 LISTS

The collection hierarchy is divided into sets and lists. Sets, as you know, do not contain duplicate elements. We now turn our attention to lists, collections that allow the occurrence of duplicate objects. Indeed, a List<E> object would never pass muster in a Springfield election.

17.4.1 The *List<E>* Interface

Figure 17.1 shows that the List<E> interface extends the Collection<E> interface. Sun provides the following description of the List<E> interface:

> The List<E> interface extends the Collection<E> interface defining an *ordered* collection that permits duplicates. The interface adds position-oriented operations, as well as the ability to work with just a part of the list.

The List<E> interface includes the following methods. Assume that x belongs to a class that implements List<E>.

- boolean add(E a)
  x.append(a) appends element a to the end of x.
- void add(int index, R a)
  x.add(index, a) inserts a into x at position index. Elements are shifted upwards.
- boolean addAll(Collection<E> c)
  x.addAll(c) appends the elements in c to the end of x.
- boolean addAll(int index, Collection<E> c)
  x.addAll(index, c) inserts the elements in c into x at position index.
- void clear()
  x.clear() makes x empty.
- boolean contains(Object a)
  x.contains(a) returns true if element a is a member of x.
- boolean containsAll(Collection<E> c)
  x.containsAll(c) returns true if the all members of c belong to x.
- boolean equals(Object a)
  x.equals(a) returns true if a is equal to x.
- E get(int index)
  x.get(index) returns the element of x at position index.
- int indexOf(Object a)
  x.indexOf(a) returns the index of the first occurrence of a in x; or –1, if a is not found.
- int lastIndexOf(Object a)
  x.lastIndexOf(a) returns the index of the last instance of a in x; or –1, if a is not found.
- boolean remove(Object a)
  x.remove(a) removes the first occurrence of a from x, returns true if successful.
- E remove(int index)
  x.remove(index) removes and returns the element at position index.
- boolean removeAll(Collection<E> c)
  x.removeAll(c) removes all elements from x that are contained in Collection c and returns true if x is altered.
- boolean retainAll(Collection<E> c)
  x.retainAll(c) retains those elements in c and returns true if x is altered.
- E set(int index, E a)
  x.set(index, a) replaces the current element, b, at position index with a and returns b.
- int size()
  x.size() returns the number of items in x.
- List subList (int start, int end)
  x.subList(start, end) returns a reference to a List consisting of the elements from position start to position (end – 1).
- ListIterator<E> listIterator()
  x.listIterator() returns a reference to a ListIterator, which like an Iterator, is used to step through x.
- ListIterator<E> listIterator(int index)
  x.listIterator(index) returns a reference to a ListIterator that begins at position index.

ListIterator<E> is an interface that extends Iterator<E>. A ListIterator<E> can be used to traverse a list forward or in reverse. Because ListIterator<E> extends Iterator<E>, ListIterator<E> has methods next(), hasNext(), and remove() of Iterator<E>. The cursor is positioned "between" the next and previous elements. The methods of a ListIterator<E> also include the following additional methods. In the descriptions of these methods, assume that the object, iter, belongs to a class that implements ListIterator<E>.

- E previous()
  iter.previous() returns the previous element in the list. This method can be used to traverse the list in reverse. A call to previous() moves the iterator back one element and returns that element.
- boolean has Previous()
  iter.hasPrevious() returns true if a listIterator has another element when proceeding in reverse.
- int nextIndex()
  iter.nextIndex() returns the index of the element that would be returned by the next call to next() and returns the size of the list if the iterator is positioned at the end of the list.
- int previousIndex()
  iter.previousIndex() returns the index of the element that would be returned by the next call to previous() and returns −1 if the iterator is at the beginning of the list.
- void set(E a)
  iter.set(a) replaces the last element returned by next() or previous() with a.
- void add(E a)
- iter.add(a) inserts a into the list before the element that would be returned by the next call to next(). In other words, if an iterator is positioned before an object o, a call to add(...) places the new element before o. A call to previous(), after an add operation, returns the newly inserted element.

The cursor or list pointer of ListIterator<E> is always positioned between the items returned by the next call to previous() or the next call to next(). If x is the list ["Harpo" "Groucho" "Zeppo" "Chico"], then Figure 17.10 shows the position of the list pointer after several calls to previous() and next().

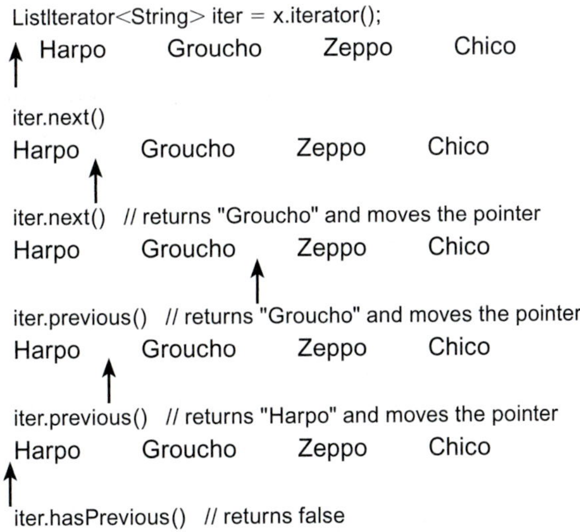

FIGURE 17.10 A *ListIterator*

The methods of ListIterator<E> throw unchecked RuntimeExceptions if an illegal operation is attempted. For example, E previous() throws a NoSuchElementException if no previous element exists.

17.4.2 The *ArrayList<E>* Class

ArrayList<E> is a concrete Java class that implements List<E>. As you know from Chapter 16, an ArrayList<E> object resizes itself, if necessary. As with an array, insertion and deletion into the middle of an ArrayList<E> is relatively inefficient because items are shifted with each insertion or deletion.

> ArrayList<E> is a good choice in situations when random access is required and/or insertion and deletion usually occur at the end of the list.

Like an array, the elements of an ArrayList<E> are indexed from 0. Example 17.4 gives a situation where ArrayList<E> is an appropriate and efficient choice.

EXAMPLE 17.4 One of the oldest and fastest methods for finding prime numbers is the Sieve of Eratosthenes. The following illustration uses this method to determine all prime numbers between 2 and 25 inclusive:

Initialize a list with the integers between 2 and 25 inclusive:

2 3 4 5 6 7 8 9 10 11 12 13 14 15 16 17 18 19 20 21 22 23 24 25

Start with $p = 2$ and cross out all numbers greater than p that are multiples of p, that is, cross out 4, 6, 8, 10 and so on.

2 × 3 × 5 × 7 × 9 × 11 × 13 × 15 × 17 × 19 × 21 × 23 × 25

Being multiples of 2, these numbers are not prime.

Now, find the next unmarked number p ($p = 3$), and again cross out all multiples of p that are greater than p (6, 9, 12, 15, . . .)

2 × 3 × 5 × 7 × × × 11 × 13 × × × 17 × 19 × × × 23 × 25

Once again, find the next unmarked number p ($p = 5$), and cross out all multiples (10, 15, 20, 25).

2 × 3 × 5 × 7 × × × 11 × 13 × × × 17 × 19 × × × 23 × ×

Continue the process. Stop when p exceeds the square root of 25. The numbers that remain unmarked (2, 3, 5, 7, 11, 13, 17, and 23) are the prime numbers less than 25.

Problem Statement Design an application that implements the Sieve of Eratosthenes. Input to the program should be a positive integer, n, that is greater than 1; output should be all prime numbers less than or equal to n.

Java Solution In our implementation, we instantiate an ArrayList<E>, sieve, and initialize each location to true (indicated by T):

T	T	T	T	T	T	T	T	T	T	T	T	T	T	T	T	T	T	T	T	T	T	T	T
2	3	4	5	6	7	8	9	10	11	12	13	14	15	16	17	18	19	20	21	22	23	24	25

To "cross out a number i," set the ith element of sieve to false (indicated by F). For example, after we cross out multiples of 2, sieve is false at positions 4, 6, 8, 10, 12, 14, 16, 18, 20, 22, and 24:

T	T	**F**	T	**F**	T	**F**	T	**F**	T	**F**	T	**F**	T	**F**	T	**F**	T	**F**	T	**F**	T	**F**	T
2	3	**4**	5	**6**	7	**8**	9	**10**	11	**12**	13	**14**	15	**16**	17	**18**	19	**20**	21	**22**	23	**24**	25

After the process terminates, sieve has the form:

T	T	F	T	F	T	F	F	F	T	F	T	F	F	F	T	F	T	F	F	F	T	F	F
2	3	4	5	6	7	8	9	10	11	12	13	14	15	16	17	18	19	20	21	22	23	24	25

If the *i*th element of sieve is true, then *i* was not eliminated and *i* is prime.

The following class implements the Sieve of Eratosthenes.

```
import java.util.*;

public class SieveOfEratosthenes
{
   ArrayList<Boolean> sieve;
   int num;

   public SieveOfEratosthenes()                    // default constructor; num = 25
   {
      num = 25;
      sieve = new ArrayList<Boolean>(26);          // need 26 spots for 0 to 25
      sieve.add(false);                            // 0 is not prime
      sieve.add(false);                            // 1 is not prime
      for (int i = 2; i <= num; i++)               // set all other positions to true
          sieve.add(true);
   }

   public SieveOfEratosthenes(int n)
   {
      num = n;
      sieve = new ArrayList<Boolean>(n + 1);
      sieve.add(false);                            // 0 is not prime
      sieve.add(false);                            // 1 is not prime
      for (int i = 2; i <= num; i++)               // set all other positions to true
          sieve.add(true);
   }

   public void getPrimes()
   {
      int p = 2;
      while(p * p <= num)                          // while p <= sqrt(num)
      {
         // j will step through multiples of p
         // setting the jth element of sieve to false
         for (int j = 2 * p; j <= num; j + = p)    // cross out multiples of p
             sieve.set(j, false);
         do             // find index of the next unmarked (non-zero) entry in sieve
         {
             p++;
         } while( (sieve.get(p)).equals(false));   // autoboxing
      }

      // print primes
      System.out.println("The primes less than or equal to " + num + " are:");
      for (int i = 1; i <= num; i++)
         if ((sieve.get(i)).equals(true))          // autoboxing
             System.out.println(i);
   }

   public static void main(String [] args)
   {
      Scanner input = new Scanner(System.in);
      System.out.print("Number: ");
```

```
        int n = input.nextInt();
        SieveOfEratosthenes s = new SieveOfEratosthenes(n);
        s.getPrimes();
    }
}
```

Output

```
Number: 50
The primes less than or equal to 50 are:
 2
 3
 5
 7
11
13
17
19
23
29
31
37
41
43
47
```

Discussion Setting values stored in sieve to false incurs no overhead. ArrayList<E> provides direct access to any location. Furthermore, the ArrayList<E>, sieve, is created by adding Boolean (uppercase "B") references to the *end* of the list. This action involves no shifting of elements. Once sieve is created and initialized, no values are added to, or deleted from, the middle of sieve. No elements need to be moved. These characteristics make ArrayList<E> an excellent choice for the Sieve of Eratosthenes.

17.4.3 The *LinkedList<E>* Class

The LinkedList<E> class, like the ArrayList<E> class, implements the List<E> interface, and consequently the Collection<E> interface.

Java's implementation of LinkedList<E> is a slightly more complicated version of the LList<E> class of Chapter 16. Like the LList<E> class of Chapter 16, LinkedList<E> is built by linking nodes together; but unlike the LList<E>, each node contains *two* references—one pointing to the next node on the list and the other pointing to the previous node. Such a list is sometimes called a *doubly linked list.* See Figure 17.11.

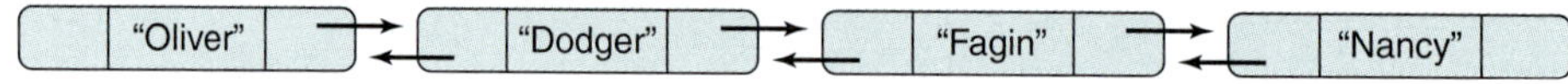

FIGURE 17.11 A *doubly linked list*. Each node has two reference fields.

> Java's LinkedList<E> class is a doubly linked list data structure in contrast to the LList<E> data structure of Chapter 16, which is singly linked.

Although the *methods* of LinkedList<E> and ArrayList<E> are functionally similar, there are some notable differences between the classes regarding implementation:

- Insertion into an ArrayList<E> at position *i* requires that *all references* in positions greater than or equal to *i* be shifted upwards one location. In contrast, insertion into the middle of a LinkedList<E> requires that a new node be allocated and at most four references adjusted. No elements are relocated. This always requires the same amount of time, regardless of the size of the list. See Figure 17.12.

1. Get a new node
2. Adjust the references to include the new node in the list

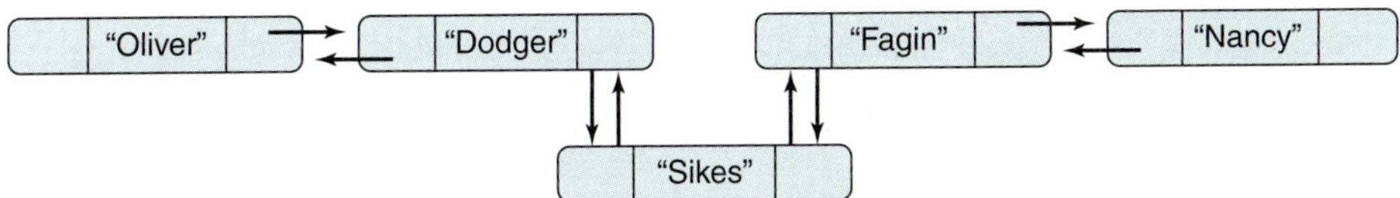

FIGURE 17.12 "Sikes" is added to the list of Figure 17.11. No data are shifted.

- Access to any element in an ArrayList<E> is immediate; an ArrayList<E> (like an array) provides *direct* access to any element. On the other hand, accessing the nth node in a LinkedList<E> involves traversing the list.

The LinkedList<E> class has the following constructors:

```
LinkedList<E> ();
LinkedList<E> (Collection<E> c);
```

Notice that there is no constructor that sets the initial size of the list. A list is initially empty, and it grows and shrinks as single items are added or deleted.

In addition to the methods of the List interface, LinkedList<E> implements the following methods that are not available to ArrayList<E> objects. The purpose of each method should be clear from the method's name and parameters.

- void addFirst(E x)
- void addLast(E x)

- E getFirst()
- E getLast()

- E removeFirst()
- E removeLast()

The solution to the next problem involves traversing a list and performing deletions. Because the solution does not require accessing an element at a particular index, LinkedList<E> holds a definite advantage over ArrayList<E>.

EXAMPLE 17.5

In the Jewish revolt against Rome, Josephus and 39 of his comrades were holding out against the Romans in a cave. With defeat imminent, they resolved that, like the rebels at Masada, they would rather die than be slaves to the Romans. They decided to arrange themselves in a circle. One man was designated as number one, and they proceeded clockwise killing every seventh man . . . Josephus (according to the story) was among other things an accomplished mathematician; so he instantly figured out where he ought to sit in order to be the last to go. But when the time came, instead of killing himself he joined the Roman side.

—from *Matters Mathematical* by Herstein and Kaplansky

Problem Statement Design an application that determines not only the position of the survivor but also the order in which the men are removed from the circle. Instead of assuming that there are 39 rebels, assume that there are n men (where $n \geq 1$) and rather than choosing every seventh man, choose every m^{th} man where n and m are supplied interactively.

For example, if $n = 9$ (9 men) and $m = 5$ (count every fifth man), the countdown is: 5, 1, 7, 4, 3, 6, 9, 2, and finally 8.

Java Solution Using the LinkedList<E> class, we can simulate "circular counting" using an iterator, as follows:

- Iterate through the list.
- When the iterator reaches the end of the list, create a new iterator positioned at the beginning of the list.

The end of the list can be detected using the hasNext() method.

```
import java.util.*;
public class Josephus
{
    LinkedList <Integer>men;
    int numMen;
    int counter;                              // number used to count off the men

    public Josephus()
    {
        men = new LinkedList<Integer>();
        numMen = 39;                          // defaults to 39 and 7
        counter = 7;
        for (int i = 1; i <= numMen; i++)     // build a list
            men.add(i);                       // autoboxing
    }

    public Josephus(int m, int c)
    // m is the number of men
    // c is the number used for counting off the men
    {
        men = new LinkedList<Integer>();
        numMen = m;
        counter = c;
        for (int i = 1; i <= numMen; i++)
            men.add(i);
    }

    public void count()
    // determines the last man alive and gives the order in which
    // the men die
    {
        ListIterator i = men.listIterator();
        Integer man;
        System.out.println("The order in which the men die is:");
        while(men.size() > 1)                 // while more than one man remains
        {
            // count out men
            for (int j = 1; j < counter; j++)
            {
                if( !i.hasNext())             // if at the end of the list
                    i = men.listIterator();   // get a new iterator
```

```
39.                 i.next();                    // next man
40.             }
41.             if (!i.hasNext())                // if at the end of the list
42.                 i = men.listIterator();      // get a new iterator
43.             System.out.print(i.next() + " ");
44.             i.remove();                      // remove the man from the list
45.         }
46.         if (i.hasNext())
47.             System.out.println ("\n" + i.next() + " " + "joins the Romans");
48.         else
49.             System.out.println ("\n" + i.previous() + " " + "joins the Romans");
50.     }

51.     public static void main(String [] args)
52.     {
53.         Scanner input = new Scanner(System.in);
54.         System.out.print("Number of men: ");
55.         int men = input.nextInt();
56.         System.out.print("Count: ");
57.         int counter = input.nextInt();
58.         Josephus josephus = new Josephus(men, counter);
59.         josephus.count();
60.     }
61. }
```

Output

```
Number of men: 9
Count: 5
The order in which the men die is:
5 1 7 4 3 6 9 2
8 joins the Romans
```

Discussion Each constructor builds a list of Integer references. Each Integer in the range 1 to numMen represents a soldier.

Lines 25–50: void count()

Line 29: A ListIterator <Integer> i is instantiated. The iterator i is used to count off the men.

Line 32: Repeat the statements on Lines 34–44 until just one man survives.

Lines 35–40: Count off the men, one by one. If the iterator reaches the end of the list before the process concludes, instantiate a new iterator positioned at the front of the list. This effectively makes the list circular.

Lines 41–43: The next man, returned by next(), is the next unlucky fellow. If the iterator has reached the end of the list, this "next man" is the first man on the list, so instantiate a new iterator positioned at the front of the list.

Lines 43–44: At this point, counter men have been marked off. A call to remove() removes the last item returned by next(). Consequently, a call to next() followed by one to remove() deletes this next man from the list.

Lines 46–49: One man remains. The cursor might be positioned so that either hasNext() is true or hasPrevious() is true. Both cases are considered.

17.5 PERFORMANCE ISSUES: CHOOSING THE RIGHT COLLECTION

We chose ArrayList<E> for the implementation of the Sieve of Eratosthenes and LinkedList<E> for the Josephus Problem. Both classes share the same interface. Both classes implement (mostly) the same methods. Could we have designed the Sieve of Eratosthenes using LinkedList<E> and the Josephus Problem with ArrayList<E>? Absolutely, but for a price.

A LinkedList<E> object can easily take the place of the ArrayList<E>, sieve, in the SieveOfEratosthenes class of Example 17.4. The changes in code are minor:

```
// replace ArrayList<E> with LinkedList<E> on lines 4, 9, and 18
Line 4: LinkedList<Boolean> sieve;
Line 9: sieve = new LinkedList<Boolean>();    // no capacity for LinkedList constructor
Line 18: sieve = new LinkedList<Boolean>();   // no capacity for LinkedList constructor
```

However, the change in performance is astounding. When computing all prime numbers less than 25,000, timed versions of the two programs produced the following results:

ArrayList Implementation	**LinkedList Implementation**
Number: 25000	Number: 25000
ArrayList: 20 ms	LinkedList: 13630 ms

The output speaks for itself.

ArrayList<E> provides direct access to an element. Access to a specific element of a LinkedList<E> requires traversing the list. Each time the LinkedList<E> implementation sets a value to false, the list must be traversed. That is not the case with the ArrayList<E> version of the program. Thus, choosing the wrong Collection class can cause a serious deterioration in efficiency.

Similarly, we compare the running time of the Josephus Problem implemented first using LinkedList<Integer>, as in Example 17.5, and then using ArrayList<Integer>:

LinkedList Implementation	ArrayList Implementation
Number of men: 100000	Number of men: 100000
Count: 13	Count: 13
LinkedList implementation: 170 ms	ArrayList implementation: 7671 ms

In this case, LinkedList<Integer> is the winner. Each time a man is removed from the list, data in the ArrayList<Integer> are moved to fill the gap. This is not the case using LinkedList<Integer>; no data are shifted by a remove() operation.

The next example utilizes ArrayList<E> in a class that adds integers comprised of an arbitrary number of digits - "big integers." However, in this application, neither ArrayList<E> nor LinkedList<E> provides any striking advantage.

EXAMPLE 17.6 The integer 2,147,483,647 is the largest value that can be assigned to a variable of type int. Similarly, 9,223,372,036,854,775,807 is the largest value of type long. Addition with larger numbers results in overflow and incorrect results.

Problem Statement Design a class BigInt with a method that adds non-negative integers of arbitrary size and returns the sum as a BigInt reference.

Java Solution A big integer consists of any number of digits, and to accommodate such numbers, the BigInt class stores an integer as a list (ArrayList<Integer>) of digits *in reverse* *order*. That is, the units digit is stored in position 0, the tens digit in position 1, and so on. See Figure 17.13. Storing the numbers in reverse order simplifies the addition process. Because addition is done beginning with the units digits, the index of the processing loop increases from 0. As you will see, this is especially convenient when adding two numbers of unequal length.

integer: 2957450818

[0]	[1]	[2]	[3]	[4]	[5]	[6]	[7]	[8]	[9]
8	1	8	0	5	4	7	5	9	2

FIGURE 17.13 The integer 2957450818 stored (in reverse) as a list of digits

To accomplish the addition of two large integers, their two corresponding digit lists are simultaneously traversed from left to right, beginning with the units digit. Digits are added in turn, first the ones digits, then the tens digits, and so on, keeping track of the "carry" values, if any.

BigInt adds two numbers exactly as you might add numbers with pencil and paper.

Figure 17.14 illustrates the addition process.

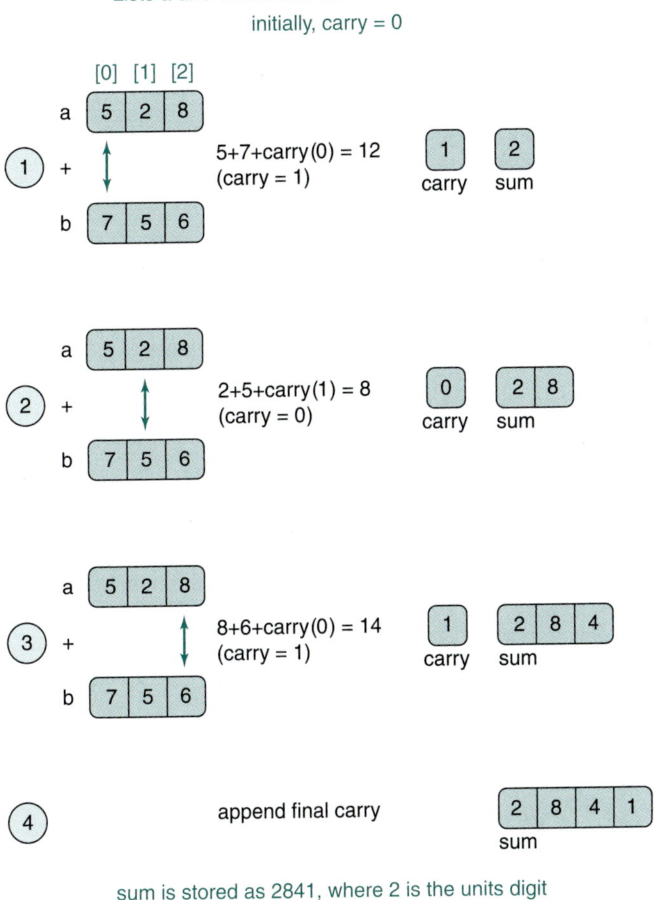

FIGURE 17.14 Add 825 + 657 and store the result in *sum*

In addition to adding large integers, the BigInt class overrides toString() so that toString() returns a String reference representing the sum, with the digits in natural order. A main(...) method demonstrates the BigInt class.

```
import java.util.*;
public class BigInt
{
   private ArrayList <Integer>num;  // holds digits in reverse order

   public BigInt()
   {
      num = new ArrayList<Integer>(1000);
   }

   public BigInt(String s) // s must be composed of digit characters '0'..'9'
   {
      num = new ArrayList<Integer>(1000);

      // convert character digits to integer digits, store digits in reverse
      for (int i = s.length() - 1; i >= 0; i--)
         num.add(s.charAt(i) - '0');
   }

   public String toString()  // override toString from Object
   {

      // appends each digit to a StringBuilder then converts to String
      StringBuilder temp = new StringBuilder(num.size());
      ListIterator <Integer> iter = num.listIterator(num.size());  // start at the end
      while (iter.hasPrevious())
         temp.append(iter.previous());
      return temp.toString();
   }

   public BigInt add(BigInt a)
   {
      BigInt sum = new BigInt();     // holds the sum

      // get two iterators for traversing each list of digits
      // the list pointer for each iterator is positioned at the
      // beginning of the list
      ListIterator <Integer> i1 = num.listIterator();
      ListIterator <Integer> i2 = (a.num).listIterator();

      int digitSum, carry = 0; // digitSum holds the sum of two digits

      // traverse each list of digits beginning with the units digit
      // the units digit is the first digit in the list, i.e., the digit at position 0
      // stop when one list has no more digits

      while (i2.hasNext() && i1.hasNext())
      {
            // add the two digits
         digitSum = i1.next() + i2.next() + carry;

            // adjust the carry digit
```

```
42.          carry = digitSum/10;

43.                // add the ones digit of the digit sum to the end of sum
44.          (sum.num).add(digitSum % 10);
45.       }

46.       // continue traversing the longer of the two lists
47.       // at most one of the following two loops executes
48.       while (i1.hasNext())
49.       {
50.          digitSum = i1.next() + carry;
51.          carry = digitSum/10;
52.          (sum.num).add(digitSum % 10);
53.       }
54.       while (i2.hasNext())
55.       {
56.          digitSum = i2.next() + carry;
57.          carry = digitSum/10;
58.          (sum.num).add(digitSum % 10);
59.       }

60.       // the final addition may have resulted in a carry value
61.       // if so, add the carry value (1) to the end of the list

62.       if (carry == 1)
63.          (sum.num).add(1);
64.       return sum;
65.    }

66.    public static void main(String [] args) // for testing
67.    {
68.       Scanner input = new Scanner(System.in);
69.       System.out.print("First number: ");
70.       BigInt a = new BigInt(input.next());
71.       System.out.print("Second number: ");
72.       BigInt b = new BigInt(input.next());
73.       System.out.println(a + " + " + b + " = " + a.add(b));
74.    }
75. }
```

Output

First number: **45676543212398765678**
Second number: **234543598787**
45676543212398765678 + 234543598787 = 45676543446942364465

Discussion

Lines 5–8: The default constructor instantiates an ArrayList<E>, num, with initial capacity of 1000. No values are inserted into num.

Lines 9–15: The one-argument constructor accepts a String, s, as a parameter. This String, made up of digit characters, represents an integer. For example, s might be "1234567890". Beginning with the last character, each character of s is converted to an integer and appended, in turn, to the end of the ArrayList<E>, num. Thus, if s is "1234567890" then num holds the digits, in reverse order, as [0,9,8,7,6,5,4,3,2,1].

Lines 16–24: toString()

Here, toString() overrides the toString() method inherited from Object so that a BigInt object can be displayed as a string of digits, rather than a memory address. The statement on line 19 instantiates a StringBuilder object, temp, large enough to hold the digits of num. Next, an iterator for num is created (line 20) so that the iterator is positioned at the end of num, and moving from right to left, each digit of num is appended to temp. Finally, temp is returned as a String. The same effect could be accomplished, though less efficiently, using the String class rather than the StringBuilder class:

```
String temp = "";
ListIterator <Integer>iter = num.listIterator(num.size());
while (iter.hasPrevious())
   temp = temp + previous();         // Each concatenation creates a new String object
                                     // This is inefficient
return temp;
```

Lines 25–65: add(BigInt a); // adds two BigInt objects

Line 27: ArrayList<E> sum holds digits of the sum in reverse order. For example, the sum of 99 and 1 (100) is stored in sum as [0,0,1].

Lines 31 and 32: Two ListIterators, i1 and i2 are instantiated: i1 for num and i2 for a.num. The list pointers for these iterators are positioned at the beginning of each list. The first item of each list represents the units digit of each number. The lists are traversed left to right, that is, beginning with the unit digits.

Line 33: Initially digitCarry is 0.

Line 37: Repeat the statements on lines 38–45 while *both* lists still have digits remaining.

Line 40: Moving left to right, add the next digit of each number plus the carry digit. Store this value in digitSum. The sum of the two digits plus the carry digit can be a number from 0 to 19, so carry is either 0 or 1.

Line 42: The carry digit is digitSum/10. For example, if digitSum is 15, then carry = 15/10 = 1; if digitSum is 8 then carry = 8/10 = 0.

Line 44: Add the units digit of digitSum to the end of the ArrayList<E>, sum.num. For example, if digitSum is 15, then the units digit is digitSum % 10 = 5.

Lines 48–64: If the two digit lists are not of equal size, exactly one of the loops, lines 48–53 or lines 54–59, executes. Each loop continues the iteration until no more digits remain. Finally, if carry equals 1, the digit 1 is added to the end of sum.num (lines 62–63). The final sum is stored in sum.num and the method returns a reference to sum.

The BigInt class could have been just as easily written using LinkedList<E> rather than ArrayList<E>. The code for the LinkedList<E> version of BigInt is virtually identical and is not reproduced here. Just substitute LinkedList for ArrayList and instantiate LinkedList<Integer>() with no initial capacity, rather than ArrayList<Integer>(1000).

Is any one implementation better than the other? Performing 10,000 additions of two 25-digit numbers produced the following results:

ArrayList: 281 milliseconds **LinkedList**: 235 milliseconds

In this case, neither collection has a large advantage, but LinkedList has a small edge in performance. On the other hand, ArrayList uses less memory because each node of a LinkedList holds data as well as two references, while an ArrayList just holds data. See Figure 17.11. We examine the results of this example in the exercises (Programming 3).

A time-space trade-off is a common theme when choosing a data structure.

17.6 THE *for-each* LOOP

Because traversing a collection is such a common task, Java 1.5 introduces the for-each loop.

The *for-each* loop is a convenience that can be used to iterate through a collection without having to explicitly instantiate an iterator.

For example, suppose that names is a collection of strings. Using an iterator, the following code displays each name in the collection, names:

```
Iterator <String> iter = names.iterator();
while (iter.hasNext())
{
        String name = names.next();
        System.out.println(name));
}
```

The collection can also be displayed using the following for-each construction:

```
for (String name : names)      // "for each" String, name, in the collection names
        System.out.println(name);
```

The for-each loop cannot be used to alter a collection.

So, for example, the following fragment is illegal.

```
for (String name : names)
        names.remove(); // ILLEGAL
```

Methods such as add(), remove(), and clear() cannot be used in conjunction with the for-each construction. However, the following iteration, which sums a list of integers and does *not* alter a collection, is fine.

```
int sum = 0;
for (Integer number : list)     // for each Integer, number, in the collection list
   sum = sum + number;          // This is legal
```

The equivalent code, using an iterator, is

```
int sum = 0;
Iterator <Integer> iter = list.iterator();
while (iter.hasNext())
     sum = sum + iter.next();
```

The *for-each* loop can make your code cleaner and easier to read. It provides a syntactic convenience.

17.7 IN CONCLUSION

The classes of the Java Collections Framework implement the Collection<E> interface. Each collection class implements many of the same methods. In spite of the similarities among the collection classes, choosing the most appropriate collection for a particular application can be crucial. The right choice demands understanding the advantages and disadvantages of each class. The wrong choice can result in an inefficient and even sluggish program. A little knowledge about the inner workings of a class implementation is all that it takes to guide your choice.

Choosing the right collection makes for efficient programs.

Just the Facts

- The Java Collections Framework is a hierarchy of classes and interfaces that manage and manipulate collections of data.
- Although the classes of the Collection hierarchy may seem redundant, the data structures underlying each one are different. Choosing the wrong class can result in a working but inefficient program.
- The Collection hierarchy divides into two interfaces, Set and List. A Set allows no duplicate entries, while a List does allow duplicates. A Set is not indexed; a List, however, is indexed from 0.
- Every interface in the Collection hierarchy declares methods that allow the manipulation of the elements in a collection. These methods provide the capability to:
  - add elements,
  - remove elements,
  - append other collections,
  - check for equality between collections,
  - check whether or not an element is a member of a collection, and
  - obtain the size of a collection.
- An iterator is an object capable of stepping through a collection. Iterators use next(), previous(), hasNext(), and hasPrevious() methods to "loop" through a collection.
- HashSet<E> is a class that implements Set<E>. No duplicate values are stored in a HashSet<E> object. HashSet<E> uses a hash function and a hash table to implement storage and retrieval.
- HashSet<E> is an appropriate choice when rapid lookup is paramount and ordering is not needed—in other words, when your objective is primarily to check whether or not some object is in a collection.
- SortedSet<E> is an interface that extends Set<E>. Unlike HashSet<E>, a class that implements SortedSet<E> is ordered and therefore must implement the Comparable interface. An object of a class that implements SortedSet<E> contains no duplicate elements.

- TreeSet<E> is a class that implements SortedSet<E>. A TreeSet<E> object stores elements in a balanced binary search tree, allowing for fast storage and retrieval.
- If a set must be kept sorted, then TreeSet<E> is an excellent choice. If objects need not be ordered, then HashSet<E> is probably a better choice.
- The Comparator<E> interface allows a class (such as TreeSet<E>) to implement a different ordering scheme on its data by implementing the compare(...) method. For classes that have no natural ordering, implementing Comparator<E> adds functionality.
- ArrayList<E> is a class that implements List<E>. An ArrayList<E> object provides direct access to any value via an index. ArrayList<E> has additional methods that insert and delete values at any index. An array is the underlying storage structure for the ArrayList<E> class..
- LinkedList<E> implements List<E>. LinkedList<E>, like ArrayList<E>, provides methods for access via an index, and for insertion and deletion of values. Like any class that implements List<E>, duplicates are allowed.
- A LinkedList<E> object accesses an element in time that increases proportionately with the number of elements in the list, but once an iterator is positioned before an element, insertions and deletions are performed in constant time. An ArrayList<E> object achieves access in constant time, but general insertions and deletions require time proportional to the number of elements in the list.
- The for-each construct is a feature of Java 1.5 that can be used for stepping through a collection without the need for an explicit iterator. This syntactic convenience works for *accessing* values, but not for *modifying* values.

Bug Extermination

- A poor choice of a particular Collection class can slow a program down. Yes, your program may run, produce correct results, and be "bug-free," but efficiency is an important consideration. So that your applications run efficiently, always choose a Collection class that suits your particular application or problem. Know how the collection operates. Don't use a Collection class with more muscle than necessary.
- When an application instantiates HashSet<SomeClass>, and SomeClass overrides equals(Object o), then SomeClass should also override hashCode(). Otherwise, the hashCode() method may produce different values for "equal" objects.
- If a class uses a Comparator<E> object, the compare(...) method should be consistent with the class's equals(...) method. This means that compare(a, b) returns 0 if and only if a.equals(b) returns 0.

EXERCISES

LEARN THE LINGO

Test your knowledge of the chapter's vocabulary by completing the following crossword puzzle.

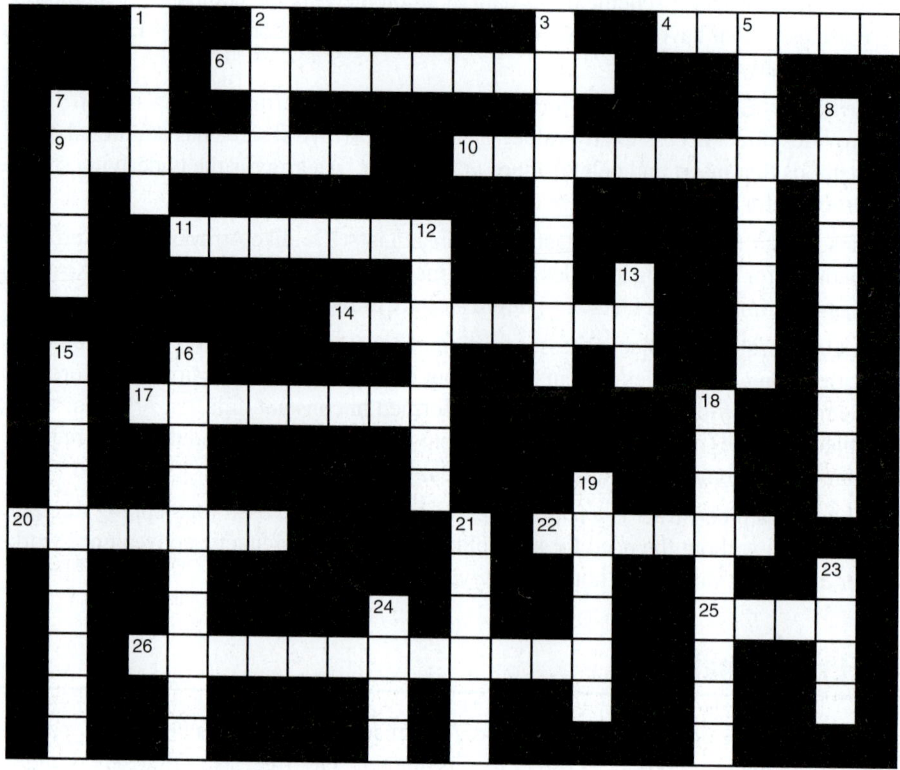

Across

4 Can be called only once for each call to next()
6 Implement to define an alternate order.
9 Used to traverse a collection
10 A group of objects considered as a single unit
11 Special loop that can be used to traverse a collection
14 Maps an object to an integer
17 Method that can be used to traverse a list in reverse
20 Returns true if there is a "next" item in a collection
22 Searching an unbalanced binary search tree is similar to a _____ search.
25 Allows duplicates
26 Extends Iterator

Down

1 Inserting into the front of an ArrayList is costly because data are ________.
2 A node on a tree with no parent
3 hashCode() maps two distinct objects to the same number.
5 The for-each loop is convenient for traversing a list but not for _____ values.
7 The Collection hierarchy is divided into Sets and ________.
8 The top tiers of the Collection hierarchy consist of ________.
12 Provides rapid lookup in an unordered collection
13 Does not allow duplicates
15 The natural ordering of a class is achieved by implementing ________.
16 Access to a specific element of a linked list involves _____ the list.
18 Provides direct access to an object
19 Searching a balanced binary search tree is similar to a _____ search.
21 hashCode() should be consistent with ________.
23 The Collection classes belong to the _____ package.
24 Tree node with no subtrees

SHORT EXERCISES

1. **True or False**

   If false, give an explanation.

   a. A collection that implements Set<E> can contain duplicate elements.
   b. An iterator is a kind of collection.
   c. An iterator has a size() method.
   d. A list *is-a* kind of set.
   e. Both lists and sets are kinds of collections.
   f. ArrayList<E> implements the List<E> interface.
   g. At most one iterator is available for each collection.
   h. A Comparator is a kind of iterator.
   i. TreeSet<E> is a good choice when sorted data is frequently accessed.
   j. HashSet<E> is better than a TreeSet<E> when data must remain sorted.
   k. The for-each construction is a syntactically cleaner way to accomplish the tasks of certain Iterator<E> methods.

2. **Hash Codes**

   Explain why, in the program of Example 17.1, using the Person class requires that the programmer override hashCode(), but using String does not, despite the fact that both classes override equals(...).

3. **Playing Compiler**

   Find and correct all the error(s) in each of the following statements. If a statement has no errors say so.

   a. test = new HashSet<int>();
   b. test1 = new TreeSet<Integer>();
      Iterator it = test1.iterator;
   c. LinkedList <Boolean> test2;
      test2 = new LinkedList(10);
   d. test3 = newArrayList <Integer> (50);
      System.out.print(test3.iterator().next());
   e. list = new LinkedList<Integer>();
      Iterator <Integer> it1 = list.iterator();
      int sum = it1.next();

4. **HashSet, TreeSet, ArrayList, and LinkedList**

   Each of the following statements applies to one or more of the four classes:

   - HashSet<E>
   - TreeSet<E>
   - LinkedList<E>
   - ArrayList<E>

   Determine the class(es) to which each statement applies.

   a. Does not allow duplicate entries.
   b. Does not allow ordering.
   c. Allows indexed access.
   d. Allows constant time insertions and deletions, that is, the time required for the insertion and deletion of an element is independent of the number of elements in the collection.
   e. Allows an arbitrary number of elements.
   f. Allows constant time access to elements, that is, the time required to access an element is independent of the number of elements in the collection.
   g. Sorting is easily accomplished.

5. **Which Collection Classes?**
For each scenario, describe which Collection class(es) you would use, how you would use the class(es), and why you choose the class(es).
    a. You want to maintain a list of foods together with the number of calories in each food. Your list should allow a user to specify a food and retrieve the number of calories for that food. You should be able to add new foods to the list.
    b. You want to maintain a list of your daily meals—foods and calories. You should be able to specify a particular day and retrieve the day's meals. You should be able to retrieve the total number of calories for any consecutive number of days.

6. **Which Collection Classes?**
For each scenario, describe which Collection class(es) you would use, how you would use the class(es), and why you chose those class(es).
    a. You keep track of all U.S. states that you have visited. Your program should have the capability to:
        - add a state to the list, and
        - determine whether or not you have visited a particular state.
    b. You store the names of all people to whom you have sent email. Your program should be able to:
        - retrieve a particular person's email address,
        - add a new name and email to the list,
        - print the list out in alphabetical order.

7. **Implementations—Time–Space Trade-offs**
    a. Explain why the LinkedList<E> implementation of BigInt (Example 17.6) performs slightly faster than the ArrayList<E> implementation.
    b. Explain why the LinkedList<E> implementation of BigInt uses more memory than the ArrayList<E> implementation.
    c. For BigInt, which do you think is more important, using less memory or having slightly faster methods? Why?
    d. When designing a class, what issues might determine whether memory usage or time usage is more important?

8. **A New Data Structure: The Priority Queue**
A *priority queue* is a data structure that allows insertion and deletion of elements. Each element in a priority queue has a unique integer priority. Unlike the queues of Chapter 16, items are deleted from a priority queue in order of priority; the element with highest priority is removed first. A waiting line in a bakery models a priority queue. As a customer enters the bakery he/she takes a ticket. The customer with the lowest-numbered ticket is served first. The lowest-numbered ticket has the highest priority.
    A priority queue should support the following methods:
    - void insert(E data, int priority);
    - E delete();
    - boolean contains(E data);

    a. Design a PriorityQueue class using one (or more) of the Collection classes.
    b. Which methods perform in constant time, that is, the time is independent of the number of elements in the priority queue? Explain your answer.

9. **Hash Functions**
   A good hash function *must* map equal objects to the same number and *should* produce as few collisions as possible. Each of the following hash functions maps a person's surname (a string) to an integer in the range 0…25? Which, if any, of these functions would you classify as a "good" hash function? Explain your answer.
   a. The sum of the ASCII values of the characters in the string, mod 26.
   b. The alphabetical position of the first character in the string; use 0 for 'A', 1 for 'B', . . . , 25 for 'Z'.
   c. The alphabetical position of the last character in the string; use 0 for 'A', 1 for 'B', . . . , 25 for 'Z'.
   d. The alphabetical position of either the first or last character in the string. The choice of first or last is random.
   e. The number of characters in the string.

10. **I Wonder Why (Challenging)**
   Did you ever wonder why Java classes are defined the way they are? Why are certain inherited methods overridden and others not? For example, the == operator compares references, as does equals(Object o) inherited from Object. However, equals(Object o) can be, and often is, overridden. String overrides equals(Object o), but StringBuilder does not. When applied to String objects, equals(Object o) compares characters but the == operator compares references. This is not the case with StringBuilder where both == and equals(Object o) compare references.
   a. Why do you think Java's designers made this choice? Justify your answer.
   b. How is this choice related to the immutability of String objects and/or the fact that the hashCode() method must assign the same value to "equal" objects. You may need to do a little research to answer this question.

PROGRAMMING EXERCISES

Programs marked **(R)** require recursive solutions.

1. **Using TreeSet<E>**
   Write a program that uses TreeSet<E> to sort a list of integers accepted from the console. End input with an integer flag, −999.
2. **Extending LinkedList**
   Create a class called NewList <E> that extends LinkedList<E> and implements an additional method,

```
void printMe()
```

   that prints the data in the list. Test your new class in main(…) by instantiating a NewList<Integer> object, filling it with the integers 1 through 100, and printing the integers using printMe().
3. **Recursively Printing the Elements of a LinkedList**
   (R) To recursively print the elements of a LinkedList, an iterator must be passed as an argument. Redo problem 2 but implement printMe() as follows:

```
public void printme()
{       recursivePrintMe(this.listIterator());
}
```

   This "wrapping" hides the ListIterator parameter needed by the recursive method and allows printMe() to maintain the same parameter-less signature as the iterative version in problem 2. To complete this problem, you should write a private tail recursive method

```
private void recursivePrintMe(ListIterator x)
```

that effects the printing.

4. **BigInt—Performance of ArrayList<E> vs LinkedList<E>**
Add a method to the BigInt class of Example 17.6 that performs subtraction of two arbitrarily long non-negative integers a and b such that $a \geq b$. Your method is easier to implement if it does subtraction as a computer subtracts rather than as you might do it with paper and pencil.
To subtract $a - b$
   1. Pad b with leading zeros (on the left) so that b has the same number of digits as a.
   2. Compute the complement of b: replace each digit k with $9 - k$.
   3. Add a to the complement of b.
   4. Add 1 to the total.
   5. Delete the leftmost digit in the answer.

   For example:
   To compute 14256789 – 3456:
   - pad $b = 3456$ with leading zeroes so that b has the form 00003456;
   - compute the complement of 00003456, which is 99996543;
   - add 99996543 to a: $a + 99996543 = 14256789 + 99996543 = 114253332$.
   - add 1 to the sum of the previous step: $114253332 + 1 = 114253333$.
   - delete the leftmost digit from 114253333, giving the final result: 14253333.

   You can check by hand that this is indeed correct.
   Implement the expanded BigInt class with ArrayList<E> and with LinkedList<E>. Time the subtractions and additions with each implementation. Discuss your results.

5. **Hash Sets**
Every pixel on your computer's screen has a unique *position* described by a pair (x, y), such that x and y are positive integers. The x-coordinate of a pixel, p, is the number of pixels from the left edge of the screen to p; the y-coordinate of p is the number of pixels from the top of the screen to p. Thus, the position of the pixel at the top left corner of your screen is (0, 0).
   Write a Position class with integer fields x and y that represent the screen position of a pixel. Override equals(Object o).
   The implementation of a video game must determine whether or not a given position is lit. When the game starts, no position is lit. A hash table is used to keep track of which positions are lit. Write a program that generates a list of 5000 random positions (x ranges from 0 to 60, and y ranges from 0 to 40). If the position is unlit, (not in the hash table) add it to the hash table (i.e., light it), and if it is lit, then remove it from the table ("unlight" it). Remember to override hashCode().
   When your program concludes, print a picture using '*'s and blanks that simulates the lit and unlit pixels. Display the number of pixels that are lit.

6. **Golf Records—Performance of ArrayList vs LinkedList**
A golfer keeps track of all the holes he/she plays during a season. For each hole, the golfer records two integers. The first integer is the par score for that hole, and the second, his/her score for that hole. Every 19th entry is the sum of the previous 18 entries. For example, if the first 18 entries are:

   3 4 4 4 5 4 4 4 3 5 4 4 4 4 3 4 4 4
   3 4 6 5 5 4 4 3 4 7 3 4 5 5 4 4 4 5

Then the 19th entry is:

71
79

Implement a class Hole that has two integer instance variables

```
int par;
int score.
```

Include the standard getter and setter methods. Override the equals(Object o) method that is inherited from Object based on score. Note that you won't need to use equals(...) in this problem, but it is good style to provide it in the class for other clients.

Write a program that creates a list of 1800 Hole references, representing 100 rounds of golf. The par value for each Hole is a random integer between 3 and 5, inclusive. The score is a random integer from two below the par value to four above it. Your program should iterate through the list, calculate the sum after every series of 18 holes, and insert that sum into the list at the correct position.

Implement your program with ArrayList<E> and also LinkedList<E>. Time both programs. Report and explain the results.

7. **An Ad Hoc Circularly Linked List**
A *circularly linked list* is a linked list in which the last element refers to the first element. One of the features of a circularly linked list is that given a list item, the entire list can be processed in order starting with that item. In the text, we created an ad hoc circularly linked list using LinkedList<E> by creating a new iterator every time the current iterator reaches the end of the list.
Write a CircList<E> class that extends LinkedList<E>. Your class should include a boolean method, display(...), which given an object e belonging to E, searches the list for e, and if found, prints all the data in the list in order starting with e, wrapping around the end of the list when necessary. The method returns true if e is found, otherwise false.

8. **Comparator and Comparable**
A Student class has a name field (String) and an array of four integer grades in the range 0 to 100. Methods include
   - String getName(), and
   - int getAverage() // returns the integer average of the four grades.

Student implements the Comparable interface so that compareTo(...) compares Student objects alphabetically by name. Student also overrides equals(Object 0) and toString().
Gradebook is a class that stores Student objects in a TreeSet, students. Gradebook has a two-argument constructor

```
public Gradebook(int num, Comparator c)
```

that populates students by prompting for num names along with four grades for each name. The parameter c may be null, in which case the TreeSet, students, is created using the natural order of Student; otherwise students is created with the order imposed by c. GradeBook also includes a method

```
public void display()
```

that iterates through students and displays each student's name and average.
The class OrderByAverage implements Comparator<Student>. The compare(...) method of Comparator compares Student objects based on average grade (an integer).

Implement each of these classes. Test them using the following class:

```
public class TestGradebook
{
        public static void main(String[] args)
        {
            Gradebook gradeBook = new Gradebook(10, null);
            gb.display();                            // alphabetical order, by name
            gradeBook = new Gradebook(10, new OrderByAverage());
            gradeBook.display();                     // sorted by average grade
        }
}
```

9. **Josephus and Recursion**

(R) Example 17.5 describes the famous Josephus Problem. If $m = 2$, that is, every other person is counted off and killed, there is a recursive formula for computing J(n), the number of the last person to be removed from the original circle of n people. Of course, J(1) = J(2) = 1.

For general n:
if n is odd then $J(n) = 2 \times J(n/2) + 1;$
if n is even then $J(n) = 2 \times J(n/2) - 1.$
Note that $n/2$ is integer division.

For example:
$J(19) = 2 \times J(9) + 1.$
$J(9) = 2 \times J(4) + 1.$
$J(4) = 2 \times J(2) - 1.$
$J(2) = 1.$

Hence, J(4) = 1, J(9) = 3, and J(19) = 7.

Write a recursive method that returns the position of the survivor in the n person Josephus Problem when $m = 2$. Time your algorithm for n = 100, 1000, 10000, and 100000. How does the running time of your algorithm compare to the running time of the program in Example 17.5?

10. **Josephus and Binary Numbers**

There is an interesting connection between the Josephus Problem where $m = 2$ and binary numbers. If you write the number of people, n, in binary format, then the number of the last surviving person can be calculated by rotating the bits once to the left.

For example, to calculate J(19), the number of the survivor from a group of 19, write 19 in binary as 10011, and rotate the bits once to the left to get 00111, which is 7. Notice that the original leftmost bit moves to the rightmost position.

Write a program that determines the survivor when $m = 2$ by converting n to binary and inserting the bits into a LinkedList<E> object. Then use the data structure to "rotate" the bits to the left, and finally, convert the resulting list of bits back to an integer.

Conversion of n to a binary number can be done iteratively or recursively:

```
convert(n) // iteratively
        while (n > 1)
        {  insert n % 2 into the front of the list;
                n = n/2;
        }
```

```
convert(n) // recursively
        if (n == 1) then insert 1 into the list and break;
        // else
        insert n % 2 into the front of the list;  // inserts rightmost digit into the list
        convert (n / 2);                          // cuts off the rightmost digit
```

Once again, *n*/2 is integer division and consequently truncates remainders.

Conversion of the bits back to a number can also be done iteratively or recursively:

```
bitsToInt(list) // iteratively
        sum = 0;
        traverse the list, left to right, starting at the front;
        for each bit b
        {       sum = 2 * sum;
                add b to sum;
        }
        return sum;

bitsToInt(list) // recursively
        b = rightmost bit;   // rear of the list
        delete the rightmost bit from the list;
        return (b + 2 * bitsToInt(list) );
```

11. **Simulating a Print Queue Using the Collections Framework**
A computer's operating system keeps track of a print queue for each printer. A print queue is a list of jobs waiting for access to a printer. A job has

- an ID number,
- a size,
- a time-stamp indicating when it was added to the queue, and
- a priority from 1 to 10.

The time-stamp is a positive integer representing the number of seconds that the computer has been operating (uptime) when the job arrived. The operating system has access to the current uptime of the computer. The size of the job is the number of seconds required to print the job. The priority of the job is a measure of the importance of the job. A priority of 10 indicates "most important."

When the current job is finished, the operating system chooses the next job. The next job is the one in the queue with the highest priority. If more than one job has the highest priority, the operating system chooses the job that has been waiting in the queue for the longest amount of time. The printer takes five seconds between jobs to reset itself and prepare for the new job. If a job remains in the queue for a long period of time, its priority increases by one (to a maximum of 10) for every 200 seconds it remains in the queue.

Write a program that reads a list of jobs from a file and prints the time at which each job started and finished printing. Your program should simulate one print queue. You will need a Job class and a PrinterQueue class. The latter should be built from classes of the Collections Framework.

12. **The Map Hierarchy**
A *map* is a collection of object pairs (key, value) such that each key object is unique. The key object is used to locate and store the value object. The key serves as an index into a map collection.

Suppose, for example, that student data consists of

ID
name
gpa (grade point average)

Several students may have the same name and, of course, gpa. However, a student's ID number is unique. Consequently, the ID number might serve as the key in a map of the form

(id, {name, gpa})

For example, the table

id (key)	name, gpa
19834	Lucy 2.1
18765	Ricky 2.7
18123	Fred 3.4
17654	Ethel 3.4
12987	Ricky 3.9

is such a map. The key for this map is the ID, and the value is a single object that holds two strings, a student's name and his/her gpa.

Since a key uniquely identifies each object, a search for any particular object is a search for a particular key value—that is, searching is based upon the key.

Like the Collection hierarchy, Java's Map hierarchy consists of a collection of interfaces and concrete classes. See Figure 17.15.

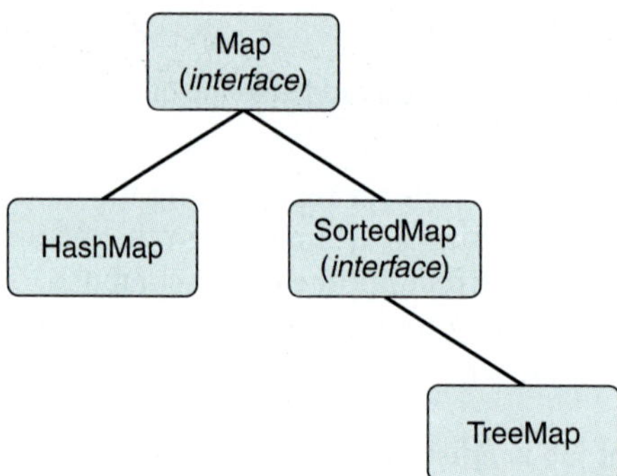

FIGURE 17.15 The *Map* hierarchy

Map<K,V> is an interface that is at the root of the hierarchy. SortedMap<K,V> is also an interface. HashMap<K,V> and TreeMap<K,V> are classes.

A few commonly used methods of the Map<K,V> interface are:

- void clear(),
  removes all objects from the map;
- boolean containsKey(Object key)
  returns true if the map contains a value for key;
- V getKey(Object key),
  returns the value associated with key;
- Set <K> keySet(),
  returns the keys of the map as a Set;

- V put(K key, V value),
  inserts the pair (key, value) into the map. If the map contains another value associated with key, replaces and returns that value. Otherwise returns null.
- int size(),
  returns the number of (key, value) pairs in the map.

The SortedMap<K,V> interface extends Map<K,V>. SortedMap<K,V> objects are stored in key order, lowest to highest.

Some additional methods of SortedMap are:

- K firstKey(),
  returns the first key in the map;
- K lastKey(),
  returns the highest key in the map;
- SortedMap<K,V> headMap(Key toKey),
  returns all (key, value) pairs as a SortedMap<V,K> object with key values less than toKey;
- SortedMap tailMap headMap(Object fromKey),
  returns all (key, value) pairs as a SortedMap<V,K> object with key greater than or equal to fromKey;
- SortedMap subMap(Object fromKey, Object toKey),
  returns all (key, value) pairs as a SortedMap<V,K> object with key greater than or equal to fromKey and strictly less than toKey.

TreeMap<K,V> is a class that implements SortedMap<K,V>. Objects are stored in a balanced tree and are ordered by the key.

HashMap<K,V> implements Map<K,V>. Objects are stored using a hash table based on the key. No order is assumed among keys.

Efficiency considerations for the HashMap<K,V> and TreeMap<K,V> classes are similar to those for HashSet<E> and TreeSet<E> classes. The following problems require the use of both Map classes.

---

a. Construct a HashMap<K,V> object that can be used to translate English to both French and Pig Latin. Your application should:

- prompt for an English word and provide the French and Pig Latin equivalents, and
- print a list of all English words (not necessarily in order).

Just in case you are unfamiliar with either French or Pig Latin, here are a few words that you can use as data.

English	**French**	**Pig Latin**
chicken	le poulet	ickenchay
pig	le couchon	igpay
money	l'argent	oneymay
hello	bonjour	ellohay
bye	au revoir	eyebay
thanks	merci	anksthay
dog	le chien	ogday
wine	le vin	ineway
hot dog	le hot dog	othay ogday

b. In general, TreeMap<K,V> operations are slower than HashMap <K,V> operations, but because keys are kept in sorted order, the TreeMap<K,V> class provides a few extra methods and gives additional functionality. Unfortunately, TreeMap<K,V> does *not* implement Collection<E> and does not supply an iterator method.

To circumvent this minor inconvenience, instantiate a Set<E> object from the (key, value) pairs of a TreeMap<K,V>, then iterate over this set. The TreeMap method that returns such a set is

```
Set<Map.Entry<K,V>> entrySet()
```

where Map.Entry<K,V> is a (key, value) pair.

The following code instantiates such an iterator for a TreeMap tree:

```
Iterator<Map.Entry<K,V>> iterator = (tree.entrySet()).iterator();
```

Implement the English-French-Pig Latin application using TreeMap<K,V> and an iterator to display the (key, value) pairs sorted by key.

c. The motor vehicle department has a system whereby each driver is given an integer rating from 9 to 40 measuring his/her safety record; 9 is the best rating. Drivers with a rating of 9 get the lowest insurance rates.

An insurance agent keeps a set of 10,000 clients, storing each client's account number and safety number. The latter is used to calculate a client's annual bill. The agent occasionally adds or deletes a driver. The agent frequently updates the safety record of a particular client by increasing the saftey number based upon citations or accidents. Once a year, the agent updates the safety records of *all* clients, subtracting 1 from each client's safety number. This lets people improve their scores during "clean" years, that is, years in which they have no accidents or tickets. Recall that the minimum safety record is 9, so during the annual update, a driver with safety record of 9 is unaffected. Also once a year, the agent prints a list of the clients ordered by increasing safety number.

Write a class, InsuranceAgent, that initializes a list with 10,000 drivers, each with an account number and randomly selected safety number. Assume that account numbers begin with 1 and increase to 10,000.

Your application should be able to:

- add a driver to the list,
- delete a driver,
- add 1 to the safety record of a particular driver,
- iterate through all the clients, subtracting 1 from each one's safety record (9 is minimum),
- sort the clients by safety number, and
- calculate the median (middle) safety record.

It makes sense to implement InsuranceAgent using a HashMap. A TreeMap would be inefficient for the updates. However, a TreeMap is appropriate when doing the annual sorting. Hence, use a HashMap and convert your HashMap to a TreeMap one time each year, after all the insertions, deletions, and modifications have been effected. Then, use TreeMap to sort and calculate the median.

Write a class that demonstrates InsuranceAgent.

THE BIGGER PICTURE

TREES

Trees form the basis of dozens of data structures, each one suited to a specific kind of task. Here we examine two of these: the binary search tree and the shortest path tree. We begin with the binary search tree, a data structure that provides efficient storage, retrieval, and management of data.

Binary Search Trees

In Section 17.3.3 we define a binary tree as well as a binary search tree. In this set of exercises, we ask you to implement a binary search tree class that includes methods that build a tree, traverse a tree, and search a tree.

As defined in this chapter, a *binary search tree* is a binary tree such that for any node *N*, all data contained in the left subtree of *N* are less than the data of *N* and all data contained in the right subtree of *N* are greater than or equal to the data of *N*. That is, a binary search tree is ordered.

Figures 17.7a, 17.8a, and 17.8b are all examples of binary search trees.

As with a linked list, we can implement a binary search tree by linking nodes. In the case of a binary tree, each node contains data as well as *two* reference fields. See Figure 17.16.

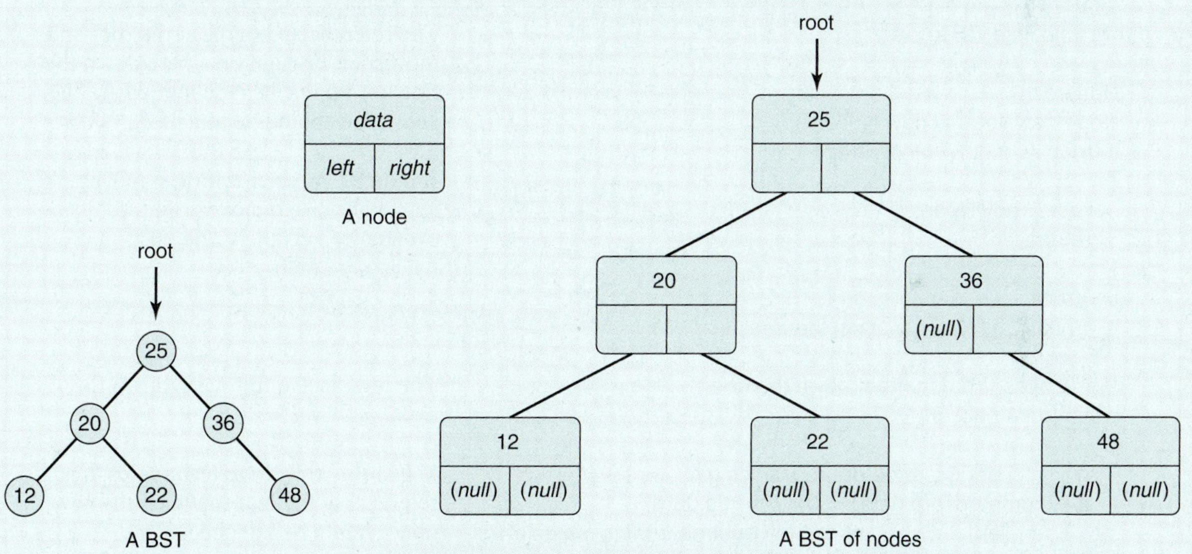

FIGURE 17.16 A binary search tree

We begin an implementation of a binary search tree class with the following code segment that includes a Node class:

```
public class BST<E extends Comparable<E>>
{
        private class Node
        {
            private E data;
            private Node left;
```

```
            private Node right;

            public Node(E x)        // Node constructor
            {
                data = x;
                left = right = null;
            }
        }
        private Node root;          // a reference to the root of the tree
        public BST()                // BST constructor
        {
            root = null;            // initially the tree is empty
        }
    }
```

Of course, to build a binary search tree, we need a method that inserts elements into the tree. The following method

```
void insert(E x)
```

places a node with value x into a binary search tree. This method can be used repeatedly to construct a tree.

<table>
<tr>
<td>

```
public void insert(E x)
{
    Node p,q;
    Node newNode = new Node(x);
    if (root == null) // empty tree
    {
        root = newNode;
        return;
    }
    p = root;
    q = null; // q follows p down the tree

    // p "moves" from the root down the tree
    while (p != null)
    {
        q = p; // set q to p before reassigning p
        if (x.compareTo(p.data) < 0)  // x < p.data
            p = p.left;        // set p to left subtree, that is move left
        else
        // x >= p.data; set p to right subtree, move right
            p = p.right;
    }
    // determine whether to place x on left or right
    if (x.compareTo(q.data) < 0)
        q.left = newNode;
    else
        q.right = newNode;
}
```

</td>
<td>
The reference p begins at the root and moves left or right on a path down the tree until p reaches the leaf where the new node should be attached.

If p.data is greater than x, p moves left; otherwise p moves right. p eventually gets the value null : (while p != null)

The reference q follows p down the tree.

When the while loop terminates, q is referencing the leaf to which the new node should be attached.
</td>
</tr>
</table>

THE BIGGER PICTURE

Exercises

1. Draw the binary search tree that is created via the following method calls:

```
BST<Integer> tree = new BST<Integer>(),
tree.insert(25),
tree.insert(16),
tree.insert(32),
tree.insert(12),
tree.insert(43),
tree.insert(1), and
tree.insert (27).
```

2. Draw the binary search tree created by the loop

```
BST<Integer> tree = new BST<Integer>()
for (int i = 1; i <= 6; i ++)
        tree.insert(i);
```

   and the tree created by

```
BST<Integer> tree = new BST<Integer>()
for (int i = 6; i <= 1; i --)
        tree.insert(i);
```

3. Devise a method

```
boolean contains(E x)
```

   that returns true if the specified object is in the tree. The method is similar to the insert(E x), method in that a reference p should move left or right down the tree until either x is found or p is null. The method can be implemented iteratively or recursively. Use iteration here.

4. Write a method

```
E search (E x)
```

   that returns the specified object, if found in the tree, otherwise null. The method can be implemented iteratively or recursively. Use iteration here.

Tree Traversal

Traversing a tree is almost as easy as traversing a list. There are a number of traversal algorithms, but the following *inorder* traversal method is particularly useful because this method displays BST data in sorted order. Although some binary search tree methods can be accomplished iteratively as easily as recursively, traversals are done more easily using recursion.

Written as a Java method, this recursive algorithm has the following compact form:

```
void traverse (Node root)
{
        if (root != null)                   // if the tree is not empty
        {
            traverse(root.left);            // recursively traverse the left subtree
            System.out.println(root.data);  // display the data of the root
            traverse(root.right);           // recursively traverse the right subtree
        }
}
```

Figure 17.17 shows a binary search tree and a corresponding *recursion* tree, which traces the execution of the traversal algorithm. Note that if a (sub)tree consists of a single node, traversal amounts to no more than printing the data of the node. In Figure 17.17, we refer to a node by the value of its data.

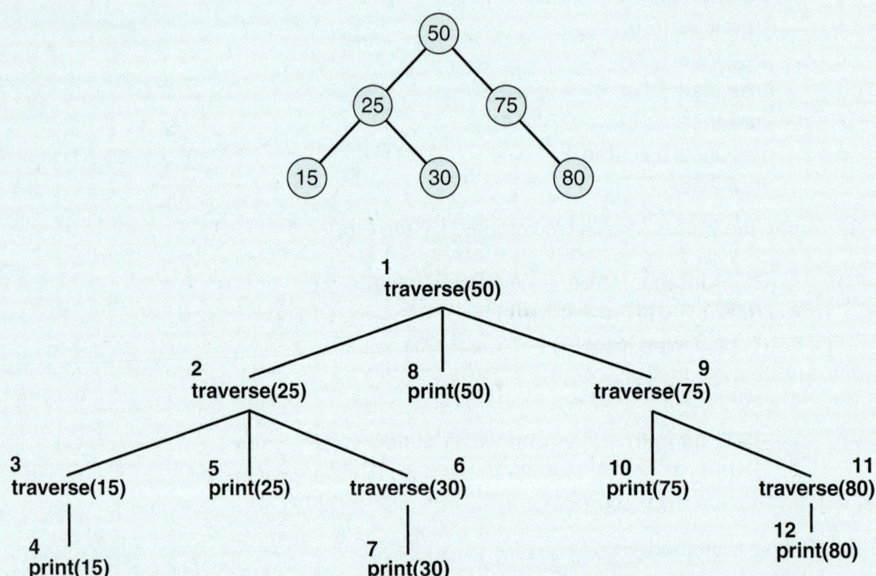

FIGURE 17.17 A binary search tree and the actions of an inorder traversal. Data is displayed in sorted order: 15, 25, 30, 50, 75, 80.

Exercises

5. Traverse the binary tree of Figure 17.18. Note that since this is *not* a BST, a traversal does *not* display data in sorted order.

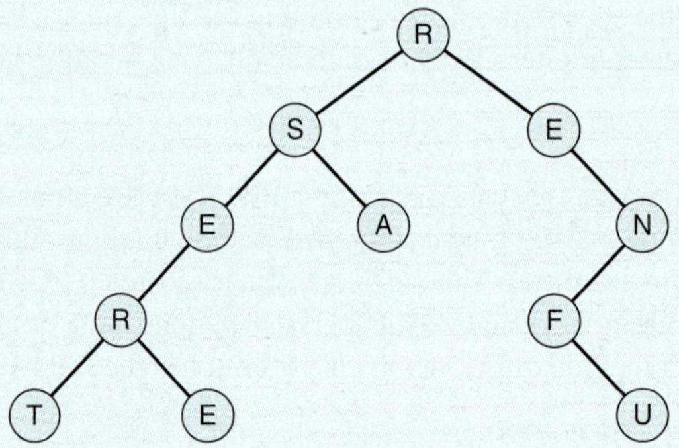

FIGURE 17.18 A binary tree that is not a search tree

6. Include the following methods in a BST<E> class:

```
public void insert(E x),
public boolean contains(E x),
public search(E x), and
private void traverse(Node root) // note that this method is private in the BST class.
```

Because the parameter of traverse(Node root) is the private field root, the method call traverse(**root**) cannot be invoked from outside the class. This presents no difficulty. Declare traverse(Node root) a private helper method and include a second *public* method traversal() that calls traverse(root).

```
private void traverse (Node root)
{
        // code as given
}

public void traversal()
{
        traverse(root);
}
```

This "wrapping" trick is common when using recursive methods, and it occurs for a variety of reasons. Another example can be found in Programming Exercise 3 of this chapter—recursively printing a linked list. You will see a number of similar examples in the following exercises.

Include a main(...) method that builds a tree with String data and demonstrates the methods of BST.

A binary search tree is a recursive data structure, and so its methods lend themselves to recursive programming. In the following exercises, we ask you to write some recursive methods.

Exercises

7. **(R)** The number of nodes in a tree can be found recursively:

```
int numNodes(Node root)
{
   // if root is null return 0
   // otherwise
   // return
   // the number of nodes in the left subtree of root +
   // the number of nodes in the right subtree of root +
   // 1 (for the root)
}
```

Add the following recursive method to BST:

```
private int numNodes(Node root) // returns the number of nodes in a tree
```

Like the traversal method, this method is private. Include a public method

```
public int size()
{
  return numNodes(root);
}
```

8. **(R)** The maximum value in a BST can be found recursively:

```
E max(Node root)
{
   // if the right subtree of the root is empty return the data in the root
   // otherwise return the maximum value of the right subtree of the root node
}
```

THE BIGGER PICTURE

Include the recursive method

```
private E max(Node root)
```

in the BST class, along with

```
public E maximum()
{
        return max(root);
}
```

9. **(R)** Add a recursive method to BST that returns the minimum value stored in a binary search tree.

10. Replace the iterative versions of the insert(...), contains(...), and search(...) methods of the BST class with their recursive counterparts.

Shortest Path Trees and Arrays

A binary search tree is a versatile data structure used for many kinds of applications, the most common being the efficient storage, retrieval, and management of data. However, there are many other types of trees used for different kinds of applications. These include red-black trees, heaps, treaps, height-balanced trees, weight-balanced trees, splay trees, decision trees, B-trees, ternary trees, *n*-ary trees, expression trees, mini-max trees, and more, with applications ranging from database systems to algorithms, caching, compilers, game playing, and decision theory.

Unlike binary search trees, *shortest path trees* have nothing to do with storing and retrieving data. Shortest path trees are used for determining the shortest path(s) between two locations on a map. Simpler than a binary search tree, a shortest path tree can be implemented with two one-dimensional arrays.

The shortest path algorithm might be the most commonly executed algorithm after perhaps sorting, searching, and Euclid's greatest common divisor. The shortest path algorithm is used each time a person requests directions from Mapquest or Google Maps. Here, we do not discuss the details of the algorithm, but instead focus on the data structures used. One of these data structures is a surprisingly simple implementation of a tree.

Given a representation of a road map, the shortest path algorithm calculates the shortest route from one place to another. For example, the network in Figure 17.19 shows the streets in a small town that connect various town attractions. For example, if A signifies the post office and B the elementary school, then the direct distance between the post office and the school is two miles. If C represents the high school, there are many paths between the high school and the elementary school. The path from C to A to B is three miles, but a shorter path (two miles) from C to B goes through G.

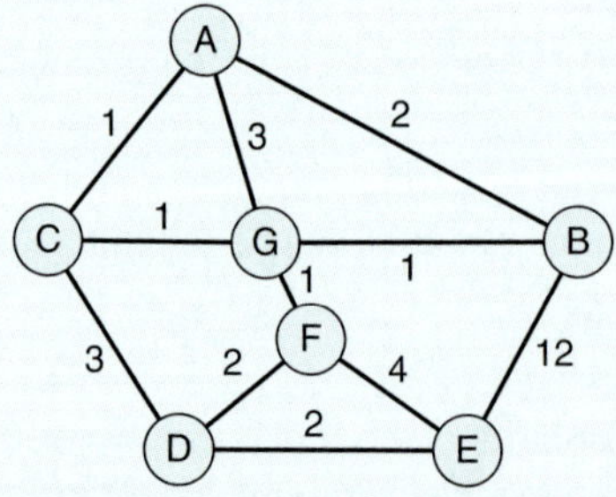

FIGURE 17.19 A network that depicts the streets of a small town

The information in this network can be stored in a table:

	A	B	C	D	E	F	G
A	0	2	1	1000	1000	1000	3
B	2	0	1000	1000	12	1000	1
C	1	1000	0	3	1000	1000	1
D	1000	1000	3	0	2	2	1000
E	1000	12	1000	2	0	4	1000
F	1000	1000	1000	2	4	0	1
G	3	1	1	1000	1000	1	0

The distance between any two *adjacent* places *i* and *j* is located in the table at position (*i, j*). For example, the entry in position (E,B) is 12, the distance between E and B. The number 1000 (any number much larger than any possible path value will do) is placed in every position (*i, j*) such that *i* and *j* are not adjacent.

We do not describe how the shortest path algorithm does its job, but we do describe the data structure used to store the solution. The shortest path algorithm computes the shortest path from A to every other location including A. The result is stored in a *shortest path tree,* with root A. A picture of this tree is shown in Figure 17.20.

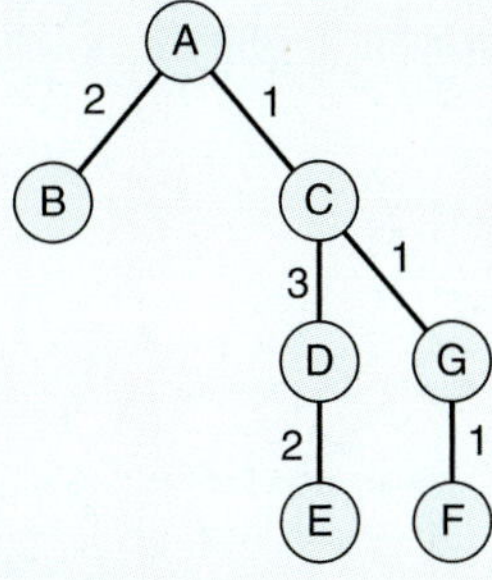

FIGURE 17.20 A shortest path tree rooted at A

Because there is a unique path between any two nodes of a tree, we can use this tree to find the shortest distance and corresponding path from any node to A. For example, the shortest distance from E to A is 6, and the corresponding path is E-D-C-A. Similarly, the shortest distance from F to A is 3, and the path is F-G-C-A.

The shortest path tree can be stored using two arrays, one holding the lengths of the shortest paths to A, and the other, the paths themselves. The latter array is sometimes called a *parent* array, because it stores the *parent* of each node. The parent of the root, A, is null; A is the *parent* of B and C; C is the parent of D and G, and so on. The two arrays of this example are shown below:

	A	B	C	D	E	F	G
Shortest Distance From A:	0	2	1	4	6	3	2

	A	B	C	D	E	F	G
Parent:	Null	A	A	C	D	G	C

The *parent* array helps determine the actual sequence of nodes in the shortest path between the root A and any given node. For example, to determine the path between A and

E, start with E, and find the parent of E. That's D. The parent of D is C, and finally the parent of C is A. Thus, the shortest path from E to A is E-D-C-A.

Exercise

11. Implement a ShortestPathTree class using two arrays. Include constructors, getter methods, and setter methods. Finally, include a method that displays the shortest distance and corresponding path from the root of the tree to any other node.

Conclusion

The shortest path tree is *not* a binary search tree. It is not even necessarily a *binary* tree; each node can have many children. Compared to a binary search tree with its linked structure, a shortest path tree is easy to store using just two arrays. Indeed, a tree representation is only as complicated as it needs to be for its intended use. If your intention is to display the shortest path between two nodes, then the simple array/parent representation of a shortest path tree is sufficient. On the other hand, operations such as storing, searching, deleting, and retrieving data call for a more complex tree representation such as a binary search tree or even a *balanced* binary search tree.

There are many kinds of tree-based data structures. Always choose the simplest one that allows an efficient solution to your problem.

PART 4

Basic Graphics, GUIs, and Event-Driven Programming

CHAPTER 18

Graphics: AWT and Swing

"It don't mean a thing if it ain't got that swing"
—Duke Ellington, Irving Mills

Objectives

The objectives of Chapter 18 include an understanding of

- Java's Component classes,
- Swing and AWT,
- frames,
- panels,
- layout managers, and
- simple graphics.

18.1 INTRODUCTION

At this point, you already know enough about programming and Java to implement applications that are challenging, interesting, and useful. Nonetheless, clever data structures, good error handling, tight code, and flexible design are not enough. With today's interactive computer applications, a user-friendly graphical interface is the norm. Windows, clickable buttons, drop-down menus, input boxes, and eye-catching graphics provide a little "razzle dazzle" and make programs fun and easy to use.

In the remainder of the book, we discuss programs that interact with a user via a graphical user interface (GUI); programs that utilize windows, menus, buttons, checkboxes, and what we generally call *widgets*. Input may come by clicking the mouse, pressing a button, selecting a menu item, or typing a string into a text box. Output can be accomplished not only with text but with images, sound, and graphics.

In this chapter, you will learn how to arrange graphical components within a window and how to use these components to display images, labels, text, and even your own graphics. In Chapter 19, we explain how to make your buttons, checkboxes, menus, and other widgets come alive and respond to user actions.

18.2 COMPONENTS AND CONTAINERS

It is probably no surprise that Java provides a hierarchy of classes that facilitates GUI programming. Part of Java's Component hierarchy is shown in Figure 18.1.

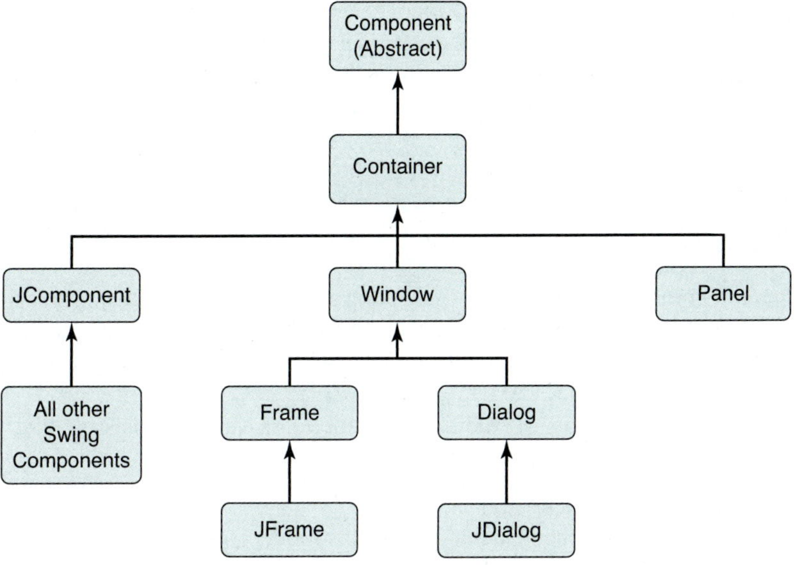

FIGURE 18.1 The *Component* hierarchy

At the top of the hierarchy is the (abstract) Component class.

> A *component* is an object that can be displayed on the screen.

For example, buttons, text boxes, checkboxes, and labels are all components. A window is also a component.

The Container class extends Component.

> A *container* is an object that holds components.

Figure 18.2 shows a *frame* that holds six buttons, three inside the frame and three on the upper border. A frame is a container and a button is a component.

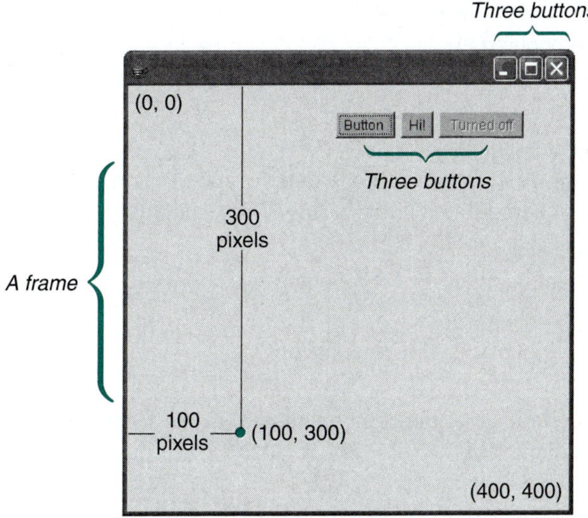

FIGURE 18.2 Six buttons in a frame

But wait. If Container extends Component, then every Container object is also a Component object. So isn't a frame both a container and a component? Yes, a frame is both a component and a container. The distinction is really semantic. The Container class indicates that an object is meant to hold other components. A frame is usually considered a container.

> Every component, such as a button, a checkbox, a text box, or a window is an object belonging to some class that extends Component. These components are placed in containers.

The upper left corner of a container is designated as position (0, 0), and (*x, y*) is the point located *x* pixels to the right of and *y* pixels down from (0, 0). For example, the dot in the frame of Figure 18.2 marks the point (100, 300), which is 100 pixels right of (0, 0) and 300 pixels down from (0, 0).

A few useful methods of the Component class and all classes that extend Component are:

- void setSize(int width, int height)
  sets the size of a component so that its width is width pixels and its height is height pixels. This method can be used to resize a button or a window.
- void setLocation(int x, int y)
  places a component at position (x, y) of the container that holds it. When a component is placed at position (x, y), the upper left-hand corner of the component is placed at (x, y). You will see that regardless of the visual shape of a component, every component has an upper left-hand corner.
- void setBounds(int x, int y, int width, int height)
  places a component at position (x, y) and resizes the component to the number of pixels specified by the parameters width and height.
- void setEnabled(boolean enable)
  enables the component if the parameter, enable, is true; disables the component if enable is false. If a button is enabled, clicking the button usually triggers some program action. For instance, clicking the "X" button of Figure 18.1 closes the frame; clicking the "-" button minimizes the frame. If a button is not enabled, clicking the button results in no action. The "turned off" button of Figure 18.2 is disabled. This is indicated by the faded, "grayed-out" label.
- void setVisible(boolean x)
  hides the component if the parameter is false; displays the component if the parameter is true.
- void setName(String name)
  sets the name of the component. For example, someButton.setName("Print Button") sets the name of someButton to the String "Print Button".
- int getHeight()
  returns the height in pixels of a component.
- int getWidth()
  returns the width in pixels of a component.
- int getX()
  returns the *x*-coordinate of the component, that is, the *x*-coordinate of the upper left corner of the component.
- int getY()
  returns the *y*-coordinate of the component, that is, the *y*-coordinate of the upper left corner of the component.

- String getName()
  returns the name of the component.
- boolean isEnabled()
  returns true if the component is enabled, false otherwise.
- boolean isVisible()
  returns true if the component is visible when its container is visible, false otherwise. Note that a visible component does not display if its parent container is not also visible.

  The Container class defines additional methods. The most important of these is

  Component add(Component c),

which places a component, c, in a container and returns c. We discuss other Container methods as needed.

18.3 ABSTRACT WINDOWS TOOLKIT AND SWING

Java provides two packages that contain the classes for graphics programming: the original Abstract Windows Toolkit (AWT) and the newer Swing package. AWT is the original class library for graphics programming. The AWT widgets use the interface elements of a particular platform. In other words, a button on a Windows machine may not look like a button on a Unix machine or an Apple. The more modern Swing library paints the components on the screen so that the look and feel of a graphical user interface is consistent from platform to platform. Swing does not replace AWT; in fact, Swing uses many AWT classes. Swing, however, does provide new user interface components (buttons, textboxes, checkboxes, menus, etc.) which are platform independent. Figure 18.3 compares Swing and AWT. The AWT classes are in java.awt and the Swing classes reside in javax.swing.

AWT in java.awt package	Swing in javax.swing package
Each component is mapped to a corresponding platform-dependent interface called a *peer*. Platform-specific and prone to platform-specific bugs. Components may look different on different platforms. Components have the look of a particular platform.	No platform-dependent peers. Code written in Java. All components look the same, regardless of the platform. Components are all prefixed with "J," e.g., JButton, JCheckbox, JLabel.

FIGURE 18.3 AWT and Swing

Swing classes are all prefixed with uppercase J. For example JButton, JCheckBox, JWindow, and JMenu are Swing classes that encapsulate buttons, checkboxes, windows, and menus—your everyday, standard components.

All Swing components except JFrame and JDialog extend JComponent.

See Figure 18.1.

18.4 WINDOWS AND FRAMES

Every GUI utilizes one or more windows. A GUI may or may not have buttons, checkboxes, or menus, but windows are indispensable.

The Window class extends Container. That is, a Window *is-a* Container and as a Container, a Window holds widgets. Of course, Window also implements all the methods of parent class Component. A Java Window is a "window" without borders and a title bar. The Frame class, a member of AWT, extends Window. A Frame *is-a* Window that includes a title bar and border. JFrame is a Swing class that extends the AWT class Frame. See Figure 18.1. A JFrame object is a container for other objects such as buttons, labels, text boxes, and checkboxes.

> A JFrame encapsulates what you normally think of as a "window," and it is the primary container used in all our applications.

JFrame is a Swing class, and we always use the Swing classes in our examples.

Two JFrame constructors are:

- JFrame()
  creates a new JFrame that is initially invisible.
- JFrame(String title)
  creates a new JFrame with title, title, that is initially invisible. When the frame is visible, the title appears on the title bar of the frame.

In addition to the methods of Component, some useful JFrame methods are:

- void setTitle(String title)
  sets the title of the frame to title.
- void setResizable(boolean x)
  if x is true, the frame can be resized by the user; if x is false, the frame cannot be resized. By default, a frame is resizable.
- void setDefaultCloseOperation(int op)
  exits the application when the user closes the frame, provided that op is the JFrame constant EXIT_ON_CLOSE. If the close operation is not set with EXIT_ON_CLOSE, when a user clicks on the x in the upper right-hand corner of the window, the window disappears but the process still runs in the background.

Adding components to a JFrame and displaying them is very common. Because a JFrame *is-a* Container, use

- the add(Component c) method of Container to add components to a JFrame, and
- the setVisible(boolean x) method of Component to make a JFrame visible.

The next example is the graphical equivalent of the traditional "Hello World" program.

EXAMPLE 18.1 **Problem Statement** Design a class that extends JFrame. Include two constructors. The default constructor sets the title to "I've been framed!" A one-argument constructor accepts a String parameter, title. The frame should be positioned at (0, 0) on the user screen. The dimensions of the frame should be 300 by 300 pixels.

Java Solution The upper left corner of the screen has coordinates (0, 0). Consequently, a call to setBounds (0, 0, 300, 300) places the upper left corner of the frame at screen position (0, 0).

```
1.  import javax.swing.*;

2.  public class MyFirstFrame extends JFrame
3.  {
4.     public MyFirstFrame ()           // creates a frame with title "I've been framed!"
5.     {
6.        super("I've been framed!");   // call the one-argument constructor of JFrame
7.        setBounds(0, 0, 300, 300);    // placed at screen position (0, 0); size 300 by 300
8.     }

9.     public MyFirstFrame (String title) // creates a frame with title title
10.    {
11.       super(title);                  // call the one-argument constructor of JFrame
12.       setBounds(0, 0, 300, 300);     // placed at (0,0); size 300 by 300
13.
14.    }
15. }
```

The following test class creates, displays, and closes a MyFirstFrame frame.

```
16. import javax.swing.*;

17. public class TestMyFirstFrame
18. {
19.    public static void main(String[] args)
20.    {
21.       JFrame frame = new MyFirstFrame ("This is a test");
22.       frame.setVisible(true);
23.       frame.setResizable(false);
24.       frame.setDefaultCloseOperation(JFrame.EXIT_ON_CLOSE);
25.    }
26. }
```

Output TestMyFirstFrame places a frame in the upper left-hand corner of the screen. See Figure 18.4. Notice the String on the title bar.

FIGURE 18.4 A frame in the upper left-hand corner of the screen

Discussion

Line 21: The reference frame is declared as a JFrame. Because MyFirstFrame extends JFrame, upcasting is acceptable.

Line 22: By default, a frame is invisible; so the call setVisible(true) is essential.

Line 23: The frame cannot be resized by the user. Notice that the center button in the upper right-hand corner of the frame has been disabled. The frame always remains 300 by 300.

Line 24: This line can also be placed in the constructor.

18.4.1 Centering a Frame

The frame of Example 18.1 appears in the upper left-hand corner of the screen. Placing the frame there is easy enough because the upper left-hand corner position is (0, 0). Suppose, however, that you would like to place a frame of size 200 by 100 pixels in the center of the screen. If the screen size (resolution) is 800 by 600, then the upper right-hand corner of the frame should be positioned at (x, y) such that

$x = (800 - 200)/2 = 300$

$y = (600 - 100)/2 = 250$

See Figure 18.5.

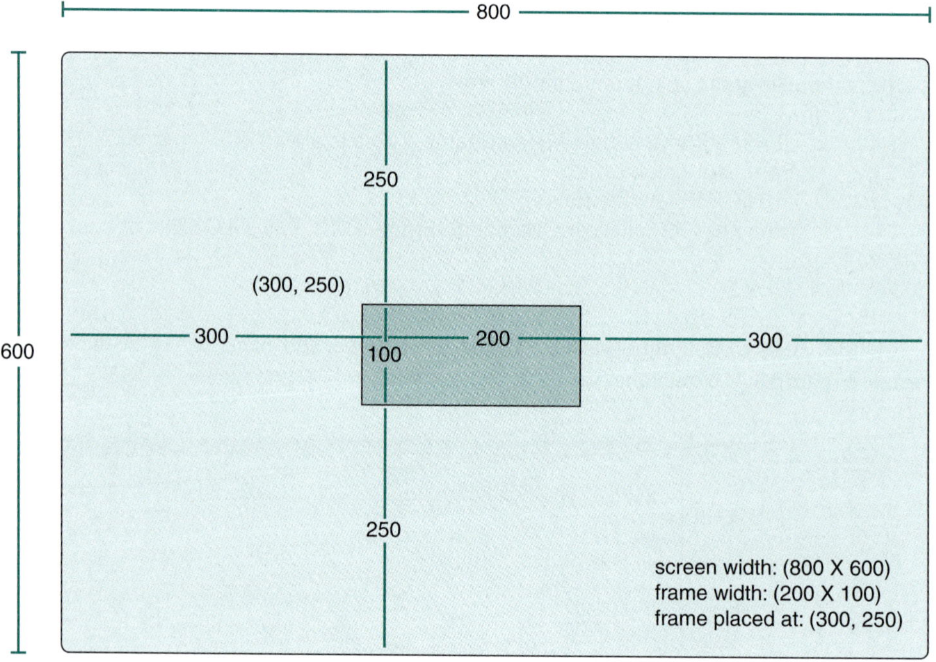

FIGURE 18.5 Centering a 200 by 100 frame

Of course, if the screen resolution is 1024 by 768 then a centered 200 by 100 frame should be positioned at:

$x = (1024 - 200)/2 = 412$

$y = (768 - 100)/2 = 334$

So if myFrame belongs to JFrame, the statement

```
myFrame.setBounds(300, 250, 200, 100);
```

centers the frame on a screen with dimensions 800 by 600. However, notice that the frame would *not* be centered on a screen with different dimensions, such as 1024 by 768.

> To center a frame on a screen of any size, use methods of Java's Toolkit and the Dimension classes (in AWT).

The Toolkit class contains a method, getScreenSize(), that returns a Dimension object. The Dimension class has two public fields, width and height, that hold the screen dimensions. The following segment uses the Toolkit and Dimension classes to obtain the screen size:

```
Toolkit toolkit = Toolkit.getDefaultToolkit();        // a static method of the Toolkit class
Dimension dimensions = toolkit.getScreenSize();   // dimensions.width is the width of the screen
                                                  // dimensions.height is the height of the screen
```

In conjunction with Toolkit and Dimension, we use Java's Point class, which encapsulates a two-dimensional point. The Point class has two public fields int x and int y that denote the horizontal and vertical coordinates of a two-dimensional point. The class has a two-argument constructor

```
Point (int x, int y)
```

that sets the values of x and y.

The following utility class CenterFrame has a single static method

```
public static Point getPosition(int frameWidth, int frameHeight)
```

that, given the width and height of a frame, returns a Point that holds the coordinates, x and y, of the position where the frame should be placed so that it is centered on the screen.

```
import java.awt.*;

public class CenterFrame // a utility class
{

    public static Point getPosition(int frameWidth, int frameHeight)
    {
        // returns a Point holding the coordinates of
        // the upper left-hand corner of the (centered) frame

        Toolkit toolkit = Toolkit.getDefaultToolkit();
        Dimension dimensions = toolkit.getScreenSize();
        int x = (dimensions.width - frameWidth)/2;    // x coordinate of upper left corner
        int y = (dimensions.height - frameHeight)/2;  // y coordinate of upper left corner
        return (new Point(x, y));                     // return coordinates as a Point object
    }
}
```

The following program centers a frame regardless of the screen resolution.

EXAMPLE 18.2

Problem Statement Create a class, AnotherFrameClass, that extends JFrame and defines four constructors.

- The default constructor does not specify a title, and it centers an untitled 300 by 300 frame.

- The three-argument constructor specifies a title and the size (width and height) of a frame. The constructor also centers the frame.
- The one-argument constructor creates a frame that fills the entire screen.
- The five-argument constructor includes a title, coordinates of the upper left-hand corner of the frame, and the size of the frame. The frame is not automatically centered.

Java Solution AnotherFrameClass uses the utility class CenterFrame to center a frame on the screen.

```
import java.awt.*;
import javax.swing.*;

public class AnotherFrameClass extends JFrame
{
   public AnotherFrameClass()
   {
      // default constructor
      // frame contains no title
      // width = 300, height = 300
      // centers frame

      super();   // call default constructor of JFrame
      final int FRAME_WIDTH = 300;
      final int FRAME_HEIGHT = 300;
      Point position = CenterFrame.getPosition(FRAME_WIDTH, FRAME_HEIGHT);
      setBounds(position.x, position.y, FRAME_WIDTH, FRAME_HEIGHT);
   }

   public AnotherFrameClass(String title, int width, int height)

   // three-argument constructor, set title, width, height, centers frame
   {
      super(title); // call the one argument constructor of JFrame

        // position gives the coordinates of the upper left corner of the frame
      Point position = CenterFrame.getPosition(width, height);
      setBounds(position.x, position.y, width, height);
   }

   public AnotherFrameClass(String title )   // one-argument constructor
   // creates a frame that fills the entire screen
   {
      super(title); // call the one argument constructor of JFrame
      Toolkit tk = Toolkit.getDefaultToolkit();
      Dimension d = tk.getScreenSize(); // d has public fields width and height
      setBounds(0, 0, d.width, d.height);
   }

   public AnotherFrameClass(String title, int x, int y, int width, int height)
   // five-argument constructor, a frame with dimensions width by height is placed at (x, y)
   {
        // (x, y) denotes the position of the upper left-hand corner of the frame
        // width is the width of the frame
        // height is the height of the frame
      super(title); // call the one argument constructor of JFrame
```

```
40.         setBounds(x, y, width, height);
41.     }
42. }
```

The following class demonstrates AnotherFrameClass.

```
43. import javax.swing.*;

44. public class TestAnotherFrameClass
45. {
46.     public static void main(String[] args)
47.     {
48.         JFrame centerFrame =
                    new AnotherFrameClass ("I'm at the center!", 200, 300);
49.         centerFrame.setVisible(true);
50.         JFrame topFrame =
                new AnotherFrameClass("I'm at the top!", 0, 0, 600, 100);
51.         topFrame.setVisible(true);
52.         topFrame.setDefaultCloseOperation(JFrame.EXIT_ON_CLOSE);
53.         centerFrame.setDefaultCloseOperation(JFrame.EXIT_ON_CLOSE);
54.     }
55. }
```

Output The output of this application appears in Figure 18.6.

FIGURE 18.6 Two frames, one at the top and one at the center

Discussion

Line 48: The three-argument constructor places a frame with the title "I'm at the center!" in the center of the screen. The method call on line 22

```
Point position = CenterFrame.getPosition(width, height);
```

returns a Point object that holds the screen coordinates of the position that centers the frame. Because the x and y fields of Point are public, they can be accessed directly with

setBounds(**position.x**, **position.y**, width, height);

Line 50: The five-argument constructor places the frame titled "I'm at the top" in the upper left-hand corner of the screen.

Using a Toolkit object (tk), the one-argument constructor (lines 25–32) creates a frame that fills the entire screen. The call tk.getScreenSize() returns a Dimension reference d where d.width and d.height are the width and height of the screen. These values are passed to SetBounds(...) on line 31.

Now that we can position a frame on the screen, we add a few widgets.

18.5 LAYOUT MANAGERS

To add components to a frame, Java provides *layout managers*.

A *layout manager* is an object that arranges components in a container such as a frame. The layout manager classes implement the LayoutManager interface.

You might think of a layout manager as an interior designer who arranges the furniture in your home. Different designers use different schemes. Different layout managers arrange widgets differently.

A layout manager is an object and consequently belongs to a class. Those classes that we discuss are:

- BorderLayout,
- FlowLayout, and
- GridLayout.

There are others. Each layout manager works differently. Each has its own scheme.

18.5.1 *BorderLayout*

BorderLayout is the default layout manager for JFrame. That is, unless you specifically instantiate a layout manager for a frame, components are placed in a frame using the BorderLayout layout manager.

The BorderLayout manager divides a frame into five areas:

NORTH WEST SOUTH EAST CENTER

See Figure 18.7.

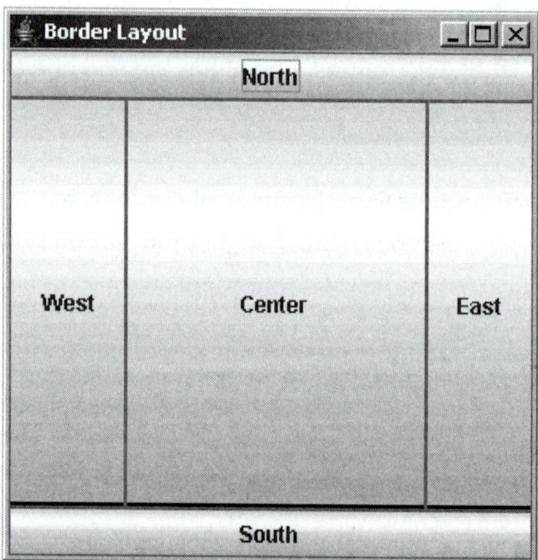

FIGURE 18.7 *BorderLayout* partitions a frame into five regions

The BorderLayout constructors are:

- BorderLayout()
- BorderLayout(int horizontalgap, int verticalgap)
  where horizontalgap and verticalgap specify horizontal and vertical space, in pixels, between components.

The method

```
add(Component c, int region)
```

places a component into a container. The parameter, region, is specified by one of the constants

```
BorderLayout.NORTH,
BorderLayout.SOUTH,
BorderLayout.EAST,
BorderLayout.WEST, or
BorderLayout.CENTER.
```

> If no region is specified, a BorderLayout layout manager places a component in the center region. Only one component can be placed in a region, and components are resized to fit the region.

The class of Example 18.3 places five buttons in a frame.

> A *button* is a widget that displays some text or image and allows some action to occur when the button is "pressed"—that is, when the mouse is clicked on the button.

For the present, we are not concerned with the functionality of a button; for now, clicking a button triggers no action. Our primary purpose here is to demonstrate the placement of components in a frame.

A button is a member of the JButton class. Three constructors of JButton are:

- JButton(),
  creates a button with no text.
- JButton(String text),
  text is text displayed on the button.
- JButton(new ImageIcon (String filename))
  displays an image on the button, where filename is the name of an image file, such as myPicture.jpg or yourPicture.gif.

  The ImageIcon class is discussed in detail in Section 18.8. To understand the following example, you do not need to know anything more about ImageIcon.

Of course, a JButton *is-a* Component; so JButton inherits the methods of Component.

EXAMPLE 18.3

Problem Statement Create a class, BorderLayoutFrame, that extends JFrame such that an object belonging to BorderLayoutFrame displays five buttons. Arrange the five buttons in the frame using the default BorderLayout layout manager. The center button should display the famous "smiley face" image stored in smiley.jpg. The other four buttons should display the word *smile* in four languages: English, French (*sourire*), Italian (*sorriso*), and Spanish (*sonrisa*).

The size of the frame should be 300 by 300 and the frame should be positioned at (0, 0). Include a main(...) method that instantiates the frame.

Java Solution The button that displays an image is instantiated as:

```
new JButton(new ImageIcon("smiley.jpg")).
```

The image file is in the same directory as the BorderLayoutFrame class.

```
import javax.swing.*;
import java.awt.*;

public class BorderLayoutFrame extends JFrame
{
   public BorderLayoutFrame()
   {
      super("BorderLayout ");            // call one-argument constructor of JFrame
      setBounds(0, 0, 300, 300);         // position and size

      // add the center button; the button displays the image in "smiley.jpg"

      add(new JButton(new ImageIcon("smiley.jpg")), BorderLayout.CENTER);

      // add four buttons to NORTH, SOUTH, EAST, and WEST

      add(new JButton("Smile"), BorderLayout.NORTH);
      add(new JButton("Sourire"),BorderLayout.SOUTH);
      add(new JButton("Sorriso"), BorderLayout.EAST);
      add(new JButton("Sonrisa"),BorderLayout.WEST);
   }

   public static void main(String[] args)      // for display purposes
   {
      JFrame frame = new BorderLayoutFrame ();
      frame.setVisible(true);
      frame.setDefaultCloseOperation(JFrame.EXIT_ON_CLOSE);
   }
}
```

Output Figure 18.8 shows the frame created by BorderLayoutFrame.

FIGURE 18.8 Five *JButtons*, one displaying an *ImageIcon*, placed with the default layout manager, *BorderLayout*

Discussion Notice that each button fills its region. If the frame is expanded, so are the buttons. That is, the buttons are resized.

The frame can hold only five components, and components can be covered by other components. For instance, if the additional statement

```
add(new JButton( ":)" ),BorderLayout.CENTER);
```

is added to the constructor at line 16, the frame would appear as in Figure 18.9.

FIGURE 18.9 Output of the *BorderLayout Frame* class with one additional statement: *add(new JButton(":)"),BorderLayout.CENTER)*;

18.5.2 *FlowLayout*

An object belonging to FlowLayout arranges components horizontally in a container, left to right, row by row, in the order in which they are added to the container.

The FlowLayout class has three constructors:

- FlowLayout()
  instantiates a FlowLayout object that center aligns components in a container.
- FlowLayout(int Alignment)
  instantiates a FlowLayout object with the specified alignment: FlowLayout.LEFT, FlowLayout.CENTER, or FlowLayout.RIGHT, with integer values 0, 1, and 2, respectively.
- FlowLayout(int Alignment, int horizontalSpace, int verticalSpace)
  instantiates a FlowLayout object with the specified alignment. Parameters horizontalSpace and verticalSpace specify horizontal and vertical space, in pixels, between components.

The JFrame method

```
setLayout(LayoutManager m);
```

sets the layout manager for a frame. For example,

```
setLayout(new FlowLayout());
```

or

```
LayoutManager manager = new FlowLayoutManager();
setLayout(manager);
```

changes the layout manager of a frame from the default BorderLayout to FlowLayout.

Example 18.4 places not five but 26 buttons in a frame using the FlowLayout class.

EXAMPLE 18.4 In one version of the game *Hangman*, a program randomly chooses a word from a list of 5000 words. A player attempts to determine the mystery word by guessing letters, one letter at a time. The player guesses a letter by clicking a labeled button. For example, if the mystery word is *ELEPHANT* and the player clicks the *E* button the computer displays

$$E * E * * * * *$$

The player made a correct guess and sees all the *E*s that occur in the secret word. The player is allowed only six incorrect guesses.

Problem Statement Create a class AlphabetFrame that extends JFrame. A frame belonging to AlphabetFrame is a container that holds 26 buttons labeled with the letters of the alphabet. Such a frame might be used as part of a GUI for a Hangman application.

Include a main(...) method that instantiates AlphabetFrame.

Java Solution

```
import java.awt.*;
import javax.swing.*;

public class AlphabetButtons extends JFrame
{

   public AlphabetButtons(int width, int height)              // height and width of frame
   {
      super("Alphabet Buttons");
      setLayout(new FlowLayout());                           // layout manager
      setBounds(0, 0, width, height);
      for (int i = 0; i < 26; i++)
      {
         Character letter = (char)(i + 'A');
         JButton button = new JButton(letter.toString());   // String parameter
         add(button);
      }
   }

   public static void main(String[] args)
   {
      JFrame frame = new AlphabetButtons(300, 300);
      frame.setVisible(true);
      frame.setDefaultCloseOperation(JFrame.EXIT_ON_CLOSE);
   }
}
```

Output Figure 18.10 shows the frame AlphabetButtons. It's not quite a Hangman game, but it's a beginning.

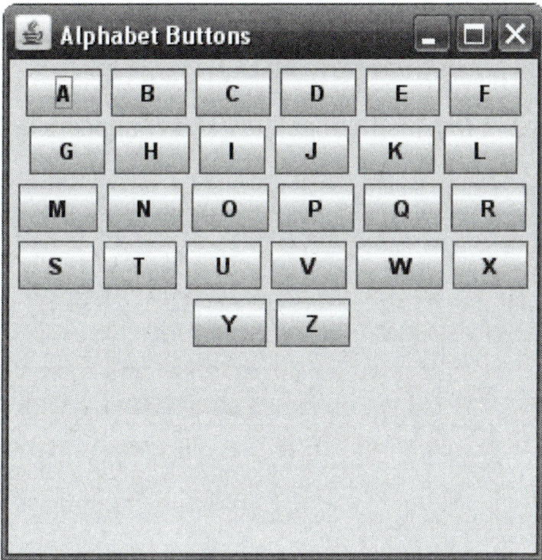

FIGURE 18.10 Twenty-six buttons placed with *FlowLayout*

Discussion In contrast to the buttons placed by BorderLayout, those arranged by FlowLayout are not stretched or resized in any way. These buttons are placed consecutively one after the other. When there is no more room in the first row, the second row begins, and so on. Each row is centered in the frame because the default constructor FlowLayout() uses center alignment.

Line 8: The frame uses FlowLayout for placement of components. The default constructor FlowLayout() is equivalent to FlowLayout(FlowLayout.CENTER). Notice that the buttons are centered in the frame.

Line 12: The expression i + 'A' gives the ASCII value of the ith letter of the alphabet, where A is the 0th letter; (char)(i + 'A') returns an upper case alphabetical character (a primitive). The variable letter is a Character reference. Thus, autoboxing occurs. The next line shows why letter is of type Character and not char.

Line 13: The JButton constructor requires a String reference as a parameter. The method call letter.toString() returns the String equivalent of the Character reference letter. If letter were of type char, the method toString() could not be applied.

Changing line 19 to

```
JFrame frame = new AlphabetButtons(100, 100);
```

produces the frame of Figure 18.11. The buttons are not resized, and there is not enough room to display every button.

FIGURE 18.11 An *AlphabetButtons* frame of size 100 by 100

When the frame is expanded, all buttons are visible in three rows. See Figure 18.12.

FIGURE 18.12 A full width frame that fills the screen

Finally, if line 8 is changed to

```
setLayout(new FlowLayout(FlowLayout.LEFT);
```

the buttons in each row are left justified and the frame appears as in Figure 18.13.

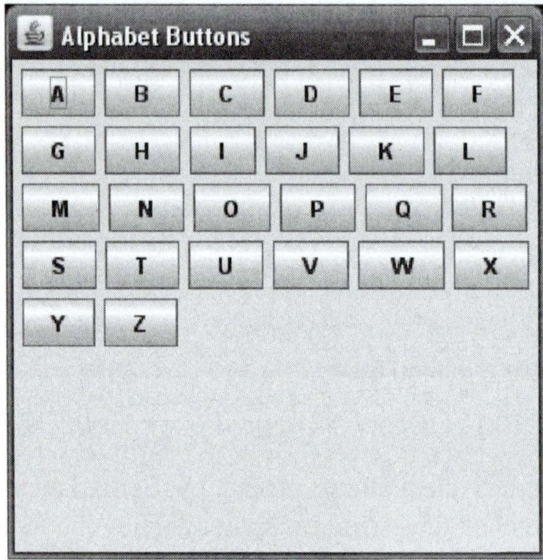

FIGURE 18.13 *FlowLayout* with *LEFT* alignment

18.5.3 *GridLayout*

The GridLayout layout manager arranges the components of a frame in a grid of specified dimensions, left to right, top to bottom, row by row.

The constructors of GridLayout are:

- GridLayout(int rows, int columns)
  where rows and columns specify the number of rows and columns in the grid.
- GridLayout(int rows, int columns, int horizontalSpace, int verticalSpace)
  where rows and columns specify the number of rows and columns in the grid and horizontalSpace and verticalSpace are the horizontal and vertical gaps between components.
- GridLayout()
  creates a grid with a single row and a column for each component.

The following example uses GridLayout rather than FlowLayout to place 26 alphabet buttons in a frame.

EXAMPLE 18.5 **Problem Statement** Place 26 "alphabet buttons" in a frame using GridLayout. The grid should have 6 rows and 5 columns.

Java Solution

```
import java.awt.*;
import javax.swing.*;
```

```
3.  import java.util.*;
4.  public class GridAlphabetButtons extends JFrame
5.  {
6.     public GridAlphabetButtons (int width, int height) // two argument constructor
7.     {                                                  // width and height are frame dimensions
8.        super("Grid Layout Alphabet Buttons");
9.        setLayout(new GridLayout(6, 5));                // 6 rows; 5 columns
10.       setBounds(0, 0, width, height);

11.       for (int i = 0; i < 26; i++)
12.       {
13.          Character alphabet = (char)(i + 'A');
14.          JButton button = new JButton(alphabet.toString());
15.          add(button);
16.       }
17.    }

18.    public static void main(String[] args)
19.    {
20.       JFrame frame = new GridAlphabetButtons (300, 300);
21.       frame.setVisible(true);
22.       frame.setDefaultCloseOperation(JFrame.EXIT_ON_CLOSE);
23.    }
24. }
```

Output Figure 18.14 shows the frame of GridAlphabetButtons.

FIGURE 18.14 A frame of size 300 by 300 created with *GridLayout*

Discussion The only difference between this application and the application of Example 18.4 is line 9:

```
setLayout(new GridLayout(6, 5));
```

Alternatively, line 9 can be written as

```
GridLayout grid = new GridLayout(6, 5);
setLayout(grid);
```

In contrast to the FlowLayout of Example 18.4, a frame of size 100 by 100 resizes and displays all 26 buttons. The letters in the buttons do not resize and are too small to be viewable, but all the buttons do appear. See Figure 18.15.

FIGURE 18.15 *GridLayout* frame of size 100 by 100

18.5.4 Placing Components in a Frame Without a Layout Manager

A layout manager is a convenience but not a necessity. You don't *need* a designer to arrange your furniture! You can place components in a frame without a layout manager.

> By default, a frame uses the BorderLayout layout manager. To disable the default layout manager and place components in a frame without any assistance, set the layout manager of the frame to null, using setLayout(null).

The application of the Example 18.6 places three buttons in a frame without the help of a layout manager.

EXAMPLE 18.6

Problem Statement Place three buttons, each of size 50 by 50, in a frame of size 300 by 300 such that:

- the first button is placed at position (30, 30),
- the second button is placed at (220, 30), and
- the third button is placed at (125, 125).

Include a main(...) method that instantiates the frame with three buttons.

Java Solution In the following application, two buttons display text and the third displays a picture.

```
import javax.swing.*;
import java.awt.*;

public class NoLayoutManager extends JFrame
{

    public NoLayoutManager()
    {
        super("No Layout manager");
        setLayout(null);                          // no layout manager
        setBounds(0, 0, 300, 300);                // for the frame
```

```
10.         // create the three buttons
11.         JButton picture = new JButton(new ImageIcon("smiley.jpg"));
12.         JButton smile = new JButton (":-)");
13.         JButton frown = new JButton (":-(");

14.         // set the position and size of each button
15.         picture.setBounds(125, 125, 50, 50);
16.         smile.setBounds(30, 30, 50, 50);
17.         frown.setBounds(220, 30, 50, 50);

18.         // add each button to the frame
19.         add(picture);
20.         add(smile);
21.         add(frown);
22.         setResizable(false);
23.     }

24.     public static void main(String[] args)
25.     {
26.         JFrame frame = new NoLayoutManager();
27.         frame.setVisible(true);
28.         frame.setDefaultCloseOperation(JFrame.EXIT_ON_CLOSE);
29.     }
30. }
```

Output Figure 18.16 shows the frame created by placing buttons without a layout manager.

FIGURE 18.16 A frame created without a layout manager

Discussion

Lines 15–17: Each button is a component and as such has a setBounds(...) method. The first two parameters set the position of the button relative to the container, that is, relative to the frame. These are frame coordinates, not screen coordinates.

Lines 19–21: Once the size and position of each button is established using setBounds(…), the statements on these lines add the buttons to the frame. Without a layout manager, it is imperative that a component invoke setBounds(…) before it is added to the frame. If setBounds(…) is not called, then the component does not display even after a call to add(...).

Line 22: The frame cannot be resized—notice the "grayed out" maximize box. If the frame were, in fact, resizable, that is, setResizable(true), then after expanding the frame, the three buttons would not resize and their positions in the expanded frame would remain the same. Without a layout manager, the buttons do not resize automatically. See Figure 18.17.

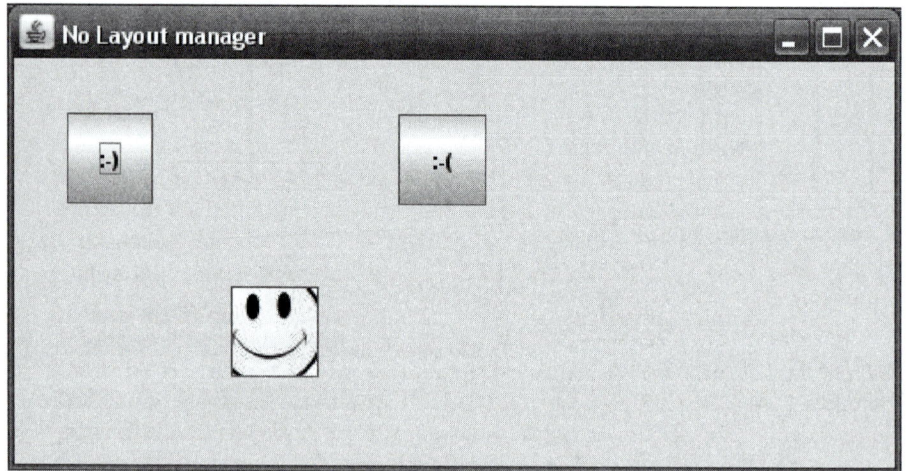

FIGURE 18.17 A resizeable *NoLayoutManager* frame maximized

18.6 PANELS

Most Swing applications do not place components directly in a frame. Instead, components are grouped together and placed in *panels*.

A *panel* is an invisible container used for arranging and organizing components.

A panel can have a layout manager. Components are placed in panels and the panels are subsequently added to a frame. For example, one panel may hold a group of buttons and another a group of checkboxes.

Placing related components in a panel adds flexibility to frame design. For instance, you might place five buttons in one panel using a FlowLayout layout manager, and in a second panel, you might arrange four text boxes using a GridLayout layout manager. Now you can place these two panels or groups of components in a frame using a BorderLayout layout manager.

Swing's JPanel class extends JComponent. See Figure 18.1. Two constructors of JPanel are:

- JPanel()
  instantiates a JPanel object with FlowLayout as the default layout manager.
- JPanel (LayoutManager layoutManager)
  instantiates a JPanel object with the specified layout manager.

FlowLayout is the default layout manager for JPanel. To use other layout managers, the setLayout(...) method is available to JPanel objects.

The application of Example 18.7 arranges 24 buttons and four *labels* in a frame.

A *label* is a component that displays text and/or an image. In contrast to a button, which can be "clicked" and utilized for input, a label is a component that is used primarily to *display* a string or an image.

The Swing class that encapsulates a label is JLabel. One JLabel constructor is

```
JLabel(String text),
```

where text is the string displayed on the label.

EXAMPLE 18.7

The game *How Good Is Your Memory?* (also known as *Concentration* or *Memory*) utilizes a frame with 20 numbered buttons. Each button hides a picture. There are 10 different pairs of identical pictures. For example, there may be a smiley face hidden by buttons 6 and 19 and question marks hidden by buttons 2 and 16. See Figure 18.18.

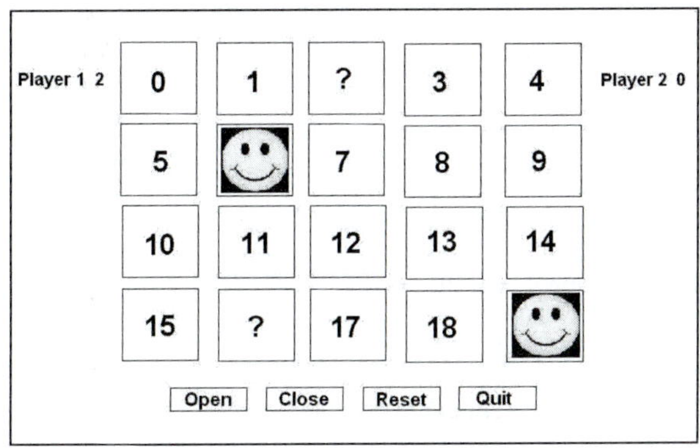

FIGURE 18.18 A Concentration game in progress

The game is played by two people. Players alternately click two buttons, and the buttons' hidden pictures are displayed. If the pictures match, the player gets a point, the pictures remain visible, and that player chooses again. If the pictures do not match, they are hidden again, and the other player chooses. When all matches have been revealed, the player with the greater number of points wins.

The frame also shows each player's score. Currently, Player 1 is leading 2 to 0. See Figure 18.18. On the bottom of the frame are four buttons:

- The Open button displays the pictures behind the last unmatched pair.
- The Close button hides the last two unmatched pictures.
- The Reset button initializes a game.
- The Quit button exits the program.

Of course, none of the actions for these buttons is implemented in this program. Here we are strictly interested in showing how to design and lay out components in a frame. Handling actions comes in Chapter 19.

Problem Statement Create a frame that can be used as an interface for *How Good Is Your Memory*?

Java Solution The program

- creates 20 numbered buttons,
- creates four labeled buttons: Close, Open, Reset, and Quit,
- creates two labels, player1 and score1, one to hold the text "Player 1" and the other to hold 0, the initial score for Player 1,
- creates two labels, player2 and score2, one to hold the text "Player 2" and the other to hold 0, the initial score for Player 2,
- creates a panel and places the numerical buttons in that panel,
- creates a second panel and places the Close, Open, Reset, and Quit buttons in the panel,
- creates a third panel and places the player1 and score1 labels in the panel,
- creates a fourth panel and places the player2 and score2 labels in the panel, and
- places the panels in a frame.

```
import java.awt.*;
import javax.swing.*;

public class HowGoodIsYourMemory extends JFrame
{
   public HowGoodIsYourMemory()
   {
      super("Let's Play How Good Is Your Memory");
      setBounds(0, 0, 600, 400);

        // Create an array of 20 buttons

      JButton[] button = new JButton[20];
      for (int i = 0; i < 20; i++)
         button[i] = new JButton(i + " ");

        // Create the four bottom row buttons

      JButton buttonClose = new JButton("Close");
      JButton buttonReset = new JButton("Reset");
      JButton buttonOpen = new JButton("Open");
      JButton buttonQuit = new JButton("Quit");

        // Labels for Player 1 and Player 1 score

      JLabel player1 = new JLabel(" Player 1");
      JLabel score1 = new JLabel("   0   ");

        // Labels for Player 2 and Player 2 score

      JLabel player2 = new JLabel("Player 2   ");
      JLabel score2 = new JLabel("   0   ");

        // Create a panel for the array of numerical buttons
        // using GridLayout, and
        // place the buttons in the panel

      JPanel numberPanel = new JPanel(new GridLayout(4, 5, 10, 10));
      for (int i = 0; i < 20; i++)
         numberPanel.add(button[i]);
```

```
30.        // Create a panel of bottom buttons
31.        // using FlowLayout, and
32.        // place the buttons in the panel
33.      JPanel bottomPanel = new JPanel(new FlowLayout());
34.      bottomPanel.add(buttonClose);
35.      bottomPanel.add(buttonOpen);
36.      bottomPanel.add(buttonReset);
37.      bottomPanel.add(buttonQuit);
38.        // Create a panel for the Player 1 labels
39.        // using FlowLayout
40.      JPanel player1Panel = new JPanel(new FlowLayout());
41.      player1Panel.add(player1);
42.      player1Panel.add(score1);
43.        // Create a panel for the Player 2 labels
44.        // using FlowLayout
45.      JPanel player2Panel = new JPanel(new FlowLayout());
46.      player2Panel.add(player2);
47.      player2Panel.add(score2);
48.        // Place all panels in the frame using the default BorderLayout layout manager
49.      add(bottomPanel, BorderLayout.SOUTH);
50.      add(numberPanel, BorderLayout.CENTER);
51.      add(player1Panel, BorderLayout.WEST);
52.      add(player2Panel, BorderLayout.EAST);
53.      setResizable(false); // cannot resize the game
54.      setVisible(true);
55.    }
56.    public static void main(String[] args)
57.    {
58.      JFrame game = new HowGoodIsYourMemory();
59.      game.setDefaultCloseOperation(JFrame.EXIT_ON_CLOSE);
60.    }
61. }
```

Output The HowGoodIsYourMemory frame is shown in Figure 18.19.

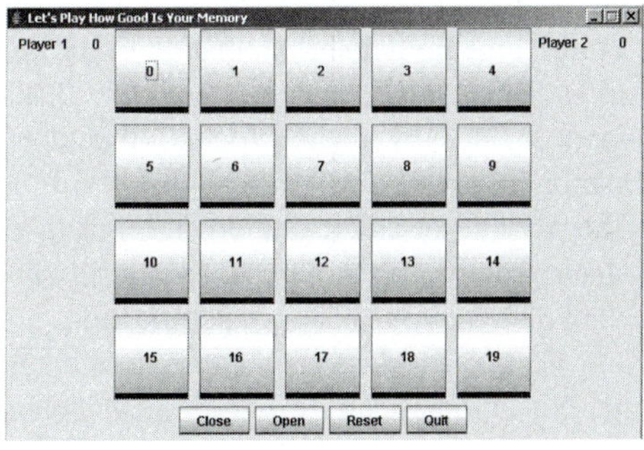

FIGURE 18.19 How Good Is Your Memory?

Discussion

Lines 10–12: The 20 numbered buttons are instantiated as an array of JButton, and each is accessible as button[i], where i is an integer between 0 and 19, inclusive.

Lines 14–17: The four buttons that make up the bottom row are instantiated.

Lines 19–20, 22–23: Two labels are created for each player. One label displays the player, "Player 1" or "Player 2". The second label shows the current score, initially 0 for each player.

Lines 27–29: These statements instantiate a panel for the numerical buttons and use a 4 by 5 GridLayout layout manager to place the buttons in the panel. The horizontal and vertical gaps between buttons are set to 10 pixels.

Lines 33–37: The statement on line 33 instantiates a panel for the Close, Open, Reset, and Quit buttons. The subsequent statements place these buttons in the panel using the FlowLayout layout manager. FlowLayout is the default for a panel, so the instantiation of FlowLayout (line 33) is not strictly necessary.

Lines 40–42, 45–47: The statements on lines 40–42 create a panel for the player1 and score1 labels and place the labels in the panel using FlowLayout. Those on lines 45–47 do the same for the player2 and score2 labels.

Lines 49–52: Here, the application uses the frame's default BorderLayout layout manager to place the four panels in the frame.

18.7 SOME BASIC GRAPHICS

No doubt you have moved a frame, minimized and restored a frame, or resized a frame. Each time that a frame is moved or changed, it must be "repainted" or redrawn on the screen. What may look like a simple task entails quite a bit of work. Fortuitously, Java provides two methods, paint(...) and paintComponent(...), that not only redraw a component that has been moved, resized, or changed but also facilitate painting your own custom, home-grown images directly on a panel or other component. Indeed, paint(...) and paintComponent(...), along with the methods of the Graphics class, provide drawing tools that DaVinci never imagined.

18.7.1 The *paint*() and *paintComponent*() Methods

The Component class defines a method, paint(...), that draws or *renders* a component on the screen. When a frame is first displayed, the system calls paint(...), and paint(...) does the drawing. Likewise, JComponent includes a method, paintComponent(...), which draws Swing components such as JButtons, JLabels, or JPanels. When a user resizes, moves, covers, or uncovers a component, the paint(...) or paintComponent(...) method redraws the component. The method call is automatic, compliments of Java. Technically, for Swing components, the system first calls paint(...), which in turn calls paintComponent(...).

For example, when a chess or checkers application first displays the frame containing the playing board, paint(…) is automatically invoked. If the board contains Swing components such as panels, buttons, and labels, then paint(…) invokes paintComponent(…) for each one of the contained components. If the user minimizes the board, covers it up with another window, or resizes the board, then the process repeats all over again.

The paint(...) and/or paintComponent(....) methods are invoked automatically whenever the system determines that a component should be drawn or redrawn on the screen.

Like the garbage collector, paint(...) and paintComponent(...) work behind the scenes. An application does not explicitly invoke paint(...) or paintComponent(...). That's done by the system.

More formally, these two methods are declared as:

```
void paint(Graphics g);
void paintComponent(Graphics g);
```

Notice that each method accepts a single parameter g, a reference to a Graphics object. The Graphics object encapsulates information about a component and includes methods that facilitate drawing on a component. Graphics is an abstract class in java.awt.

18.7.2 The *Graphics* Context

The Graphics parameter, g, supplies paint(...) and paintComponent(...) with information about how to draw a particular component. For example, certain information about the font, drawing color, and location are encapsulated in g.

> Every component that can be drawn on the screen has an associated Graphics object that encapsulates information about the component such as color and font. When a component is drawn, the JVM automatically retrieves and passes the component's Graphic object, g, to paint(...) and paintComponent(...). The Graphics object g is not explicitly instantiated using a constructor.

A component's Graphics object is also called the component's *graphics context.*

The paint(...) and paintComponent(...) methods use the information encapsulated in the Graphics parameter g to render a component. So, when the system calls paint(...) or paintComponent(...), it also sends along the graphics context of the particular component via the parameter g.

For example, if a JFrame object, myFrame, is resized then myFrame must be repainted. Consequently, the system automatically invokes myFrame.paint(g), where g is the graphics context associated with myFrame. This parameter g supplies information to paint(...) so that paint(...) knows how to draw myFrame. Indeed, without the graphics context g, paint(...) cannot do its job; paint(...) needs information. It's all done rather covertly, behind the scenes.

The paint(...) and paintComponent(...) methods are called by the system; they work in the background, and that's that. But if these methods are always invisible to the programmer, we would have little reason to discuss them here. In fact, the programmer can override these methods to display custom, homemade images. If an application must draw an image on a panel, be it a complex 3-dimensional surface, colorful text, or a simple stick figure, an understanding of these methods, in conjunction with methods of Graphics, is indispensable. You will soon see how a programmer overrides paint(…) and paintComponent(…) to create custom images, pictures, and stylized text.

The following methods of Graphics are among the most useful of more than three dozen methods that can be invoked by the Graphics object of a component.

- void drawString(String message, int x, int y)
  draws message on the component, starting at position (x, y).
- void setColor(Color c)
  sets the color of a component. Color is a class in java.awt.
- void setFont(Font f)
  sets the font to be used when drawing characters on a component. Font belongs to java.awt.

- void drawImage(Image img, int x, int y, ImageObserver observer)
  draws an image on the component such that img is an image file (e.g., .jpg or .gif), x and y designate the position of the image, and observer is the object on which the image is drawn—usually this.

Because these methods use the Color class and Font class, some explanation is in order.

18.7.3 The *Color* Class

As its name suggests, the Color class is used to encapsulate a color. One constructor for the class is

```
Color(int red, int green, int blue)
```

where parameters red, green, and blue range from 0 to 255 inclusive.

The colors red, green, and blue form the basis for every possible color. The parameters indicate how much of each color goes into the mix. The higher the parameter value, the greater the amount of the corresponding color in the red-green-blue mix. For example,

```
Color color = new Color(255, 0, 0)      // full red, no green, no blue.
Color color = new Color(0, 0, 0)        // no red, no green, no blue; that's white.
Color color = new Color(150, 0, 150)    // an equal mix of red and blue; that's purple.
Color color = new Color(255, 255, 255)  // this is black.
```

The Color class also defines a number of class constants:

RED, WHITE, BLUE, GREEN, YELLOW, BLACK, CYAN, MAGENTA, PINK, ORANGE, GRAY, LIGHTGRAY, and DARKGRAY.

These colors are accessed with the class name, e.g., Color.RED.

Every component implements two methods:

- setBackground(Color c)
  sets the background color of a component. The parameter can be null, in which case the background color is the background color of the parent.
- setForeground(Color c)
  sets the foreground color of a component. The foreground color is the color used for drawing and displaying text.

18.7.4 The *Font* Class

An object belonging to Font encapsulates the properties of the font used to display text. The class constructor is

```
Font(String name, int style, int size)
```

where name is the name of a standard font such as Courier or Arial, style is a combination of Font class constants:

Font.PLAIN, Font.BOLD, Font.ITALIC, or Font.BOLD + Font.ITALIC,

with values 0, 1, 2, and 3, respectively, and size is the point size of a character.

For example, to create a 12 point Courier font that is both bold and italic, use

```
Font font = new Font("Courier", Font.BOLD + Font.ITALIC, 12);
```

Since Font.BOLD + Font.ITALIC = 1 + 2 = 3, the same Font object can be also instantiated as

```
Font font = new Font("Courier", 3, 12);
```

The methods of Font are:

- public String getName()
  returns the name of the font.
- public boolean isPlain()
  returns true if the style is Font.PLAIN.
- public boolean isItalic()
  returns true if the style is Font.ITALIC.
- public boolean isBold()
  returns true if the style is Font.BOLD.
- public int getStyle()
  returns 0 if the style is PLAIN.
  returns 1 if the style is BOLD.
  returns 2 if the style is ITALIC.
  returns 3 if the style is BOLD + ITALIC.
- public int getSize()
  returns the font size.

18.7.5 "Painting" on Panels

Custom "painting" is usually done on a panel. To paint or draw on a panel,

- extend the JPanel class, and
- override the paintComponent(Graphics g) method so that the redefined paintComponent(...) renders the panel with some customized image or text.

Images and text are drawn by invoking methods of the Graphics object g, which is passed to paintComponent(...), as illustrated in Example 18.8.

EXAMPLE 18.8

Problem Statement Create a panel with a gray background that displays the familiar Star Wars quotation, "May the Force be with you." The quote should be drawn in black on a gray background, with point size 24, using the exotic Flat Brush font. Position the quote at (50, 50). Include a main(...) method that places the panel in frame. See Figure 18.20.

Java Solution The following application

- defines the class StarPanel, which extends JPanel,
- overrides JPanel's paintComponent(...) method so that paintComponent(...) paints the message "May the Force be with you" on a StarPanel object.

Notice that the Graphics object g, which is passed to paintComponent(...), invokes the setColor(...) and setFont(...) methods. As you know, the parameter g is provided automatically, courtesy of Java.

```
import javax.swing.*;
import java.awt.*;

public class StarPanel extends JPanel
{
   public void paintComponent(Graphics g)
   {
      super.paintComponent(g);       // Call the paintComponent method of the parent
      g.setColor(Color.BLACK);       // Use black for drawing in the panel
      Font font = new Font("Flat Brush", Font.BOLD, 24);
      g.setFont(font);               // Uses the Flat Brush font when drawing a String
```

```
11.         setBackground(Color.GRAY);
12.         g.drawString("May the Force be with you", 50, 50);
13.     }
14.     public static void main(String [] args)
15.     {
16.         JFrame frame = new JFrame("Star Wars Quotation");
17.         frame.setBounds(0, 0, 400, 200);
18.         StarPanel panel = new StarPanel();
19.         frame.add(panel);
20.         frame.setVisible(true);
21.         frame.setDefaultCloseOperation(JFrame.EXIT_ON_CLOSE);
22.     }
23. }
```

Output The frame is displayed in Figure 18.20.

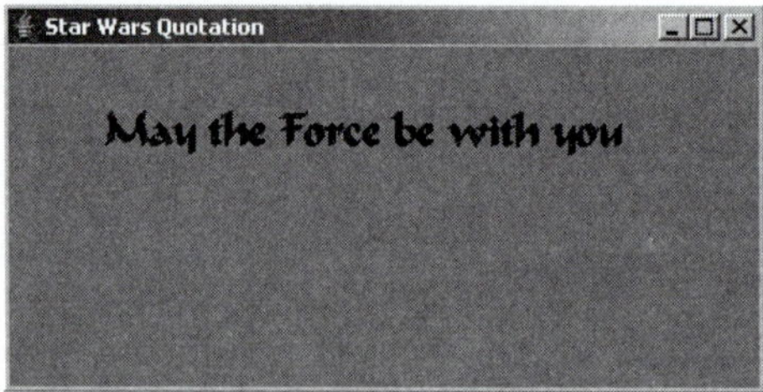

FIGURE 18.20 Painting a *String* on a panel

Discussion

Line 3: StarPanel extends JPanel. Thus StarPanel *is-a* JPanel . . . and more.

Line 5: Override the paintComponent(Graphics g) method of JPanel. The overridden version of paintComponent(...) is invoked each time that a StarPanel panel must be (re)painted.

Line 7: This statement is a call to the paintComponent(...) method of JPanel, the parent class. Such a call paints a generic panel with no frills. When you override paintComponent(...), you should include this statement.

Line 8: Invokes the Graphics method that sets the color of the graphics context to black so that all Graphics actions are done using black.

Line 9: Instantiates a Font object font using type Flat Brush, style Bold, and point size 24. (Note: the type Flat Brush may not be available on all systems.)

Line 10: Invokes the Graphics method that sets the font of the graphics context to font (from line 9), so that all Strings are painted using font.

Line 11: The background color of a StarPanel object is gray. Notice that setBackground(...) is *not* a Graphics method; it is a JPanel method inherited from JComponent.

Line 12: Paints the string on the panel using the color and font encapsulated by the graphics context.

The main(...) method creates a frame, adds the StarPanel object panel to it, and displays the frame.

The paint(...) method of JFrame and the (overridden) paintComponent(...) method of StarPanel are automatically invoked when the frame is first displayed or when it needs to be repainted. The parameter g is never explicitly instantiated. The graphics context of each frame and panel is automatically passed to paint(...) and paintComponent(...), respectively. The overridden version of paintComponent(...) invokes three methods of g (lines 8, 10, and 12).

18.7.6 Drawing Shapes

The Graphics class also defines a number of methods that facilitate drawing various shapes on a panel. Among the most commonly used methods are:

- void drawLine(int startx, int starty, int endx, int endy)
  draws a line segment from point (startx, starty) to point (endx, endy).
- void drawRect(int x, int y, int width, int height)
  draws a rectangle with upper left-hand corner positioned at (x, y). The width and height of the rectangle are width and height, respectively.
- void fillRect(int x, int y, int width, int height)
  draws and fills the specified rectangle.
- void drawOval(int x, int y, int width, int height)
  draws an ellipse that fits within the boundary of the rectangle specified by the parameters x, y, width, and height. See Figure 18.21. If width and height are equal, the figure is a circle.

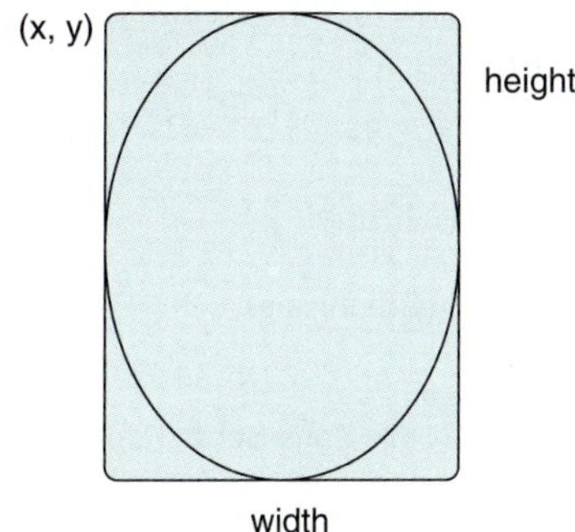

FIGURE 18.21 An oval with bounding rectangle

- void fillOval(int x, int y, int width, int height)
  draws and fills the specified oval.
- void drawArc(int x, int y, int width, int height, int startAngle, int arcAngle)
  draws an arc using the oval inscribed in the rectangle specified by parameters x, y, width, and height. The arc begins at startAngle and spans arcAngle. Angles are given in degrees. See Figure 18.22.

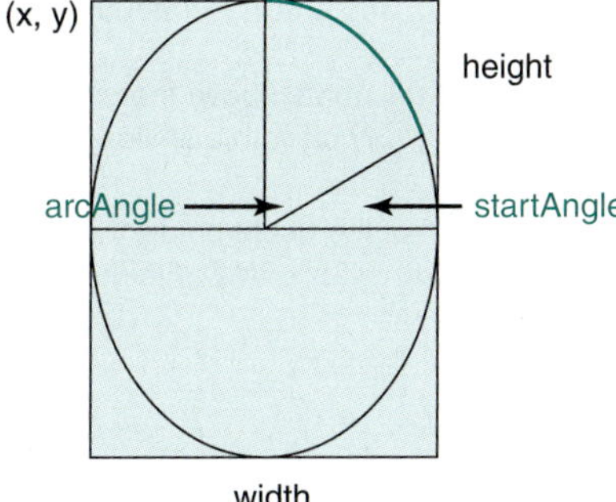

FIGURE 18.22 The arc drawn by the *drawArc*() method

Example 18.9 uses the methods of Graphics to draw a *not-so-smiley* face.

EXAMPLE 18.9 **Problem Statement** W. C. Fields is reputed to have said, "Start every day off with a smile—and get it over with." Create a frame that displays not a smiley face but the rather glum face of Figure 18.23. Include Fields' quotation.

FIGURE 18.23 A not-so-smiley face

Java Solution The FacePanel class extends JPanel and draws the face and quotation on the panel. This is done by overriding the paintComponent(Graphics g) method of JPanel. The second class, FaceFrame, creates a FacePanel object panel and adds it to a frame. The FaceFrame class includes a main(...) method.

```
import java.awt.*;
import javax.swing.*;

public class FacePanel extends JPanel
{
    public void paintComponent(Graphics g)
    {
        super.paintComponent(g);
        Font font = new Font("Comic Sans Serif", Font.BOLD, 16); // set the font
        g.setFont(font);
        setBackground(Color.white);         // a method of Component
        g.setColor(Color.YELLOW);           // color for the face, the traditional color
        g.fillOval(50, 50, 200, 200);       // face position (50, 50), a circle of radius 200
        g.setColor(Color.black);            // color for eyes, nose, and mouth
        g.fillOval(100, 100, 25, 25);       // left eye, position (100, 100), circle of radius 25
        g.fillOval(150, 100, 25, 25);       // right eye, position(150, 100), circle of radius 25
        g.drawLine(125, 135, 100, 160);     // upper nose, line from (125, 135) to (120, 160)
        g.drawLine(100, 160, 120, 160);     // lower nose, line from (120, 160) to (100, 160)

            // mouth–the bounding rectangle is positioned at (75, 175) with width 100 and
            // height 40. The start angle is 350 degrees and the span is 200 degrees
        g.drawArc(75, 175, 100, 40, 350, 200);   // mouth

            // Draw the first part of the quote above the picture
        g.drawString("\"Start every day off with a smile--", 20, 20);

            // Draw the second part of the quote below the picture
        g.drawString("and get it over with\"-- W.C. Fields", 20, 300);
    }
}
```

The FaceFrame class uses FacePanel.

```
public class FaceFrame extends JFrame
{
    public FaceFrame(String title)
```

```
    {
        super(title);
        setBounds(0, 0, 400, 400);
        FacePanel panel = new FacePanel();
        add(panel); // uses the default BorderLayout; places at center
        setResizable(false);
        setVisible(true);
        setDefaultCloseOperation(JFrame.EXIT_ON_CLOSE);
    }

    public static void main(String[] args)
    {
        JFrame frown = new FaceFrame("Unhappy Face");
    }
}
```

Output Figure 18.24 shows the rather unhappy fellow.

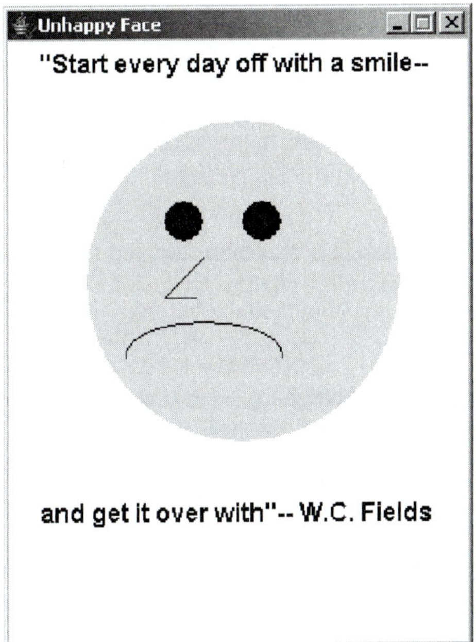

FIGURE 18.24 An unsmiley face

Discussion The FacePanel class extends JPanel and overrides the paintComponent (Graphics g) method of JPanel. The class uses the Graphics methods to draw the face as well as the string. Each circle that makes up the face is placed in the frame by specifying the location of the upper left-hand corner of a bounding rectangle. Figure 18.25 lays out the frame with the bounding rectangles and the points where each part of the face is positioned.

The second class, FaceFrame, extends JFrame. The class instantiates a FacePanel and adds that panel to the frame using the default BorderLayout layout manager. This places the panel in the center of the frame and fills the whole frame.

When the frame is first painted or repainted, the paintComponent(...) method of FacePanel is invoked by the system, not by the application.

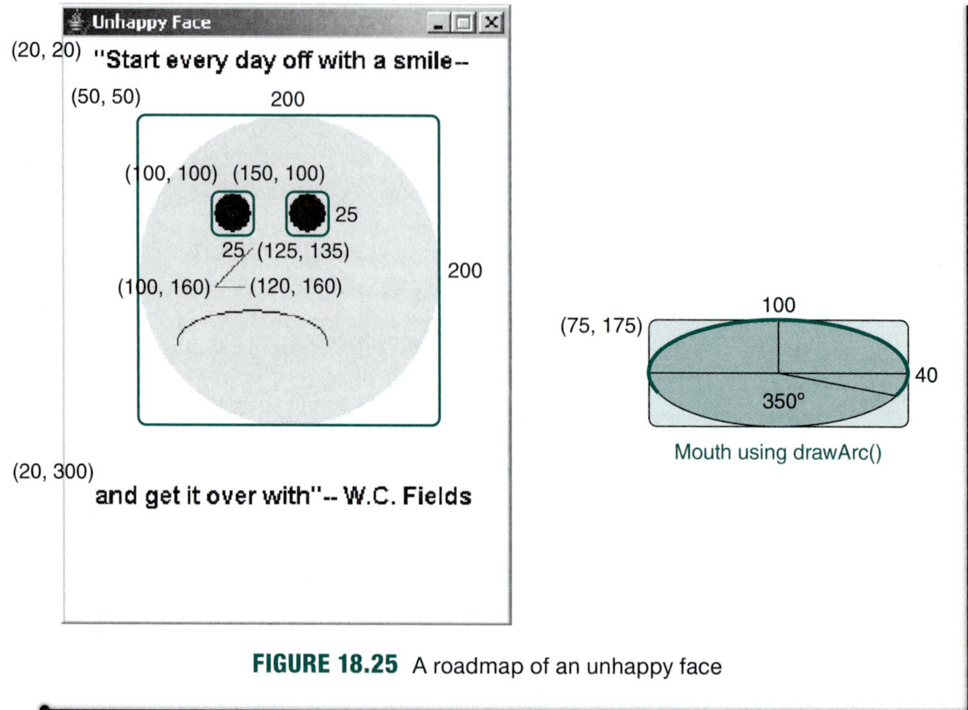

FIGURE 18.25 A roadmap of an unhappy face

EXAMPLE 18.10 **Problem Statement** Design an application that draws the "megaphone of circles" in a frame. See Figure 18.26.

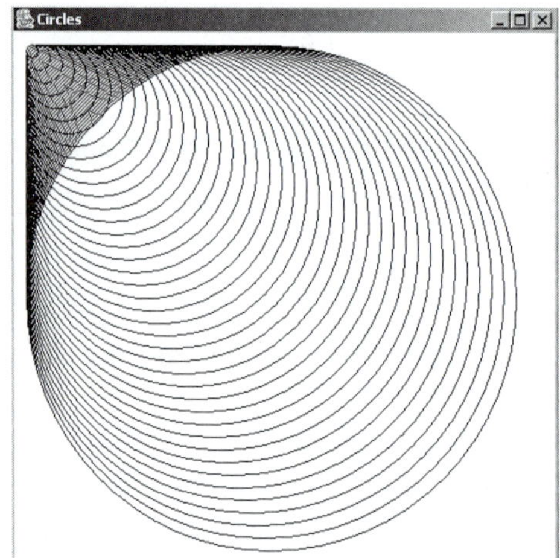

FIGURE 18.26 A megaphone of sorts

Java Solution The following application uses two classes:

- CirclesPanel extends JPanel and overrides paintComponent(Graphics g), and
- CircleFrame extends JFrame, instantiates CirclePanel, and adds a CirclesPanel object to the frame. The CircleFrame class includes a main(...) method.

```
1.  import javax.swing.*;
2.  import java.awt.*;
3.  public class CirclePanel extends JPanel
4.         // Displays 39 circles. The bounding rectangle for each circle is positioned at (10, 10).
5.         // The circles range in radius 10 to 400 pixels.
6.         // A frame size of at least 440 by 440 is recommended.
7.  {
8.     public void paintComponent(Graphics g)
9.     {
10.        super.paintComponent(g);
11.        g.setColor(Color.black);
12.        setBackground(Color.white);
13.        for (int radius = 400; radius > 0; radius -= 10) // draw 39 circles of decreasing radius
14.           g.drawOval(10, 10, radius, radius);
15.    }
16. }
17.    import javax.swing.*;
18. public class CircleFrame extends JFrame
19. {
20.    public CircleFrame(String title)
21.    {
22.        super(title);
23.        setBounds(0, 0, 450, 450);
24.        JPanel circles = new CirclePanel();
25.        add(circles);
26.        setVisible(true);
27.        setDefaultCloseOperation(JFrame.EXIT_ON_CLOSE);
28.    }
29.    public static void main(String[] args)
30.    {
31.        JFrame frame = new CircleFrame("Circles");
32.    }
33. }
```

Output See Figure 18.26.

Discussion The CirclePanel class extends JPanel and overrides paintComponent (Graphics g). By invoking drawOval() 39 times, the for-loop of lines 13 and 14 draws 39 circles. The bounding rectangle for each circle is positioned at (10, 10). The radii of the circles range from 400 to 10 pixels.

The constructor of CircleFrame, which extends JFrame,

- creates a frame of size 450 by 450 pixels,
- instantiates a CirclePanel object circles, and
- adds circles to the frame using the default BorderLayout layout manager.

Thus, the panel is placed in the center of the frame.

The main(...) method of the CircleFrame method instantiates the frame.

18.7.7 Recursive Drawing

The next example uses recursion to draw a famous fractal. Figure 18.27 is a picture of *Sierpinski's Triangle*.

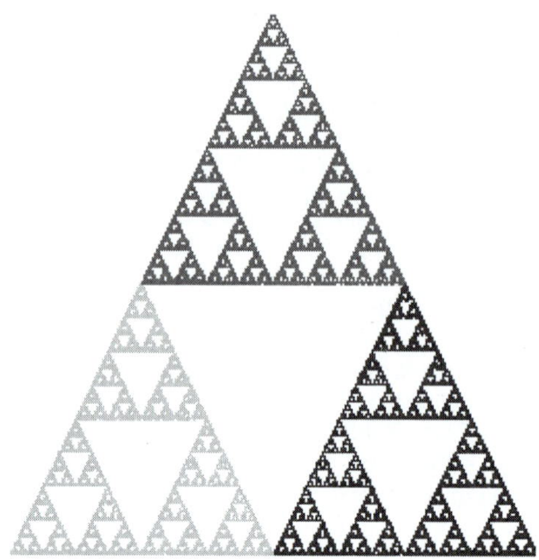

FIGURE 18.27 Sierpinski's Triangle

Sierpinski's Triangle is a *fractal*. A fractal is a geometrical figure that is *self-similar*. That is, if you magnify any small piece of the figure, the magnified image looks like the whole figure. Take a closer look at Figure 18.27. There are Sierpinski Triangles inside Sierpinski Triangles inside Sierpinski Triangles. Each little piece of Sierpinski's Triangle looks just like the whole triangle. This self-similarity is what makes recursion a natural choice for drawing the triangle. An iterative version is more complicated. See Programming Exercises 12 and 13 for examples of iterated fractals.

To generate Sierpinski's Triangle, begin with an equilateral triangle such as the triangle of Figure 18.28.

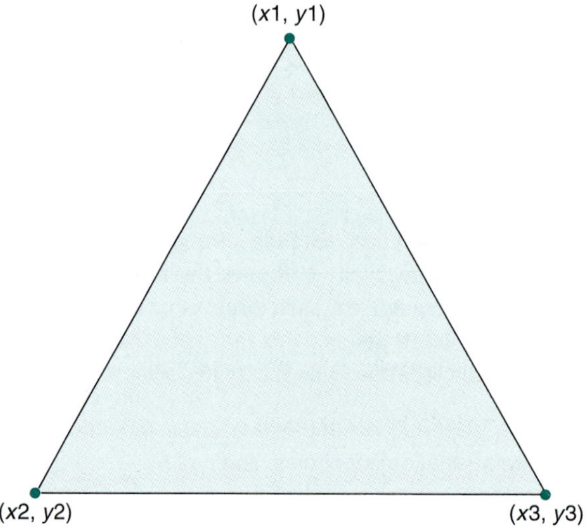

FIGURE 18.28 The beginning of a Sierpinski Triangle: an equilateral triangle

Next, find the midpoint of each side and form three more triangles, as shown numbered in Figure 18.29. Disregard the triangle in the center.

The midpoint of the side joining ($x1$, $y1$) and ($x2$, $y2$) is the point:

$$([x1 + x2]/2, [y1 + y2]/2).$$

For example, the midpoint of the line segment joining (10, 20) and (100, 200) is

$$([10 + 100]/2, [20 + 200]/2) = (110/2, 220/2) = (55, 110).$$

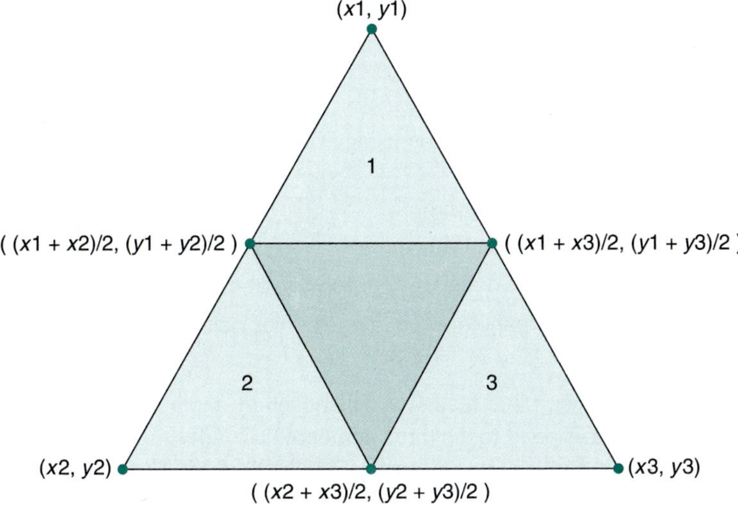

FIGURE 18.29 Form three triangles from the midpoints of the three sides

Repeat the process, giving nine numbered triangles. See Figure 18.30.

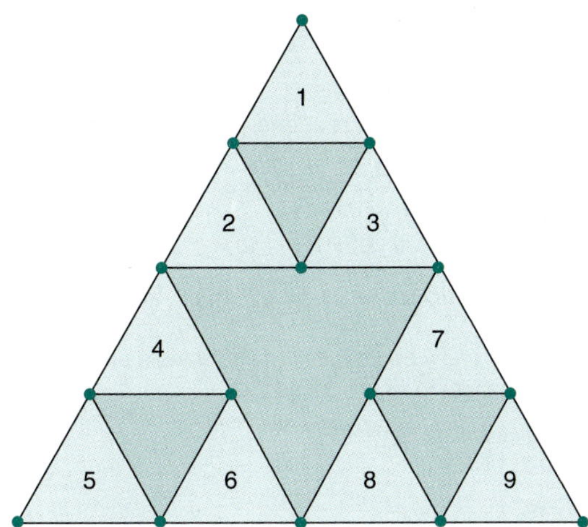

FIGURE 18.30 Continuing the process

Continue the process forever, producing 1, 3, 9, 27, 81, 243, 729, . . . triangles. Sierpinski's Triangle is the set of points that result if the process is carried out indefinitely. If the process is carried out for *n* iterations, the figure is called a Sierpinski Triangle of depth *n*.

The program of Example 18.11 draws a Sierpinski Triangle of specific depth on a panel.

EXAMPLE 18.11

Problem Statement Draw a Sierpinski Triangle of depth 10 on a JPanel. Include a main(...) method that places the panel in a frame.

Java Solution To draw a Sierpinski Triangle of depth *n*, it is necessary to first draw a triangle. We can certainly do this using the drawLine() method of Graphics. However, Java provides a Polygon class that makes drawing a triangle, a rectangle, a pentagon, or any polygon a snap.

To draw a triangle:

- instantiate an "empty" polygon:

```
Polygon triangle = new Polygon();
```

- add three points (x, y) to the polygon using Polygon's addPoint(int x, int y) method:

```
triangle.addPoint(0,0);
triangle.addPoint(100,100);
triangle.addPoint(50, 150);
```

- draw the polygon using the drawPolygon(Polygon p) method of Graphics:

```
g.drawPolygon(triangle)   // g is a Graphics object
```

That's all there is to it.

After the triangle is drawn, three recursive calls, each of depth $n - 1$, are made. The three recursive calls correspond to the three numbered triangles in Figure 18.29.

In the following application, SierpinskiPanel extends JPanel and overwrites paintComponent(...). The paintComponent(...) method invokes sierpinski(...), which draws the figure recursively. The recursive method includes a parameter depth that is used to stop the recursion. Each time a recursive call is made, depth is decremented, and the recursion stops when depth equals 0. The initial value of depth is 10.

A main(...) method instantiates a frame and adds a SierpinskiPanel object to the frame.

```
import javax.swing.*;
import java.awt.*;

public class SierpinskiPanel extends JPanel
{
   // (x1, y1), (x2, y2), and (x3, y3) determine a triangle
   private int x1, y1, x2, y2, x3, y3;
   private final int RECURSIVE_DEPTH = 10;

   public SierpinskiPanel(int a1, int b1, int a2, int b2, int a3, int b3)
   {
      // accepts the x and y coordinates of the triangle points
      // and assigns them to x1, y1, x2, y2, x3, y3
      x1 = a1;
      y1 = b1;

      x2 = a2;
      y2 = b2;

      x3 = a3;
      y3 = b3;
   }

   public void paintComponent(Graphics g)
   {
      super.paintComponent(g);
      g.setColor(Color.black);
      setBackground(Color.white);
      // pass the coordinates of the initial triangle, along with g
      sierpinski(x1, y1, x2, y2, x3, y3, RECURSIVE_DEPTH, g);
   }

   public void sierpinski(int x1, int y1, int x2, int y2, int x3, int y3, int depth, Graphics g)
   {
      // draw the triangle specified by (x1, y1), (x2, y2), and (x3, y3)

      if (depth > 0)      // stops recursion
      {
```

```
            depth--;
            Polygon triangle = new Polygon();      // make a triangle
            triangle.addPoint(x1, y1);
            triangle.addPoint(x2, y2);
            triangle.addPoint(x3, y3);
            g.drawPolygon(triangle);

            // recursively draw three triangles using one "original" point and two midpoints

            // Initially, Triangle 1 of Figure 18.29 – the triangle formed by (x1, y1)
            // and midpoints of sides joining (x1, y1) & (x2, y2) and (x1, y1) & (x3, y3)

            sierpinski(x1, y1, (x1 + x2) / 2, (y1 + y2) / 2, (x1 + x3) / 2, (y1 + y3) / 2, depth, g);

            // Initially, Triangle 2 of Figure 18.29 – the triangle formed by (x2, y2)
            // and midpoints of sides joining (x2, y2) & (x1, y1) and (x2, y2) & (x3, y3)
            sierpinski((x1 + x2) / 2, (y1 + y2) / 2, x2, y2, (x3 + x2) / 2, (y3 + y2) / 2, depth, g);

            // Initially, Triangle 3 of Figure 18.29 – the triangle formed by (x3, y3)
            // and midpoints of sides joining (x3, y3) & (x1, y1) and (x3, y3) & (x2, y2)

            sierpinski((x1 + x3) / 2, (y1 + y3) / 2, (x3 + x2) / 2, (y3 + y2) / 2, x3, y3,depth, g);
        }
    }

    public static void main(String[] args)
    {
        JFrame frame = new JFrame("Sierpinski's Triangle");
        // instantiate a panel with the Sierpinski Triangle

        // instantiate panel with triangle points (x1, y1), (x2, y2) & (x3, y3)
        // and a maximum depth: points:(210,10), (10, 410), (410, 410);

        SierpinskiPanel sp = new SierpinskiPanel(210, 10, 10, 410,  410, 410);

        // add the panel to the frame
        frame.add(sp);
        frame.setBounds(0, 0, 450, 450);
        frame.setVisible(true);
        frame.setDefaultCloseOperation(JFrame.EXIT_ON_CLOSE);
    }
}
```

Output The frame with the depth 10 Sierpinski Triangle is shown in Figure 18.31.

FIGURE 18.31 Sierpinski's Triangle in a *JFrame*

Discussion

Line 6: The points (x1, y1), (x2, y2), (x3, y3) specify a triangle.

Lines 8–18: The constructor assigns values to the coordinates x1, y1, x2, y2, x3, and y3.

Lines 19–26: Override the paintComponent(Graphics g) method. After setting the colors for the drawing, this method passes the triangle points and graphic context to the recursive method sierpinski(...), which draws Sierpinski's Triangle.

Lines 27–49: sierpinski(...)

Line 30: Technically, drawing Sierpinski's Triangle is an infinite process; like the Energizer bunny, it goes on forever. However, programs must stop, so we draw a Sierpinski Triangle of depth 10. According to the condition on line 30, when the recursive depth reaches 0, the recursion stops. On each invocation of sierpinski(...) the depth is reduced by 1 (line 32).

Lines 33–37: Construct a triangle using the Polygon class, and draw the triangle.

Lines 41, 44, and 47: These lines exhibit three recursive calls. The parameters of each call are the coordinates of one of the three triangles carved out of the larger triangle. Each of these calls again draws the appropriate triangle and then makes three more recursive calls with three smaller triangles. This continues until the triangles are very small. The condition on line 30 prevents infinite recursion.

The recursive sierpinski(...) method invokes itself many times. Initially, with depth set to 10 (line 7), sierpinski(...) draws a single triangle (see Figure 18.28) and makes three recursive calls with depth 9. Eventually, *each* of these three calls draws a triangle (see Figure 18.29) and *each* makes three additional recursive calls with depth 8. That's nine calls to sierpinski(...). Similarly, *each* of these nine calls draws a triangle (see Figure 18.30) and each makes three additional recursive calls (that's 27), and so on. This continues until 3^{10} recursive calls are eventually made with depth 0. In all, the number of triangles drawn is $3^0 + 3^1 + 3^2 + 3^3 + ... + 3^9 = 29{,}524$, and the number of recursive calls is $3^0 + 3^1 + 3^2 + 3^3 + ... + 3^9 + 3^{10} = 88{,}573$.

As an experiment, run the program first with the recursive depth set to 1, then to 2, then to 3, and so on. The corresponding pictures show how the fractal takes shape. Could we get a reasonable picture with the depth set less than 10? At what depth can you no longer distinguish any new triangles?

Even when you can no longer distinguish new triangles with the naked eye, you could magnify the picture to see the extra detail provided by higher depths. Of course, there is a practical limit to the depth that has nothing to do with the picture's resolution. Higher depths mean more computing time. What is the practical limit on the depth before the program takes too much time? See Short Exercise 10.

18.7.8 The *getGraphics*() Method

Each displayable component has an associated Graphics context. This object is automatically created and passed to paint(Graphics g) or paintComponent(Graphics g). However, the Graphics context of a component can also be accessed, not by a constructor, but via the method

```
Graphics getGraphics().
```

This method, declared in Component and inherited by concrete Component classes such as JButton and JFrame, returns a component's Graphics context if the component is displayable, or null if the component is not displayable. The following small class uses the getGraphics() method to obtain the Graphics context of a JFrame and set the drawing color to red.

```
1.  import javax.swing.*;
2.  import java.awt.*;

3.  public class GetGraphicsDemo extends JFrame
4.  {
5.     public static void main(String[] args)
6.     {
7.        GetGraphicsDemo frame = new GetGraphicsDemo();
8.        Graphics g;

9.        g = frame.getGraphics();
10.       System.out.println(g);

11.       frame.setVisible(true);
12.       g = frame.getGraphics();
13.       g.setColor(Color.RED);
14.       System.out.println(g.getColor());
15.    }
16. }
```

The output of this small program is

```
null
java.awt.Color[r=255,g=0,b=0]
```

Before the frame is made visible, the call

```
frame.getGraphics() (line 9)
```

returns null. When the frame is made visible (line 11), the method returns the Graphics object associated with the displayable frame. On line 13, the Graphics color is set to red, and the statement on line 14 prints the RGB version of red (i.e., r = 255, g = 0, b = 0).

Because the JVM automatically passes the requisite Graphics object to paint(...) or paintComponent(...) we have no need to invoke getGraphics() in the programs of the previous examples. However, in Chapter 19, the method does come in handy.

18.8 DISPLAYING AN IMAGE

An *icon* is a small picture that can be displayed on a component. You can place an icon on a frame or panel directly. You can even display an icon on a button or label. Java's Icon interface declares the following methods for working with icons:

- int getIconHeight(),
- int getIconWidth(), and
- void paintIcon(Component c, Graphics g, int x, int y), where (x, y) denotes a position in component c.

The ImageIcon class, found in Swing, implements the Icon interface. The constructor

ImageIcon(String filename)

creates an icon from the specified image file.

The following example displays a vintage US Army photo of two women manually programming the ENIAC, one of the world's first computers. Needless to say, they did not use Java. The image is stored in the file eniac.gif.

EXAMPLE 18.12 **Problem Statement** Display the image stored in eniac.gif in a frame.

Java Solution We design two classes. The first class, PicturePanel, extends JPanel. The constructor accepts the name of an image file. PicturePanel overrides paintComponent(...) so that paintComponent(...)

- instantiates ImageIcon, and
- paints the image on the panel.

The second class, ShowPicture, instantiates a JFrame and a PicturePanel. The panel is added to the frame.

```
import java.awt.*;
import javax.swing.*;

public class PicturePanel extends JPanel
{
   private String image;                         // a filename
   public PicturePanel(String filename)
   {
      image = filename;
   }
   public void paintComponent(Graphics g)
   {
      super.paintComponent(g);
      ImageIcon picture = new ImageIcon(image);
      picture.paintIcon(this, g, 0, 0);          // this means "this panel"
   }
}

import javax.swing.*;
public class ShowPicture extends JFrame
{
   public ShowPicture()
   {
      super("Two women programming the Eniac ");
      setBounds(0, 0, 650, 450);
      PicturePanel picPanel = new PicturePanel("eniac.gif");
      add(picPanel);
      setVisible(true);
      setDefaultCloseOperation(JFrame.EXIT_ON_CLOSE);
   }

   public static void main(String[] args)
   {
```

```
31.                 JFrame frame = new ShowPicture();
32.         }
33.  }
```

Output Figure 18.32 shows the frame created by ShowPicture.

FIGURE 18.32 Programming, B.J., that is, before Java
Source: U.S. Army Photo

Discussion

Line 13: With the name of an image file as a parameter, the constructor instantiates an ImageIcon object. If the file is not found, no picture is displayed, but the program does not crash.

Line 14: The parameter this indicates that the image is painted on "this panel" and not another component.

Line 23: The frame size (width 650, height 450) accommodates the entire image. The image eniac.gif has height 417 pixels and width 640 pixels. You can determine the height and width of an image file in pixels using:

```
ImageIcon image = new ImageIcon("eniac.gif");
System.out.println(image.getIconHeight() + " " + image.getIconWidth());
```

18.9 THE *repaint*() METHOD

In each of the previous examples, calls to paint(...) and paintComponent(...) have been system generated. When a component or its container is first displayed or subsequently resized, the system automatically paints/repaints the component. No work is required from the programmer. On the other hand, the JVM does not *always* know when a component needs to be redrawn. If component A is painted using components B and C, and B or C is changed, the system has no way to know exactly when to repaint A. In general, the system will *not* automatically repaint A at all. The programmer, in these cases, must take control and explicitly direct the application to repaint the component.

Surprisingly, your program does not invoke paint(...) or paintComponent(...) to redisplay a component, but another method of the Component class:

```
void repaint().
```

The repaint() method, in turn, calls paint(...). The following example uses repaint() to change a message displayed on a panel.

EXAMPLE 18.13 **Problem Statement** Devise an application that paints a message on a panel, prompts for a new message, and repaints the panel showing the new message.

Java Solution The following Message class extends JPanel and overrides paintComponent(...) so that a new version of paintComponent(…) paints a String on the panel.

The FrameWithAMessage class, which demonstrates Message,

- interactively prompts a user for a message (a string),
- interactively reads the message using the Scanner method next(),
- instantiates a frame and a Message panel,
- adds the panel to the frame,
- paints the user's message on the panel,
- prompts for a second message, and
- repaints the panel so that the new message is displayed.

```
import javax.swing.*;
import java.awt.*;

public class Message extends JPanel
{
   String message;
   public Message()
   {
      super();                          // call the default constructor of JPanel
      message = "";
      setBackground(Color.WHITE);
   }

   public void paintComponent(Graphics g)   // override paintComponent(…) of JPanel
   {
      super.paintComponent(g);          // first call paintComponent(...) of JPanel
      Font font = new Font("ARIAL", Font.BOLD, 14);
      g.setFont(font);
      g.drawString (message, 30, 30);   // display the message
   }

   public void setMessage(String msg)   // set the value of message
   {
         message = msg;
   }
}

import java.util.*;                     // java.util.* is needed for Scanner
import javax.swing.*;                   // java.awt is not necessary for this class

public class FrameWithAMessage
{
   public static void main(String[] args)
   {
      Scanner input = new Scanner(System.in);
      System.out.print("Enter Greeting: ");
      String message = input.next();

      JFrame frame = new JFrame();      // create a frame
      frame.setBounds(0, 0, 200, 200);
      Message panel = new Message();    // create a panel
```

```
36.         panel.setMessage(message);
37.         frame.add(panel);              // add the panel to the frame
38.         frame.setVisible(true);        // triggers system call to paintComponent(...)

39.         System.out.print("Enter Greeting: ");
40.         message = input.next();        // get a new message
41.         panel.setMessage(message);     // make the new message the panel's message

42.         panel.repaint();               // repaint the panel with the new message
43.         frame.set DefaultCloseOperation(JFrame.EXIT_ON_CLOSE);
44.     }
45. }
```

Output Figure 18.33a shows the frame after line 38 executes; Figure 18.33b shows the frame after line 42.

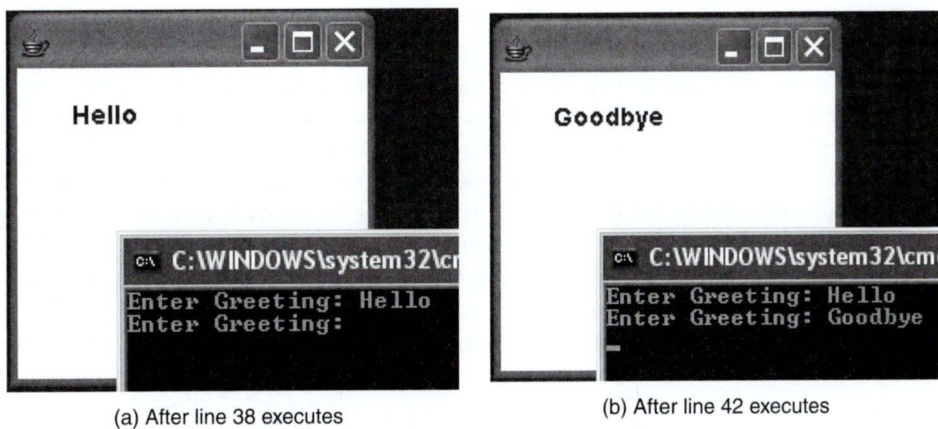

(a) After line 38 executes

(b) After line 42 executes

FIGURE 18.33 Output following lines 38 and 42

Discussion The Message class is straightforward and requires no explanation. In the FrameWithAMessage class, the Message object panel is painted twice:

line 38: when setVisible(...) is called and the frame and panel are first displayed, and also

line 42: when panel.repaint() is called, and the panel is redrawn.

Without the call to panel.repaint() on line 42, the panel would not be redrawn, and after line 41 the frame would remain as shown in Figure 18.33a. Of course, if you minimize, resize, move, cover, or uncover the frame after line 41 executes, the system automatically repaints the frame (and all components contained in the frame). Consequently, new message *would* be shown even without the explicit repaint() on line 42.

You can also explicitly repaint the whole frame rather than just one panel in a frame. Repainting a frame will automatically repaint each panel contained in the frame. For example, if you invoke **frame.repaint()** rather than **panel.repaint()** on line 42, the program displays the same output. In general, if only a single panel has been changed, it is better style to repaint the panel. Repainting a frame is useful when the frame contains many panels, each of which has been modified.

Finally, note that any changes that result from adding (or removing) components are shown immediately, provided that the container is *visible*. When adding or removing components, no call to repaint() is necessary (see Short Exercise 6).

Why repaint()? Why not call paint(...) or paintComponent(...) directly? The answer is subtle and has to do with the system's efficient management of graphical resources. The system wants to control any call to paint(…) and may, for various reasons, delay its execution. Because the system may have other tasks of higher priority than repainting a panel, execution of paint(...) may not be immediate. At the risk of oversimplification, we say that repaint() calls paint(…), and paint(...) executes "as soon as possible."

You have seen a similar situation with garbage collection. The garbage collector runs when it is expedient to do so. Similarly, a call to repaint() results in a call to paint(...), but the system decides when to execute paint(...). Using repaint() gives the system, and not the programmer, control over graphical resources.

In Chapter 19, we use repaint() in a few more examples.

18.10 IN CONCLUSION

You now know how to place components in a frame as well as how to draw a few simple figures using AWT and Swing. There are many, many more classes and methods in both of these libraries. Indeed, the Component class declares more than 100 methods. Nonetheless, if you study the examples in the chapter and do the exercises, you will have a good understanding of how components are placed in a frame. Once you know the basics, the learning curve flattens out a bit. Yes, there are other layout managers and other drawing methods. Yes, each class implements many more methods. However, you can get along quite well for a while using the subset presented here. When you need to expand your repertoire, excellent documentation for all Swing and AWT classes can be found on Sun's Java website. As you create more complex programs and gain experience, you will find Sun's documentation invaluable.

Just the Facts

- The Swing classes provide GUI capabilities that are platform independent.
- The AWT classes provide GUI capabilities that are platform dependent.
- All graphical output is displayed in frames. A frame is a window with borders and a title bar. Frame is an AWT class. Frame extends Window which extends Container which extends Component.
- JFrame is Swing's version of a frame. JFrame extends Frame.
- Frames may contain components. Components can be buttons, labels, menus, images, etc. Place a component in a frame using the add(…) method of Component.
- To assist with adding components to a frame, Java provides layout managers.
- Each layout manager is a class that implements the LayoutManager interface.
- Layout managers include BorderLayout, GridLayout, and FlowLayout. BorderLayout is the default layout manager for JFrame.
- A layout manager is not necessary. You can place components at any location in a container. To place components in a frame without a layout manager, use setLayout(null) and specify locations with the setBounds(…) method.
- A panel is an invisible container used for grouping components before they are added to a frame. A panel can have a layout manager. The Swing class that encapsulates a panel is JPanel.
- The default layout manager for a JPanel object is FlowLayout. This is in contrast to JFrame with default layout manager BorderLayout.

- Panels allow nested levels of layout control, providing great flexibility in the design of graphical output. Components are placed in panels and the panels are then placed in a frame.
- A label is a component used to display some text or an image. A button is another kind of component that displays text or an image (ImageIcon). The difference between a label and a button is that pressing a button usually triggers an action. The Swing classes that encapsulate labels and buttons are JLabel and JButton.
- To draw on a panel, extend JPanel and override paintComponent(Graphics g). When overriding paint Component (Graphics g) begin with the statement super.paintComponent(g).
- The paint(...) and paintComponent(...) methods are automatically invoked when a frame or panel is first displayed, or needs to be redisplayed due to resizing, moving, covering, or uncovering. If you need to explicitly redraw a panel or frame, use repaint().
- Repainting a frame or panel will automatically repaint each of its components. For example, if you wish to redisplay the contents of all the panels in a frame, repaint the frame.
- The parameter g of paint(g) and paintComponent(g) is a Graphics object. The Graphics class provides methods for setting colors, displaying text of various sizes and fonts, and drawing lines, rectangles, polygons, and ovals.
- A Graphics object g that is passed to paint(...) or paintComponent(...) is not explicitly created using a constructor. Instead, it is instantiated behind the scenes.
- The Graphics context of a component can be explicitly accessed using the getGraphics() method.
- Recursion is a powerful technique for drawing fractal images. Fractals can also be drawn with iterative techniques using stacks and/or queues.
- JPG and GIF images stored in files can be directly added to panels and frames (with or without labels or buttons) using the ImageIcon class of Swing.
- ImageIcon implements Icon, which provides methods for accessing information about an image file, and for painting an image onto a component such as a button, panel, or frame.

Bug Extermination

- Remember that *visible* components contained in a frame or in other components will only display if their container is also visible. Use the setVisible(Boolean visible) method to be sure.
- Panels and frames have different default layout managers. Sometimes what you expect is not what you get. Be sure that you understand how each layout manager positions components, and choose the one you want.
- When overriding a paint(g) or paintComponent(g) method, begin the method by invoking the paint(g) or paintComponent(g) method of the parent class, that is, super.paint(g) or super.paintComponent(g).
- Don't forget to use repaint() when you explicitly change any part of a component that you want displayed. Without an explicit repaint() request, the system cannot guess when the program has made a change to a component that warrants repainting.
- Don't forget to close a frame using:

```
frame.setDefaultCloseOperation(JFrame.EXIT_ON_CLOSE);
```

EXERCISES

LEARN THE LINGO

Test your knowledge of the chapter's vocabulary by completing the following crossword puzzle.

Across

1 FlowLayout arranges components _____ in a container.
5 Font class constant
7 Class that extends component
8 To place components in a frame with no layout manager, set the frame's layout manager to _______.
9 Method places a component in a container
10 BorderLayout divides a frame into _____ regions (number).
12 Implements the Icon interface
14 The x and y fields of Point are _______.
16 Graphical user interface
19 Default layout manager for a frame
21 Original graphics package
23 Components are often grouped together and placed in _______.
24 Positions a component at (*x*, *y*) and resizes the component
25 Newer graphics package
26 Called automatically whenever a component has to be drawn on the screen

Down

2 Every frame is initially _______.
3 Used to display text or an image
4 Bottom BorderLayout constant
6 Method used to draw a circle
11 A small picture that can be displayed on a component
13 Layout manager that uses a two-dimensional array structure
15 Any object that can be displayed on the screen
16 Every component that can be drawn on the screen has an associated _____ object.
17 Used to get the dimensions of the screen
18 A _____ is a window.
20 Default layout manager for a panel
22 A button, label, checkbox, for example (a "nickname")

SHORT EXERCISES

1. **True or False**
   If false, give an explanation.
   a. Swing is a subset of AWT.
   b. Swing is an earlier version of AWT.
   c. The names of all Swing classes begin with the uppercase letter J.
   d. A Frame *is-a* Container *is-a* Window.
   e. A JFrame *is-a* Frame *is-a* Container *is-a* Component.
   f. A panel is used to group objects together before placing them in a frame.
   g. A layout manager is required when placing objects in frames or panels.
   h. The paint(g) method is called automatically when a frame is made visible.
   i. The paintComponent(g) method is called automatically when a frame is made visible.
   j. A JButton *is-a* JComponent *is-a* Component.
   k. The Container and Component classes are abstract.
   l. A Swing method cannot be called by a recursive method.
   m. Any panel placed in a frame must use the same layout manager as the frame.
   n. An ImageIcon obtains an image stored in a file.
   o. A Graphics object is not instantiated explicitly using a constructor.

2. **Which Layout Manager?**
   For each of the following, describe how many panels (if any) you would use, which layout manager (if any) you would use for each panel, and which layout manager you would use for the frame. Explain your reasoning.
   a. A picture of a chess board.
   b. A picture of a pinball machine.
   c. A logo for your favorite sports team.
   d. An online poker GUI with tables, chairs, bets, and cards.
   e. A *Jeopardy* game including the board, along with scores and icons for each player.
   f. An image of the first page of a US passport.
   g. An image of your driver's license.

3. **Playing Compiler**
   Find the errors in the following program, which is supposed to display a picture of a smile with the heading "Smile".

```
import javax.swing.*;
public class MySecondFrame extends JFrame
{
   public MySecondFrame ()
   {
      add(new JButton("Smile"), BorderLayout.NORTH);         // adds image of smile
      add(new IconImage("smile.jpg", BorderLayout.CENTER);  // in center with heading
      setBounds(0,0,300,300);                                // below
   }
   public MySecondFrame (String title)
   {
      super(title);
      setBounds(0, 0, 300, 300);
   }
}
```

The following test class creates, displays, and closes a MySecondFrame frame.

```
import javax.swing.*;
public class TestMySecondFrame
{
   public static void main(String[] args)
   {
      JFrame frame = new MySecondFrame ("This is a test");
      frame.setVisible(true);
      frame.setResizable(false);
      frame.setDefaultCloseOperation(JFrame.EXIT_ON_CLOSE);
   }
}
```

4. **Playing Compiler**
   The following program is supposed to display an image on one panel, and the word "huh?" on another, without using layout managers. In fact, the program contains several syntax errors. When the errors are corrected, the program displays an empty frame. Find and correct the syntax errors. Explain why the program displays an empty frame, and then fix the program. *Hint*: The panels and buttons did not call the setBounds(…) method.
   To test your solution, use an image of your choice stored in a file called test.jpg.

```
import javax.swing.*;
import java.awt.*;

public class NoLayoutManagers extends JFrame
{

  public NoLayoutManagers()
  {
    super("No Layout Managers");
    setLayout(null);                        // no layout manager
    setBounds(0, 0, 300, 300);              // for the frame

    JPanel panel1 = new JPanel (null);   // no layout manager for the panel
    JButton picture = new JButton(new ImageIcon("test.jpg"));
    picture.setBounds(125, 125, 50, 50);
    panel1.add(picture);
    panel1.setResizable(false);
    setResizable(false);
    JPanel panel2 = new JPanel (null);  // no layout manager for the panel
    JButton button = new JButton(new String "huh?");   // add the word "huh?"
    panel.add(button);
    panel.setBounds(20, 20, 60, 60);
    add(panel);
  }

  public static void main(String[] args)
  {
     JFrame frame = new NoLayoutManager();
     frame.setVisible(true);
     frame.setDefaultCloseOperation(JFrame.EXIT_ON_CLOSE);
  }
}
```

5. **Playing Compiler**
   Find and correct the syntax and logic errors in the following program, which is supposed to display an image in the center of a frame, the words "huh?" and

"what?" in the EAST and WEST sections of the frame, respectively, the digits 0 through 9 from left to right in the NORTH section, and the digits 9 through 0 from left to right in the SOUTH section.

```
import javax.swing.*;
import java.awt.*;

public class BorderLayoutExample extends JFrame
{

  public BorderLayoutExample()
  {
    super("Border Layout Example");

    setBounds(0, 0, 300, 300);   // for the frame

    JPanel bottomPanel = new JPanel (new (GridLayout()) );
    JPanel topPanel = new JPanel (new (GridLayout()) );
      for (int i = 0; i < 10; i++)
           {
             bottomPanel.add (new JLabel(i));
             bottomPanel.add (new JLabel(10 – i));
           }
    add(bottomPanel, BorderLayout.SOUTH);
    add(topPanel, BorderLayout.NORTH);
    add(new String ("huh?"), BorderLayout.EAST);
    add(new String ("what?"), BorderLayout.WEST);

    JLabel picture = new JLabel(new ImageIcon("test.jpg"));
    add(picture, BorderLayout.CENTER);
  }

  public static void main(String[] args)
  {
    JFrame frame = new BorderLayoutExample();
    frame.setVisible(true);
    frame.setDefaultCloseOperation(JFrame.EXIT_ON_CLOSE);
  }
}
```

6. **What's the Output?**
   The remove(...) method of the Container class removes a specified component from its container. Suppose that, in Example 18.7, *How Good Is Your Memory*? the following lines are inserted after line 54:

   ```
   numberPanel.remove(button[0]);
   numberPanel.remove(button[1]);
   numberPanel.add(button[0]);
   numberPanel.add(button[1]);
   ```

   Describe the changes to Figure 18.19.

7. **Components and Containers**
   Answer each of the following questions:

   a. How does the use a label differ from that of a button? Do labels and buttons look different?
   b. What is the difference between a frame and a panel?

c. Why do you think there is a setResizeable(...) method for the JFrame class but not for the JPanel class?
d. What is the difference between Panel and JPanel?

8. **Panels and Frames**
The following question was posted on a Java Developer Forum. Be the "expert," and explain why this user sees only one panel on his/her frame.
"Trying to add two JPanels in one JFrame but only ever get one JPanel and it's always the last. Can someone please explain this to me? Thanks"

```
import java.awt.*;
import javax.swing.*;

// Program modifed for anonymity and clarity
// Original posted program was less concise and poorly formatted

public class query
{
        public static void main(String[] args)
        {

                JFrame myFrame = new JFrame("Anonymous");
                myFrame.setDefaultCloseOperation(JFrame.EXIT_ON_CLOSE);
                myFrame.setSize(800, 300);

                JPanel panel_1 = new JPanel(new GridLayout(2, 3, 5, 5));

                panel_1.add(new JButton("Main"));
                panel_1.add(new JButton("Help"));
                panel_1.add(new JButton("Save"));

                JPanel panel_2 = new JPanel(new GridLayout(2, 3, 5, 5));

                panel_2.add(new JButton("1"));
                panel_2.add(new JButton("2"));
                panel_2.add(new JButton("3"));
                panel_2.add(new JButton("4"));
                panel_2.add(new JButton("5"));
                panel_2.add(new JButton("6"));

                myFrame.add(panel_1);
                myFrame.add(panel_2);
                myFrame.setVisible(true);
        }
}
```

9. **Images**
An ImageIcon, stored as a JPG or GIF file, can be attached to a button or label, which, in turn, can be added to a frame or panel.
a. Consult Sun's documentation and confirm that an ImageIcon may *not* be added directly to a frame or panel. Describe in your own words what you have discovered.
b. How might you display an image in a panel or frame without using an intermediate button or label?

10. **A Time Complexity Experiment**
Run the Sierpinski program of Example 18.11 for various depths.

a. Find the smallest depth for which the program takes more than 1 minute to finish running.
b. Estimate the depth at which the program would take more than an hour. *Hint*: The number of recursive calls plus the number of triangles drawn approximately triples with each new depth.

11. **Opaque Containers**
When a container paints itself, it first paints its background and then triggers an avalanche of "component painting." That is, each component paints itself before any of the components it contains. This ensures that the background of a panel is visible only where it is *not* covered by one of its components.
Containers can either be opaque or transparent. This property is set using setOpaque(true) or setOpaque(false), respectively. Painting, as described above, occurs when a container is *opaque*. But when a container is transparent, something more complicated and time intensive occurs.
What extra work is needed when a container is *transparent*?

12. **Double Buffering**
A common problem when running graphic-intensive applications is *flicker* or jumpiness. A computer monitor typically redraws the screen approximately 60 times every second. Any kind of drawing that takes more than a 60th of a second occurs over more than one *redraw*, and that causes the image to flicker. Flickering makes an application look amateurish at best and can render a program too annoying to use. Swing drawing methods solve this problem using a trick called *double buffering*.
Look up the term and explain how double buffering reduces flicker.

PROGRAMMING EXERCISES

1. **An ID Card**
Using BorderLayout, design an ID card with your picture in the center, your name on the top, and your personal information (height, weight, eye color, address) split left and right. The bottom section of the card should display "Java Programmer Identification Card". The ID card should be the size of a typical driver's license positioned in the center of the screen with no resizing allowed.

2. **Hangman Revisited**
Add three additional panels to the frame of Example 18.3, the Hangman example. These new panels should display the player's name, a picture of the gallows, and a sequence of stars with one star for each letter in the secret word. For example, if the secret word is "hangman", the frame should show seven stars:

```
* * * * * * *
```

Include a two-argument constructor:

```
Hangman(String playerName, String secretWord)
```

Implement a class that displays the frame. The gallows can look like Figure 18.34, but you may prefer to use your own artwork.

3. **A Checkers Board**
Create a frame using Grid Layout that displays a picture of a checkers board. The board should have 64 panels. Each panel should have the appropriate background color, green or white; see Figure 18.35. Checkers, should not be placed on the board. The board is not resizable.

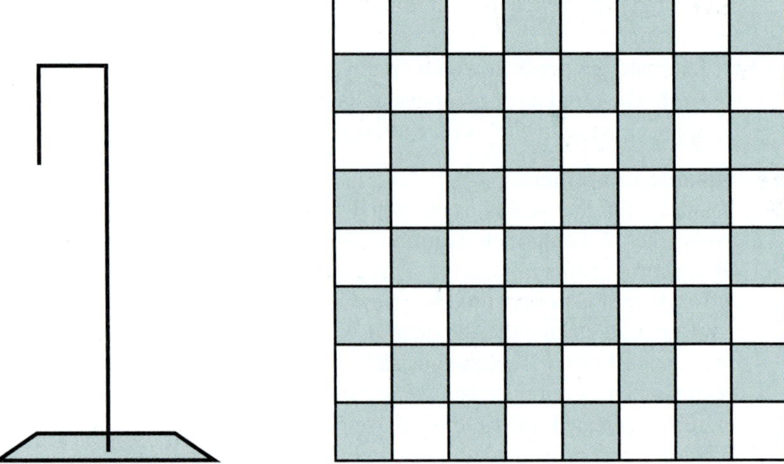

FIGURE 18.34 Gallows for a Hangman game

FIGURE 18.35 A checkers board

4. **A Fancier Checkers Board**
   Create a frame using GridLayout that makes a picture of a checkers board. The board should have 64 panels. Each panel should have the appropriate background color, green or white. Three red checkers should be drawn in random green positions on the board. The board is not resizable. See Figure 18.36.

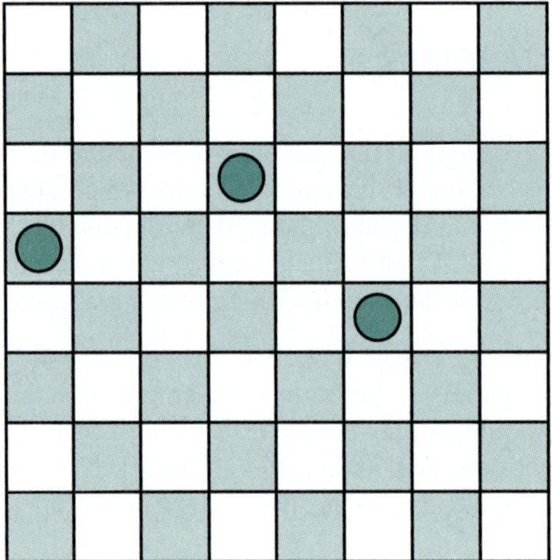

FIGURE 18.36 A checkers board with three "red" checkers

5. **A Checkers Board with a Data Model**
   Create a class CheckerBoard that extends JFrame. Using GridLayout, a CheckerBoard object displays a picture of a checkers board. The board should have 64 panels. Each panel should have the appropriate background color, green or white, and contain either a red or black checker, or no checker.
   Include two constructors:
   - The default constructor should set up the normal starting configuration for checkers. See Figure 18.37.

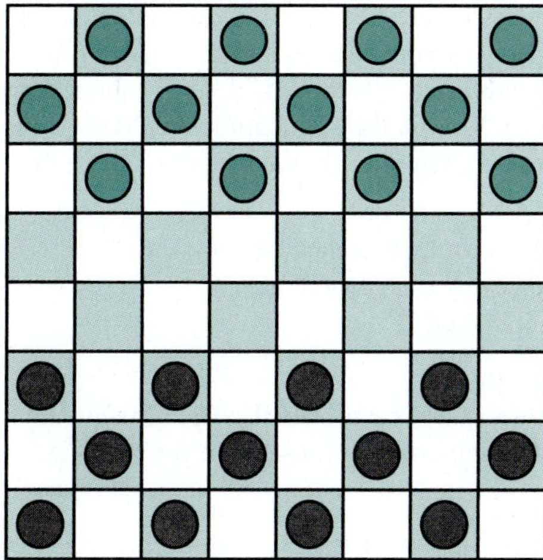

FIGURE 18.37 A checkers board with a normal starting configuration

- A one-argument constructor CheckerBoard(char [][] checkers) accepts a two-dimensional array of char that stores the board positions of the checkers: 'r' for red, 'b' for black, and 'e' for empty. The array determines the position of each checkers piece.

6. **A Personal Logo**
   Write a program that draws your own personal logo. Design the logo so that it can be used as a "splash screen" for your programming assignments. Include images, drawings, and whatever else you want, but make sure that the logo, in some way, shows your identity.

7. **Dice**
   Create a frame with two panels. On each panel draw a picture of a die with one to six spots. The number of spots on each die should be chosen randomly. Use any layout manager you like, and display the dice with your own colors and design.

8. **Faces**
   Create a frame with three buttons in the NORTH section of the frame. The buttons should be labeled with the names of three of your favorite TV or movie characters such as Moe, Larry, and Curly, or Bart, Homer, and Marge, or perhaps Sleepy, Dopey, and Grumpy.

   Place a label in the CENTER section of the frame. It would be nice if, when you click a button, a picture of the corresponding character appears on the label. However, button-clicking is a topic for Chapter 19. For the present, the constructor should place a randomly chosen image of one of the three characters in the CENTER section of the frame. Because the image is randomly chosen, the same picture does not show each time the frame is instantiated. In the SOUTH section of the frame, include a quotation from the character or caption about the character.

   Include a main(...) method that instantiates your frame.

9. **A Tic-Tac-Toe Board**
   Create a class TicTacToe that extends JFrame. TicTacToe contains an array of nine panels arranged as a 3 by 3 Tic-Tac-Toe board. The panels display the numbers 1 through 9. Your implementation should define a panel class, which extends JPanel, and has methods x() and o() that draw X's and O's, respectively, on the panel. A reset() method should erase whatever is in the panel.

Write another class that tests TicTacToe. Input consists of a character, X, O, or E, along with an integer between 0 and 9, inclusive. Digits 1–9 represent squares 1–9, respectively, and 0 indicates "all squares." Use a scanner for interactive input.

If a user enters an X or O, the application should draw that character on the corresponding square(s). On input E, the program erases the indicated square(s). For example,

- O 3 places an O in upper right corner (square 3),
- X 0 draws an X on every square, and
- E 0 erases the entire board.

10. **Recursive Megaphone**
(**R**) Rewrite Example 18.10 recursively. Use a tail recursive helper method inside the overridden paintComponent(…) instead of the for loop.

11. **Tunnel Vision**
Create a class TunnelVision that extends JFrame. Include a one-argument constructor TunnelVision (int numSquares) that draws numSquares squares nested one inside the other. The outermost square should be drawn at the perimeter of the frame, and each inner square should have its four corners at the midpoints of the previous square. The area of each inner square is half the area of the square in which it is inscribed. For example, TunnelVision(3) should display a drawing like the one in Figure 18.38.

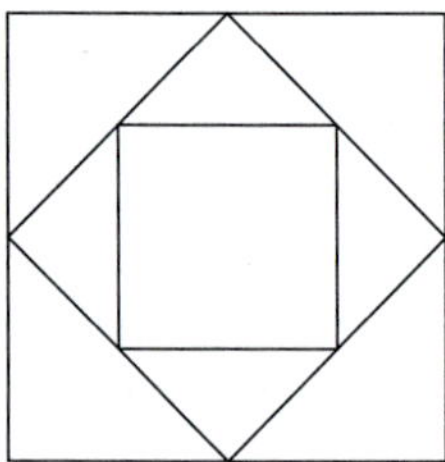

FIGURE 18.38 A square inside a square inside a square

Test the method with different values. You can write this program recursively or iteratively.

12. **The von Koch Snowflake**
The Swedish mathematician Niels Fabian Helge von Koch (1870–1924) introduced the *Koch curve* in 1904. To construct the Koch curve,

- Draw a line segment with endpoints labeled A and E. See Figure 18.39.

FIGURE 18.39 The first step in the construction of the Koch curve.

- Divide the segment into three equal-length segments, AB, BD, and DE, and replace the middle segment BD with two segments BC and CD, with lengths equal to BD. This is called applying the Koch rule. Note that BCD forms an equilateral triangle. See Figure 18.40.

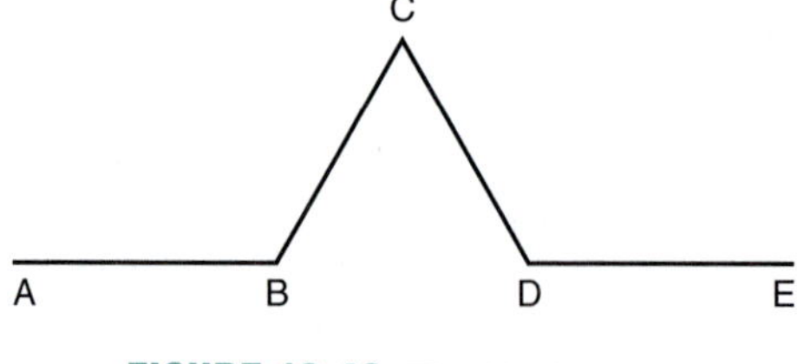

FIGURE 18.40 The Koch curve

- Apply the Koch rule to each of the four resulting segments. See Figure 18.41.

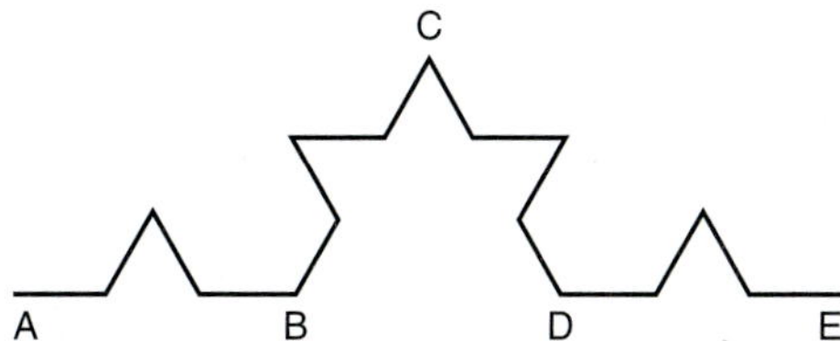

FIGURE 18.41 The Koch curve continued

After an infinite number of applications of the Koch rule, the result is a figure with an infinite perimeter.

The Koch Rule

If AE is a segment with endpoints A = (x, y) and E = (u, v), the points B, C, and D of Figure 18.40 are calculated as follows:

$$\mathrm{B} = \left(\frac{2x+u}{3}, \frac{2y+v}{3}\right),$$

$$\mathrm{C} = \left(\frac{1}{2}(u+x) - \frac{\sqrt{3}}{6}(v-y), \frac{1}{2}(v+y) + \frac{\sqrt{3}}{6}(u-x)\right), \text{ and}$$

$$\mathrm{D} = \left(\frac{x+2u}{3}, \frac{y+2v}{3}\right)$$

Note that this calculation works even if the segment AE is not horizontal. The new triangle appears on the left side of the segment, where your orientation is looking from A toward E; see Figure 18.40. Of course, if you reverse A and E then the triangle ends up on the other side of the segment.

The von Koch Snowflake

A *von Koch snowflake* is a fractal constructed from von Koch curves. To draw the von Koch snowflake, start with an equilateral triangle, and apply the construction described above to each side of the triangle in clockwise order. If you process points in clockwise order around the triangle, the new triangles will always be constructed correctly, that is, toward the outside rather than the inside.

Figure 18.42 shows the first four iterations of the von Koch snowflake.

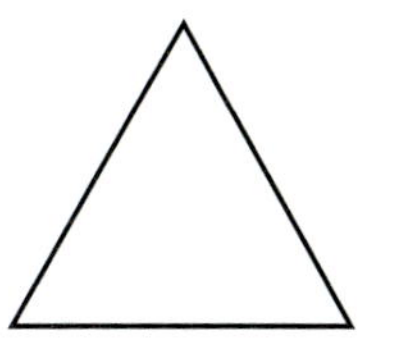

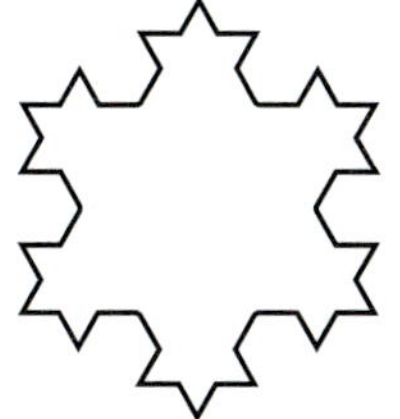
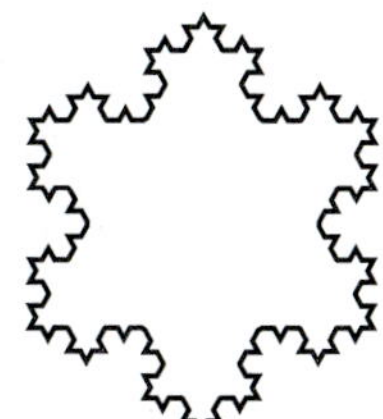

FIGURE 18.42 Building the von Koch snowflake

An *n-iteration von Koch snowflake* is the picture resulting from *n* iterations of this process. The *von Koch snowflake* is the resulting picture after an infinite number of iterations. The snowflake has some unusual properties. You may be surprised to learn that the von Koch snowflake has an infinite perimeter, but a finite area!

Programming Exercise: Exhibit an n-iteration von Koch snowflake in a frame. Extend JFrame and include a one-argument constructor with parameter n. Test your program with n = 5.

Programming Hints and Suggestions

There are a number of ways to draw the von Koch snowflake. Here is one suggestion that uses a queue and iteration. See Chapter 16. The algorithm draws each iteration of an n-iteration snowflake.

Initialize a queue Q with a set of four points such that the first three points form an equilateral triangle in clockwise order, and the last point, identical to the first, is used as a flag or marker. For example, you can start with the points:

$$(200, 200\sqrt{3}), (300, 100\sqrt{3}), (100, 100\sqrt{3}), (200, 200\sqrt{3}).$$

These points determine a large equilateral triangle. Note that, although these points are given as floating-point numbers, to use them as screen coordinates you must round them to integers.

The algorithm is short but not simple. It processes all the points in the queue, drawing lines between each consecutive pair, and while doing so, it adds those points plus the new intermediate points to the rear of the queue (for the next iteration). For example, if the initial points in the queue are A, B, C, and A, after the first iteration, three lines are be drawn: AB, BC, and CA. And, the new list of points in the queue for the next iteration is A, x, y, z, B, u, v, w, C, p, q, r, A, where the lowercase letters represent the intermediate points created by applying the Koch rule on AB, BC, and CA, respectively.

On the next iteration, apply the Koch rule to every point that was added to the queue in the previous iteration. The algorithm terminates after reaching the last point in the last iteration. Here is the pseudocode:

```
Repeat n times
{
   ClearScreen;
   A = Q.delete();
   Q.insert(A);
   E = 0;
   while( E is not (200, 200√3))
   {
      E = Q.delete();
      Draw a line joining A and E;
      Q.insert(B);         // B, C, and D computed as described in "The Koch Rule"
      Q.insert (C);
      Q.insert (D);
      Q.insert (E);
      A = E;
   }
}
```

Alternatively, the von Koch snowflake can be programmed recursively in a manner similar to the Sierpinski example of this chapter. The choice of recursion or iteration, and the details of the recursive method, are left to you.

13. **The Square Koch Curve and the Squareflake**

This exercise is similar to the von Koch snowflake of Exercise 12. The square Koch curve uses a square bump on each line segment instead of a triangle. See Figure 18.43.

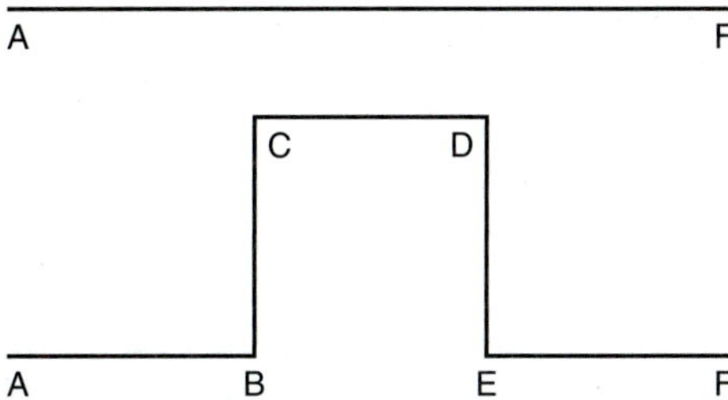

FIGURE 18.43 The square Koch curve

The *n-iteration von Koch squareflake* starts with a square and uses the "square Koch rule" on each side in each iteration. For a segment AF, if A = (x, y) and F = (u, v), then:

$$\text{B} = \left(\frac{2x + u}{3}, \frac{2y + v}{3}\right), \text{C} = \left(\frac{2x + u + y - v}{3}, \frac{2y + v + u - x}{3}\right),$$

$$\text{D} = \left(\frac{x + 2u + y - v}{3}, \frac{y + 2v + u - x}{3}\right), \text{ and E} = \left(\frac{x + 2u}{3}, \frac{y + 2v}{3}\right).$$

The new square appears on the left side of the segment AF, where your orientation is looking from A toward F; see Figure 18.42. This calculation works regardless of the angle of segment AF, that is, whether or not AF is horizontal.

Programming Exercise: Design a class that extends JFrame that exhibits an *n*-iteration von Koch squareflake. Include a one-argument constructor with parameter *n*, and test your program with $n = 4$.

The same hints given in Programming Exercise 12 apply here. You can start with points (100, 100), (100, 200), (200, 200), (200, 100), (100, 100) that form a square in clockwise order.

14. **The Chaos Game**

Write a program that implements the following iterative algorithm, known as "The Chaos Game."

> "Hardwire" into your program three points of an equilateral triangle (x_1, y_1), (x_2, y_2), and (x_3, y_3). These should be screen coordinates.
> Let *w* be one of the three vertices, chosen at random.
> Repeat forever // 10000 drawn points is enough
> {
> Pick one vertex, (x_1, y_1), (x_2, y_2), or (x_3, y_3), at random. Call this point *v*.
> Draw a point *p* exactly halfway between *w* and *v*.
> Set *w* equal to *p*.
> }

a. Describe the figure.
b. Try it again with a right triangle.
c. Explain how the algorithm might have produced such figures.

Note: Java does not provide a method that draws a single point (x, y). To draw a point, use:

```
void drawRectangle(x, y, 1, 1) or void drawOval(x, y, 1, 1).
```

THE BIGGER PICTURE

FRACTALS AND COMPUTER GRAPHICS

The set of exercises at the end of this section requires some familiarity with *complex* numbers. A short introduction appears in the appendix at the end of this section. The appendix also includes two Java classes that may be useful when completing the exercises. With just a little mathematics and a few Java methods, you will be amazed at the beautiful and colorful images that you can create.

The Sierpinski triangle of Example 18.11 is a *fractal*. So are the von Koch snowflake and squareflake of Programming Exercises 12 and 13. Mathematician Benoit Mandelbrot describes a fractal as "a rough or fragmented geometric shape that can be subdivided in parts, each of which is (at least approximately) a reduced size copy of the whole."

Fractals can model objects such as leaves, clouds, ferns, mountains, or even the coastline of England—objects more complex than those constructed from the rigid lines, circles, and spheres of Euclidean geometry. Fractals have found their way into the realms of abstract art. Fractal images have even been used in science fiction films: *Star Trek II* used fractal images to create computer-generated images of outer space. Figure 18.44 shows a few pictures of these strange, but beautiful, geometric objects called fractals.

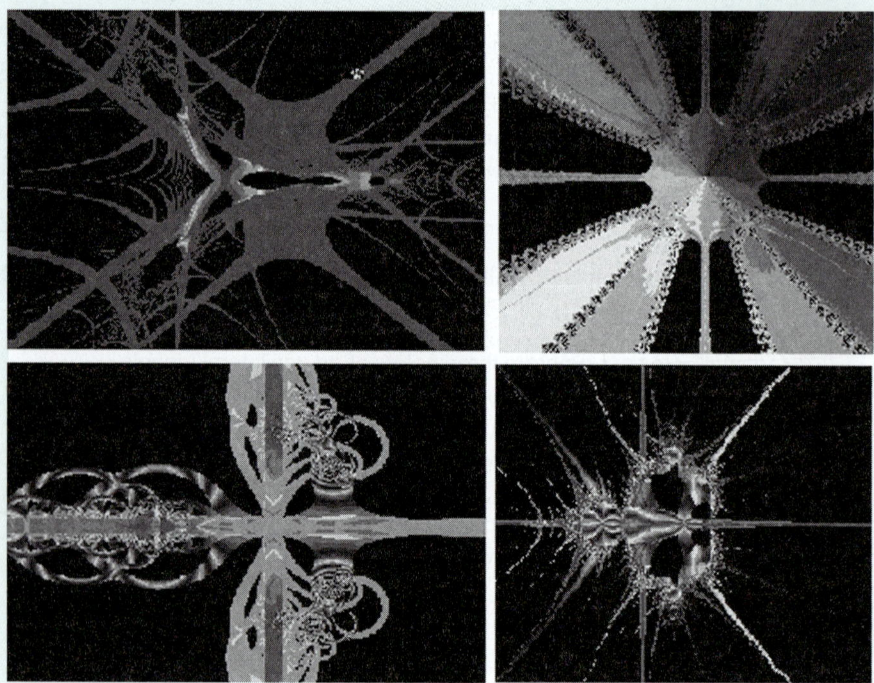

FIGURE 18.44 Some fractals

Obviously, fractals are detailed, intricate objects. One particularly remarkable property of a fractal is "self-similarity," a characteristic described above by Mandlebrot and more precisely by Ivars Peterson in *The Mathematical Tourist*:

> Fractal objects contain structures nested within one another. Each small structure is a miniature, though not necessarily identical, version of the

larger form. The mathematics of fractals mirrors this relation between patterns seen in the whole and patterns seen in parts of the whole.

As we have already noted, the Sierpinski triangle is a fractal image; the von Koch snowflake is another. And, although the Sierpinski triangle simply and effectively illustrates the notion of self-similarity, there are more striking illustrations. The last decade has produced some amazing, and quite beautiful, computer-generated pictures of fractals. In the upcoming exercises, you are asked to write programs that draw fractal images more exotic and colorful than either the Sierpinski triangle or the von Koch snowflake.

Some Colorful Fractals

Two of the most famous fractal images are the Julia set and the Mandelbrot set. See Figure 18.45.

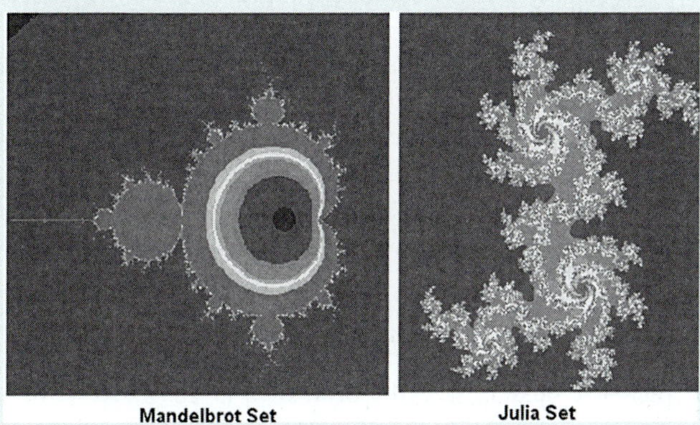

FIGURE 18.45 Two famous fractals

Ivars Peterson describes the Mandelbrot set:

> It has the appearance of a snowman with a bad case of warts. . . . On superficial inspection, the Mandelbrot set looks like a self-similar fractal, with infinitely many copies of itself within itself. On detailed investigation, however, the set is extraordinarily complicated. The baby Mandelbrot sets within the parent Mandelbrot sets are fuzzier than the original. They have more *hair* and other curious features. . . . Fractals such as the Mandelbrot set are called nonlinear fractals. For self-similar fractals, lines that show up within a figure, whether blown up or reduced in size, remain lines. For nonlinear fractals such a change in scale doesn't preserve the straightness of individual lines.

In the following exercises, we ask you to write applications that draw pictures like those of Figure 18.45. But before you can paint the Julia and Mandelbrot sets on a frame, we take a short but easy mathematical side trip.

Iterated Algorithms and Fractals

In his award-winning play *Arcadia,* Tom Stoppard, through the voice of his character Valentine, gives an intuitive and reasonable explanation of an *iterated algorithm*:

> You have some *x* and *y* equation. Any value for *x* gives you a value for *y*. So you put a dot where it's right for both *x* and *y*. Then you take the next value of *x,* which gives you another value for *y,* and when you've done that a few times you join up the dots and that's your graph of whatever the equation is, [however] what she's doing is, every time she

works out a value for y, she's using *that* as her next value for x. And so on. Like a feedback.

We illustrate this process with $y = x^2$, or equivalently, the function $f(x) = x^2$. First, choose an initial value, say, $x_0 = 2$. Now, compute some values of $y = f(x)$ starting with $x = 2$:

$f(2) = 2^2 = 4$; 4 is the "next x"
$f(4) = 16$; 16 is the "next x"
$f(16) = 256$; 256 is the "next x"
$f(256) = 65{,}536$;
$f(65536) = 4{,}294{,}967{,}296$; etc.

Notice every time we "work out a value for y [we are] using that as the next value for x. Like a feedback." You can see that the computed values of our example are growing larger and larger. That is, the computed values are *unbounded*. However, this is not always the case. Depending on the initial value x_0 the computed values may behave quite differently. Figure 18.46 shows the values computed by $f(x) = x^2$ for several different choices of x_0. Remember, each computed "y-value" becomes the next "x-value."

Orbits, Escape Sets, and Prisoner Sets

Let $y = f(x)$, and x_0 be some initial value for an iterative process.

The set $\{\boldsymbol{x_0}, y_1, y_2, y_3, \ldots\}$, where $y_1 = f(x_0)$, $y_2 = f(y_1)$, $y_3 = f(y_2)$, . . . , and $y_{n+1} = f(y_n)$, is called the *orbit* of x_0.

For example, if $f(x) = x^2$ and $x_0 = 2$ the orbit of 2 is {2, 4, 16, 256, 65536, ...}; see table 5 in Figure 18.46.

The tables of Figure 18.46 provide several other examples:

$x_0 = 0$ orbit of 0 = {0} (table 1)
$x_0 = -1$ orbit of 1 = {1, −1} (table 2)
$x_0 = 0.5$ orbit of .5 = {0.5, 0.25, 0.0625, 0.00390625, . . .} (table 3)

It is not too difficult to see that for $f(x) = x^2$

if x_0 is greater than 1 or less than −1, then the orbit of x_0 is unbounded, and
if x_0 is between −1 and 1, inclusive, then the orbit of x_0 is bounded.

The set of all points with unbounded orbits is called the *escape set* for $f(x)$.
The set of points with bounded orbits is called the *prisoner set* for $f(x)$.

Thus for $f(x) = x^2$,

the prisoner set is $\{ x \mid -1 \leq x \leq 1\}$, and
the escape set is $\{x \mid x < -1 \text{ or } x > 1\}$.

So, −3, 27, and −231 are members of the escape set of $f(x) = x^2$, but −0.3, 0.222, and 0.9999 belong to the prisoner set of $f(x) = x^2$.

All this mathematics, but where are the pretty pictures? Patience and you will soon see.

Complex Numbers

The story becomes a bit more interesting when we consider *complex* rather than *real* numbers. If you are unfamiliar with complex numbers, read the short introduction that appears in the appendix at the end of this section.

Let's use the same quadratic function, $f(z) = z^2$, but now assume that z is a complex variable, that is, a variable that holds a complex number. Suppose that we iterate with initial

Initial value $x_0 = 0$

x	y
0	0
0	0
0	0
0	0
0	0
0	0
0	0
0	0
0	0
0	0

Table 1: The computed values are all 0.

Initial value $x_0 = -1$

x	y
−1	1
1	1
1	1
1	1
1	1
1	1
1	1
1	1
1	1

Table 2: The computed values are all 1.

Initial value $x_0 = .5$

x	y
0.5	0.25
0.25	0.0625
0.0625	0.00390625
0.00390625	1.52588e-05
1.52588e-05	2.32831e-10
2.32831e-10	5.42101e-20
5.42101e-20	2.93874e-39
2.93874e-39	8.63617e-78
8.63617e-78	7.45834e-155
7.45834e-155	5.56268e-309

Table 3: The computed values get closer and closer to 0 (notice the exponent: −309).

Initial value $x_0 = .99$

x	y
0.99	0.9801
0.9801	0.960596
0.960596	0.922745
0.922745	0.851458
0.851458	0.72498
0.72498	0.525596
0.525596	0.276252
0.276252	0.076315
0.076315	0.00582398
0.00582398	3.39187e-05
3.39187e-05	1.15048e-09
1.15048e-09	1.3236e-18
1.3236e-18	1.75192e-36

Table 4: The computed values approach 0.

Initial value $x_0 = 1.01$

x	y
1.01	1.0201
1.0201	1.0406
1.0406	1.08286
1.08286	1.17258
1.17258	1.37494
1.37494	1.89046
1.89046	3.57385
3.57385	12.7724
12.7724	163.134
163.134	26612.6
26612.6	7.08229e + 08
7.08229e + 08	5.01588e + 17
5.01588e + 17	2.5159e + 35

Table 5: The computed values grow without bound.

Initial value $x_0 = 2$

x	y
2	4
4	16
16	256
256	65536
65536	4.29497e + 09
4.29497e + 09	1.84467e + 19
1.84467e + 19	3.40282e + 38
3.40282e + 38	1.15792e + 77
1.15792e + 77	1.34078e + 154

Table 6: The computed values grow without bond.

FIGURE 18.46 Values of $f(x) = x^2$ using various starting points x_0

value $z_0 = i$. Remember $i^2 = -1$, so

$$f(i) = i^2 = -1,$$
$$f(-1) = 1,$$
$$f(1) = 1,$$
$$f(1) = 1, \text{ etc.}$$

And the orbit of i is $\{i, -1, 1\}$, a bounded set. Consequently, because the orbit of i is bounded, i is a member of the prisoner set of $f(z) = z^2$

Now, suppose that $z_0 = 1 + i$:

$$f(1+ i) = (1+i)(1+i) = 2i,$$
$$f(2i) = (2i)(2i) = -4,$$
$$f(-4) = 16,$$
$$f(16) = 256, \text{ etc.}$$

Thus the orbit of $1 + i$ is $\{1 + i, 2i, -4, 16, 256, \ldots\}$ which grows without bound.

In this case the orbit of $z_0 = 1 + i$ is unbounded or "escapes to infinity." Thus, $1 + i$ is a member of the escape set.

There is a theorem that can help to determine whether or not a starting or initial point is in the escape set of $f(z) = z^2 + c$, where c is a complex number

> Theorem: Let $f(z) = z^2 + c$, and let z_0 be an initial point in an iterative process. If *any* point in the orbit of z_0 has absolute value greater than max(abs(c), 2), where abs(c) is the *absolute value* of c, then z_0 is in the escape set of $f(z) = z^2 + c$.

In other words, if the absolute value of *any one point* in the orbit of z_0 exceeds max(abs(c), 2), then the orbit escapes to infinity, it is unbounded, and z_0 is in the escape set. For a complex number $z = x + yi$, the absolute value, abs(z), is defined as $\sqrt{x^2 + y^2}$.

Let's look again at $f(z) = z^2$ with $z_0 = -2 + i$. Here $c = 0$, so max(abs(0), 2)) = 2. Thus,

$$f(-2 + i) = 3 - 4i. \text{ And, abs}(3 - 4i) = \sqrt{3^2 + 4^2} = 5 > 2.$$

So, by the theorem, we know that $z_0 = -2 + i$ is in the escape set of $f(z) = z^2$. We do not have to compute any additional values in the orbit of $-2 + i$.

Similarly, if

$$f(z) = z^2 + (3 + 4i) \text{ with } z_0 = i,$$

then

$$c = 3 + 4i \text{ and abs}(c) = \sqrt{3^2 + 4^2} = 5.$$

so

$$\text{max(abs}(c), 2) = \text{max}(5, 2) = 5.$$

The theorem states that if *any* value in the orbit of $z_0 = i$ has absolute value greater than 5, then $z_0 = i$ is in the escape set of $f(z)$. So we begin computing the orbit of $z_0 = i$:

$$f(i) = -1 + (3 + 4i) = 2 + 4i. \text{ And, abs}(2 + 4i) = \sqrt{2^2 + 4^2} = \sqrt{20} = 4.47;$$

$$f(2 + 4i) = -9 + 20i. \text{ And, abs}(-9 + 20i) = \sqrt{9^2 + 20^2} = 21.9 > 5.$$

Stop. No further values need be computed; $z_0 = i$ is in the escape set of $f(z) = z^2 + (3 + 4i)$.

For the following exercises, you may find the Complex and ComplexFunctions classes in the appendix of this section helpful.

Exercise

1. Use the Complex class and the ComplexFunctions class (in the appendix of this section) to iterate the function $f(z) = z^2$, first with $z_0 = 0.5 + 0.5i$, and then with $z_0 = 1 + i$. Determine the orbit of each point.

The Julia Set

Let $f(z) = z^2 + c$, where z is a complex variable and c is some complex constant. For example, $f(z) = z^2 + (2 + 3i)$, $f(z) = z^2 + 7$ or $f(z) = z^2$.

The *Julia set* is the boundary of the escape set of $f(z)$. In other words, the Julia set is the boundary of the set of starting points z_0 whose orbits escape to infinity.

In the next exercise, you are asked to paint the Julia set on a frame, point by point. Java, however, does not come equipped with a drawPoint() or drawPixel() method. Nonetheless, you can paint or draw a single point (x, y) using:

```
void drawRect(x, y, 1, 1) or void drawOval(x, y, 1, 1).
```

Exercises

2. Write a computer application that paints the Julia set for $f(z) = z^2$ on a frame. Here, $c = 0$. Your application should color all points in the prisoner set of

THE BIGGER PICTURE

$f(z) = z^2$ black and vary the colors in the escape set depending on how fast the iterations tend to infinity. See the hints below.

Your program should examine only those complex numbers that lie in the shaded square of Figure 18.47 and determine which are in the prisoner set of $f(z) = z^2$ and which are in the escape set. Notice the lower corner of the square is at $-2 - 2i$ and the upper corner at $2 + 2i$.

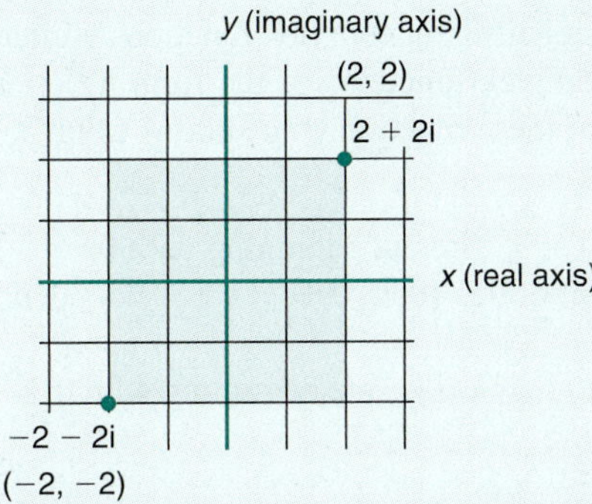

FIGURE 18.47 A portion of the complex plane

Of course, the complex numbers in the shaded section of Figure 18.47 are not specified as screen coordinates. You must map each complex number that you process to some point in your frame.

Hints:

Because the collection of complex numbers in Figure 18.47 is infinite, you must limit your application to a finite subset. The following loop does precisely that:

```
for (double x = −2; x < 2; x += 0.005)
   for (double y = −2; y < 2; y += 0.005)
      // Determine whether or not z = x + yi is in the escape set
      // or the prisoner set of f(x) = z²;
```

If no point in the orbit of z exceeds max(abs(c), 2) = max(0, 2) = 2 after, say, 50 iterations, assume that z is in the prisoner set. Of course, there is always the chance of an error if it takes more than 50 iterations to exceed 2, but usually 50 is enough. If *any* point in the orbit of z exceeds 2, then you know (by the theorem) that z is in the escape set.

Here is the fun part. Color each point z. If z is in the prisoner set, color it black. If it is in the escape set, color it with RGB (red, green, blue) values based on the number of iterations it took before "escaping." For example, let color = 50 − the number of iterations before escaping.

Here is a one possibility for calculating the color:

```
int red = (color * 24 % 256);   // a number from 0 to 255
int green = (color * 6 % 256);
int blue = (color * 13 % 256);
Color c = new Color(red, green, blue);
```

You might experiment with the constants 24, 6, and 13. Every combination will give a picture with different hues and colors.

3. The picture from Exercise 2 was not too exotic. Using a different value for c in the function $f(z) = z^2 + c$, you can get some pretty neat fractals. Draw the Julia set for each constant c.

THE BIGGER PICTURE

a. $c = 0.3 - 4i$, i.e., use $f(z) = z^2 + (0.3 - 4i)$

b. $c = -1 + 0i$, i.e., use $f(z) = z^2 - 1$

c. Try your own constant c.

The Mandelbrot Set

The Julia set considers different starting points of a fixed complex function. In contrast, the Mandelbrot set considers different complex functions with a fixed starting point. Consider the collection of all complex functions of the form $f(z) = z^2 + c$, where c is a complex constant. Iterate each of these function with starting point $z_0 = 0$.

For example,

if $c = 0, f(z) = z^2$. Iterate beginning with 0:
The orbit of 0 is $\{0, 0, 0, 0, \ldots\}$ – bounded,

if $c = i, f(z) = z^2 + i$. Iterate beginning with 0:
$f(0) = i$
$f(i) = -1 + i$
$f(-1 + i) = -2i$
$f(-2i) = 4 + i$

The orbit of 0 is $\{0, i, i - 1, -2i, 4 + i, \ldots\}$ – unbounded, and

if $c = 1 + i, f(z) = z^2 + (1 + i)$. Iterate beginning with 0:
$f(0) = 1 + i;$
$f(1 + i) = 1 + 3;$
$f(1 + 3i) = -7 - 7i;$

The orbit of 0 is $\{ 0, 1 + i, 1 + 3i, -7 - 7i, \ldots\}$ – unbounded.

For each constant c and function $f(z) = z^2 + c$, if 0 is in the prisoner set of $f(z)$, then c is a member of the Mandelbrot set.

Exercises

4. Write an application that paints the Mandelbrot set on a frame.
Let $f(z) = z^2 + c$, such that $c = a + bi$ with $-1 < a < 2$, and $-1.5 < b < 1.5$. For each c, determine whether 0 is in the escape set or the prisoner set of $f(z)$, and paint the point c with an appropriate color. Make points in the Mandelbrot set black. Vary the colors of the other points as in the Julia set program. You will get some really incredible pictures!

Use an increment value of 0.01.

5. The Mandelbrot set considers different complex functions with a fixed starting point. Normally, the starting point is 0, as in Exercise 4. Redo Exercise 4 using a variety of complex starting points. Report and explain your results.

APPENDIX: COMPLEX NUMBERS

A *complex number* is a number of the form

$$a + bi$$

where a and b are real numbers and $i^2 = -1$. For example, $4 + 3i$, $-5 - 8i$, and $6i$ are complex numbers. So are $7 = 7 + 0i$ and $0 = 0 + 0i$.

If $z = a + bi$ is a complex number, a is called the *real part* of z and b is called the *imaginary part* of z. For example, 4 is the real part of $4 + 3i$ and 3 is the imaginary part.

A complex number can be visualized as a two-dimensional point in the *complex plane* as shown in Figure 18.48.

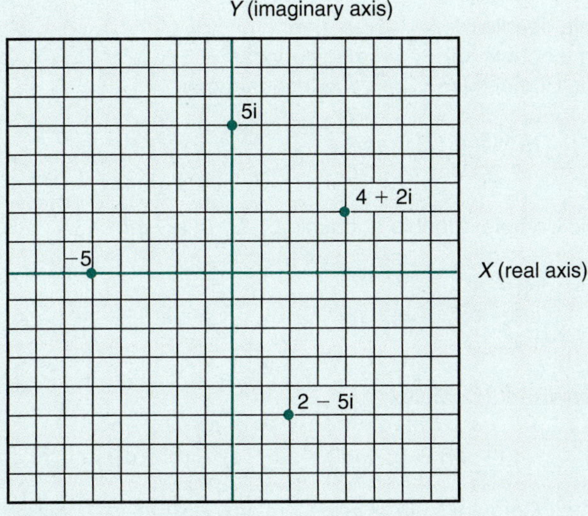

FIGURE 18.48 Four complex numbers shown in the complex plane

Notice that $4 + 2i$ is identified with the point (4, 2), $5i$ with the point (0, 5), and -5 with the point $(-5, 0)$.

Complex Arithmetic

Arithmetic on complex numbers is performed as follows:

Addition:

$(a + bi) + (c + di) = (a + c) + (b + d)i$

For example, $(3 + 4i) + (9 - 2i) = (3 + 9) + (4 - 2)i = 12 + 2i$

Subtraction:

$(a + bi) - (c + di) = (a - c) + (b - d)i$

For example, $(3 + 4i) - (9 - 2i) = (3 - 9) + (4 - (-2))i = -6 + 6i$

Multiplication:

Multiplication is accomplished just as you would multiply $(a + bi)(c + di)$, keeping in mind that $i^2 = -1$.

$$\begin{gathered}(a + bi)(c + di) = \\ ac + bdi^2 + cbi + adi = \\ ac + bd(-1) + (cb + ad)i = \\ (ac - bd) + (cb + ad)i\end{gathered}$$

For example, $(2 + 3i)(7 + 2i) = (2)(7) - (3)(2) + [(3)(7) + (2)(2)]\, i = 8 - 25i$

Absolute value:

The absolute value of a complex number $a + bi$ is the distance from (0, 0) to the point $a + bi$. This is calculated using Pythagoras's theorem.

That is, $\text{abs}(a + bi) = \sqrt{a^2 + b^2}$.

For example, $\text{abs}(4 + 3i) = \sqrt{3^2 + 4^2} = 5$;

THE BIGGER PICTURE

A *Complex* Class

The following class encapsulates a complex number:

```
public class Complex
{
        private double re;        // real part
        private double im;        // imaginary part
        public Complex()          // default constructor
        {
                re = im = 0;
        }

        public Complex(double a, double b)        // a + bi
        {
                re = a;
                im = b;
        }

        Complex add(Complex z)
        {
                // (a + bi) + (c + di) = (a + c) + (b + d)i.

                Complex sum = new Complex();
                sum.re = re + z.re;
                sum.im = im + z.im;
                return sum;
        }

        Complex sub(Complex z)
        {
                // (a + bi) − (c + di) = (a − c) + (b − d)i.

                Complex difference = new Complex();
                difference.re = re − z.re;
                difference.im = im − z.im;
                return difference;
        }

        Complex mul(Complex z)
        {
                // (a + bi) * (c + di) = (ac − bd) + (cb − ad)i
                Complex product = new Complex();
                product.re = re * z.re − im * z.im; // (ac − bd)
                product.im = re * z.im + im * z.re; // (cb − ad)
                return product;
        }

        double abs()
        {
                return Math.sqrt(re * re + im * im);
        }

        double real()
        {
                return re;
        }
```

```
        double imaginary()
        {
                return im;
        }
}
```

Complex Functions

Just as the function $f(x) = x^2$, where x is a real number, pairs a real number, x, with its square, the complex valued function $f(z) = z^2$ pairs a complex number z with its square. For example,

$$f(i) = i^2 = -1$$
$$f(2 + 3i) = (2 + 3i) * (2 + 3i) = (4 - 9) + (6 + 6)\, i = -5 + 12i$$
$$f(3 + 7i) = (3 + 7i)(3 + 7i) = -40 + 42i$$

Similarly, if $f(z) = z^2 + (3 + 2i)$, then

$$f(i) = i^2 + (3 + 2i) = -1 + (3 + 2i) = 2 + 2i$$
$$f(2 + 3i) = (2 + 3i)(2 + 3i) + (3 + 2i) = (-5 + 12i) + (3 + 2i) = -2 + 14i$$

For example, a complex function such as $f(z) = z^2$ and $f(z) = z^2 + (3 + 2i)$ can be implemented as:

A *ComplexFunctions* Class

```
public class ComplexFunctions
{
        public static Complex f(Complex z)
        {
                // f(z) = z * z
                return z.mul(z);
        }

        public static Complex g(Complex z)
        {
                // f(z) = z * z + (3 + 2i)
                Complex constant = new Complex(3, 2);     // 3 + 2i
                return (z.mul(z)).add(constant);          // z * z + (3 + 2i)
        }
}
```

THE BIGGER PICTURE

CHAPTER 19

Event-Driven Programming

"Life happens at the level of events, not words."
—Alfred Adler

"What wonderful things are events!"
—Disraeli

"The face of Garbo is an idea, that of Hepburn an event."
—Ethel Barrymore

Objectives

The objectives of Chapter 19 include an understanding of

- event-driven programming,
- the event delegation model,
- button events,
- radio button events,
- mouse events,
- menu events,
- checkbox events,
- text fields,
- text areas,
- labels, and
- dialog boxes.

19.1 INTRODUCTION

Webster's Dictionary defines an *event* as:

> an occurrence, an episode, a happening, an incident, an occasion.

(a) (b)

FIGURE 19.1
Clicking a button generates an event

In terms of programming, an event may not be an episode or an occasion, but an event is certainly an occurrence. Pressing a button or selecting a checkbox is an event. Choosing an item from a menu is also an event. Simply moving the mouse is an event. Events happen.

Clicking the X button that you see in the upper right-hand corner of a window and also in Figure 19.1a *generates* or *fires* an event.

The system *responds* to this event by closing the window. In a word processing environment, clicking the button of Figure 19.1b generates an event. The response sends a document to the printer.

An application can ignore an event or respond to an event. In any program, many events occur but only some are significant. For example, each mouse click generates an event, but only some clicks warrant a response.

Programs that respond to events are called *event-driven programs*. Almost all popular commercial programs are event-driven, including word processors, video games, and spreadsheets. Event-driven programming is the focus of this chapter.

19.2 THE DELEGATION EVENT MODEL

The *delegation event model* is Java's mechanism for handling events.

> The delegation event model specifies that when some *source*, such as a button or the mouse generates an event, the response is delegated or handed over to some other object.

For example, when a user presses an Exit button (the event source), the button object does not close the application; another object carries out or handles the response. The source passes the buck, so to speak. The source creates the event, an "event object," and then the JVM sends or passes the event object to another object for processing. More specifically:

- Whenever an event is generated, an *event object* belonging to the EventObject class is automatically instantiated. This event object encapsulates information about the event, including the *source* of the event—a button, the mouse, a checkbox, a menu item—along with other pertinent information such as the number of mouse clicks, the current screen position of the mouse, or whether or not a checkbox is checked.
- The event object generated by the source object is passed to one or more *listeners*.

  > A *listener* is an object with methods that process or handle the event.

  The listeners do the work. For example, when you click a printer button, an event object is instantiated, and that object is sent to a listener, which then sends a message to the printer. It's not the button that notifies the printer; a listener does that. When you click an Exit button, a listener issues the command such as System.exit(0). The listener is a servant, patiently waiting to respond to events.
- A listener object waits until an event is passed to it. When the listener receives an event, the listener responds to the event.

Thus, the principal actors of the event delegation model are three: the source, the event, and the listener. We discuss each of these in a bit more detail.

19.2.1 The Source Object

> The *source* object is the component that generates an event.

The event source may be a button, a textbox, a list, a mouse, a checkbox, a radio button, a key, a scroll bar, a menu item, or some other component.

19.2.2 The Event Object

As you know, when an exception occurs, such as "array index out of bounds" or "file not found," an object belonging to some Exception class is automatically created. The exception object may belong to NullPointerException, IOException, ArithmeticException, or any other class that extends Exception. The Exception object encapsulates information about the particular exception that has occurred. Exceptions are automatically generated by the JVM but handled by the programmer.

Event objects are similar to exception objects: event objects are generated automatically; they encapsulate information about the event, and the programmer chooses whether to handle or ignore the event.

> When an event occurs, such as clicking a button, checking a checkbox, or pressing a key, an object belonging to a class that extends EventObject is automatically instantiated.

When a button is clicked or a menu item selected, an ActionEvent object is created; when a checkbox is checked or unchecked, an ItemEvent is instantiated; when a key is pressed, a KeyEvent is generated. A partial view of the EventObject hierarchy is shown in Figure 19.2.

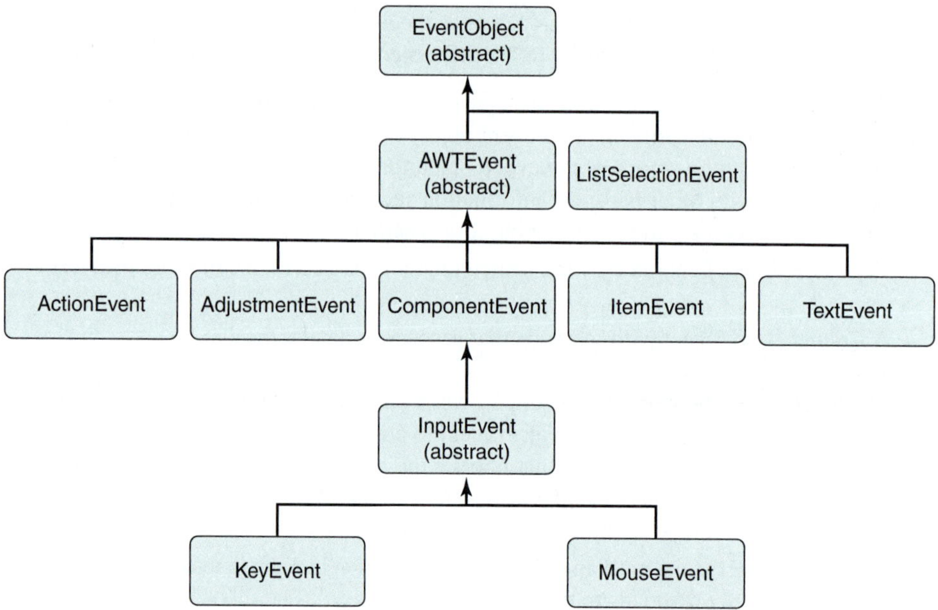

FIGURE 19.2 A partial view of the *EventObject* hierarchy

An object belonging to EventObject encapsulates information about the event, such as the source of the event. EventObject, which belongs to the java.util package, also defines two important methods:

- Object getSource()
  returns the source of the event, such as a reference to a particular button or checkbox, and
- String toString()
  returns a string equivalent of the event.

So, when you press a button or choose a menu item, an object belonging to ActionEvent is created by the JVM and subsequently passed to a listener object. The listener can invoke getSource() to determine the source component that generated the event.

19.2.3 The Listener

A listener waits or "listens" for an event to occur. A listener is automatically notified when certain events occur.

For example, when a button is pressed, a listener associated with the button is notified and responds; when the mouse is clicked, a "mouse listener" is sent a message and responds.

As you might guess, a listener is an object and, as such, every listener belongs to a class. It is the programmer's responsibility to define listener classes for each event that requires a response. The methods of a listener class perform the actions that handle events. A listener, however, is not an independent agent.

Every listener must implement one or more listener interfaces.

Thus, a listener is required to implement the methods declared in some interface. Every listener is under contract. For example, when a button is pressed, an ActionEvent object is generated and passed to a listener. The listener responsible for the button event must implement the ActionListener interface in the java.awt.event package:

```
public interface ActionListener
{
        public void actionPerformed(ActionEvent e);
}
```

Similarly, when a checkbox is clicked, an ItemEvent is generated and sent to a listener that implements the ItemListener interface. ItemListener declares a single method

```
void itemStateChanged(ItemEvent e).
```

So that a listener can receive events from a source, a connection must be established between the source and a listener. If no connection is established, the listener listens forever while the source generates unprocessed events. It is the source's job to *register* the listener by invoking a "registration method." Not registering the listener is a common source of errors.

We discuss the details of listener registration a bit later.

Figure 19.3 shows how the event delegation model plays out. A user action causes a source to generate an event. An event object encapsulating the details of the event is automatically created by the JVM and passed to a listener object registered by the source. When an event object is received by a listener, the listener handles the event. Each listener must implement the appropriate interfaces.

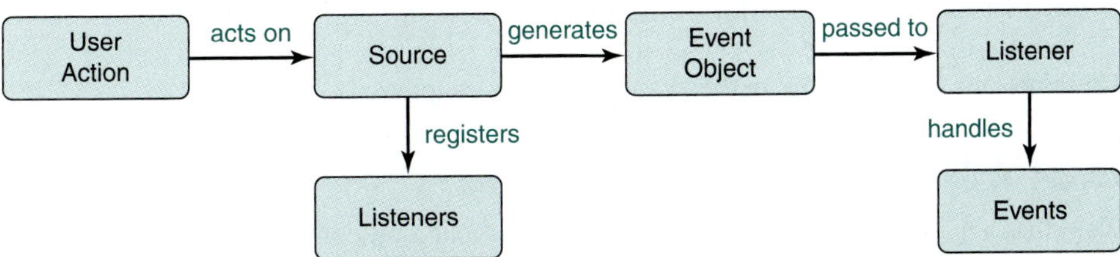

FIGURE 19.3 The event delegation model

Figure 19.4 lists some of the most common user actions along with the source, the class of the event object, and the required listener interface. This table provides a quick and easily accessible reference.

Action	Source of Event	Event Class	Listener Interface	Listener Methods to Implement
Button clicked	JButton	ActionEvent	ActionListener	actionPerformed(ActionEvent e)
Menu item selected	JMenuItem	ActionEvent	ActionListener	actionPerformed(ActionEvent e)
Press Enter in a text field	JTextField	ActionEvent	ActionListener	actionPerformed(ActionEvent e)
Click a checkbox	JCheckBox	ActionEvent ItemEvent	ActionListener ItemListener	actionPerformed(ActionEvent e) itemStateChanged(ItemEvent e)
Click a radio button	JRadioButton	ActionEvent ItemEvent	ActionListener ItemListener	actionPerformed(ActionEvent e) itemStateChanged(ItemEvent e)
Mouse moved, dragged, pressed, released, clicked, entered, exited	Component	MouseEvent	MouseListener MouseMotionListener	mousePressed(MouseEvent e) mouseReleased(MouseEvent e) mouseEntered(MouseEvent e) mouseExited(MouseEvent e) mouseClicked(MouseEvent e) mouseDragged(MouseEvent e) MouseMoved(MouseEvent e)

FIGURE 19.4 Java user actions and events, and their corresponding listeners

Thus, event handling is a two-step process:

1. Create a class that implements the appropriate listener interface(s) (see Figure 19.4). Code *all* the methods of the listener interface to effect the appropriate action for the event. For example, clicking a button generates an ActionEvent event. To handle the response, define a class that implements the ActionListener interface. Similarly, checking a check-box generates an ItemEvent event. The listener class must implement ItemListener.
2. Register the listener objects with the event source by using the "*addEventtype-Listener*" methods (e.g., addActionListener(...), addItemListener(...), addMouse-Listener(...), addKeyListener(...), etc.). This registration makes the connection between the listener and the source.

The event delegation model is very flexible.

- A source object may register many listeners.
- Different source objects may register the same listener.
- A listener may implement more than one listener interface.
- If a listener implements more than one listener interface, a source may register that listener multiple times, once for each interface.

These options are illustrated in the examples of this chapter.

19.2.4 A Simple Example—Hello Goodbye

Well, that's the general picture. A little too general and a bit confusing? No doubt! But a simple example should clear things up.

EXAMPLE 19.1

Problem Statement Design a GUI application consisting of a single frame with three buttons labeled Hello, Goodbye, and Exit. Pressing the Hello button displays the string "Hello" in the frame, pressing the Goodbye button displays "Goodbye", and pressing the Exit button closes the frame and terminates the application. When the program begins, the frame is empty. See Figure 19.5.

FIGURE 19.5 A frame with three buttons

Java Solution We implement the application in three steps.

1. **Set up the GUI.** That's easy. Chapter 18 is all about setting up GUIs.
   - Extend JFrame.
   - Instantiate three buttons.
   - Place the three buttons on a panel.
   - Place the panel in the SOUTH area of the frame.
   - Override paint(Graphics g) so that the method paints a string ("Hello" or "Goodbye") in the frame.

Here is the code that sets up the frame.

```
import java.awt.*;
import javax.swing.*;
public class HelloAndGoodbye extends JFrame
{
   private JButton helloButton;
   private JButton goodbyeButton;
   private JButton exitButton ;
   private String message;

   public HelloAndGoodbye()   // constructor
   {
      helloButton = new JButton("Hello");
      goodbyeButton = new JButton("Goodbye");
      exitButton = new JButton("Exit");
      message = ""; // initializes message to the empty string, so that if no button
                    // is pressed, nothing appears on the screen
```

```
        setTitle("Hello and Goodbye");
        setBounds(0, 0, 300, 300);

        JPanel buttonPanel = new JPanel();
        buttonPanel.add(helloButton);                // add buttons to panel
        buttonPanel.add(goodbyeButton);
        buttonPanel.add(exitButton);
        add(buttonPanel,BorderLayout.SOUTH);         // add panel to the frame
        setVisible(true);
    }

    public void paint (Graphics g)                   // override paint()
    {
        super.paint (g);
        Font f = new Font("Arial", Font.BOLD, 16);
        g.setFont(f);
        g.drawString(message, 100, 100);
    }

    public static void main(String[] args)
    {
        HelloAndGoodbye frame = new HelloAndGoodbye();
        frame.setDefaultCloseOperation(JFrame.EXIT_ON_CLOSE);
    }
}
```

2. **Design a listener class that implements the appropriate listener interface(s).** Refer to Figure 19.4. Clicking a button *always* generates an ActionEvent object. The appropriate listener interface is ActionListener. Thus to handle an ActionEvent:
   - Declare a listener class that implements the ActionListener interface.
   - Implement the single method of ActionListener

     void actionPerformed(ActionEvent e)

   The following code segment includes an inner class, ButtonListener (line 18), that responds to a button event. Recall that an inner class is a class that is defined within another class. An inner class can access the variables and methods of its surrounding class, but the surrounding class can access the data and methods of an inner class only via an object. See Section 16.6.2 for a brief discussion of inner classes.

   This inner class is the listener and, by contract, ButtonListener must implement the method

     void actionPerformed(ActionEvent e).

   The package java.awt.event must be imported.

```
1.  import java.awt.*;
2.  import javax.swing.*;
3.  import java.awt.event.*;

4.  public class HelloAndGoodbye extends JFrame
5.  {
6.      private JButton helloButton;
7.      private JButton goodbyeButton;
8.      private JButton exitButton ;
9.      private String message;

10.     public HelloAndGoodbye()
```

```
    {
        // as above
    }

    public void paint(Graphics g)
    {
        // as above
    }

    // the ButtonListener class, an inner class that handles button events.
    private class ButtonListener implements ActionListener  // the listener
    {
        public void actionPerformed(ActionEvent e)         // must implement this method
        {
            if (e.getSource() == helloButton)              // event source is helloButton
            {
                message = "Hello";                          // change the message String
                repaint();                                  // repaint the frame
            }
            else if (e.getSource() == goodbyeButton)       // source is goodbyeButton
            {
                message = "Goodbye";                        // change the message string
                repaint();                                  // repaint the frame
            }
            else                                            // the source is exitButton
                System.exit(0);
        }
    }

    public static void main(String[] args)
    {
            // as before
    }
}
```

3. **Register the listener, that is, make a connection between the button and the listener.**
   Because a button generates an **ActionEvent** object, registration is effected by the method

   void add**ActionListener**(ActionListener listener).

   The complete program follows.

```
import java.awt.*;
import javax.swing.*;
import java.awt.event.*;

public class HelloAndGoodbye extends JFrame
{
    private JButton helloButton;
    private JButton goodbyeButton;
    private JButton exitButton ;
    private String message;

    public HelloAndGoodbye()
    {
        helloButton = new JButton("Hello");
        goodbyeButton = new JButton("Goodbye");
        exitButton = new JButton("Exit");
        message = "";
```

```
16.         setTitle("Hello and Goodbye");
17.         setBounds(0, 0, 300, 300);
18.         JPanel buttonPanel = new JPanel();
19.         buttonPanel.add(helloButton);                        // add buttons to panel
20.         buttonPanel.add(goodbyeButton);
21.         buttonPanel.add(exitButton);
22.         add(buttonPanel,BorderLayout.SOUTH);

23.         // register the listener with each button

24.         helloButton.addActionListener(new ButtonListener());
25.         goodbyeButton.addActionListener(new ButtonListener());
26.         exitButton.addActionListener(new ButtonListener());

27.       setVisible(true);
28.     }

29.     public void paint(Graphics g)
30.     {
31.         super.paint(g);
32.         Font f = new Font("Arial", Font.BOLD, 16);
33.         g.setFont(f);
34.         g.drawString(message, 100, 100);
35.     }

36.     private class ButtonListener implements ActionListener   // the listener
37.     {
38.         public void actionPerformed(ActionEvent e)           // must implement this method
39.         {
40.             if (e.getSource() == helloButton)                // event source is helloButton
41.             {
42.                 message = "Hello";                           // change the message String
43.                 repaint();                                   // repaint the frame
44.             }
45.             else if (e.getSource() == goodbyeButton)         // source is goodbyeButton
46.             {
47.                 message = "Goodbye";                         // change the message string
48.                 repaint();                                   // repaint the frame
49.             }
50.             else                                             // the source is exit Button
51.                 System.exit(0);
52.         }
53.     }

54.     public static void main(String[] args)
55.     {
56.         HelloAndGoodbye frame = new HelloAndGoodbye();
57.         frame.setDefaultCloseOperation(JFrame.EXIT_ON_CLOSE);
58.     }
59. }
```

Output See Figure 19.5.

Discussion

Line 3: The ActionListener interface is defined in the package java.awt.event. The statement

```
import java.awt.*;
```

does *not* import the java.awt.event package. An explicit

```
import java.awt.event.*;
```

is necessary.

Lines 6–8: Declare the three JButton references.

Line 9: The String reference message refers to either "Hello" or "Goodbye".

Lines 10–28: The Constructor

Lines 12–14: Instantiate the three JButton objects

Line 15: Initially message refers to the empty string.

Lines 18–21: Instantiate a panel, and add the buttons to the panel using JPanel's default layout manager (FlowLayout).

Line 22: Place the panel in the frame using the JFrame's default layout manager (BorderLayout).

Line 24–26: Register the listener with the three buttons. The listener class is the inner class ButtonListener (lines 36–53). A connection must be set up between each event source (a button) and the listener. The JButton method

```
void addActionListener (new ButtonListener())
```

makes this connection. The listener must be registered with *each* of the buttons. This registration can also be accomplished with the following statements:

```
ButtonListener buttonListener = new ButtonListener();
helloButton.addActionListener(buttonListener);
goodbyeButton.addActionListener(buttonListener);
exitButton.addActionListener(buttonListener);
```

Notice that all three buttons register the same listener, ButtonListener, which handles events emanating from any of the three buttons.

Lines 29–35: Override the paint(Graphics g) method of JFrame so that each time the frame is repainted, the string referenced by message is drawn. Sometimes this string is "Hello" and other times "Goodbye".

Lines 36–53: The ButtonListener class (an inner class)

Line 36: ButtonListener must implement the ActionListener interface. See Figure 19.4.

Line 38: The only method of the ActionListener interface is

```
public void actionPerformed(ActionEvent e)
```

By contract, ButtonListener implements this method.

Line 40: The object e belongs to ActionEvent, which extends EventObject. ActionEvent inherits

```
Object getSource()
```

which returns the object that triggered the event. Thus getSource() can return a reference to helloButton, goodbyeButton, or exitButton.

Lines 41–44: If the event source is helloButton, change message to "Hello" and repaint the frame. The repaint() method calls paint(Graphics g).

Lines 45–49: If the event source is goodbyeButton, change message to "Goodbye" and repaint the frame.

Line 51: The event source is exitButton. Exit the application.

In Example 19.1, the listener class, ButtonListener, is an inner class, that is, a class defined inside another class. Although a listener can be an external public class, using a private inner class is more secure, efficient, and semantically clear.

In the remaining sections, we discuss some commonly used components and provide a few simple applications that demonstrate how these components are used. There are many components not explicitly discussed in this chapter. However, once you understand the event delegation model, the learning curve becomes a bit flatter and using new and different components is a snap.

19.3 COMPONENT AND JCOMPONENT

The hierarchy of Figure 19.6 shows that most Swing components inherit from Component and JComponent. JFrame extends Component and Container, but not JComponent.

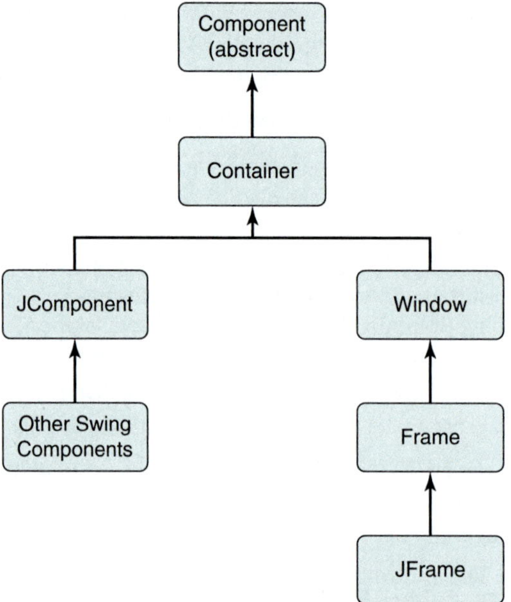

FIGURE 19.6 All Swing classes derive from *Component*

As a subclass of Component, each Swing component inherits a multitude of methods defined in Component, including:

- void setSize(int width, int height)
- void setLocation(int x, int y)
- void setBounds(int x, int y, int width, int height)
- void setEnabled(boolean b)
- void setVisible(boolean b)
- void setName(String s)
- void setFont(Font f)
- void setBackground(Color c)
- void setForeground(Color c)
- void resize(int width, int height)
- void repaint()

- int getHeight()
- int getWidth()
- int getx()
- int gety()
- int getName()
- Color getBackground()
- Color getForeground()
- boolean isEnabled()
- boolean isVisible()

Moreover, all components also inherit

- Component add(Component c), and
- void setLayout(LayoutManager layoutManager)

from Container.

A button is certainly one of the most commonly utilized Components. And, because we have already used buttons in several layout applications, JButton is a good place to start our discussion of Swing components. Like every class that extends Component and Container, JButton inherits the methods of these two superclasses.

19.4 BUTTONS

Buttons come in all shapes, sizes, and colors. Some display images and others text. Buttons generate action events, and a "button listener" might send a document to a printer, copy or paste text, save a file, open a file, or change a font style. And those are just a few actions related to a word processor. There are Exit buttons, Go buttons, Submit buttons, Clear buttons, and Resume buttons. Buttons are part of almost every GUI. Buttons are almost a necessity.

Here are the basics of the JButton class:

Class: JButton

Generates: ActionEvent

Listener: Must implement ActionListener

Listener method to implement: void actionPerformed(ActionEvent e)

Register a listener: void addActionListener(ActionListener a)

Constructors:

- JButton()
  instantiates a JButton object that displays neither text nor image.
- JButton(String text)
  instantiates a JButton object that displays text.
- JButton(Icon icon)
  instantiates a JButton object that displays an image;
  can be invoked as JButton button(new ImageIcon(String filename)),
  where filename is the name of a graphic file such as zap.gif.
- JButton(String text, Icon icon)
  instantiates a JButton object that displays text as well as an image.

Some JButton Methods:

- public void setHorizontalAlignment(int alignment)
  sets the horizontal alignment of the text and/or image on the button. The alignment parameter is a Swing constant:

SwingConstants.LEFT	(numerical value: 2)
SwingConstants.RIGHT	(numerical value: 4, default)
SwingConstants.CENTER	(numerical value: 0)

- public int getHorizontalAlignment()
  returns the horizontal alignment.
- public void setVerticalAlignment(int alignment)
  sets the vertical alignment of the text and/or image on the button. The alignment parameter is a Swing constant:

SwingConstants.TOP	(numerical value: 1)
SwingConstants.BOTTOM	(numerical value: 3)
SwingConstants.CENTER	(numerical value: 0, default)

- public int getVerticalAlignment()
  returns the vertical alignment.
- void setText(String text)
  sets the text that is displayed on the button.
- String getText()
  returns the text displayed on the button.
- void setIcon(Icon image) // e.g., setIcon(new ImageIcon("zap.gif"));
  sets the icon that is displayed.
- Icon getIcon()
  returns a reference to the button's icon.

There are many more JButton methods that can add some pizzazz to a GUI. One such method is the setRolloverIcon(Icon image) method that sets a mouse rollover image. Another useful JButton method is setMnemonic(int mnemonic), which assigns a key sequence such as ALT-P to a button so that pressing ALT-P performs the same function as the button. The preceding methods together with those inherited from Component and Container are a beginning. Once you are comfortable with these methods, you should explore Sun's website and discover many more additional methods available to a JButton object.

Example 19.2 uses several buttons as part of the implementation of an interactive Tic-Tac-Toe board.

19.4.1 JButton in Action—Tic-Tac-Toe

EXAMPLE 19.2 **Problem Statement** Design an interactive Tic-Tac-Toe board. The board should initially show nine empty squares. See Figure 19.7.

Two players, X and O, alternately click on empty squares. Each time a player clicks a square, the appropriate symbol (X or O) appears in the square and that square (button) is disabled. See Figure 19.8.

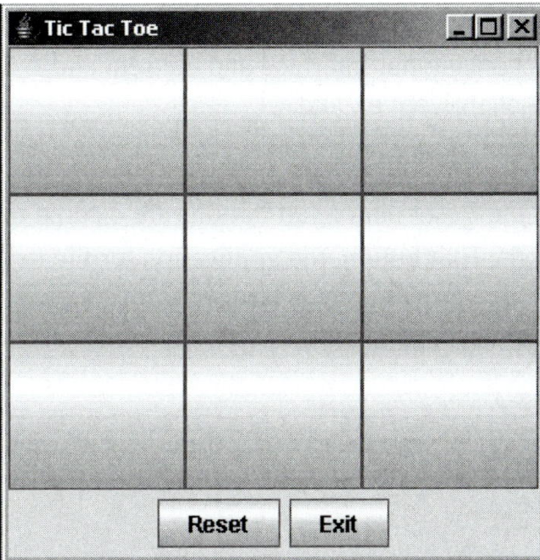

FIGURE 19.7 A Tic-Tac-Toe board

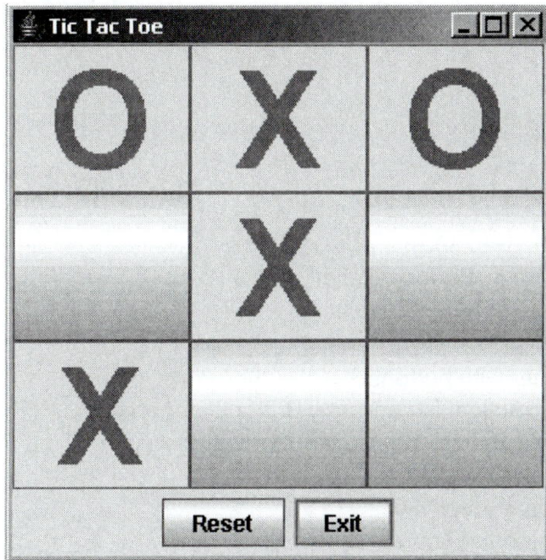

FIGURE 19.8 The Tic-Tac-Toe board after five moves

A Reset button clears the board. An Exit button terminates the application. In our application, X always makes the first move.

Java Solution The following application extends JFrame. The constructor, which builds the GUI,

- instantiates two JButton objects: resetButton and exitButton,
- registers a listener (ButtonListener) with each button,
- places the buttons in a panel,
- creates an array of nine JButton objects, one for each square of the Tic-Tac-Toe board,
- registers a listener (ButtonListener) with each of the nine array buttons,
- places the nine buttons in a panel using the GridLayout layout manager, and
- places the two panels of buttons in the frame.

The inner class, ButtonListener, responds to button events. This inner class

- implements the ActionListener interface and consequently actionPerformed(ActionEvent e), and
- determines the source of an event:

  if the source is the Reset button, all buttons are cleared of text and enabled;

  if the source is the Exit button, the application terminates;

  if the source is one of the nine board buttons, that button's text is set "X" or "O", and the button is disabled.

The application follows.

```
import java.awt.*;
import javax.swing.*;
import java.awt.event.*;

public class TicTacToeBoard extends JFrame
{
   private JButton resetButton;                    // clear board
   private JButton exitButton ;                    // ends game
   private JButton[] board;                        // as a 3 by 3 grid of buttons
   private int turn;                               // 1 for "X" and 0 for "O"

   public TicTacToeBoard()                         // constructor builds the GUI
   {
      turn = 1;                                    // for "'X'"
      setTitle("Tic Tac Toe");
      setBounds(0, 0, 300, 300);
      resetButton = new JButton("Reset");
      exitButton = new JButton("Exit");

      // register listener with buttons
      resetButton.addActionListener(new ButtonListener());
      exitButton.addActionListener(new ButtonListener());

      // add buttons to a panel and
      // add the panel to the bottom of the frame
      JPanel bottomPanel = new JPanel();
      bottomPanel.add(resetButton);
      bottomPanel.add(exitButton);

      // instantiate a Panel for the board
      // use the GridLayout layout manager (3 by 3) for the board

      JPanel boardPanel = new JPanel();
      boardPanel.setLayout(new GridLayout(3, 3));
      board = new JButton[9];

      for (int i = 0; i < 9; i++)
      {
         board[i] = new JButton();
         board[i].setFont(new Font("Arial", Font.BOLD, 72));

         // register the listener for each button

         board[i].addActionListener(new ButtonListener());
         boardPanel.add(board[i]);
      }
```

```
38.       // add both panels to the frame

39.       add(bottomPanel,BorderLayout.SOUTH);
40.       add(boardPanel,BorderLayout.CENTER);
41.       setVisible(true);
42.       setDefaultCloseOperation(JFrame.EXIT_ON_CLOSE);
43.    }

44.    private class ButtonListener implements ActionListener  // responds to button event
45.    {
46.       public void actionPerformed(ActionEvent e)          // ActionListener Interface method
47.       {
48.          if (e.getSource() == resetButton)                // Reset button?
49.             for(int i = 0; i < 9; i++)
50.             {
51.                // remove X's and O's
52.                board[i].setText("");

53.                // enable all board buttons
54.                board[i].setEnabled(true);
                   turn = 1;
55.             }
56.          else if (e.getSource() == exitButton)
57.             System.exit(0);

58.          else
59.             for (int i = 0; i < 9; i++)                    // for each board square
60.                if (e.getSource() == board[i])
61.                {
62.                   if (turn == 1)                          // X's turn
63.                         board[i].setText("X");            // put an "X" on the board
64.                   else                                    // O's turn
65.                      board[i].setText("O");               // put an "O" on the board
66.                   board[i].setEnabled(false);             // disable or "gray-out" the button
67.                   turn = (turn + 1) % 2;                  // change turn designator, toggles 0 and 1
68.                   return;                                 // source determined; return
69.                }
70.             }
71.    }
72.    public static void main(String [] args)
73.    {
74.       TicTacToeBoard frame = new TicTacToeBoard();
75.
76.    }
77. }
```

Output See Figures 19.7 and 19.8 for typical output

Discussion

Lines 6–8: The Declarations

resetButton clears the board; exitButton terminates the program, and the nine buttons of the board array comprise the game board.

Line 9: The variable turn keeps track of the current player. A value of 1 indicates that it is X's turn to move; 0 indicates that it is O's turn.

Line 12: Player X makes the first move.

Line 18–19: The inner class ButtonListener (lines 44–71) responds to events generated by JButton objects. To respond to an event, a listener class must register with the event source. The buttons resetButton and exitButton register the ButtonListener via the method calls:

```
resetButton.addActionListener(new ButtonListener());
exitButton.addActionListener(new ButtonListener()).
```

and consequently, establish a connection.

Lines 22–24: These statements create a JPanel, buttonPanel, and place resetButton and exitButton in the panel using the default layout manager, FlowLayout.

Lines 27–28: Here, the code instantiates a panel with layout manager GridLayout (3, 3). This panel holds the nine buttons that constitute the game board.

Lines 30–37: For i = 0 to 8 the application

- creates a button, board[i], without text or icon (line 32);
- sets the font to Arial, Bold, 72 point (line 33);
- registers the listener, ButtonListener, with the new button via the method call addActionListener(Action Event) (line 35);
- places the button on the panel using GridLayout (line 36).

Each of the 11 buttons (board[0]...board[8], resetButton, and exitButton) registers the same listener, ButtonListener.

Lines 39–40: Two panels have been created, bottomPanel and boardPanel. The constructor places these two panels in the frame using the default BorderLayout layout manager.

Lines 44–71: The ButtonListener class
The inner class ButtonListener must implement the ActionListener interface. See Figure 19.4. Thus, ButtonListener must implement the sole method of the ActionListener interface:

```
void actionPerformed(ActionEvent e).
```

When a button is pressed, an ActionEvent object is generated and passed as a parameter to actionPerformed(...), which handles the event as follows:

If the source of the event is resetButton (line 48),
remove the text from all buttons (line 52), and enable all buttons (line 54).

This action refreshes the board.

If the source of the event is exitButton (line 56),
call System.out.exit(0) and terminate the application (line 57).

If the source of the event is one of the board buttons,

- set the button text to "X", if it is X's turn; otherwise set the button text to "O";
- disable the button (line 66);
- change the value of turn (line 67). If turn is 1 then (1 + 1) % 2 = 0; if turn is 0 then (0 + 1) % 2 = 1.

19.5 LABELS

A *label* is an area that can be used to display text or images. A label is *not* a source of events.

Here are the basics:

Class: JLabel

Constructors:

- JLabel()
  instantiates a JLabel object that displays neither text nor an image.
- JLabel (String text)
  instantiates a JLabel object with text, text.
- JLabel(Icon icon) // e.g., JLabel label = new JLabel(new ImageIcon("pic.jpg"))
  instantiates a JLabel object that displays icon.
- JLabel(String text, int horizontalAlignment)
  instantiates a JLabel object that displays text. Alignment is determined by one of the Swing constants: LEFT, RIGHT, CENTER
- JLabel(Icon icon, int horizontalAlignment)
  instantiates a JLabel object that displays icon. Alignment is determined by one of the Swing constants: LEFT, RIGHT, CENTER
- JLabel(String text, Icon icon, int horizontalAlignment)
  instantiates a JLabel that displays text and icon. Alignment is determined by one of the Swing constants: LEFT, RIGHT, CENTER

The JLabel class provides the same getters and setters as JButton, such as setText(String text) and setAlignment(int alignment).

Example 19.3 uses buttons and labels to create an electronic photo album. The buttons generate the source events. The labels are used for display.

19.5.1 A Photo Album—*JLabel* in Action

EXAMPLE 19.3

Travelin' Tina has recently returned from an Italian vacation with an extensive collection of full-size digital photos as well as a small "thumbnail" version of each photo. She has saved the large photos in files named photo0.jpg, photo1.jpg, photo2.jpg, and so on. The pictures in the thumbnail collection are appropriately named thumbnail0.jpg, thumbnail1.jpg, etc.

Problem Statement Devise an application that displays nine thumbnail pictures in a single frame so that when Tina clicks on any thumbnail, a full size version shows in another frame. The lower panel of the thumbnail frame contains two buttons, a Next button and an Exit button. When the Next button is clicked, the next batch of nine thumbnail pictures comes into view. After the last thumbnail is shown, the display cycles around and the first thumbnail is once again displayed. The Exit button terminates the application. Figure 19.9 shows the first "tray" of thumbnails.

Java Solution The following solution consists of three interacting classes:

1. **PhotoAlbum**
   - PhotoAlbum maintains two ArrayList<ImageIcon> objects: one list holds full-size photos, the other thumbnails.
   - PhotoAlbum provides methods that return the number of photos, the ith photo, or the ith thumbnail.

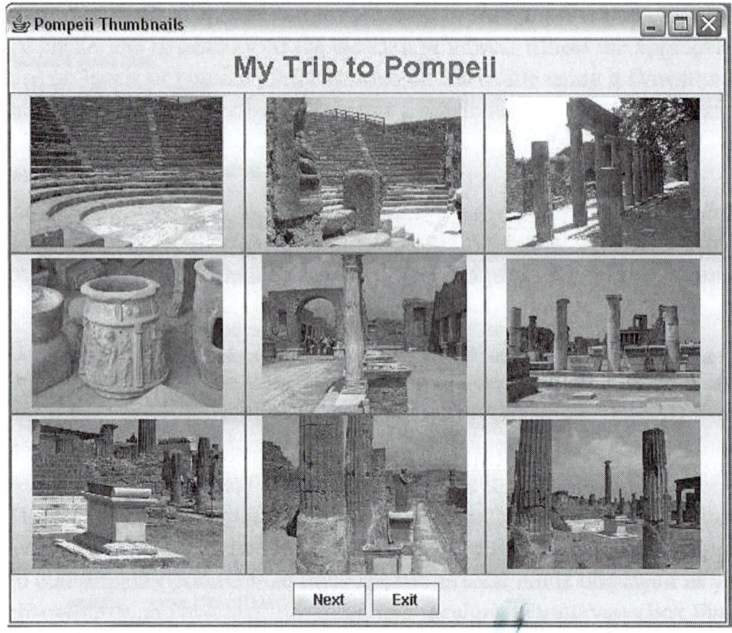

FIGURE 19.9 Nine thumbnail pictures displayed in a frame

This class is not part of the GUI. The class strictly maintains the data of the application.

2. **PictureFrame**
   - PictureFrame extends JFrame, displays a single picture on a label, and places the label in the center of a frame.
   - PictureFrame also provides a method that changes the picture.

   Figure 19.10 shows this frame.

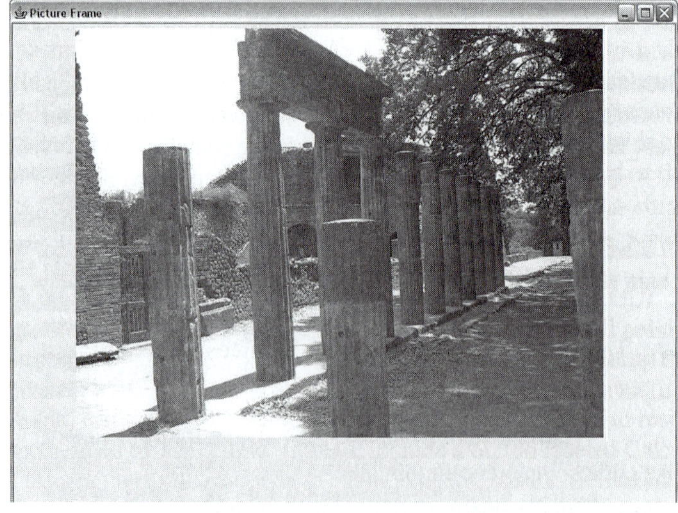

FIGURE 19.10 A full-size photo

3. ManagePhotos

- ManagePhotos extends JFrame and contains three panels in the NORTH, CENTER, and SOUTH sections of the frame. This is the frame shown in Figure 19.9.
- The NORTH panel holds a label that displays a title string. The title string of Figure 19.9 is "My Trip to Pompeii".
- The CENTER panel is a grid of nine buttons. Each button displays one thumbnail. Clicking a button displays the corresponding full size photo in a PictureFrame object.
- The SOUTH panel contains two buttons, Next and Exit. Clicking the Next button changes the nine pictures in the center grid. The Next button is disabled if there are fewer than 10 pictures.

  In the exercises, we ask you to add a Previous button that allows a user to move backward as well as forward through the pictures (see Programming Exercise 3).

ManagePhotos includes a call to validate(), which is defined in Container. Sun's documentation states:

> AWT uses validate() to cause a container to lay out its subcomponents again after the components it contains have been added to or modified.

Contrast this method with repaint(), which does *not* lay out components again, but instead calls paint(g) to render each component again. The latter method is used when component features like color or text on a label have changed, but no new layout is necessary—that is, the size and location of the components stays fixed.

////////////////////////// PhotoAlbum class //////////////////////////

```
import java.awt.*;
import javax.swing.*;
import java.util.*;                                          // for ArrayList
import java.io.*;

public class PhotoAlbum
{
   ArrayList<ImageIcon> thumbnails;                          // holds thumbnail pics
   ArrayList<ImageIcon> photos;                              // holds full size pics

   public PhotoAlbum()            // constructor, adds the photos and thumbnails to the ArrayLists
   {
      thumbnails = new ArrayList<ImageIcon> ();              // set initial capacity
      photos = new ArrayList<ImageIcon>();
      int picNum = 0;

      while((new File("Pompeii/thumbnail" + picNum + ".jpg").exists()))     // for each photo
      {
         ImageIcon thumb = new ImageIcon("Pompeii/thumbnail" + picNum + ".jpg");  // thumbnail0.jpg, etc.
         ImageIcon full = new ImageIcon("Pompeii/photo" + picNum + ".jpg");    // photo0.jpg, etc.
         thumbnails.add(thumb);                              // adds to the end of the ArrayList
         photos.add(full);
         picNum++;
      }
   }

   public ImageIcon getPhoto(int i)                          // returns the ith photo
   {
      return photos.get(i);
   }
```

```

    public ImageIcon getThumbnail(int i)          // returns the ith thumbnail
    {
       return thumbnails.get(i);
    }

    public int numPhotos()                        // returns the number of photos in the album
    {
       return photos.size();
    }
}
```

//////////////////////////// PictureFrame class ////////////////////////////

```
import java.awt.*;
import javax.swing.*;

public class PictureFrame extends JFrame
{
    private JLabel pictureLabel;
    private JPanel picturePanel;
    public PictureFrame()                         // default constructor
    {
       super("Picture Frame");                    // invoke parent constructor
       JFrame PictureFrame = new JFrame();

       // Make the frame fill the entire screen
       Toolkit tk = Toolkit.getDefaultToolkit();
       Dimension dim = tk.getScreenSize();        // returns screen width, height
       setBounds(0,0, dim.width, dim.height);

       // place a label in a panel; place the panel in the frame
       pictureLabel = new JLabel();
       picturePanel = new JPanel();
       picturePanel.add(pictureLabel);
       add(picturePanel, BorderLayout.CENTER);
    }

    public void changePhoto(Icon icon)
       // change the picture displayed in the frame by changing
       // the picture displayed in the label
    {
       pictureLabel.setIcon(icon);
    }
}
```

//////////////////////////// ManagePhotos class ////////////////////////////

```
import java.awt.*;
import javax.swing.*;
import java.awt.event.*;

public class ManagePhotos extends JFrame
{
    private JButton nextButton;                   // to show the next nine thumbnails
    private JButton exitButton;                   // exit application
    private JPanel buttonPanel;                   // for the next and Exit buttons

    private PhotoAlbum album;                     // holds photos and thumbnails
    private JButton[] display;                    // one button for each thumbnail
    private JPanel displayPanel;                  // holds 9 thumbnail buttons
```

```
    private JLabel titleLabel;                           // displays title of the display
    private JPanel titlePanel;                           // holds the title label

    private PictureFrame PictureFrame;                   // displays one large photo
    int nextPicture;                                     // number of next thumbnail placed in the display

    public ManagePhotos()                                // default constructor
    {
      setTitle("Pompeii Thumbnails");
      setBounds(0, 0, 600, 500);
      album = new PhotoAlbum();

      // create the title label and place it in a panel
      titleLabel = new JLabel();
      titleLabel.setFont(new Font("Comic Sans Serif", Font.BOLD, 24));
      titleLabel.setForeground(Color.RED);
      titleLabel.setText("My Trip to Pompeii");
      titlePanel = new JPanel();
      titlePanel.add(titleLabel);

      // create the buttons and place them in a panel
      nextButton = new JButton("Next");
      if (album.numPhotos() <= 9)
         nextButton.setEnabled(false);
      exitButton = new JButton("Exit");
      buttonPanel = new JPanel();
      buttonPanel.add(nextButton);                       // add the two buttons to the panel
      buttonPanel.add(exitButton);

      // register the listener for the buttons
      nextButton.addActionListener(new ButtonListener());
      exitButton.addActionListener(new ButtonListener());

      // create a button for each thumbnail
      // register a listener with each button
      display = new JButton[album.numPhotos()];          // instantiate the array
      for (int i = 0; i < album.numPhotos(); i++)
      {
         display[i] = new JButton(album.getThumbnail(i));       // populate the array
         display[i].addActionListener(new ButtonListener());    // register a listener for each thumbnail
      }

      displayPanel = new JPanel();                       // panel holds 9 buttons that display thumbnails
      displayPanel.setLayout(new GridLayout(3, 3));

      // place the thumbnails in a panel
      for (int i = 0; i < 9; i++)                        // for the first nine thumbnails
      if (i < album.numPhotos())
         displayPanel.add(display[i]);

      // place the three panels in the frame
      add(titlePanel, BorderLayout.NORTH);
      add(buttonPanel,BorderLayout.SOUTH);
      add(displayPanel, BorderLayout.CENTER);

      // reset nextPicture
      if (album.numPhotos() < 9)
         nextPicture = 0;
      else
         nextPicture = 9;

      setVisible(true);
```

```
126.         // create an empty PictureFrame object that displays a photo
127.         PictureFrame = new PictureFrame();
128.     }
129.     // responds to button events
130.     private class ButtonListener implements ActionListener
131.     {
132.         // method in the ActionListener interface
133.         public void actionPerformed(ActionEvent e)
134.         {
135.             if (e.getSource() == nextButton)
136.             {
137.                 remove(displayPanel);                // the current display of thumbnails
138.                 displayPanel = new JPanel();
139.                 displayPanel.setLayout(new GridLayout(3, 3));
140.                 for(int i = 1; i <= 9; i++)          // display next 9 thumbnails
141.                 {
142.                     displayPanel.add(display[nextPicture]);
143.                     // increment nextPicture and wrap around to 0
144.                     nextPicture = (nextPicture + 1) % album.numPhotos();
145.                 }
146.                 add(displayPanel, BorderLayout.CENTER);
147.                 validate();                 // layout the components of the frame again
148.             }
149.             else if (e.getSource() == exitButton)
150.             {
151.                 System.exit(0);
152.             }
153.             else  // determine which thumbnail button was clicked
154.                 for(int i = 0; i < (album.numPhotos()); i++)
155.                 {
156.                     if (e.getSource() == display[i])             // clicked on a thumbnail
157.                     {
158.                         PictureFrame.changePhoto(album.getPhoto(i)); // change the large photo
159.                         PictureFrame.setVisible(true);
160.                         return;
161.                     }
162.                 }
163.         }
164.     }
165.     public static void main(String[] args)
166.     {
167.         ManagePhotos frame = new ManagePhotos();
168.     }
169. }
```

Output Figure 19.9 shows the initial tray of thumbnail pictures. Clicking the third picture in the first row displays the frame of Figure 19.10.

Discussion

Lines 1–36: The PhotoAlbum Class

Lines 14–21: The photos and thumbnails are added to the appropriate lists. The photos are stored in files conveniently named photo*i*.jpg and thumbnail*i*.jpg. The condition of the while loop on line 14:

```
new File("Pompeii/thumbnail" + picNum + ".jpg").exists()
```

returns true if a file with the name thumbnail*i*.jpg, where *i* = 0, 1, 2, . . ., exists. After loading the last pair of thumbnail and full-size photos, the condition on line 14 returns false and the loop terminates.

Lines 37–63: The PictureFrame Class

This class is very simple. Its purpose is to display a single image. Initially, an empty label is placed in a panel, which in turn is placed in the CENTER section of a frame. The method changePhoto(ImageIcon image) places image in the label. See Figure 19.10.

Lines 64–169: The ManagePhotos Class

This class extends JFrame. Figure 19.9 shows a frame created using this class. The frame has three panels.

In the NORTH section of the frame is a panel, titlePanel, which is declared on line 76 and holds a label, titleLabel, declared on line 75. The panel and label are instantiated in the constructor on lines 85–90. The statements on lines 85–90 also set the font and foreground color of the label.

The CENTER section of the frame shows a 3 by 3 grid of nine buttons. Each button displays a thumbnail version of a larger photo. The statement on line 73 declares display as an array of thumbnail buttons, and the statement on line 74 declares the panel, displayPanel, that holds the buttons. The array referenced by display is created on line 104 and populated with JButton references on line 107. On line 108, each button registers a listener.

The loop on lines 113–115 adds (at most) nine buttons to the panel.

The SOUTH section of the frame of Figure 19.9 holds a panel, buttonPanel, with two buttons, nextButton and exitButton. These JButton references are declared on lines 70–71 and instantiated in the constructor (lines 92 and 95). If there are nine or fewer pictures, the nextButton is disabled (lines 93–94). Each button registers a listener (lines 100–101).

The three panels are placed in the frame using the default BorderLayout layout manager (lines 117–119).

In addition to the components of the frame, a PictureFrame reference is declared on line 77 and a PictureFrame object instantiated on line 127. This frame holds one large photo. Initially, this frame is not visible.

The inner class ButtonListener (lines 130–163) responds to button events.

If the source of an event is nextButton, the listener handles the event by

- removing the panel of thumbnails currently displayed in the frame (line 137),
- creating a new panel (lines 138 and 139),
- placing the next nine thumbnail buttons in the panel (lines 140–145),
- adding the panel to the frame (line 146), and
- *validating* the frame, that is, laying out the frame's components again (line 147).

The integer variable nextPicture (declared on line 78) holds the number of the next picture that is placed in the display panel. Initially nextPicture is 0. After the first nine pictures are placed, nextPicture has the value 9. Note that the first nine pictures are numbered 0 through 8. The variable nextPicture is updated on line 144. The value of nextPicture returns to 0 after it reaches the number of the last photo. This is accomplished with the % operator (line 144).

If the event source is exitButton the application exits (lines 149–152). Otherwise, the event source is one of the thumbnail buttons. When the particular button is determined (line 156), a new photo is placed in the frame referenced by PictureFrame, and that frame is made visible (lines 158–159).

19.6 TEXT FIELDS

A *text field* holds one line of text (a string) and can be used for input or output.

See Figure 19.11.

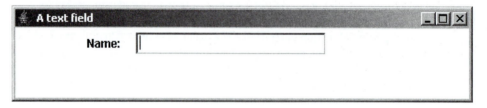

FIGURE 19.11 A text field in a frame

Here are the basics:

Class: JTextField

Generates: ActionEvent when a user presses the Enter key.

Listener: Must implement ActionListener

Listener method to implement: void actionPerformed(ActionEvent e)

Register a listener: void addActionListener(ActionListener a)

Constructors:

- JTextField(int numColumns)
  creates a JTextField object with numColumns columns that are visible. The initial string of the text field is the empty string, that is, the string with no characters.
- JTextField(String text)
  creates a JTextField object and initializes the text to text, which is shown with enough columns to display the entire string.
- JTextField(String text, int numColumns)
  creates a JTextField object with numColumns columns and initial text, text.

Methods:

- void setText(String text)
  places text in the text field.
- String getText()
  returns the text in a text field.
- void setEditable(boolean editable)
  if editable is false, the string in the text field is read-only, that is, it cannot be changed.
- boolean isEditable()
  returns false if the text field is read-only.

- void setColums(int numColums)
  sets the number of columns that are displayed by the text field.
- int getColumns()
  returns the number of columns that are displayed by the text field.
- void setFont(Font font)
  set the font to font.
- void setHorizontalAlignment (int alignment) alignment is
  JTextField.LEFT, JTextField.RIGHT, or JTextField.CENTER. The default is LEFT.

Example 19.4 uses a text field for input.

19.6.1 A Loan Calculator—*JTextField* in Action

EXAMPLE 19.4

The following formula determines the monthly payment on a loan such that:

- *amount* is the amount borrowed,
- *interest* is the yearly percent interest rate (e.g., 6.5), and
- *years* is the duration of the loan in years.

$$payment = amount\left[\frac{interest/1200.0}{1-\left(1+\dfrac{interest}{1200.0}\right)^{-12\,(years)}}\right]$$

Problem Statement Design an application that accepts

- the amount of a loan,
- the duration (in years) of the loan, and
- the yearly interest rate
  and calculates the monthly payment. Use three text fields for input and an additional text field for output.

Java Solution The following solution utilizes two classes:

- LoanPayment, a utility class with a single static method

  double getPayment(double amount, double interest, double years)

  that calculates and returns the monthly payment, and
- LoanCalculator, a class that extends JFrame, with three text fields for input and one for output. See Figure 19.12.

```
// A utility class with a static method that returns a loan payment rounded to two decimal places //
public class LoanPayment
{
   public static double getPayment(double amount, double interest, double years)
   {
      double payment =
            amount * ((interest / 1200.0) / (1 – Math.pow(1 + interest/1200.0, –years * 12)));
      return(Math.round(payment * 100)) / 100.00;          // rounds to 2 decimal places
   }
}
```

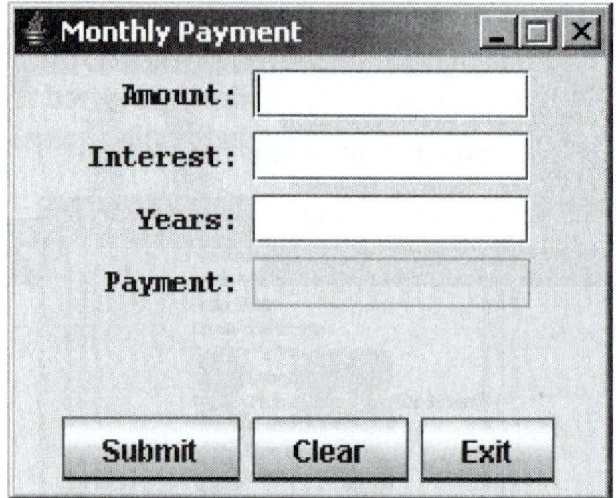

FIGURE 19.12 A loan calculator GUI

////////////// Loan Calculator Class //////////////

```
import java.awt.*;
import javax.swing.*;
import java.awt.event.*;

public class LoanCalculator extends JFrame
{
   private JTextField amountField;
   private JTextField interestField;
   private JTextField yearsField;
   private JTextField paymentField;
   private JButton submitButton;
   private JButton clearButton;
   private JButton exitButton;

   public LoanCalculator()                              // constructor
   {
      super("Monthly Payment");
      setBounds(0, 0, 250, 200);
      JPanel panel = new JPanel();                       // for text fields and labels

      // make a label for each text field
      // add the labels and text fields to the panel

      JLabel amountLabel = new JLabel();
      amountLabel.setFont(new Font("Courier", Font.BOLD, 12));
      amountLabel.setText("   Amount:");
      amountField = new JTextField(10);
      panel.add(amountLabel);                           // place the label in the panel
      panel.add(amountField);                           // place the text field in the panel

      JLabel interestLabel = new JLabel();
      interestLabel.setFont(new Font("Courier", Font.BOLD, 12));
      interestLabel.setText("Interest:");
      interestField = new JTextField(10);
      panel.add(interestLabel);
      panel.add(interestField);

      JLabel yearsLabel = new JLabel();
      yearsLabel.setFont(new Font("Courier", Font.BOLD, 12));
```

```
        yearsLabel.setText("   Years:");
        yearsField = new JTextField(10);
        panel.add(yearsLabel);
        panel.add(yearsField);

        JLabel paymentLabel = new JLabel();
        paymentLabel.setFont(new Font("Courier", Font.BOLD, 12));
        paymentLabel.setText(" Payment:");
        paymentField = new JTextField(10);
        panel.add(paymentLabel);
        panel.add(paymentField);
        paymentField.setEditable(false);                  // read-only

        add(panel, BorderLayout.CENTER);                  // add the panel to the frame

        // add three buttons to the bottom of the frame

        JPanel buttonPanel = new JPanel();                // holds the buttons
        submitButton = new JButton("Submit");             // calculates
        exitButton = new JButton("Exit");                 // ends application
        clearButton = new JButton("Clear");               // clears all fields
        buttonPanel.add(submitButton);                    // add buttons to buttonPanel
        buttonPanel.add(clearButton);
        buttonPanel.add(exitButton);
        add(buttonPanel, BorderLayout.SOUTH);             // add buttonPanel to bottom of frame

        // register a listener with each button

        submitButton.addActionListener(new ButtonListener());
        clearButton.addActionListener(new ButtonListener());
        exitButton.addActionListener(new ButtonListener());

        setResizable(false);
        setVisible(true);
        setDefaultCloseOperation(JFrame.EXIT_ON_CLOSE);
    }

    private class ButtonListener implements ActionListener    // responds to the button events
    {
        public void actionPerformed(ActionEvent e)        // method of ActionListener
        {
            if (e.getSource() == submitButton)            // calculates payment
                try                                       // DoubleParseDouble() throws NumberFormatException
                {
                    // retrieve data from the text fields; the data are strings
                    // use Double.parseDouble(..) to convert the strings to numbers
                    double amount = Double.parseDouble(amountField.getText());
                    double interest = Double.parseDouble(interestField.getText());
                    double years = Double.parseDouble(yearsField.getText());
                    double payment = LoanPayment.getPayment(amount, interest, years);
                    // setText() requires a String reference, payment + "" returns a String
                    paymentField.setText(payment + "");
                }
                catch(NumberFormatException ex)           // if a text field has bad data
                {
                    paymentField.setText("Illegal Input");
                }

            else if (e.getSource() == clearButton)        // clear all fields
```

```
92.            {
93.                amountField.setText("");
94.                interestField.setText("");
95.                yearsField.setText("");
96.                paymentField.setText("");
97.            }
98.            else
99.                System.exit(0);
100.       }
101.   }

102.   public static void main(String[] args)
103.   {
104.       LoanCalculator frame = new LoanCalculator();
105.   }

106. }
```

Output Figure 19.13 shows the results of running the program twice, once with good data in and once with illegal data.

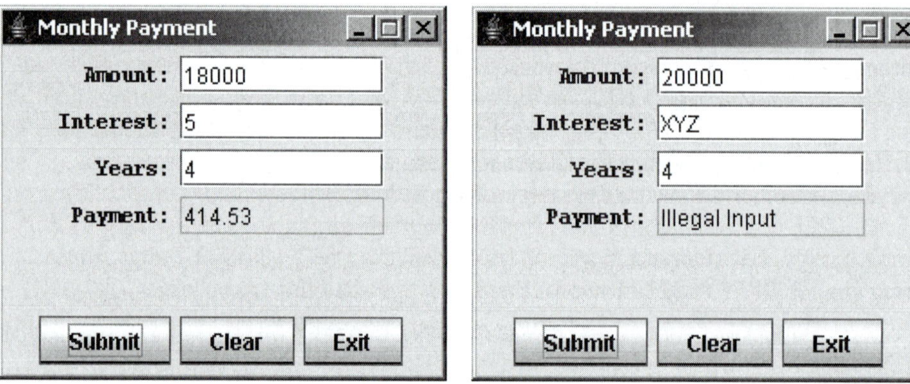

FIGURE 19.13 *LoanCalculator*: with legal and illegal data

Discussion

Lines 1–8: The LoanPayment class provides a single utility method that returns the monthly payment (double) when values are supplied to parameters amount, interest, and years. The return value is rounded to two decimal places (line 6). For example, if

payment = 1000.**34**8456765, then
payment * 100 = 1000**34**.8456765, and
round(payment * 100) = round(100034.8456765) = 1000**35**, and finally
round(payment * 100) / 100.00 = 100035/100.00 = 1000.**35**.

Lines 14–20: These statements are the declarations for the components that are shown in Figure 19.12.

Lines 21–70: The default constructor
Figure 19.12 shows four labeled text fields. Consequently, there are four groups of statements that instantiate the four text field/label pairs, set the

characteristics, and place the components in the panel that is instantiated on line 25. The statement groups are lines 28–33, 34–39, 40–45, and 46–51. Each statement group

- instantiates a label (lines 28, 34, 40, 46)
- sets the font for the label (lines 29, 35, 41, 47)
- sets the name of the label (lines 30, 36, 42, 48)
- instantiates a text field (lines 31, 37, 43, 49)
- places the label in a panel (lines 32, 38, 44, 50)
- places the text field in a panel (lines 33, 39, 45, 51)

The payment field is not editable (line 52).
Finally, the panel is added to the frame (line 53).

The visual layout of the labels and text fields consists of four rows because the width of the panel is just large enough to hold a single label/text field pair. Because the panel is not resizable, its width is constant. If the panel were resizable, the four labels and four text fields might stretch into longer and fewer rows.

Lines 55–62 handle the buttons that are shown in Figure 19.12. That is, three JButton objects are created and placed in a panel. The panel is then added to the SOUTH section of the frame. Finally, a listener is registered with each button (lines 64–66).

Lines 71–101: The ButtonListener class

To respond to a button-generated event, ButtonListener must implement the ActionListener interface and consequently the ActionPerformed(ActionEvent e) method. When an event occurs, an ActionEvent object is passed to ActionPerformed(...), which handles the response. The event source can be submitButton, clearButton, or exitButton.

The code on lines 75–90 handles the response to an event generated by submitButton. The listener responds by:

- retrieving the values in the text fields labeled Amount, Interest, and Years (lines 80–82),
- passing these values to the getPayment(...) method belonging to LoanCalculator (line 83), and
- placing the return value in the text field labeled Payment (line 85).

To calculate the monthly payment, the three strings returned by getText() must be converted to numerical (double) data. This is done via calls to Double.parseDouble(String s) (lines 80–82).

If a user enters faulty data such as "100x" into one of the text fields, Double.parseDouble(String s) throws a NumberFormatException exception. The exception is caught by the catch block of lines 87–90.

The response to an event generated by clearButton is handled by the code of lines 91–97. The response is simple: all text fields are set to the empty string.

The response to an exitButton event is a call to System.exit(0) (line 99).

Finally, note that the listener does not receive events generated by the text field. Indeed, the text field does not register any listener. If the Enter key is pressed, an event is generated but no listener responds. Only an event fired by a button merits a response.

19.7 TEXT AREAS

A text field holds a single line of data; a *text area* holds multiple lines.

The number of lines and the length of each line of a text area are defined in the constructor. Moreover, a text area can also display horizontal and vertical *scroll bars*, if desired. See Figure 19.14.

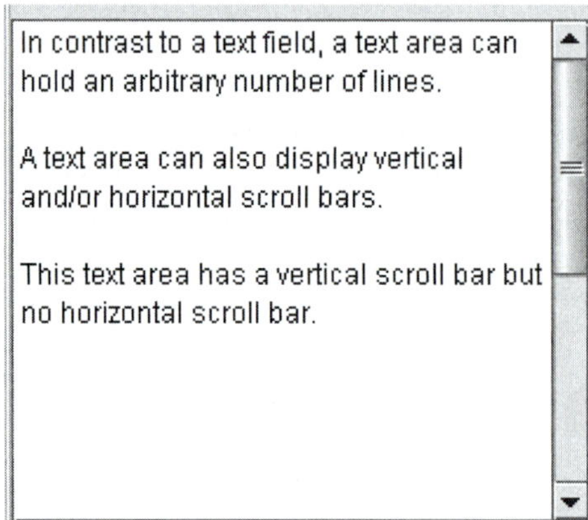

FIGURE 19.14 A text area with a vertical scroll bar

Here are the basics:

Class: JTextArea

Generates: ActionEvent when a user presses the Enter key.

Listener: Must implement ActionListener.

Listener method to implement: void actionPerformed(ActionEvent e)

Register a listener: void addActionListener(ActionListener a)

Constructors:

- public JTextArea()
  instantiates a JTextArea object that displays no initial text.
- public JTextArea(String text)
  instantiates a JTextArea object that displays the string text.
- public JTextArea(int rows, int cols)
  instantiates a JTextArea object with rows rows and cols columns and displays no initial text.
- public JTextArea(String text, int rows, int cols)
  instantiates a JTextArea object with rows rows and cols columns and displays the string text.

The methods of JTextField are also applicable to JTextArea. Additionally, the following methods are also available:

- void append(String text)
  appends text to the end of a text area.
- void insert (String text, int place)
  inserts text at position place.

- void replaceRange(String text, int start, int end)
  replaces the characters from position start to position end with text.
- void setLineWrap(boolean wrap)
  if wrap is set to true, lines that exceed the allocated number of colums of a text area will wrap to the next line. The default is false.
- boolean getLineWrap()
  returns true if line wrapping is enabled.
- void setWrapStyleWord(boolean wrap)
  if line wrap is enabled and wrap is set to true then lines wrap only at whitespace. That is, no single word appears on two lines.
- boolean getWrapStyleWord()
  returns true if word wrapping is enabled.
- void setRows(int rows)
  sets the number of rows of a text area to rows.
- int getRows()
  returns the number of visible rows.
- int getLineCount()
  returns the number of lines displayed in a text area. Lines are determined by the newline character. A wrapped line does not constitute two lines.

In addition to the text area methods, JTextArea and JTextField inherit the following methods familiar to anyone who has used a word processor or text editor. These methods are inherited from JTextComponent.

- void copy()
  copies selected text to the system clipboard. Text is selected as you normally select text when using an editor or a word processor.
- void cut()
  removes the selected text from the text area (field) and moves the text to the system clipboard.
- void paste()
  places the contents of the system clipboard into the text area (field). If text in the component has been selected, that text is replaced. If text is not selected, the clipboard text is inserted at the position of the cursor.
- void selectAll()
  marks as selected all the text in the component.

Finally, even if you have not read Chapter 15 (Stream I/O), you can easily use the following two methods that read data from a file into a text area and write the data of a text area to a file.

- read (Reader in, Object o) throws IOException

  initializes the text area using the Reader stream in. For our purposes, o should be set to null. The following statements read the contents of myFile.txt into text area textArea:

  ```
  FileReader in = new FileReader("myFile.txt");
  textArea.read(in, null);    // the contents of myFile.txt is read into the text area.
  in.close();
  ```

  Because FileReader *is-a* Reader, the upcast causes no problem.
- write (Writer out) throws IOException

writes the contents of a text area to the Writer stream. The following segment writes the contents of textArea to a text file, output.txt:

```
FileWriter out = new FileWriter("output.txt");
textArea.write(out);
out.close();
```

19.7.1 Scroll Bars

Scroll bars are often a necessary addition to a text area.

> You can add a scroll bar to a text area by placing a text area in a *scroll pane*.

Although we do not discuss the JScrollPane class in any detail, the following code segments demonstrate how you can add scroll bars to a text area. If you prefer that horizontal and vertical scroll bars appear only when necessary (the default), pass a JTextArea reference to JScrollPane:

```
private JTextArea textArea = new JTextArea();
JScrollPane scrollArea = new JScrollPane(textArea);
```

Or, you can set the scroll bar policy with the following segment:

```
private JTextArea textArea = new JTextArea();
JScrollPane scrollArea =
    new JScrollPane(textArea, int verticalPolicy, int horizontalPolicy);
```

where verticalPolicy is one of:

- ScrollPaneConstants.VERTICAL_SCROLLBAR_AS_NEEDED
- ScrollPaneConstants.VERTICAL_SCROLLBAR_ALWAYS
- ScrollPaneConstants.VERTICAL_SCROLLBAR_NEVER

and horizontalPolicy is one of:

- ScrollPaneConstants.HORIZONTAL_SCROLLBAR_AS_NEEDED
- ScrollPaneConstants.HORIZONTAL_SCROLLBAR_ALWAYS
- ScrollPaneConstants.HORIZONTAL_SCROLLBAR_NEVER

Example 19.5 uses two text areas, one text field, and four buttons to decipher a coded message.

19.7.2 Encryption with GUI—Using *JTextArea*

EXAMPLE 19.5 A *Caesar cipher* is an encryption method that replaces each letter of some text with another letter that is a fixed number of positions farther down in the alphabet. For example, a *3-shift* replaces A with D, B with E, W with Z, and cycling back, X with A, Y with B, and Z with C. So, a 3-shift encodes CAESAR as FDHVDU; but a 15-shift encodes CAESAR as RPTHPH.

Breaking a Caesar cipher requires trying up to 25 different shifts. While that may have been a tedious task for Roman cryptographers, it is no challenge at all for modern-day Java programmers.

Problem Statement Write an application that displays two text areas, a text field, and five buttons. A user enters a character shift number (0–25) in the text field and, in one text area, a message, either coded or uncoded. If the message is uncoded, the user clicks a button labeled Encode and a coded version appears in the second text field. An uncoded message may contain punctuation and whitespace that will be removed when encoded. Encoded messages are comprised of uppercase letters with no punctuation or whitespace. If the original message is a coded message, the Decode button produces a version of the message using the supplied shift number. The decoded message may make sense or it may not, depending on whether or not the shift value is correct.

A Move button transfers a message from the output area to the input area. This allows you to transfer a coded message to the input box without retyping the message. A Clear button clears all text areas. See Figure 19.15.

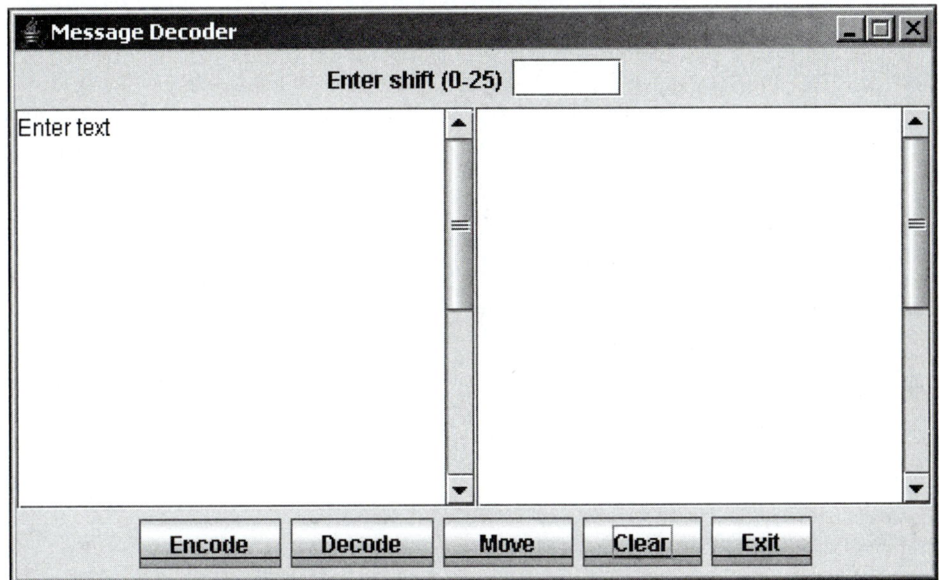

FIGURE 19.15 The left text area is for input, the right for output

Java Solution The following solution consists of two classes:

- The CaesarCipher class is a utility class that consists of two static methods: one method encodes a string using a shift in the range 0–25. The second method decodes a message.
- The Decoder class extends JFrame and sets up the GUI shown in Figure 19.15. The constructor sets up the GUI and an inner class, ButtonListener, responds to events generated by the five GUI buttons. The Encode button invokes CaesarCipher.code(String msg, int shift) and the Decode button CaesarCipher.decode(String msg, int shift).

```
public class CaesarCipher
{
  public static String code(String msg, int shift)
  {
     // Encodes msg using the supplies shift
     // Shift must be an integer in the range 0 – 25
     // Returns the encoded message

     String codedMessage = new String();
     msg = msg.toUpperCase();                    // change all letters to uppercase
     for (int i = 0; i < msg.length(); i++)      // for each letter of the message
     {
```

```
            char ch = msg.charAt(i);
            if (ch >= 'A' && ch <= 'Z')                // do not include punctuation or whitespace
            {
                int oldPositionInAlphabet = ch - 'A';     // 0 to 25
                int newPositionInAlphabet = (oldPositionInAlphabet + shift) % 26;            // %26 enables cycling
                codedMessage = codedMessage + (char)(newPositionInAlphabet + 'A');  // ASCII value
            }
        }
        return codedMessage;
    }

    public static String decode(String msg, int shift)
    {
        // Decodes msg using the supplies shift
        // Shift must be an integer in the range 0 - 25
        // Returns the decoded message

        String decodedMessage = new String();
        for (int i = 0; i < msg.length(); i++)                        // for each letter of the message
        {
            char ch = msg.charAt(i);
            int oldPositionInAlphabet = ch - 'A';                     // 0..25
            int newPositionInAlphabet = (oldPositionInAlphabet - shift);
            if (newPositionInAlphabet < 0)
                newPositionInAlphabet = newPositionInAlphabet + 26;
            decodedMessage = decodedMessage + (char)(newPositionInAlphabet + 'A');
        }
        return decodedMessage;
    }
}

import java.awt.*;
import javax.swing.*;
import java.awt.event.*;

public class Decoder extends JFrame
{
    private JTextArea inputTextArea;
    private JTextArea outputTextArea;
    private JTextField shiftTextField;
    private JButton encodeButton;
    private JButton decodeButton;
    private JButton clearButton;
    private JButton moveButton;                          // move text from output area to input area
    private JButton exitButton;

    public Decoder() // constructor
    {
        super("Message Decoder");
        setBounds(0, 0, 500, 300);
        JPanel topPanel = new JPanel();      // for the text field
        JLabel shiftLabel = new JLabel("Enter shift (0-25)");
        shiftTextField = new JTextField(5);
        topPanel.add(shiftLabel);
        topPanel.add(shiftTextField);

        JPanel buttonPanel = new JPanel();
        encodeButton = new JButton("Encode");
        decodeButton = new JButton("Decode");
        moveButton = new JButton(" Move ");
        clearButton = new JButton("Clear");
        exitButton = new JButton("Exit");
        buttonPanel.add(encodeButton);
```

```
        buttonPanel.add(decodeButton);
        buttonPanel.add(moveButton);
        buttonPanel.add(clearButton);
        buttonPanel.add(exitButton);

        JPanel textPanel = new JPanel(new GridLayout(1, 2));       // two text areas
        inputTextArea = new JTextArea("Enter Text", 25, 20);       // include directions in the input area
        outputTextArea = new JTextArea(25, 20);
        inputTextArea.setLineWrap(true);
        outputTextArea.setLineWrap(true);
        outputTextArea.setEditable(false);

        // Get Scroll Panes for the TextAreas

        JScrollPane inputPane = new JScrollPane(inputTextArea);   // scroll bars if necessary
        JScrollPane outputPane = new JScrollPane(outputTextArea);
        textPanel.add(inputPane);
        textPanel.add(outputPane);

        // Place the three panels in the frame

        add(topPanel, BorderLayout.NORTH);
        add(buttonPanel, BorderLayout.SOUTH);
        add(textPanel, BorderLayout.CENTER);

        // register listener with the buttons

        encodeButton.addActionListener(new ButtonListener());
        decodeButton.addActionListener(new ButtonListener());
        moveButton.addActionListener(new ButtonListener());
        clearButton.addActionListener(new ButtonListener());
        exitButton.addActionListener(new ButtonListener());

        setResizable(false);
        setVisible(true);
        setDefaultCloseOperation(JFrame.EXIT_ON_CLOSE);
    } // end of constructor

    // Listener class for the buttons
    private class ButtonListener implements ActionListener
    {
        public void actionPerformed(ActionEvent e)
        {

            if ( e.getSource() == encodeButton)
                try                                 // shift must be an integer, 0..25, or an exception is thrown
                {
                    int shift = Integer.parseInt(shiftTextField.getText());
                    if (shift > 25 || shift < 0)
                        throw new Exception();
                    String inputText = inputTextArea.getText();
                    String outputText = CaesarCipher.code(inputText,shift);
                    outputTextArea. setText(outputText);
                    inputTextArea.cut();
                }
                catch(Exception ex)
                {
                    outputTextArea.setText("Illegal shift");
                }
            else if ( e.getSource() == decodeButton)
                try                                 // shift must be an integer, 0..25, or an exception is thrown
                {
                    int shift = Integer.parseInt(shiftTextField.getText());
```

```
                if (shift > 25 || shift < 0)
                   throw new Exception();
                String inputText = inputTextArea.getText();
                String outputText = CaesarCipher.decode(inputText, shift);
                outputTextArea.setText(outputText);
             }
             catch (Exception ex)
             {
                outputTextArea.setText("Illegal shift");
             }
          else if (e.getSource() == clearButton)
             // clears text areas and the text field
          {
             outputTextArea.setText("");
             inputTextArea.setText("Enter text");
             shiftTextField.setText("");
          }
          else if (e.getSource() == moveButton)
             // move text from outputTextArea to inputTextArea
          {
             inputTextArea.setText(outputTextArea.getText());
             outputTextArea.setText("");
          }
          else
             System.exit(0);
       }
    }
    public static void main(String[] args)
    {
       Decoder frame = new Decoder();
    }
}
```

Output The message displayed in the left text area of Figure 19.16 is an English version of a message that Julius Caesar reportedly sent to his good friend, Mark Antony. Trusting no one, Caesar encrypted his message using a 13 character shift. The encoded message appears in the second text area.

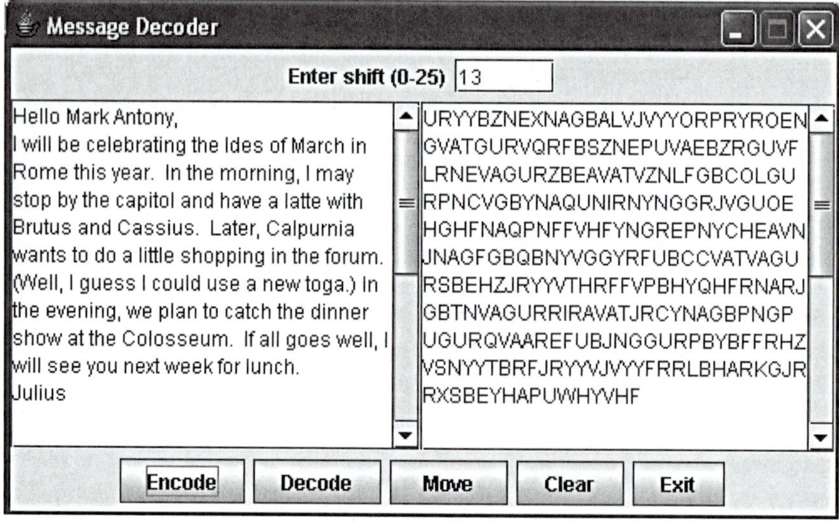

FIGURE 19.16 An uncoded and a coded message

Clicking the Move button transfers the encoded message to the left text area. Then, clicking the Decode button, with shift 13, decodes the message back to the original, but without punctuation or whitespace. See Figure 19.17.

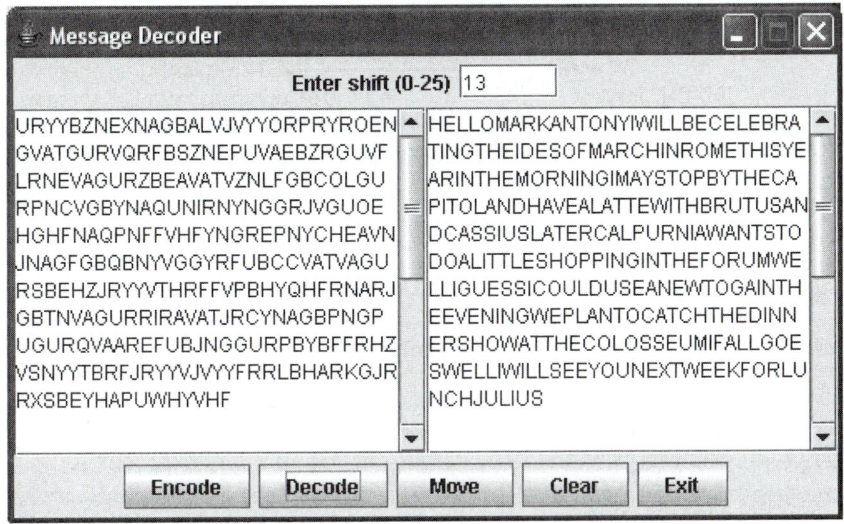

FIGURE 19.17 The coded message of Figure 19.16 now decoded

Discussion

Lines 53–97: The Constructor

The statements on lines 57–61:

- create a panel, a label ("Enter shift (0–25)") and a text field, and
- place the two components in the panel.

The statements on lines 62–72:

- create a panel for the five buttons,
- instantiate five JButton objects, and
- place the buttons in the panel.

The statements on lines 73–83:

- create a panel, two text areas, and two scroll panes that provide the text areas with scroll bars as needed, and
- place the scroll panes in the panel.

The statements on lines 85–87 add the three panels to the frame.
The statements on lines 89–93 register a listener with each button.

Lines 98–152: The ButtonListener class

The ButtonListener class responds to the events generated by the five buttons placed at the SOUTH section of the frame. Because a button generates an action event, the ButtonListener class implements the ActionListener interface with its single method, actionPerformed(ActionEvent e). There are five buttons, and consequently actionPerformed(...) has five distinct code sections, each of which respond to a particular event.

- The statements on lines 103–117 handle an event generated by encodeButton. Notice the try-catch construction. If the text field has an illegal entry such as a number out of the range 0–25 or an ill-formed integer such as *XIII,* the method throws an exception. The single statement of the catch block displays "Illegal shift" in the output text area. If no exception occurs, the text displayed in inputTextArea and the number shown in shiftTextField are passed to CaesarCipher.encode(String msg, int shift). The encoded string is displayed in outputTextArea. Because encode(…) is static, the method can be invoked using the class name, CaesarCipher.

- The statements on lines 118–131 respond to an event generated by decodeButton in much the same way as the code of lines 103–117.
- The statements on line 132–138 respond to an event generated by clearButton by setting the text of outputTextArea and shiftTextField to the empty string and resetting inputTextArea to "Enter text."
- The statements on lines 139–144 respond to a moveButton event by invoking getText() to retrieve the text displayed in outputTextArea, and setText(...) to place that text in the input area. Finally, the text of outputTextArea is set to the empty string.
- Line 146, a call to System.exit(0), is a response to an event generated by exitButton.

19.8 DIALOG BOXES

A *dialog box* is a pop-up window that is used for both input and output.

Dialog boxes provide specific but simple functionality that could otherwise be built from labels, buttons, and listeners but with more effort (see Short Exercise 5). However, dialog boxes effect input and output without your having to deal with events and listeners. Figure 19.18 shows a typical, and perhaps familiar, dialog box.

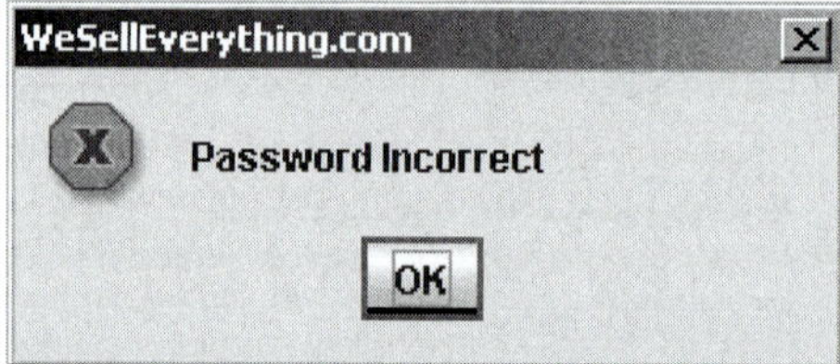

FIGURE 19.18 A message dialog box

Swing's JOptionPane class provides a few useful dialog boxes, including

- message dialog box,
- confirmation dialog box, and
- input dialog box.

19.8.1 The Message Dialog Box

A *message dialog box* displays a message and does nothing else.

Figure 19.18 shows a message dialog box. To incorporate a message dialog box into an application, invoke one of the static methods of JOptionPane:

- public static void showMessageDialog(Component parent, Object message);
- public static void showMessageDialog(Component parent, Object message, String title, int messageType);
- public static void showMessageDialog(Component parent, Object message, String title, int messageType, Icon icon);

such that

- parent is the parent component of the dialog box. Use null to signify the default component.
- message is the object that the dialog box displays. Technically, message can be any object: a button, a label, a text field. However, for the most part, message is a string.
- title is the text displayed on the title bar.
- messageType is one of the following constants:
  - JOptionPane.ERROR_MESSAGE (numerical value: 0)
  - JOptionPane.INFORMATION_MESSAGE (numerical value: 1)
  - JOptionPane.PLAIN_MESSAGE (numerical value: –1)
  - JOptionPane.WARNING_MESSAGE (numerical value: 2)
  - JOptionPane.QUESTION_MESSAGE (numerical value: 3)
- icon is an image that can be displayed on the dialog box.

The message dialog box of Figure 19.18 is the result of the following statement:

```
JOptionPane.showMessageDialog(null, "Password Incorrect",
                 "WeSellEverything.com", JOptionPane.ERROR_MESSAGE);
```

The icon displayed by the message is Java's standard icon that is displayed when messageType is passed:

```
JOptionPane.ERROR_MESSAGE.
```

Whenever messageType is passed by one of the JOptionPane constants, the system uses a standard icon in the dialog box. These are shown in Figure 19.19.

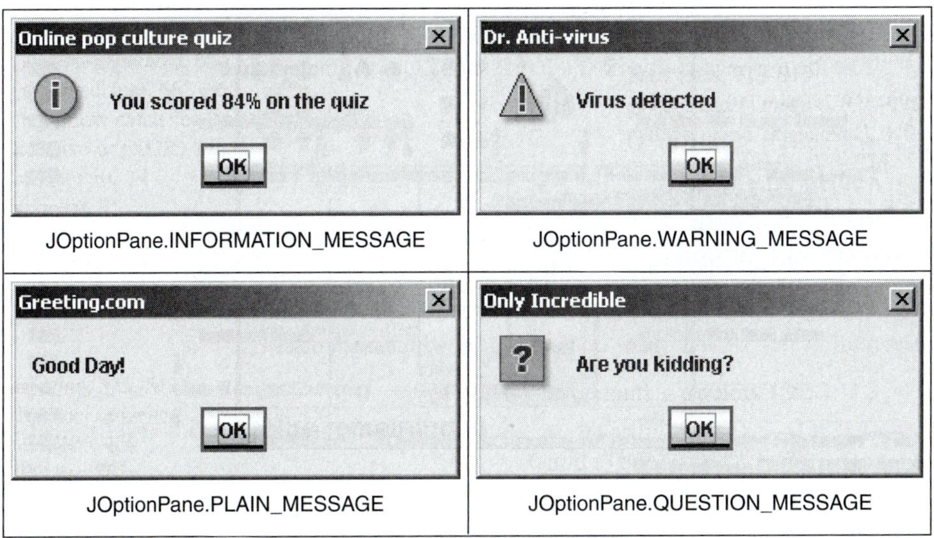

FIGURE 19.19 Four message dialog boxes

19.8.2 Confirmation Dialog Box

A *confirmation dialog box* displays a question, expects a reply, and returns an integer value.

See Figure 19.20.

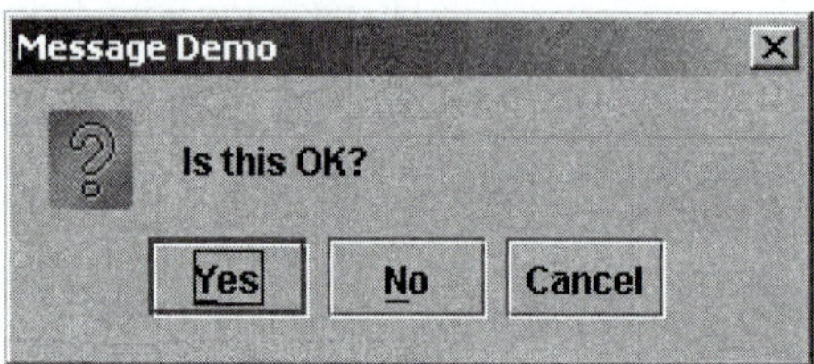

FIGURE 19.20 A confirmation dialog box

As with a message dialog box, you can use a confirmation dialog box by calling one of the static methods of JOptionPane:

- public static int showConfirmDialog(Component parent, Object message);
- public static int showConfirmDialog(Component parent, Object message, String title, int optionType);
- public static int showConfirmDialog(Component parent, Object message, String title, int optionType, int messageType);
- public static int showConfirmDialog(Component parent, Object message, String title, int optionType, int messageType, Icon icon);

The optionType parameter determines the options that appear as buttons. The parameter accepts one of the following JOptionPane constants:

- YES_NO_OPTION (numerical value: 0)
- YES_NO_CANCEL_OPTION (numerical value: 1)
- OK_CANCEL_OPTION (numerical value: 2)

If no option type is specified, the YES_NO_CANCEL_OPTION is the default.

Like the message dialog box, the messageType parameter can be one of the following constants:

- ERROR_MESSAGE
- INFORMATION_MESSAGE
- PLAIN_MESSAGE
- WARNING_MESSAGE
- QUESTION_MESSAGE

The return value, an integer, is one of the following constants:

- CANCEL_OPTION (numerical value: 2)
- CLOSED_OPTION (numerical value: –1, dialog closed without choosing one of the options)
- NO_OPTION (numerical value: 1)
- OK_OPTION (numerical value: 0)
- YES _OPTION (numerical value: 0)

A constant can be accessed as

JOptionPane.YES_NO_OPTION, or JOptionPane.YES_OPTION, etc.

The following segment uses the confirmation dialog box and the message dialog box to ask a question and get a reply. Figure 19.21 shows the dialog when a user chooses the "No" option.

```
int answer = JOptionPane.showConfirmDialog
                (null, "Are you having a good day?",
                "Greeting",   JOptionPane.YES_NO_CANCEL_OPTION,
                JOptionPane.QUESTION_MESSAGE);
if (answer == JOptionPane.NO_OPTION)
     JOptionPane.showMessageDialog(null, "Sorry about that", "Greeting",
                          JOptionPane.PLAIN_MESSAGE, new ImageIcon("frown.jpg") );
else if (answer == JOptionPane.YES_OPTION)
     JOptionPane.showMessageDialog(null,"I'm glad to hear that!",
                          "Greeting", JOptionPane.PLAIN_MESSAGE, new
ImageIcon("smiley.jpg") );
```

FIGURE 19.21 A confirmation dialog box and a message dialog box

19.8.3 Input Dialog Box

An *input dialog box* can be used to obtain string input from a user.

The available JOptionPane methods are:

- public static String showInputDialog(Object message),
- public static String showInputDialog(Component parent, Object message), and
- public static String showInputDialog(Component parent, Object message,
  String title, int messageType)

The parameters have the same meaning as the parameters of the message dialog box and the confirmation dialog box.

Indeed, you can substitute an input dialog box for a Scanner object in any of the interactive programs of the previous chapters. However, unlike the Scanner methods nextInt() or nextDouble(), an input dialog box always returns a String reference. The string returned by an input dialog box is either the string supplied by the user or null if the user chooses Cancel or closes the dialog box. This string can be converted to a numerical value, if necessary.

For example, the text-based segment

```
1.   Scanner input = new Scanner(System.in);
2.   System.out.println("Enter a number");
3.   try // if user supplies bad data
```

```
{
    double number = input.nextDouble();
    System.out.println("The square root of "+ number + "is "+ Math.sqrt(number));
}
catch (Exception e) // actually InputMismatchException
{
    System.out.println("Input Error");
}
```

can be rewritten using dialog boxes as

```
// get input from the user via an input dialog box; input is returned as a String reference
String numberString = JOptionPane.showInputDialog(null,
                                        "Enter a number:", "Square Root Calculator",
                                        JOptionPane.QUESTION_MESSAGE);
if (numberString != null)               // Cancel or Close option returns null
{
   // convert to double
   try    // if parseDouble() throws an exception
   {
       double number = Double.parseDouble(numberString);
       // display result with a message dialog box
       JOptionPane.showMessageDialog(null, "The square root of " + number + " is "
                                        + Math.sqrt(number),"Square Root Calculator",
                                        JOptionPane.INFORMATION_MESSAGE);
   }
   catch (NumberFormatException e)
   {
       JOptionPane.showMessageDialog(null, "Input error: " + numberString,
                              "Square Root Calculator", JOptionPane.ERROR_MESSAGE);
   }
}
```

Figure 19.22 shows dialogs that occur when the previous segment executes twice.

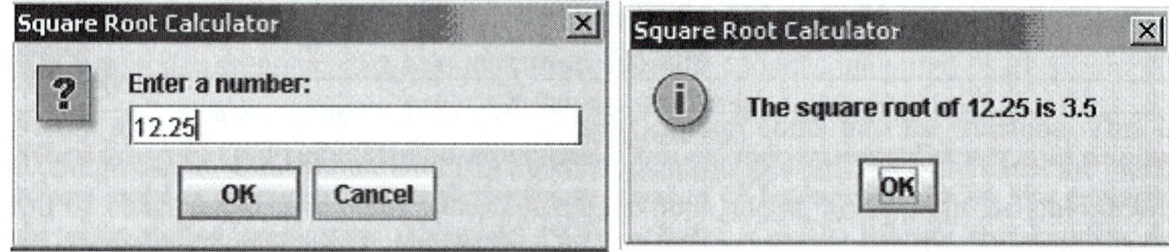

(a) Correct Input

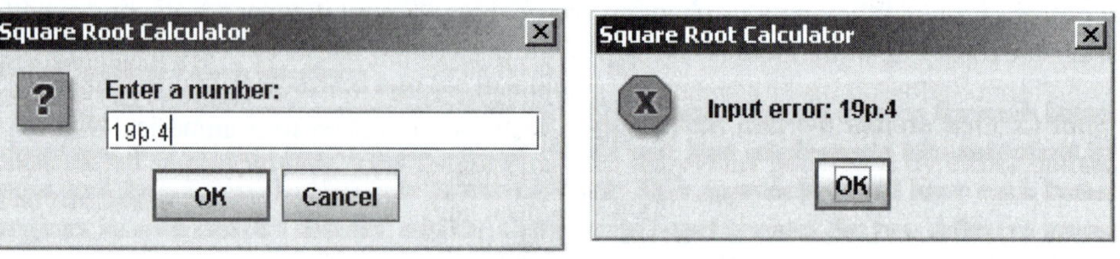

(b) Incorrect Input

FIGURE 19.22 Two dialogs: one using correct data, the other incorrect data

Swing also provides a version of the input dialog box that allows selection from a drop-down list of options. See Figure 19.23.

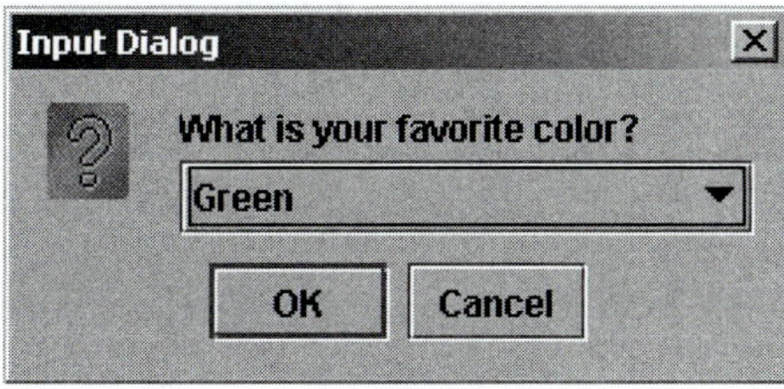

FIGURE 19.23 Input dialog box with a list of options

The JOptionPane method that displays an option dialog is:

```
public static Object showInputDialog(Component parent,
                                     Object message,
                                     String title,
                                     int messageType,
                                     Icon icon,
                                     Object [] options,
                                     Object selected)
```

The array, options, is a list of choices that appears in the drop-down box. This array can be an array of references to objects of any class, but it is usually an array of String references. The parameter selected gives the values that initialize the input. For the dialog box of Figure 19.23, selected is Green. The value of selected can be null. The value of icon can also be null. The return value belongs to Object and is usually cast to String.

The following short segment that utilizes an input dialog box and a message dialog box administers a personality test, of sorts.

```
String[] colors = {"Yellow", "Green", "Blue", "Red", "Orange"};          // options array

String choice = (String)JOptionPane.showInputDialog(null,"What is your favorite color",
                 "Psychology Test", JOptionPane.QUESTION_MESSAGE, null, colors,"Green");

if (choice ! = null)                             // can be null if user cancels or closes dialog box
{
   String personality = new String();
   if (choice .equals("Blue"))
      personality = " You are calm and compassionate";
   else if (choice .equals("Green"))
      personality = " You are sincere and sociable";
   else if (choice .equals("Yellow"))
      personality = " You are wise with a good business sense";
   else if (choice .equals("Red"))
      personality = " You are outgoing and ambitious";
   else if (choice .equals("Orange"))
      personality = " You are flamboyant and dramatic";
   JOptionPane.showMessageDialog(null, personality,
                      "Personality diagnosis", JOptionPane.INFORMATION_MESSAGE);
}
```

The logic of the fragment is simple. Notice that, on line 2, the return value is cast to String. Figure 19.24 illustrates a typical dialog.

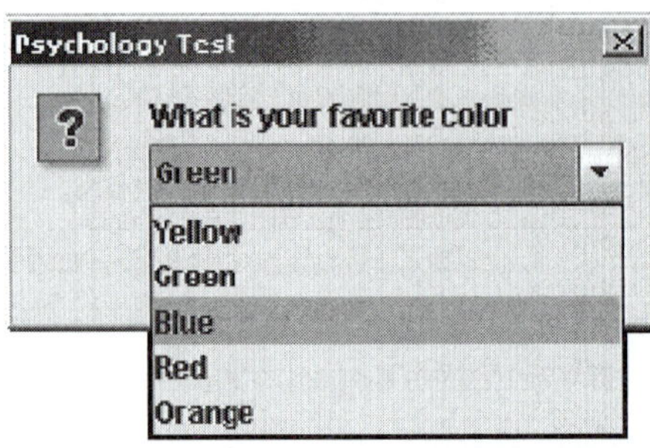

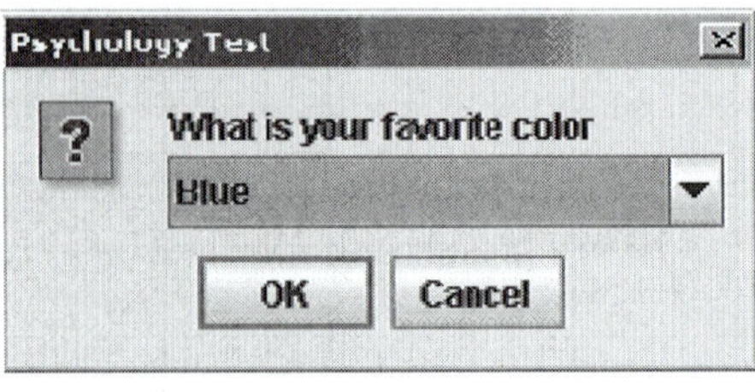

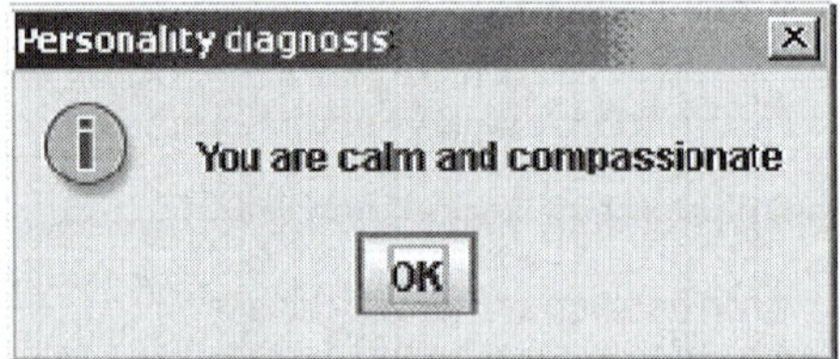

FIGURE 19.24 An input dialog using a drop-down list

19.9 MOUSE EVENTS

In previous examples, clicking a JButton object with the mouse results in an ActionEvent generated by the *button* rather than the mouse. Although the ActionEvent was triggered by clicking the mouse, this event is *not* the same as a MouseEvent. A MouseEvent is caused by any pressing, releasing, dragging, or moving the mouse, independent of the events generated by "clicked components." Processing MouseEvents facilitates drawing or dragging components on the screen.

A listener class that handles events fired by dragging and moving the mouse implements the MouseMotionListener interface with methods:

- void mouseDragged(MouseEvent e) and
- void mouseMoved(MouseEvent e)

A listener class that handles events generated by clicking the mouse, pressing the mouse, releasing the mouse, entering a component, or exiting a component implements MouseListener with methods:

- void mouseClicked(MouseEvent e)
  mouse is pressed and released
- void mouseEntered(MouseEvent e)
  mouse enters a component
- void mouseExited(MouseEvent e)
  mouse leaves a component
- void mousePressed(MouseEvent e)
  mouse is pressed
- void mouseReleased(MouseEvent e)
  mouse is released

The following small class that implements MouseListener changes the text on a label whenever the mouse enters or exits the label. The class implements the five methods of MouseListener, but three of these methods are empty. The label registers the listener.

```
public class MouseDemo extends JFrame
{
    JPanel panel;
    JLabel label;
    public MouseDemo()
    {
        setBounds(0, 0, 300, 300);
        panel = new JPanel();
        label = new JLabel("Start");
        panel.add(label);
        add(panel);
        setVisible(true);
        label.addMouseListener(new MouseHandler()); // label registers listener
        setDefaultCloseOperation(JFrame.EXIT_ON_CLOSE);
    }

    private class MouseHandler implements MouseListener
    {
        public void mousePressed(MouseEvent e){}      // empty methods
        public void mouseReleased(MouseEvent e){}
        public void mouseClicked(MouseEvent e){}

        public void mouseEntered(MouseEvent e)
        {
            label.setText("Mouse Entered");
        }
        public void mouseExited(MouseEvent e)
        {
            label.setText("Mouse Exited");
        }
    }
}
```

A few useful MouseEvent methods are:

- Component getComponent()
  returns component where the MouseEvent occurred.
- int getX()
  returns the horizontal coordinate of the event.
- int getY()
  returns the vertical coordinate of the event.
- Point getPoint()
  returns a reference to a two-dimensional Point object such that the public fields x and y hold the horizontal and vertical coordinates of the event.

Example 19.6 uses these methods to implement a simple paint program.

19.9.1 A Simple Paint Program

EXAMPLE 19.6 Graphics programs such as Microsoft Paint provide tools for drawing all types of predefined shapes as well as "freehand" sketches using the mouse. Paint provides "pencil drawing" as well as thick-lined paintbrush drawing and spray paint drawing. Each of these options utilizes the mouse like a pencil, a paintbrush, or a can of spray paint. Although we are not quite ready to build an entire graphics drawing application, we can implement a simple system that provides pencil drawing. All we need to do is respond to mouse events. The following application defines three listener classes, MouseButtonListener, MoveMouseListener, and ButtonListener, which implement MouseListener, MouseMotionListener, and ActionListener, respectively.

Problem Statement Implement a rather primitive drawing application that allows a user to pencil-draw figures by dragging the mouse. Drawing can be done using one of three colors chosen via an input dialog box. The application should also provide an Erase button that clears the screen. Figure 19.25 shows a pencil-drawn masterpiece.

FIGURE 19.25 A pencil-drawn masterpiece

Java Solution The artwork is accomplished by drawing tiny line segments that join "close" points. When the mouse is pressed, a "starting point" is recorded. As the user drags the mouse, lines are drawn from the start point to the current mouse position, then from that point to the next mouse position, and so on. For example, if the mouse is pressed at starting position (38, 32) and then dragged over (39, 32), (40, 32), (41, 33), and (41, 34), *very* short line segments are drawn connecting

(38, 32) and (39, 32),
(39, 32) and (40, 32),
(40, 32) and (41, 33), and
(41, 33) and (41, 34).

When the mouse button is released, line-drawing stops. The process involves three events,

mouse pressed, mouse dragged, and mouse released,

each of which requires a response.

The application defines three new classes: ColorPoint, PointData, and PencilDrawing, the GUI.

ColorPoint encapsulates a single screen point. A ColorPoint has three components:

- x, the horizontal coordinate,
- y, the vertical coordinate, and
- a color.

The class has three fields as well as the standard getter and setter methods.

PointData does all the bookkeeping for the application. PointData registers the starting point when the mouse is initially pressed and also keeps a list of every point over which the mouse is dragged, a history of points. Why do we need to save every point? Suppose, for example, that the frame is minimized and later restored. As you already know, when a frame is restored, paint(...) is automatically invoked. So that paint(…) can restore the frame *exactly* as it was, the application must override the default paint(...) method with a version that recreates the last drawing. If the application does not override paint(…), then whenever the frame is minimized and restored, the default paint(…) method paints an empty frame.

To accomplish this restoration correctly, an ArrayList of those points used to create the drawing is maintained. Each time the mouse is pressed, the program saves all the points over which the mouse is subsequently dragged. When the mouse is released, a null is inserted into this list of points, and no new points are saved until the mouse is pressed again. The null value marks a break between points so that no line is drawn between the last point of the one sequence of points and the first point of the next sequence. The overridden paint(…) method uses this ArrayList of points to repaint the image. The paint(…) method plays "connect the dots" with all of the points of the last drawn image, with the exception of the points separated by null.

The methods of the PointData class are the standard getter and setter methods along with a method that returns the number of saved points.

PencilDrawing extends JFrame and contains three inner classes:

- ButtonListener, which respond to button events,
- MoveMouseListener, which responds to "mouse dragged" events by drawing tiny line segments from point to point as the mouse is moved, and
- MouseButtonListener, which responds to events that occur when the mouse is pressed or released.

In addition to the listeners and constructors, PencilDrawing overrides paint(…) so that whenever a frame is repainted, the drawn image is not erased.

The frame fills the entire screen and is not resizable. However, the frame can be minimized and restored.

```
import java.awt.*;
import javax.swing.*;
import java.awt.event.*;
import java.util.*;

public class ColorPoint
{
   private Color color;
   private int x;                 // horizontal coordinate
   private int y;                 // vertical coordinate
   public ColorPoint()            // default constructor
   {
      color = Color.BLACK;
      x = 0;
      y = 0;
```

```
    }

    // three-argument constructor
    public ColorPoint(int x, int y, Color color)
    {
        this.x = x;
        this.y = y;
        this.color = color;
    }

    public void setX(int x)
    {
        this.x = x;
    }

    public void setY(int y)
    {
        this.y = y;
    }

    public void setColor(Color c)
    {
        color = c;
    }

    public void setColor(String c)   // set Color from a String description
    {                                // lists just a few possible colors
        if (c.equals("Red"))
            color = Color.RED;
        else if (c.equals("Blue"))
            color = Color.BLUE;
        else if (c.equals("Black"))
            color = Color.BLACK;
        else if (c.equals("Green"))
            color = Color.GREEN;
        else if (c.equals("Magenta"))
            color = Color.MAGENTA; // etc
    }

    public int getX()
    {
        return x;
    }

    public int getY()
    {
        return y;
    }

    public Color getColor()
    {
        return color;
    }
}
```

///////////////////////////// The PointData class /////////////////////////////

```
import java.util.*;     // for ArrayList
import java.awt.*;

public class PointData
```

```
{
   private ArrayList <ColorPoint> pointHistory;   // drawn points
   private final int capacity = 1000;             // initial capacity of ArrayList
   private ColorPoint startPoint;
   public PointData()
   {
      pointHistory = new ArrayList<ColorPoint>(capacity);
      startPoint = new ColorPoint();
   }

   public ColorPoint get(int i)
   {
      return pointHistory.get(i);
   }

   public void setColor(Color c)
   {
      startPoint.setColor(c);
   }

   public void setColor(String c)
   {
      startPoint.setColor(c);
   }

   public void add(ColorPoint p)
   {
      pointHistory.add(p);
   }

   public void setX(int x)
   {
      startPoint.setX(x);
   }

   public void setY(int y)
   {
      startPoint.setY(y);
   }

   public int getX()
   {
      return startPoint.getX();
   }

   public int getY()
   {
      return startPoint.getY();
   }

   public Color getColor()
   {
      return startPoint.getColor();
   }

   public int size()
   {
      return pointHistory.size();
   }

}
```

```
///////////////////////// The PencilDrawing class /////////////////////////

import java.awt.*;
import java.awt.event.*;
import javax.swing.*;

public class PencilDrawing extends JFrame
{
  private JButton eraseButton;                  // clears screen
  private JButton colorButton;                  // changes color
  private JButton exitButton;                   // ends application
  private JPanel paper;                         // the drawing surface
  private JPanel buttonPanel;                   // holds 3 buttons
  private PointData points ;                    // manages the data for the application

  public PencilDrawing()                        // default constructor
  {
     super("Pencil Draw");

     Toolkit tk = Toolkit.getDefaultToolkit();  // so that frame fills the screen
     Dimension dim = tk.getScreenSize();
     setBounds(0, 0, dim.width, dim.height);
     points = new PointData();

     // place buttons
     buttonPanel = new JPanel();
     eraseButton = new JButton("Erase");
     colorButton = new JButton("Color");
     exitButton = new JButton("Exit");
     buttonPanel.add(eraseButton);
     buttonPanel.add(colorButton);
     buttonPanel.add(exitButton);
     add(buttonPanel, BorderLayout.SOUTH);

     // place the drawing panel in the frame
     paper = new JPanel();
     add(paper);

     // register the mouse listeners
     addMouseListener(new MouseButtonListener());
     addMouseMotionListener(new MoveMouseListener());

     // register the button listeners
     eraseButton.addActionListener(new ButtonListener());
     colorButton.addActionListener(new ButtonListener());
     exitButton.addActionListener(new ButtonListener());
     setResizable(false);
     setVisible(true);
     setDefaultCloseOperation(JFrame.EXIT_ON_CLOSE);
  }

  public void paint(Graphics g)
  {
     buttonPanel.repaint();
     // get the graphics context for the drawing panel
     g = paper.getGraphics();
     // recreate the image from the PointHistory object points
     for (int i = 0; i < points.size() -1; i++)
     if (points.get(i + 1)! = null && points.get(i)! = null)
     {
        g.setColor(points.get(i).getColor());
```

```
            g.drawLine(points.get(i).getX(), points.get(i).getY(),
                    points.get(i + 1).getX(), points.get(i + 1).getY());
        }
    }

    private class ButtonListener implements ActionListener
    {
        public void actionPerformed(ActionEvent e)
        {
            String options[] = {"Black", "Red", "Blue", "Green", "Magenta"};
            if (e.getSource() == colorButton)
            {
                String drawColor =
                (String) JOptionPane.showInputDialog(null, "Choose a color",
                                "ColorChooser",JOptionPane.QUESTION_MESSAGE,null,
                                options,   "BLACK");

                if (drawColor != null) // cancel returns null
                  points.setColor(drawColor);
            }
            else if (e.getSource() == eraseButton)
            {
                points = new PointData();      // empty the history
                paper.repaint();               // repaint the single JPanel
            }
            else
                System.exit(0);                // exitButton
        }
    }

    private class MouseButtonListener implements MouseListener
    {
        public void mouseClicked (MouseEvent e)
        {}                      // required by MouseListener interface but does nothing
        public void mouseEntered (MouseEvent e)
        {}                      // required by MouseListener interface but does nothing
        public void mouseExited (MouseEvent e)
        {}                      // required by MouseListener interface but does nothing
        public void mouseReleased (MouseEvent e)
        {
            // add a null ColorPoint to the points
            // to signify the end of a continuous
            // section when redrawing the image
            points.add(null);
        }

        public void mousePressed (MouseEvent e)
        {
            // this is where drawing starts
            points.setX(e.getX());
            points.setY(e.getY());
        }
    }

    private class MoveMouseListener implements MouseMotionListener
    {
        public void mouseMoved(MouseEvent e)
        { }
        public void mouseDragged(MouseEvent e)
        {
            Graphics g = paper.getGraphics();
            g.setColor(points.getColor());
```

```
220.            int x1 = points.getX();          // get start point
221.            int y1 = points.getY();
222.            int x2 = e.getX();               // get current mouse-over point
223.            int y2 = e.getY();
224.            g.drawLine(x1, y1, x2, y2 );
225.            // add the last point to the list of points
226.            points.add(new ColorPoint(x1, y1, points.getColor()));

227.            points.setX(x2);                 // update the start point with the last point
228.            points.setY(y2);
229.        }
230.    }

231.    public static void main(String[] args)
232.    {
233.        PencilDrawing d = new PencilDrawing();
234.    }
235. }
```

Output When the program begins, a blank frame with three buttons fills the entire screen. The user draws on the frame by pressing the mouse button while he/she drags the mouse, creating a picture, hopefully better than the one in Figure 19.25.

Discussion Although the application may appear long, the logic is easy to follow. The methods of the auxiliary classes, ColorPoint and PointData, are mostly getter and setter methods and require no explanation.

Lines 119–124: The PencilDrawing declarations include three button references, two panel references—one for the buttons and the other for a drawing panel, and a PointData reference, points. A PointData object holds the current start point as well as a list of all points in the last drawn image.

Lines 125–154: The constructor of PencilDrawing creates the GUI and registers listeners. Nothing in the constructor is new, just the usual suspects: button and panel instantiations as well as the requisite add...Listener() method calls.

Lines 155–168: Overrides the paint(..) method. See the explanation at the end of this section.

Lines 169–189: ButtonListener is an inner class that provides the response to each of three button events. If the event source is colorButton, a call to JOptionPane.showInputDialog (…) displays a pop-up window that presents the user with a list of colors (line 177). The response to eraseButton instantiates an empty list of previously drawn points, effectively disposing of the old list, and then calls repaint(). When the frame is repainted, the list of previously drawn points is empty, so the call to repaint() paints an empty frame. Unlike a professional graphics program, our application cannot erase sections of a picture. It's all or nothing. Indeed, our erase procedure more closely resembles an *Etch-A-Sketch* toy plotter than a realistic paint program.

Lines 190–211: Because the inner class MouseButtonListener implements the MouseListener interface, by contract, the MouseButtonListener class must implement the five methods:

- void mouseClicked (MouseEvent e),
- void mouseEntered (MouseEvent e),

- void mouseExited (MouseEvent e),
- void mouseReleased (MouseEvent e), and
- void mousePressed (MouseEvent e).

For this application, only the mouse pressed and released events are of interest. Nonetheless, all five methods require implementation, even if three perform no actions (lines 193, 195, 197). The five methods are part of the MouseListener interface and, by contract, require implementation.

The mousePressed (ActionEvent e) method records the point where the mouse is first pressed. This location is the starting point for the next tiny line segment that is drawn (lines 208–209). The call e.getx() returns the *x*-coordinate of this point, and e.gety() returns the *y*-coordinate. The calls to

```
points.SetX(e.getx()) and points.SetY(e.gety())
```

store the starting point coordinates in the PointData object. The method

```
void mouseReleased (MouseEvent e)
```

performs a single action:

```
points.add(null) (line 203).
```

This method adds a null reference to the ArrayList of previously drawn points. The null reference signals that a segment of the drawing is complete and that the mouse has been released. For example, suppose that you

- first drag the mouse over the points (53, 24), (60, 39), . . . **(65, 45),** then
- release the mouse, and
- begin drawing again with the point sequence **(122, 48),** (123, 48), . . ., (152, 149).

The list of saved points (technically, a list of point references) includes a null reference between (65, 45) and (122, 48):

(53, 24), (60, 39), . . ., **(65, 45), null, (122, 48),** (123, 48), . . ., (152, 149).

The null value indicates that (65, 45) and (122, 48) are not connected when the frame is repainted. See Figure 19.26a. Without including the null reference or some other type of flag, when the frame is minimized and restored, paint(...) connects (65, 45) and (122,48) and "restores" a picture that is different than the original. See Figure 19.26b.

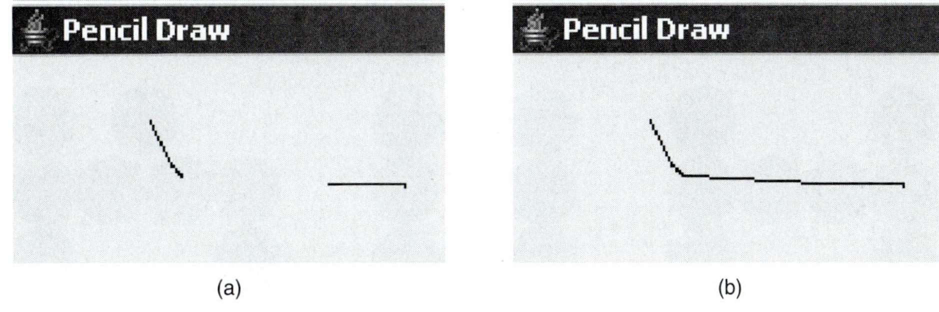

FIGURE 19.26 Without the null reference, (a) is repainted as (b)

Lines 212–230: The second listener class is MoveMouseListener, which implements the MouseMotionListener interface. Although the

MouseMotionListener interface has two methods, one method, mouseMoved(MouseEvent e), is of no interest to the application, and consequently has no statements. The mouseDragged(MouseEvent e) is the method that draws the tiny line segments between close points. After retrieving the graphics object for the panel and setting the color to the color of the start point (lines 218–219), the method

- retrieves the start point (x1, y1) which is stored in the points object (line 220–221),
- gets the coordinates of the point over which the mouse is being dragged (x2, y2) (line 222–223),
- draws a line segment from (x1, y1) to (x2, y2) (line 224),
- adds a point with coordinates (x2, y2) to the "point history" list (line 226), and
- sets the new start point to (x2, y2) (lines 227–228).

Lines 155–168: The overriden paint(...) method redraws the image on the frame when the frame is repainted. This is done in the for loop on lines 161–167. The list of saved points is used to once again draw the same tiny line segments. A value of null in the list signals that the mouse had been released and no segment connects the points before and after null. The method points.get(i) returns the *i*th point on the list.

19.9.2 A Coin Sliding Puzzle

The next example uses the mouse to move or drag images on a screen.

EXAMPLE 19.7 Figures 19.27a and b show two different arrangements of eight coins that are placed on a flat surface such as a table. One arrangement is in the shape of the letter H and the other in the shape of an O. A classic coin sliding puzzle, described by Harry Langman in *Scripta Mathematica*,[1] challenges a player to transform the configuration of Figure 19.27a to that of Figure 19.27b by sliding just four coins, one at a time, to new positions. When one slides a coin, no other coin on the table can be moved or disturbed in any way. No coin may be picked up. Furthermore, when a coin is repositioned, it must be moved into a position such that it touches *exactly* two other coins. Figure 19.27c shows the resulting arrangement of coins after sliding the left uppermost coin in Figure 19.27a. Notice that the relocated coin touches exactly two other coins.

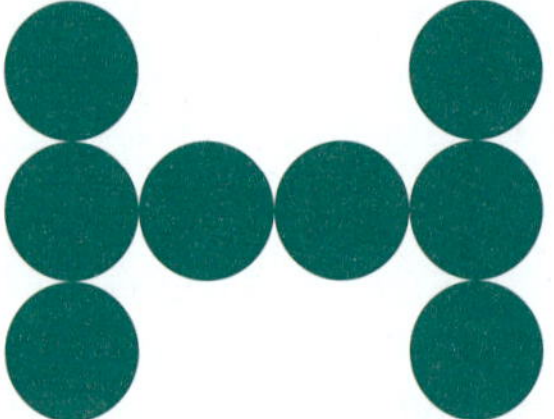

(a) An "H" Configuration

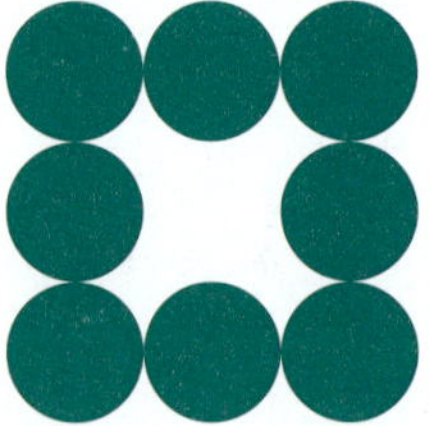

(b) An "O" Configuration

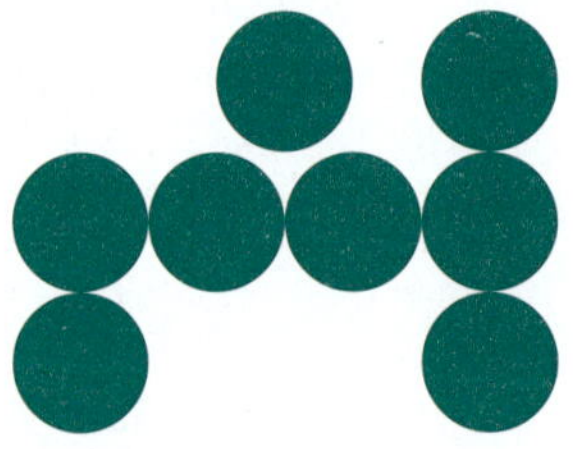

(c) One Coin Is Moved

FIGURE 19.27 Transform (a) to (b) using four coin-slides

[1] Harry Langman. Curiosa 342: Easy but not obvious. *Scripta Mathematica*, 19(4):242, December 1953.

The output displayed in Figure 19.29 shows one solution to this puzzle. Surprisingly, rearranging the coins from the O pattern back to the H requires six moves.

Problem Statement Design a GUI-based application that allows a user to solve the puzzle by interactively moving ("sliding") coins displayed in a frame. When the application begins, a frame should display the arrangement of numbered coins as shown in Figure 19.28. A user can slide a coin to a new position by dragging the coin with the mouse. The GUI should have a Reset button that restores the coins to the original configuration and also an Exit button.

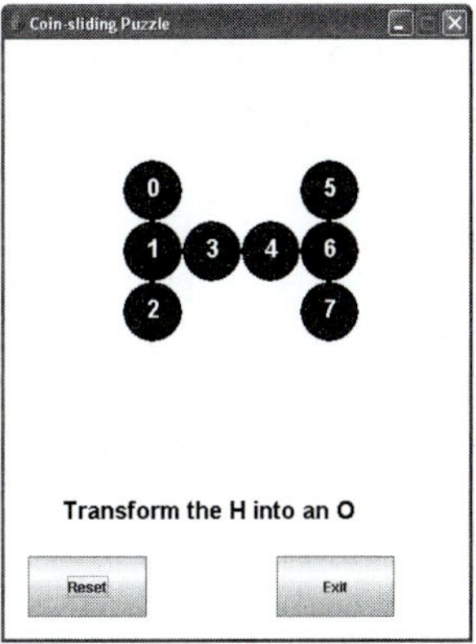

FIGURE 19.28 A GUI for the coin-sliding puzzle

The following program does *not* enforce the rules of the puzzle. Indeed, the program allows you to drag a coin through other coins, and place it anywhere. You can even leave one coin on top of another! It is the player's responsibility to follow the rules and not cheat. Adding code to implement and enforce the rules is left as an exercise (see Programming Exercise 13).

Java Solution The solution consists of two classes: CoinPuzzle and CoinFrame.

CoinPuzzle extends JPanel and builds the GUI shown in Figure 19.28. To draw the eight circles that represent coins, CoinPuzzle overrides PaintComponent(...) and uses the fillOval(...) method of Graphics. Two inner classes handle mouse events and button events. Note that the MouseHandler listener class implements two interfaces, MouseListener and MouseMotionListener.

CoinFrame, which extends JFrame, instantiates a CoinPuzzle panel. CoinFrame also includes the main(...) method of the application.

```
import java.awt.*;
import javax.swing.*;
import java.awt.event.*;
public class CoinPuzzle extends JPanel
// A GUI for the H --> O coin puzzle
{
   // (x[i],y[i]) is the corner point of a bounding square for circle i
   private int[] x = {100, 100, 100, 150, 200, 250, 250, 250};
   private int[] y = {100, 150, 200, 150, 150, 100, 150, 200};

   private final int RADIUS = 50;      // radius of each coin
   private JButton reset,exit;
```

```
    int circleNumber;                        // −1 for no circle

    public CoinPuzzle()
    {
        setLayout(null);                 // no layout manager for the panel
        setBackground(Color.WHITE);

        reset = new JButton("Reset");
        reset.setBounds(20, 500, 100, 50);

        exit = new JButton("Exit");
        exit.setBounds(230, 500, 100, 50);

        add(reset);
        add(exit);
        circleNumber = −1;               // No circle

        // register listeners
        addMouseListener(new MouseHandler());
        addMouseMotionListener(new MouseHandler());

        reset.addActionListener(new ButtonHandler());
        exit.addActionListener(new ButtonHandler());
    }

    public void paintComponent(Graphics g)
    {
        super.paintComponent(g);
        g.setColor(Color.BLACK);
        g.setFont(new Font("Arial", Font.BOLD, 20));
        g.drawString(" Transform the H to an O", 20, 470);

        // Draw 8 circles
        // Upper left corner of bounding box for circle-i is (x[i], y[i])

        for(int i = 0; i < 8; i++)
            g.fillOval(x[i], y[i], RADIUS, RADIUS);

        g.setColor(Color.WHITE);

        // Make labels for the coins
        String[] numbers = {"0", "1", "2", "3", "4", "5", "6", "7"};
        // Place a number on each coin
        for(int i = 0; i < 8; i++)
            g.drawString(numbers[i],x[i] + 20, y[i] + 30);
    }

    private class ButtonHandler implements ActionListener
    {
        public void actionPerformed(ActionEvent e)
        {
            if (e.getSource() == reset)   // reset corner points to the original arrangement
            {
                x[0] = 100; x[1] = 100; x[2] = 100; x[3] = 150; x[4] = 200; x[5] = 250; x[6] = 250; x[7] = 250;
                y[0] = 100; y[1] = 150; y[2] = 200; y[3] = 150; y[4] = 150; y[5] = 100; y[6] = 150; y[7] = 200;
                circleNumber = −1;
```

```
                repaint();
            }
            if (e.getSource() == exit)
                System.exit(0);
        }
    }

    private class MouseHandler implements MouseListener, MouseMotionListener
    {
        public void mouseReleased(MouseEvent e)
        {
            circleNumber = -1;                          // done dragging a circle
        }

        public void mousePressed(MouseEvent e)
        {
            int newX = e.getX();
            int newY = e.getY();
            for (int i = 0; i < 8; i++)
                // if the mouse is in the bounding square of a circle
                if (newX <= x[i] + 50 && newX >= x[i] && newY >= y[i] && newY <= y[i] + 50)
                {
                        circleNumber = i;               // circle i can be dragged
                        break;
                }
        }

        public void mouseDragged(MouseEvent e)
        {
            if (circleNumber >= 0)
            {                                           // change the upper corner of the bounding rectangle
                x[circleNumber] = e.getX();
                y[circleNumber] = e.getY();
                repaint();
            }
        }
        public void mouseMoved(MouseEvent e){}         // empty method
        public void mouseEntered(MouseEvent e){}       // empty method
        public void mouseExited(MouseEvent e){}        // empty method
        public void mouseClicked(MouseEvent e){}       // empty method
    }
}

public class CoinFrame extends JFrame
{
    public CoinFrame()
    {
        super("Coin-sliding Puzzle");                  // call one-argument constructor of JFrame
        setBounds(0, 0, 400, 600);
        CoinPuzzle panel = new CoinPuzzle();
        add(panel);                                     // uses the default BorderLayout; places at center
        setResizable(false);
        setVisible(true);
        setDefaultCloseOperation(JFrame.EXIT_ON_CLOSE);
    }

    public static void main(String[] args)
    {
        JFrame frown = new CoinFrame();
    }
}
```

Output Figure 19.29 gives a solution to the coin-sliding problem. Four moves are required. The realignment is accomplished without moving a coin through, across, or above another coin.

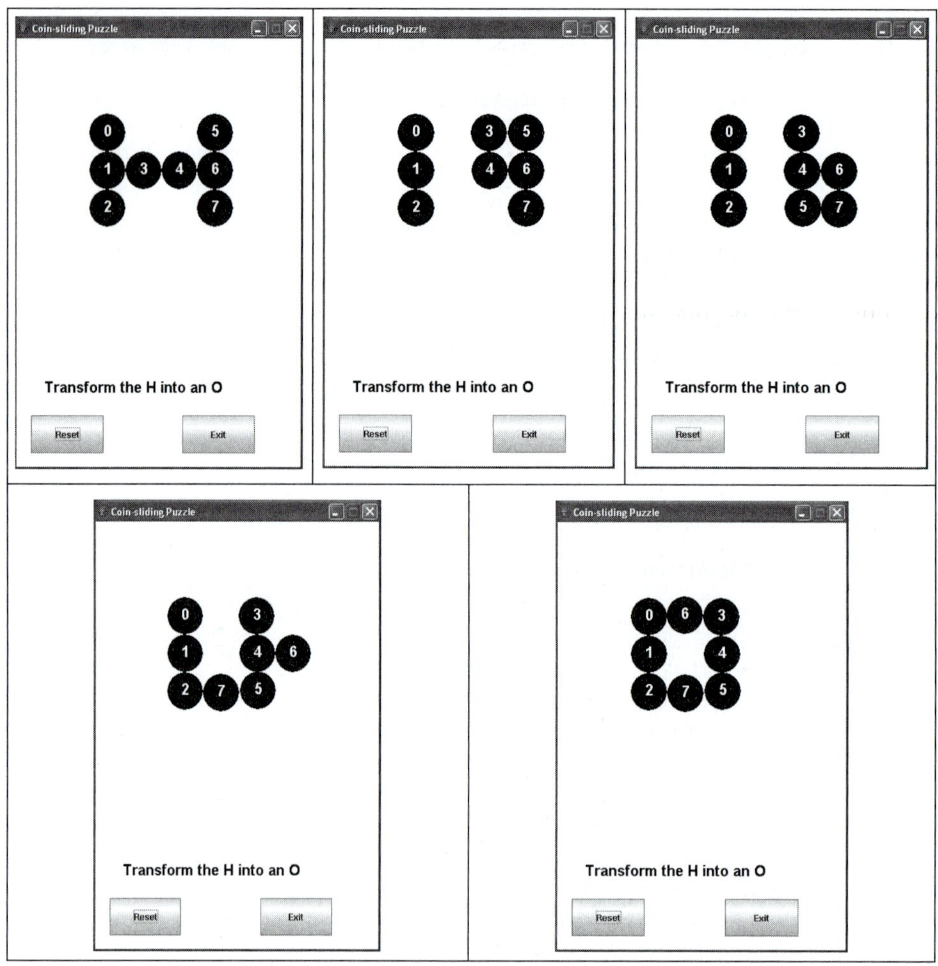

FIGURE 19.29 A solution to the H-O coin-sliding problem. A coin cannot be dragged over another coin.

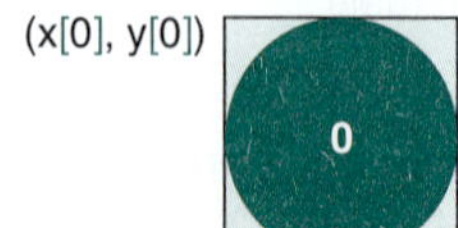

FIGURE 19.30 A circle shown within a bounding square

Discussion

Lines 8–9: Each circle that is drawn on a panel is specified by an invisible bounding square. The points (x[0], y[0]), (x[1], y[1])...(x[5], y[5]) represent the coordinates of the upper left-hand corners of the bounding squares for the initial configuration of six circles. Figure 19.30 shows one such circle situated inside a bounding square. The point (x[0], y[0]) is the location of the upper left-hand corner of the square.

Lines 13–29: The Constructor
The statements on lines 15–22 instantiate and place the two buttons in the panel. Notice that there is no layout manager (line 15); the buttons are place using setBounds(...).

On line 23, the instance variable circleNumber is initialized to −1, indicating that no circle is currently selected. As long as circleNumber has the value −1, dragging the mouse accomplishes nothing.

The statements on lines 25 and 26 register the mouse listeners and those on lines 27 and 28 register the button listeners. It is necessary that CoinPuzzle registers MouseHandler twice, once for each interface, MouseListener and MouseMotionListener.

Lines 30–46: paintComponent(Graphics g)
The statement on line 32 is a call to the paintComponent(…) method of JPanel. The statements on lines 33 and 34 set the font and color of the Graphics object. The assigned font and color are used whenever a Graphics method paints on the panel.

Line 35: The Graphics object g paints user instructions on the panel beginning at position (20, 470). The for loop of lines 38 and 39 paints six circles. The upper left corner of the bounding square of circle *i* is situated at (x[i], y[i]).

The for loop on lines 44 and 45 paints a number on each circle.

Lines 47–61: The ButtonHandler class

Line 47: private class ButtonHandler implements ActionListener
Because ButtonHandler implements ActionListener, ButtonHandler is bound, by contract, to implement actionPerformed(ActionEvent e).

Lines 49–61: actionPerformed(ActionEvent e)
The actionPerformed(...) method listens for events generated by the Reset and Exit buttons. The statements on lines 51–57 implement a response to events generated by the Reset button: the arrays x and y are reset to their original values and the panel is repainted. The statements on lines 58 and 59 realize a response to the Exit button: the application terminates.

Lines 62–93: The MouseHandler class
To handle mouse events, MouseHandler implements two interfaces, MouseListener and MouseMotionListener (line 62). This necessitates the implementation of seven different methods.

Lines 64–67: mouseReleased(MouseEvent e)
When the mouse is released, dragging has terminated and a circle is no longer selected. Deselection is indicated by assigning −1 to circleNumber. No circle can be moved if circleNumber is −1.

Lines 68–79: mousePressed(MouseEvent e)
The coordinates of the point where the mouse is pressed are recorded in newX and newY. If the point (newY, newY) resides within one of the bounding squares, circleNumber is assigned the number of the corresponding circle and, as long as the mouse remains pressed, that circle can be dragged.

Lines 80–88: mouseDragged(MouseEvent e)
If circle i is currently selected (line 82), the coordinates of the current mouse position are assigned to x[i] and y[i], thus changing the coordinates of the bounding square. The circle is repainted within the new bounding square, that is, the circle is moved to the position of the mouse.

Lines 89–92: Four empty but necessary methods
Because MouseHandler implements MouseListener and MouseMotionListener, these methods must be included. They are empty methods; although by contract they are necessary, they do nothing.

If the user presses the mouse anywhere within the bounding square, the associated circle can be dragged. The square fits tightly around the circle, and this approximation is not a major problem. As an exercise, you might implement mousePressed so that, to move a circle, the user must press the mouse within the boundary of the circle (see Programming Exercise 13).

19.10 CHECKBOXES AND RADIO BUTTONS

Two components that can be used for simple input are checkboxes and radio buttons. See Figure 19.31.

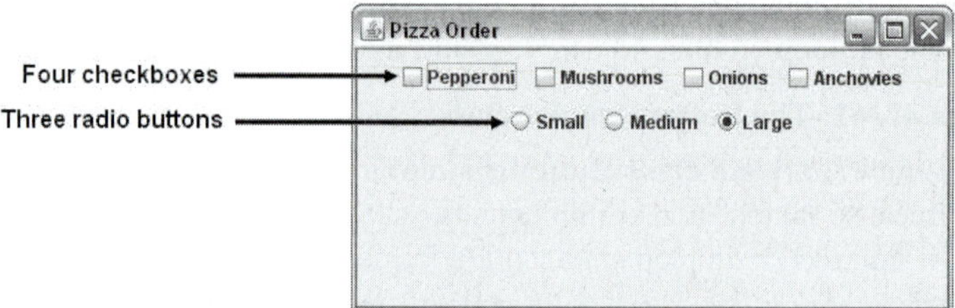

FIGURE 19.31 Four checkboxes and a group of three radio buttons

Checkboxes and radio buttons differ in that you may check or select any number of checkboxes in a group but only one radio button.

We begin with checkboxes.

19.10.1 *JCheckBox*

A *checkbox* is a component that can be either selected or not—that is, switched or toggled on or off.

If a checkbox, with only two possible states, seems like a button, it should be no surprise that JCheckBox extends AbstractButton.

Here are the basics:

Class: JCheckBox

Generates: ActionEvent and ItemEvent when the state of a checkbox changes.

Listener: Must implement ActionListener to respond to an ActionEvent and ItemListener to respond to an ItemEvent.

Listener method to implement: void actionPerformed(ActionEvent e) for ActionListener
void itemStateChanged(ItemEvent e) for ItemListener

Register a listener: void addActionListener(ActionListener a) // for ActionListener interface
void addItemListener(ItemListener i) // for ItemListener interface

Constructors:

- JCheckBox()
  creates an unselected checkbox with no text.
- JCheckBox(String text)
  creates an unselected checkbox with accompanying text, text.
- JCheckBox(String text, boolean selected)
  creates a checkbox with text, text. If selected is true, the checkbox is initially selected.
- JCheckBox(Icon image)
  creates an unselected checkbox with picture image and no text.
- JCheckBox(Icon i, boolean selected)
  creates a checkbox with picture image. If selected is true, the checkbox is initially selected.
- JCheckBox(String text, Icon i)
  creates an unselected checkbox with picture image and text, text.
- JCheckBox(String text, Icon i, boolean selected)
  creates an unselected checkbox with picture image and text, text. If selected is true, the checkbox is initially selected.

Methods:

- boolean isSelected()
- void setSelected(boolean selected)
- void addActionListener(ActionListener ActionListener)
- void addItemListener(ItemListener ItemListener)

The following class extends JFrame and uses four checkboxes to record a pizza order. The checkboxes are shown in Figure 19.31.

```
public class PizzaOrder extends JFrame
{
   private JCheckBox pepperoniCB;
   private JCheckBox mushroomCB;
   private JCheckBox onionCB;
   private JCheckBox anchovyCB;
   private String toppings = "";

   public PizzaOrder()
   {
      // instantiate checkboxes
      pepperoniCB = new JCheckBox("Pepperoni");
      mushroomCB = new JCheckBox("Mushrooms");
      onionCB = new JCheckBox("Onions");
      anchovyCB = new JCheckBox("Anchovies");

      // add checkboxes to the frame
      setLayout(new FlowLayout());
      add(pepperoniCB);
      add(mushroomCB);
      add(onionCB);
      add(anchovyCB);
```

```
        // register listeners for checkboxes
        pepperoniCB.addItemListener(new CheckBoxListener());
        mushroomCB.addItemListener(new CheckBoxListener());
        onionCB.addItemListener(new CheckBoxListener());
        anchovyCB.addItemListener(new CheckBoxListener());
    }

    // implement listener class for checkboxes
    private class CheckBoxListener implements ItemListener
    {
        public void itemStateChanged(ItemEvent e)
        {
            if (e.getSource() == pepperoniCB  || e.getSource() == mushroomCB ||
                        e.getSource()== onionCB   || e.getSource() == anchovyCB)
            {
                toppings = "";
                if (pepperoniCB.isSelected())
                    toppings = toppings + " " + "pepperoni";
                if (mushroomCB.isSelected())
                    toppings = toppings + " " + "mushrooms";
                if (onionCB.isSelected())
                    toppings = toppings + " " + "onion";
                if (anchovyCB.isSelected())
                    toppings = toppings + " " + "anchovies";
            }
        }
    }
}
```

19.10.2 *JRadioButton*

Next to the four checkboxes of Figure 19.31 is a group of three radio buttons. A user may check one, two, three, or all four checkboxes but may select only one of the three radio buttons. These radio buttons are members of a "button group," and turning on one button in the group turns off the others. That is, one and only one member of a button group may be selected at any time. An application may include any number of button groups. For example, the frame of Figure 19.31 might include a second button group consisting of two buttons labeled Eat-in and Take-out.

> When you include radio buttons in an application, create a *button group* and add the radio buttons to the button group. This ensures that only one radio button in the group is ever selected.

Here are the basics:

Class: JRadioButton

Generates: ActionEvent and ItemEvent when the state of a radio button changes.

Listener: Must implement ActionListener to respond to an ActionEvent and ItemListener to respond to an ItemEvent.

Listener method to implement: void actionPerformed(ActionEvent e)
void itemStateChanged(ItemEvent e)

Register a listener: void addActionListener(ActionListener a)
void addItemListener(ItemListener i)

Constructors:

- JRadioButton()
- JRadioButton(String text)
- JRadioButton(String s, boolean selected)
- JRadioButton(Icon i)
- JRadioButton(Icon i, boolean selected)
- JRadioButton(String text, Icon i)
- JRadioButton(String text, Icon i, boolean selected)

Methods:

- void setSelected(boolean selected)
- boolean isSelected()
- addActionListener(ActionListener a)
- addItemListener(ItemListener a)

The ButtonGroup class encapsulates a group of radio buttons.

Constructor for ButtonGroup: ButtonGroup()

Method that adds a radio button to a button group: void add(JRadioButton radioButton)

The following addition to PizzaOrder adds the group of three radio buttons shown in Figure 19.31. The additional code

- creates three radio buttons,
- add the buttons to the frame,
- creates a ButtonGroup object,
- adds the radio buttons to the button group,
- registers listeners, and
- implements a listener class that implements the ItemListener interface.

```
public class PizzaOrder extends JFrame
{
   private JCheckBox pepperoniCB;
   private JCheckBox mushroomCB;
   private JCheckBox onionCB;
   private JCheckBox anchovyCB;
   private String toppings = "";
   private double price;

   private JRadioButton smallRB;
   private JRadioButton mediumRB;
   private JRadioButton largeRB;          // default selection

   public PizzaOrder()                    // default constructor

   {
      // instantiate checkboxes
      pepperoniCB = new JCheckBox("Pepperoni");
      mushroomCB = new JCheckBox("Mushrooms");
      onionCB = new JCheckBox("Onions");
```

```
        anchovyCB = new JCheckBox("Anchovies");

        // instantiate the radio buttons
        smallRB = new JRadioButton("Small",false);
        mediumRB = new JRadioButton("Medium",false);
        largeRB = new JRadioButton("Large",true );              // default selection
        setLayout(new FlowLayout());
        add(pepperoniCB);
        add(mushroomCB);
        add(onionCB);
        add(anchovyCB);

        // add the radio buttons to the frame
        add(smallRB);
        add(mediumRB);
        add(largeRB);

        // create a button group
        ButtonGroup pizzaSizes = new ButtonGroup();

        // add buttons to the button goup
        pizzaSizes.add(smallRB);
        pizzaSizes.add(mediumRB);
        pizzaSizes.add(largeRB);

        // register a listener with each checkbox
        pepperoniCB.addItemListener(new CheckBoxListener());
        mushroomCB.addItemListener(new CheckBoxListener());
        onionCB.addItemListener(new CheckBoxListener());
        anchovyCB.addItemListener(new CheckBoxListener());

        // register a listener with each button
        smallRB.addItemListener(new PizzaButtonListener());
        mediumRB.addItemListener(new PizzaButtonListener());
        largeRB.addItemListener(new PizzaButtonListener());
    }

    // implement listener class for checkboxes
    private class CheckBoxListener implements ItemListener
    {
        public void itemStateChanged(ItemEvent e)
        {
            if (e.getSource() == pepperoniCB   || e.getSource() == mushroomCB ||
                e.getSource() == onionCB   || e.getSource() == anchovyCB)
            {
                toppings = "";
                if (pepperoniCB.isSelected())
                    toppings = toppings + " " + "pepperoni";
                if (mushroomCB.isSelected())
                    toppings = toppings + " " + "mushrooms";
                if (onionCB.isSelected())
```

```
63.                 toppings = toppings + " " + "onion";
64.             if (anchovyCB.isSelected())
65.                 toppings = toppings + " " + "anchovies";
66.         }
67.     }
68. }

69. private class PizzaButtonListener implements ItemListener
70. {
71.     public void itemStateChanged(ItemEvent e)
72.     {
73.         if (e.getSource() instanceof JRadioButton)
74.         {
75.             if (smallRB.isSelected())
76.                 price = 8.75;
77.             else if (mediumRB.isSelected())
78.                 price = 10.75;
79.             else
80.                 price = 15.75;
81.         }
82.     }
83. }

84. public static void main(String[] args)
85. {
86.     PizzaOrder frame = new PizzaOrder();
87.     frame.setTitle("Pizza Order");
88.     frame.setBounds(0, 0, 400, 200);
89.     frame.setVisible(true);
90. }
91. }
```

The condition on line 73

```
if (e.getSource() instanceof JRadioButton)
```

can also be implemented as

```
if ( (e.getSource() == smallRB) || (e.getSource() == mediumRB) || (e.getSource() == largeRB) )
```

19.11 MENUS

If you have used a text editor or a word processor, no doubt, you have used a menu. A GUI application that includes menus requires the use of three Swing classes:

- JMenuBar,
- JMenu, and
- JMenuItem.

Figure 19.32 shows a menu bar and two different menus, the Edit menu and the File menu. The menu bar is the bar, or thin strip, on which the two menus reside. Clicking on a menu reveals several menu items. For example, clicking on the File menu or the Edit menu shows the menu items of Figure 19.32.

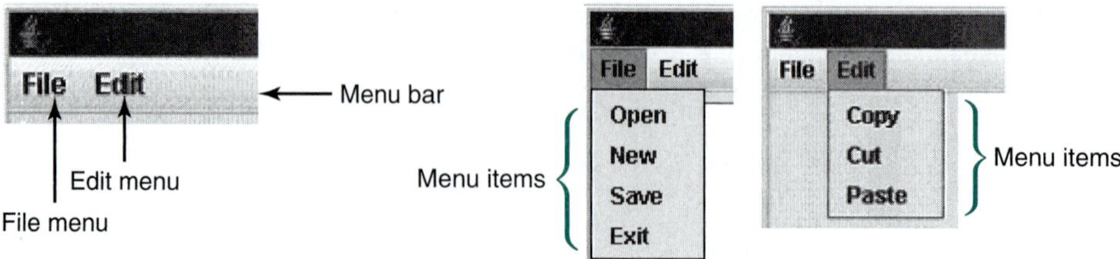

FIGURE 19.32 A menu bar, two menus, and seven menu items

Adding one or more menus to a GUI is a three-step process:

1. Create a menu bar.
2. Create each menu and add each to the menu bar.
3. Create the menu items and add them to the appropriate menus.

1. **Create the menu bar.**

   To create a menu bar, use the constructor

   ```
   JMenuBar().
   ```

   To place a menu bar in a frame, use the JFrame method

   ```
   void setJMenuBar(JMenuBar menuBar).
   ```

   Within the constructor of a JFrame, you can add a menu bar to a frame using the statements:

   ```
   JMenuBar menuBar = new JMenuBar();
   setJMenuBar(menuBar);
   ```

   Otherwise, you can add a menu bar as follows:

   ```
   JFrame frame = new JFrame();
   JMenuBar menuBar = new JMenuBar();
   frame.setJMenuBar(menuBar);
   ```

2. **Create each menu and add each menu to the menu bar.**

   Here, the appropriate constructor is

   ```
   JMenu(String menu),
     where menu is the name of the menu.
   ```

   To add a menu to a menu bar, use the JMenuBar method

   ```
   JMenu   addJMenu(JMenu m),
   ```

   which adds a menu, m, to the end of a menu bar.

   For example, the following segment adds two menus to the menu bar:

   ```
   JMenuBar menuBar = new JMenuBar();    // create a menu bar
   JMenu fileMenu = new JMenu("File");   // create a File menu
   JMenu editMenu = new JMenu("Edit");   // create an Edit menu
   menuBar.add(fileMenu);                // add the File menu to the menu bar
   menuBar.add(editMenu);                // add the Edit menu to the menu bar
   ```

In fact, you can add any component to a menu bar with the Container method:

```
Component add(Component c).
```

3. **Create the menu items and add the items to the appropriate menu.**

As you might expect, the JMenuItem constructor is

```
JMenuItem(String item)
```

To add a menu item to a menu, use the JMenu method

```
JMenuItem add (JMenuItem menuItem)
```

The following segment, embedded in an application, creates the menus shown in Figure 19.32.

```
JFrame frame = new JFrame();
frame.setBounds(0, 0, 500, 500);

// create the menu bar
JMenuBar menuBar = new JMenuBar();
frame.setJMenuBar(menuBar);   // add menu bar to frame

// create a menu ("File")
JMenu fileMenu = new JMenu("File");

// add the file menu to the menu bar
menuBar.add(fileMenu);

// create four menu items–Open, New, Save, and Exit
JMenuItem openMenuItem = new JMenuItem("Open");
JMenuItem newMenuItem = new JMenuItem("New");
JMenuItem saveMenuItem = new JMenuItem("Save");
JMenuItem exitMenuItem = new JMenuItem("Exit");

// add the three menu items to the File menu
fileMenu.add (openMenuItem);
fileMenu.add (newMenuItem);
fileMenu.add(saveMenuItem);
fileMenu.add (exitMenuItem);

// create a second menu, "Edit"
JMenu editMenu = new JMenu("Edit");

// add the Edit menu to the menu bar
menuBar.add(editMenu);

// create three menu items, Copy, Cut, and Paste
JMenuItem copyMenuItem = new JMenuItem("Copy");
JMenuItem cutMenuItem = new JMenuItem("Cut");
JMenuItem pasteMenuItem = new JMenuItem("Paste");

// add the Cut and Paste menu items to the Edit menu
```

```
editMenu.add(copyMenuItem);
editMenu.add(cutMenuItem);
editMenu.add(pasteMenuItem);

frame.setVisible(true)
```

Useful methods available to JMenuItem and JMenu are:

- boolean isSelected()
  returns true if the menu or menu item is selected.
- void setSelected(boolean selected)
  sets the status of the menu or menu item.
- void doClick()
  clicks the menu via the code, not the mouse.
- String getActionCommand()
  returns the text or label of a menu item.

Selecting a menu item generates an ActionEvent object. A response requires that the programmer:

- create an event listener class that implements the interface ActionListener and the actionPerformed(ActionEvent) method, and
- register the listener with the appropriate source via the method
  void addActionListener(...).

19.11.1 A Simple Text Editor with Menus, Checkboxes, and Radio Buttons

The application of Example 19.8 uses menus, checkboxes, radio buttons, and dialog boxes to implement a rudimentary text editor.

EXAMPLE 19.8 A word processor such as Word or WordPerfect produces formatted documents with numerous fonts, type sizes, and type styles. Format information is saved using "characters" that are not part of the ASCII (or any other standard) character set. These *binary* files are readable only by programs that know how to interpret the special encoding of the file. In contrast, a text editor, such as Notepad, produces standard text files that any other program can read. A text file is a sequence of characters encoded using the ASCII character code.

Problem Statement Implement a simple text editor. The application should have:

- functioning File and Edit menus as seen in Figure 19.32,
- the capability to display text in bold or italics, and
- the capability to display text in one of three fonts : Times New Roman, Courier, or Arial.

Although the text can be viewed in three fonts and two styles, the text is saved strictly as a sequence of ASCII characters. In this application, the text is treated as a single group of characters that share the same style and font. It would require a bit more work to allow each character to have its own style and font.

Java Solution The following application contains no difficult algorithms or complex logic. Indeed, you may be surprised by how easy it is to build a text editor using Swing components.

```
import java.awt.*;
import java.awt.event.*;
import javax.swing.*;
import java.io.*;

public class Editor extends JFrame
{
   JMenuBar menuBar;
   JMenu fileMenu, editMenu;
   JMenuItem openMenuItem, newMenuItem, saveMenuItem, exitMenuItem;
   JMenuItem copyMenuItem, cutMenuItem, pasteMenuItem;

   JTextArea text;                         // the area that holds all text
   JPanel textPanel;                       // for the text area
   JScrollPane scrollPane;                 // provides scroll bars for the text area

   JCheckBox boldCB, italicCB;             // checkboxes for bold and italic

   ButtonGroup buttonGroup;                // a group of radio buttons that control font style
   JRadioButton timesRB, courierRB, arialRB; // New Times Roman, Courier, Arial

   public Editor() // default constructor, sets up GUI
   {
      setBounds(0, 0, 500, 500);
      // create the menu bar
      // place the menu bar in the frame
      menuBar = new JMenuBar();
      setJMenuBar(menuBar);

      // create a File menu
      fileMenu = new JMenu("File");

      // add the File menu to the menu bar
      menuBar.add(fileMenu);

      // create four menu items : Open, Close, Save, and Exit
      openMenuItem = new JMenuItem("Open");
      newMenuItem = new JMenuItem("New");
      saveMenuItem = new JMenuItem("Save");
      exitMenuItem = new JMenuItem("Exit");

      // add the four menu items to the File menu
      fileMenu.add(openMenuItem);
      fileMenu.add(newMenuItem);
      fileMenu.add(saveMenuItem);
      fileMenu.add(exitMenuItem);

      // create the Edit menu
      editMenu = new JMenu("Edit");

      // add the Edit menu to the menu bar
      menuBar.add(editMenu);

      // create three menu items, Copy, Cut, and Paste
      copyMenuItem = new JMenuItem("Copy");
      cutMenuItem = new JMenuItem("Cut");
      pasteMenuItem = new JMenuItem("Paste");

      // add the Copy, Cut, and Paste menu items to the Edit menu
      editMenu.add(copyMenuItem);
      editMenu.add(cutMenuItem);
```

```
        editMenu.add(pasteMenuItem);

        // place a text area in a scroll pane and in a panel
        textPanel = new JPanel();
        text = new JTextArea(30,50);
        text.setFont(new Font("Times New Roman", Font.PLAIN, 12));      // initial font
        scrollPane = new JScrollPane(text);
        text.setLineWrap(true);
        text.setWrapStyleWord(true); // wrap at whitespace
        textPanel.add(scrollPane);
        add(textPanel,BorderLayout.CENTER);

        // checkboxes control Bold an/or italic type
        boldCB = new JCheckBox("Bold");
        italicCB = new JCheckBox("Italic");

        // Use 3 radio buttons for the font style
        buttonGroup = new ButtonGroup();                    // first make a button group
        timesRB = new JRadioButton("Times New Roman");
        courierRB = new JRadioButton("Courier");
        arialRB= new JRadioButton("Arial");
        buttonGroup.add(timesRB);                           // add to button group
        buttonGroup.add(courierRB);
        buttonGroup.add(arialRB);
        timesRB.setSelected(true);

        // place the checkboxes and the radio buttons
        // on a panel and place the panel in the SOUTH
        // section of the frame

        JPanel viewPanel = new JPanel();
        JLabel viewLabel = new JLabel(" View Text ");       // separate boxes and buttons
        viewPanel.add(boldCB);
        viewPanel.add(italicCB);
        viewPanel.add(viewLabel);
        viewPanel.add(timesRB);
        viewPanel.add(courierRB);
        viewPanel.add(arialRB);
        add(viewPanel, BorderLayout.SOUTH);

        // register listeners for the checkboxes and radio buttons
        ClickListener clickListener = new ClickListener();
        boldCB.addItemListener(clickListener);
        italicCB.addItemListener(clickListener);
        timesRB.addItemListener(clickListener);
        courierRB.addItemListener(clickListener);
        arialRB.addItemListener(clickListener);

        // register listeners for the menu items
        MenuListener menuListener = new MenuListener();
        openMenuItem.addActionListener(menuListener);
        newMenuItem.addActionListener(menuListener);
        saveMenuItem.addActionListener(menuListener);
        exitMenuItem.addActionListener(menuListener);
        copyMenuItem.addActionListener(menuListener);
        cutMenuItem.addActionListener(menuListener);
        pasteMenuItem.addActionListener(menuListener);
        setVisible(true);
        setDefaultCloseOperation(JFrame.EXIT_ON_CLOSE);
    }
```

```
    // Listener for the checkboxes and radio buttons
    // Listener responds to ItemEvent objects, not ActionEvent objects
    // Constants: PLAIN = 0; BOLD = 1; ITALIC = 2; BOLD + ITALIC = 3

    private class ClickListener implements ItemListener
    {
        public void itemStateChanged(ItemEvent e)
        {
            int fontStyle = Font.PLAIN;

            if (boldCB.isSelected())
                fontStyle = fontStyle + Font.BOLD;
            if (italicCB.isSelected())
                fontStyle = fontStyle + Font.ITALIC;

            // determine font style
            if (timesRB.isSelected())
                text.setFont(new Font("Times New Roman", fontStyle,12));
            else if (courierRB.isSelected())
                text.setFont(new Font("Courier", fontStyle, 12));
            else if (arialRB.isSelected())
                text.setFont(new Font("Arial", fontStyle, 12));
        }
    }

    private class MenuListener implements ActionListener
    {
        public void actionPerformed(ActionEvent e)
        {
            if (e.getSource() == openMenuItem)
            {  // get the name of the input file
                String fileName = JOptionPane.showInputDialog(null, "Enter File name", "File",
                                                        JOptionPane.QUESTION_MESSAGE);

                if (fileName == null || fileName.equals(""))       // user chooses Cancel or X (close)
                    return;
                try
                {  // create a FileReader object to read the text file
                    FileReader in = new FileReader(fileName);
                    text.read(in, null);
                    in.close();
                }
                catch (IOException ex)                              // if the file is not found
                {
                    JOptionPane.showMessageDialog(null, "File not Found", "Input Error",
                                                    JOptionPane.ERROR_MESSAGE);
                }
            }
            else if (e.getSource() == newMenuItem)
            {
                text.setText("");                                   // clear the text area
            }
            else if (e.getSource() == saveMenuItem)
            {
                String fileName = JOptionPane.showInputDialog(null, "Enter File name","File",
                                                        JOptionPane.QUESTION_MESSAGE);

                if (fileName == null || fileName.equals(""))       // cancel or close
                    return;
                try
```

```
        {
            FileWriter out = new FileWriter(fileName);
            text.write(out);
            out.close();
        }
        catch (IOException ex)      // if file cannot be opened or some other error occurs
        {
            JOptionPane.showMessageDialog(null, "File cannot be saved", "Output Error",
                                                         JOptionPane.ERROR_MESSAGE);
        }
      }
      else if (e.getSource() == exitMenuItem)
      {
        System.exit(0);
      }
      else if (e.getSource() == copyMenuItem)
      {
        text.copy();                          // copies selected text to the system clipboard
      }
      else if (e.getSource() == cutMenuItem)
      {
        text.cut();                           // cuts selected text; copies text to clipboard
      }
      else if (e.getSource() == pasteMenuItem)
      {
        text.paste();                         // pastes text from the system clipboard
      }
    }
  }

  public static void main(String [] args)
  {
    Editor ed = new Editor();
  }
}
```

Output Two screens of output are shown in Figure 19.33.

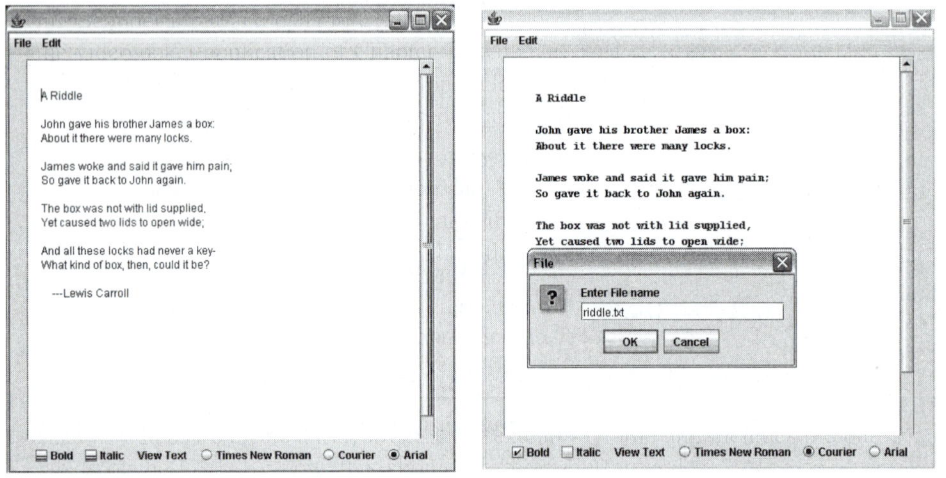

FIGURE 19.33 Choosing the Save menu item. Text is displayed in plain Arial on left, and bold Courier on right screen.

Discussion

Lines 7–16: The declarations

Although the application may seem a bit long, it is indeed rather simple. The declarations (lines 7–16) specify the components of the GUI as seen in Figure 19.33: two menus: File and Edit, a text area with scroll bars, two checkboxes, and a group of three radio buttons.

Lines 17–101: The constructor

The constructor lays out the GUI and registers listeners with various components:

Lines 22–23: These statements create a menu bar and place the menu bar in the frame.

Lines 24–27: The File menu is instantiated and placed on the menu bar.

Lines 28–32: Four menu items are created.

Lines 33–37: The four menu items are added to the File menu.

Lines 38–49: The Edit menu is set up in a manner similar to the File menu.

Lines 50–58: A text area, text, is instantiated and passed to a scroll pane. This ensures that the text area has scroll bars as needed. The scroll pane is placed in a panel, and the panel is placed in the center of the frame.

Lines 59–61: Two checkboxes are created: one indicates whether or not the font is **bold**, and the other indicates *italic*.

Lines 62–70: A button group is created for three radio buttons. The radio buttons indicate the font style: New Times Roman, Courier, or Arial. The radio button timesRB is initially selected (line 70).

Lines 71–82: The checkboxes are placed in a panel, and a label View Text follows the checkboxes; then the radio buttons are placed in the panel. The panel of boxes and buttons is placed in the SOUTH section of the frame.

Lines 83–89: Register the inner class, ClickListener, as a listener class for the checkboxes and radio buttons. ClickListener implements the ItemListener interface.

Lines 90–98: Register MenuListener with the menu items.

The constructor is nothing more than a direct layout of the GUI components.

Lines 105–122: ClickListener, a listener class that implements ItemListener

ClickListener responds to events that occur whenever a radio button is clicked or a checkbox is (un)checked. To respond to an item event, a listener class must implement the ItemListener interface, which has a single method

```
void itemStateChanged(ItemEvent e).
```

If any of the boxes or buttons generates an event, the same code executes. First, the type of font, plain, bold, italic, or combination bold and italic is determined (lines 109–113). Suppose, for example, that both boldCB and italicCB are selected:

The variable fontStyle is initialized to 0 (PLAIN)

Because the Bold checkbox is selected, fontStyle = fontStyle + BOLD = 0 + 1 = 1.

Because the Italic checkbox is selected, fontStyle = fontStyle + ITALIC = 1 + 2 = 3.

The value 3 indicates a bold and italic font.

Next, a sequence of if-else statements determines which type of font has been chosen (lines 115–119). Finally, the font property of the text area is reset (line 120).

Lines 123–179: MenuListener, a listener class that implements ActionListener. Menu items generate action events, and a class that handles an action event must implement the ActionListener interface. As you already know, ActionListener declares just a single method

void actionPerformed(ActionEvent e).

Lines 127–141: Selecting the Open menu item triggers an action event. In response, the method queries the user, via an input dialog box, for the name of an input file (line 129). If the user clicks Cancel or closes the dialog box, the method returns. No file name is supplied; no action is taken (130–131). However, if the user supplies a file name, a FileReader is instantiated, the read(...) method of JTextArea reads the contents of the file into the text area, text, and, subsequently, the stream is closed (lines 134–136).

Of course, any time that a program attempts to open a file there is the chance of an IOException exception. Because of this possibility, the statements on lines 134–136 are enclosed by a try block. The corresponding catch block (lines 139–141) handles an exception by issuing an error message via a pop-up message dialog box.

Lines 143–146: If a user selects the New menu item, the application responds by setting the text of the text area to the empty string. This action clears the text box.

Lines 147–161: Selecting the Save menu item triggers an event similar to the one generated when choosing the Open menu item.

Lines 167–178: These lines show the responses to the menu items Copy, Cut, and Paste. In each case, a JTextArea method is invoked. For example, if the Cut menu item is selected, the cut() method, shown on line 173, moves all selected text from the text area to the system clipboard.

19.12 DESIGNING EVENT LISTENER CLASSES

When designing listener classes, a programmer has options: an event listener may respond to any number of events and implement any number of listener interfaces. For example, the coin sliding application (Example 19.7) includes a single listener that handles the events generated by both the Reset and the Exit buttons. Both buttons register this listener. A second listener, which responds to mouse events, implements two listener interfaces: MouseListener and MouseMotionListener, and the CoinPuzzle panel registers this listener twice, once for each interface.

An alternative implementation might include separate listener classes for each button event and two distinct listeners for mouse events: one that implements MouseMotionListener and another that implements MouseListener. This approach would have each button register its own distinct listener, and the CoinPuzzle panel register the two different mouse event listeners.

Still other implementations are possible. All button and mouse events might even be handled within a single class. However, one listener class that responds to every mouse and button event may be cumbersome, difficult to maintain, and not logically organized.

No rules, other than good style and common sense, govern the organization of your listener classes. In our examples, we usually create a separate class for each *kind* of event listener. But determining which events are of the same kind can be tricky. Too few or too many listener classes can result in complex, inefficient, and hard to maintain code. As you gain experience and develop your own style, you will find the right balance.

19.13 IN CONCLUSION

This chapter gives a brief introduction to event-driven programming and specifically Java's event delegation model. Events are generated by components and, in this chapter, you have seen just a handful of Swing components. The documentation on Sun's website includes many more components than we can possibly include in a single chapter. Try experimenting. Start with JScrollBar, JComboBox, or JList. Once you master a few components, working with others becomes easier. Like any set of tools, however, knowing how to use each one is only half the battle. It takes practice and experience to decide which combination of components is the simplest, most efficient, and most effective.

Just the Facts

- An *event* is an occurrence to which a program may respond.
- There are dozens of possible events, including pressing a button, clicking and dragging the mouse, choosing a menu item, or selecting a checkbox.
- The *delegation event model* is Java's mechanism for handling events.
- Java's event delegation model uses three objects: the source, the event object, and the listener.
  - The source is the object that generates the event, be it the mouse, a button, a textbox, or a menu.
  - The event object encapsulates information about the event.
  - Event objects are passed to a listener object registered by the source.
  - Using information encapsulated by the event object, the listener object handles the event.
- Every listener must implement at least one listener interface. Each listener interface declares methods that handle certain kinds of events. A listener may implement more than one interface.
- To handle an event, a connection must be established between the source and a listener. The source must *register* each listener. The source effects registration via a method call such as addActionerListener(...) or addMouseListener(...).
- A source may register more than one listener. Indeed, if a listener implements more than one listener interface, a source may register that listener multiple times, once for each interface.
- More than one source can register the same listener.

- It is good style to declare listener classes as private inner classes, though this is not necessary.
- Designing listener classes involves choosing how many and which events are handled by the class. A common style organizes listener classes by kind—for example, one listener might handle all button-generated events.
- There are dozens of source objects (components) that generate events. In this chapter, we discuss only a few.
- JButton is a commonly used class of objects that generate events. Many simple applications can be built using buttons. A button listener class implements ActionListener.
- Use a label to display an image or text on a panel when you do not need to process an event. A label does not generate events. That is, a label is an output object. A label does not necessitate a listener. A label object belongs to JLabel.
- A text field is an object that holds a single line of text. A text field can be used for input or output and is appropriate for programs such as calculators or spreadsheets. A text field generates an action event when Enter is pressed. A text field belongs to JTextField.
- A text area is similar to a text field except that a text area can hold more than one line of text. A text area, placed in a scroll pane, can exhibit scroll bars when necessary.
- Dialog boxes provide specific but simple functionality that could otherwise be built from labels, buttons, and listeners, albeit with more effort. However, dialog boxes effect input and output without your having to deal with events and listeners. Dialog boxes belong to JOptionPane.
- Mouse movements and mouse clicks generate events. The listeners that respond to mouse-generated events implement MouseListener and MouseMotionListener.
- Checkboxes and radio buttons are two components used for input. A user may check any number of checkboxes but select only one radio button in a group. Both objects may implement one or both of two interfaces—ActionListener and ItemListener.
- Menus are built from three classes, JMenu, JMenuBar, and JMenuItem. Menu bars hold menus, which in turn, hold menu items. A menu item listener implements ActionListener.

Bug Extermination

- The source object must register every listener to which it sends events. Neglecting to register listeners is a common error.
- There are many ways to implement interactive input and output. When in doubt, it is best to use the simplest tool that does the job. In order of simplicity, try dialog boxes, text boxes, buttons, radio buttons or checkboxes, menus, and finally the mouse.
- Every listener must implement the appropriate interface(s) required by the sources that register the listener. For example, a listener that responds to a button event must implement ActionListener, and not, for example, ItemListener. If appropriate, a listener may implement more than one interface. See Example 19.7.

- Each listener must fulfill its contract by implementing *every* method of each interface that it implements. If the listener has no relevant action for an interface method, then implement that method with an empty block, { }.
- If two or more sources register the same listener, that listener must implement all appropriate interfaces and be able to respond to events from each source. To determine the source of an event, use getSource().
- If a listener implements more than one interface, a source must register the listener multiple times, once for each different interface that implements a response to events fired by that source. See Example 19.7, lines 25–26.
- It may be tricky to choose between validate() and repaint() when redisplaying a frame or panel after modifying its components. The AWT validate() method lays out components after the components have been modified. Contrast this method with repaint(), which does *not* lay out components again, but instead calls paint(g) to render each component again. The repaint() method is used when component features have changed, but no new layout is necessary, that is, the size, location, and number of the components stays fixed. The validate() method is necessary when the component layout has changed.

EXERCISES

LEARN THE LINGO

Test your knowledge of the chapter's vocabulary by completing the following crossword puzzle.

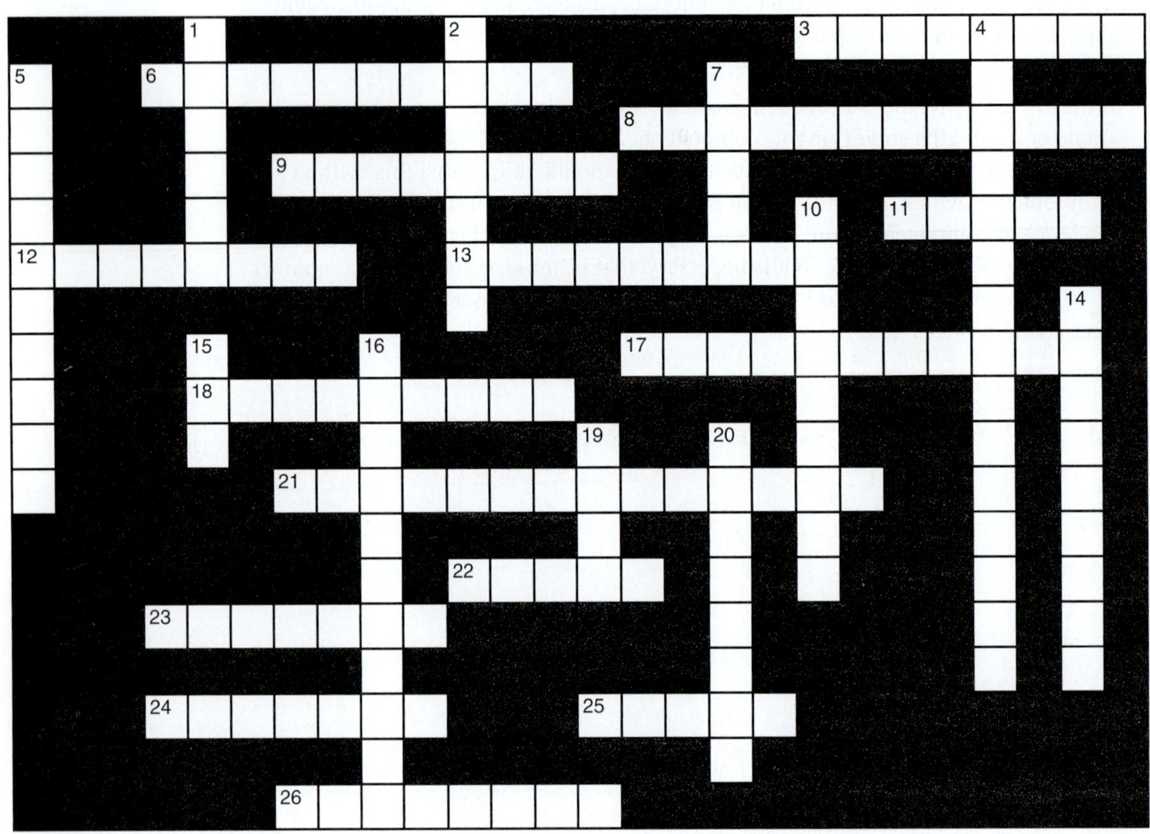

Across

3 Holds multiple lines of text
6 Dragging or moving the mouse over a component generates a ________.
8 A ______ dialog box can have buttons Yes, No, and Cancel.
9 A listener must ______ with a source.
11 Radio buttons should belong to a ________.
12 Responds to events.
13 Method that identifies the source of the event.
17 Event class
18 A pop-up window
21 A button listener must implement ________.
22 Pressing ______ in a text field generates an event.
23 A "!" in a dialog box indicates a ______ message.
24 A menu is added to a ________.
25 Component used for output but not input
26 Component that can be selected or not

Down

1 An event is generated by some ________.
2 A ______ dialog box is incapable of input.
4 When a button is pressed, an event object is generated and passed as a parameter to ________.
5 Provides scroll bars to a text area
7 A listener is usually implemented as a(n) ______ class.
10 Holds a single line of text
14 Clicking a checkbox generates a(n) ________.
15 A component registers a listener with a method that has the prefix ________.
16 Class that defines dialog boxes
19 When implementing the MouseListener interface, a listener must implement ______ methods.
20 A ______ is added to a menu.

SHORT EXERCISES

1. **True or False**
   If false, give an explanation.
   a. Every listener also generates events.
   b. Every component requires at least one listener.
   c. Event objects are automatically generated whether or not there is a listener.
   d. There is no need for a source to register a listener if the listener is the default listener.
   e. A listener that implements a particular interface must implement every method declared in that interface.
   f. Every GUI contains both input and output components.
   g. An input dialog box and a text field are functionally equivalent.
   h. A text field and a message dialog box are functionally equivalent.
   i. Dialog boxes do not require listeners.
   j. A menu contains menu bars that in turn contain menu items.
   k. A listener class may implement only one interface.
   n. A source may register only one listener.
   m. A listener class may handle events from only one source.

2. **What's Wrong?**
   Determine whether or not there is an error in each of the following statement groups. If there is an error, correct it.
   a. `JPanel x = new JFrame();`
   b. `JFrame y = new JFrame(); y.setTitle("Oops");`
   c. `JButton b = new JButton("Oops"); JFrame z = new JFrame(); z.add(b, BorderLayout.SOUTH);`
   d. `JButton c = new JButton(); c.addActionListener(new ActionListener());`
   e. `private class W implements MouseListener, ActionListener`

3. **Event Delegation Model Review**
   Give an example of each the following, and justify your answers.
   a. A source that never needs to register a listener (i.e., generates no events).
   b. A listener interface requiring the implementation of five methods.
   c. A Swing class that is used only for output, never for input.
   d. A source that generates events from more than one event class.
   e. An event class whose events are naturally handled by a listener that implements two different listener interfaces.

4. **GUI Design**
   Determine whether you would use a button, a dialog box (specify: message, confirmation, or input), or a text field when designing a GUI for the following features of a chess program. Justify your choice for each feature.
   The chess game should allow a player to:
   a. repeatedly undo the last move,
   b. choose to play again or quit when the game is over,
   c. click on the piece that he/she wishes to move,
   d. choose whether or not he/she wishes to move first, and
   e. warn a player when he/she attempts to make an illegal move.

5. **Simulation**
   Java offers many different tools and features. Some of these are absolutely necessary, and some are merely convenient. For example, because a `switch`

statement can be realized with nested if-then-else statements, a switch statement is a convenience, not a necessity. Not all GUI features are necessary. Explain how you might simulate the component in column A with the corresponding components and objects in column B.

A	B
A button	A label and a mouse listener
An input dialog box	A text field and a listener
A confirmation dialog box	A button and a listener
A radio button	Buttons, labels, and listeners
A checkbox	Buttons, labels, and listeners

6. **Debugging**
The following program is supposed to display two buttons—Switch and Exit. When Switch is pressed, the two buttons switch their text (Switch becomes Exit and vice versa). When Exit is pressed, the program terminates. As written, the program has numerous syntax and semantic errors, some careless and some more serious. Debug the program and fix it so that it works correctly.

```
import java.awt.*;
import javax.swing.*;

public class Switch extends JFrame
{
   private JButton switchButton;
   private JButton exitButton ;

   public Switch()          // constructor
   {
      switchButton = new JButton("Switch");
      exitButton = new JButton("Exit");

      setTitle("Switch");
      setBounds(0, 0, 300, 300);

      switchButton.addActionListener(new ButtonListener());
      exitButton.addActionListener(newButtonListener());
      JPanel buttonPanel = new JPanel();
      buttonPanel.add(switchButton);                    // add buttons to panel
      buttonPanel.add(exitButton);
      add(buttonPanel,BorderLayout.CENTER);             // add panel to the frame
      setVisible(true);
   }

   private class ButtonListener implements ActionListener    // the listener
   {
      public void actionPerformed(ActionEvent e)        // must implement this method
      {
         if (e.getSource() == switchButton)
         {
            if (switchButton.getText() = "switch")
            {
               switchButton.setText() = "exit";
               exitButton.Text = "switch";
               repaint();                               // repaint the frame
            }
            else
               if (exitButton.text == "switch")         // the source is exit Button
```

```
                {
                    switchButton.text = "switch";
                    exitButton.text = "exit";
                }
            else
                System.exit(0);
        }
    }

    public static void main(String [] args)
    {
        Switch frame = new Switch();
        frame.setDefaultCloseOperation(JFrame.EXIT_ON_CLOSE);
    }
}
```

7. **More Debugging**
   Can you determine what the following program is supposed to do? Find and correct the errors so that the program performs correctly.

```
import java.awt.*;
import javax.swing.*;

public class Mystery extends JFrame
{
    private JButton aButton;

    public Mystery()      // constructor
    {
        aButton = new JButton("mystery");
        setTitle = "Mystery";
        setBounds(0, 0, 300, 300);
        JPanel buttonPanel = new JPanel();
        buttonPanel.add(aButton);                          // add button to panel
        buttonPanel.add(buttonPanel, BorderLayout.CENTER); // add panel to the frame
        aButton.addActionListener(new ButtonListener());   // register the listener
        aButton.setVisible(true);
    }

    private class ButtonListener implements ActionListener      // the listener
    {
        public void actionPerformed(ActionEvent e)               // must implement this method
        {
          // Do not react to the event
        }
    }

    public static void main(String [] args)
    {
        Mystery frame = new Mystery();
        frame.setDefaultCloseOperation(JFrame.EXIT_ON_CLOSE);
    }
}
```

8. **Listener Trade-Offs: Code Simplicity and Efficiency**
   A GUI displays a 10 by 20 grid of images. Clicking on an image triggers some action. Here are three ways to design the GUI.

   a. Use 200 JButton objects with a grid layout. Create a listener to handle button clicks, and register the listener with each button.

b. Use 200 JLabel objects with a grid layout. Register a single mouse listener to check for clicks, and depending on the location of a click, follow the appropriate action.
c. Use no labels or buttons. Draw images on the frame using g.DrawImage(…), where g is a Graphics object. Register a single mouse listener to check for clicks, and depending on the location of a click, follow the appropriate action, and call repaint().

What are the advantages and disadvantages of each method with respect to simplicity and efficiency? Be specific. Consider the number of objects that you define, the number of events that must handled, and the difficulty of implementing the listener methods that handle the events.

9. **GUI Design**
Without writing any code, describe those components and listeners (if any) that you would use to design the following GUIs. Sketch a picture of the GUI.

a. **A purchase order form for online shopping.**
A store sells 50 different items and allows you to order any number of each item. The prices and pictures of each item are shown. You are asked to choose a state of residence so that tax can be computed. You are asked to choose a shipping method so that shipping costs can be calculated. The total bill is displayed as you make changes, but you can undo anything and recalculate until you click Finished.

b. **A solitaire blackjack program.**
A player is dealt cards face up, and the computer (dealer) is dealt two cards face down. The player may ask for another card if the total of his/her hand is under 21. The player has a bankroll that is displayed, along with his/her current bet.

PROGRAMMING EXERCISES

1. **Rise to Vote Sir**
Write a program that displays three buttons with the names or images of three candidates for public office. Imagine that a person votes by clicking the button that shows the candidate of his/her choice. Display the current number of votes above each button. Include a Finished button that erases the images of the losers and displays only the winner's image with a message of congratulations. Be sure to consider a tie.

2. **A Two-Way Listener**
Write an application with a GUI that displays a button labeled Reverse and two text fields. The first text field accepts a string, and the second displays the string in reverse. The reverse string should be displayed either when the cursor is in the first text field and the Enter key is pressed, or when the Reverse button is clicked. That is, your listener must handle events generated by either the text field or the button.

3. **A Modified Photo Album**
Modify the photo album (Example 19.3) in this chapter so that there is a Previous button, which allows the user to scroll back through the previous nine thumbnails.

4. **Fixed GPA Calculation—One Listener**
Write a program that calculates the grade point average (GPA) of up to five letter grades, each of which can be A, B, C, D, or F. Use five separate text fields for grade input, and a label for output. Your program does not need to respond to events generated by a text field. Instead, include a button labeled Calculate along with a listener class that responds to a button event. Handle erroneous data with an appropriate message. When calculating the GPA, a value of 4 is assigned to A, 3 to B, 2 to C, and so on.

5. **Fixed GPA—No Listeners**
   Rewrite the program of Exercise 4 using input dialog boxes. Each box should provide a drop-down list of grades. You do not need to implement any listeners.

6. **Fixed GPA—Two Listeners**
   Rewrite the program of Exercise 4 using radio buttons. Why are radio buttons more appropriate than checkboxes?

7. **General GPA Calculation**
   Write a program that calculates the GPA of up to 100 letter grades A through F. Use one text area for all the grades, and add scroll bars to the text area. You may ignore any symbols other than A, B, C, D, or F. However, if other symbols are encountered, a warning should be displayed stating that only the letters A, B, C, D, and F were processed.

8. **General GPA Calculation**
   Rewrite the program of Exercise 7 without using a text area. Use the simplest components that get the job done without sacrificing clarity of the interface.

9. **Stop and Go**
   Write a program that displays two buttons at the bottom of a frame: one reads STOP and the other GO. When STOP is clicked, the application should display a red circle above the buttons, and when GO is clicked, a green circle.

10. **Weakling Point**
    Write a program that can be used as a visual aid for a short three-slide presentation—like PowerPoint but without the muscle and versatility. Your program should have a frame that is split vertically into two panels: the right panel holds a text area with scroll bars, and the left displays a label with an image. Place three buttons beneath the two panels. Each button should display the title of a "slide." When you click on a button, an image associated with that slide should appear on the label, and related text should appear in the text area to its right. The text should be read from one or more files.

11. **123-Nim**
    Write a program that allows a person to play 123-Nim against the computer. The initial configuration of 123-Nim consists of a pile of 5 to 50 sticks. Each player may take 1, 2, or 3 sticks on his/her turn, hence the name "123-Nim." The player who takes the last stick wins the game. The player should be shown the initial pile of sticks and given the opportunity to go first or second. The computer and player alternate turns until the game is over. When the game is over, a message appears stating who won, and the player may choose to quit or play again. A running total of the number of games played and the number won by the player is kept in some area of the screen.

    A perfect strategy for this game has the computer choosing `n % 4` sticks, where `n` is the number of sticks remaining in the game, and `n % 4` is not zero. If `n % 4 == 0`, then the computer randomly chooses 1, 2, or 3 sticks.

12. **Extending the Text Editor**
    The text editor program of Example 19.8 is very rudimentary. Most text editors include Find and Replace functions. Add these functions to the Editor class.

13. **Enhancing the Sliding Coins Simulator**
    Implement any or all of the following enhancements to the Sliding Coins program of Example 19.7. Each enhancement is independent of the others.

    a. A coin may not be dragged over any other coin.
    b. A coin may only be dropped if it is touching exactly two other coins.
    c. A running total of the number of coin slides is displayed.

d. Unlimited "undos" are allowed.

e. The mousePressed() method is implemented so that, to move a circle, the user must press the mouse strictly within the boundary of the circle.

14. **A Simple Calculator**
Write a program that simulates a very simple, but unconventional, calculator. The application's GUI should include two text fields, F1 and F2, for numerical input and also a label for output. So, to compute 23 + 56, a user enters 23 into F1 and 56 into F2. There should be four buttons labeled +, −, *, and / . When button **B** is pressed, the operation (F1) **B** (F2) is computed and the result displayed on the label. If a button is pressed and a field F1 or F2 is empty, then the program should display an error message.
   Include a button that copies the result of the computation to F1 and another that copies the result to F2. These buttons facilitate subsequent computation using the result of the previous computation.
   Use exceptions to catch any ill-formed input in the text fields. A Quit button ends the program.

15. **More Coin Sliding**
Expand Example 19.7 to include two additional coin-sliding games. Instead of a Reset button, the GUI should display three buttons: the first resets the H-O game of the example, and the second and third buttons show different starting configurations.
   One of the new games displays a pyramid of six coins as the initial configuration. See Figure 19.34a. The player must slide the coins into the configuration of Figure 19.34b using a minimum number of moves. As usual, any coin that is moved must be placed in a position touching two other coins. This can be done with seven moves.

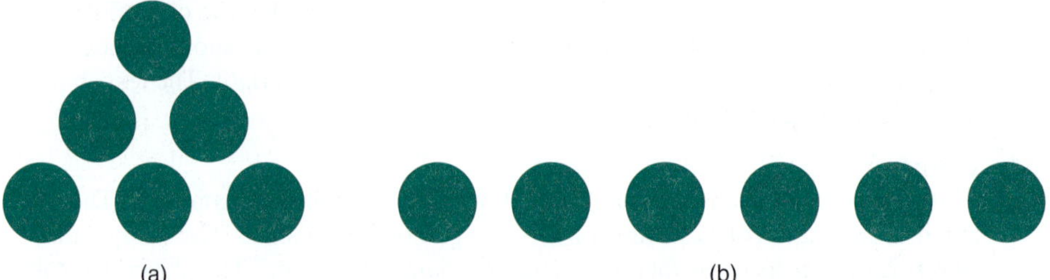

FIGURE 19.34 Change (a) to (b)

A second game transforms the arrangement of Figure 19.35a to that of Figure 19.35b. This can be done by moving just three coins.

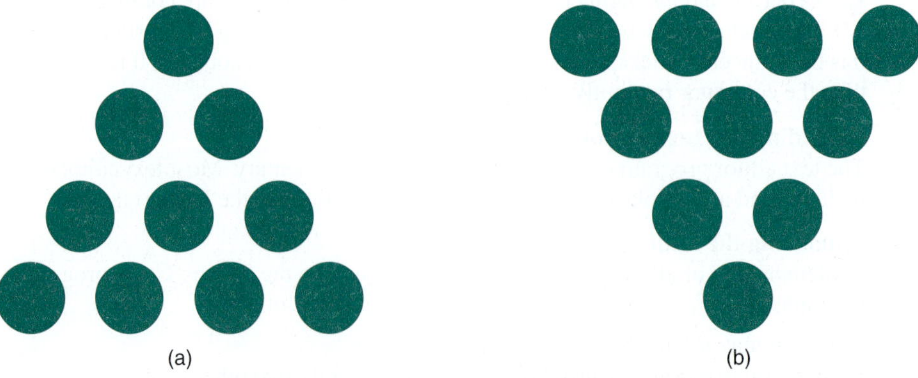

FIGURE 19.35 Make the arrow point down

16. **Extending the Sketch Pad**
The sketch pad implemented in Example 19.6 is bare-bones. Modify the sketch pad program to include the option of drawing ovals/circles. Add two buttons, Line and Circle, at the bottom. When Line is clicked, the program works as it did originally. When Circle is clicked, circles/ovals are drawn instead of lines.

Only one of the two buttons should be enabled at any time. You can achieve this effect by disabling a button after it has been clicked, and enabling it when the other (enabled) button is pressed. The program begins in the line drawing mode, that is, with the line button disabled. An alternative implementation uses a group of two radio buttons.

To draw an oval, follow this procedure:
When the mouse button is pressed, a start point (x, y) is recorded, and when the mouse is dragged and subsequently released, an end point (u, v) is recorded. An oval is drawn with width $|x - u|$ and height $|y - v|$ by invoking

```
drawOval(x, y, width, height).
```

17. **Multiplication Quiz Generator**
Write a program that displays 10 multiple choice questions, one question at a time, each with four possible answers labeled A, B, C, and D. When the user answers one question, the next question appears. The application should display the number of questions that have appeared and the number that have been answered correctly. There should be a menu or button option to quit and restart.

The multiple choice questions should be randomly generated multiplication problems using numbers between 0 and 99. One of the choices should be the correct answer. It is a good idea to generate all 10 questions first and store them in an array (or ArrayList). This allows a clean separation of data and GUI. Use a radio button group for the answers to each question.

18. **A Trivia Quiz Generator**
Write a program that displays 10 multiple choice trivia questions, each with four possible answers labeled A, B, C, and D. The questions can come from one of three categories such as horror movies, classic TV, and rock and roll, or action heroes, cereal brands, and nursery rhymes. Choose three categories that interest you. Be imaginative. The questions along with the correct answers are stored in three text files, one for each category. Each file has at least 25 questions, but additional questions make the application more interesting.

With a button click, a user selects a category and 10 questions from that category are randomly chosen and displayed on the screen. When the user has answered the questions, he/she clicks a Finished button, the quiz is scored, and the results are displayed.

Use a radio button group for the answers to each question. There should be a menu or button option to quit and restart.

As an optional feature, you might include three levels of questions so that a user can select either beginner, intermediate, or advanced.

19. **Car or Goat?**
The Monty Hall Problem derives its name from a classic TV game show, "Let's Make a Deal" starring perennial host Monty Hall. During the show, a contestant is shown three closed doors labeled 1, 2, and 3. Behind one of the doors is a new sports car and behind each of the other doors is a rather handsome goat. Of course, Monty knows which door conceals the car.

After the contestant selects a door (1, 2, or 3), Monty opens one of the other two doors revealing a goat. Two doors now remain closed; one hides a car, the other a goat. The contestant is now given an option: stick with his/her original choice or switch to the other closed door.

Should the contestant switch doors? Keep the original door? Stay or switch, does it make a difference? How often does the contestant go home with the car and how often with a goat? You may be surprised by the answer.

Write an application that simulates this game. Use a random number to choose the door (1, 2, or 3) that hides the car.

The GUI should display three doors labeled 1, 2, and 3. A player chooses a door by clicking on the door. After a player chooses a door, one of the other doors is opened, revealing the picture of a goat, or perhaps just the word Goat. The player now has a choice: click on the original door again or switch doors by clicking on the other closed door. The player clicks on one of the two doors and the door is opened revealing the prize, a car or a goat.

Your GUI should also provide a Reset button allowing a contestant to play again. Include labels that show the number of times the game is played, the number of times the contestant switches doors, the number of times a player wins the car, and the number of times the player chooses the goat. Include an Exit button.

Play the game many times, always switching doors. Then play a series of games in which you never switch. What have you discovered?

Note: In the actual game show, Monty knows the location of the grand prize, and does *not always* open up a second door. His choice of whether or not to show another door is based on the contestant's first guess, and his instincts about the contestant's personality—is he/she more likely to stay or switch? This gives Hall a huge advantage, compared to what can be expected with our simulation.

20. **Binary Nim**
Write a GUI program to play Binary-Nim. Binary-Nim begins with three to eight piles of sticks, such that each pile contains at most 10 sticks. The number of piles and the number of sticks in each pile should be chosen randomly. Each pile may have a different number of sticks. At each turn, a player may remove any number of sticks, but only from a single pile. The player who removes the last stick wins.

The computer and player alternate turns until the game is over. A player should be given the choice of going first or second after he/she sees the initial configuration. When the game is over, the application should display a message stating who won. A running total of the number of games won and lost should be displayed in some area of the screen. After each game, a player may choose to quit or play again.

Random play is fine, but you won't enjoy the game very much because the player can win too easily. There is a perfect but complex winning strategy that involves binary numbers. The data model for the perfect strategy uses a two-dimensional array with one row for each pile. Each row holds the digits (0's and 1's) of the binary number representing the number of sticks in that pile. The bits are right justified. You might research this strategy and incorporate it into your program, or else devise your own strategy. Whatever you do, it is good style to separate the computer's game strategy from the GUI.

21. **(R) Graphical Tower of Hanoi**
The famous Tower of Hanoi problem is frequently used to demonstrate recursion. The basic version of the puzzle consists of three pegs, two of which are empty. The third peg contains a stack of disks, piled on top of each other in size order, with the largest disks at the bottom. See Figure 19.36.

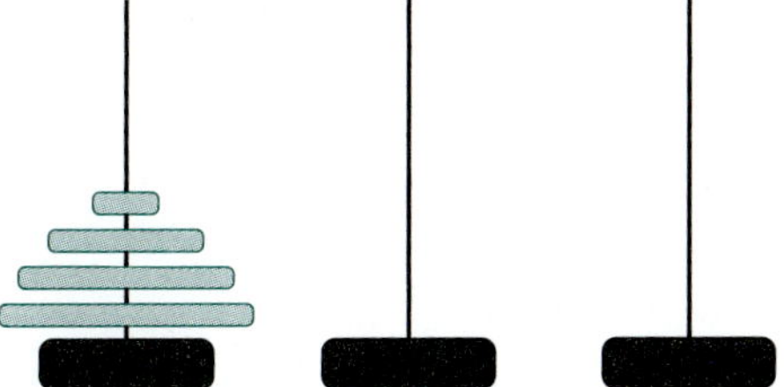

FIGURE 19.36 An initial configuration for the Tower of Hanoi with four disks

The task is to move all the disks to one of the other pegs, with the caveat that you may never move more than one disk at a time, and you may never place a larger disk on top of a smaller one.

The Famous Recursive Solution
A simple and elegant recursive solution follows:

```
TowerHanoi(n, Start, Using, Finish)
// n is the number of disks
// Start is the peg with n disks
// Finish is the peg to which the n disks must be moved
// Using is the extra peg

        void TowerHanoi(n, Start, Using, Finish)
        {
            if n is 0 then exit
            // otherwise
            TowerHanoi(n − 1, Start, Finish, Using)
            Move one disk from Start to Finish
            TowerHanoi(n − 1, Using, Start, Finish)
        }
```

This solution not only works, but it transfers the disks using the minimum number of steps.

The Obscure Iterative Solution
It is not as well known, but there is a simple and elegant iterative solution. Color the base of the Start peg black, and color the disks alternately white and black, so that no two disks (or disk and base) of the same color are touching. Next, color the bases of the Finish and Using pegs black and white, respectively. If you add the rule that two disks (or disk and base) of the same color may never touch, then every move is uniquely determined and, like the recursive solution, this unique set of moves transfers n disks from Start to Finish using the minimum number of steps.

As the number of disks increases, the minimum number of moves required to solve the puzzle grows *exponentially*. That is, the number of moves approximately doubles with each additional disk. For example, a tower of three disks requires at least seven moves, a tower of size four requires 15, and for 25 disks the minimum number of moves is 33,554,431. In general, transferring n disks from one peg to another requires at least $2^n - 1$ moves.

a. Program both methods and verify that each solves the problem for $n = 4$ and $n = 5$.
b. Make a GUI for Tower of Hanoi, so that a user may specify the number of disks (up to eight), and by clicking buttons, move forward and backward through the

solution. The application should display each move graphically with a picture of all three pegs and the disks on each. Your program should display four buttons:

- Reset,
- Next,
- Previous, and
- Exit.

Hints: One way to design the program is to run the solution in advance and store the solution in an array (or ArrayList). A more efficient way that does *not* require preprocessing an exponential time computation is to use the iterative algorithm and create a method that calculates the unique next move from the current configuration.

Depending on your design, the data model will utilize a representation of the current configuration, or an array of configurations. A single configuration with n disks can be stored as an array of size n containing values from the set $\{1, 2, 3\}$. The ith value in the array is the number of the peg (1, 2, or 3) on which the ith largest disk is currently sitting. For example, the starting configuration for five disks is an array of five 1's, since all five disks are on peg 1. If the four smallest disks are on peg 2 and the largest on peg 1, the array would have the form $\{1, 2, 2, 2, 2\}$.

The GUI should draw a picture of a given configuration. To do this, the GUI can query the data model for the current configuration.

22. **The Combo Box—Another Component**

A *combo box* is a familiar component that offers a selection of items such that a user may choose exactly one item. Figure 19.37 shows a combo box that presents a user with a choice of four colors.

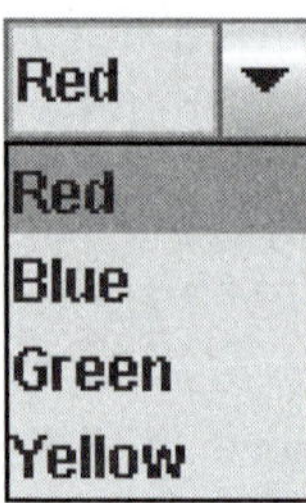

FIGURE 19.37 A combo box displays one item unless the arrow is clicked

Here are the basics:

Class: JComboBox

Generates:

- ActionEvent when an item is selected;
- two ItemEvents when a new item is selected—one for deselecting the *old* item, and one for selecting the *new* item.

An ItemEvent object has two additional methods:

- Object getItem(), and
- int getStateChanged()
  returns an integer: ItemEvent.SELECTED or ItemEvent.DESELECTED with respective integer values 1 and 2.

Listener: Implements ActionListener and/or ItemListener.

Listener method to implement: void actionPerformed(ActionEvent e)
void itemStateChanged(ItemEvent e)

Register a listener: void addActionListener(ActionEvent a)
void addItemListener(ItemEvent i)

Constructors:

- JComboBox()
- JTComboBox(Object[] options)
  creates a combo box, initialized with options. The parameter options may be an array of any Object, but is usually an array of String.

Methods:

- Object getSelectedItem()
  returns the selected item or null if no value is selected.
- int getSelectedItemIndex()
  returns the selected index or −1 if no item is selected.
- int getItemCount()
  returns the number of options.
- void addItem(Object x)
  adds an item to the end of the list of options.
- void removeItemAt(int i)
  removes the item at index i.
- void removeItem(Object s)
  removes item s from the list of options.
- void removeAllItems()
  removes all options.
- void addActionListener(ActionListener x), and
- void addItemListener(ItemListener x)

The following segment instantiates a combo box called colorOption with the choices Red, Blue, Green, and Yellow:

```
public class ComboColorDemo extends JFrame
{
    private JComboBox coloroption;
    private String[] colors = new String[4];
    ...
    public ComboColorDemo()
    {
        panel.setBackground(Color.red);

        colors[0] = "Red";      // initialize names to be displayed
        colors[1] = "Blue";
        colors[2] = "Green";
        colors[3] = "Yellow";

        colorOption = new JComboBox(colors);
        ...
    }
    ...
}
```

Write a program that places the colorOption combo box in a panel with a red background. Whenever a color is selected from the combo box, the background of the panel should change appropriately.

23. **The List Box—One More Component**
A list box is similar to a combo box but allows the user to choose more than one value. That is, list box is to combo box as checkbox is to radio button. Like a combo box, a list box displays more that one value. See Figure 19.38.

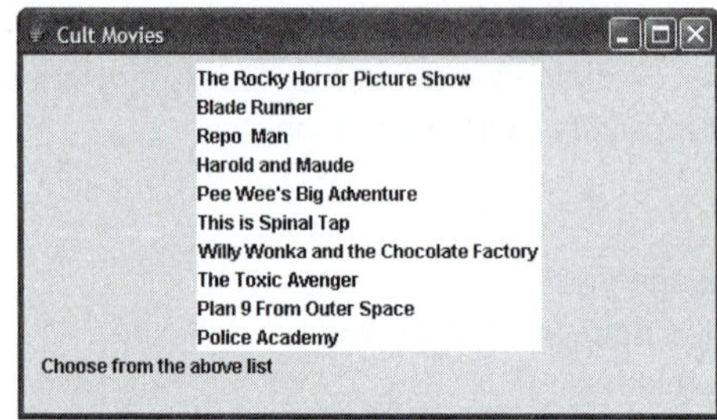

A list box without scroll bars

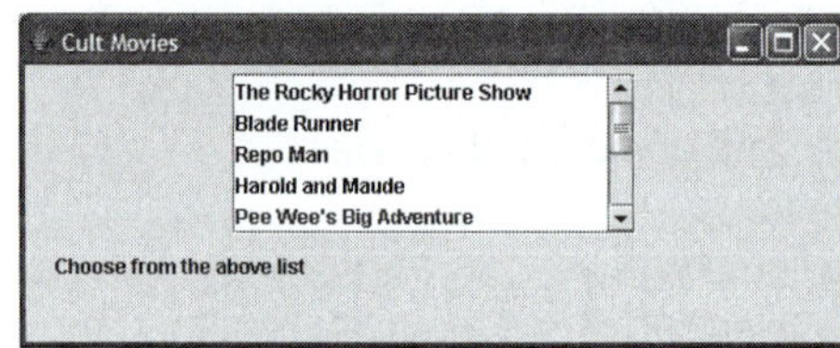

A list box with scroll bars

FIGURE 19.38 Two list boxes

Here are the basics:

Class: JList
Generates: ListSelectionEvent
Listener: ListSelectionListener
Method to implement: void valueChanged(ListSelectionEvent e).
Register a listener: void addListSelectionListener(ListSelectionListener l)

Constructor:

public JList(Object [] choices) // choices is usually an array of String

Methods

- Object getSelectedValue()
returns the first selected item or null if no value is selected.
- int getSelectedIndex()
returns the index of the first selected item or −1 if no item is selected.
- Object[] getSelectedValues()
returns an Object array of selected items.
- int[] getSelectedIndices()
returns an array of all selected indices.
- boolean isSelected(int x)
returns true if the item with index x is selected.
- void setVisibleRowCount(int n)
sets the number of rows displayed, used when a list box is displayed in a scroll pane.
- void setSelectionMode(int n)
sets to single or multiple selection mode using the constants from the ListSelectionModel:
    - ListSelectionModel .SINGLE_SELECTION, (value 0),

- ListSelectionModel .SINGLE_INTERVAL_SELECTION, (value 1),
- ListSelectionModel .MULTIPLE_INTERVAL_SELECTION, (value 2).

Of course, numerous additional methods are detailed on Sun's website.

Write a program that creates a list box containing your name and the names of 10 of your closest friends. The list should be placed in a panel and then in a frame. An array of empty labels should be placed in a second panel and added to the frame. When you select any name(s) from the list, the corresponding phone number(s) should be displayed in the labels. The names and phone numbers should be read from a file when the program begins.

24. **Submenus—One Last Feature**
A *submenu* is a menu that drops down from a menu item. See Figure 19.39.

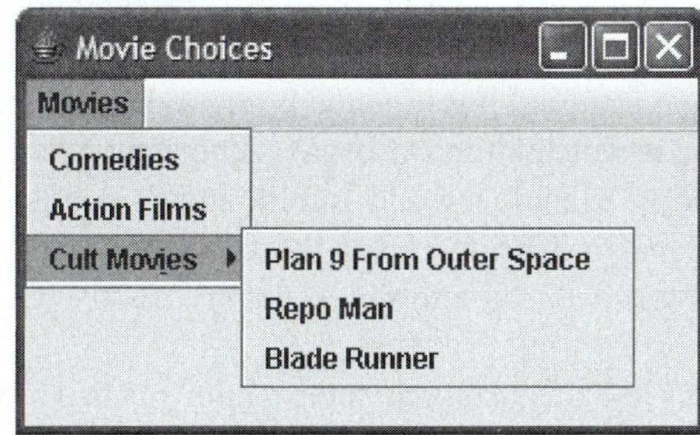

FIGURE 19.39 A submenu of cult films

That's right, menu items can be menus. Thus, if movies and cultMovies are both menus, that is, both belong to JMenu, then movies.add(cultMovies) creates a submenu such as the one displayed in Figure 19.39. Theoretically, there is no limit to the level of nested menus. Of course, more than two or three levels may be somewhat excessive.

Create a frame with a Format menu containing two submenus Color and Font. Pick four colors for the menu items of the Color menu and three fonts for the Font menu. The application should initially display a label Test Me, in a default font, on a white background. The font and the background should change as the user makes menu selections.

THE BIGGER PICTURE

ARTIFICIAL INTELLIGENCE

Artificial Intelligence (AI) is a special area of computer science dealing with devices and applications that exhibit human intelligence and behavior, including the ability to learn and adapt from experience. AI is interdisciplinary—a mix of computer science, cognitive science, psychology, and engineering. Current research in AI includes:

- machine vision—applications in automated camera/video focus, and autonomous vehicles,
- knowledge based (expert) systems—applications in medical diagnosis, oil exploration,
- speech recognition—applications in automated phone systems,

- natural language processing—applications in automated translation, and
- game playing—applications in chess programs, poker, as well as other games.

Success in these areas has been both academic and commercial. And in some cases the successes have been dramatic. Nevertheless, AI suffers somewhat unfairly from an identity crisis. The distinction between artificial intelligence and clever engineering is not always clear. Before programs could play chess, most of the AI community agreed that a chess playing program would demonstrate artificial intelligence. But now that that a chess program routinely holds its own against a world champion human player, that perception has changed. Indeed, a championship chess program owes its success to advances in algorithms, parallel hardware architectures, speed and memory, and chess knowledge. Are these advances in AI, or in algorithms, hardware, and software? That depends on your perspective. But, regardless of your point of view, it is safe to say that AI research has contributed greatly to advances in all areas of computer science.

A complete history of artificial intelligence is beyond the scope of this short "bigger picture," but a quick look is worthwhile. AI began, according to some, with Alan Turing's famous article "Computing Machinery and Intelligence," published in *Mind* magazine (October 1950). In this paper, Turing raises the question "can machines think?" and defines the famous "Turing Test," an attempt to define exactly what is considered artificial intelligence.

The Turing test works like this: a human interrogator sits in a room with two terminals, one connected to a human subject and one to a machine (or program). The interrogator types questions at either terminal. Are the responses coming from a human or a machine? If the interrogator cannot determine the identity of the human subject more than 50% of the time, then the program exhibits artificial intelligence.

There have been many debates about the validity of this test, both philosophical and practical. However, since it is difficult to produce reasonable alternatives, for better or worse, the Turing Test stands as the measure of artificial intelligence. In fact, in 1990, Dr. Hugh Loebner at the Cambridge Center for Behavioral Studies in Massachusetts offered a prize of $100,000, as well as the solid 18-carat gold medal shown in Figure 19.40, for any program that could pass the Turing Test.

Courtesy Dr. Hugh Loebner

FIGURE 19.40 The two sides of the solid 18-carat gold medal pledged as part of the Loebner prize

Since no program has ever come close to passing the test, or is likely to win the prize in the near future, a competition is held each year and a $2000 consolation prize is awarded to

THE BIGGER PICTURE

the creator of the most "human-seeming" entry. When/if any program ever passes the Turing Test, the author will win the prize of $100,000 along with the solid gold medal, after which the Loebner Prize competition will dissolve. If this ever happens, it would not be so surprising if the winning program were to protest this policy, arguing intelligently, of course, that the program itself should win the prize rather than its author—a science fiction drama, to be sure.

Although no computer program is likely to pass an unrestricted Turing Test anytime soon, machines have already passed Turing tests in restricted domains. For example, a chess master frequently cannot determine whether an opponent is a world-class human player or a world-class program.

In the following experiment you will ascertain whether or not you can write a program that exhibits artificial intelligence in a restricted game domain. Can you distinguish between the play of your program and that of a human? Can your program beat the play of its author?

An AI Experiment

In this exercise, you develop a GUI for a one-person game called SameGame (pronounced sa-me-ga-me). And, in the process, you will see how human intuition combined with a computer algorithm allows a program to play better than its creator. Whether you consider this genuine AI or just clever software design is a moot point. Regardless of your opinion, the experiment captures the style and flavor of an AI problem coupled with a dose of event-driven programming.

SameGame

The game begins with a 10 by 15 grid filled with colored circles, each of which is randomly chosen to be one of three colors. Figure 19.41 shows a typical starting configuration.

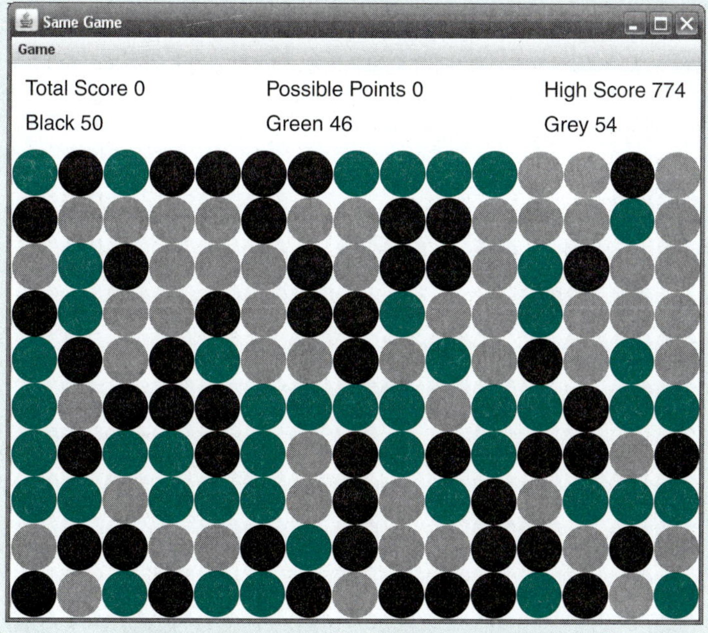

FIGURE 19.41 A starting SameGame configuration

A player clicks on one circle and all circles of the same color "connected" to that circle are highlighted. One circle is connected to another via up-down or left-right connections (not diagonal connections). The picture in Figure 19.42 shows a group of highlighted green circles. This connected group is the result of the player clicking on one of the highlighted circles.

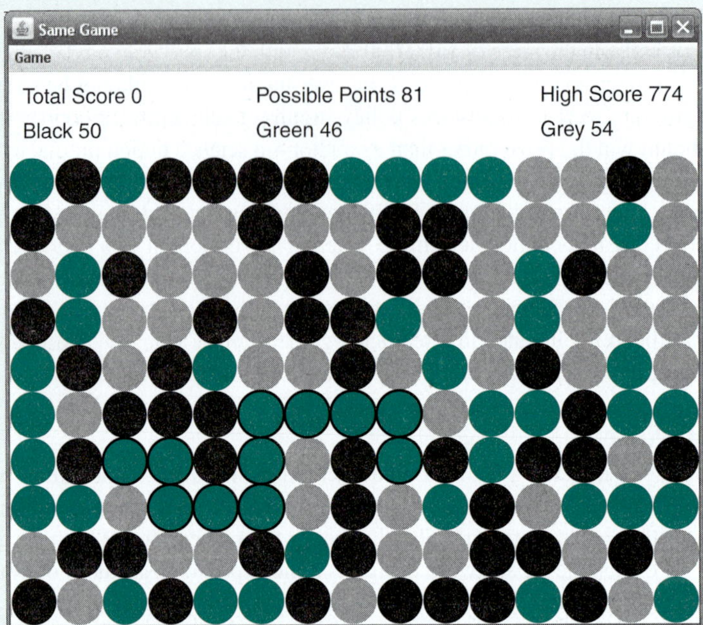

FIGURE 19.42 The highlighted green group is selected

When the mouse button is released, the highlighted group is removed from the picture, and the other circles cascade downward, filling the empty slots. Only connected groups of two or more may be deleted. Single circles may *not* be clicked and deleted. Figure 19.43 shows the board after the green group of Figure 19.42 is deleted.

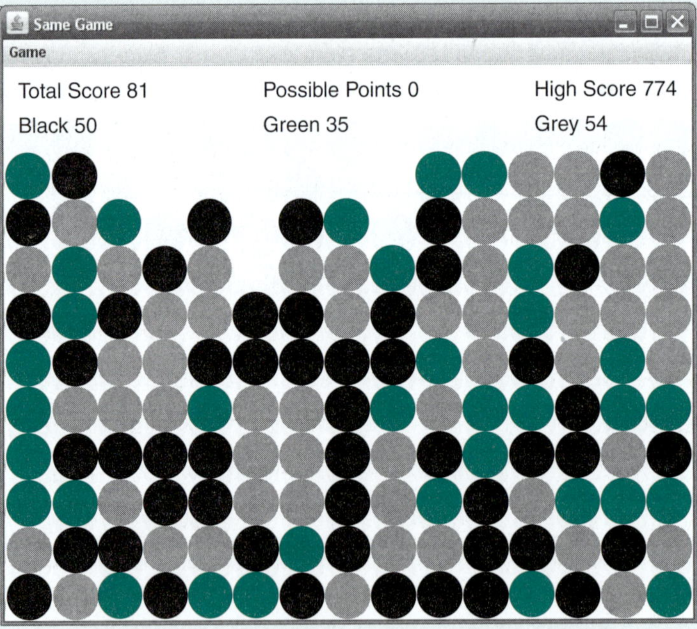

FIGURE 19.43 The pieces fall downward into the gaps left by the deleted green pieces

Depending on the locations of the deleted pieces, empty slots can occur in several places in any column. Every column must be compacted downward until all the empty slots are filled with colored circles.

If a column is emptied, then the columns to the right of the missing column shift to the left. See Figures 19.44 and 19.45.

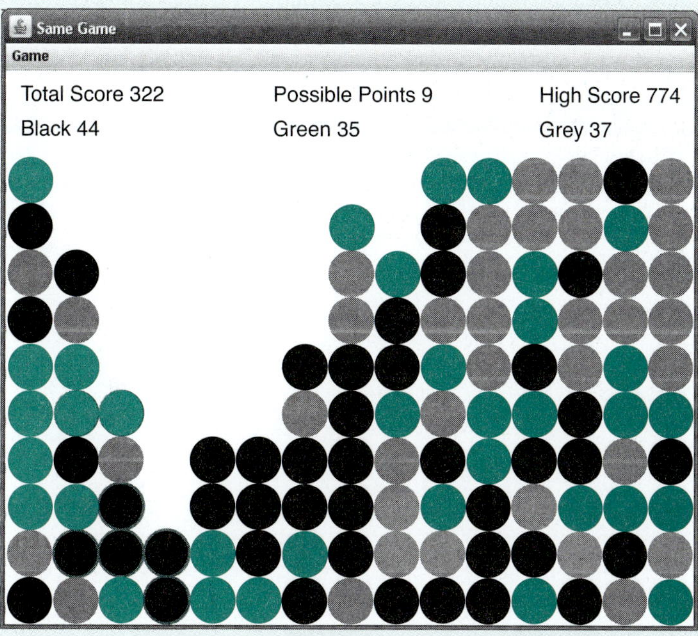

FIGURE 19.44 A small group of black pieces is selected. When it is deleted, the board collapses left to fill in the missing column.

FIGURE 19.45 The black highlighted pieces are deleted, and since a whole column disappears, the board collapses left

Scoring works as follows: Each deleted group of circles earns points, and the more circles in a group, the more points earned. In particular, a group of k circles earns $(k - 2)^2$ points.

So, a two-circle group earns nothing, but a 32-circle group earns $(32 - 2)^2 = 900$ points. There is also a bonus of 1000 points if no circles remain at the end of the game.

For example, when the highlighted green group of Figure 19.46 is deleted, the player earns $(6 - 2)^2 = 16$ points and the player's score increases from 725 to 741. The new board configuration is shown in Figure 19.47.

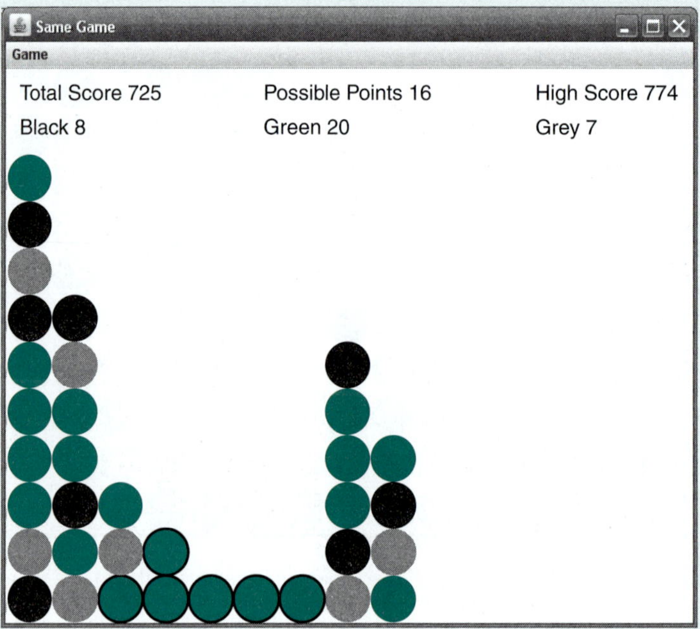

FIGURE 19.46 The selected group earns 16 points

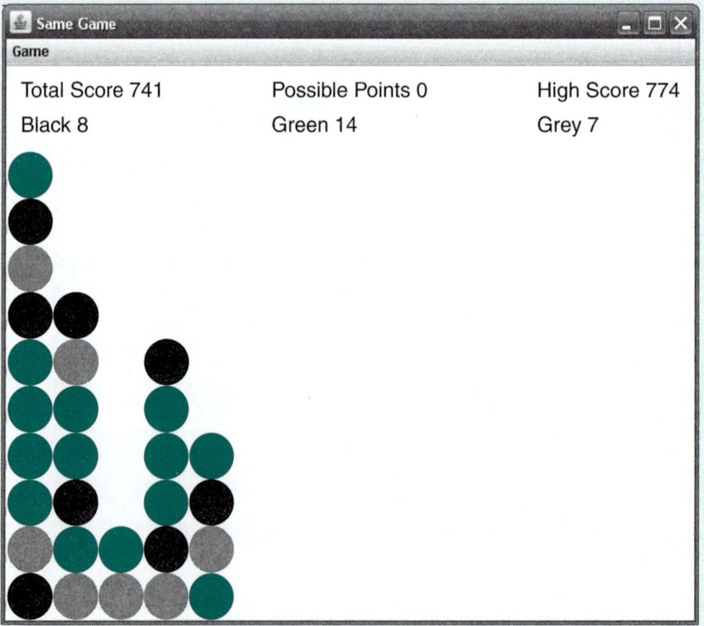

FIGURE 19.47 The deletion of six circles selected in Figure 19.46 results in a number of columns disappearing, and the board collapses leftwards. The score increases by 16 from 725 to 741

Design—The View and the Data Model

When designing the program that plays SameGame, or any visual game, separate the *view* from the *data model*.

The data model consists of the data and logic of the program. The data model keeps track of the locations of the pieces and the current score. The data model also determines the connected groups, and how the board collapses when a group is deleted. Indeed, the data model is responsible for almost all of the program's functionality.

The *view* processes input through mouse clicks and scroll-down menus. The view displays the board and other relevant information, such as a player's score. That is, the view is in charge of the GUI. The view sends messages to the data model so that the data model can update its data structures, and the data model provides information about what the board should look like. The view is very much a client of the data model, but not vice versa.

The View

Certainly, a GUI for this game includes a Start button and a Quit button. Allowing a single "undo" is a nice option, and unlimited "undos" is an even nicer feature.

With the assistance of the data model, the GUI draws the colored circles on the board. The circles can be realized with buttons, labels, or graphics. Choose three images to your liking: three differently colored circles, three distinguishable smiley faces, or, if you prefer, pictures of three friends. To allow highlighting of connected groups, it is helpful to have three additional similar, but highlighted, images. This second set of images is used on a *mouseover*, that is, when the mouse rolls over a spot but no clicking occurs.

Use labels to display the score, high score, and the numbers of each color remaining. Another nice feature is a Possible Points label. This label, on a mouseover, displays the potential points gained if the mouse were to be clicked. For example, on a mouseover, the green group of circles in Figure 19.46 is potentially worth $(6 - 2)^2 = 16$ points; the Possible Points label would show 16.

The Data Model—Data Structure and Algorithms

The data model represents the board and, since the board is a two-dimensional grid, the obvious choice of data structure is a two-dimensional array of integers, with a different integer signifying each color and a blank space. In fact, you may want to use more than one two-dimensional array. You might use one array for the original data, another as a temporary copy that can be "marked up" while finding connected groups, and still another to help implement "undo" features. You decide.

The data model requires a method that accepts a position (row, column) in the array and computes the set of all "color-connected" positions. If you have difficulty with this method, revisiting Example 16.4 (The Lady or the Tiger) might help.

Another method determines the new board configuration after a color group is deleted. It is all too easy to write an erroneous version of this method. Make sure that your method works when:

- a single column has more than one block of circles that are deleted, and when
- multiple columns completely disappear.

It is easier to avoid bugs by first compacting each column and then, if necessary, sliding columns over to the left, rather than first sliding columns to the left and then compacting. Finally, compacting a single column should be done efficiently with a single loop, and not with nested loops.

Exercise

1. **The Game Program**
   Design an interactive SameGame application. On a mouseover, the connected group of pieces should be highlighted, and on a mouseclick, the group should be deleted. The current score and high score for the session should be displayed. Optionally, the GUI might display the number of each different type of piece (e.g. black, gray and green circles) remaining.

How to Teach Your Computer to Play SameGame

Once you have implemented a version of SameGame for a human player, you can teach a computer to play the game.

Computer Strategy—The Algorithm

A very simple strategy tries every move and chooses the one that earns the most points. This method of play is called the *greedy strategy,* and the greedy strategy is sometimes successful. However, any experienced SameGame player will tell you that the greedy strategy is usually not the best way to play the game. There is a way to improve the greedy strategy by looking ahead. Indeed, if the program looks ahead until no more moves are possible, the program plays perfectly!

The following recursive algorithm, recScore(...), accepts a board and returns the maximum possible score attainable. When the algorithm returns, parameter move references the move that leads to that score. Board is a class that stores a board configuration; Board has a field currentScore.

```
int recScore(Board board, Move move)       // move references the best move
{
    (if board is empty)
      return board.currentScore            // there is no more looking ahead.

    else
    {
        int max = 0;
        move = null;
        for each move m
        // m is any non-empty spot on board
        {
            Board newBoard = the board configuration after making move m
            newBoard.currentScore = board.currentScore + score from making move m
            tempScore = recScore(newboard, m);
            // tempScore is the best we can do from newBoard
            if (tempScore > max)
            {
                max = tempScore;
                move = m;
            }
        }
    }

    return max;
}
```

The problem with this algorithm is that the number of possible configurations is astronomical and the program cannot run to completion within your lifetime. Nonetheless, you can use a restricted version of the same algorithm.

As you look ahead, count the levels of recursion. Pass each recursive call an additional parameter, level. The value of level starts at 0, and level + 1 is passed to any subsequent recursive call. When level reaches some predetermined value (you can experiment with this), the program stops recursing. In other words, stop the recursion after n levels, where n is some predetermined constant.

At this point, the algorithm returns currentScore *plus* an estimate of the best score possible from this particular non-empty configuration. The method that calculates this "guestimate" is called an *evaluation function*. If the program reaches an empty board within its n level horizon, no estimate is necessary: the current score is precise; the evaluation function is not needed. Otherwise, an evaluation function is useful, and its usefulness increases as the depth of look-ahead increases.

Estimating a Configuration with Heuristics—The Evaluation Function

An *evaluation function* is a method that estimates, *without looking ahead,* the best score from a particular position. A simple evaluation function for SameGame might add up the squares of the number of remaining circles of each color.

For example, if the numbers of remaining red, green, and yellow circles are 8, 12, and 3, respectively, then this evaluation function returns $8^2 + 12^2 + 3^2 = 217$. This particular evaluation function naively assumes impossibly high scores; a player cannot achieve these scores even if he/she removes all the remaining circles of each color at once. Nonetheless, the function *does* distinguish one position from another in a way that hopefully has some bearing on reality, that is, the higher-evaluated positions offer better scoring opportunities.

Develop your own evaluation function. Use your intuition developed through experience to quantitatively capture the essence of your own style of play. Your evaluation function should somehow mirror your skill and expertise. These ad hoc ideas that form your evaluation are called *heuristics*—rules of thumb that work well but imperfectly.

Exercise

2. The Experiment

Modify your SameGame program so that the computer suggests a move at each turn. Store an initial random starting configuration and play the game without using any computer help. Play again using only the computer's suggestions. Then play the game a third time using the computer's suggestions only when you feel they might help. Play with different starting configurations and see which method gives the highest overall scores. Tabulate and analyze your results.

CHAPTER 20

A Case Study: Video Poker, Revisited

"There are few things that are so unpardonably neglected in our country as poker."
—Mark Twain

"I must complain the cards are ill shuffled till I have a good hand."
—Jonathan Swift

Objective

This chapter presents a case study focusing on the design and implementation of a GUI for the video poker game developed in Chapter 11.

The objective of this chapter is an understanding of the design principle that entails the separation of the data model from the interface, or more simply, the *model* from the *view*.

20.1 INTRODUCTION

Chapter 11 guides you through the design and implementation of a video poker game. From the problem specification, to the determination and responsibilities of the classes, to implementation and testing, the case study illustrates a methodology for program design.

The video poker game of Chapter 11, while functional and even fun, gives the player a text-based interface. Input is accomplished with a Scanner object; output with System.out.println(). In this chapter, we replace the rather bland user interface developed in Chapter 11 with a more visual GUI that utilizes buttons, labels, and pictures. Even if you have forgotten the implementation details of Chapter 11, you may be surprised at how easily we can accomplish this task.

> The separation of model from view that was underscored in the case study of Chapter 11 enables us to plug in a new graphical interface with minimal effort.

For non-players, the rules of poker are explained in Section 11.2.

20.2 A QUICK REVIEW

The poker application of Chapter 11 consists of seven interacting classes: Player, PokerGame, Bet, Deck, Card, Hand, and Bankroll. The details of these classes are summarized in Figure 11.5, and the classes are implemented in Section 11.9.

The Player class provides a text-based user interface. It is the Player class that we reimplement here, replacing text-based input and output with a GUI of buttons, labels, and pictures.

Replacing the text-based UI of Chapter 11 with a GUI does not require knowledge of the implementation details of the other classes.

To replace the old user interface with a GUI, all that you need is information about the objectives and methods of some of the classes. Figure 20.1 lists those classes and methods that we use in creating a new GUI-based poker game. The information summarized in Figure 20.1 and a few methods that we discuss in the chapter are all that you need. Except for the Player class, which handles all input and output, no class needs alteration.

Class	Purpose	Constructor	Method	Method
Bankroll	Manages the number of coins in the machine	**Bankroll();** Sets initial coin number to 0	**void alterBankroll(int n);** Adds n coins to the number of coins in the machine	**int getBankRoll();** Returns the number of coins currently in the machine
Hand	Maintains a hand of five cards	**Hand();** Creates an empty hand	**String[] getHand();** Returns an array of five String references that describes a hand, e.g., {"Ace of Hearts", "2 of Spades", "3 of Diamonds",…}	
Bet	Manages the current bet or wager	**Bet(int n);** Sets the bet to n coins	**int getBet();** Returns the current bet	**void setBet(int n);** Sets the bet to n coins
PokerGame	Plays the game: deals and updates the hands, maintains the list of discarded cards	**PokerGame(Bet bet, Bankroll bankroll, Player player);** Initializes the bet and bankroll for a player	**void viewInitialHand( );** Requests a hand of five cards via hand.getHand() Asks the player to display the hand via the message player.displayHand(hand)	**void discardOrHoldCards();** Queries the player for the list of discarded cards: player.getDiscard(…); Updates the hand; Requests that the player display the new hand: player,displayHand() Evaluates the hand; determines the winnings/losses; updates the bankroll; Asks the player to display the results: player.displayResults()

FIGURE 20.1 A few video poker classes and methods

20.3 A VISUAL POKER GAME

Figure 20.2 shows a screenshot of a video poker game. The GUI is not a text menu but a display of buttons, labels, and images. Figure 20.2 shows that the player was dealt a hand of two pair. A hand of two pair pays 2 to 1, the bet is three coins, so the payout is six. The current bankroll is 12 coins.

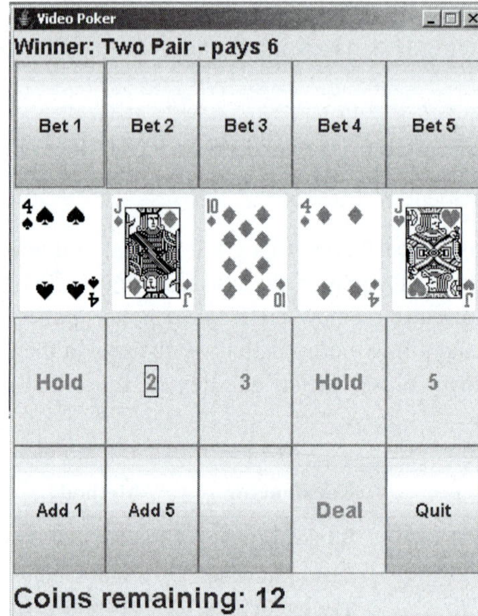

FIGURE 20.2 A video poker GUI

Before playing a hand of poker, a player must insert coins into the machine. This action is simulated by clicking the Add 1 or the Add 5 button. These buttons can be clicked repeatedly. Each time a player clicks one of these buttons, either 1 or 5 coins are "inserted" into the machine. The bottom panel of the GUI displays the current number of coins, that is, the bankroll. Figure 20.3 gives a screenshot of the game after a player has inserted three coins into the machine by clicking the Add 1 button three times.

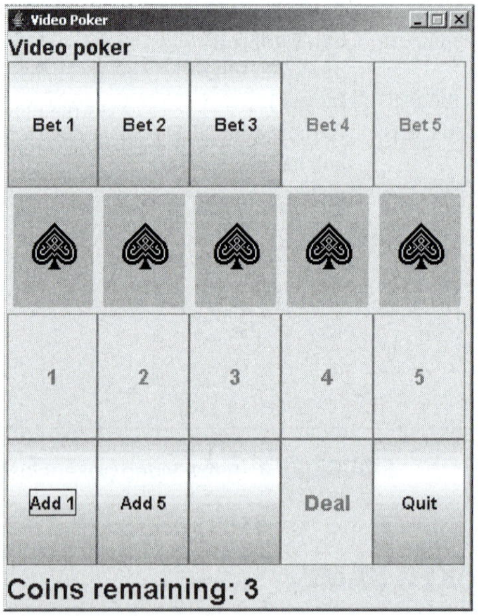

FIGURE 20.3 A player inserts three coins

Once a player inserts a few coins into the machine, he/she clicks one of the five Bet buttons, thus placing a bet from one to five coins, but not more than the number of coins in the machine. Subsequently, a hand of five cards is dealt. Figure 20.4 shows a typical poker hand displayed as five card images. The bet of two coins is displayed in the upper left-hand corner of the frame.

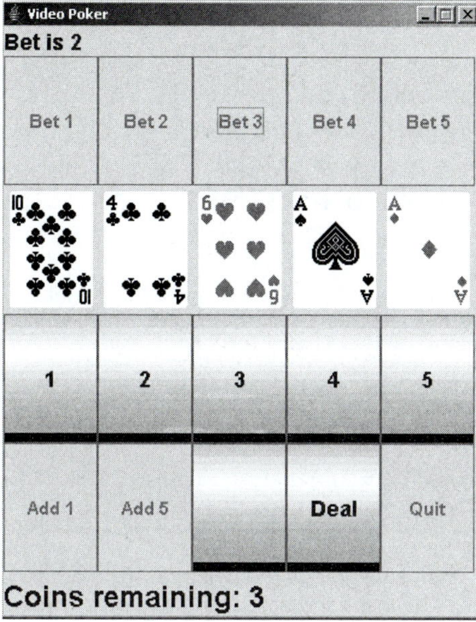

FIGURE 20.4 A player bets two coins and a hand is dealt

After the initial hand is dealt, a player has the option of keeping or discarding any of those five cards. To "hold" or keep a card, a player clicks the number that is displayed below the card, and that number is replaced by the word Hold. The two aces of Figure 20.5 are designated Hold.

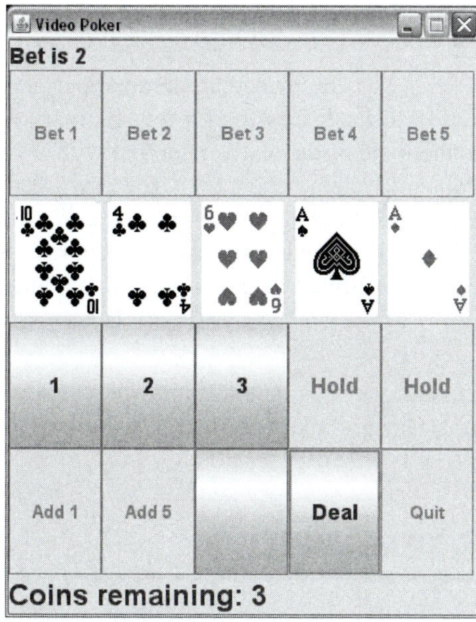

FIGURE 20.5 Two cards are marked Hold

After deciding which cards are to be kept and which discarded, a player clicks the Deal button, and those cards that the player chooses to discard are replaced with different cards. The hand is scored and the number of coins updated. See Figure 20.6.

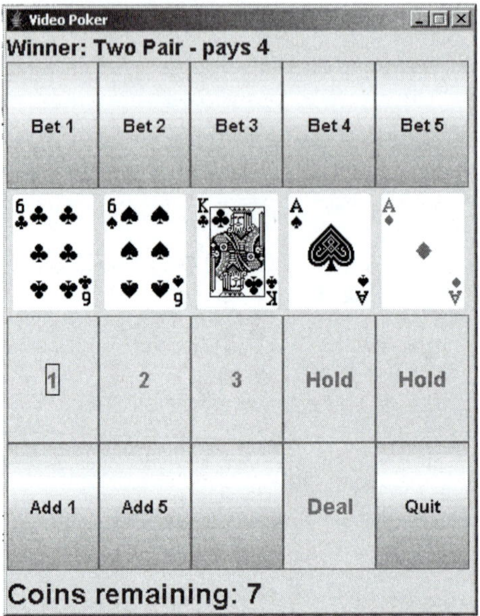

FIGURE 20.6 The player keeps the two aces. The other three cards are replaced, resulting in a hand containing two pair, which pays 2 to 1.

The game of Figure 20.6 is a winner. The final hand includes two pair paying 2 to 1. Consequently, the initial bet of two coins pays back four coins, and the bankroll increases from three to seven coins. All winning hands and the corresponding payoffs are enumerated in Section 11.2.

In the following sections, we develop a new Player class, one that is graphical and uses Swing components for input and output. Figures 20.2 through 20.6 serve as a model.

We begin the new Player class by extending JFrame and placing buttons and labels in the frame. Next, we add a listener class and a few auxiliary methods. The graphical version of Player reflects the logic of the text version but with Swing components replacing Scanner input and calls to System.out.println(). The new interface plugs directly into the video poker application of Chapter 11 with surprising ease. Among the classes of the video poker application, Player is the only class that we replace. No other classes need to be changed, added, deleted, or modified in any way. All input and output is handled by a Player object.

Because the design of the poker game in Chapter 11 separates the data model from the user interface, it is easy to replace the text based interface with a new GUI.

20.4 LAYING OUT THE FRAME

As a first step, we create a Player class that extends JFrame and includes the buttons and labels of the GUI. By now, this should be a straightforward task. The following code builds a nonfunctioning GUI, that is, a GUI with no listeners. Figure 20.3 provides a blueprint and guide for component layout. When instantiated, a Player object duplicates Figure 20.3.

////////////// Player class, a GUI for video poker //////////////

```
public class Player extends JFrame
{
   private JLabel resultLabel;              // label displays the type of hand and the payout
   private JLabel[] cardLabel;              // an array of 5 labels that display card images
   private JButton[] holdButton;            // click to keep a particular card
   private JButton add1Button;              // add 1 coin
   private JButton add5Button               // clicking adds 5 coins;
   private JLabel bankrollLabel;            // label that displays the current number of coins
   private JButton quitButton;              // exit the application
   private JButton dealButton;              // click to display the updated hand
   private JButton[] betAndPlayButton;      // clicking any of these buttons makes a bet and begins play

   public Player()                          // default constructor, places all components
   {
      super("Video Poker");
      setBounds(0, 0, 400, 500);

      // the label at the top of the frame
      resultLabel = new JLabel();
      resultLabel.setFont(new Font("Arial", Font.BOLD, 18));
      resultLabel.setText("Video poker");

      // The five card images; the initial image is "Back.gif," which is a dummy card
      cardLabel = new JLabel[5];
      for (int i = 0; i < 5; i++)
         cardLabel[i] = new JLabel(new ImageIcon("Back.gif"));

      // the five hold/discard buttons
      holdButton = new JButton[5];
      for (int i = 0; i < 5; i++)
      {
         holdButton[i] = new JButton("" + (i + 1));                // initially these have numbers
         holdButton[i].setFont(new Font("Arial", Font.BOLD, 18));
         holdButton[i].setEnabled(false);                          // initially turned off
      }

      // the five bet and play buttons
      betAndPlayButton = new JButton[5];
      for (int i = 0; i < 5; i++)
      {
         betAndPlayButton[i] = new JButton("Bet " + (i + 1));
         betAndPlayButton[i].setEnabled(false);                    // initially turned off
         betAndPlayButton[i].setFont(new Font("Arial", Font.BOLD, 15));
      }

      // the deal button, initially turned off
      dealButton = (new JButton("Deal"));
      dealButton.setFont(new Font("Arial", Font.BOLD, 18));
      dealButton.setEnabled(false);

      // the quit button
      quitButton = new JButton("Quit");
      quitButton.setFont(new Font("Arial", Font.BOLD, 15));

      // label that displays current number of coins, the bankroll
      bankrollLabel = new JLabel();
      bankrollLabel.setFont(new Font("Arial", Font.BOLD, 24));
      bankrollLabel.setText("Coins remaining: " + 0);             // initially no coins

      // two buttons that add 1 or 5 coins to the machine
      add1Button = new JButton("Add 1");
```

```
        add5Button = new JButton("Add 5");
        add1Button.setFont(new Font("Arial", Font.BOLD, 15));
        add5Button.setFont(new Font("Arial", Font.BOLD, 15));

        // panel that holds play buttons, card labels, hold buttons, deposit buttons, deal and quit
        JPanel centerPanel = new JPanel(new GridLayout(4,5));
        // add the five bet buttons
        for (int i = 0; i < 5; i++)
           centerPanel.add(betAndPlayButton[i]);

        // add the five labels that display the card images
        for (int i = 0; i < 5; i++)
           centerPanel.add(cardLabel[i]);

        // add the five hold buttons
        for (int i = 0; i < 5; i++)
           centerPanel.add(holdButton[i]);

        // add the two deposit buttons, a blank button, the deal and quit buttons
        centerPanel.add(add1Button);
        centerPanel.add(add5Button);
        centerPanel.add(new JButton());                  // a blank button as a separator
        centerPanel.add(dealButton);
        centerPanel.add(quitButton);

        // add the label that displays the results to the NORTH section of the frame
        add(resultLabel, BorderLayout.NORTH);
        // add the label that displays the coin count to the SOUTH section of the frame
        add(bankrollLabel, BorderLayout.SOUTH);

        // add the panel with the buttons and card labels to the CENTER section of the frame
        add(centerPanel, BorderLayout.CENTER);

        setResizable(false);
        setVisible(true);
    }
}
```

With the frame of the new GUI in place, we now animate a few components and provide listeners that respond to events.

20.5 ADDING COINS

Before playing a hand of poker, a player must deposit coins into the machine. This is accomplished by clicking the Add 1 button or Add 5 button. Each click increases the bankroll by either one or five coins. Once coins have been added, the appropriate Bet buttons are enabled. For example, if a player deposits three coins, the buttons labeled Bet 1, Bet 2, and Bet 3 are enabled but Bet 4 and Bet 5 are not. The Bet 4 and Bet 5 buttons are disabled because you cannot bet four or more coins when there are just three coins in the machine! If a player deposits seven coins, then all five buttons are enabled. A Bankroll object manages the number of coins deposited into the machine.

Clicking Add 1 or Add 5 generates an action event that we handle with an inner class called ButtonHandler. This listener handles the events generated by either button. The following code

- declares and initializes a Bankroll reference, bankroll, and
- implements ButtonListener, an inner class that responds to events generated by add1Button and add5Button.

The response of ButtonListener necessitates:

- incrementing the bankroll,
- displaying the number of coins in the machine on the label referenced by bankrollLabel, and
- enabling the appropriate Bet and Play buttons.

Figure 20.3 shows the game after three coins have been "inserted" into the machine. Notice that some buttons are enabled and others disabled.

```
public class Player extends JFrame
{
   private JLabel resultLabel;                // label displays the type of hand and the payout
   private JLabel[] cardLabel;                // an array of 5 labels that display card images
   private JButton[] holdButton;              // click to keep a particular card
   private JButton add1Button;                // clicking adds 1 coin
   private JButton add5Button;                // clicking adds 5 coins
   private JLabel bankrollLabel;              // label that displays the current number of coins
   private JButton quitButton;                // exit the application
   private JButton dealButton;                // click to display the updated hand
   private JButton[] betAndPlayButton;        // clicking buttons makes a bet and private begins play
   Bankroll bankroll;                         // manages the number of coins in the machine

   public Player()                            // constructor, places all components, registers listeners
   {
        // as above
      bankroll = newBankroll();
      add1Button.addActionListener(new ButtonListener());     // register listener
      add5Button.addActionListenet(new Button Listener());    // register listener
   }

   private class ButtonListener implements ActionListener     // responds to button events
   {
      public void actionPerformed(ActionEvent e)
      {
         if ((e.getSource() == add1Button) ||
                       (e.getSource() == add5Button))
         {
            if (e.getSource() == add1Button)
               bankroll.alterBankroll(1);                      // add one coin to the bankroll
            else
               bankroll.alterBankroll(5);                      // add 5 coins

            int br = bankroll.getBankroll();                   // total number of coins deposited
            bankrollLabel. setText("Coins remaining: "+ br );  // display total coins on label

                                                               // enable the appropriate bet buttons
               for (int i = 0; i < 5; i++)
                    if (br >= (i + 1))
                         betAndPlayButton[i].setEnabled(true);
            return;
         }
      }
   }
```

20.6 THE FIRST HAND

After a player inserts coins, he/she is ready to play a hand of poker. Now, the player clicks one of the buttons labeled Bet 1, Bet 2, . . . , Bet 5. Clicking one of these buttons determines the current bet and deals the initial poker hand. To the Player class we add code that:

- registers the ButtonListener class with each of the five Bet buttons, and

- responds to the Bet button events by:
  - instantiating and setting the bet,
  - displaying the bet on the label referenced by resultLabel,
  - instantiating a new PokerGame with bet, bankroll, and player as parameters,
  - displaying images of the cards that make up the hand,
  - enabling the Hold and Deal buttons, and
  - disabling the Bet buttons, the Add 1 and Add 5 buttons, and the Quit button.

Figure 20.4 shows the GUI after a hand has been dealt. At this stage of play, only the Hold and Deal buttons are enabled.

```
public class Player extends JFrame
{
   private JLabel resultLabel;           // label displays the type of hand and the payout
   private JLabel[] cardLabel;           // an array of 5 labels that display card images
   private JButton[] holdButton;         // click to keep a particular card
   private JButton add1Button;           // add 1 coin
   private JButton add5Button            // clicking adds 5 coins;
   private JLabel bankrollLabel;         // label that displays the current number of coins
   private JButton quitButton;           // exit the application
   private JButton dealButton;           // click to display the updated hand
   private JButton[] betAndPlayButton;   // clicking any of these buttons makes a bet and begins play
   Bankroll bankroll;                    // maintains number of coins in the machine
   PokerGame pokerGame;
   Bet bet;
   Hand hand;

   public Player()                       // default constructor, lays out components, registers listeners
   {
      // as previously coded

    for (int i = 0; i < 5; i++)          // register ButtonListener with each button
         betAndPlayButton[i].addActionListener(new ButtonListener());
   }

   private class ButtonListener implements ActionListener
   {
      public void actionPerformed(ActionEvent e)
      {
         if ((e.getSource() == add1Button) ||
                        (e.getSource() == add5Button))
         { // as previously coded }

         for (int i = 0; i < 5; i++)                     // respond to betAndPlayButton[i]
            if (e.getSource() == betAndPlayButton[i])
            {
               bet = new Bet();
               bet.setBet(i + 1);                       // set the bet for this hand
               resultLabel.setText("Bet is " + (i + 1)); // display the bet on the label
               pokerGame = new PokerGame(bet, bankroll,Player.this); // instantiate PokerGame
               pokerGame.viewInitialHand();             // ask pokerGame to deal the first hand
               for (int j = 0; j < 5; j++)              // for each hold button
               {
                  holdButton[j].setText("" + (j + 1));   // display the card number
                  holdButton[j].setEnabled(true);       // enable the button
               }
               dealButton.setEnabled(true);             // enable the deal button
               add1Button.setEnabled(false);            // disable add1Button..
               add5Button.setEnabled(false);            // disable add5Button
               quitButton.setEnabled(false);            // disable quitButton
               for (int j = 0; j < 5; j++)              // disable all betAndPlayButtons
                  betAndPlayButton[j].setEnabled(false);
```

```
48.                 return;
49.             }
50.         }
51.     }
```

Notice that the response to a betAndPlayButton event includes sending a message to pokerGame (line 36):

```
pokerGame.viewInitialHand()
```

The viewInitialhand() method of PokerGame consists of two method calls:

```
public void viewInitialHand()
{
      hand.newHand();
      player.displayHand(hand);
}
```

The call to newHand() creates a new hand of five cards. This method works correctly regardless of the interface. However, the second call is a Player method, displayHand(hand).

The text-based version of Player implements displayHand(Hand hand) as:

```
public void displayHand(Hand hand)
{
   String [] handString = hand.getHand();
   for(int i = 0; i < 5; i++)
      System.out.println((i + 1) + ". " + handString[i]);
}
```

That is, a hand is displayed on the screen as a list of strings:

Ace of Hearts
Queen of Clubs
Queen of Hearts
3 of Spades
4 of Hearts

Of course, textual output is inappropriate for our new version of Player. Instead, we incorporate a similar method into our new graphical Player class that displays five card images rather than five lines of text. To accomplish this we use a collection of 52 card images, conveniently named Ace of Hearts.gif, Ace of Spades.gif, . . . , 10 of Hearts.gif, 10 of Spades.gif, and so on.

Moreover, the Hand method

```
String[] getHand()
```

returns an array of five strings, e.g., {"Ace of Spades", "Queen of Clubs", "Queen of Hearts", "3 of Spades", "4 of Hearts"}.

A revised displayHand() for a revised Player class can be written as:

```
public void displayHand(Hand hand)
{
   String[] handString = hand.getHand();
   for (int i = 0; i < 5; i++)
   {
         String name = handString[i] + ".gif";               // name is an image file name
         cardLabel[i].setIcon(new ImageIcon(name));          // display images on labels
   }
}
```

Thus, in addition to the constructor and the inner class ButtonListener, the GUI version of Player, like the text version, implements the displayHand(Hand hand) method. Both accomplish the same task: one with words, the other with pictures; one with System.out.println(), the other with labels.

20.7 HOLD THOSE CARDS

A player has the option of holding or discarding any or all of his/her five cards. To retain a card, a player presses the numbered button shown directly below the card. The response to pressing any one of these buttons changes the button's text from a number to the string "Hold" and disables the button. Figure 20.5 shows that two buttons have been marked Hold and disabled.

To register a listener with each such button, we add the following statement to the constructor:

```
for (int i = 0; i < 5; i++)
    holdButton[i].addActionListener(new ButtonListener());
```

To respond to events generated by these buttons, we add code to ButtonListener that changes a button's text to "Hold" and disables the button:

```
for (int i = 0; i < 5; i++)
    if (e.getSource() == holdButton[i])  // source is button[i]
    {
        holdButton[i].setText("Hold");
        holdButton[i].setEnabled(false);
        return;
    }
```

Once a player clicks a Hold button, the button is disabled and the decision cannot be reversed. You could certainly add a mechanism that allows a player to change his/her mind, but we opt for simplicity.

20.8 THE NEW HAND

After a player decides which cards to hold and which to discard, he/she clicks the Deal button. This action generates an event. The response to this event

- invokes pokerGame.discardOrHoldCards(),
- disables the Deal and Hold buttons, and
- enables the other buttons.

Figure 20.6 shows a game configuration after the Deal button has been clicked. In addition to registering ButtonHandler as a listener for dealButton, we add the following if statement to the ButtonHandler class to handle a Deal button event:

```
if (e.getSource() == dealButton)
{
    pokerGame.discardOrHoldCards();  // discardOrHoldCards() does the work

    // enable and disable the appropriate buttons
    dealButton.setEnabled(false);
    for(int j = 0; j < 5; j++)
        holdButton[j].setEnabled(false);
```

```
    for (int i = 0; i < 5; i++)
        if (bankroll.getBankroll() >= (i + 1))
            betAndPlayButton[i].setEnabled(true);
    add1Button.setEnabled(true);
    add5Button.setEnabled(true);
    quitButton.setEnabled(true);
}
```

The PokerGame method discardOrHoldCards() defined in Chapter 11 manages the updated hand.

```
public void discardOrHoldCards();
{
        player.getDiscard(holdCards);
        hand.updateHand(holdCards);
        player.displayHand(hand);
        int payoff = hand.evaluateHand();
        int winnings = updateBankroll(payoff);
        player.displayResults(payoff, winnings);
}
```

Notice that discardOrHoldCards() invokes three Player methods:

- void getDiscard(boolean[] holdCards),
- void displayHand(Hand hand), and
- void displayResults(int payoff, int winnings).

The getDiscard(boolean[] holdCards) method of the text-based Player class sets holdCards[i] to true if the player opts to keep the ith card and false otherwise. That is, the Player method getDiscard(…) tells the caller which cards to keep and which to discard. The new GUI Player class must do likewise. When a player retains a card, the corresponding Hold button is disabled. Consequently, getDiscard(boolean[] holdCards) can be implemented by checking whether or not a Hold button is enabled:

```
public void getDiscard(boolean[] holdCards)
{
    for (int i = 0; i < 5; i++)          //check whether or not the Hold button is enabled
        if (holdButton[i].isEnabled())   // button was not clicked
            holdCards[i] =false;
        else                             // button was clicked and enabled
            holdCards[i] = true;
}
```

We have already implemented displayHand(Hand hand) in the GUI Player class, so that leaves just displayResults(int payoff, int winnings).

The text-based version of Player implements this method as:

```
public void displayResults(int payoff, int winnings)
{
    String nameOfHand = "Lose";
    if (payoff == 250)
        nameOfHand = "Royal Flush";
    else if (payoff == 50)
        nameOfHand = "Straight Flush";
```

```
    else if (payoff == 25)
        nameOfHand = "Four of a Kind";
    else if (payoff == 9)
        nameOfHand = "Full House";
    else if (payoff == 6)
        nameOfHand = " Flush";
    else if (payoff == 4)
        nameOfHand = "Straight ";
    else if (payoff == 3)
        nameOfHand = "Three of a Kind";
    else if (payoff == 2)
        nameOfHand = "Two Pair";
    else if (payoff == 1)
        nameOfHand = " Pair of Jacks or Better";

    if (winnings > 0)
    {
        System.out.println("Winner: " + nameOfHand);
        System.out.println("Payoff is " + winnings + " coins.");
    }
    else
        System.out.println("You lost your bet of " + bet.getBet());
        System.out.println("Current Bankroll is " + bankroll.getBankroll());
        System.out.println();
}
```

Indeed, this method can be incorporated into the new Player class with minimal change. The game's outcome is displayed on two labels rather than in a text-based window using System.out.println(). The only code that must be altered is the final if-else statement:

```
// use a label rather than println() for output
if (winnings > 0)
        resultLabel.setText("Winner: " + nameOfHand + " – pays " + winnings);
else
        resultLabel.setText("You lost your bet of " + bet.getBet());
        bankrollLabel.setText("Coins remaining: " + bankroll.getBankroll());
```

20.9 THE COMPLETE *Player* CLASS

The new Player class has the following skeletal form that includes a constructor, three methods, and a private inner class:

```
public class Player extends JFrame
{
        //      The Constructor
        public Player()
        {
                sets up the components of the GUI
                registers listener with buttons
        }

        //      Three Methods
        public void displayHand(Hand hand)
```

```
{
        displays images of the five cards in hand
}

public void getDiscard(boolean[] holdCards)
{
    holdCards[i] = true if the ith Hold Button is disabled
}

public void displayResults(int payoff, int winnings)
{
        displays the outcome of a hand
}

//      Listener—an Inner Class
private class ButtonListener implements ActionListener
{
        public void ActionPerformed(ActionEvent e)
        {
                responds to events generated by GUI buttons
        }
}
```

The complete class, although rather lengthy, is direct and uncomplicated. The card images are assumed to be in a folder, Cards, which is in the same directory as the Player class.

```
import javax.swing.*;
import java.awt.*;
import java.awt.event.*;

public class Player extends JFrame
{
   private JLabel resultLabel;              // label displays the type of hand and the payout
   private JLabel[] cardLabel;              // an array of 5 labels that display card images
   private JButton[] holdButton;            // click to keep a particular card
   private JButton add1Button;              // add 1 coin
   private JButton add5Button;              // clicking adds 5 coins;
   private JLabel bankrollLabel;            // label that displays the current number of coins
   private JButton quitButton;              // exit the application
   private JButton dealButton;              // click to display the updated hand
   private JButton[] betAndPlayButton;      // clicking makes a bet and begins play

   private Bankroll bankroll;
   private PokerGame pokerGame;
   private Bet bet;
   private Hand hand;

   public Player() // constructor
   {

      super("Video Poker");
      bet = new Bet();
      bankroll = new Bankroll();
      setBounds(0, 0, 400, 500);

      // the label places at the NORTH area of the frame
```

```
resultLabel = new JLabel();
resultLabel.setFont(new Font("Arial", Font.BOLD, 18));
resultLabel.setText("Video poker");

// Display five card images, the initial image is "Back.gif" – a dummy card
cardLabel = new JLabel[5];
for (int i = 0; i < 5; i++)
     cardLabel[i] = new JLabel(new ImageIcon("Cards/Back.gif"));

// the five hold/discard buttons
holdButton = new JButton[5];
for (int i = 0; i < 5; i++)
{
   holdButton[i] = new JButton("" +(i + 1));                  // initially display numbers 1 – 5
   holdButton[i].setFont(new Font("Arial", Font.BOLD, 18));
   holdButton[i].setEnabled(false);                           // initially turned off
}

// the five "bet and play" buttons
betAndPlayButton = new JButton[5];
for (int i = 0; i < 5; i++)
{
     betAndPlayButton[i] = new JButton("Bet " + (i + 1));     // display Bet 1, Bet 2,...Bet 5
     betAndPlayButton[i].setEnabled(false);                   // initially turned off
     betAndPlayButton[i].setFont(new Font("Arial", Font.BOLD, 15));
}

// the deal button, initially turned off
dealButton = (new JButton("Deal"));
dealButton.setFont(new Font("Arial", Font.BOLD, 18));
dealButton.setEnabled(false);

// the quit button
quitButton = new JButton("Quit");
quitButton.setFont(new Font("Arial", Font.BOLD, 15));

// label that displays current number of coins, i.e., the "bankroll"
bankrollLabel = new JLabel();
bankrollLabel.setFont(new Font("Arial", Font.BOLD, 24));
bankrollLabel.setText("Coins remaining: " + 0 );              // initially no coins

// two buttons that either add 1 or 5 coins to the machine
add1Button = new JButton("Add 1");                             // displays "Add1"
add5Button = new JButton("Add 5");
add1Button.setFont(new Font("Arial", Font.BOLD, 15));
add5Button.setFont(new Font("Arial", Font.BOLD, 15));

// panel holds bet buttons, card labels, hold buttons, deposit buttons, deal and quit
JPanel centerPanel = new JPanel(new GridLayout(4,5));

// add the five bet buttons
for (int i = 0; i < 5; i++)
   centerPanel.add(betAndPlayButton[i]);

//add the five labels that display the card images
```

```
        for (int i = 0; i < 5; i++)
           centerPanel.add(cardLabel[i]);

        // add the five hold buttons
        for (int i = 0; i < 5; i++)
           centerPanel.add(holdButton[i]);

        // add the two deposit buttons, a blank button, the deal and quit buttons
        centerPanel.add(add1Button);
        centerPanel.add(add5Button);
        centerPanel.add(new JButton());                  // a blank button as a separator
        centerPanel.add(dealButton);
        centerPanel.add(quitButton);

        // add the label that displays the game results to the NORTH section of the frame
        add(resultLabel, BorderLayout.NORTH);
        // add the label that displays the coin count to the SOUTH section of the frame
        add(bankrollLabel, BorderLayout.SOUTH);

        // add the panel that holds the buttons and card labels to the CENTER section of the frame
        add(centerPanel, BorderLayout.CENTER);

        // register listeners, one inner class does all listening
        add1Button.addActionListener(new ButtonListener());
        add5Button.addActionListener(new ButtonListener());
        dealButton.addActionListener(new ButtonListener());
        quitButton.addActionListener(new ButtonListener());

        for (int i = 0; i < 5; i++)
           betAndPlayButton[i].addActionListener(new ButtonListener());

        for (int i = 0; i < 5; i++)
           holdButton[i].addActionListener(new ButtonListener());
        setResizable(false);
        setVisible(true);
     }

     public void displayHand(Hand hand)                  // displays images of five cards
     {
        String[] handString = hand.getHand();
        for (int i = 0; i < 5; i++)
        {
           String name = "Cards/" + handString[i] + ".gif"; // name is a file name.
           cardLabel[i].setIcon(new ImageIcon(name));
        }
     }

     public void getDiscard(boolean[] holdCards)         // maintains hold/discard information
     {
        for (int i = 0; i < 5; i++)
        {
           if (holdButton[i].isEnabled())                // card is discarded
              holdCards[i] = false;
           else                                          // card is retained
              holdCards[i] = true;
        }
     }
```

```
public void displayResults(int payoff, int winnings)      // displays the final outcome on a label
{
   String nameOfHand = "Lose";
   if (payoff == 250)
     nameOfHand = "Royal Flush";
   else if (payoff == 50)
     nameOfHand = "Straight Flush";
   else if (payoff == 25)
        nameOfHand = "Four of a Kind";
   else if (payoff == 9)
     nameOfHand = "Full House";
   else if (payoff == 6)
     nameOfHand = " Flush";
   else if (payoff == 4)
     nameOfHand = "Straight ";
   else if (payoff == 3)
     nameOfHand = "Three of a Kind";
   else if (payoff == 2)
        nameOfHand = "Two Pair";
   else if (payoff == 1)
     nameOfHand = " Pair of Jacks or Better";

   if (winnings > 0)                                    // display outcome on resultLabel
        resultLabel.setText("Winner: "+ nameOfHand + " – pays " + winnings);
   else
     resultLabel.setText("You lost your bet of " + bet.getBet());

   bankrollLabel.setText("Coins remaining: " + bankroll.getBankroll());
}

private class ButtonListener implements ActionListener      // respond to button events
{
   public void actionPerformed(ActionEvent e)
   {
     if ((e.getSource() == add1Button) || (e.getSource() == add5Button))    // click Add 1/ Add 5
     {
        if (e.getSource() == add1Button)
          bankroll.alterBankroll(1);
        else
          bankroll.alterBankroll(5);

        int br = bankroll.getBankroll();
        bankrollLabel. setText("Coins remaining: " + br);
        for (int i = 0; i < 5; i++)
          if (br >= (i + 1))
             betAndPlayButton[i].setEnabled(true);
        return;
     }
     if (e.getSource() == quitButton)                 // click the Quit button
        System.exit(0);

     for (int i = 0; i < 5; i++)                     // click one of the five bet buttons
        if (e.getSource() == betAndPlayButton[i])
        {
          bet = new Bet();
```

```
                bet.setBet(i + 1);
                resultLabel.setText("Bet is " + (i + 1));
                pokerGame = new PokerGame(bet, bankroll, Player.this);
                pokerGame.viewInitialHand();

                for(int j = 0; j < 5; j++)                    // enable the hold buttons
                {
                    holdButton[j].setText("" + (j + 1));
                    holdButton[j].setEnabled(true);
                }

                // enable and disable other buttons
                add1Button.setEnabled(false);
                add5Button.setEnabled(false);
                quitButton.setEnabled(false);
                dealButton.setEnabled(true);
                for (int j = 0; j < 5; j++)
                    betAndPlayButton[j].setEnabled(false);
                return;
            }

            for (int i = 0; i < 5; i++)                       // respond to a Hold button event
                if (e.getSource() == holdButton[i])
                {
                    holdButton[i].setText("Hold");
                    holdButton[i].setEnabled(false);
                    return;
                }

            if (e.getSource() == dealButton)                  // respond to a Deal button event
            {
                pokerGame.discardOrHoldCards();
                dealButton.setEnabled(false);
                for(int j = 0; j < 5; j++)
                    holdButton[j].setEnabled(false);

                for (int i = 0; i < 5; i++)
                    if (bankroll.getBankroll() >= (i + 1))    // enough coins ?
                        betAndPlayButton[i].setEnabled(true);

                add1Button.setEnabled(true);
                add5Button.setEnabled(true);
                quitButton.setEnabled(true);
            }
        }
    }

    public static void main(String[] args)
    {
        Player pm = new Player();
    }
}
```

Figures 20.3 through 20.6 give screenshots of the GUI as it changes during one complete game.

20.10 IN CONCLUSION

The video poker application, as presented here and also in Chapter 11, emphasizes an important program design principle:

Separate the interface from the data model.

Because of this separation of interface and model, we can easily replace the original text-based interface with a GUI or even add an additional interface. Poker-playing algorithms are not intertwined with Player class logic. A Player object sends messages to the objects of the other classes, and likewise the other classes send messages to Player. Information is passed back and forth between classes. A programmer can easily design a new interface without understanding the implementation details of the game. The division of labor is clear, and that makes the task easier.

WHAT'S NEXT?

This chapter has no short exercises, no crossword puzzle, no true-false questions, no compiler playing, and no Bigger Picture. Instead, we suggest a few longer projects. Each of these projects gives you the opportunity to synthesize what you have learned, gain experience, and hone your problem-solving and programming skills.

When you have completed a few projects, here's what to try next:

- **Read other programmers' code.**
  This will help you develop opinions about good and bad programming style. You will see how other people think. You may discover a new trick or two, and you may even learn what you do *not* want to do.
- **Design your own projects.**
  Design your own projects from scratch. Think of a favorite game or application, and build it. Beginners get little practice with the progression from conception to design to final implementation. Explore this process fully.
- **Push ahead.**
  You have reached the end of the text, but hardly the end of Java. Java is a large and practical language with features that extend beyond the contents of this introductory text. Network programming, servelets, threads, and database programming are a few of the features that enable you to write practical commercial programs. At this point you should be able to learn the rudiments of these features. Don't be afraid to try.
- **Have fun.**
  Java is playdough for grown-ups—a tool to help mold ideas. Play with Java. Better yet, get paid to play with it.

PROJECTS

1. **Tic-Tac-Toe**
   You know how to play. Create a GUI for a Tic-Tac-Toe game that pits a human player against the computer. The computer should never lose, and it should win if the player makes an error. That is, the computer should play perfectly. Allow the player to choose whether or not to play first. Keep a running total of the wins, losses, and ties. After each game, the player may play again or quit.

2. **An Electronic Photo Album**
   Design a program that maintains an electronic photo album. The program should display the photos sorted by name, four per page, and allow user to move forward or backward through the album. Store the actual photos (jpg images) in a directory, and maintain a sorted file with the names of the images currently in the photo album. Options to add and delete photos should be available. There are file exceptions that can occur with this project, so be sure to catch them.

3. **A Calculator**
   Create a version of the calculator supplied with Windows. See Figure 20.7.

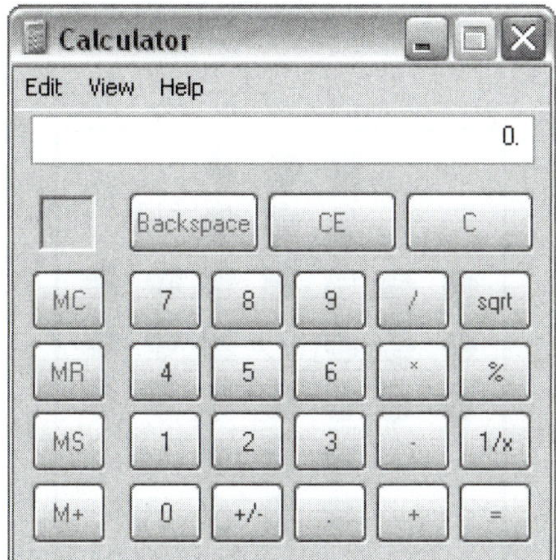

FIGURE 20.7 A calculator GUI

The data model should keep track of the memory, the last number entered, the current number, and the last operation. Use a separate class for the GUI.

4. **An Artist's Palette**
   Design a program that simulates an artist's color palette. A frame should display three color buttons: Red, Green, and Blue. Another part of the frame shows a surface, initially white, for mixing colors. When the artist clicks on a color, that color is "added" to the color displayed in the mixing area. Adding a color to the "current color" is accomplished by a 1 to 9 weighted average. That is, if you click on color *A* and the current color is *P*, the new color is $.1A + .9P$. Note that since the palette starts white, it takes a number of color additions before dark colors appear.

   For example, if the current color is a shade of light purple with RGB values (128, 0, 128) and you click on green (0, 255, 0), then the new color is .9(128, 0, 128) + .1(0, 255, 128) = (115, 26, 115), a deeper shade of purple.

   Similarly, adding green (0, 255, 0) to white (255, 255, 255) results in

$$
\begin{aligned}
&.9(255, 255, 255) + .1(0, 255, 0) = \\
&(230, 230, 230) \quad + \quad (0, 25, 0) \quad = \\
&(230, 255, 230).
\end{aligned}
$$

   This is a very light shade of green. Of course, the RGB numbers are rounded to the nearest integer.

   The artist should be able to store the current palette color. Use a menu with a Store item. When a color is stored, a new button, showing the stored color, appears along with the original Red, Green, and Blue buttons and any other stored colors.

Stored colors can also be used to mix colors. Allow a maximum of six stored colors. The menu should also include a Remove option that allows the artist to remove any stored color.

The program should also allow the artist to undo up to 10 previous actions and provide the artist with the option of saving the stored colors in a file, which is loaded when the program starts.
It will be helpful to use the getGreen(), getRed(), and getBlue() methods of the Color class.

5. **Peg Solitaire**
Design a computer version of Peg Solitaire. Peg Solitaire is a game consisting of a wooden board with 33 holes, each big enough to hold a small wooden or plastic peg. Initially, each hole, except the center hole, contains a peg. See Figure 20.8.

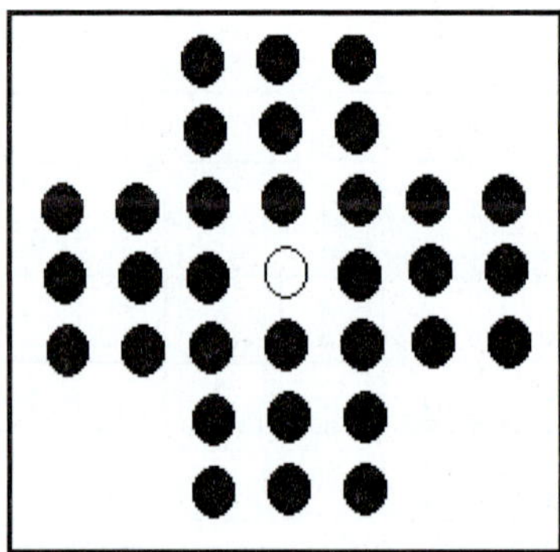

FIGURE 20.8 Peg solitaire. The center hole is empty.

A player can move a peg into an unoccupied hole by "jumping over" another peg. The peg that is "jumped over" is removed from the board. The object of the game is to remove as many pegs as possible. A perfect game removes all pegs except one, with the remaining peg occupying the center hole. When there are no more jumps possible, the program should inform the player, display the final number of pegs remaining, and ask the user if he/she wants to play again or quit. The best score achieved so far should be displayed.

Include three buttons that handle the following options:

- unlimited undos (*Hint*: keep a stack of "jumps" in the data model),
- quit the game, and
- reset the board.

6. **Solitaire Concentration (a.k.a. Memory)**
Solitaire Concentration, also known as Memory, is played on a 4 by 6 grid hiding 12 pairs of images. Each cell of the grid displays a number from 1 to 24. Hidden behind each cell is one of the 24 images. The images can be anything you like: playing cards, smiley faces, a picture of Bart Simpson, or birds of the Northwest. The starting board configuration is shown in Figure 20.9.

When a player clicks a cell, the hidden image is revealed. After the player sees that image, he/she clicks on another cell and the image hidden by that cell is displayed. If the two images match, as they do in Figure 20.10a they remain visible, and the player chooses two more cells without penalty. Otherwise, the two unmatched images are hidden again, and the player continues but with one mark against him/her. The number of marks against the player is displayed prominently on the frame.

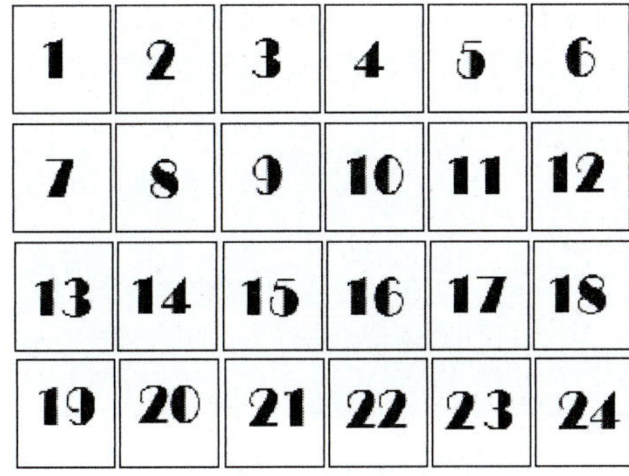

FIGURE 20.9 An initial configuration for solitaire concentration

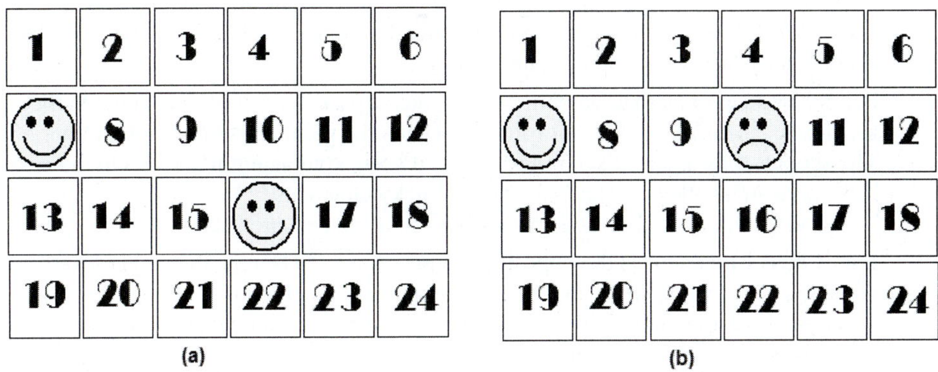

FIGURE 20.10 Clicking 7 and 16 reveals matched images. Clicking 7 and 10 does not.

When all 24 images have been matched, the player may quit, or play again. The best score for a session is also displayed.

On a mouseover, light up a button. This lets the player know that it is okay to click. The setRolloverIcon(Icon image) method of JButton allows you to do this without an extra listener or class.

7. **An Interior Design Aid**
Write a program that aids in the placement of objects such as furniture or audio equipment in a room. Assume that the shape of each object is rectangular. By clicking and dragging the mouse, a user creates rectangles of different sizes that remain in place when the mouse is released. Rectangles should not be permitted to overlap.
In the data model, a rectangle can be stored by its coordinates. All currently displayed rectangles should be stored. The user should be able to move an object and/or erase it.

8. **A Craps Table**
The craps table of Figure 20.11 shows the many bets that a player can make.
The simplest of these bets is a "pass line" bet. To make a pass line bet, a player places one or more chips on the table in the area marked "pass line." A pass line bet always pays 1 to 1. Once all bets are placed, a "shooter" rolls the dice. This is called the "come out" roll.

- If the come out roll shows 7 or 11, the pass line bet wins and the game is over.
- If the come out roll shows 2, 3, or 12, the pass line bet loses and the game is over.

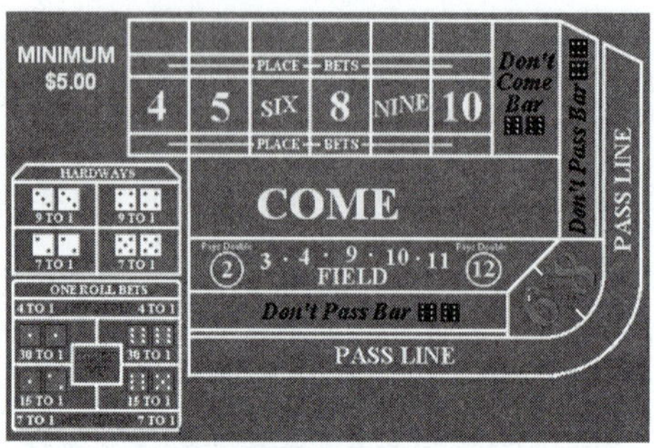

FIGURE 20.11 A craps table

- If the come out roll shows 4, 5, 6, 8, 9, or 10, that number is the called the "point," and the shooter rolls again and continues to roll until he rolls the point or a 7. If the shooter rolls a 7, the pass line player loses his bet and the game is over. If the shooter rolls the point, the player wins, and the game is over.

For example, assume that Gamblin' Gus makes a pass line bet of one chip. On the first toss of the dice, the shooter rolls a 5. That's the point. Gus hopes for another 5. The shooter rolls again. It's a 3. And again; it's a 6. And again; it's a 12. On the next roll the shooter rolls a 5. That's the point. Lucky Gus wins.

In addition to pass line bets, some other possible bets are:

Don't Pass Line: This is the opposite of a pass line bet. That is, the player loses when the pass line bet wins and wins when the pass line bet loses, except if a 12 is rolled on the come out roll. When this occurs, the game is a tie and the player takes back his/her wager. The payoff is 1 to 1.

Place Bets: A place bet is made *after* the point has been established. To make a place bet, place one or more chips on 4, 5, 6, 8, 9, or 10. If your number is rolled before a 7, you win. If a 7 is rolled before your number, you lose. Unlike the pass line bet, these bets do not pay 1 to 1. If you bet on 4 or 10, the payoff is 9 to 5. That is, you win 9 chips for every 5 chips that you bet. If you bet on 5 or 9, the payoff is 7 to 5. And if you bet on 6 or 8, the payoff is 7 to 6.

Field Bets: A field bet is a one-roll bet. A player bets that the next roll of the dice will be a 2, 3, 4, 9, 10, 11, or 12. A 2 pays 2 to 1, a 12 pays 3 to 1, and each of the other numbers pays 1 to 1.

These are just a few of the many possible bets.

Design an interactive video craps game that includes pass line bets, don't-pass bets, place bets, and field bets as well as any other type of bet that you may wish to include. Indeed, there are many websites that enumerate and describe all the rules and bets of craps. Take a look.

The GUI should display a picture of a craps table. To make a one-chip pass line, place, field, or don't-pass bet, the player clicks in the appropriate area of the table. Each time the player clicks, the bet increases by one chip. For example, clicking the pass line three times makes a pass line wager of three chips.

Your application should obviously include a Roll Dice button and a Quit button. On each roll of the dice the GUI should display the results. A picture of two dice would be nice. The program should also query the player for an initial bankroll and display and update the bankroll after every game. Include a mechanism to add chips to the bankroll.

9. **An Arithmetic Tutor**

Design and implement a program that helps a third grade student to learn his/her multiplication tables. The program should display a table such as the table in

Figure 20.12. To practice multiplication, the student clicks on a cell and types the product of the row value and the column value. At any time, he/she can press a Check button, and all correct answers are displayed in bold black, while incorrect answers are displayed in red. Empty cells are left empty. There should also be an Answers button that, when clicked, fills in all the answers in bold black.

x	**1**	**2**	**3**	**4**
2				
3				

FIGURE 20.12 A multiplication table

The student can vary the range of digits that appear in the table, one range for the rows and one for the columns. In Figure 20.12, the row range is 2 to 3 and the column range 1 to 4.

10. **A Graphical Mastermind Program**

Mastermind is a game for two players. Each player chooses a secret code consisting of four colors. Each color can be chosen from a set of six colors, {Red, Green, Blue, Yellow, Black, White}. A player may choose duplicate colors. Each player attempts to guess the other player's secret code.

Let's call the two players Mack and Mabel. In order to discover Mabel's secret code, Mack makes a guess at Mabel's four-color code. Mabel responds by telling Mack

a. the number of exact matches between Mack's guess and her secret code, and

b. the number of inexact matches between Mack's guess and her secret code.

An exact match means the codes match color and position. An inexact match means that the codes match color, but they are not in the correct position. No match is counted twice, and exact matches take precedence over inexact matches. Consequently, the total number of matches, exact or inexact, is between zero and four.

For example, if Mabel's secret code is:

(Red, Red, Green, White)

then the match responses for the following guesses are shown below:

(Red, Blue, Black, Green)	1 Exact 1 Inexact
(Red, Red, Red, Black)	2 Exact 0 Inexact
(Green, Red, Red, White)	2 Exact 2 Inexact
(Black, Yellow, Red, Green)	0 Exact 2 Inexact
(Green, Red, Red, Red)	1 Exact 2 Inexact

The players alternate making guesses and giving responses until one of them guesses the other's secret code.

The Project Design a program that pits the computer against a human in a game of Mastermind. There are many design issues, the most difficult having to do with the computer's strategy. We make a few suggestions on the more difficult problems, but otherwise leave the design to you.

A ColorCode Class Before detailing the computer's strategy, let's take a closer look at a color code. A skeletal ColorCode class might be defined as:

```
public class ColorCode
{
        private int[] code;          // each color has a code number
        // 0 = Red, 1 = Green, 2 = Blue, 3 = Yellow, 4 = Black, 5 = White
```

```
        public ColorCode(int [] colors)                  // constructor
        {
                code = new int[4];
                for (int i = 0; i < 4; i++)
                        code[i] = colors[i]
        }

        public ColorCode(String [] colors)               // constructor
        {
                code = new int[4];
                for (int i = 0; i < 4; i ++)
                    if (colors[i] .equals("Red")
                       code[i] = 0;
                    else if (...)
        }

        int exactMatch (ColorCode c)
        {
                // returns the number of exact matches between this and c
        }

        int inexactMatch (ColorCode c)
        {
                // returns the number of inexact matches between this and c
        }

        String toString()
        {
                // returns a string version of the code
        }

        // also include necessary getter and setter methods
}
```

Computer Strategy When formulating a guess, many people use an ill-defined intuitive approach that tries to identify the code piece by piece. This naïve approach guesses codes that cannot possibly be correct in order to obtain more information about what might actually be correct. This method can be effective and is by no means a bad strategy. However, by its very nature this technique is impossible to simulate on a computer. A strategy that is better suited to computer simulation, but not so well suited to a human, is described below. This strategy usually uncovers a code in six guesses or less, which beats all but the best and luckiest players.

At the beginning of the game, every color code is a viable candidate. There are $6^4 = 1296$ possible codes, (six colors for each of four positions). A human opponent secretly selects a code and the computer attempts to guess that code. The computer employs a strategy that keeps track of those codes that remain consistent with all previously acquired information. That is, the computer never chooses a guess unless the possibility exists that the guess is the correct one.

The computer begins with a random guess because any code is possible at this point. This guess might be accomplished with four random numbers between 0 and 5, inclusive, which represent a four-color code. After making this initial guess, all subsequent guesses are carefully planned. How does the machine continue?

Suppose, for example, that the computer's first guess scored 2 exact matches and 0 inexact matches. Then the only remaining possibilities are those codes that match 2 exact and 0 inexact with the computer's first guess. All other codes are permanently eliminated. The computer generates all the possible codes and tests each one against its first guess. If a code matches 2 exact and 0 inexact with the first guess, then that code is a viable candidate and must be remembered. So, add that code to a HashSet object h, where h holds all viable candidate codes.

For its second guess, the computer chooses some object from h, perhaps the last object added, or one chosen at random and retrieved via an iterator. Remember, a HashSet is not ordered. The second guess is compared to the secret code. If, for example, the second guess has 1 exact and 1 inexact match, the computer iterates through h and eliminates all the codes that this information rules out. That is, all codes in h that do not match up 1 exact and 1 inexact with the second guess are deleted.

With each subsequent guess, more codes are deleted from h. The process continues until just a single code remains in the hash set. Here is the strategy in action:

Guess	Exact	Inexact
(Red, Red, Green, White)	2	0
The next guess must match 2-0 with the first guess.		
(Red, Red, Black, Yellow)	1	1
The next guess must match 2-0 with the first guess and 1-1 with the second guess.		
(Red, Yellow, Green, Blue)	0	3
The next guess must match 2-0 with the first guess, 1-1 with the second guess, and 0-3 with the third guess.		
(Blue, Red, Yellow, White)	2	2

Now the process becomes more difficult for a human because there are so few candidate codes still viable. How many and which ones? Your program's hash set holds the answer to this question. What is difficult for humans is a snap to a computer.

Design As always, separate the GUI from the data model. The data model must keep track of the codes, the guesses, and the HashSet. In other words, the data model handles the computer strategy. The GUI should give the human player a pretty color picture of the guesses and the replies, as well as some type of scorecard and the options to quit, start over, and play again.

11. **Chess and Checkers**
Design an application that allows two people to play chess or checkers. Whenever a player moves a piece, the application should check the validity of the move.

12. **Your Own Game**
Design a GUI-based program based on a game that you enjoy. It might be your version of a commercial board game such as Monopoly or Scrabble, a card game such as Black Jack or Texas Hold 'Em, or perhaps a television game such as Deal or No Deal, Jeopardy!, or Wheel of Fortune. Start simple. Begin with just a few features and gradually add more.

13. **The Check Please**
Design a GUI-based program that can be used in a restaurant to generate a customer's check. Assume that the menu consists of:

- appetizers
- salads
- pasta courses
- entrees
- side dishes
- desserts
- drinks

Initially, the program reads the day's menu from a text file. Each item is stored on three lines of the file:

1. category (see choices above),
2. item description (any text), and
3. price (double).

Each item should be displayed graphically under the appropriate category. The server selects any number of items from the menu and the application generates a bill. The bill includes 5% sales tax.

Use the following typical no-frills bill as a template for your bill:

2 Shrimp Cocktail	12.50
1 Caesar Salad	5.00
1 Spinach Salad	4.50
1 Seafood pasta	18.50
1 Swordfish	23.00
2 Coffees	4.00
Total	67.50
Tax (5%)	3.38
Total	70.88

Number of guests: 2
Server: Maurice

Of course, your bill should include the restaurant name and be a bit fancier. Your program should write the bill to another file so that the bill can be printed.

You can use menus or buttons for the GUI as long as the server has a clear way to select items.

14. **The Convex Hull Problem—A Geometric Algorithm**
This is a challenging problem that uses more complex algorithms than do the other problems in this chapter. The problem considers a set of two-dimensional points, *S*, and determines a subset of these points called the *convex hull*, which intuitively serves as an outer boundary.

Imagine that a nail is hammered into each point of *S* and a rubber band stretched around all the nails and then released. The convex hull of *S* is the set of those points touched by the rubber band. See Figure 20.13.

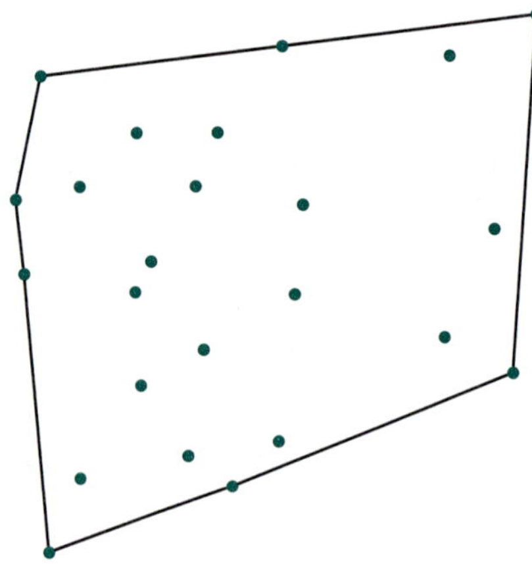

FIGURE 20.13 The convex hull is the set of points that are joined by the lines

The convex hull is used to determine the outer border of a set of points, and it is useful in many geometric applications. Convex hull is the "sorting" of geometric algorithms. Like sorting, convex hull is fundamental, and just as there are dozens of algorithms for sorting, so it is for convex hull.

The Graham Scan Algorithm The particular algorithm that we discuss is due to Ron Graham, who discovered it in 1972. Graham Scan, as it is called, works by picking the lowest point *p*, that is, the one with the minimum *y*-value (note this must be on the convex hull), and then scanning the rest of the points in counterclockwise order with respect to *p*. As this scanning is done, the points that should remain on the convex hull are kept and the rest are discarded, leaving only the points in the convex hull when the algorithm terminates.

To visualize the algorithm, imagine first that, by luck, all the points are actually in the convex hull, that is, no points get discarded. In this case, each time we move to the next point, we make a left turn with respect to the line determined by the last two points of the hull. Of course, normally this does not happen and a right turn occurs. These right turns are what cause points to be discarded.

As the points are considered in counterclockwise order, Graham Scan checks whether or not we make a left turn. When a move is a left turn, we store the new point. If the move is *not* a left turn, then the algorithm backtracks to the first pair of points from which the turn *would* be a left turn and discards all points over which it backs up. Because Graham Scan involves storing points and backtracking, we choose to implement the algorithm with a stack of points.

Let's look at an example. Suppose that an initial set of points, *S* is contained in an array P:

i	P[i]
0	(0, 0)
1	(−5, −2)
2	(−2, −1)
3	(−6, 0)
4	(−3.5, 1)
5	(−4.5, 1.5)
6	(−2.5, −5)
7	(1, −2.5)
8	(2.5, .5)
9	(−2.2, 2.2)

See Figure 20.14.

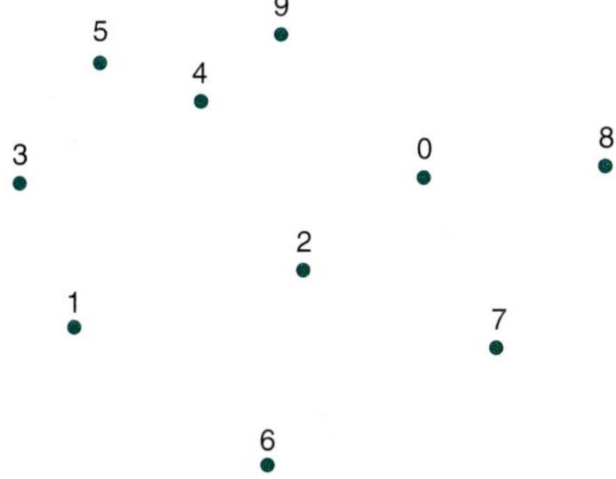

FIGURE 20.14 An initial set of two-dimensional points stored in an array. Each point is labeled by its index in the array.

First, the lowest point is swapped into position 0 of the list. That is, the point (−2.5, −5) is now in position 0 and the point (0, 0) occupies position 6. See Figure 20.15.

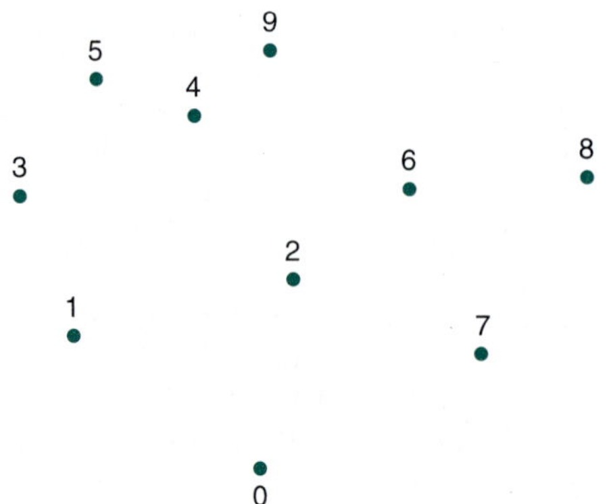

FIGURE 20.15 The lowest point is in position 0 of the array

The points are then sorted by their polar angles with respect to the lowest point, so that they can be considered in counterclockwise order. That is, the points are rearranged in the array as:

i	P[i]
0	(−2.5, −5)
1	(1, −2.5)
2	(2.5, 5)
3	(0, 0)
4	(−2, −1)
5	(−2.2, −.2)
6	(−3.5, 1)
7	(−4.5, 1.5)
8	(−6, 0)
9	(−5, −2)

See Figure 20.16.

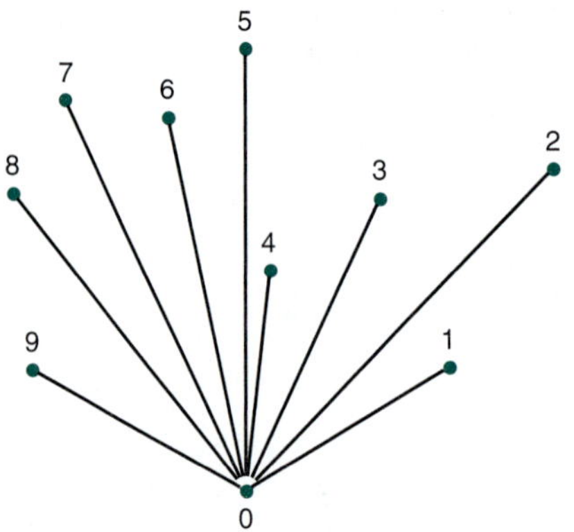

FIGURE 20.16 The points are sorted into counterclockwise order

The turn from line 0–1 to point 2 is left, from 1–2 to 3 is left, and from 2–3 to 4 is left. At this stage, points 0, 1, 2, 3, and 4 have been pushed on a stack, with 4 the top element. This "partial hull" is shown in Figure 20.17.

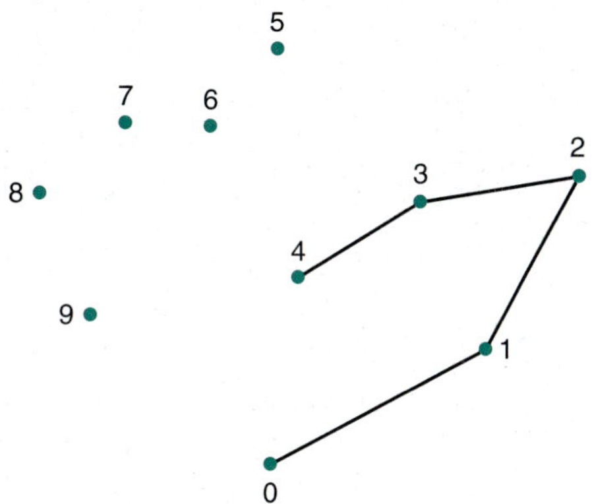

FIGURE 20.17 The beginning

The turn from line 3–4 to point 5 is a right turn, so pop the stack. The turn from 2–3 to 5 is also a right turn, so, once again, pop the stack. The turn from 1–2 to 5 is a left turn, so push 5 onto the stack. The stack now holds points 0, 1, 2, and 5. See Figure 20.18.

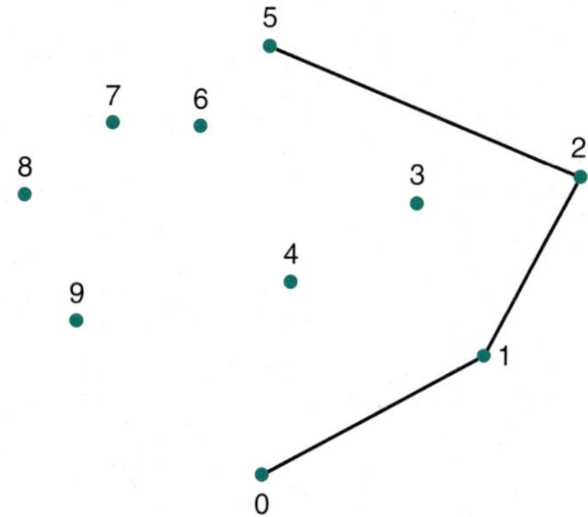

FIGURE 20.18 Backtracking and discarding points 3 and 4

The turn from line 2–5 to 6 is left, so push 6 onto the stack. Next, the turn from 5–6 to 7 is right, so pop 6 and push 7 because the turn from line 2–5 to 7 is left. The remaining turns are left, so push 8 and 9. The final stack contains 0125789 and the convex hull is shown in Figure 20.19.

The Graham Scan Algorithm

Input: An array of two-dimensional points, P.
Output: The convex hull of P.

1. Find the lowest point p, (the point with the minimum *y*-coordinate). If there is more than one point with the minimum *y*-coordinate, then use the leftmost one.
2. Sort the remaining points in counterclockwise order around p. That is, sort them by increasing angle with respect to p and the horizontal. If any points have the same angle with respect to p (they all lie on the same line), then sort them by increasing distance from p.
3. Push the first three points onto a stack.

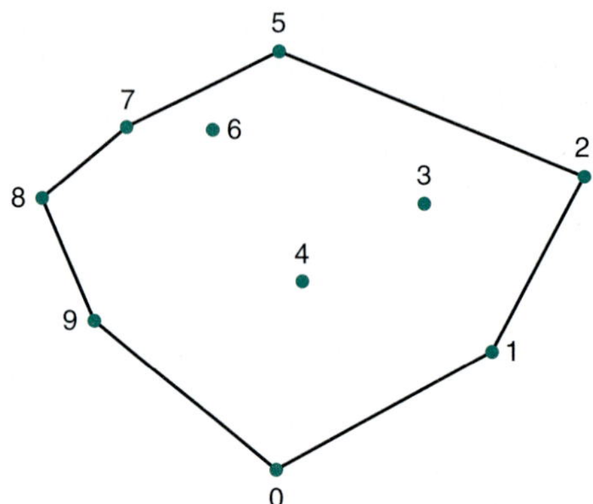

FIGURE 20.19 The convex hull

4. For each remaining point c in sorted order, do the following:

```
b = the point on top of the stack.
a = the point below b on the stack.
while a left turn is not made in moving from line a-b to point c do        // See below
{
        pop the stack.
        b = the point on top of the stack.
        a = the point below b on the stack.
}
Push c onto the stack.
```

The convex hull is the set of points remaining on the stack.

The Problem Design a visual application that determines the convex hull for a set of two-dimensional points. Like the poker game of this chapter, this program consists of two parts. The data model is somewhat technical; the GUI is entertaining and fun. Let's look at the GUI first.

Initially, a user selects a set of points by clicking the mouse at several screen locations. The GUI draws each point on the screen. A point can be "drawn" with a small circle, using g.drawOval(). After all points have been selected, the user runs the algorithm. When a new point is pushed onto the stack, a line should be drawn from the point previously on top of the stack to the new point. Whenever a point is popped from the stack, the line from that point to the point on the top of the stack should be erased.

The GUI animates the Graham Scan algorithm and makes the computation intuitive. In order to see the algorithm perform step by step, have a Next button that runs the algorithm until the next time the stack is modified.
Figures 20.17 through 20.19 might give you some ideas for the GUI.

Because we are using screen coordinates, we assume that all points have integer coordinates. Moreover, recall that the point lowest on the screen has the largest y-coordinate. You can use Java's Polygon class to implement the GUI, but that is not necessary.

The Data Model Create a class CHPoint that extend Java's Point class (in java.awt .Point). CHPoint contains a very important but difficult method:

```
int leftOrRight(Point b, Point c),
```

that returns 1, −1, or 0 depending upon whether the "sweeping movement" from the line this-b to the line this-c goes clockwise (1), counterclockwise (−1), or neither (0). The result is clockwise when a right turn is made, counterclockwise when a left turn is made, and neither when this, b, and c are collinear.

This method is necessary for deciding whether a left or right turn is made when moving from line a-b to point c in step 4 of the Graham Scan algorithm. The method is also used for sorting points by their polar angles in step 2 of the algorithm. To compare two points, b and c, with respect to the lowest point p, use p.leftOrRight(CHPoint b, CHPoint c). The CHPoint class should implement the Comparable interface.

The implementation of leftOrRight(Point b, Point c), is not obvious, and it stems from the cross product of two vectors. Even if you know nothing about vectors and cross products, you can use the following if-statements to implement leftOrRight(Point b, Point c).

Let a, b, and c be three two-dimensional points such that a.x is the *x*-coordinate of a and a.y the *y*-coordinate.

if (c.x – a.x)(b.y – a.y) > (c.y – a.y)(b.x – a.x)
then the movement from line *a-b* to line *a-c* is clockwise.

if (c.x – a.x)(b.y – a.y) < (c.y – a.y)(b.x – a.x)
then the movement from line *a-b* to line *a-c* is counterclockwise.

Otherwise the three points are collinear.

Why the Math Works—Just in Case You're Interested To gain an intuitive understanding, concentrate on the case where the lines a-b and a-c both have positive slope. A clockwise motion implies that the line a-b has a steeper (greater) slope than line a-c. This means that (b.y – a.y)/(b.x – a.x) > (c.y – a.y)/(c.x – a.x). Multiply this inequality by (c.x – a.x)(b.x – a.x) to get the inequalities above.

The reasons for performing the multiplication and using this "cross product" rather than the division version are twofold:

1. to avoid having to check for division by zero, and
2. so that the inequality works consistently for the cases where both slopes are not positive.

APPENDICES

APPENDIX A

Java Keywords

abstract	assert	boolean	break	byte
case	catch	char	class	const*
continue	default	do	double	else
enum	extends	final	finally	float
for	goto*	if	implements	import
instanceof	int	interface	long	native
new	package	private	protected	public
return	short	static	strictfp	super
switch	synchronized	this	throw	throws
transient	try	void	volatile	while

*Keywords const and goto are currently not used.
The words true, false, and null signify literals and may not be used as identifier names.

APPENDIX B

The ASCII Character Set

Control Characters

Character	Value (Decimal)	Control key	Interpretation
NUL	0	^@	Null character
SOH	1	^A	Start of heading
STX	2	^B	Start of text
ETX	3	^C	End of text
EOT	4	^D	End of transmission
ENQ	5	^E	Enquiry
ACK	6	^F	Acknowledge
BEL	7	^G	Bell
BS	8	^H	Backspace
HT	9	^I	Horizontal tab
LF	10	^J	Line Feed
VT	11	^K	Vertical tab
FF	12	^L	Form Feed
CR	13	^M	Carriage Return
SO	14	^N	Shift Out
SI	15	^O	Shift In
DLE	16	^P	Data link escape
DC1	17	^Q	Device control 1
DC2	18	^R	Device control 2
DC3	19	^S	Device control 3
DC4	20	^T	Device control 4
NAK	21	^U	Negative acknowledge
SYN	22	^V	Synchronous idle
ETB	23	^W	End transmission block
CAN	24	^X	Cancel
EM	25	^Y	End of medium
SUB	26	^Z	Substitute
ESC	27	^[	Escape
FS	28	^\	File separator
GS	29	^]	Group separator
RS	30	^^	Record separator
US	31	^_	Unit separator

Printing Characters

Character	Value (Decimal)	Character	Value (Decimal)	Character	Value (Decimal)
Space	32	A	65	a	97
!	33	B	66	b	98
"	34	C	67	c	99
#	35	D	68	d	100
$	36	E	69	e	101
%	37	F	70	f	102
&	38	G	71	g	103
`	39	H	72	h	104
(	40	I	73	i	105
)	41	J	74	j	106
*	42	K	75	k	107
+	43	L	76	l	108
,	44	M	77	m	109
-	45	N	78	n	110
.	46	O	79	o	111
/	47	P	80	p	112
0	48	Q	81	q	113
1	49	R	82	r	114
2	50	S	83	s	115
3	51	T	84	t	116
4	52	U	85	u	117
5	53	V	86	v	118
6	54	W	87	w	119
7	55	X	88	x	120
8	56	Y	89	y	121
9	57	Z	90	z	122
:	58	[	91	{	123
;	59	\	92	|	124
<	60	]	93	}	125
=	61	^	94	~	126
>	62	_	95	DEL	127
?	63	`	96		
@	64				

APPENDIX C

Operator Precedence

High

Operator	Associativity
() [] •	left to right
++ (postfix) −− (postfix)	right to left
! ++ (prefix) −− (prefix) + (unary plus) − (unary minus) (*type*) ~	right to left
* / %	left to right
+ −	left to right
<< >> >>> (bitwise operators)	left to right
< <= > >= instanceof	left to right
== !=	left to right
& (bitwise AND)	left to right
^ (bitwise exclusive OR)	left to right
| (bitwise inclusive OR)	left to right
&&	left to right
||	left to right
&: (ternary conditional operator)	right to left
= += −= *= /= %= &= ^= |= <<= >>= >>>=	right to left

Low

(*type*) signifies the cast operator.
The operators

~, <<, >>, >>>, &, ^ , | , &:, &=, ^=, |=, <<=, >>=, and >>>=

are not discussed in this book.

APPENDIX D

Javadoc

Introduction

Sun provides extensive online documentation for each Java class in the form of HTML documents that are accessible using any web browser. If you have not already viewed Sun's documentation, you might use Google or some other search engine to locate this extensive archive.

Documentation Comments

By including *documentation comments* in your own classes, you can generate HTML documents, complete with hyperlinks and readable through a browser, that describe your own classes and methods.

A documentation comment begins with the compound symbol /**, ends with */, and immediately precedes a public item such as a class, method, or field. Like ordinary comments, documentation comments may contain any text you wish to include.

Documentation comments may also include *tags*. Each tag appears on a separate line and includes special information. Common tags are:

- @param *parameterNameAndDescription*,

  gives the name and a description of a parameter.
- @return *description*,

  gives a description of the return value of a method.
- @throws *exceptionTypeDescription*

  gives a description of the types of exceptions that are thrown by a method.
- @author *author*

  gives the name of the author.
- @version *version*

  gives the version number of the class.

A Javadoc Example

The following example shows a simple class hierarchy that includes documentation comments containing various tags.

```
/**
    An employee of a company.
    An employee has a name and salary
    @author John Doe
    @version 1.42
*/
public class Employee
{
        protected String name;
        protected double salary;
/** default constructor */
        public Employee()
        {
                name = "";
                salary = 0.0;
        }
/** Two-argument constructor
@param n name (String)
@param s salary (double) */
        public Employee(String n,double s )
        {
                name = n;
                salary = s;
        }
/** Changes salary
@param s salary (double) */
        public void setSalary(double s)
        {
                salary = s;
        }
/** Changes name
@param n name (String) */
        public void setName( String n)
        {
                name = n;
        }
/** @return salary (double) */
        public double getSalary()
        {
                return salary;
        }
/** @return name (String) */
        public String getName()
        {
                return name;
        }
}
```

```
/**
    The manager of a department;
    Manager extends Employee,
    A Manager has a department.
*/
public class Manager extends Employee
{
        private String dept;

        /** default constructor */

        public Manager()
        {
                super();
                dept = "";
        }

        /** Two-argument constructor
        @param n name of the manager
        @param s salary of the manager
        @param d department of the manager */

        public Manager(String n, double s, String d)
        {
                super(n, s);
                dept = d;
        }

/** sets the name of the department
@param d department name */

        public void setDept(String d)
        {
                dept = d;
        }

/** @return name of the department */

        public String getDept()
        {
                return dept;
        }
}
```

The documentation comments are used to create HTML documents that describe Employee and Manager.

To generate documentation for a particular class, enter "javadoc classname.java" from the command prompt. The result is an HTML file, classname.html, constructed in the style of Sun's online documentation.

For example, the commands

javadoc Employee.java and javadoc Manager.java

generate the files

Employee.html and Manager.html.

These files are accessible with any browser. In addition to these files, the *javadoc* command produces a number of auxilary files such as help-doc.html and overview-tree.html that are linked to Employee.html and Manager.html.

The Employee.html and Manager.html files are shown in the list that follows.

Employee.html

Package **Class** **Tree** **Deprecated** **Index** **Help**
PREV CLASS NEXT CLASS　　**FRAMES** **NO FRAMES**　　**All Classes** **All Classes**
SUMMARY: NESTED | FIELD | CONSTR | METHOD　　DETAIL: FIELD | CONSTR | METHOD

Class Employee

```
java.lang.Object
  └ Employee
```

```
public class Employee
extends java.lang.Object
```

An employee of a company. An employee has a name and salary.

Field Summary	
protected java.lang.String	**name**
protected double	**salary**

Constructor Summary
Employee() default constructor
Employee(java.lang.String n, double s) Two-argument constructor

Method Summary

`java.lang.String`	**`getName`**`()`
`double`	**`getSalary`**`()`
`void`	**`setName`**`(java.lang.String n)` Changes name
`void`	**`setSalary`**`(double s)` Changes salary

Methods inherited from class java.lang.Object
`clone, equals, finalize, getClass, hashCode, notify, notifyAll, toString, wait, wait, wait`

Field Detail

name

`protected java.lang.String` **`name`**

---

salary

`protected double` **`salary`**

Constructor Detail

Employee

`public` **`Employee`**`()`

default constructor

Employee

```
public Employee(java.lang.String n,
                double s)
```

Two-argument constructor

Parameters:

`n` - name (String)

`s` - salary (double)

Method Detail

setSalary

`public void` **`setSalary`**`(double s)`

Changes salary

Parameters:

`s` - salary (double)

---

setName

```
public void setName(java.lang.String n)
```

Changes name

Parameters:

`n` - name (String)

---

getSalary

```
public double getSalary()
```

Returns:

salary (double)

---

getName

```
public java.lang.String getName()
```

Returns:

name (String)

Package **Class** **Tree** **Deprecated** **Index** **Help**
PREV CLASS NEXT CLASS **FRAMES** **NO FRAMES** **All Classes** **All Classes**
SUMMARY: NESTED | FIELD | CONSTR | METHOD DETAIL: FIELD | CONSTR | METHOD

Manager.html

Package **Class** **Tree** **Deprecated** **Index** **Help**
PREV CLASS NEXT CLASS **FRAMES** **NO FRAMES** **All Classes** **All Classes**
SUMMARY: NESTED | FIELD | CONSTR | METHOD DETAIL: FIELD | CONSTR | METHOD

Class Manager

```
java.lang.Object
  └ Employee
      └ Manager
```

```
public class Manager
extends Employee
```

The manager of a department; Manager extends Employee. A Manager has a department.

Field Summary

Fields inherited from class Employee
`name, salary`

Constructor Summary

`Manager()` default constructor
`Manager(java.lang.String n, double s, java.lang.String d)` Two-argument constructor

Method Summary

`java.lang.String`	**getDept**()
`void`	**setDept**(java.lang.String d) sets the name of the department

Methods inherited from class Employee
`getName, getSalary, setName, setSalary`

Methods inherited from class java.lang.Object
`clone, equals, finalize, getClass, hashCode, notify, notifyAll, toString, wait, wait, wait`

Constructor Detail

Manager

```
public Manager()
```

default constructor

Manager

```
public Manager(java.lang.String n,
               double s,
               java.lang.String d)
```

Two-argument constructor

Parameters:

`n` - manager's name (String)

`s` - manager's salary (double)

`d` - manager's department (String)

Method Detail

setDept

```
public void setDept(java.lang.String d)
```

sets the name of the department

Parameters:

`d` - department name (String)

getDept

```
public java.lang.String getDept()
```

Returns:

department name(String)

Package Class **Tree** **Deprecated** **Index** **Help**

PREV CLASS NEXT CLASS

SUMMARY: NESTED | FIELD | CONSTR | METHOD

FRAMES **NO FRAMES** **All Classes** **All Classes**

DETAIL: FIELD | CONSTR | METHOD

APPENDIX E

Packages

Packages and the *import* Statement

A *package* is a named collection of classes and interfaces.

Packages are used to organize related classes. Every Java class in Sun's extensive library is contained in some package. Scanner, HashSet, and Random belong to java.util; the Swing classes belong to javax.swing; the stream classes are found in java.io; and Math, String, System, and the wrapper classes are located in java.lang.

A class's package name tells the compiler how to locate the class. For example, if a class instantiates a Scanner object, the Java compiler must be directed to the package that contains the Scanner class, that is, to java.util. This can be accomplished in several ways, but in this text, our choice is the import statement

```
import java.util.*; // Scanner belongs to the java.util package
```

Without the information provided by this statement, the compiler cannot locate the Scanner class and issues an error message:

```
C:\JavaPrograms\NoImport.java:5: cannot find symbol
symbol : class Scanner
location: class NoImport
                    Scanner input = new Scanner(System.in);
```

To utilize Scanner, either one of the following two import statements works equally well:

- import java.util.*;
- import java.util.Scanner;

A class that includes the first statement can use *all* the classes in the java.util package, such as Random, TreeSet, and HashSet. A class that includes the second version can use the Scanner class and only the Scanner class. Neither import statement is more efficient than the other, and the choice does not affect the size of the compiled class file.

In general, to use SomeClass belonging to somePackage, use one of the import statements:

- import somePackage.*; // imports all classes in somepackage
- import somePackage.SomeClass; // imports only SomeClass

The java.lang package, which contains the Math, String, and System classes, is automatically imported into every application, so no explicit import statement is required when using the classes of this package.

Packages and the Fully Qualified Name of a Class

An import statement is simple and convenient but not necessary. Without an import statement, you can still utilize any Java class by using its *fully qualified name.*

The *fully qualified name* of a class consists of its package name, followed by a period, followed by the class name.

For example, the fully qualified name of the Scanner class is **java.util.**Scanner; the fully qualified name of String is **java.lang.**String; and the fully qualified name of JButton is **java.swing.**JButton.

Although the following program does not include an import statement, the program compiles.

```
public class NoImport Necessary
{
        public static void main(String[] args)
        {
                java.util.Scanner input = new java.util.Scanner(System.in);
                int number = input.nextInt();
        }
}
```

Here, the fully qualified name java.util.Scanner provides the compiler with the information needed to locate the Scanner class. An import statement would be redundant.

The Default Package

Although it may not be apparent, the classes in the examples of this text belong to a package, the *default package.*

If you do not specifically place your classes in a package, your classes are automatically placed in the *default package* of the current directory.

For small applications, you can certainly keep all classes in the default package. However, if you are working on a large project that involves dozens of classes, it is often wise to organize related classes by placing them into your own named packages.

How to Create Your Own Packages

It is not difficult to create your own packages.

You can instruct the Java compiler to place a class file into a package by including a *package statement* of the form

package *packagename*;

as the first statement of a class definition.

The following three classes are all members of the animal package:

package animal;
import java.util.*;
public class Baboon
{
....
}
	package animal;
	import java.util.*;
	public class Sardine
	{
	....
	}
		package animal;
		import java.util.*;
		public class Cobra
		{
		....
		}

If a class belongs to a named package, the name of the package is part of the class's fully qualified name, that is, the complete class name is *packagename.classname*. For example, the full names of the classes belonging to the animal package are:

animal.Baboon,
animal.Sardine, and
animal.Cobra,

just as the Scanner and JButton classes are fully named java.util.Scanner and javax.swing.JButton, respectively.

Packages, Package Names, and Directories

A package name is usually comprised of lowercase letters. The name of a package can be a single word or several words separated by periods, such as java.util or java.awt.event.

When a package is created, the compiled class files belonging to the package must be placed in a specific directory that mirrors the name of the package. For example, consider the following Baboon class:

```
package animal.primate;
public class Baboon
{
}
```

The class file, Baboon.class, must be stored in a directory of the form

...\animal\primate\

If you normally store all your Java programs in a directory such as c:\javaprograms, then the Baboon.class must be saved below c:\javaprograms as

c:\javaprograms**animal\primate**\Baboon.class.

To locate animal.primate.Baboon.class, the JVM must know where to begin its search, that is, the JVM needs to know about c:\javaprograms, the *root directory* for your Java programs. Once the system knows the name of the root directory, the full classname

animal.primate.Baboon.class

supplies the remainder of the complete address of the file, which is:

c:\javaprograms\animal\primate\Baboon.class.

To set the root directory to c:\javaprograms, you must add it to the *class path* of your system.

The class path tells the JVM where to begin looking for class files.

The class path gives a starting point. The class path contains the name of the root directory.

The root directory for your Java classes can be any directory at all, such as c:\javaprograms, or c:\myprograms. The procedure for adding a root directory to the class path is system dependent and varies according to your operating system. Check the documentation of your operating system to determine how to do this.

Example

The following example guides you through the creation of a package animal.primate that contains two class files, Baboon.class and Gorilla.class. In the example, we assume that the root directory for all Java classes is

c:\javaprograms

1. If it is not already there, add c:\javaprograms to the class path of your system.
2. Create a directory under c:\javaprograms named animal.
   You now have a directory

   c:\javaprograms\animal\

3. Create a directory under c:\javaprograms\animal named primate.
   You now have a directory

   c:\javaprograms\animal\primate

4. Use a package statement with each class. Define and compile your classes.

```
package animal.primate;
public class Baboon
{
    // code for baboon
}

package animal.primate;
public class Gorilla
{
    // code for Gorilla
}
```

5. Place the compiled class files into the directory c:\javaprograms\animal\primate.
   (If you are already working in this directory, then, of course, this step is automatic.)

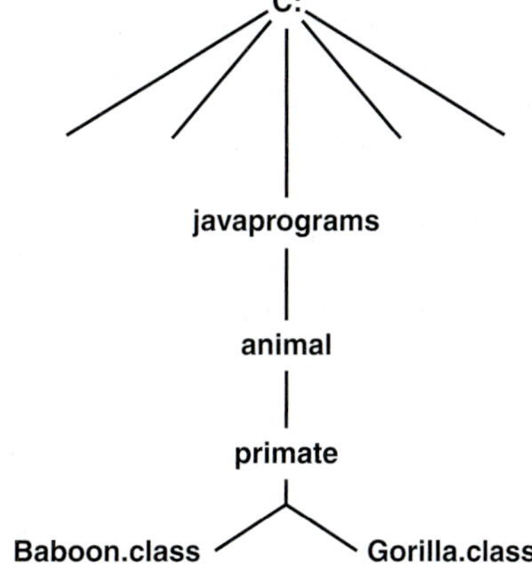

You now have a package containing two classes. Another class can conveniently use either of the two classes in this package by including an import statement

```
import animal.primate.*;
```

Alternatively, a class can import just a single class from the package, say Baboon, using

```
import animal.primate.Baboon;
```

Package Documentation

Using the javadoc tool (see Appendix D) it is possible to generate documentation for an entire package. To do this you must be in the directory *above* the package directory. From that directory, issue the command

javadoc –d *targetDirectory package*

where *targetDirectory* is the directory into which the documentation should be placed and *package* is the name of the package.

For example, to generate documentation for the animal.primate class, you must be in the c:\javaprograms\animal directory. From this directory, issue the command

```
javadoc –d c:\myjavaprograms\myJavadocs animal.primate
```

INDEX

N

O

P

Q

R

S

T

Y

Z